September 17–21, 2011
Beijing, China

Association for Computing Machinery

Advancing Computing as a Science & Profession

UbiComp'11

Proceedings of the 2011 ACM Conference on Ubiquitous Computing

Sponsored by:

ACM SIGCHI & ACM SIGMOBILE

In cooperation with:

ACM SIGSPATIAL

Supported by:

Microsoft Research, Shanda Innovations, HTC, Qualcomm, IGRS, Google, Nokia, Intel, National Science Foundation, Autodesk, National Natural Science Foundation of China, Opzoon, & Telezone

Association for
Computing Machinery

Advancing Computing as a Science & Profession

The Association for Computing Machinery
2 Penn Plaza, Suite 701
New York, New York 10121-0701

Notice to Past Authors of ACM-Published Articles
ACM intends to create a complete electronic archive of all articles and/or other material previously published by ACM. If you have written a work that has been previously published by ACM in any journal or conference proceedings prior to 1978, or any SIG Newsletter at any time, and you do NOT want this work to appear in the ACM Digital Library, please inform permissions@acm.org, stating the title of the work, the author(s), and where and when published.

ISBN: 978-1-4503-0630-0

Additional copies may be ordered prepaid from:

ACM Order Department
PO Box 11405
New York, NY 10286-1405

Phone: 1-800-342-6626 (USA and Canada)
+1-212-626-0500 (all other countries)
Fax: +1-212-944-1318
E-mail: acmhelp@acm.org

Proceedings Prepared in the USA.

Printed in China.

Foreword

On behalf of the organizing committee, it is our great pleasure to welcome you to the 13th International Conference on Ubiquitous Computing. This is the third time the UbiComp conference series has come to Asia. This year's conference in Beijing, China, follows Seoul, Korea (2008) and Tokyo, Japan (2005). UbiComp is a conference that truly captures the wide variety of research activities in the diverse field of ubiquitous computing, encompassing research from, e.g., Human-Computer Interaction, Mobile Computing, Location and Sensing Technology, Machine Learning, Middleware and Systems, and Programming Models and Tools.

September 2011 also marks a historic date in the history of Ubicomp. It is exactly 20 years from when Dr. Mark Weiser's historic article, "The Computer for the Twenty-First Century," appeared in *Scientific American*. This article is acclaimed for widely publicizing the idea of Ubicomp in the research community and setting the goals for the early years of the field. We will mark this historic occasion with a special panel in tribute to the late Dr. Weiser. Our panel of luminaries, including those who worked with Dr. Weiser at Xerox PARC, as well as his contemporaries who were influenced by his work at the time, will reminisce on Mark's predictions as well as present their view of where the field should move going forward.

Each UbiComp conference represents a snapshot of our field, capturing the state-of-the-art in technology, the research challenges we are addressing, as well as the people that form the UbiComp community. Each year's proceedings represent an opportunity to learn about new areas and identify upcoming research opportunities, and this year is no exception. UbiComp 2011 continues the tradition of a single-track program that allows participants to experience the entire program in a variety of sessions, ranging from context awareness to location sharing, from home infrastructures to novel interactions, and from persuasive computing to sensing.

This year our international Program Committee, composed of 28 of the leading researchers in the field, evaluated a record number of 302 submissions — 234 full papers and 68 notes. Using a multi-phase review process, initially each submission was reviewed by at least one member of the PC and three or more external reviewers. Of the 302 submissions, 118 were evaluated by 1-2 additional PC members and discussed at a 2-day PC meeting held on the campus of the University of California, Berkeley. In total, the Program Committee and 531 external reviewers spent countless hours to provide feedback to the authors through 1343 reviews. After this rigorous process, a total of 50 submissions — 44 full papers and 6 notes — were accepted for publication in these proceedings, representing an overall acceptance rate of 16.6%. We feel our selective review process has resulted in a high-quality set of published papers. A sub-committee discussed and selected five of the 50 accepted papers to be recognized in these proceedings for their particular level of quality. Of these five, one stood out as the best paper of UbiComp 2011.

This year also sees a high quality adjunct program, accepting 22 demos, 9 videos, and 33 posters, for a total of 55 accepted adjunct papers out of 85 submissions (note that several accepted adjunct submissions appear in multiple categories, but are only counted once in the acceptance numbers). Continued from UbiComp 2010, we encouraged authors of accepted full papers and notes to also submit a poster, video, or demo of their work, to better engage the audience and stimulate discussion. To properly reflect the significance of the work represented in the adjunct program, these submissions also see a tighter integration in the main program, with video presentations interspersed with the technical presentations of the main track, and posters and demos presented during lunch breaks.

The workshop program has 12 workshops that cover both traditional Ubicomp topics (e.g., context awareness, location-based services, mobile sensing, health, and design) and newer topics (e.g., crowdsourcing and urban computing). This year, we launched the first tutorial program in UbiComp conference history. We offered five tutorials by leading experts on the topics of activity recognition, Android development, evaluation, ubicomp research in the wild, and urban sensing. We also experimented with a new Visions of Ubicomp Film Contest.

Last but not least, Jan Chipchase's keynote will offer a provocative look at the future of ubiquitous computing in new settings.

We hope you find this year's program interesting, useful and enjoyable. Several organizations and people contributed to the success of UbiComp 2011 and we are grateful for their support. First, we would like to thank Tsinghua University for hosting and helping to organize UbiComp. We also appreciate the sponsorship of ACM SIGCHI, ACM SIGMOBILE and ACM SIGSPATIAL. Finally, the conference could not occur without the kind financial support of our benefactors Microsoft Research, Shanda, NSFC, NSF, Qualcomm, Google, IGRS, HTC, Nokia, Intel, AutoDesk, Opzoon, and Telezoon.

Putting together UbiComp 2011 has been a team effort and we would like to thank a series of people. First of all, the local organizers, Yu Chen, Silvia M. Lindtner and Yu Zheng have been working hard to put it all together in Beijing. At ACM, Ashley Cozzi provided efficient and prompt support. As chair of the steering committee, James Scott has been supportive in answering our questions about the conference history. We are also thankful to those helping organize the practical matters required to pull off such an important event, including the web masters Guoliang Li and Yue Suo, the publicity chairs Jiannong Cao and Henriette Cramer, the student volunteer chairs Sidhant Gupta and Jia Jia, the access chairs Jennifer A. Rode and Qiong Wu, the industrial exhibition chair Yuan Dong, and the treasurer Pin Tao.

We also want to thank the technical program committee, including the workshop chairs Katie Siek and Zhiwen Yu, the posters chairs Mike Chen and Tim Sohn, the demos chairs Darren Edge and Yongqiang Lv, the doctoral colloquium chairs Anind Dey and Cho-li Wang, the video chairs Jiming Guo, Julie Maitland and Gang Pan, the tutorials chairs Cecilia Mascolo and Daqing Zhang, the panel chair Beth Mynatt, and the film festival chairs Ian Li and Jun Fei. Finally, a special thanks to our publication chairs Beihong Jin and Sian Lindley, assisted by Lisa Tolles from Sheridan Printing Company, all of whom have processed the papers in a timely manner.

Finally, we wish to thank all the UbiComp 2011 attendees for supporting the conference and making it one of the most prestigious events in this field. We hope that you will find this program interesting and thought-provoking and that the conference will provide you with a valuable opportunity to share ideas with other researchers and practitioners from institutions around the world.

Donald J. Patterson, Yvonne Rogers, and Xing Xie
UbiComp 2011 Program Chairs
University of California, Irvine, USA, Open University, UK, and Microsoft Research Asia, China

James Landay and Yuanchun Shi
UbiComp 2011 General Chairs
University of Washington, USA / Microsoft Research Asia, China, and Tsinghua University, China

Table of Contents

Session 3: On the Move

Session 4: Near and Far

Session 5: How Close?

Session 6: DIY and Design

Session 7: Home and Away

Session 8: Energy and Networking

UbiComp 2011 Conference Organization

General Chairs: James Landay (*University of Washington, USA & Microsoft Research Asia, China)*
Yuanchun Shi (*Tsinghua University, China)*

Program Chairs: Donald J. Patterson (*University of California, Irvine, USA*)
Yvonne Rogers *(Open University, UK)*
Xing Xie *(Microsoft Research Asia, China)*

Workshop Chairs: Katie Siek *(University of Colorado at Boulder, USA)*
Zhiwen Yu *(Northwestern Polytechnical University, China)*

Poster Chairs: Mike Chen *(Taiwan University, China)*
Tim Sohn *(Lab126, USA)*

Demo Chairs: Darren Edge *(Microsoft Research Asia, China)*
Yongqiang Lv *(Tsinghua University, China)*

Video Chairs: Jiming Guo *(Qualcomm, China)*
Julie Maitland *(National Research Council of Canada, Canada)*
Gang Pan *(Zhejiang University, China)*

Doctoral Colloquium Chairs: Anind Dey *(Carnegie Mellon University, USA)*
Cho-li Wang *(The University of Hong Kong, China)*

Student Film Festival Chairs: Ian Li *(Carnegie Mellon University, USA)*
Jun Fei *(Central Academy of Fine Arts, China)*

Panels Chair: Elizabeth Mynatt *(Georgia Institute of Technology, USA)*

Proceedings Chairs: Beihong Jin *(Institute of Software, Chinese Academy of Sciences, China)*
Sian Lindley *(Microsoft Research, UK)*

Local Arrangements Chairs: Yu Chen *(Tsinghua University, China)*
Silvia M. Lindtner *(University of California, Irvine, USA)*
Yu Zheng *(Microsoft Research Asia, China)*

Publicity Chairs: Jiannong Cao *(Hong Kong Polytechnic University, China)*
Henriette Cramer *(Mobile Life Centre in Stockholm, Sweden)*

Treasurer & Registration Chair: Pin Tao *(Tsinghua University, China)*

Student Volunteer Chairs: Sidhant Gupta *(University of Washington, USA)*
Jia Jia *(Tsinghua University, China)*

Tutorial Chairs: Cecilia Mascolo *(University of Cambridge, UK)*
Daqing Zhang *(Institute TELECOM SudParis, France)*

Access Chairs: Jennifer A. Rode *(Drexel University, USA)*
Qiong Wu *(Tsinghua University, China)*

Industrial Exhibition Chair Yuan Dong *(Tsinghua University, China)*

Web Masters Guoliang Li *(Tsinghua University, China)*
Yue Suo *(Tsinghua University, China)*

Steering Committee Chair: James Scott *(Microsoft Research, UK)*

Steering Committee: Jeffrey Hightower *(Google, USA)*
Elaine M. Huang *(University of Zurich, Switzerland)*
Jakob Bardram *(IT University of Copenhagen, Denmark)*
Marc Langheinrich *(Università della Svizzera Italiana, Switzerland)*
Patrik Floreen *(Helsinki Institute for Information Technology, Finland)*
Antonio Krueger *(Saarland University, Germany)*
Sunny Consolvo *(Amazon, USA)*
Hans Gellersen *(Lancaster University, UK)*
A.J. Brush *(Microsoft Research, USA)*
Hideyuki Tokuda *(Keio University, Japan)*
Joe McCarthy *(University of Washington, Tacoma, USA)*
Adrian Friday *(Lancaster University, UK)*
Aaron Quigley *(University of St. Andrews, UK)*
Gregory Abowd *(Georgia Tech, USA)*
Thomas Strang *(University of Innsbruck and German Aerospace Center, Germany)*
Anthony LaMarca *(Intel, USA)*
Khai Truong *(University of Toronto, Canada)*
Paul Dourish *(University of California, Irvine, USA)*

Program Committee: A.J. Brush *(Microsoft Research, USA)*
Leah Buechley *(Massachusetts Institute of Technology, USA)*
John Canny *(University of California, Berkeley, USA)*
Tanzeem Choudhury *(Dartmouth College, USA)*
Hao-hua Chu *(Taiwan University, China)*
Anind K. Dey *(Carnegie Mellon University, USA)*
Parisa Eslambolchilar *(Swansea University, UK)*
Ling Feng *(Tsinghua University, China)*
Adrian Friday *(Lancaster University, UK)*
Minyi Guo *(Shanghai Jiao Tong University, China)*
Steve Hodges *(Microsoft Research Cambridge, UK)*
Jason I. Hong *(Carnegie Mellon University, USA)*
Eva Hornecker *(University of Strathclyde, UK)*
Elaine M. Huang *(University of Zurich, Switzerland)*
Julie Kientz *(University of Washington, USA)*
John Krumm *(Microsoft Research, USA)*
Youn-Kyung Lim *(KAIST, Korea)*
Yang Li *(Google, USA)*
Patrick L. Oliver *(Newcastle University, UK)*
Oscar Mayora *(CREATE-NET Research Center, Italy)*
Shwetak Patel *(University of Washington, USA)*
Scott Saponas *(Microsoft Research, USA)*
Johannes Schöning *(German Research Centre for Artificial Intelligence, Germany)*
Sri Subramanian *(University of Bristol, UK)*
Hideyuki Tokuda *(Keio University, Japan)*
Woontack Woo *(GIST, Korea)*
Qiang Yang *(Hong Kong University of Science and Technology, China)*
Yu Zheng *(Microsoft Research Asia, China)*

UbiComp 2011 Additional Reviewers

Gregory Abowd *(Georgia Institute of Technology)*
Joana Abreu *(MIT Portugal Program)*
Mark Ackerman *(University of Michigan)*
Eytan Adar *(University of Michigan)*
Stefan Agamanolis *(Akron Children's Hospital)*
Sharad Agarwal *(Microsoft Research)*
Yuvraj Agarwal *(University of California, San Diego)*
Jason Alexander *(University of Bristol)*
Dzmitry Aliakseyeu *(Philips Research)*
Simo Ali-löytty *(Tampere University of Technology)*
Jalal Al-muhtadi *(King Saud University)*
Florian Alt *(University of Duisburg-Essen)*
Saleema Amershi *(University of Washington)*
Shahriyar Amini *(Carnegie Mellon University)*
Margarita Anastassova *(CEA LIST, LISA)*
ken anderson *(Intel Research)*
Paul André *(University of Southampton)*
Michael Angermann *(German Aerospace center (DLR))*
Daniel Arnitz *(Graz University of Technology)*
Bert Arnrich *(Swiss Federal Institute of Technology Zurich)*
Daniel Ashbrook *(Georgia Institute of Technology)*
Mark Ashdown *(Thales Research and Technology UK)*
Juan Carlos Augusto *(University of Ulster)*
Adam Aviv *(University of Pennsylvania)*
Daniel Avrahami *(Intel)*
Seok-Hyung Bae *(KAIST)*
Madeline Balaam *(Culture Lab, Newcastle University)*
Rajesh Balan *(Singapore Management University)*
Aruna Balasubramanian *(University of Washington)*
Rafael Ballagas *(Nokia Research Center)*
Magnus Bang *(Linkoping university)*
Richard Banks *(Microsoft Research)*
Jakob Bardram *(IT University of Copenhagen)*
Louise Barkhuus *(University of California, San Diego)*
John Barton *(IBM Almaden)*
Sumit Basu *(Microsoft Research)*
Karin Bee *(Augsburg University)*
Bo Begole *(PARC)*
Michael Beigl *(TU Braunschweig)*
Frank Bentley *(Motorola Applied Research)*
Carlos Bento *(Universidade de Coimbra)*
Alastair Beresford *(University of Cambridge)*
Mario Berges *(Carnegie Mellon University)*
Michael Bernstein *(Massachusetts Institute of Technology)*
Jordan Besnoff *(Duke University)*
Dominik Bial *(Paluno - The Ruhr Institute for Software Technology)*
Robert Biddle *(Carleton University)*
Jacob Biehl *(FX Palo Alto Laboratory, Inc.)*
Jeffrey Bigham *(University of Rochester)*
Aras Bilgen *(Intel)*
Jon Bird *(The Open University)*
Alan Blackwell *(University of Cambridge)*
Ulf Blanke *(Max Planck Institute für Informatik)*
Matthias Böhmer *(DFKI)*
Susanne Boll *(University of Oldenburg, Germany)*
Dirk Börner *(Open Universiteit Nederland)*
Nis Bornoe *(University of Copenhagen)*
V. Michael Bove Jr *(MIT Media Lab)*
Jose Bravo *(Castilla-La Mancha University)*
Margot Brereton *(Queensland University of Technology)*
Gregor Broll *(Ludwig-Maximilians-Universität München)*
Barry Brown *(University of California, San Diego)*
Amy Bruckman *(Georgia Institute of Technology)*
Pascal Bruegger *(University of Fribourg)*
George Buchanan *(City University London)*
Michael Buettner *(University of Washington)*
Hung Bui *(SRI International)*
Andreas Bulling *(University of Cambridge and Lancaster University)*
Kelly Caine *(Indiana University)*
Paul Cairns *(University of York)*
Tiago Camacho *(Madeira Interactive Technologies Institute (M-ITI))*
Andrew Campbell *(Dartmouth College)*
Andy Carle *(University of California, Berkeley)*
Jessica Cauchard *(University of Bristol)*
James Caverlee *(Texas A&M University)*
Manuel Cebrian *(MIT)*
Ranveer Chandra *(Microsoft Research)*
Kerry Chang *(Carnegie Mellon University)*
Tsung-Hsiang Chang *(Massachusetts Institute of Technology)*
Kenghao Chang *(University of California, Berkeley)*
Keng-hao Chang *(University of California, Berkeley)*
Haibo Chen *(Fudan University)*
Tom Chen *(Swansea University)*
Jianwen Chen *(Tsinghua University)*
Yunan Chen *(University of California, Irvine)*
Marshini Chetty *(Georgia Institute of Technology)*
Keith Cheverst *(Lancaster University)*

Krishna Chintalapudi *(Microsoft Research)*
Eun Kyoung Choe *(University of Washington)*
Jesse Cirimele *(Stanford University)*
Adrian Clear *(Lancaster University)*
Andy Cockburn *(UoC)*
Gabe Cohn *(University of Washington)*
Sunny Consolvo *(Intel Research Seattle)*
Diane Cook *(Washington State University)*
Cristina Costa *(CREATE-NET)*
Tim Coughlan *(The Open University)*
Scott Counts *(Microsoft Research)*
Landon Cox *(Duke University)*
Henriette Cramer *(Mobile Life @ SICS)*
Meg Cramer *(University of California, Irvine)*
Jon Crowcroft *(University of Cambridge)*
Ali Dada *(SAP)*
Florian Daiber *(DFKI GmbH)*
Peter Dalsgaard *(Aarhus University)*
Elizabeth Daly *(IBM Research)*
Sarah Darby *(University of Oxford)*
Scott Davidoff *(Carnegie Mellon University)*
Fernando De la Torre *(Carnegie Mellon University)*
Eyal de Lara *(University of Toronto)*
Alexander De Luca *(University of Munich)*
Francesco De Pellegrini *(CREATE-NET)*
David Dearman *(University of Toronto)*
Gerald DeJean *(Microsoft Research)*
Franca Delmastro *(IIT-CNR)*
Tangjian Deng *(Tsinghua University)*
Tamara Denning *(University of Washington)*
Charlie DeTar *(MIT)*
Travis Deyle *(Georgia Institute of Technology)*
Tawanna Dillahunt *(Carnegie Mellon University)*
Carl Disalvo *(Georgia Institute of Technology)*
Ellen Yi-Luen Do *(Georgia Institute of Technology)*
Mianxiong Dong *(The University of Aizu)*
Afsaneh Doryab *(IT University of Copenhagen)*
Paul Dourish *(University of California, Irvine)*
Steven Dow *(Georgia Institute of Technology)*
Matt Duckham *(The University of Melbourne)*
Henry Been-Lirn Duh *(National University of Singapore)*
Adam Dunkels *(SICS)*
Lucy Dunne *(University College Dublin)*
Paul Dunphy *(Newcastle University)*
Prabal Dutta *(University of Michigan)*
Felix Duvallet *(Carnegie Mellon University)*
Florian Echtler *(Munich Univ. of Applied Sciences)*
Jens Edlund *(KTH Speech, Music and Hearing)*
Mike Eisenberg *(University of Colorado)*
Rana el Kaliouby *(MIT Media Lab)*
mark feldmeier *(massachusetts institute of technology)*
Diego Felix *(University of Victoria)*
Ylva Fernaeus *(SICS)*
Mirko Fetter *(University of Bamberg)*
Andrea Finke *(Bielefeld University)*
Joel Fischer *(The Mixed Reality Laboratory)*
Daniel Fitton *(University of Central Lancashire)*
Elizabeth FitzGerald *(University of Nottingham)*
Sean Follmer *(MIT)*
Mike Fraser *(University of Bristol)*
Jon Froehlich *(University of Washington)*
Kaori Fujinami *(Tokyo Univ. of Agriculture and Technology)*
Jürgen Fuss *(Upper Austria University of Applied Sciences)*
Silvia Gabrielli *(CREATE-NET)*
Krzysztof Gajos *(Harvard University)*
Peter Gallagher *(Newcastle University)*
Raghu K Ganti *(IBM T J Watson Research Center)*
Daniel Gatica-Perez *(Idiap Research Institute)*
Yong Ge *(Rutgers University)*
Sven Gehring *(German Research Center for Artificial Intelligence)*
Darren Gergle *(Northwestern University)*
Gabriel Ghinita *(Purdue University)*
lewis girod *(MIT)*
Ben Greenstein *(Intel Research Seattle)*
Andrea Grimes Parker *(Georgia Institute of Technology)*
Mark Gross *(Carnegie Mellon University)*
Marco Gruteser *(Rutgers University)*
Yukang Guo *(Lancaster University)*
Song Guo *(University of Aizu)*
Arpit Gupta *(North Carolina State University)*
Sidhant Gupta *(University of Washington)*
Josh Hailpern *(University of Illinois at Urbana-Champaign)*
Jonna Häkkilä *(Nokia Research Center)*
Daniel Halperin *(University of Washington)*
Jaap R.C. Ham *(Eindhoven University of Technology)*
Raffay Hamid *(Georgia Institute of Technology)*
Nils Hammerla *(Culture Lab, School of Computing Science, Newcastle University)*
Bo Han *(University of Maryland)*
Thomas Riisgaard Hansen *(University of Aarhus)*
Ramaswamy Hariharan *(AT&T Interactive Research)*
Robert Harle *(University of Cambridge)*
Chris Harrison *(Human-Computer Interaction Institute, Carnegie Mellon University)*
Steve Harrison *(Virginia Polytechnic Institute and State University)*

Kirstie Hawkey *(Dalhousie University)*
Eiji Hayashi *(Carnegie Mellon University)*
Gillian Hayes *(University of California, Irvine)*
Mike Hazas *(Lancaster University)*
William Hazlewood *(Indiana University School of Informatics)*
Jennifer Healey *(Intel Labs)*
Brent Hecht *(Northwestern University)*
Eric Hekler *(Stanford University)*
Peter Henry *(University of Washington)*
Alex Hill *(Georgia Institute of Technology)*
Benjamin Mako Hill *(Massachuetts Institute of Technology)*
Jesse Hoey *(University of Waterloo)*
Tiffany Holmes *(The School of the Art Institute of Chicago)*
Jin-Hyuk Hong *(Carnegie Mellon University)*
Juan Pablo Hourcade *(University of Iowa)*
Gary Hsieh *(Michigan State University)*
Derek Hao Hu *(Hong Kong University of Science and Technology)*
Yan Huang *(University of North Texas)*
Duke Hutchings *(Elon University)*
Liviu Iftode *(Rutgers University)*
Tom Igoe *(New York University)*
Kori Inkpen *(Microsoft Research)*
Stephen Intille *(MIT)*
Mihaela Ion *(CREATE-NET)*
Iulia Ion *(ETH Zurich)*
Pourang Irani *(University of Manitoba)*
Masayuki Iwai *(Tokyo Denki University)*
Dan Jackson *(Newcastle University)*
Seiie Jang *(Nagoya University)*
Chandrika Jayant *(University of Washington)*
YI JI *(UNIVERSITY OF TECHNOLOGY, SYDNEY)*
Xiaofan Jiang *(Microsoft Research)*
Lei Jing *(University of Aizu)*
Wendy Ju *(Stanford)*
Ata Kaban *(University of Birmingham)*
Eric Kabisch *(University of California, Irvine)*
Matthew Kam *(Carnegie Mellon University)*
Masayuki Kanbara *(NAIST)*
Shaun Kane *(University of Washington)*
Jong Hee Kang *(Microsoft)*
Ashish Kapoor *(Microsoft Research)*
Karrie Karahalios *(University of Illinois, Urbana-Champaign)*
Amy Karlson *(Microsoft Research)*
Aniket Kate *(Max Planck Institute for Software Systems (MPI-SWS))*
Nobuo Kawaguchi *(Nagoya University)*
Yoshihiro Kawahara *(The University of Tokyo)*
Fahim Kawsar *(Lancaster University)*
Jofish Kaye *(Nokia Research Center)*
Patrick Gage Kelley *(Carnegie Mellon University)*
Azam Khan *(Autodesk Research)*
Omar Khan *(University of California, Berkeley)*
Sunyoung Kim *(Carnegie Mellon University)*
Hyungsin Kim *(Georgia Institute of Technology)*
Minkyong Kim *(IBM)*
Ig-jae Kim *(Korea Institute of Science and Technology)*
Yungeun Kim *(Mobile Embedded System Lab. Yonsei University)*
Sehwan Kim *(University California at Santa Barbara)*
Donnie Kim *(University of California, Los Angeles)*
Younghun Kim *(University of California, Los Angeles)*
Hiroaki Kimura *(Waseda University)*
Tim Kindberg *(HP Labs, Bristol)*
Irwin King *(AT&T Labs Research)*
Dan Kirschen *(University of Washin)*
Mikkel Baun Kjærgaard *(Aarhus University)*
Predrag Klasnja *(University of Washington)*
Bart Knijnenburg *(University of California, Irvine)*
Shoubin Kong *(Tsinghua University)*
Shinichi Konomi *(University of Tokyo)*
Stephan Kopf *(University of Mannheim)*
Gerd Kortuem *(Computing Department, Lancaster University)*
Vassilis Kostakos *(University of Madeira)*
Marek Kowalkiewicz *(SAP Research)*
Matthias Kranz *(Technische Universität München)*
Sven Kratz *(Deutsche Telekom Laboratories, TU Berlin)*
Robin Kravets *(University of Illinois)*
Antonio Krüger *(Uni Münster)*
Werner Kuhn *(University of Muenster)*
Anuj Kumar *(Carnegie Mellon University)*
Bob Kummerfeld *(University of Sydney)*
Sri Kurniawan *(University of California Santa Cruz)*
Stacey Kuznetsov *(Carnegie Mellon University)*
Haewoon Kwak *(KAIST)*
Tsung-te Lai *(National Taiwan University)*
Anthony LaMarca *(Intel Research Seattle)*
Nicholas Lane *(Dartmouth College)*
Marc Langheinrich *(University of Lugano (USI))*
Eric Larson *(University of Washington)*
Neal Lathia *(University College London)*
Celine Latulipe *(UNC Charlotte)*
Steven Lavalle *(University of Illinois)*
Shaun Lawson *(University of Lincoln)*
Christopher Le Dantec *(Georgia Institute of Technology)*

Youngho Lee *(GIST U-VR Lab.)*
Geehyuk Lee *(Information & Communications University)*
Bongshin Lee *(Microsoft Research)*
Ben Leong *(National University of Singapore)*
Jonathan Lester *(University of Washington)*
Julie Letchner *(Microsoft)*
Kevin Li *(AT&T Labs - Research)*
Ian Li *(Carnegie Mellon University)*
Bin Li *(Institut TELECOM SudParis)*
Wu-Jun Li *(Shanghai Jiao Tong University)*
Zhuo Li *(State Key Laboratory for Novel Software and Technology, Nanjing University)*
Yunqiu Li *(Swansea University)*
Yiping Li *(Tsinghua University)*
Fei Li *(TUW, Vienna University of Technology)*
Lihong Li *(Yahoo! Research)*
Chieh-Jan Mike Liang *(Microsoft Research)*
Lin Liao *(Google Inc.)*
Xiaofei Liao *(Huazhong University of Science and Technology, Wuhan, China)*
Brian Lim *(Human-Computer Interaction Institute, Carnegie Mellon University)*
Jialiu Lin *(Carnegie Mellon University)*
Mu Lin *(Dartmouth College)*
Siân Lindley *(Microsoft Research Cambridge)*
Janne Lindqvist *(Carnegie Mellon University)*
Silvia Lindtner *(University of California, Irvine)*
Heather Lipford *(UNC Charlotte)*
Nathan N. Liu *(Hong Kong University of Science and Technology)*
Jie Liu *(Microsoft Research)*
Qingwei Liu *(Tsinghua University)*
Markus Löchtefeld *(DFKI)*
Emily Lovell *(MIT Media Lab)*
Hong Lu *(Dartmouth College)*
Hao Lü *(University of Washington)*
Christopher Lueg *(University of Tasmania)*
Paul Luff *(King's College London)*
paul lukowicz *(university of passau)*
Ping Luo *(HP Labs China)*
Kent Lyons *(Intel Research)*
Jun Ma *(aGraduate Department of Computer and Information Systems, University of Aizu)*
Hao Ma *(Microsoft Research)*
Anmol Madan *(MIT Media Lab)*
Angela Mahr *(DFKI)*
Apostolos Malatras *(University of Fribourg)*
Clara Mancini *(The Open University)*
Regan Mandryk *(University of Saskatchewan)*
Natalia Marmasse *(Google)*
Nicolai Marquardt *(University of Calgary)*
Paul Marshall *(The University of Warwick)*
Mark Marshall *(University of Bristol)*
Tom Martin *(Virginia Tech)*
Cecilia Mascolo *(University of Cambridge)*
Michael Massimi *(University of Toronto)*
Aleksandar Matic *(CREATE-NET)*
Yutaka Matsuo *(University of Tokyo)*
Tara Matthews *(IBM Research, Almaden)*
Rene Mayrhofer *(Upper Austria University of Applied Sciences)*
Justin Mazola Paluska *(MIT)*
Joe McCarthy *(Nokia Research Center)*
David McGookin *(University of Glasgow)*
Don McMillan *(University of Glasgow)*
Yevgeniy Medynskiy *(Georgia Institute of Technology)*
David Mellis *(MIT)*
Nemanja Memarović *(University of Lugano)*
Florian Michahelles *(ETH Zurich)*
Takashi Miyaki *(Karlsruhe Institute of Technology)*
Iqbal Mohomed *(University of Toronto)*
Mark Moll *(Rice University)*
Andreas Möller *(Technische Universität München)*
Tentori Monica *(CICESE)*
Marc-Antoine Mouilleron *(France Telecom Orange)*
Frederick Muench *(Mobile Health Interventions)*
Hans Jörg Müller *(University of Münster)*
Steven Murdoch *(University of Cambridge)*
Roderick Murray-smith *(University of Glasgow)*
Mirco Musolesi *(University of St Andrews)*
Miguel Nacenta *(University of Calgary)*
Tatsuo Nakajima *(Waseda University)*
Jin Nakazawa *(Keio University)*
Vinod Namboodiri *(Wichita State University)*
Jason Nawyn *(Massachusetts Institute of Technology)*
Carman Neustaedter *(Kodak Research Labs)*
Lionel Ni *(Hong Kong University of Science and Technology)*
Laurence Nigay *(University of Grenoble 1)*
Nobuhiko Nishio *(Ritsumeikan University)*
Helen Nissenbaum *(NYU)*
Petteri Nurmi *(Helsinki Institute for Information Technology HIIT)*
Ian Oakley *(University of Madeira, Carnegie Mellon University)*
William Odom *(Carnegie Mellon University)*
Yoosoo Oh *(GIST CTI)*
Alice Oh *(Korea Advanced Institute of Science and Technology)*

Kenton O'Hara *(CSIRO)*
Timo Ojala *(University of Oulu)*
Daniel Olguin Olguin *(MIT Media Laboratory)*
N Oliver *(Telefonica Research)*
Eleanor O'Neill *(Trinity College Dublin)*
Eamonn O'neill *(University of Bath)*
Venet Osmani *(CREATE-NET)*
Kaoru Ota *(University of Aizu)*
Antti Oulasvirta *(Helsinki Institute for Information Technology HIIT)*
Joe Paradiso *(MIT Media Lab)*
Miguel Pardal *(Instituto Superior Técnico, Technical University of Lisbon)*
Pablo Paredes *(University of California, Berkeley)*
Kurt Partridge *(PARC)*
Eric Paulos *(Carnegie Mellon University)*
Stephen Payne *(University of Bath)*
Wen-Chih Peng *(National Chiao Tung University)*
Trevor Pering *(Intel Research)*
Mark Perry *(Brunel University)*
Matthai Philipose *(Intel Research)*
James Pierce *(Carnegie Mellon University)*
Anne Marie Piper *(University of California, San Diego)*
Thomas Ploetz *(Georgia Institute of Technology)*
Johan Plomp *(VTT)*
Matthew Plumlee *(University of New Hampshire)*
Erika Poole *(The Pennsylvania State University)*
Andrei Popleteev *(CREATE-NET)*
Rehmi Post *(MIT Center for Bits and Atoms)*
Sara Price *(Institute of Education, London)*
Blaine Price *(The Open University)*
Bodhi Priyantha *(Microsoft Research)*
Alessandro Puiatti *(University of Applied Science of Southern Switzerland)*
Zhuzhong Qian *(Nanjing University)*
Kiran Rachuri *(University of Cambridge)*
Hayes Raffle *(Nokia Research Center, Palo Alto)*
Ahmad Rahmati *(Rice University)*
Nishkam Ravi *(NEC Labs)*
Janet Read *(UCLan)*
Madhu Reddy *(The Pennsylvania State University)*
Sasank Reddy *(University of California Los Angeles)*
Stuart Reeves *(University of Nottingham)*
Katharina Reinecke *(Harvard School of Engineering and Applied Sciences)*
Xiaofeng Ren *(Intel Labs)*
Matt Reynolds *(Duke University)*
Ali Rezafard *(Afilias)*
Andrew Rice *(University of Cambridge)*
jochen Rick *(Saarland University)*
Jukka Riekki *(University of Oulu)*
Alejandro Riera *(Starlab Barcelona SL)*
Simon Robinson *(Swansea University)*
Carsten Röcker *(RWTH Aachen University)*
Johnny Rodgers *(Simon Fraser University)*
Daniel Roggen *(ETH Zürich)*
Michael Rohs *(University of Munich)*
Mario Romero *(Georgia Institute of Technology)*
Teemu Roos *(Helsinki Institute for Information Technology HIIT)*
Stephanie Rosenthal *(Carnegie Mellon University)*
Daniela Rosner *(University of California, Berkeley)*
Philip Ross *(Eindhoven University of Technology)*
Romit Roy Choudhury *(Duke University)*
Enrico Rukzio *(Lancaster University)*
Giovanni Russello *(CREATE-NET)*
Hideo Saito *(Keio University)*
Alessandra Sala *(University California at Santa Barbara)*
Pedro Santana *(University of Colima)*
Andy Sarroff *(Dartmouth College)*
Gerhard Schall *(Graz University of Technology)*
Bernt Schiele *(TU Darmstadt)*
Chris Schmandt *(MIT Media Lab)*
Dominik Schmidt *(Lancaster University)*
Michael Schmitz *(DFKI)*
Michelle Scott *(Madeira Interactive Technologies Institute)*
James Scott *(Microsoft Research)*
Orit Shaer *(Wellesley College)*
Steve Shafer *(Microsoft)*
David Ayman Shamma *(Yahoo! Inc.)*
Ehud Sharlin *(University of Calgary)*
Yanming Shen *(Dalian University of Technology)*
Victor Sheng *(University of Central Arkansas)*
Choonsung Shin *(Carnegie Mellon University)*
Beat Signer *(Vrije Universiteit Brussel)*
Itiro Siio *(Ochanomizu University)*
Chris Smith *(Newcastle University)*
Josh Smith *(University of Washington)*
Timothy Sohn *(Lab126)*
Erin Solovey *(Tufts)*
Erik Stolterman *(Indiana University)*
Matt Studley *(university of the west of england)*
Kazunori Takashio *(Keio University)*
Iwamoto Takeshi *(Toyama Prefectural University)*
Anthony Tang *(Georgia Institute of Technology)*
John Tang *(Microsoft)*
Jie Tang *(Tsinghua University)*
Karen Tang *(University of California, Irvine)*

Lei Tang *(Yahoo! Labs)*
Alex Taylor *(Microsoft Research)*
Anuj Tewari *(University of California, Berkeley)*
Frederic Thiesse *(University of Wuerzburg)*
Stewart Thomas *(Duke University)*
Bruce Thomas *(University of South Australia)*
Yoshito Tobe *(Tokyo Denki University)*
Tammy Toscos *(Indiana University)*
Khai Truong *(University of Toronto)*
Janice Tsai *(Microsoft)*
Manfred Tscheligi *(University of Salzburg)*
Xuping Tu *(huazhong university of science of technology)*
Joe Tullio *(Motorola)*
Alireza Vahdatpour *(University of California, Los Angeles)*
Kristof Van Laerhoven *(TU Darmstadt)*
Aad van Moorsel *(sadas)*
Alexander Varshavsky *(AT&T Labs)*
Elina Vartiainen *(Nokia Research Center)*
Harsh Vathsangam *(USC)*
Jo Vermeulen *(Hasselt University)*
Chi Thanh Vi *(University of Bristol)*
Vikram Vijayaraghavan *(Stanford University)*
Nicolas Villar *(Microsoft Research)*
Dan Vogel *(Mount Allison University)*
Ron Wakkary *(Simon Fraser University)*
Bruce Walker *(Georgia Institute of Technology)*
Lorna Wall *(Sony Computer Entertainment)*
Simon Walton *(Swansea University)*
Licai Wang *(Beijing University of Posts and Telecommunications)*
Yang Wang *(Carnegie Mellon University)*
Guojun Wang *(Central South University)*
Hao Wang *(Tsinghua University)*
Jun Wang *(Tsinghua University)*
Matt Weber *(Georgia Institute of Technology)*
Evan Welbourne *(University of Washington)*
Jianshu Weng *(HP Labs Singapore)*
Jens Weppner *(University of Passau)*
Jason Wiese *(Carnegie Mellon University)*
Daniel Wigdor *(Microsoft)*
Amanda Williams *(Concordia University)*
Max Wilson *(Swansea University)*
Raphael Wimmer *(University of Munich)*
Martin Wirz *(Wearable Computing Lab., ETH Zurich)*
Adam Wolisz *(Technical University Berlin (TUB); University of California, Berkeley (UCB))*
Lok Woo *(Newcastle University)*
Oliver Woodman *(University of Cambridge)*
Peter Wright *(University of Newcastle)*
Min Wu *(Oracle)*
Danny Wyatt *(University of Washington)*
Susan Wyche *(Virginia Tech)*
Guang Xiang *(Carnegie Mellon University)*
Hui Xiong *(Rutgers University)*
Wenwei Xue *(Nokia Research Center, Beijing)*
Shuicheng Yan *(National University of Singapore)*
Svetlana Yarosh *(Georgia Institute of Technology)*
Koji Yatani *(University of Toronto)*
Baoliu Ye *(Nanjing University)*
Jie Yin *(CSIRO ICT Centre)*
Takuro Yonezawa *(Keio University)*
Hyoseok Yoon *(Gwangju Institute of Science and Technology)*
Chuang-wen You *(Academia Sinica)*
Zhiwen Yu *(Northwestern Polytechnical University)*
Jing Yuan *(Microsoft Research Asia)*
Li Yuanping *(Tsinghua University)*
Nicola Yuill *(University of Sussex)*
Tae-Jung Yun *(Georgia Institute of Technology)*
Jose Zagal *(DePaul University)*
Joy Zhang *(Carnegie Mellon University)*
Liang Zhao *(Tsinghua University)*
Vincent Zheng *(Hong Kong University of Science and Technology)*
Long Zheng *(University of Aizu)*
Lin Zhong *(Rice University)*
JIngyu Zhou *(Shanghai Jiao Tong University)*
Changqing Zhou *(University of Minnesota)*
Yin Zhu *(Hong Kong University of Science and Technology)*
Zhenyun Zhuang *(Oracle Corporation)*
Brian Ziebart *(Carnegie Mellon University)*

UbiComp 2011 Sponsors & Supporters

Sponsors:

In cooperation with:

Benefactors:

Smiling Makes Us Happier: Enhancing Positive Mood and Communication with Smile-Encouraging Digital Appliances

Hitomi Tsujita
The University of Tokyo
Hongo, Bunkyo-ku Tokyo 113-0033, Japan
tsujita@acm.org

Jun Rekimoto
The University of Tokyo & Sony Computer Science Laboratories, Inc.
rekimoto@acm.org

ABSTRACT
William James, the noted psychologist and philosopher, believed that smiling has a positive effect on our mind. James' view, which was confirmed by several psychological studies, was that we become happier when we laugh. In this paper, we propose a new digital appliance that encourages the act of smiling in our daily lives. This system is designed for people who may not always realize when they are in low spirits and/or have difficulty with smiling. In addition, we believe that this system will foster casual conversation and prompt communications with other people. Our appliance, called the HappinessCounter, combines visual smile recognition, user feedback, and network communication. We conducted two trials of the HappinessCounter system, the first with a single occupant and the second with a couple living together. The system had positive effects on user's mood and prompted communication among family members, thereby increasing their positive mood as well.

Author Keywords
Smile, Happiness, Mental mood, Health, Communication, Daily life

ACM Classification Keywords
H5.m. Information interfaces and presentation (e.g., HCI): Miscellaneous.

General Terms
Design, Human Factors

INTRODUCTION
William James said, "We don't laugh because we're happy – we're happy because we laugh." [2] His theory, called the James-Lange theory of emotion, states that life experiences produce a direct physiological response via the human autonomic nervous system, including increased muscle tone and heart rate, perspiration, and dryness of the mouth. Therefore, emotions occur because of these physiological changes, rather than being their cause. Tomkins mentions that facial movement can influence one's emotional experience [12][13]. For example, an individual who feels compelled to smile during a social event will actually come to find the event more enjoyable. Kleinke *et al.* [3] conducted an experiment on the influence of facial expressions on mood. They found that the participants in the study experienced an increase in positive mood when they created positive facial expressions, and a decrease in positive mood when they created negative facial expressions, even when the facial expressions were only mimicked. Kleinke *et al.* also found that these effects were enhanced when the participants viewed themselves in a mirror. Based upon these results, we believe that putting a smile on one's face, even when one is not in a good mood, may lead to a more positive disposition.

On the other hand, many people live alone for various reasons, including social situations, age, and diseases such as autism and depression. There are more than 31 million one-person households in the United States, which amounts to roughly 27% of all households [16]. For those people, it may be difficult at times to realize when they are in low spirits and do not have a smile on their faces. Without positive reinforcement, this condition could lead to more serious mental health problems. Medication might be one treatment option, but there are often side effects that should be considered.

To address these problems, we propose a new system called the HappinessCounter. This device facilitates the act of smiling in one's daily life and thus promotes a more positive mood. By providing feedback to users about their smile in combination with other tools [e.g., communication tools, social networking services (SNS), or applications], the system makes it easy for users to smile and thus leads to happiness. Moreover, the benefits extend to family members living together; the system may help to improve relationships with other family member by increasing their positive mood and enhancing communication.

UbiComp'11, September 17–21, 2011, Beijing, China.

HAPPINESSCOUNTER

The HappinessCounter detects a user's smile, counts the number of smiles, and records the user's mental state. After detecting a smile, the system displays visual feedback in the form of a "smile" icon in the corner of a mirror, as seen in Figure 1. If users do not smile regularly, the system notifies them by displaying a "sad" icon. As previously mentioned, Kleinke [3] pointed out that the effects were enhanced when participants viewed their smile in a mirror. We believe that if users are provided with feedback about their smile, they will be able to understand their feelings better. In other words, users will realize what is making them feel bad or good based on their corresponding smile response.

Figure 1. The HappinessCounter encourages users to smile in their daily lives by providing feedback about their smile and combining other reinforcing tools. The system detects a user's smile using the smile-recognition engine, and it displays the smile icon as visual feedback in the corner of a mirror.

We developed the "HappinessCounter Box" for this purpose. We enclosed a digital camera, an LED matrix display, and a light sensor inside the box. These devices enable the system to detect a user's smile and provide the necessary visual feedback, as seen in Figure 2. Moreover, we attached the HappinessCounter box behind a one-way mirror, as seen in Figure 3, to detect the user's smile throughout his or her daily life. By incorporating the tools that most people use on a daily basis, such as a vanity mirror, we established an environment in which the system would be used in a natural and sustained manner, thus encouraging the user to smile regularly.

However, depending on the user's mental state, he or she may not smile positively when provided with only visual feedback. Combining the system with other tools, therefore, encourages the user to smile more frequently and helps the user to be happier. Several applications can be combined with the HappinessCounter system.

We use this system in two modes. The first mode, called "Smile Awareness," simply recognizes and acknowledges when people smile to increase their awareness of smiling. The second mode, called "Smile Gateway," promotes a user's smile more actively. The system places light limits on certain routine actions performed in daily life, such as opening a door or turning on a TV, until the user's smile is detected.

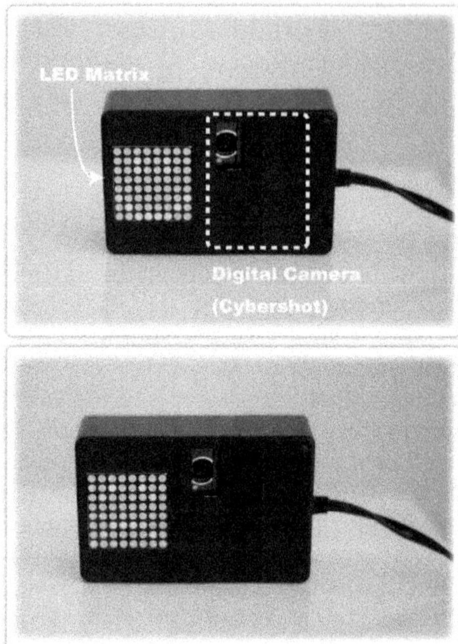

Figure 2. The HappinessCounter Box consists of a digital camera, LED matrix display, and light sensor.

Figure 3. If the user has not recorded many smiles, the system displays a "sad" icon. When the user smiles, the system displays a "smile" icon accompanied by a happy sound. Note that the mirror is half-silvered; the camera attached behind the mirror can see through it for facial recognition.

SMILE AWARENESS

In our proposed system, Smile Awareness mode provides a supportive method that encourages smiles. Positioning the HappinessCounter in a commonly used location, such as a vanity mirror, and combining it with the following applications, leads to a natural and sustained use of the system. This, in turn, will encourage the user to smile regularly.

Sound feedback:

When the system detects a user's smile and displays the smile icon, the system will provide audio feedback in the form of a happy piece of music. This cheerful music, combined with the visual feedback, may make the user feel better and happier. The music player can be set up to play the user's favorite music only when a smile is registered. Encouraging smiling by using sound feedback may cause the user actively to produce more smiles.

Send the smile picture to a digital photo frame:

The system can be connected with other communication tools and automatically send out a picture of the user smiling. When the user tallies enough smiles, the system will take a picture of her smiling face and automatically send it to family members' digital picture frame and/or e-mail. Because the system does not require complex operations, even elderly people living alone who are unfamiliar with a PC can send their pictures to their family just by smiling. The system also enables an elderly person's family to monitor his activity or mental health easily. When a picture is sent, it may prompt other forms of contact, such as a telephone call. Thus, the elderly have an incentive to smile because it will encourage communication with their family members. Young people living apart from their parents may feel that it is a bother to contact them too frequently. At the same time, parents worry about their children and wonder if they are staying healthy. By using this system, children can reassure their parents about their well-being without much hassle, and their parents will feel relieved.

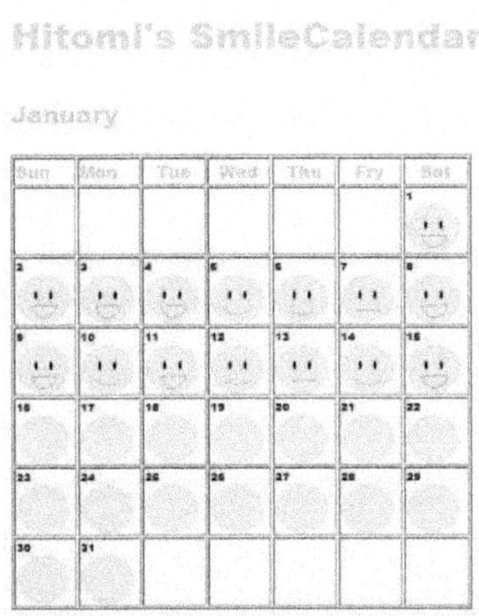

Figure 4. Screen shot of the smile calendar. Users can use their smile icon to keep track of how many times they have smiled.

Display the smile results on a calendar:

After the user's smiles and the number of actual smiles per day are recorded, the results can be displayed on a Web-based calendar application, as seen in Figure 4. The user's smiles are represented with three icons—happy, normal, or unhappy—depending on the number of smiles counted on a particular day. In addition, when the icon is clicked, the user can see the particular smiles recorded that day. By viewing his smile results on the calendar, the user (and potentially his social network) can easily understand how often he smiles, and how he felt on a given day compared to the previous day, week, and/or month. This organized feedback-based trend line may also lead the user to a more positive self-assessment.

Post on SNS (e.g., Twitter):

Connecting the system to an SNS will enhance interaction, and a user can easily share her feelings and emotional state with family or friends. The HappinessCounter system will automatically check the number of smiles for the day/week. For example, the system could automatically post a tweet such as, "Alice laughed 20 times today!" If the user does not have enough smiles recorded for the week, the system could automatically post a tweet such as, "Alice seems to be feeling blue." When family members or friends read such a message, they can call or send a message to the user. When another person provides this sort of encouragement, the user may feel better and be able to smile under conditions in which she could not smile by herself. Furthermore, the user could compare the number of her smiles to that of a friend. Thus, the system may motivate the user to smile more. The system may also lead to a new form of communication through smiles. For example, for elderly people living alone, the ease with which they can share this information with people around them may lead to a reduced burden on all individuals, thus leading to a more effective treatment in which the elderly can ultimately feel more reassured.

Smile Gateway

Smile Gateway mode provides a method in which access to something can be forcibly limited. Depending on the individual or his mental state, he may not positively make smiles under normal situations. Therefore, by creating an inconvenient situation, we believe the system may prompt smiling more effectively. Thus, we focus on the following method.

Disallowing use of a daily appliance or piece of furniture without first smiling:

To create an inconvenient situation, we focused on the appliances and furniture that people use frequently in their daily lives. If there is a shortage of smiles, the system notifies the user by making furniture and other appliances more difficult to use. We assume that the user will smile more positively when provided not only with visual feedback but also with a sense of force. As examples of daily appliances/furniture, we propose a door, refrigerator, cabinet, TV, and electric pot. These are central items in our daily lives, and the system can make them harder to use when there is no smile registered. For example, the system can make it slightly harder to open items such as doors, refrigerators, and cabinets, and it can make it harder to turn on the TV. The system controls them until the user smiles, at which point the system returns them to their normal state (Figure 5). Obviously, the system does not go so far as to make these things completely unusable, as that could actually make the user feel sadder or even angry. In this type of inconvenient situation, when the user can use the desired items smoothly, she feels lucky or happier; conversely, when she cannot use these items easily, she will be made aware of her feelings and the fact that she is not smiling enough on their own.

Several applications, beyond the ones mentioned above, can be connected with the HappinessCounter system. Along these lines, through this research we will try to determine the best method to use to generate as many smiles as possible by determining when rate-limiting and -encouraging applications should be used and what order and frequency the stimuli should be applied.

Figure 5. We combined the HappinessCounter Box with an electric magnet and attached it to the refrigerator door.

Usage Scenario

When this system is utilized, the following scenarios can be envisioned.

Scenario 1: A grandmother living apart from her family. She notices that she has not smiled recently based on the icon displayed on the mirror. When she tries to make a smile, the system automatically detects her smile and sends her smile picture to her family to be displayed on their digital photo frame. When the family sees it, they feel happier because her smile looked good. Afterward, they call her and have a conversation. The grandmother feels happier because she was able to communicate with her grandchild.

Scenario 2: A wife had only a little time due to housework. She was very busy and did not realize she looked cranky. When she tried to open the refrigerator, she could not open it smoothly. At that time, she noticed that she had not smiled. She "woke herself out of her trance" and made a smile. She could then open the refrigerator smoothly. After making a smile, she felt better than before. Minutes later, she met her husband, who had just come home. He said, "Did you have a good day today? You look great." When she heard that, she felt happy.

IMPLEMENTATION

We developed the HappinessCounter system to detect a user's smile in daily life and make it easier for the user to smile regularly. The HappinessCounter system consists of two components—the "Smile Awareness" system and the "Smile Gateway" system, which control an appliance and/or a door using an electric magnet.

Smile Awareness System

We developed the HappinessCounter Box to detect a user's smile and provide visual feedback. We enclosed a digital camera, an LED matrix display, and a light sensor inside the box. We enclosed a Sony Cyber Shot digital camera[1] in the box because it has a built-in smile-recognition engine. In addition, we enclosed an LED matrix display[2] to show the happy or sad icon. This LED matrix is connected to a computer via an Arduino[3].

We used a light sensor to detect when the system takes a picture in real time. Thus, sensors are connected to a computer via a Phidgets Interface Kit[4]. By attaching the sensor behind the camera display, we can monitor the brightness of the display (Figure 6). We put the CyberShot digital camera in the "smile shutter mode," in which the camera automatically takes a picture when a smile is recognized. Thus, we can detect when it takes a picture because the brightness of the camera's display changes significantly after the shutter is pressed, as seen in Figure 6. Using this function, when the system detects a user's smile, the system displays the smile icon on the LED matrix and plays a happy sound.

We also attached a servo motor into the HappinessCounter Box to enable constant use of the "smile shutter mode" (Figure 6). We found that the smile shutter mode timed out automatically over a certain period, and we therefore developed a mechanism to constantly re-enable the mode. For this purpose, the servo motor continually selects the smile shutter mode icon on the camera touch panel. This

---

[1] Sony Cyber-Shot DSC-T99

[2] http://www.sparkfun.com/products/759

[3] http://www.arduino.cc/

[4] http://www.phidgets.com/

servo motor is connected to a computer via an Arduino[5] interface.

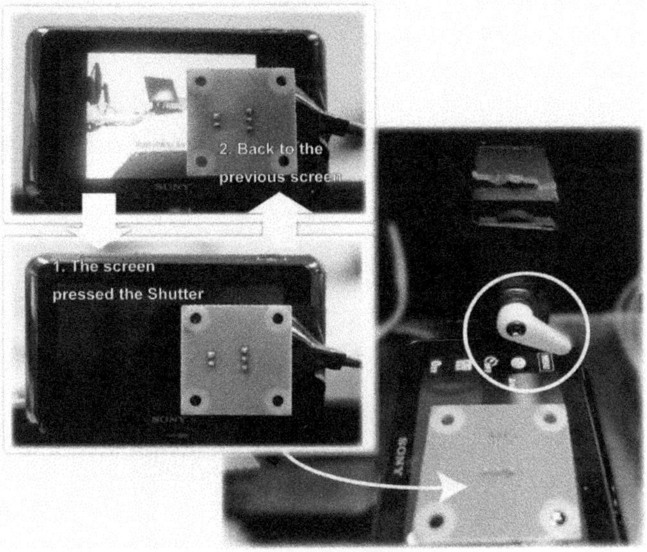

Figure 6. For facial recognition, we attached a light sensor to a camera's monitor screen. When the camera detects a smile and automatically triggers a shutter, the brightness of the monitor screen also changes, and this change can be detected by the light sensor. In addition, we attached a servo motor into the HappinessCounter Box to enable constant use of the "smile shutter mode." The servo motor continually selects the smile shutter mode icon.

Moreover, using an Eye-fi card,[6] the system automatically takes a picture and transmits the image wirelessly to a PC, which is then uploaded to Flickr[7]. The system counts the user's smile for the day. After a certain number at the end of the day, the system uploads these states to a Web server. The system logs the user's smile status while the other applications refer to the state on the Web server.

After recording the user's smile and the number of actual smiles per day, we displayed the result on a Web-based calendar application, as seen in Figure 4. The user's smiles are represented as three icons—happy, normal, or unhappy—depending on the number of smiles recorded on that particular day. We decided that if the number of smiles is more than 10, the icon is happy; if the number of smiles is fewer than five, the icon is unhappy. Anything else is considered normal. In addition, when the icon is clicked, the user can see the particular smile pictures taken that day. These pictures are retrieved from Flickr[8] and displayed on the Web-based page. By viewing his smile results on the calendar, the user can easily understand how often he smiles, and how he felt on a given day compared to the previous day, week, and/or month.

Smile Gateway System

As an example of a method by which we can limit access to something, we developed a system that can control the refrigerator door using an electric magnet. If the user does not have enough smiles, the system makes the refrigerator door harder to open by using an electric magnet to hold down the door. An X10[9] controller is used in this device. The X10 uses the power line as a means of communication and can easily control AC powered devices. Given that the X10 uses the power line as a means of communication, any electrical device within a residence can be conveniently controlled via this method.

Likewise, other devices such as room lights, fans, and air filters can be potentially controlled using this method. The host program monitors the Web server state. By smiling, the user unlocks the refrigerator door, allowing it to be opened smoothly.

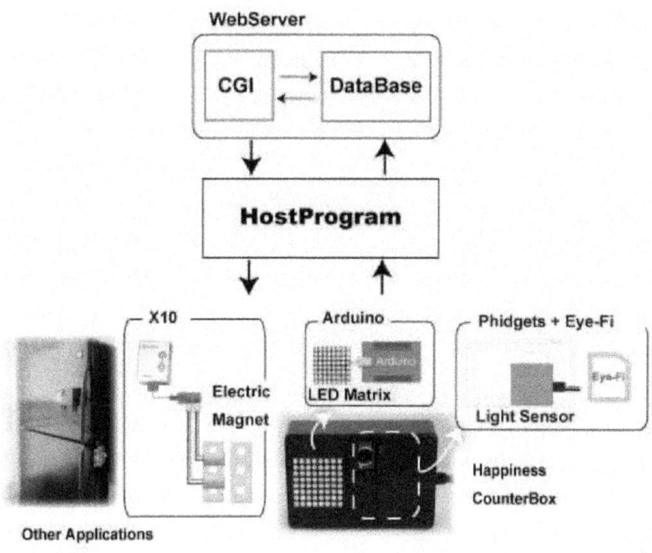

Figure 7. Overview of the HappinessCounter components.

FIELD TEST

To determine the effectiveness of the system, we conducted two field tests, one with a person living alone and the other with a couple living together. Both tests used an application that limited access to a refrigerator. We wanted to know how the system was received and how limiting access would change a user's behavior, whether the subject was a person living alone or a couple living together.

---

[5] http://www.arduino.cc/

[6] http://www.eye.fi/

[7] http://www.flickr.com/

[8] http://www.flickr.com/

[9] http://www.smarthome.com/2000.html POWERLINC SERIAL/TW523

Field Test with a Person Living Alone

To determine the effectiveness of the system in daily life, we conducted the following field test in an actual home during a two-day trial.

The aim of the field test

The aim was to investigate the following:

· How will the system work with a person living alone in daily life?

How the field tests were conducted

We attached the HappinessCounter Box and an electric magnet to a refrigerator door. In this scenario, if the user did not smile at the box, the refrigerator door became somewhat harder to open. It only became possible to open the door normally when the user smiled, at which point he also saw the smile icon and heard the smile chime.

For this field test, we installed the system in a home with one occupant (a participant), a 39-year-old male. He used the system for two days in his home. During this time, the participant used the refrigerator naturally several times a day.

Observations

During the field test, the number of recognized smiles totaled 33, with an average of 16.5 smiles per day in front of the refrigerator door. The participant cooked on both days and used the refrigerator most often in the morning and evening. He was surprised by the number of smiles because he thought he usually did not smile that often (we describe this in detail in the DISCUSSION section).

Field Test with a Couple Living Together

To determine the effectiveness of the system in everyday family life, we conducted the following field test in an actual home during a 10-day trial.

The aim of the field test

The aim was to investigate the following:

· How will the system work with a couple living together in an everyday family setting?

· Did the system prompt other forms of communication?

How the field tests were conducted

The participating family was comprised of two participants, participant A (male, 64 years old) and participant B (female, 62 years old). The participants are rarely at home during the day because they work outside the home.

We attached the HappinessCounter Box and an electric magnet to their refrigerator door (Figure 8). In addition, we installed the smile calendar system so the participants could check how many smiles they made during the day by watching the calendar on the web. We asked the participants to keep a daily journal to provide feedback on the system. We recorded separate detailed system logs of the field test.

Figure 8. We attached the HappinessCounter Box with an electric magnet to the participant's refrigerator door.

During the trial period, we asked the participants to use the refrigerator naturally. The participants mainly used the refrigerator in the morning and night because they usually had breakfast and dinner at home.

Observations

This section presents the findings from the captured log data.

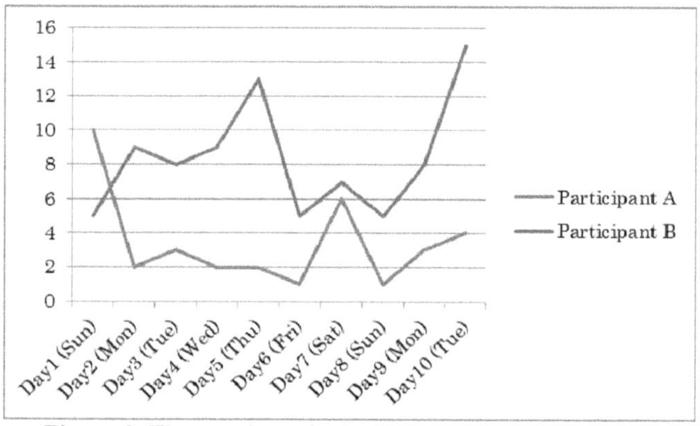

Figure 9. The number of recognized smiles per day and average.

Figure 9 shows the number of recognized smiles per day and the average number per day during the field test period.

As can be seen from the figure, the number of recognized smiles from participants A and B per day did not change dramatically during the field test.

During the field test, there was an average of 3.4 smiles per day for participant A and 8.4 smiles for participant B.

Participant B had a larger number of smiles than participant A. Participant B cooked every day and therefore used the refrigerator more often. Participant A usually used the refrigerator to get drinks such as milk or beer.

On days 1 and 7, the number of smiles by participant A increased more than any other day. On these days, participant A stayed home all day and therefore had more chances to use the refrigerator. In addition, participant A sometimes used the refrigerator intentionally like a game (we describe this in detail in the DISCUSSION section).

On days 6 and 8, the number of both participants' smiles was lower. This was due to the participants eating out and spending a lesser amount of time at home, which meant they did not use the refrigerator as frequently.

Figure 10 shows the participants' pictures taken during the field test. Pictures A and B were taken on day 1. Pictures A' and B' were taken on day 10. As seen in the figure, it looks like both participants initially forced an artificial smile expression. However, by the end of the trial, they made smile expressions naturally (we describe this in detail in the DISCUSSION section).

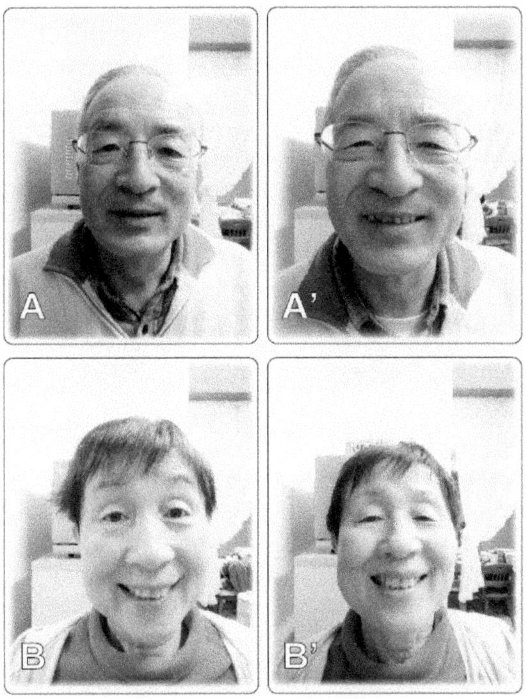

Figure 10. A part of the participants' pictures taken during the field test. Pictures A and B were taken on day 1. Pictures A' and B' were taken on day 10. We found that the participants' smiles became more natural compared with those recorded earlier in the field test. At first, participants smiled by forcing themselves. Eventually, however, they could smile unconsciously.

Discussion

We will discuss the results of the field tests and the method by which they matched the original predictions.

How did the system work for a person who lives alone?

As described in the Observation section, the person living alone was surprised by the number of smiles because he usually did not smile that often. In the interview, the participant mentioned that it was good exercise for his facial expression. He also said the following:

"I tried to make more smiles than usual because I felt happy when I heard the smile sound and saw the smile icon after making a smile."

At first, the participant made a smile as a form of good exercise. Eventually, however, he felt happy by continually trying to make smiles. Although this test was very small in scale and duration, we think the idea of facilitating smiles for a person living alone has potential.

How did the system work for a couple living together?

In the interview, the participants mentioned that they tried to make more smiles than before the field test. When we informed the participants of the number of recognized smiles during the field test, they were a little surprised because they thought they had made more smiles. Participant A, in particular, felt that he had made more smiles than the actual number recorded. For that reason, we considered the possibility (as we will discuss in detail later) that participant A had made smiles in the general vicinity without actually standing in front of the refrigerator. Therefore, although participant A attempted to smile, the system did not recognize his smiles.

In addition, participant B mentioned her change in feelings as follows:

"When I felt a bit down, not in a good mood, or was busy with things to do, I stood up in front of the refrigerator and found myself trying to feel good. I then changed my feeling by making a smile and recovered my presence of mind and could continue cooking." (Participant B)

Participant B also said the refrigerator had become a place to smile.

"Early in the field test, I didn't know how I should smile and therefore made smiles intentionally. However, by making a lot of smiles in front of the refrigerator, I became used to making smiles and learned how I should make a smile. Eventually, when I stood up in front of the refrigerator, I could make smiles naturally. Therefore, I began to associate the refrigerator as a place to feel relieved." (Participant B)

As seen in Figure10, we found that participant B's smiles became more natural compared to those recorded earlier in the field test. At first, participant B made a smile by forcing herself. Eventually, however, she could make smiles unconsciously. Although participant A did not mention it, it is clear that participant A's smiles started looking more natural.

As Kleinke *et al.* [3] mentions, we think the results show that the participants experienced an increase in positive mood when they created positive facial expressions and a decrease when they created negative facial expressions. However, even if the facial expressions were only mimicked, the participants could eventually make smiles naturally.

We believe that the Smile Gateway mode worked well for the participants as it encouraged making smiles and improved their positive mood.

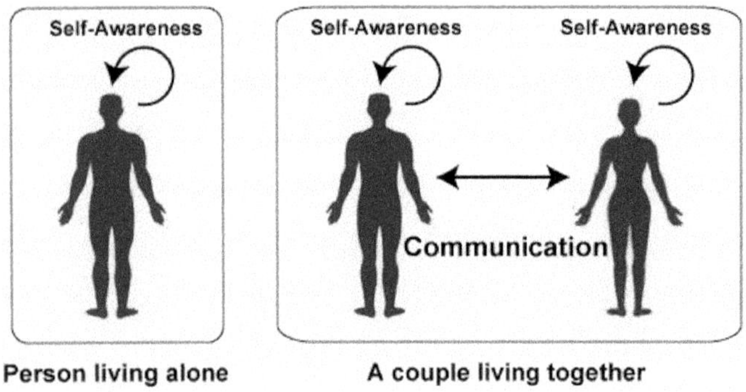

Figure 11. The person living alone made more smiles and thus felt that his mood was improved. For the couple living together, making more smiles prompted communication among family members, thereby increasing their positive mood as well.

Did the system prompt other forms of communication?
The participants' journals indicated that the system led to the start of conversations. Participant A mentioned the following:

"I was happy to hear the smile sound when my wife made smiles and therefore started talking to her." (Participant A)

When participant A was in the living room, he could hear the sound. Although he was not in front of the refrigerator, he felt good and started conversations such as, "What's for dinner?"

Moreover, in the interview, participant B mentioned that at first the system did not recognize her smile at times. When participant B said, "Um, the system doesn't recognize my smile," participant A then came in front of the refrigerator and said, "I can do that instead of you." This led to another conversation. In addition, participant B said:

"When we used the system together we had fun, like a sense of playing a game together."(Participant B)

"I thought my husband had fun with the system like a game. After starting the field test, he came to the refrigerator more often without having anything to do."(Participant B)

In the interview, participant A mentioned he didn't think his behavior changed. However, as pointed out by participant B, the data log (Day 1 and Day 7) displayed in Figure 9 shows that the number of recognized smiles increased. We believe that when the system was used with multiple people, it prompted communication among family members, thereby increasing their positive mood.

Other
In the field test involving the person living alone, sometimes the system took a little longer to recognize the participant's smile, and thus he had to wait before seeing the smile icon and hearing the chime. During these times, he felt a little stressed by this delay. Furthermore, he did not want to give up until his smile was detected. Based on this finding, we need to improve the detecting technology using other tools and/or methods. It is very important that the user's smile be detected immediately.

In the field test involving a couple living together, participant A also mentioned wanting feedback about how he was smiling.

"I want to get feedback about how I am smiling, such as with a mirror, because I don't know what kind of facial expression I am making now."(Participant A)

At times, the system did not recognize the participant's smile even though he thought he made one. He wanted to know what kind of smile was receptive to the system. Depending on the person, we found that there were types of faces that were easily recognized and others that were harder to recognize. Although we developed a system combined with a mirror, the version installed on the refrigerator did not include a mirror. Based upon the results, it may be appropriate to attach a mirror to all systems in order to provide feedback. Moreover, we used the built-in smile-recognition engine from the camera mentioned in this paper. However, in the future we hope to use technologies for detecting smiles in which we can adjust the level of smile detection based on the person.

In the interview, the participants mentioned that the smile calendar was not used very often. In fact, participant B never saw it, because she did not use the computer in everyday life and thus had no chance to see the calendar. In addition, participant A only saw it once or twice. We considered that it might be appropriate to display the smile calendar in the same place as the HappinessCounter Box so that the user can see it without using a PC.

The participants also expressed some concern about privacy issues. Specifically, they were both used to using the refrigerator after taking a bath. Participant A did not wear any clothes on his upper body and worried a little about pictures being taken of him in such situations. However, the participants became less concerned about this issue as time went on. We need to consider such privacy issues and ensure that the system takes pictures of only the user's face.

"Smile Awareness" and "Smile Gateway" mode

In these field tests, we chose a "Smile Gateway" application that limited access by creating an inconvenient situation if the appropriate smiles were not made. As a result, the system had positive effects on the user's mood. However, depending on the user's mental state, the system may not have the desired positive effect. For example, when users are having a bad day, they may not make smiles and the system may lead to the user feeling worse. In this situation, it might be more appropriate to assist the user by, for example, having the refrigerator door open automatically. On the other hand, when the user does not make smiles, the system could make these things completely unusable and make the user feel even angrier. Because there are several approaches, as mentioned above, we need to consider the best method to generate as many smiles as possible by determining when rate-limiting and -encouraging applications should be used, in what order, and what frequency the stimuli should be applied.

POTENTIAL

This system architecture may have potential uses in therapy situations. As previously mentioned, the researcher Strack [11] pointed out that facial expressions affect one's emotions. Some people focus on these theories and describe "smile therapy" to encourage and make smiles in daily life. In addition, some people describe the effects of "laughter yoga," which refers to traditional physical, mental, and spiritual disciplines that originated in India. We believe that making smiles continually in daily life may improve mental health.

This system architecture will also enable us to create various kinds of smile-inducing appliances. The following are some examples of interactions that are connected with existing products based on this architecture.

Built-in HappinessCounter system into a digital photo frame or Chumby-like device:

By attaching a camera to a digital photo frame or Chumby [10] device and installing the HappinessCounter system, a user can easily send smile pictures to the digital picture frames of remote family or friends and/or a remote Chumby device by just making a smile. Users can exchange their daily feeling and may inform others of their health and mental state as determined by the picture of their smile.

Using the camera on a tablet or mobile phone:

By using the existing camera on a tablet or mobile phone, the HappinessCounter system can control access to phone calls or e-mail with a "smile gateway." For example, only the user is required to smile before being allowed to call another person. In addition, when the user does not smile enough, e-mail they send or receive may be delayed. Conversely, when the user smiles a lot, they are allowed to send/receive e-mail normally.

PC-based interaction:

The HappinessCounter system installed on a user's PC will use the PC's Web camera to monitor the number of smiles the user makes while using the computer. If the number of smiles the user makes is below normal or not enough, the system can alert the user or force another action. For example, if the smile count is below normal, applications can become noticeably slower. This type of feedback system is not only useful at home but also within the workplace. For example, the HappinessCounter system can be attached in front of a meeting room of a workplace. When the user makes a smile, that user can then enter the meeting room.

Increasing the number of smiles in the workplace will enhance the atmosphere for everyone. Conversely, if someone is irritated or bothered by something, slowing the system down will allow the user to calm down and reconsider before doing something he might regret later. By making the user smile in this situation, it will help him to overcome whatever made him angry in the first place.

RELATED WORK

There are many research projects related to smile detection [5][17]. We used the built-in smile-recognition engine from the camera mentioned in this paper, but in the future, we will use these technologies, and we believe we can install and combine several applications without a special camera. McDuf *et al.* [7] proposed a system that could measure health indicators just by putting a person in front of a low-cost camera. Relax to Win [6] is a game that measures the player's galvanic skin response and uses the data during the playing of the game. Emotional Flowers [8] also harnesses the player's emotions. Within the game, the player's facial expression or emotion is used to control the growth of a flower. We try to enhance mental happiness by encouraging users to smile in daily life.

EyeCatcher [15] is a system that helps photographers capture a variety of natural-looking facial expressions of subjects by presenting images or videos (e.g., friends or animation characters) on the display attached to the front of the camera. Cheese Cam [4] uses a camera that can induce unconscious facial reactions in a photography subject by displaying a small facial expression icon on its screen. Based on this research, Samsung released a digital camera (DualView TL225) [10]. These studies aimed to make several natural facial expressions when the user takes pictures by using several previously displayed images or icons. We focused on increasing smiles in daily life to increase happiness.

Several researchers have focused on monitoring the activities of the elderly for the benefit of their family. Digital Family Portrait [9] is an electronic picture frame

[10] http://www.chumby.com/

that can display the daily activities of an elderly person who lives far from his/her family. I-pot [18] is an electric pot that sends an e-mail to family members when the power switch is turned on or the water is being poured. Family Planter [1] is a pair of artificial flowerpots with sensors, lights, and actuators that indicate the proximity of people in houses that are located far apart. SocialMedicineBox [14] is a communication system for the elderly that uses a medicine chest and notifies family members of the status of the elderly person taking medicines, as well as sending pictures to the family. These devices use e-mail to inform the family members of an elderly person as to his or her behavior or activity. Our research used the "smile" as a trigger and led to an enhancement of other communication.

CONCLUSION AND FUTURE PLAN

In this paper, we proposed a system called the "HappinessCounter," which facilitates smiling and improves positive mood. After detecting the user's smile, it provides visual and auditory feedback. In addition, the system can be connected to other applications that can prompt the user to make a smile. We conducted two field tests, one with a person living alone and the other with a couple living together. Both tests were conducted in actual homes. In both tests, the system limited access to the refrigerator. Both sets of participants mentioned that they tried to make more smiles than before the field test and thus felt that it improved their mood. In addition, the system prompted communication among the family members, thereby increasing their positive mood as well. Our field test was small in scale, so the participants may have been positively biased toward the system. Nevertheless, our test managed to deliver results, and we hope this will help others to enhance their systems to better support and improve users' feelings and prompt communication among family members.

Currently, we can only detect a user's smile in a specific location. In the future, we would like to detect smiles nonintrusively, automatically, and combine the system with various potential applications.

ACKNOWLEDGMENTS

This work was partially supported by the Ministry of Education, Science, Sports and Culture (MEXT), and by a Grant-in-Aid for Japan Society for the Promotion of Science (JSPS) Fellows.

REFERENCES

1. AItoh, Y., Miyajima, A., and Watanabe, T. "TSUNAGARI" communication: Fostering a feeling of connection between family members. *Ext. Abstracts CHI 2002*, ACM Press (2002), 810-811.
2. James, W. *The Principles of Psychology* (Vol. 2). Dover Publications, New York, USA, (1950).
3. Kleinke, C.L., Peterson, T.R., and Rutledge, T.R. Effects of self-generated facial expressions on mood. *Journal of Personality and Social Psychology*, 74 (1998), 272-279.
4. Lee, B. and Lee, W. Cheese cam: Unconscious interaction between humans and a digital camera. In: *Ext. Abstracts CHI2009*, ACM Press (2009), 4285-4290.
5. Deniz, O., Castrillon, M., Lorenzo, J., Anton, L., and Bueno, G. Smile detection for user interfaces. *In Proceedings of ISVC '08 (2008)*, 602-611.
6. Philips Relax to Win Sensor: http://www.dexigner.com/news/4480
7. Poh, M.Z., McDuff, D.J., and Picard, R.W. Non-contact, automated cardiac pulse measurements using video imaging and blind source separation. *Optics Express*, 18, no. 10 (2010), 10762-10774.
8. Bernhaupt, R., Boldt, A., Mirlacher, T., Wilfinger, D., and Tscheligi, M. Using emotion in games: Emotional flowers. *In Proceedings of the International Conference on Advances in Computer Entertainment Technology (ACE '07)*. ACM, New York (2007), 41-48.
9. Rowan, J. and Mynatt, E.D. Digital family portrait field trial: Support for aging in place. *Ext. Abstracts CHI 2005*, ACM Press (2005), 521-530.
10. Samsung Dualview TL225, http://www.samsung.com/us/tl225 (2009).
11. Strack, F., Martin, L.L., and Stepper, S. Inhibiting and facilitating conditions of the human smile: A nonobtrusive test of the facial feedback hypothesis. *J. Pers. Soc. Psychol.* 54 (1988): 768-777.
12. Tomkins, S. S. *Affect, imagery, consciousness: Vol. 1. The positive affects*. Springer, New York, USA, (1962).
13. Tomkins, S. S. *Affect, imagery, consciousness: Vol. 2. The negative affects*. Springer, New York, USA, (1963).
14. Tsujita, H. and Abowd, D.G. SocialMedicineBox: A communication system for the elderly using medicine box, in *Proceedings of Ubicomp 2010*, 2010, 437-438.
15. Tsukada, K. and Oki, M. EyeCatcher: A digital camera for capturing a variety of natural looking facial expressions in daily snapshots, *Proceedings of Pervasive 2010*, Springer LNCS 6030 (2010), 112-129.
16. U.S. Census Bureau. America's Families and Living Arrangements (2007).
17. Tian, Y.-L., Kanade, T., and Cohn, J. Facial expression analysis, in *Handbook of face recognition*, S. L. and Jain, A., ed. Springer, October (2003).
18. Zojirushi i-pot http://www.mimamori.net/

How to Nudge *In Situ*: Designing Lambent Devices to Deliver Salient Information in Supermarkets

Vaiva Kalnikaitė[1], Yvonne Rogers[1], Jon Bird[1], Nicolas Villar[2], Khaled Bachour[1], Stephen Payne[3], Peter M. Todd[4], Johannes Schöning[5], Antonio Krüger[5], Stefan Kreitmayer[1]

Pervasive Interaction Lab[1], Open University, Milton Keynes, UK
vaiva@interactables.com, {y.rogers, j.bird, k.bachour, s.kreitmayer}@open.ac.uk

Microsoft Research[2]
Cambridge, UK
nvillar@microsoft.com

University of Bath[3]
Bath, UK
s.j.payne@bath.ac.uk

Indiana University[4]
Bloomington, USA
pmtodd@indiana.edu

DFKI GmbH[5]
Saarbrücken, Germany
{schoening, krueger}@dfki.de

ABSTRACT
There are a number of mobile shopping aids and recommender systems available, but none can be easily used for a weekly shop at a local supermarket. We present a minimal, mobile and fully functional lambent display that clips onto any shopping trolley handle, intended to nudge people when choosing what to buy. It provides salient information about the food miles for various scanned food items represented by varying lengths of lit LEDs on the handle and a changing emoticon comparing the average miles of all the products in the trolley against a social norm. When evaluated *in situ,* the lambent handle display nudged people to choose products with fewer food miles than the items they selected using their ordinary shopping strategies. People also felt guilty when the average mileage of the contents of their entire shopping trolley was above the social norm. The findings are discussed in terms of how to provide different kinds of product information that people care about, using simple lambent displays.

Author Keywords
Decision-making, in-the-wild study, persuasive technology, tangible embedded interaction, mobile devices, nudging

ACM Classification Keywords
H5.2. Information interfaces and presentation (e.g., HCI): User Interfaces – user-centered design, evaluation /methodology, prototyping.

General Terms
Design, Experimentation, Human Factors

INTRODUCTION
Increasingly, we are being told about the costs and benefits of food choices. Consumer surveys also indicate that shoppers are taking heed, wanting to know more about the global consequences of their consumer decisions [28]. In response, a flood of information is becoming available in a variety of forms: online, on food labels, in information leaflets and books, and now appearing as smartphone apps, aimed at informing the consumer so that better decisions can be made while shopping. But all this information risks overwhelming the shopper trying to navigate a complex store environment in a hurry, possibly leading to the opposite outcome – poor decisions made without the proper input. How can product information be consolidated, pruned down, and presented to supermarket shoppers in an easy-to-understand and meaningful form that will actually help them make better choices on the basis of values they care about? How might UbiComp technologies be designed to provide this?

We are interested in how everyday decisions can be nudged using simple technologies that are *lambent* (that is, those that have lights that flicker gently over a surface).

Figure 1. Shopper making a decision with respect to the origin and organic properties of a product by scanning the barcode on a block of cheese in her right hand while holding an alternative brand in her left

The goal is to provide just enough salient information about certain product properties to help shoppers make more informed purchasing decisions in supermarkets. Our aim is to develop a mobile, easy-to-use display that can convey relevant information that is difficult to find on a label *in situ* when doing a weekly shop in a supermarket. In the research presented here, we chose to display information about food miles (i.e. how far the food product has travelled to arrive at the supermarket) as well as information on whether or not the product is organic.

Our approach starts from the perspective of ecological rationality, which explains how people make reasonable decisions given the constraints of limited time, information and computational resources that characterize most real-world situations [20, 23]. Research shows that many decisions are made using „fast and frugal' heuristics – short-cut strategies where people simply ignore most available information and focus on the highly useful and prominent information, processing it quickly. Example strategies used for *in situ* decision tasks include: making choices on the basis of what is recognized [3]; looking for options until one finds one that is „good enough' [24]; and choice heuristics that seek as little information as possible to determine which option should be selected [12]. Often people make a decision based on a single reason as this strategy is quick and simple and avoids having to weigh up trade-offs between multiple and potentially conflicting options [6]. For example, in a supermarket shoppers tend to make snap judgments based on just a few salient cues (low price, recognized brand and attractive packaging) and they rarely take time to read product information labels [25].

Taking this real-world behavior into account, we developed a novel lambent display that provides product information in a brief, highly salient and „glanceable' form. Our design approach was born out of the need for an embedded device that is mobile, self-contained and easy to use in a supermarket. For this we built a fully functional independent device that clips on to a shopping handle and comprises a small display, a series of LEDs that are connected to an embedded barcode reader and other electronics (Figure 1). When a shopper scans a product, relevant information is displayed together with feedback that shows how the averaged aggregate of the entire shopping trolley compares to a social norm. An in-the-wild study was conducted to evaluate how shoppers used the lambent display to inform their selection of food items. We describe here the design process used in developing the lambent handle and our study findings.

RELATED WORK

Ubiquitous computing approaches for augmenting the shopping experience are abundant. They range from simple applications available on popular smart phone platforms to full-fledged hardware setups integrated into supermarket trolleys. On the mobile side, several apps currently exist that enable shoppers to scan product RFID tags or barcodes on enabled mobile devices and receive information, reviews and recommendations, such as the Mobile Sales Assistant [14], Mobile Prosumer [15], APriori [16], GoodGuide [4], Google Shopper [5] and RedLaser [13]. These applications provide the user with star ratings and price comparisons as the primary decision making inputs. While it is sometimes helpful to receive such information when one is making a purchase decision, at other times it can be overwhelming to be exposed to this flood of often contradictory advice from other consumers. The iGrocer [18] takes this approach a step further and provides the user with personalised recommendations based on the user's own predefined health concerns. It is particularly suited for elderly users and those with critical health requirements such as allergies.

Other apps have been designed based around shopping lists. Nurmi et al. [11] developed a system that maps shopping lists written in natural language with actual products in a grocery store. They developed the system using nine months of shopping basket data from a large Finnish supermarket. A prototype for creating shopping lists using multiple input devices such as desktops, smart phones, and landline phones in multimodal formats such as text, audio, still images, video, and annotated media was introduced by Jain et al. [7]. Wu et al. designed a new architecture enabling efficient integration between mobile phone applications and web services to implement a mobile shopping assistant [27].

Recently, hardware-based shopping assistants have also begun appearing. The IRL SmartCart [9] is a fully implemented augmented shopping trolley that assists the user by facilitating navigation and making it easier to find the products they are looking for. The Context-Aware Shopping Trolley [1] assists a user in finding the products on their shopping list. All products in close proximity to the user's shopping cart are highlighted on a map and the shopping list gets automatically reordered so that the nearest products are at the top of the list. If the user is near to an item on their shopping list, they get an acoustic signal as a notification.

These systems provide users with interactive information meant to guide them to the products they want and aid them in making their decisions. A different approach to augmenting the shopping experience is to provide users with information meant to nudge them towards making a decision they would have not otherwise have made. For this type of augmentation, detailed displays of information that require complex user interaction may be ineffective in real-world settings, as users would likely ignore them. Systems that hope to *change*, rather than facilitate, a user's behaviour are thus more likely to succeed when they provide a very simple mechanism for interaction and display a very limited amount of information that targets specific desired behaviour and is difficult to ignore.

An example of such a system is the iCart [10], an augmented handle bar built into a shopping trolley that provides simplified nutritional information to the user about the products they put into their shopping cart. The iCart aggregates nutritional properties of each product and tells the user which of three health categories it falls into. It was implemented using a Wizard of Oz technique, and an evaluation of the device showed that by providing simple recommendations at the right moments, users were susceptible to changing their decisions.

Recommendations aim to change behaviour by influencing what people consciously think about. Nudging is an alternative behavioural change technique which works by altering the context in which people act. Recommendations stimulate conscious reflection, whereas nudges typically influence the automatic brain system and operate unconsciously [22]. A number of other systems have been developed to nudge people towards behaving in a particular way in contexts other than the supermarket. Rogers et al. [17] showed how an ambient display using a combination of a kinetic sculpture and twinkling LEDs can push people to take the stairs rather than use an elevator when moving between floors in an office building. Other examples target energy consumption [19] and physical exercise habits [2].

THE LAMBENT SHOPPING HANDLE

We begin by describing the motivation for and design of our clip-on lambent shopping trolley device. Then we describe details of an *in situ* user evaluation that took place in one of the main supermarket chains in the UK.

Handle Design

The lambent shopping handle is a tangible mobile shopping device that has been designed for *in situ* use within the supermarket environment. Figure 1 shows how the device directly clips onto any supermarket shopping trolley. In contrast to the iCart [10], the lambent shopping display makes salient information which is difficult or impossible to determine from a product's label, such as food miles or whether it is organic. Furthermore, it uses simple and subtle nudging effects, rather than providing recommendations, to influence consumer behaviour: i) providing a few pieces of salient information about a product's properties; ii) showing how the average food miles of all the selected items in the shopping trolley relates to a norm. Thus, nudging in this context means providing additional information in a low-cost way, naturally embedded in the decision task, so as to influence behaviour in that task.

The design focus was to create a fully functional device in a self-contained portable shell which could easily be used in a supermarket. In essence, the device is a digital shopping trolley handle. It is designed to clip onto any shopping trolley and display information while still functioning as a graspable handle. The limited space required us to develop a compact design. We chose to build the trolley handle using .NET Gadgeteer – a modular hardware platform. This platform is based on a small but powerful embedded processing unit to which a number of electronic modules can easily be connected. Modules provide additional capabilities for input, output, power, display, sensing and actuation. They can be connected and disconnected using a standardized interconnection mechanism, making the hardware very flexible. We programmed the hardware using the high-level C# object-oriented language.

In large part, the lambent device was built with the hardware modules pictured in Figure 2: the *Battery* is connected to the *Power* module, which can be used to recharge the battery through a *USB connector*, and provides a mechanism to program the device from a PC; the *LED* module can be programmed to display a set colour, or to fade between different colours; the *Button* is used to provide a way for the user to indicate that a previously scanned product has been removed from the basket; the *Barcode Scanner* is used to scan in product barcodes; the *Mainboard* provides core processing functionality; the *SD Card* stores and references the product database; the *Ultrasonic Sensor* activates the *Barcode Scanner* when objects are within range; the *Display* module provides a 128x128 pixel resolution graphical TFT display.

All these modules are standard components of .NET Gadgeteer, except for the Barcode Scanner. For this prototype we adopted an off-the-shelf OPR-3201 laser barcode scanner, which we adapted to work as a custom module. The scanner communicates with the Mainboard through a USB interface, appearing to the Mainboard as a USB keyboard. An additional digital output on the Mainboard is connected to the scanner as a control signal to start and stop the barcode scanning process.

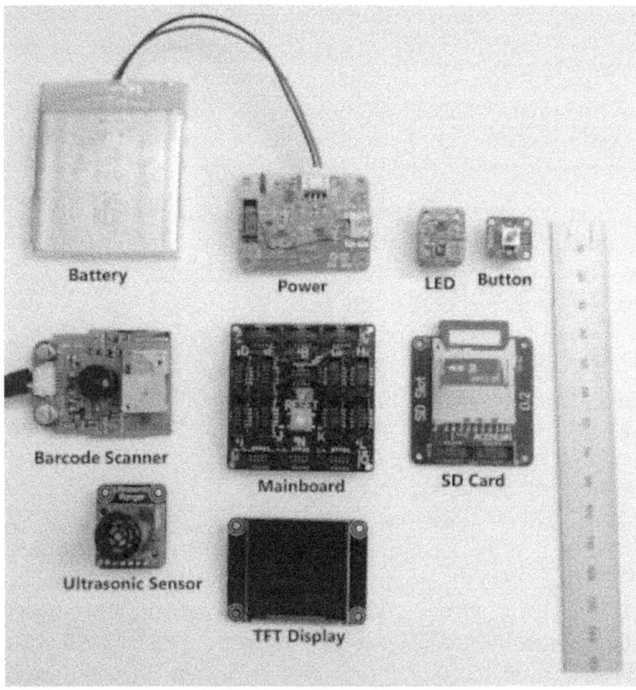

Figure 2. .NET Gadgeteer components and bespoke barcode scanner hardware used in the lambent handle

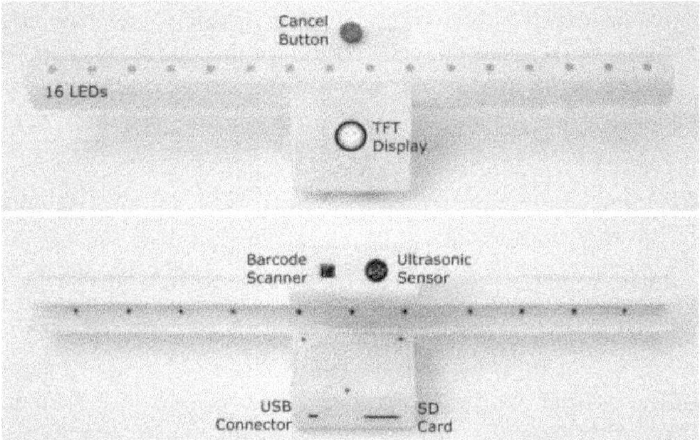

Figure 3. Clip-on lambent shopping handle shell 3D-printed in high definition with embedded electronics: interaction model (top), hardware modules visible (bottom)

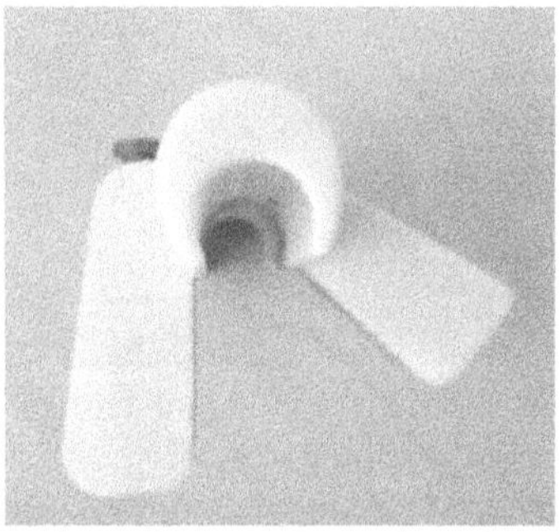

Figure 4. A side view of the lambent shopping device showing how it clips on standard supermarket trolleys

The assembled system contains 16 of the LED modules configured as shown in Figure 3. The LED modules can be daisy-chained in series and individually addressed. In our prototype, the LED chain is used as a simple one-dimensional display providing user feedback. The prototype is fully functional and was designed to clip onto an ordinary supermarket trolley handle (see Figure 4).

Handle Interaction Model and Design Rationale

We chose to use the lambent device in our first *in situ* study to display information about a product's food miles (how far a product travelled to the store) as well as whether or not it is organic. The rationale for this choice derives from a pilot study we carried out to help us understand how people shop [8]. Eleven participants (25 to 60 years of age, 4 female, 7 male) took part in this pilot study where we observed people carrying out their weekly shop. These participants reported that price was the most important factor in their decisions, but the majority also reported a concern with the origin and organic properties of products. They described the origin in terms of three categories: local, not far (often from countries in Europe) and far away (countries that were outside Europe). We applied this classification to our lambent device design. In addition to displaying an individual product's mileage using the LEDs, we also displayed an iconic representation of how the average mileage of all the products in the trolley compares to a predetermined social norm.

The lambent device was thus programmed to provide information about four product properties:

1. *Individual Product Mileage* – represented as a number of orange or green LEDs (see dimension 3 below) momentarily fading in from left to right whenever a product is scanned. The first five LEDs represented local products; the next five indicated that the product came from somewhere within Europe, and the rightmost five indicated that the product travelled from further parts of the world, e.g., South America or the Far East. The precise number of LEDs corresponded to an approximate mileage between the UK and the country of origin; for example, France would have six lights whereas Spain would have eight (see Figure 5).
2. *Average Trolley Mileage* – represented as a number of orange LEDs statically lit up from left to right in-between the product scans. The lambent handle continuously calculated and displayed the average mileage of all the products scanned and added to the trolley (see Figure 5). (The *Cancel Button* was pushed when the user wanted to remove the last scanned item from the trolley – see Figure 3, top.)
3. *Organic* – indicated by green LEDs lighting up for the product's *Individual Product Mileage,* with orange LEDs used for non-organic products (Figure 5, bottom).
4. *Social Norm* – indicated by an emoticon corresponding to the relation between a social norm and the *Average Trolley Mileage*. We pre-programmed this to fit the study scenarios described below: There are 3 modes – happy, neutral and sad – and by default, at the start of the study all participants began with the happy emoticon. If the average trolley mileage reached 10 LEDs, the social norm display would show an emoticon of a neutral face, while if there were 13 lit LEDs, the emoticon display would become a sad face. The participants were thus encouraged by the emoticon display to maintain an average mileage that corresponded to nine LEDs or less (see Figure 6).

The rationale for using LEDs as a way to show distance rather than using another representation such as whole numbers is because we believe shoppers can understand the mapping from LEDs to distance better than other displays. People are already overloaded with information and having another number to look at would not be so effective. The traffic light product goodness measure displayed by supermarkets on food labels has not yet proven successful either.

We constructed a database that contained all the product varieties in our shopping lists, described below. We used an off-the-shelf barcode scanner to scan in product barcodes. In total we scanned in 113 barcodes of products in our chosen supermarket and then used the supermarket website to generate annotations for individual products detailing its food miles and whether it was organic.

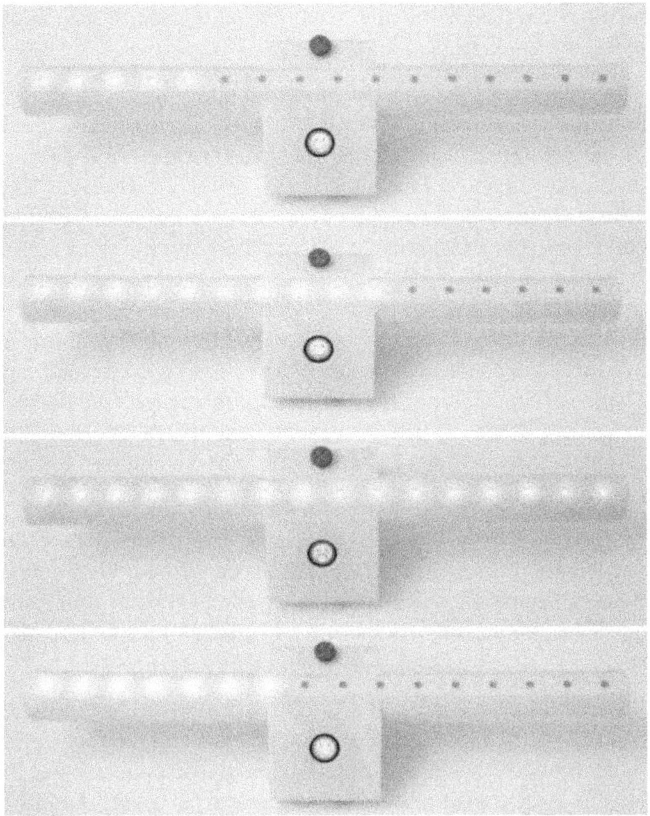

Figure 5. The LEDs light up from left to right to indicate product mileage (origin), in green when the product is organic or in orange if not. From top to bottom: local (UK), not far (European), far away (rest of the world), organic European

EVALUATION

We asked 18 people to go shopping in a large local supermarket from a well-known UK chain. We observed how they shopped and how they made decisions *in situ*. Each participant was asked to shop in two different ways: (i) using an ordinary shopping trolley; and (ii) using the same shopping trolley with our clip-on lambent device. We compared the two conditions to see whether using the lambent device nudged people into buying different products than when they used an ordinary shopping trolley.

The specific research questions we aimed to address were as follows:

- Do people use the lambent shopping handle when it is available to help them make decisions?
- Does the lambent display nudge shoppers towards more environmentally friendly product choices or do shoppers continue to choose the products they habitually buy?
- If the lambent device does change consumer behaviour, is the nudge a result of the social norm, the salience of the product information or a combination of the two?

Participants

Eighteen participants took part (8 female and 10 male, aged 23 to 65 years). Participants were recruited via a public notice board and came from a wide variety of backgrounds: librarians, catering staff, lecturers, researchers and other professionals. None of the participants had any prior experience of using the lambent device. Participants received a £10 gift card on completion of the experiment.

Procedure

We conducted a semi-controlled within-subjects study in a large 7000m^2 supermarket in the UK. In the nudge condition participants shopped using the lambent shopping handle. In the control condition participants shopped using an ordinary unmodified shopping trolley. Each participant completed two shopping trips, one in each condition, with the order of conditions counterbalanced across the participants.

We generated two average-length shopping lists (12 items each) as shown below. When selecting items for the shopping lists, we tried to pick products that varied in their food miles and organic properties. For each product on our shopping lists, there were at least two choices for origin, for example, local (UK) and close (European) or local (UK) and very far (rest of the World). However, we also had a few products where the country of origin was less important, such as Brie cheese where all the alternatives came from France.

Since the participants were not shopping for themselves, we created a short scenario to go with each shopping list to give a context and purpose to their shopping trip:

Scenario 1: *"You have some friends coming over to stay for the weekend who run a website promoting an environmentally aware and organic lifestyle. They are very particular about what they eat. You have offered to stock your fridge and pantry with food for them during their stay and they have mentioned that they would like the following things. Please make your decisions as you normally would when shopping, but consider the needs of your guests."*

Your shopping list is as follows:

1. *Sparkling water (1 bottle up to 2L)*
2. *Cranberry cordial (1 bottle)*

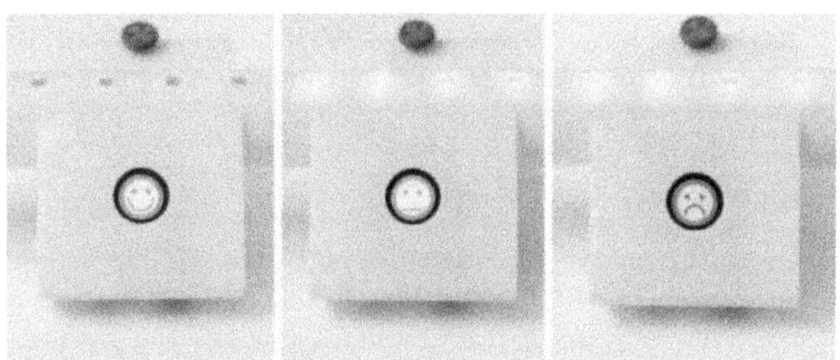

Figure 6. The TFT screen displays an emoticon showing how the participant's choice behaviour compares to the social norm. Left to right: below norm level, at norm, above norm

3. *Yeast extract (spread – 1 jar)*
4. *Maple syrup (1 bottle)*
5. *Anchovy fillets in olive oil (1 small jar)*
6. *Brie cheese (1 piece)*
7. *Full fat spreadable soft cheese (1 tub)*
8. *Demerara sugar (1 bag)*
9. *Canned prunes (1 jar)*
10. *Cucumber (1 piece)*
11. *Chillies (1 bag)*
12. *Dark chocolate (1 bar)*

Scenario 2: *"You have an older relative coming over to stay with you for a few days. She is a member of the Green Party and always shops for organic food. You have offered to stock your fridge and pantry with food for her during her stay and she has told you that she would like the following things. Please make your decisions as you normally would when shopping bearing in mind your relative's interests."*

Your shopping list is as follows:

1. *Still water (1 bottle up to 2L)*
2. *Fresh cranberry juice (1 carton)*
3. *Clear honey in a 340g or smaller jar*
4. *Chocolate spread with hazelnut (1 tub)*
5. *Tuna in spring water (1 can)*
6. *Fresh Mozzarella (1 piece)*
7. *Unsalted butter (1 cube)*
8. *Crunchy peanut butter (1 jar)*
9. *Pears (1 bag)*
10. *Spring onions (1 bunch)*
11. *Mushrooms (1 box)*
12. *Chocolate Ice Cream (500ml tub)*

Each participant used both shopping lists, one in each condition. The lists and conditions were counterbalanced so that half the participants used the one list for the nudge condition, and the other half used that list for the control condition. The participants found the scenarios to be quite realistic and some could even think of a real friend or a relative who fit these descriptions quite closely. Some participants even went further than we expected in the role designated for them in the scenario saying, *"I don't want the guests to see that I bought them the cheapest bottled water"* when asked why they went for a branded product. In addition users were asked to consider their own shopping habits and how much they would be prepared to compromise for their guests. For example, one participant said, *"I don't buy unsalted butter usually, so since I'm buying for a guest, I'm getting the cheapest because I don't know how much I'm gonna use."*

Prior to the study, we asked the participants 20 questions based on the Food Choice Questionnaire [21], including some that focused on their attitudes towards buying local and organic products.

After a quick demo and a 5-minute hands-on tutorial on how to use the lambent shopping handle, participants had no problem following the scenarios and shopping lists or using the lambent device.

We recognize that locally grown food is not necessarily „greener'. For example, growing food in less than ideal local conditions can sometimes result in more carbon emissions than importing food. [29]. However, CO2 emissions are not yet included on UK product labels, and to carry out this evaluation study we had to choose product information that is currently displayed on product labels. Importantly, the lambent device is not restricted to displaying information about food miles and whether a product is organic; it is a far more general system and can display one piece of ordinal product information (the degree to which it has a property) and one piece of nominal product information (whether or not it has a certain property).

In total, we conducted 36 shopping trips, two with each participant, and each trip lasted between 20 and 50 minutes. The participants were not required to check out and purchase their items, which were instead returned to the shelves at the end of each shopping trip.

We captured audio, images, and occasionally video, in both conditions. We automatically logged all interactions with the lambent device and noted what participants chose to buy in both conditions. However, due to a combination of human and software error, the control condition product choices made by one participant were not recorded and could not be recovered. In addition, given the *in situ* nature of the study, real world conditions caused some data collection problems such as certain types of products being sold out during some shopping trips. However, the majority of products chosen by participants were successfully logged, which was sufficient for our analysis.

RESULTS

We were interested to see whether people would use the lambent shopping device to help them make decisions or would continue with their usual shopping practices, which could involve reading the label or purchasing items they have purchased before. Contrary to our original expectations, we observed some differences in participant consumer behaviour when they used the device. In particular, when participants were given the lambent shopping handle, for every two items they chose to scan and place in their trolley, they also scanned at least one additional item on average to make sure it did not have lower mileage (people made about 1.5 scans per each product they chose to purchase). The reason often given was that users were unable to spot the product origin on the label: *"I wouldn't know just by reading the label how far it has travelled."* Based on what they discovered with the lambent shopping handle, they sometimes changed their mind (*"I changed my mind about the Lurpak butter"*) and chose more local.

Participants whose experimental sequence involved completing the nudge condition first and then following it with the control condition had an interesting reflex effect, whereby they leaned towards their trolleys trying to scan the product only to discover that the lambent shopping handle was no longer clipped onto their trolley. After this discovery, we expected most participants would simply read the label to find the information that the trolley would have shown. However, to our surprise, they tended not to rely on the label, instead choosing products by price, taste or brand recognition, and ignoring food mile information.

In order to run more reliable quantitative analysis on our data we dropped the data for those products that had been compromised. For example, products where at least one product alternative was frequently sold out, thus limiting participant choice, and products for which there was a large number of missing data due to other sources of error. In total we removed six products, three from each scenario. These were: cranberry cordial; cucumbers; prunes; chocolate ice cream; mozzarella cheese; and spring onions.

Decision Making *In Situ*

We initially compared the average food miles for each of the 16 products across the two conditions. One item, still water, had the same average food miles in both conditions, but all other products showed a difference. A binomial test showed that 13 products had significantly lower mean mileage in the lambent device condition (p=0.05) than in the control condition (Table 1). Thus with most products there was a significant nudge effect to select items with lower food miles when using the lambent shopping handle compared to the control condition.

Products	*Mean food miles (using lambent device) max = 16*	*Mean food miles (control - normal trolley) max = 16*
Anchovies	10.4	12.4
Sugar	5.9	14.1
Butter	3.4	7.5
Cranberry Juice	4.5	10.8
Honey	5.9	12.3
Brie cheese	10.6	10.5
Soft cheese	11.0	11.1
Dark chocolate	12.0	10.6
Sparkling water	5.3	6.0
Still water	4.3	4.3
Chocolate spread	5.0	5.8
Peanut butter	9.3	10.0
Mushrooms	5.0	9.1
Pears	12.3	13.5
Tuna	15.6	15.5
Chillies	15.0	15.2
Maple syrup	6.9	5.4
Yeast extract	3.4	3.9

Table 1. Differences in mean food miles for each product in the two conditions – measured in terms of the number of LEDs lit up on the lambent device

The largest differences between the conditions were for products where there was a bimodal choice of food miles. For example, the type of sugar that users were asked to pick was harvested either in New Zealand or in the UK – there were no mid-range alternatives that originated in Europe. Similarly for cranberry juice, there was a choice of local produce or North American.

Two products that displayed similarly diverse mileage ranges but displayed no significant nudge effect in user choice were maple syrup and yeast extract. From our observations, we noted that participants usually had strong opinions about these products: *"[Picked the largest jar of Marmite brand yeast extract on the shelf]...it has got to be Marmite, because it has the right taste and I love it! I tried Vegemite [the alternative brand] when I was in Australia, but it has a strange aftertaste...and I picked the largest jar because this is the one I normally buy."* Similarly with maple syrup, people who liked it or had used it before picked the authentic Canadian brand over the local British one: *"I only buy this for Pancake Day, but I always get the proper [Canadian] one."*

Products where there was only a small difference in food miles between available choices displayed no significant differences between the two conditions in the average food miles of the chosen items. However, we did observe participants making item choices on the basis of a difference of only a few LEDs. For example, soft cheese from France (6 LEDs) and Germany (7 LEDs) only had a difference of 1 LED on the display and participants tended to choose the item with fewer LEDs, unless a large difference in price was seen.

We did not observe any significant difference in the choice of fruit and vegetables between the two conditions. This could be because their origin was often clearly marked on the front of the packaging, unlike for other products where origin information was typically written in small print, if at all, and often on the back of the item.

Nudge Effect

The nudge at individual product level was more prominent in situations where labelling on the origin of the product was more discreet, in small print or absent. With the lambent shopping handle we made this often discreet information more prominent and salient, creating a nudge effect whereby people were making more informed decisions based on the very simple ambient display. As one participant noted: *"Products that light up too much make me think twice"*.

Most food mileage decisions were made at the level of how many "lights lit up". Participants either scanned alternative products if they thought there were too many lights or they were simply curious about mileage for other similar products. Often people would choose the products with fewer lights and then consider other factors such as organic properties, the price and the overall quality and appearance of the product: *"Picked cranberry juice because it is close and half the price."* and *"Picked the local mushrooms which were not much more expensive."*

We found no nudge effect for organic products based on LED colour (see Table 2). There was a significant effect for honey but in the opposite direction: People bought organic honey less often in the nudge condition. This is due to the fact that the only organic honey available came either from Mexico or from New Zealand. Since organic products are much more prominently labelled as organic, participants in both conditions found it very easy to find organic honey. In the nudge condition, once participants scanned in organic honey, they discovered that it came from far away, and this is when many of them opted for non-organic but local honey instead. Indeed, it was rare that a participant would use the lambent shopping handle to determine if a product was organic or not. One participant highlighted this by saying that: *"Lights for organic weren't very useful."*

In Situ Appropriation

All the participants were happy using the lambent shopping handle. Some particularly liked it and thought it would be useful for their own weekly shop: *"This is ideal for my age [64 female]: it helped not to have to look at the tiny print on the labels. The [lambent shopping handle] also influences my decisions, and I discovered a few new things that I didn't know before, e.g. about British butter."* Others commented on how the lambent shopping handle influenced their shopping behaviour: *"I took the trolley with me into the aisles to scan which I don't normally do."* But people also noted that the device increased the time it took them to select products on the shopping list because they were scanning and checking more items than they normally would: *"... [the lambent shopping handle] slowed me down a bit. I scanned more things."* Overall, the trolley did seem to have an effect on how people shopped and felt about their product choices: *"I did feel really bad sometimes - when the trolley showed high distance."*

The lambent device was less useful for the few participants who always read product labels when shopping: *"I was not using the trolley to get information. I was looking at the distance on the label rather than the trolley."* Participants' choices were also influenced by other properties such as recyclable packaging: *"I chose these spring onions because they were not packaged"* and *"...these mushrooms were in a recyclable box."*

Products	% Organic (nudge)	% Organic (control)
Honey	12.5	75
Dark chocolate	50.0	90.0
Peanut butter	85.7	100
Mushrooms	71.4	28.6
Pears	25.0	50.0

Table 2. User choices for organic products where available

Other participants were very specific in the brands they chose, and so ignored the lambent device and suggested changes to the shopping list. For example, asked to buy chocolate ice cream, one participant said: *"They don't have Haagen-Dazs chocolate ice cream. I'd rather get another flavour in Haagen-Dazs than chocolate ice cream of another brand."* Price was the predominant factor affecting participants' product choices. Our participants were well versed in looking for bargains and offers and were familiar with the way that this particular supermarket chain displayed price information: "*[Chocolate spread] I chose the closest that looks greener. It's also on offer which is what got my attention."* But despite the influence of all these different factors, people seemed to be able to prioritize and objectively assess what was important to them and how much they were prepared to compromise for their guests in our scenarios: *"Got the local cucumber over organic"* or *"Scanned mushrooms and picked the local which was not much more expensive."* or *"Peanut butter: more expensive but organic."* On the other hand, when no other criterion exists for the decision, people would simply pick the produce with the fewest food miles: *"I don't know the brands, and neither is organic, so I followed the recommendation of the [trolley]."*

Social Norm Influence

The two shopping scenarios emphasised that the guests for whom the participants were shopping were environmentally aware. We configured the lambent device to display how the average food miles of the contents of participants' shopping trolleys related to the guests values, that is, the social norm was relatively low average food miles. We anticipated that if the average trolley food miles were above the social norm, and the participants saw a sad face on the display, then this might lead to them exchanging some of the items in their trolley.

Participants tended to be above the food mile norm at the beginning of their shopping trips, particularly when they began by scanning in high mileage items such as chillies (all of which came from Africa). When they were not below the food miles norm, participants tended to scan in and check the mileage on more products. The emoticons did have an effect on the participants' mood as they continued to shop from that point on: *"The smiley face made me happy and the sad face bothered me"*. Participants did not like the norm feedback when they did not feel that they could change it by selecting different items: *"...it was not useful when there was no choice – it just made me feel bad."*

All participants completed their shopping trips with below average food miles (indicated by smiley icons), and in general they were *"pleased to see that [they were] below the average."*

Usability

Initially, we anticipated that people might have difficulties with the handle interaction, in particular having to rescan the items again before they could remove them from their shopping trolleys. However, there did not seem to be any usability issues with this, except that sometimes people forgot which products they have scanned in and which they no longer needed, and thus had to rescan items that were not in the trolley only to remove them again with the „Cancel' button.

There was one usability issue related to the „Cancel' button that emerged: occasionally, when participants were leaning over their handle to place their items into the trolley, this button was accidentally pressed, removing the last scanned item. This is easily addressable by moving the „Cancel' button to another location on our lambent shopping handle.

DISCUSSION AND CONCLUSIONS

Overall, we found that the lambent shopping handle generated a significant nudge effect, influencing what products people selected. When using the device, 72% of the products had lower mean food mileage than the products chosen when using a normal shopping trolley.

Most nudging seemed to occur instantly as soon as people scanned in the product and glanced at the number of lights that lit up across the surface of the shopping handle. In addition, participants frequently had interesting and strong emotional reactions to the emoticon feedback comparing the social norm to the averaged aggregate of their trolley mileage. On occasions where the social norm was neutral or negative, they were nudged whereby they tried to scan in and check mileage on alternative product choices. Contrary to our expectations we observed no nudging effect for the organic property of products, but this could be because organic products are clearly marked on the label. So there is less need for this information to be made more salient.

Interestingly, while product food miles had a significant effect on consumer decisions, other everyday factors continued to have an influence on the choices participants made. There were frequent trade-offs between choosing an organic product or a non-organic low food miles alternative, as well as between low food miles items and lower priced high mileage items. If items were on special offer, people calculated the trade-off of those, too, for example, choosing a larger jar of Marmite over a smaller more expensive one (in terms of price per unit volume).

The use of cell phones to augment shopping experiences has not been as successful. Commercial applications such as Google Shopper [5], GoodGuide [4] and RedLaser [13] are not useful for supermarket shopping [8]. However, these applications may be more effective when shoppers are looking to immediately purchase a relatively expensive item, such as a DVD player, and they are prepared to spend several minutes getting comparative price data and general reviews. In this situation the demands on a person's attention and the requirement for holding the phone in one of their hands is perfectly acceptable. However, this is not the case when supermarket shopping where decisions are made rapidly and people often use both hands for picking and comparing different products [26]. Barcode scanning using mobile phone cameras is also slower than with purpose built barcode scanners and this could be a further reason why mobile shopping applications have not really been effective.

Product labels do provide some useful information but a number of factors limit their usefulness for shoppers. First, label information is often not salient enough to enable shoppers to make quick purchase decisions. Second, product labels do not provide information on some product properties, for example, CO2 emissions or food miles. Third, reading every product label is both time-consuming and tedious. For these reasons, shoppers typically make their purchases based on price, brand or packaging. As we have explored here, augmented shopping trolleys that push the right information to the user at the appropriate time could be a better solution for improving immersed user shopping experiences and providing a gentle nudge towards better decisions. Issues of information representation (e.g., bars of LEDs versus pie charts or numbers) and aggregation of data (one product at a time, or the whole cart at once?) need further exploration.

Our future work will focus on understanding not only effective information representation, but also what information in supermarkets would help inform shoppers and nudge them towards the right choices, while also allowing them to decide what these right choices are. This could include individual preferences related to food allergies or other health concerns. Factors such as seasonality, fat, salt content and cost would also be considered. The food mileage that we focused on here for reasons of availability does not necessarily reflect what people care most about; for instance, locally grown food does not necessarily mean a ‚greener' choice, especially when it comes to carbon emissions [29]. As more and more information becomes available about carbon footprints of products, studies like ours are needed to determine just how this information can be conveyed to shoppers in ways that influence them without overwhelming them.

In sum, our study has shown that once the information people care about is salient enough, people are generally very good at making the right decisions for themselves – they do not want to see yet another recommender system. What is key in nudging shopping decisions is balancing information frugality and simplicity with enough feedback to enable people to change their choices in a way that they find rewarding and motivating.

ACKNOWLEDGMENTS

The research is partially funded by the EPSRC grant "CHANGE: Engendering Change in People's Everyday Habits Using Ubiquitous Computing Technologies" (number XC/09/043/YR). We would like to thank all our participants and ASDA supermarket. We would also like to thank Charlie Snelling and other colleagues in the Design School at the OU for helping out with the 3D printing of the lambent device.

REFERENCES

1. Black, D. Clemmensen, N.J. and Skov, M.B. Supporting the supermarket shopping experience through a context-aware shopping trolley. In *Proc. of the 21st Annual Conference of the Australian Computer-Human Interaction Special Interest Group,* ACM Press (2009), 33-40.
2. Consolvo, S., Klasnja, P., McDonald, D. W., Avrahami, D., Froehlich, J., LeGrand, L., Libby, R., Mosher, K. and Landay, J. Flowers or a robot army?: Encouraging awareness and activity with personal, mobile displays. In *Proc. of UbiComp'08*, ACM Press (2008), 54-63.
3. Goldstein, D.G. and Gigerenzer, G. Models of ecological rationality: the recognition heuristic. *Psychological Review,* 109, (2002), 75-90.
4. Goodman, J., Brewster, S. and Gray, P. Using field experiments to evaluate mobile guides. In Schmidt-Belz, B. and Cheverst, K., editors, *Proc. of HCI in Mobile Guides, workshop at Mobile HCI 2004,* Glasgow, UK: Springer (2004), 38-48.
5. Google Shopper (retrieved on 17th Feb 2011): http://www.google.com/mobile/shopper/
6. Iyengar, S. *The Art of Choosing*. Twelve, 2010.
7. Jain, J., Ghosh, R. and Dekhil, M. Multimodal shopping lists. In *Proc. HCI '09*, Berlin, Heidelberg, Springer-Verlag (2009), 39-47.
8. Kalnikaitė, V. Bird, J. and Rogers, Y. Decision-making in the aisles: insights from field studies for the design of mobile shopping devices (under review).
9. Kahl, G., Spassova, L., Schöning, J., Gehring, S. and Krüger, A. IRL SmartCart - a user-adaptive context-aware interface for shopping assistance. In *Proc. of IUI'11,* ACM Press (2011), 359-362.
10. Kallehave, O., Skov, M. B., Tiainen, and N. Persuasion in-situ: shopping for healthy food in supermarkets. In *Proc. PINC 2011 Workshop at CHI* (2011).
11. Nurmi, P., Lagerspetz, E., Buntine, W., Floréen, P. and Kukkonen, S J. Product retrieval for grocery stores. In In *Proc. SIGIR '08,* ACM press (2008), 781-782.
12. Payne, J. W., Bettman, J. R. and Johnson, E. J. The Adaptive Decision Maker. Cambridge University Press, Cambridge, UK, 1993.
13. RedLaser, http://redlaser.com/ (retrieved 17th Feb 2011)
14. Resatsch, F., Karpischek, S., Sandner, U. and Hamacher, S. Mobile sales assistant: NFC for tetailers. In *Proc. of Mobile HCI'07,* ACM Press (2007), 313 – 316.
15. Resatsch, F., Sandner, U., Leimeister, J. M. and Krcmar, H. Do point of sale RFID-based information services make a difference? Analyzing consumer perceptions for designing smart product information services in retail business. *Electronic Markets* 18(3), (2008), 216-231.
16. Reischach, F., Guinard, D., Michahelles, F. and Fleisch, E. A mobile product recommendation system interacting with tagged products. In *Proc. PerCom'09* (2009), 1-6.
17. Rogers, Y., Hazlewood, W., Marshall, P., Dalton, N. S., Hertrich, S. Ambient influence: can twinkly lights lure and abstract representations trigger behavioural change? In *Proc. Ubicomp'10*, (2010), 261-270.
18. Shekar, S., Nair, P. and Helal, A. iGrocer: a ubiquitous and pervasive smart grocery shopping system. In *Proc. of* SAC '03, ACM Press (2003), 645-652.
19. Shultz, W., Nolan, J., Cialdini, R., Goldstein, N. and Griskevicius, V. The constructive, destructive and reconstructive power of social norms. *Psychological Science,* 18, (2007), 429-437.
20. Simon, H.A. Invariants of human behaviour. *Annual Review of Psychology,* 41, (1990), 1-19.
21. Steptoe, A., Pollard, T.M. and Wardle, J. The development of a measure of the motives underlying the selection of food: the food choice questionnaire. *Appetite*, 25 (1995), 267-284.
22. Thaler, R.H. and Sunstein, C.R. Nudge: improving decisions about health wealth and happiness. Penguin (Non-fiction), 2009.
23. Todd, P.M. and Gigerenzer, G. Environments that make us smart: ecological rationality. *Current Directions in Psychological Science,* 16(3), (2007), 167-171.
24. Todd, P.M. and Miller, G.F. From pride and prejudice to persuasion: satisficing in mate search. In: Gigerenzer, G., Todd, P.M. and the ABC Research Group (eds.), Simple Heuristics That Make Us Smart. Oxford University Press (1999), 287-308.
25. Todd, P.M. How much information do we need? *European Journal of Operational Research,* 177, (2007), 1317-1332.
26. Underhill, P. Why we buy: the science of shopping. Simon and Schuster: New York, 2009.
27. Wu, H. and Natchetoi, Y. Mobile shopping assistant: integration of mobile applications and web services. In *Proc. WWW '07,* ACM Press, (2007), 1257-1260.
28. EDS IDG Shopping report 2007: shopping choices: attraction or distraction? http://www.eds.com/industries/cir/downloads/EDSIDG Report_aw_final.pdf
29. Sustainability of local food. (retrieved on 4th July 2011) http://melbourneurbanist.wordpress.com/2010/07/11/is-local-food-more-sustainable/

CoDine: An Interactive Multi-sensory System for Remote Dining

Jun Wei[1,3], Xuan Wang[1,3], Roshan Lalintha Peiris[1,3], Yongsoon Choi[2], Xavier Roman Martinez[1], Remi Tache[1], Jeffrey Tzu Kwan Valino Koh[1,3], Veronica Halupka[2], Adrian David Cheok[1,2,3]

[1]Keio-NUS CUTE Center
IDM Institute
National University of Singapore

[2]Keio-NUS CUTE Center
Keio University
Yokohama-city
Japan

[3]NUS Graduate School for Integrative Sciences and Engineering
Singapore

{weijun,wangxuan,roshan,goodsoon96}@mixedrealitylab.org
{xroman,remitache,jeffrey,veronica,adriancheok}@mixedrealitylab.org

ABSTRACT
The pervasiveness of computing has extended into domestic realms, including the dining room. Beyond simply a place to consume food, the dining room is a social hub where family members meet and share experiences. Yet busy lifestyles can make it difficult to spend social time with your family. To provide a new solution for family bonding, this paper presents the CoDine system, a dining table embedded with interactive subsystems that augment and transport the experience of communal family dining to create a sense of coexistence among remote family members. CoDine connects people in different locations through shared dining activities: gesture-based screen interaction, mutual food serving, ambient pictures on an animated tablecloth, and the transportation of edible messages. Rather than focusing on functionality or efficiency, CoDine aims to provide people with an engaging interactive dining experience through enriched multi-sensory communication.

Author Keywords
kitchen, co-dining, interactive media, tangible interface, multisensory, family communication, co-presence.

ACM Classification Keywords
H.5.2 Information interfaces and presentation (e.g., HCI): User Interfaces, Prototyping, User-centered design.
H.5.3 Group and Organization Interfaces: Synchronous interaction, Web-based interaction.

General Terms
Design, Experimentation, Human Factors.

INTRODUCTION
Our world is increasingly populated with a profusion of digital devices designed to assist and automate more human tasks and activities. In addition, the physical world is being increasingly digitally instrumented and strewn with embedded sensor-based and control devices [30]. The kitchen and dining room, places for family cooking and dining, have been a target environment of many ubiquitous computing prototypes that investigate the use of technologies in real-world situations. Previous research to bring technology into the domestic realm has focused on improved efficiency and automation [6, 14, 15].

While technology has arguably made everyday life more convenient, human relationships are going through a transformation as lifestyles are becoming more complex and busier than ever before. The speedy pace of modern life has decreased the opportunities for families to have meals together, especially dual-income families and those who live away from their grandparents. A recent survey showed that families want to eat dinner together, but lack the time or resources to achieve their desires [29]. For at least the past three decades, the ideal in the United States and Western Europe has been for family members to come together for the evening dinner [20]. Unfortunately, advances in technology are dragging people into the digital lifestyle, full of virtual communication, but lacking a sense of warmth and intimacy.

Food, cooking, and kitchens are often associated with an important set of experiences in Western, as well as non-Western cultures [7]. Dinnertime is often a special moment in family life. For many, dinner around the table is a time to reaffirm cultural and familial identity, values, and ideals [29]. Many of us have the memory of eating, talking and laughing when dining together with parents and grandparents. As Rae-Espinoza observed, "The family that eats together stays together" [25].

The social importance of dinnertime inspires our vision: reconnecting family through a computerized dining environment that enhances co-presence, which we call co-dining.

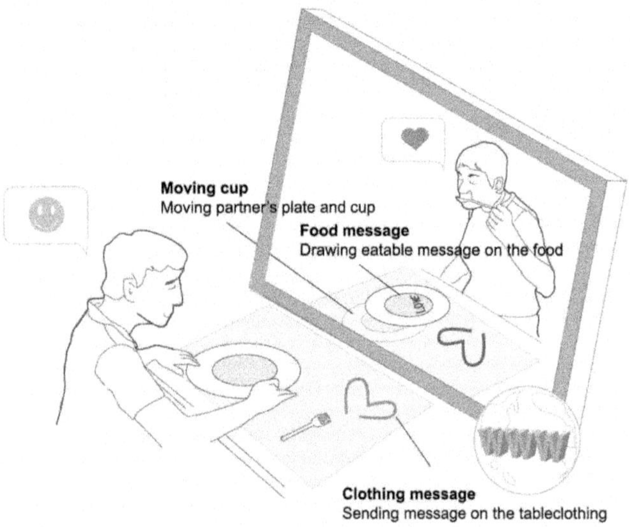

Figure 1. CoDine system scenario.

While families have a strong desire to connect with their loved ones over distance, most communication technologies, like phone and email, fail to provide the same feelings of connectedness that one feels when physically with family members [16]. As an exploration of new modalities to reconnect, the CoDine system is inspired by design research with family members who lived apart, but desired to maintain a close sense of emotional connection. Through a connected dining table, together with expressive and physical interaction, CoDine engages people in shared dining activities and physically embodied affection, to create a sense of intimacy and co-presence between distant family members.

The contribution of this work is the development of the CoDine system, as an extended approach for family eating and socializing. CoDine integrates: (1) an Interaction Screen that enables gesture-based control and interaction in front of the dining table; (2) a Hosting Table that can move the partner's dishes remotely to serve food, showing respect and care; (3) an Ambient Tablecloth that displays animated message on fabric, expressing love and warmth physically; and (4) Food Teleportation to transmit digital messages and self-designed gifts by reproducing them using edible food materials at the remote location. CoDine aims to support a range of mealtime interactions for remote families. Through these mediated communicative activities during mealtime, people can engage in a variety of interactions including creating, sharing and transmitting personalized messages visually or physically through food.

Figure 1 is a conceptual illustration of the co-dining scenario. In this scenario, two persons are enjoying dinner together although physically apart. Using the CoDine system, they can interact through the tangible dinnerware, together with the edible food, to achieve the feeling of a shared dining experience. With integrated sensing and computation, the CoDine system allows one table surface to reflect and respond to the dining activity at a distant location, supporting video conferencing, gesture interaction, food serving, fabric display sharing, and food gifting to facilitate the natural and affective communication between two connected households.

In the rest of the paper, we first describe related projects on intelligent and interactive kitchens to show existing research has not focused on interactive dining. Next, we explain the design approach we applied when designing the system. We then provide a comprehensive description of the system configuration, followed by detailed description of the functionalities for each module, and their integrated application into the whole system. Finally, we conclude by discussing future work on designing interactive media to facilitate effective communication and emotional sharing, taking the advantage of technology embedded in everyday environments.

RELATED WORK

A growing number of domestic, digital and intelligent appliances are appearing, due to the advancement in ubiquitous computing and smart devices. Currently most research has focused on various aspects of the "smart kitchen", for instance to obtain increased functionality, efficiency and security. In parallel, a sizeable body of research has emerged regarding computer-aided systems for interactive cooking, mainly based on numerous displays, webcams, speakers, and sensors [15].

Smart Kitchen

The "smart kitchen" is embedded within the smart house and typically presupposes a digital lifestyle, with the purpose of automating the services and obtaining increased safety and security, comfort, communication and technical management [7].

A number of academic research institutions have been developing robotic and assistive services in the kitchen environment. In the Assistive Kitchen project, researchers developed a service robot that operates autonomously in a sensor-equipped kitchen. The system supports and assists people in their household chores through physical action and monitors health at the same time, using cognitive technical systems [6, 26]. Similarly, the Intelligent Kitchen project uses a human activity recognition system to infer the next action based on previously observed human behaviours. This system also includes an LCD touch panel to display a recipe with pictures and a mobile robot to suggest the next action using voice and gestures [18, 19].

In the U-kitchen system, smart devices communicate with each other and share the context via a kitchen server, including RFID tags in appliances so the system can identify appliances being used, and ubiquitous services which help the user with the grocery management, cooking and give healthy dining advice [4]. The Ambient Kitchen integrates data projectors, cameras, RFID tags and readers, object mounted accelerometers, and under-floor pressure sensing, to construct a supportive environment for food planning, preparation and cooking [21]. Cooking Navi [14], another cooking assistant, aims to help an inexperienced user to cook without failure.

Augmented Reality Kitchen implemented multimedia projections to enrich a conventional kitchen by projecting intuitive displays to reveal the status of tools and surfaces, concentrating on creating interfaces that inform activity without interfering with tasks [17]. Also, researchers have developed nutrition-aware cooking, a kitchen that intelligently senses cooking activities and provides real-time nutritional information to help facilitate healthy cooking [9].

All of this previous research primarily focuses on smart facilities and assistive appliances. While these projects represent one approach to integrating technology into kitchens, we feel this perspective ignores the social element of cooking and dining that could be supported through technology.

Interactive Cooking and Dining

Ubiquitous computing has also been applied to interactive cooking as a social event. The Kitchen Stories project developed a new digital kitchen appliance which allows a user to record, annotate and play back cooking sessions, to make the cooking process explicitly recordable and shareable [31]. The "Kitchen of the Future" is a computer-augmented kitchen environment with embedded video cameras, displays, microphones, switches, sensors and network, to assist the self-recording and replaying of the cooking process, as well as storing interactive multimedia content to provide cooking guidance for others to achieve an enjoyable cooking experience [28]. The Semantic Cookbook [27], automatically captures, and annotates making a recipe using sensors, cameras, and networked kitchen appliances. The captured cooking session can be shared with others.

While some research has focused on dining, remote co-dining, our scenario of interest, has not been explored to the same extent. For example, DinnerWare [11], explored the eating as a medium for computation and aesthetic expression using a dining service electronically equipped to react to the properties of food. Gamelunch [24], a sonically augmented dining table, mapped the usual dining actions like cutting and slicing onto physically-based sound synthesis. Specifically for family dining, the e-Care dining table is designed as an interactive and educational tool for family leisure and educational activity [10]. CU-Later, another communication system that connects two remote dining tables, records and transmits the remote video after a time shift, to allow people to share their conversation while eating despite time difference [32]. However, none of these systems enable the synchronous sharing of dining experience through connected dining table and dining activities.

In contrast, our approach to enable the co-dining experience through physical dining interactions differentiates CoDine from other existing intelligent cooking and dining-based interactive systems. The goal of this research was not to increase the quantity and quality of kitchen-unit activity or event awareness, but rather to support relationship-building activities and extend them to distant dining situations. With CoDine we want to support family bonding, communication, and social togetherness during family dining with remote participants.

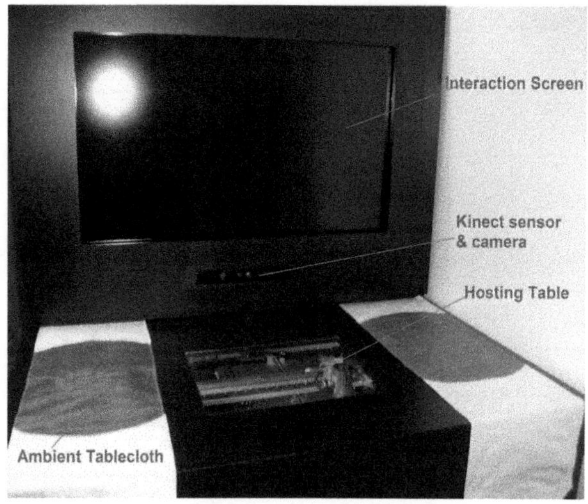

Figure 2. Prototype of CoDine system in dining room.

DESIGN FOCUS: EXPERIENCE SHARING

Technologies for connecting distant family members have typically involved information exchanges and purposeful messaging systems, rather than experience sharing. With the onset of affordable digital media and information and communication devices, communication takes many forms. In face to face situations people are able to use their full range of expression: language, expressions, gestures, and interaction with the artefacts and space. On the contrary, mediated communication has to rely on a more limited range text, sound, image, and video alone or in any combination [5], when face-to-face is not available.

In our system, we concentrate on mediated co-presence, which means "social togetherness" for remote partners [13] during dining. To support co-dining, we were inspired by the concept of co-experience, which is driven by social needs of communication and maintaining relationships. Co-experience takes place as experiences are created together, or shared with others [12].

Interactive technology can play a large role in supporting co-experience, by providing mediated communication channels and the possibility of shared physical activities. This can lead to an increase in feelings of connectedness by providing availability awareness and opportunities for sharing everyday life [8]. In the specific context of family dining, our approach was to better understand what people usually do while dining together from our experience, and extend those activities into remote, but synchronous situations. Moreover, rather than depending heavily on the digital format like video and audio, we believe that interaction with the physical environment can be an important aspect for enriched and multi-sensory communication, which might contribute to the feeling of co-presence.

Based on these principles, we designed a dynamic and interactive environment that draws on and learns from the rich cultural routines of family dinner, and above all, focuses on the human experience. We brainstormed several social activ-

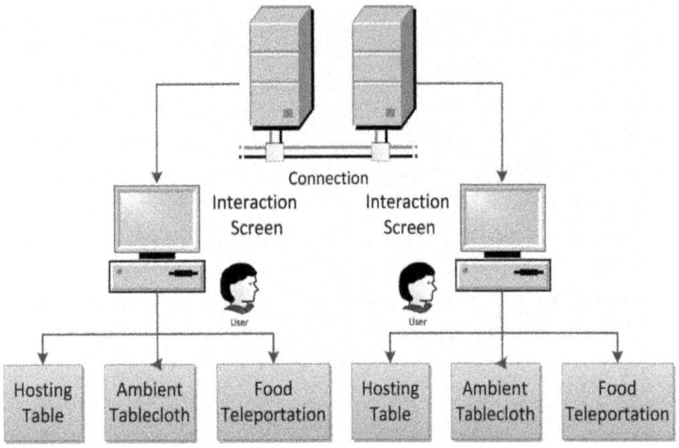

Figure 3. System configuration of CoDine system.

Figure 4. Gesture Interaction with screen to choose icons.

Subset module	Icon	Scenario Functionality	System Action in remote location
Hosting Table		Serving soup	Bowl with soup moves automatically to user
		Serving rice	Bowl with rice moves automatically to user
		Serving Pickles	Bowl with pickles moves automatically to user
Ambient Tablecloth		Expressing Love	Animated heart shape appears on tablecloth
		Expressing Happiness	Animated smiling face appears on tablecloth
		Expressing excitement	Animated exclamation mark appears on tablecloth
Food Teleportation		Sending food message	Food-made message "LOVE" printed on toast

Figure 5. Dining activities the user can select.

ities around the dining table to facilitate synchronous interactions, as shown in Figure 1. Beyond video conferencing, we included activities like serving food, expressing emotions, sending messages, and integrated them into the CoDine system in a tangible and shared manner. By augmenting the dining table, tablecloth and dinnerware with computerized devices, we model the multi-sensory dining experience with embodied extensions of communication, supporting the enhanced sense of engagement and co-existence. Figure 2 shows the actual set up of the CoDine system.

CODINE SYSTEM CONFIGURATION

As explained in Figure 3, the CoDine system consists of four modules. The Interaction Screen, embedded with Microsoft Kinect sensor [1] and camera, works as the hub of the system, enabling the real-time interaction between the remote users. The three activity modules, the Hosting Table, Ambient Tablecloth and Food Teleportation module, are connected with and controlled by the Interaction Screen wirelessly through Bluetooth. When people are dining at the table, their images, together with the dining table surface, are displayed on the screen to achieve normal video conferencing. To initiate any remote physical interaction, people move their hands to choose icons on the screen. Figure 4 shows the gesture interaction with the screen to choose different icons and Figure 5 shows the list of possible dining activities. CoDine tracks the user's hand movement and transmits the icon chosen across the internet to the paired table at the remote location. This triggers the corresponding module of the system on the other side to serve food, to display pattern on tablecloth, or create edible food. Compared with pure video and audio communication, this system provides a wider range for affective expression and interaction. It is through these shared physical messages and social activities that people engage themselves into the shared dining experience, in a reciprocal fashion.

CODINE SYSTEM DESCRIPTION AND IMPLEMENTATION

In this section, we will go through the detailed design and implementation of each module, and explain how they integrate together to achieve the co-presence dining experience.

Hosting Table

One of the shared dining activities in the CoDine system is serving dishes using the Hosting Table module. In many Asian cultures, serving food is considered as an important aspect of the dining etiquette, to show respect, love and intimacy to family members and guests as well. Before the dinner starts, the younger people show their respect and gratitude to the elderly by offering a choice morsel from their bowls. This tradition has been part of everyday activities in our culture, something that we regularly and unconsciously engage in. However, fewer and fewer of the younger generation are aware of this practice as a result of the decreased opportunity for them to dine together with their parents or grandparents. Using this Hosting Table, we aim to bring back the rituals and routines of family dining, even when people are unable to share the same dining table.

To support remote food serving, we designed a remote moving mechanism and embedded it into the normal dining table. The mechanism applies the basic principle of magnetic attraction, combined with two-axis linear movement. Permanent magnets are attached on the bottom of the dishes, including bowls and plates. By controlling the movement of electro-magnet component underneath, we can control the movement of dinnerware on the table. We chose to use magnets because they are simple to implement, easy to control,

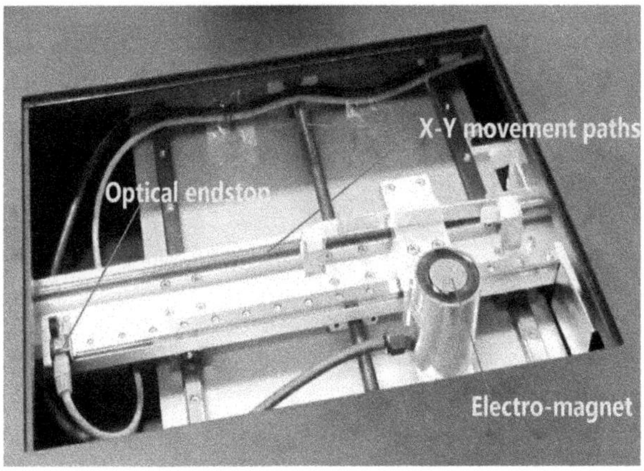

Figure 6. Mechanism of Hosting Table.

and require no wires. When the master controller receives the activation signal, the motors and magnets are activated accordingly to execute the remote moving of dishes on the table surface.

The structure under the table is essentially an electromagnet component installed on an x-y plotter structure (Figure 6). Both axes have two optical limit switches for safety reasons, also for initial position recognition. The movements of motors, activation of electromagnets and wireless communication with the screen are controlled by an 8-bit microcontroller from the master board, embedded with a Bluetooth module.

The Hosting Table, installed as part of the dining table, is integrated with visual interface through Bluetooth protocol, achieving a user-friendly interactive experience based on gesture. For the prototype, it is designed to serve three different dishes. At the beginning, three bowls with different food are put along the farther side of the table, and the electro-magnet in its initial position. When user on the other side selects one of the dish icons from the screen, let's say, serving the rice dish on their partner's table, the electro-magnet will move directly to the position of that dish, activate the magnet, and drag the rice smoothly towards the user on the table surface. Figure 7 shows the actual dish serving after the user selected the serving rice icon.

In the current implementation, the electromagnet component attached to the Hosting Table is designed to move smoothly in x-y dimensions, with a range of 300mm and 400mm respectively. For the purpose of dishes serving, the speed and smoothness of movement are key factors to simulate the natural feeling. Many experiments were conducted on different surfaces, matched with the suitable magnet force and moving speed. A glass surface was finally used to reduce the friction and avoid wiggling effect. To keep the balance between the speed and the natural sense, we set the speed to 16mm/sec in both x and y dimensions, which means that the dish can be served to the user in about 15 seconds.

Compared to interacting in a virtual environment, we be-

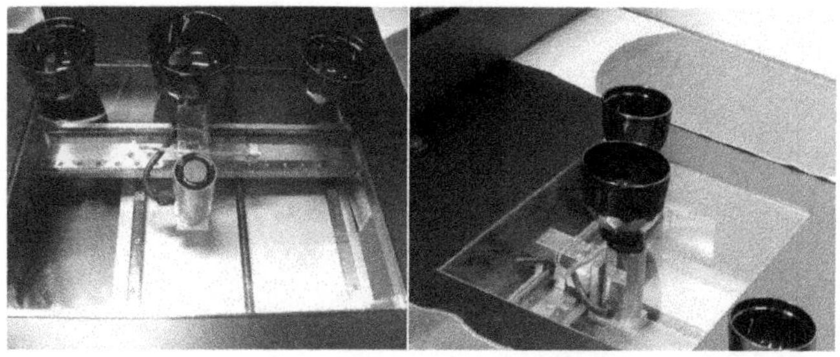

Figure 7. Actual result of hosting table: serving dishes remotely.

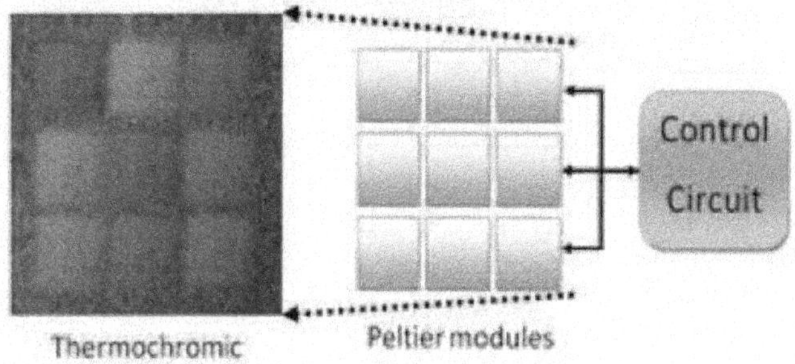

Figure 8. Basic mechanism for the fabric display.

lieve these physical movements of plates or cups physically on dining table convey more delicate human emotions and stronger feeling of warmth, which contributes to the enhanced sense of co-presence when user take the served dish from their remote dining partner, even though they do not share the same physical dining table.

Ambient Tablecloth

The Ambient Tablecloth extends the remote co-dining experience to another component of the dining table, the tablecloth. By introducing the dynamically colour-changing and interactive tablecloth, CoDine further enhances the communication experience around the dining table.

The tablecloth is implemented to display various slow-rate animations through controlled colour changing on fabric. The special-designed tablecloth is placed on top of the dining table, to display different patterns triggered by the messages from the interaction process. We use a non-emissive display technology that can display images on the fabric, while avoiding the effect of unnatural displays on the tabletop.

To achieve this functionality, we are currently using thermo chromic inks combined with Peltier semiconductor elements [22]. The basic structure is depicted in Figure 8. Our tablecloth combines Peltier semiconductor modules and thermo chromic leuco dye ink technologies using a closed loop control system, employing a PI (proportional, integral) controller in order to accurately control the colour. As thermo chromic inks are thermally actuated to change colour, we chose the Peltier semiconductor modules due to its rapid thermal actuation capabilities within a wide range of temperatures. The current inks actuate at 32 degrees (colourless) and regain the original colour of brown at 24 degrees. In addition, Peltier

Figure 9. Matrix arrangement of Peltiers for the tablecloth display.

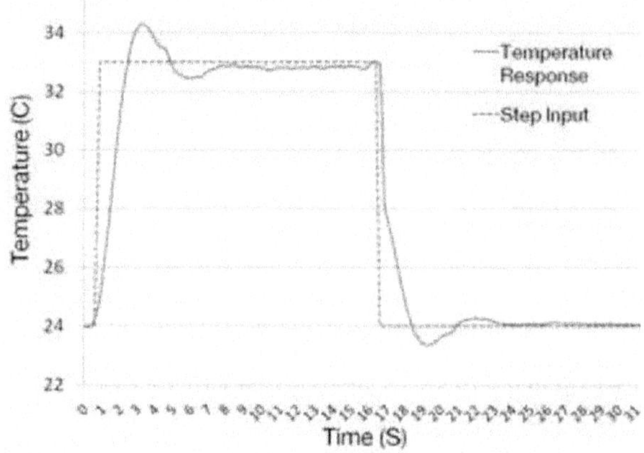

Figure 10. Transient response of one Peltier element.

elements can reverse their function from heating to cooling or vice versa by reversing the polarity of the supply voltage. This allows both heating and cooling of the fabric (a screen printed with thermo chromic ink) dynamically, to achieve a subtle and fast animation effect. This is an advantage compared to most current technologies using thermo chromic inks which only include a heating function. Without a cooling function, cooling must be done naturally, slowing down the bi-directional colour change process and preventing the bi-directional animations of the fabric possible with our approach.

In the current implementation, a pixel display mechanism is applied to achieve accurate display of various patterns. As shown in Figure 9, 60 Peltier modules (1.5cmx1.5cm each) are arranged in a 6x10 pixel display pattern, and the whole display is 20cmx12cm. Fifteen control circuits with each circuit individually controlling four Peltiers are connected to a master controller using I2C protocol. Each controller uses a single microcontroller with the internal oscillator running at 8MHz. Four PWM (Pulse-width modulation) signals are generated using internal timer interrupts at 100Hz. The duty cycle of each PWM signal is controlled by the PID control (proportional, integral, derivative) module implemented in the microcontroller with the four temperature feedbacks. In this way each of the four Peltiers is accurately controlled for temperature using a single controller circuit. The master controller connects to the screen interface wirelessly using the Bluetooth. Once the display patterns are received, the master controller issues commands to each of the control circuits to turn on or off one or one set of Peltiers according to the specific pattern.

The quality of response for Peltier element is quite essential to achieve animated display and pattern changing accurately. Figure 10 depicts the transient response of a single Peltier element. The rest of the Peltiers in the arrangement behave similarly. As observed, the rise time of the system is approximately 1.5s (to go from an ambient temperature of 25 degrees to 32 degrees). In addition, the cooling time of the system also takes approximately 1.5s which is an important characteristic for allowing subtle bidirectional animations on

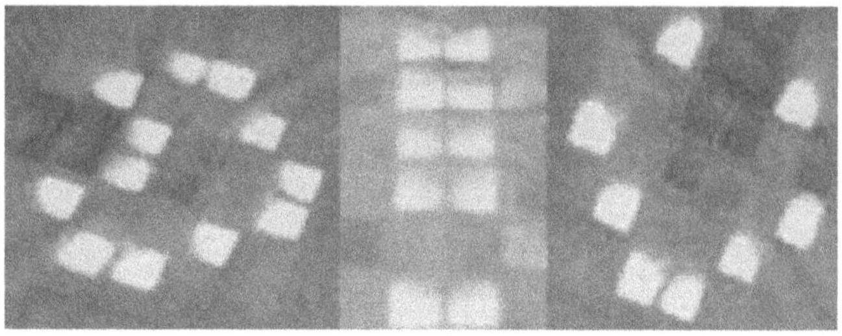

Figure 11. Different pattern display on Ambient Tablecloth:(a) Heart pattern (b) Exclamation mark (c) Smiley.

fabric. Some of the resulting patterns are as shown in the Figure 11.

This ambient tablecloth provides another channel for information sharing and emotion expression between family members in dining situations. It allows users to convey their particular messages in an animated, but tangible way. We feel receiving an animated display on your tablecloth would be surprising and pleasant, and stimulate an enhanced feeling of co-presence beyond receiving plain text or words.

Food Teleportation

Dinner cannot exist without food, of course. The Food Teleportation module is inspired by the importance of food in the kitchen and dining context, and its symbolic character for social bonds. Besides dishes and tablecloth, we believe edible food can also be an affective medium to enhance the emotional connectedness for remote families. Although it is almost effortless to send Short Message Service (SMS), photos or digital gift, these intangible messages miss out the physical and emotional sense of care. Instead, imagine receiving an edible "Hello" from your remote family members during dinner. Food Teleportation achieves this by reproducing the digital greetings (i.e. messages and gift) using edible food materials, which makes tangible the digital messages, creating personalized greetings in edible format.

To transport food, people select the Food Teleportation icon on the Interaction Screen . The user's selection triggers the remote food teleportation module, and prints out a digital

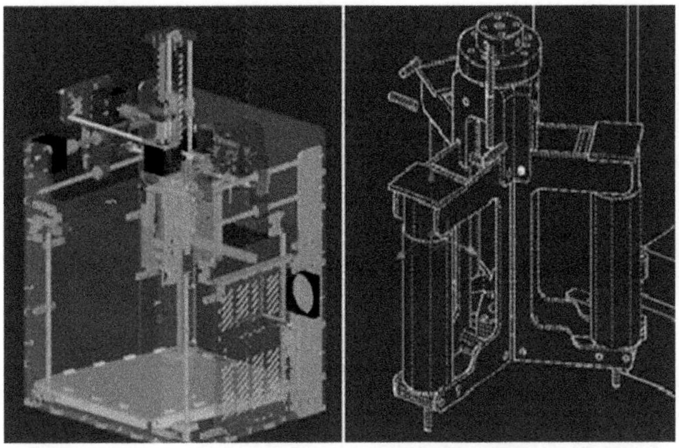

Figure 12. Structure assembly:(a) The whole subsystem (b) Food deposition component.

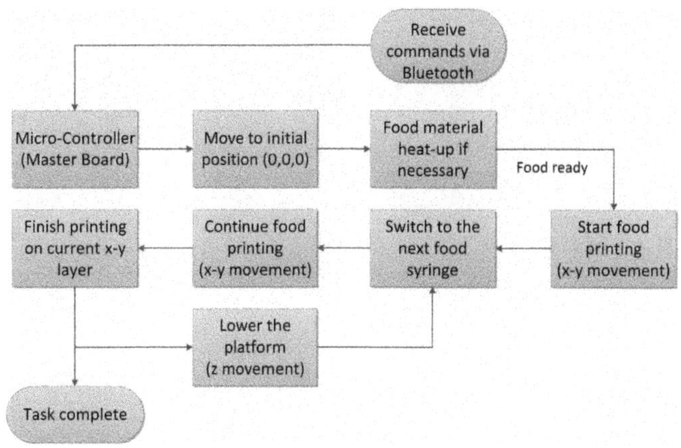

Figure 13. Flowchart of the food teleportation subsystem.

message in edible food synchronously. This message-embedded food is received by loved ones as a unique gift, showing greetings and care physically. Compared with plain text, or digital message like SMS or twitter, transmission through organic food can convey a stronger sense of presence it is more than simply saying "I love you" or "I miss you", it is a physical embodiment of care and affection of one person to others [23], not only visually, but also with smell and taste.

Although currently selecting the Food Transportation icon sends a single message, "LOVE", the Food Transportation subsystem is designed to craft with multiple food materials, not only to make the food message colourful visually and more tasty, but also enable the creation of contextual messages with changed color, smell and flavor, to represent different emotions or feelings. We have experimented with different kinds of food such as chocolate cream (pure black chocolate, white chocolate and milk chocolate), sugar-water mixture, Kaya jam, peanut cream, etc. We also included the most important staple food for Asian households, rice. Food here is the multisensory medium for family communication, and each flavour can be translated into a corresponding emotional state or special experience from one's memory. This flavour-changed eating experience of food gift acts as an intuitive and meaningful way for emotional expression.

Structure Description

The mechanical structure of the subsystem contains two main parts: (Figure 12)

1. 3-axis mechanical structure, with robotic carriage.

2. Food depositing component with 3 syringes .

The mechanical structure is a custom-built 3-axis model of Cartesian X, Y, and Z type. Essentially, the model is designed to use 3-degree freedom robotic carriage to move the food depositing component along the x and y axis and the platform up and down to form z coordinate of the system. The accurate and smooth movement of each axis is achieved through lead-screw coupling powered by step motor, controlled by microchip PIC32MX340F256H from the master board.

The food depositing component is designed exclusively to enable food heating, extrusion and material change while moved by the robotic carriage. A flexible heater can be attached around the syringe and connected with the master board, to heat up the food material that needs to be liquefied before been dispensed. Also, in order to know the exact volume of food material at each beginning of a new material, tiny limit switches are installed under the pushing pad and connected to the master board for position sensing.

This mechanism, connected with the CoDine system, will allow users to reproduce personal digital messages in a remote location using normal food and present to their preferred recipients physically. After receiving the user's chosen message from the interaction, the coordination of the starting point and the motion path for the pattern are interpreted and sent to the food teleportation module on the other side, to be re-produced layer by layer. When finishing crafting the top layer, the platform will move down a certain distance to continue with the next layer. Through this layer-by-layer printing, a 3-dimensional food message or tiny gift could be constructed. Figure 13 illustrates the working flow of the Food Teleportation mechanism.

In building the Food Transportation prototype we had to consider a range of issues. For the mechanical design, we experimented with the diameter of syringe pinhead, coordinate speed of the 3-axis moving motors with piston pushing motor, and the distance between food platform and food droplet, etc. We also had to consider the characteristics of the food to achieve accurate crafting, for example the viscosity and density of different foods at different temperatures.

In our prototype, we experimented with different food materials iteratively to improve the accuracy and resolution, without sacrificing crafting speed. Initially, the message of "LOVE" was crafted with Kaya sauce. With the finalized parameters regarding the mechanical issues, the mechanism crafts with the speed of 5mm/s - 7.2mm/s, taking about 3

Figure 14. Actual result of food teleportation module.

Figure 15. Photo showing user interacts with the integrated system.

minutes to craft the "LOVE" message, and achieves resolution of 1-2mm. We then implemented multiple-layer printing with changed materials, and composed the heart-shape image using ketchup. Rice is also implemented to configure the "HI" character. Figure 14 shows some of the outcomes from the experiments. We have also experimented with melted chocolate which achieved high resolution for food crafting, but have not yet attached the heating feature to the syringe.

Integrated into the CoDine system, people can achieve affective message transmission during dinner, either by printing the chocolate-made message on a piece of toast located in their grandparents' kitchen, or teleport a muffin with different food materials in each layer to express their complicate and indescribable feeling, or sending a message using different natural colored rice. The richness of the message content was much increased with the inclusion of other senses, like colour, image, even smell and taste, not only because they provide a richer, multisensory description of reality, but because the elements together provided more possibilities for interpretation: emotion, mood and humour [5]. We believe the transmission of physical and multi-sensory message is quite promising to contribute to the feeling of co-presence for remote family members.

Interaction Screen

The Interactive Screen integrates these three activities seamlessly to achieve intuitive interaction experience. It is designed to allow the user easily select the activities he/she wanted to perform while dining. Figure 5 showed the dining activities implemented in the CoDine prototype. Using hand gestures towards the Interaction Screen, people can choose to serve dish, display a fancy pattern on tablecloth, or send edible greetings.

Several interaction methods were considered, including a touch screen and buttons. As the screen is about 1m away from the user, the distance makes the use of a touch screen inappropriate. In addition, the table is to be used for dining purpose, so placing buttons on the table is not user-friendly either, since the user may press the buttons accidentally. Hiding the buttons at the bottom or on the side of the table would make it difficult for the user to see and select the buttons. After comparison, we decided that the most natural interaction in this scenario was to use gesture recognition together with the on-screen display, so that the user can select an action using simple and natural gestures.

The Interactive Screen module includes a Kinect sensor bar and gesture-based on-screen menu selection. One RGB camera inside the Kinect sensor supports traditional video conferencing, allowing the user to see his/her remote dining partner and the partner's dining table. It captures image at 8-bit VGA resolution (640 x 480) at 30 Hz. The stereoscopic 3D camera embedded into Kinect is used to capture and compute the depth of the current frame image. A gesture-based menu selection allows the user to easily select and perform the actions on the remote side. The signals received from tracking the user are transmitted to the remote location, triggering the corresponding subsystem through Bluetooth, which supports food serving, ambient tablecloth display and food messaging.

The gesture detection is achieved by using a Kinect sensor bar, the OpenNI [2] 1.0.0 API and PrimeSense's [3] NITE 1.3.0 Middleware. The API provides some methods to easily detect and track the user's hand. Various gestures can be detected. In this module, we choose to use the following three gestures based on their naturalness and recognition accuracy.

1. Raise-hand gesture: User raises his/her hand.

2. Hold gesture: User holds his/her hand at a certain position for 2 seconds.

3. Push gesture: User pushes his/her hand towards the camera.

Besides the hand tracking and gesture recognition, different colours have been mapped to different cursor states to improve the user's understanding of what is currently happening. Colours make the visual system much friendlier while enhancing the overall comprehension.

The screen interaction is designed as follows:

1. To select an action, a user performs the Raise-hand gesture. When his or her hand is detected and tracked, a blue point shows up on the screen, indicating the user's control pointer. The Interaction Screen implements an offset shifting mechanism to make sure the user can reach the whole screen without too much movement.

2. By default the menu icons are translucent to avoid distracting the user from the video conferencing. When a user moves his or her hand over an icon, the icon lights up to give user the feedback of interaction.

3. If the user wants to select an icon, he/she can perform a Hold gesture by focusing the blue pointer on the icon for 2 seconds. The pointer will turn green, indicating it is now waiting for the confirmation gesture.

4. To confirm the selection, user performs a Push gesture towards the camera. After a successful push, the control pointer changes to red and a message is displayed on the top left corner of the screen to verify which action has been chosen. This signal will be transmitted through the network to the remote location, and trigger the corresponding subsystem via Bluetooth. Alternatively, the user can cancel the choice by moving away from the button area.

5. After the desired icon has been selected, other interactions are possible while the previous selected action happens remotely (e.g. serving food, transporting food, displaying picture on tablecloth) is still continuing. The interactive session ends when the user rests his/her hand on the table, ending hand tracking. Then, the menu automatically disappears, returning the Interaction Screen to the normal video conferencing mode.

Overall, the integrated CoDine system provides a mediated platform to enrich the mealtime interactions for remote families, with the purpose of enhancing the feeling of co-presence while dining in different locations. Through embedding computerized devices into normal dining table, a series of intuitive and interactive activities under dining context are accomplished to support the feeling of social connectedness. Figure 15 is a photo taken during the prototype testing which gives an overview of how the system works. The testing was conducted to verify the functionalities and robustness of the CoDine system.

CONCLUSION AND FUTURE WORK

In this paper, we present the design and implementation of the CoDine table system as an exploration of using interactive media in dining space to reconnect people. Inspired by our desire to facilitate co-dining, the system augments and transports the experience of communal family dining. Through shared dining activities, including serving dishes remotely, transmitting animated textile display and physical edible message, CoDine aims to provide a new solution to connecting the dining experience between people in remote locations, creating a sense of co-existence among family members who may be physically apart.

While we have conducted prototype tests during the implementation to verify the CoDine modules function, our next step is a user study to assess whether CoDine enhances engagement between fellow co-diners. This will also help us to better define and improve the user experience and user interface. Certain combinations of modules might lead to more successful feelings of connectedness between co-diners. Feedback from users will help us better understand the novel interactions that push the experience of using CoDine beyond that of video conferencing.

Our research explores how interaction with familiar but intelligent everyday environment and artefacts can be used to enhance meaningful interactions in dining situation, going beyond ambient sensing and computing, to the level of subconscious connection between human beings. As we move towards the era of intelligent environment everywhere, it is important that researchers adequately understand the power interactive media and ubiquitous computing have to increase the richness of human experience. We hope the CoDine system will provide insights on designing context-aware interfaces that emphasize experience over efficiency and shared interaction over information.

ACKNOWLEDGEMENTS

This research is carried out under CUTE Project No. WBS R- 7050000-100-279 partially funded by a grant from the National Research Foundation (NRF) administered by the Media Development Authority (MDA) of Singapore, and No. WBS R705-000-101-597 funded by NEC C&C Innovation Research Laboratories in Osaka, Japan.

ADDITIONAL AUTHORS

Jose Sepulveda (National University of Singapore,
email: pepe.sepulveda.sanchis@gmail.com),
Daishi Kato, Maiko Kamata, Tomoharu Yamaguchi,
Kazuo Kunieda, Keiji Yamada
(NEC C & C Innovation Research Laboratories in Japan,
email: daishi@cb.jp.nec.com)

REFERENCES

1. Microsoft Xbox Kinect
`http://www.xbox.com/kinect.`
2. OpenNI `http://www.openni.org/.`
3. PrimeSense `http://www.primesense.com/.`
4. J. Ali, W.-S. Yoon, J.-H. Kim, and W.-D. Cho. U-kitchen: application scenario. In *Software Technologies for Future Embedded and Ubiquitous Systems, 2004. Proceedings. Second IEEE Workshop on*, pages 169 – 171, May 2004.
5. K. Battarbee. Defining co-experience. In *Proc. DPPI '03*, pages 109–113. ACM, 2003.

6. M. Beetz, F. Stulp, B. Radig, J. Bandouch, N. Blodow, M. Dolha, A. Fedrizzi, D. Jain, U. Klank, I. Kresse, A. Maldonado, Z. Marton, L. Mosenlechner, F. Ruiz, R. Rusu, and M. Tenorth. The assistive kitchen - a demonstration scenario for cognitive technical systems. In *Proc. RO-MAN '2008*, pages 1 –8, 2008.

7. G. Bell and J. Kaye. Designing technology for domestic spaces: A kitchen manifesto. *Gastronomica: The Journal of Food and Culture*, 2(2):46–62.

8. M. Canton. The presence table: a reactive surface for ambient connection. In *Proc. TEI '11*, pages 401–402. ACM, 2011.

9. J.-H. Chen, P.-Y. Chi, H.-H. Chu, C.-H. Chen, and P. Huang. A smart kitchen for nutrition-aware cooking. *Pervasive Computing, IEEE*, 9(4):58 –65, 2010.

10. L.-E. Cheng, C.-H. Tseng, and C.-L. Lu. Design of interactive e-care dining table for smart kitchen. In *Proc. CASoN '2010*, pages 179 –182, sept. 2010.

11. M. Coelho. Dinnerware: why playing with food should be encouraged. In *Proc. CHI EA '09*, pages 3505–3506. ACM, 2009.

12. J. Forlizzi and K. Battarbee. Understanding experience in interactive systems. In *Proc. DIS '04*, pages 261–268. ACM, 2004.

13. D. Gooch. Socialising presence. In *Proc. CHI EA '11*, pages 1049–1052. ACM, 2011.

14. R. Hamada, J. Okabe, I. Ide, S. Satoh, S. Sakai, and H. Tanaka. Cooking navi: assistant for daily cooking in kitchen. In *Proc. MULTIMEDIA '05*, pages 371–374. ACM, 2005.

15. R. Iglesias, I. Ibarguren, N. G. de Segura, J. Ugalde, L. Coello, and M. Iturburu. Foodmanager: a cooking, eating and appliance controlling support system for the elderly. In *Proc. PETRA '10*, pages 38:1–38:6. ACM, 2010.

16. T. K. Judge, C. Neustaedter, and A. F. Kurtz. The family window: the design and evaluation of a domestic media space. In *Proc. CHI '10*, pages 2361–2370. ACM, 2010.

17. C.-H. Lee, L. Bonnani, and T. Selker. Augmented reality kitchen: enhancing human sensibility in domestic life. In *ACM SIGGRAPH 2005 Posters*, SIGGRAPH '05. ACM, 2005.

18. Y. Nakauchi, T. Fukuda, K. Noguchi, and T. Matsubara. Intelligent kitchen: cooking support by lcd and mobile robot with ic-labeled objects. In *Proc. IROS '2005*, pages 1911 – 1916, 2005.

19. Y. Nakauchi, T. Suzuki, A. Tokumasu, and S. Murakami. Cooking procedure recognition and inference in sensor embedded kitchen. In *Proc. RO-MAN 2009*, pages 593 –600, 27 2009-oct. 2 2009.

20. E. Ochs and M. Shohet. The cultural structuring of mealtime socialization. *New Directions for Child and Adolescent Development*, 2006(111):35–49, 2006.

21. P. Olivier, G. Xu, A. Monk, and J. Hoey. Ambient kitchen: designing situated services using a high fidelity prototyping environment. In *Proc. PETRA '09*, pages 47:1–47:7. ACM, 2009.

22. R. L. Peiris, A. D. Cheok, J. K. S. Teh, O. N. N. Fernando, W. Yingqian, A. Lim, P. Yi, D. Polydorou, K. P. Ong, and M. Tharakan. Ambikraf: an embedded non-emissive and fast changing wearable display. In *ACM SIGGRAPH '09 Emerging Technologies*, pages 1:1–1:1, New York, NY, USA, 2009. ACM.

23. M. Perry and D. Rachovides. Entertaining situated messaging at home. *Computer Supported Cooperative Work (CSCW)*, 16:99–128, 2007. 10.1007/s10606-007-9042-7.

24. P. Polotti, S. Delle Monache, S. Papetti, and D. Rocchesso. Gamelunch: forging a dining experience through sound. In *Proc. CHI EA '08*, pages 2281–2286. ACM, 2008.

25. H. Rae-Espinoza. Family mealtime as a context of development and socialization. larson, reed w., angela r. wiley, and kathryn r. branscomb, eds. new directions for child development, number 111. san francisco, ca: Wiley periodicals, inc. 2006. 110pp. *Ethos*, 38(1):1–3, 2010.

26. R. B. Rusu, B. Gerkey, and M. Beetz. Robots in the kitchen: Exploiting ubiquitous sensing and actuation. *Robotics and Autonomous Systems*, 56(10):844 – 856, 2008. Network Robot Systems.

27. M. Schneider. The semantic cookbook: sharing cooking experiences in the smart kitchen. In *Proc. IE '07*, pages 416 –423, sept. 2007.

28. I. Siio, R. Hamada, and N. Mima. Kitchen of the future and applications. In *Proc. HCI'07*, pages 946–955. Springer-Verlag, 2007.

29. M. Snyder, J. Zimmerman, and J. Forlizzi. Your dinner's calling: supporting family dinnertime activities. In *Proc. DPPI '07*, pages 485–489. ACM, 2007.

30. Stefan Poslad. *Ubiquitous computing: smart devices, environments and interactions.* John Wiley and Sons, Ltd, Queen Mary, University of London, UK, 2009.

31. L. Terrenghi, O. Hilliges, and A. Butz. Kitchen stories: sharing recipes with the living cookbook. *Personal and Ubiquitous Computing*, 11:409–414, 2007. 10.1007/s00779-006-0079-2.

32. H. Tsujita, S. Yarosh, and G. D. Abowd. Cu-later: a communication system considering time difference. In *Proc. Ubicomp '10*, pages 435–436. ACM, 2010.

Promoting Intergenerational Communication Through Location-Based Asynchronous Video Communication

Frank Bentley[1], Santosh Basapur[1], Sujoy Kumar Chowdhury[2]

[1]Motorola Mobility Applied Research Center
Libertyville, IL USA
{f.bentley, sbasapur} @motorola.com

[2]Missouri Western State University
St. Joseph, Missouri USA
schowdhury@missouriwestern.edu

ABSTRACT

We describe the design and field evaluation of the Serendipitous Family Stories system, a web and mobile service that allows for videos to be saved in user-specified real-world locations, shared with friends and family, and then serendipitously discovered as those people approach the location of a story. Through a twenty-participant field evaluation, we discovered how this new form of location-based asynchronous communication can be used to strengthen family relationships by encouraging communication across generations and enhancing users' relationships with everyday places in their lives.

Author Keywords

Intergenerational communication, video sharing, mobile, reminiscing, storytelling, evaluation

ACM Classification Keywords

H.4.3 Communications Applications

H.5.1 Multimedia Information Systems

H5.m. Information interfaces and presentation (e.g., HCI): Miscellaneous

General Terms

Design, Experimentation, Human Factors

INTRODUCTION

Sharing stories is a core part of being human. People reminisce and discuss stories from their past with family, friends, neighbors, and new acquaintances. A story is a performance that brings together family members and creates lasting memories [11]. Stories serve as a way to get to know others and to build stronger ties through these shared memories.

Traditionally, stories are told face-to-face, and through our research we've found that holidays, family parties, and other in-person get togethers are still the main occasion for the telling of stories from a family's history. However, families are moving apart from each other. As of 1993, 43% of American adults lived more than an hour away from their parents [10]. This number is growing as the workforce becomes more mobile and retirement destinations increasingly attract older adults to locations far from family. As it has been shown that communication decreases when families move apart [12], we see a need for new communications tools to keep family members connected.

We are interested in connecting older adults to their children over a distance through the sharing of location-based video stories. We believe that the visual nature of video, which allows recipients to literally see their older relatives, combined with the serendipity and asynchronous nature of location-based discovery together form a strong platform for the sharing of memories. This experience then encourages recipients to be aware of places of family importance in their own lives and to initiate communication about these family stories across generations.

By making the creation, sharing, and receiving of video narratives simple, we hoped to turn seniors into creators of mobile media and to engage the whole family in the process of creating, viewing, and talking about family history. We have observed use in daily life through our study and are encouraged by the ways our participants became more aware of their family history and the lives of their relatives as well as the increase in communication reported during the month of use.

RELATED WORK

This system draws on work from a variety of disciplines. Intergenerational communication has been studied in anthropology and gerontology domains. Mobile video use and storytelling have been explored in ethnographic-style studies as well as through the fielding of new experimental systems in this space. We will introduce this work to better ground the design of our system in the research that preceded it.

Intergenerational Communication

Treas' study in 1975 [24] explored a concept he termed "intimacy at a distance" in that older adults preferred to keep their own homes and have specific scheduled times of interaction with their adult children. He found that married

UbiComp '11, September 17–21, 2011, Beijing, China.

children keep in touch with their parents more often than unmarried children and that daughters communicate with parents more than sons.

More recent study of intergenerational communication has been focused on communication between grandparents and their grandchildren. Ballagas et al studied current practices in this domain and found that video is a strong way to engage young children who are not yet able to understand the concept of a voice coming through a telephone [2]. From these insights, their group created the Family Story Play system that added live video of a relative to a book so that stories could be read together over a distance.

Yarosh et al [26] reviewed the literature on communication between parents and young children as well as describe five mobile systems to support communication with children while their parents are out of town. We are working in a complementary space by addressing communication between generations after children are grown and independent.

In the spring of 2010, our group conducted a study that addressed communication between older adults and their adult children over a distance [4]. Through this work, we observed tensions between generations about bothering each other too much with phone calls as well as observed storytelling behaviors and how one person's context could bring about a shared story between generations. For example, one participant in our study was walking past a theater while talking to her mom on the phone. She remembered that her grandfather used to dance in that theater when he was in the military on leave. She mentioned this to her mom and they had a conversation about the importance of this place in the life of the family. We were intrigued by this contextual cue that prompted storytelling between generations and this led to the design idea for the Serendipitous Family Stories system.

Mobile Video Use

Currently, the sharing of mobile video is growing in popularity. The ability to upload video to social network services, such as Facebook, directly from a mobile device lowers barriers to sharing video with others. Mobile video streaming services such as Bambuser and Qik allow people to live-stream video to the web from their mobile devices. However, in a 2010 study of these services, Julhin et al found that the majority of streams were tests or had very low production value [13]. One of our goals with this system was to lower the barrier to mobile video creation while increasing the quality and memorability of the resulting clips.

Dougherty studied the use of mobile video for political purposes. She found civic videos to be longer on average than typical videos posted to the Qik system [6]. She found that older users were more likely to use mobile broadcasting for civic reasons compared to younger users who focused more on friends and family.

Reminiscing and Storytelling Systems

Over the past decade, several research systems have been created to encourage reminiscing and storytelling, both for one's own remembrance and for sharing with others.

Olsson et al explored requirements for creating systems to record and share life memories [15]. They observed the importance of time, event, and place in stories and in using these attributes to retrieve the media. In a later study, they observed motivations for sharing stories with close friends and family including strengthening relationships, creating a feeling of community and belonging, and bonding over geographical distance [14]. We sought to use the rich medium of video in the context of the world to achieve these goals of sharing stories.

Peesapati et al created a system called Pensieve for supporting everyday reminiscence [17]. One of their design goals was to make the act of reminiscing more serendipitous and they achieved this through randomly sending emails to users containing content from their own online media accounts. By seeing old pictures or music that was played in the past, users could reflect on these times in their life when prompted by the system.

Location-Based Content Delivery

Several systems have been created that deliver content to users automatically based on their location. Sohn et al's Place-Its system [23] delivered location-based reminders to users when they entered or left a location, such as remembering to take out the garbage when one gets home. Ballagas et al's REXplorer [3] was a pervasive game in Regensburg, Germany that notified visitors about important locations in the city's history as they walked about.

Pan et al created a system called M-Studio for creating and experiencing location-aware stories [16]. Through M-Studio, professionals could create stories that spanned multiple physical locations. An iPAQ client was developed for users to view the content as they walked around campus receiving the stories. The client would send its current location to the server each second and retrieve any related media for that location. Systems like this inspired our work, and we wanted to make it easy for anyone to create such location-based stories without the need for a complex story creation tool and for the stories to be more personal instead of more professionally produced films.

THE SERENDIPITOUS FAMILY STORIES SYSTEM

As mentioned above, the Serendipitous Family Stories (SFS) system was created based on findings of an earlier study on intergenerational communication over a distance [4]. We observed how a person's current location could trigger conversations over the phone about past family stories that occurred in that place. From this, we wanted to create a system that made reminiscing about stories in a particular place easier and would increase communication between generations over a distance.

From our study, we had three main design implications. The main implication was that new technology for inter-generational distance communication should "re-create feelings of being together and doing things together." We wanted our Serendipitous Family Stories system to put the recipient literally face-to-face with their family members by seeing the video of them telling a story. Because the story is viewed in the location where it occurred, we wanted to re-create the feeling of actually being in that space with the relative.

The next implication was that "communication needs to fit into daily life." We observed how older adults often felt as if they were interrupting the busy lives of their adult children, and because of this, did not communicate as much as they wanted to. We also observed that the adult children do welcome communication, but want it to be more on their schedule. Because the Serendipitous Family Stories system delivers communication asynchronously and allows for video to be viewed immediately or again at later times, we believe it fits better into the patterns of daily life. Parents can create as many videos as they would like, and recipients receive them over time, one at a time.

Finally, we saw a need for communication to evoke and share family memories. This served as the core concept for our system, as the story is the central component. We hoped that receiving stories would encourage further conversation among family members about the stories themselves as well as other events in their lives. This is supported by our data, as discussed below.

The system contains two user-facing components. First, the Family Stories website allows for users to record video stories using the webcam in their computer and to save them to a spot on a map. Stories can be shared with friends and family members through this web interface. We use a Flash component in the web page to automatically find the camera and audio source to make it as easy as possible to record videos. As our goal was to turn seniors into video-creators, we wanted this process to be as simple as possible.

Figure 2: The mobile application allows friends and family to receive notifications when they approach the location of a story that is shared with them. Users can then watch the video of any story that is unlocked.

The second component is the mobile application, which currently runs on any Android phone with OS version 1.6 or higher. This application automatically connects to our server and downloads the stories shared with that device's phone number. It then monitors the location of the device through network location (to minimize battery drain and work indoors) in the background. When the device nears the location of a story that has not been found before, it will vibrate three times to get the user's attention. If the user is within a pre-defined radius of the story location, they can "unlock" the story and view the video. Otherwise, they are given a map to the story location. Once a story is unlocked, its videos can be viewed again from any location facilitating the ability to share with others or watch again in a quieter environment. Each story page contains shortcuts to call or text message the creator as well as a button to "like" the story. When users return to locations where stories are located, no vibration will occur, but a silent notification will be placed in their status bar so that they can be reminded of previously viewed stories in that area if they happen to glance at their device.

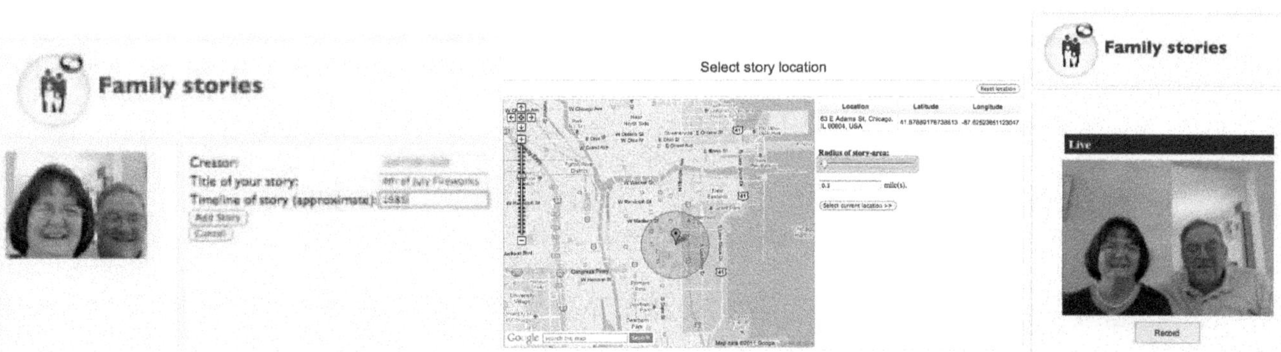

Figure 1: The web interface allows for users to record video stories and save them in a place on a map. Users first create a new story (left), then choose a location (center) and finally record their video (right) to create a new story. Even older seniors found this to be a simple process and were able to create new stories with little assistance.

A "hint" on the main page of the application also tells users the rough cardinal direction and distance to the nearest unfound story. This design creates the potential for a game dynamic in which users seek to find all of the stories that are shared with them.

METHOD

We used a professional recruiting agency to recruit 20 diverse participants to use the system. Ten participants were adults in their 20s-40s living in Chicago and would be receiving stories on their Android phones. The other ten participants were their older relatives (parents, grandparents, aunts), five of whom lived in South Florida (about 1200 miles away) and five of whom lived in the Chicago area, but not with the main participant. These participants ranged in age from their 50s through mid-80s and had all lived in Chicago for some part of their adult lives. They would be creating stories in the system to share with their younger relative.

We met with the older adults first for them to record stories using our web interface. We brought a laptop with a webcam to their homes and, after a brief explanation of the system and a few icebreaker questions, we let the participants create as many videos as they would like (minimum of 5) for their younger relatives using our system's web site. The choice of content, location, and storytelling style was up to them. After creating stories, we conducted a short interview on previous storytelling and communication patterns in their family.

Later, we met with the younger participants in their homes and either installed our application on their existing Android phone or moved their SIM card into a new Android phone with the application preinstalled. Participants were asked to keep the application installed for four weeks and to call our voicemail diary system whenever they found a story to report on their experience. Their older relative was also asked to call if they received any communication about the stories. After a quick demonstration of the system, we conducted a short semi-structured interview with the younger relatives about their story sharing and communication practices.

In addition to the interviews and voicemail diary entries, we also logged information from the mobile application including times when a story was nearby, when it was viewed, when a story video was played, and when communication was initiated from the application. These logs were automatically uploaded to our server nightly.

LIMITATIONS

There are several limitations to the method that we employed. First, in only allowing the older adults to create videos in one sitting, we were only able to observe the types of videos that the participants initially thought would be interesting to their younger relatives. There was no ability to form a feedback loop and have more stories created as the study went on. We found it difficult to recruit participants meeting our other criteria (diverse ages, occupations, parts of the city, ethnic backgrounds, relatives who also wanted to participate, etc.) and finding older adults who also had webcams was seen to be too difficult. We will be conducting a deeper content analysis this fall on a wider, more natural deployment.

It is also hard to quantify the number of families who are in the situation where one person lives in a place where the other has memories. Haas et al calculate that over two million adults over 60 have permanently relocated within the US [7]. In addition, Smith and House found that over 700,000 older adults temporarily move to Florida each winter and return home to the North in the summers [22] where they presumable spend time with relatives and friends that remain there. They also reference high numbers of "snowbirds" in Arizona, Spain, and Mexico.

CONTENT OF STORIES

The older adults in our study produced between five and ten stories each in the time provided during the initial interview. This led to 78 stories in total, including our pilot participant. Since no major changes were made to the system after the pilot participant, the following content analysis will include the videos from all ten study participants plus the pilot.

Videos ranged from twenty seconds to three minutes and twenty seconds in length, as shown in Figure 3. Two main clusters occurred around 0:30 and 1:10. This fit with two common narrative styles employed by our participants. For stories that were already well-known to the recipient, often just the salient points of the story were mentioned, making these stories shorter. Participants would use constructs such as "remember when" to set the stage, knowing that the recipient knew the context of the story well. Longer stories were often from farther back in the creator's life and events that were not as well known to the recipient. In these stories, the stage had to be set in the video, resulting in longer durations. In general, these shorter lengths fit well with mobile video consumption as they could easily be watched while on the go in a variety of circumstances as described below without requiring a major interruption in activity. All videos are significantly shorter than the videos typically posted to mobile streaming sites such as Bambuser and Qik [6].

As shown in Figure 4, stories ranged over many years in our participants' lives. Two main peaks occurred during the 1940s when many of our participants were young and growing up and in the 1980s when they were starting families and their children were small. When asking follow up questions with participants about the stories that they remembered most in their lives, we observed a great number of these to have come from the time when they were growing up. Memories of trips, youth sporting events, and friends from their neighborhoods dominated stories in

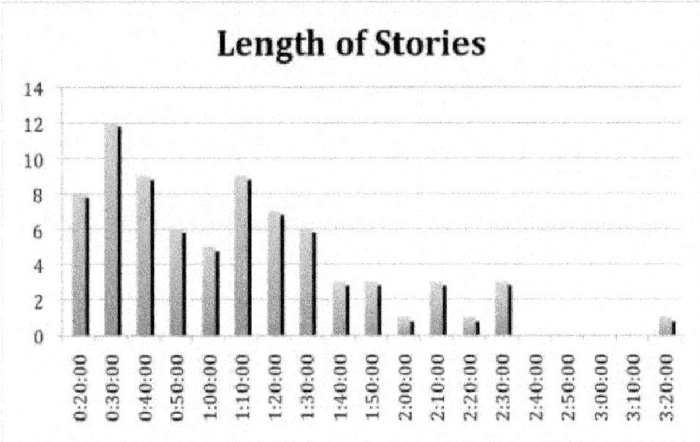

Figure 3: Typical stories averaged 1:10 in length with some quite longer stories created.

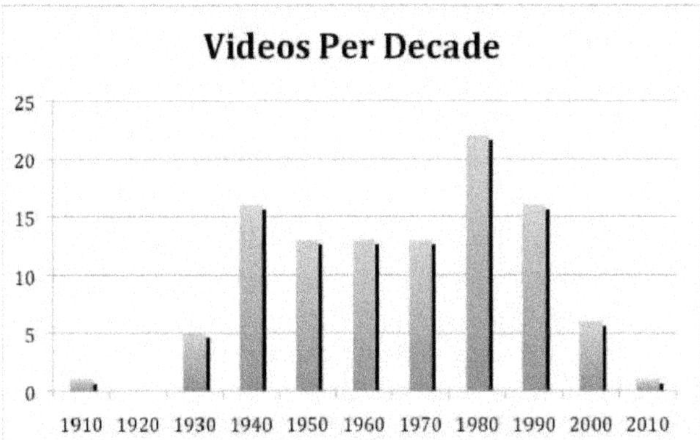

Figure 4: Stories were created from many time periods in our participants' lives, peaking on times when they were growing up or when their children were growing up.

this grouping. These, often idyllic, times of youth are events that people enjoy reliving as they get older.

There were a variety of characters in each of the stories that was created. Almost all stories included one of the creators as a primary character in the story. Other family members also featured prominently in the stories. One third of the stories included the recipient as a character in the story, and most of these stories were about events that occurred as a family while the participant was growing up, but a few covered recent family events and outings such as trips to a musical or sporting event. Public figures were featured in 14 of the stories where participants told stories about interactions with politicians, famous singers, talk show hosts, and sports players.

Story Locations

Stories were created in all parts of the city and a few surrounding suburbs. Stories created within the city can be seen in Figure 5. Twenty-six of the seventy-eight stories were created in the central business district of Chicago (the "Loop") with other clusters around major sporting event sites (e.g. Wrigley Field) and in neighborhoods where our

Figure 5. Stories were saved throughout the city, although many were concentrated in the "loop" central business district. 83% of stories were found by participants during study period and are shown with red pins.

participants grew up. Since our participants were from diverse parts of the city, these stories are spread out in many of Chicago's neighborhoods. In total, 83% of the stories that were created were found during the four weeks of the study. We will have a larger discussion on the process of findings stories below.

Stories covered a variety of location types. Nineteen percent of stories were saved in private places such as homes or workplaces while the rest were saved in public places such as parks, museums, restaurants, and retail establishments. Due to the neighborhood layout of Chicago, this meant that many of the residential stories were created in the outer parts of the city and many of the work or public location stories were created in the city center. There were some exceptions to this such as neighborhood parks and theaters outside of the central business district.

QUALITATIVE DATA

From our interviews and the voice mail diaries, we learned about the experience of using the system in daily life. Data from the interviews and voicemail were analyzed in a grounded theory affinity. We present those qualitative findings in this section where each point that is discussed is supported by data from multiple study participants.

Finding Stories

By the end of the four weeks, our participants had discovered 83% of the stories that were created for them. Some participants found all of their stories while others only found as few as two out of five. Serendipitous discovery of stories was seen by participants as "a cute little treat" (C3) and an experience "that will make you feel happy or bring a smile to your face" (P6). As seen in Figure 7, stories were discovered fairly regularly for the first three weeks of the study, but no new videos were found during the final week. Participants continued to use the system to show the stories to others, but reported not traveling to many new places that week due to the cold (high of -7C) temperatures during that time.

Participants discovered some stories in unexpected places. C2 was picking up a marriage certificate at the courthouse and found a story from his aunt at the mall across the street. "I was surprised. I was not intentionally going to the location to see the story but it was a surprise for me ... and then this thing was right there!" (C2) Other times, participants came across stories and received notifications that they were close by, but not close enough to view the video. In these cases, participants had to change course to find the story. While this was not often possible, and sometimes frustrating in a busy morning commute, when participants had more flexibility they reported opening up the map interface and finding the exact location.

Other stories were in the places where participants expected to find them. Based on family history and common stories that are told, they thought stories would appear in certain places. C7's father-in-law was an attorney for many years in Chicago. C7 told us: "I went over to the Daley Center because that's where he did a lot of his court cases." In the initial interview C3 told us that she was "anxious because I know when I start to use it I'll start getting notifications right away because I work right next to Macy's or Marshall Fields." She told us of her mom telling her of a holiday tradition of seeing the windows at Fields "ever since I can remember." For these participants, getting these familiar stories helped strengthen the tie of stories to places in their daily lives and reminded them of memories from their past.

The system made receiving stories "fun" as reported by several participants and "being places where other people were" (C4) brought an added dimension to the hearing of family stories. While not all stories were found during the month of the study, many participants expressed an interest in continuing to use the system to find the remaining stories and the system becoming a part of their lives to discover content over months and years. We were unable to support this due to our server power being off over the holidays, but we gave all participants their remaining videos after the final interview.

Strong Memories and Emotions

One of our most interesting findings was observing the

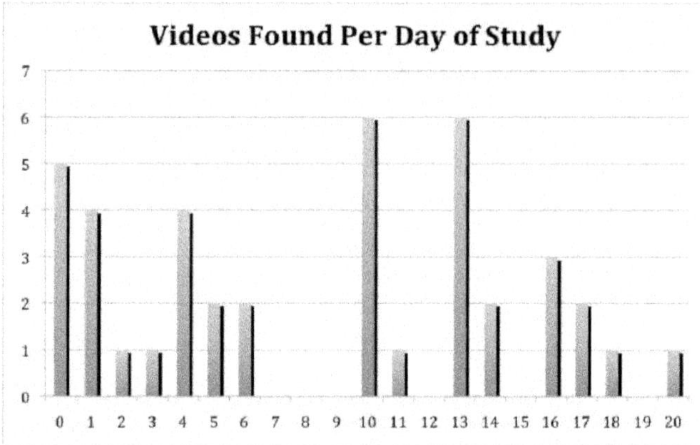

Figure 6: Videos were found fairly regularly throughout the first three weeks of the study as participants lived their lives. Spikes occur on weekend days when participants were more likely to visit new places or go hunting for a story.

wide range of deep emotions that the system evoked in our participants. We had expected just a general enjoyment of the system and an increase in communication, but our participants reported laughing, crying, and getting choked up upon receiving a story or discussing it later with family.

P6 told us of a phone call she received from her daughter-in law. She called "to say that I made her cry that she was so touched by the stories. And she thought they were funny, the first ones I told her about." In this case, the story that was shared was about C6 meeting the parents of her now husband back when she was in high school.

C10 reported laughing about many of the stories that were created by his mom and brothers: "After that [watching the two new stories] I called both my mom and my brother and I laughed about the situation cause it was pretty funny what they said." Laughing about stories was a common reaction, both alone when receiving a story and again later when discussing it with the creator or other friends and family.

Evoking strong and personal emotions demonstrated the ability of our system to re-create some of the feeling of being together and of experiencing places together. The range and depth of emotions demonstrate the potential richness of this new medium of location-based asynchronous video communication.

Ramping Communication

We observed a pattern of ramping communication [19], where initial lighter-weight asynchronous communication through text messages or "likes" led to deeper communication over the phone or in person at later times. This style of communication matches what has been previously observed in studies of social TV systems [9] and we believe is a key way to build social engagement with systems that involve interaction at a distance. One example was C6: I "did end up texting my mother and telling her how sweet it was. Brought back a lot of memories, which was nice. And she called me back and we actually laughed about it."

In the end, participants reported feeling closer to their family because of their participation. P4: "This has really brought us closer together because we've been more communicative." P5 called the intergenerational communication that the system created "a minor miracle" since her daughter did not previously show an interest in family history. Here, two factors may have acted together to reach the 'tipping point' for an audience previously uninterested in reminiscence activities: the serendipity achieved through the receipt of the story in everyday settings, and the asynchronicity offered by the deferred delivery. We found in our first study that intergenerational communication is often inhibited for fear of interrupting the other family member when s/he is busy. In SFS, both the obtrusiveness and the social pressure of attending to a face-to-face reminiscence activity are avoided.

Extending Storytelling to Family/Friends

The communication that the system generated was not limited to the creator and recipient. In many cases, both the creator and recipient talked to others about the stories that they discovered or showed videos directly from their phone to friends and family after the initial viewing. As shown in Figure 7, many videos were played multiple times with an average view count of 1.8 views per video.

In some instances, participants were not alone when receiving stories. In these cases, discovering which story was about to appear and watching the video became a group activity. C6 received several videos while she was in the car which led to conversation among all present and the sharing of more details of the story: "My husband was watching it with me, we were in the car. So we were in the car and he was watching it with me and was laughing. I don't remember word for word what we were talking about and then my kids starting asking us questions about it, I know that. He wanted to see the video and they got all involved in it too."

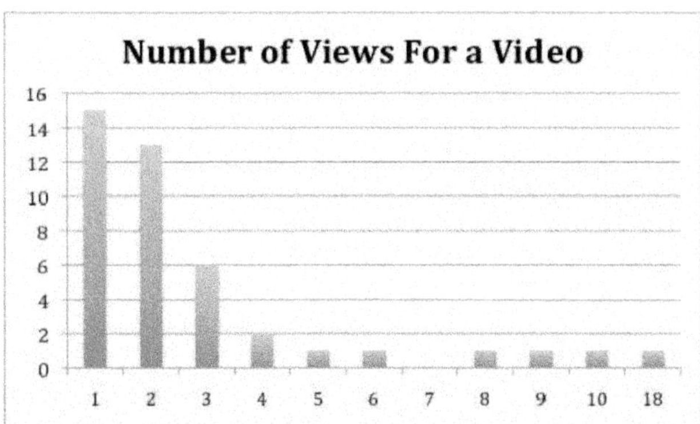

Figure 7: While most videos were only viewed once or twice, many were shown repeatedly to friends and family after the initial viewing.

Some participants would also show many of the videos to their significant others. This was especially common when the participant was a son- or daughter-in-law of the creator and wanted to get to know more about a side of the family that was less familiar. C7 "watched them all one day when I was on the way home and then I watched them again with [my wife]. Showed them to her cause she wanted to see them and wanted to see what her dad had said." C2's wife works where her mom used to work and C2 "talked with [her] about it and then she gave [her husband] the feedback on how different it is at her workplace today." In these cases, the stories served as conversation starters to learn more about the family and its rich history.

Our study ran over the holiday of American Thanksgiving, which is a common time to have large family gatherings. In the voicemail diaries, almost all of our participants reported sharing stories with family members during this holiday. C4: "Oh yeah, I showed everyone at Thanksgiving. Which was nice because it was Thanksgiving and everybody was together. My mom started talking about the stories then and it was great!" C6's son wanted to tell others about all of the stories they had been receiving in the car: "My son brought it up actually so he brought it up there. It was before a few of my other family members came and they were like, mom, show tio [uncle] the stories and stuff."

Other times when visiting family served as opportune times to share stories. C5 "was hanging out with my cousin. And I was telling him about this app … And I was like, look! Look! It's mom and dad and they recorded stories and they geolocated them. So I showed him the stories and he was like woah, that's cool."

Having stories of relatives accessible on a mobile device allowed for conversation starters when around other people. Especially when those people knew the family well, conversations around these stories often emerged and extended well beyond the creator and recipient.

Re-engaging with the city via family history

Serendipitous Family Stories allowed our participants to engage with the city in new ways. Previously everyday locations took on added meaning as participants learned about the significance of those places in their family history. While some stories were familiar, many stories were new to our participants, and they saw the importance of these places in their parents' or grandparents' lives when they were growing up. This caused participants to engage with their 'regular' places differently as they learned about the stories and other historical tidbits about their city.

Some stories were very 'visual' and gave their recipients a chance to visualize the experiences enjoyed by their older generations. P7 left a story about the times when the lights would go out at his office in the Sears Tower each evening. Upon discovering the story, the son-in-law said "It was interesting to hear about [father's] office in that building and how when the lights went off the whole city lit up, otherwise you couldn't see anything. It was very dark up there. That was an interesting story."

C4 commented on receiving the stories in the places that her grandmother used to frequent decades ago: "Just being other places that other people were is neat." Often, participants learned about how these places have changed over the years. C4 learned of an old amusement park where her grandmother used to go on dates. It was torn down in the 1960s and she drove past the site everyday. As she told us: "I had no idea there was even an amusement park there." C3 learned about an old TV dance show called Ray Reiner that used to be filmed in Chicago and that her aunt had participated in: "It was a story about her being on the dance show and how they took video and used to go on boat rides. I had never heard of Ray Reiner, but I guess everybody else has because when I talked about it with people from my office they all said that oh yes, Ray Reiner is very popular. … [My aunt and I] just talked about who Ray Reiner was and how he was kind of like a Dick Clark."

Through these stories, our participants not only engaged with their family history, but they also learned about the city's past and the importance of the places that they pass by each day.

Creating stronger family bonds through storytelling

Sharing stories allowed our participants to create stronger relationships with their family members. Recipients learned about aspects of their relatives' lives that they had not known before and also reminisced about shared family experiences in their past.

C4 learned a lot about her grandmother's life growing up. "I didn't know that they didn't have a car. She never had a car growing up. So everything they did they took a bus or the train and things like that." Stories like this helped the younger generation to imagine a life very different from their own and see older relatives as they were in their younger lives. As her grandmother put it, "She got a big kick out of the things that I did tell her though! And I guess she never knew her grandmother was human."

Often, the lives of older relatives remain mostly unknown to younger generations. C3 learned a lot about her aunt during the study, even though they are fairly close and talk regularly. "Yes, she said that she never realized that I worked at Carson Pirie Scott. And she said that she also didn't realize that I was pregnant when I worked there. She was so surprised to hear that. So she says, 'Were you married!?' ... And said that she didn't realize that I was a Jr Executive with Carson Pirie Scott. She thought I was just always just a little sales clerk."

C7 learned a lot about his father-in-law's interests: "I didn't realize that so much [father's interest in architecture] Cause I thought he was more into, he does a lot of work for like legal funds and stuff, and I didn't know he was so into the architecture of things. I talked to him about it. I talked to [my wife] about it too."

This learning was not just one-way from the creator to the recipient. P3 reported learning a lot about her niece through using the system: "And she learned things about me that she didn't know too. We learned things about each other. And that's really cool, you know."

Families also reminisced about shared experiences in their past, and this helped to increase feelings of connectedness between the generations and reinforce the good times that they had spent together. P6 left a story for her daughter about going to see a musical in downtown Chicago. "Cause it was my daughter and my other daughter, it was a girls' night out. … That was the first time we went out to see a play so that was just great." Her daughter talked to her about the story and planned another theater event when reminded of the good times they had on the first outing. "We talked about how that was fun and how we want to do that again."

Reliving memories of old sporting events was another common topic for stories that brought back fond memories of childhood both for the creator and the recipient. C10 was reminded of times when the whole family would go ice skating together: "That one was something that we used to do back in the day with my mother which was going ice skating and we used to love doing that. And she just talked about how … every different person in the family would try to ice skate, who would fall. And that was the one time that my little brother was good at something I wasn't athletically." This memory prompted a call to his mother where they talked about old memories in the park playing baseball as well as the ice skating outings.

C1 was able to relive memories about taking a boat out on the river when he was young: "When I was a kid we used to have a small boat … and I think we had my grandparents with us and we … took the channel all the way down to the Chicago River and we showed them, they had never seen the buildings from the Chicago River before. So that was kind of neat to hear. Cause I didn't really remember it too much from when I was a kid, but hearing my parents tell it, you know they were real happy that they were able to do that and show my grandparents that." Through hearing this story, C1 was able to reconnect with a bit of his past and relatives across three generations.

Through using the system both to create and receive stories, participants strengthened their family bonds. Both through learning about new experiences from the past and by reliving times that the family had experienced together, our participants were able to be stronger families through their participation. The conversations that occurred and the events that were planned occurred directly as a result of using the system and receiving these asynchronous stories.

DISCUSSION

We believe that the mobile device is an ideal platform for fostering reminiscing experiences and increasing feelings of connectedness in families. While "measurements, metrics, and methodologies" for establishing connectedness are "not well established" [25], we have seen an increase in the frequency and duration of communication as well as an increase in communication that focuses on details of the family from users of this system. In addition, when asked for any final comments on using the system, several participants explicitly spoke of feeling more connected to and informed about family members. These stronger connections and knowledge will hopefully continue into deeper relationships in the future. If this can be validated, it demonstrates the power of a few mobile experiences during a four-week period to dramatically enhance family relationships. We see this as similar to the power of a weekend trip or other time spent together in strengthening bonds among friends and family. The experience provides a multitude of topics and common interests among those involved which we have observed being used to inspire future communication and activities to engage in together. P6 and C6 are already planning more outings together as a direct result of reminiscing that came from one of the stories shared in the system.

Our observations in the study have shown initial results that mobile interfaces that support ramping communication fidelity can indeed increase communication about family history and strengthen family relationships. Getting a story, liking it or texting the sender, and then moving on to deeper phone or in-person communication about the story and other topics of family history was a successful communication path for almost all of our participants. We are encouraged by these findings and would like to see how this style of usage can extend beyond the immediate family to sharing stories with friends and acquaintances.

Virtual Placemaking

This system has also demonstrated a new way for people to connect with a city and become aware of the importance of the places that they visit everyday in the lives of others or in history of the city itself. Previous location-based media systems have focused on delivering professionally produced content [16] or advertising [1] to users in certain locations. By sharing content of direct importance to close social relations in the context of the city, the system thus makes those places more meaningful and memorable in a very personal way.

Current discussions on the concept of "Placemaking" focus on physical changes to a place in order to make them more amenable to the needs of people who spend time there [21]. Location-based media systems can create a form of "virtual Placemaking" where in they making places more meaningful for people through the delivery of personally meaningful digital information about that place, thus transforming people's perceptions of that place.

Location-based asynchronous media delivery is a new and interesting way to communicate with those in our lives. We are interested in other applications of this technology that can help make people more aware of their surroundings and the places where friends and family have visited or enjoyed.

Improving the production quality of mobile video

One of our goals with this work was to create a system that promotes the production of high quality content in mobile video. By focusing on storytelling, we chose a domain that centers on performance. Telling stories is an art where the performer wants to entertain as well as inform and recipients want to understand and be engaged. [11] This creates a high incentive for story creators to produce higher quality video with more engaging content. Because of this, stories were also kept short, allowing for easy mobile viewing between, or in parallel with, other tasks the recipient was involved in while navigating the city. The narrative quality of the videos that we observed was much higher than the content observed through studies of mobile video streaming services [13]. We believe this is largely due to the focused and performative nature of storytelling to a small audience. Recipients all enjoyed watching the video content that was produced explicitly for them.

Turning older adults into media creators

Often, older adults see video recording and other interactive technologies as too complicated to learn. By creating a system that allowed for simple video recording through a webpage, we hope to encourage more seniors to get involved in the process of creating media and sharing stories with others. All of the older participants in our study commented on the ease of creating new stories in the system and most participants were able to use the system with little guidance from the research team. We hope that by engaging older adults, it will be easier to create historical records of past eras and that families will feel closer to each other because of the stories that are shared.

CONCLUSION

Our initial findings demonstrate that location-based asynchronous video communication can enhance relationships and create feelings of togetherness over a distance. We are encouraged by these findings and have created a more scalable version of the system that will be released publicly. We are interested in comparing results from this larger scale deployment to findings from this study and in investigating other uses of the system that emerge beyond intergenerational storytelling. Some of our participants were quite interested in using the system to leave location-based messages for loved ones at their work or at a distant airport to receive when they land. Participants also mentioned wanting travel tips from friends in other cities so that they could stumble upon restaurants and attractions as they roam the city. We are interested in how a single system could support these uses in addition to the type of family stories that were created for this trial. Most of all, we hope that this new communication medium can work to create stronger bonds across a distance in the lives of many users and better connect people to the cities in which they live. To study this, we will soon be releasing the system as a public beta at http://www.storyplace.me to study emergent uses of this new form of communication.

ACKNOWLEDGMENTS

We would like to thank all of our participants for their time, our reviewers for their comments on the paper, and Gunnar Harboe, Pallavi Kaushik, and Elaine Huang for their work on the study that led to this concept.

REFERENCES

1. Aalto, L., Göthlin, N., Korhonen, J., and Ojala. T. 2004. Bluetooth and WAP push based location-aware mobile advertising system. In Proc. MobiSys '04.
2. Ballagas, R., Kaye, J., Ames, M., Go, J., and Raffle, H. "Family communication: phone conversations with children." Proceedings of IDC '09
3. Ballagas, R., Walz, S.P., Kratz, S., Fuhr, C., Yu, E., Tann, M., Borchers, J., and Hovestadt. L. 2007. REXplorer: A Mobile, Pervasive Spell-Casting Game for Tourists. In CHI '07: Extended Abstracts.
4. Bentley, F., Harboe, G., and Kaushik, P. Involving Seniors in Ethnographic-style Work: Initial findings from a study on long-distance communication. CHI 2010 Workshop on Senior-Friendly Technologies: Interaction Design for the Elderly. April, 2010.
5. Bidwell, N.J., Reitmaier, T., Marsden, G., and Hansen, S. 2010. Designing with mobile digital storytelling in rural Africa. In Proc CHI 2010.
6. Dougherty, A. 2010. New Medium, New Practice: Civic Production in Live-Streaming Mobile Video. Masters thesis in Comparative Media Studies, MIT.
7. Haas, W., Bradley, D., Longino, C., Stoller, E., Serow, W. 2006. In Retirement Migration, Who Counts? A Methodological Question With Economic Policy Implications. The Gerontologist (2006) 46 (6): 815-820.
8. Hart,P .The Reverse Geocache Puzzle. http://arduiniana.org/projects/the-reverse-geo-cache-puzzle/ Accessed June 18, 2010.
9. Harboe, G., Metcalf, C., Bentley, F., Tullio, J., Massey, N., Romano, G. (2008) Ambient Social TV: Drawing People into a Shared Experience. Proc CHI 2008.
10. He, W., Sengupta, M., Velkoff, V., and DeBarros. K. 65+ in the United States: 2005. US Department of Health and Human Services and US Census Bureau. http://www.census.gov/prod/2006pubs/p23-209.pdf
11. Huisman. D.M.. 2008. Telling a Family: Family storytelling, family identity, and cultural membership. PhD dissertation, University of Iowa.
12. Lawton, L., Silverstein. M., Bengtson, V. Affection, Social Contact, and Geographic Distance between Adult Children and Their Parents. Journal of Marriage and the Family, Vol. 56, No. 1. (Feb., 1994), pp. 57-68.
13. Juhlin, O., Engström, A., and Reponen, E. 2010. Mobile broadcasting: the whats and hows of live video as a social medium. In Proc Mobile HCI 2010.
14. Olsson, T., Soronen, H., and Väänänen-Vainio-Mattila, K. 2008. User needs and design guidelines for mobile services for sharing digital life memories. In Proc Mobile HCI 2008.
15. Olsson, T., Lehtonen, M., Pavel, D., and Väänänen-Vainio-Mattila, K. 2007. User-centered design of a mobile application for sharing life memories. In Proc Mobility '07.
16. Pan, P., Kastner, C., Crow, D., and Davenport, G. 2002. M-Studio: an authoring application for context-aware multimedia. In Proceedings ACM Multimedia (MULTIMEDIA '02).
17. Peesapati, S.T., Schwanda, V., Schultz, J,. Lepage, M., Jeong, S., and Cosley, D. 2010. Pensieve: supporting everyday reminiscence. In Proc. CHI 2010..
18. Ballagas, R., Revelle, G., Horii, H., Follmer, S., Go, J., Reardon, E., Mori, K., Kaye, J., and Spasojevic, M. 2010. Family story play: reading with young children (and elmo) over a distance. In Proc CHI 2010.
19. Rhodes, B. and Maes, P. (2000) Just-in-time information retrieval agents. IBM Systems Journal 39(3–4).
20. Riley, M. W. and Foner, A. Aging and Society. Russell Sage, NY, 1968.
21. Lynda H. Schneekloth, Robert G. Shibley. 1995. Placemaking: The Art and Practice of Building Communities. Wiley.
22. Smith, S., and House, M. 2005. Snowbirds, Sunbirds, and Stayers: Seasonal Migration of the Elderly in Florida. Presented at the annual meeting of the Population Association of America, 2005.
23. Sohn, T., Li, K.A., Lee, G., Smith, I., Scott, J., Griswold, W.G. Place-Its: A Study of Location-Based Reminders on Mobile Phones. In Proc. Ubicomp 2005. Tokyo, Japan, pp. 232-250 2005.
24. Treas, J. Aging and the Family. In D. Woodruff and J. Birren (eds.), Aging: Scientific Perspectives and Social Issues. Van Nostrand. Ny, 1975.
25. Yarosh, S. 2010. Poster of the outcomes of the "Designing and Evaluating Affective Aspects of Sociable Media to Support Social Connectedness" workshop at CHI 2010.
26. Yarosh, S, Davis, H., Modlitba, P., Skov, M., and Vetere, F. Mobile Technologies for Parent/Child Relationships. In: Allison Druin, editor, Mobile Technology for Children. Boston: Morgan Kaufmann, 2009, pp. 285-306.

Living in a Glass House: A Survey of Private Moments in the Home

Eun Kyoung Choe[1], Sunny Consolvo[2], Jaeyeon Jung[3*], Beverly Harrison[4*], Julie A. Kientz[1, 5]

University of Washington
[1]The Information School
[5]Human Centered Design & Eng.
{eunky, jkientz}@uw.edu

[2]Intel Labs Seattle
sunny@consolvo.org

[3]Microsoft Research
jjung@microsoft.com

[4]Lab126
beverly_harrison
@yahoo.com

ABSTRACT

As advances in technology accelerate, sensors and recording devices are increasingly being integrated into homes. Although the added benefit of sensing is often clear (e.g., entertainment, security, encouraging sustainable behaviors, etc.), the home is a private and intimate place, with multiple stakeholders who may have competing priorities and tolerances for what is acceptable and useful. In an effort to develop systems that account for the needs and concerns of householders, we conducted an anonymous survey (N = 475) focusing on the activities and habits that people do at home that they would not want to be recorded. In this paper, we discuss those activities and where in the home they are performed, and offer suggestions for the design of UbiComp systems that rely on sensing and recording.

Author Keywords Privacy, home, sensors, sensing, capture and access, survey, self-report, Mechanical Turk, postcard.

ACM Classification Keywords H5.m. Information interfaces and presentation (e.g., HCI): Miscellaneous.

General Terms Human Factors.

INTRODUCTION

Sensors and recording devices are increasingly being integrated into homes. It is common for homes today to have smart thermostats, wireless smoke detectors, or home security systems. Consumer electronics such as Microsoft's Kinect and Samsung televisions already have built-in sensing, such as an RGB camera, depth sensor, or a light sensor. These types of sensors have been used for numerous applications, such as providing controller-free interaction experiences in entertainment platforms, monitoring the safety of elders in assisted living facilities, monitoring children's activities at home [4], or providing householders with detailed resource use reports for sustainability purposes [10].

However, recent work by Srinivasan et al. has shown that private activities in the home such as cooking, showering, and toileting can be inferred by eavesdropping on the wireless transmissions of data coming from off-the-shelf sensors installed in homes [11]. Furthermore, although the added benefit of sensing is often clear, the home is a private and intimate environment with multiple stakeholders (e.g., members of the household, visitors, overnight guests, and service people) who may have competing priorities and different tolerances for what is acceptable and useful—independent of concerns over eavesdroppers.

Discussions around privacy concerns over emerging technologies are not new, including Warren and Brandeis' classic article from 1890 [14] when instantaneous photographs taken by newspapers began to invade private life. Such invasion has only become more convoluted in ubiquitous computing (UbiComp) environments, which has led several researchers to investigate the intersection of privacy and technology. Some have proposed principles and guidelines to build privacy-sensitive UbiComp systems [5] or theoretical tools such as privacy risk models [3], while others have focused on identifying user tensions with privacy management [8] or attempted to understand perceptions toward recording technologies *in situ* [2,6].

While our work shares similar goals to the work above, we focus on privacy concerns around sensing and recording technologies *in the home*. Despite considerable research into many aspects of the home using ethnographic approaches or field studies of technology prototypes (e.g., [12,13]), privacy in the home has received less attention. One exception is work by Neustaedter et al. exploring privacy concerns of always-on video in the context of telecommuters working at home [7]. They created scenarios where one's privacy may be at moderate-to-extreme risk and employed privacy/awareness questionnaires. Their focus was evaluating the effectiveness of video blurring filters in balancing privacy and awareness, whereas our focus is to understand activities that people do not want recorded.

In an effort to develop systems that account for the needs and concerns of householders, we investigated the types of activities that occur in the home that could cause concern if they were to be recorded. However, studying such concerns depends on householders being willing to disclose sensitive information about their private lives—precisely the type of information they may not want to reveal to others. To address this issue, we conducted an anonymous survey. In this paper, we present results from the survey ($N = 475$), focusing on activities and habits that people do at home that they would not want to be recorded. Our analysis focuses on the activity/task (e.g., nose picking) and location in the home (e.g., in the kitchen). Our work provides an empirical basis for privacy concerns in the home.

SURVEY

We conducted an anonymous survey using online and offline recruiting methods. We iterated the survey questions using Amazon's Mechanical Turk (MTurk), an online crowdsourcing system. We conducted 7 iterations with 114 pilot respondents before deriving the final questions and scenarios that are presented here. We compensated MTurk participants—in both the pilot and final version of the surveys—$0.10 USD per survey, but paid nothing for the offline methods due to the need to preserve anonymity.

Recruiting

We distributed the final version of the survey online through MTurk, the researchers' personal networks, and Craigslist. In addition, we distributed 150 physical postcards with nearby drop boxes and another 150 prepaid postcards returnable via U.S. Mail at local places such as coffee shops and medical center waiting rooms. MTurk workers who accepted the task were redirected to an external survey page. To protect their anonymity, no direct link was made between the worker ID and their responses. The survey was available only to U.S. residents with at least a 95% approval rating (a screening option that MTurk provides). We also posted the survey link to the volunteer section of nine U.S. cities on Craigslist.org and sent emails to our personal networks asking people to forward the link to others who were *not* students or engaged in technology-related jobs.

Survey Content

To help respondents imagine how sensors might be embedded in their homes, we provided the following scenario:

> *Imagine a future where you live in a smart home in which security cameras and microphones are used to protect you, the other members of your household, and your household itself. These devices would be integrated into every room in your home except for the bathroom(s).*

Through our pilot testing, we found that the scenario worked best when it was neither too vague nor too specific; a vague description of sensing technologies (e.g., "a system capable of detecting activities" instead of "a camera or microphone") did not provide a frame of reference for the average respondents to understand sensor context. On the other hand, very specific scenarios (e.g., "protection of the elderly or infirm") were often too emotionally charged and thus introduced certain response bias. Therefore, we were deliberate in choosing an example ("security cameras and microphone") that was specific, less emotionally loaded, and still generally understandable to laypeople today. Respondents could only react meaningfully to questions with respect to certain positive properties that the system was supposed to have, and thus we illustrated in the scenario that the cameras and microphones are installed for the householders' security—for their own use. We also included a statement that only the members of the household would be in control of the data. Because we offered minimal to no compensation for participating, we kept the survey brief. We asked people to describe "*at least three regular habits*" that they do at home that they would not want to have recorded. We also asked them to include *where* in the home they do the activities. Extra space was provided for anyone willing to provide additional activities. We also collected basic demographic information such as gender, age, occupation, housing structure, home ownership, and other householder members. We included a screening question at the end of the MTurk survey to filter out respondents who did not take the survey seriously [1].

Respondents

We received a total of 489 surveys, 475 of which we considered valid. We eliminated empty responses and responses from people who were under the age of 18 or lived outside of the U.S. Of the 468 respondents who provided their gender, 71.6% were female and 28.4% were male. Respondents identified themselves as students (20.9%), homemakers (11.8%), unemployed (6.3%), and having IT-related jobs (5.2%). Other occupations included attorney, writer, artist, cashier, teacher, marketer, statistician, professor, consultant, and so on. The majority of the 475 surveys came from MTurk ($n = 405$), though we note that others have found that young, female, highly educated people are overrepresented in U.S. MTurk workers [9]. An additional 30 surveys came from the physical postcards, 24 from Craigslist.org, and 16 from our personal networks.

RESULTS

We collected a total of 1433 activity descriptions that respondents reported doing in their homes that they would not want recorded. We analyzed the activities using affinity diagramming and developed a category scheme for *activity type* creating 19 high-level and 75 sub-categories. Using this category scheme, we had a total of 1533 coded activities. The activities were also analyzed based on *location* in the home. We discuss results in terms of the *types of activities* that were reported and *where in the home* the activities tend to be performed. We note that the frequencies that we report are not necessarily reflective of the *importance* or *sensitivity* of the activities, though it does indicate what was important enough for respondents to mention.

Types of Activities

The most frequently reported activities that respondents do in their homes that they would not want recorded fall into the categories of self-appearance, intimacy, cooking & eating, media use, and oral expressions. We discuss each category, include quotes to describe the activities in the respondents' own words, and discuss the influence of respondents' demographics on the types of activities that they reported.

Self-appearance. Activities in this category included walking around in underwear, partially dressed, or in the nude; the act of getting dressed & undressed; putting on makeup or lotion; and having a makeup-less face. Activities performed while partially nude or naked were frequently reported along with other activities, such as right before or after taking a shower. For example, one respondent commented,

> *"I take off my clothes in the bathroom, but then really quick nip out around the corner and toss them in the washer. It is only a foot and a half to step around the corner to the washer in the hallway. Still, I don't want anybody looking at me."*—62, F, homemaker, lives with spouse & child(ren)

Intimacy. Many respondents did not want intimate activities, including sexual activities with a partner, masturbating, and other activities such as kissing or cuddling to be recorded. A respondent explained,

> *"Having sex with my husband. We have sex in the bedroom, and since we live with children and grandchildren I would not want them to have access to recordings of that."*—56, F, legal assistant, lives with spouse & child(ren)

Cooking & Eating. Activities in this category included eating, snacking, eating sweets or junk food in particular, drinking soda, eating or drinking directly from a food or beverage carton, preparing food, and occasional binge eating. While some respondents did not want any form of eating or cooking to be recorded, it was often eating or cooking with questionable manners or in unusual places and times that was the problem. For example, respondents did not want to be recorded while eating in bed, eating in front of the computer or TV, overeating, eating with fingers, or eating ice cream at 3am. One respondent shared,

> *"If I am cooking in the kitchen and something falls on the floor, sometimes I will still use the food (though I rinse it off)."*—53, F, faculty, lives with a spouse

Media Use. The activities in this category included watching TV or movies, watching pornography, using a computer, listening to music, playing video games, and reading. Concerns focused on the possibility that other household members could find out what the respondent was watching, the ability to figure out for oneself how much time he or she was wasting by watching TV, and that passwords might be exposed if a camera could see what he or she was typing. One respondent clarified,

> *"Watching bad tv. I generally watch at least a couple hours a day of tv that I don't want people to know about because they'll mock me."*—21, F, student, lives with parents

Oral Expressions. This category included activities such as singing, having a personal conversation, talking on the phone, talking to oneself or to a pet, and crying. Respondents were concerned about recordings of conversations regarding anything from surprise birthday presents for other householders to being frustrated with other members of the family to financial plans to politics. As one explained,

Activity Type	%	Examples of sub categories
Self-appearance	22.5%	Nudity, walking in underwear, no makeup
Intimacy	18.3%	Sex, masturbating, kissing
Cooking & Eating	9.3%	Eating, snacking, binging, cooking
Media Use	8.3%	Watching TV/movies/porn, computer use
Oral Expressions	8.0%	Singing, conversation, phone calls, crying
Socially Awkward Acts	5.9%	Nose picking, scratching
Personal Hygiene	5.0%	Grooming, toileting, showering, weighing
Physical Activity	4.8%	Dancing, exercising, yoga
Sleep	4.6%	Sleeping, snoring, napping, staying up late
Home Keeping	3.4%	Being messy, cleaning, sniffing clothes
Contentious Acts	2.5%	Arguing, swearing, yelling, disciplining
Bodily Functions	1.7%	Passing gas, blowing nose, belching
Alcohol & Tobacco use	1.4%	Drinking alcohol, smoking
Unwinding	1.2%	Lounging, relaxing, killing time
Working	0.8%	Working, writing, creating artwork
Intentional sneaky acts	0.8%	Sneaking into the kitchen, hiding, stealing
Illegal behavior	0.5%	Illegal drug use
Spirituality	0.5%	Praying, reading bible
Miscellaneous	0.4%	Anything, everything

Table 1. Breakdown of activity types for 1433 activity descriptions (1533 coded activities) and examples

> *"Singing 80s songs with my cats' names substituted into the lyrics."*—29, F, consultant, lives with a spouse

Other categories. As Table 1 shows, the data that we collected can be described as a long tail. We briefly report some of the other private moments that were reported here. Several respondents did not want *Socially Awkward Acts* such as nose picking (the 5th most frequently mentioned sub-category overall) or scratching to be recorded. *Personal Hygiene* activities, such as grooming, toileting, and showering, were also considered private (e.g., *"Trimming toenails. For some reason, this should take place in the bathroom but always happens in the bedroom."*). Many respondents would not want *Physical Activity* recorded either—they explained that it *"would just feel weird"* to be recorded while dancing or doing uncommon exercises such as yoga while naked or the "air bike" abdominal exercise. Related to *Oral Expressions* discussed above, several respondents reported activities related to heated conversations and emotions—that is, *Contentious Acts.* These included arguing or fighting with one's spouse, swearing, yelling, disciplining children or pets, and making rude hand gestures. Finally, many respondents would not want *Bodily Functions* recorded, such as passing gas, sneezing, or belching (e.g., *"When I sneeze while watching tv in the living room and wipe snot off myself with a napkin."*).

Demographics in Relation to Activity Type

We observed that respondents' demographic information such as gender and household structure affected reported activity types. A chi-square test of independence was performed to examine the relation between gender and activity type, and household structure and activity type. The relationship between gender and activity type was significant, χ^2 (4, N = 1006) = 14.71, p = .005. As shown in Table 2, male respondents were more likely to report activities in the *Intimacy* and *Media Use* categories than female respondents, while female respondents were more likely to report activities in the *Self-appearance* and *Oral Expressions* categories. The relationship between household structure and

	Gender		Household Structure	
	Male	Female	Live alone	Live with Child(ren)
# of coded activities	287	719	117	320
Self-appearance	30.0%	35.6%	32.5%	39.4%
Intimacy	32.1%	25.9%	22.2%	29.1%
Kitchen & Eating	12.2%	14.3%	14.5%	11.3%
Media Use	16.7%	10.7%	18.8%	10.6%
Oral Expressions	9.1%	13.5%	12.0%	9.7%

Table 2. Breakdown of the 5 most frequently reported activity types across gender and household structure

activity type was only marginally significant, χ^2 (4, N = 437) = 8.22, p = .084.

Locations in the Home

Some locations in the home were thought to be more private than others, which is an important consideration when deploying in-home sensing systems[†]. Though 20.3% of the activities mentioned did not report a location, of the 79.7% that did, the *bedroom* was the most frequently mentioned place (33.7% of activities that included a location). The types of activities that occur in the bedroom were often related to sexual activities, sleeping, and the act of getting dressed and undressed. *Anywhere in the home* (16.2%) was another common response and often involved family arguments and private conversations, walking around in underwear, nose picking, bodily functions, and intimacy. The *living room* (13.9%) was often mentioned with activities regarding Media Use, Physical Activity, and Oral Expressions. Of the activities that included a location, 5.2% involved *a specific path or sequence* in the home such as bedroom to bathroom, bathroom to laundry, and to and from the shower. These paths often involved activities regarding Personal Hygiene (e.g., putting clothing in the laundry before taking a shower) and Self-appearance (e.g., walking around in the nude, changing clothes).

DISCUSSION AND LIMITATIONS

The results of this study about familiar and everyday activities in the home may look obvious. However, despite their unsurprising nature, we feel that privacy concerns around sensing and recording technologies in the home have not been previously studied in detail in this context and that many of these concerns are not being accounted for in current systems. For example, Microsoft's Kinect sensor can take photos or videos of people when they are playing games. It is quite possible that shirtless game players or bystanders in the camera's field of view might accidently have their photos taken by the Kinect sensor, which could raise serious privacy concerns. Thus, we want to help designers and developers become better aware of the types of activities that their potential users consider private. It is not our intention to define privacy by generic categories of activity and location. We rather show that relatively 'safe' activities such as cooking could suddenly become a sensitive activity by subtle changes in context. Now that this work has provided a better understanding of the types of activities householders would like to keep private, our next step is to explore how particular sensing modalities (e.g., data processing techniques, retention periods, etc.) may affect people's privacy concerns.

CONCLUSION

In this paper, we presented the results of an anonymous survey (N = 475) of activities that householders do at home that they would *not* want to be recorded by an in-home sensing system. We discussed our results in terms of the types of activities as well as where in the home the activities tend to occur. This work has provided a better understanding of the types of private moments that occur in the home, which can help designers and developers of in-home sensing systems be more mindful of the types of activities that need to remain private.

REFERENCES

1. Downs, J.S. et al. (2010). Are your participants gaming the system? Screening Mechanical Turk workers. *CHI '10,* 2399–2402.
2. Hayes, G.R. et al. (2007). Physical, social, and experiential knowledge in pervasive computing environments. *IEEE Pervasive Computing, 6*(4), 56–63.
3. Hong, J.I., Ng, J.D., Lederer, S., & Landay, J.A. (2004). Privacy risk models for designing privacy-sensitive ubiquitous computing systems. *DIS '04*, 91–100.
4. Kientz, J.A., & Abowd, G.D. (2009). KidCam: Toward an effective technology for the capture of children's moments of interest. *Pervasive '09,* 115–132.
5. Langheinrich, M. (2001). Privacy by design—Principles of privacy-aware ubiquitous systems. *UbiComp '01*, 273–291.
6. Massimi, M. et al. (2010). Understanding recording technologies in everyday life. *IEEE Pervasive Computing, 9*(3), 64–71.
7. Neustaedter, C. et al. (2006). Blur filtration fails to preserve privacy for home-based video conferencing. *ACM TOCHI, 13*(1), 1–36.
8. Palen, L., & Dourish, P. (2003). Unpacking "privacy" for a networked world. *CHI '03*, 129–136.
9. Paolacci, G., Chandler, J., & Ipeirotis, P.G. (2010). Running experiments on Amazon Mechanical Turk. *Judgment and Decision Making, 5*(5), 411–419.
10. Patel, S.N. (2008) Infrastructure mediated sensing. Ph.D. diss., Georgia Institute of Technology.
11. Srinivasan, V. et al. (2008). Protecting your daily in-home activity information from a wireless snooping attack. *UbiComp '08*, 202–211.
12. Taylor, A. et al. (2007). Homes that make us smart. *J.of Personal Technologies, 11*(5), 383–393.
13. Tolmie, P., & Crabtree, A. (2008). Deploying research technology in the home. *CSCW '08*, 639–648.
14. Warren, S., & Brandeis, L. (1890). The right to privacy. *Harvard Law Review, 4*(1), 193–220.

---

[*] Work done while the author was at Intel Labs Seattle.

[†] Our scenario specified that sensors were not in the bathroom.

Leveraging Conductive Inkjet Technology to Build a Scalable and Versatile Surface for Ubiquitous Sensing

Nan-Wei Gong[1,2], Steve Hodges[2], Joseph A. Paradiso[1,2]

[1]MIT Media Lab
Responsive Environments Group,
Cambridge, USA
{nanwei|joep}@media.mit.edu

[2]Microsoft Research Cambridge,
Sensors and Devices Group,
Cambridge, UK
shodges@microsoft.com

ABSTRACT
In this paper we describe the design and implementation of a new versatile, scalable and cost-effective sensate surface. The system is based on a new conductive inkjet technology, which allows capacitive sensor electrodes and different types of RF antennas to be cheaply printed onto a roll of flexible substrate that may be many meters long. By deploying this surface on (or under) a floor it is possible to detect the presence and whereabouts of users through both passive and active capacitive coupling schemes. We have also incorporated GSM and NFC electromagnetic radiation sensing and piezoelectric pressure and vibration detection. We report on a number of experiments which evaluate sensing performance based on a 2.5m x 0.3m hardware test-bed. We describe some potential applications for this technology and highlight a number of improvements we have in mind.

Author Keywords
Sensate skin surface, flexible electronics, location tracking, distributed sensor network.

ACM Classification Keywords
C.3 Special-Purpose And Application-Based Systems: Microprocessor /microcomputer applications; Real-time and embedded systems; Signal processing systems. H.5.2 User Interfaces: Input devices and strategies.

General Terms
Design, Experimentation, Human Factors

INTRODUCTION
Traditional electronic fabrication techniques are based on rigid planar substrates – namely mass-produced low-cost printed circuit boards (PCBs). This constrains the associated circuitry not only in terms of physical flexibility, but also in terms of surface area – because they are rigid, PCBs larger than around 30cm x 30cm are typically impractical because they are hard to manufacture, transport and deploy. Research into materials and mechanics for flexible and stretchable electronics [1-4] promise an exciting future but are still far away from full-scale mass production. However, recent advancements in manufacturing based on flexible films coupled with conventional rigid components are opening up new possibilities in the design of a large, flexible and cheap substrate for circuitry. Indeed, flexible substrates with customized printed conductive traces are now becoming readily accessible and have potential applications in a number of ubiquitous computing application scenarios.

In this paper, we explore the use of a recently commercialized technology known as conductive inkjet printing [5] (e.g. conductiveinkjet.com) as an enabler for the goal of building low cost, large area flexible sensate surfaces which can detect and localize users in an indoor environment. We present a prototype sensing 'surface' based on a flexible substrate with custom-printed conductive traces which provide natural electrodes and antennas for capacitive and electromagnetic sensing.

RELATED WORK
Our prior work has explored dense networks of hardwired sensor modules (termed *Sensate Media*) as a scalable sensor substrate [6-7], and low cost, dense sensing environments have been explored by many research groups, often as sensate floors for interactive media applications. Unlike computer vision based tracking, this approach requires minimal computing power, can be quite low cost, and can also provide good range-independent resolution depending on the sensor density. A flexible sensor floor can be quickly rolled out and hooked up anywhere without constraints on lighting or issues of camera occlusion. One of the methods is to use load cells at the corners of a surface that can estimate the changes in weight and position of an object and

[1] This work was undertaken at Microsoft Research Cambridge, UK

further identify people based on their footstep force profiles [8-9]. Other projects, including the Magic Carpet (piezoelectric wires) [10], Litefoot (optical proximity sensors) [11] and ISA floor (FSR) [12], create pixilated surfaces using larger numbers of sensors. The Z-tiles used Force sensing resistors (FSRs) in networked modular sensing units for easy installation and reconfiguration [13]. Recent projects in the area of floor sensing evolved quickly in the direction of multi-modal sensor fusion, especially those combining vision tracking for off-floor three-dimensional movement and interaction [14-16].

In this work, we want to leverage the latest advances in flexible electronics substrate manufacture to create a sensing floor. Three major types of manufacturing technique can be used to fabricate a flexible sensing surface. The first one is fabrication by roll-to-roll processing [17-18]. Roll-to-roll lithography is capable of very high resolution conductor placement on flexible substrate materials, but at a relatively high cost. Another manufacturing method for fabricating large-area, low cost flexible materials is additive printing of noble-metal conductors, organic conductors, and even semiconductors [17-18]. However, the electrical and mechanical characteristics of the resulting materials do not make them an adequate substitute for more conventional manufacturing techniques. The third approach centers around methods for printing metallic conductors from nanoparticles – these techniques are currently being developed, hence few are yet main-stream. The main contenders appear to be copper-on-kapton substrate (e.g. www.allflexinc.com), conductive inkjet flex technology (e.g. www.conductiveinkjet.com) and metallic nanoparticle inkjet printing (e.g. t-ink.com).

SYSTEM OVERVIEW

Overall Architecture and Construction

Our prototype sensate surface is based on a matrix of sensing 'tiles' that is formed by printing a specific copper pattern onto a thin, flexible plastic substrate using conductive inkjet technology. Each sensing tile is around 0.3m x 0.3m and contains four printed electrodes of approximately 0.12m x 0.12m for capacitive sensing and two additional printed RF antennas – one for detection of cellular GSM UHF electromagnetic radiation and another for Near Field Communication (NFC) pickup in the HF band.

Whilst it is possible to attach surface mount electronic components directly to the printed substrate, using either low-temperature solder or conductive adhesive, this process is not straightforward and does not yield high enough performance to support the circuitry needed to process the signals picked up by the printed electrodes and antennas. For this reason, we decided to implement the required circuitry on a small but separate conventional FR4 glass fiber printed circuit board (PCB). This is reminiscent of the architecture proposed by Wagner et al. [19] for an elastomeric skin that carried rigid islands housing active sub-circuits. In our case, the PCB forms a signal conditioning and processing module, which is itself attached to the flexible substrate. One such module is attached per tile, in the center of the four capacitive electrodes. Figure 1 shows photos of these components. Details about the operation of the various sensing modes supported by the electronic hardware are described in the following section.

In addition to performing the necessary signal processing, the PCB modules also contain a microcontroller unit (MCU), which is able to sample the detected waveforms and communicate this information with a PC over a shared I^2C bus that runs along the length of the substrate. In order to minimize any cross-coupling between the data lines, each is separated by a grounded trace. The MCU can also be instructed to excite the electrodes with a predefined waveform – for this, synchronization between the adjacent squares is required, and this is achieved using one additional line that distributes a global clock to all tiles and their associated MCUs.

Power is distributed to each PCB using dedicated power and ground lines running along the left and right edges of the substrate. Wider tracks are used for this to lower trace impedance and hence power drop. The conductive inkjet printing process results in a sheet resistance of printing 200 mΩ per square, and the resulting power drop across each sensing tile was measured at ~0.18V with all sensing modules fully powered on. The power rails run at 18V nominally (for 8 units), and a smoothed linear regulator fitted to each PCB is used to generate a 5V supply locally.

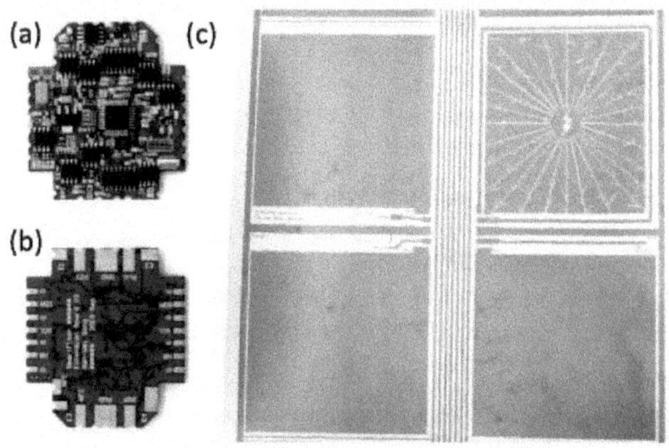

Figure 1. (a) The top view of the signal processing PCB module shows the electronic components, whilst (b) shows the surface-mount pads on the underside of the PCB module, which are used to connect with the substrate below. (c) The substrate is made up from sensing tiles like the one shown. The 2x2 matrix of printed electrodes is clearly visible; note that the top-right electrode incorporates a pattern of breaks in the copper designed to minimize Eddy currents because the NFC HF antenna is printed around it (just visible in the photo). The GSM UHF antenna is just above the bottom-right hand capacitive electrode.

Figure 2 shows what the sensing floor looks like when the PCB modules are attached to the flexible substrate. Our test-bed is based on a 2.4m length of 0.3m wide printed film, which has 8 tiles along its length. In our prototypes the width of the substrate was limited to a single tile because the conductive inkjet process was only available to us on a 30cm wide roll at the time of manufacture, although our supplier's manufacturing facility is theoretically capable of printing on substrate up to around 2m wide. The length of substrate is only constrained by the size of the roll; a single piece tens of meters long is entirely feasible. The PCB modules are soldered to the substrate with low temperature solder (we used $Sn_{42}Bi_{58}$ tin-bismuth solder: melting point 138°C, tensile strength 55.2 MPa). We also attached a piezoelectric pickup element directly to the substrate.

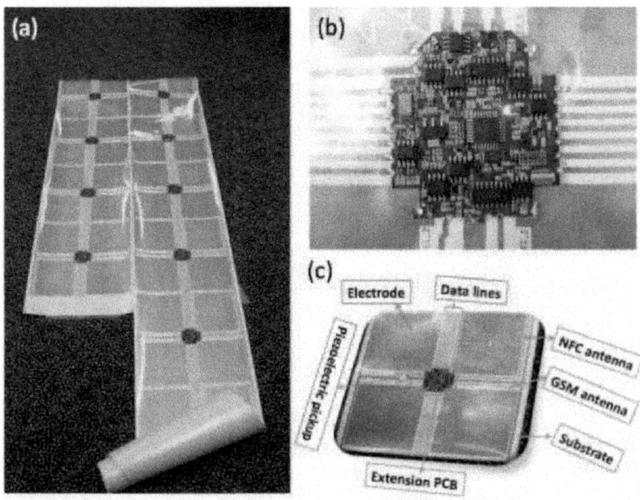

Figure 2. (a) A roll of the substrate with multiple sensing PCB modules fitted and (b) a close-up of one PCB module. (c) A single sensing tile consists of the substrate plus the corresponding PCB module.

PCB module circuitry

Having made the decision to mount the electronic components on a 'PCB module' rather than directly to the flexible substrate, we decided to make the circuitry as versatile as possible. To that end, each PCB module in the system uses an Atmel Atmega368 microcontroller to coordinate global and local communication, manage sensor I/O and perform basic data processing. Global communication is achieved by a two-wire I^2C protocol that is coordinated by a master microcontroller, which interfaces between the end of the substrate and a PC.

Figure 3 shows a block diagram of the sensing operation of each unit. There are five major modalities: passive capacitive sensing, active capacitive sensing, GSM UHF detection, NFC HF detection, and vibration/pressure sensing from the piezoelectric sensor. This wide range of approaches was chosen to allow us to explore the use of printed conductors for sensing as extensively as possible. The raw signal from each printed detector is passed through some signal conditioning circuitry and then into a multiplexer (CD4052) for selective analog to digital conversion (ADC) sampling on the microcontroller. The sampling rate was set to fast mode (400 kHz) with 6 channels of 10-bit ADC. The electrode size in our design (~12cm x 12cm) seems to work well for resolving detail down to the size of a human foot. It would be possible to design a higher or lower resolution floor to match different needs for tracking and localization.

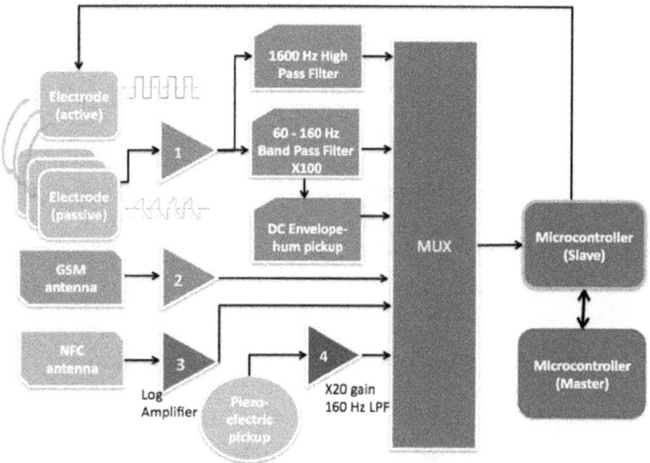

Figure 3. Block diagram of operation for each sensing tile. From left to right, signals picked up by the electrodes/ antennae are then filtered by analog circuits and finally sampled by the microcontroller. Each microcontroller acts as a slave device to a master microcontroller, which controlled the entire floor via a two wire communication protocol.

Figure 4 below illustrates the basic operation of the firmware for power management on each slave sensor unit. Each operation starts after receiving "start" command from the master MCU and then enters Idle mode after it successfully joins the I^2C network. Idle mode is the low power mode where the MCU stays in sleep state and the most power-hungry analog circuits (e.g. the NFC log amp) are disabled to save power. The slave units will wake on interrupts from the passive sensor signals, piezo pickup (or optionally on the passive capacitive or GSM/NFC signals), indicating nearby activity. If verified, every unit in proximity wakes up and enters passive capacitive sensing mode.

In the passive capacitive sensing mode, we can easily locate the presence of a person and start the active (interaction) mode. If nothing is detected (event completion), passive mode will eventually time out in favor of idle mode. However, if presence is detected, the operation enters active sensing mode. In this stage, the slave MCU repeatedly excites one of the electrodes with a 5V square wave pattern and samples adjacent electrodes for coupled pick-up, transmitting signal strength information back to the master node. It also samples for signals that are potentially generated by mobile devices the detected user may be carrying or interacting with, namely GSM and NFC signals.

After the interaction stops, the master node sends out a stop command, and slave units return to low power mode until further movements are picked up. Details about how each sensing modality works are described in the following section.

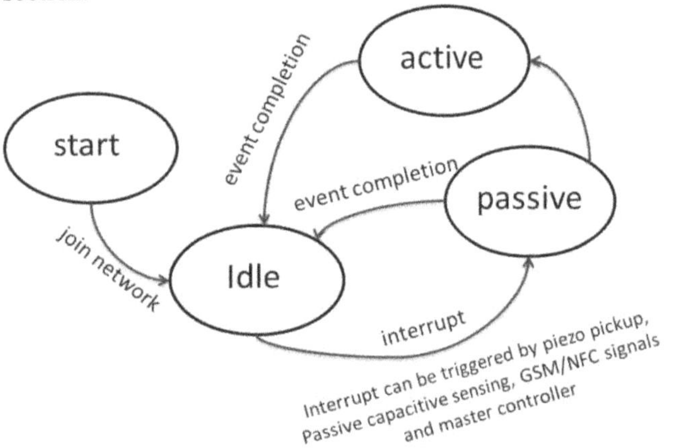

Figure 4. Basic operation of each slave sensor unit.

Physical topology

As mentioned above, our prototype is based on a relatively narrow roll of substrate due to current limitations of the production process we used, as shown in Figure 2(a). In order to cover a wider area with a single strip of sensing substrate, we explored the use of folding – which is possible given the flexible nature of our prototype. In this way, it is possible to cover large areas and also non-flat geometries without the need to cut or re-connect different pieces of the substrate. Examples of this are shown in Figure 5.

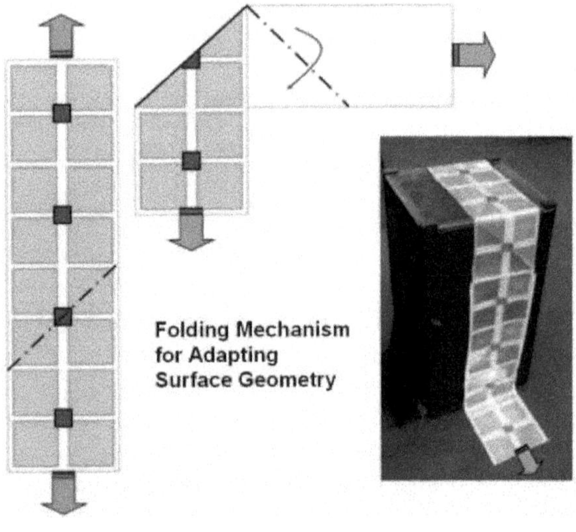

Figure 5. Example folding schemes that allow wider and non-flat areas to be covered using a single piece of the substrate without any cutting or joining. Blue arrows indicate the direction of connecting units.

SENSING MODALITIES

Analog active filtering circuits were designed to detect all of the supported signal types mentioned previously. Each is described in more detail here.

Passive Mode Capacitive Sensing

Passive mode turns out to be both the simplest and the most power-efficient mode for tracking people moving across the surface. In passive mode, the floor detects signals from the environment, such as power line hum (usually 50 or 60 Hz). These signals are coupled into electrodes much more strongly when a person stands on them. We implemented circuits for detecting and sampling this electric hum. The raw signal was first fed into a band-limit filter, made from a pair of first-order filters - a 50Hz high-pass followed by 160 Hz low-pass with x100 gain. The filter output can be selected for ADC sampling by the microcontroller, or alternatively it is also passed through a DC envelope-detector that gives an easily-sampled smooth output reflecting hum amplitude. Because there was a 2.5 V offset on the electrodes, they worked as condenser microphones, and were very sensitive to impacts. Although this was mainly filtered out by our conditioning circuitry, it could be used as another sensing modality as well.

Active Mode Capacitive Sensing

In active mode, one of the floor electrodes on each tile transmits a signal that is detected by adjacent electrodes when a person's body bridges any two of those electrodes. Any of the four electrodes can serve as the transmitter by emitting a 0V to 5V square wave. The other three electrodes are set up as receivers via trans-impedance front-end current-voltage converters that amplify coupled transmit signals. This process is illustrated in Figure 6.

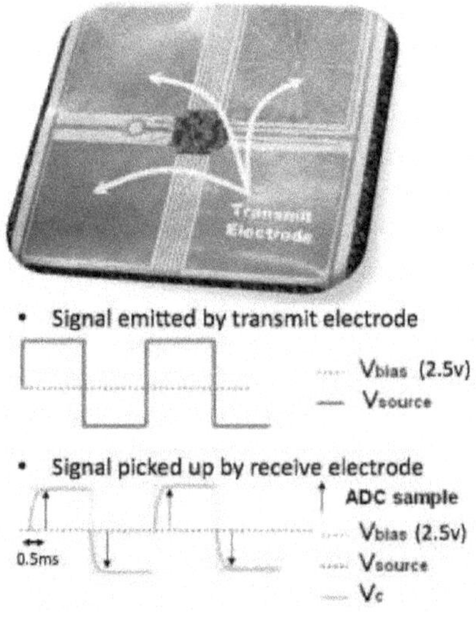

Figure 6. Active capacitive sensing: one of the electrodes serves as a transmitter by way of a series of rising and falling edges that act as an excitation waveform (Vsource). The neighboring electrodes pick up this signal (Vc). The amplitude of Vc is proportional to the capacitive coupling between transmit and receive electrodes.

Signals from the receive electrodes were connected to a high pass filter (1600Hz cut-off frequency) with 10x gain and then sampled by the built-in microcontroller ADC after each changing edge of the transmit electrode (ADC sampling rate ~9600Hz), once the receive signal stabilized (around 0.5ms in our case). As seen in Figure 6, we sampled the charging and discharging amplitude change (voltage) for 32 cycles and averaged their difference.

It is important to note that with a tiled setup like our floor system, there is very likely to be cross talk between tiles during active mode. This means the transmit electrode of any one tile is likely to generate a signal that is picked up by electrodes on neighboring tiles. In our prototype, we alleviate this issue by ensuring all tiles operate in sync when running in active capacitive sensing mode. We do this by running a global clock synchronization line to each tile. Accordingly, with proper synchronization, sensing between a transmitter attached to one microcontroller and receiver on an adjacent microcontroller is possible.

There are two possible scenarios when a user's body comes into the electric field between transmit and receive electrodes – these are known as transmit mode and shunt mode [20-21]. In transmit mode, the signal is coupled through the person, effectively increasing the amplitude of the signal on receive electrodes. The user or object has to be very close to the transmit conductor, hence is acting like an extension of the transmit electrode. Conversely, in shunt mode, the object or body of the user is not connected to the transmit electrode. Instead, it blocks the electrical field between electrodes, i.e., the coupling between the person and the room ground dominates.

The relative dominance of transmit and shunt modes depends on aspects of the physical configuration of the floor and the user walking across it – things like the position of the user's foot relative to the transmit electrode and the distance between the somewhat dielectric floor surface and the capacitive electrodes below it. In transmit mode, the strength of the detected signal will increase as the foot approaches the floor, and in shunt mode it will drop. Nonetheless, it is possible to use either to detect the user's presence.

In addition to localization and identifying people, an active capacitive sensing floor can be further used as a platform for communication between different devices or users by transmitting signals through the user's body as in [23-24]. For example, we have demonstrated this with a small circuit clipped on a shoe with inner side electrode to local ground (against the body) and outer electrode transmitting/receiving a digital signal to and from the floor (Fig. 15).

UHF and HF Sensing

We implemented two antenna designs to pick up signals from a cellular phone. The first type is a ¼ wave GSM antenna, which is designed to pick up both 900MHz and 1800MHz emissions from a GSM cellular handset. The design is a simple 8 cm by 0.3 cm trace on the flexible substrate that feeds a Schottky diode detector followed by a low-pass filter with gain.

NFC signal detection was achieved by constructing a square loop antenna designed to be resonant at 13.56 MHz around one electrode. The electrode was cut into sectors as shown in Figure 1(c) in order to eliminate Eddy currents that would decrease performance. The signal is amplified and detected with an AD8307 log amp in order to produce an easily sampled output response.

Piezoelectric pickup

In addition to printing electromagnetic pick-ups on the substrate in the form of capacitive sensing electrodes and UHF/HF antennas, we also integrated flat contact piezoelectric pick-up sensing elements onto the substrate, adjacent to each PCB as shown in Figure 2(c). Each sensor was soldered onto the ground line of the substrate and was also glued in place to ensure it would be physically coupled to any vibration around the area, as well as responding to dynamic pressure applied from above. Signals were conditioned with a 160Hz active x20 gain low pass filter.

EVALUATION

Here, we report the capability of our system operating under various types of inputs and conditions. We seek to demonstrate the potential of printed conductive technology as a basis for sensing the presence and location of users in a low-cost, highly flexible sensing system.

Detecting users with passive mode

First, we evaluate the ability of our system to sense users via the electric hum, which is coupled into the electrodes using the passive capacitive sensing circuit outlined above. Without any stimulus, the output from the signal conditioning circuitry is centered at the bias voltage of just under 2.5V. When a user steps on the sensing surface, different intensities of electric hum coupled via the body were picked up based on the contact area and proximity.

In Figure 7, we demonstrate footstep detection over time on 4 individual sensing units. As we can see from these traces, the interaction patterns are clean and consistent. It is also worth observing that we can detect the user's foot approaching from a range of 15-20cm in passive mode.

In Figure 8, signals from each of the electrodes in a single tile are plotted separately. Three major signatures of the three typical signal patterns – heel strikes, forefoot strikes and mid-swings between steps – can be differentiated.

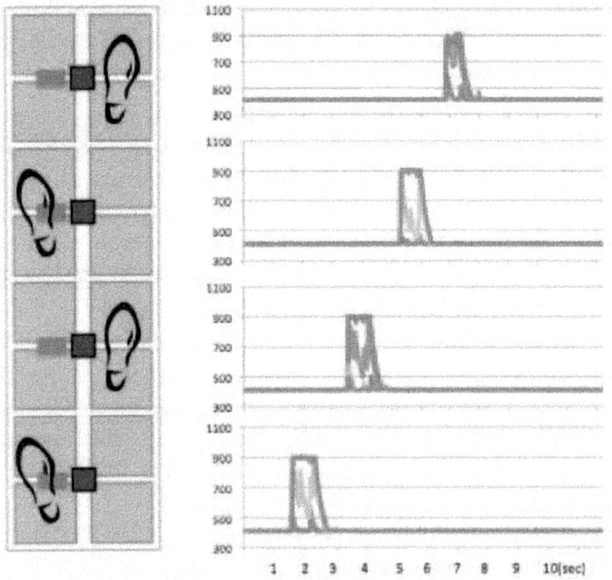

Figure 7. Footstep patterns detected by electrodes embedded in the floor in passive capacitive sensing mode. The four different colors in the right-hand figures represent the signals from the four different electrodes in one sensing tile.

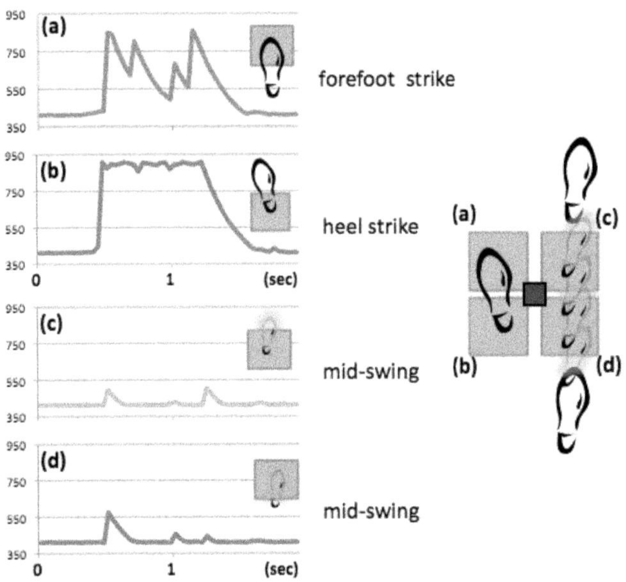

Figure 8. Different signatures typically detected with the passive capacitive sensing method. (a) Forefoot strike, (b) heel strike pattern (left feet), (c) and (d) mid-swing between steps (right feet), detected by adjacent electrodes. The decay time is from the RC response of the envelope detector.

Sensing with active mode

As mentioned above, depending on the distance between users' body and the transmit electrode, two possible effects can be observed during active capacitive sensing, namely transmit mode and shunt mode. We therefore tested the active mode in these two conditions.

Firstly, a user interacted with one unit by directly touching the transmit electrode (4) and approaching the receive electrode (1), see Figure 9(b). From the resulting signal distribution in Figure 9(c), it can be seen that adjacent electrodes picked up the signals as well. To demonstrate the range versus signal response of transmit mode, we tested and plotted signal strength based on 5 sets of interactions per sensing distance. The result shown in figure 9(a) indicates that signal strength decays smoothly with distance. This not only demonstrates transmit mode, but also suggests that signals can be easily capacitively coupled into and out of the body, enabling the body to be used as a conduit for electronic messaging via touch.

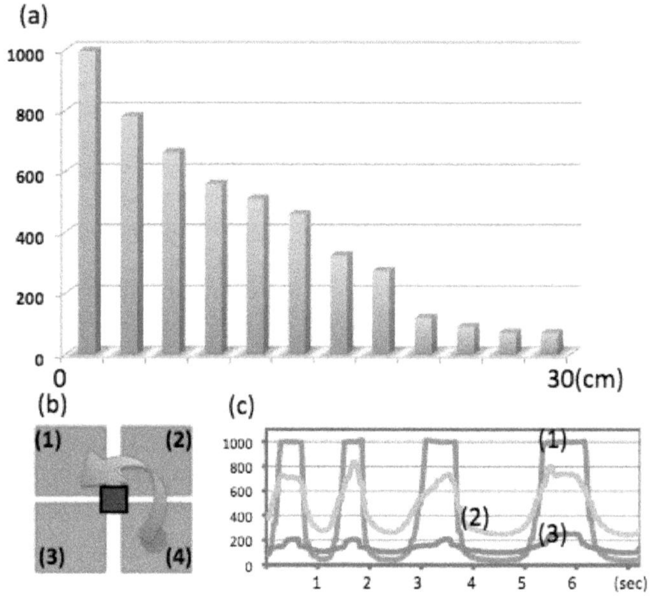

Figure 9. The effectiveness of active capacitive sensing mode. (b) Shows the electrode pattern of a single tile, where the electrode marked by the red dot served as the transmitter. The user was bridging two electrodes, namely transmit electrode (4) and receive electrode (1). (a) The user was touching the transmit electrode and moved from towards electrode (1). The strength of the signal pick-up is plotted as a function of distance. (c) Signal pickup on all the receive electrodes as a function of time, as the user repeatedly bridges electrodes (4) and (1) – significant signals are picked up by adjacent electrodes (2) and (3) as well as electrode (1).

The second condition involves detecting walking signals on the floor in shunt mode. The testing environment was set up on the floor, with ~4cm of high-dielectric constant foam on top of the sensors. The test subject walked over the receive electrodes as indicated in Figure 10, thereby avoiding transmit mode. Again, the red dots in the figure represent the transmit electrodes, and the results plotted show how the signal picked up by the electrodes adjacent to the transmit electrode demonstrate a noticeable attenuation through the shunt effect. Although this effect is less marked than the passive sensing results, it none-the-less shows around 4 bits of resolution. Signals from each electrode are marked with numbers – patterns from the steps were consistent across four units: (a) heel strikes and (b) mid-swings. Better shunt-mode response can be attained by lifting the electrodes a few cm above a conducting floor (e.g. by putting a piece of wood below the sensing strip).

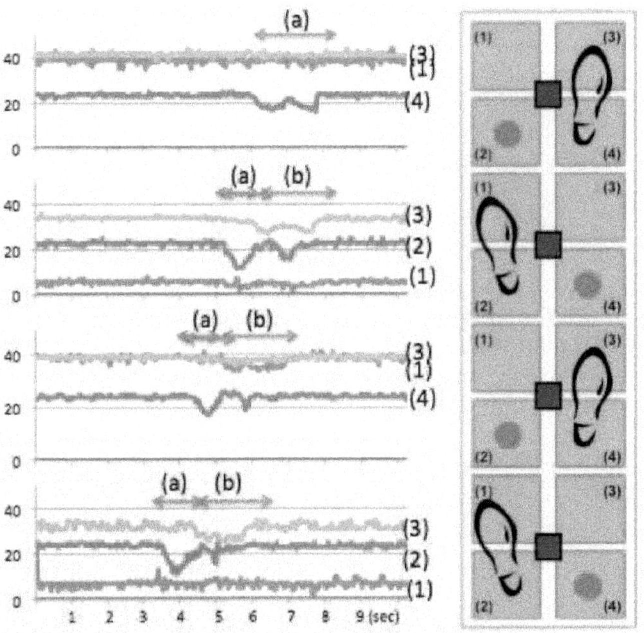

Figure 10. Walking patterns detected by shunt mode. During each step, the user effectively blocks the electromagnetic field flux, hence the signal drop: (a) heel strikes and (b) mid-swing. The red dots mark the transmit electrodes.

Piezoelectric sensor

We integrated piezoelectric sensors into our system for several reasons. First, like passive capacitive sensing mode, piezoelectric sensors do not require active pulsing, and can therefore be operated with relatively low power consumption. Additionally, a piezoelectric sensor can sense vibration and strain on the surface, so activity at distance can be detected as well as dynamic pressure applied directly to the sensor. In this way, we can easily use the signal from a piezoelectric element to trigger wake up of the microcontroller from a low power sleep mode. The piezo signal also yields dynamics that might roughly infer the weight of a person and provide insight into gait dynamics [27].

We evaluated the effectiveness of vibration and pressure detection in a similar manner to the previously reported tests of capacitive sensing. Figure 11 shows the signals picked up by our system. When a user walks along the floor, vibrations that match their footsteps are detected by the nearest sensor; smaller amplitude vibrations are also detected by adjacent sensors.

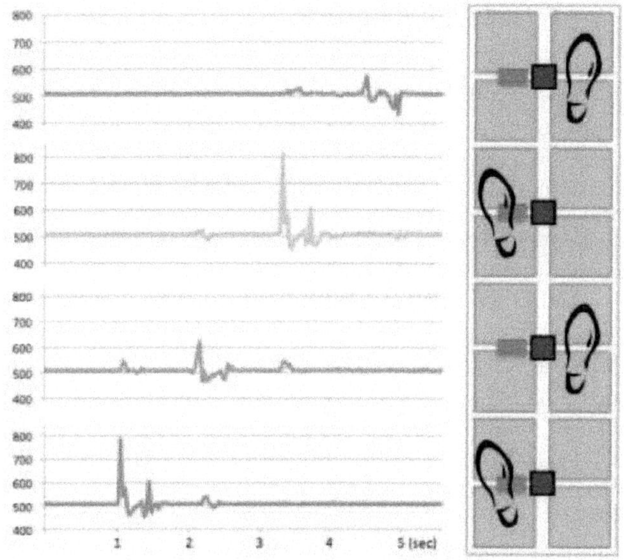

Figure 11. Signals picked up from the piezoelectric sensors. Red rectangles mark the location of each sensor within the sensing surface. Walking patterns were consistent with the other experiments reported in this paper. Note that vibration from adjacent units is also perceptible.

Cellular signals versus localization and identification

In our system, we included two types of RF antennas, namely 13.56MHz NFC and 900/1800MHz GSM. We used a Nokia 6212 phone to test the signal strength of both NFC and GSM emissions across the platform. Figure 12 shows the typical signal patterns picked up by our system.

The signal response from the NFC output of our logarithmic amplifier circuit is consistent and can be mapped to the distance – Figure 13(d) shows this. GSM signals are both stronger and more complex. The signal versus distance relationship can be related more easily by filtering & averaging the signal patterns.

Figures 13(b) and 14(b) show the experimental setup. We tried to evaluate the effectiveness of our platform in terms of identifying the exact unit the user was standing on or near, and the detection range over which cellular signals could be used. Each data point was taken and averaged according to five measurements.

To demonstrate signal propagation across the whole floor system, we plotted the signal response across the tiles in Figure 13(a) when the NFC device was held 30 cm away from the surface. The peak value was reported from the tile directly under the NFC reader as expected, and the signal strength drops off in all directions, enabling the location of the handset to be determined via the NFC signal. We further tested range versus signal strength by taking data from only one tile, recording measurements at various distances. The red circle in figure 13(b) indicates the location of NFC antenna used for this. Results are shown in Figure 13(d). The NFC signal is good for detecting short-range signal emissions, up to around 90 cm in our tests.

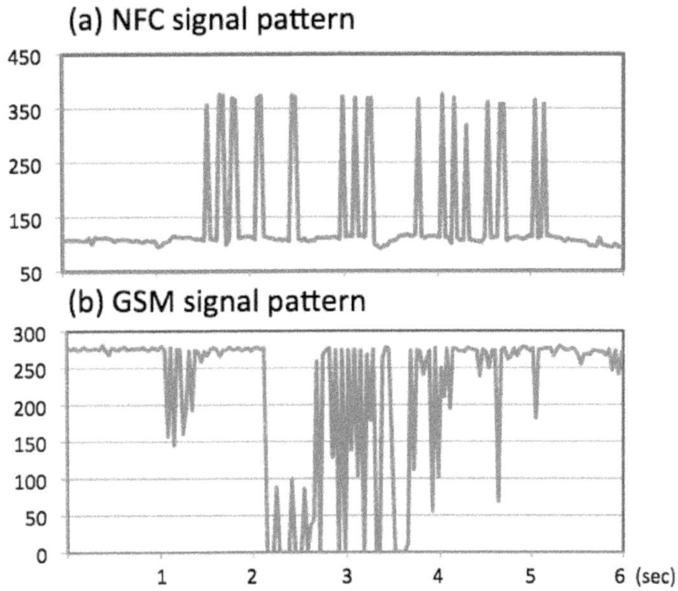

Figure 12. Signals picked up by antennas printed on the sensing substrate. (a) NFC signal pattern. The pattern and signal strength of NFC are consistent and can easily be used to determine range by measuring peak thresholds. (b) GSM signals have stronger signal response that can infer longer distance tracking by integrating and averaging the signal patterns.

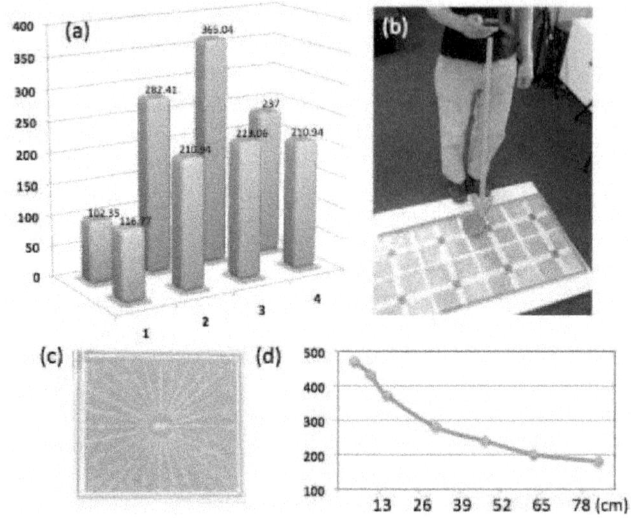

Figure 13. (a) Signal response versus sensing unit location when a NFC device is held 30cm from the surface. (b) Illustration of the experimental setup. (c) Close up of the NFC square loop antenna printed on each tile. (d) NFC signal strength versus distance.

We performed a similar experiment with GSM signal detection. When communicating with the cell tower, a cellphone generates a strong signal in the GSM band, which turns out to be readily detectable by the floor tiles from some distance via our simple circuit. Figure 14(a) shows the signal strength distribution across our platform when the mobile device is held about 1m away from the sensing surface as shown in Figure 14(b). The signal strength was integrated and averaged from a 6-second long GSM connection. As seen in figure 14(a), the peak value fell off in adjacent tiles in a similar manner to the NFC signal. We again recorded signal strength versus range as described above, and illustrated the result in Figure 14(d). This shows that the GSM signal strength drops off with distance in a similar manner to NFC and it is apparent that either could be used as a basis for determining range.

Both NFC and GSM signal strengths are directionally sensitive and could be affected by the way a user holds the mobile device. We have seen the GSM pickup to be fairly resilient, however, and the NFC detection range has been over a meter when the NFC antennae on the floor are isolated from magnetic material below – e.g., by putting a piece of magnetic shielding under the antenna or raising the floor up by a cm or two atop a nonconductor (e.g., piece of wood).

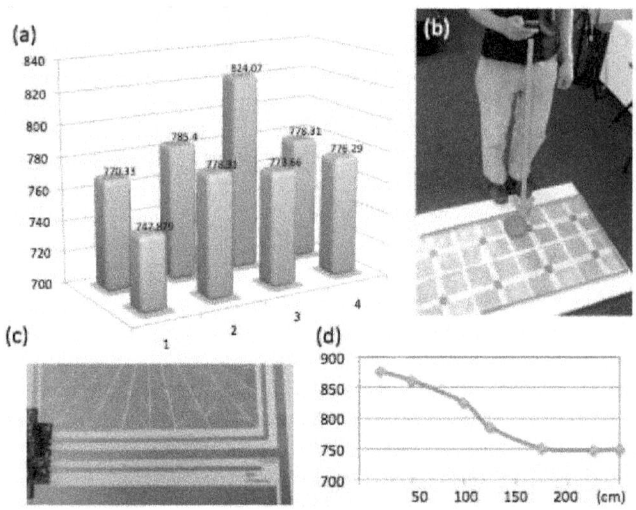

Figure 14. (a) Signal response versus sensing unit location when a GSM device is held 1m from the surface. (b) Illustration of the experimental setup. (c) Close up of the tile GSM antenna. (d) GSM signal strength versus distance.

OBSERVATIONS, EXTENSIONS AND APPLICATIONS

Passive mode is the simplest sensing method to integrate and implement with minimum electronic components, and it is yet one of the most powerful modes for localization. Crosstalk between different electrodes was unnoticeable. The received signal patterns could be used to distinguish walking direction, strikes and mid-swing – all useful information for gait analysis.

In order to minimize system power consumption (in our full system deployment, each unit consumes ~25 mA when it's actively scanning for each sensor input), we combined both active and passive modes as a low power hybrid mode. The floor defaults to sleep mode and interrupted only when a vibration occurred at the nearby surface and immediately entered passive mode. Upon confirmation from the passive mode, the floor switches to active mode (see Figure 5). Interrupts can also be triggered by the passive capacitive sensing mode or GSM or NFC pickups. It is possible to form a larger network if the current drain is managed properly to avoid excessively loading the power bus lines.

Whilst the sensate floor described in this paper can detect and locate users, it is not intrinsically capable of identifying specific users. However, substantial studies of locomotion and especially gait structure analyses [24-26] suggest that it is possible to use the difference in a person's unique walking motion for identification. Given the gait data presented in Figures 7, 8 and 10 we believe these techniques may be applicable here. It may also be possible to combine additional sensing and identification modalities. For example, if a user is positively identified when they are logged into a desktop computer or when they make use of an electronic access control system, it may be possible to track them subsequently using the floor and maintain the correct association between identity and current location.

Besides localizing and identifying people, it may also be possible to use this technology to sense hands interacting with a surface such as a desktop or wall, and to associate these with the corresponding feet using active transmit mode coupling between the two surfaces through the user's body in a DiamondTouch–like manner [23]. It may also be possible to instrument more complex surface structures by folding or forming a conductive printed substrate in more sophisticated ways than we have presented here. In active capacitive sensing mode, the signal strength is strong enough to be used as a way of transmitting digital information from a body-worn device to the floor sensing system. For example, it would be possible put small tags on users' shoes that transmit unique identification signals for each person with a transmit electrode outside and local ground electrode inside against one's sock and sending the ID of a user (see Figure 15).

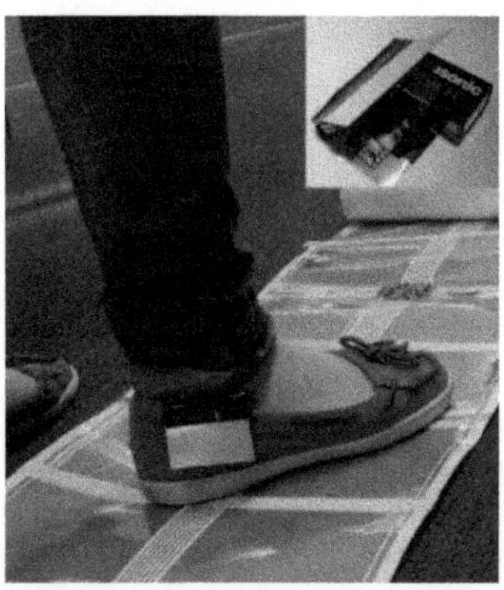

Figure 15. Illustration of transmitting/receiving into the floor – from clip on shoe to floor.

Our future work will focus on integrating this system into a building environment to form a ubiquitous computing platform. In addition to evaluating and extending the system further, this will give us an opportunity to investigate potential applications, including smart floor sensing for motion tracking, localization, identification, gesture recognition, gait analysis and a variety of human-computer interaction and ubiquitous computing scenarios.

CONCLUSIONS

In this paper we have presented what we believe to be a scalable and versatile distributed sensate surface based on a new conductive inkjet printing technology, which we believe will become increasingly well established. We constructed a 2.5m x 30cm hardware test-bed to demonstrate and evaluate the potential of this approach. Our design incorporates many different sensing capabilities based on the ability to create a large-scale non-rigid substrate with conductors printed onto it at a relatively low cost. This was not previously practical - it now opens the possibility of easily deploying a large-area surface sensing system. We described the design and implementation of passive and active capacitive sensing, coupled with GSM and NFC RF signal pickup – all based on copper electrodes and antennas printed on the substrate. We also demonstrated a way of incorporating piezoelectric sensors into the system.

Whilst we have not yet built or deployed any real-world applications of this technology, we have presented the results of our extensive evaluation of a range of sensing modalities that we built into our first prototype. We feel that we have proven the possibility of using conductive printing technology to build scalable and versatile generic surfaces for ubiquitous sensing. We also believe that it will be possible to further simplify the electronic circuitry which we currently use in conjunction with the flexible substrate through a design-for-manufacture process. Ultimately we believe that this technology has the potential to change the way we think about covering large areas with sensors and associated electronic circuitry – not just for floors but potentially desktops, walls and beyond – and we seek to inform such work with these early results.

ACKNOWLEDGMENTS

We would like to thank members of Sensors and Devices Group at Microsoft Research Cambridge, especially James Scott, Nicolas Villar, Shahram Izadi and Alex Butler for their help and support during the development of this project. We also thank Rich Fletcher for advice on the NFC detector and Nokia Research in Cambridge UK for lending us the NFC phone.

REFERENCES

1. Keun Soo Kim et al., Large-scale pattern growth of graphene films for stretchable transparent electrodes. *Nature* 457 (7230), 706-10 (14 Jan 2009)
2. Tsuyoshi Sekitani et al., A Rubberlike Stretchable Active Matrix Using Elastic Conductors. *Science* 321 (5895), 12 Sep 2008
3. John Rogers, Takao Someya, and Yonggang Huang, Materials and Mechanics for Stretchable Electronics *Science* 327 (5973), (26 Mar 2010)
4. Bok Y. Ah et al., Omnidirectional Printing of Flexible, Stretchable, and Spanning Silver Microelectrodes. *Science* 20 March 2009: 323 (5921), 1590-1593.
5. Paul Calvert, Inkjet Printing for Materials and Devices, *Chem. Mater.*, 2001, 13 (10), pp 3299–3305
6. Mistree, B.F.T., and Paradiso, J.A., ChainMail – A Configurable Multimodal Lining to Enable Sensate Surfaces and Interactive Objects, in Proc. of *TEI 2010*, pp. 65-72.
7. Paradiso, J.A., Lifton. J., and Broxton, M., Sensate Media - Multimodal Electronic Skins as Dense Sensor Networks, *BT Technology Journal*, Vol. 22, No. 4, October 2004, pp. 32-44.
8. Orr, R. J. and Abowd, G. D., The Smart Floor: A Mechanism for Natural User Identification and Tracking. Proc. *CHI 2000*.
9. Schmidt, A., Strohbach, M. et al., Context Acquisition Based on Load Sensing. Proc. *UbiComp 2002*.
10. Paradiso, J., Abler, C., et al., The Magic Carpet: Physical Sensing for Immersive Environments. Ext. Abstracts *CHI 1997*. ACM Press, pp.277-278.
11. Griffith, N. and Fernström, M., LiteFoot: A floor space for recording dance and controlling media. In: Proceedings of *ICMC 1998*, pp. 475–481 (1998)
12. Kidané, A., Rodriguez, A., Cifdaloz, O., Harikrishnan, V., ISA floor: A high resolution floor sensor with 3D visualization and multimedia interface capability. *AME Program*,AME-TR-2003-11p (2003)
13. Richardson, B., Leydon, K., Fernström, M., Paradiso, J., Z-Tiles: building blocks for modular, pressure-sensing floor spaces. In: Extended Abstracts of the *2004 conference on Human factors and computing systems*, Vienna, Austria, pp. 1529–1532 (2004)
14. Sankar Rangarajan et al., The design of a pressure sensing floor for movement-based human computer interaction. In Proceedings of the 2nd European conference on Smart sensing and context (*EuroSSC'07*)
15. Lee Middleton et al., A Floor Sensor System for Gait Recognition. In Proceedings of the Fourth IEEE Workshop on Automatic Identification Advanced Technologies (*AUTOID '05*). IEEE Computer Society, Washington, DC, USA, 171-176.
16. Y.-T. Chiang et.al., "Interaction Models for Multiple-Resident Activity Recognition in a Smart Home," In *IEEE RSJ International Conference on Intelligent Robots and Systems*, Taipei Taiwan, pp. 3753 – 3758 (2010)
17. William S. Wong (Editor), Alberto Salleo, Flexible Electronics: Materials and Applications, William S. Wong (Editor), Alberto Salleo, 2009
18. Jain, K., Klosner, M., Zemel, M., Raghunandan, S. Flexible Electronics and Displays: High-Resolution, Roll-to-Roll, Projection Lithography and Photoablation *Processing Technologies for High Throughput Production (2005)* Proc IEEE 93:1500-1510
19. Sigurd Wagner et al. Electronic skin: architecture and components, *Physica E: Low-dimensional Systems and Nano structures* Volume 25, Issues 2-3, November 2004, Pages 326-334
20. Zimmerman, T., Personal Area Networks: Near-field intrabody communication, *IBM Systems Journal*, Vol. 35, No. 3&4, 1996.
21. Joseph A. Paradiso and Neil Gershenfeld, Musical Applications of Electric Field Sensing Sensing Joseph A. Paradiso and Neil Gershenfeld, *Computer Music Journal 21(2)*, Summer 1997, pp. 69-89.
22. Rekimoto, J., Smartskin: An infrastructure for freehand manipulation on interactive surfaces. Proceedings of *CHI2002*, 113-120. (2002).
23. Dietz P and Leigh D,: DiamondTouch: a multi-user touchtechnology, in Proc of *ACM UIST 2001*, Orlando, Florida, USA, pp 219—226 (November 2001).
24. M. S. Nixon and J. N. Carter, Automatic recognition by gait, *Proc. IEEE*, vol. 94, no. 11, pp. 2013–2024, Nov. 2006
25. L. Lee and W. Grimson, Gait analysis for recognition andclassification, *in Proc. 5th IEEE Int. Conf. Autom. Face Gesture Recog.*, 2002, pp. 148–155.
26. T. Chau, A review of analytical techniques for gait data. Part 1: Fuzzy, statistical and fractal methods, *Gait Posture*, vol. 13, no. 1, pp. 49–66,Feb. 2001
27. Bamberg, S.J.M. et al, Gait Analysis Using a Shoe-Integrated Wireless Sensor System, *IEEE Transactions on Information Technology in Biomedicine*, Vol. 12, No. 4, July 2008, pp. 413-423.

HeatProbe: A Thermal-based Power Meter for Accounting Disaggregated Electricity Usage

Bo-Jhang Ho[1], Hsin-Liu (Cindy) Kao[1], Nan-Chen Chen[1], Chuang-Wen You[2], Hao-Hua Chu[1], Ming-Syan Chen[2]

[1]Department of Computer Science and Information Engineering, National Taiwan University
1, Sec. 4, Roosevelt Rd., Taipei 106, Taiwan
{b96118, b95701241, b97006, hchu}@csie.ntu.edu.tw

[2]Research Center for Information Technology Innovation, Academia Sinica
128, Sec. 2, Academia Rd., Taipei 115, Taiwan
{cwyou, mschen}@citi.sinica.edu.tw

ABSTRACT
To promote energy-saving behavior, disaggregating electricity usage is critical for increasing consumer awareness of energy usage behavior. This study proposes HeatProbe, a thermal-based power meter system that uses thermal imaging to track disaggregated appliance usage. We have designed, prototyped, and tested the HeatProbe system. Results show that HeatProbe successfully senses individual appliance operating durations with an average error of 125.03 seconds, achieving 80.2% appliance power accounting accuracy in different appliance usage scenarios.

Author Keywords
Power Consumption Monitoring, Per-appliance Power Disaggregation.

ACM Classification Keywords
H5.m. Information interfaces and presentation (e.g., HCI): Miscellaneous.

General Terms
Design, Experimentation.

INTRODUCTION
Energy conservation has recently become a significant concern [1], and has long been an important goal of UbiComp research on promoting energy consumption awareness [2, 3, 4]. Since utility bills aggregate electricity usage, it is difficult to determine disaggregated energy consumption. If individuals can be made aware of their major energy consuming behaviors (e.g., the type and operating duration of the consuming appliance), they can explore ways to make positive changes in their energy usage. As emphasized by Stern [17], this information awareness on appliance usage behavior and incentives for changing environmentally significant consumer behavior can have synergistic effects to conserve energy.

This study proposes the HeatProbe system to track the energy consumed by individual appliances. The proposed system disaggregates total power usage from a master power meter into individual appliance power usage by tracking the heat patterns generated by running appliances. This approach is based on indirect sensing. Rather than directly sensing the power line connecting to each appliance, HeatProbe uses a thermal camera and thermal imaging algorithms to recognize heat patterns from appliance usage. Figure 1 shows heatmaps of appliances captured at two different time points. The upper heatmap (Fig. 1(a)) shows the appliance surface near room temperature in the power-off state. The lower heatmap (Fig. 1(b)) shows that a user has entered the space and turned on various appliances whose surface temperature exceeds room temperature. Since appliances produce heat as a byproduct of their operation, HeatProbe determines changes in an appliance's power state by tracking its surface temperature. A rising surface temperature implies that the appliance has been turned on, while a falling surface temperature implies the appliance has been turned off.

Several recent power metering systems, such as ElectriSense [2], Viridiscope [3], and contactless EMF sensing method [4], allow the tracking of *per-appliance* electricity consumption by analyzing the electro-magnetic signals of each appliance in the home. However, these systems require per-home calibration or a training process to determine the parameters (e.g., calibrated parameters for estimating power consumption or electro-magnetic fingerprints) of different appliances. Recognizing the difficulty of these calibration/training efforts, this study proposes the HeatProbe system. This system aims to automate the tracking of disaggregated appliance energy usage footprints by indirectly sensing the runtime temperature-changing trends on appliance surfaces. Since all electric appliances generate heat during operation, individual appliance usage can be inferred from the detected appliance on/off events.

The main contribution of this study is its novel thermal approach to disaggregate whole electric energy usage into appliance-level energy consumption. This study presents thermal imagining algorithms to recognize heat patterns from appliance surfaces and human body surfaces, thus accounting for individual appliance electricity usage. Experimental results showed that the proposed thermal approach sensed individual appliance operating durations with an average error of 125.03 seconds and achieved 80% appliance power accounting accuracy in different appliance usage scenarios.

RELATED WORK

Existing studies on monitoring electric energy consumption

Commercial electricity monitoring solutions, such as Cent-a-Meter [5] and TED [6], provide aggregated whole-home electricity usage with a single-point inline power meter. These solutions produce accurate aggregated power monitoring results. Jiang *et al.* [7] designed a wireless sensor network to monitor AC power usage with customized *ACme* nodes. All nodes in this system route the power readings back to a server over the IP network. All collected power data is then processed on the server and can be visualized by users, who view their individual real-time energy consumption using a Web interface. Considering the installation difficulty for end-users, Patel *et al.* [16] designed an easily deployable power meter that consists of a sensor unit with wireless radio interface attached to the electrical breaker panel and a calibration device plugged in to each electrical outlet. This system computes real-time power consumption by sensing the anisotropic magnetoresistive (AMR) effect caused by changing magnetic fields and collecting information from the plug-in devices on outlets.

Many researchers have investigated various ways to monitor appliance-level power consumption. By analyzing power readings from in-line power meters, Non-Intrusive Load Monitoring (NILM) [8, 9] identifies the sudden changes in the voltage or current readings caused by the state changes of appliances. Based on these detected appliance on/off events, NILM disaggregates whole-home power consumption into appliance-level components. Rowe *et al.* [4] exploited an electromagnetic field (EMF) sensor to assist the training phase of NILM. However, a machine learning procedure is required to learn models for specific appliances. ViridiScope [3] proposed an indirect-sensing approach to estimate current power consumption based on the magnitude of the sensed magnetic field near an appliance. Intermediate appliance state changes can also be detected using light and acoustic sensors. ElectriSense [2] enables the tracking of different appliance usages by analyzing the continuously high frequency electromagnetic interference (EMI) signals generated when an appliance is running. By extracting the features embedded in the emitted EMI signals, ElectriSense can classify the usage of different appliances using a machine learning toolkit. In contrast, HeatProbe captures the runtime heatmaps using a thermal camera to segment appliance heat and detect significant heat increases/decreases on the appliance surfaces. Using this data, the system infers the appliance operating duration

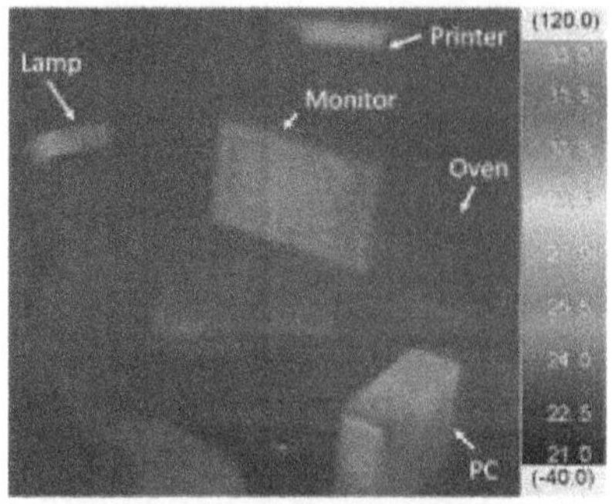

(a) Before turning on appliances

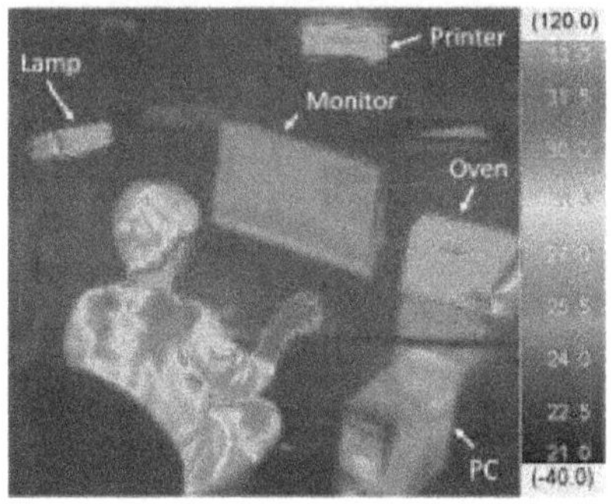

(b) After turning on all appliances

Figure 1. Two frames captured (a) before and (b) after all appliances are turned on. These five appliances are a lamp, a monitor, and oven, a PC and a printer.

and power usage without performing calibration/training steps.

Prior Work Using Thermal Sensing

Previous researchers have explored various possibilities on applying thermal imaging in the HCI research. StressCam [10] presents a method to detect people's stress level using thermal cameras. Based on the correlation between people's stress level and their forehead temperature, StressCam measure their physiological stress based on the temperature of their foreheads. Yun *et al.* [11] extended this thermal imaging method to observe players' physiological stress level while playing games. Based on the detected stress level, the system can infer the difficulty level in a game faced by individual players and then adjust the difficulty of the game dynamically based on players' skill levels. HeatWave [12] explores thermal sensing to enhance user surface interaction. Using a thermal camera to track residential heat traces left on an interactive surface, their system detects various finger gestures such as hovering, touching, target selection, etc.

THEORY OF OPERATION

The HeatProbe system infers per-user power consumption using one in-line power meter and one thermal camera. According to the electric circuit theory [15], the rate of electrical energy dissipation (P) due to resistance is proportional to the current (I) and resistance (R) and based on the following equation:

$$P = I^2R \tag{1}$$

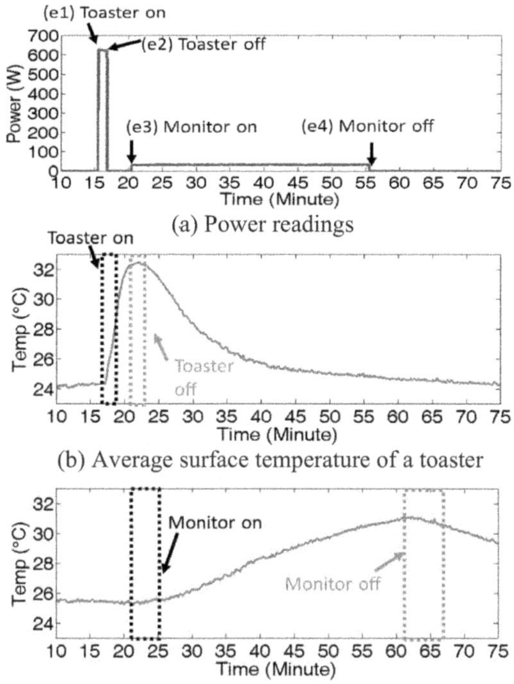

(a) Power readings

(b) Average surface temperature of a toaster

(c) Average surface temperature of a monitor

Figure 2. Resulting average surface temperature of two exemplar appliances (a toaster and a monitor) when the appliance is turned on/off. These two cases show that surface temperature increases (decreases) when the appliance turned on (off).

Dissipated energy due to the internal resistance of an appliance is converted into the form of thermal energy, i.e., heat, which causes the temperature on the appliance surface to rise.

HeatProbe uses a thermal camera to capture this temperature change on appliance surface. Figure 1 shows the temperature difference between two heatmaps captured at two time points. The upper heatmap (Fig. 1(a)) shows the appliance surface near room temperature in the power-off state. The lower heatmap (Fig. 1(b)) shows that a user has entered the space and turned on appliances, including a desk lamp, an LCD monitor, a printer, a PC, and an oven. The surface temperature of these appliances rises, exceeding room temperature. HeatProbe uses the change in the appliance surface temperature to infer the appliance on/off state. This heat-producing phenomenon is universal to almost all electric-powered appliances.

Assumptions and Limitations

The current HeatProbe system works based on the following assumptions. (1) The system tracks electricity usage from appliances that are plugged into the building circuit such that the inline master power meter can sense their electricity usage. For example, the system cannot track electricity consumed by mobile devices that run on their own batteries. (2) The system cannot track an appliance whose surface is not within view of the thermal camera, e.g., appliances that are hidden underneath a desk. (3) The system recognizes only appliance on/off binary state. However, some appliances, such as refrigerators, have multiple power states. Since an intermediate power state change often produces a small temperature change, the current thermal camera cannot detect heat-changing events caused by the intermediate appliance state change. Thus, the current system implementation assumes that the appliance consumes constant amount of power. However, most shared appliances have limited operating states and tend to be used for a limited amount of time. Thus, the amount of under- (or over-) estimated power consumption should be relatively insignificant over a longer monitoring period.

SYSTEM DESIGN

Figure 3 presents the HeatProbe system design. HeatProbe implements five inference modules to derive appliance power consumption from the raw heatmaps and power readings: (1) heatmap segmentation, (2) power event detection, (3) appliance usage detection, (4) appliance operating duration resolution, and (5) appliance power accounting. This section first provides a brief description of how these five inference modules operate in the HeatProbe system.

(Step 1). *Heatmap segmentation* processes each heatmap and partitions it into multiple segments, each of which corresponds to either a heated (running) appliance or a human body. For example, after segmenting the heatmap in Fig. 1(b), HeatProbe locates six heat segments corresponding to five appliances and one human body. HeatProbe then computes the surface temperature of each appliance segment. By continuously computing the surface temperature of each appliance segment over time, the system determines temperature changes on the appliance surface. Rising (falling) temperature indicates a *heat event* with an on (off) appliance power state change. HeatProbe also identifies and tracks the human bodies by continuously analyzing heatmaps.

(Step 2). *Power event detection* analyzes aggregated power readings obtained from the master power meter and identifies *power events* correlated to changes in an appliance's on/off power state. For example, Fig. 2(a) shows

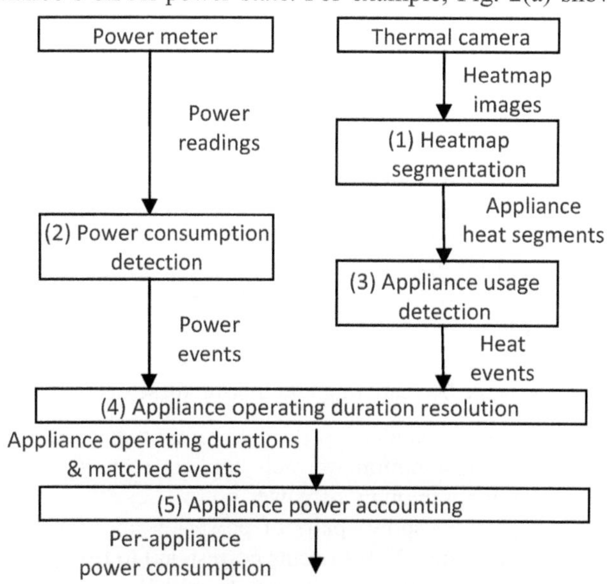

Figure 3. HeatProbe system design.

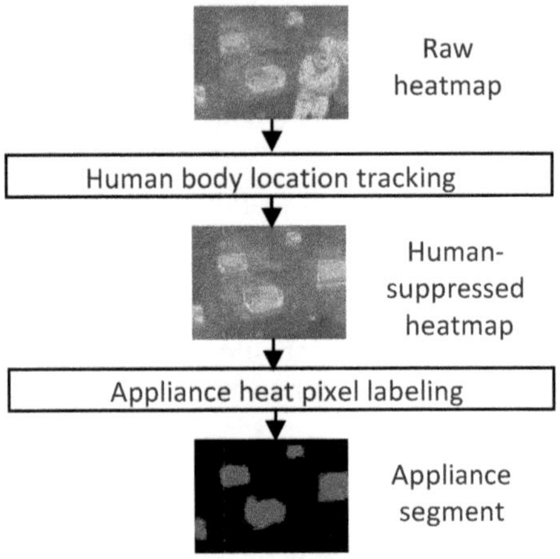

Figure 4. Steps in the heatmap image segmentation module.

the aggregated power readings including two pairs of power-on and -off events. They correspond to (e1) power-on of a toaster at the 16th minute, (e2) power-off of the toaster at the 17th minute, (e3) power-on of an LCD monitor at the 20th minute, and (e4) power-off of the LCD monitor at the 56th minute.

(Step 3). *Appliance usage detection* monitors any significant temperature increases/decreases for each appliance segment. Because electric energy dissipates on the internal resistance as a form of thermal heat, the generated heat will cause a noticeable temperature increase on the surface of an appliance. For example, Fig. 2 shows significant temperature increases occurring at the 16th and 21th minutes. After the toaster (monitor) turns off, the surface temperature drops back to the room temperature, as indicated at the 22th (56th) minute in Fig. 2 (b) and (c). This allows the system to infer an appliance on/off state change by detecting significant temperature increases/decreases in an appliance segment.

(Step 4). *Appliance operating duration resolution* captures the relationship between an appliance's power-on event (the cause) and its surface temperature increase event (the effect). Similarly, this step captures the relationship between an appliance's power-off event (the cause) and the subsequently temperature decrease event (the effect). For example, Fig. 2 shows the matching of four pairs of power-on (-off) and heat-rising (-falling) events. The first pair occurs around the 16th minute, when the user switches on the toaster. This action produces a power-on event at the 16th minute, and the heat-rising event from the image segment of the toaster from the 16th to the 19th minute. Three other event pairs occur at the 21th, 22th, and 56th minutes. The system determines the starting/ending times of each appliance's usage by matching and linking these events.

(Step 5). *Appliance power accounting* estimates the average power consumption of each appliance based on the power changing amounts of power-on (off) events. For example, Fig. 2 (a) shows pairs of power-on and power-off events for a toaster. These events correspond to (e1) power-on of a toaster at the 16th minute (a 600 Watt power increase), (e2) power-off of the toaster at the 17th minute (a 600 Watt power decrease). The appliance power consumption can be approximated by the amount of energy consumed in an average power (600 Watt) over the entire appliance usage session.

The following sections describe each module in details as follows.

In-line Power Meter and Thermal Camera

The system uses two sensors: an in-line power meter and a long-wavelength infrared (LW-IR) thermal camera. Existing power meters installed by the utility providers can provide data on aggregated power consumption.

The infrared/thermal camera measures the quantity of infrared (far-infrared, F-IR, or long-wavelength infrared, LW-IR) radiation emitted by any object. Based on Planck's law, the electromagnetic radiation from a room-temperature object falls mainly in the IR spectrum, with the radiation intensity directly proportional to the fourth power of the object's absolute temperature. By measuring the radiation intensity emitted in the IR spectrum, the thermal camera can passively generate a heatmap of an object in the view range without any illumination sources. This approach is unlike the *reflected* infrared operating in the near-infrared (N-IR) spectrum.

Heatmap Segmentation

Figure 4 shows a sequential block diagram of the heatmap segmentation module, which includes the following steps: (1) human body location tracking, and (2) appliance heat pixel labeling steps. These two steps are described as follows.

Human body location tracking: Given raw heatmaps, the human body location tracking component finds moving heating sources (i.e., humans) by identifying pixels with sudden temperature changes. Because the temperature values of human bodies are significantly higher than room temperature, the movement of a human body should cause abrupt temperature increases/decreases on pixels in or near human bodies between two time-adjacent frames. By identifying pixels with abrupt temperature changes, it is possible to segment out a body area by drawing a bounding contour for a clustered region of pixels with sudden temperature changes. The same procedure can be repeated for all time-adjacent heatmaps to find a corresponding human mask, which labels all pixels in bounding contours as human-type pixels. Subsequent modules can use this human mask to retrieve the location of a user, which is given by the coordinates of all pixels within the selected human body area.

Appliance heat pixel labeling: To locate the regions of running appliances, the system uses the human-suppressed heatmaps to find heated appliance pixels with temperatures above the room temperature (24.3 ℃). First, the system dynamically selects a cut-off temperature in each heatmap to segment out appliance heat pixels. The system then analyzes the temperature distribution of pixels in each heatmap.

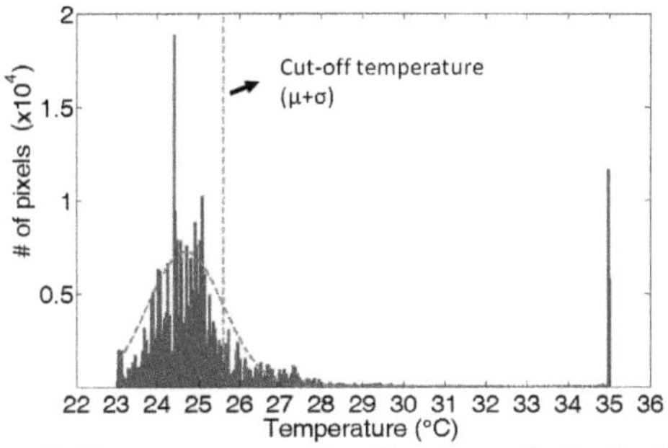

Figure 5. Temperature distribution of all pixels in a frame. The peak (red dotted line) is fit by the Gaussian distribution, with a mean value of μ and a standard deviation of σ.

Figure 5 shows an example temperature distribution of a heatmap. Due to the thermal camera's limited temperature sensing range (23 ℃ ~ 35 ℃), all temperature values are limited within the sensing range. All pixels with temperatures higher (lower) than maximum (minimum) sensing temperature are set to the maximum (minimum) value. This results in large number of pixels at the minimum (23 ℃) and maximum (35 ℃) temperature. This temperature distribution also has a peak located around the room temperature (24.3 ℃). The whole distribution is fit by a Gaussian function to extract the mean (μ) and variance (σ^2) parameters shown as the red dotted line in Fig. 5. The cut-off temperature is set as the mean value (around the room temperature) plus one standard deviation, $\mu+\sigma$. After determining the cut-off temperature for a heatmap, it is possible to label all pixels with temperature values greater than the cut-off temperature as appliance-type pixels in a corresponding labeling frame, as indicated the middle row of Fig. 6. Repeating the same procedure for each raw heatmap identifies the corresponding appliance heat pixels. The resulting appliance heat pixels are then used to generate appliance masks for detecting the appliance usages.

Power Usage Detection

The raw power readings in Fig. 2(a) are measured by an in-line power meter that samples the power consumption of appliances once per second. These raw power readings can be smoothed using a median filter with a sliding window of five samples. The starting (or ending) time of a power-on (or -off) event can be determined by finding a significant change in the value of the smoothed power curve, which is caused by turning on (off) an electric load. A significant change of a power event of the ith appliance usage session, defined as Δp_i, gives the power demand of that appliance. For example, Fig. 2 (a) shows that the power readings increase (decrease) at the 20th (56th) minute when the LCD monitor is turned on (off), with an increasing (decreasing) amount of 25 (25) Watts. Therefore, a power event is defined as power changing vectors $P_i = (t_i, \Delta p_i)$, where t_i, and Δp_i are the starting (ending) time, and the increasing (decreasing) amount of the power readings of the power on (off) event of the ith appliance usage session, respectively.

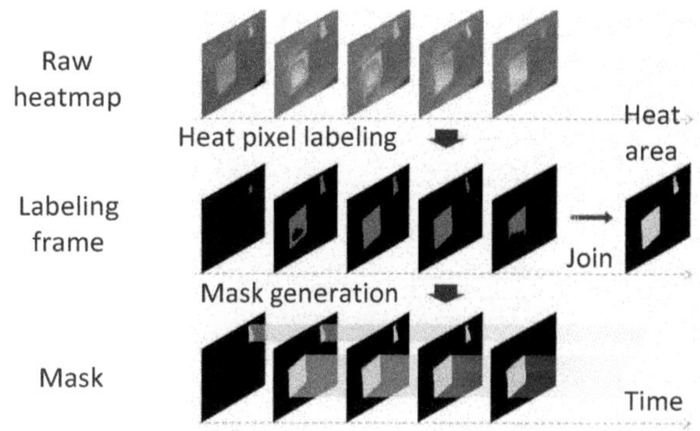

Figure 6. Appliance mask generation steps. The top row includes raw heatmaps captured in five adjacent times. The middle and lowest rows represent the corresponding labeling frames and masks. The right-most frame contains the resulting appliance heat areas for a lamp and a monitor.

Appliance Usage Detection

This module involves the following four steps: (1) temperature-based spatial smoothing, (2) appliance heat mask generation, (3) heat-rising event detection, and (4) heat-falling event detection.

Temperature-based spatial smoothing: The temperature-based spatial smoothing step first performs noise reduction on the observed temperature. Each frame is smoothed by finding the average temperature of each 3x3 neighborhood of pixels. The same procedure is repeated for all pixels in a heatmap, generating a smoothed heatmap. These smoothed heatmaps are processed in subsequent steps to detect heat events.

Appliance heat mask generation: This step obtains the appliance heat masks corresponding to different appliance usage sessions, which indicate the pixel locations of running appliances. During appliance operating, the number of heat pixels (i.e., whose temperature is above the room temperature) of an appliance might vary due to temperature increases (decreases) on the appliance surface or appliance form changes caused by usage behaviors (e.g., opening/closing the LCD monitor of a laptop). To locate an appliance's pixels, the system joins all heat pixels during an appliance operating session to form a union area, called an *appliance heat area.* This appliance heat area can effectively monitor the temperature-changing trends during the appliance operating. This area appears in the rightmost frame of the middle row of Fig. 6. An appliance mask for a specific time can be generated by unmasking pixels in appliance heat areas for all appliances running at that time. Repeating the same procedure for each time instance produces a series of time-ordered appliance masks, as shown in the lowest row of Fig. 6. The subsequent steps of this module use this appliance mask series to retrieve the coordinates of all pixels within each appliance.

Heat-rising event detection: This step analyzes the smoothed heatmaps to detect the heat-rising events of all appliances. Turning on an appliance should persistently dissipate electric energy, and thus cause a noticeable tem-

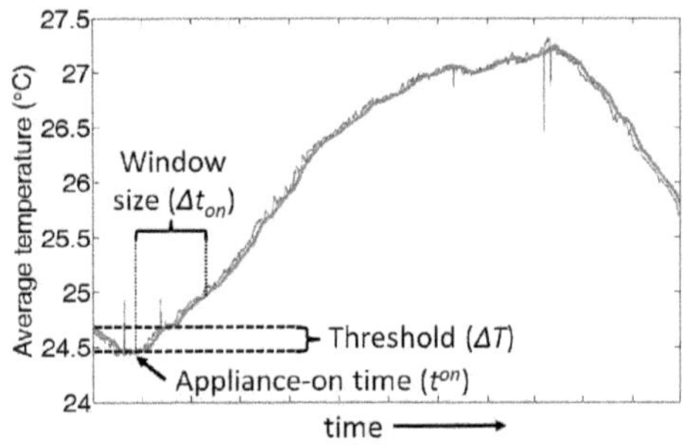

Figure 7. The average temperature for an appliance heat area. The blue line is the original data curve, and the red line is the smoothed curve after applying a low-passed filter.

perature increase on the appliance surface. The heat-rising process shows a slow but persistent temperature increase. Thus, the proposed system takes the average temperatures of all pixels for each appliance (i.e., all pixels in each appliance heat area) every second, producing the temperature trend depicted in Fig. 7. To detect the rising trends, the raw average temperature is smoothed using a low-pass filter (the red line in Fig. 7). The smoothed signal is then analyzed with a sliding window (Δt_{on}) of 60 samples or 1 min of sensed average temperature.

The occurrence of a heat-rising event corresponds to a condition in which the temperature difference between the beginning and ending time in the sliding window exceeds a threshold ΔT = 0.2°C, indicating a slow but substantial change. This is determined by the average heat-rising rate observed from the empirical results of the appliances in our experiment. After the starting time of an event, the temperature changing rate (r_i) of an event of the ith appliance usage session is equal to the maximum slope in the sliding window. This value represents the heat generation characteristic of the appliance when turned on.

Heat-falling event detection: The proposed system detects the occurrence of a heat-falling event by monitoring the major temperature-changing trend of all pixels. Due to the thermal conductivity of the materials surrounding the appliances (e.g., the air, the surface of the desk, etc.), it takes some time to disperse the generated heat left inside an appliance. This makes the surface temperature fall at a slow rate after an appliance is turned off. The heat-falling rate is not uniform across the appliance surface. To detect the temperature changing trend of each pixel, the system calculates the temperature difference (T_{diff}) of a pixel between the current temperature and the previous temperature recorded 60 seconds earlier (a time interval long enough to reflect the falling trend). The system can then classify each pixel into one of three temperature-changing categories: a temperature-rising pixel ($T_{diff} > T$), a temperature-falling pixel ($T_{diff} < -T$), and a temperature-fixed pixel ($-T \leqq T_{diff} \leqq T$). The temperature threshold, T, is determined by the temperature resolution of the thermal camera (T=0.3°C in the current implementation). A heat-falling event occurs when there are more temperature-falling pixels than temperature-rising pixels in an appliance heat area. A trend indicator (TD) calculates the difference between the percentage of temperature-rising pixels and the percentage of temperature-falling pixels in an appliance area. Fig. 8 shows when an appliance is turned off, TD drops below zero because the number of temperature-falling pixels exceeds the number of temperature-rising pixels. After the surface temperature of the appliance returns to the room temperature, TD also goes near zero. The system calculates TD for each appliance heat area in every second interval (Fig. 8). A low-pass filter smoothes the TD samples (the red line in Fig. 8) with a sliding window (Δt_{off}) of 90 TD samples over one and a half minutes. An appliance-off event corresponds to a drop in TD below zero in the sliding window exceeding a threshold (ΔTD) of 10%. This means the percentage of temperature-falling pixels exceeds the percentage of temperature-rising pixels by 10%.

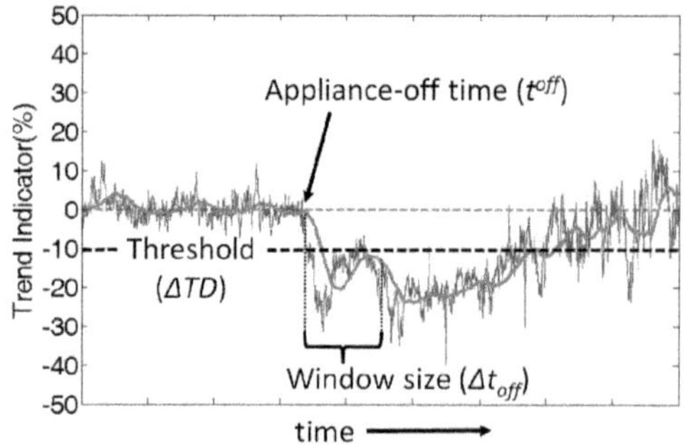

Figure 8. The trend indicator for an appliance heat area. The blue line is the original data curve, and the red line is the smoothed curve after applying a low-passed filter.

Appliance Operating Duration Resolution

This module resolves the appliance-on (-off) time and operating duration of each appliance usage session. Each appliance-on (-off) state change generates a pair of power and heat events that are correlated with each other in event occurrence time. Therefore, this module infers the appliance-on (-off) times by finding the optimal matched pairs of power and heat events based on time proximity, which can be formulated as an event assignment problem [13]. Each operating duration can then be obtained by calculating the time difference between on and off time. This module involves the following three steps: (1) appliance-on time, (2) appliance-off time, and (3) operating duration resolution steps.

Appliance-on time resolution: The appliance-on time is determined by power-on and heat-rising events matching algorithm. Appliances requiring a pre-heating step in preparation for further action (e.g., printing papers) tend to consume a larger amount of power (i.e., a larger Δp value). This pre-heating step also causes the appliance surface temperature to increase rapidly (i.e., at a higher heat-rising rate r_i) when entering the full operating mode, and thus instantly triggers a significant temperature increase. Based on this observation, the initial matching stage selects power events with a large Δp value and thermal events with a high heat-

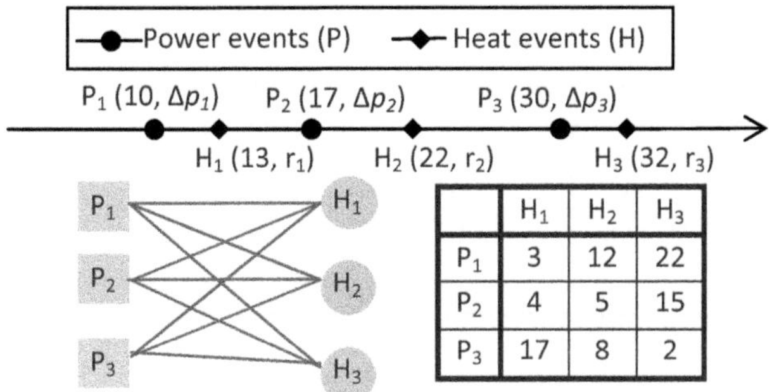

	H_1	H_2	H_3
P_1	3	12	22
P_2	4	5	15
P_3	17	8	2

(a) The graph (b) The edge costs

Figure 9. An example power-heat matching graph. In (a), three power events (P_1, P_2, and P_3) are connected with three heat events (H_1, H_2, and H_3) with edges with costs listed in (b).

rising rate. To identify appliances with high power consumption, the system computes the average power-changing amount from all power-on events and then identify high-power events whose Δp is above the average value. Similarly, the system designates heat-rising events with temperature changing rates above the average rate. After obtaining these high-power (-heat) events, the system performs matching to join heat and power events. Figure 9 shows an example in which high-power and high-heat events are represented as two types of vertices: power and heat vertices. A heat vertex represents an ith heat event ($H_i^{on}(t_i^{on}, r_i^{on})$) occurring on t_i^{on} with a heat-rising rate r_i^{on}. A power-type vertex representing a jth power event ($P_j^{on}(t_j^{on}, \Delta p_j^{on})$) occurring on t_j^{on} with the power-changing amount Δp_j^{on}. An edge connecting a heat vertex to a power vertex has a matching likelihood weight (or cost) set as the time difference ($|t_i^{on} - t_j^{on}|$) between the ith heat and j^{th} power events. By adding these edges between heat and power vertices creates a weighted bipartite graph.

In the next step, the system applies an event assignment algorithm [13] to find the optimal event assignment in which the sum of cost from edges is minimum. After performing the high-power and -heat event matching, the same algorithm is performed to join all remaining power-on and heat-rising events. The resulting matched on-event pair of the kth appliance usage session is defined as $E_k^{on}(t_k^{on}, \Delta p_k^{on})$, where t_k^{on} and Δp_k^{on} are the corresponding appliance-on time and power changing amount of this on-event pair, respectively. Because the power-on time and heat-rising time given by events of an event pair may differ, the appliance-on time t_k^{on} is set as the power-on time of the power event included by the matched event pair.

Appliance-off time resolution: After the on-event matching step, the appliance-off time is determined by matching power-off and heat-falling events using the weighted bipartite graph and event assignment algorithm described in the previous paragraph. However, the edge cost used in the off-event matching is calculated differently, as explained below. Given an on-event pair of the kth appliance usage session matched by the previous step, the edge cost between a mth heat-falling event, $H_m^{off}(t_m^{off}, r_m^{off})$, and a nth power-off event, $P_n^{off}(t_n^{off}, \Delta p_n^{off})$, is calculated as follows:

$$cost_{mn} = w_t \times time\_cost_{mn} + w_p \times power\_cost_n \quad (2)$$

$$where \quad time\_cost_{mn} = \frac{|t_m^{off} - t_n^{off}|}{max_{mn}|t_m^{off} - t_n^{off}|} \times 100 \quad (3)$$

$$power\_cost_n = \frac{|\Delta p_n^{off} - \Delta p_k^{on}|}{max_n |\Delta p_n^{off} - \Delta p_k^{on}|} \times 100 \quad (4)$$

where $time\_cost_{mn}$ measures the time proximity between the mth heat-falling event and the nth power-off even, and $power\_cost_n$ reflects the correlation of the power-changing amount between the current n^{th} power-off and the value inferred from previous matched power-on events. Thus, the $time\_cost_{mn}$ is proportional to the time difference between the power and heat events ($|t_m^{off} - t_n^{off}|$). The $power\_cost_{mn}$ is proportional to the difference of the power-changing amount between power -on and -off events ($|\Delta p_n^{off} - \Delta p_k^{on}|$). To simultaneously consider these two sets of parameters measured in different units, both *time_cost* and *power_cost* are rescaled to a unified cost range of 0~100. The weights, w_t and w_p, are set as 0.8 and 0.2, respectively, to rate the time-based cost (i.e., $time\_cost_{mn}$) at a higher rank than the other cost term $power\_cost_n$. After the off-event matching step, the resulting matched off-event pair of the kth appliance usage session is defined as $C_k^{off}(t_k^{off}, \Delta p_k^{off})$, where t_k^{off}, Δp_k^{off} are the corresponding appliance-off time and power changing amount of this off-event pair, respectively. Similarly, the inferred appliance-off time (denoted as t_k^{off}) of the matched off-event pair of the kth appliance usage session is given by the time of the matched power-off event.

Operating duration resolution: The appliance operating duration (T_k) of the kth appliance usage session is calculated from the time difference between on and off time instances (i.e., $t_k^{off} - t_k^{on}$). For those appliance usage session with only matched on- (off-) event pair, the system uses an off (on) time recovery scheme to further improve resolution accuracy. Most appliances are turned on by a switch on the appliance body. Although some appliances are remotely-controlled, users often interact with or touch these appliances during usage (e.g., take printed papers from the printer). Therefore, the system uses both human-appliance interaction hints and event times of un-matched thermal events to infer missing on (off) times. The system searches for the most likely human triggering action closest to a reference time indicated by the event time of a time-adjacent un-matched thermal event. The missing appliance-on (-off) time t_k^{on} (t_k^{off}) is given by the time instance of the triggering action that a human body area touches (or is in closest location proximity to) the appliance heat area.

Appliance Power Accounting

The appliance power accounting module estimates the average power consumption for each appliance by the matching results provided in the previous step. Based on the pre-

(a) Thermal camera

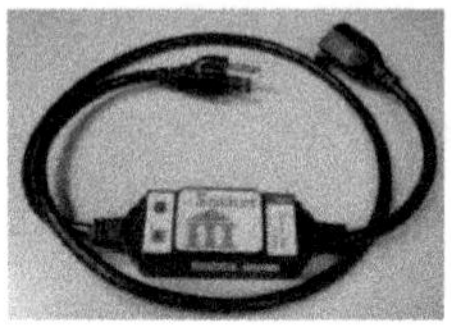
(b) Power meter

Figure 10. The prototype sensor components. The thermal camera (a) is mounted on the ceiling. The power meter (b) communicates with the data receiving module wirelessly.

vious matched power-on (-off) event pair of the kth appliance usage session, the average power (P_k) can be approximated by the average of power changing amount given by the on- and off-events (Δp_k^{on} and Δp_k^{off}) using the following formula.

$$P_k = \frac{\Delta p_k^{off} + \Delta p_k^{on}}{2} \quad (5)$$

Take the monitor usage session in Fig. 2(a) as an example: Δp_k^{on} and Δp_k^{off} are 20 Watts in the 21th minute and 20 Watts in the 56th minute, respectively. The appliance-level power consumption in the kth appliance usage session can then be approximated by the electric energy consumed in an average rate of P_k over the entire session (with session duration equal to T_k).

IMPLEMENTATION DETAILS

The current HeatProbe implementation consists of (1) a NEC TH7102MX thermal camera and (2) a wireless inline power meter (Fig. 10). The camera was mounted to the ceiling to monitor a space, e.g., cubicle spaces, public rooms, or kitchen spaces. The thermal imaging signals captured by the camera were sent through an 1394 port to a backend data processing server. In the current prototype, the server records and processes sensor data. Our thermal imaging processing software is developed based on the OpenCV libraries [14].

As for power monitoring, the inline power meter transmits power readings to the server through the Zigbee radio every second. A corresponding wireless Zigbee-based data receiving module attached to the server receives power readings. The server records power readings for subsequent processing by the power usage detection module.

EVALUATION

To measure accuracy of the HeatProbe system, this study conducts experiments involving three appliance usage scenarios with multiple users.

Appliance Usage Scenarios

Table 1 lists three appliance usage scenarios. These scenarios differ on the operating appliances, the number of participants, and the number of appliance usage events. For each scenario, we scripted a sequence of appliance usage actions for the participants to perform. The following sections describe these scripted action sequences in detail. We recruited a total of six participants for these experiments. All participants were graduate students in our

Environment	(1) cubicle spaces	(2) room spaces	(3) kitchen spaces
Participating Appliances	2 PCs 2 monitors 2 desk lamps 1 heater 1 toaster 1 printer	2 Notebooks 2 desk lamps 1 television 1 shredder 1 bug zapper	1 water heater 1 toaster 1 electric oven 1 microwave 1 television
# of participants for each round	2 people	2 people	3 people
# of on/off events per round	20	14	18

Table 1. Experimental appliance usage scenarios for three types of environments.

department. For each set of scenarios, there were several experimental rounds with different pairs of participants: there were 5, 2, and 2 rounds for scenario #1, #2, and #3, respectively. 82 different appliance usage sessions (with durations ranging from one to 60 minutes, with an average length of about 22 minutes) were collected in these usage scenarios.

Appliance usage scenario #1 (office cubicles)

Two participants worked in two adjacent cubicle spaces, and a thermal camera mounted on the ceiling monitored their electricity usage. Appliances included two PCs, two LCD monitors, and two desk lamps. Additionally, one heater, one toaster, and one printer were placed between the two cubicles. The appliance usage script for participant #1 was (1) turn on/off a PC, (2) turn on/off a LCD monitor, (3) turn on/off a desk lamp, and (4) print documents from the shared printer. The appliance usage script for participant #2 was (1) turn on/off a PC, (2) turn on/off a LCD monitor, (3) a desk lamp, (4) a heater, and (5) toast bread using a toaster.

Appliance usage scenario #2 (a meeting room)

Two participants discussed their project in a meeting room where a thermal camera mounted on the ceiling monitored their electricity usage. Appliances included two notebook PCs, two desk lamps, one TV-size screen, one paper shredder, and one bug zapper. The appliance usage script for participant #1 was (1) turn on/off his/her notebook PC, (2) turning on/off a desk lamp, and (3) the TV-size screen. The appliance usage script for participant #2 was (1) turn on/off a notebook PC, (2) a desk lamp, (3) a paper shredder, and (4) a bug zapper.

Appliance usage scenario #3 (a kitchen)

Three participants operated various appliances in a kitchen where a thermal camera mounted on the ceiling monitored their electricity usage. Appliances included a water boiler, a toaster, an electric oven, a microwave, and one TV. The appliance usage script for participant #1 was (1) boil water using an electric water heater, (2) toast bread using a toaster, and (3) heat food in a microwave. The appliance usage script for participant #2 was (1) heat a microwave oven and (2) heat food in an electric oven to heat their food, and (3) watch some TV. The appliance usage script for participant

Event Type	P-On	P-Off	P-All	H-Rising	H-Falling	H-All
Ground-truth	82	82	164	82	82	164
True positive	77	82	159	81	78	159
False positive	2	4	5	6	5	11
Average time diff (S.D.)	4.70 (7.67)	3.43 (6.79)	4.06 (7.25)	114.67 (156.59)	108.69 (125.97)	112.25 (142.37)
Accuracy	0.94	1	0.97	0.99	0.95	0.97
Precision	0.97	0.95	0.96	0.93	0.94	0.94

Table 2. Experimental results for three scenarios. P-On (or H-Rising) indicates the power-on (heat-rising) type of events. And, P-Off (or H-Falling) indicates power-off (heat-falling) type of events. P (H) -All means the overall summary of all power (heat) events. In the 5th row, the standard deviation of the time difference is indicated by values inside of the parentheses.

#3 was (1) make toast with the toaster, and (2) heat food in an electric oven.

Evaluation Metrics

This study defines the following metrics to measure the accuracy of event detection, matching algorithms, and the appliance power accounting results.

- *Event time detection error:* This measures the time difference between the system-detected power/heat event and the actual, ground-truth event.
- *Event detection accuracy and precision.* This measures how accurately the HeatProbe system detects power and heat events.
- *Matching accuracy.* This measures how accurately the HeatProbe system matches power events to corresponding heat events.
- *Appliance operating duration resolution error.* This measures how accurately the HeatProbe system monitors appliance operating duration. The resolution error calculates the amount of error in the HeatProbe-detected appliance operating duration and the actual ground-truth operating duration.
- *Appliance power accounting error.* This measures how accurately the HeatProbe system accounts for appliance energy consumption. The accounting error calculates the amount of error (in percentage) in the HeatProbe-detected appliance power consumption and the actual groud-truth appliance power consumption.

Results

HeatProbe-detected events were collected and compared with the ground-truth events labeled by humans observing the heatmap video recordings.

Event detection accuracy and precision

Table 2 presents statistics of the HeatProbe's accuracy performance from three experimental scenarios. True (false) positives mean the number of correctly (incorrectly) detected events by the HeatProbe system. The table also shows the average time difference between the HeatProbe-detect events and the ground-truth events.

Event Type	On event	Off event	All
# of Ground-truth event pairs	82	82	164
# of correctly matched event pairs	61	65	126
Accuracy	74%	79%	77%

Table 3. Summary of the event matching accuracy.

The average accuracies for detecting power-on, power-off, heat-rising, and heat-falling events are 94%, 100%, 99%, and 95%. The average precisions for detecting power-on, power-off, heat-rising, and heat-falling events are 97%, 95%, 93%, and 94%. All average detection accuracies are above 90%. The average event time detection errors for power-on, power-off, heat-rising, and heat-falling events are 4.7, 3.43, 114.67, and 108.69 seconds. The reason for the large errors in detecting times of heat events is an inherent delay between the time when an appliance is powered on/off and the time when an appliance surface exhibits a noticeable temperature change. For example, it takes a few minutes after powering on a PC to heat up its surface enough for the thermal camera to notice a temperature difference. The large standard deviations in the event time error are due to some appliances, such as a desk lamp and a heater, that increase their surface temperature more rapidly than that of other appliances.

Appliance operating duration resolution accuracy

Table 3 summarizes the number of ground-truth events, the number of correctly matched events by our matching algorithm, and the average event matching accuracy. The overall accuracy is 0.77. The matching error is caused primarily by a few seriously-delayed heat-rising (-falling) and/or false-positive events with a large time difference from the ground truth starting (ending) time. Because the current matching algorithm maps one heat-rising (-falling) event to a power-on (-off) event based on time proximity, a seriously-delayed heat-rising (-falling) event tends to match an incorrect power event (temporarily called e_1). This mismatched result might force another heat event (which should be matched with e_1) to pair with another incorrect power event, resulting in a series of mismatched pairs.

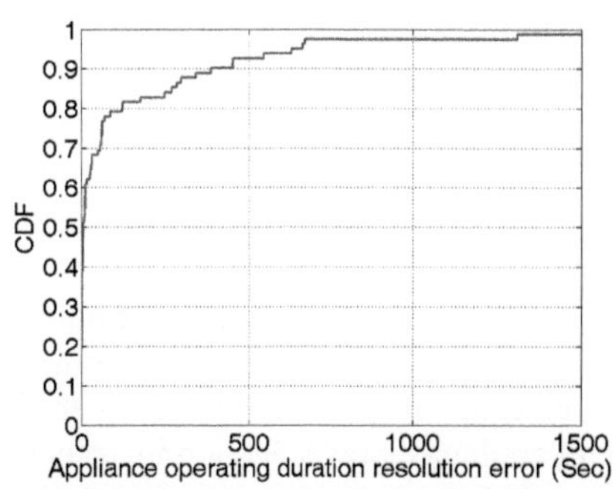

Figure 11. Cumulative distribution of the appliance operating duration resolution error.

Scena-rios	Appliance	True Power [W]	Estimated Power [W] (Error)
1	PC #1	86.09	79.25 (7.94%)
	PC #2	79.91	74.45 (6.83%)
	LCD Monitor #1	27.86	40.08 (43.88%)
	LCD Monitor #2	26.94	39.34 (46.04%)
	Lamp #1	80.03	110.42 (37.97%)
	Lamp #2	29.61	82.04 (177.05%)
	Printer	256.23	286.42 (11.78%)
	Toaster	629.09	616.10 (2.06%)
	Heater	411.76	353.11 (14.24%)
2	Notebook #1	32.26	35.08 (8.77%)
	Notebook #2	29.86	29.80 (0.20%)
	Lamp #1	80.23	82.20 (2.45%)
	Lamp #2	82.44	88.11 (6.89%)
	TV	121.14	121.54 (0.33%)
	Bug zapper	33.65	30.32 (9.91%)
	Shredder	76.86	75.75 (1.45%)
3	Water heater	433.98	417.55 (3.79%)
	Microwave oven	733.15	741.23 (1.10%)
	Toaster	540.63	631.93 (16.89%)
	TV	121.28	121.61 (0.27%)
	Oven	547.85	457.87 (16.42%)

Table 4. Appliance power accounting error for all scenarios. True (Estimated) column means the true (estimated) power.

Figure 11 shows the statistics of the appliance operating duration resolution error of the HeatProbe system. The x-axis represents the amount of operating duration resolution error between the detected and actual operating durations, while the y-axis represents the cumulative distribution function of the operating duration resolution error. From the usage durations inferred from the previous matching results, 80% of duration errors are less than 120 seconds, with an average error of 125.03 seconds.

Overall appliance power accounting accuracy

Table 4 presents the average appliance power accounting accuracy. The ground-truth (estimated) powers for each appliance are averaged and listed in the table. The overall average error between the estimated power and the ground-truth power is 19.8%. Most errors are less than 10%. However, there are a few cases in Scenario #1 where the error rates are above 30%, e.g., LCD Monitors #1 and #2, and Lamps #1 and #2. These large errors are due to mismatched on/off events. For example, the 177.05% inaccuracy of Lamp #2 in Scenario #1 is caused by mismatching Lamp #2 events to the power amount of a heater. The two appliances greatly differ in power consumption, resulting in a significant energy accounting error.

CONCLUSION

This study presents HeatProbe, a novel thermal-based energy meter system to disaggregate total energy consumption. Experiments conducted on three multi-user scenarios showed that the overall appliance power accounting accuracy reached an average of 80.2%. The system successfully monitored appliance usage durations with an average error of 125.03 seconds. Moreover, 80% of the measured usage durations were under 120 seconds.

We believe that the HeatProbe system offers an alternative and promising thermal-sensing approach to tackle the problem of disaggregating electricity usages. In the future, we will improve disaggregation accuracy and explore the possibility of accounting per-user energy footprints by incorporating human identification schemes.

REFERENCES

1. Behavior, Energy, and Climate Change Conference. http://www.beccconference.org/
2. Gupta, S., Reynolds, M.S., and Patel, S.N. ElectriSense: Single-point Sensing using EMI for Electrical Event Detection and Classification in the Home. In *Proc. Ubicomp 2010*, ACM Press (2010), 139-148.
3. Kim, Y., Schmid, T., Charbiwala, Z.M., and Srivastava, M.B. ViridiScope: Design and Implementation of a Fine Grained Power Monitoring System for Homes. In *Proc. Ubicomp 2009*, ACM Press (2009), 245-254.
4. Rowe, A., Berges, M., and Rajkumar, R., Contactless Sensing of Appliance State Transitions. In *Proc. BuildSys 2010*, ACM Press (201 0), 19-24.
5. Cent-a-Meter, http://www.centameter.com.au/
6. TED: The Energy Detective, http://www.theenergydetective.com/
7. Jiang, X., Dawson-Haggerty, S., Dutta, P., and Culler, D. Design and Implementation of a High-fidelity AC Metering Network. In *Proc. IPSN 2009*, IEEE Computer Society (2009), 253-264.
8. Hart, G. Nonintrusive appliance load monitoring. In *Proc. the IEEE*, 80, 12 (1992), 1870-1891.
9. Norford, L. K. and Leeb, S. B. Non-intrusive electrical load monitoring in commercial buildings based on steady-state and transient load-detection algorithms. *Energy and Buildings*, 24, 1 (1996), 51-64.
10. Puri, C., Olson, L., Pavlidis, I., Levine, J., and Starren, J., StressCam: non-contact measurement of users' emotional states through thermal imaging. *Ext. Abstracts CHI 2005*, ACM Press (2005), 1725-1728.
11. Yun, C., Shastri, D., Pavlidis, I., and Deng, Z., O' game, can you feel my frustration?: improving user's gaming experience via stresscam. In *Proc. CHI 2009*, ACM Press (2009), 2195-2204.
12. Larson, E.C., Cohn, G., Gupta, S., Ren, X., Harrison, B., Fox, D. and Patel, S.N. HeatWave: Exploring the Feasibility of Thermal Imaging for Surface User Interaction, In *Proc. CHI 2011*, ACM Press (2011), 2565-2574.
13. Bayati, M., Shah, D., Sharma, M. Maximum Weight Matching via Max-Product Belief Propagation, In *Proc. ISIT 2005*, ARXIV (2005), 1763-1767
14. Bradski, G., Kaehler, A., *Learning OpenCV: Computer Vision with the OpenCV Library*, O'Reily Media (2008).
15. Nilsson J. W., and Riedel S. *Electric Circuits, 8th Edition*, Prentice Hall (2007).
16. Patel, S.N., Gupta, S., Reynolds, M.S. The design and evaluation of an end-user-deployable, whole house, contactless power consumption sensor. In Proc. *CHI 2010*. ACM Press (2010), 2471-2480.
17. Stern, P.C. Information, incentives, and proenvironmental consumer behavior. *Journal of Consumer Policy*, 22, 4 (1999), 461-478.

LightWave: Using Compact Fluorescent Lights as Sensors

Sidhant Gupta[1], Ke-Yu Chen[1], Matthew S. Reynolds[2], Shwetak N. Patel[1]

[1]Computer Science & Engineering,
Electrical Engineering,
UbiComp Lab
University of Washington, Seattle 98195
{sidhant, kychen, shwetak}@uw.edu

[2]Electrical and Computer Engineering
Duke University
Durham, NC, 27708
matt.reynolds@duke.edu

ABSTRACT
In this paper, we describe LightWave, a sensing approach that turns ordinary compact fluorescent light (CFL) bulbs into sensors of human proximity. Unmodified CFL bulbs are shown to be sensitive proximity transducers when they are illuminated. This approach utilizes predictable variations in electromagnetic noise resulting from the change in impedance due to the proximity of a human body to the bulb. The electromagnetic noise can be sensed from any point along a home's electrical wiring. This allows users to perform gestures near any CFL lighting fixture, even when multiple lamps are operational. Gestures can be sensed using a single interface device plugged into any electrical outlet. We experimentally show that we can reliably detect hover gestures (waving a hand close to a lamp), touches on lampshades, and touches on the glass part of the bulb itself. Additionally, we show that touches anywhere along the body of a metal lamp can be detected. These basic detectable signals can then be combined to form complex gesture sequences for a variety of applications. We also show that CFLs can function as more general-purpose sensors for distributed human motion detection and ambient temperature sensing.

Author Keywords
Capacitive sensing, EMI, CFLs, interaction, gesture, proximity sensing.

ACM Classification Keywords
H5.m. Information interfaces and presentation (e.g., HCI): Miscellaneous.

General Terms
Algorithms, Experimentation, Measurement.

INTRODUCTION AND MOTIVATION
Developing easy-to-deploy sensing approaches has long been a focus of ubiquitous computing research. In particular, home environments are very challenging to instrument because they demand sensing solutions that are unobtrusive, low-cost and easy to maintain. The desire for new types of sensors in home environments also extends to a need for new interaction modalities that can be enabled by these easily deployed sensing infrastructures.

Figure 1: A user performing a hover gesture (left) near a compact fluorescent light (CFL) lamp, and a user touching the metallic base of a lamp (right). Both of these gestures can be detected using a single plug-in module.

In a typical sensing solution, one sensing system is required at each interaction point in the interaction space. For example, capacitive touch sensors can be used to turn any surface into an interaction point; however, an individual capacitive sensor is required on *each* interaction surface. Recently, video and depth cameras have been used to dramatically expand the interaction space; however, the user can only interact directly in front of the camera, and therefore many cameras are needed to allow interaction anywhere within a large space. Although many of these natural user interaction systems may be low-cost on a per sensor basis, the number of sensors required to instrument an entire interaction space make these systems potentially cost-prohibitive, as well as time-consuming to install and setup, and difficult to maintain, in the case of battery powered devices.

To alleviate some of these challenges, past solutions have looked at leveraging the existing infrastructure for sensing [3,14,7,8,10,13,14,15]. Some approaches have used the motion sensors found in alarm systems [1] and the changes in airflow through the HVAC system for detecting human motion [15]. Some have eliminated the need to instrument the environment by requiring the user to carry or wear a sensor-enabled device [9,11,12]. However, the need to wear sensing devices may make these approaches undesirable in the home setting. Another approach is to take advantage of the existing devices in the home and *repurpose* them as sensors. For example, researchers have shown how ordinary LEDs can be used as a both light emitters as well as light detectors [6].

In this work, we build on this general concept by introducing an approach that repurposes existing compact fluorescent lamps (CFL) as human proximity sensors. This approach requires *no modification to* the CFL bulbs, the lamp fixtures, or the human body, and many CFL fixtures can be used as sensors using only a *single* interface device plugged into any available electrical outlet. Our approach uses variations in the electromagnetic interference (EMI) generated by all CFL bulbs. We show that these "signals of opportunity" generated by the CFL's built-in power supply contains a characteristic pattern of fundamental and harmonic components that vary with the proximity of a human hand or body. These variations result from the change in CFL bulb-circuit impedance as a human body or another conductive object approaches the lamp. Thus, in essence, it can be thought of as an already-ubiquitous capacitive sensor (see Figure 1)

We demonstrate this phenomenon by evaluating it in the context of sensing and detecting a variety of basic gestures performed by a user, including: (1) *hover*: the passing of a hand near a CFL-equipped lamp, (2) lamp *shade touch*: touching the lamp shade with one or more fingers, and (3) *bulb touch*: touching the bulb with one or more fingers. Note that CFL bulbs operate at very low power compared to incandescent bulbs and as a result they do not get dangerously hot when installed in an open fixture (40 degrees Celsius for a 13W lamp). We mainly explored touching the glass on the bulbs to better understand the possible gamut of observed signals and their properties. Touching the bulb itself is one possible interaction technique, even though it may not be appropriate for all lamps. We anticipate that hovering or touching the lampshade or metallic base will prove to be more useful gestures in most cases.

Although our focus is initially the detection of simple gesture events, we use it to show the robustness and significance of using CFLs as a sensor. We have also observed other interesting properties of the CFL and its built-in power supply that could be used as a more general purpose distributed sensor, such as monitoring the changes in ambient temperature, detecting distance of user's hand from the lamp, or human motion detection.

An important implication of our approach is that each CFL in a home can be thought of as a low-cost general-purpose sensor that is inherently networked since all bulbs are connected to the power line. Only a single power line interface is needed to observe all of these CFLs. Since CFLs are also becoming increasingly ubiquitous due to their much higher efficiency compared to incandescent lamps, longer lifespan, and potential cost savings from reduced electricity consumption, we can expect them to be installed in many locations in a home already. Modern commercial and residential buildings looking to comply with certain "green" certifications, such as the LEED building certification system, require that the lighting be Energy Star® compliant (in the US, and similar programs across the world). Additionally, many utilities and power companies have programs that subsidize the purchase of or give away CFL for residential customers[1].

The specific contributions of this paper are:

1) The novel use of CFLs as capacitive sensors that require no additional instrumentation of the bulb, light fixture, or human.
2) A set of experiments that show the reliability of detecting hand gestures across different people as well as different CFL bulb brands, shapes, styles, and lighting fixture types. Additionally, we show that multiple CFLs (even of similar brands) can be distinguished when operating simultaneously.
3) We also show how CFLs could be used for human proximity detection and general ambient temperature sensing.

RELATED WORK

Capacitive and Electric Field Sensing

The fundamental phenomenon that LightWave leverages is variations in the observed EMI generated by the built-in CFL power supply. This EMI varies in response to changes in the impedance of the CFL bulb circuit due to variations in the local electric fields surrounding the bulb. These electric field variations are caused by the movement of grounded conductive objects in the space near the bulb. When the bulb is illuminated, the ionized gases within the bulb are conductive and they form the sensing electrode of a capacitive sensor.

Capacitive sensing has a long history in sensing human proximity. The first popular use of electric field (EF) sensing for machine control, or 'performing gestures' was Leon Theremin's musical instrument. The Theremin instrument is played by moving the body with respect to two antennas, one to control the pitch of sound and other to control the amplitude. This allows the performer to play music without making physical contact with the device. The capacitance between the human body and the Theremin's antenna is small, on the order of hundreds of femtofarads to a few picofarads. This capacitance detunes an L-C oscillator inside the Theremin causing an easily detectable frequency shift. EF sensing based on a similar concept has

[1] EU mandate to adopt CFLs. http://europa.eu/rapid/pressReleasesAction.do?reference=IP/08/1909

since been applied to graphical and human computer user interfaces for sensing touch and 2-D motion gestures as well as for sensing the position of a person in a room. These systems can operate in shunt mode where the human shunts an electric field to ground, or transmit mode, where the human conducts the electric field to a receiving electrode [17,18].

The key requirement for EF sensing is the presence of an electric field created by a high frequency oscillator. In prior work, such a field is explicitly generated by dedicated circuitry, which is installed at each point where sensing is desired. Cooley et al. demonstrated a human proximity system that uses modified fluorescent lamps as capacitive sensors, by monitoring distortions in the lamp's EF over time depending upon how people move under it. Though electromagnetically similar to our work, Cooley et al.'s approach requires that the lamp be instrumented with additional circuitry to measure the EF [5]. LightWave on the other hand does not require any additional instrumentation, since it does not measure the change in EF directly, but instead its effect on the variations in existing conducted EMI, which can be measured from anywhere in the home. Other work in the defense community has exploited ionized gases in fluorescent tubes as plasma-based radio frequency communication antennas that "disappear" when the voltage that ionizes the gas is removed [2].

EMI Sensing in a Home

Researchers have considered using the EMI generated from switch mode power supplies (SMPS) to infer the use of electronic devices in the home, including CFLs [10]. Although our approach uses a similar method of monitoring the power line for this EMI noise signal, prior work has largely focused on the presence or absence of this noise over the power line. In addition, the signal characterization was focused on identifying stable, environment-invariant signal features such as center frequency, bandwidth, and variance whereas LightWave examines the EMI noise signal much more closely to detect small changes in the CFL's operating parameters. Gupta et al. also showed that it is possible to differentiate among similar devices in the home using a single monitoring point, which implies that one could use a collection of CFLs already installed in a home as distributed sensors.

Recent work has also examined the use of radiated electromagnetic noise for gestural interaction by looking at the amount of noise coupled onto the human body, by using the body itself as a receiving antenna. The amount of noise picked up by the body is then used to infer physical touch points in the home [4]. One drawback of this approach is that it requires the user to carry a custom device for detecting this EM noise being coupled to the human body. In a way, our approach is the reverse since the human body is changing the characteristic EMI of the CFLs attached to the power line, and does not require the instrumentation to be carried by the human.

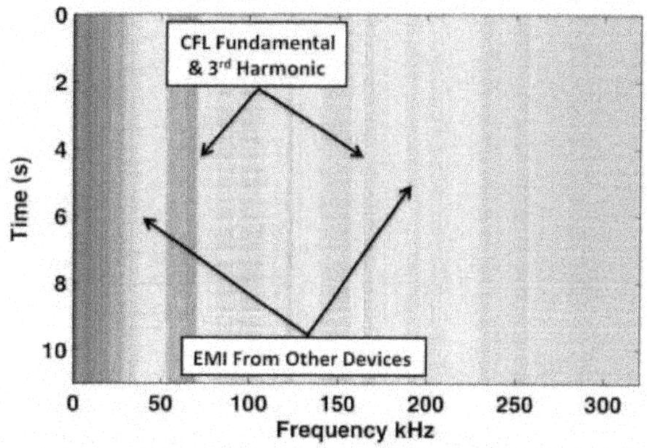

Figure 2: Spectrogram showing electromagnetic interference that various devices produce as observed on a power line. Only part of the full spectrum (500 kHz) is shown for clarity.

BACKGROUND AND THEORY OF OPERATION

Electromagnetic Interference On the Power line

Electrical noise present on a power line when a device is operational is called conducted electromagnetic interference, which can be classified into two types: transient and continuous. Transient noise is characterized by the short duration for which it can be observed, generally tens of nanoseconds to a few milliseconds. Transient noise is most often observed in conjunction with a switch open or close event. Continuous noise on the other hand can be observed for as long as the device is operational. A CFL bulb is an example of a device that generates continuous noise, which is then conducted onto the power line due to its physical connection with the power line. Since a home's electrical infrastructure is interconnected in parallel, conducted EMI coupled onto the power line at one location propagates throughout a home's electrical infrastructure. Figure 2 shows EMI observed on a typical power line infrastructure.

Continuous noise is usually intrinsic to the device's operation and internal electronics. A CFL lamp, for example, generates EMI at frequencies that are harmonically related to its power supply's internal high frequency oscillator.

Variations in CFL's Line-Conducted EMI

When a human is in proximity to a CFL, the conducted EMI changes in amplitude, fundamental frequency, and the distribution of harmonic energy among the harmonics. LightWave detects these changes in amplitude and shifts in frequency to infer when a human is in proximity to the lamp, and determine what kind of interaction took place. To better understand how the EMI changes as a result of human proximity, it is essential to understand the basic operation of a CFL. Figure 3 shows a highly simplified block diagram of a typical CFL.

A CFL has two main components: a gas filled tube (e.g., the bulb), and an electronic circuit called a ballast. In a CFL, the ballast is integrated with the bulb into a single unit; however, in other styles of fluorescent fixtures the ballast is

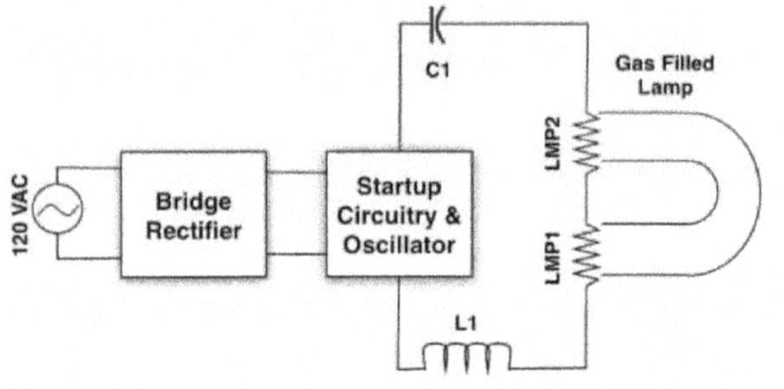

Figure 3: Simplified block diagram of a CFL. L1-Lamp-C1 forms a series resonant circuit. Human proximity causes the effective capacitance to change and detune the oscillator.

separate from the bulb. The ballast is connected to the line voltage (120V/ 60 Hz AC in the US), which is rectified and stepped up by a high frequency switching power converter to around 300 V AC, which drives the fluorescent tube. The reason for using high switching frequencies, typically around 40 kHz, is the increased efficiency of the power converter circuit as well as the smaller size of components, thus making the entire CFL unit both compact and more efficient. This high frequency can be achieved by a variety of methods – from simple L-C resonant oscillators in cheaper lamps to microcontroller-controlled oscillators in others. Irrespective of the mechanism to generate the high frequency, the purpose of the resonant circuit is to stabilize the current through the fluorescent tube as the bulb warms up, and then maintain equilibrium in lamp current and voltage. Thus during operation, the oscillator is at resonance with the L1-Lamp-C1 series network as shown in Figure 3.

This equilibrium can be disturbed in many ways, including changes in the supply voltage, current, or failure of a component. Additionally the bulb's equilibrium state is disturbed by capacitive and/or ambient temperature changes in and around the lamp. This state change can be detected in the bulb's EMI signature.

The bulb itself serves as a sensing electrode because the CFL's electronic ballast generates a strong electric field inside the bulb to ionize the internal gases and produce light. However, this process also produces a strong electric field around the periphery of the bulb, because the ionized gases act like a single equipotential electrode. The field that results is similar in essence to electric fields that are explicitly generated for capacitive proximity sensing [18], with the difference that, the former is a *by-product* of the way CFLs functions and latter is intentional.

By moving a hand in the vicinity of the CFL, the electric field surrounding the bulb is disrupted and there is an increase in the effective capacitance in the lamp circuit since the human body is essentially a capacitor to ground. In a traditional capacitive proximity sensor, this change in capacitance results in a change in displacement current, which is sensed directly. In contrast, the displacement current being coupled from a CFL results in a small

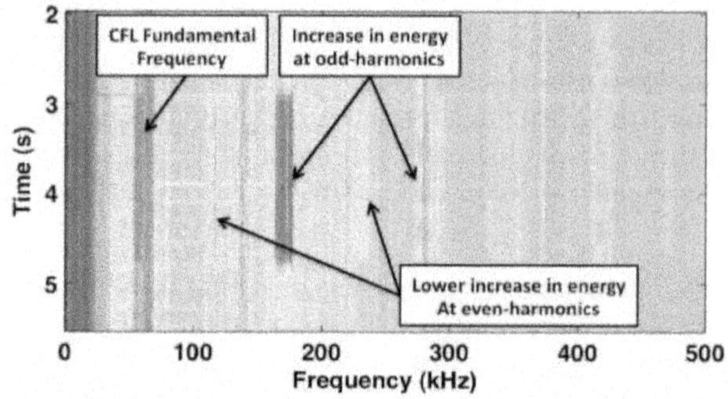

Figure 4: Spectrogram showing change in observed EMI as a result of touching the CFL bulb, which causes a large capacitive change resulting in increased energy.

imbalance in the oscillator and bulb equilibrium, resulting in a shift of the CFL's fundamental resonant frequency by 1–5%. A balanced oscillating circuit tends to suppress even-order harmonic products, while unbalancing it tends to enhance odd-order products. Figure 4 shows how the energy at odd-harmonics increases when a bulb is touched – creating an even more significant imbalance than that created by human proximity. It should be noted that multiple similar CFL bulbs could be operating simultaneously in an environment or on a common electrical circuit without effecting LightWave's ability to detect the change in energy. This is because, the harmonic energy only increases when the capacitance changes, thus two lamps could be on, but neither could be generating increased energy at the odd-harmonics.

When a user brings their hand close to the CFL lamp, it causes an increase in energy at the harmonics, but the change is much smaller and harder to visualize on a spectrogram. These changes are only reliably detectable after significant filtering and post processing as described in the following section.

SYSTEM DESCRIPTION AND IMPLEMENTATION

Electromagnetic interference conducted onto the power line by various electrical devices can be measured by sampling the voltage on the power line at appropriate frequencies. Since the power line has a very strong 60 Hz signal (50 Hz in Europe and Asia) meant to power electrical appliances, it is necessary to reject this 60 Hz component using high dynamic range analog circuitry. Our prototype system makes use of an analog high-pass front end, similar to one described by Gupta et al. in [10], but modified for a wider frequency response (corner frequency of 5.3 kHz). The signals from the front end are then digitized using USRP-1 (Universal Software Radio Peripheral), a general purpose, software configurable FPGA-based digitizer equipped with a 12-bit dual-channel ADC. The digitizer is configured to sample the voltage at 1 MS/s and compute a 16,384-point Fast Fourier Transform (FFT), yielding 61.03 FFT vectors per second. The magnitude in dB of each FFT vector is then computed before it is fed into the signal processing chain (see Figure 5), for further processing and detection of events.

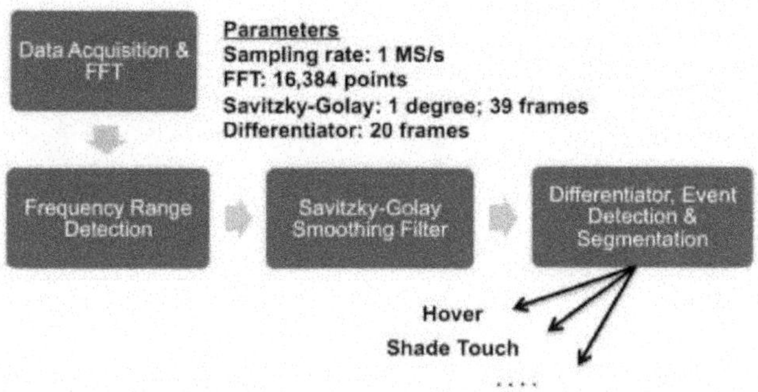

Figure 5: Stages of the signal processing chain that condition the input signal, apply differentiators, detects and segments events.

We define events as instants in time when a human is in proximity to a CFL and performing a gesture. Since our input signal is real valued and we are only interested in the magnitude, the magnitude FFT vectors are symmetric around baseband, and hence half of the bins are redundant. These are truncated, reducing the number of points in the FFT vectors to 8192 across a spectral width of 500 kHz.

Frequency Range Detection

As described earlier, human proximity to a CFL appears as increased energy in harmonics of the fundamental frequency at which the CFL produces EMI. Thus, the first step is to identify the fundamental and harmonic frequencies. Though most CFLs have a switching frequency between 40 kHz and 120 kHz, it can vary from one brand to another and thus setting a global range for all lamps is not practical. If the range to monitor is set too wide, the aggregate noise power from other sources reduces the overall signal to noise ratio. This makes the detection of changes in harmonic energy less reliable. Thus, a potential solution is to setup multiple narrow ranges specific to each CFL lamp and monitor each simultaneously.

Earlier prototypes of LightWave required that these frequency ranges be set manually for each lamp. This manual approach was later discarded in favor of a simple one-time calibration step, which involves switching each lamp on and off twice. By turning the lamp on and off, LightWave can detect the fundamental and its harmonic by looking for presence and absence of EMI on the power line.

Actual measurement of the frequency of the fundamental is made only during the second on/off sequence, since during first interval the CFL bulb could be warming up, during which the frequency changes until the bulb reaches thermal equilibrium with its environment.

Once the frequency range for the desired bulb's 3rd harmonic is identified, a sum across this entire band is computed. For each FFT vector in time, a sum of energies in this range of frequencies is computed. Figure 6 (left), shows such a running sum plotted over time for a lamp. When the energy in this range increases as a result of a gesture or human proximity, the sum also increases. The reason a sum over a frequency band is computed instead of tracking individual frequency bins over time is because even when the CFL is in equilibrium, its fundamental frequency shifts a few kHz over time due to temperature changes. Tracking a range of frequencies (in tens of kHz) is immune to such small shifts.

Smoothing the Summed Energy

As evident from Figure 6 (left), the tracked sum over time is quite noisy and cannot be directly used for reliable event detection. In addition to EMI noise from other appliances, occasional broadband noise also plagues the signal. The source of such broadband noise could be from flicking mechanical switches [14], noise from dimmers, or other switch mode power supplies. Prior to taking the sum in a range of frequencies, we discard FFT vectors where the sum across the entire spectrum is more than 4 standard deviations greater than the running mean over 15 FFT vectors.

To smooth the summed energy time series data, we experimented with several filters, beginning with the standard averaging FIR filters and a moving window Gaussian smoothing filter, but found that not only did they not remove the high frequency noise, but also 'smoothened out' the peak from the gesture event itself, making it flatter and more difficult to detect. We found that the Savitzky-Golay smoothing filter with a degree of 1 and frame length of 39 to be most effective (see Figure 6 (center)). Not only does it remove the high frequency noise, but it also maintains the underlying shape of the peak. We apply two passes of the same filter on the summed data, which

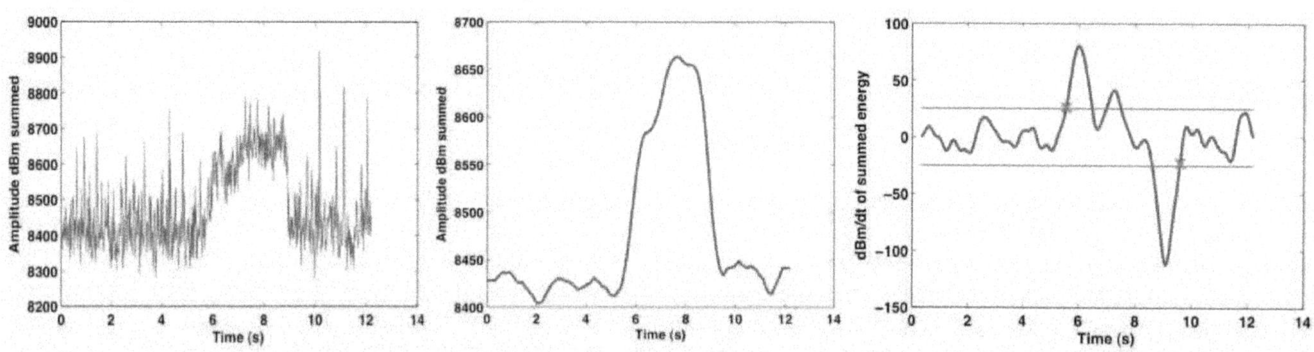

Figure 6: Summed energy in band over time shows increase in energy as a result of a hover (left), filtered summed energy (middle) and first derivative waveform along with start and stop of the hover event as detected (right).

minimizes noise and makes the event detection more reliable.

Event Detection and Segmentation

We make use of a moving window first order derivative filter with a frame size of 20 to obtain a signal that gives us an indication of any abrupt changes in the signal. Since small abrupt changes also cause the derivative filter's output to generate a peak, it is necessary to set a rejection threshold. That is, we only want to consider changes in summed energy that are abrupt as well as large in magnitude. We chose a threshold value of 25 dB/dt (dt = 20 frames, 0.327s), which has good sensitivity to detecting hovers and other gestures while still maintaining a low false positive rate. The ROC curve characterizing the tradeoff between true positive rate and false positive for different threshold values is described later in the paper. It should be noted that this single threshold works across all people and all lamps that we tested. Figure 6 (right), the red lines show the threshold.

When a hand approaches the lamp there is an increase in the summed energy signal producing a large positive spike from the derivative filter. As the hand moves away from the lamp, the summed energy signal decreases back to its baseline level, producing a comparable negative spike in the derivative filter. We leverage this phenomenon in finding the beginning and ending of an event.

We also leverage the expectation that a large positive derivative should be directly followed by a large negative derivative to prevent the algorithm from over-segmenting a single event. This is necessary because during the event the summed energy signal is larger than normal, resulting variations in the signal that are also more intense – for example, when a user's hand naturally moves closer or farther while performing a gesture. These subtle variations can also result in shifts in the derivative signal. An example is shown in Figure 6 (right). The signal rises above the positive threshold, falls below it and rises again (due to variation in signal *during* the event). We wish to ignore the second positive threshold crossing to avoid overly segmenting a single event. This is easily achieved by building hysteresis into our threshold values.

Events that surpass the derivative threshold must also meet a set of specific constraints. First, a positive derivative, which surpasses threshold, must be followed by a negative derivative value that surpasses threshold at least after 600 ms, but no more than 5 seconds. Second, the peak derivative value of a positive spike and magnitude of the negative spike must be within 30% of each other. This ensures that dissimilar spikes are not matched. Third, when two or more consecutive positive spikes are followed by a negative spike, the process is repeated for each spike, in chronological order. If a match is made, the remaining positive spikes are discarded and the algorithm moves on, begins searching for another positive spike after the matched negative spike. It should be noted that the maximum duration only limits the time for each gesture, not the time between them or the total duration of a complex gesture. For example, one can perform three hovers one after another forming a single complex gesture (at an application level) that lasts 6 seconds and each hover will be detected. Points marked with an 'x' in Figure 6 (right) show the start and end of a segment as found by this search algorithm. These segments are then outputted as events.

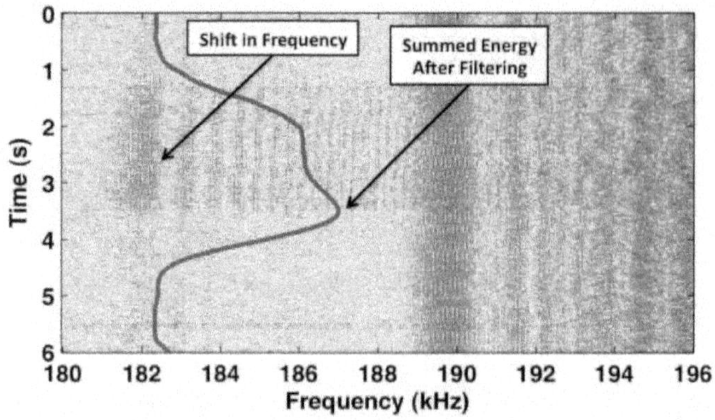

Figure 7: Summed energy in band (blue line) tracked over time overlaid with the spectrogram showing EMI from CFL. Notice the bump in blue line and increase in harmonic energy at 182 kHz in the spectrogram as a user hovers for 2.5 seconds.

OBSERVABLE SIGNALS AND USING THE CFL AS A SENSOR

In this section, we detail the variations that LightWave can observe in the EMI signal from a CFL and the potential uses of it as a "sensor." Since not all of the minute changes in the EMI are visually apparent on a spectrum analyzer, our signal-processing pipeline was critical in identifying some of these signal variations.

Hover

As described previously, when a human is in proximity to a CFL lamp it can cause changes in capacitance of the resonating circuit resulting in variations in the observed EMI. This allows LightWave to sense hover gestures. Thus, when a person passes their hand close to a CFL lamp, it produces a detectable change in the energy levels of the EMI. This 1-bit binary information of whether a hand is near or not, coupled with timing information (time duration of the energy increase) can be used as a basis for complex gestures. Figure 7 shows how the EMI changes when a person hovers their hand close to a CFL. Observe how the energy in the 182–189 kHz band increases as a result. The small bumps are the slight movement of the person's hand under the bulb.

Touches on Lamp Shade, Bulb, and Base

Much like a hover, touching the lampshade or the bulb also causes an increase in the harmonics energy. Since CFL bulbs are not dangerously hot like incandescent bulb, especially when installed in an open fixture, we decided to experiment with touching the bulb as well. We measured the temperature of the bulb and found it to be around 40 °C

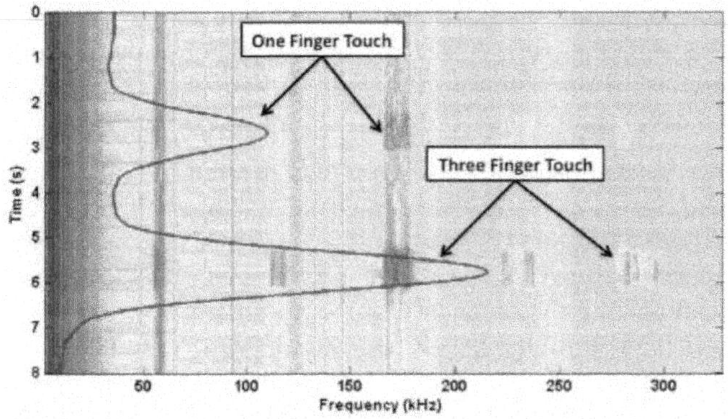

Figure 8: Notice the difference in amplitude of energy between a one finger touch on bulb and a three finger touch. Blue line is filtered sum of these energies over time.

for a 13W CFL. The key difference in a hover and touch is the amplitude of the energy increase.

A hover event produces the smallest capacitive coupling, followed closely by touching the lampshade and bulb touch produces the most coupling. An interesting signal observed with touch gestures is that the amplitude of the signal is proportional to the surface area of the contact. That is, the energy amplitude of the signal observed is much higher when the bulb is touched with three fingers than when touched with one. Figure 8 shows an overlay of energy tracked over time for one-finger and three-finger touch on top of the spectrogram. Notice the amplitude difference between the first touch and the second. Also, for metallic lamp fixtures, it is even possible to detect touches on the base of the lamp (see Figure 1), which produce a similar response to the lampshade being touched.

Changes in Proximity

The change in proximity of a user's hand to the CFL, that is, whether the hand is moving away from the lamp or towards the lamp can be detecting by observing the slope of the signal. When the hand is moving towards the lamp, instead of seeing an abrupt increase in energy, a gradual increase is seen since the amplitude depends on how far the user's hand from the lamp is. Figure 9 shows an instance where the hand is moved towards the lamp and then abruptly removed. From our experience, the hand can be as far as 30 cm from the CFL bulb and be detected.

Detecting Ambient Temperature Change

In addition to variations in EMI as a result of capacitive changes from touches and human proximity, we also observe changes in EMI when the temperature of the CFL bulb or the ambient temperature around it changes. Instead of an increase in harmonic energy, changes in temperature cause the frequency to shift up to tens of kHz. Tracking the fundamental frequency over time can give an indication of changes in ambient temperature around the lamp. If calibrated, we can measure the true ambient temperature.

We observed that when the ambient temperature around the lamp is increased, it causes the frequency at which the CFL's EMI is observed to shift to a lower frequency. To

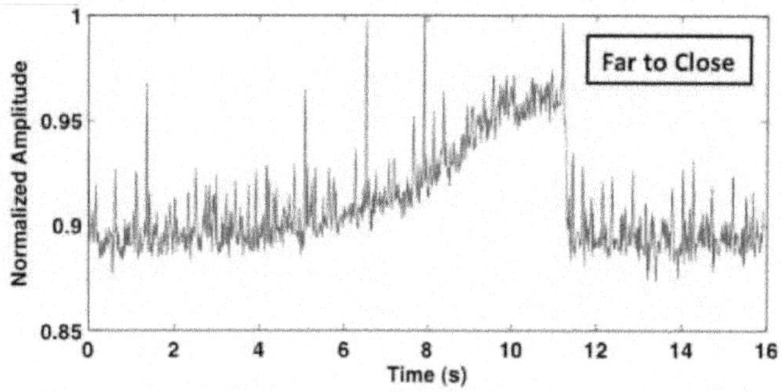

Figure 9: Amplitude of the observed energy depends on the proximity to the lamp. Amplitude gradually rises when a hand is brought closer over time.

verify this phenomenon, we performed two experiments. In both experiments, we put a CFL bulb on a tray along with a thermocouple based digital temperature sensor. We let the bulb stay on for 10 minutes to reach room temperature (temperature of environment at time was 27 °C). In the first experiment, we used a heated chamber whose inside temperature was around 65 °C. We then introduced the tray with the bulb and the temperature sensor into the chamber. The second experiment was similar, but instead of a heated chamber, we used a small refrigerator, with an internal temperature of 18 °C. Figure 10 shows the change in frequency as a result of the heated chamber experiment. The change in the CFL's fundamental frequency tracks closely with the change in ambient temperature.

With these preliminary experiments we wanted to confirm that EMI changes as the ambient temperature around the lamp changes. This change in frequency with temperature opens up the possibility of using CFLs in a home as distributed temperature sensors. This technique could also be used to monitor large or abnormal increases in lighting temperature to detect potential safety hazards. We also observed that the CFL as a temperature sensor has an incredibly fast response time, which can be used as an air movement or air convection sensor. For instance, this can

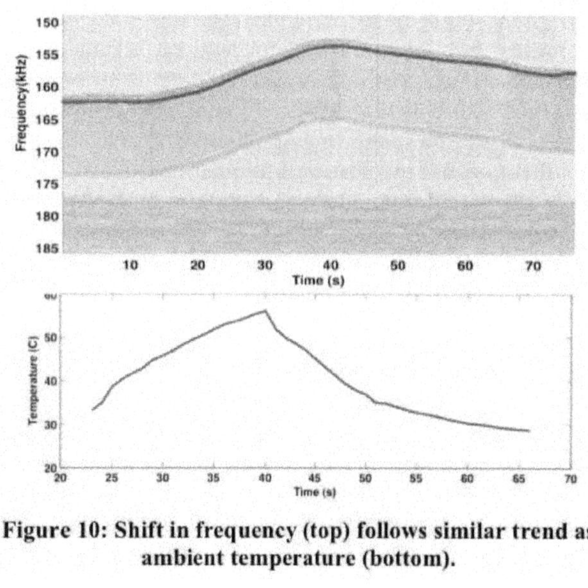

Figure 10: Shift in frequency (top) follows similar trend as ambient temperature (bottom).

be used for detecting air drafts, opening windows or doors, or potentially air movement created by people passing by.

CORE EXPERIMENTS

For our core experiments, we decided to evaluate the ability to build simple gesture event detectors using CFLs as proximity sensors. To validate our approach, and confirm its applicability across various people, different brands of CFLs and lamp fixture styles, we conducted experiments with 10 participants (7 males, 3 females). This was conducted in a simulated home environment in our lab with 6 lamps. We also conducted feasibility experiments with a subset of those participants and lamps in 2 actual homes.

Figure 11: Lamps that we used for our experiments. Two lamps (top left, top middle) were chosen to be similar for comparison. All lamps were on during the experiment.

We collected data for a variety of different lamp fixtures (see Figure 11) that included lamps with metal shade (3), glass shade (1), plastic shade (1) and no shade (1). The CFL bulbs used also varied in brand: GE (1), Energy Star certified GreenLite/Sylvania (1), Commercial Electric (1), ProLume (1) and a generic brand (2) from a local home improvement store. This collection of bulbs we used also varied in wattages from 12W to 26W (mean 16W).

Data Collection Procedure

Our simulated home setup included 6 lamps placed randomly throughout the lab space. The lamps were powered through separate residential style power source (a 60 Hz split single phase transformer). It should be noted that despite this isolating transformer, EMI from a large number of devices running in the building were observed, which made this have at least comparable EMI levels that would typically be found in a home environment. Our own data collection and monitoring equipment produced EMI, as well as the many computers and measurement equipment that operated in the lab space. Figure 2 is a spectrogram generated from EMI observed on our setup. Notice the large number of EMI from other devices.

Each participant in our experiment performed 5 different gestures, with each gesture repeated 4 times. The gestures included: a hover, touching the lampshade with two fingers, touching the lampshade with hand, touching the glass part of the bulb with one and three fingers. These 20 gestures were performed on each lamp one after another. To ensure consistency in where participants touched the lamp, we marked a spot on each lampshade. For one lamp that did not have any lampshade, instead of the two gestures involving touching the lampshade, we instead had the participants perform a hover to the left of the lamp and to the right of the lamp.

We built a data collection tool that allowed us to label the gestures as the users performed them. For each lamp, the software randomly ordered the sequence in which the gestures were required to be performed, in addition to randomizing the order in which each lamp was tested. This was done to minimize any temporal biases. Additionally, to minimize any effects from when the CFL lamps were turned on relative to start of the experiment, we turned the lamps off and only turned them on 5 minutes prior to each experiment. The entire experiment with each participant was repeated twice, on separate days to validate the stability over time. Each experiment took 45-50 minutes. The entire experiment ran for a period of two weeks during which we collected a total of 2400 events (120 per person, per session).

Feasibility in Homes

We randomly chose two lamps, and performed the same set of experiments in two different homes to confirm that the approach extends to an actual home. The homeowners were asked to continue their daily routine, thus lights and devices were being turned on and off as we collected the data.

RESULTS

Analysis of Hit Rate Accuracy

We chose a threshold of 25 dBm/dt (dt = 0.3277s) after plotting a ROC curve that characterizes the tradeoff between true positive rate and the false positive rate over the entire dataset (see Figure 12). The choice of 25 dBm/dt was based on maintaining good sensitivity (91.2%) towards detecting events while having a low (6%) false positives rate. All the results presented here on use this threshold.

Table 1 summarizes the hit rate for event detection and segmentation that we obtained for each lamp. Since hover events have the lowest energy change relative to other touch-based gestures and are more challenging to detect and segment, we show the hit rate for hover events from the first session across lamps for each user. Means for each session for all gestures are also shown. Overall, hovers had

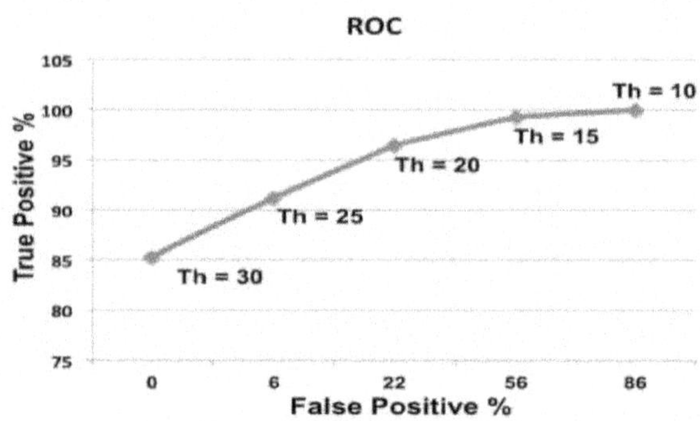

Figure 12: ROC showing tradeoff between the true positives rate and false positives rate for different threshold values.

Lamp	Hover												Bulb Touch One Finger		Bulb Touch Three Fingers		Shade Touch One Finger		Shade Touch with Hand	
	P1	P2	P3	P4	P5	P6	P7	P8	P9	P10	Mean 1st run	Mean 2nd run	Mean 1st run	Mean 2nd run	Mean 1st run	Mean 2nd run	Mean 1st run	Mean 2nd run	Mean 1st run	Mean 2nd run
L1	1	0.75	0.75	1	1	1	1	1	1	1	0.95	0.9	1	1	1	1	0.65	0.75	0.75	0.85
L2	1	1	1	1	1	1	1	1	1	1	1	0.95	1	1	1	1	0.725	0.775	0.8	0.85
L3	1	1	1	1	0.75	1	1	1	1	1	0.975	0.9	1	1	1	1	0.825	0.875	0.975	0.9
L4	1	0.75	1	1	0.75	0.25	1	0.75	0.75	1	0.825	1	1	1	1	1	*	*	*	*
L5	1	0.25	1	1	1	0	1	0.5	0.25	1	0.7	0.85	1	1	0.975	1	1	1	1	1
L6	1	1	1	1	1	1	1	1	1	1	1	0.9	1	0.975	1	1	1	0.975	1	1
Avg.											**0.908**	**0.917**	**1**	**0.996**	**0.996**	**1**	**0.84**	**0.875**	**0.905**	**0.92**

Table 1: Hit rate for each gesture. For hover events, per user (P1-P10) hit rate for 1st run and means are shown, while for others only means are presented across different participants.

an average hit rate of 90.8% for the first session and 91.7% for second. A key observation is that the mean hit rates we calculated are across all lamps and all users, suggesting the robustness of using a CFL as a "capacitive sensor." This hit rate suggests that is possible to build complex gesture from sequence of these basic gesture events. If a particular application can tolerate a higher false positive rate, then a lower threshold could be used to increase the overall accuracy.

Touches on bulb itself were easily detectable (100% and 99.6% between the two sessions), which can be attributed to the large energy change that passes the various event detection and segmentation checks. The average energy for bulb touch with three fingers events were 82.7 dB/dt (44.3 for one finger touches), roughly three times our set rejection threshold.

We expected lampshade touches to perform well, but relative to both hover and bulb touches some of the lamps exhibited a lower hit rate. In particular, we found that L1 performed poorly (see Table 1). This lamp has a plastic lampshade (black frame with white shade in Figure 11). Lamp L3, which has a metal frame and a glass shade performed better than L1. The best performers were lamps L5 and L6, both of which have a metal body and metal shade. Clearly, the metal and glass shades are far more conductive, and hence easier to detect (see Table 2). In the case of L4, which did not have a lamp shade around the bulb and we found that there were no noticeable differences if the hand gestures or hovers occurring on the top, right or left of the illuminated bulb.

Interestingly, metal fixtures actually made the entire metal surface conductive and thus a touch gesture could occur anywhere on the stem or base. For example, the lamp on the right in Figure 1 with a stainless steel frame can be touched anywhere along the body, thus expanding the interactive area on the lamp. If a metal lamp was placed on another metallic surface, then that surface would also become a potential touch surface to some extent. Other metallic lamps exhibit this same behavior, where the entire lamp surface can act as a capacitive touch sensor. This was particularly evident in L2, which is the same style lamp as L6, but it performed worse because it was placed on a metallic table and appeared always grounded. The metal surface produces a grounding effect on the signal, thus touches to lamp had noticeably small increase in energy. When we placed L2 on a non-conductive surface, we found that the effect went away and the increase in energy was comparable to L6.

Overall, we found that we could reliably detect both touch and proximity gestures with a CFL. Much of the variations in performance were not due to the person or differences in CFL, but the style of the lamp itself (metal, plastic, glass, etc). This implies that even though the CFL bulbs act consistently, the various lamp styles can add some variation to what gesture can be reliably sensed.

	Hover	Bulb Touch One Finger	Bulb Touch 3 Fingers	Shade Touch One Finger	Shade Touch with Hand
L1	6.671	25.937	62.828	4.86	5.038
L2	6.155	43.521	77.853	8	8.837
L3	5.343	43.036	83.028	4.6	6.428
L4	6.23	40.114	69.43	*	*
L5	9.402	55.577	104.51	14.9	16.776
L6	6.594	45.201	85.4486	9.12	10.353
Avg.	**6.53**	**44.35**	**82.78**	**9.12**	**10.353**

Table 2: Average energy change (dB/dt) for each lamp and gesture. Notice the difference between the energy values for a hover vs. bulb touches vs. shade touches. Shade touch energy for L2 is low due to the grounding effect of the metal surface.

In-home Experiments

Table 3 summarizes the results of the in-home experiments. We found that our initial evaluation shows promising results for our approach extending to a home environment. The results are actually similar to those found in the lab. Given the lab scenario was likely noisier in terms of additional EMI noise on the powerline, these results seem plausible.

DISCUSSION AND FUTURE WORK

The use of CFL as a capacitive proximity detector by monitoring the variations in its conducted EMI appears to be a promising sensing approach. Our core experiments reveal that EMI signal is temporally stable across people. A single segmentation algorithm was developed to isolate and

	Hover	Bulb Touch One Finger	Bulb Touch Three Fingers	Shade Touch One Finger	Shade Touch with Hand
Home1	0.875	1	1	1	1
Home2	0.875	0.875	0.75	0.875	0.875
Avg.	**0.875**	**0.9375**	**0.875**	**0.9375**	**0.9375**

Table 3. Hit rate from the two in-home experiments.

detect the various gesture events across all of the different participants and various brands of CFLs. We also found that multiple CFLs (even those of similar brands) operating simultaneously can still be distinguished using our approach. There is enough of a difference in the operating frequency between two similar bulbs, that the odd harmonics are also distinguishable. If two CFLs do happen to have the exact same operating frequency and are operating simultaneously, as long as only one is interacted with at a time, LightWave will be able to detect events but may confuse the source lamp from which the events are being generated.

Although our methods primarily consider the 3rd harmonic, we found that there is an increase in energy not only at the 3rd but also the 5th and 7th harmonics. Our algorithm can potentially be improved by tracking energy in multiple higher order harmonics. This could also alleviate a key limitation of LightWave, which is the potential for a strong interfering device to mask the smaller energy changes from the CFL. Because the fundamental frequency of the CFL changes based on the ambient temperature (the temperature sensor effect), the location of the odd harmonics also changes. Thus, to use the CFL as both a temperature sensor and a capacitive proximity sensor, both the fundamental and its odd harmonics need to be tracked while it is operating. In any case, this would be good practice in general because of the slight fluctuations in ambient temperature could cause some sort of frequency shift.

To confirm that this phenomenon is exhibited by as many CFLs, we acquired 6 additional (different) bulbs of various wattages and found that all exhibited similar responses as the ones used in the core experiment.

Of course, LightWave's methods require that the CFL bulb be illuminated (and thus generating EFs and EMI) for it to be used as a sensor. This limitation could be in some cases seen as a feature, because the sensing system can be turned off on demand.

CONCLUSION

We present a new sensing approach that turns ordinary compact fluorescent light (CFL) bulbs into human proximity sensors. In addition, we present evidence that CFLs can also be used for more general purpose sensing applications, such as monitoring the changes in ambient temperature, human motion detection (if a person is in range of a CFL), or as a sensor for incipient failure of CFL failure. All of these new uses are enabled by monitoring the EMI over the power line from a single point. By using the CFL as a proximity sensor, we showed that simple gestures (waving the hand near the bulb, touching the bulb, touching the lamp shade, and touching the base of a metal lamp) performed near a CFL lamp can be robustly detected and segmented in the presence of other CFLs and electrical noise sources on the power line. This was confirmed both in the lab in and in actual homes. The growing popularity of CFLs and the increasing mandates on the use of CFLs for lighting may provide an opportunity to potentially scale some of these simple sensing approaches throughout the home with little installation effort.

REFERENCES

1. ADT QuietCare. www.gehealthcare.com/quietcare.
2. Borg, G.C., J. H. Harris, D.G. Miljak, and N.H. Martin, "Applications of Plasma Columns to Radiofrequency Antennas", Appl. Phys. Lett. 74, 3272 (1999)
3. Chen, J., Kam, A.H., Zhang, J., Liu, N. and Shue, L.: Bathroom Activity Monitoring Based on Sound. In: Pervasive Computing 2005.
4. Cohn, G., Morris, D., Patel, S.N., Tan, D.S. Your Noise is My Command: Sensing Gestures Using the Body as an Antenna. In the Proceedings of CHI 2011.
5. Cooley, J.J.; Avestruz, A.-T.; Leeb, S.B.; Norford, L.K.; , "A Fluorescent Lamp with Integral Proximity Sensor for Building Energy Management," Power Electronics Specialists, 2007
6. Dietz, P.H.; Yerazunis, W.S.; Leigh, D.L., "Very Low Cost Sensing and Communication Using Bidirectional LEDS", In UbiComp 2003.
7. Fogarty, J., Au, C. and Hudson, S.E.: Sensing from the Basement: A Feasibility Study of Unobtrusive and Low-Cost Home Activity Recognition. In: UIST 2006.
8. Froehlich, J., Larson, E., Campbell, T., Haggerty, C., Fogarty, J., Patel, S.N.: HydroSense: infrastructure-mediated single-point sensing of whole-home water activity. In UbiComp 2009.
9. Fukumoto, M. and Tonomura, Y. Body Coupled FingeRing: Wireless Wearable Keyboard. Proc ACM CHI 1997.
10. Gupta, S., Reynolds, M.S., Patel, S.N. ElectriSense: Single-Point Sensing Using EMI for Electrical Event Detection and Classification in the Home. Proc ACM Ubicomp 2010.
11. Harrison, C., Tan, D. Morris, D. Skinput: Appropriating the Body as an Input Surface. Proc ACM CHI 2010.
12. Kim, J., Jiasheng He , Kent Lyons , Thad Starner, The Gesture Watch: A Wireless Contact-free Gesture based Wrist Interface. In Wearable Computers 2007.
13. Kim, Y., Schmid, T., Charbiwala, Z., Srivastava, M.B.: ViridiScope: design and implementation of a fine grained power monitoring system for homes. In UbiComp 2009.
14. Patel, S.N., Robertson, T., Kientz, J.A., Reynolds, M.S. and Abowd, G.D.: At the Flick of a Switch: Detecting and Classifying Unique Electrical Events on the Residential Power Line. In: UbiComp 2007.
15. Patel, S.N., Reynolds, M.S., Abowd, G.D. Detecting Human Movement by Differential Air Pressure Sensing in HVAC System Ductwork: An Exploration in Infrastructure Mediated Sensing. In Pervasive 2008..
16. Saponas, S., Tan, D., Morris, D., Balakrishnan, R., Turner, J., Landay, J. Enabling Always-Available Input with Muscle-Computer Interfaces. Proc ACM UIST 2009.
17. Smith, J.R. Field Mice: Extracting hand geometry from electric field measurements. IBM Systems Journal, (1996).
18. Zimmerman, T., Smith, J., Paradiso, J., Allport, D., Gershenfeld, N. Applying Electric Field Sensing to Human-Computer Interfaces. Proc ACM CHI 1995.

Interactive 3D Modeling of Indoor Environments with a Consumer Depth Camera

Hao Du[1], Peter Henry[1], Xiaofeng Ren[2], Marvin Cheng[1], Dan B Goldman[3], Steven M. Seitz[1], Dieter Fox[1,2]

[1]Department of Computer Science and Engineering, University of Washington, Seattle, WA, USA
{duhao,peter,kaiwen,fox,seitz}@cs.washington.edu

[2]Intel Labs Seattle, Seattle, WA, USA
xiaofeng.ren@intel.com

[3]Adobe Systems, Seattle, WA, USA
dgoldman@adobe.com

ABSTRACT
Detailed 3D visual models of indoor spaces, from walls and floors to objects and their configurations, can provide extensive knowledge about the environments as well as rich contextual information of people living therein. Vision-based 3D modeling has only seen limited success in applications, as it faces many technical challenges that only a few experts understand, let alone solve. In this work we utilize (Kinect style) consumer depth cameras to enable non-expert users to scan their personal spaces into 3D models. We build a prototype mobile system for 3D modeling that runs in real-time on a laptop, assisting and interacting with the user on-the-fly. Color and depth are jointly used to achieve robust 3D registration. The system offers online feedback and hints, tolerates human errors and alignment failures, and helps to obtain complete scene coverage. We show that our prototype system can both scan large environments (50 meters across) and at the same time preserve fine details (centimeter accuracy). The capability of detailed 3D modeling leads to many promising applications such as accurate 3D localization, measuring dimensions, and interactive visualization.

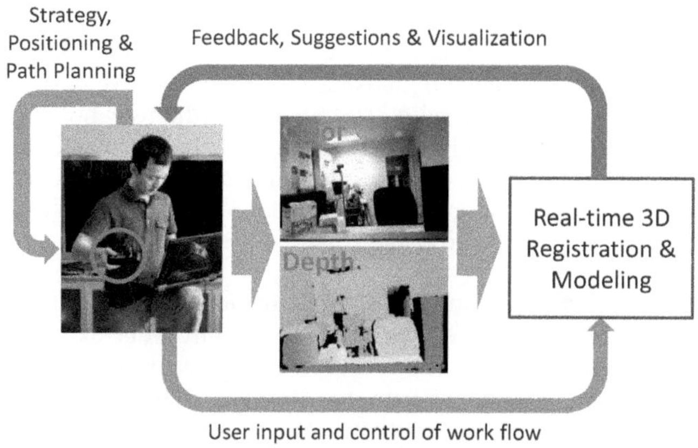

Figure 1. Interactive 3D mapping: color and depth frames from a consumer depth camera are aligned and globally registered in real time. The system alerts the user if the current data cannot be aligned, and provides guidance on where more data needs to be collected. The user can "rewind" and resume the process, and also check the quality and completeness of the 3D model on-the-fly.

Author Keywords
3D mapping, localization, depth camera, user interaction.

ACM Classification Keywords
H.5.m Information interfaces and presentation: Miscellaneous.

General Terms
Algorithms, Design, Experimentation, Measurement.

INTRODUCTION
Detailed 3D visual models of indoor spaces, from walls and floors to objects and their configurations, can provide extensive knowledge about the environments as well as rich contextual information of people living therein and how they interact with the environment. As cameras become ubiquitous and see fast growing usage, accurate 3D visual models will be a cornerstone of future context-aware applications.

Accurate 3D models are difficult to build and thus have rarely been used in applications. Most existing 3D scanning products work only on small objects. Scanning an indoor environment is possible but costly, usually requiring heavy-duty laser scanners on special platforms such as robots [30]. These systems are far from accessible to average consumers.

Recently, image-based 3D modeling has become feasible, with Photo Tourism [28] being a prominent example how 3D structures can be recovered by analyzing and matching photos. There has been research work showing promising results on city-scale outdoor scenes [24, 1]. On the other hand, indoor personal spaces remain difficult due to many technical challenges such as low lighting and textureless surfaces. Limited successes have been reported, including the use of the Manhattan world assumption [8], trading 3D geometric accuracy for robustness in a constrained setting.

In this work, we present a prototype mobile system that enables a non-expert user to build dense and complete models for his/her personal environments, running on a laptop in real-time and interacting with the user on-the-fly. One technology that makes this feasible is the wide availability of affordable depth cameras, such as those deployed in the Microsoft Kinect system [19, 25]. These cameras directly provide dense color and depth information. However, their field of view is limited (about 60°) and the data is rather noisy and low resolution (640×480). Henry et al [12] showed that such cameras are suitable for dense 3D modeling, but much was left to be desired, such as robustness for use by non-experts, or complete coverage of the environment including featureless or low-light areas.

The key idea behind our work is that, by running 3D modeling in real-time on a mobile device, the system can explore the space together with the user and take advantage of online user interaction and guidance (see Figure 1). We design an interactive 3D modeling system so that the user holds a depth camera in-hand to freely scan an environment and get feedback on-the-spot. Online user interaction, with a freely moving depth camera, solves many of the challenging issues in 3D environment modeling:

Robustness: We compute 3D alignments of depth frames on-the-fly, so that the system can detect failures (due to many reasons such as fast motions or featureless areas) and prompt the user to "rewind" and resume scanning. The success of 3D registration of consecutive frames is thus "guaranteed".

Completeness: A 3D environment model is constructed on-the-fly. The user can check the model in 3D at any time for coverage and quality. The system also automatically provides suggestions where the map may yet be incomplete.

Dense coverage: Largely due to the use of a depth sensor, our system produces visual models that are dense in 3D space, even in textureless areas, comparing favorably to most existing work in vision- or laser-based modeling. A dense model reveals fine details of the environment.

Our system is capable of scanning large-scale indoor spaces, such as office buildings of 50 meters across, with centimeter-level details accurate in both 3D geometry and color appearance. We show a variety of models built with our online mobile system covering different sizes and types, when used by both expert and non-expert users. We compare our interactive system to traditional offline approaches and demonstrate how user interaction makes the system robust enough to be accessible to everyone with a depth camera[1].

How can we use such a detailed 3D map? We demonstrate three promising directions: (1) localization in 3D space approaching decimeter accuracy; (2) measuring dimensions of spaces and objects; and (3) photorealistic visualization of 3D environments applicable to virtual remodeling and furniture shopping. We believe that a consumer-friendly 3D modeling system will open up many more opportunities for interesting applications that may benefit from a rich 3D context.

[1]Supplemental videos demonstrating our interactive system can be found at: `http://www.cs.washington.edu/robotics/projects/interactive-mapping/`

RELATED WORKS

Geometrically modeling a physical environment is a problem of general importance, and for a long time it was done manually by specialists using specialized tools. Automatically mapping an environment is challenging, and one success story is that of using a laser scanner on a mobile robot [7, 30]. Robot mapping has been shown to be robust, but is mostly limited to 2D maps and relies on expensive hardware.

In the Ubiquitous Computing community, much attention has been devoted to a closely related problem: localization. A variety of signals has been used in indoor localization [13, 17, 2], such as 802.11 [3], GSM [22], and recently powerline signals [23]. There is a limit on the localization accuracy using these low-rate signals, the state of the art being around 0.5 meters [32]. Many efforts have been made on how to simplify and avoid extensive calibration [18].

Vision-based 3D modeling techniques have been gaining popularity in recent years. Building on multi-view geometry [11] and in particular bundle adjustment algorithms [31], 3D structures can be recovered from a set of 2D views. PhotoTourism [28] is an example where sparse 3D models are constructed from web photos. There has been a lot of work on multi-view stereo techniques [26]. The patch-based framework [10], which has been most successful on object modeling, has also been applied to environment modeling. The work of Furukawa et al. [9] built on these works and obtained dense indoor models using the Manhattan world assumption.

There have been successful efforts to build real-time systems for 3D structure recovery. Davison et al. built real-time SLAM (simultaneous localization and mapping) [5] systems using monocular cameras. Klein et al. built the Parallel Tracking and Mapping (PTAM) [15] system which applies SLAM for tracking. Pollefeys et al. [24] proposed real-time solutions for street-view reconstruction. Newcombe et al. [20] recently used PTAM and optical flow techniques to compute dense depths. Many real-time systems are limited to small-scale spaces.

Due to the difficulties of indoor modeling such as low lighting and lack of texture, interactive approaches have been proposed to utilize human input. [6] was an early example showing very impressive facade models and visualizations with manual labeling. [29] used interactions to extract planes from a single image. [27] was a recent example combining user input with vanishing line analysis and multi-view stereo to recover polygonal structures. Our approach to interactive mapping is different in nature, as we enable online user interaction, utilizing user input on-the-fly for both capturing data and extracting geometric primitives.

The arrival of consumer depth cameras such as Kinect [19] and Primesense [25] is significant. We believe these affordable depth cameras will soon see extensive uses in applica-

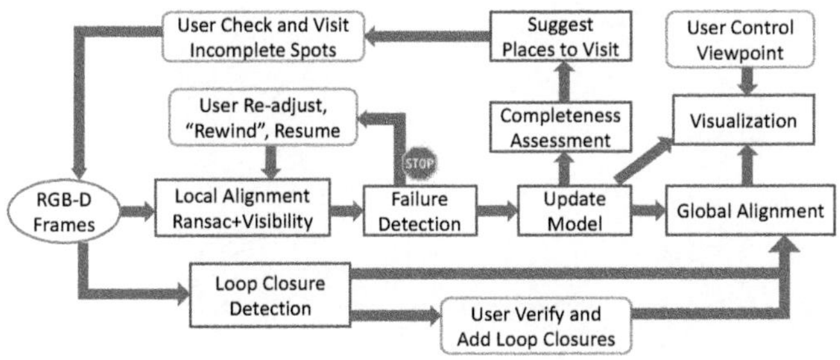

Figure 2. Detailed system overview: frame alignment, loop closure detection, and global alignment are performed in real time. Green boxes represent user interactions. The user is alerted if alignment fails, is notified of suggested places to visit, and can verify and improve the model quality via manual loop closure.

tions beyond gaming, in particular in 3D modeling, making it accessible to consumers. The work by Henry et al. [12] is the most relevant as a pioneer of 3D modeling using consumer depth cameras. They carried out experimental studies of alignment algorithms and combinations using both color and depth. Our work aims at making such a depth-camera-based modeling system work in real-time, incorporating various aspects of user interaction to make 3D modeling robust, easy to use, and capable of producing dense, complete models of personal spaces.

SYSTEM OVERVIEW

Figure 2 shows an overview of the design of our interactive mapping system. The base system follows a well-established structure of 3D mapping, which partitions the registration of RGB-D (color+depth) frames into *local alignment* plus *global alignment*. Local alignment, or *visual odometry* [21], is a frame-to-frame registration step matching the current frame to the most recent frame. The current frame is also matched to a subset of "keyframes" in the system to detect "loop closure" [16, 12, 4], i.e. whether this is a revisit to a known scene. Global alignment uses loop closure information to jointly optimize over all the RGB-D frames to produce globally consistent camera poses and maps.

User feedback and interaction is enabled at multiple levels in our system. First, if local alignment fails, i.e. the current frame cannot be registered into the map, the system alerts the user and pauses the mapping process. The user re-orients the camera with suggestions from the system, until local alignment succeeds and the mapping resumes. Second, the user has control over loop closure detection by verifying and adding links that are difficult decisions for an automatic algorithm. Combining both, our system is robust to algorithm failures or human errors, making it "guaranteed" to produce globally consistent maps given sufficient user supervision.

In our system, the globally aligned map is visualized on-the-fly, as shown in Figure 3. The user can see how the 3D map grows in real-time, freely change the 3D viewpoint to check for inconsistencies and completeness, and plan the camera path accordingly to ensure a complete and consistent map. To facilitate, the system continuously checks the completeness of the current map, provides visual feedback about incomplete areas, and guides the user to locations from which the view could bring added map coverage.

By closely integrating the user into the data collection phase and making him/her fully aware of the state of the process, our interactive system avoids many pitfalls in 3D mapping and achieves robustness and completeness even in challenging cases. As can be seen in Figure 1 and the supplemental video, our prototype system runs on a laptop, and is fully mobile. We envision that, in the near future, such a system can be integrated and packaged to a portable form factor with a touch interface and become accessible to everyone.

ROBUST RGB+DEPTH REGISTRATION

In this section we describe the core of our real-time 3D registration algorithm. The *3-Point* matching algorithm is used to compute full 6-D transformations between frame pairs [14]. A novel matching criterion is used to combine RANSAC inlier count with *visibility* conflict. Combining the visibility criterion, matching is much more robust in difficult cases where the inlier count is small and becomes unreliable.

RANSAC and 3-Point Matching

Following the RGB-D alignment approach in [12], we detect visual features in the color frame using the GPU implementation of the standard SIFT features [33], find matches using the SIFT ratio test, and use RANSAC to prune outliers and find the camera pose transform between two frames. It is worth noting that since we have depth information for the visual features, only 3 point pairs are needed in RANSAC search, making it much more robust and efficient than the classical 7-point solution. Moreover, the 6-D full transform can be computed without scale ambiguity.

Consider N pairs of initial feature matches between Frame F_1 and F_2, represented by 3D coordinates (X_1^i, X_2^i) in their respective reference systems. RANSAC samples the solution space of (R, T) (rotation and translation) and estimates its fitness by counting the number of inliers, f_0,

$$f_0(F_1, F_2, R, T) = \sum_i^N L(X_1^i, X_2^i, R, T), \qquad (1)$$

where,

$$L(X_1^i, X_2^i, R, T) = \begin{cases} 1, & e = \|RX_1^i + T - X_2^i\| < \epsilon \\ 0, & otherwise \end{cases}$$

and ϵ is the threshold beneath which a feature match (X_1^i, X_2^i) is determined to be an inlier. RANSAC chooses the transform consistent with the largest number of inlier matches.

Combining RANSAC with Visibility

The RANSAC framework above only accesses depth values at the SIFT feature points. To make use of dense depth information available at all pixels, we introduce a visibility confliction term and combine it with the RANSAC inlier count. Consider the 2D example shown in Figure 4 (left), showing two camera views. The circles and stars are the depth maps sampled at the camera pixels. When (R, T) is

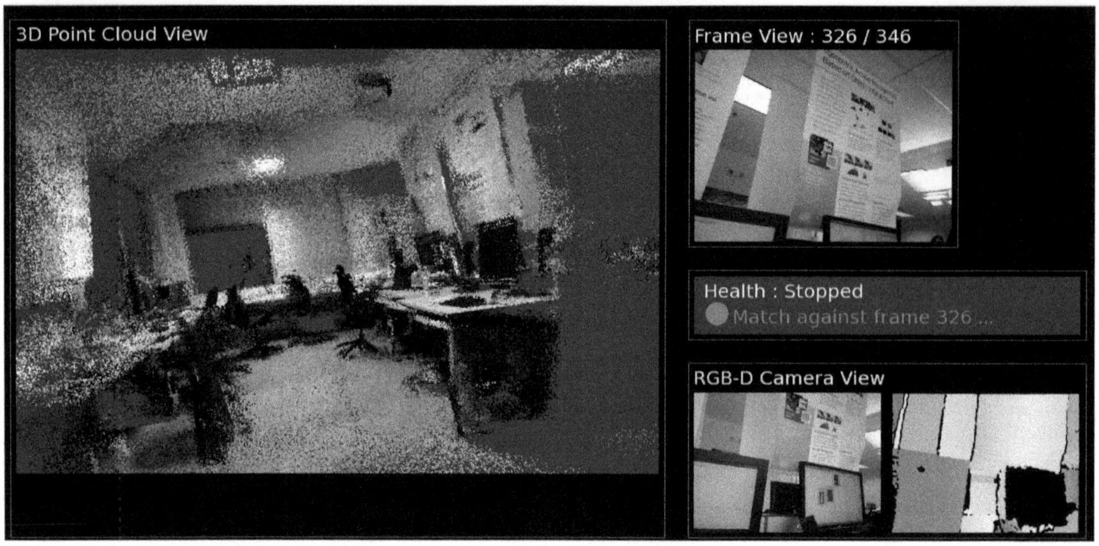

Figure 3. Real time visualization of the mapping process: The left panel provides a 3D view of the globally aligned map. The health bar in the center right panel indicates the current quality of frame alignment. In a failure case, as is shown, the user is guided to re-orient the camera with respect to a target frame registered in the map. The upper right panel shows this target frame, and lower right panel indicates the current camera view.

the genuine relative transformation, the two scenes overlap perfectly. When (R^*, T^*) is a wrong relative transformation, shown in Figure 4 (right), overlaying the point clouds from both cameras, it is possible to see visibility conflicts – when a camera captures a scene point in 3D, the space along its viewing line should be completely empty; if there exist points from the other camera in between due to a incorrect (R^*, T^*), there is a conflict.

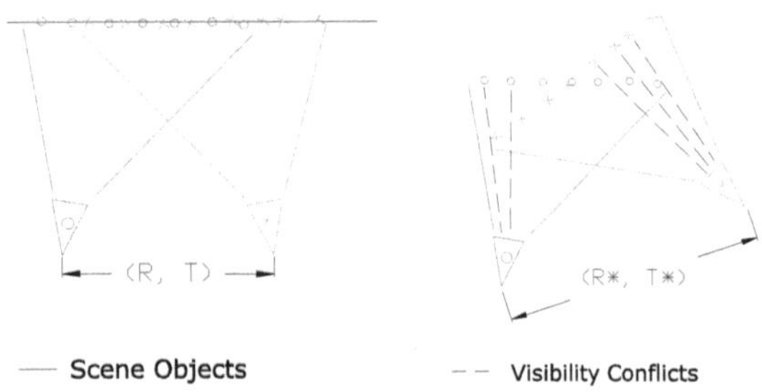

Figure 4. Visibility conflicts. Left: what a surface should look like from two depth camera views. Right: inconsistent camera poses lead to visibility conflicts, useful information for RANSAC search.

We compute visibility conflict by projecting the point cloud C_1 from frame F_1 onto the image plane of F_2, and vice versa. If the depth of a pixel of C_1 is smaller than the depth of the F_2's pixel at the corresponding location (larger than a varying threshold equal to depth uncertainty), it is counted as a visibility conflict. We compute the following quantities: number of visibility conflicts (f_1); average squared distance of points with visibility conflicts (f_2); number of visibility inliers (f_3) by counting those pixels where no visibility conflicts both ways of projections. We use a linear function to combine these with the RANSAC inlier count:

$$g(F_1, F_2, R, T) = \sum_{i=0}^{m} \alpha_i f_i \quad (2)$$

where m is the number of quantities involved, and the weights α_i are learned through linear regression.

INTRODUCING USER INTERACTION

User interaction has been utilized in 3D modeling to overcome the incompetency of automatic algorithms in hard cases (e.g. [27]). Existing work typically views user interaction as a post-processing step: after all the data have been acquired, the user sits down at a desktop computer, and then marks up and corrects structures in the model.

Our approach utilizes interaction in a different nature – involving user interaction early in the image data acquisition stage as well as in post-processing. Decent source data is crucial for a successful reconstruction, and user interaction can significantly help data capture. We envision that a compact mobile system/device can be developed for a user to hold in his/her hand, freely move it to scan scenes, and interact with the system as the 3D map is being built. We view data acquisition and model construction as one integrated process that happens on-the-spot.

As shown in Figure 2, our prototype system incorporates three types of user interactions to achieve robustness and completeness in 3D mapping: (1) failure detection and rewind/resume; (2) scene completeness guidance; and (3) user-assisted loop closure.

Rewind & Resume and Failure Tolerance

In the case of indoor 3D mapping, each camera view or frame usually covers a small area of the entire scene, so it is crucial to align the frames together and merge them. Since consecutive frames have the most similar views, a typical approach is to align neighboring frames first.

Frame-to-frame matching, however, can fail for many reasons, especially at the hand of a non-technical user who does not have any understanding of the mechanisms and limits of vision-based mapping. For example, if the user moves the camera too fast, motion blur will fail the matching. Even if the user is careful, matching can fail when the field of view does not contain sufficient color and geometric features. As we will see in the experiments, even with a state-of-the-art RGB-D mapping approach, failures can be frequent.

We design our system to be robust to matching failures, with what we call *Rewind and Resume*. When a frame fails to register with the previous frame, the system raises an alert, pauses the mapping process, and waits for a new frame that can successfully register (Figure 3). The system shows the user what frame it expects, so the user can move the camera to match the expected view. Moreover, it is not limited to the most recent frame: the user can either "undo" and drop the most recent frames (say to remove frames of an intruding person), or "rewind" to any previous frame in the system and "resume" at a different point. This results in a tree-structured data flow and makes the system more flexible and usable. The user can save the partial map to disk, and resume on a different day from any scene that is already captured.

Model Completeness

Capturing a complete 3D model of the scene is desired, because large missing areas in an incomplete 3D model significantly lower the visual quality. A missing area exists in the scene either because the area has never been captured or the frames that did contain the area did not get depth values, for reasons such as camera range or surface slant.

We consider the completeness in a user-defined manner. Using a passive capturing system, it can be very difficult for the user to be aware of which parts of the scene have been captured. With an online system, the user can view the current reconstruction in real time, view the up-to-date 3D model, and directly see which areas are missing.

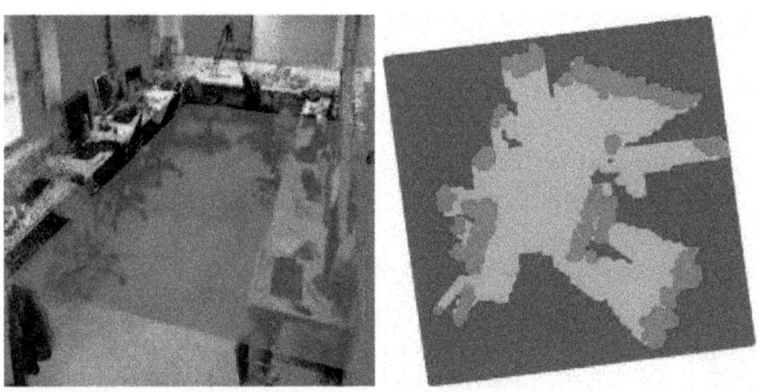

Figure 5. Completeness Guide. At the user's request, our system displays the classification of voxels from a user specified 2D slice in the 3D point cloud. Green: the voxel is guaranteed to be "empty"; Red: it is "occupied"; Blue: "unknown" area.

In order to further assist users in finding uncaptured areas, our system is able to estimate completeness. Consider a bounding box that contains the currently reconstructed point cloud. The inside of the bounding box can be represented by 3D grid voxels. Each grid voxel is classified into one of the three categories: (1) "occupied": there is at least a scene point in that voxel; (2) "empty": there must be no scene point in the voxel; (3) "unknown": none of the above. All voxels are initialized in Category (3). A voxel is set as Category (1) when there exists a scene point. A voxel is set as Category (2) when it is not (1) and the voxel has been seen through by any of the existing camera viewing line.

Figure 5 shows the classification of voxels from a user specified 2D slice in the 3D point cloud. Green: the voxel is guaranteed to be "empty"; Red: it is "occupied"; Blue: "unknown" area. The user's goal is then to paint all areas in either green or red by exploring the 3D space.

Interactive Loop Closure

Loop closure (global pose optimization based on frame-pair matches captured at different times) helps to fix the accumulated errors originating from sequential frame-to-frame matching. Automatic loop closure is hard as there may be large differences between scene frames over a loop [12]. A single matching outlier due to low lighting or few features could cause the whole loop to be inconsistent.

A decent loop closure does not require matches between many pairs of frames. When combined with frame-to-frame alignments, a few matches over key frames can well constrain the entire loop and facilitate global consistency. This provides us an opportunity to involve user supervision. Our system runs an automatic matching algorithm to select candidate frame pairs, ranks them using the proposed visibility criterion, and then suggests frame pairs with large visibility conflicts. The user can select any frame pair to perform a RANSAC or ICP based alignment to add a loop closure constraint, inspect the resulting map, and then decide to accept or reject the newly added constraint.

3D MAPPING EVALUATIONS

In this section, we present experimental results of our 3D mapping system. We show three types of evaluations: (1) how our RGB-D RANSAC utilizes dense depth information and outperforms classical computer vision solutions; (2) how user interaction plays an essential role in making mapping successful; and (3) how our results compare to the state of the art in vision-based 3D modeling. We also show examples of the 3D models that we have scanned with the system.

We use a PrimeSense camera [25] with resolution 640-by-480 and an effective range of $0.5m$ to $5m$. The depth uncertainty, needed for visibility conflict, is calculated from camera specifications ($7.5cm$ baseline, 570 pixel focal length), approximately $0.03cm$ at a distance of $0.3m$ and $7cm$ at $5m$. All the computations and visualizations are done on an Intel i7-720qm laptop at 3 to 4 frames per second.

RGB-D RANSAC for Visual Odometry

We compare the accuracy of the 3-point RANSAC solution on RGB-D frames to that of the 7-point algorithm [11]. We generate feature pairs via bidirectional matching, considering a pair matched if they are both the best matching feature to the other, and the second best match has significantly higher distance in the feature descriptor space (ratio > 1.25).

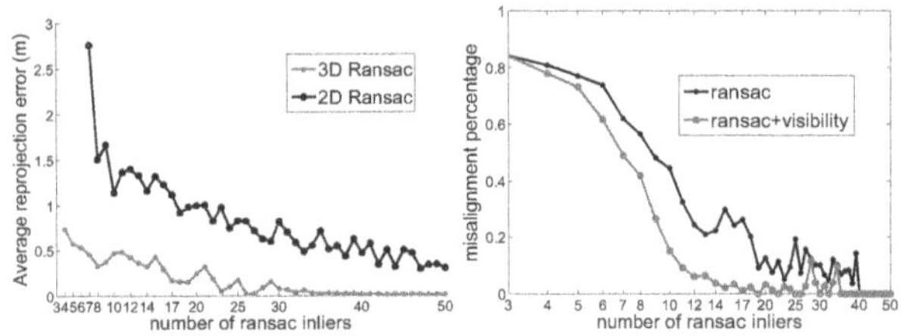

Figure 6. (Left) Alignment errors of 7 point 2D RANSAC and 3 point 3D RANSAC versus number of inliers. (Right) Percentage of misaligned frames of 3D RANSAC vs 3D RANSAC+Visibility.

2D versus 3D RANSAC. We collect a long RGB-D sequence in the lab through slow motion and use our system to generate a globally optimized map, shown in the bottom left panel of Figure 12. Visual inspection shows that the resulting map is highly consistent, and we use the globally optimized poses as groundtruth. We randomly sample frame pairs from this dataset and compare the 7-point 2D RANSAC (without further optimization after obtaining 7-point algorithm) solution and the 3-point 3D RANSAC solution. 2D RANSAC finds $15,149$ valid pairs (≥ 7 inliers), with an average reprojection error of 0.69m. 3D RANSAC finds $15,693$ valid pairs (≥ 3 inliers) with an error of 0.31m. Figure 6(left) shows the reprojection error versus the number of inliers in the solution. Using depth information within RANSAC (3D RANSAC) clearly reduces reprojection errors and generates good results even for a small number of inliers.

3D RANSAC with Visibility Features. We also compare the accuracy of 3-Point RANSAC with and without incorporating the visibility conflict criterion. We collect a dataset by placing the depth camera at 12 different locations, measure their ground truth distances, and rotate the camera at each location to take 100 depth frames. We randomly pick pairs of camera frames, and randomly split the set into training (linear regression for weights) and testing. Figure 6 (right) shows the results using a threshold of $0.1m$ on camera translation for determining a misalignment. "RANSAC + Visibility" produces more accurate camera poses and is capable of working with a lower threshold on RANSAC inliers.

The Importance of User Interaction

To evaluate the capability of our interactive system to generate improved visual odometry data, we performed a small study in which four persons were tasked to collect data for a map of a small meeting room. A 3D map generated with our system is shown in Figure 7. For each of the four people, we determined if (s)he was able to collect data that can be consecutively aligned for visual odometry. Two of the people were "expert users" who had substantial experience in using the depth camera for mapping purposes. Two persons were "novice users" who had not studied mapping. The different mapping runs collected between 357 and 781 frames. In all cases, the users were able to complete the mapping process using the interactive system.

The results for this small-scale user study are shown in Table 1. We evaluate the mapping process using several quantities: for offline mapping (similar to the setup in [12]), we can

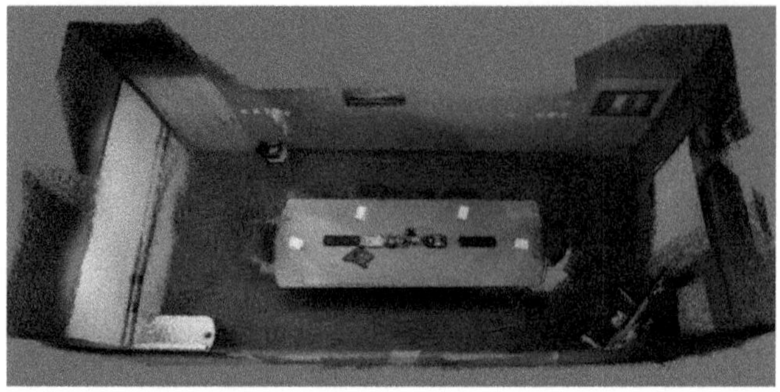

Figure 7. Top down view of 3D map of meeting room used to evaluate the benefits of interactive mapping.

detect failures in the mapping algorithm (when RANSAC fails). The first time (frame number) when failure occurs is a measure of how far a user can go into the process, or how complete a map he can expect, if there is no feedback and the user blindly continues data collection. Similarly, the average number of frames between failure is a measure of how often failure occurs and how large a map can grow in offline mapping. For online interactive mapping, the system reports failures directly and recovers from them, so we can count the number of failures when users finish. Finally, we ask the user to start and finish on a table, so the groundtruth heights of the start and end poses are the same (vertical distance zero). We compute the vertical distance of the estimated camera poses and use it as a measure of alignment error.

While the sample size may be too small to be conclusive, we do see patterns and trends in these results showing the promise of interactive mapping. We see that failures occurred often, and for a moderately difficult scenario like the conference room (low lighting and many textureless areas), the users failed early in the process using the offline system, and could only complete 3 to 10 percent of the process. The mean time between failure was only seconds. On the other hand, the online interactive system always "worked": the users all managed to recover from the failures and completed the process by going from the assigned starting point to the end. That is also reflected in the vertical alignment error – the offline errors are much larger than online errors, suggesting that offline mapping failed and interactive mapping had reasonable successes.

Comparison to Bundler and PMVS

We compared our system, using cheap depth cameras, to that of the state-of-the-art approach of using Bundler [28] and PMVS [9] which reconstruct dense 3D models from photo collections. We collected a depth camera sequence (PrimeSense) and a collection of high-res camera images (Canon 5D Mk II) of a wall and a textured white board standing in front of it. Figure 8 shows a zoom into the white board part of the reconstruction achieved by our system (left) and by Bundler+PMVS using the high-res images. Even with a lot of texture and super high-res photos, PMVS failed to produce a dense model, leaving many holes. Our system captured entire areas densely without holes.

Metrics	Offline (novice)	Interactive (novice)	Offline (expert)	Interactive (expert)
#frame at 1st failure (offline)	15.0	-	66.5	-
Mean #frame to failure (offline)	9.9	-	9.6	-
#failure (interactive)	-	9.0	-	17.0
Alignment Error (m)	1.14	0.11	1.12	0.05

Table 1. A small-scale user study of 4 users, 2 expert (who know 3D mapping) and 2 non-expert (do not know 3D mapping), comparing interactive mapping with state-of-the-art offline mapping. While the sample size may be too small to draw any conclusion, these results do strongly suggest that interactive mapping has great potential and can make the mapping process robust and error-tolerant.

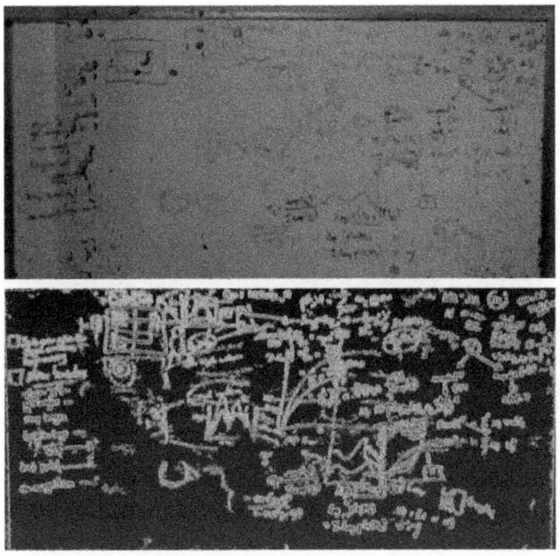

Figure 8. 3D reconstruction by our interactive system (top) and by Bundler+PMVS using high-res camera images (bottom). Blue indicates areas without any reconstruction.

Acquired Models of Large Indoor Environments

Figure 12 shows examples of maps we built with our interactive system. These results were achieved by collecting good visual odometry data using the failure detection and relocalization process. For large maps, automatic loop closure ran into troubles, and the interactive system allowed us to add loop closure constraints manually. The globally consistent map shown at the top was generated with 25 manual loop closure links merging with automatic loop closure.

3D MAPPING APPLICATIONS

What can detailed 3D models be used for if everyone can scan their personal spaces into 3D? As can be seen in the map visualizations and the supplemental video , our interactive system produces accurate 3D models that contain a large amount of detail, from large architectural elements (e.g. walls and floors) to small-sized objects situated in 3D settings. There are a multitude of possible applications, especially in context awareness and wearable computing, where the 3D map, along with objects inferred from it, provides rich context for users and their activities.

We briefly explore and demonstrate three potential applications: (1) 3D localization, locating a camera view in a precomputed map; (2) measuring dimensions, obtaining lengths and sizes in the virtual map; and (3) free exploration and photorealistic rendering of the environment, with connections to virtual furniture shopping. We leave rigorous developments and evaluations of the applications to future work.

Accurate 3D Localization

Once we have a 3D model constructed, we can turn our system into a localization mode, where new camera views are continuously registered but the map is no longer updated. This simple change allows us to localize a depth camera in 3D space, comparing to typical 2D localization.

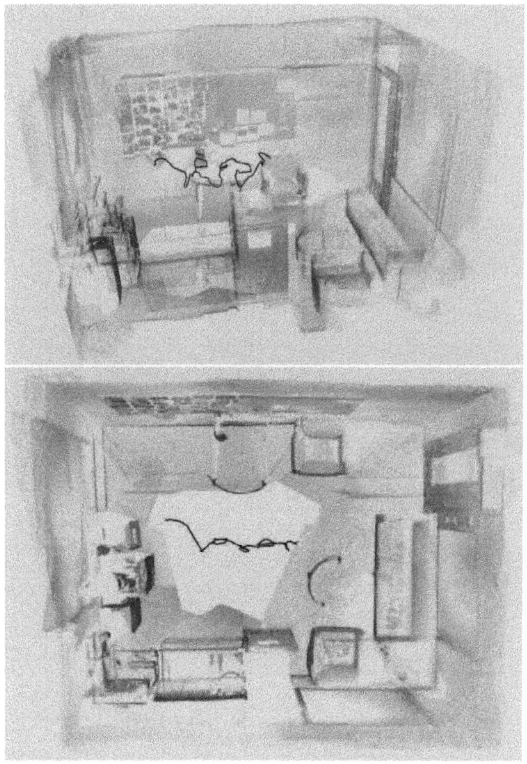

Figure 9. 3D localization: using a pre-computed 3D map captured on a different day, our system localizes itself in 3D (position+orientation). Shown is the path of (3D) camera poses from two viewpoints.

Figure 9 shows an example of how 3D localization works with our approach. The map shown is built from a separate set of data captured on a different day. When we run the mapping system on a new day, new RGB-D frames are registered into the existing map through loop closure, and then continuously tracked over time in 6-D pose. The path of camera poses, of about 100 views, is shown at the center of the map from two view points. More details can be found in the supplemental video.

Although we do not have groundtruth for camera poses, it should be clear from the camera path that (1) our approach can localize in 3D, both in translation and in rotation, not just in a flat 2D plane; (2) a vision-based localization approach, using a detailed 3D map, can achieve localization accuracy that is much higher than using other sensing modalities such as Wi-Fi. While $0.5m$ accuracy is normal for a Wi-Fi based system [32], our approach has the potential to achieve decimeter or even centimeter level accuracy. Such high-accuracy localization, possibly done with a wearable camera, can be useful for many location-based applications and also in robotics. An RGB-D approach like ours will also be robust to lighting conditions and textureless areas.

Measuring Dimensions of Spaces and Objects

A second application, directly derived from the geometric correctness of the 3D models, is to measure dimensions and sizes of spaces and objects virtually. Imagine a person goes into an environment, moves the camera and scans it into 3D. Now he has all the 3D information in the virtual model, and he can measure the dimensions of anything later. If a person builds a 3D model of his home, if there is any need for measurements, for instance when shopping for furniture, he can easily do it on a mobile device in his virtual home.

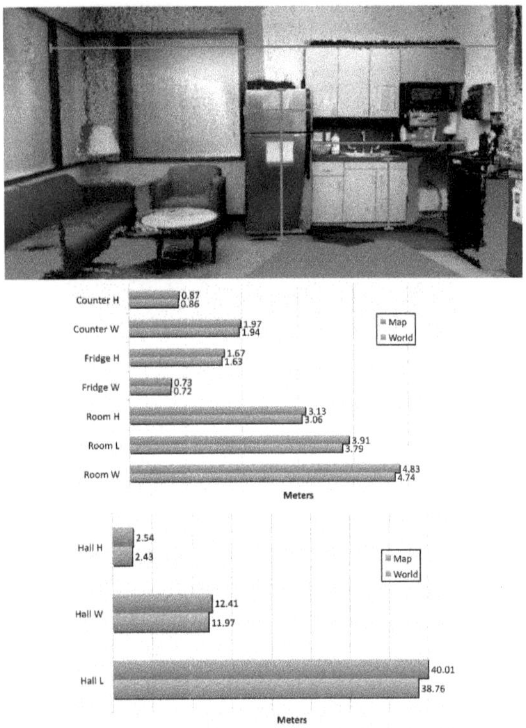

Figure 10. Measuring dimensions of objects (length, width, height) in a virtual model (top). We show quantitative evaluations of the measured virtual dimensions comparing those in the physical world (bottom).

Figure 10(top) shows an example of the dimensions that we measure from a virtual model of the Espresso Room. A single 3D model contains many details such as distances between walls and sizes of objects, which can be easily measured. In Figure 10(bottom) we compare measurements in the virtual models (espresso room and building hallway) to that done in the physical world (with a laser meter). We see that the measurements in the 3D model is accurate, with errors typically under one percent. We also notice that there is a systematic bias in these measurements, suggesting that the measurement accuracy may still improve with better calibration and/or better camera hardware.

Interactive Visualization and Furniture Shopping

One can take the furniture shopping application further: with a detailed 3D model, not only can we measure dimensions in the virtual model to see if a piece of furniture fits, we can potentially visualize, photo-realistically, how the furniture may fit into the home. The rendering can incorporate different arrangements of furniture, different colors, and changing illuminations.

Figure 11. A gesture-controlled flythrough system running on a 3D TV. The user uses hand gestures to navigate through a virtual space being rendered in real-time; he can also use gestures to place a downloaded sofa model into the constructed model.

Toward this goal, we have developed a prototype interactive visualization system, as shown in Figure 11, on a 3D TV. The system has a gesture control interface using the same type of depth camera: the user uses hand gestures to control up, down, left, right, forward and backward. The gestures are used to navigate through the virtual space while it is rendered at real-time, using level-of-detail control and hierarchical culling. The same gestures can also be used in a furniture placement mode, where a pre-downloaded furniture model (e.g. from Google 3D Warehouse) is rendered into the constructed environment model.

DISCUSSIONS AND FUTURE WORK

We have presented a prototype mobile system for 3D mapping and modeling that introduces and extensively uses online user feedback and interaction. We allow the user to freely move a camera through an indoor space, track the 3D mapping process, recover from (inevitable) registration failures, and achieve complete coverage through visual inspection and automatic guide. We have successfully scanned a variety of indoor spaces using the system, including large spaces up to 50 meters across with centimeter level details.

How may such a detailed and accurate 3D model be useful? We have briefly shown and discussed three applications: 3D localization with the potential of centimeter level accuracy; measuring dimensions of spaces and objects with 99% accuracy; and photorealistic visualization of personal spaces, with possible applications in virtual furniture shopping. These are all promising directions, and we plan to explore them in depth in future work.

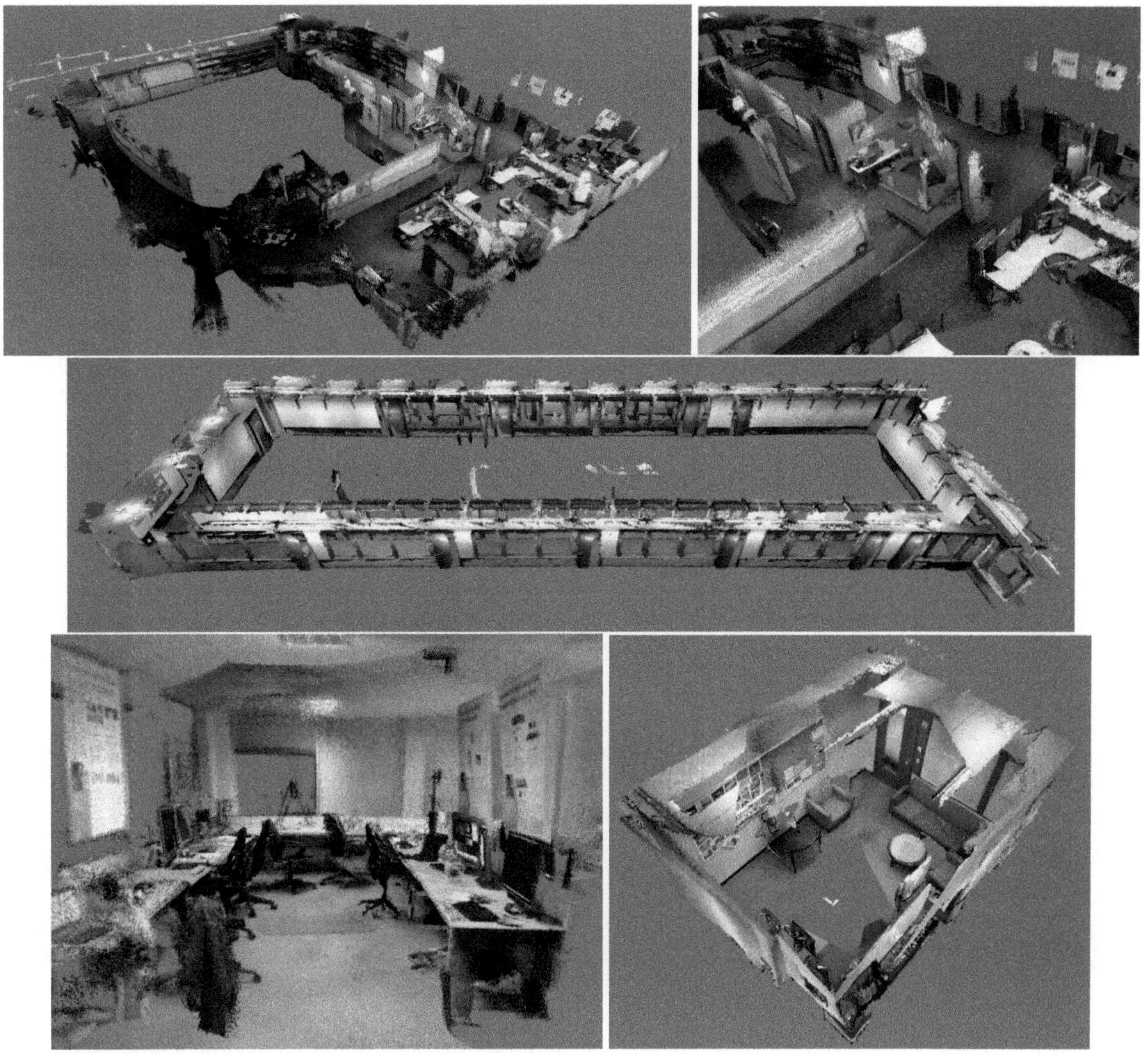

Figure 12. A variety of indoor spaces that we have captured using our 3D mapping system. (top) a large office space (50 meters across), with a detailed zoom-in view. (middle) another office building structure with repetitive offices and long hallways. (bottom) a (small-size) office and a (small-size) coffee room with furnitures and details.

Our work shows great promises for personal 3D mapping and opens up many possible applications. While 3D modeling is traditionally known to be hard, consumer depth cameras, real-time mapping, and user interaction have great potential to make it accessible to everyone. Our vision is that we can soon build compact mobile devices that allow a consumer to build 3D models for personal spaces. As shown in localization, such a 3D model can provide rich information for many applications that benefit from spatial contexts.

A lot more information can be extracted from such detailed 3D models other than spatial dimensions and layout. As seen from the maps in Figure 12, rich details show opportunities for semantic analysis, such as finding walls and floors, extracting objects, and learning human-object interactions.

Acknowledgments. We thank Matthai Philipose and Keith Mosher for their gesture work using PrimeSense. This work was supported by an Intel grant, and partially by ONR MURI grant N00014-09-1-1052, by the NSF under contract IIS-0812671, and through collaborative participation in the Robotics Consortium sponsored by the U.S Army Research Laboratory under Agreement W911NF-10-2-0016.

REFERENCES

1. S. Agarwal, N. Snavely, I. Simon, S. Seitz, and R. Szeliski. Building Rome in a Day. In *Computer Vision and Pattern Recognition (CVPR)*, pages 72–79, 2010.

2. M. Azizyan, I. Constandache, and R. Roy Choudhury. Surroundsense: Mobile Phone Localization via Ambience Fingerprinting. In *International Conference on Mobile Computing and Networking*, pages 261–272. ACM, 2009.

3. P. Bahl and V. Padmanabhan. RADAR: An In-building RF-based User Location and Tracking System. In *INFOCOM 2000*, volume 2, pages 775–784. IEEE, 2000.

4. L. Clemente, A. Davison, I. Reid, J. Neira, and J. Tardós. Mapping Large Loops with a Single Hand-Held Camera. In *Robotics Science and Systems (RSS)*, 2007.

5. A. Davison, I. Reid, N. Molton, and O. Stasse. MonoSLAM: Real-time Single Camera SLAM. *IEEE Transactions on Pattern Analysis and Machine Intelligence (PAMI)*, pages 1052–1067, 2007.

6. P. Debevec, C. J. Taylor, and J. Malik. Modeling and Rendering Architecture from Photographs: A Hybrid Geometryand Image-based Approach. In *SIGGRAPH*, 1996.

7. D. Fox, W. Burgard, F. Dellaert, and S. Thrun. Monte Carlo Localization: Efficient Position Estimation for Mobile Robots. In *AAAI*, pages 343–349, 1999.

8. Y. Furukawa, B. Curless, S. Seitz, and R. Szeliski. Manhattan-world Stereo. In *Computer Vision and Pattern Recognition (CVPR)*. IEEE, 2009.

9. Y. Furukawa, B. Curless, S. M. Seitz, and R. Szeliski. Reconstructing Building Interiors from Images. In *Intl. Conference on Computer Vision (ICCV)*, 2009.

10. Y. Furukawa and J. Ponce. Accurate, Dense, and Robust Multi-view Stereopsis. *IEEE Transactions on Pattern Analysis and Machine Intelligence (PAMI)*, 2009.

11. R. Hartley and A. Zisserman. *Multiple View Geometry in Computer Vision*. Cambridge University Press, 2003.

12. P. Henry, M. Krainin, E. Herbst, X. Ren, and D. Fox. RGB-D Mapping: Using Depth Cameras for Dense 3D Modeling of Indoor Environments. In *Intl. Symposium on Experimental Robotics (ISER)*, 2010.

13. J. Hightower and G. Borriello. Location Systems for Ubiquitous Computing. *Computer*, 34(8):57–66, 2001.

14. B. K. P. Horn. Closed-form Solution of Absolute Orientation using Unit Quaternions. *J. Opt. Soc. Am. A*, 4(4):629–642, 1987.

15. G. Klein and D. W. Murray. Parallel Tracking and Mapping for Small AR Workspaces. In *Intl. Symposium on Mixed and Augmented Reality*, 2007.

16. K. Konolige, J. Bowman, J. D. Chen, P. Mihelich, M. Calonder, V. Lepetit, and P. Fua. View-Based Maps. *Intl. Journal of Robotics Research (IJRR)*, 29(10), 2010.

17. A. LaMarca, Y. Chawathe, S. Consolvo, J. Hightower, I. Smith, J. Scott, T. Sohn, J. Howard, J. Hughes, F. Potter, J. Tabert, P. Powledge, G. Borriello, and B. Schilit. Place Lab: Device Positioning using Radio Beacons in the Wild. *Pervasive Computing*, pages 116–133, 2005.

18. A. LaMarca, J. Hightower, I. Smith, and S. Consolvo. Self-mapping in 802.11 Location Systems. *Ubiquitous Computing (UbiComp)*, pages 87–104, 2005.

19. Microsoft Kinect. `http://www.xbox.com/en-US/kinect`, 2010.

20. R. A. Newcombe and A. J. Davison. Live Dense Reconstruction with a Single Moving Camera. In *Computer Vision and Pattern Recognition (CVPR)*, 2010.

21. D. Nistér, O. Naroditsky, and J. Bergen. Visual Odometry. In *Computer Vision and Pattern Recognition (CVPR)*. IEEE, 2004.

22. V. Otsason, A. Varshavsky, A. LaMarca, and E. De Lara. Accurate GSM Indoor Localization. *Ubiquitous Computing (UbiComp)*, pages 141–158, 2005.

23. S. Patel, K. Truong, and G. Abowd. Powerline Positioning: A Practical Sub-room-level Indoor Location System for Domestic Use. *Ubiquitous Computing (UbiComp)*, pages 441–458, 2006.

24. M. Pollefeys, D. Nister, J.-M. Frahm, A. Akbarzadeh, P. Mordohai, B. Clipp, C. Engels, D. Gallup, S.-J. Kim, P. Merrell, C. Salmi, S. Sinha, B. Talton, L. Wang, Q. Yang, H. Stewenius, R. Yang, G. Welch, and H. Towles. Detailed Real-Time Urban 3D Reconstruction From Video. *Intl. Journal on Computer Vision (IJCV)*, 72(2):143–67, 2008.

25. PrimeSense. `http://www.primesense.com/`.

26. S. Seitz, B. Curless, J. Diebel, D. Scharstein, and R. Szeliski. A Comparison and Evaluation of Multi-view Stereo Reconstruction Algorithms. In *Computer Vision and Pattern Recognition (CVPR)*, volume 1, pages 519–528, 2006.

27. S. Sinha, D. Steedly, R. Szeliski, M. Agrawala, and M. Pollefeys. Interactive 3D architectural modeling from unordered photo collections. *ACM Transactions on Graphics (TOG)*, 27(5):1–10, 2008.

28. N. Snavely, S. M. Seitz, and R. Szeliski. Photo Tourism: Exploring Photo Collections in 3D. In *SIGGRAPH*, 2006.

29. P. Sturm and S. Maybank. A Method for Interactive 3D Reconstruction of Piecewise Planar Objects from Single Images. In *British Machine Vision Conference (BMVC)*, pages 265–274, 1999.

30. S. Thrun, W. Burgard, and D. Fox. *Probabilistic Robotics*. The MIT Press, 2005.

31. B. Triggs, P. McLauchlan, R. Hartley, and A. Fitzgibbon. Bundle Adjustment: A Modern Synthesis. *Vision Algorithms: Theory and Practice*, pages 153–177, 2000.

32. O. Woodman and R. Harle. Pedestrian Localisation for Indoor Environments. In *Ubiquitous Computing (UbiComp)*, pages 114–123. ACM, 2008.

33. C. Wu. SiftGPU: A GPU implementation of scale invariant feature transform (SIFT). `http://cs.unc.edu/~ccwu/siftgpu`, 2007.

Tactile Feedback without a Big Fuss: Simple Actuators for High-Resolution Phantom Sensations

Hendrik Richter, Benedikt Blaha, Alexander Wiethoff, Dominikus Baur, Andreas Butz
University of Munich, Germany
{hendrik.richter, alexander.wiethoff, dominikus.baur, andreas.butz}@ifi.lmu.de

ABSTRACT
Multi-touch screens and surfaces for manipulating digital content play a crucial role in mobile and ubiquitous computing. Augmenting these interactive surfaces with tactile feedback has been found to increase interaction speed, reduce operating errors and minimize visual and cognitive load. Communicating detailed tactile characteristics of virtual elements, however, requires complex electromechanical or electrostatic actuator setups. This increase in complexity makes tactile interfaces intricate, costly or poorly scalable.

In order to provide sophisticated tactile sensations with simple actuator technology, we exploit a haptic psychophysical phenomenon called Phantom Sensation. We present a comparison of three standard tactile actuator technologies to see which one can recreate the Phantom Sensation with maximum effect. Our results show the way to a simple and scalable implementation of illusion-based tactile feedback for interactive surfaces. We explore the notion of the Phantom Sensation and its possible applications within a ubicomp scenario.

Author Keywords
interactive surfaces, tactile feedback, actuator technology

ACM Classification Keywords
H5.2: User Interfaces. - *Haptic I/O.*

General Terms
Experimentation, Human Factors.

INTRODUCTION
Research in mobile interaction, pervasive and physical computing shows that users substantially benefit from tactile feedback on interactive surfaces [6, 9]. This holds true for both objective measures and emotional aspects of the interaction [4].

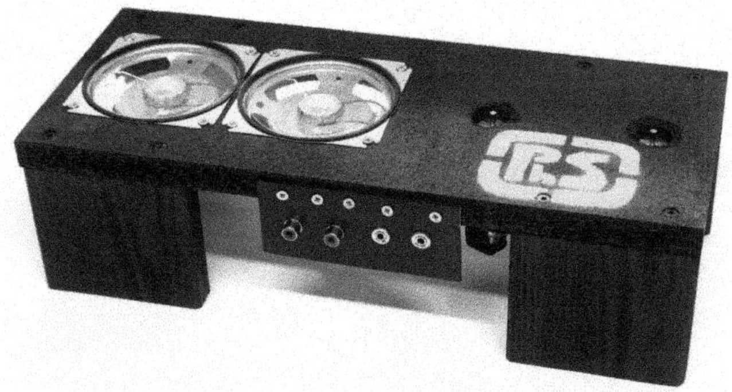

Figure 1: We used a prototypical tactile interface to compare three different actuator technologies.

In order to create tactile feedback, developers tend to reduce the size of tactile technology and increase the number of individual actuator elements to improve resolution and richness of tactile communication [5]. This approach, however, entails high mechanical complexity, often resulting in poor scalability and costly hardware.

Using so-called tactile illusions promises to reduce this complexity of actuators. Kato et al. [8], for example, first hinted at utilizing the Phantom Sensation, where a tactile stimulus can be produced and continuously moved between only two adjacent actuators. This tactile illusion has been thoroughly analyzed and reproduced in psychology and perceptual research since the 1950s [3]. But while research on psychophysical and perceptual aspects is widely available, the discussion of actual technical aspects is slim, even though prototypical implementations exist [11]. Information for practitioners on how to integrate such tactile feedback for interactive surfaces with readily available hardware is needed.

We present the results of a user study in which we identified the most effective commonly used actuator technology to recreate the effect (see Figure 1). Our findings allow the simple and cheap implementation of tactile stimulators to reproduce the Phantom Sensation. In addition, we discuss how our findings can be used in the context of interactive surfaces.

Figure 2: We compared three actuator technologies in a user study: (a) Eccentric vibrational motors (integrated in an elastic arm sleeve) (b) solenoids (c) voice coil actuators

RELATED WORK

Electromechanical actuators are commonly used to communicate tactile information to the user of an interactive surface. A variety of technical solutions have been investigated, e.g., the vibration of the entire device or screen [7], the segmentation of a touch surface into individually movable 'tactile' pixels [12] or the use of TUIs atop the interactive surface [10]. The tactile characteristics that are communicated by these systems either simulate physical attributes (form, malleability) or encode abstract states (progress bar, zoom level) of an interactive element. Increasing the tactile resolution requires complex hardware setups with large numbers of actuators. We propose the use of tactile illusions to improve these limitations.

PHANTOM SENSATION

Phantom Sensations stem from the effect that "*two equally loud stimuli presented simultaneously to adjacent locations on the skin are not felt separately but rather combine to form a sensation midway between the two stimulators*" [1]. A Phantom Sensation is affected by two parameters, the *amplitude inhibition* and the *temporal inhibition*. Amplitude inhibition happens when two stimuli are applied simultaneously to the skin and both have equal sensation magnitudes. The Phantom Sensation appears midway between the two actuators. By varying the relative amplitudes of both stimuli, the apparent sensation can be moved towards the louder actuator. Two equally loud stimuli occurring in close succession cause temporal inhibition. A single Phantom Sensation is created between the two actuators. The position of this apparent stimulus can be adjusted by modifying the interstimulus time interval. The illusionary stimulus is shifted towards the earlier stimulus for interstimulus intervals up to 8-10 ms [1].

TEST SETUP

In order to compare different technologies for their ability to create a stable Phantom Sensation, we built a low-cost test setup (see Figure 1 and 2). Békésy [3] suggests the use of the glabrous skin on the user's forearm to apply the tactile sensations, because the mechanoreceptors in that area of the skin are very evenly distributed. In order to make our results comparable to existing studies, we decided to use the same stimulus area. Other properties of the system, such as the distance between actuators (80mm / 3.1in), interstimulus intervals (0-8ms) or stimulus length (333ms), were designed in accordance with related work in psychology and perception [1,3].

Our prototype comprises three common types of tactile electromechanical actuators (see Figure 2): eccentric vibrational motors, linear magnetic solenoids and voice coil speakers. We chose these three types for three reasons: (1) they are commonly used in the field (for an overview see [5]), (2) they are readily commercially available, (3) they differ in the characteristics of the stimuli they create. With the goal to produce the illusion in the most distinct and comparable way, we modified the contact pressure of every actuator by adjusting countersink on the components.

Vibrational Motors

A flat or cylindrical motor is spinning an eccentric mass causing the housing to vibrate. We used the Lily Pad Vibe Boards[1].With different driving voltage amplitudes, different velocity plateaus can be reached. Vibratory frequency and amplitude are linked and cannot be addressed individually. The stimulation is diffuse and affects a larger area of the skin than the other two actuator types. We attached these tactile actuators to the forearm with a fixed distance of 80mm / 3.1in using an adaptable arm-sleeve.

Solenoids

A solenoid consists of a magnetic coil that applies forces to a ferrous plunger. A solenoid can solely by switched up or down by applying voltage. It is not possible to control the amplitude independently. The top of the plunger provides a punctual stimulation with a high steady-state force. Although the movement is not linear, it only takes 2-8 ms to reach full amplitude.

Voice Coils

The third type of actuator can be described as a hybrid between the two aforementioned. A cone is moved by the reaction of copper coil in a magnetic field to a current passing through. We used Visaton SL 87 XA Speakers[2]. Dedicated voice coil actuators exist, but did not fit our needs in terms of amplitude, size and pricing. With our actuators, we are able to generate vibrations on a spatially limited area of the skin and amplitude and frequency of the stimuli can be varied independently.

STUDY

In the user study, we evaluated which technology created the most distinct and clearly perceivable tactile illusion. We used 3 technologies, each in time inhibition mode and amplitude inhibition mode, except the solenoids, with which amplitude inhibition is not possible. Accordingly, we compare 5 combinations of actuator-funneling-modes (AFM-combinations).

---

[1] arduino.cc/en/Main/ArduinoBoardLilyPad

[2] visaton.de

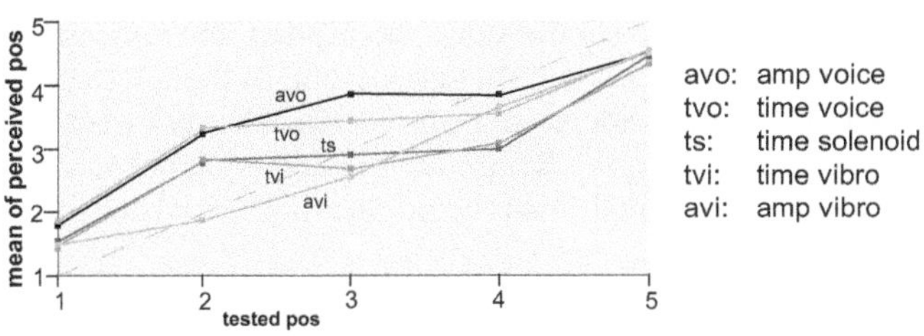

Figure 3: Perceived positions of Phantom Sensation for every triggered position (discrete values connected for readability)

Subjects

Fifteen computer literate persons (5 male, 10 female) served as paid subjects, all of them were right-handed. Ten persons stated that they had used tactile interfaces such as game-controllers before.

Apparatus

All participants were sitting at a table with their left forearm resting on the device. Based on existing research [2] we decided on discrete positions and depicted a scale from 1 to 5 next to the user's arm. Position 1 represents the distal actuator near the wrist, position 5 the proximal actuator near the elbow (compare Figure 2).

Procedure

After a short period of training, in which the participants could familiarize themselves with the tactile stimuli, the testing procedure began. The order of AFM-combinations was counterbalanced using a non-balanced Latin Square. A stimulus was given and the participant was asked to indicate the perceived position on the depicted scale. If more than one stimulus was perceived, the participant was requested to indicate the stronger one. Within an AFM-combination, every position was tested 3 times; the order within a set of 5 positions each was randomized. The tactile stimuli were communicated using the actuators mounted near the participant's wrist. The prototype was turned around when changing actuator technology (cf. Figure 1).

After each of the 5 AFM-combination trials, the participants were asked to fill in a questionnaire with 9 questions on prototype, stimulus and stimulus effect. Every participant was asked to mark his opinion on 7-point Likert scales (1=totally disagree, 7=totally agree). We think that these emotional aspects are very important for the acceptance of a tactile technology.

RESULTS

Each position was tested 225 times (15 participants, 5 AFM-combinations, 3 repetitions). For a start, we measured the frequencies of occurrence for each perceived position for all participants and techniques. The mean of perceived positions is 3.09. This result shows that a stable Phantom Sensation was produced with every one of the 5 AFM-combinations.

Figure 3 shows the mean perceived positions for each AFM-combination. Especially the AFM-combination vibrotactile amplitude inhibition (*avi)* shows a stable Phantom Sensation with spatial deviations less than 1 for each position.

We aggregated the data by creating a *mean input deviation (MID)* index. For each AFM-combination we had 15 data sets per participant (5 positions, 3 iterations each). The mean of spatial deviation was calculated for each position over all trials. The MID index was created by calculating the mean of the resulting 5 values and Figure 4 shows the results. The lower the MID index value, the more distinct the perception of the Phantom Sensation.

Based on Kolmogorv-Smirnov and Shapiro-Wilk, we used one-way repeated-measure ANOVA. It was found that the type of AFM-combination had a significant effect on the MID index ($F_{(4,56)}=8.45$, $p<0.001$). The Post-Hoc-Test with Bonferroni corrections showed significant differences between Time Vibro (MID=0.9) and Amplitude Vibro (MID=0.68) ($p<0.001$). The same holds true for Amplitude Voice Coil (MID=0.92) and Amplitude Vibro (MID=0.68) ($p<0.014$). All other comparisons showed no significant differences ($p>0.05$).

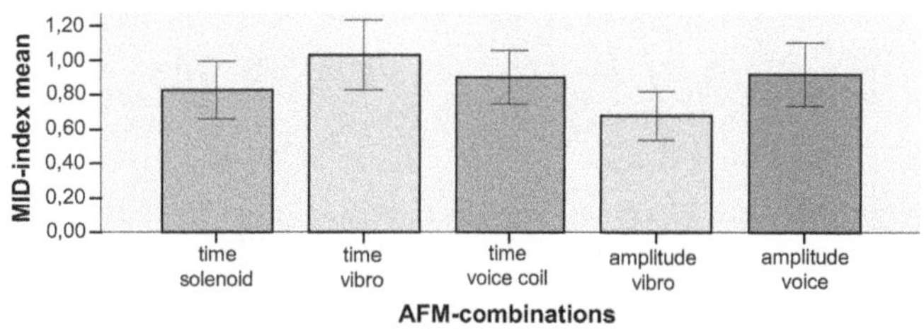

Figure 4: Mean Input Deviation (MID) for each AFM-combination.

Based on these findings, we excluded Time Vibro and Amplitude Voice Coil. Due to the high deviations in the distal position of illusions created by the voice coils (see Figure 3), we also excluded the AFM combination Time Voice Coil.

For the remaining AFM combinations (Time Solenoid and Amplitude Vibro), we consulted the results of the questionnaire. With Amplitude Vibro, the question "Do you think the generated stimulus is comfortable?" was answered with a mean of 4.47 (1=totally disagree, 7=totally agree). Accordingly, the question "Did you feel intimidated by the stimulus?" was answered with a mean of 1.00. In comparison, the results for Time Solenoid – 3.27 and 2.73, respectively – show a clear preference of the participants for the vibrotactile actuators using amplitude inhibition.

In summary, we can state that based on quantitative and qualitative results, the vibrotactile actuators using amplitude inhibition created the most distinct and stable Phantom Sensations. Additionally, this AFM combination was stated as creating stimuli being least disturbing and intimidating, but most comfortable.

DISCUSSION

The small, cheap and simple to control vibrational actuators turned out to be the appropriate means for creating stable tactile illusions. Despite their technological simplicity, they allow the creation and utilization of the Phantom Sensation. In general, we used prototypical and inexpensive technology to build our system. This has an influence on size and noise of the device. Currently, the user has to put his forearm atop the device, thus preventing bimanual input. To collect data comparable to existing studies we only tested 5 discrete positions. The Phantom Sensation, however, can be applied with a higher resolution [8] which is preferable in actual usage scenarios.

APPLICATION SCENARIOS

Vibrational motors are small and simple to control, thus making it easy to integrate them into wearable interfaces or implement them in the direct environment to guarantee reliable contact with the user's skin.

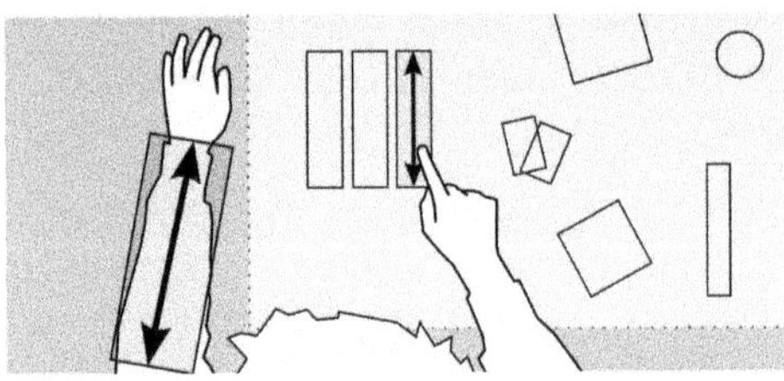

Figure 5: The Phantom Sensation may be used to convey the position of a virtual fader's knob to the user's forearm.

Figure 5 shows a potential scenario of use for the stimuli generated using the Phantom Sensation: The user is touching a fader widget on the interactive surface with the dominant hand. In reaction, the vibrotactile interface implemented in the table's border provides a tactile signal to the user's non-dominant forearm using a pair of actuators. The fader area is enlarged and mapped to the user's forearm to reduce visual load. Using the Phantom Sensation, only two actuators are needed even for high-resolution feedback.

Synchronized tactile illusions during touch interactions could convey the orientation, size and shape of interactive elements that are manually explored by the user. For example, the Phantom Sensation could be used to depict the position of a fader (see above) or the state of a pressure sensitive widget. One could also think of communicating abstract information, semantics or additional parameters not visually depicted in the interface. Examples may be the conveyance of a zooming level or a progress bar.

CONCLUSION AND FUTURE WORK

We have compared three actuator technologies to create a stable and repeatable Phantom Sensation. The vibrotactile actuator with amplitude inhibition mode turned out to be the most effective in terms of both quantitative and qualitative measures. Based on these findings, we presented scenarios for the utilization of vibrotactile Phantom Sensations.

Future evaluations should cover perceptual and conceptual aspects such as the role of the orientation of the interface in relation to the widget and the drawbacks of wearable actuator technology. Real life scenarios incorporating cognitive and visual load could identify drawbacks and opportunities.

In summary, the remote application of Phantom Sensations can help in creating interactions with rich tactile feedback. Complexity and effort for building these interfaces can be greatly reduced. Novel forms of tactile interfaces based on tactile illusions may help us in enhancing and enriching the interaction with ubiquitous environments.

REFERENCES

1. Alles, D. Information Transmission by Phantom Sensations. *IEEE Transactions on Man Machine Systems 11, 1* (1970), 85-91.
2. Barghout, A., Cha, J., El Saddik, A., Kammerl, J., and Steinbach, E. Spatial resolution of vibrotactile perception on the human forearm when exploiting funneling illusion. *IEEE International Workshop on HAvEG (2009)*, 19-23.
3. Bekesy, G. Funneling in the nervous system and its role in loudness and sensation intensity on the skin. The *Journal of the Acoustical Society of America 30*, (1958), 399.
4. Chang, A. and O'Sullivan, C. Audio-haptic feedback in mobile phones. *Proc. CHI 2005*, 1264–1267.
5. Hayward, V. and Maclean, K. Do it yourself haptics: part I. *IEEE Robotics & Automation Magazine 14*, 4 (2007), 88-104.
6. Hoggan, E., Brewster, S.A., and Johnston, J. Investigating the Effectiveness of Tactile Feedback for Mobile Touchscreens. *Proc. CHI 2008*, 1573.
7. Kaaresoja, T., Brown, L.M., and Linjama, J. Snap-Crackle-Pop. *Proc. Eurohaptics 2006* , 565–566.
8. Kato, H., Hashimoto, Y., and Kajimoto, H. Basic Properties of Phantom Sensation for Practical Haptic Applications. *Haptics: Generating and Perceiving Tangible Sensations 6191*, (2010), 271–278.
9. Leung, R., MacLean, K., Bertelsen, M.B., and Saubhasik, M. Evaluation of Haptically Augmented Touchscreen GUI Elements under Cognitive Load. *Proc. ICMI 2007*, 374–381.
10. Marquardt, N., Nacenta, M., Young, J., Carpendale, S., Greenberg, S., and Sharlin, E. The Haptic Tabletop Puck. *Proc. ITS 2009*, 93-100.
11. Richter, H., Hang, A., Blaha, B., The PhantomStation: Towards funneling remote tactile feedback on interactive surfaces. *Proc. AH*, 2011.
12. Poupyrev, I., Nashida, T., Maruyama, S., Rekimoto, J., and Yamaji, Y. Lumen. *Proc. SIGGRAPH* 2004, 17.

Urban Computing with Taxicabs

Yu Zheng[1], Yanchi Liu[1,2], Jing Yuan[1], Xing Xie[1]
[1]Microsoft Research Asia, Beijing, China
[2]University of Science and Technology Beijing, Beijing, China
{yuzheng, v-jinyua, xingx,}@microsoft.com, liuyanchi@manage.ustb.edu.cn

ABSTRACT
Urban computing for city planning is one of the most significant applications in Ubiquitous computing. In this paper we detect flawed urban planning using the GPS trajectories of taxicabs traveling in urban areas. The detected results consist of 1) pairs of regions with salient traffic problems and 2) the linking structure as well as correlation among them. These results can evaluate the effectiveness of the carried out planning, such as a newly built road and subway lines in a city, and remind city planners of a problem that has not been recognized when they conceive future plans. We conduct our method using the trajectories generated by 30,000 taxis from March to May in 2009 and 2010 in Beijing, and evaluate our results with the real urban planning of Beijing.

Author Keywords
Urban computing, urban planning, GPS trajectory, taxicab

ACM Classification Keywords
H.2.8 [**Database Management**]: Database Applications - *data mining, Spatial databases and GIS*;

General Terms
Algorithms, Experimentation.

INTRODUCTION
Ubiquitous computing has largely been applied either in relatively homogeneous rural areas, where researchers have added sensors in places such as forests and glaciers, or in small-scale, well-defined patches of the built environment, such as smart houses or rooms [7]. Attention has recently been shifting to urban areas, which are regarded as the third place between rural areas and houses, or the public place between home and work [12]. Urban areas are more complex and interesting spaces than the other two, as they are navigated both through physical movement and interpretations of social context. Though urban settings tend to be far more dynamic in terms of what and who would participate in an application or system, urban spaces also bring us a lot of opportunities in exploring novel systems and applications facilitating people's life and serving the city. Emerging in this circumstance, urban computing comes up with the new ubiquitous computing concept where every sensor, person, vehicle, building, and street in urban areas can be used as a computing component for serving the people and the city.

Urban computing for urban planning is one of the most significant application scenarios in the urban spaces [7][12]. The advance of human civilization has given rise to the need for urban planning that integrates land use planning and transportation planning to improve the built, economic and social environments of communities. Urbanization is increasing at a faster pace than ever in many developing countries, while some modern cities in developed countries are engaging in urban reconstruction, renewal, and sub-urbanization. Therefore, we need innovative technologies that can automatically and unobtrusively sense urban dynamics and provide crucial information to urban planners.

Naturally, big cities faced with the challenges to urban planning usually have a large number of taxicabs traversing in urban areas. For example, the numbers of taxis in Mexico City, Beijing, Tokyo and Seoul are all over 60,000 respectively. Meanwhile, there are approximated 30 cities, including New York City, Shanghai, Hong Kong, London, and Paris that have more than 10,000 licensed taxis individually. To enable efficient taxi dispatch and monitoring, taxis are usually equipped with GPS sensors, which enable them to report on their location to a centralized server at regular intervals, e.g., 1~2 minutes. In other words, a lot of GPS-equipped taxis already exist in major cities around the world, generating huge volumes of trajectories everyday [5][6][15].

Essentially, GPS-equipped taxicabs can be viewed as ubiquitous mobile sensors constantly probing a city's rhythm and pulse, such as traffic flows on road surfaces and city-wide travel patterns of people. For instance, Beijing has approximately 67,000 licensed taxis generating over 1.2 million occupied trips per day (in terms of the recorded taxi trajectories). Supposing each taxi transports 1.2 passengers per trip on average, there are about 1.44 million personal trips generated by these taxis in Beijing per day. This figure is 4.2% of the total personal trips (35 million) created by all kinds of transportations including buses, subways, taxis and private vehicles within the Six Ring Road of Beijing City (reported by Beijing transportation bureau July 2010). 4.2 percent is a significant sample reflecting people's travel in the city. Meanwhile, the traffic flow on a road can be well modeled by the mobility of taxis traveling on the road together with a large number of private vehicles and buses.

In this paper we aim to detect the flawed and less effective urban planning in a city according to the GPS trajectories of taxicabs recorded in a certain period, such as 3 months. There are two main challenges involved in this work: 1) Modeling the city-wide traffic and travel of people using taxi trajectories; 2) Embodying the flawed planning to reveal the relationship among these flaws. In our method, we first partition a city into some disjoint regions using major roads. Then, we project the taxi trajectories of each day into these regions and formulate transitions between each pair of regions. Later, we detect the salient region pairs having heavy traffic beyond the capacity of the existing connections between them. The region pairs frequently detected across many days will be regarded as the flawed planning. At the same time, we associate the individual flaws into a series of graphs reflecting the global defects of the urban planning according to the spatial and temporal properties of these flaws. The contribution of this report lies in three aspects:

- *Traffic modeling*: We model the city-wide traffic of taxis of each day using a matrix of regions. Each item in the matrix consists of a set of features representing the effectiveness of the connection between two different regions. The values of these features are derived from the taxi traces passing the two regions.
- *Flaw detection*: We seek the possibly flawed region pairs (called a skyline) from the matrix of each day using a skyline operator. We associate the skylines (of a day) into some graphs (representing global flawed planning), and mine the frequent sub-graph patterns from the graphs across a certain number of days. The mined results consist of both flawed planning and the relationship between them.
- *Real evaluation*: We evaluate our method using a series of large-scale real GPS trajectories generated by 30,000 taxis in Beijing from March to May in 2009 and 2010. As a result, we find strong data from the real urban planning of Beijing, justifying the effectiveness of our method.

The rest of the paper is organized as follows. Section 2 overviews the problem and our solution. Section 3 presents the process for modeling city-wide traffic. Section 4 describes the detection of the flawed planning. In Section 5 we evaluate our work. After summarizing the related work in Section 6, we draw our conclusions in Section 7.

OVERVIEW

Definition 1 (*Taxi Trajectory*): A taxi *trajectory* Tr is a sequence of time-ordered GPS points, $Tr: p_1 \rightarrow p_2 \rightarrow \cdots \rightarrow p_n$, where each point consists of a geospatial coordinate set, a timestamp, and a state of occupation (with passengers or not), e. g., $p = (lat, long, t, o)$.

Definition 2. (*Region*): The map of a city is partitioned into disjoint regions (r) bounded by high level (i.e. major) roads. Each region may consist of a number of road segments and lands. Refer to Figure 2 for an example.

Definition 3. (*Transition*): Given a trajectory $Tr: p_1 \rightarrow p_2 \rightarrow \cdots \rightarrow p_n$, a directional transition $s: r_1 \rightarrow r_2$ is generated between r_1 and r_2 if p_i is the first point (from Tr) falling in region r_1 and p_j is the first point (from Tr) falling in region r_2 $(i < j)$. A transition s is associated with a leaving time $(p_i.t)$, an arriving time $(p_j.t)$, and a travel distance d and speed v calculated according to Equation 1 and 2.

$$d(p_i, p_j) = \sum_{i \le k < j} Dist(p_k, p_{k+1}), \quad (1)$$

$$v = d(p_i, p_j)/|p_j.t - p_i.t|, \quad (2)$$

$Dist(p_k, p_{k+1})$ denotes the Euclidian distance between two consecutive GPS points.

Figure 1 presents the architecture of our method, which consists of two major components: 1) modeling city-wide traffic based on taxi trajectories and 2) detecting flawed planning. We will detail each step of these two components in the following two sections respectively.

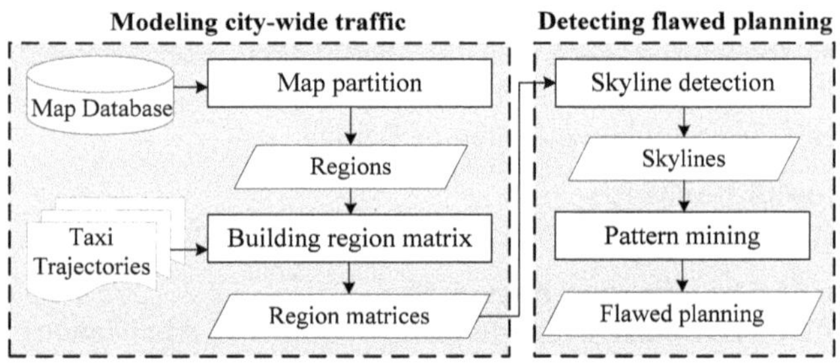

Figure 1. The architecture of our method

MODELING CITY-WIDE TRAFFIC

This component first partitions a map of a city into some regions, and then builds a set of region matrices that correspond to different time of day and day of week.

Map Partition

As shown in Figure 2, we partition the urban area of Beijing into disjoint regions using major roads (like the red and blue roads). Each region stands for a community including some neighborhoods and low-level road segments (denoted as gray polylines). The partition method carries more semantic meanings of people's travel than using a uniform grid-based partition. At the same time, we conduct our research based on regions instead of road segments for two reasons. First, traffic problems appearing on roads are just observations, while regions carrying rich knowledge about people's living and travel are the source of the problem. Second, flaws represented by regions contribute to both land use and transportation planning. However, the road segments can only help transportation planning. For instance, if the connection between two regions are determined to be less-effective, the possible solution for fixing this flaw could be building new roads between them (pertaining to transportation planning), or adding some local businesses, e.g., shopping malls, in the region outsourcing people (i.e., land use planning).

Here, we employ Connected Components Labeling (an image segment method) [11] to segment a map into regions effectively and efficiently, as the problem of subdivisions in a polygonal region is NP-complete.

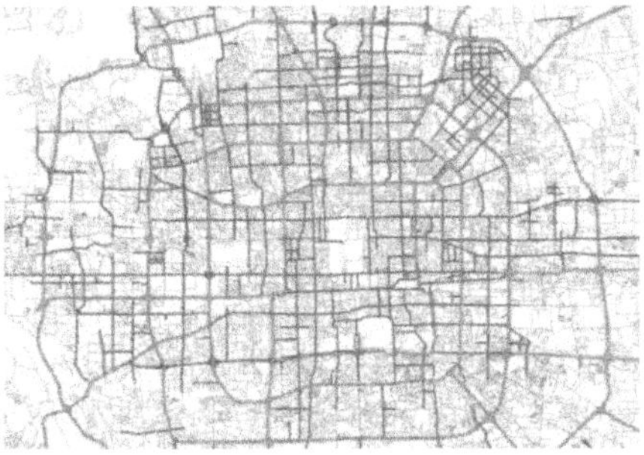

Figure 2. Heat map of the partitioned regions in Beijing

Building Region Matrix

This process is comprised of the following three steps.

1) *Temporal partition*: In this step, we first partition the taxi trajectories into two parts according to workday and rest day (consisting of weekends and public holidays) since people's travel on these two types of days are different. Then, we further segment time of day into some slots in terms of the traffic conditions in the city.

First, in the same time slot, the traffic conditions and the semantic meaning of people's travel are similar. For example, Figure 3 A) shows the average travel speed of all the taxis (with passengers) in Beijing at different times of workdays. The average travel speed of the entire city of Beijing as defined previously in time slot 7:00-10:30am is lower than that of the entire day. This matches the generally accepted assumption that people are going to work during the morning rush hours. Likewise, the time slot of 4pm-7:30pm corresponds to the evening rushing hour in the workday when people go home. Second, if we do not respectively explore the trajectories from different time slots, we will miss some actually flawed planning as the detected results could be dominated by some regions only having heavy traffic in a particular time slot. Third, the time partition enables us to explore the temporal relations between the results detected from continuous time slots, helping us deeply understand the flaws. We will further justify the temporal partition later.

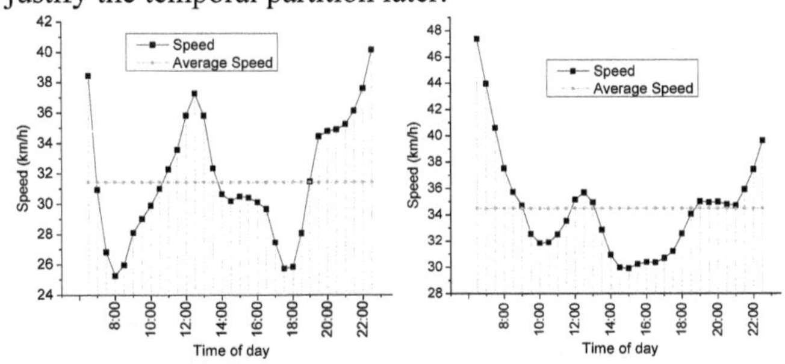

A) Workday B) Rest day

Figure 3. Traffic conditions in Bejing changing over time

According to Figure 3, we obtain the time slots shown in Table 1. Later, we build a region matrix for each time slot of each day (refer to the following paragraphs).

Time	Work day	Rest day
Slot 1	7:00am-10:30am	9:00am-12:30pm
Slot 2	10:30am-4:00pm	12:30pm-7:30pm
Slot 3	4:00pm-7:30pm	7:30pm-9:00am
Slot 4	7:30pm-7:00am	

Table 1. Time partition for workdays and rest days

2) *Transition construction*: We pick out the effective trips with passengers from taxi trajectories in terms of the occupancy state associated with a sample (a weight sensor is embedded in a taxi to detect whether there are additional persons beside a driver in the taxi). So, an effective taxi trajectory represents a passenger's trip. Then, we project these trajectories onto the map and construct transitions between two regions according to definition 3. As demonstrated in Figure 4, two trajectories, Tr_1 and Tr_2, respectively traversing $r_1 \rightarrow r_3$ and $r_1 \rightarrow r_2 \rightarrow r_3$, formulate four transitions: $r_1 \rightarrow r_3$, $r_1 \rightarrow r_2$, $r_2 \rightarrow r_3$, and $r_1 \rightarrow r_3$, denoted as the blue arrows. Note that, a trajectory discontinuously traversing two regions, such as $r_1 \rightarrow r_3$ in Tr_2, still formulate a transition between the two regions. The distance d of this transition is $\sum_{4 \le k < 8} Dist(p_k, p_{k+1})$, and the travel speed is approximately $d/(p_8.t - p_4.t)$.

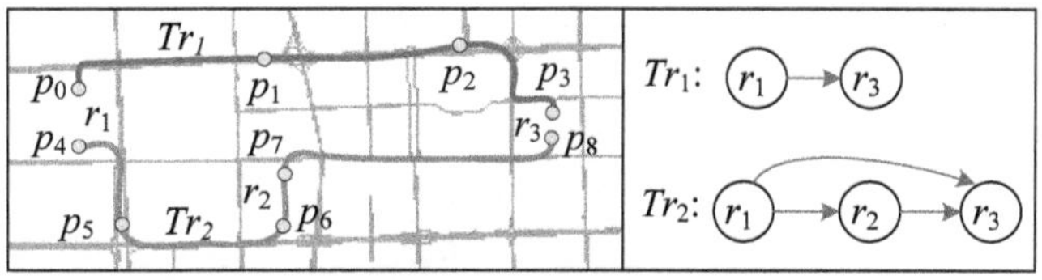

Figure 4. Transfer a trajectory into transitions

***Definition** 4 (Region Pair)*. A region pair is a pair of regions ($r_1 \rightarrow r_2$) having a set of transitions (between them). By aggregating the transitions, each region pair is associated with the following three features: 1) volume of traffic between these two regions, i.e., the count of transitions $|\boldsymbol{S}|$, and 2) expectation of these transitions' speeds $E(V)$, and 3) ratio θ between the expectation of the actual travel distance $E(D)$ and the Euclidian distance between the centroids of two regions, $CenDist(r_1, r_2)$.

$$E(V) = \frac{\sum_{s_i \in S} s_i.v}{|S|}, \quad (3)$$

$$E(D) = \frac{\sum_{s_j \in S} s_j.d}{|S|}, \quad (4)$$

$$\theta = E(D)/CenDist(r_1, r_2), \quad (5)$$

Where $\boldsymbol{S}$ is the collection of transitions between r_1 and r_2.

Figure 5 plots the region pairs from a time slot 7-10:30am in a workday in the $< |\boldsymbol{S}|, E(V), \theta >$ space. A black point represents a region pair. The projections of these region pairs on XZ and YZ spaces are also visualized with green and blue plots. Note that the value of a given θ could be smaller than 1 as taxis might cross two adjacent regions with a distance shorter than that between the two centroids.

Some might be concerned with the transitions generated by the trajectories discontinuously passing two regions, e.g.,

Tr_2 traveling from r_1 to r_3 in Figure 4, in which a taxi visited several other regions before reaching r_3. We can analyze this problem from two perspectives. First, the connectivity of the two regions should be represented by all the possible routes between them instead of the fast (or direct) transitions. Sometimes, reaching a region through a roundabout route passing other regions is also a good choice to avoid traffic jams. Second, these discontinuous transitions do not bias the $E(V)$ and θ. If there is an effective shortcut between two regions (e.g., Tr_1), most taxis intending to travel from r_1 to r_3 will still take the shortcut instead of the roundabout route. That is, the mount of discontinuous travel is only a small portion in the transition set. As a result, $E(V)$ and θ are still close to the real travel speed and ratio that people could travel from r_1 to r_3. On the contrary, if all the taxis have to reach r_3 by passing additional regions, e.g., r_2, that means the route directly connecting r_1 and r_3 is not very effective.

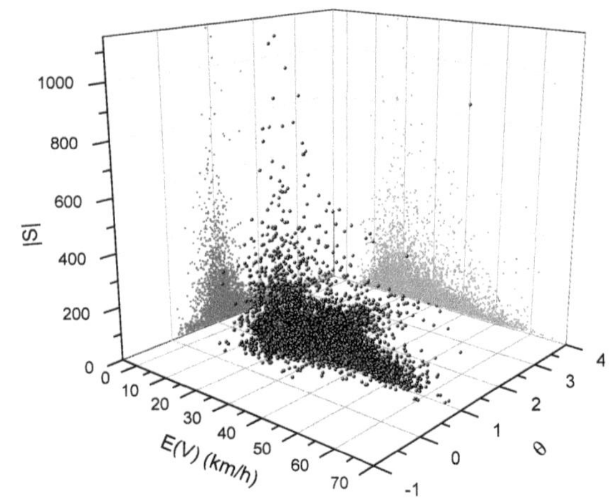

Figure 5. Distribution of region pairs in the workday

3) *Build region matrix*: We formulate a matrix of regions $\boldsymbol{M}$, as demonstrated in Figure 6, for each time slot in each day. An item in the matrix is a tuple, $a_{i,j} =< |\boldsymbol{S}|, E(V), \theta >$, denoting the number of transitions, expectation of travel speed, and θ between region r_i and r_j. Supposing there are x workdays and y rest days, $4x + 3y$ matrices will be built if using the scheme of the time slots shown in Table 1.

$$\boldsymbol{M} = \begin{array}{c} \\ r_0 \\ r_1 \\ \vdots \\ r_i \\ \vdots \\ r_{n-1} \\ r_n \end{array} \begin{array}{c} \begin{array}{cccccc} r_0 & r_1 & \cdots & r_j & \cdots & r_{n-1} \quad r_n \end{array} \\ \begin{bmatrix} \phi & a_{0,1} & \cdots & & & a_{0,n} \\ a_{1,0} & \phi & \cdots & & & a_{1,n} \\ & & \cdots & & & \\ a_{i,0} & a_{i,1} & \cdots & a_{i,j} & \cdots & a_{i,n} \\ & & \cdots & & & \\ a_{n-1,0} & & \cdots & & \phi & a_{n-1,n} \\ a_{n,0} & & \cdots & & & \phi \end{bmatrix} \end{array}$$

Figure 6. Region matrix and the properties of each item

DETECTING FLAWED URBAN PLANNING

We first detects the skyline of each region matrix in terms of the values of each tuple. Then, we mine graph patterns representing flawed planning from these skylines.

Skyline Detection

$< |\boldsymbol{S}|, E(V), \theta >$ will model the connectivity and the traffic between two regions. Specifically, θ captures the geometric property of the connection between a pair of regions. A region pair with a big θ means people have to take a long detour traveling from one region to the other. $E(V)$ and $|\boldsymbol{S}|$ represent the features of traffic. A big $|\boldsymbol{S}|$ and small $E(V)$ imply heavy traffic carried by the existing routes between two regions. In this step, we aim to retrieve the region pairs with a big θ, small $E(V)$ and large $|\boldsymbol{S}|$, which indicate flawed urban planning.

We first select the region pairs having the number of transitions above the average from a matrix $\boldsymbol{M}$. Then, we find the skyline set $\boldsymbol{L}$ from these selected region pairs according to $E(V)$ and θ, using skyline operator [1].

***Definition** 5.* (*Skyline*): The skyline is defined as those points which are not dominated by any other point. A point dominates another point if it is as good or better in all dimensions and better in at least one dimension.

Specifically, in our application, each $a_{i,j} \in \boldsymbol{L}$ is not dominated by others, $a_{p,q} \notin \boldsymbol{L} \wedge a_{p,q} \in \boldsymbol{M}$, in terms of $E(V)$ and θ. That is, there is no region pair $a_{p,q} \notin \boldsymbol{L}$ having a lower speed and bigger θ than $a_{i,j} \in \boldsymbol{L}$. Figure 7 A) depicts an example of the skyline set $\boldsymbol{L}$ using a blue dash line where a point denotes a region pair. Clearly, no blank points simultaneously have a smaller $E(V)$ and bigger θ than the points from the $\boldsymbol{L}$.

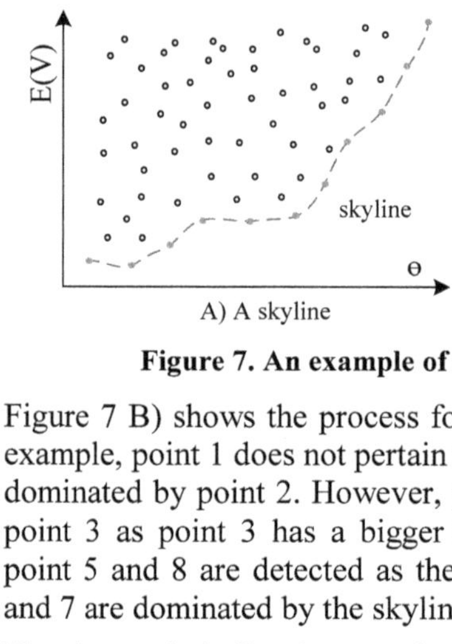

A) A skyline

point	E(V)	θ
1	24	1.6
2	20	2.4
3	30	2.8
4	22	2.0
5	18	1.4
6	34	2.4
7	30	2.0
8	36	3.2

B) Seeking a skyline

Figure 7. An example of skyline detection

Figure 7 B) shows the process for seeking the skyline. For example, point 1 does not pertain to the skyline because it is dominated by point 2. However, point 2 does not dominate point 3 as point 3 has a bigger θ than point 2. Likewise, point 5 and 8 are detected as the skyline while point 4, 6, and 7 are dominated by the skyline.

The detected skyline is comprised of three kinds of region pairs. 1) A region pair with a very small $E(V)$ and θ, illustrated in Figure 8 A). This means two regions are connected with some direct routes while the capacity of these routes are not sufficient as compared to the existing traffic between the two regions. The small $E(V)$ and θ also indicate that people have no other choice (even if it is a detour) but to take these ineffective routes for traveling between the two regions. Otherwise, the θ will become bigger. 2) A region pair with a small $E(V)$ and big θ, shown in Figure 8 B). This denotes that people have to take detours for travelling between two regions while these detours suffer from heavy traffic leading to a slow speed. This is the worst case among these three situations. 3) A region pair with a big $E(V)$ and big θ, depicted in Figure 8 C). These two values imply that people travel between two regions by taking some far detours which are fast, e.g., a high way. Though the speed is not slow, the long distance will cost people a lot of time and gas. So, the connectivity between such kinds of regions still has flaws.

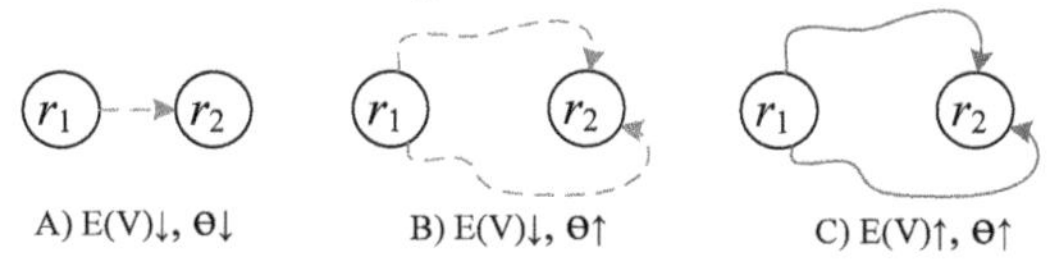

Figure 8. Three kinds of region pairs in a skyline

Note that we focus on finding the most salient flawed urban planning instead of all the poor ones. Seeking the skyline from the region pairs with a large volume of traffic ($|\boldsymbol{S}|$ is above the average), we guarantee 1) the detected skyline is related to many people's travel and 2) each $(E(V), \theta)$ is calculated based on a large number of observations.

Pattern Mining from Skylines

In this step, we first build a skyline graph for each day by connecting the region pairs in the skylines of different time slots. Then, we detect the sub-graph patterns from these graphs using a graph pattern mining algorithm [13].

1) *Formulating skyline graphs*: As demonstrated in Figure 9, there is a skyline in each time slot (denoted as a row) of each day (represented by a column). Two region pairs from two consecutive slots are connected if they are spatially close to each other. For example, in Day 1 we connect the region pair $(r_1 \rightarrow r_2)$ from slot 1 to $(r_2 \rightarrow r_8)$ from slot 2, because these two region pairs share the same node r_2 and appear in the consecutive time slots of the same day. Likewise, $(r_4 \rightarrow r_5)$ to $(r_5 \rightarrow r_7)$ from these two slots are connected. However, $(r_4 \rightarrow r_5)$ from slot 1 and $(r_8 \rightarrow r_4)$ from slot 3 cannot be connected as they are not temporally close. The built skyline graphs are shown in the fourth column. Note that, there could be multiple isolated graphs pertaining to a day like day 2.

2) *Mining frequent sub-graph patterns*: We mine the frequent sub-graph patterns from the skyline graphs $\mathbb{G}$ across a certain number of days for two reasons. One is to avoid any false alteration. Sometimes, a region pair with effective connectivity could be detected as a part of skyline because of some anomaly events, such as traffic accidents. The other is to provide a deeper understanding of the flawed planning. By associating individual region pairs, we can find the causality and relation among these regions, which is more valuable for understanding how a problem is derived. The bottom of Figure 9 shows the mined skyline patterns using different supports. Here, the support of a sub-graph pattern g is calculated as Equation 6, where G is a skyline graph containing the sub-graph g and $\mathbb{G}$ is the collection of skyline graphs across days. The denominator denotes the number of days that the dataset across.

$$Support(g) = \frac{|\{G|g \subseteq G, G \in \mathbb{G}\}|}{num\ of\ days}, \quad (6)$$

For instance, the support of $(r_4 \rightarrow r_5)$ is 1 since it appears in the skyline graphs of all three days while that of $(r_3 \rightarrow r_6)$ is 2/3 as it only appears in Day 2 and Day 3. Given a threshold δ we can choose the patterns with the support $\geq \delta$. These patterns represent the flawed urban planning which is salient and appears frequently.

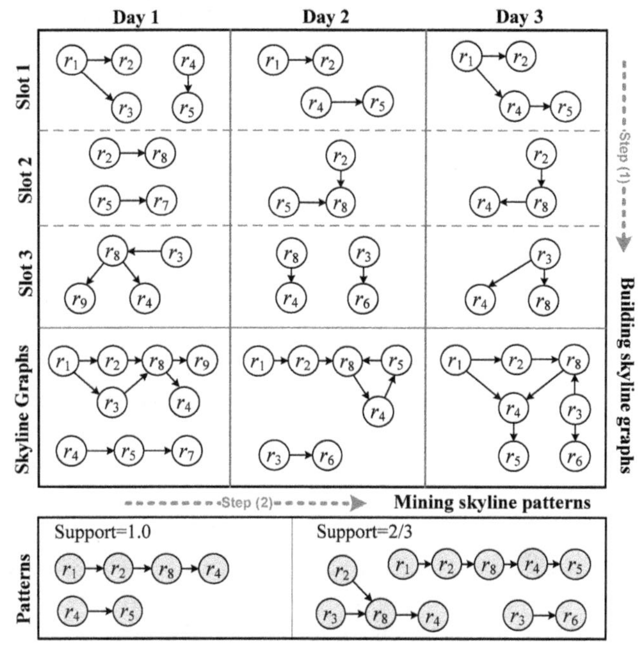

Figure 9. Mining frequent skyline patterns

Besides, we mine the association rules among these patterns according to Equation 7 and 8 where $|g_1 \cup g_2|$ denotes the number of days that g_1 and g_2 co-occurred and $|g_1|$ means the number of days having g_1. Two patterns formulate an association rule, denoted as $g_1 \Rightarrow g_2$, if the support of $g_1 \Rightarrow g_2 \geq \delta$ and its confidence $\geq \theta$ (a given threshold).

$$Support(g_1 \Rightarrow g_2) = \frac{|g_1 \cup g_2|}{num\ of\ days}, \quad (7)$$

$$Confidence(g_1 \Rightarrow g_2) = \frac{|g_1 \cup g_2|}{|g_1|}. \quad (8)$$

For example, as depicted in Figure 9, $(r_4 \rightarrow r_5) \Rightarrow (r_3 \rightarrow r_6)$ whose support is 2/3 and confidence is 2/3, while the confidence of $(r_3 \rightarrow r_6) \Rightarrow (r_4 \rightarrow r_5)$ is 1.

The mined association rules can consist of over 2 patterns. For instance, $g_1, g_2 \Rightarrow g_3$, i. e., g_3 has a very high probability (conditioned by δ and θ) to occur when g_1 and g_2 appear simultaneously. Meanwhile, these association rules may not be geospatially close to each other, hence revealing the causality and correlation between the flawed planning that seems to have no relationship in the geo-spaces. The experiments include more examples.

EVALUATION

Settings

In this section, we carry out our method with a large-scale taxi trajectory dataset generated in Beijing in the past two years, and evaluate the detected results based on the real urban planning published by the government of Beijing.

Taxi trajectories: Table 2 shows the properties of the two trajectory datasets that we used for evaluating our method. We select the data from the same time span within a year in case people have different travel patterns in different seasons. The latter is slightly larger and denser as some expired taxis are replaced by new taxis with better facilities.

Datasets		**2009. 3-5**	**2010.3-6**
Number of taxis		29,286	30,121
Effective days		89	116
Number of points	Total	679M	1,730M
	Per taxi/day	306	528
Distance (KM)	Total	310M	600M
	Per taxi/day	128	171
Average sampling rate (s)		100	74
Ave. dist. between two points (m)		457	349

Table 2. Two datasets of taxi trajectories used for evaluation

Map data: We use the road network data of Beijing, which has 106,579 road vertices and 141,380 road segments. We pick out 25,262 major road segments with level 0, 1, and 2 (0 is the highest level representing highways, 6 is the lowest denoting small streets) to partition the urban area of Beijing into some regions. As a result, we obtain 444 regions.

We verify the detected flaws in the following two ways:

1) We select some urban planning, such as new subway lines and roads, which has been implemented for use between the times of the two datasets, and study whether the carried out planning reduces the flaws existing in the former dataset.

2) We check if some flaws that have been detected in both two datasets by our method embodied in the future urban planning of Beijing (i. e., the problem of these regions has been recognized by the city planner).

We compare our approach with a baseline method which retrieves the top hottest regions in Beijing according to the following metric q, where l denotes the road segments falling in the region r.

$$q = \frac{number\ of\ taxis\ ending\ at\ r}{|time|\cdot\sum_{l\in r} l.length}; \quad (9)$$

This metric represents the density of taxis sending people to a region in a unit time slot (hour). Here, the total length of road (in a region) makes more sense beyond the area size of the region since the length (and capacity) of roads reflect the real spaces that vehicles can travel. Meanwhile, we do not differentiate the capacities of the road segments in a region any longer as all of them are local streets. We will show the heat maps of Beijing in terms of this metric later.

Results

Figure 10 and 11 present the distributions and trends of $< |S|, E(V), \theta >$ changing over time of day in the urban area of Beijing on workdays and rest days respectively. The value shown in each figure is an average result across a number of days (from the dataset of 2010). The trends and distributions of 2009 are similar to those of 2010, though the exact values have minor differences. So, we do not show them in our paper. The two sets of figures present two aspects of information. First, they demonstrate the clear differences (of distributions and trends) between workdays and rest days and among different time slots, justifying the importance of temporal partition. Second, the three features (we used to detect flawed planning) well reflect on people's mobility patterns and traffic at a city-wide level. A lot of commonsense knowledge and interesting stories can be found in these figures, validating their effectiveness.

For example, as illustrated in Figure 10 A) and Figure 11 A), the morning rush hour on the rest days comes 2 hours later than workdays, which denotes that on average people start outdoor activities on the rest days (in Beijing) 2 hours later than on the workdays. However, the rest days and work days have the same evening rush hours at 6pm. This denotes people always keep their time for dinner which is important to them no matter the day of the week and when they get up. Meanwhile, workdays have a slightly heavy traffic in the morning rush hours than in the evening one; on the contrary, the rest days have an opposite result. Figure 10 C) contains two clear peaks (at 10am and 5pm) where the number of region pairs with a θ greater than 1.2 increases rapidly, while those where θ<1 remain stable. This denotes that more taxi drivers have to take a slight detour to reach a destination quickly during rush hours instead of choosing the shortest path as they can at other times (since the direct paths become crowded). That could mean the taxi fare increases during rush hours.

			2009	**2010**
Workdays	**Average # of region pairs in a skyline**	Time slot 1	7.65	9.09
		Time slot2	7.40	7.05
		Time slot 3	7.35	7.29
		Time slot4	6.70	7.82
	Skyline graphs	# of nodes	12.93	16.18
		# of links	8.40	10.81
Rest days	**Average # of region pairs in a skyline**	Time slot 1	6.68	7.97
		Time slot2	6.68	7.66
		Time slot 3	6.66	7.37
	Skyline graphs	# of nodes	11.91	14.49
		# of links	7.05	8.86

Table 3. Properties of the detected skylines and skyline graphs

Table 3 shows the properties of the skylines detected from each time slot and the graph formulated for a day. The values are averages across a number of days. First, the size of the skylines and graphs becomes slightly larger in 2010 as compared to 2009. For instance, the skyline of time slot 1 (7am-10:30am) in a workday contains on average 7.65 region pairs in 2009 while this number reaches 9.09 in 2010. At the same time, the number of nodes, i.e., regions (refer to Figure 9 for an example) in a skyline graph also increased from 12.93 (in 2009) to 16.18 (in 2010) in the workdays. These results indicate that the traffic conditions in Beijing become worse in 2010 than 2009 (the figures of these two years are comparable since the number of taxis in these two years are similar and we have divided the counts by days, i.e., irrelevant to the period of time). Second, the skylines of workday have a bigger number of region pairs than the rest days, leading to a larger size of skyline graph in workday as well. This trend occurs in both years, denoting that people's mobility is relatively more focused on rest days (shopping and entertainment areas are more likely to be the destinations) while they would travel to a variety of locations on workdays for more purposes.

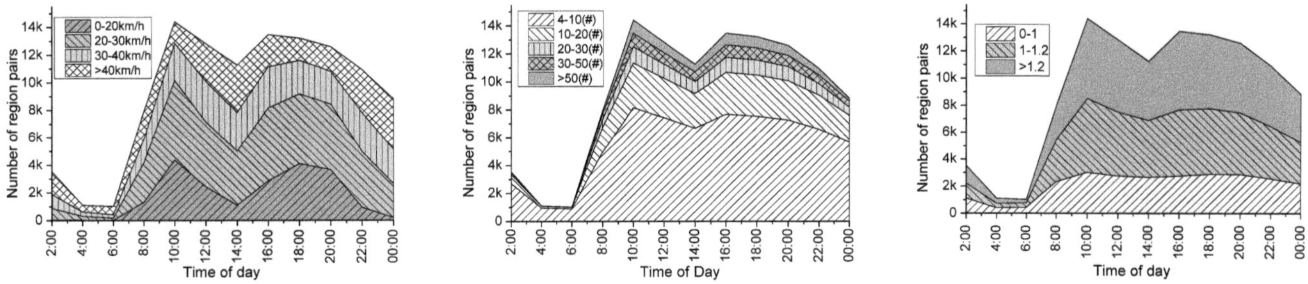

A) E(V) B) |S| C) θ

Figure 10. Distribution and trend of workday changing over time of day (in urban areas of Beijing): In these figures Y axis is the number of region pairs. For instance, as shown in Figure 10 A), at 10am on work days, there are about 4,000 (4k) region pairs whose E(v)≤20km/h and 6k regions pairs with a 20km/h< **E(V)** ≤30km/h.

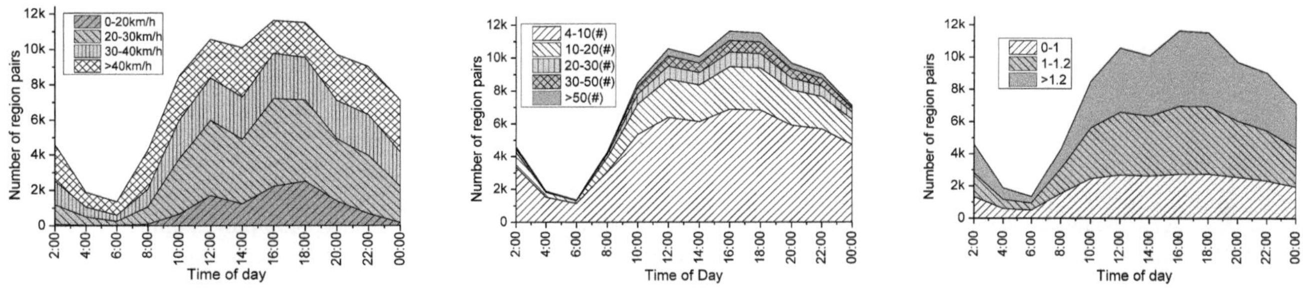

A) E(V) B) |S| C) θ

Figure 11. Distribution and trend of the rest days changing over time of day (in urban areas of Beijing): In these figures Y axis is the number of region pairs. For instance, as demonstrated in Figure 11 B), at 6pm on rest days, there are approximately 6k region pairs whose 4≤|S|<10 and 3k region pairs having 10≤|S|<20.

Table 4 presents the number of trips (with passengers) that a taxi generated in different time slots in 2009 and 2010 respectively. Clearly, the numbers of 2010 become smaller than those of 2009, which means taxi drivers took fewer passengers than before. The major reason causing this is that the average travel speed of a taxi sending a passenger to a destination becomes lower, increasing the travel time of a single trip (as shown in the two bottom rows of Table 4). In short, the traffic conditions of Beijing become worse in 2010 (compared with 2009). It is not difficult to understand this result given that the number of auto mobiles in Beijing has reached 4.8 million with a rapid growth of 800,000 from 2009 to 2010, reported by Beijing Traffic Management Bureau. At the same time, the number of residents in Beijing exceeded 19 million in 2010 with a growth of over 560,000 from 2009. Moreover, as Beijing has been becoming an advanced city, a significant number of flowing population (e.g., 184 million tourists, i.e., over 0.5 million per day) have traveled to Beijing in 2010, generating addition traffic. The other reason is that some newly built transportation systems, such as subway lines, change the transportation modes of some people who took taxis previously in some regions. Also, a few people traveling by taxis before bought their own private cars in 2010. But, the number of people expecting to take a taxi may not decrease in Beijing as the added population could be larger than the number reduced by the second reason.

		Workday				Rest days		
	Slots	1	2	3	4	1	2	3
Trip	**2009**	3.1	4.6	3.2	3.8	2.0	5.0	4.3
	2010	2.7	4.4	2.9	3.7	1.7	4.5	3.9
Speed km/h	**2009**	29.6	34.2	29.1	42.3	33.4	32.8	41.7
	2010	28.0	32.7	28.3	40.8	32.9	32.0	41.0

Table 4. Number of trips per taxi per day and average speed: The actual number of trips could be slightly bigger as we remove some trips with sensor signal error. Both years have a similar portion of such data, hence the gap is correct.

The indication derived from Table 3 and 4 is also embodied by the heat maps of Beijing shown in Figure 12, where the color of most regions becomes shallower in 2010 than 2009, especially in some hot areas. This denotes that the number of passengers that reach a region in a unit time decreased. Actually, the transportation and land use of these hot regions do not change while the population of Beijing increased in 2010. In short, the number of people expecting to take a taxi should increase in these areas. The only reason leading to this result is that the travel speed of taxis in these regions decreased. However, a few regions, like Wangjing area located in the East-West corner of the 4th Ring Road, have attracted more people with its recent development (many companies, shopping malls and restaurants have been built here), becoming deeper in color.

However, the hot regions may not be the defects in urban planning though very likely to be, while some regions which are not that hot could have flaws. Additionally, the heat map does not reveal the relation between the flawed regions. To address these issues, Figure 13 presents the flawed urban planning (frequent sub-graph patterns) determined by our method in 2009 and 2010 respectively. Clearly, there are some regions, which are not very hot, that have been detected as flawed planning (we will evaluate these regions later). By comparing these two sets of figures, we observe the following two aspects:

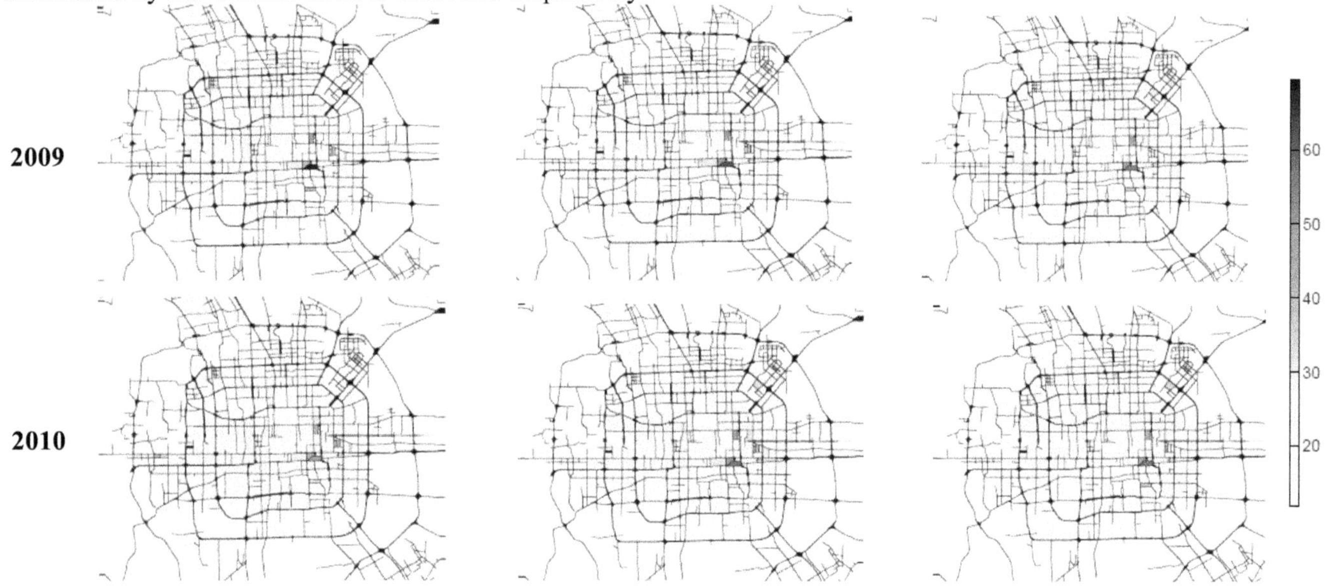

A) 7:00am-10:30am B) 10:30-4:00pm C) 4:00pm-7:30pm

Figure 12. Heat maps of Beijing of the same workday from different two years 2009/5/12 and 2010/5/12 according the *q*: The depth of color filling a region stands for the number of people reaching a region by taxis in an hour (refer to Equation 9 for details).

Figure 13. The flawed urban planning detected based on the taxi trajectories of 2009 and 2010 in the workdays and rest days: The color of a region denotes the frequency that a region has been detected as a flaw (the deeper means more frequent), and the arrows represent the direction of transition between two regions. The first row shows the results of 2009 and the second row stands for 2010. Figures in the left column pertain to workdays and the other column belongs to the rest days. The results are frequent sub-graph patterns with a support ≥0.06. Clearly, a hot region shown in Figure 12 might not be the region with frequent traffic problem, vice versa.

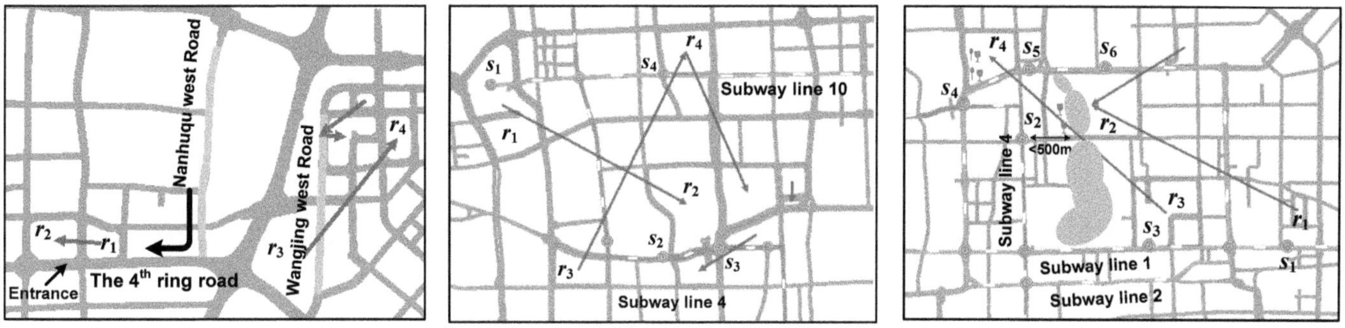

A) New roads built around Wangjing area **B) The launch of the Subway line 4** **C) The central part of Beijing**

Figure 14 Illustration on the flawed planning that appeared in 2009 while disappearing in 2010

1) *Some flawed planning occurring in 2009 disappeared in 2010.* As shown in Figure 14 A), some region graphs like ($r_1 \rightarrow r_2$) disappeared in 2010 because of the two newly built roads (depicted as the yellow lines). These two roads were opened between the times of the two datasets. Before the launch of Nanhuqu west road in August 2009, people living in the areas above the 4th ring road in this figure had to enter the 4th Ring Road (a high way) using the only entrance located in r_2. Now, a significant portion of people can reach the 4th Ring Road by taking the Nanhuqu west road directly; hence not necessarily travel to r_2 by passing r_1. Similarly, regions like ($r_3 \rightarrow r_4$) disappeared in Wangjing area with the launch of the Wangjing west road, as people have additional ways for traveling among them.

Other examples demonstrated in Figure 14 B) and C) reveal the effect of subway line 4 (launched in September 2009) on urban planning in Beijing. Before the launch, ($r_1 \rightarrow r_2$) shown in Figure 14 B) had traffic problems according to the results of our method. However, with the subway line 4 more people can reach r_2 by taking subway systems with a one-stop transfer (e.g., starting at subway station s_1 in line 10 and ending at s_2 or s_3 in line 4). This transport mode is faster and cheaper than by taxi. Similar explanations can also be applied to other flawed urban planning having disappeared in Figure 14 B). Figure 14 C) illustrates two interesting stories, reflecting on how the subway line 4 affects the traffic of the central part of Beijing, where r_1 belongs to central business district and regions within the subway line 2 contains a lot of famous tourist attractions, such as Houhai bar street along Houhai lake in r_2 and Wangfujing pedestrian street in r_3. Previous, many people went to Houhai bar street from r_1 by taxis after finishing their business. Though there is a subway station $s_6$on line 2 close to r_2, most bars are located in the west side of the lake, leading to a 20-minute walk distance to a traveler. After the launch of the subway line 4, there is a subway station s_2 with a distance smaller than 500 meters to the bar street. Consequently, people have additional choices for their trips. A similar story can be found in the disappeared flaw ($r_3 \rightarrow r_4$), where people travel to r_4 for diner after visiting r_3 while most restaurants are located close to s_4.

2) *The number of regions having defects increased in 2010 beyond 2009 and some flaws occurring in 2009 still exist.* Figure 15 demonstrates some flawed planning (represented by frequent sub-graph patterns) that still exists in 2010. The blue polyline shown in Figure 15 A) is the subway line 15 (which was partially launched in Dec. 2010 after the time of the trajectory data), and the green one stands for line 14 (which is still under construction). The planning of these two subway lines denotes that the urban planner has recognized the problem existing in the regions, justifying the validity of the results generated using our method. Furthermore, we specify the linking structure between these regions. For example, region r_1, r_2, and r_3 formulate a graph pattern, which means that they often appear together. Such kind of graph patterns reveals the relation between individual flawed regions and presents a comprehensive view on the defects of a plan. So, when designing a new plan, a city planner cannot only discover regions with problems but also understand the flaws systematically.

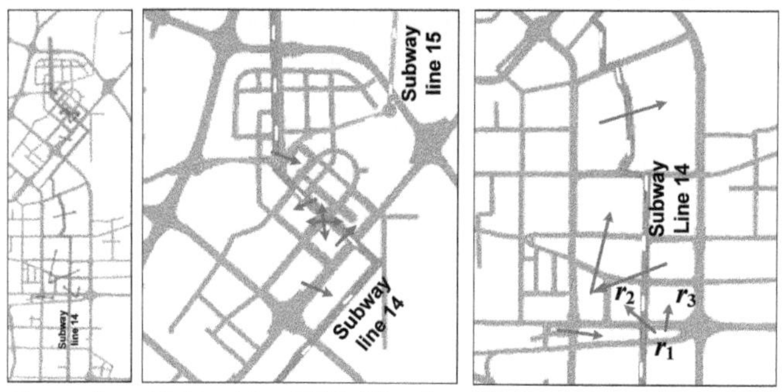

A) overview B) Line 14 and 15 in Wangjing C) Line 14 passing New CBD

Figure 15. Subway Lines 14 and 15 and related existing flaws

From the result presented in Figure 13, we also find some association rules between the detected graph patterns. Figure 16 illustrates an example, $(r_1 \rightarrow r_2) \Rightarrow [(r_2 \rightarrow r_4), (r_1 \rightarrow r_3)]$ with support=0.05 and confidence=0.7. In short, ($r_2 \rightarrow r_4$) and ($r_1 \rightarrow r_3$) have a probability of 0.7 to appear if ($r_1 \rightarrow r_2$) occurs. This pattern suggests that many people leaving r_1 are heading to regions r_3 and r_4 while r_2 becomes the bottle-neck of these transitions. Such kind of implied problem is not easy to find (without using our method), as sometimes the detected regions may not be geospatially close. For instance, r_3 is not close to r_2, and r_4 is not adjacent to r_1. Due to the limited spaces, we will show more interesting results and a live demo during the presentation at the conference.

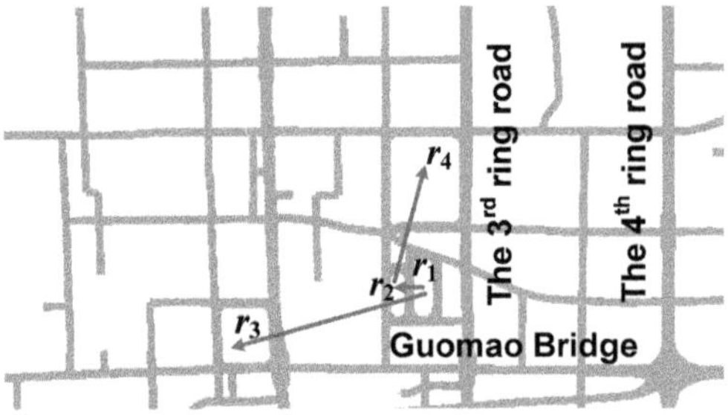

Figure 16. Association rules mined from the data of 2010

RELATED WORK

Mining Taxi Trajectories

A significant number of published documents have presented work aiming to mine the trajectories of taxicabs since the trajectory data has recently become widely available. They [5][10] studied taxi drivers' pick-up behavior in creating higher profit (e.g., how to easily find passengers) by analyzing fleet trajectories. Paper [16] presents some probabilistic models predicting a driver's destination and route based on historical GPS trajectories. Paper [6] estimates the real-time traffic flows on some road segments in terms of the recently received taxi trajectories. Yuan et al. [14][15] learn the practical, driving path to a destination from taxi trajectories, considering that taxi drivers are experienced drivers. Different from the above-mentioned work, we mine taxi trajectories for supporting urban planning instead of for an end user. We are the first team to carry out such studies for this purpose.

Urban Computing

The advances of ubiquitous computing technology have brought considerable attention to urban computing in recent years [7][12]. Most literature discusses the urban computing from the perspective of social computing in the urban area, e.g., estimating the similarity between users in terms of their location histories [2][3][9], extracting social structures from mobile phone data [4], enabling friend and location recommenders in the real world [17][18], and studying the influence of pervasive systems on people in urban spaces [8]. Different from these studies, we explore the urban computing from the perspective of urban planning, sensing people's mobility in a city unobtrusively with taxis and detect flaws with implicit engagement of citizens.

CONCLUSION

In this paper, we detect the flaws in the existing urban planning of a city using the GPS trajectories of taxis traveling in the urban areas. The detected results are comprised of two sets of findings. One is the frequent sub-graph patterns consisting of region pairs with salient traffic problems and the linking structure among these regions. The other is the association relations between these patterns. These results can first evaluate the effectiveness of the carried urban planning, and second provide a comprehensive view on the existing problem for decision-making when city planners conceive future plans. We executed our method based on real data generated by 30,000 taxis in Beijing in 2009 and 2010, and evaluated the validity of our results using real urban planning of Beijing, including the newly built subway lines and roads and city projects that are still under construction. Some interesting discoveries are revealed from the data as well.

In the future, we might analyze how the detected flaws are derived from the existing urban planning by 1) studying the geographic features of a region, such as the road segments and points of interests, and 2) the purpose of people's travel, e.g., for shopping, sports, work etc.

REFERENCES

1. Börzsönyi, S., Kossmann, D., Stocker, K. The skyline operator. In *Proc.* ICDE 2001. IEEE Press: 421-430.
2. Cranshaw, J., Toch, E., Hong, J. Kittur, A., Sadeh, N. Bridging the gap between the Physical Location and Online Social Networks. In *Proc.* Ubicomp'10, ACM Press (2010): 119-128.
3. Eagle, N., and Pentland, A. Reality mining: sensing complex social systems. *Personal Ubiquitous Computing*, 10, 4 (2006): 255–268.
4. Eagle, N., Montjoye, Y. D., and Bettencourt, L. Community Computing: Comparisons between Rural and Urban Societies using Mobile Phone Data, IEEE Social Computing, 144-150.
5. Ge, Y., Xiong, H., Tuzhilin, A., Xiao, K., Gruteser M., Pazzani M. J. An Energy-Efficient Mobile Recommender System. In *Proc.* KDD 2010, ACM Press (2010): 899-908.
6. Guehnemann A., Schaefer R. P., Thiessenhusen K. U., Wagner P. Monitoring traffic and emissions by floating car data. Institute of transport studies Australia; 2004.
7. Kindberg, T., Chalmers, M., Paulos, E. Gest editors' introduction: Urban computing. Pervasive computing. 6, 3 (2007), 18-20.
8. Kostakos V., O'Neill, E. Cityware: Urban computing to bridge online and real-world social networks. Handbook of Research on Urban Informatics, 2008.
9. Li, Q., Zheng, Y., Xie, X., Chen, Y., Liu, W., Ma, W.Y. Mining user similarity based on location history. In *Proc.* GIS 2008, ACM Press (2008): 1-10.
10. Liu, L., Andris, C., Biderman, A. and Ratti, C. Uncovering cabdrivers' behavior patterns from their digital traces. Computers, Environment and Urban Systems, 2010.
11. Rosenfeld, A. Connectivity in digital pictures. Journal of the ACM (JACM), 17, 1(1970): 146-160.
12. Shklovski, I., Chang, M. F. Urban Computing-Navigating Space and Context. IEEE Computer Society. 39, 9 (2006), 36.
13. Yan, X., and Han, J. Discovery of frequent substructures. Wiley-Interscience, 2007. 99-113
14. Yuan J., Zheng Y., Xie, X., Sun, G. Driving with Knowledge from the Physical World. In *Proc.* KDD 2011, ACM Press 2011.
15. Yuan J., Zheng Y., Zhang C. Y., Xie, W., Xie, X., Sun, G. and Huang, Y. T-Drive: Driving Directions Based on Taxi Trajectories. In *Proc.* GIS 2010. ACM Press (2010), 99-108.
16. Ziebart, B., Maas, A., Dey, A. and Bagnell, J. Navigate like a cabbie: Probabilistic reasoning from observed context-aware behavior. In *Proc.* Ubicomp 2008, ACM Press (2008): 322.
17. Zheng, Y., Xie, X. and Ma, W. Y. GeoLife: A Collaborative Social Networking Service among User, Location and Trajectory. IEEE Date Engineer Bulletin, 33, 2 (2010), 32-40.
18. Zheng, Y., Zhang, L., Ma, Z., Xie, X., and Ma, W. Y. Recommending friends and locations based on individual location history. ACM Trans. on the Web, 5, 1 (2011), 1-44.

iBAT: Detecting Anomalous Taxi Trajectories from GPS Traces

Daqing Zhang[†], **Nan Li**[‡,♮], **Zhi-Hua Zhou**[‡], **Chao Chen**[†], **Lin Sun**[†], **Shijian Li**[♭]
[†] Institut TELECOM SudParis, France
{daqing.zhang, chao.chen, lin.sun}@it-sudparis.eu
[‡] National Key Laboratory for Novel Software Technology, Nanjing University, China
{lin, zhouzh}@lamda.nju.edu.cn
[♮] School of Mathematical Sciences, Soochow University, China
[♭] Department of Computer Science, Zhejiang University, China shijianli@zju.edu.cn

ABSTRACT
GPS-equipped taxis can be viewed as pervasive sensors and the large-scale digital traces produced allow us to reveal many hidden "facts" about the city dynamics and human behaviors. In this paper, we aim to discover anomalous driving patterns from taxi's GPS traces, targeting applications like automatically detecting taxi driving frauds or road network change in modern cites. To achieve the objective, firstly we group all the taxi trajectories crossing the same source-destination cell-pair and represent each taxi trajectory as a sequence of symbols. Secondly, we propose an Isolation-Based Anomalous Trajectory (*iBAT*) detection method and verify with large scale taxi data that *iBAT* achieves remarkable performance (AUC>0.99, over 90% detection rate at false alarm rate of less than 2%). Finally, we demonstrate the potential of iBAT in enabling innovative applications by using it for taxi driving fraud detection and road network change detection.

Author Keywords
Anomalous trajectory detection, GPS trace, isolation-based anomaly detection, taxi

ACM Classification Keywords
H.2.8 Database applications: Data mining.

General Terms
Algorithms

INTRODUCTION
With recent advances in sensing, communication, storage and computing, the digital traces left by people while interacting with cyber-physical spaces are accumulating at an unprecedented rate. The scale and richness of different digital traces provides us with new opportunities to understand society behaviours and community dynamics in different contexts, showing great potential to revolutionize the services in various areas ranging from public safety, urban planning to transportation management [10, 27].

In modern cities, more and more vehicles, such as taxis, have been equipped with GPS devices for localization and navigation. Gathering and analyzing the large-scale GPS traces have provided us a great opportunity to reveal the hidden "facts" about the city dynamics and human behaviors, enabling diverse innovative applications [22, 13, 18, 30, 26, 21, 23, 28, 24]. Recent years have witnessed an increasing interest in trajectory anomaly detection [14, 6, 9], which aims to detect suspicious moving objects automatically. However, while several aspects of abnormality of moving objects have been investigated, there are very few works on discovering anomalous driving patterns by mining GPS traces with practical applications examined. In this paper, we intend to motivate our research on anomalous taxi driving trajectory detection with the following potential applications:

EXAMPLE 1. Many people, mostly tourists, are victims of taxi driving frauds committed by greedy taxi drivers who overcharge passengers by deliberately taking unnecessary detours. To ensure quality taxi services, it is crucial to detect and penalize such frauds. Currently, detecting taxi driving frauds is often done by experienced staff via manually checking the GPS trajectories corresponding to the taxi rides, based on complaints from passengers, but this is costly and not very effective because many frauds are not even noticed by passengers. As the traces of driving frauds often significantly deviate from normal ones, it is possible to automatically detect the anomalous driving trajectories by mining taxi GPS traces and hence taxi driving frauds.

EXAMPLE 2. Urban road networks often change over time in developing cities, it is important to update these changes in the digital map. If this is done manually by digital map providers, it would be expensive and also difficult to capture the changes in time. If GPS-equipped taxis are viewed as moving sensors probing the real-time information about urban road network, then the taxi traces accumulated in a new and different area might indicate a sudden road network

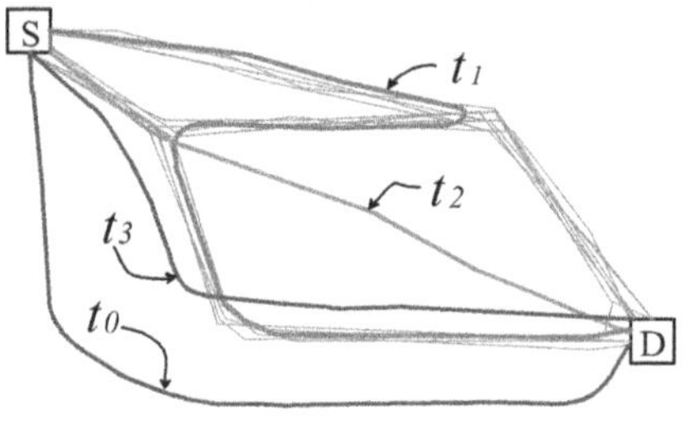

Figure 1. An illustration of taxi trajectories between S and D.

change, *i.e.* a newly-built or blocked road segment nearby. Hence, detecting anomalous taxi driving trajectories can be helpful in identifying road network changes promptly.

Consider the taxi trajectories between two places S (source) and D (destination) as shown in Fig. 1. Assume that the three clusters of trajectories between the $(S;D)$ pair are defined as normal ones, then the four trajectories (t_0, t_1, t_2, t_3) are considered as anomalies since they are "*few*" and "*different*" from the normal ones. Detecting driving anomalies is a non-trivial task because of the following challenging issues.

- First, as shown in Fig. 1, there might be different sets of normal trajectories between each $(S;D)$ pair and these trajectory clusters usually have different densities or distance distributions. If we exploit traditional anomaly detection techniques [14, 6, 9] based on distance or density, it is hard to choose the parameters and identify all anomalous trajectories.
- Second, multiple normal routes between each $(S;D)$ pair also mean different driving distances. If we directly model driving distance for anomalous trajectories detection, it is not able to discover those anomalies whose driving distance is close to that of the normal trajectories (like t_3).
- Third, the road network often changes over time in developing cities: a new (anomalous) route may become normal and an old road can be blocked. Hence, it is important to be able to detect an emerging cluster of anomalous trajectories and incorporate these changes in the model.
- Finally, some traditional anomaly detection methods often require that the taxi trajectories be represented as fixed-length feature vectors. However, the real taxi trajectories are variable-length sequences of points, thus traditional methods can not be directly used. If we transform them into fixed-length feature vectors, spatial information can be lost. Moreover, GPS traces often suffer from the low-sampling-rate problem since GPS devices usually send data at a low and changing frequency.

In this paper, we aim to propose a novel anomalous driving trajectory detection method which addresses the four challenges above. Firstly, we extract valid taxi rides from all the taxi GPS traces, split the city map into grid-cells of equal size, group all the taxi rides crossing the same source-destination cell-pair, and augment and represent each taxi trajectory in each source-destination pair as an ordered sequence of traversed cell symbols. In such a way, the problem of anomalous driving trajectory detection is converted to that of finding anomalous trajectories from all the trajectories with the same source-destination cell pair. Secondly, for all the taxi trajectories between a certain source-destination cell-pair, we define those trajectories that are "*few*" and "*different*" from the normal trajectory clusters as anomalies. Instead of profiling the normal trajectories and detecting the anomalies by employing the similarity or density measure, this paper proposes an Isolation-Based Anomalous Trajectory (*iBAT*) detection method which exploits the property that anomalies are susceptible to a mechanism called *isolation* [20]. Finally, we perform an empirical evaluation of *iBAT* with real-world taxi GPS data and show how the two applications (*i.e.*, taxi driving fraud detection and road network change detection) can be enabled by using *iBAT*. In summary, the main contributions of this paper include:

- We identify a new kind of anomalous trajectory detection problem based on two motivating applications with taxi GPS traces. We further propose a series of techniques to transform the problem of anomalous driving trajectory detection into an easy-to-solve form: finding anomalous trajectories from all the trajectories with the same source-destination cell pair, with each taxi trajectory represented as a sequence of cell symbols.
- To solve the above mentioned problem, we propose an Isolation-Based Anomalous Trajectory (*iBAT*) detection method which exploits the property that anomalies are susceptible to a mechanism called *isolation*. To our best knowledge, this is the first work applying the isolation mechanism in the trajectory anomaly detection.
- We evaluate *iBAT* with real-world GPS traces collected from 7,600 taxis for one month. It achieves remarkable detection rate with low processing-time, it also outperforms the density-based method as a baseline approach in terms of AUC (*i.e.*, the Area Under the ROC Curve) [4].
- By using two examples (*i.e.*, taxi driving fraud detection and road network change detection), we show how innovative applications can be achieved by using *iBAT*.

RELATED WORK

In this section, we briefly review the related work which can be grouped into three categories. The first category includes the work on analyzing or exploiting GPS traces with research issues other than anomaly detection. For instance, Patterson, Liao, et al. [22, 18] used GPS traces to infer an individual's mode of transportation and daily routine, providing reminders for persons with mild cognitive disabilities when they, for instance, take the wrong bus; Krumm et al. [13, 8] showed it is possible to predict the destination and entire route of a vehicle based on historical GPS traces, and recently reported further results building routable road networks from raw GPS traces [7]. Based on the observation that taxi drivers are experienced in finding the best route to a destination, Ziebart et al. [30] and Yuan et al. [26] designed *PROCAB* and *T-Drive*, respectively, providing driving direction guidance by leveraging taxis' GPS traces. Zheng et al. [29] gave travel location recommendation to new visitors by mining GPS data left by previous tourists. Liu et al. [21] developed a novel methodology to reveal taxi drivers' operation patterns by analyzing their GPS traces. Zheng et al. [28] mined GPS traces to discover interesting locations and possible activities that can be performed there for recommendations. Phithakkitnukoon et al. [23] derived a model to predict vacant taxis. Qi et al. [24] measured social functions of city regions by analyzing taxi's GPS traces. Li et al. [15] studied the passenger-finding strategies of taxi drivers. While these works target research problems different from ours, they have inspired us to motivate our research with innovative applications using taxi GPS traces.

The second category focuses on anomalous trajectory detection, which is highly related to our work. In the literature, some solutions for trajectory outlier detection have already been reported, each addressing certain aspects of abnormality. For instance, Lee et al. [14] proposed the partition-and-detect framework to detect outlying sub-trajectories, they used both distance and density for anomaly detection. For a similar problem to Lee et al.'s, Ge et al. [9] detected the evolving trajectory outliers by computing the outlying score, based on the evolving direction and density of trajectories. Bu et al. [6] presented an outlier detection framework for monitoring anomalies over continuous trajectory streams. The key idea is to build local clusters upon trajectory streams and detect anomalies by a cluster join mechanism. Li et al. [17], instead, developed a temporal outlier detection approach for vehicle traffic data, which aimed to discover the abnormal traffic change in the road network. In addition, there are also some learning-based approaches reported [16, 25, 19], but they all require training data which is expensive to label. In contrast, we define a different trajectory anomaly problem from previous ones, *i.e.*, given all the taxi trajectories between a certain source-destination cell-pair, our objective is to discover those trajectories that are *"few"* and *"different"* from the normal trajectory clusters.

The third category includes anomaly detection methods that are not designed for trajectory data. This category of work has its deep roots in database, data mining, computer vision, etc. The proposed methods range from supervised approaches [1] to distance-based [12, 3], density-based [5], and model-based methods [11], each having a specific formulation of the problem with different anomaly measures and notions. Among these approaches, one new and fundamentally different anomaly detection method directly inspiring this work is *iForest* [20]. By assuming anomalies are *"few and different"*, they found that anomalies are susceptible to a mechanism called *"isolation"*, with which *iForest* can detect anomalies without employing any distance or density measure. It has been shown that *iForest* outperforms the state-of-the-art outlier detection techniques like ORCA, one-class SVM, LOF, one-class SVM and Random Forest in terms of AUC and processing time, at a low time and space complexity. It also deals with the effects of swamping and masking effectively. However, as *iForest* is designed for anomaly detection problems with fixed-length feature vector as input, it can not be directly applied to handle the trajectory data. In this paper, we first adapt the idea of *iForest* to trajectory data, and improve it further by considering the characteristics of the sequence of trajectories so that it can manage more anomalous cases.

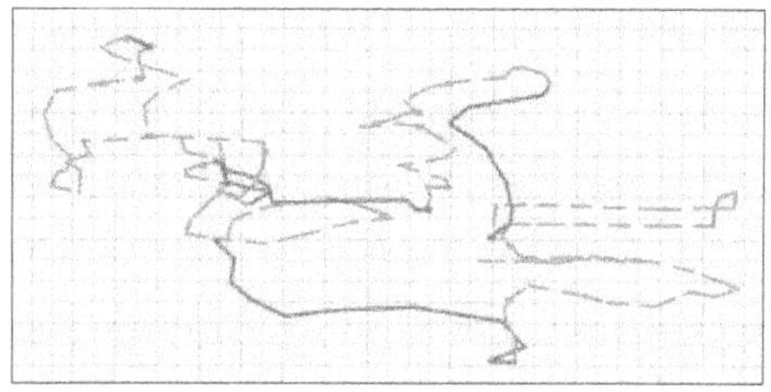

Figure 2. One taxi's GPS trace in two hours, where red (solid) or green (dashed) indicates the taxi is occupied or vacant.

PROBLEM STATEMENT

A taxi's GPS trace consists of a sequence of GPS points (*i.e.*, latitude and longitude) generated by the taxi GPS device, the time stamp, the estimated speed and the operation status (*i.e.*, vacant or occupied) associated with each time stamp. On a two dimensional plane, a taxi's moving trajectory over a time interval can be depicted by connecting these GPS points. For instance, Fig. 2 shows one taxi's moving trajectory in two hours, where red (solid) lines and green (dashed) lines correspond to the taxi's occupied and empty status, respectively. As the taxi driving fraud occurs only when the taxi is occupied by passengers, in this paper we only consider the taxi trajectories corresponding to the taxi rides (red lines, where taxi's operation status is occupied).

DEFINITION 1. A *taxi trajectory* is a sequence of GPS points pertaining to an occupied taxi ride, *i.e.*,

$$t:\ p_1 \to p_2 \to \ldots \to p_n\ ,$$

where p_i's are GPS points, p_1 and p_n are *source* and *destination* of the trajectory, respectively.

By extracting valid taxi rides from all the taxi GPS traces based on operation status, we can obtain a large collection of taxi trajectories. If we split the city map into equal sized grid-cells and group all the taxi trajectories crossing the same source destination cell-pair, then we can have many taxi trajectories between two cells (*e.g.*, S and D) as shown in Fig. 1. Assume that the three clusters of trajectories (the majority of trajectories with similar routes) correspond to normal taxi rides, the rest of the scattered trajectories are considered to be anomalous. The anomalous trajectories can be long detours made by greedy taxi drivers like $t_0$and t_1 in Fig. 1, they can also be short-cuts or new routes taken by experienced drivers like t_2 and t_3. Our goal is to find these anomalous trajectories, based on which new applications can be enabled. Formally, the problem is defined as follows.

PROBLEM. Given a set of trajectories $T = \{t_1, t_2, \ldots, t_n\}$ between two locations S and D, find those in T that are significantly different from the majority.

In this paper, by exploiting the *"few and different"* properties of anomalous trajectories, we propose an isolation-based anomalous trajectory detection method.

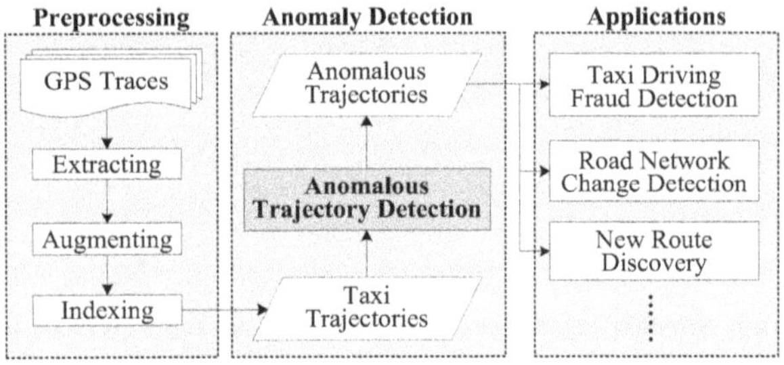

Figure 3. Overview of our approach.

OUR PROPOSED APPROACH

A Three-Step Procedure

As shown in Fig. 3, our approach to detecting anomalous taxi trajectories consists of three main steps. In the first step, after extracting taxi trajectories from GPS traces, we split the city map into grid-cells of equal size, then we group all taxi trajectories crossing the same source-destination cell-pair, augment and represent each trajectory as a sequence of traversed cells.In the second step, we present our *iBAT* method to discover anomalous trajectories for a specific source destination cell-pair. Specifically, we exploit the *"few and different"* properties of anomalous trajectories, and apply the isolation mechanism to detect anomalous trajectories. Finally, we perform further analysis on detected anomalous trajectories, and demonstrate their effectiveness in enabling the two innovative applications, *i.e.*, taxi driving fraud detection and road network change detection. We describe each step of our approach below.

Preprocessing GPS traces

Extracting and Augmenting Taxi Trajectories

Given a large collection of GPS traces, our first task is to extract taxi ride trajectories by partitioning GPS traces according to the taxi operation status. As we split the city map into grid-cells of equal size, then each taxi trajectory is mapped to the cell grid and become a sequence of traversed cells.

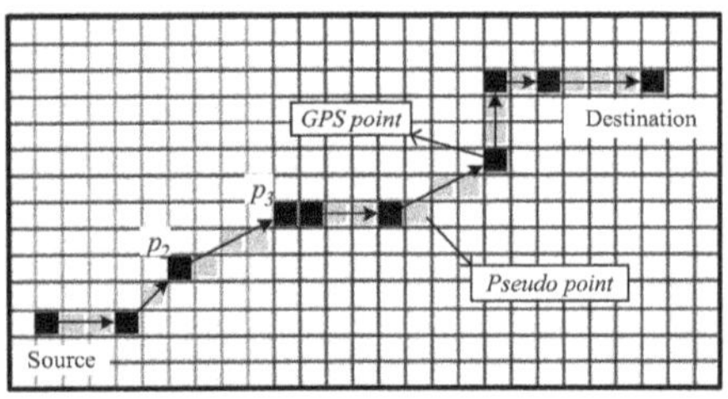

Figure 4. An illustrative example of augmenting trajectory.

In practice, GPS devices usually report data at a low frequency, for example, about one record per minute in our real-world dataset. This results in a non-detailed representation of taxi trajectories, because one taxi may traverse multiple consecutive cells without GPS points recorded. As shown in Fig. 4, due to the low-sampling-rate problem, a taxi trajectory often consists of a series of GPS points (shown as black cells) which are not adjacent to each other (like p_2 and p_3). In such a way, if two taxis take the same route, their trajectories can be different. In order to ensure that same taxi trajectories are represented equally in the system, we need to argument the trajectory. In this paper, we take a simple method to augment taxi trajectories. That is, along the line defined by two GPS cells, we insert pseudo cells between them. For example, in Fig. 4, three pseudo cells (shown as gray cells) are inserted between p_2 and p_3 . Eventually, such an augmenting process will allow us to obtain a cascaded cell sequence for the representation of each trajectory.

Finding Trajectories between a Source-Destination Cell-Pair

In practice, the extracted taxi trajectories have various sources and destinations. Given a source-destination cell-pair, we need to find all the related taxi trajectories. For a given period of time and grid cell size, we may face the problem that there are not sufficient taxi trajectories between certain source-destination pairs to form "normal" trajectory clusters. To alleviate this problem, we not only count the set of taxi trajectories with exactly the same source-destination pair we also add all those taxi trajectories which pass through the source-destination cell-pair. For example, given two taxi trajectories

$$t_1 : p_1 \to p_2 \to p_3 \to p_5,$$
$$t_2 : p_3 \to p_1 \to p_4 \to p_5 \to p_2,$$

both of them will be counted if we want to find trajectories with p_1 and p_5 as source and destination (for t_2, only the segment $p_1 \to p_4 \to p_5$ is included). To achieve this, we employ the inverted index mechanism [31], which is popularly used in information retrieval, to index all the taxi trajectories, As an analogy, the taxi trajectory and cell correspond to the document and word [31], respectively. As an illustrative example, given t_1 and t_2 as above, we have the inverted index as

$$p_1 : \{(t_1, 1), (t_2, 2)\}, \quad p_2 : \{(t_1, 2), (t_2, 5)\},$$
$$p_3 : \{(t_1, 3), (t_2, 1)\}, \quad p_4 : \{(t_2, 3)\},$$
$$p_5 : \{(t_1, 4), (t_2, 4)\},$$

where, for instance, $p_1 : \{(t_1, 1), (t_2, 2)\}$ means that p_1 appears in t_1 and t_2 at the 1st and 2nd place, respectively. Then, if we want to get trajectories whose source and destination are p_1 and p_5, both t_1 and t_2 will be sorted out because both p_1 and p_5 appear in t_1 and t_2 in the correct order (*i.e.*, $1 < 4$ and $2 < 4$); but if p_1 and p_3 are the concerned source and destination, only t_1 will be returned because the order of p_1 and p_3 is incorrect in t_2 although they both appear in in t_1 and t_2.

As the number of taxi trajectories between two cells is a function of time given a fixed cell size, apparently another effective way to get more taxi trajectories is to use more historical data (with longer period of time). As the focus of the paper is on the anomalous trajectory detection method, here we just simply assume that we have sufficient taxi trajectories to form "normal" routes between our interested source and destination cell-pair. Moreover, we can further alleviate this problem by using more historical data. It is worth noting that all above operations allow online updates, thus newly generated taxi trajectories can be easily incorporated.

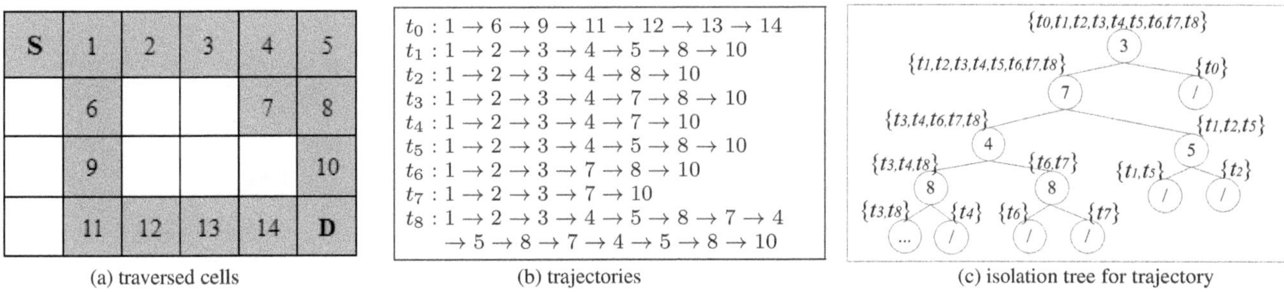

Figure 5. An illustrative example of isolation tree for trajectories partition. (a) cells that are traversed by trajectories (gray, 1 to 14); (b) nine trajectories from S to D, where t_0 and t_8 are significantly different from others; (c) an isolation tree, where the randomly selected cell is shown at each node, the anomalous trajectory t_0 has much shorter path length than other trajectories.

$$
\begin{aligned}
&t_0 : \{t_1, \ldots, t_8\} \xrightarrow{12} \emptyset \\
&t_8 : \{t_0, \ldots, t_7\} \xrightarrow{5} \{t_1, t_5\} \xrightarrow{7} \emptyset \\
&t_3 : \{t_0, t_1, t_2, t_4, \ldots, t_8\} \xrightarrow{3} \{t_1, t_2, t_4, \ldots, t_8\} \\
&\quad \xrightarrow{2} \{t_1, t_2, t_4, \ldots, t_8\} \xrightarrow{7} \{t_4, t_6, t_7, t_8\} \\
&\quad \xrightarrow{8} \{t_6, t_8\}
\end{aligned}
$$

Figure 6. An example of eliminating trajectories by randomly selecting cells from the concerned trajectory, where at each step only the ones that passed the selected cell (superscript of arrow) are kept.

Isolation-Based Anomalous Trajectory Detection

Now, we present our proposed *iBAT* (*i.e.*, Isolation-Based Anomalous Trajectory detection) method.

Characterizing Anomalous Trajectories

Before trying to detect anomalous trajectories, we need to characterize anomalous trajectories precisely. This is not straightforward in practice, because anomalous trajectories can be varied and normal ones can fall into several different clusters (as illustrated in Fig. 1).

Instead of using distance or density measure, we exploit the following two intrinsic properties of anomalous trajectories:

1. anomalous trajectories are *few* in number ;
2. they are *different* from the majority, in particular, they pass *different* locations, or pass similar locations in *different* orders.

Since anomalous trajectories are "*few and different*", normal ones are "*many and similar*". Hence, it is not difficult to find that separating a normal trajectory from the rest requires more effort, since there are "*many*" "*similar*" ones; while anomalous trajectories are easier to be separated from the majority of the trajectories, *i.e.*, they are susceptible to *isolation*. This constitutes the basis of our proposed method.

Adapting iForest for Trajectory Data

Isolation Forest (*iForest*) [20] is a novel anomaly detection method, which adopts a fundamentally different approach to take advantage of anomalies' intrinsic properties of being "few and different". It applies a data-induced random tree to partition all the instances until all of them are isolated (*iTree*). This random partitioning produces noticeable shorter paths for anomalies and long paths for normal instances. When a forest of *iTree*s collectively produce shorter path lengths for some particular points, then these instances are highly likely to be anomalies. By exploiting sub-sampling, *iForest* achieves state-of-the-art performance with low linear time-complexity and small memory-requirement. Unfortunately, *iForest* is designed in the traditional anomaly detection framework where instances are fixed-width vectors, thus it cannot be directly used for anomalous trajectory detection.

Noting that anomalous trajectories often contain points (cells) that are not always contained by other trajectories, we adapt *iForest* to handle our trajectory data based on this property. Specifically, we use a randomly selected cell to recursively divide the trajectories in each node of the *iTree* until the node has only one trajectory or all trajectories at the node are the same. The trajectories that have short path lengths in *iTree* are suspicious to be anomalous. For example, Fig. 5 (b) shows a set of nine trajectories, among which t_0 is significantly different from others; Fig. 5 (a) shows all the 14 cells (gray) that traversed by at least one trajectory; Fig. 5 (c) shows an adapted *iTree*, where a cell is randomly selected at each node for partition. If the trajectory contains this cell, it falls into its left child node, else right child node. For instance, the cell 3 is selected at root node, then t_0 falls to its right child node since it does not pass the cell 3. Finally, we can obtain an *iTree* in Fig. 5 (c), where the path length of the anomalous trajectory t_0 is 1, much smaller than other trajectories. Consequently, after such an adaption, *iForest* can be used for anomalous trajectory detection.

This adapted *iForest* can detect anomalous trajectories that traverse different cells from the majority; but it fails if anomalous trajectories detour in cells that are always contained by other trajectories. For example, the trajectory t_8 is definitively an anomalous trajectory since it detours a lot in the top right area of Fig. 5 (a); but if we build *iTree* as Fig. 5 (c), the path length of t_8 will be not smaller than any other trajectory, which suggests it is a normal trajectory. Obviously, this result is not correct, and a better method is needed.

iBAT: Applying Isolation in a Lazy Learning Manner

Now, we present the *iBAT* method which improves the adapted *iForest* via lazy learning [2]. Lazy learners do not train a model until presented with a test sample, they usually achieve

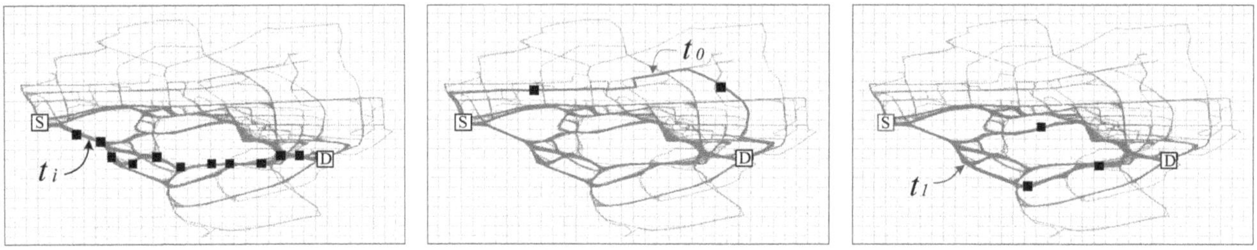

(a) Isolating normal trajectory t_i (b) Isolating anomalous trajectory t_O (c) Isolating anomalous trajectory t_1

Figure 7. Anomalous trajectories are easier to be isolated. In each sub-figure, the test trajectory is highlighted in solid red, while others are in dashed gray. Given a set of 593 trajectories from S to D, (a) a normal trajectory t_i requires 11 randomly selected cells (solid black cells) to be isolated; (b) the anomalous trajectory t_O requires only 2 randomly selected cells to be isolated. (c) the anomalous trajectory t_1 requires only 3 cells.

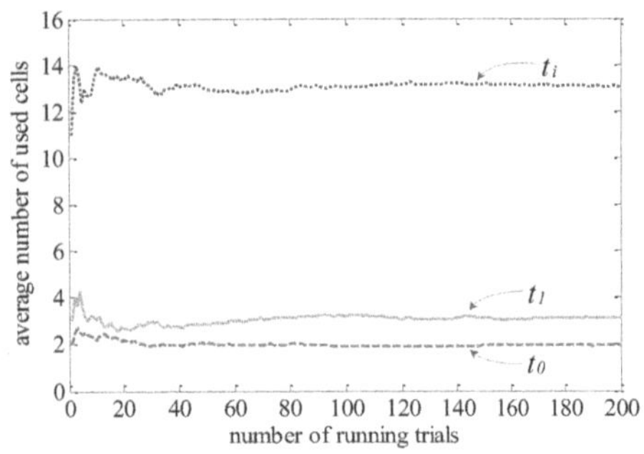

Figure 8. Average number of cells used for isolation, where as in Fig. 7, t_i is a normal trajectory, t_O and t_1 are anomalous.

competitive performance in practical problems, and can trivially adapt to evolving training data.

In particular, rather than building *iTree* based on all the trajectories at hand, *iBAT* focuses on the test trajectory, and tries to separate it from the rest of trajectories by randomly selecting cells solely from the test trajectory. For example, let $T = \{t_0, \ldots, t_8\}$ where t_i's are defined in Fig. 5 (b). If t_0 is a test trajectory, we randomly select one cell from t_0 and remove the trajectories that do not pass the selected cell from the set $T \backslash \{t_0\}$, this process is repeated until no trajectory is left or all the trajectories left contain all the cells t_0 has. As shown in Fig. 6, t_0 is separated from other trajectories after one test; t_8 is isolated after two tests; while t_3 is not separated even after selecting four cells. This indicates that t_0 and t_8 are anomalous, while t_3 is normal. Thus, we can see that the proposed method properly addresses the problem of detecting anomalous trajectories that detour in cells that are always contained by other trajectories (like t_8). In addition, for the loop detours, like t_8 that loops at 4, 5, 8, 7 and $t_9 = 1 \rightarrow 2 \rightarrow 3 \rightarrow 2 \rightarrow 3 \rightarrow 2 \rightarrow 3 \rightarrow 4 \rightarrow 5 \rightarrow 8 \rightarrow 10$ that loops at 2, 3, it is easy to detect them simply by counting the number of each passed cell beforehand.

In Fig. 7, we show a real-world example of isolating trajectories, where the isolation is performed by randomly selecting cells from the test trajectory. It can be observed that a normal trajectory t_i requires 11 randomly selected cells to be isolated, while anomalous trajectory t_O requires only two cells and another anomalous trajectory t_1 requires three cells to be isolated. In particular, t_O requires less cells to be isolated because it contains cells that are not always contained by other trajectories, t_1 is easy to be isolated because it passes cells in a quite different order although these cells are always contained by other trajectories. Subsequently, we denote the number of cells used for isolating the trajectory t as $n(t)$.

Since each cell is randomly selected in each individual isolation process, we estimate the expected number of used cells by averaging the number of used cells over multiple isolation processes. Fig. 8 shows that the average number of used cells for t_i, t_O and t_1 when the number of isolation processes increases. After repeating the random isolation process for 200 times, we can see that the average number of cells needed to isolate t_i converges to 13.11, while those of t_O and t_1 are both less than 3. This shows that the average number of cells used for isolating anomalous trajectories is less than the average used for that of isolating normal ones.

Following [20], we define the *anomaly score* of a trajectory t as a normalization of the average number of used cells, *i.e.*,

$$s(t, N) = 2^{-\frac{E(n(t))}{c(N)}}, \quad (1)$$

where $E(n(t))$ is average number of cells used for isolating t, N is the number of trajectories from which we separate t, and $c(N)$ is the average of $n(t)$ given N (it equals to the average path length of unsuccessful searches in a binary search tree). In particular,

$$c(N) = 2H(N-1) - 2(N-1)/N,$$

where $H(i)$ is the harmonic number that can be estimated as $ln(i) + 0.57721566$ (Euler's constant). Obviously, when $E(n(t)) \rightarrow 0$, $s(t,N) \rightarrow 1$, meaning that t is definitely an anomalous trajectory; when $E(n(t)) > c(N)$, $s(t,N) < 0.5$, meaning that t can safely be categorized as a normal trajectory.

In practice, given a large number of taxi trajectories, we do not need to isolate our trajectory t from the rest, and the isolating process is able to work well with a small sub-sample of all trajectories. Specifically, given one trajectory, our *i-BAT* method repeats the isolation process on different sub-samples of all trajectories and computes the anomaly score according to Eq. 1. The pseudo code of the *iBAT* method is summarized in Algorithm 1. Besides the test trajectory t and the set of trajectories T, it has two parameters, *i.e.*, number of running trials m and sub-sample size ψ. Unless otherwise stated, we use $m = 100$ and $\psi = 256$ in our experiments.

Algorithm 1 The *iBAT* method

Input: t – test trajectory
T – set of trajectories to be separated from
m – number of running trials
ψ – sub-sample size
Process:
let n be a vector of m zeros (n_i's are zeros)
for $i = 1$ to m **do**
$T' \leftarrow$ randomly sample ψ trajectories from T
repeat
$n_i \leftarrow n_i + 1$
randomly choose a cell p from t
$T' \leftarrow$ select the trajectories that include p from T'
until T' is empty
end for
compute $s(t, \psi)$ according to Equation 1
Output: anomaly score $s(t, \psi)$

An analysis on these two parameters can be found in the evaluation section which shows that the performance is nearly optimal at this setting and insensitive to a wide range of values. Furthermore, as each isolation process is independent, *iBAT* can be implemented with parallel techniques.

Discussion

By applying the isolation mechanism in a lazy learning manner, our proposed *iBAT* method solves the problem of anomalous trajectory detection with the following characteristics:

- By exploiting anomalous trajectories' intrinsic properties of being *"few and different"*, it is able to detect different kinds of anomalous trajectories.
- By applying the isolation mechanism, it provides a simple but effective way for detecting anomalous trajectories, no distance or density measure is needed.
- By working in a lazy learning manner, it naturally incorporates newly-generated taxi trajectories, thus can detect an emerging cluster of anomalous trajectories and hence the road network change promptly.
- By utilizing sub-sampling, it has the capacity to handle very large-scale set of trajectories, whilst keeping high performance and low processing-time..

Applications Based on Anomalous Trajectory Detection

With the anomalous trajectories detected and the characteristics of *iBAT*, different applications can be developed. For instance, if the travel distance of an anomalous trajectory is close to or shorter than that of the normal trajectories, then the route can be recommended to mission critical drivers in emergency cases; if the route is detected as a new path with many similar trajectories accumulating, then it can be used to update the road network change in the digital map. If the travel distance is much longer than normal ones, it is suspicious to be a driving fraud; further evidences can be collected to see if the case is caused by a traffic jam, or unfamiliarity with the area, or intentional fraud. Two potential applications will be further elaborated in next section.

EMPIRICAL EVALUATION

In this section, we provide an empirical evaluation of our proposed approach, and demonstrate its potential to enable practical applications.

Experimental Setup

In the experiments, we use a real-world taxi GPS dataset, which is collected from more than 7600 taxis served in a large city in China (Hangzhou) for one year (actually, the data in March 2010 has been used and found sufficient for this experiments). In this dataset, each taxi is equipped with a GPS device with a sampling-rate of about one record per minute. For each record, there are four fields: *latitude*, *longitude*, *passenger status* and *timestamp*. For the sake of simplicity in computation and visualization, we restrict our interest within the metropolitan area of Hangzhou with longitude [120.0°E, 120.5°E] and latitude [30.15°N, 30.40°N], the invalid records and those beyond this area are discarded. We discretize the area into a 100 × 200 grid cells, each corresponding to a $250m \times 250m$ square.

To provide a quantitative evaluation, we pick up five source-destination cell-pair[1], and ask three volunteers to *manually* label whether the trajectories are anomalous or not, in particular, if one volunteer thinks a taxi trajectory is anomalous, it is labeled to be anomalous. The datasets are summarized in Table 1, and visualized in Fig. 9.

Table 1. Datasets used in our experiments.

	# Trajectories	# Anomalies	Ratio
T-1	1418	41	2.89%
T-2	895	58	6.48%
T-3	593	43	7.25%
T-4	669	33	4.93%
T-5	649	36	5.55%

Table 2. The contingency table.

		Real Value	
		Anomalous	*Normal*
Detection Result	*Anomalous*	TP	FP
	Normal	FN	TN

For comparison purposes, we use the density-based method as a baseline, whose basic idea is to rank trajectories according to its density. Specifically, the density of a trajectory is the averaged density of all its cells, and the density of a cell is the number of trajectories that pass through it.

The evaluation criteria we use is AUC (Area Under ROC Curve) [4]. In practice, detection rate (dr, *i.e.*, the fraction of anomalous trajectories that are successfully detected) and false alarm rate (flr, *i.e.*, the fraction of normal ones that are predicted to be anomalous) are two important measures to evaluate the performance of an anomaly detection method. Based on Table 2, they are defined as

$$dr = \frac{TP}{TP + FN} \quad \text{and} \quad flr = \frac{FP}{FP + TN}.$$

[1]The source and destination are $500m \times 500m$ grid-cells.

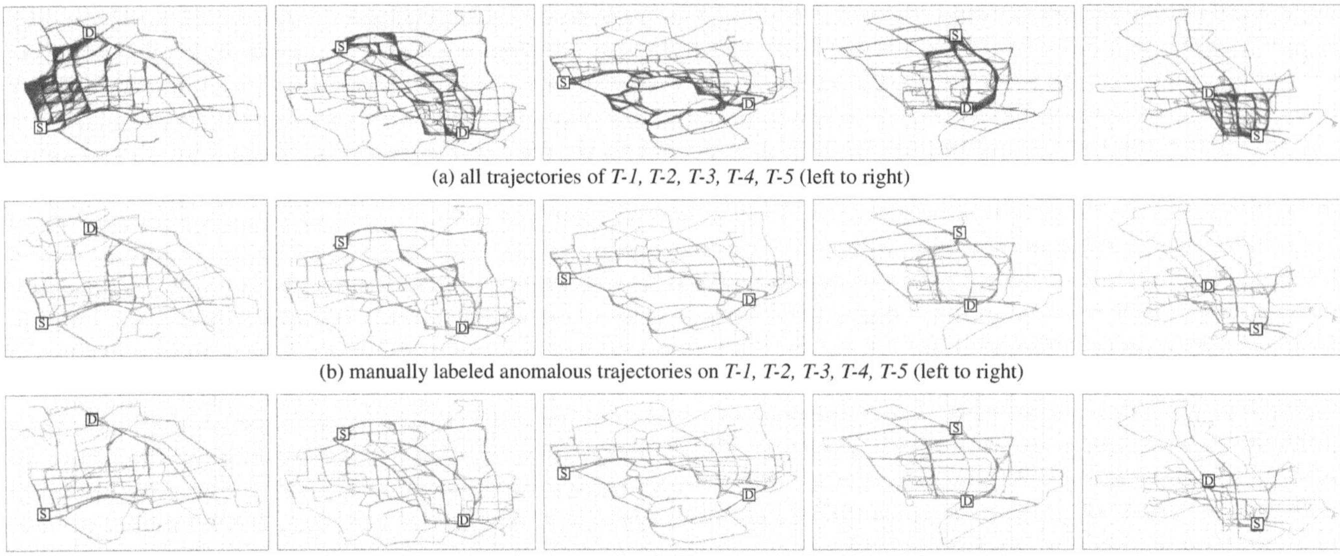

(a) all trajectories of *T-1, T-2, T-3, T-4, T-5* (left to right)

(b) manually labeled anomalous trajectories on *T-1, T-2, T-3, T-4, T-5* (left to right)

(c) anomalous trajectories detected by iBAT on *T-1, T-2, T-3, T-4, T-5* (left to right)

Figure 9. Visualization of taxi trajectories, where S and D are source and destination. (top row: all trajectories; center row: manually labeled anomalous trajectories; bottom: anomalous trajectories detected by iBAT, with the same number of manually labeled anomalies)

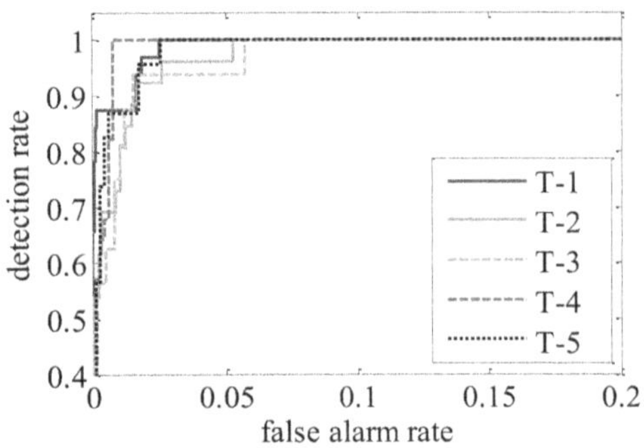

Figure 10. The ROC curves of *iBAT*. For better illustration, the ranges of false alarm rate and detection rate are set to [0, 0.2] and [0.4, 1].

Obviously, a good anomaly detection method should have both high detection rate and low false alarm rate. The ROC curve shows the detection rate (y-axis) against the false alarm rate (x-axis), and the AUC value is defined as the area under the ROC curve. As a statistical explanation, the AUC value is equal to the probability that a randomly chosen anomalous trajectory is ranked higher than a randomly chosen normal one. Obviously, if the AUC value is close to 1, the anomaly detection method is of high quality.

The experiments are run in Matlab on an Intel Xeon W3500 PC with 4GB RAM running Windows 7.

Experimental Results

We first provide a visualization of the detection results in Fig. 9, where manually labeled anomalous trajectories and the anomalous trajectories detected by *iBAT* (the same number of manually labeled anomalies) are depicted. We can see that the visualization of detected results are very similar to that of manually labeled data, which indicates that *iBAT* is effective in detecting anomalous trajectories.

Table 3. The AUC value of *iBAT* and density-based method.

	T-1	*T-2*	*T-3*	*T-4*	*T-5*
iBAT	0.9972	0.9936	0.9923	0.9970	0.9958
Density	0.9448	0.9491	0.9435	0.9712	0.9386

Fig. 10 depicts the ROC curves of *iBAT* on each dataset. We can find that *iBAT* is able to achieve high detection rate whilst keeping low false alarm rate. For all datasets, over 90% of anomalous trajectories can be detected at the false alarm rate of 2%; especially on *T-4*, 100% detection rate is achieved at the false alarm rate of less than 1%.

Table 3 compares the AUC value of *iBAT* with that of the density-based method. We can see that *iBAT* achieves quite high AUC values (>0.99 on all datasets) and the density-based method achieves lower AUC values (<0.95 on 4 datasets, 0.97 on *T-4*), suggesting that *iBAT* makes a better ranking than the density-based method. This is not difficult to understand, because the density-based method can only detect trajectories that pass through low-density cells and it ranks trajectories that detour on high-density cells lower, but our proposed method can detect both these two types of anomalous trajectories. In fact, this is also the reason why the density-based method achieves relatively higher AUC value on *T-4* than on other datasets, because there are less anomalous trajectories that detour on high-density cells.

In addition, we study *iBAT*'s performance and time efficiency in relation to the number of running trails m and sub-sampling size ψ. Specifically, we run experiments on the largest dataset *T-1*, and record the AUC value and processing time for $m \in [1, 200]$ and $\psi \in \{2, 4, 8, 16, \ldots, 1024\}$. Fig. 11 shows how the AUC value and processing time change with respect to m, where ψ is set to 256. It can be seen that

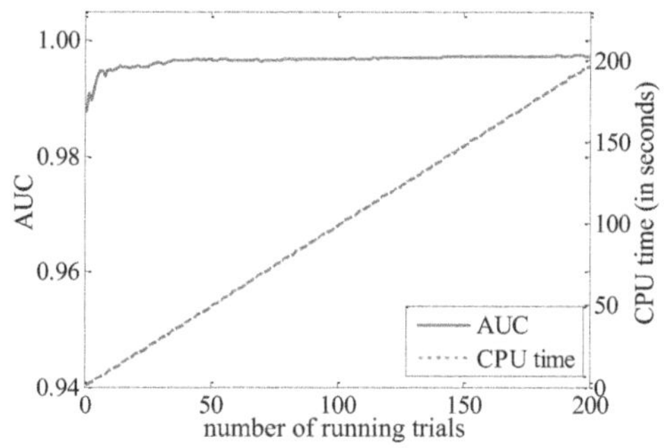

Figure 11. The AUC value (left y-axis, red solid) converges at a small m (x-axis), and processing time (right y-axis, green dashed) increases linearly with m.

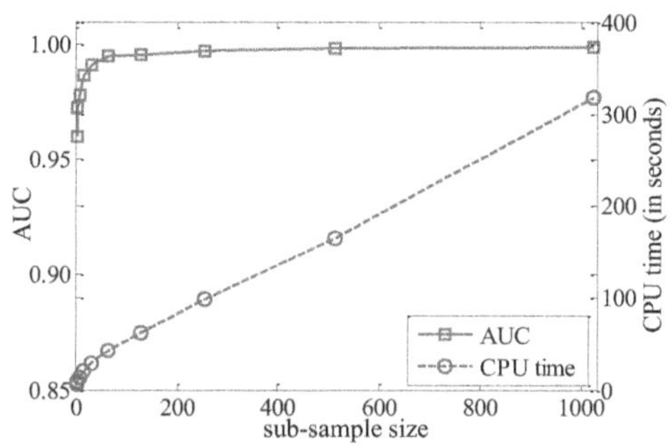

Figure 12. A small sub-sampling size provides both high AUC (left y-axis, red solid) and low processing time (right y-axis, green dashed).

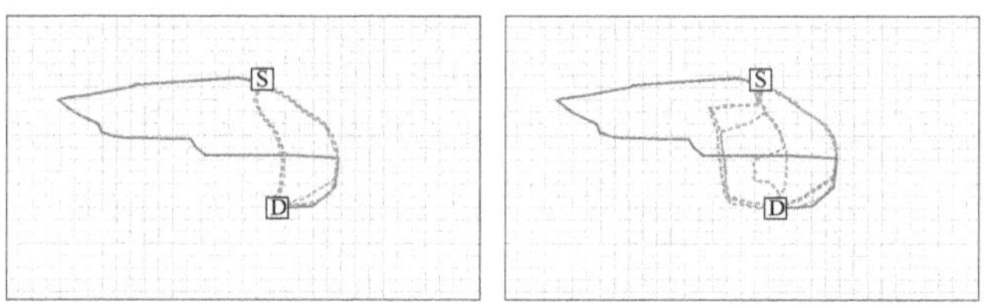

(a) (b)

Figure 13. Avoiding excuses for taxi driving fraud detection. (a) the anomalous trajectory (red solid) is compared with previous trips of the same driver (green dashed); (b) the anomalous trajectory is compared with trajectories in the same time slot (green dashed).

the AUC value converges at a small m, and processing time increases linearly with m. Also, *iBAT* is quite efficient, for instance, when $m = 100$ the overall precessing time is about 100 seconds, about 0.07 second per trajectory. Of course, this can be further improved by parallel computing since every trial of *iBAT* is independent. In Fig. 12, we show how the performance changes with respect to ψ, where m is set to 100. It can be seen that both high AUC and low processing time can be obtained at a small sub-sample size.

Taxi Driving Fraud

As Fig. 9 shows, many detected anomalous trajectories are long-distance detours, which may correspond to taxi driving frauds. Therefore, detecting anomalous taxi trajectories can help building taxi driving fraud detection systems.

For detecting taxi driving frauds, a practical challenge is that some taxi drivers, responsible for anomalous taxi trajectories, may be truly unfamiliar with this area and some cunning drivers may use this as an excuse. Moreover, for some suspected frauds, someone may argue that they took a different route due to unexpected car accidents or heavy traffic. In this case, more evidence is needed to verify the fraud. Here, since we have all taxi trajectories between source and destination, if an anomalous trajectory is detected, we can get all previous trajectories of the corresponding driver to check whether he used to travel frequently in this area; meanwhile, we can also find all the trajectories that took place around the same time to check the traffic related excuses. For example, given an anomalous trajectory (red solid) in Fig. 13 (a), we compare it with the driver's previous trips (green dashed) between the same source and destination in Fig. 13 (b) and can see that this driver often operates in this area. Meanwhile, in Fig. 13 (b) we compare it with all the trips (green dashed) that happened around that time, and can see many other drivers did not detour. Based on these, we can deny possible excuses and confirm the fraud.

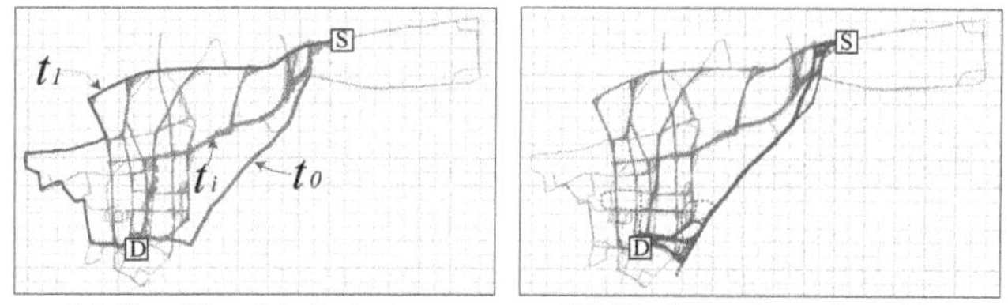

(a) Considered trajectories (b) Similar trajectories with t_0

Figure 14. Trajectories considered for road network change detection. (a) three trajectories considered: two anomalous trajectories t_0 and t_1 (red solid and blue solid), one normal trajectory t_i (green dashed); (b) 160 trajectories (dark red dashed) that are similar to t_0.

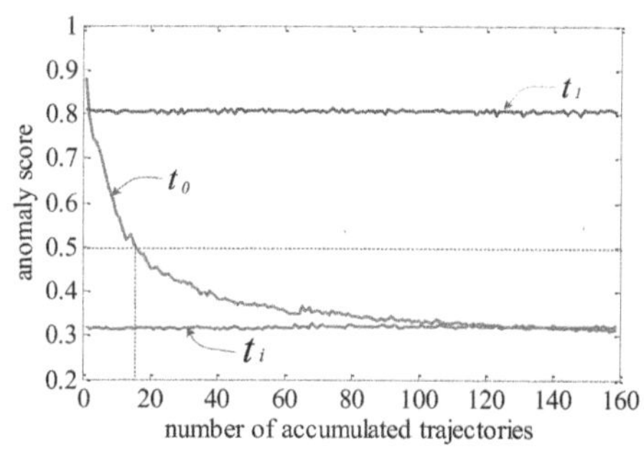

Figure 15. The anomaly score of t_0 decrease rapidly when similar trajectories are accumulating, but that of t_1 and t_1 keeps almost the same.

Road Network Change

As mentioned before, if more and more similar anomalous trajectories are accumulating, it may be an indication that a new road has been built or an old road is blocked in the area. We explain this via an example. As shown in Fig. 14 (a), we consider two anomalous trajectories t_0 and t_1 and one normal trajectory t_i. In addition, Fig. 14 (b) depicts a set of 160 trajectories that are similar to t_0. Then, to see the impact of accumulating trajectories, we add these 160 trajectories into the original trajectory set one by one, and study how the anomaly score of t_0, t_1 and t_i changes. The result is shown in Fig. 15, where we can see that the anomaly score of t_1 and t_i remain basically unchanged, while that of t_0 is reduced from about 0.9 to 0.3, which means that t_0 has definitively become a normal trajectory from an anomalous one. In particular, after adding 18 similar trajectories, the anomaly score is reduced from 0.9 to 0.5. Hence, in real-world applications, if an anomalous trajectory becomes normal, like t_0, it corresponds to a change in the road network.

CONCLUSION AND FUTURE WORK

In this paper, we have investigated the problem of detecting anomalous driving trajectories from taxi's GPS trace, which is motivated by the fact that anomalous trajectories can reveal many hidden "facts" about the city dynamics and human behaviors and thus can be used to enable innovative applications. To solve the problem, we first grouped taxi trajectories crossing the same source-destination cell-pair and represented each taxi trajectory as a sequence of symbols. We then proposed the *iBAT* method to detect anomalous trajectories. Specifically, instead of profiling the normal trajectories or utilizing the distance or density measure, *iBAT* exploits anomalous trajectories' intrinsic properties of being *"few and different"*, and applied the isolation mechanism to detect anomalous trajectories. We validate our approach in real-world taxi GPS data, and show that it achieves remarkable performance (AUC>0.99, detecting over 90% of anomalous trajectories at the false alarm rate of less than 2%). Furthermore, we show the potential of anomalous trajectories in enabling innovative applications, by two examples: taxi driving fraud detection and prompt road network change detection.

In the future, we plan to broaden this work in several directions. First, we will attempt to exploit other information enclosed in GPS traces such as driving speed for anomalous trajectories detection. Second, we would like to develop practical taxi driving fraud detection and road network change detection systems. Third, we are interested in detecting anomalous trajectories before the trips are complete.

ACKNOWLEDGEMENTS

The authors want to thank anonymous reviewers for helpful comments and Pablo S. Castro for comments and inputs. This research was supported by the Institut TELECOM "Futur et ruptures" Program, the Paris-Region SYSTEM@TIC Smart City Program, NSFC (61021062, 60803109), JiangsuSF (BK2008018), 973 Program (2010CB327903), 863 Program (2009AA011900). This work was done when Nan Li was visiting Institut TELECOM SudParis, France.

REFERENCES

1. N. Abe, B. Zadrozny, and J. Langford. Outlier detection by active learning. In *Proc. KDD 2006*, pages 504–509, 2006.
2. D. Aha. *Lazy Learning*. Springer, 1997.
3. F. Angiulli and F. Fassetti. Dolphin: An efficient algorithm for mining distance-based outliers in very large datasets. *ACM-TKDD*, 3(1), 2009.
4. A. P. Bradley. The use of the area under the ROC curve in the evaluation of machine learning algorithms. *Pattern Recognition*, 30(7):1145 – 1159, 1997.
5. M. M. Breunig, H.-P. Kriegel, R. T. Ng, and J. Sander. LOF: Identifying density-based local outliers. In *Proc. SIGMOD 2000*, pages 93–104, 2000.
6. Y. Bu, L. Chen, A. W.-C. Fu, and D. Liu. Efficient anomaly monitoring over moving object trajectory streams. In *Proc. KDD 2009*, pages 159–168, 2009.
7. L. Cao and J. Krumm. From GPS traces to a routable road map. In *Proc. GIS 2009*, pages 3–12, 2009.
8. J. Froehlich and J. Krumm. Route prediction from trip observations. In *Proc. SAE 2008*, pages 1031–1038, 2008.
9. Y. Ge, H. Xiong, Z.-H. Zhou, H. Ozdemir, J. Yu, and K. C. Lee. Top-Eye: Top-k evolving trajectory outlier detection. In *Proc. CIKM 2010*, pages 1733–1736, 2010.
10. M. C. Gonzalez, C. A. Hidalgo, and A.-L. Barabasi. Understanding individual human mobility patterns. *Nature*, 453(5):779–782, 2008.
11. Z. He, X. Xu, and S. Deng. Discovering cluster-based local outliers. *Pattern Recognition Letters*, 24(9-10):1641–1650, 2003.
12. E. M. Knorr, R. T. Ng, and V. Tucakov. Distance-based outliers: Algorithms and applications. *VLDB Journal*, 8(3-4):237–253, 2000.
13. J. Krumm and E. Horvitz. Predestination: Inferring destinations from partial trajectories. In *Proc. Ubicomp 2006*, pages 243–260, 2006.
14. J.-G. Lee, J. Han, and X. Li. Trajectory outlier detection: A partition-and-detect framework. In *Proc. ICDE 2008*, pages 140–149, 2008.
15. B. Li, D. Zhang, L. Sun, C. Chen, S. Li, G. Qi, and Q. Yang. Hunting or waiting? discovering passenger-finding strategies from a large-scale real-world taxi dataset. In *MUCS'11 in conjunction with PerCom 2011*, pages 63–68, 2011.
16. X. Li, J. Han, S. Kim, and H. Gonzalez. ROAM: Rule- and motif-based anomaly detection in massive moving object data sets. In *Proc. SDM 2007*, pages 273–284, 2007.
17. X. Li, Z. Li, J. Han, and J.-G. Lee. Temporal outlier detection in vehicle traffic data. In *Proc. ICDE 2009*, pages 1319–1322, 2009.
18. L. Liao, D. J. Patterson, D. Fox, and H. Kautz. Learning and inferring transportation routines. *Artificial Intelligence*, 171(5-6):311–331, 2007.
19. Z. Liao, Y. Yu, and B. Chen. Anomaly detection in GPS data based on visual analytics. In *Proc. VAST 2010*, pages 51–58, 2010.
20. F. T. Liu, K. M. Ting, and Z.-H. Zhou. Isolation forest. In *Proc. ICDM 2008*, pages 413–422, 2008.
21. L. Liu, C. Andrisa, and C. Rattia. Uncovering cabdrivers' behavior patterns from their digital traces. *Computers, Environment and Urban Systems*, 34(6):541 – 548, 2010.
22. D. J. Patterson, L. Liao, D. Fox, and H. A. Kautz. Inferring high-level behavior from low-level sensors. In *Proc. Ubicomp 2003*, pages 73–89, 2003.
23. S. Phithakkitnukoon, M. Veloso, C. Bento, A. Biderman, and C. Ratti. Taxi-aware map: Identifying and predicting vacant taxis in the city. In *Proc. AmI 2010*, pages 86–95, 2010.
24. G. Qi, X. Li, S. Li, G. Pan, and D. Zhang. Measuring social functions of city regions from large-scale taxi behaviors. In *Proc. PerCom 2011*, pages 21–25, 2010.
25. R. R. Sillito and R. B. Fisher. Semi-supervised learning for anomalous trajectory detection. In *Proc. BMVC 2008*, pages 1035–1044, 2008.
26. J. Yuan, Y. Zheng, C. Zhang, W. Xie, X. Xie, G. Sun, and Y. Huang. T-drive: Driving directions based on taxi trajectories. In *Proc. GIS 2010*, pages 99–108, 2010.
27. D. Zhang, B. Guo, and Z. Yu. The emergence of social and community intelligence. *IEEE-Computer*, July:21–28, 2011.
28. V. W. Zheng, B. Cao, Y. Zheng, X. Xie, and Q. Yang. Collaborative filtering meets mobile recommendation: A user-centered approach. In *Proc. AAAI 2010*, 2010.
29. Y. Zheng, L. Zhang, X. Xie, and W.-Y. Ma. Mining interesting locations and travel sequences from GPS trajectories. In *Proc. WWW 2009*, pages 791–800, 2009.
30. B. D. Ziebart, A. L. Maas, A. K. Dey, and J. A. Bagnell. Navigate like a cabbie: probabilistic reasoning from observed context-aware behavior. In *Proc. Ubicomp 2008*, pages 322–331, 2008.
31. J. Zobel and A. Moffat. Inverted files for text search engines. *ACM Computing Surveys*, 38(2), 2006.

Where to Find My Next Passenger?

Jing Yuan[1,2], Yu Zheng[2], Liuhang Zhang[1,2], Xing Xie[2] and Guangzhong Sun[1]
[1]University of Science and Technology of China
[2]Microsoft Research Asia
yuanjing@mail.ustc.edu.cn, {yuzheng,xing.xie}@microsoft.com

ABSTRACT
We present a recommender for taxi drivers and people expecting to take a taxi, using the knowledge of 1) passengers' mobility patterns and 2) taxi drivers' pick-up behaviors learned from the GPS trajectories of taxicabs. First, this recommender provides taxi drivers with some locations and the routes to these locations, towards which they are more likely to pick up passengers quickly (during the routes or at these locations) and maximize the profit. Second, it recommends people with some locations (within a walking distance) where they can easily find vacant taxis. In our method, we learn the above knowledge (represented by probabilities) from GPS trajectories of taxis. Then, we feed the knowledge into a probabilistic model which estimates the profit of the candidate locations for a particular driver based on where and when the driver requests for the recommendation. We validate our recommender using historical trajectories generated by over 12,000 taxis during 110 days.

Author Keywords
Taxicab, recommender, parking place

ACM Classification Keywords
H.2.8 Database Management: data mining, spatial databases and GIS.

General Terms
Algorithms, Design, Experimentation, Performance

INTRODUCTION
Taxicabs play an important role in people's commute between public and private transports. A significant number of people are traveling by taxis in their daily lives around the world. According to a recent survey about the taxi service of New York City [7], 41% people take a taxi per week and 25% of the respondents take a taxi everyday. However, on one hand, to facilitate people's travel, major cities, like New York, Tokyo, London, and Beijing, have a huge number of taxis traversing in urban areas. The vacant taxis cruising on roads not only waste gas and time of a taxi driver but also generate additional traffic in a city. Thus, how to improve the utilization of these taxis and reduce the energy consumption effectively poses an urgent challenge. On the other hand, many people feel frustrated and anxious when they are unable to find a taxicab after waiting for a long time.

To address this issue, we propose a recommender for both taxi drivers and passengers using a huge number of historical GPS trajectories of taxis. Specifically, on one hand, given the geo-position and time of a taxicab looking for passengers, we suggest the taxi driver with a location, towards which he/she is most likely to pick up a passenger as soon as possible and maximize the profit of the next trip, as demonstrated in Figure 1 A). This recommendation helps to reduce the cruising (without a fare) time of a taxi thus saves energy consumption and eases the exhaust pollution as well as helps the drivers to make more profit. On the other hand, we provide people expecting to take a taxi with the locations (within a walking distance) where they are most likely to find a vacant taxicab, as shown in Figure 1 B). Using our recommender, a taxi will find passengers more quickly and people will take a taxi more easily; therefore, reduces the above-mentioned problem to some extent.

A) Taxi recommender B) Passenger recommender

Figure 1. Recommendation scenario

Recently, in many big cities, like New York, Beijing and Singapore, taxicabs are equipped with GPS sensors for dispatching and safety. Typically, these taxis will report their present locations to a data center in a certain frequency, e.g., 2 minutes [12]. Besides a geo-position and timestamp, the occupancy information of a taxi is also recorded (using some weight sensor or by connecting a taxi meter with the embedded GPS device). Therefore a large number of such GPS trajectories with occupancy information are being generated everyday. Intuitively, these taxi trajectories contain two aspects of knowledge. One is passengers' mobility, i.e., where and when passengers get on and off a taxi. The other is taxis' pick-up behaviors. For example, where the high-profit taxi drivers usually go and how they can find passengers quickly. With these two aspects of knowledge, we can recommend locations with high-probability to pick up a passenger to the taxi driver and suggest locations where a passenger is easy to find a vacant taxi.

The major contribution of this work lies in the following aspects:

- We propose an approach for accurately detecting *parking places* from the GPS trajectories of a large number of taxis. These parking places stand for the locations where taxi drivers usually wait for passengers with their taxis parked. From these parking places, we can calculate the probability of picking up a passenger if the driver goes towards a parking place (including the situation that the driver picks up a passenger when cruising), hence, enable the recommender for taxi drivers.
- We devise a probabilistic model to formulate the time-dependent taxi behaviors (pick-up/drop-off/cruising/parking), both on road segments and in parking places, based on which, we build the recommendation solution for taxi drivers and passengers. We devise a partition-and-group framework to learn the citywide statistical knowledge so as to provide just-in-time recommendations with time varying information learned from the historical data.
- We evaluate our method using a large number (12,000 taxis during 110 days) of historical GPS trajectories generated by taxicabs. The evaluation results validate that our method can effectively suggest the taxi drivers with locations towards which the driver can make more profit and save cruising time.

OVERVIEW

Preliminary

DEFINITION 1 (ROAD SEGMENT). A *road segment* r is a directed edge that is associated with a direction symbol $r.dir$ (one-way or bidirectional), two terminal points $r.s$ and $r.e$, road level $r.level$ (e.g., level-0 roads are mainly highways), as well as the travel time $r.t$.

DEFINITION 2 (ROUTE). A *route* R is a sequence of connected road segments, i.e., R: $r_1 \rightarrow r_2 \rightarrow \cdots \rightarrow r_n$, where $r_{k+1}.s = r_k.e$, $(1 \leq k < n)$. The start point and end point of a route can be represented as $R.s = r_1.s$ and $R.e = r_n.e$.

DEFINITION 3 (STATE). We consider three states for a working taxi: *occupied* ($\mathcal{O}$), *cruising* ($\mathcal{C}$) and *parking* ($\mathcal{P}$), detailed in Table 1. The taxi is *non-occupied* for both cruising and parking states.

State	Taxi Status
Occupied ($\mathcal{O}$)	A taxi is occupied by a passenger.
Cruising ($\mathcal{C}$)	A taxi is traveling without a passenger.
Parking ($\mathcal{P}$)	A taxi is waiting for a passenger.

Table 1. The states of a taxi

Note that the "parking" state proposed in this paper is the status that taxi drivers wait somewhere for business, i.e., stay and/or queue for a while with the intention to get a passenger on-board. This status is frequently found at airports, hotels, shopping centers, etc. We call these places where the taxis frequently wait for passengers as *parking places*. Note the parking place here does not merely imply a parking lot for private vehicles (which is the typical definition for "parking place").

DEFINITION 4 (TRAJECTORY and TRIP). A taxi *trajectory* is a sequence of GPS points logged for a working taxi, where each point p has the following fields: time stamp $p.t$, latitude $p.lat$, longitude $p.lon$, located road segment (provided by map matching algorithms [13]) $p.r$, state $p.s$ (The raw GPS trajectory only indicates whether a point is occupied or non-occupied). A taxi *trip* is a sub-trajectory which has a single state, either cruising (need to be inferred) or occupied. Refer to Figure 2 for an example. Note that a taxi could generate multiple trips between two parking places.

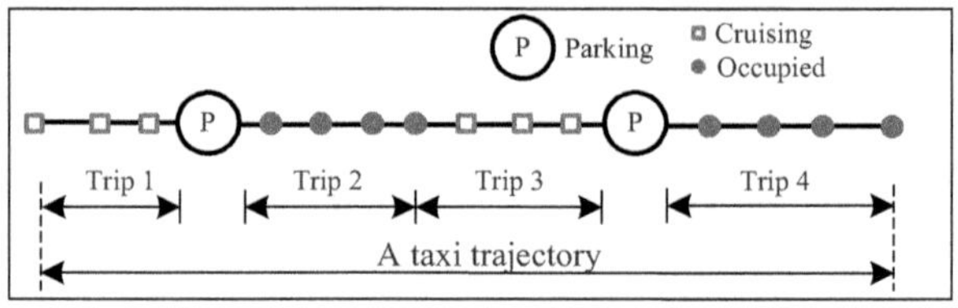

Figure 2. Taxi trajectory and taxi trip

Motivation

Different from other public transports like buses or subways, which follow the fixed routes everyday, taxi drivers plan their own routes once they drop off a passenger. This is the main reason that different drivers get discrepant incomes. Figure 3 reveals some statistics w.r.t. 12,000 taxicabs during 110 days. As shown in Figure 3(a), the profit of a taxi driver can be measured by the fare (occupied) distance per unit working time, based on which, we divide the taxi drivers into 3 groups, the top 10% are regarded as high-profit drivers, the bottom 10% are considered as the low-profit drivers and the rests are medium part.

There is no doubt that at peak hours, the taxicabs are easy to find passengers. i.e., the taxis are often in short supply. However, at off-peak hours, the gap between the high-profit drivers and the low-profit drivers becomes obvious. Figure 3(b) further shows the time-variant occupied ratio (the quotient between the occupied distance and the whole distance) pertaining to the high/low-profit taxi drivers as well as the overall occupied ratio changing during a day. It's clear that from 10am to 3pm, the gap between the high-profit drivers and low-profit drivers is more significant. The critical factor determining the profit of a taxi driver depends on two folds.

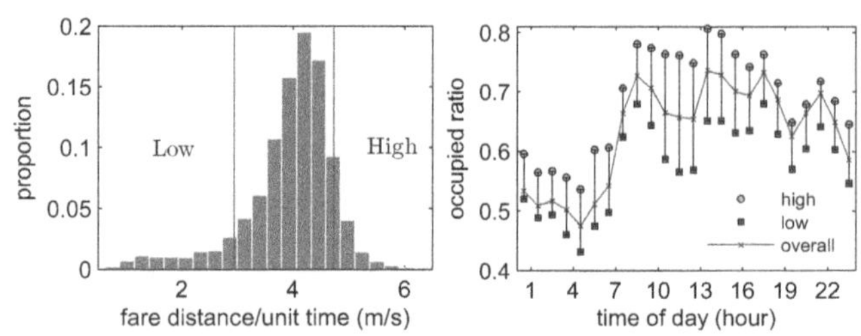

(a) Distribution of profit (b) Occupied ratio during a day

Figure 3. Statistics on the profit distribution and occupied ratio

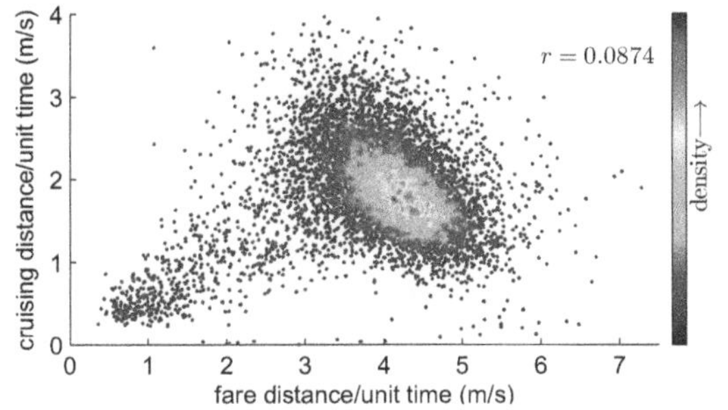

Figure 4. Density scatter of cruising distance/unit time w.r.t. profit

One is that the driver should know the places where he/she can pick up passengers quickly given a particular time of day. The other is the length of the typical trips that originate from a pick-up place. As we know, transportation terminals, shopping centers and hotels all generate demand for taxi service. A professional taxi driver usually knows when certain planes and trains arrive, when the movie is over at a local theater and even what time shifts change at certain businesses.

Typically, for experienced local drivers, instead of random cruising, they usually have a place to go with the intention to pick up new passengers after dropping off a passenger. Figure 4 presents an informative density scatter of the cruising distance per unit time w.r.t. the profit (measured by fare distance per unit time) for the time interval 10am to 3pm. The Pearson correlation coefficient of these two variables is only 0.0874 according to the plotted data. The color indicates the density of a point. This figure shows us that cruising more does not mean earning more. Instead, waiting at some right places may bring more chance to pick up a passenger. As shown in the figure, quite a few drivers cruise more than the majority (the points on the upper left corner of the hot kernel), however, their profit is lower. The right bottom parts (of the hot kernel) are the drivers who earn more but cruise less than the majority. We also conduct a survey among more than 10 local taxi drivers. According to their answers, after they drop off a passenger, 8 of them often have an intentionally nearby destination (the parking place we defined) to go, especially at off-peak hours. Based on their experience, rather than wasting gas when random cruising, they prefer to wait at a parking place with more chance to get a passenger.

Framework

The framework is illustrated in Figure 5. We develop an approach to detect the parking places from GPS trajectories and segment the GPS trajectories according to Definition 4, then map-match the GPS trajectories to road networks using the IVMM algorithm [13], which outperforms other approaches for low-sampling-rate GPS trajectories. Later, we utilize the detected parking places and the mapped trajectories to learn the time-dependent taxi behaviors. These processes are performed offline and will be repeated only when the trajectory data is updated. Leveraging the learned statistical results, we formulate a probabilistic model to integrate the taxi behaviors on each road segment and parking place as well as the mobility patterns of passengers. Based on this model, we perform real-time recommendations to taxi drivers and passengers, given their locations and current times.

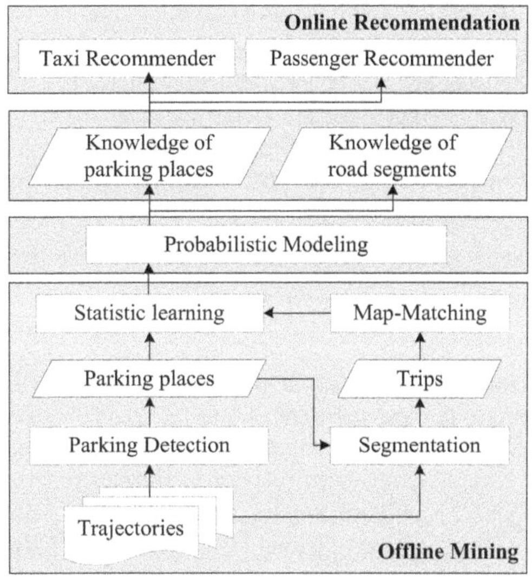

Figure 5. System Overview

MODEL DESCRIPTION

Taxi Recommender

The taxi recommender aims to *provide the taxi drivers with the best parking places and the routes to these parking places*. But how to define a "good" parking place? After a taxi drops off a passenger at time T_0, what the driver hopes is to find a new passenger as soon as possible. It would be best that the next trip is as long as possible, thus the driver can earn more money from the next trip. So a good parking place should bring a *high probability* (during the routes or at the parking places) to get a passenger, a *short waiting time* and a *long distance* of the next trip.

DEFINITION 5 (ACTION Λ_{RP}). *Assume P is a certain parking place and $R : r_1 \to r_2 \to \ldots \to r_n$ is a route to P. We say the driver takes action Λ_{RP} if he/she drives along R until finding a new passenger and waits at P for at most $t_{\max}$ time if he/she fails to pick up a passenger along R.*

In this subsection, the model of taxi recommender is described by answering the following questions:

1. How likely will the driver pick up a passenger if he/she takes the action Λ_{RP}?
2. If the driver takes action Λ_{RP} and succeeds in finding a new passenger, what is the expected duration from T_0 to the beginning of the next trip?
3. If the driver takes action Λ_{RP} and succeeds in finding a new passenger, how long is the expected distance/travel time of the next trip ?

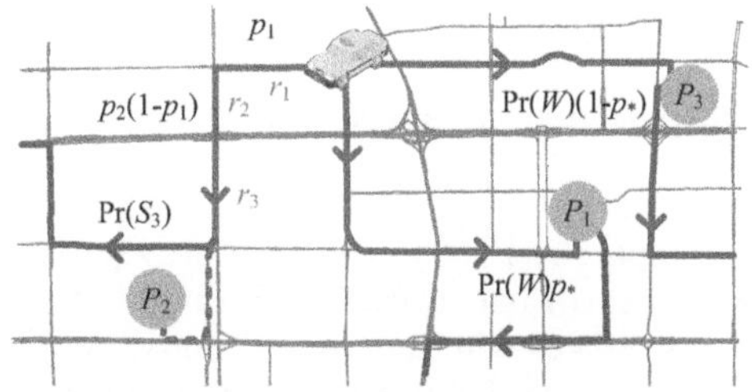

Figure 6. Taxi recommendation model

The Probability of Picking up the Next Passenger

As shown in Figure 6, if the driver takes action Λ_{RP}, he may pick-up a passenger on R; or pick-up a passenger at P; or fail to pick-up a passenger after waiting at P for $t_{\max}$ time. Let S be the event that the driver *succeeds* in picking up the next passenger if he/she takes the action Λ_{RP} and $\overline{S}$ be the opposite situation (fails to get the next passenger). Then we have

$$S = \bigcup_{i=1}^{n+1} S_i, \tag{1}$$

where S_i for $i = 1, 2, \ldots, n$ is the event that the driver picks up a passenger at road segment r_i, and S_{n+1} is the event that the driver picks up a passenger at the parking place. Note that both S and S_i are with respect to the current time T_0. Let $t_i = \sum_{j=1}^{i} r_j.t$, i.e., the travel time from the start point to r_i. Denote the probability that a cruising taxi picks up a passenger at road segment r_i and at time $T_0 + t_i$ by

$$p_i = \Pr(\mathcal{C} \rightsquigarrow \mathcal{O} | r_i, T_0 + t_i). \tag{2}$$

Let

$$p_* = \Pr(\mathcal{P} \overset{(0,t_{\max}]}{\rightsquigarrow} \mathcal{O} | T_0 + t_n) \tag{3}$$

be the probability that a taxi succeeds in picking up a passenger at parking place P and waiting time $T_P \in (0, t_{\max}]$ if the driver reaches P at $T_0 + t_n$. Then

$$\Pr(S_i) = \begin{cases} p_1, & i = 1 \\ p_i \prod_{j=1}^{i-1} (1 - p_j), & i = 2, 3, \ldots, n, \\ p_* \prod_{j=1}^{n} (1 - p_j), & i = n + 1. \end{cases} \tag{4}$$

Now the answer of question 1 is clear:

$$\boxed{\begin{aligned} \Pr(S) &= 1 - \Pr(\overline{\bigcup_{i=1}^{n+1} S_i}) \\ &= 1 - (1 - p_*) \prod_{j=1}^{n} (1 - p_j). \end{aligned}} \tag{5}$$

The factor $\prod_{j=1}^{n}(1 - p_j)$ in Equation 5 is the probability that the driver fails to find a passenger along R. We denote this event by $\overline{S_R}$. Note the route from the current position of the driver to P is not unique. Should we suggest the driver with the route that has the minimum $\Pr(\overline{S_R})$? It's obviously absurd since the driver can traverse all the road network in that case. In practice, we can provide the fastest route or a route with the minimum $\Pr(\overline{S_R})$ conditioned by that the distance does not exceed a threshold. This can be implemented by a simple generalization of the constrained shortest path problem [14].

Figure 7(a) plots the $\Pr(S)$ of three nearby parking places around Rear Sea (a bar district of Beijing). It's clear the probability fluctuates with time significantly. At peak hours (8-9am, 5-6pm) the probability is relatively higher than other time intervals for all these parking places.

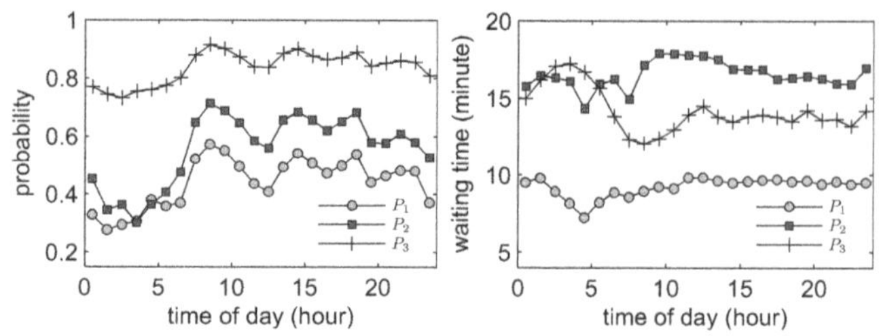

(a) $\Pr(S)$ (b) $E[T|S]$

Figure 7. $\Pr(S)$ **and** $E[T|S]$ **changing over time**

Duration Before the Next Trip T

Let random variable T be the duration from current time T_0 to the beginning of the next trip, given that the taxi driver takes the action Λ_{RP}. Then T is a summation of two random variables: the cruising time along R, denoted by T_R and the waiting time at P, termed as T_P, i.e.,

$$T = T_R + T_P. \tag{6}$$

Note that T_R and T_P are not independent. Actually,

$$\begin{cases} T_P = 0, & \text{if } T_R \le t_n, \\ T_R = t_n, & \text{if } T_P > 0. \end{cases} \tag{7}$$

Based on Bayes rules, the probability mass function is given by

$$\begin{aligned} &\Pr(T_R = t_i | S) \\ =&\Pr(T_R = t_i, S) / \Pr(S) \\ =&\begin{cases} \Pr(S_i) / \Pr(S), & i = 1, 2, \ldots, n - 1, \\ \dfrac{\Pr(S_n) + \Pr(S_{n+1})}{\Pr(S)}, & i = n, \end{cases} \end{aligned} \tag{8}$$

thus the conditional expectation of T_R is

$$\begin{aligned} \mathbf{E}[T_R | S] &= \sum_{i=1}^{n} t_i \Pr(T_R = t_i | S) \\ &= \frac{1}{\Pr(S)} \left(\sum_{i=1}^{n} t_i \Pr(S_i) + t_n \Pr(S_{n+1}) \right). \end{aligned} \tag{9}$$

Let W be the event that the driver waits at P, we have

$$\Pr(W) = \prod_{j=1}^{n} (1 - p_j). \tag{10}$$

To learn the distribution, we break the interval $(0, t_{\max}]$ into m buckets. Specifically, let

$$\begin{cases} t_0 = 0, \\ \Delta t^* = t_{\max}/2m, \\ t_j^* = (2j - 1)\Delta t^*, \ j = 1, 2, \ldots, m, \end{cases} \tag{11}$$

where t_j^* is the average waiting time for the j-th bucket. Denote the probability that the taxi succeeds in picking up a passenger and the waiting time T_P belongs to the j-th bucket by

$$p_*^j = \Pr(\mathcal{P} \overset{(t_j^* - \Delta t^*, t_j^* + \Delta t^*]}{\rightsquigarrow} \mathcal{O} | T_P > 0, T_0 + t_n). \tag{12}$$

Actually, recall Equation 3, we have $p_* = \sum_{j=1}^{m} p_*^j$.

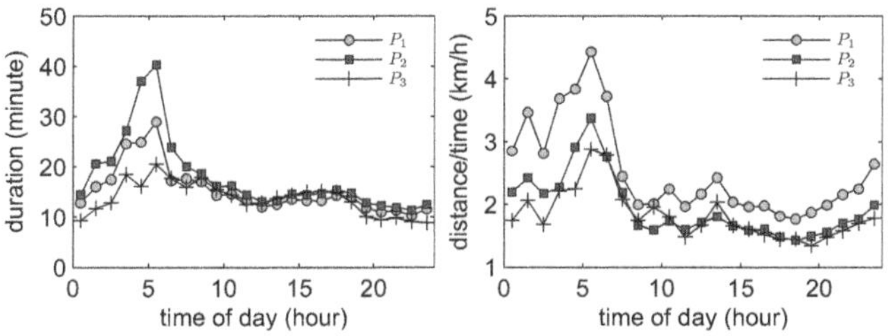

(a) $\mathbf{E}[T_N|S]$ (b) $\mathbf{E}[D_N|S]/E[T+T_N|S]$

Figure 8. Expected duration of next trip and expected profit w.r.t. time

The conditional probability

$$\Pr(T_p = t_j^*|S) = \begin{cases} \dfrac{(1-\Pr(W))}{\Pr(S)}, & j = 0, \\ \dfrac{\Pr(W)p_*^j}{\Pr(S)}, & 1 \le j \le m. \end{cases} \quad (13)$$

Therefore, the conditional expectation of T_P is

$$\mathbf{E}[T_P|S] = \frac{\Pr(W)}{\Pr(S)} \sum_{j=1}^{m} p_*^j t_j^*. \quad (14)$$

Then, the conditional expectation of T is

$$\begin{aligned} &\mathbf{E}[T|S] \\ =&\mathbf{E}[T_R|S] + \mathbf{E}[T_P|S] \\ =&\frac{\sum_{i=1}^{n} t_i \Pr(S_i) + t_n \Pr(S_{n+1}) + \Pr(W)\sum_{j=1}^{m} p_*^j t_j^*}{\Pr(S)}. \end{aligned} \quad (15)$$

As shown in Figure 7(b), the values of $\mathbf{E}[T]$ of the three parking places (using the same query point as Figure 7(a)) are depicted, changing over time. Note that the parking place P_1 has the shortest expected duration, yet has the lowest $\Pr(S)$.

Distance/Travel Time of the Next Trip D_N, T_N

Let random variable D_N be the distance of the next trip if the driver takes the action Λ_{RP} conditioned by that S happens. Let q_i^j be the probability that the distance of the first trip satisfies $d_{j-1} < D_N \le d_j$, when S_i happens (note the time at that moment is $T_0 + t_i$), i.e., $\forall i = 1, 2, \dots, n+1$,

$$q_i^j = \Pr(d_j - \triangle d < D_N \le d_j + \triangle d | S_i, T_0 + t_i). \quad (16)$$

Here,

$$\begin{cases} d_0 = 0, \\ \triangle d = d_{\max}/2s, \\ d_j = (2j-1)\triangle d, \quad j = 1, 2, \dots, s, \end{cases} \quad (17)$$

where $d_{\max}$ is the maximum distance of the first trip. Then, the conditional probability distribution is given by:

$$\Pr(D_N = d_j|S) = \sum_{i=1}^{n+1} \Pr(S_i) q_i^j / \Pr(S), \quad (18)$$

for $j = 1, 2, \dots, s$. Thus, the conditional expected distance of the next trip is

$$\begin{aligned} \mathbf{E}[D_N|S] &= \frac{1}{\Pr(S)} \sum_{j=1}^{s} \left(d_j \sum_{i=1}^{n+1} \Pr(S_i) q_i^j \right) \\ &= \frac{1}{\Pr(S)} \sum_{i=1}^{n+1} \Pr(S_i) \left(\sum_{j=1}^{s} d_j q_i^j \right). \end{aligned} \quad (19)$$

Note that the conditional expected travel time of the next trip $\mathbf{E}[T_N|S]$ is computed in exactly the same way as $\mathbf{E}[D_N|S]$, thus we omit the detail. Figure 8 plots the expected duration and distance of the next trip w.r.t. time of day. As we stated above, this area is the bar district. People mainly come to this area at night and stay until the dawn of the next day. Mostly, people who go to this place live not so close to this area, thus both the expected duration and distance of the next trip at pre-dawn period is higher than other time of day.

Passenger Recommender

Different from the taxis, the passengers do not want to walk too long for hailing a taxi. If a passenger is close to at least one parking place, we suggest him to go to the nearest parking place. Otherwise, we suggest the passenger with the most possible road segments nearby on which they can find a vacant taxi. This is much easier than the taxi recommendation problem. Let $\Pr(\mathcal{C}; r|t)$ be the probability that there is a vacant taxi on road segment r at time t, given the passenger's current position, we suggest the road segments, which have the highest $\Pr(\mathcal{C}; r|t)$ among a reachable region Ω of the passenger, i.e.,

$$r = \operatorname*{argmax}_{r \in \Omega} \Pr(\mathcal{C}; r|t). \quad (20)$$

Later, we discuss in detail how to learn the needed probabilities proposed in this section.

OFF-LINE MINING

Parking Places Detection

This section details the process for detecting parking status from a *non-occupied trip* and accordingly finding out the parking places in the urban area of a city based on a collection of taxi trajectories.

Candidates Detection

Figure 9 demonstrates the parking candidate detection approach, given a non-occupied trip $p_1 \to p_2 \to \cdots \to p_7$. We

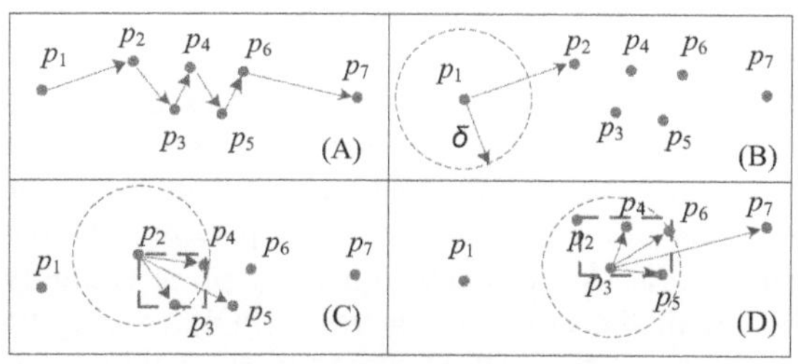

Figure 9. Parking candidates detection

Algorithm 1: ParkingCandidateDetection

```
Input: A road network G, a trajectory Tr, distance threshold δ, time
       threshold τ
Output: A set of parking candidates ℙ = {P}
i ← 0, M ← ||Tr||, P ← ∅, ℙ ← ∅;
while i < (M − 1) do
    j ← i + 1; flag ←false;
    while j < M do
        dist ←Distance (p_i, p_j);
        if dist < δ then j ← j + 1;flag =true;
        else break;
    if p_{j−1}.t − p_i.t > τ and flag =true then
        foreach point p ∈ Tr[i, j) and p ∉ P do
            P.Add(p);/* build a candidate */
        if i = j − 1 then
            ℙ.Add(MB (P)); P ← ∅;
            /* add the minimum bounding box of P
               into ℙ */
        i ← i + 1;
    return ℙ
```

first keep on checking the distance between the current point and the latter point until the distance is smaller than a threshold. As depicted in Figure 9 B), since $dist(p_1, p_2)$ exceeds the distance threshold δ, we move next, fixing p_2 as the "pivot" point and find that $dist(p_2, p_3) < \delta, dist(p_2, p_4) < \delta$ while $dist(p_2, p_5) > \delta$ (Figure 9 C). If the time interval between $p_2.t$ and $p_4.t$ is larger than the time threshold τ, the three points that form a small cluster represent a possible parking candidate. Next, we fix p_3 as the pivot point and keep on the procedure to check latter points. Finally, as shown in Figure 9 D), we detect $(p_2, p_3, p_4, p_5, p_6)$ as a parking candidate because we cannot expand this group any further, i.e., all the points in this group have a distance farther than δ to p_7. The pseudocode is provided in Algorithm 1.

Filtering

Essentially, the candidate detection algorithm finds out the locations where the GPS points of a taxi are densely clustered, with spatial and temporal constraints. However, a parking candidate could sometimes be generated by taxis stuck in a traffic jam, or waiting for signals at a traffic light, instead of a real parking. To reduce such false selections, we design a supervised model for picking out the true parking status from the candidate sets, using the following features:

- *Spatial-Temporal features* including 1) Minimum Bounding Ratio (MBR). As shown in Figure 10(A),B)), MBR is the area ratio between the bounding box of the road segment (MBRr) and the bounding box of the GPS points (MBRc) in the candidate set. 2) AverageDistance. The average distance d_c between points in the candidate set and their nearest road segments, as shown in Figure 10 C). 3) CenterDistance. The distance between center point in MBRc of the candidate set and the road segments. 4) Duration. The parking duration of a candidate. 5) LastSpeed. The speed of the last point leaving a parking candidate.
- *POI feature.* As we know, a parking place is highly relevant with the points of interests (POI) around it, e.g., subway exits, theaters, shopping malls within 50 meters, shown in Figure 10 C). We employ the *term frequency-inverse document frequency* (tf-idf)[10] to measure the importance of a POI to a parking place. Specifically, for a given parking place, we formulate a POI vector, $\langle v_1, v_2, \ldots, v_k \rangle$ where v_i is the tf-idf value of the i-th POI category, given by:

$$v_i = \frac{n_i}{N} \times \log \frac{||\mathbb{P}||}{||\{P \in \mathbb{P} | \text{the } i\text{-th POI category} \in P\}||},$$

  where n_i is the number of POIs belonging to the i-th category and N is the number of POIs lying around the parking candidate. The idf item is calculated using the quotient of the number of parking candidates divided by the number of parking candidates which have the i-th POI category, and then taking the logarithm of that quotient.
- *Collaborative feature.* For a real parking place, other drivers should also park historically at that place. Otherwise, it's not a common parking place. So we use the number of parking candidates within 50 meters in the past 7 days of a candidate as a collaborative feature to enhance the classifier.

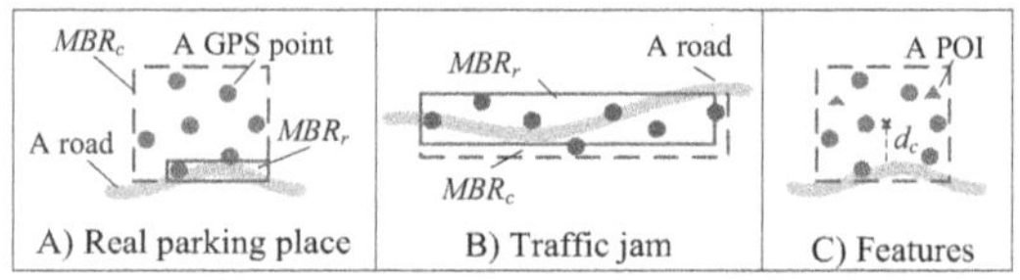

Figure 10. Parking candidates filtering

We use a human-labeled dataset to learn the threshold and train a bagging [2] classifier model to guarantee the high precision and recall of the detected parking candidates (The results will be shown later in the evaluation part). Then we utilize the model to inference whether a candidate is a really parking or a traffic jam.

Parking Place Clustering

The parking status is detected for each trajectory separately. However, the parking place detected from a single trajectory is only a portion of a real parking place. Thus different parking places may be actually the same one. We use a density based clustering method OPTICS [1] aiming to discover the essentially same parking places. The reason for using this method is that it outperforms other methods when the clustered region may have an arbitrary shape and the points inside a region may be arbitrarily distributed. As shown in Figure 11, the left figure plots all the parking candidates in the area of Beijing West Railway Station and the right one shows the results after filtering and clustering, with the color indicating the number of candidates in a cluster.

Learning the Time-dependent Probabilities

In practice, we assume the probability is stable during time interval $[t, t + \triangle t]$, where $\triangle t$ is a fixed threshold. This is reasonable, since the probability changes gradually instead of sharply. For computing the time-dependent probability, a common way is to partition a day into fixed slots (e.g., one hour a slot), and calculate the result for each slot beforehand. Different from this method, we develop a *partition-and-group* approach so as to compute this probability "just-in-time" and enable real-time recommendation. More con-

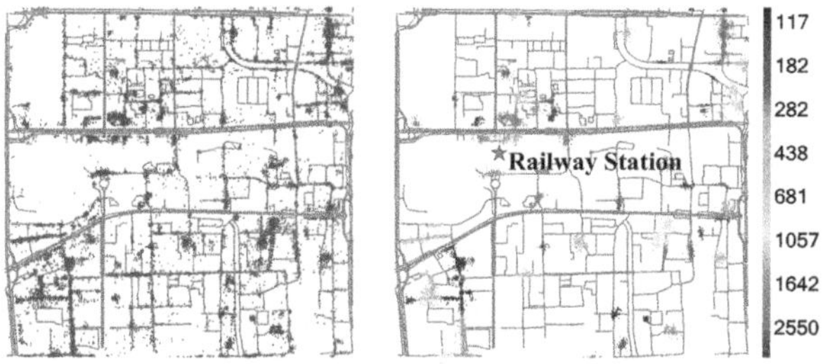

Figure 11. Candidate parking places (left) and clustered parking places (right) in the area of Beijing West Railway Station. The color indicates the number of parking candidates detected for each cluster.

cretely, we partition one day into K small time intervals, the length of each interval is τ (where $\triangle t$ can be divisible by τ, e.g., $\tau = 5$ minutes, $\triangle t = 30$ minutes). Thus, the k_{th} interval is

$$I_k = [(k-1)\tau, k\tau],\ k = 1, 2, \ldots, K. \tag{21}$$

Then we count the instances pertaining to each I_k (for needed probabilities) offline. In the online phase, when the time t of a taxi driver/passenger is input, we retrieve the corresponding intervals (i.e., a set of I_k) which belong to $[t, t+\triangle t]$, then compute the corresponding probability using the statistical results obtained from all the retrieved intervals. The intuition of this partition-and-group approach is much like the Riemann Integral. The advantage of the above "just-in-time" way compared to the fixed slot method is that we can avoid the discontinuity when crossing the boundary of a interval (e.g., the probability at 10:59 am may entirely different with the one at 11:00am if 11:00am is the boundary of a fixed time slot) as well as make the most use of the sparse data in each small interval.

The Probabilities w.r.t. Road Segments

For computing the probability on a road segment, we need to detect all the state transitions. Due to the *low sampling rate* [13] problem, the exact point that the transition occurs may not be observed from the data. In this situation, we adopt the convention that the transition happens at the road segment on which the previous state is observed, i.e., if

$$\begin{cases} p_i.s \neq p_{i+1}.s, \\ p_i.r \neq p_{i+1}.r, \end{cases} \tag{22}$$

we insert a p'_i between p_i and p_{i+1} on $p_i.r$, with state $p_{i+1}.s$.

Instead of computing the probability on each road segment, we first conduct a road segment clustering to integrate the road segments with similar features so as to tackle the data sparseness problem and accelerate the online computing. We identify the following features (as input for road segment clustering), which are derived from the underlying road structure and POIs.

- L: The actual length of a road segment.
- L/E: The ratio between L and the Euclidean length (between the terminal points) E of a road segment. The larger the value is, the more tortuous the road segment is.
- *dir*: The direction of a road segment (one-way/two-way).
- *Lanes*: The number of lanes in a given road segment.
- *degree*: The in/out-degree of a given road segment.
- *POI*: The POI features used are similar with the ones used in parking place detection.

As a result, we obtain a collection of clusters, each of which contains a set of road segments with similar features. Then the statistical learning is performed in terms of each cluster. Let $\widetilde{r}$ be the cluster road segment r belongs to, and $\widetilde{R}$ be the set of all the clusters. Let $\#_k(\mathcal{C};\widetilde{r})$ be the number of trips that the taxis once have been at the $\mathcal{C}$ state during I_k on all the road segments within cluster $\widetilde{r}$, versus $\#_k(\mathcal{O};\widetilde{r})$ for the occupied state. Then the probability that there exists a taxi cruising on r at time t is computed by:

$$\Pr(\mathcal{C}; r|t) = \frac{\sum_{k=\lfloor t/\tau \rfloor}^{\lfloor (t+\triangle t)/\tau \rfloor} \#_k(\mathcal{C};\widetilde{r})}{\sum_{k=\lfloor t/\tau \rfloor}^{\lfloor (t+\triangle t)/\tau \rfloor} \sum_{\widetilde{r}\in\widetilde{R}} (\#_k(\mathcal{C};\widetilde{r}) + \#_k(\mathcal{O};\widetilde{r}))}. \tag{23}$$

The probability $\Pr(\mathcal{O}; r|t)$ can be similarly computed.

Let $\#_k(\mathcal{C}\rightsquigarrow\mathcal{O};\widetilde{r})$ be the number of trips that the taxis transfer from the cruising state to occupied state, i.e., pick up a passenger during I_k when cruising on all road segments within cluster $\widetilde{r}$, then

$$\Pr(\mathcal{C}\rightsquigarrow\mathcal{O}|r, t) = \frac{\sum_{k=\lfloor t/\tau \rfloor}^{\lfloor (t+\triangle t)/\tau \rfloor} \#_k(\mathcal{C}\rightsquigarrow\mathcal{O};\widetilde{r})}{\sum_{k=\lfloor t/\tau \rfloor}^{\lfloor (t+\triangle t)/\tau \rfloor} (\#_k(\mathcal{C};\widetilde{r}))}. \tag{24}$$

With regard to the distance D_N,

$$\Pr(d_a < D_N \leq d_b|r, t) = \frac{\sum_{k=\lfloor t/\tau \rfloor}^{\lfloor t+\triangle t/\tau \rfloor} \#_k(d_a, d_b;\widetilde{r})}{\sum_{k=\lfloor t/\tau \rfloor}^{\lfloor (t+\triangle t)/\tau \rfloor} \#_k(0, d_{\max};\widetilde{r})}, \tag{25}$$

where $d_{\max}$ is the maximum distance of a trip and $\Pr(t_a < T_N \leq t_b \mid r, t)$ is similarly computed.

The Probabilities w.r.t. the Parking Places

For each cluster of the parking places, we have a set of trajectories which are at the parking state with varied arriving time and leaving time. Let $\#_k(t_a, t_b, \mathcal{P}\rightsquigarrow\mathcal{O}; P)$ be the number of trips that originate from parking place P when the taxis arrive at P during I_k and finally become occupied with the waiting time $T_P \in (t_a, t_b]$. Let $\#_k(\mathcal{P}\rightsquigarrow\mathcal{O}; P)$ be the number of trips that originate from P after the taxis arrive at P during I_k and become occupied when leaving P, versus $\#_k(\mathcal{P}\rightsquigarrow\mathcal{C}; P)$ denotes the taxis which are still non-occupied (cruising) when leaving P. Then the probability that the waiting time $T_P \in (t_a, t_b]$ when reaching P at t can be calculated by

$$\Pr(\mathcal{P}\overset{(t_a,t_b]}{\rightsquigarrow}\mathcal{O}|T_P > 0, t) = \frac{\sum_{k=\lfloor t/\tau \rfloor}^{\lfloor t+\triangle t/\tau \rfloor} \#_k(t_a, t_b, \mathcal{P}\rightsquigarrow\mathcal{O}; P)}{\sum_{k=\lfloor t/\tau \rfloor}^{\lfloor (t+\triangle t)/\tau \rfloor} (\#_k(\mathcal{P}\rightsquigarrow\mathcal{O}; P) + \#_k(\mathcal{P}\rightsquigarrow\mathcal{C}; P))}. \tag{26}$$

ONLINE RECOMMENDATION

In this stage, given the location and time of a taxi driver/passenger, we provide real-time recommendation based on the proposed probabilistic model and the derived statistical knowledge.

For the taxi recommender, we first perform a range query according to the location of the taxi, and then retrieve a set of potential parking places. For each parking place P, we generate the route R with the minimum $\Pr(\overline{S_R})$ constrained by a distance threshold ($1.5\times$ distance of the shortest path) using a dynamic programming recursion [14] in parallel. Then we compute the probability $\Pr(S)$ and the conditional expectations: $\mathbf{E}[T|S]$, $\mathbf{E}[D_N|S]$, $\mathbf{E}[T_N|S]$ according to the query time. Later, we rank the candidate parking places with (but not limited to) the following strategies (S1–S3) and accordingly recommend top-k parking places to the driver in real-time. The thresholds P_θ, D_θ and F_θ can either be learned from the training data or be set by the user.

S1. $Topk_{\max}\{\mathbf{E}[D_N|S]/\mathbf{E}[T+T_N|S] : \Pr(S) > P_\theta\}$. The candidate parking places of this strategy are restricted to the ones which have a $\Pr(S)$ larger than a threshold P_θ, among which, we provide the taxi driver with the top-k profitable parking places, i.e., the driver can earn the most money per unit time by traveling to these k parking places.

S2. $Topk_{\min}\{\mathbf{E}[T|S] : \Pr(S) > P_\theta, D_N > D_\theta\}$. This strategy retrieves k parking places which have the minimum expected duration before picking up a new passenger and have at least P_θ possibility to pick up a passenger as well as D_θ distance of the next trip.

S3. $Topk_{\max}\{\Pr(S) : \mathbf{E}[D_N|S]/\mathbf{E}[T+T_N|S] > F_\theta\}$. This strategy provides the parking places, towards which the drivers are most likely to pick up a passenger and has a guaranteed profit (at least F_θ).

For the passenger recommender, we also perform a range query so as to obtain a region, which is within a walking distance of the passenger. If this region contains parking places, we suggest the passenger with the k nearest parking places. Otherwise, according to Equation 20, we return the road segments with k largest probability of having a vacant taxi.

VALIDATION

Settings

Dataset

Road network: We evaluate our method using the road network of Beijing, which contains 106,579 road nodes and 141,380 road segments.

Trajectory: The dataset contains the GPS trajectory recorded by over 12,000 taxis in a period of 110 days. The total distance of the data set is more than 200 million kilometers and the number of points reaches to 577 million. After trip segmentation, there are in total 20 million trips, among which 46% are occupied trips and 54% are non-occupied trips. We use 70 days' (random selected) data to build our system and evaluate the method using the rest (40 days) data.

Evaluation on Parking Place Detection

We first evaluate the effectiveness of filtering, i.e., whether our method can identify a taxi is parking or is stuck in a traffic jam. We ask three local people to label 1000 parking candidates (True/False). The precision and recall w.r.t. the features we used for the classifier is presented in Table 2. As a result, we get a 91% precision and 89% recall which are enough for detecting the true parking places and clustering.

Features	Precision	Recall
Spatial	0.695	0.670
Spatial+POI	0.716	0.696
Spatial+POI+Collaborative	0.725	0.706
Spatial+POI+Collaborative+Temporal	0.909	0.889

Table 2. Results of parking place filtering

We evaluate the performance of parking place clustering by two methods: 1) We conduct a survey towards more than 20 users and ask them for submissions of parking places they know/have seen. We received over 70 parking places which basically uniformly distributed in the urban area of Beijing. Then we use this labeled data to test the recall of parking places generated by our parking place clustering approach. The recall of the labeled parking places reaches to 81%, i.e., 81% of the labeled parking places are involved in the clustered parking places. 2) We check the ratio of positive instances compared with all the parking candidates (using the test set) for each clustered parking place. The mean value of the ratio is around 89%.

Evaluation on Statistical Learning

Based on our model, we calculate the overall time-dependent distribution for both the parking places (Figure 12) and the road segments (Figure 13). For example, as shown in Figure 12(a), the average waiting time T_P is mostly less than 10 minutes. During the midnight, the distribution of waiting time is comparatively decentralized while after 8am, the waiting time trends to be shorter. That means, the driver can get a passenger with a shorter waiting time than in midnight, which is quite accord with the common sense. Figure 13(a) depicts the average probability (for each level of road segments) that a taxi transfer from the cruising status to the occupied status changing over time. Since the level-0 roads and level-1 roads are mainly high-ways or main roads, the probability is reasonable lower compared with level-2/3.

Evaluation on Online Recommendation

For preprocessing the test set, we extract the trajectories of the detected high profit drivers and segment them to occupied/cruising/parking trips. Before each parking or occupied trip, we randomly select 10 points which are less than 3km faraway (which is the radius of our range query for retrieving the parking places) to the next pick-up point/parking place as the query points. For each query point, the groundtruth contains the following information: query ID, query time, geo-position, the routes before next pick-up point, and the parking places they've gone to before next pick-up point (ordered by timestamps). Then we evaluate the performance of our method using three ranking strategies (S1–S3) as well as two baselines: B1) suggest the top-k nearest parking places and B2) recommend the top-k parking places which have the largest overall probability of picking up a passenger). We measure the effectiveness of these methods using three criterion:

1) *Precision and Recall.* The precision is the ratio between number of hits and the number of recommendations. The recall measures the fraction of the parking places the drivers actually go to that are suggested.

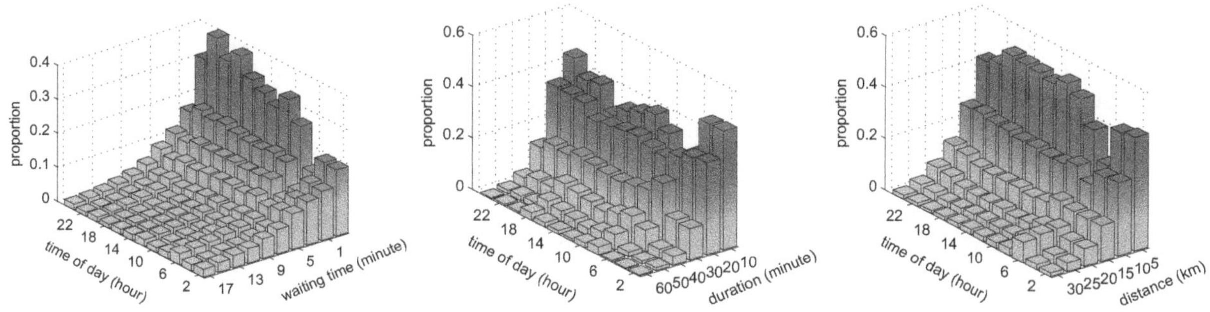

(a) waiting time (b) duration of the first trip (c) distance of the first trip

Figure 12. Distribution in parking places (overall)

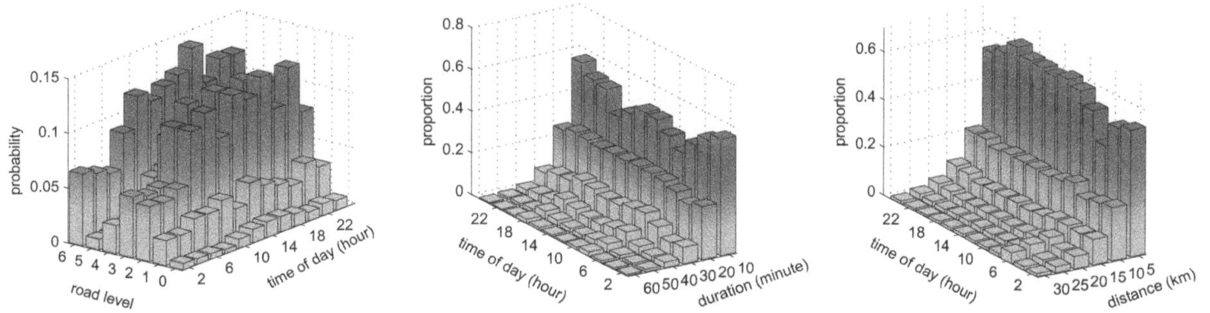

(a) $\Pr(\mathcal{C} \rightsquigarrow \mathcal{O})$ (b) duration of the first trip (c) distance of the first trip

Figure 13. Statistics results of road segments (overall)

2) *Normalized Discounted Cumulative Gain at the k-th position [4] (nDCG$_k$).* $nDCG_k = \frac{DCG_k}{IDCG_k}$, where $DCG_k = \sum_{i=1}^{k} \frac{S(i)}{\log(1+i)}$ and $IDCG_k$ denotes the DCG_k value for an ideal ranking, given $S(i)$ is the scoring function for the i-th recommendation. Given a driver's position and time, we recommend him/her with top-k parking places and the corresponding routes. Let (R_j^*, P_j^*), $j = 1, 2, \dots, m$ be the routes the driver actually traversed, and the parking places the driver waited at, before he/she picked up the next passenger (note that the driver may wait at several parking places or didn't wait at any parking place). Assume the top-k parking places we recommend to a driver are denoted by (R_i, P_i), $i = 1, 2, \dots, k$. The scoring function for (R_i, P_i) is determined according to Table 3. For routes R_i and R_j^*, we consider them to be the same if there is a significant overlap (90%, say) between R_i and R_j^*. Then we compute the $nDCG_k$ for each query point and take the average $nDCG_k$ among all the queries as the overall $nDCG_k$.

3) For the hit parking places (the driver went to the suggested parking places and picked up a passenger finally), we further study the precision of the predicted value, i.e., T, D_N and T_N measured by *Relative Mean Error* (RME), e.g., given the real duration before the next trip T^* , then

$$RME[T] = \mathbf{E}\left[(T^* - \mathbf{E}\left[T|S\right])/T^*\right].$$

Rule	Condition	Score
(i)	$R_i = R_1^*$ and the driver picks up a passenger on R_1^*	3
(ii)	$R_i = R_1^*$ and $P_i = P_1^*$	3
(iii)	(i),(ii) do not hold, but $R_i = R_1^*$ or $P_i = P_1^*$	2
(iv)	(i),(ii),(iii) do not hold, but $\exists j$ s.t., $R_i = R_j^*$ or $P_i = P_j^*$	1
(v)	none of the above holds	0

Table 3. Scoring rules

Figure 14 plots the nDCG changing over k. We visualize the average nDCG value of S1, S2, and S3 as the nDCG for our method. Overall, our approach has a 0.1 improvement than the competing methods in terms of nDCG$_2$. Table 4 presents the other results obtained from the evaluation. The S3 strategy has the best performance in terms of precision and S2 is the best for the recall. The overall error of our method, measured by *RME*, is less than 3% for D_N and T_N and 15% for T.

RELATED WORK

Dispatching Systems

Taxi dispatching systems are attracting growing attention from researchers with the development of intelligent transportation systems and the popularization of GPS sensors [5]. Most existing dispatching systems assign a task to taxi drivers based on nearest neighbor principle in terms of distance or time. Phithakkitnukoon et al. [8] use the naive Bayesian classifi-

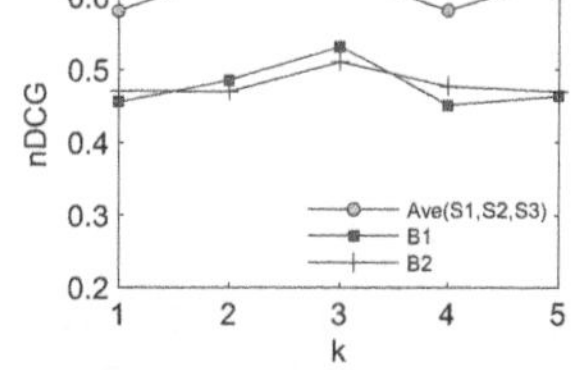

Figure 14. nDCG

	S1	S2	S3	B1	B2
Precision	0.63	0.66	0.67	0.60	0.61
Recall	0.59	0.65	0.64	0.57	0.52
$RME(T)$			0.15		
$RME(D_N)$			0.02		
$RME(T_N)$			0.03		

Table 4. RME, precision and recall

er with developed error-based learning approach to infer the number of vacant taxis at a given time and location which can be used to enhance the dispatching system. Yamamoto et al. [11] propose a fuzzy clustering and adaptive routing approach to improve dispatching system by assigning vacant taxis adaptively to the locations with high expectation of potential customers.

Different from the centralized dispatching, our recommendation system provide suggestions to taxi drivers/passengers and let them make their own decisions. Typically, for a dispatching system, the customers need to book a taxi by telephone/internet in advance, and it is usually not free of charge. Most passengers hail a taxi along the road or stand where the taxis are available instead of booking a taxi. Besides, our method aims to maximize the profit for a particular taxi driver instead of balancing the income of all the taxi drivers, which is usually a goal of a dispatching system. In addition, our approach can be combined with a dispatching system so as to complement each other.

Location Recommendation For Taxi Drivers

Ge et al. [3] present a model to recommend a taxi driver with a sequence of pick-up points so as to maximize a taxi driver's profit. This work formulates the target problem by a mobile sequential recommendation (MSR) problem. Li et al. [6] study the passenger-finding strategies (hunting/waiting) of taxi drivers in Hangzhou. In this work, L1-Norm SVM is used to select features for classifying the passenger-finding strategies in terms of performance. Recently, Powell et al. [9] propose an approach to suggest profit (grid-based) locations for taxi drivers by constructing a Spatio-Temporal Profitability map, on which, the nearby regions of the driver are scored according to the potential profit calculated by the historical data.

Our approach is different from the above methods in the following aspects: 1) We provide recommendations to both taxi drivers and passengers, which mobilizes them and reduces the disequilibrium of the demand and supply. 2) Instead of a grid/cell-based partition of the map, our recommendation is provided on road-segment level, which enables more accurate and meaningful understanding of the taxi drivers' behaviors as well as a more practical recommendation for both the taxi drivers and the passengers. 3) We focus on the off-peak hours to help the driver make the first step decision whenever and wherever they want to decide a destination to go. In practice, the "first step" recommendation would be more effective since usually the drivers are not willing to remember a sequence of places. 4) We develop an algorithm to distinguish the parking status from traffic jams and propose a solution to detect the parking places in an urban area. 5) We target the challenges when building the system based on sparse data and facilitate the on-line recommendation with a partition-and-group framework.

CONCLUSION

Leveraging the pick-up behaviors learned from the high-profit taxi drivers and the mobility patterns of passengers, we build a recommendation system for both the taxi drivers and passengers. In this paper, motivated by the behaviors of discovered high-profit taxi drivers, an elaborate probabilistic model is devised to maximize the profit of a taxi driver and the possibility to find a vacant taxi for a passenger. We evaluate our method using a large number of GPS trajectories of taxicabs. The results show that our method can effectively provide the taxi drivers with high-profit locations, e.g., the $nDCG_2$ of our method has a 10% improvement than the baseline methods and the precision of the recommendation reaches to 67%. By mobilizing the drivers and passengers, our system can ease the supply/denamd disequilibrium problem to a certain extent. Furthermore, this recommender reduces the cruising distance of a taxi driver such that saves energy consumption and lighten the transportation pressure of a city.

In the future, we will incorporate the real-time traffic information to provide better routes towards the parking places and investigate the user equilibrium model for the proposed recommendation system.

REFERENCES

1. M. Ankerst, M. M. Breunig, H.-P. Kriegel, and J. Sander. Optics: Ordering points to identify the clustering structure. In *SIGMOD 1999*, pages 49–60. ACM Press, 1999.
2. L. Breiman. Bagging predictors. *Machine learning*, 24(2):123–140, 1996.
3. Y. Ge, H. Xiong, A. Tuzhilin, K. Xiao, M. Gruteser, and M. Pazzani. An energy-efficient mobile recommender system. In *Proc. KDD 2010*, pages 899–908.
4. K. Järvelin and J. Kekäläinen. Cumulated gain-based evaluation of ir techniques. *ACM Transactions on Information Systems (TOIS)*, 20(4):422–446, 2002.
5. D. Lee, H. Wang, R. Cheu, and S. Teo. Taxi dispatch system based on current demands and real-time traffic conditions. *Transportation Research Record: Journal of the Transportation Research Board*, 1882(-1):193–200, 2004.
6. B. Li, D. Zhang, L. Sun, C. Chen, S. Li, G. Qi, and Q. Yang. Hunting or waiting? discovering passenger-finding strategies from a large-scale real-world taxi dataset. In *Pervasive Computing and Communications Workshops (PERCOM Workshops), 2011 IEEE International Conference on*, pages 63 –68, march 2011.
7. New York City Taxi and Limousine Commission. Taxi of Tomorrow Survey Results, Feb 2011.
8. S. Phithakkitnukoon, M. Veloso, C. Bento, A. Biderman, and C. Ratti. Taxi-aware map: Identifying and predicting vacant taxis in the city. In *Proc. AMI 2010*, page 86.
9. J. Powell, Y. Huang, F. Bastani, and M. Ji. Towards reducing taxicab cruising time using spatio-temporal profitability maps. In *Proceedings of the 12th International Symposium on Advances in Spatial and Temporal Databases*, SSTD '11, 2011.
10. H. Wu, R. Luk, K. Wong, and K. Kwok. Interpreting TF-IDF term weights as making relevance decisions. *ACM Transactions on Information Systems (TOIS)*, 26(3):1–37, 2008.
11. K. Yamamoto, K. Uesugi, and T. Watanabe. Adaptive routing of cruising taxis by mutual exchange of pathways. In *Knowledge-Based Intelligent Information and Engineering Systems*, pages 559–566. Springer, 2010.
12. J. Yuan, Y. Zheng, C. Zhang, W. Xie, X. Xie, G. Sun, and Y. Huang. T-drive: driving directions based on taxi trajectories. In *Proceedings of the 18th SIGSPATIAL International Conference on Advances in Geographic Information Systems*, GIS '10, pages 99–108, New York, NY, USA, 2010. ACM.
13. J. Yuan, Y. Zheng, C. Zhang, X. Xie, and G. Sun. An interactive-voting based map matching algorithm. In *Proc. MDM 2010*, pages 43–52.
14. M. Ziegelmann. *Constrained Shortest Paths and Related Problems*. PhD thesis, Universität des Saarlandes, 2001.

Out of the Lab and Into the Woods: Kinematic Analysis in Running Using Wearable Sensors

Christina Strohrmann, Holger Harms, Gerhard Tröster
Wearable Computing Lab.
ETH Zurich, Switzerland
{strohrmann,harms,troester}@ife.ee.ethz.ch

Stefanie Hensler, Roland Müller
Institute of Human Movement Sciences and Sport
ETH Zurich, Switzerland
{shensler,muelrola}@ethz.ch

ABSTRACT
Injuries in running are often provoked by fatigue or improper technique, which are both reflected in the runner's kinematics. State of the art research on kinematics in sports is using optical motion capture systems that are inaccessible to most athletes. This paper demonstrates the potential of wearable sensors for runners' kinematics analysis. We present a user study including 21 subjects of different running experience that performed an exhausting run on a conventional outside track wearing ETHOS units. For performance level assessment, training assistance, and fatigue monitoring we extracted the foot contact duration, the foot strike type, and the heel lift as kinematic parameters. A questionnaire revealed that subjects perceived the sensors as comfortable to wear and would use them on a regular basis. We concluded that wearable sensors provide a valuable tool for runners, from beginners to experts, for running technique assessment.

Author Keywords
Sports, wearable system, performance evaluation.

ACM Classification Keywords
I.5.4 Pattern Recognition: Applications—*Signal Processing*

General Terms
Algorithms, Experimentation, Measurement.

INTRODUCTION
Long distance running has become a popular sport for the masses, alone in the US about two Marathon competitions are carried out per day[1]. The motivation for runners to pursue this sport is not limited to improvement of the personal record performance, a query revealed that running is "like therapy, or an antidepressant". However, everybody can run but might not do it properly. About 65 % of runners are injured in an average year[2]. Poor running technique and fatigue increase the risk of injury [1]. Both are reflected in the runner's kinematics which is traditionally monitored and analyzed using optical motion capture systems [2, 9]. The high costs of such systems and marginal availability restrict assessments to professional runners in a constrained environment [2].

However, continuous advances in sensing technology emerged miniature sensors enabling body worn sensing and analysis of human motion [7]. Following this trend, we developed a small and lightweight inertial measurement unit (IMU), specifically optimized for long-term, out of the lab measurements.

In this work, we demonstrate the potential of ETHOS for kinematic parameter assessment in endurance running, which makes great demands especially on wearability and comfortable sensor attachment. We present a user study, in which each runner wore 12 ETHOS units throughout an exhausting run. We extracted kinematic features from the sensors to assess the three main application areas skill level assessment, fatigue monitoring, and training assistance. From our observations we found that kinematic features from two sensors, on the foot and on the shin, suffice to cover these. In this work, we present the kinematic feature extraction and evaluation based on these two sensors. Table 1 illustrates the kinematic features, congruent sensor position, and the covered application areas.

		application		
		skill level assessment	fatigue monitoring	training assistance
kinematic feature	Foot Contact (foot sensor)	x	x	
	Foot Strike Type (foot sensor)		x	x
	Heel Lift (shin sensor)	x	x	

Table 1. Overview of calculated kinematic features and corresponding application areas.

ETH ORIENTATION SENSOR (ETHOS)
ETHOS constitutes an inertial measurement unit (IMU), which is optimized for long-term, out of the lab recordings [3]. Each unit comprises a 3D accelerometer, a 3D gyroscope, and a 3D magnetic field sensor. The central processing unit of ETHOS is a 16-bit dsPIC. Sampled data can be stored to a local 2 GB microSD card, or be transmitted via USB. Wireless connectivity is provided by an integrated ultra low power ANT+ module that allows for interfacing of other ETHOS units or sampling of data provided by external ANT+ compatible devices such as heart rate belts or GPS re-

[1]http://www.runningintheusa.com/More/Default.aspx
[2]http://www.sportsinjurybulletin.com/

UbiComp'11, September 17–21, 2011, Beijing, China.

ceivers. Each ETHOS unit is equipped with a real time clock (RTC) for synchronization of multiple devices.
Its elongated design (WxLxH = 14 mm × 45 mm × 4 mm) is optimized for attachment along human body limbs. We developed flat and bracelet housings (compare Fig. 1), that contain the sensor, a battery, and a switch. The overall system weighs 27 g for the round housing and 22 g for the flat housing, respectively.
In a typical ETHOS use case, in which data are sampled at a frequency of 128 Hz and stored locally, a system runtime of seven hours is achieved. The orientation is calculated from sensor data by fusing acceleration, gyroscope, and magnetic field data using a state of the art complementary filter [10]. While its low computational requirements permit an online implementation on the sensor, it shows sufficient accuracy for most applications. We achieved an average RMS error in 3D orientation of 1.17° for all axes during experimental characterization, wherein an optical motion capture system (Vicon) was utilized as a reference.

EXPERIMENT DESIGN

Respective data used for assessment of kinematic parameters was recorded during a 45 min run on an outside track. 21 healthy subjects (13 men, 8 women) with an average age of 33.8 ± 8.4 years participated in the experiment. Table 2 details information on the subjects including weekly training amount, which was ground truth for classification into skill level groups. Chosen participants showed a balanced skill level distribution ranging from beginners to competitive runners.

skill level group	training [km/week]	speed [km/h]	number of subjects
beginner	0–5	9–10.5	6
intermediate	5–25	10.5–12	6
advanced	25–45	12–14.5	6
expert	> 45	14.5–17.8	3

Table 2. Skill level groups, their amount of training per week, the speed range during the 45 min run, and the number of subjects participating in this study of the individual performance group.

Subjects were instructed to maintain a speed of 75–85 % of their maximum aerobic speed to provoke a change in running kinematics due to fatigue. Maximum aerobic speed was conducted preliminary to the study in a standardized endurance test on a treadmill. The run was performed on an outside track commonly used by runners, speed was monitored by GPS. The track showed a circular shape with a total length of 550 m, which allowed for permanent supervision of the subjects by an assistant for safety reasons. Subjects were filmed with a video camera at a defined checkpoint and a turn-based feedback on the lap time was provided.
Figure 1 depicts the attachment and the positions of the two ETHOS units on the foot and the shin used for analysis in this work. ETHOS data were sampled at 100 Hz and stored to a local microSD card for subsequent offline analysis. Temporal alignment of simultaneously recorded data was guaranteed by a dedicated hub that synchronizes the onboard real time clocks (RTC) of attached ETHOS units.
The presented experiment design was authorized by an ethics commission. Subjects signed an informed consent before participation.

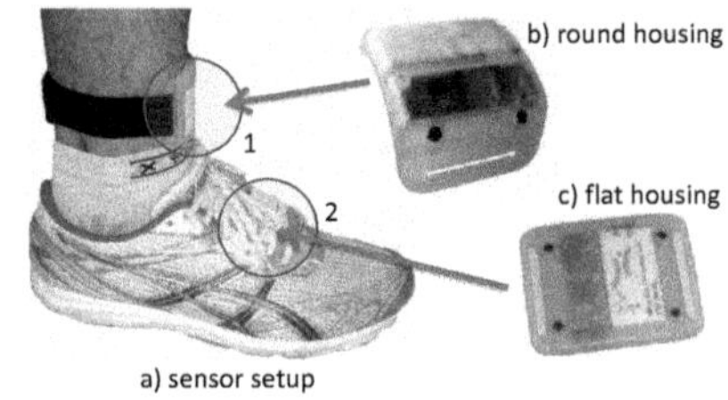

Figure 1. Runner equipped with ETHOS devices (encircled) on foot and shin (a). Close up of the two housing types (round (b) and flat (c)).

FOOT CONTACT DURATION

The normalized foot contact duration (NFC) denotes the percentage of time one foot is on the ground during one step cycle. NFC decreases with increasing skill level, since shorter contact allows for faster running [2].
Figure 2 depicts the magnitude of the right foot's acceleration (sensor 2, Fig. 1) for one step and subdividing step phases. As depicted in Fig. 2 the (absolute) foot contact duration of step k corresponded to the time interval in which the magnitude of the foot's acceleration remained stable below a defined threshold after a foot strike ($FS(k)$). During this time, the foot was on the ground and was not exposed to dynamic accelerations as it occurred when the foot became airborne. The subsequent toe off ($TO(k)$) was thus detected when the acceleration magnitude exceeded a defined threshold of 2 g.
The normalized foot contact duration is calculated by dividing the foot contact duration ($TO(k) - FS(k)$) by the step cycle duration ($FS(k+1) - FS(k)$).

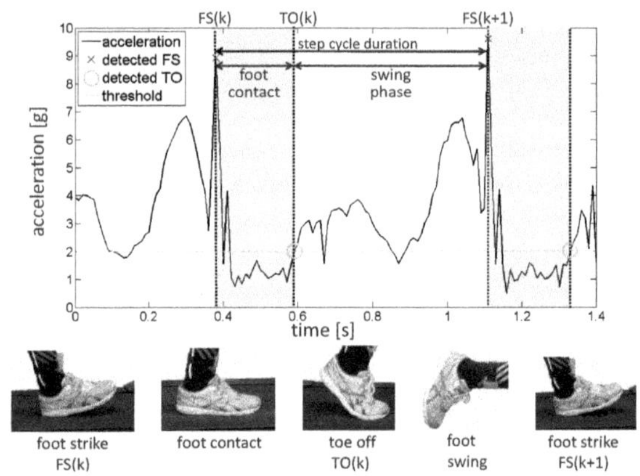

Figure 2. Acceleration magnitude of the foot mounted sensor (sensor 2, see Fig. 1). Detected foot strikes $FS(k)$ are indicated by 'x'. Each step cycle is subdivided into foot contact and swing phase. The toe off ($TO(k)$, indicated by 'o') separates both phases and is detected by a threshold (dashed horizontal line).

Figure 3 depicts NFC of a beginner and an expert runner during the whole run. We observed that the expert's foot contact is shorter, which is congruent with related work [2]. Additionally, the beginner's NFC showed greater variations throughout the run compared to the expert, and increases over time, probably due to fatigue. From GPS measurements we observed that the beginner runner was not able to maintain her individual speed. Since step duration was kept stable, we concluded that flying phase was shortened.
Moreover, our results indicated that an analysis of the normalized foot contact duration shows potential for skill level assessment and fatigue monitoring.

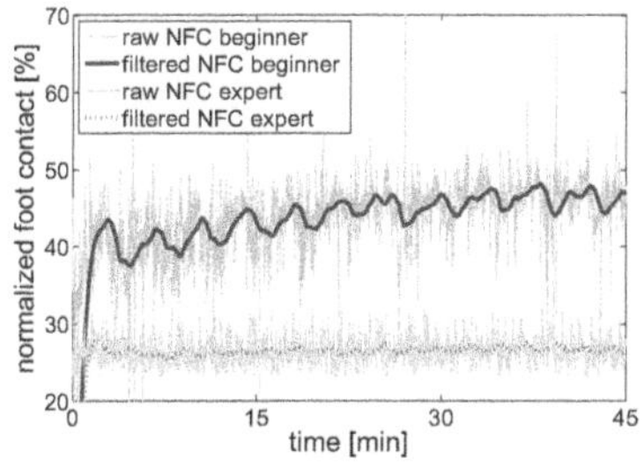

Figure 3. *NFC* of beginner and expert during the 45 min run. *NFC* constitutes the time the foot is on the ground during one step. It is lower for the better runner. For the beginner, an increase of *NFC* can be observed over the course of the run.

FOOT STRIKE TYPE

Depending on an individual history of injuries and training distance, most runners train to maintain a specific foot strike type. Automated assessment of the foot strikes provides valuable information to runners of all skill levels. While it presents a diagnostic tool for ambitious runners, it can be used for beginners as a basis for instructions on stretching after the workout to help prevent injuries.

Three different foot strike types are common, named after the part of the foot that touches the ground first: (1) heel, (2) midfoot, or (3) toe strike. Each of the strike types has advantages and disadvantages. Heel strikers have less stress on their calves and Achilles tendon but are slowed down. As the knee is not bent during the strike it experiences high impact stresses, which promotes injuries over time [4]. Midfoot runners experience more stress on the calves and Achilles tendon but absorb shock better since the knee is bent. Most long distance runners are midfoot runners. Toe striking contributes to a better form and faster running but it keeps calf muscles contracted contributing to various injuries [8]. However, toe strikers experience less stress on knees and ankles.

The analysis of the foot strikes was performed stepwise based on the gyroscope data recorded by the right foot mounted sensor (sensor 2, Fig. 1). Foot strikes were characterized by the forward-backward rolling characteristics of the foot, which correspond to a rotation about the lateral axis of the sensor. Figure 4 displays a calibrated gyroscope signal for a typical heel, midfoot, and toe striker. The ground truth of foot strike type was derived from video observations. A heel striker showed a high negative peak in rate of turn at foot strike, which indicated the rolling of the foot from heel to toe. The midfoot striker showed a lower rate of turn in both directions, and the toe striker showed a higher positive peak around foot strike evoked by rolling from toe to heel.

For discrimination of the strike type, we spotted the minimum and maximum peak of the unfiltered foot's pitch rate of turn in a 0.2 s window around foot strike (*FS*). Figure 5 depicts a scatter plot of these features for the whole duration of the experiment of a typical heel, midfoot, and toe runner. The plot indicates that the two features are sufficient for discrimination of the foot strike type. This cluster forming can be observed for any runner combinations of the individual foot strike types. Figure 6 details the chronological development of the strikes during the 45 min run by an expert runner. The plot indicates a slight tendency towards midfoot striking over time, since the mean of a 5 min sliding window moves from the upper right to the lower left (compare

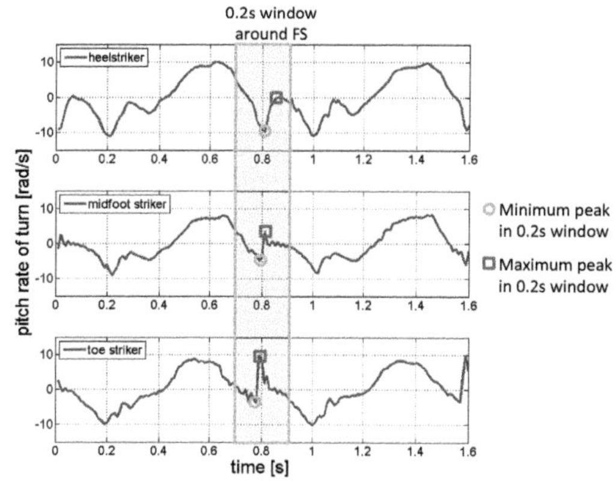

Figure 4. Foot's pitch rate of turn of a typical heel, midfoot, and toe striker (sensor 2, Fig. 1). For classification, minimum and maximum peak within a 0.2 s around foot strike were detected.

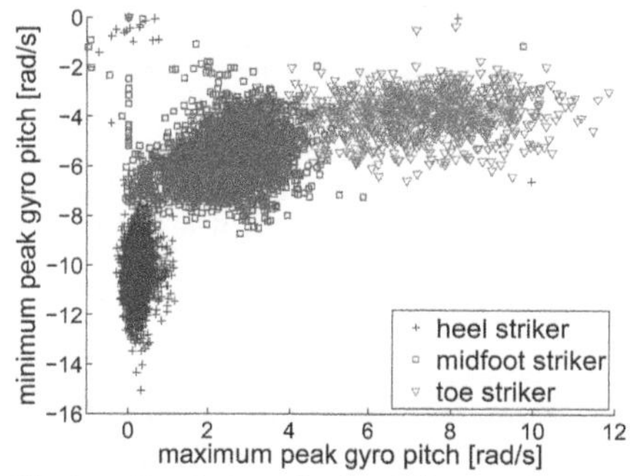

Figure 5. Clusters discriminate heel, midfoot, and toe striker. The two features are minimum and maximum peak of foot's pitch rate of turn within a 0.2 s window around foot strike.

Fig. 5). This trend indicated muscle fatigue and could be utilized for retrospective assessment of the training quality. We conclude that foot strike type analysis enables training assistance and fatigue monitoring.

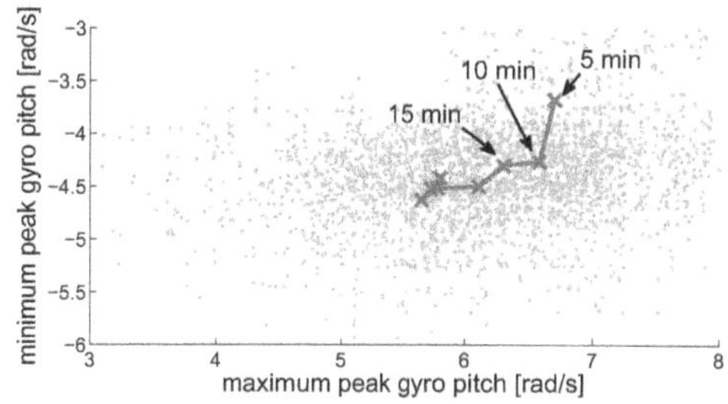

Figure 6. Traveling center of toe striker toward a more midfoot striking during the 45 min run. Mean travels from upper right to lower left.

HEEL LIFT

The Heel Lift (*HL*) denotes the amount of foot lifting, hence, flection of the knee during the swing phase. An increased heel lift decreases the effective leg length, leading to a decreased moment during forward swing. Research concluded that high heel lift allows for energy efficient and fast running [6]. Moreover it was shown that heel lift increases with speed, and tends to decrease during exhaustive runs owing to muscle fatigue.

We derived the *HL* metric from orientation data of the sensor attached to the right shin (sensor 1, Fig. 1). It was calculated as the maximum pitch angle of the shin during individual step cycles. An angle of 0° equals normal standing, i.e. the shin is vertical to the ground.

Figure 7 details the averaged heel lift for skill level groups for the first, the middle, and the last 5 min of the run. The bars indicate that participants of higher skill level groups performed heel lift to a greater extent (Fig. 7). Our observation was congruent to movement sciences' findings that heel lift increases with speed and indicates an efficient running technique [6]. Independent of the skill level, heel lift decreased through the course of the run due to progressive muscle fatigue. Since fatigue promotes the risk of injuries, an indicator providing feedback on exhaustion could help to assess running technique and prevent injuries.

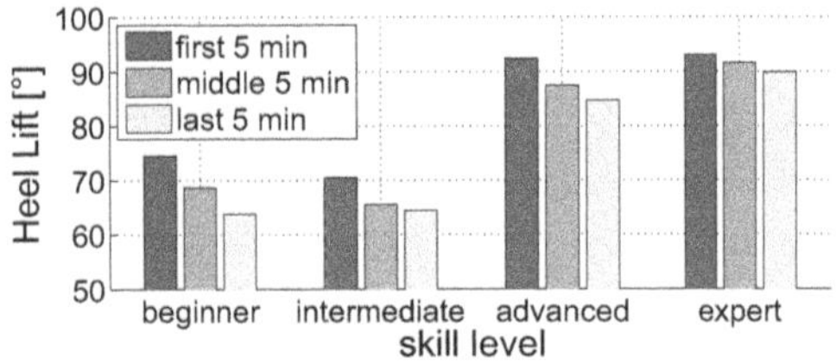

Figure 7. Heel lift of the right shin (sensor 1, Fig. 1) of the different skill level groups during the exhaustive outside run. Bars indicate the change of *HL* from the first 5 min to the middle and last 5 min of the run.

FEEDBACK ON SENSOR WEARABILITY

Subsequently to the experiments all subjects were asked to complete a questionnaire concerning wearability of sensors. Evaluation was based on the Comfort Rating Scales (CRS) introduced by Knight et al. [5]. Knight found that comfort should be assessed over multiple dimensions, including emotional, perceptive and physical components. In a self-administered assessment, subjects graded the following aspects from 0 (low) to 10 (high):

Emotion: I am worried about how I look when I'm wearing this device. I feel tense or on edge because of wearing the device.
Attachment: I can feel the device on my body. I can feel the device moving.
Harm: The device is causing me some harm. The device is painful to wear.
Perceived Change: Wearing the device makes me feel physically different. I feel strange wearing the device.
Movement: The device affects the way I move. The device inhibits or restricts my movements.
Anxiety: I do not feel secure wearing the device.

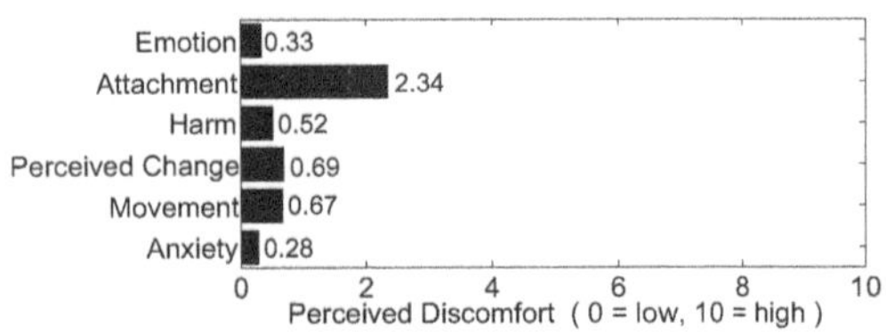

Figure 8. Mean CRS of sensor wearability for all subjects.

Figure 8 depicts results of the CRS. The attachment dimension scored the highest CRS with an average of 2.34, while the anxiety dimension obtained the lowest with 0.28.
In addition to the CRS subjects were asked if they would wear ETHOS on a regular basis as a personal trainer, and achieved an average rating of 8.2 (0 equals "no", 10 equals "yes").

We concluded from the CRS that ETHOS units were perceived as comfortable to wear, and did not constrain movements of the subjects during running. User acceptance could possibly be further improved by removal of spare sensors that were not considered in this study or integrating sensors in shoes or clothes.

CONCLUSION

In this work, we demonstrated the potential of wearable technology for assessment of kinematic parameters using the example of running. We introduced a miniature IMU that was designed for long-term monitoring of human movement outside the lab. We investigated wearability and assessment of established kinematic parameters in a user study with 12 runners of different skill levels. Each runner wore a set of 12 ETHOS units and performed an exhausting run on an outside track for a duration of 45 min. We found that from the 12 units a minimal set of two units attached to the foot and shin is sufficient to cover the desired application areas skill level assessment, fatigue monitoring, and training assistance. Inference of kinematic parameters using wearable devices enables a transition from subjective self-assessment to objective assessment. The automatically calculated parameters can be provided to doctors or athletes for post training analysis.
The significance of our approach was confirmed by a questionnaire, in which subjects stated that the experienced wearing comfort approves the acceptance of sensors. We concluded that wearable technology opens possibilities for technique improvement and injury risk reduction to a wide spectrum of athletes.

REFERENCES

1. J. Abt, T. Sell, Y. Chu, M. Lovalekar, R. Burdett, and S. Lephart. Running kinematics and shock absorption do not change after brief exhaustive running. *The Journal of Strength & Conditioning Research*, 2011.
2. P. Fleming, C. Young, S. Dixon, and M. Carré. Athlete and coach perceptions of technology needs for evaluating running performance. *Sports Eng.*, 13:1–18, 2010.
3. H. Harms, O. Amft, R. Winkler, J. Schumm, M. Kusserow, and G. Tröster. ETHOS: Miniature Orientation Sensor for Wearable Human Motion Analysis. In *IEEE Sensors*, 2010.
4. W. Kim, A. S. Voloshin, and S. H. Johnson. Modeling of heel strike transients during running. *Human Movement Science*, 13:221 – 244, 1994.
5. J. Knight, C. Baber, A. Schwirtz, and H. Bristow. The comfort assessment of wearable computers. In *The Sixth International Symposium on Wearable Computers*, 2002.
6. T. F. Novacheck. The biomechanics of running. *Gait & Posture*, 7:77 – 95, 1998.
7. A. Sabatini, C. Martelloni, S. Scapellato, and F. Cavallo. Assessment of walking features from foot inertial sensing. *Biomedical Engineering, IEEE Transactions on*, 52(3):486 –494, march 2005.
8. M. F. Weisenfeld and B. Burr. *The runner's repair manual*. St. Martin's Griffin, 1981.
9. K. R. Williams and P. R. Cavanagh. Relationship between distance running mechanics, running economy, and performance. *Journal of Applied Physiology*, 63:1236–1245, 1987.
10. A. Young. Comparison of orientation filter algorithms for realtime wireless inertial posture tracking. In *BSN 2009. Sixth International Workshop on*, 2009.

Route Classification Using Cellular Handoff Patterns

Richard A. Becker, Ramon Caceres, Karrie Hanson, Ji Meng Loh, Simon Urbanek, Alexander Varshavsky and Chris Volinsky
AT&T Labs - Research
180 Park Ave., Florham Park, NJ, USA
rab, ramon, karrie, loh, urbanek, varshavsky, volinsky @research.att.com

ABSTRACT

Understanding utilization of city roads is important for urban planners. In this paper, we show how to use handoff patterns from cellular phone networks to identify which routes people take through a city. Specifically, this paper makes three contributions. First, we show that cellular handoff patterns on a given route are stable across a range of conditions and propose a way to measure stability within and between routes using a variant of Earth Mover's Distance. Second, we present two accurate classification algorithms for matching cellular handoff patterns to routes: one requires test drives on the routes while the other uses signal strength data collected by high-resolution scanners. Finally, we present an application of our algorithms for measuring relative volumes of traffic on routes leading into and out of a specific city, and validate our methods using statistics published by a state transportation authority.

Author Keywords

Handoff patterns, route classification

ACM Classification Keywords

K.8.m Personal Computing: Miscellaneous.

General Terms

Algorithms, Experimentation, Measurement

INTRODUCTION

Urban planners are interested in understanding the mobility patterns of the people who live in and use their cities. This understanding facilitates effective solutions to problems with traffic congestion, parking, vehicular and pedestrian safety, and other aspects of urban living. To gain some knowledge of mobility patterns, planners currently use a combination of census data and vehicle counting. However, the expense of these methods typically results in infrequent data collection and/or small population samples.

Cellular telephone networks have the potential to provide near real-time information about human mobility on a large scale and at a low cost. These networks must know the approximate locations of all affiliated cell phones in order to provide the phones with voice and data services. Since people usually carry their cell phones with them, the location of a phone is a good proxy for the location of its owner.

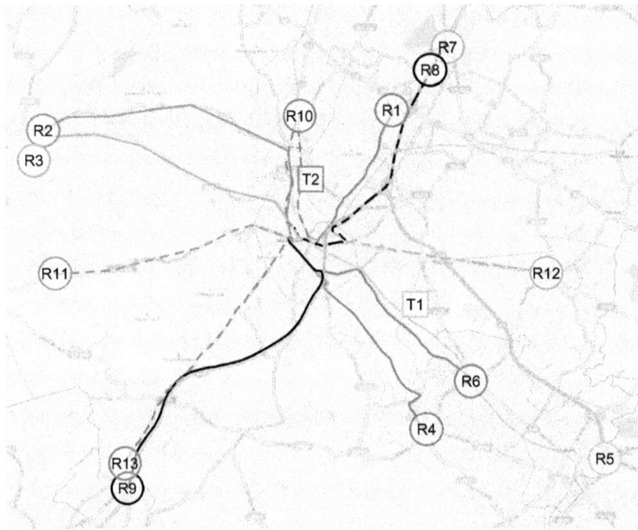

Figure 1. Thirteen driving routes (R1-R13) and two train routes (T1-T2) leading to the center of Anytown. R5, R7, R8, and R9 are freeways; the remainder are other principal commuting routes into town.

This paper explores the use of cellular handoff patterns to identify which routes people take through a city. A handoff pattern is the sequence of cellular antennas that a moving phone uses while engaged in a voice call. However, it is not obvious whether these patterns can be translated into useful route information. The main challenge is location inaccuracy due to the large geographic areas covered by individual antennas, which are often larger than one square mile. Therefore, knowing which antenna a phone is connected to does not immediately reveal what route the phone's owner is traveling on. However, it is possible that knowing sequences of antennas can yield enough information to reveal these routes.

Specifically, we investigate the use of handoff patterns extracted from anonymized Call Detail Records (CDRs). CDRs are collected when a phone is involved in a call, and may contain the full sequence of antennas used by the phone during that call. CDRs are routinely collected by network operators for all active cellular phones, which number in the hundreds of millions in the US and billions worldwide. Furthermore, CDRs are already used for network operation and planning, so additional uses incur little marginal cost. Another advantage of CDRs is that they are generated inside the network and thus do not place any extra burden on the limited resources of mobile phones, particularly their batteries. Despite the fact that our data is restricted to records of phones actively making calls while in transit, the ubiquity and scale of CDR records combined with the likelihood that we will observe a call in a moving vehicle provides us with sufficient data to apply our methods, even in a mid-sized suburban city. We defer the discussion of the limitations of our approach to a later section of the paper. We note, however, that our route identification techniques are independent of how cellular handoff patterns are recorded, whether by the network or by the phones.

Our work explores the following research questions:

1. Are handoff patterns stable across a wide enough range of conditions to be used for identifying routes?
2. Can we devise algorithms that reliably match handoff patterns to routes?
3. Can we derive reliable route utilization statistics from cellular network data?

To answer these questions, we undertook an experimental study of 15 driving and train routes leading into Anytown, a suburban city with roughly 20,000 residents. Figure 1 shows these routes. We used cellular phones to maintain active voice calls while we drove a car and rode the train on these routes. Later, we obtained CDRs from our calls, and used the corresponding handoff patterns to evaluate different route classification techniques. Finally, we applied our best performing techniques to 60 days of anonymized CDRs for all calls handled by one cellular carrier in the Anytown area.

This paper makes the following contributions:

1. We show that cellular handoff patterns are stable across different routes, speeds, directions, phone models, and weather conditions.
2. We propose two algorithms for matching handoff patterns to routes and show that they are accurate. The first uses nearest neighbor classification based on Earth Mover's Distance [8, 9]. The second uses signal strength data to compute the likelihood that a given handoff pattern occurs on a particular route.
3. We show how CDRs, in combination with our algorithms, can be used to determine the relative traffic volumes on roads. We validate these results against statistics published by a state transportation authority.

STABILITY OF HANDOFF PATTERNS

In this section, we show that cellular handoff patterns on a given route are stable over time and across a wide range of conditions. This stability allows us to capture the "typical" handoff pattern for a given route at one time and use it for route classification at another time.

We use the following terminology throughout the rest of this paper. A cell *tower* is a physical structure holding radio antennas and located at a particular latitude and longitude. A *sector* corresponds to a direction from a given cell tower. Each sector is covered by one or more antennas. An *antenna* is a physical device that communicates with mobile phones. Each antenna services a particular cellular technology (e.g., UMTS) and frequency (e.g., 2.1 GHz). Finally, a *handoff pattern* for a call consists of the list of antennas that handled that call, together with the time intervals during which the phone was communicating with each of those antennas. More formally, a handoff pattern for a call handled by n antennas can be expressed as $H = \{(a_i, t_i), i = 1, \ldots, n\}$, where a_i is the identifier of the ith antenna that handled the call and t_i is the duration (in seconds) the call spent on the antenna a_i.

Route Stability Data Collection

To test the stability of handoff patterns on a route, we collected data on a 3-mile stretch of road located in a residential area with many traffic lights and mostly two story buildings. In total, we collected 39 traces under the following varying conditions:

Time Eight months, from September, 2010 to April, 2011.

Phone Model iPhone 3GS, Nokia N95, Samsung Captivate (Android), HTC Aria (Android).

Route Direction North to South and the opposite.

Call Direction Calls originated and received.

Weather Sunny, cloudy, raining, snowing.

Traffic No traffic to heavy traffic.

During each drive, there were one or two pairs of phones in the car, with a call always active between the phones in each pair. In addition, the car's true route was captured using an iPhone application we developed for this purpose. The application recorded the car's location every 10 meters using the iPhone Location API, and uploaded the captured time-stamped locations to a server. We later obtained the handoff patterns of all the calls we made during our drives from the network operator's CDRs.

Stability Analysis

Figure 2 shows the geographic map of the area around the 3-mile route. The lines connecting cell sectors to the route represent locations on the route where a call was handed off to the corresponding sector during any of our 39 drives along this route. Portions of the route that do not show handoffs represent areas consistently covered by a single sector.

Figure 3 plots the handoff patterns of the same 39 drives in a way that allows side-by-side comparison. Each horizontal strip represents one drive along the route. Each color represents a different cell sector, using the colors from Figure 2. The drives are sorted by time, with the white strip separating

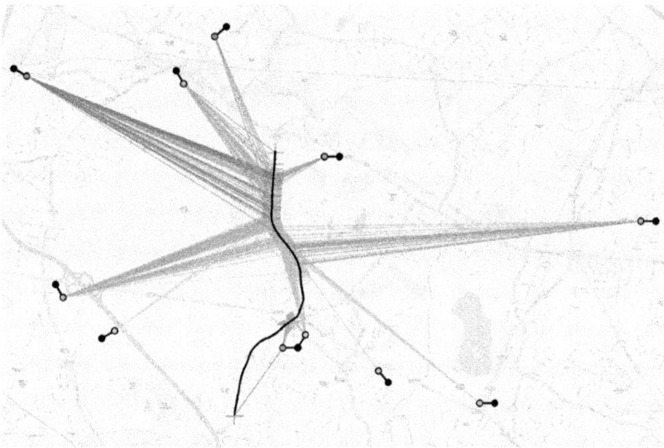

Figure 2. Handoff Stability. The black line marks the 2.8-mile route we drove repetitively to monitor the stability of handoffs under varying conditions. Black dots show the location of cell towers; these are connected to open circles showing the angle of an associated sector. Each thin colored line extends from a point on the route where a handoff occurred to the sector that received the call.

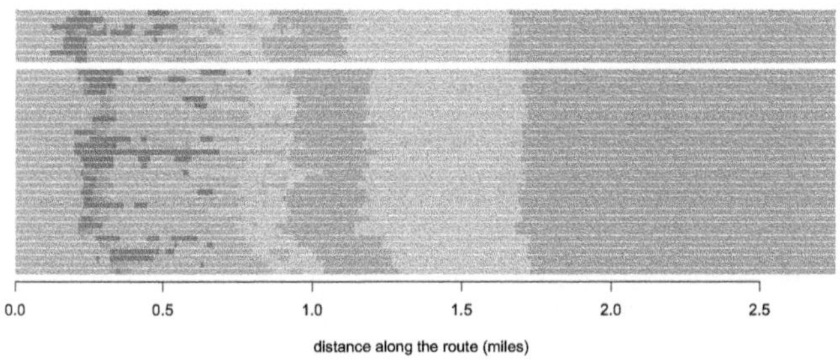

Figure 3. Side-by-side route coverage chart. Each horizontal strip represents one drive along the route. Colors represent sectors covering that portion of the route. The top section (8 calls) were for drives in one direction; the rest in reverse. Note that the handoffs happen at roughly the same locations along the route, and that the set of sectors covering each drive is almost identical.

drives in the two opposite directions. To directly compare the drives in both directions, we reversed the handoff patterns of drives in one direction.

We expect the geographic area for a handoff between two antennas to be roughly the same, regardless of the direction travelled. Indeed, we see each cell sector "covering" a certain geographic area. However, the locations of handoffs during drives in one direction appear to consistently lag relative to drives in the other direction. We believe this is due to the cellular network's desire to keep the phone connected to the current antenna as long as possible to avoid spurious handoffs. Other visualizations (not included in this paper for space reasons),permute the strips in Figure 3 using different grouping variables, and show that handoff patterns are relatively stable across all conditions. The same sectors cover the same road segments consistently, regardless of the phone model, weather conditions, traffic conditions and time.

Note that Figure 3 plots handoff patterns as a function of travelled distance. If plotted as a function of time, however, handoff patterns on the same route show greater differences because the phone may spend different amounts of time on each sector, due, for example, to varying traffic conditions. A good route classification algorithm must handle these time fluctuations.

ROUTE CLASSIFICATION USING NEAREST NEIGHBORS

The stability of handoff patterns across repeated drives on a given route is only part of the story. To match handoff patterns to routes requires that the handoff patterns of those routes are unique, even if the routes are geographically close. In order to assess our ability to classify handoff patterns into actual routes, we identified 15 common routes into and out of Anytown to form the basis of our experimental study. Each route either originates or terminates in the center of the city. We then developed and evaluated two methods for classifying handoff patterns on these routes. The first method uses handoff patterns collected from test drives as the training data for nearest-neighbor classification algorithms, and the second method uses signal-strength data collected on the routes as training data.

Test Drive Data Collection

We collected data on 13 commuter routes and 2 train routes leading into Anytown, a suburban city with approximately 20,000 residents. These routes represent all major ways to get in and out of the city. The route lengths vary from 3 to 6 miles. Many of the routes either partially overlap (e.g., routes R7 and R8) or lay very close to each other (e.g., routes T2 and R10). Overlapping or nearby routes serve to both stress-test our classification algorithms and to reflect reality. Figure 1 shows the 15 routes.

We travelled each route four times, two in each direction, primarily in the Fall of 2010, with a few fill-in drives and train rides in March of 2011. During each drive, there were two phones of different models in the car, one calling the other. As before, we obtained the handoff patterns of all calls from the network operator's CDRs. In total, we collected $4 \times 2 \times 15 = 120$ handoff patterns.

Distance Metrics and Classification Algorithm

Our classification is done via a nearest-neighbor algorithm. For each route, we split the 8 test drives randomly into equal sized training and test sets. For each instance in the test set, we assign the route label of the nearest instance from the training set. We evaluated four different distance metrics, as this choice is crucial for determining the nearest neighbor.

Common Subset Distances

Distances between two handoff patterns can be defined by measuring how much the two patterns have in common [13]. These distances are based on attributes of antennas in the handoff patterns. The larger the intersection between these sets of attributes, the more similar the handoff patterns. We refer to these distances as *common-subset* distances. We defined three common-subset distances that compare these attributes at different levels of granularity: cell towers, sectors, and antennas. The *Common Antennas* distance between two handoff patterns is the number of antennas that appear in

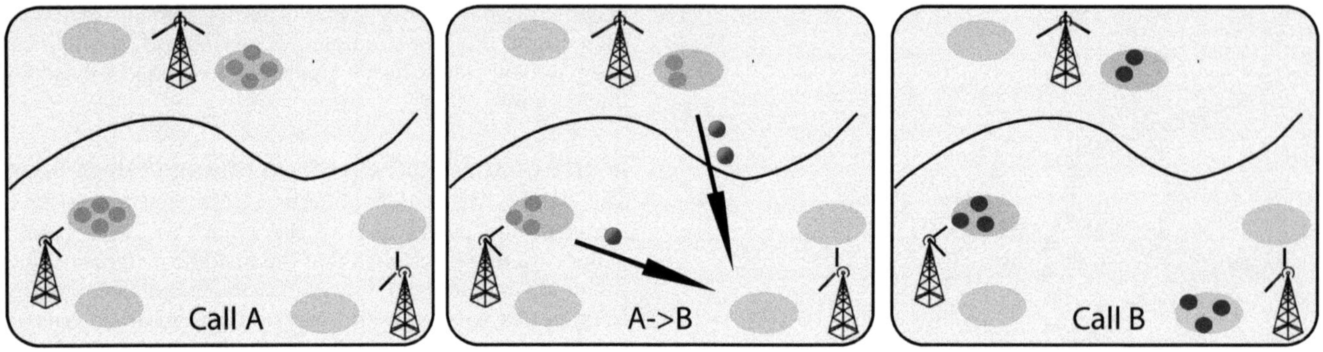

Figure 4. What is the Earth Mover's Distance between call A and call B? Each colored dot represents one minute of connect time to a specific sector (gray ovals). Both calls are 8 minutes long, but distributed differently across sectors. The curved black line represents a road. A->B shows the EMD metric optimally redistributing the minutes from sector to sector, turning call A into call B. The number of minutes moved between each pair of sectors is multiplied by the the Euclidean distance between that pair, summed for all pairs, and divided by total minutes moved, yielding the EMD.

both handoff patterns. Similar definitions apply to *Common Sectors* and *Common Towers* distances.

Classification algorithms based on these common subset distances compute the number of common entities between a handoff pattern in the test set and each of the handoff patterns in the training set. The training route with the highest number of common entities is selected as the best matching route. In the case of a tie, the training handoff pattern with the higher actual number of matching items (as opposed to the common set size) wins.

Earth Mover's Distance

Although common subset distances are good for baselines, they do not account for three important characteristics of the handoff pattern. First, the sequential nature of the handoff pattern is lost, basically reduced to an unordered set of entities to be used in the calculation. Second, temporal information on how long the call spends on each tower is not used by these algorithms. Finally, the cell tower location is not accounted for. Two patterns that differ only by towers that are close to each other should be considered close patterns.

We propose a variant of *Earth Mover's Distance* (EMD) as a distance metric that accounts for all of these characteristics. EMD is traditionally used to measure the differences between images. It was introduced as a technique for image retrieval in the computer vision community, although its roots are far older, [8, 9] and has previously been applied to wireless signals [3]. In the statistical literature, EMD is known as Mallows distance [6] or Wasserstein distance and is used as a distance metric for probability density functions.

Conceptually, imagine a pair of two dimensional images, where each pixel's brightness value is represented by a pile of dirt on that pixel. Pixels with similar brightness have similar amounts of dirt. Now, consider the energy needed to transform one image into the other by moving the piles of dirt. EMD is defined as the minimal energy needed to move the mass of dirt of one image into the locations that result in the target image. One only needs to define how that energy is calculated. Similarly, EMD is defined for arbitrary probability distributions as the mass of probability that needs to be moved to turn one distribution into another,

Figure 4 illustrates a simplified example of how we apply EMD to cellular call data. Given handoff patterns of calls A and B, the figure shows how much and what "work" needs to be performed to convert call A into call B.

More formally, let us define a handoff pattern as a sequence P, with elements $\mathbf{p}_i$ representing the locations of cell sectors in the sequence, and w_{p_i} representing a weight on each of those sectors. Then, let P and Q be two handoff patterns:

$$P = \{(\mathbf{p}_1, w_{p_1}), (\mathbf{p}_2, w_{p_2}), \ldots, (\mathbf{p}_m, w_{p_m})\} \quad (1)$$

$$Q = \{(\mathbf{q}_1, w_{q_1}), (\mathbf{q}_2, w_{q_2}), \ldots, (\mathbf{q}_n, w_{q_n})\}, \quad (2)$$

and let $D = [d_{ij}]$ be the geographical ground distance between points $\mathbf{p}_i$ and $\mathbf{q}_j$. Define the flow, f_{ij} as the amount of mass transported between points $\mathbf{p}_i$ and $\mathbf{q}_j$. We want to find $F = [f_{ij}]$, that minimizes the overall cost

$$W(P, Q, F) = \sum_{i=1}^{m} \sum_{j=1}^{n} f_{ij} d_{ij} \quad (3)$$

Let $[f^*_{ij}]$ be the optimal flow that minimizes Equation 3. Then, the Earth Mover's Distance is defined to be

$$EMD(P, Q) = \frac{\sum_{i=1}^{m} \sum_{j=1}^{n} f^*{}_{ij} d_{ij}}{\sum_{i=1}^{m} \sum_{j=1}^{n} f^*{}_{ij}} \quad (4)$$

In our case, the spatial locations $\mathbf{p}_i$ and $\mathbf{q}_j$ are given by the physical location (latitude and longitude) of sectors. We allow for the directionality of sectors by adjusting this location by a radius r in the direction of the azimuth of the sector. We set the weights w_i to be the duration spent on the particular sectors. We use Euclidean distance

$$d_{ij} = \sqrt{(x_i - x_j)^2 + (y_i - y_j)^2 + (\rho t_i - \rho t_j)^2} \quad (5)$$

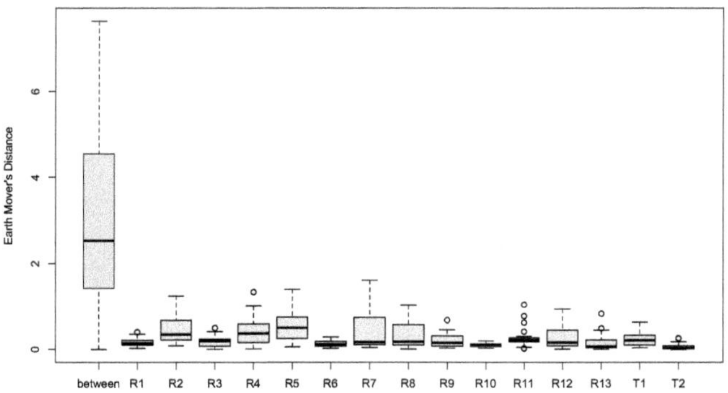

Figure 5. Boxplots show the within-route variation of handoff patterns, as computed by EMD distance. For each route, the within-route distance distribution is much smaller than the between-route distances. This figure shows within-route handoff pattern consistency and that the routes are different from one another and thus can be distinguished.

as our ground distance. In order for d_{ij} to operate on both space and time, we introduce a factor ρ as a conversion factor between the two dimensions to put them on a similar scale. In this way, EMD defines the distance between two distinct calls (handoff patterns), while accounting for temporal and spatial similarity.

One complexity of using EMD for our data is that handoff patterns can have varying length, both in duration and in the sequence of cell sectors, even on the same route (e.g., due to traffic lights). However, even in the extreme case where one sequence is a subset of another, EMD is still an effective distance metric. The imbalance would not contribute to the measure as the excess portion of the longer sequence will not be 'moved' and thus not included in any flow f_{ij}. A by-product of this feature is that the resulting measure is not commutative and hence no longer a proper distance metric. To adjust for this, we use the minimum of EMD(P, Q) and EMD(Q, P) as our distance measure.

Applying EMD in a nearest-neighbor classification task is a straightforward calculation of EMD between the test instances and our training set, then selecting the route label of the nearest one. However, we need one more adjustment to account for situations where the routes of interest are nested, or nearly nested (as in our R2 and R10). In this case, a fraction of a drive along the longer route could be matched well by the shorter route even though the longer route would account for more mass. Hence, for classification, we penalize short matches by adjusting EMD by a multiplicative factor equal to the quotient of the masses $\sum_i w_{p_i} / \sum_j w_{q_j}$, where p_i represents the test sequence and q_i the training sequence.

In this implementation of EMD, both r and ρ are free parameters in our classification algorithm, and so we optimize them using a grid search and cross-validation. The resulting values are $r = 660\text{m}$ and $\rho = 5\text{m/s}$, although the classification is not overly sensitive to the exact values. Our source code is available as the R package `emd` from CRAN.

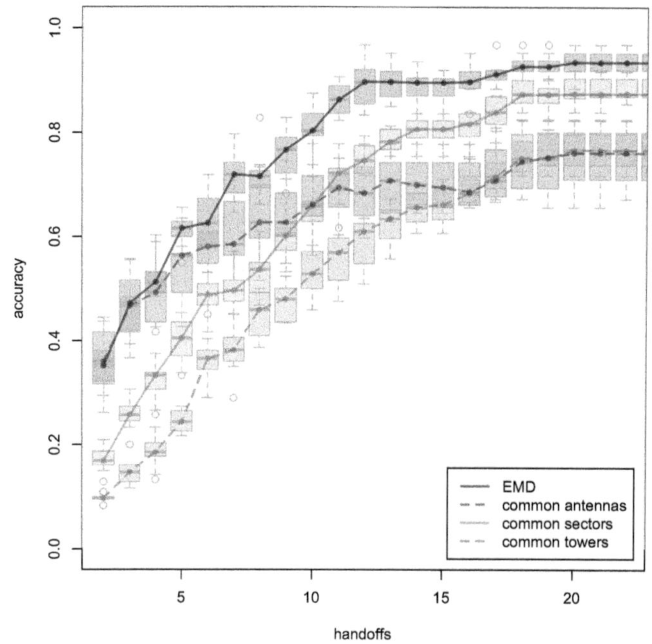

Figure 6. A comparison of nearest-neighbor classification using four distance metrics, with four handoff patterns as training and four as testing per route. Accuracy is shown as a function of the number of handoffs per drive. The boxplots show the range of accuracy over 10 randomly chosen training sets and the colored lines connect the medians of those sets. The EMD metric out-performs the others.

Variability of Handoff Patterns

We assessed the variability of handoff patterns based on the EMD distance metric by calculating all pairwise EMD distances for all of the drives on each of our 15 routes, and compared them to the pairwise distances for drives on different routes. Using the statistical concept of analysis of variance (ANOVA), we expect that the variance among handoff patterns for different drives on the same route to be significantly smaller than the variance between handoff patterns of different routes. Figure 5 shows the distribution of within-route distances plotted as boxplots above each route name, as well as a boxplot for all between-drive pairwise distances.

The figure gives us a good indication of the varying stability of the different drives. It shows that some routes (R1, R6, R10) are extremely stable, with consistently small distances across all pairwise calculations. Other routes are somewhat less stable, showing a wider spread in the boxplot and perhaps a few outliers. However, in all cases the within-route variation is much smaller than the between-routes variation, providing evidence that EMD will be able to differentiate between the routes well.

Performance of the Classification Algorithms

To show that we are effectively able to classify handoff patterns to our defined routes, we split our data into training and test sets, with four randomly selected drives for each route in each set. We fit each test instance to its nearest neighbor in the training set using our four distance metrics, EMD and the three common subset distances, repeating this procedure for 10 different random selections of the training set.

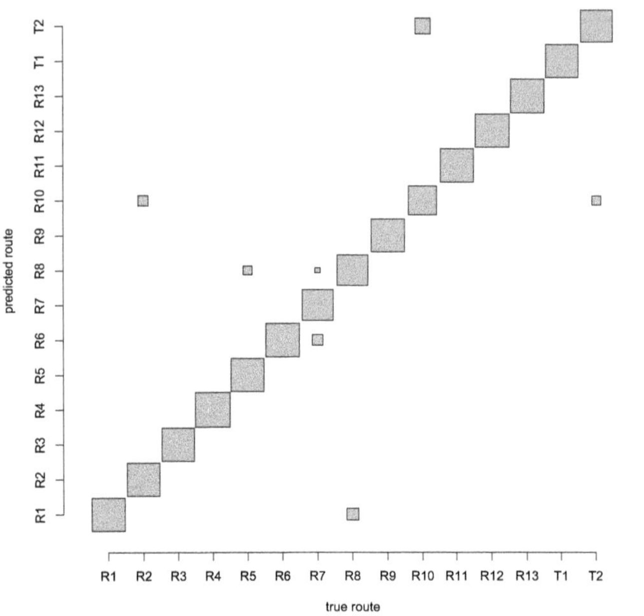

Figure 7. The confusion matrix for EMD algorithm with four training drives shows that most drives were classified correctly. The horizontal axis is the true route and the vertical axis is the predicted route. Correctly identified drives lie on the diagonal; off-diagonal squares are mis-classified. The area of the square is proportional to the number of drives.

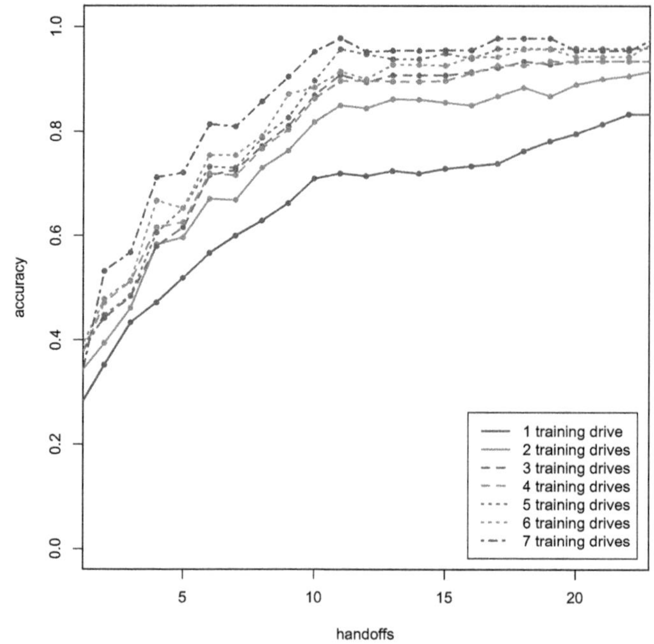

Figure 8. EMD's classification accuracy improves with the number of training samples.

We are also interested in measuring how much information is needed on a single drive in order to classify it correctly. Since all of our routes emerge from the center of Anytown, we assessed the accuracy of our algorithms for a call starting in the center of Anytown as a function of the number of handoffs the algorithm is allowed to observe. Figure 6 shows these results, with boxplots representing the accuracy across all replications for each distance metric and number of handoffs. Colored lines connect medians of the boxplots.

Figure 6 shows that, in general, the prediction accuracy increases as the number of handoffs increases up to a saturation point for all metrics. That is, the farther away the phone moves from the Anytown center, the easier it is to differentiate between routes. The EMD metric performs the best, achieving a median classification accuracy of 90% after 12 handoffs (corresponding roughly to 2 miles). The Common Towers metric performs the worst because it cannot differentiate between handoffs occurring between antennas on the same cell tower. Interestingly, the Common Antennas metric outperforms the Common Sectors metric for up to 10 handoffs, but then performs worse because sometimes phone calls on the same route are handled by different antennas pointing in the same direction.

Figure 7 shows the confusion matrix for the EMD algorithm (the nearest-neighbor classification using the EMD metric) with four training drives using complete test routes. The area of the squares is proportional to the number of drives represented by the square. Squares on the diagonal indicate correctly classified drives, whereas off-diagonal squares are misclassified. Not surprisingly, most of mis-classifications come from overlapping or nearby routes, such as R10 and T2 or R2 and R10 (see Figure 1).

Finally, we studied the effect the number of training drives has on the classification accuracy of the EMD algorithm. Figure 8 shows the performance as we vary the number of training drives from 1 to 7. The results indicate that performance increases with the number of training drives, as the larger training set allows the EMD algorithm to capture more variance on each route. However, we see that with as few as two training drives, performance is quite high, achieving median accuracy of more than 80% after only 12 handoffs. In summary, we showed that the EMD algorithm is well suited to classify handoff patterns under realistic conditions.

ROUTE CLASSIFICATION USING SIGNAL STRENGTHS

The previous section showed that a nearest-neighbor classification algorithm using EMD does a good job matching handoff patterns to routes, requiring as few as two training drives. However, training the algorithm required time-consuming test drives on every target route, and the use of EMD as a distance metric is computationally complex. Although that methodology can be valuable for targeted small deployments where collecting traces of handoff patterns on routes is feasible, a large-scale deployment requires a different approach.

Luckily, cellular network operators routinely use high-resolution scanners to collect GPS-stamped signal-strength measurements from all observable antennas along all major and some minor roads. This process is done for network engineering and maintenance purposes, and it is often referred to as *wardriving* in the research community [5].

In this section, we show that signal-strength data collected by scanners can be used for matching handoff patterns to routes, eliminating the need for training drives. We also present a novel classification algorithm that uses the signal strength data for training and compare its performance with that of the nearest-neighbor classification using EMD.

Scanner Data

We obtained access to scanner traces collected around the Anytown area primarily on September 3, 2010. The traces include GPS-stamped measurements (one per second) along most of our routes. Each measurement contains a list of antennas that were observed at a given location along with the Signal-to-Noise Ratios (SNR), expressed logarithmically in decibels (dB). Unfortunately, we had no scanner data from the train routes.

Although the scanner data did not always correspond exactly to our routes, it did cover the region systematically and we were able to stitch together various parts of the data to match the routes. Since the scanner data is collected at regular intervals throughout the year, we have an opportunity to see how it changes over time, reflecting any changes in network configuration as well as any seasonal differences.

Signal Strength Route Classification Algorithm

The signal strength algorithm classifies a given handoff pattern to one of the routes and it has two stages. In the first stage, it creates a matrix of the maximum SNR values observed on each route from each antenna. If a given antenna has not been observed on a route, the appropriate matrix cell gets a low value of -30dB [1]. We experimented with lower floor values and found no effects on our results. More formally, the algorithm builds a matrix $S = \{(s_{i,j}) : i = 1, \ldots, n; j = 1, \ldots, m\}$, where s_{ij} is the maximum SNR value seen on route i from antenna j.

In the second stage, the algorithm estimates the likelihood of a given handoff pattern appearing on each route by summing up, separately for each route, the maximum SNR values of the antennas appearing in the handoff pattern. The handoff pattern is assigned to the route with the largest likelihood. The intuition is that the antennas with the strongest signals on a route are likely the ones that will appear in the handoff patterns for that route. For example, if a handoff pattern contains three antennas: a_1, a_3, a_5 and there are a total of two routes r_1, r_2, the algorithm computes $S_{r_i} = s_{i,1} + s_{i,3} + s_{i,5}$ for i of 1 and 2, corresponding to the two routes. Summing the SNR logarithms is similar to adding log likelihoods to get the log likelihood of multiple independent events, ignoring any dependence of antennas on one another.

This approach is a weighted variation of the Common Antennas algorithm from the previous section, but the weights and antennas come from the scanned signal-strength data, not from CDRs for our own test drives. Therefore, there is no "training" to be done – the weights take the place of a multitude of test drives.

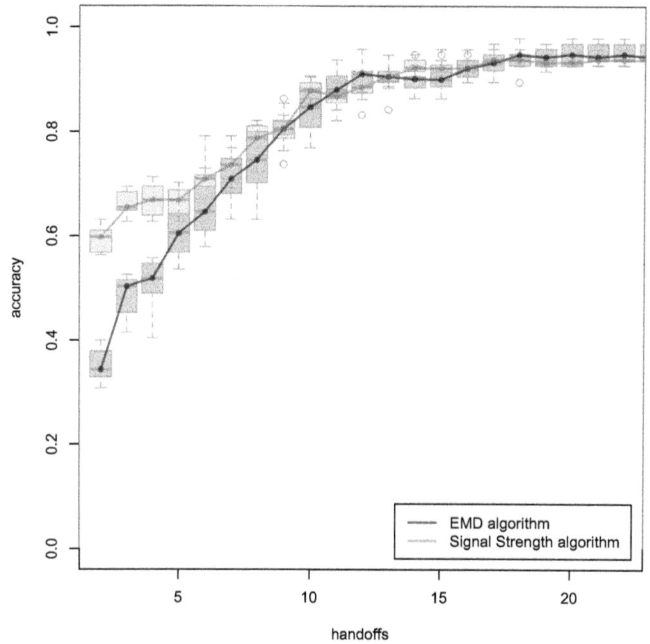

Figure 9. Classification accuracy of the EMD algorithm and the Signal Strength algorithm over 10 random runs.

Figure 9 compares the performance of the Signal Strength and EMD algorithms. Although the Signal Strength algorithm outperforms EMD until up to 8 handoff patterns, the two perform comparably with 9 or more handoff patterns on a drive, achieving more than 90% accuracy. This is a strong result, showing that we can achieve similar accuracy for route classification using two very different approaches.

ESTIMATING RELATIVE TRAFFIC VOLUMES

In this section, we show how our route classification algorithms can be used in practice. Specifically, we show that anonymized CDRs from a network provider, together with our route classification algorithms, can be used to estimate the relative volume of traffic on our Anytown routes.

We had several meetings with urban planners in Anytown, who showed great interest in estimating the flow of traffic along certain routes into and out of the city. When they see congestion in the town center, they do not know where the cars are coming from or headed. And although they can get traffic counts at stationary points from traffic meters, learning about routes entails costly and error-prone surveys of individuals who travel in the area. Detailed route information might help planners to design better traffic signaling and to plan future public transportation infrastructure.

We next describe our CDR collection methodology, the steps we took to protect people's privacy and the limitations of our approach. We then present our estimates for relative traffic volumes on each route. Finally, we compare our estimates to publicly available traffic count data from the Anystate Department of Transportation.

CDR Data Collection

We collected anonymized CDRs from the cellular network of a large US communications service provider. These CDRs capture calls carried by the 35 cell towers located within 5 miles of the center of Anytown, a suburban city with approximately 20,000 residents. These 35 cell towers house approximately 300 antennas pointed in various directions and supporting various radio technologies and frequencies. Our goal was to capture cellular traffic in and around the city and choosing the 5-mile radius allowed us to cover both Anytown proper and its neighboring areas.

In place of the phone number of the person involved in a voice call, each CDR contains an anonymous identifier consisting of a unique integer. Each CDR also contains the starting time and duration of the call, and the locations and azimuths of the cell tower antennas associated with the event. The CDRs contain no information about the second party involved in the call.

We collected voice traffic for 60 days between November 29, 2009, and January 27, 2010, resulting in 15 million voice CDRs for 475,000 unique phones.

Privacy

Given the sensitivity of CDR data, we took several steps to ensure the privacy of individuals. First, only anonymous records were used in this study. The data was collected and anonymized by a party not involved in the data analysis. Personally identifying characteristics were removed from our CDRs. CDRs for the same phone are linked using an anonymous unique identifier, rather than a telephone number. No demographic data is linked to any cell phone user or CDR.

Second, all our results are presented as aggregates. That is, no individual anonymous identifier was singled out for the study. By observing and reporting only on the aggregates, we protect the privacy of individuals.

Finally, each CDR only included location information for the cellular antennas associated with a phone during a voice call. The phones were effectively invisible to us outside those times, and we only knew those phone locations at the granularity of an antenna's coverage area, often greater than one square mile.

Limitations

Our CDR data is limited to devices that are actively making a phone call. A US Department of Transportation study [12] estimates that 9% of drivers are using mobile devices while they are driving, but underestimates hands-free usage and omits passenger phone usage. It is possible that this factor differs according to time of day or length of trip, which could skew our results. Nonetheless, combining the 9% usage factor with our carrier's significant market share in the region of the study and the large volume of the overall data provides confidence that our sample sizes are large enough to estimate the traffic flows correctly. This confidence would only increase if we run our algorithms in a market with a larger subscriber base.

Applying our algorithms in areas without the nice hub-and-spoke layouts will require a more careful designation of the roads of interest and is likely to result in different accuracy numbers. However, we believe that our algorithms are applicable to environments of any complexity or size.

Analysis

In the previous sections, we tested our route classification algorithms on handoff patterns known to correspond to one of our selected city routes. In practice, however, it is a challenge to determine whether a voice call was conducted while driving on one of our routes. We used two heuristics to select an appropriate subset of calls. First, we filtered out all CDRs for calls that do not begin or end at the cell tower located at the center of Anytown. Second, we filtered out all CDRs whose handoff patterns include antennas from fewer than 5 distinct cell towers. Although the second step may be too conservative, we wanted to make sure that the remaining CDRs belong to calls made from moving vehicles. After filtering, we were still left with tens of thousands of CDRs.

Figure 10 plots relative traffic volumes as estimated by the EMD algorithm, overlaid on our map of routes into and out of Anytown. The counts are normalized to a count per 1000 cars. The thickness of the line represents the volume estimated on that route. The plot allows comparing the relative number of people who access the town from north and south on the interstate (the black lines) vs. the relative number of people who enter and leave Anytown on secondary state or county roads. The relative traffic volumes as computed by the Signal Strength route classification algorithm are similar and are not included due to space considerations.

Both of our route classification algorithms can deal with calls that are not on any of the target routes. When this happens, the EMD distance will be too large or the signal-strength likelihood too small, and we can set a threshold that indicates that the call does not match. After applying the thresholds on our data, we saw no noticable impact on the relative traffic distributions.

Validation

We present our results as relative volumes instead of absolute volumes since there are many factors that play into whether we will see a particular traveling vehicle: the phone must be active, the user must be a customer of the cellular provider that supplies the data, the phone must use five unique towers, and so on. Because of this, validation of our numbers against readily available government traffic count data is challenging. An additional challenge is that the government traffic data is typically collected using in-street traffic meters or human car counters. Both methods give a count at a static point, while our methods are estimating traffic along a particular route made up of many sequential points.

Nonetheless, we attempted to validate our data with available traffic count information from the Anystate Department of Transportation (DOT). The DOT has a multitude of data available at strategic places around town from traffic meters over the years 2004-2010 [7]. This data allows us to see how

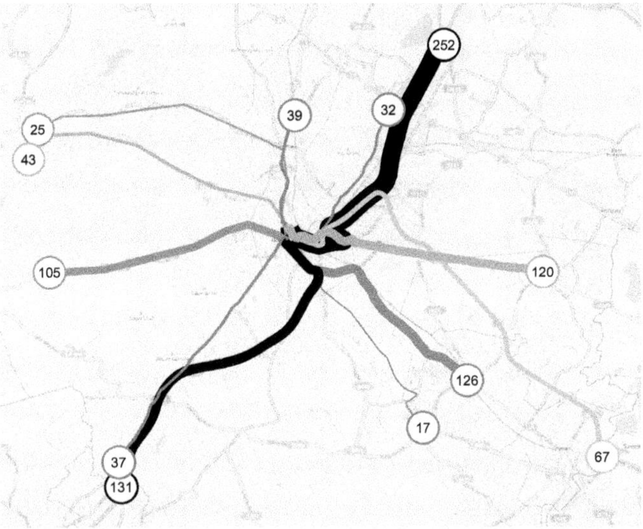

Figure 10. Predicted traffic distribution of 1000 calls. Both the EMD and Signal Strength algorithms were used to estimate traffic volumes on the 13 commuter routes into Anytown. The EMD results are shown as flows into Anytown, with the line width proportional to the estimated volume; the Signal Strength algorithm results are similar.

much daily traffic there is on specific spot on a road. Most of our routes had multiple traffic measurements available at different locations along the route.

Because Anytown is a local hub (it is the largest city in its county), we made the simplifying assumption that all of the traffic on the secondary roads heading into town either originated or terminated at the town center. Since this assumption could not be true for the main interstate running through town, we did not include those routes (R7,R8, and R9) in this analysis. Also, we did not have any traffic counts for any part of R10 that was unique to R10, so we excluded that route as well. Additionally, if a route had multiple measurements of daily traffic at different locations, we selected the minimum of these counts. In most cases, this minimum count was at the furthest point from Anytown, and hence was the best estimate of the number of cars that had travelled the entire length of the route. Finally, we removed a single data point from the DOT data that was highly suspicious as an outlier; it was incongruous with nearby data points in a way that made it appear to be erroneous.

Figure 11 shows a scatterplot of EMD-estimated traffic counts vs. the DOT-supplied traffic counts. The figure shows that the two estimates are closely related, with a correlation coefficient of 0.77. We believe that this result validates our methodology.

To summarize, we showed how CDR data together with our route classification algorithms can be used to estimate relative traffic volumes. We validated this methodology using Anystate DOT traffic counts. The main advantage of our technique vs. simply using Anystate DOT estimates is that we can provide relative traffic estimates much more frequently due to the low cost of our approach. For instance,

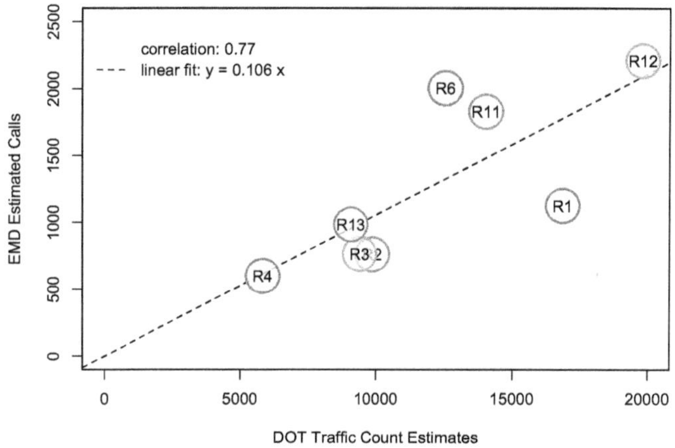

Figure 11. Comparison of traffic volumes estimated by our EMD algorithm against corresponding values obtained from the Anystate Department of Transportation.

we could generate figures similar to Figure 10 for different days of the week, times of day, or for special events like a town parade or a holiday.

RELATED WORK

Mobile phone localization has been an active research topic during the past decade [14]. Placelab [5, 2] was the first system to demonstrate the feasibility of using WiFi and GSM signals for localizing mobile devices. That effort has inspired several follow-up commercial products [15, 16]. Instead of localizing mobile devices, this paper addresses the problem of identifying the route a phone has taken based on cellular handoff patterns.

Krumm et al. [4] developed a Hidden Markov Model (HMM) algorithm for map matching using frequently sampled GPS data. VTrack [11] is a system for travel time estimation using WiFi-based and GPS-based location predictions. VTrack estimates travel times by first mapping location estimates obtained from WiFi and GPS to road segments using a HMM-based algorithm. In contrast to those efforts, we use infrequent changes to the currently associated cellular antenna to match drives to routes.

In a parallel effort to ours, Thiagarajan et al. [10] have developed CTrack, a system for trajectory mapping using cellular base-station fingerprints. Using a two phase HMM-based algorithm and a pre-existing database of location-stamped GSM fingerprints, CTrack is able to match a stream of new GSM fingerprints to road segments with a median accuracy of 75%. CTrack can also utilize information from an accelerometer and a compass to improve its accuracy further. In contrast, our method doesn't require new software to be installed on mobile phones, as we are using the information collected by cellular network operators for billing and maintenance purposes. In addition, our algorithms use only a single cellular antenna at a time, whereas CTrack uses ID and RSSI from up to seven antennas per location. Finally, we analyzed the stability of handoff patterns and showed how to estimate relative traffic volumes on roads.

CONCLUSIONS

CDRs represent perhaps the most abundant records of human mobility available in the world today, and are routinely gathered by cellular network operators for operation and planning. Identifying the trajectories of mobile devices using this CDR data is of great interest to sociologists, civil engineers, and urban planners. In this paper, we showed how to use CDRs to identify which routes people take through a city.

Specifically, we first measured the variability inherent in repeated drives of the same route, and showed that the handoff patterns are relatively stable across different routes, speeds, directions, phone models, and weather conditions. We also employed a novel metric for measuring route variability, based on Earth Mover's Distance, and used it to quantify variability across repeated drives of the same route and between routes.

We then proposed two algorithms for matching handoff patterns to routes and showed their accuracy. The first uses nearest-neighbor classification based on Earth Mover's Distance. The second uses signal strength data to compute the likelihood that a given handoff pattern occurs on a particular route. We showed that the two algorithms have comparable results, with accuracies over 90% for classifying new handoff patterns with only 12 handoffs. Note that although we use handoff patterns extracted from CDRs in our study, our algorithms could be used with cellular handoff patterns captured by the devices themselves. With more and more handsets providing rich programming APIs, the ability to collect this data from the handsets themselves is likely to increase.

Finally, we showed how CDRs, in combination with our algorithms, can be used to estimate the relative traffic volumes on roads, and we validated these estimates against statistics published by a state transportation authority, showing excellent correlation. Currently, such estimates can only be done by laborious placement of in-road or human traffic monitors or by expensive and inaccurate surveys. Conversely, CDRs come in real time and allow studying effects of weather and other disruptions in ways the current sporadic measurements cannot. Our preliminary discussions with urban planners indicate that if proven effective, CDR-based traffic volume estimation could bring significant changes in how they do community planning.

ACKNOWLEDGEMENTS

We thank Mike Orth for providing us with the Nova RF data and Colin Goodall and Siva Prakasam for collecting and anonymizing the CDR data we used in this paper.

REFERENCES

1. A. Buvaneswari, J. M. Graybeal, D. A. James, D. Lambert, C. Liu, and W. M. MacDonald. A statistical view of the transient signals that support a wireless call. *Technometrics*, 49, 2007.
2. M. Y. Chen, T. Sohn, D. Chmelev, D. H. J. Hightower, J. Hughes, A. LaMarca, F. Potter, I. Smith, and A. Varshavsky. Practical metropolitan-scale positioning for gsm phones. In *Proc. of the 8th Int. Conference on Ubiquitous Computing*, Irvine, California, Sept. 2006.
3. K. Kleisouris, B. Firner, R. Howard, Y. Zhang, and R. P. Martin. Detecting intra-room mobility with signal strength descriptors. In *Proc. of the 11th ACM Int. Symposium on Mobile Ad Hoc Networking and Computing*, MobiHoc '10, pages 71–80, 2010.
4. J. Krumm, J. Letchner, and E. Horvitz. Map matching with travel time constraints. In *Society of Automotive Engineers (SAE) 2007 World Congress*, April 2007.
5. A. LaMarca, Y. Chawathe, S. Consolvo, J. Hightower, I. Smith, J. Scott, T. Sohn, J. Howard, J. Hughes, F. Potter, J. Tabert, P. Powledge, G. Borriello, and B. Schilit. Place lab: Device positioning using radio beacons in the wild. In *Proc. of the 3rd Int. Conference on Pervasive Computing*, Lecture Notes in Computer Science. Springer-Verlag, May 2005.
6. E. Levina and P. Bickel. The Earth Mover's Distance is the Mallows Distance: Some Insights from Statistics. In *ICCV 2001*, pages 251–256, 2001.
7. NJ Department of Transportation. Roadway information and traffic counts. www.state.nj.us/transportation/refdata/roadway/traffic.shtm.
8. Y. Rubner, C. Tomasi, and L. J. Guibas. A metric for distributions with applications to image databases. In *Proceedings of the Sixth International Conference on Computer Vision*, ICCV '98, pages 59–, Washington, DC, USA, 1998. IEEE Computer Society.
9. Y. Rubner, C. Tomasi, and L. J. Guibas. The earth mover's distance as a metric for image retrieval. *Int. J. Comput. Vision*, 40:99–121, November 2000.
10. A. Thiagarajan, L. S. Ravindranath, H. Balakrishnan, S. Madden, and L. Girod. Accurate, Low-Energy Trajectory Mapping for Mobile Devices. In *8th USENIX Symp. on Networked Systems Design and Implementation (NSDI)*, Boston, MA, March 2011.
11. A. Thiagarajan, L. S. Ravindranath, K. LaCurts, S. Toledo, J. Eriksson, S. Madden, and H. Balakrishnan. VTrack: Accurate, Energy-Aware Traffic Delay Estimation Using Mobile Phones. In *7th ACM Conference on Embedded Networked Sensor Systems (SenSys)*, Berkeley, CA, November 2009.
12. US Department of Transportation. Driver electronic device use in 2009. *Traffic Safety Facts Research Note*, DOT HS 811-372, September 2010.
13. A. Varshavsky, D. Pankratov, J. Krumm, and E. de Lara. Calibree: Calibration-free localization using relative distance estimations. In *Proc. of the 6th International Conference on Pervasive Computing*, May 2008.
14. A. Varshavsky and S. Patel. chapter 7: Location in ubiquitous computing. *Ubiquitous Computing Fundamentals*, 2010.
15. SkyHook Wireless, http://www.skyhookwireless.com.
16. Navizon, http://www.navizon.com.

Reflections on the Long-term Use of an Experimental Digital Signage System

Sarah Clinch[1], Nigel Davies[1], Adrian Friday[1], and Christos Efstratiou[2]

[1]Lancaster University, Lancaster, UK
[2]University of Cambridge, Cambridge, UK

ABSTRACT
In this paper we reflect on our long-term experiences of developing, deploying and supporting an experimental digital signage system. Existing public display systems almost always feature a single point of control that is responsible for scheduling content for presentation on the network and provide sophisticated mechanisms for controlling play-out timing and relative ordering. Our experiences suggest that such complex feature-sets are unnecessary in many cases and may be counter productive in signage systems. We describe an alternative, simpler paradigm for encouraging widespread use of signage systems based on shared 'content channels' between content providers and display owners. Our system has been in continuous use for approximately 3 years. We reflect and draw lessons from how our user community has adopted and used the resulting public display network. We believe that these reflections will be of benefit to future developers of ubiquitous display networks.

Author Keywords
Public display, digital signage, long-term deployments, HCI

ACM Classification Keywords
H1.2 User / Machine Systems: Human information processing

General Terms
Design, Experimentation, Human Factors

INTRODUCTION
Digital public displays have long been an area of interest in both commercial and academic settings. As display hardware costs have fallen, digital displays have become increasingly prevalent, appearing in many public and semi-public spaces. In parallel there has been an increase in research in the area, with a particular focus on user interaction with public displays. Our own work is driven by the desire to eventually create open display networks in which viewers can appropriate displays for their own purposes—shifting the focus of display networks away from pushing advertising at unreceptive audiences and towards a key role as part of our future global computing and communications infrastructure.

In 2004 we began an intensive research programme in this area—a key part of which was the creation of a large scale testbed for public display research. In order to justify the cost and disruption associated with its deployment and to help reduce the novelty factor associated with the displays we considered it important that the testbed would also serve as a general digital signage solution for our institution—while as researchers we have many exciting ideas for how to use public display networks it is inescapable that for many people these same displays need to fulfil a more conventional signage role.

We initially experimented with a range of commercial signage offerings but soon found that the feature set offered by these systems did not fit well with our user community nor did they encourage an 'open system' with content coming from the diverse small groups we aimed to support. As a result we designed, developed and deployed our own signage system on top of an experimental systems infrastructure. At the time of writing our system has been in operation for approximately three years and in this paper we reflect on our own and our users' long-term experiences. In particular, we make the following contributions:

- We present a novel design for a simplified signage control system based on a separation of content producers and display owners.
- We provide detailed insight into the system's continued daily use for approximately 3 years.
- We provide lessons for designers of future ubiquitous display systems.

We believe these contributions will be of significant value to future developers of ubiquitous display systems.

EARLY EXPERIMENTS
Overview
In order to support conventional "signage" functionality in our organisation we initially explored the use of two distinct methods of managing and scheduling content within our campus-based display network.

UbiComp'11, September 17–21, 2011, Beijing, China.

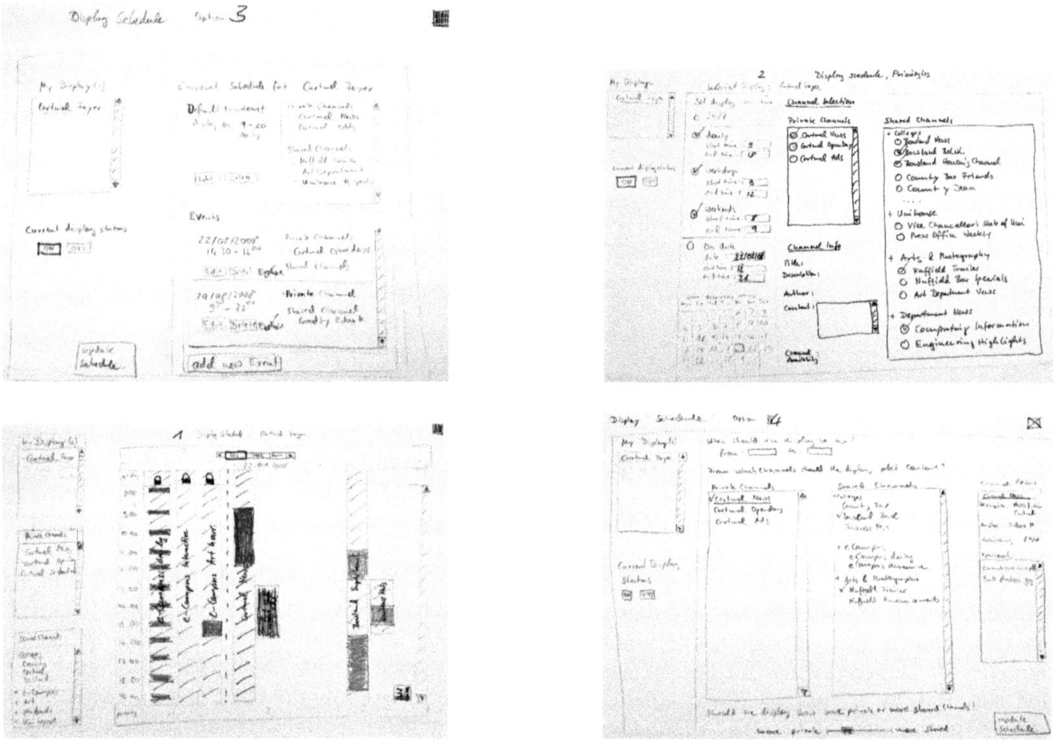

Figure 1. Sketch of a possible UIs for sharing content across University campus. From left to right, exploring (a) daily content vs. overriding 'events', (b) associating dates and times with content, (c) a calendar timeline view, and (d) presenting private and shared (public) channels.

A commercial signage system

Deploying and controlling large scale networks of public displays is commonplace in the commercial world and scheduling and managing content is a key part of any modern public display system (e.g. [16]). We deployed a common commercial signage system that provides software for content creation and scheduling, content transfer, content play-out and monitoring of software and hardware on play-out devices. The system provides the ability to ingest content into the display network. Content that is to be scheduled has to be arranged into multi-track timelines that are called "playlists". Finally the user can specify which "channels" to schedule the content in. Channels, in this context, represent pre-defined sets of play-out devices. We provided access to several key user groups such as the marketing department, colleges and public arts.

A drop-box system

For more casual content providers we built a "drop-box" solution. This system was a simple web-based workflow that allowed content providers to request the publication of a piece of content they uploaded. The system notified the Display Management Team when and on which displays that piece of content should be displayed and allowed the team to accept and reject content easily. In most cases, the team then used a commercial signage system to add the content to the displays' playlists.

These two systems were deployed and used to support routine scheduling of content within our deployment.

Analysis

The commercial signage system and the drop-box system provided two very different ways of managing content on a network of public displays. The commercial system offered a highly configurable 'TV schedule' like environment that allowed content creators to decide exactly when their content should be displayed, in what sequence and on which displays. The system assumes a model of the world in which a small number of well trained operators are responsible for scheduling content and the learning curve for the system is relatively steep.

The "drop-box" approach was much simpler for the content providers, but relied on a centralised administrator to decide the scheduling patterns of individual pieces of content. This placed a significant burden on a busy team behind the scenes, often leading to a perception of unresponsiveness.

After a period of 16 months during which people had the opportunity to experiment with both mechanisms we performed a set of interviews with selected major users of the system in the public arts, colleges and a marketing department. The aim of these interviews was to discuss their experiences with the two systems and identify the requirements for a new system of managing content distribution on the public display network. The resulting observations were:

- *Too much flexibility hampers usability.* Only very few people in the University environment were willing to schedule content using the commercial system (mainly in the public arts who required more flexibility for scheduling their content). Most interviewees believed the system not well suited to non-technical users. In fact, most people used the "drop-box", despite having access to the full system.

- *Users want to control their own displays.* People affiliated with colleges and departments expressed a need to assume ownership of displays in their environment. Although it was clear that the displays belong to a University wide infrastructure, the fact that a display is located in a particular building raised the issue of control from the people that are affiliated with that location.
- *Users want their content to appear on other displays across campus.* An obvious requirement for any public display system—people from different groups across the University expressed the need to publish announcements or publicity content on multiple displays. Combining this requirement with the desire for display ownership requires us to balance control and sharing of content on displays.
- *Users want real-time responses to changes in their content.* Our "drop-box" approach meant that content providers would have to create or modify content and then wait (sometimes days) before a member of the Display Management Team could respond to their request. In practice we found that they often wanted to make changes to content at the last minute and wanted real-time responses to their requests!

During the interviews we had the opportunity to discuss alternative interfaces for a replacement system (see prototype designs in Figure 1). Designs that were discussed ranged from those based on calendars and timelines, to interfaces where playback of each content item could be fine-tuned.

The interviews gave us clear indications drawn from our users' past experience: people liked the simplicity of the "drop-box" approach, but they required coarse-grained control over content scheduling. It was clear that too much detailed scheduling control was considered burdensome, but no control over what was displayed was equally undesirable.

THE E-CHANNEL SYSTEM

Based on our early experiences our aim was to develop a system that provided a simple way of enabling users to distribute content to their own and others' displays and also to control the content on their own display. The resulting system is called *the e-Channel system*. Our key technical insight was to *maintain a separation between content providers and display owners*. To support this separation we enable users to adopt the following roles—that of a *content provider* or that of a *display owner*:

1. Content providers generate content in a wide range of formats (images, videos, web pages, live video streams) and organize their content in logical containers called "Channels". A content provider has full ownership of their Channels and is able to add and remove content at any time, schedule the times that a channel is active, suspend it from use, or delete it. Content providers are not affiliated with displays in the infrastructure and have no control on where or when content is displayed. Instead, their channels can be shared and their content is displayed when display owners subscribe to them.
2. Display owners are linked to a number of physical displays in the infrastructure, typically, those in a 'local' physical space. For example, College officers are considered display owners for displays located within the College's premises and departmental administrators are owners of the displays in their own department. A display owner controls the content on their own displays by means of channel subscriptions. They can subscribe or unsubscribe to channels at any time and decide when the display should be scheduled to be on or off.

The two roles are completely separate from one another although certain users are *both* content providers and display owners. For example, a college officer may be a display owner controlling the displays in the college, and at the same time a content provider to those displays creating content for a 'college news' channel. In such cases users can create "private channels" with content only available for displays under their control.

The general architecture of the e-Channel system imposes no restrictions on how content is published through channels and how display owners subscribe to them. A channel provider may change the content of a channel at any time. There is no way for a subscriber to preview the content—they must rely on the channel description and the reputation of the channel source to inform their subscription decisions.

The e-Channel system provides two user interfaces: *a file system interface* that allows content providers to add and remove channel content, and *a web interface* that allows content providers and display owners to manage channel scheduling parameters, subscriptions and display availability.

Content providers can use the web interface to create channels and access a dedicated folder on a networked file system associated with the channel. Once a channel has been created, content providers are able to add content to the channel by dragging and dropping media files into this shared folder. The aim was to maintain the benefits of the "drop-box" approach without the need to upload via a web browser. Users find manipulating content using the file system substantially less cumbersome than a web-based approach, especially for large video files and operations involving many pieces of content. Conceptually, the model is also very simple to grasp: users know that files in the folder correspond to their channel's content; they simply drag them out or delete them to take them out of the system. Content providers are able to limit the availability of their channels to certain public displays, and to certain dates and times using the web interface (see Figure 2).

Display owners subscribe their displays to one or more channels using the web interface. The system produces a schedule for each display based on the set of content items from

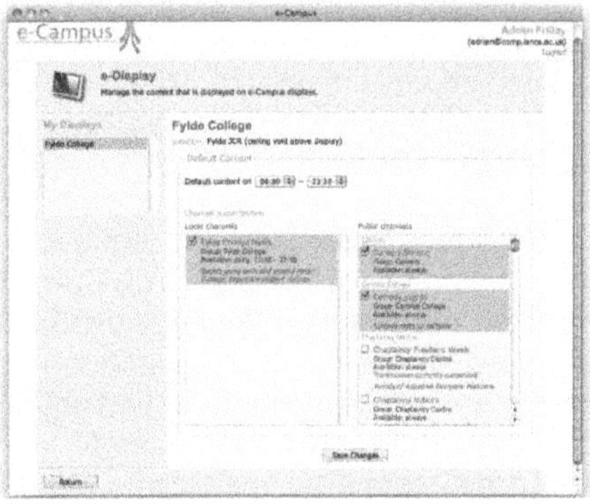

(a) Controlling subscriptions on a display.

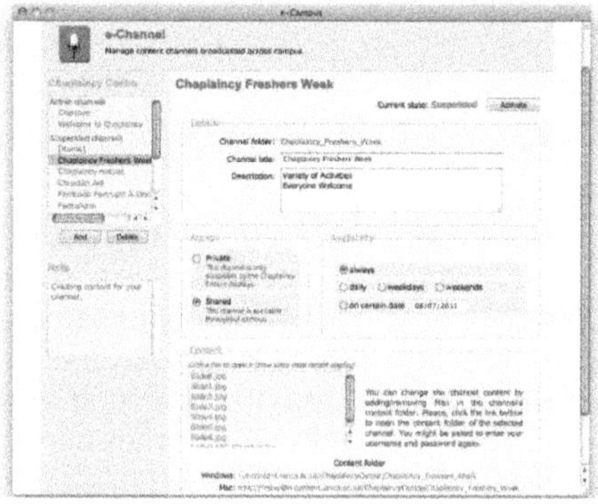

(b) Controlling channel availability.

Figure 2. Screenshot showing the UI that display owners use to control their subscriptions (left), and content creators to control their channels (right).

all of the channels that the display is currently subscribed to. Our scheduling policy treats all channels equally, although we prioritise newer content and specific types of content (such as emergency alerts and interactive applications[1]).

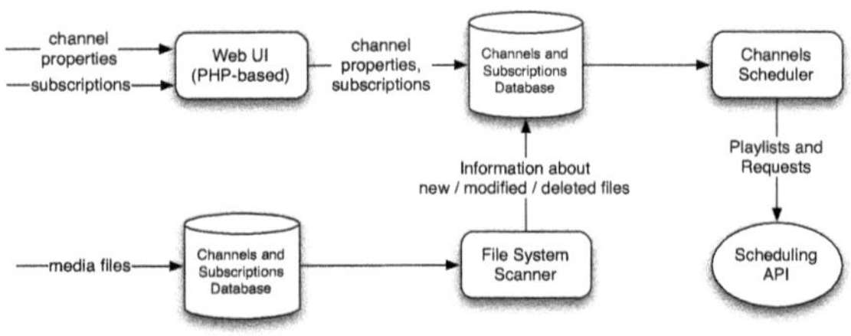

Figure 3. Overview of the e-Channel architecture.

Figure 3 shows an overview of the implementation of the channels system. The web-based parts of the channels system are built using PHP. Information about channels and subscriptions to channels are stored in a MySQL database. A Python process periodically scans the folder structure containing the channel folders and records changes to the file system in the MySQL database.

Each channel includes user-defined availability constraints that are inherited by the content in the channel. These are expressed in the form of repeating times slots such as "*every weekday from 8:00 to 17:00*", "*every day from 12:00 to 15:00*". In the same manner, each display has similar time constraints for its hours of operation. The e-Channel scheduler scans all of the subscriptions in the system and extracts the intersection of these time constraints for every channel-display combination. These form the constraints for when each content item should be shown. The available content is pooled together and ordered by the scheduler then displayed in a round-robin fashion. The duration of videos is extracted from the media file, while static media items, such as web pages and images, are shown for a fixed amount of time (currently 10 seconds each).

[1]Discussion of these features are regrettably outside the scope of this paper.

In the following sections we reflect in detail on our long-term experiences of the e-Channel system.

REFLECTIONS ON HOW CHANNELS ARE USED

The e-Channel system has been in open use since May 2008. The first non-test content was added by a user on 14th May and the most recent (at the time of writing) on 11th April 2011 (1,062 content days, or about 2.9 years duration). During this time the channels system has grown to 81 individual users in 33 groups who've created 3,700 content items (1,796 unique items) in 102 channels. Figure 4 shows the duration of each user's involvement with the e-channels system. The current live status of the system is 64 active channels containing 511 files. 40 of these channels are marked private, so are not available to displays other than those controlled by the owner. There are 24 public channels available (188 content items) that any display owner can subscribe to. Over the lifetime of the system there are almost exactly equal proportions of shared and private channels.

Use and sharing of channels

There are considerable differences in the practices of the different user groups and how they use channels, especially when it comes to sharing content for other displays (shared channels). The modal number of active channels is 1, but the maximum is 8 and half the groups have more than 1 channel (median 2). Content providers typically have few suspended channels (58% have 1 or more), but in one case (our heaviest channel user) there are 13 suspended and only one active channel. Looking deeper we find that this content provider has a remit of observing religious events and each channel is named after a particular festival. All of these channels are marked private rather than shared, so the channels are just serving as a tool for organising and controlling the release of their content.

Another content provider which represents the students interests, has 2 active channels and 4 suspended ones, all their channels are marked shared. In this case it appears that the channels reflect the evolving organisational sub-units and their remits: new channels have been created and the old ones suspended, as the unit has rebranded itself. Rather

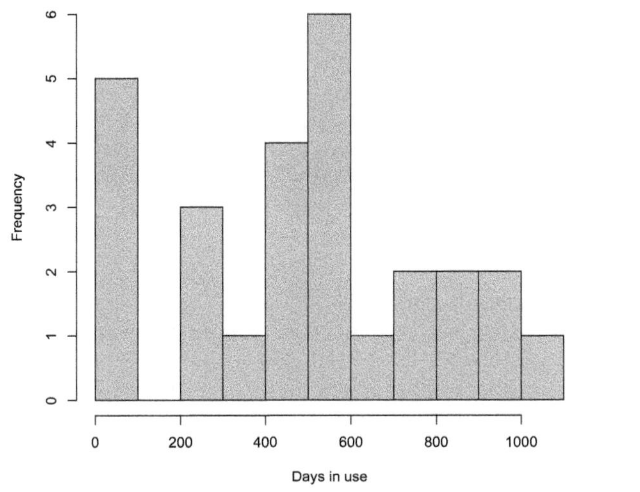

Figure 4. Breakdown of length of use of the channels system (from date of first piece of content to most recent). Note more than half the active users have used the system for 1 year or more, 8 or so over 2 years and new users continuing to join (active in the last 100 days).

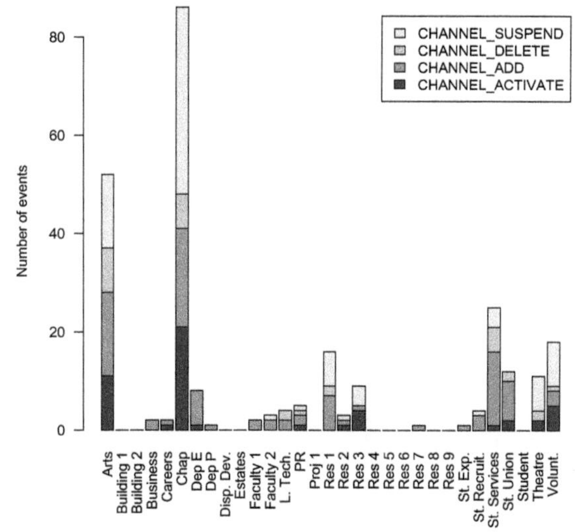

Figure 5. Summary of channel related operations per user group (adding, deleting, suspending and activating from suspension).

than create new channels, when an update is made content is changed within the existing channels. This has the associated implication that display owners aren't burdened with subscribing to get the new content. It also highlights that once signed up to a channel, the content in that channel may change—a display owner is very much trusting the source of the content to continue to meet their expectations.

From Figure 5 we see the relative numbers of operations on channels logged by the system (note that these are accumulated over different usage periods as outlined above). We observe that significantly more channels are added than deleted. Instead of removing the channels, users seem to prefer 'suspending' them, which removes their content from the schedule without discarding the channel and its contents. Groups *Chap* and *Arts* make very active use of this mechanism: from the detailed logs we see two other forms of behaviour exemplified. Firstly, channels are often suspended for a few days while content is updated and then activated again. Secondly, a channel is created, immediately suspended, then 'made live when ready'.

Adjusting the content displayed

Users who can both create channels and have control of a display's subscriptions also exhibit different patterns of behaviour, as illustrated in Figure 6. The chart represents each user group's activity in a horizontal strip with channel adjustments, display subscription adjustments and file system activity (triangles, crosses and dots respectively). There are several different patterns: the press office (*PR*) and college residence (*Res 5*) make frequent adjustments to their content but rarely create channels for it and only infrequently adjust their displays' subscriptions. *Theatre* created a channel, very regularly reviewed their subscriptions and no further content appears for nearly 1 year: this was a change of personnel and a restructuring (*Theatre* becomes *Arts*)—note how *Arts* uses channels more actively than her predecessor. *Res 1* experimented with the system at the beginning (burst of content and channel manipulation), then continues to manipulate channels periodically, rarely adjusts subscriptions directly, but provides new content every 6 weeks or so via the file system. Department (*Dep E*) displays a burst of activity, adds content burstily for 1 year then use of the system stops entirely (the person who learnt the system left, but did not pass the role on).

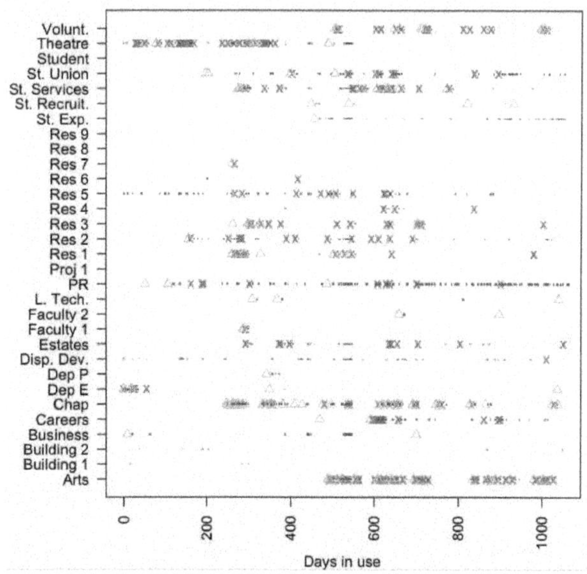

Figure 6. Adjusting channels (triangles), adjusting display subscriptions (crosses) and modifying content in channels (dots)

Overall, the amount of content added daily is typically small

(10s of files), but there are exceptions (Figure 7). Spikes, such as the peak exceeding 200 files around day 500, are normally slide decks saved as galleries of images or (as in this case) a library of photographs added for an open day. Content either has a short lifetime, most commonly 7–10 days or lasts for many weeks. There is a second peak at around 120 days, corresponding to the teaching cycles of the University. The third, lesser, peak is roughly bi-monthly. These peaks closely match the content validity periods we identify (see the following section), in which 12% of content images have a validity of up to 1 week (a further 11% between 1 week and 1 month) and 7% a validity of 2–3 months.

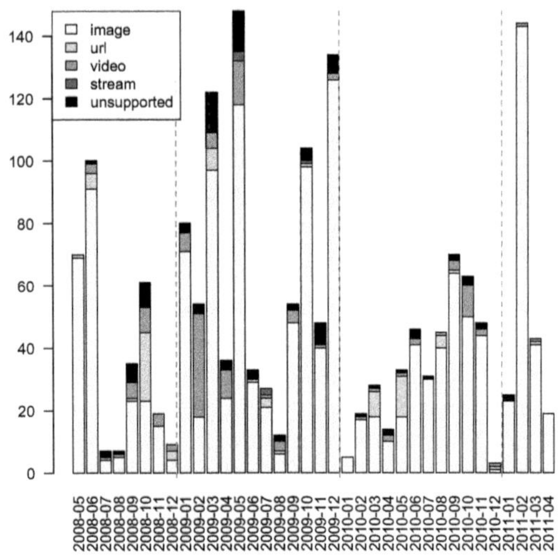

(a) Profile of files and file types added per month

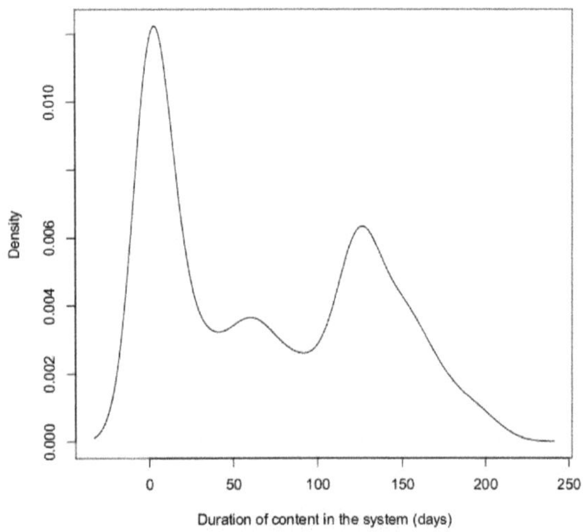

(b) Length of time content is in the system

Figure 7. Volume and lifetime of content

Gaming the system

One surprise for us when we analysed the content in the system was that over the lifetime of the system we found several duplicate files (affecting 11% of the content), not just in separate channel folders, but within the same channel. In exceptional cases we have found as many as 6 copies of the same file. This appears to be users deliberately trying to manipulate the system to offer 'implicit priorities' so that their content appears more often (which it will!). Even though only a very small number of content providers seem to do this systematically, our instinctive reaction was to plan measures to prevent this behaviour e.g. based on content fingerprinting, but we have since noticed that the most replicated item was an important health message that needed more air time—so our instinct would've been too hasty.

Usage lessons learned

- *User engagement follows very varied patterns.* We note that even within our user community there are very different patterns of engagement and usage. In particular, we note that the frequency of content generation varies dramatically and that for many users the system needs to be optimised for occasional use. This suggests that our approach of a very simple interface is likely to be of benefit to many of our users.
- *Users develop a sophisticated understanding of the system's behaviour.* The existence of gaming techniques suggests that some users develop fairly sophisticated mental models of how the system behaves and are able to manipulate the scheduling algorithms for their own benefit. Addressing this may have unintentional consequences as we discovered—but equally it is clear that signage systems that can be manipulated by sophisticated users will be.
- *The perceived lifetime of content is bi-polar—very short term or very long term.* While our sampling of content suggested a range of times for which content might be valid the behaviour of users indicated content was either very short or very long lived. This suggests that in practice users either create content for a very specific event or they create content for an event in the future and essentially forget about the content once it is in the system. Mechanisms for indicating the lifetime of content at creation time would help to overcome this problem which manifests itself as out of date content appearing on screens.

REFLECTIONS ON CONTENT IN E-CHANNELS

Reflecting on the types of content people add to the system, we find that of the 1,796 unique content items (Figure 8), there are 1,494 images, 128 videos, 73 web pages, 6 live video streams and 95 unsupported files.

Images

Images are clearly the most popular content type and this is unchanging throughout the duration of the deployment (Figure 7). In fact, it seems that over time the diversity of content types is reducing—perhaps due to the extra effort involved in developing other forms of content—increasing the domination of images as the primary content format. We examined a random sample of 100 images for format, time and location-sensitivity, intended audience, provider identity and purpose. 95 of the sampled images appeared to have been intentionally added to the channel. 5 of the items appeared to

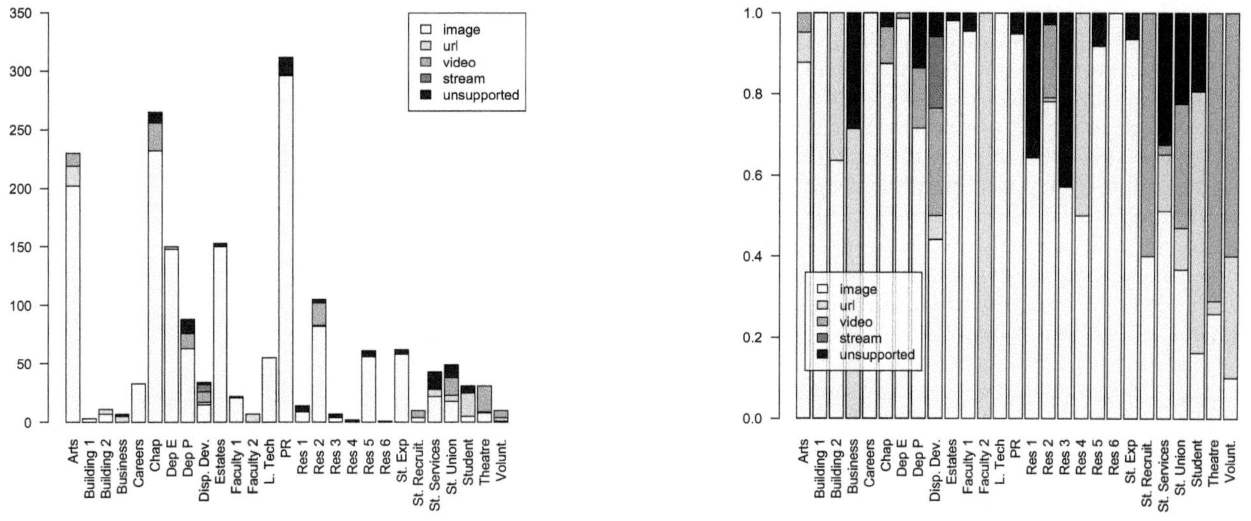

(a) (b)

Figure 8. (a) Content items added to the channel system by provider group and (b) ratio of content types by provider group.

have been accidentally introduced, these included 'a button image' that had presumably been saved as a supporting image for a webpage, without the realisation that it would be scheduled as an independent content item.

Formatting. The files were largely in JPEG format (94%) and were in a resolution and aspect ratio appropriate to the deployed displays suggesting that they had been created with the specific display in mind (80%). 76% of items were designed with some common style or identity (although only 55% of content items contained a textual or iconic reference explicitly telling the viewer who the identity belonged to).

Temporal and locative properties. 40% of content items had no obvious time constraints, of the remaining items 17% had a validity of one day (although these typically referred to an event that might be repeated—an open day or theatre performance, extending the validity), 12% had a validity of up to week, 11% up to a month, 7% a validity of 2-3 months and 6% a validity of 1 year. The remaining 7% were valid for the duration of a building project (typically up to one year in length). 95% of the content appeared to be University specific (the remaining external 5% was still targeted to a University audience rather than, e.g. referring to local or national events or news, as commonly seen on digital signage). The majority of items were not tailored to particular display location (approximately 20% of the deliberately placed images would have made little sense outside of their intended locations).

Purpose and audience. The majority of images had a single clear purpose: only 3 of the 100 images appeared to serve multiple purposes and the purpose of 6 further images could not be identified. Purpose was closely tied with audience: 59% of the identified purposes concerned raising internal awareness of things within the university; the remaining items were more broadly directed, containing items that may be of interest to visitors as well as members of the University (Table 1). Some content items were directed at subgroups within the University but these were typically large subgroups (e.g. 3 to all teaching staff, 8 to all students) rather than smaller ones (e.g. 4 to members of a particular college).

Raise awareness of an event (future)	16%
Raise awareness of an event (past)	4%
Raise awareness of service	9%
Raise awareness of departmental project	6%
Raise awareness of building project	11%
Information about student experience	11%
Press Release	23%
Theatre information	4%
Other	11%
Unknown	5%

Table 1. Breakdown of image purposes.

Microsoft Office/Open Office files	62
iTunes video (.m4v)	6
PDF	1
Windows shortcut files (.lnk)	1
Supporting files (.swf/.js)	11
Windows thumbnail cache (.db)	14

Table 2. Table of unsupported file types

Video

Of the 27 channel providers, 11 (41%) had submitted videos to the channel system. Typically the number of videos per provider was significantly smaller than the quantity of images, but for three providers (the theatre, student recruitment and a volunteering unit) videos represented over 50% of the content they produce for the system. In the case of the theatre this is clearly due to the utility of the format for showing trailers and excerpts from upcoming/previous performances. Student recruitment used video to produce student profiles. The volunteering unit primarily used video to highlight their rebranding: in this final case, the videos were also used to extend the content beyond its normal length—animations of approximately 15 seconds were looped for 1.5 minutes. The median video length was 96 seconds in length (1st quartile: 43 seconds, 3rd quartile: 180 seconds) and the longest video submitted was 13 minutes long. All of the longer videos (over 5 minutes in length) were created either by the theatre or from public (performing) arts—again demonstrating the usefulness of video for performance-related purposes. 61% of the files were in the appropriate aspect ratio for the displays (16:9) and 33% were in 4:3.

Web Pages

Web pages were submitted by 13 channel providers (of which 3 used this as the dominant format for their content) either in the form of HTML files dropped directly into the file system or (more commonly) as web URLs contained within .url or .webloc files. A sample of 15 files was analysed. Web pages were the only content format to include non-University specific items but these still only accounted for 3 files (20%) and one of these was still of local interest (a location specific weather report), the remaining two files were national news and the web page of a catalogue shopping company. Of the remaining pages 25% were locally relevant pages on popular social networking sites (e.g. a welcome video uploaded to YouTube or departmental Twitter page) and the remaining pages were typically those belonging to the department or other entity owning the channel. One page produced a 404 error and we have also observed other HTTP errors during the time the system has been deployed—a risk for this kind of content that does not apply to other medias (particularly risky when the web pages themselves are not under the control of the content provider). Furthermore, whilst Web content created for other purposes can easily be recycled as a source of content for the e-Channel system this is obvious when the content appears on the display. Unlike the images and videos, only 20% of the Web content was obviously created with the displays in mind and two of these were videos. Scheduling videos via the Web in this way also creates additional problems: firstly, that Web content is shown on the display for a default period of 10 seconds, most likely clipping the video content within the page (unlike videos dropped into the file share which are shown for the duration of the video). Secondly, that many web pages with embedded videos are not set to 'autoplay' when the page is loaded, meaning that the video does not play at all: this leaves viewers looking at the title and/or initial frame.

Live video streams

All 6 streams were submitted by the development team on behalf of content providers who were unsure of how to create and submit this type of content. All were used for live events (sports competitions, graduations and a 'freshers fair').

Unsupported Files

Unsupported content within the channel system can be divided into two groups: deliberately placed unsupported files for (85%), such as those created by office applications (in these cases it is assumed that the user was unaware that the file would not be supported) and invisible operating system or application files (where the user was unaware that the file was being transferred) (Table 2). Figure 7 suggests that whilst unsupported content continues to be dropped into the system, the quantity does seem to be gradually reducing as content providers determine which content formats actually appear on their displays.

Content moderation

To our recollection, there have been only two instances where we've been asked to remove 'inappropriate' content. Once where a video sound track was disturbing an exam in progress; and another, where a college principal was concerned the audience would mistakenly assume his college was advocating a particular anti-religious message. More generally, as system administrators we approve the addition of new users to the system and rely on these users to assume responsibility for moderating the content in their channels.

Content lessons learned

- *Content is localised but rarely display specific.* We found that while most content created was specifically targeted at sub-sections of the University population it was rare for content to be specialised for a specific display.

- *Web pages make for poor signage content.* While it should be obvious that general purpose web pages will not be particularly compelling sources of content for a signage system we found that many new user's first idea of how to create content for a signage system is to simply show web pages—often from external sources. Over time they appear to recognise that this is not appropriate and focus on the use of images created specifically for the displays.

REFLECTIONS ON DEPLOYMENT & ACQUISITION

The deployment of the e-Channel system started in early 2008. This was a slow process that involved progressive addition of new user groups into the system over the period of the next 12 months. Initially we carried out significant testing and monitoring for each new user that we added but as the system matured adding users became a simple and reliable task. We can use the channel system itself to manage the user groups, often adding them in response to an email or alongside a user through a web browser. We took the time to prepare a detailed user guide that has proved worth its weight in gold in saving time-consuming training (although we still provide some to those less comfortable with web-based systems and technology generally). Normally there is a colleague to show them how to use the system, it is conceptually simple, so there is rarely the need for extra support and the user guide is often sufficient on its own.

The challenge for content providers, and where we often have to advise, is finding a tool-chain that allows them to generate content that they are happy with aesthetically and in a format that the system supports. The most readily available tool both in terms of institutional licensing and support, and familiarity for our users is Microsoft Office. It is unsurprising that posters created with Powerpoint are quite prevalent in the system. Keener users have purchased specialist products to allow them to produce more sophisticated and attention grabbing content, such as animations and videos. New users often try putting office documents directly into the system. We can quickly spot this and guide them to export appropriate formats. Initially we thought not offering support for office formats placed an unnecessary burden on content providers, but we now appreciate this forces them to deliberately create content specifically designed and formatted for the screens rather than reusing existing documents.

Over time deploying the software became synonymous with hardware acquisition as most new users were also installing hardware at the same time. During this process we noticed a particular focus on the cost of hardware purchase while totally failing to adequately take into account the cost of content production. We went to some lengths to alert them to this issue but it remains a concern with new deployments—typically hardware is well budgeted for while content production and the responsibility for producing content is a real cost that is not well catered for.

Deployment lessons learned

- *System deployment took place over an extended period of time.* While we did not expect the system to be widely deployed and adopted overnight we did not anticipate a deployment period lasting many months. However, the complexity of hardware deployment and, more significantly, role changes within organisational units can easily lead to these sorts of delays. This is likely to be the case for many similar Ubicomp deployments.
- *Users fail to appreciate the significance and cost of content.* We found that our users consistently underestimated the time and expense required to create content. In practice many also lacked the appropriate skills and training in this area and careful use of templates becomes a requirement to ensure a satisfactory level of presentation.

RELATED WORK

As display hardware costs have fallen large-scale advertising networks have emerged [13, 15] and numerous signage systems to support digital signage installations (e.g. [16, 14]).

Research in public and semi-public displays began in the 1980s with the development and installation of long-lived audio and video connections between physically separated spaces to raise awareness between co-workers (e.g. [2]). Collaboration and awareness continue to be significant themes [6, 8, 1] and much of our content analysis suggests this is true for our display network also—the provision of the e-Channel system to easily support content from multiple departments (and even multiple contributors within a department) does make them a useful tool for raising awareness between otherwise separated members of the university. A trend towards multi-user systems is also seen in recent digital signage solutions [14].

In the context of public displays in a University setting, Müller et al. [11] have deployed the iDisplay system. Motivated by similar requirements that have led to the design of the e-Channel system, the iDisplay system is designed to offer explicit support for pre-defined content types, termed "actionables" (posters offering people to take a specific action). In the design of the e-Campus system there are no explicit assumptions about the intended use of the public display system, leaving such mechanisms to be defined by the content providers and display owners. We believe that this approach allows more flexibility, enabling users to appropriate the system for a wider range of purposes.

One key issue for public and semi-public displays (particularly commercially) is that of relevance and user attention: Huang et al. observed 46 public displays in a variety of public spaces and reported infrequent, brief glancing [7] whilst Müller et al. [12] studied user expectation and its impact upon the attention users give to displays. They found that people typically attended to displays only when they expected the content to be of interest to them (and that typically, advertisements were not of interest to them—suggested 'interesting' content included local news, events and information and sports and entertainment). People were also more likely to expect interesting content in a university context than within a commercial premises. Our work considers one such university display network in which many of the previously suggested content types are scheduled for user viewing on a daily basis. We hope that systems such as ours can help to reduce the barrier to entry for content creators helping to increase the amount of interesting content in display networks.

More recent research in displays focusses on novel display technologies [4], interaction [9, 5] and mechanisms for improving the content relevance [10, 3]. Whilst this work is interesting and useful it does not reflect current everyday digital signage use. Correspondingly, research into the everyday usage process for commercially deployed signage systems in common use is understandingly lacking. In this paper we attempt to address this gap by providing insight into the usage of an experimental digital signage system from the point of view of the content providers and display owners.

CONCLUSIONS

Universities, like many large businesses, are made up of diverse stakeholders with differing needs to communicate with many audiences. In this paper we have reflected on our experiences of a highly successful, long-lasting Ubicomp system to support digital signage on a University campus. The system is open to content from a variety of sources whose needs and uses have emerged and evolved over a 3 year period, and continues to be in everyday use. We have reflected on how the system is used in detail (content and use related practices) and provided a set of lessons for designers of future Ubicomp public display systems.

Key to the system's success is its parsimony and conceptual simplicity: it features a simple, flexible design based on 'channels' of content and a separation of concerns between content providers and display owners. A web-based system offers the stakeholders control, rather than the centralised authority found in many conventional signage systems. The simplicity of marrying the web interface with a file system interface greatly simplifies everyday use of the system and many content providers update and manage their content this way. The ability to split between private and shared channels has enabled them to choose which content is for their display and which for a more general audience. Activation and suspension of channels provides simple coarse-grained control over content exposure—and content providers make extensive use of this when they update and prepare their content.

One note on usability can be made here. In an environment where non-technical people are asked to be involved in the management of a content dissemination infrastructure "less is more". The limited control offered by the e-Channel system makes it a lot easier for users to exploit the display network. However, finding the golden ratio between usability and control is always difficult. Certain content providers require more control over the scheduling of content within each channel and potentially even the priority of the content itself, while at the same time a small number of them still feel that the e-Channel system is somehow difficult to control. An observation based on experience is that it is always easier to argue for more features and flexibility than to champion simple elegant designs. We hope that lessons from our work can be taken forward to help other Ubicomp system designers achieve long lasting and usable systems.

ACKNOWLEDGEMENTS

We would like to acknowledge the support of European Union Seventh Framework Programme (FP7/2007-2013), grant ref. 244011 and Lancaster University. Thanks to Oliver Storz for his contribution to the e-Campus infrastructure, and our anonymous reviewers for their constructive remarks.

REFERENCES

1. BARDRAM, J., HANSEN, T., AND SOEGAARD, M. Awaremedia - a shared interactive display supporting social, temporal and spatial awareness in surgery. In *CSCW '06* (2006), pp. 109–118.
2. BLY, S., HARRISON, S., AND IRWIN, S. Media spaces: bringing people together in a video, audio, and computing environment. *Commun. ACM 36*, 1 (1993), 28–46.
3. BUZECK, M., AND MÜLLER, J. Twittersigns: microblogging on the walls. In *Proceedings of the international conference on Multimedia* (NY, USA, 2010), MM '10, ACM, pp. 819–822.
4. CHANDLER, A., FINNEY, J., LEWIS, C., AND DIX, A. Toward emergent technology for blended public displays. In *Proceedings of the 11th international conference on Ubiquitous computing* (2009), Ubicomp '09, pp. 101–104.
5. ERBAD, A., BLACKSTOCK, M., FRIDAY, A., LEA, R., AND AL-MUHTADI, J. Magic broker: A middleware toolkit for interactive public displays. In *Proceedings of the 2008 Sixth Annual IEEE International Conference on Pervasive Computing and Communications* (Washington, DC, USA, 2008), IEEE Computer Society, pp. 509–514.
6. GREENBERG, S., AND ROUNDING, M. The notification collage: Posting information to public and personal displays. In *CHI 2001* (2001).
7. HUANG, E., KOSTER, A., AND BORCHERS, J. Overcoming assumptions and uncovering practices: When does the public really look at public displays? In *Pervasive 2008* (2008).
8. HUANG, E., TULLIO, J., COSTA, T., AND MCCARTHY, J. Promoting awareness of work activities through peripheral displays. In *CHI 2002 (Extended Abstracts)* (NY, USA, 2002), ACM, pp. 648–649.
9. MÜLLER, J., ALT, F., MICHELIS, D., AND SCHMIDT, A. Requirements and design space for interactive public displays. In *Proceedings of the international conference on Multimedia* (NY, USA, 2010), MM '10, ACM, pp. 1285–1294.
10. MÜLLER, J., EXELER, J., BUZECK, M., AND KRÜGER, A. Reflectivesigns: Digital signs that adapt to audience attention. In *Pervasive '09* (2009), Springer.
11. MÜLLER, J., PACZKOWSKI, O., AND KRÜGER, A. Situated public news and reminder displays. In *Proceedings of the 2007 European conference on Ambient intelligence* (Berlin, Heidelberg, 2007), AmI'07, Springer-Verlag, pp. 248–265.
12. MÜLLER, J., WILMSMANN, D., EXELER, J., BUZECK, M., SCHMIDT, A., JAY, T., AND KRÜGER, A. Display blindness: The effect of expectations on attention towards digital signage. In *Pervasive '09* (Berlin, Heidelberg, 2009), Springer-Verlag.
13. NEO BOOKING SA. Bookingdooh-digital-out-of-home online planning and booking platform. `http://static.bookingdooh.com/`, 2009-2011.
14. REMOTE MEDIA LIMITED. digital signage software — signagelive delivering media to your screen. `http://www.signagelive.com/`, 2011.
15. SEESAW NETWORKS INC. Place-based digital video advertising. `http://www.seesawnetworks.com`, 2011.
16. SONY CORPORATION. Ziris digital signage. `http://www.sony.co.uk/biz/content/name/ms-ziris-landing-0308`, 2004–2011.

Haptic Reassurance in the Pitch Black for an Immersive Theatre Experience

Janet van der Linden[1], Yvonne Rogers[1], Maria Oshodi[2], Adam Spiers[3], David McGoran[4], Rafael Cronin[5], Paul O'Dowd[3]

[1]Pervasive Interaction Lab
The Open University
Milton Keynes, UK
{j.vanderLinden, y.rogers}@open.ac.uk

[2]Extant
Oval House Theatre
52-54 Kennington Oval
London, UK
ExtantAD@btconnect.com

[3]Bristol Robotics Laboratory,
University of Bristol, UK
{Adam.Spiers, Paul.oDowd}@brl.ac.uk

[4]Faculty of Creative Arts,
University of the West of England, UK
DavidMcGoran@gmail.com

[5]Indiana University,
Bloomington, IN.
USA
rafaelcronin@yahoo.com

ABSTRACT
An immersive theatre experience was designed to raise awareness and question perceptions of 'blindness', through enabling both sighted and blind members to experience a similar reality. A multimodal experience was created, comprising ambient sounds and narratives – heard through headphones – and an assortment of themed tactile objects, intended to be felt. In addition, audience members were each provided with a novel haptic device that was designed to enhance their discovery of a pitch-black space. An in the wild study of the cultural experience showed how blind and sighted audience members had different 'felt' experiences, but that neither was a lesser one. Furthermore, the haptic device was found to encourage enactive exploration and provide reassurance of the environment for both sighted and blind people, rather than acting simply as a navigation guide. We discuss the potential of using haptic feedback to create cultural experiences for both blind and sighted people; rethinking current utilitarian framing of it as assistive technology.

Author Keywords
Haptic feedback, in-the-wild user study, immersive theatre, visually impaired, blind, sensory augmentation

ACM Classification Keywords
H5.2 Information interfaces and presentation: User Interfaces. Haptic I/O.

General Terms
Design, Human Factors

INTRODUCTION
'Dining In The Dark' restaurants are appearing throughout the world where diners eat in absolute darkness. Sighted (and blind) people can come and eat while being served by blind waiters and waitresses [24]. The experience is a great leveler, with sighted people fumbling with their knifes and forks trying to fathom out what they are eating, while the blind servers move effortlessly knowing their way around every inch of the restaurant. An outcome is for sighted people to begin to understand some of the aspects of what it means to be blind and to share this with blind people. For the blind person the eating experience is the same but the dining experience is transformed as they share the same perceptual affordances with sighted people.

How might we go further by providing blind and sighted people with other more equivalent experiences of the world? For example, what would it take for blind people to enjoy a painting, a film or a play in a similar way to those who can see them? How could new technologies be designed to facilitate comparable cultural experiences that are accessible by all?

While there has been much interest in developing cultural experiences for visually impaired and blind people[1], efforts so far have focused largely on compensatory measures, such as the use of audio descriptions, tactile artifacts, raised images or through social interaction with sighted people. The experiences are limited, often depending on an accompanying sighted describer helping out, making it difficult for blind and partially sighted people to access the work directly by themselves [11,13,14].

Alternatively, we propose that the design and application of innovative ubiquitous technologies can open up the arts for visually impaired audiences to experience them in similar and even enhanced ways compared with how they are experienced by sighted people. Our approach is based on *sensory augmentation* – a philosophical perspective that considers whether and how it is possible to extend our senses. By building novel augmentation devices, it seeks to explore sensory, bodily and cognitive extensions [2,4,21]. In particular, the aim is to extend the body's ability to sense aspects of the environment that are not normally perceivable by the body in its natural state.

Informed by sensory augmentation, we developed an "immersive" theatre experience for blind and sighted audiences. Instead of a performance taking place on a stage (which cannot be seen by blind audience members), the

[1] The degree of blindness people can have varies from partial to total blindness. We use the two terms as and where appropriate.

dramatic action was moved within the bodily experience of each audience member. Our overarching goal was for it to be experienced by both on a more level playing ground. Specifically, a handheld haptic device was created to encourage enactive exploration [9] of a pitch-black space that was filled with objects to touch and sounds and narratives to hear. A novel form of haptic feedback was provided in relation to how people moved in the space. The idea was to give all audience members the opportunity to experience a 'felt' presence of the environment that would transcend their actual perception [cf 6].

We were interested in discovering how sighted and blind audience members perceived and understood this kind of enactive exploration when in a theatre setting. Would the haptic device become an extension of their own body, augmenting their sensation of experiencing and moving in the dark? If so, how would it feel and would it differ for the blind and the sighted? To address these questions, we conducted an in-the-wild study for a week of public performances held in Battersea Arts Centre in London, where 150 sighted and blind audience members took part. Below, we describe the design of the immersive theatre experience and our analysis of the performances that took place within it.

BACKGROUND

Ubiquitous computing offers new opportunities for augmenting experiences for both sighted and blind audiences. A number of projects have developed new experiences to enhance exploration and navigation.

Augmenting exploration

One of the earliest forays into using pervasive technologies to promote exploration of a mixed reality environment was the 'Hunting for the Snark' [23]. An assortment of mobile and sensor-based devices was developed, including probing devices, as part of an adventure game. Children had to hunt an elusive, virtual creature, called the Snark, who kept changing its shape, appearing and disappearing, depending on the physical actions of the children (e.g., feeding it, flying with it, dancing with it). The sensor-based devices detected movements and responded by revealing aspects of the Snark's personality, likes and dislikes. For example, a 'snooper' handheld device, that used ultrasonic sensing, enabled them to discover invisible 'virtual' objects, which they then fed to the Snark. A main finding was that the *less* direction the children were given as to what to do and how to find the Snark the *more* they explored the mixed reality space.

More recently, a haptic device, Momo, was developed in the shape of a large furry egg intended to be held in both hands [18]. The device was used as a tour guide to indicate the direction someone should take, through leaning forwards or backwards, as well as vibrating. Preprogrammed GPS coordinates set up in a number of parks in New York, enabled visitors to explore the city, without a map, from one destination to another at their own leisurely pace.

Another technological augmentation that has been used *in situ* to transport people to another time or to enhance their experience is audio. For example, Riot!1831 was designed as a historical experience to simulate the riot that took place outside in a town square in Bristol in the UK [22]. Participants wearing headphones, strolled around the square, listening to riotous scenes, such as shouting, screaming and gunshots, at different locations. Aspects of the augmented experience were recounted by one participant as *"deemed to be both moving and memorable and thus are those that people really value"* [22]. In another setting, called Scratch, participants wandered around familiar surroundings, such as their local park, while listening to various narratives, again through headphones, but this time not using location-based cues. The idea was instead to enable them to make associations between their local surroundings and the narrative using their imagination [19].

Most well known, are Benford *et al's* [3] series of mixed reality games played in the streets and online by audiences and choreographed by the theatre company Blast Theory. Various technologies were designed and orchestrated to provide audiences with complex user experiences, to enable them to traverse the digital and the physical in innovative ways. These included Desert Rain and Uncle Roy All Around You. The resulting trajectories extended over space and time involving multiple roles and interfaces.

Most of the novel augmented user experiences have been developed for sighted people. An exception was a 'soundscape' based on a Roald Dahl story, that comprised a tapestry of dialogue, music, sound effects and soundmarks (a unique sound played in one location) where blind and sighted audiences used spatiality to understand, follow and enjoy the narrative [14].

Augmenting navigation

Wearable devices have also been developed as real-time navigation aids using either audio or haptic feedback. These devices primarily aim to help people who have difficulty finding a location in an unfamiliar place. For example, pedestrians and cyclists find it problematic to look at detailed information on small screens while 'on the go' [10]. For blind people, such devices provide extra sensory cues as to the presence of obstacles, such as buildings and kerbs, as well as directions as to where to go next.

Audio interfaces, however, can make it difficult for the person to distinguish between the sounds from the system and those of the environment [26]. Wearing headphones can also prevent visually impaired pedestrians from hearing other sounds [1]. In contrast, haptic interfaces provide feedback that is more distinguishable from the environment, using vibrotactile stimulation on the body. A number of wearable devices, such as a headband [5], a vest [20] and belts [7,8] have been designed. Participants wearing the Haptic Radar headband [5] were able to 'see' objects coming from behind them. The headband sensed range information and provided spatial feedback that buzzed around the head. The Tactile Wayfinder [20], was a torso display that provided tactile location information that was mapped onto the wearer's body, letting them know the next direction they needed to take (e.g., two buzzes on the right indicates 'turn right at the next crossing'). This enabled the wearer to know in advance how the route would continue when reaching a waypoint. Kinesthetic feedback has also been used to generate a force sensation that contrasts with the buzzing associated with vibrotactile feedback, by 'pulling' a pedestrian in a particular direction [1].

The effectiveness of these types of haptic technologies is usually described in terms of whether the (blind) pedestrian is able to locate a specific target or follow a pre-determined route. However, there has been little consideration of the quality of the experience for the wearer when using it to guide their walking. Anecdotal evidence suggests they can be uncomfortable or even annoying to wear and hence may not be acceptable for long-term use.

Sensory augmentation

A number of novel sensory substitution devices have been built to investigate aspects of 'enactive' perception. This refers to where movement of the body in the environment is considered central to how we perceive. Most notable was the TVSS vision-to-tactile system [2]. This essentially consisted of a camera hooked up to an array of tactile stimulators, located on the torso or tongue of a person's body, to enable blind people to perceive the world as if seen through a camera. After some training with the system, some people reported that the experience of being buzzed through the tactile patterns became 'externalized', with a phenomenological feeling that was in many respects similar to vision.

Since this pioneering work in the 60s, research on sensory augmentation has largely focused on how vibrotactile feedback can be applied to a person's body (e.g., head, torso, legs), while they moved through an environment. An alternative approach is to provide a person with something to hold, such as a stick, a ball or a torch, whilst walking. The difference is that holding something affords more distal perception, akin to practical tool use [6]. It is well known that bodily transformations happen through practical tool-use, such as changes in body schema and body image after pointing with sticks, etc., [17]. This suggests that holding something can have a different phenomenological effect on a person than when haptic feedback is applied directly to their body. In particular, people have more control over where to point and move the handheld device. The enactive torch was developed with this in mind, enabling people to 'see' objects by moving their holding arm and pointing at objects in the environment [6]. The device provided a continuous stream of vibrotactile feedback to their hand; the strength of stimulation relative to the distance to the object being pointed at. Similarly, the Haptic Laser was developed to enable people to feel and discriminate between physical objects in a room from a distance [12]. As well as providing a new approach to investigating enactive perception, providing haptic feedback about the transitions between objects, such as tables and bodies, may prove to be more comfortable for people to use.

AIMS AND OBJECTIVES

The goal of our research was to explore whether a handheld haptic device could enhance blind and sighted people's experience of an environment, devoid of visual stimuli but rich in other multi-modal experiences. The objective was to engender sensory augmentation within the dramatic action of a theatre space. A device was designed to provide haptic feedback as to where someone was in relation to spatially located objects and sounds and that the space be pitch black so no-one could see. It was deliberately designed to be suggestive rather than directive to encourage enactive exploration for both sighted and blind people [9].

DESIGN OF THE IMMERSIVE HAPTIC THEATRE EXPERIENCE

The theatre experience, called the Question [25], was developed by Extant, a professional performing arts company of visually impaired people. It comprised a number of different components: (i) a narrative heard through headphones, (ii) sound effects to enhance the narrative, (iii) a tactile set that provide stimuli to be touched and felt, (iv) a live (blind) actor speaking about being blind and (v) the haptic device, to augment the audience members experience through the space.

The narrative, written by the blind Artistic Director, sought to dramatically engage with the issue of blindness both in content and in form. It was inspired by the book 'On Blindness', that describes the dialogues between sighted philosopher Bryan Magee and blind philosopher Martin Milligan [16]. Milligan disputed Magee's claim that the blind person's knowledge of reality differs from that of the sighted person due to their experiental knowledge. Specifically, it was developed as a fragmented path following the thoughts and experiences of a blind geometer, Kalabi. Kalabi is struggling with scientific, philosophical and cultural perspectives on the question of knowledge through sensory translation, and what ultimate impact this has on an individual's identity.

The narrative was enhanced with various recorded sounds: the clunking sound of a person walking through a building, cars crashing into each other, creaking doors that are opening and closing, and fingers tapping on a keyboard. Some of these audio effects were intended to be heard in the background and at a distance, while others at close proximity to provide a more complex and rich feel to the imagined space.

The tactile set comprised four different zones, each based around a particular theme consisting of a set of objects and shapes (e.g., a ruler, a cube). The idea was that an audience member would feel with their hands the shapes and objects in each zone, while listening to audio through their headphones. A further level of complexity was provided through a blind actor who moved through the set and spoke occasionally, while using a gong to mark specific moments in the narrative. Finally, the haptic device, intended to be held in one hand, was designed to augment the way both sighted and blind audience members experience and move about in the dark.

DESIGN OF THE HAPTIC DEVICE

The haptic device evolved from an initial concept of a handheld object that would open and close in response to being near or far from sensor detectors situated in a space. Central to the design was that it should feel comfortable and would facilitate audience members in exploring the pitch-black space. We also took into account how visually impaired and sighted people move in the dark using their existing perception and appreciation of the environment. A conceptual model was used, based on a simple hot/cold metaphor that is often used in games, where people have to find or move to a target: warm is near, cold is far.

Given that the device would be used in live performances in an actual theatre setting, the aesthetics of the experience were considered important. This included the feel of the device in terms of its smoothness and roundedness of corners, and also the experience of using it. The choice of feedback initially considered was vibrotactile feedback. However, the blind members of the design team expressed that this would not be appropriate for the theatre setting, as it felt 'strangely empty' and 'cold'. Instead, we chose to design something that opened and closed – which the blind members of the team felt had a more aesthetic feel about it. A handheld device was envisioned that would be shaped like a lotus flower that could be held in one hand. As a person moved through a physical space the 'flower' would open and close its petals in response to how near that person was to one of the tactile zones.

Prototype I: The air freshener

Figure 1 shows an early prototype for a handheld device, where the casing of a standard air freshener was used as the shell of the device. A mechanical mechanism was added to enable it to open and close. Feedback was provided through feeling the device changing shape and size when holding it.

The opening and closing of the prototype was tested. A series of beacons, that emitted infrared signals in a downward cone were attached to the ceiling of our lab. Each beacon was associated with a number; the proximity of a beacon to a 'target location' determined the number that was transmitted, where zero represented a beacon that is at a target location. The prototype contained infrared sensors that pointed at the ceiling, receiving the infrared proximity information and transforming this into the opening/closing action. By moving the prototype from beacon to beacon, a person is able to determine if they are getting closer or further away from the target zone. The conceptual metaphor was instantiated by providing 'hot' or 'cold' feedback: as a person wanders through a room the device indicates warmer (nearer the target) or colder (further away from the target) by opening and closing.

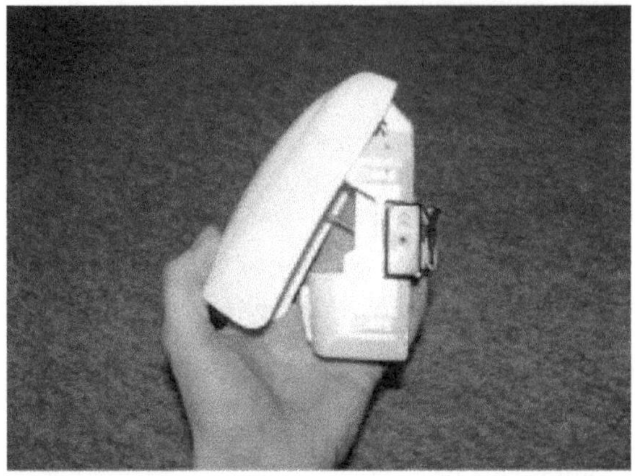

Figure 1. The first prototype for the sensory augmentation device using an air freshener case shown in its opened state

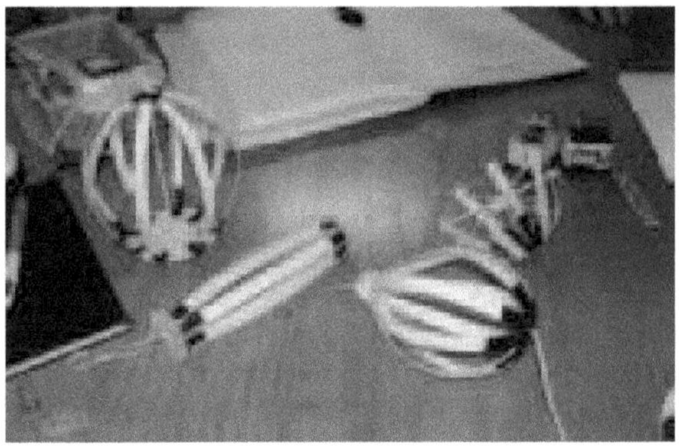

Figure 2. Shapes explored using low-tech materials for the second prototype

Figure 3. The final Haptic Lotus device that was developed

During a brainstorming meeting, which had three blind team members present, the early prototype was handed around. The prototype expanded and decreased in size in reaction to an infrared signal from the beacon that was placed on the table. A mix of reactions was evoked from the team members on first holding the device and exploring it through touch. For example, one blind person commented: "*it's a dog. It lifts up its head when it's interested*", while another said: "*It perks up, basically. It's intuitive*". One sighted person remarked that the device was up-side down from how she had imagined it. Instead she suggested it rest in the palm of her hand and to open and close its flaps more like a flower. The device was also compared to a stapler, going up and down, and an insect, that was opening its wings. However, the feel and shape of the device itself were considered too clunky for the envisioned theatre experience.

Prototype II: The Haptic Lotus

The idea of a flower opening and closing became the starting point for the second iteration of the device. Suitable types of materials were sourced that would make it pleasing to hold and enable people to perceive both opening and closing movements. A puppeteer technician joined the project team, who came up with potential designs for the device and devised the mechanics for expanding and contracting it. Figure 2 shows the different shapes considered. Eventually, a design was selected based on a trade off between expansion, requiring torque, and the necessary space for putting the electronics and sensors in. The second prototype is shown in Figure 3, having the form of a lotus flower, with petals opening and closing in response to the signals from the beacons.

The final Haptic Lotus device was coupled with an infra-red potential field emitted by beacons. The beacons were located on a grid of scaffold poles placed above the theatre space. Figure 4 shows the layout of the grid of beacons. Each Haptic Lotus contains three infra-red receivers, each with a viewing angle of approximately 30 degrees. The receivers are located on top of the central section of a Haptic Lotus, with one facing directly upwards and the two others at 20 degrees to this. This increases the overall viewing angle while also accounting for variation in hand posture.

The infra-red data transmitted from the beacons to a Haptic Lotus is modulated at 30Hz. The modulation and demodulation of the infra-red signal provides robustness against ambient infra-red, such as sound signals and camera light sources. The data sent by the beacons are RS232 encoded, alpha-numeric characters. After being received by the sensors, data is interpreted by an Arduino Pro Mini embedded device, located in each haptic lotus. Each alpha-numeric character corresponds to a position of the lotus petals. There are eight possible petal positions ranging from fully open to fully closed. The petals (which are made of flexible plastic sheet) are actuated by a single high-torque servo, controlled by the Arduino.

The Haptic Lotus 'remembers' the last value received over the infra-red, thus preventing the device from assuming an arbitrary (and possibly misleading) position when no beacon is in sight. A pack of AAA batteries is located in a flexible pouch, which fits under a person's hand. The Haptic Lotus and batteries together weigh approximately 280 grams. The weight and location of this power supply acts as a ballast, keeping the lotus pointing upwards, which benefits the infra-red sensors.

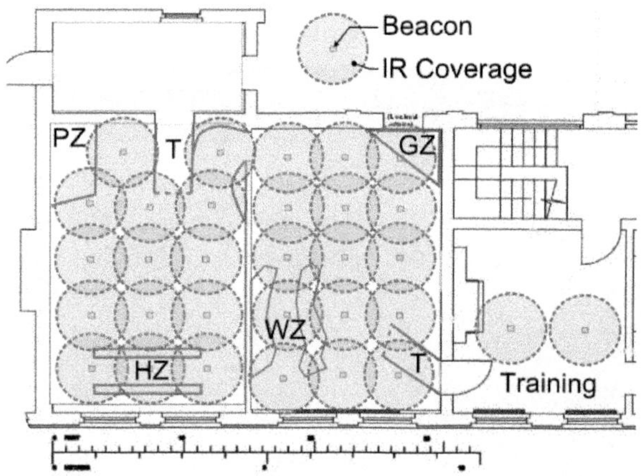

Figure 4. Layout of the beacon grid for the theatre space

THE SET-UP

Two adjacent rooms of equal size, approximately 5 by 8 meters and one smaller room of 4 by 5 meters were used for the performance (see Figure 4). Initial testing of the Haptic Lotus and beacons showed that 2.4 meters was an ideal ceiling height for the array of beacons. A total of 29 beacons were placed on a scaffolding structure at this height. A pattern was used that allowed the beacons to be matched to four themed zones positioned in the space.

The zones were philosophy (PZ), geometry (GZ), history (HZ) and work (WZ). A variety of relevant objects were placed in each zone, and the idea was that on entering a zone an audience member would be able to feel the objects and make connections with what they were hearing through their headphones about a particular theme. For example, in the philosophy zone two philosophers, one sighted and one blind, could be heard arguing with each other about the essence of what it means to be blind. Their philosophical debate is portrayed as a boxing match, with the sound of the roaring crowd in the background and the bell ringing for the start of the next round in this match. Against the backdrop of these various sounds, a number of philosophers can be heard sparring about whether blind people have equivalent experiences and what it means to know and know about.

The tactile set for the philosophy zone was built like a boxing ring, and people could feel the ropes of the ring, the bell, as well as boxing gloves. All the objects in the zones were either made from soft materials or secured in such a way and at such a height that they could not cause harm.

The two largest rooms were used for the performance, while the smaller room was used to prepare member of the audience before entering the rooms and to train them in the use of the Haptic Lotus.

THE PERFORMANCE

The performances took place over a period of a week. Audience members booked online to attend a performance and were assigned a specific time. It was not possible to control for equal numbers of sighted and blind people since it was publically advertised as a live theatre performance,

Figure 5. Two audience members (one sighted and one blind) exploring the geometry zone

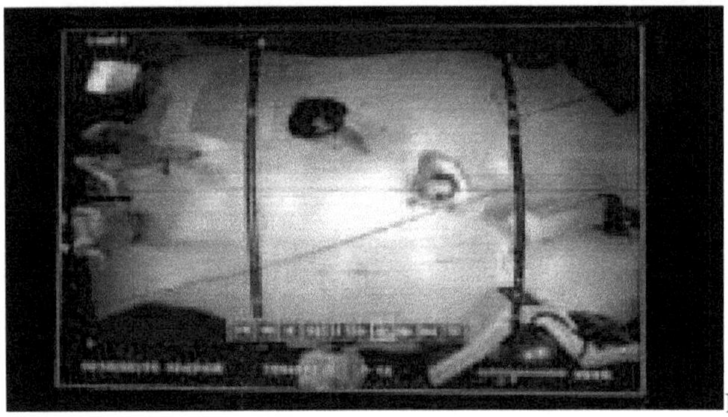

Figure 6. A screenshot taken from the CCTV footage in which members of the audience are being monitored (from above) for their own and each other's safety

so the audience members who took part were those who wanted to come. In the end, of the members of the audience that took part, 82 indicated that they were sighted, 6 were partially sighted and 10 were blind.

Each day, five to six sessions took place, lasting 30 minutes. For each session, a group of up to six participants took part. In total, about 150 audience members took part. Before entering the dark space, the audience members were taken into the semi-dark room near the entrance of the dark space, given a short introduction about the nature of the performance they were about to experience, and told to explore, listen, and to feel with their hands. They were then each provided with a Haptic Lotus, a pair of headphones and were given a short training session on how to use the haptic device using the two test beacons in the first room. The audience members were then lead one by one into the dark space, and left alone in it to explore.

Figure 5 shows a sighted (background) and blind (foreground) member of the audience taking part in a performance; one is holding the haptic device and the other touching an object encountered in a zone. Figure 6 shows a bird's eye view of the space from an infra-red CCTV camera. The safety of the audience in the dark environment was paramount and so this camera system was installed to enable someone to continuously monitor the members of the audience during the performances to check if anyone was in distress or having difficulty. Participants were told to raise their arm if they wanted assistance or felt uncomfortable.

EVALUATION

During the week of the performances we conducted a user study to evaluate the immersive theatre experience. We used a mix of methods, comprising observations from the CCTV cameras, questionnaires, 30 open-ended interviews with one or two audience members after each performance and a further five interviews with members of the theatre company. Our focus was on explicating how the haptic form of sensory augmentation worked in an immersive theatre context for both sighted and blind audiences. Below, we describe our findings in terms of:

(i) The phenomenological experience

(ii) Exploration with the Haptic Lotus device

(iii) Arm gestures and ways of moving around the space

(i) The phenomenological experience

The audience members' responses to the overall immersive experience were very positive. Many commented on how much they enjoyed the experience and how it made them reflect upon what it means to explore a novel rich multi-media space using the four senses of sound, touch, smell and taste. For the sighted members, it provided a heightened awareness of these. For the blind, it offered them a way of exploring a rich textured world, akin to a child let free in a candy store, in ways that were not usually permissible or possible.

In the interviews, the blind and sighted members of the audience raised different issues about their immersive theatre experiences. The sighted members became more aware of using these senses to find their way around and discover what was there. For example one mentioned: *"I definitely thought it was about how to rethink about spaces and shapes, and a heightening of my other senses."* Others noted how their perceptions of people around them had changed, even treating them as part of the installation, having a very different experience of how they normally behave around people. Many also lost all sense of time.

There was a notable difference between the sighted and blind people's emotional response to the experience. Some of the sighted people mentioned their struggles in the dark: "*At first it was fun, but as time passed I became a bit unnerved and disorientated*" and "*I was initially nervous, and on hearing those sounds first I jolted.*" One audience member gave an account of a particularly unhappy scene: "*I was trapped in a corner. I thought I was curtained in, (.....)*

I tried to break out of this corner and made several efforts". As might be expected, some sighted people strongly missed their lack of vision.

None of the blind members of the audience, however, talked about these kinds of struggle. On the contrary, most blind members of the audience gave accounts of increased freedom and delight, for example: "*To be in an environment where the point is that you are feeling around you the whole time - that is really interesting and liberating because I am blind, and I can't see at all. So I am constantly feeling around and it is my way of looking around. Often when you are in a shop, or most normal environments where it is probably a bit odd, as body language, and you may get told off not to feel the whole time...*". Another blind member of the audience spoke of his excitement when interacting with the zones, mentioning the profound effect when making connections between the narrative and what he felt: *"I was so disproportionately excited when I found something that I recognized. So even though I found it, I can imagine another person would think: "I found a boxing glove...great. But no, when I found it, I was like "I found a boxing glove! It's a boxing glove! Ah!"*

Several blind members of the audience gave extraordinary detailed accounts of what they had felt. One recounted that he had felt: "*a cube with different letters on its four faces, there were geometric shapes on flat surface, there was a bit of plastic film in a like a strip wound over itself, an inflatable dolphin, a smaller cube hanging up. There was a big bouncy rubber ball on the floor, there was a strange rubber creature hanging up with strange rubber fur, and maybe two eyes on it ...*". In contrast, most sighted people talked more generally about their experience of feeling objects, and only occasionally mentioned a specific object, like a coffee cup, that they had come across, but never with the same level of detail that blind people provided.

The blind audience members were also able to relate to the overall narrative and integrate the different sounds and narratives they heard with the objects they felt. This was much more of a challenge for sighted people. One sighted woman mentioned that: "*I wanted to hear the space. I think it was a bit of an overload by taking my audio and sight away*". Another said how it made her reflect on the way she usually made use of her senses: "*It made me think about how usually when I listen, I am also processing something visual. Whereas here I couldn't process it all at once. I had to stop from touching things if I was listening to the audio, because I couldn't do both of them at the same time.*" For a number of sighted people, therefore, the coordination of their senses in the dark had been the main focus of their experience, meaning they had less attention for the narrative.

There were also a large number of sighted audience members who enjoyed the challenge of being in the dark and how it imposed on their sensory systems. One person gave an account of how she had actively been exploring using her other senses: *"I remember feeling around the space, and then suddenly I got a strong whiff of rubber. I then went down on the floor and noticed several rubber tiles".* Another participant explained that "*the deprivation of sight did seem to bring out different ways of understanding or perception in a way that seemed to wake up a dormant part of the brain.*"

In discussions between blind and sighted participants, there were indications that there was an increased understanding or awareness of what it means to be blind. One sighted participant talked about her bewilderment when, as part of the audio for the performance, she heard that she was asked for directions. She hadn't known what to do or say as the encounter felt very real, but she wasn't sure where she was. Her blind companion was clearly amused by this, as this accurately described something that happened quite regularly to him as a blind person.

(ii) Exploration with the Haptic Lotus device

In the interviews with participants after the performance it became apparent that the Haptic Lotus had provided an experience that is not normally witnessed by blind or sighted people – that could only be experienced through holding the device itself. In particular, their comments suggested that the Haptic Lotus provided them with reassurance and comfort when exploring the space. For example, one person said: "*the device didn't really guide me to the zones but confirmed their location. It 'reassured' me to feel/look more closely in an area and move around in the small area to find things*". Another commented that: *"The Haptic Lotus gave me something to focus on. I wanted to believe that it guided me to the zones"* and "*The device felt like a little friend. I felt safe, and I guess I might've felt unsafe without it*". One noted "*I enjoyed feeling like it was communicating with me. It added interest.*" Hence, the device added special meaning to their felt experience, providing a friendly, reassuring presence.

Many people also commented on the Haptic Lotus as being like an animate object: being alive, pulsating and having a mind. For example, one noted: "*I liked the vibrating beat of that (the lotus)*"; another pointed out that the: "*The device was like a purring cat, or a pet.*' and "*It felt like it knew things. Like things about the space it was in*". One participant even commented: *"It was interesting to have something 'alive' in your hands. It was companionable."*

When asked about their experience of using the Haptic Lotus device, 50% of the audience said that they did not feel it had led them directly to the zones. Furthermore, the respondents were more or less equally divided as to whether they thought the device was helpful (28%), somewhat helpful (36%), and not helpful (37%).

In order to get a clearer picture of whether and how they had used the opening and closing movement of the Haptic Lotus, we asked participants how they had negotiated the dark space and how they reached their first and second zones. Their answers revealed that they had used a number of strategies to find the zones, including 'by chance', 'by touch', 'through following walls', 'following sounds', 'listening to the actor', and 'by using the Haptic Lotus'. Only a small proportion of people said that they had used the Haptic Lotus to guide them through the zones (13% mentioned Haptic Lotus for reaching their first zone, and 25% for their second zone). The diversity of answers suggests that people used a number of different strategies to move around the space, often not being aware of the haptic device directly guiding them to a zone. This suggests that the device may have become an extension of their bodily senses providing a holistic phenomenological experience, that made it difficult for people to put into words how they had reached the zones. Moreover, we noticed that audience members often talked about their experience of moving through the dark space by making a gesture as if they were still holding the device, with their palms turned upwards, their fingers gently moving as if touching the flower with its petals. It appears this gesture had become strongly associated with the experience of using the device.

(iii) Arm gestures and ways of moving around

To examine in more detail how people moved and explored the space we analysed and classified their arm gestures using the CCTV footage. We identified a number of distinct styles for moving around and making sense of the space while holding the Haptic Lotus.

Figure 7a) shows a person with both arms stretched forward and (b) a person moving their arm, that is not holding the Haptic Lotus, to feel the space. The arm movements for (a) and (b) can be seen as fairly standard ways of moving in a dark space, where people seek to avoid bumping into obstacles and are looking for walls or other points to hold onto. Most sighted people demonstrated the arm gestures of (a) and (b) on first entering the space.

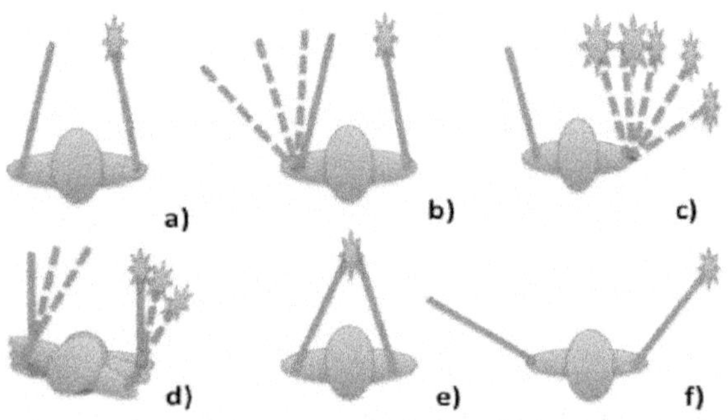

Figure 7. Arm gestures and styles of moving with the Haptic Lotus

After a short time in the area, many people demonstrated a distinct arm gesture with the Haptic Lotus, shown in Figure 7(c). The hand with the Haptic Lotus probed the space, similar to an elephant using its trunk, by moving from left to right and probing high and low. This sweeping movement was used while standing still and when walking. A variation on this was 7(d) where people pivoted around on their own axis, making the whole body move with arm plus Haptic Lotus out, in order to get a feel for the area. People were also often seen circling around themselves with the Haptic Lotus stretched out in front of them, before setting off in a direction.

A smaller number of audience members were also seen bringing their free hand towards the Haptic Lotus, as shown in Figure 7(e), possibly to feel its petals move and check their position. One person was seen flinging their arms wide out in Figure 7(f), moving through the space with great energy until they accidentally caught another person.

These exaggerated bodily movements and arm gestures are not within people's usual repertoire. Styles (c) and (d) were especially unusual and directly associated with holding the Haptic Lotus. They show how some participants were much more physical when exploring a dark space. By using the Lotus as an extended probing tool, the participants appeared to be creating a relationship between their own body and the space around it. However, from our observations of the CCTV footage, we noticed that this way of moving and probing was much more marked in the sighted compared with the blind audience members. The blind audience members were observed mostly walking using style (a) movements, and only moderately using the other probing gestures with the Haptic Lotus. Moreover, they did not appear to use their free arm to avoid obstacles, as in (b). Instead, they appeared to locate the zones by listening, or by hitting their foot against an obstruction which would made them halt to explore the area with their free arm.

To illustrate these differences between blind and sighted enactive exploration, two short vignettes are presented. Figure 8 (left) shows a blind person entering the space at location 1 coming out of the curtained entrance (T). She walked holding the Haptic Lotus in front of her with her free arm hanging to one side. At location 2 she hit with her foot an obstacle. This is the wall of the work zone, which is waist high and has various objects embedded in the structure and top of the wall.

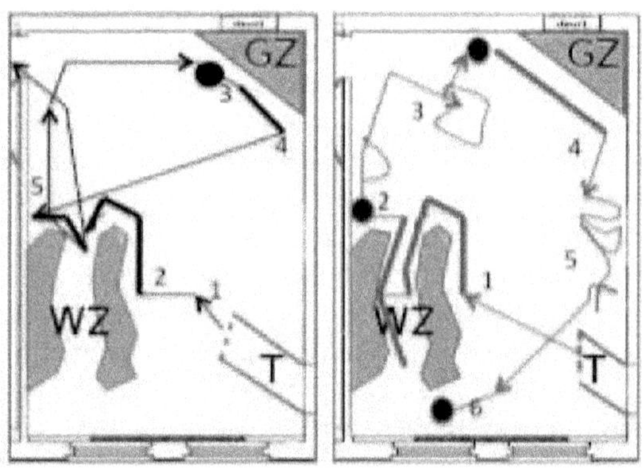

Figure 8. A blind person (left) and a sighted person (right) wandering through the dark space between two zones (Thin lines indicate walking, bold lines indicate exploring objects with hands and dark circles indicate the person standing still)

She then proceeded to inspect the various tactile elements, while slowly moving around the wall structure. She then walked away from this zone, and found herself near the next zone. At location 3 she stood completely still for about three minutes - not moving, presumably listening intently to the narrative through her headphones. She eventually moved on a few steps and noticed more objects, feeling them with her free arm for a while in a tentative manner. She then crossed the room, back to her first zone, where she explored the tactile set, vigorously pulling and tugging at the various objects. Finally, she moved away from the zone and appeared to head straight for the exit of the room.

Figure 8 (right) shows a sighted person entering the same room: he walked slowly, holding the Haptic Lotus in front of him, while carefully feeling with his free arm until he felt the walls. He tentatively explored the objects, moving around the wall structure. He then discovered the adjacent wall structure and continued to explore the tactile set, groping vigorously at the objects. At location 2 he stood still for about one minute, apparently listening. He then moved forward, and while walking quite slowly used the Haptic Lotus by waving it around in big semi-circles. While waving the Haptic Lotus around, he eventually made his way to location 3, where he circled around himself, moving his whole body in a pivoting action (cf Figure 7(d)). He stood still, again presumably listening, but was also seen to gently touch, playfully, the objects in zone GZ. He then shuffled slowly along the edge of this zone towards location 4, all the time feeling objects in the zone. He then moved away, while actively exploring where he was in the dark space, first by feeling the wall, and then bouncing himself towards the centre of the room, using the Haptic Lotus to probe around. He eventually moved away again from this spot, and while gesturing with the Haptic Lotus made for location 6, where he stood still listening.

These two vignettes show contrasting ways of moving around, typical of sighted and blind participants. The blind people appear to have a fairly accurate sense of the shape of the room, remembering where they had been before, and how to find the exit (presumably from hearing people enter the room through that door) – whereas sighted people often spent considerable amounts of time circling around themselves, probing the space. However, on occasions the blind people also used the Haptic Lotus, gently probing it into the space around them, feeling its shape with their free hand (as in Figure 7(e)), and bringing it close to their face.

The sighted person's movements demonstrate an active embodied exploration using the Haptic Lotus. From the way they moved, it seems that they used it to gain an awareness of where they were. Even though several sighted and blind people explicitly said in the interviews that the device hadn't been particularly helpful for finding zones, our observations of their actual behaviour showed them actively using the Haptic Lotus to explore the space.

DISCUSSION

Our findings have shown how haptic feedback can be designed to provide novel sensory experiences as part of an immersive theatre setting. Instead of using it as an assistive technology to help people move from one location to another – as previous research into haptic devices has largely focused on – our research has begun to rethink haptics as a form of sensory augmentation, and as part of a novel cultural experience. Our study showed that using haptic feedback in this broader context enabled both sighted and blind audience members to have equivalent and different cultural experiences. But importantly, the differences were not in terms of one being better than another but in how enabling both to focus on enactive exploration, and not seeing or substituting seeing, resulted in other ways of experiencing the world. Through physically exploring the space with the Haptic Lotus acting as a distal tool, both gained an increased awareness of and connection with the space they were in. Hence, the differences were in how sighted and blind people immersed themselves in the darkness. Being more at ease in the dark, the blind audience members were observed to use the Haptic Lotus in quite subtle ways. Furthermore, upon reaching a zone, they spent considerable time systematically feeling the different objects and making connections between them and the audio narrative they were listening to. In contrast, the sighted people appeared to experience the space in a more random way, as and when they happened upon something in a zone, or bumped into another audience member or the actor. Moreover, they tended to use the haptic device more vigorously and dramatically, waving their arms more to probe the space, suggesting that they were developing compensatory strategies for their temporary lack of vision. They also found the device to be reassuring when wandering in a strange dark space.

The positive experiences recounted by all audience members suggest that enactive exploration could be developed further in other cultural settings, such as museums, galleries, outdoor parks and gardens, to provide sighted people with quite different ways of experiencing them in order to understand what it means to be blind and to share this with blind people. Moreover, it suggests novel sensory experiences can be experimented with by everyone, through designing an assortment of ubiquitous technologies that engender different ways of perceiving and being in the world. Just as in the book 'On Blindness' they could encourage discussions between sighted and blind people about what they experience when augmented with various forms of haptic feedback.

CONCLUSIONS

While much research on haptic navigation has mainly focused on directly buzzing a person on their body, usually on their skin, and on measuring the efficiency of such devices for helping people get from A to B, our study has shown that haptic feedback can be used in a quite different way to enhance the experience of what it means to perceive, sense and move about in a space. In particular, it can enhance the holistic experience of connecting and moving between objects in a space. This suggests that distal haptic devices, such as the Haptic Lotus, can be used in a wide range of cultural settings, to enhance and extend both sighted and blind people's encounters with them. In sum, haptic feedback offers new opportunities for supporting enactive exploration that moves beyond simply navigation aids, by enabling alternative kinds of cultural experiences that are accessible by all.

ACKNOWLEDGEMENTS

We would like to acknowledge the Technology Strategy Board and the Arts Council England for supporting the project. We are grateful to Battersea Arts Centre for hosting the event. We would also like to thank all our partners who contributed to the Question, especially Terry Braun, Alex Eisenberg, Peter Bosher, Lyn Cox, Jo Paul, Gemma Riggs, Mary Paterson, the audience members, the volunteers and the guide dog, Penny.

REFERENCES

1 Amemyia, T., Sugiyama, H. Haptic handheld wayfinder with pseudo-attraction force for pedestrians with visual impairments. In *Proc. Assets '09: Computers and accessibility*, (2009), 107-114.

2 Bach-y-Rita, P., Collins, C.C., Saunders, F.A., White, B. and Scadden, L. Vision Substitution by Tactile Image Projection, *Nature*, 221 (1969) 963-964.

3 Benford, S., Giannachi, G., Koleva, B. and Rodden, T. From Interaction to Trajectories: Designing Coherent Journeys Through User Experiences. In *Proc. CHI'09 (2009)*, ACM, 709-718.

4 Bird, J., Marshall, P. and Rogers, Y. Low-Fi Skin Vision: A Case Study in Rapid Prototyping a Sensory Substitution System. In *Proc. HCI'09* (2009), 55-64.

5 Cassinelli, A., Reynolds, C. and Ishikawa, M. Augmenting Spatial Awareness with Haptic Radar. In *Proc IEEE International Symposium on Wearable Computers,* (2006), 61-64.

6 Chrisley, R. Froese, T. and Spiers, A. Engineering Conceptual Change: The Enactive Torch. Abstract of talk given November 11th, 2008, at the Royal Academy of Engineering, *Workshop on Philosophy and Engineering.*

7 van Erp, J., van Veen, H., Jansen, C. and Dobbins, T. Waypoint navigation with a vibrotactile waist belt. *ACM Transactions Applied Perception,* Vol. 2, (2005), 106-117.

8 FeelSpace. http://feelspace.cogsci.uni-osnabrueck.de/en/

9 Grespan, L., Froese, T., Di Paolo, E.A., Seth, A. K., Spiers, A. and Bigge, W. Investigating the role of movement in the constitution of spatial perception using the Enactive Torch. In *ENACTIVE08*, (2008).

10 HaptiMap, Haptic, Audio and Visual Interfaces for Maps and Location Based Services, at http://www.haptimap.org/

11 Howell, C. and Porter, D. Re-Assessing Practice: Visual Art, Visually Impaired People And The Web. *Proc. Museums and the Web*, (2003). Downloaded from http://www.archimuse.com/mw2003/papers/howell/howell.html

12 Iannacci, F., Turnquist, E., Avrahami, D., and Patel. S.N. The haptic laser: multi-sensation tactile feedback for at-a-distance physical space perception and interaction. In *Proc. CHI'11 (2011)* ACM, 2047-2050.

13 vom Lehn, D. Discovering 'Experience-ables': Socially including visually impaired people in art museums, *J. of Marketing Management,* (2010) 26: 7, 749-769.

14 Lopez, M. J. and Pauletto, S. The Design of an Audio Film For the Visually Impaired. In *Proc. 15th International Conference on Auditory Display*, 2009.

15 Kaklanis, N., Tzovaras, D and Moustakas, K. Haptic Navigation in the World Wide Web. Universal access in human-computer interaction. *Lecture Notes in Computer Science, 2009,* Volume 5616 (2009) 707-715.

16 Magee, B. and Milligan, M. *On Blindness: Letters between Bryan Magee and Martin Milligan*. Oxford University Press (1995).

17 Maravita, A. and Iriki, A. Tools for the body (schema). *Trends in Cognitive Sciences*, (2004), Vol. 8: 79-85.

18 Momo, by Che-wei Wang and Kristin O'Friel. Downloaded from http://www.kofriel.com/momo/index.php

19 Parry, N., Bendon, H., Boyd Davis, S. and Moar, M. Scratch: Video Documentation of Translocational Radio Drama, In *Adjunct Proc. Pervasive 2010.*

20 Pielot, M. and Boll, S., Tactile Wayfinder: Comparison of Tactile Waypoint Navigation with Commercial pedestrian navigation Systems. In *Proc. Pervasive Computing*, LNCS (2010), 76-93.

21 O'Regan, J. K. and Noë, A. A sensorimotor account of vision and visual consciousness. *Behavioral and Brain Sciences* (2001), 24: 939-973.

22 Reid, J., Hull, R., Cater, K. and Fleuriot, C. Magic moments in situated mediascapes. In *ACE '05, Proc. Advances in Computer Entertainment Technology*, (2005), 290-293.

23 Rogers, Y., Scaife, M., Harris, E., Phelps, T., Price, S., Smith, H., Muller, H., Randall, C., Moss, A., Taylor, I., Stanton, D., O'Malley, C., Corke, G. and Gabrielli, S. (2002) Things aren't what they seem to be: innovation through technology inspiration. In *Proc. DIS'02*, 373-379.

24 Saerberg, S. The Dining In the Dark Phenomenon, *RELOADED Disability Studies Quarterly*, (2007), Vol. 27, No.3.

25 The Question, Website for the Immersive Theatre Experience project, accessed June 2011, http://www.thequestion.org.uk/

26 Wilson, J., Walker, B., Lindsay, J., Cambias, C. and Dellaert, F. Swan: System for wearable audio navigation. In *Proc. Int. Conference on Wearable Computing*, IEEE Computer Society, (2007), 91-98.

When Recommendation Meets Mobile: Contextual and Personalized Recommendation On The Go*

Jinfeng Zhuang †, Tao Mei ‡, Steven C. H. Hoi †, Ying-Qing Xu ‡, Shipeng Li ‡
† Nanyang Technological University, 50 Nanyang Avenue, Singapore 639798
‡ Microsoft Research Asia, Beijing 100080, P. R. China
{zhua0016, chhoi}@ntu.edu.sg, {tmei, yqxu, spli}@microsoft.com

ABSTRACT
Mobile devices are becoming ubiquitous. People use their phones as a personal concierge discovering and making decisions anywhere and anytime. Understanding user intent on the go therefore becomes important for task completion on the phone. While existing efforts have predominantly focused on understanding the explicit user intent expressed by a textual or voice query, this paper presents an approach to context-aware and personalized entity recommendation which understands the *implicit* intent without any explicit user input on the phone. The approach, highly motivated from a large-scale mobile click-through analysis, is able to rank both the entity types and the entities within each type (here an entity is a local business, e.g., "I love sushi," while an entity type is a category, e.g., "restaurant"). The recommended entity types and entities are relevant to both user context (past behaviors) and sensor context (time and geo-location). Specifically, it estimates the generation probability of an entity by a given user conditioned on the current context in a probabilistic framework. A random-walk propagation is then employed to refine the estimated probability by mining the temporal patterns among entities. We deploy a recommendation application based on the proposed approach on Window Phone 7 devices. We evaluate recommendation performance on 10 thousand mobile clicks, as well as user experience through subjective user studies. We show that the application is effective to facilitate the exploration and discovery of surroundings for mobile users.

ACM Classification Keywords
H.3.5 Online Information Services: Web-based services

General Terms
Algorithms, Experimentation, Performance

Author Keywords
Entity recommendation, local search, mobile application

* This work was performed at Microsoft Research Asia.

UbiComp'11, September 17–21, 2011, Beijing, China.

(a) user and sensory context (b) rank of entity types (c) rank of restaurant entities

Figure 1. The interface of mobile recommendation application *easylife* developed based on the proposed approach. A user named "clark" gets the recommendation of entity types in (b) when he was in the context of (a), and then can check the ranked entities in (c) by selecting a specific entity type (e.g., nearby restaurants that favor his taste in the entity type of restaurant). The entity type and the entities within each type are ranked according to the relevance to user and sensor context. The proposed contextual and personalized recommendation facilitates the exploration of and decision making on the go.

INTRODUCTION
Mobile devices are becoming ubiquitous and playing vital roles in our daily life. While on the go, people are using their phones as a personal concierge discovering what is around and deciding what to do. Therefore, mobile phone has become a recommendation terminal customized for the individuals (i.e., capable to recommend contextually relevant and personalized entities and simplify the accomplishment of tasks). As a result, it is important to understand user intent through the rich context (both user and sensory context) available on the phone.

Existing research has predominantly focused on recommendation by understanding the intent expressed by text (or the text recognized from voice). For example, previous research tries to estimate user's search intent by detecting meaningful entities from a textual query [7, 13, 15, 25]. However, typing is always a tedious job on the phone and thus intrusive to be used to express intent. An alternative is to leverage speech recognition techniques to support voice as a way of expressing intent. For example, the popular mobile search engines enable a voice-to-search mode [1] [2]. Siri is one of the most popular applications that further structurizes a piece of speech to a set of entities [24]. However, the voice as an expression of user intent has some limitations: 1) it relies on a good recognition engine and usually works well only in a relatively quiet environment, and 2) understanding a long textual query still remains a challenge. Although there exists extensive research on general recommendation [3], most of them do not consider the rich context (e.g, time and location) on the mobile devices. From this perspective, the recommendation is not context-aware and personalized.

Based on our analysis of a large-scale real-world mobile search click-through data, we found that the intent on the mobile is typically context-aware, personalized, and local (i.e., driven by exploration of local business). Therefore, we present in this paper a probabilistic approach to support mobile recommendation without requiring any user input. The approach leverages the rich context signals on the mobile device (i.e., user and sensory context, such as user click-through, geo-location, and time) to ranks the entities (i.e., local business) tailored to user's interest anywhere and anytime. The approach consists of three key components on the cloud: 1) entity crawler which collects entities with attributes (e.g., cuisine for restaurant) from the Web, 2) entity extraction which detects and recognizes entities from a query or click-through, and 3) entity ranking which ranks the entities in a context-sensitive and personalized way without requiring any input. Specifically, we propose a probabilistic entity ranking algorithm in spirit of hybrid recommendation algorithm [3], which models the generating probability of an entity by the user conditioned on the mobile context, followed by a random-walk refining process. To summarize, this paper makes the following contributions:

- We conduct an analysis on a real-world large-scale click-through data collected from a commercial mobile search engine, which motivates the proposed approach. The analysis provides a good knowledge for motivating related research on mobile platforms.
- We propose a probabilistic entity recommendation approach to understand user's implicit intent on the phone. The approach is able to rank both entity types (e.g., categories such as restaurant, hotel, etc.) and entities (i.e., specific local businesses within each type) which are relevant to user and sensory context. This approach actually builds a personal model for each user on the cloud.
- We develop a real application based on this approach on a Windows Phone 7 device and conduct both objective and subjective evaluations to validate its effectiveness.

Figure 1 shows the user interface of the application (called *easylife*) developed based the proposed recommendation.

RELATED WORK

The related research to mobile recommendation includes query suggestion, vertical/local search, and recommendation.

Query Suggestion

The most basic motivation of our approach is to reduce the effort for typing textual queries with a mobile keyboard. Query suggestion and auto-completion are devised to achieve this goal [5, 11, 12, 14, 20]. It completes the query automatically such that a user does not need to type the whole query. However, the user still has to view the returned list of links and find his desired information.

Our approach shares the same goal of reducing user's input effort. However, the scenario and target function are quite different. First, we do not require any user input at all but return a list of sorted entities directly. The mobile user can click these entities to view details in a push model. Therefore, it will reduce user's effort for typing queries and looking up the returned links. We can implement this because the search purpose on mobile platform is often entity-oriented, while the limitation is that we cannot handle general query purpose that does not relate to entities directly. The research in this paper also relates to *intent prediction* [4, 18]. However, it is well known that user intent on mobile devices is quite different from that on desktop PC. The rich context is regarded as a key to solve user intent on the phone.

Object-Level Vertical/Local Search

Instead of general search, our approach extracts predefined categories of entities and recommends them to mobile users. This function connects to object-level vertical search [16, 21] and local search [15]. A vertical search engine focuses on a specific segment of online content which distinguishes from a general search engine. Typical examples include travel, academy, and product search engines. Lane *et. al.* propose to use context signals to improve local search performance [15]. Our approach is also vertical in the sense that it provides entities and their attributes only involving the local business facilities. It does not intend to improve general search function. Moreover, it works at the object level as it extracts entities automatically without requiring users to browse the original web pages related to the entities. The entity extraction plays a fundamental role for the system. However, it is different from vertical search engines because it is not designed to handle explicit user input. Instead, it returns the ranked entities directly according to the user's implicit intent. In this way, the user's input effort is minimized.

Recommendation System

Our goal is to generate a ranked list of entities to satisfy user intent on the go, which is essentially related to a recommendation system [3, 10]. The approach is inspired by an investigation of the recommendation methodologies: content-based, collaborative, and hybrid [3]. The proposed entity/type ranking approach is in spirit to the hybrid recommendation method. That is, we make use of not only user's own query history, but also the history data from other users.

Compared with traditional recommendation systems [3], the proposed approach is also personalized and more context sensitive (sensitive to location and time of the day). Researchers have proposed various recommendation techniques to handle such systems [6, 17, 19]. However, due to the unique characteristics of our entity ranking task, the conventional hybrid recommendation algorithm summarized in [3] cannot be directly applied here. First, the attributes of an entity do not make much sense when determining its position in the ranked list. The query history of a user is not long enough to detect a meaningful pattern to reflect the user's

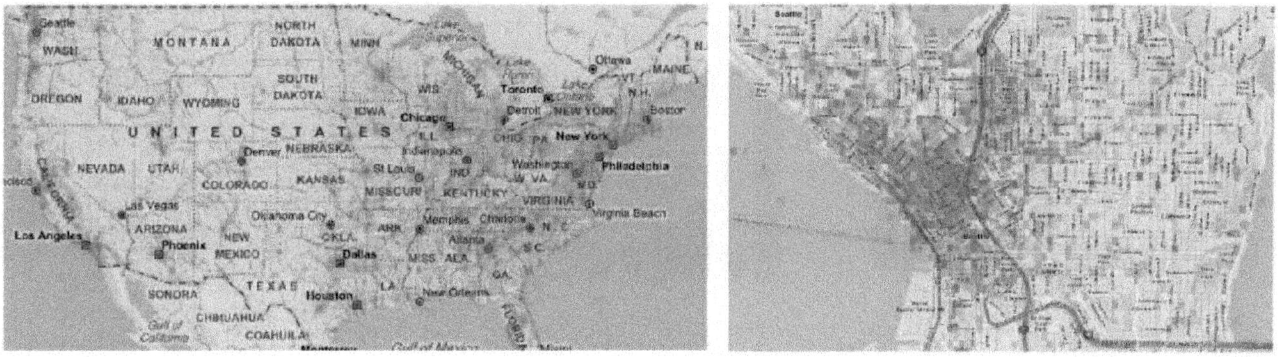

Figure 2. The query distribution with different locations. The depth of the red color is proportional to the number of queries conducted at locations. Left: query map of United States. We observe that big cities are "hot" (red color) areas of mobile search. Right: query map of Seattle city. One can see that mobile search is more popular in downtown areas.

#raw query	#user	#entity query	#entity user
75,221,037	13,711,497	11,492,382	4,012,030

Table 1. The statistics of the queries. #raw query **is the number of collected mobile queries,** #user **is the number users who conducted these raw queries,** #entity query **is the number of queries related to entities, and** #entity user **is the number of users involved in entity queries.**

preference. Moreover, as the recommendation is performed in real time and the database is large-scale (could be more than 10 million query records), complex machine learning algorithms with heavy computational costs may not work here (e.g., [26]). As a result, we consider a simple yet efficient probabilistic approach for modeling the conditional probability of generating some entities for a user. We further refine the ranking by a random walk procedure.

ANALYSIS OF MOBILE CLICK-THROUGH DATA

We collected a large-scale query log data from a commercial mobile search engine. We conduct an analysis to investigate the characteristics of mobile search query, which motivates our recommendation approach and *easylife* application.

The time range of our query database is from 2009-09-30 to 2010-03-28. All these queries were conducted in United States. During the six months, the number of *raw queries* is up to 75,221,037, which were issued by a total of 13,711,497 users, corresponding to 417,895 queries per day. Table 1 lists the query statistics. Each query log consists of "user id" (anonymous without any user identity information), "time," "GPS location," "query," and "URL."

Search via Mobile Phone is Popular

Figure 2 shows the distribution of mobile queries in US. The depth of the red color on the map is proportional to the number of queries conducted in this area. We can intuitively find the hot areas where mobile search is popular. For example, queries in Seattle and New York are significantly more than those in Nontana and North Dakota. Figure 3(a) shows the detailed #query in eight cities. We can conclude that *mobile search is becoming pervasive, especially in big cities.*

Mobile Search Query Is Short

Figure 3(b) shows the number of queries (#word) with different lengths. We observe that #query decreases sharply with #word. About 62.3% of the queries contain less than three words (three excluded), and 76.8% queries contain less than four words. On average, each query contains 2.52 words. Figure 3(c) shows the distribution of queries with different length measured by #letter. Each query contains 18.76 letters on average. These results confirm the assumption that *search queries on mobile platform are usually short.* Users are not willing to type long sentences on the keyboard of very limited size. Therefore, it would reduce user's effort significantly if we can design systems to avoid time consuming user-phone interaction.

Mobile Search Is Local and Context-Sensitive

The left map in Figure 2 shows the query distribution in US. We can see that #query is diverse in different cities. The right map in Figure 2 shows the query distribution in the city of *Seattle*. We can observe that the mobile search activity is very sensitive to location. For commercial areas, since there are a lot of local businesses like shopping centers, restaurants, and so on, people in these locations are more likely to conduct entity-related search. Figure 3(d) shows #query in different time slot (of the day). The highest peak occurs near to 5–6 pm, when the search on mobiles tends to be active. One possible reason is that people are about to get off work. The lowest point occurs at about 2–3 am. This is reasonable as few people are active in the midnight. The above observation implies that *mobile search is usually context-aware* [15]. Using entity extraction technique, we can detect the *entity query*, i.e., the queries target at searching entities. The ratio of #entity query to #raw query is 15.28% (the ratio depends on the recall of an entity extraction algorithm). This verifies that search on mobile is *local and entity-oriented.*

The above characteristics of mobile query motivates the design of a recommendation system that is *context-aware, personalized,* and *without requiring any typing of queries.* Due to the abundant attributes of extracted entities (as shown and Figure 1), a user can get a quick glance of his information need without typing a query explicitly.

APPROACH

In this section, we introduce the proposed recommendation approach, which consists of two key components: 1) entity extraction which detects and recognizes entities from a tex-

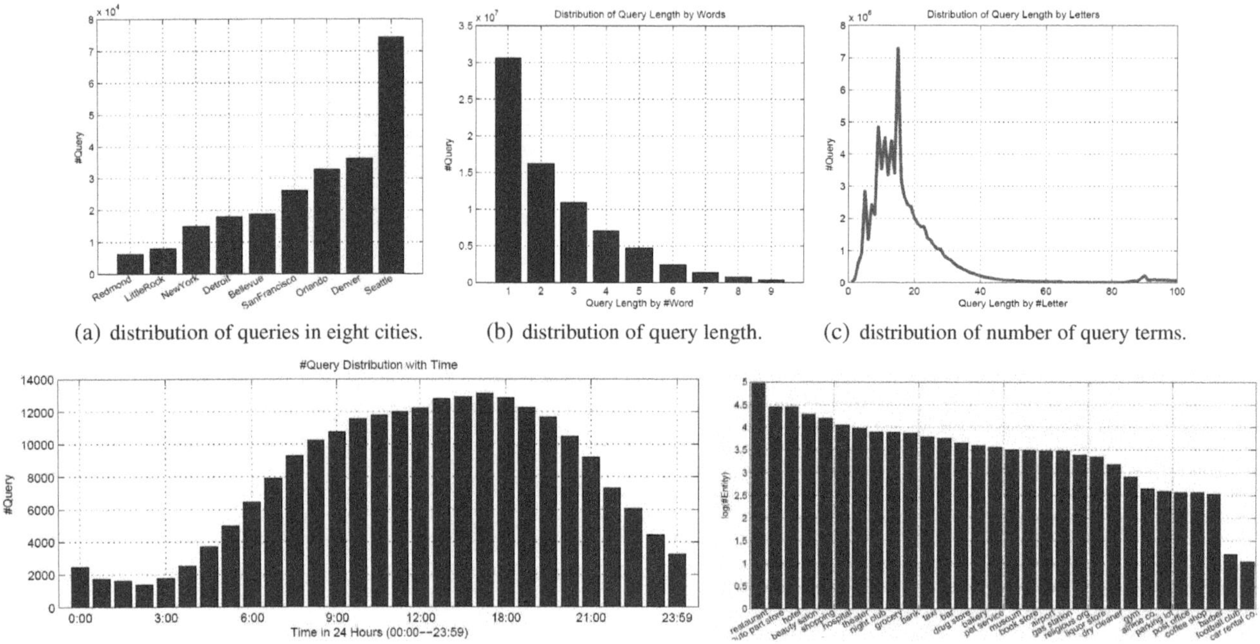

(a) distribution of queries in eight cities. (b) distribution of query length. (c) distribution of number of query terms.

(d) distribution of query time (time of the day). (e) distribution of entities within 30 entity types.

Figure 3. The statistics of user click distribution in our database.

Table 2. The common attributes of extracted entities from three examples. Each entity type has its unique attributes. The right picture in Figure 1 shows an example of a restaurant *spotlight*.

Name	Country	Region	Locality	Address	EntityType	Latitude	Longtitude	Phone
Starbucks	U.S.	CA	Irivne	115 Fortune Dr	Coffee Shop	33.6504	-117.7461	(617)277-0087
FrenchDress	U.S.	MA	Boston	49 River St	shopping	42.3572	-71.0703	(617)723-4968
Walmart	U.S.	UT	HeberCity	435 Airport Rd	shopping	40.4827	-111.4207	(435)654-6436

tual query log, and 2) entity ranking which ranks a candidate set of entities and the corresponding entity types to the user. We pay more attention to the entity ranking algorithm.

Entity Extraction

We build a database of extracted entities from several major local business sites on the Web. The extraction algorithms are similar to the previous entity extraction system *KnowItAll* [8], where the key techniques are rule-based. That is, the first step of entity extractor is to automatically create a collection of extraction rules for each kind of entity types. Beyond of the extraction rule of entities, we make a further step to extract the attributes of entities as well. Please refer to [8] for detailed components of rules. This step aims to get a high recall of entities and the corresponding attributes. After obtaining the initial extracted ones, we can pass them to a search engine to retrieve more entities. Then a pattern learner is employed to filter out high-quality entities for expansion. In summary, we extract 5,457,192 entities under 37 entity types.

Table 2 lists three entities with some extracted common features. Besides the common features, each entity type has a unique set of attributes. For example, a restaurant has the price level and cuisine type as the major features. Due to the limited space, we do not introduce the detailed features of each type here. After obtaining the results by entity extractor, we can design the query parser which maps a query to a specific entity. This can be implemented by supervised classification techniques or topic models [9].

Probabilistic Entity Ranking

In this section, we present the algorithm for the probabilistic entity ranking. Table 3 lists the key notations used in this paper. Figure 4 shows the framework of building a personal user model based on the user click-through data. The key component is an entity ranker that can estimate the conditional probabilities of entities and entity types for a given user under certain context. Given a user $u \in \mathcal{U}$ and his context information (location and time) $\langle l, t\rangle$, the basic idea is to first find the queries issued in this context, and then weight these queries according to the user similarity graph $\mathbf{S}$. To consider the co-occurrence of entities in a query session (e.g., a bar is usually queried after restaurant in a short period of time), the generating probability of entity will be smoothed and propagated on an entity similarity graph $\mathbf{W}$. The two similarity matrices $\mathbf{S}$ and $\mathbf{W}$ can be computed offline, while the other steps can be processed on the fly.

Problem Formulation

By using entity extractor and query parser, we can obtain a query database $\mathcal{Q} = \{q_1, \ldots, q_m\}$, where m is the number of mobile queries containing entities in our database. Each *mobile query* is a 5-dimensional tuple:

$$Q := \langle E, Z, U, L, T\rangle,$$

Table 3. List of key notations.

Symbol	Description
$\mathbb{N}_u$	$\{1, \ldots, u\}$, a set of integers up to u
N_u	$\lvert\mathbb{N}_u\rvert$, the cardinality of $\mathbb{N}_u$
$\mathcal{U}$	$\{\mathbf{u}_i : i \in \mathbb{N}_u\}$, a collection of N_u users
$\mathcal{Q}$	the collection of all the queries
U, E, Z, T, L	represents user, entity, entity type, time, location, respectively
$a.B$	the attribute B of object a

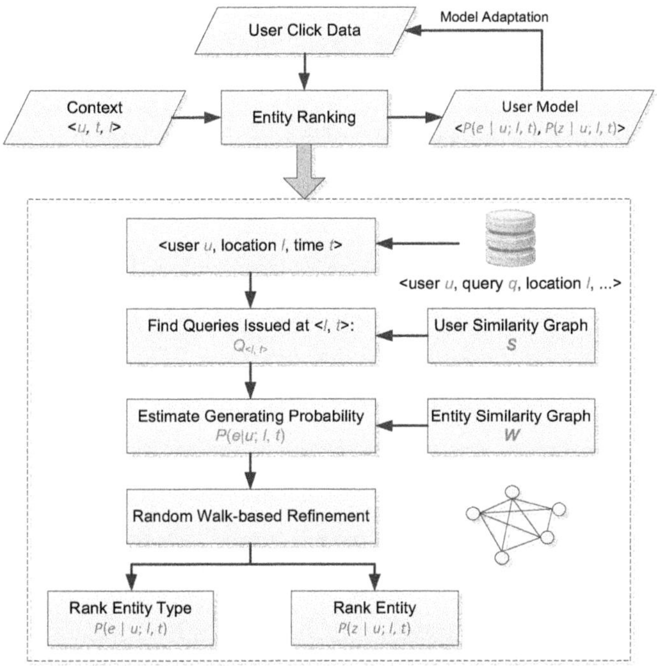

Figure 4. The pipeline of the probabilistic entity ranking algorithm. The components in the rectangle shows the details for "entity ranking."

where $E \in \mathcal{E}$ is the entity searched in Q, Z indicates the entity category of E, $U \in \mathcal{U}$ is the user who conducted the query , L and T are the context, i.e., the location and time when Q was generated, respectively. We use $\mathcal{E}$ to denote the whole collection of extracted entities.

Each *mobile user* U consists of a history of queries:

$$U := \mathcal{Q}_u = \{q_1, \ldots, q_u\}.$$

Given a user $u \in \mathcal{U}$ in the context $\langle l, t\rangle$, the task *entity ranking* is to rank the entities in $\mathcal{E}$ such that the higher ranked entity has a larger probability of being queried by u.

Probabilistic Ranking Algorithm

We first consider the probability of generating the entity e_j by user u_i with the context $\langle l, t\rangle$. The entities in $\mathcal{E}$ are ranked by the conditional probability $P(E|U; L, T)$, i.e., we consider E is generated by the user U conditioning on the context $\langle l, t\rangle$. We assume the final ranking score of a specific entity is proportional to this conditional probability. To this end, we introduce a variable Z to indicate the user's intent. For example, if Z indicates "eat" for the time being, probably the user intends to go to a restaurant. With this intuition, the possible choice of Z is determined by the number of entity categories N_z. We deem $P(E|Z)$ as the popularity of some E under the category Z, and $P(Z|U)$ proportional to the frequency of querying Z by U. We have the conditional probability

$$P(e_j|u_i; l, t) = \sum_{k=1}^{N_z} P(e_j|z_k; l, t)P(z_k|u_i; l, t).$$

Due to the limited query history of U, it is common that some entity types have never been queried by U. Assigning a zero conditional probability of these entity types are apparently not proper. To overcome this problem, we leverage the idea of collaborative recommendation techniques [3]. That is, we introduce the query record of other users to help estimate the probability. If other users similar to u_i have queried an entity before, u_i also has the possibility of searching for the entity. Thus we have

$$P(e_j|u_i; l,t) = \sum_{k=1}^{N_z} P(e_j|z_k, u_n; l,t)\sum_{n=1}^{N_u} P(z_k|u_n; l, t)P(u_n|u_i)$$
$$\propto \sum_{k=1}^{N_z} P(e_j|z_k; l,t)\sum_{n=1}^{N_u} P(z_k|u_n; l,t)s(u_n,u_i), \quad (1)$$

where $s(\cdot, \cdot) : \mathcal{U} \times \mathcal{U} \rightarrow \mathbb{R}_+$ is a function measuring the similarity between two users. The intuition here is the transition probability $P(u_n|u_i)$ is proportional to the similarity between them.

We now instantiate the components in (1). We first query $\mathcal{Q}$ with the context $\langle l, t\rangle$. Denote the returned query set as $\mathcal{Q}_{\langle l,t\rangle}$. Then for $\mathcal{Q}_e, \mathcal{Q}_z \subset \mathcal{Q}_{\langle l,t\rangle}$ we have

$$P(e_j|z_k;l,t) := \frac{|\mathcal{Q}_e : \forall q \in \mathcal{Q}_e, q.E = e_j, q.Z = z_k, q.L = l, q.T = t|}{|\mathcal{Q}_z : \forall q \in \mathcal{Q}_z, q.Z = z_k, q.L = l, q.T = t|}$$

where $|\mathcal{Q}|$ is the number of queries in the query set $\mathcal{Q}$ belonging to category z_t. Similarly, we have

$$P(z_k|u_n;l,t) := \frac{|\mathcal{Q}_z : \forall q \in \mathcal{Q}_z, q.Z = z_k, q.U = u_n, q.L = l, q.T = t|}{|\mathcal{Q}_u : \forall q \in \mathcal{Q}_u, q.U = u_n, q.L = l, q.T = t|}$$

It is intuitive to model the probability of each search intent using their frequency.

User Similarity

Now we focus on the similarity $s(\cdot, \cdot)$ defined on the user space, in which each user can be represented by a query history record. Depending on how to represent users with the query records, a three-level similarity function can be adopted here: *entity-based*, *entity-type-based*, and *entity-attribute-based* similarity.

We first convert the query history into a fixed-length vector akin to the term frequency-inverse document frequency (*tf-idf*) scheme in text processing [23]. Here each "document" implies a single user U, while each term refers to either a specific entity or the entity type. In the former case, the representation is strict in the sense that two users are similar only if they used to query the same entity. The term frequency of E with U is the frequency E has been searched by U. Specifically,

$$tf(e,u) = |\mathcal{Q}_u : \forall q \in \mathcal{Q}_u, q.E = e \text{ and } q.U = u|.$$

The inverse document frequency is

$$idf(e) = |\mathcal{U} : \forall u \in \mathcal{U}, \exists q \in \mathcal{Q}_u, q.E = e|.$$

Thus, we construct the feature vector of u_i by $\mathbf{x}_i \in \mathbb{R}^d$ using tf-idf weighting, i.e., the k-th component is computed by

$$[\mathbf{x}_i]_k = tf(e_k, u_i) \log \frac{1}{idf(e_k)}.$$

Then, we have

$$s_1(u_i, u_j) := \frac{\mathbf{x}_i^\top \mathbf{x}_j}{\sqrt{(\mathbf{x}_i^\top \mathbf{x}_i)(\mathbf{x}_j^\top \mathbf{x}_j)}}.$$

The measure s_1 may not be always optimal in real case. For example, considering two users, one of them is interested in *McDonalds*, the other always prefers *KFC*. When they come to a district where only *BurgerKing* is available, they may both like it since they both need *fast food*. Therefore, entity-type based tf-idf weighting can be complementary to entity based representation because of the coarser granularity. We just need to use the constraint $q.Z = z$ (now Z is the term instead of E) instead of $q.E = e$ when computing the term frequency of E in $\mathcal{Q}_u$. The inverse document frequency becomes the number of users who used to search that entity type. We denote the cosine similarity with entity-type based representation by s_2. We evaluated the effectiveness of both s_1 and s_2 in the experiment.

Remark. In the above methods, the attributes of entities are ignored. One might expect that such attributes can indicate the preference of users. For example, if two users both like Chinese cuisine, they are similar to some extent even if they never search the same Chinese restaurant before. However, each user could have searched different kinds of entities, it is difficult to measure entities of different types directly. Due to the defection of entity crawling process, the entity attributes are often missing. Moreover, the online entity ranking must be effective. Similarity between sets of entities cannot meet this requirement.

Ranking Refinement by Random Walk

The similarity computation in last section ignores the sequential information between queries. Considering the meeting of some friends, they probably query the restaurants before dinner. After having dinner, they may be interested in the bars nearby for night life. In this situation, temporal patterns (restaurant→bar here) exist and make sense in characterizing the relation among entities. Note that sequential co-occurrence depends on the length of time interval. Here we name the time interval by *session*. The longer the session, the more sequential co-occurrence would be detected, and vice versa. We use the number of users that exhibit temporal patterns to measure the transition probability between two entities, i.e.,

$$\begin{aligned} w(e_i, e_j) &= |\mathcal{U} : \forall u \in \mathcal{U}, \exists q, q' \in \mathcal{Q}_u, q.E = e_i \text{ and} \\ &\quad q'.E = e_j \text{ and } q'.T - q.T < \epsilon|, \end{aligned}$$

where ϵ is the upper bound of the length of the session. The constraint of $\mathcal{U}$ here is there exists at least one session in each user $u \in \mathcal{U}$ such that e_i and e_j are queried sequentially. Thus we can construct the matrix $\mathbf{W} \in \mathbb{R}_+^{N_e \times N_e}$ with $[\mathbf{W}]_{ij} := w(e_i, e_j)$ to measure the possibility of transferring from one entity to another. We can further to normalize $\mathbf{W}$ such that $\forall i \in \mathbb{N}_e \sum_{j \in \mathbb{N}_e} W_{ij} = 1$.

Suppose the ranking score obtained from above step is $\mathbf{p}_0$. Then we refine it by random walk with transition probability matrix $\mathbf{W}$ iteratively:

$$\mathbf{p} = \alpha \mathbf{W}^\top \mathbf{p} + (1 - \alpha)\mathbf{p}_0.$$

One can prove the iteration converges to a fixed point $\mathbf{p}^* = (1-\alpha)(\mathbf{I} - \alpha \mathbf{W}^\top)^{-1}\mathbf{p}_0$. We use the score $\mathbf{p}^*$ to rank the entities.

Ranking Entity Type

As shown in Figure 1, the returned entities are organized by entity types. Besides ranking entities, we also need to rank the types as the left diagram in Figure 1 to facilitate user's browsing purpose. To this end, we consider the scheme akin to the probabilistic framework of entity ranking:

$$P(z|u; l, t) \propto \sum_{n=1}^{N_u} P(z|u_n; l, t) s(u_n, u).$$

We organize the entities by ranked types with ranking score $P(Z|U; L, T)$. The entities under each category are sorted by $P(E|U; L, T)$.

Remark. We can collect the user click-through data to help rectify the ranking score. The more frequently clicked entities have larger probability to be clicked again. The relevance feedback techniques can be employed to automatically adjust the distributions $P(E|U; L, T)$ and $P(Z|U; L, T)$ [22].

EXPERIMENTS

Data and Setting

We build the user similarity graph and entity similarity graph based on the mobile click-through data from the first five months, while adopting the data in the last one month for test. We randomly selected 2,000 users and use their queries in the March of 2010 as test data, which contains a total of 58,111 query records. We denote this test set by $\mathcal{Q}_t$.

For each test query record $q \in \mathcal{Q}_t$, we use its location l and time t as the search context and call the system to recommend the entities to its user u. We split the time into 7 intervals: 0:00~5:00, 6:00~7:00, 8:00~11:00, 12:00, 13:00~17:00, 18:00~19:00, 20:00~23:00. We extract a set of queries from the query database with the context $\langle l, t \rangle$. Then we sort the entities contained in these queries by entity ranker. To this end, we extract the queries conducted within five kilometers to u and fallen into the same time interval as t.

Let $\mathcal{E}_t$ denote the set of the ranked entities, we can measure the top-k accuracy of $\mathcal{E}_t$ by counting the position $\pi(q.E)$ of $q.E$ in $\mathcal{E}_t$. For each $q \in \mathcal{Q}_t$, if $\pi(q.E)$ is less than k, we

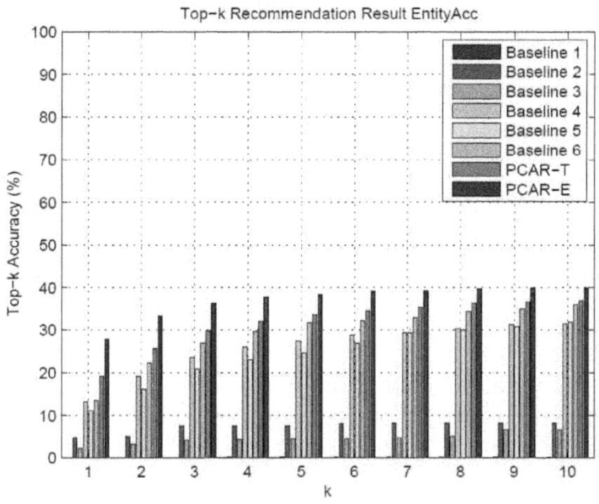

(a) Accuracy of entity ranking

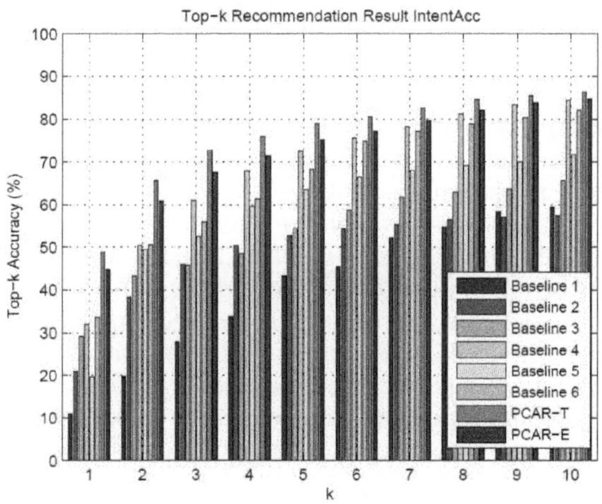

(b) Accuracy of intent ranking

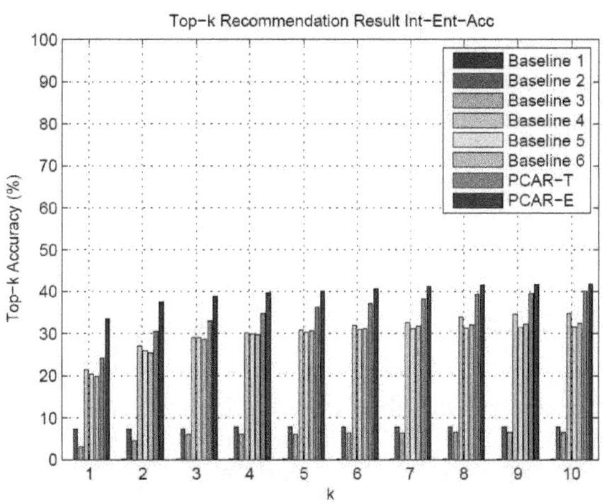

(c) Accuracy of intent-entity ranking with $t = 3$.

Figure 5. The accuracy of the proposed entity ranking.

have correctly recommended entity E. Formally the top-k accuracy of the whole test set $\mathcal{Q}_t$ is computed by

$$Accuracy(\mathcal{Q}_t, k) = \frac{\sum_{q \in \mathcal{Q}_t} \mathbb{I}(\pi(q.E) \leq k)}{|\mathcal{Q}_t|},$$

where $\mathbb{I}(c)$ returns 1 if c is true and 0 otherwise.

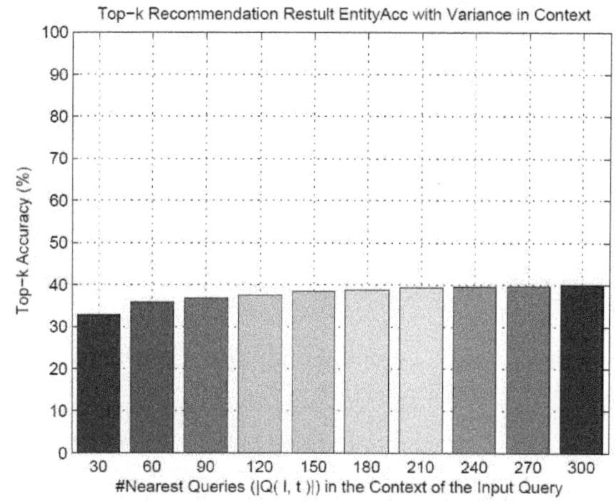

(a) Top-10 EntityAcc with different $|\mathcal{Q}_{\langle l,t \rangle}|$

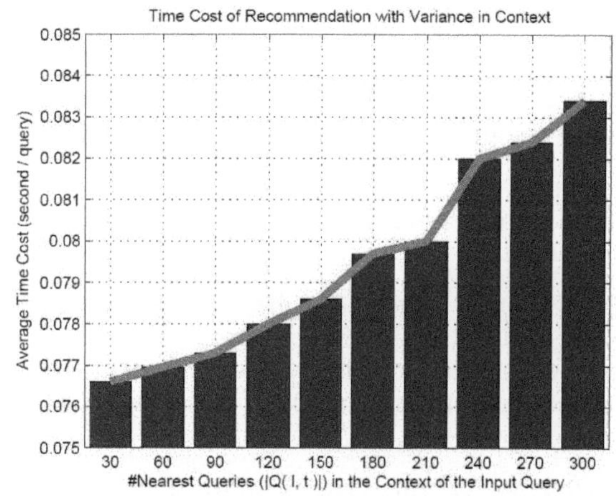

(b) Average time cost of each query with different $|\mathcal{Q}_{\langle l,t \rangle}|$.

Figure 6. Sensitivity of entity ranking to the context.

We measure accuracy of three kinds of recommendation:

- **EntityAcc**: the top-k accuracy of the recommended entities;
- **IntentAcc**: the top-k accuracy of the recommended entity type. It reflects the intent of the users at the query location;
- **IntEntAcc**: the accuracy of the top-k entities in each of the top-t entity types, i.e., $t \times k$ entities are contained in $\mathcal{E}_t$.

The recommendation results have a two-level organization (refer to Figure 1). According to the definition, EntityAcc should always be less than IntentAcc. The abbreviation of the examined schemes are summarized as follows [1]:

- **Baseline 1** $\langle l \rangle$: recommend entities according to their distance to the user's current location, and rank them by distance to the user;

[1] The result of traditional content-based recommendation (CBR) is not presented here. In most cases, a user has not searched an entity before a new context. Thus the accuracy of CBR approaches to 0.

Table 4. The recommended entity type (RcmndtnInt in the table) of 4 users.

Name	Jennifer	Peter	Peter	Pok	Miranda	Miranda
Latitude	40.7441	40.7441	40.7441	37.7896	37.7896	37.7896
Longitude	-74.0135	-74.0135	-74.0135	-122.4061	-122.4061	-122.4061
Time	18:26	18:26	15:26	22:15	22:15	13:36
Location	NewYork	NewYork	NewYork	SanFrancisco	SanFrancisco	SanFrancisco
RcmndtnInt	Bank(2.32) Shopping(0.17) Clubs(0.17)	Bank(2.33) Restaurant(0.23) Shopping(0.22)	PetService(0.66) Restaurant(0.54) Hotel(0.19)	Restaurant(4.01) Hotel(1.01) Theater(0.80)	Bank(1.03) Restaurant(0.69) Theater(0.53)	Restaurant(0.51) Bank(0.18) Shopping(0.13)

- **Baseline 2** $\langle l, p \rangle$: recommend entities as **Baseline 1**, but rank them by the popularity p [2];
- **Baseline 3** $\langle l, p, t \rangle$: recommend entities as **Baseline 1**, but rank them by their popularity in current time slot;
- **Baseline 4** $\langle l \rangle$: recommended entities that have been queried in current location, and rank them by their distance to the user;
- **Baseline 5** $\langle l, p \rangle$: recommend entities as **Baseline 4**, but rank by popularity;
- **Baseline 6** $\langle l, p, t \rangle$: recommend entities that have been queried in both current location and time slot, then rank by popularity;
- **PCAR-T** $\langle u, l, t \rangle$: the Personalized Context-Aware entity Ranking (PCAR) algorithm proposed in this paper. It is essentially a hybrid recommendation algorithm. The tf-idf representation of users for building user similarity graph is entity-type based;
- **PCAR-E** $\langle u, l, t \rangle$: the same as PCAR-T except the tf-idf representation of users are entity-based.

It is worth noticing that **Baseline 1–3** and **Baseline 4–6** can be categorized into two groups: the first group only considers the entities whose *physical locations* are close to user's current location, while the second only considers the entities which are *queried* in user's current location.

Experiment I: Top-k Recommendation Accuracy

Figure 5 shows the recommendation accuracy of the evaluated schemes. We can draw several observations from this figure. First, among all the baseline methods 1-6, baseline 4-6 reports significantly better results than baseline 1-3. Note that baseline 1-3 deem all the existing entities as candidates when recommending to users, while baseline 4-6 only use the entities that have been queried in current context as candidates. Therefore, we conclude entities used to be searched are more likely to be searched again. Baseline 5-6 are slightly better than baseline 4, which implies: 1) popularity is more important than geometric distance, and 2) time is a effective context for recommendation.

Second, PCAR produces significantly higher accuracy than all the Baseline methods. PCAR not only considers the popularity of entities through $P(E|Z)$, but only leverages the information of each individual user through the generating probability $P(Z|U)$ and the transition probability $P(Z|Z')$.

[2] The *popularity* p of an entity is the number of times it has been queried.

Besides the context, the entity-oriented search depends on the user in nature. For example, when searching a restaurant, different users may have different cuisine preference. People who like Chinese food may conduct totally different queries comparing with people who favor Western food. Therefore, it is important to make the preference personalized. The proposed PCAR system yields the accuracy of 10% higher than that of baselines. Thus we conclude that personalization exists in entity-oriented search.

Third, comparing the two user representation schemes, PCAR-E is better than PCAR-T for entity recommendation, while PCAR-T is better than PCAR-E for type recommendation. It implies that the tf-idf representation for users when computing user similarity graph is task-dependent. The top-10 EntityAcc is 40% and IntentAcc approaches to 90%. This high accuracy confirms the efficacy of the proposed probabilistic entity ranking algorithm. It also verifies the importance of taking context and personalization into account. It is observed that the accuracy of intent-entity ranking is around 30%, which leaves much room for improvement in our future work.

Experiment II: Sensitivity to Context

The first step of entity ranker retrieves a set of candidate queries $\mathcal{Q}_{\langle l,t \rangle}$ at the current context $\langle l, t \rangle$. Then it essentially ranks the entities contained in $\mathcal{Q}_{\langle l,t \rangle}$ by a probabilistic estimation of $P(E|U; L, T)$. Therefore, the performance of entity ranker relies on the quality of $\mathcal{Q}_{\langle l,t \rangle}$. In the implementation, we sort each candidate query $q \in \mathcal{Q}$ according its distance to the user. We extract the nearest-n queries (i.e., $|\mathcal{Q}_{\langle l,t \rangle}| = n$) as candidates for recommendation. We evaluate how sensitive of entity ranker to the number n. The results are shown in Figure 6.

First, we observe that the EntityAcc increases with n. When n is a small value (e.g., 30), the accuracy is merely about 32%. This is because a large portion of valuable candidate queries are ignored. The most expected entity may not be selected as candidate at all. In this case, no matter how good the ranking algorithm, it never leads to the good performance. As n increases, more entities are involved into the ranking process. When n is larger than 200, the further gain of accuracy seems marginal. When $n = 300$, the accuracy approaches to 40%. We believe that the performance would be improved with the ongoing collection of the queries.

We also emphasize that, even the accuracy is not too high, the recommended entity list is still meaningful in the sense that it provides a suggestion about the nearby entities. By re-

(a) entity type ranked by user model (b) entity ranked by user model (c) entity ranked by distance (d) entity ranked by user rating

Figure 7. The different recommended entity lists shown in user study.

viewing the attributes of the top ranked entities, the activity of users may be affected positively or guided by the recommendation results.

The average time cost of each test query is in the interval $[0.075, 0.085]$ sec with n ranging from 30 to 300. We conclude it is efficient enough for real-time application. From the flowchart in Figure 4, the computational costs in the perpendicular direction include: find candidate queries, estimate generating probability, and random walk-based refinement. As n is typically less than 300, these steps can be done very quickly. The cost on building user similarity graph and entity similarity graph can be very heavy. However, these two steps can be finished in an offline phase.

To further show the context-awareness and personalization, the two key characteristics of our approach, we sample four users (*Jennifer, Peter, Pok, and Miranda*) to show their recommendation results in different contexts in Table 4. The recommendation results exhibit the personalized characteristics clearly. At the same context, for example, NewYork at 18:26PM, the top recommended entity types of Jennifer are different from the ones of Peter. So is the case of Pok and Miranda. This verifies the personalization target of *easylife*, that is, the recommendation results should be diverse for different users even if the context is the same.

For the same user Miranda, the recommendation results at 22:15 are different from the ones at 13:36 even if the location is the same. Thus our proposed recommendation approach is flexible to meet the user's demand. This fact shows it works in a context-aware manner. Moreover, the three most frequently searched entity types of Miranda are bank, shopping, and restaurant. Depending upon the context, the system can rank them in a proper order. The result in Figure 5(b) has shown the disadvantages of the simple frequency based ranking.

Experiment III: User Study

We developed a real application called *easylife* on a Windows Phone 7 device, based on the proposed contextual recommendation approach. The application is able to automatically recommend both entity types (as shown in Figure 1 (b)) and entities within each type (Figure 1 (c)). The entities come from a dataset with 700 million local businesses and 30 entity types in U.S. We evaluate *easylife* by a series of user studies.

As our approach is built on a large-scale mobile query log data, we randomly selected 12 users frequently conducted mobile searches from our database. As "user id" is anonymous without any identity information (for privacy consideration), we invited 12 subjects to participate in the role play study. Each subject was assigned a user id and asked to play as the role of that user. The subjects were provided the search history (each search record consists of "time," "location," and "query"), and then asked to fill a form to estimate the profile of this user (e.g., age range, interested entity events, residence, etc.). Then, each subject was asked to select two time slots and two locations (one is residence, the other is somewhere else). Based on the selected context (time and location, as well as user id), we provide four ranked recommendation results to this subject: 1) entity types ranked by the built user model, 2) entities ranked by user model which belongs to the top ranked entity type (supposing user will click the "best bet" entity type in *easylife*), 3) entities ranked by distance to current location (without considering user model), and 4) entities ranked by user rating (collected from users without user model). Figure 7 shows the example of four recommendation results. Each subject was asked to give a satisfaction score of each list in a scale of 1—5: the higher the score, the more satisfied the subject is toward the recommended list. As a result, there are 192 scores ($12 \times 4 \times 2 \times 2$) in total, with each recommendation list associated with 48 scores. We computed the average satisfaction scores for each ranked list across different subjects.

Table 5. Subjective evaluation of four recommendation schemes.

Recommendation	Entity type	User model	By distance	By rating
Satisfaction score	4.31	4.00	2.79	2.54

Table 5 lists the evaluation results. The satisfaction score of entity type recommendation is the highest. Among the three entity recommendation schemes, user model achieves a better performance than the recommendations by distance and by rating (the rating data were collected from a popular commercial local business site). This shows that our recommendation technique by user model (i.e., the proposed contextual and personalized approach) is more user-friendly. Moreover, it is a little surprising that user rating is even worse than recommendation by distance. It is partially because user rating may ignore the location context for recommendation, which is critical for daily life. This observation is also confirmed by our analysis on mobile click-through data. The recommendation by user model is significantly better than that by distance. It shows that personalization is important for recommendation task on the mobile devices.

CONCLUSION

In this paper, we first conduct an analysis on a large-scale mobile click-through data collected from a commercial mobile search engine. Our observations indicate that the queries conducted on mobile devices are typically short, context-aware, and local. Motivated by these observations, we propose a query-free entity recommendation approach to understand implicit user intent on the mobile devices. The proposed approach is capable to rank relevant entity types (e.g., restaurant, hotel, bar, etc.) and entities within each type (e.g., "I love sushi" and "MacDonalds" in the type of "restaurant"). We developed a real recommendation application based on the proposed approach on Windows Phone 7 devices and evaluated it through both objective and subjective experiments. The evaluations shows our proposed approach achieves the best user experience than the traditional location and rating-based recommendation schemes.

Our future works include: 1) exploring other machine learning techniques for a better recommendation, such as learning to rank, matrix factorization, and so on; 2) leveraging social signals for improving user similarity (e.g., using the friendship in social media community such as Facebook); and 3) collecting real-world click-through data through the developed mobile application and performing the real-world evaluation on these data.

ACKNOWLEDGEMENTS

We would like to thank Peng Bai, Zheng Chen, Xuedong Huang, Xin Lin, Xiaochuan Ni, Jian-Tao Sun, Peng Xu, Bo Zhang, and Zhimin Zhang, for their insightful discussions. We also thank the subjects involved in our user studies.

REFERENCES

1. http://www.discoverbing.com/mobile/index.html.
2. http://www.google.com/mobile.
3. G. Adomavicius and A. Tuzhilin. Toward the next generation of recommender systems: A survey of the state-of-the-art and possible extensions. *IEEE Trans. Knowl. Data Eng.*, 17(6):734–749, 2005.
4. H. Cao, D. H. Hu, D. Shen, D. Jiang, J.-T. Sun, E. Chen, and Q. Yang. Context-aware query classification. In *SIGIR*, pages 3–10, 2009.
5. H. Cao, D. Jiang, J. Pei, Q. He, Z. Liao, E. Chen, and H. Li. Context-aware query suggestion by mining click-through and session data. In *KDD*, pages 875–883, 2008.
6. W. Chu and S.-T. Park. Personalized recommendation on dynamic content using predictive bilinear models. In *WWW*, pages 691–700, 2009.
7. K. Church, B. Smyth, K. Bradley, and P. Cotter. A large scale study of european mobile search behaviour. In *Mobile HCI*, pages 13–22, 2008.
8. O. Etzioni, M. J. Cafarella, D. Downey, A.-M. Popescu, T. Shaked, S. Soderland, D. S. Weld, and A. Yates. Unsupervised named-entity extraction from the web: An experimental study. *Artif. Intell.*, 165(1):91–134, 2005.
9. J. Guo, G. Xu, X. Cheng, and H. Li. Named entity recognition in query. In *SIGIR*, pages 267–274, 2009.
10. I. Guy, N. Zwerdling, I. Ronen, D. Carmel, and E. Uziel. Social media recommendation based on people and tags. In *SIGIR*, pages 194–201, 2010.
11. M. Kamvar and S. Baluja. The role of context in query input: using contextual signals to complete queries on mobile devices. In *Mobile HCI*, pages 405–412, 2007.
12. M. Kamvar and S. Baluja. Query suggestions for mobile search: understanding usage patterns. In *CHI*, pages 1013–1016, 2008.
13. M. Kamvar, M. Kellar, R. Patel, and Y. Xu. Computers and iphones and mobile phones, oh my!: a logs-based comparison of search users on different devices. In *WWW*, pages 801–810, 2009.
14. D. Kelly, K. Gyllstrom, and E. W. Bailey. A comparison of query and term suggestion features for interactive searching. In *SIGIR*, pages 371–378, 2009.
15. N. Lane, D. Lymberopoulos, F. Zhao, and A. Campbell. Hapori: Context-based local search for mobile phones using community behavioral modeling and similarity. In *Proc. of ACM International Conference on Ubiquitous Computing*, pages 109–118, 2010.
16. J. Lee, S. won Hwang, Z. Nie, and J.-R. Wen. Query result clustering for object-level search. In *KDD*, pages 1205–1214, 2009.
17. L. Li, W. Chu, J. Langford, and R. E. Schapire. A contextual-bandit approach to personalized news article recommendation. In *WWW*, pages 661–670, 2010.
18. X. Li, Y.-Y. Wang, D. Shen, and A. Acero. Learning with click graph for query intent classification. *ACM Trans. Inf. Syst.*, 28(3), 2010.
19. Z. Lu, D. Agarwal, and I. S. Dhillon. A spatio-temporal approach to collaborative filtering. In *RecSys*, pages 13–20, 2009.
20. E. Meij, P. Mika, and H. Zaragoza. An evaluation of entity and frequency based query completion methods. In *SIGIR*, pages 678–679, 2009.
21. Z. Nie, J.-R. Wen, and W.-Y. Ma. Object-level vertical search. In *CIDR*, pages 235–246, 2007.
22. Y. Rui, T. S. Huang, M. Ortega, and S. Mehrotra. Relevance feedback: A power tool in interactive content-based image retrieval. *IEEE Trans. CSVT*, 8(5):644–655, Sept. 1998.
23. F. Sebastiani. Machine learning in automated text categorization. *CoRR*, 2001.
24. Siri. http://siri.com/.
25. X. Yin and S. Shah. Building taxonomy of web search intents for name entity queries. In *Proceedings of WWW*, pages 1001–1010, 2010.
26. K. Yu, J. D. Lafferty, S. Zhu, and Y. Gong. Large-scale collaborative prediction using a nonparametric random effects model. In *ICML*, 2009.

Getting Closer: An Empirical Investigation of the Proximity of User to Their Smart Phones

Anind K. Dey, Katarzyna Wac*, Denzil Ferreira, Kevin Tassini, Jin-Hyuk Hong & Julian Ramos
Human-Computer Interaction Institute
Carnegie Mellon University
*Institute of Services Science
University of Geneva

ABSTRACT

Much research in ubiquitous computing assumes that a user's phone will be always on and at-hand, for collecting user context and for communicating with a user. Previous work with the previous generation of mobile phones has shown that such an assumption is false. Here, we investigate whether this assumption about users' proximity to their mobile phones holds for a new generation of mobile phones, smart phones. We conduct a data collection field study of 28 smart phone owners over a period of 4 weeks. We show that in fact this assumption is still false, with the within arm's reach proximity being true close to 50% of the time, similar to the earlier work. However, we also show that smart phone proximity within the same room (arm+room) as the user is true almost 90% of the time. We discuss the reasons for these phone proximities and the implications of this on the development of mobile phone applications, particularly those that collect user and environmental context, and delivering notification to users. We also show that we can accurately predict the proximity at the arm level and arm+room level with 75 and 83% accuracy, respectively, with features simple to collect and model on a mobile phone. Further we show that for several individuals who are almost always within the arm+room level, we can predict this level with over 90% accuracy.

Author Keywords
Proximity, mobile devices, mobility, smart phone.

ACM Classification Keywords
H.m. Information systems: Miscellaneous.

General Terms
Experimentation, Human Factors

INTRODUCTION

It is without question that we are living in a world where emerging mobile personal devices and high-capacity wireless networks are enabling new and innovative applications that compliment many different aspects of daily life. Over the past decade, mobile computing has become ever more present in our society, particularly as smart phones become more prevalent. By December 2010, 31% of U.S. mobile phone users had smart phones [14] and this figure is expected to cross 50% by the end of 2011 [7]. This trend holds worldwide, with almost 300 million smart phones being sold in 2010 [5] and another 500 million predicted for 2012 [4].

In keeping with this trend, there has been an underlying assumption in much of the work in ubiquitous computing that a phone is always with its owner. This assumption, if true, means that ubiquitous computing systems can use the phone as a medium for collecting data from users and communicating information to users, at any time. Further, this means that the mobile phone is an accurate proxy to collect contextual information on users' location and activity. This assumption was investigated in 2006 [20] when mobile devices were not as robust and feature-filled as they are today. At that time Patel *et al.* found that when participants had their phones on (81% of the time), they kept their phone within arm's reach 58% of that time, which was less than the participants perceived themselves as doing, and the phone was within the same room as participants an extra 20% of the time.

Since this study, five years ago, we have seen the introduction and mass adoption of Apple's iPhone and the Android platform that have redefined the mobile computing experience, and the operating systems and capabilities of mobile devices that are available to the average user. We now live in an era of so-called "smart" phones. These mobile devices have progressed far beyond a means of making and receiving phone calls, and for many, have become an almost indispensable tool to access information, complete tasks, be entertained and communicate in a wide variety of ways (*e.g.*, Skype, instant messenger, email). As a whole, it seems reasonable then to presume that people rely on their mobile phones far more than they used to and are thus likely to keep it more accessible as well. Based on the widespread availability of smart phones, it is important to re-investigate the assumption (and Patel *et al.*'s findings) about users' proximity to their phones, to determine if the smart phone is as ubiquitous a device as we believe.

Using a series of surveys and interviews, as well as by employing an application on Android mobile devices, we have gathered both quantitative and qualitative data from 28 participants over 4 weeks of real-world behaviors with their own smart phones. For this study we looked at participants'

UbiComp'11, September 17–21, 2011, Beijing, China.

proximity to their smart phone via Bluetooth monitoring. In addition we automatically collected a wide range of sensor data from their phones. Supplementing this objective field data are interviews, surveys and day reconstruction exercises with users that help to give a sense of context. Beyond these 28 participants, we also surveyed 367 smart phone users about their perceived proximity to their smart phones and their habits surrounding smart phone use.

The contribution of this paper is three-fold. The first is to present empirical evidence to understand the degree to which current smart phones are an accurate proxy for their owners' location and context. Second, we identify themes that help explain these results, providing implications for future application development. Finally, we demonstrate that we can build accurate predictive models of proximity using readily available features about user activity. We begin with a discussion of related work.

RELATED WORK

As mobile phones become smaller and more powerful computing devices, they have also become more prevalent in the world at large [5,14]. The evolution of the mobile phone has led it to move far beyond a simple communication device and now is a versatile tool for connecting people to their digital lives on various social networks and e-mail, providing them with access to the Internet, and even for entertaining them by supporting the playing of games, music, and video. This evolution has even lent itself to referring to these robust devices as *smart phones*. The potential for the use of smart phones in ubiquitous computing has not gone unexplored over the past decade.

Leveraging the capabilities of smart phones, data can now be captured that would have previously required carrying customized hardware or a large number of specialized devices [22]. Examples of new applications enabled by the convergence of functionality in smart phones include healthcare [9,12,21], support for the elderly [18], augmenting advertising [16], understanding social networks and behavior [6,17], among many others.

Knowing that a user has her smart phone on and nearby (or tends to) is useful for ubiquitous computing and mobile application development, as the smart phone offers the unique ability to communicate information to a user and collect information from a user, regardless of location or time. However, it is not just knowing that the phone is nearby that can offer a meaningful contribution. There is a whole field of research and design that has arisen from being able to leverage the mobile phone as a means to gather contextual information and build an understanding of human behavior and the environment at large. Related work in this area includes activity sensing endeavors such as UbiFit [1], SenSay [15], and MotionBand [9] that leverage context-sensing to support people's day-to-day actions.

In 2006 Patel *et al.* studied people's proximity to their mobile phone as well as their perceived proximity to their phone and found that people had higher expectations of their availability to their phone then was found to be the case in actuality [20]. On average they found that the phone was on 81% of the time. When it was on, it was within arm's reach 58% of the time, and within the same room as their owners an additional 20% of the *on* time, leaving 23% when the phone was on and considered "unavailable" to the user. In actuality, the true unavailable time should include the time when the phone was off, equaling 38% of the day, on average. Trends that were noted upon by Patel include a small, not statistically significant variance on cell phone proximity between weekday (59%) and weekends (53%), waking versus sleep (61% awake, 52% asleep, and home and away (est. 50% to 71%). Furthermore they explored whether a proximity relationship between users and their mobile phones could be *predicted* by applying classifiers to context data that could be easily acquired from the phones themselves. With one week of training data, their classifiers determined whether the phone was within arm's reach with 86% accuracy.

The findings of this research, and its implications for how the data gathered on a mobile phone can be leveraged to give insights into the user's context, have been cited in numerous subsequent articles. While some have referenced it as evidence that mobile phones *can* serve as a reasonably accurate proxy for a user's location and context [8,19,23], others interpret the paper's findings as the opposite: the phone is *not* a good proxy for a user's location [1,12,16]. Not surprisingly, the true interpretation depends on the application, users, and context of use being designed for.

The question we want to explore in this paper is whether with the evolution of the smart phone (and all the services and apps now available) over the past five years since the Patel *et al.* paper was published, users' proximity to their phone has changed. Smart phones have become not only more commonplace, but more powerful computing devices used to connect people to their e-mail, social networks, and entertainment, through a wide variety of available apps. In investigating user behavior at this stage of mobile technology, we explore implications for mobile applications that can inform developers, researchers, and technologists as they innovate and envision new uses and applications for mobile phones.

EXPERIMENTAL DESIGN

We now describe the design of our experiment in which we sought to understand how users' proximity to their phones has changed with the availability of smart phones.

Overview

In order to accurately replicate the proximity study from Patel *et al.* [20], we contacted the authors of this paper and requested the experimental instruments they used and asked for additional details on their experimental setup. By doing so, we were able to closely replicate the original study. We briefly describe that study and the instruments used, and highlight differences in our study.

In keeping with the original experimental setup, we used mixed methods: surveys to collect information about subjects' perceptions about their phone use and phone proximity, and a 4-week long deployment of data collection software on subjects' *own* Android phones to collect both proximity information and a wide variety of contextual information. We also conducted weekly interviews to provide additional context to this data. Our study differs from the original study, which provided mobile phones to subjects, and included 16 participants for 3 weeks.

Surveys

The original survey instrument asked questions about the respondents' age and occupation, how they thought they used their phones and how close they thought they kept their phones in different situations. We adapted this survey to collect additional information on mobile applications they use and their frequency of use, what applications they would be interested in using, as well as their general experience with the phone and expectations being met (or not) with respect to mobile communications. We also collected detailed socio-economic status information of respondents, including education level, experience with mobile technologies (year started using).

We used the responses to the survey to select subjects for our study of smart phone proximity. Subjects were randomly selected from those respondents having an Android phone with an unlimited data plan and being willing to participate in the 4-week long study.

Mobile Users Data Collection Study

Interview

Participants selected for our study came to our lab, where we explained our study and what we expected of them in detail. We also deployed our proximity monitoring and context data capturing framework on their Android phone, provided them with a Bluetooth device to collect proximity information, and collected some proximity calibration data. We describe our automated data collection process below.

Android AWARE Data Collection Framework

Sensors and Internet connectivity in mobile devices provide researchers an opportunity to capture real-life context information from the owners of the mobile devices and to collect information on the proximity of the phones to their owners. We developed the AWARE Android framework, to help gather this information. The framework was developed using Android SDK 2.1, was tested and then deployed on a variety of Android devices throughout our user study. In consideration of space, we only present the sensing modules in the framework that are relevant to our exploration of phone proximity. While some of these modules may not seem relevant to proximity, we erred on the side of sensing completeness in order to identify as many factors as possible that impact proximity.

Activity Manager: Every 3 seconds, this module collects information about the active, inactive and background processes, current active activity on the screen, CPU and memory usage by application and system by querying the Android API Activity Manager.

Battery Manager: This module logs battery-related events with information such as percentage, temperature, health, voltage, technology and uptime (amount of time without charging), when the phone was plugged in and unplugged to the power supply (USB and AC).

Bluetooth Manager: The framework scans each minute for Bluetooth devices in the vicinity, keeping a record of their MAC address, friendly name and Received Signal Strength Indication (RSSI) value.

Call Manager: This module keeps track of incoming, missed and outgoing calls, including call duration, time of call and phone number.

Phone Manager: This module captures the phone's carrier information on the device, such as tower location, whether the phone has an active data plan, IP address, the device ID (IMEI for GSM devices and MEID for CDMA devices), the device's phone number, neighbor cell towers, network country, network operator, network type (CDMA, GSM, UMTS, *etc.*) and roaming status. It also provides information about the software running on the device, including version, manufacturer and device model.

Location Manager: This module collects the device's location (latitude, longitude, bearing, altitude, speed and accuracy), using network triangulation and GPS coordinates. As per the Android's developer recommendation, a one-minute interval is used for polling for GPS and Network-provided coordinates. The *Location Manager* first acquires a network-provided location, as it requires less battery power to quickly get the mobile device's location. Once a preliminary location is acquired, a GPS location is requested, as network location is less accurate. If the acquisition of GPS location fails for some reason (*e.g.*, user is indoors, phone failed to acquire satellite GPS signal, GPS turned off), the network location is logged. If the user is moving, a new location is requested for every ten meters of motion on GPS or for every 100 meters through the network location.

Network Manager: This module logs network traffic (received and sent) on available network interfaces (Wi-Fi, Carrier network) and assigned IP address for each network interface, along with network connections/disconnections.

Screen Manager: This module detects when the user turns On/Off the screen and unlocks/locks the screen.

Sensor Manager: This module logs sensor events from all the available sensors on the device, such as the accelerometer, ambient light sensor, magnetometer, pressure sensor, gyroscope, orientation sensor and temperature sensor. It also captures the vendor, precision, power consumption and sensor range values for each.

Messaging Manager: This module logs SMS and MMS messages received/sent (including time and phone number).

Weather Manager: Each time the device's location changes, the weather forecast for the current day and location is gathered from Weather.com.

Wi-Fi Manager: Every minute, this module logs the current Wi-Fi state (active, inactive) and access point information (connected and neighbor access points), such as MAC addresses, broadcasted SSID, hidden SSID, link speed, RSSI values, network capabilities, and each channel's frequency.

WatchDog: The WatchDog monitors the framework operation each minute, verifying that all the data logging modules are running and restarts any that are not. It also pings our server every 5 minutes to indicate that the framework is still alive and collecting data. A separate server process notifies the study participant by email to check her phone (and eventually reboot it), if it does not receive this ping for more than 30 minutes.

We stored all logged data into an SQLite database on the mobile's phone external storage (*i.e.* miniSD card), rather than using the phone's internal memory. Offloading the data from internal to external memory kept the phone's memory available for the proper operation of the device, reducing the influence of the framework on the device's operation.

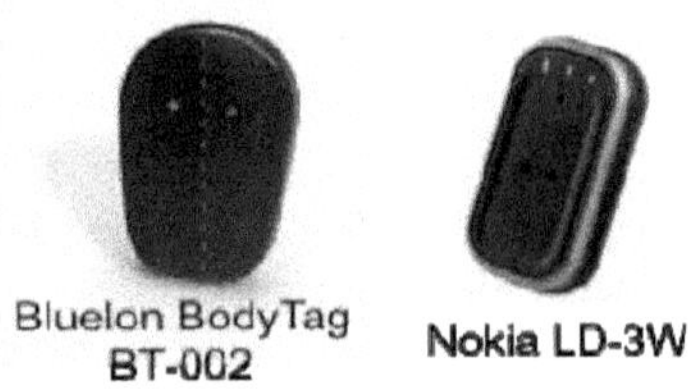

Figure 1. Bluetooth tags given to participants

Proximity Data Collection

To collect data on the proximity of users to their smart phones, we provided Bluetooth devices to our subjects, as in the original Patel paper. However, unlike the original work, we did not have enough of a single type of Bluetooth device, so we used a combination of BlueLon Bluetooth tags (3) and Nokia Bluetooth GPS devices (25) (Figure 1). We provided lanyards to each participant to wear the device around their neck. Every morning, participants received an automated email, reminding them to wear their device.Similar to the original study, the Bluetooth Manager in the AWARE framework performs a Bluetooth scan every 60 seconds, and determines the distance of the phone from the provided Bluetooth device using RSSI measurements. However, because we did not provide smart phones to our subjects and because we used a variety of Bluetooth devices, we collected calibration data for each user (smart phone-Bluetooth device pair). We collected a few minutes of RSSI data for each of the following: within arm's reach (1-2 meters), within the same room (5-6 meters) and unavailable (beyond 6 meters). After removing outlier RSSI values (using a quartile approach), we identified the range of valid RSSI values for each of our 3 distances. We do note that even when using the same model of phone and the same model of Bluetooth tag, calibration was necessary, as different combinations of the same models resulted in different RSSI ranges.

Table 1: Demographic information, percentage data lost to framework errors. Also, ignoring lost data, percentage phone off and proximity without (and with) off data

	Gender	Profession	% bad data	% off data	% arm	% arm + room
1	F	Software eng.	4	16	47 (40)	95 (80)
2	M	Owner, moving company	25	24	45 (34)	78 (59)
3	M	Admin. Asst.	21	21	27 (22)	94 (75)
4	M	Driver	8	31	76 (52)	89 (61)
5	M	Student	16	21	76 (60)	99 (79)
6	M	AP coordinator	6	21	85 (68)	97 (77)
7	F	Designer	19	8	48 (44)	90 (83)
8	M	Web developer	54	17	53 (44)	72 (60)
9	M	PC technician	17	21	25 (19)	87 (68)
10	F	Software eng.	7	6	87 (82)	100 (94)
11	M	Graphic designer	14	23	30 (23)	68 (53)
12	M	Paramedic	15	31	65 (45)	99 (68)
13	M	Program manager	53	23	54 (41)	100 (77)
14	F	Researcher	16	23	32 (24)	44 (33)
15	M	Salesman	11	15	26 (22)	80 (68)
16	M	Collections agent	18	9	38 (34)	99 (91)
17	F	Librarian	9	8	74 (68)	96 (88)
18	M	Software eng.	5	7	47 (44)	100 (93)
19	F	Photo lab tech	22	16	51 (42)	66 (56)
20	M	Advertising agent	13	13	96 (83)	99 (86)
21	M	Software eng.	7	38	68 (42)	98 (60)
22	M	Systems analyst	11	21	43 (34)	86 (68)
23	M	Student	51	33	67 (45)	99 (66)
24	M	Teacher	18	54	38 (17)	82 (38)
25	F	Therapist	0	42	36 (21)	78 (46)
26	M	Social worker	7	16	38 (32)	93 (78)
27	M	Software analyst	37	30	34 (24)	84 (58)
28	F	Manager	9	18	73 (59)	99 (81)

Weekly Interviews

When our deployment subjects returned to our office each week over the 4-week study, we interviewed them for ground truth about their proximity to their mobile phone. This information was compared to the data automatically logged by the AWARE framework. Similar to the original study, participants completed a diary of the previous 24-

hour period wherein they record their activity and the relative location of their mobile phone, as suggested by the Day Reconstruction Method [13]. This method breaks the day into episodes described by activities, locations and time intervals, and the location of the phone during these times. During the interview, users explained, in more detail, the factors influencing their proximity. This way causalities and relations between proximity and user behavior could be identified, and any inconsistencies in the AWARE framework data could be clarified. As well, they indicated when they forgot the phone/tag, or took the tag off.

SUBJECTS

Thirty subjects were recruited using Internet advertisements in <city removed> using the survey described above as a screener. We compensated subjects with $250 each for participating in the entire study. Subjects' ages ranged from 18 to 45, and included 9 females and 21 males. They came from a range of ethnic and cultural backgrounds and had varying income levels and occupations (see Table 1). Two subjects withdrew from the study: one on the second day of data collection and the other after completing only the first 2 weeks. In the following section, we present the results of our analysis of the collected data from the remaining 28 participants, using Droid, Droid X and Nexus One phones.

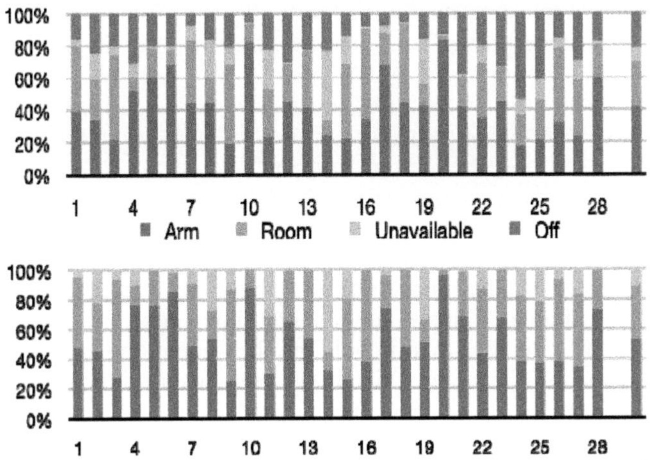

Figure 2. Distribution of proximity levels for each of the 28 participants, with (upper) and without (lower) off data, with the last bar representing the average across all participants.

RESULTS

Participants ranged in their participation from 27 to 30 days. On average, our phone failed to collect Bluetooth proximity data (but collected other data) 18% (std. dev. 15%) of the time. This number is high particularly because for some subjects we only noticed that there was a data collection error at the weekly interview, and that no data was collected that week. The remainder of our results and analyses will not include this data. Of the remaining time, users either turned their phone or just our application off for an average of 22% of the time (Figure 2). One reason this was so high is that users turned their phones off to conserve battery when they did not think they would use them or could not use them. One subject, S24 was a teacher who turned off her phone during school hours and at night. S17 was pregnant and turned off her phone in the evening and night. Despite our attempts to keep the AWARE framework's energy footprint low by making it mostly event-driven, some of our subjects complained about the impact it had on their phone battery and having to recharge more frequently.

Proximity Results

We acquired between 13430 and 37564 proximity samples (*i.e.*, number of minutes) from our subjects, with the average being 26474. Because not all subjects participated for the same number of days, these results are best viewed as percentages of participation (not including framework data acquisition errors, but including time when the phone was turned off) range from 46 to 94%, averaging 78%.

In *contrast* to our hypothesis that users of smart phones carry their phones with them (*i.e.*, within arm's reach) more than users of the previous generation of mobile phones, we found that our participants had their phones within arm's reach on average for only 53% of the time when the phone was on. This is similar to what Patel *et al.* found in 2006: 58% (see Table 2 for proximity percentages that include the time the phone was off). However, participants' perceptions were that their phone was within arm's reach 91% of the time. While most participants grossly overestimated their proximity, there were 3 subjects (S1, S26, S27) whose estimation was ~58%, much closer to the actual proximity.

However, while there was not an increase in the amount of time the phone was within arm's reach, we did find a *substantial increase* in the amount of time that our subject's smart phones were outside of arm's reach but were in the same room as them: 35% in our study vs. 20% from the previous study. Combining both within arm's reach and within the same room (arm+room) results in a total of 88% for our smart phone study and 78% for Patel *et al.*'s mobile phone study.

Table 2: Comparison of proximity between original study and ours, not including (and including) off time

	Arm's Reach	Room level	Arm + Room
Original	58% (47)	20% (16)	78% (63)
Our study	53% (42)	35% (28)	88% (69)

Proximity and Contextual Factors

We also examined the impact of different contextual factors such as day of week, time of day, and location. There were no differences in the proximity of the phone between weekdays and weekends: 53% and 52% within arm's reach for weekdays and weekends, respectively; and 89% and 87% for within room (and arm's) reach, respectively. This matches participants' perceptions that there was little difference between weekends and weekdays. The original paper reported similar results of 59% and 53% for within arm's reach for the weekdays and weekends, respectively.

The phone was within arm's reach 56% of the time when subjects were sleeping (estimated between 11pm and 7am), and 51% of the time, at other times of the day, whereas the

Table 3: Comparison of proximity at different times of day

	Arm	Room	Arm + Room
Morning (7-9am)	57% (46)	30% (23)	87% (69)
Daytime (9am-6pm)	51% (40)	36% (28)	87% (68)
Evening (6-11pm)	48% (37)	40% (31)	88% (68)
Night (11pm-7am)	56% (46)	33% (26)	89 %(72)
Not Night (7am-11pm)	51% (40)	37% (29)	88% (69)

Patel paper showed a different trend with percentages being 52% and 61%, respectively. There was less distinction at the arm+room proximity: 89% while sleeping and 88% at other times. Table 3 shows the distribution of proximity for different times of the day.

The phone was within arm's reach 46% of the time when subjects were home (Patel: 50%), and 54% of the time (Patel: 71%) when in named locations other than home, and within room and arm's reach cumulatively 83% (Patel: 77% when at home), and 85% (Patel: 82% when not at home), respectively. Table 4 shows the distribution of proximity for different categories of locations that our subjects identified in our initial interview. While proximity at the arm level varied, proximity at the arm+room level stayed relatively stable. Most subjects reported that their proximity to their phone was not different between work and home, and that perception bears true.

We also checked to see if there was a correlation between proximity at the arm or arm+room level with either time spent talking on the phone or the number of SMS/MMS sent. However, these factors were not correlated.

Table 4: Comparison of proximity in different locations

	Arm	Room	Unavailable	Arm + Room
Home	46%	36%	17%	83%
Not Home	54%	31%	15%	85%
Work	48%	33%	18%	82%
Shopping	62%	20%	17%	83%
Leisure	50%	37%	13%	87%
Family	56%	33%	10%	90%
Friends	51%	30%	18%	82%
Gas	74%	3%	22%	78%

Factors Affecting Phone Proximity

We now discuss factors that impact users' proximity to their phone, based on qualitative information collected from the 28 participants in our data collection study, as well as the 339 additional subjects who responded to our survey but were not selected. Like the original study, we derived our factors using affinity clustering to group the self-reported factors from our interviews and surveys into themes, and from the features that contained the most information gain from our predictive models of phone proximity.

During the weekly interviews, as part of the day reconstruction method, we asked participants to describe their activities and the proximity of their phone over the past 24 hours. We asked them for additional detail about why their phone was in a particular location throughout this day. We first used this information and the survey data to identify the themes in the original study that we did and did not (light grey text below) have evidence for, and then to identify new themes.

1. *Routine*: The phone's proximity was linked to users' flow of usual activities, *e.g.*, a) at home, leaving phone in a fixed/central position such as on a coffee table or shelf or at work, leaving it on their desk; b) at home, the phone is with the user to support using different applications substituting for a PC or to call a spouse inside a big house; c) outside the home, carrying the phone in a pocket or on a belt clip by a male, and in a purse or bag by a female (depending on her outfit).
2. *Environment*: The phone's proximity is related to the physical constraints of the space. For example, at home, users kept their phones in the same rooms as them, while in the car, the phone was most often within arm's reach.
3. *Physicality of person/activity*: The phone's proximity is related to the physicality of the person or the person's activity. For example, while playing sports or exercising, we found that users chose to keep their phones with them to listen to music. While the theme matches that of Patel *et al.*, we find the opposite result.
4. *Disruption to others*: In contrast to the original study, we have not identified any evidence suggesting that a user's phone proximity is based on how it might affect other people or the environment. This could be because social norms around cell phone use have evolved over the last 5 years [1].
5. *Disruption of self*: The phone's proximity takes into account the impact of proximity on the user. For example, at home, users kept phones in central places with the idea that it could get their attention regardless of their location. Others who responded to our survey reported that they put their phones "away" on weekends so as not to be bothered.
6. *Regulations*: We identified a number of situations where users turned off their phones in certain locations due to legal or other specific regulations preventing use. For example, one subject was a teacher who had to turn off her phone in school. Similarly, others turned off their phones in churches and hospitals, and in other locations where camera phones were forbidden.
7. *Use of phone by self*: Users made choices about the phone proximity based on their anticipated use of the phone. Unlike the earlier study, rather than keeping them close for making a phone call, our subjects did this for access to data, *e.g.*, carrying the phone inside the house to be able to check something quickly on the Internet. In addition, from our survey respondents, we saw that some people used their mobile phones to check their private email accounts while at work.
8. *Use of phone by others*: The phone's proximity was affected by the idea that someone else would want to

contact the subject. For example, users would keep their phone in a fixed/central location in their home to hear phone calls (similar to the previous study), or be notified about email/SMS arrivals (new in our study).

9. *Use of phone both by self and by others*: We primarily saw evidence of this theme through descriptions of coordination efforts. For example, some kept the phone close by to make it easier to coordinate efforts for going out with friends on the weekend, while the moving company owner did it to coordinate his staff.
10. *Use of handset by others*: We did not identify any evidence suggesting that a user would make a choice about the phone proximity based on the expectation that somebody else would physically use the device. This could be because smart phones and cell phones have become widely available [4,14] and, therefore, are becoming more personal devices.
11. *No need for use of phone*: When users believed they were not going to use their phones soon, users were willing to be further away. While only about one-half of our subjects had a landline phone, for those who did, the expectation that a caller could reach them using this line, was evidence of this theme. While at work, having access to a PC for relevant data/Internet supplanted use of the phone and affected its proximity.
12. *Technical resources*: The phone's proximity is impacted by technical considerations inherent to limitations of the phone. We saw evidence of this theme when users limited the mobility of their phone when charging (USB or AC adapter). In addition, survey respondents physically moved with their phone to acquire improved signal reception in their home.
13. *Quick trips*: Unlike the previous study, we found that users did not leave their phones behind when taking quick trips. Our subjects tended to take their phones with them when going on a coffee break and when going to the bathroom. This may be related to theme #19 about the use of the phone during idle periods.
14. *Memory and forgetfulness*: We saw multiple instances where users simply forgot their phone at home or work or left/forgot it someplace temporarily.
15. *Protection of phone from others*: Similar to the previous study, we saw that users made choices about phone proximity to protect the phone from tampering. For example, users put their phone out of reach while playing with children. Similarly, survey respondents reported leaving their phones behind when going out for fear their expensive smart phones would be stolen.

In addition to the analysis of the 15 themes identified in the original paper, we identified 5 new emergent themes:

16. *Costs associated with usage*: The phone's proximity is associated with monetary costs related to phone usage. While everyone in our study had an unlimited data plan, they still had to pay for data usage when traveling abroad. As such, the few subjects that left the U.S. during our study tended to keep their phone off.
17. *Personal Utility applications*: The phone's proximity is related to use of its applications in a given context. For example, phones were often used as an alarm in the bedroom while subjects were sleeping, to support nutrition or sports training in the gym, and to replace the use of a PC at home.
18. *Data privacy on the phone*: The phone's proximity is related to access of data applications holding or accessing private data on the device, *e.g.*, checking private email on phone while at work and having access to a corporate network while not at work.
19. *Idle time in between activities*: The phone's proximity is related to time spent on mobile data applications while waiting for some activity to start. For example, users checked their email or accessed the web while waiting for a friend, waiting for a bus, or even while on the toilet.
20. *Applications for planning or scheduling coordinated tasks*: The phone's proximity is related to tasks requiring the management of coordination and cooperation. For example, some users used shared grocery lists or to-do lists with a partner, used Google Calendar to add new group events, and then accessed this information at later times.
21. *Protection of phone from environment*: The phone's proximity was affected by users' beliefs that the phone had the potential to be damaged. Survey respondents reported leaving their phones behind when going fishing (wary about water damage) and when cooking in the kitchen (wary about water and heat damage).

PREDICTING USERS' PHONE PROXIMITY

Similar to the Patel paper, we also investigated whether we could predict users' phone proximity using information that are already available on the phone, rather than using our extra Bluetooth tag. For each subject, we use our Bluetooth tag proximity information as ground truth, and attempt to predict whether the phone was within arm's reach, or within arm+room. using the contextual information we collected with our AWARE framework. If the predictions are accurate, application developers can use our prediction models to determine when they can use the phone to collect contextual information from phone owners (arm's reach) or to collect contextual information about the owner's environment and deliver information to them (arm+room).

We created models that could classify phone proximity. We used a decision tree classifier using the ID3 algorithm so we could interpret the resulting trees and determine which features were most important to the classification task. Features near the root of decision trees usually have high predictive power and can be treated as important features.

We formulated the model building as two supervised learning problems, in which the class labels are three (arm vs. room vs. unavailable) and two (arm+room vs. unavailable) levels of proximity. Each data instance is a feature vector extracted with a one minute time window from the logged contextual data. We used three different feature sets to build our models. We ranked features for each subject using the Greedy Stepwise search method with Consistency Subset evaluation method from Weka [10], and used the top 3, 5 and all features. Figure 3 shows the 10-fold cross validation results using all the data from each subject for our 2 classification problems. We achieved 75 and 83% accuracy for the 3-class and 2-class problems, respectively, with large variations across our subjects.

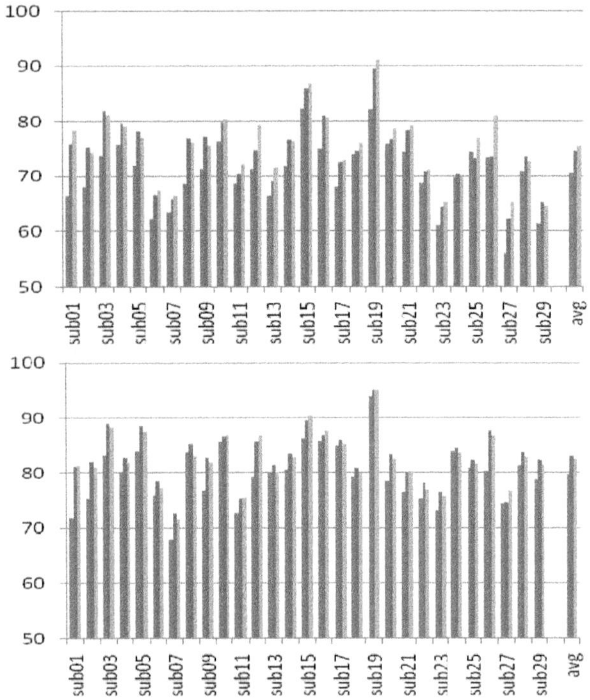

Figure 3. Classification accuracy for 3-class (upper) and 2-class (lower). Blue, red, green represent 3, 5 and all features, S3 (only 2 weeks of data) is included for completeness.

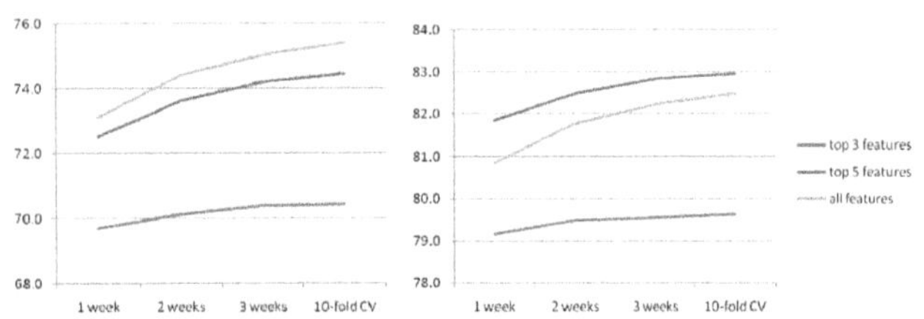

Figure 4. Analysis of the number of weeks of training required for accurate 3 –class (arm vs. room vs. unavailable) and 2-class (arm+room vs. unavail) models.

To determine how many weeks of data were needed to build a reliable model, we trained 3 additional models on the first one, two, and three weeks of data, testing on the remaining data using 10-fold cross validation. Figure 4 shows that while 3 weeks of data may not be enough for producing accurate models in the 3-class problem, 1 week of training provides reasonably high accuracy in the 2-class problem. Also, exploiting more features requires more training data to model their relationship with proximity.

We also analyze the features selected using the search method (Feature in Table 5) and the features at and near the root of the decision trees (DT). Similar to the original study, we found hour of day and time of day to be quite predictive of proximity. However, location was not very useful. The other features we found to be useful were very related to activities that the user performs and interaction with the phone: acceleration, application used, battery level, battery temperature and screen status. Battery temperature is particularly interesting as high values are correlated with close proximity: carried in a pocket next to a warm body, or being used for CPU-intensive applications.

Table 5: Predictive features for 3-class and 2-class prediction problems. Number of participants using each feature from the search method (Feature) and decision trees (DT).

	arm+room vs. other		arm vs. room vs. other	
	Feature	**DT**	**Feature**	**DT**
mean acceleration (acc)	8	2	15	2
std deviation of acc.	5	0	12	3
application used	4	8	4	8
battery level	18	20	15	22
mean battery temp.	24	19	24	17
tower ID for CSDMA	0	3	0	0
day of the week	29	27	26	29
tower ID for GSM	1	0	1	0
hour of the day	28	24	28	26
screen status (on, off)	21	4	12	2
ringer status (on, off)	2	6	0	2
weather	5	1	3	3

DISCUSSION

We now discuss our hypothesis about the proximity of smart phones, the results of our study, and our analysis.

Actual Phone Proximity

We were very surprised to see that there was no increase in the proximity of users to their mobile phones, with the availability and widespread use of smart phones. Our intuition led us to believe that access to the Internet, the use of smart phones as entertainment devices, and the huge uptake in apps would increase proximity. In fact, we saw a slight decline at the arm's reach from 58% to 53%.

However, we did see a considerable increase in proximity at the room level from 20% to 35%, resulting in an overall increase at the arm+room level from 78% to 88%. We first describe the implications of this increase and then discuss the possible reasons for it.

Many ubicomp systems make the assumption that users always have their smart phones with them. If that assumption were true, it would allow these systems to:

- Collect user context (*e.g.*, motion, activity)
- Collect user's environment context (*e.g.*, sound)
- Get the user's attention at any time and present information (*e.g.*, notifications)
- Provide an always-available service for the user

However, our work and Patel's earlier work showed that users don't have their phones with them at all times. However, our work does demonstrate that users often are in the same room (or very close by) to their phones. While only a little more than half the time can the phone be used as a proxy for the user's physical context, almost 90% of the time, it can be used as a proxy for environmental context, a mechanism for getting the user's attention, and a medium for delivering always-available services.

From our interviews, surveys and our analysis of themes, we have a better understanding of why this change occurs in users' proximity to their phones. We heard several examples from each of our participants of placing their phone down on a table or desk, to keep the phone close by and easily reachable, but not immediately at-hand. It was enough to have the phone easily reachable in the case of notifications or phone calls, to look something up on the Internet or to use an app for a short period of time. None of these require the phone to be within arm's reach. Almost all the themes discussed (Patel's orginal and our new ones) help provide evidence for why people keep their phones nearby, but not necessarily within arm's reach: routine, environment, disruption of self, use of phone by self, use of phone by others, use of phone by self and others, use of handset by others, no need for use of phone, technical resources, quick trips, memory, personal utility applications, data privacy on the phone, idle time in between activities, applications for planning, and protection of phone from environment.

Perception of Phone Proximity and Individual Difference

On average, most of our participants believed they were in close proximity to their smart phones almost 22 hours a day! Half of our participants said they were *always* next to their phones. As we have shown, this number is closer to 10 hours a day, when taking *off time* into account. Users clearly tend to greatly overestimate their proximity. However, users are within arm+room level almost 16.5 hours per day, when considering off time. We do see considerable individual differences. From Table 1, 16 of our participants keep their phone at the arm+room level over 90% of the time the phone is on, with 13 of those at 95% or above. The remaining participants have arm+room levels ranging from 44 to 89% and average 76%.

For the 16 participants that keep their phones nearby almost all the time, it is unclear whether a prediction system is necessary for determining when the phone is nearby. With proximity rates of more than 90%, assuming the phone is nearby (arm+room) could be more accurate than many learned models of proximity. There are 7 users whose proximity at the arm level is 75% or greater, and the same statement can be made for them.

Phone Proximity By Context

Just as we were surprised by the lack of increase in proximity at the arm level with smart phones, we were also surprised that there was no difference in proximity between weekdays and weekends. There were some however, interesting differences in proximity at the arm level by location. Users were less likely to keep their phones within arm's reach at home, work, places of leisure, and at friends' residences. In contrast, they were more likely to keep their phones within arm's reach while shopping, buying gas, and visiting with family. The difference between proximity from home to other locations defined and geo-located by our participants was 46 to 54%. From our interviews with our participants, we found that in places where they were most comfortable and familiar, they tended to leave their phones further away from them: close by so they could use them, but not within arm's reach. As well, the 3 locations where phones were closer, tend to involve activities that allow for smart phone interaction during short idle periods.

Similarly, we saw differences in proximity by time of day. While proximity at the arm+room level was independent of this factor, proximity at the arm level was not. Participants tended to have their phones closer during sleeping hours than during other hours (56 vs. 51%). This can partly be explained by the use of smart phones as an alarm clock. Users were also closer to their phones during the morning hours (7-9am). Participants explained that they used their phones to check email and other Internet resources shortly after waking up, and during their commute to work. The times with the lowest proximity are the work hours and the time at home after work and before sleeping. Combined with the location results just described, the lower proximity values are not surprising. Both differences in location and time of day offer opportunities for designers of mobile phone applications to use the phone as a proxy for the user and their environment, and for communicating with users.

Predicting Phone Proximity

We produced models of proximity that used contextual factors from phone sensors that could predict when the phone was within arm's reach with 75% accuracy, and within arm+room with 83% accuracy. These models are not computationally intensive and can be executed quite easily on today's smart phones. There was large variability in accuracy by users, and in the features that were most predictive. This implies that a single population model or a small number of population models (as suggested by Patel *et al.*) may not be possible. It is interesting that all the most predictive features are directly related to user activities, both those in the real world (*e.g.*, movement) and those on the phone (*e.g.*, phone usage as measured by battery level and temperature). Perhaps by collecting information on the active applications on the phone and using more sophisticated features related to user activity we can improve the accuracy of our models. Certainly by taking into account those that were almost always within the arm+room level, and combining with the predictive models (taking the maximum accuracy for each subject), we can reach an overall predictive accuracy of 92%.

Limitations

As with the original study, our study has some limitations. We studied a limited population (28) of smart phone users for a limited period of time (4 weeks). As such, it may be difficult to generalize these findings to other populations of smart phone users. We provide this detailed exploration of how smart phone users use their phones and their proximity to their phones to illustrate the challenges and opportunities for designers of phone applications looking to use the mobile phone as a proxy for user context and attention.

One issue with our study was the amount of data we lost data due to issues with our data collection framework. We discovered that some of our participants had an automated task killer app on their phone. A task killer app removes processes (in our case, modules from our framework) that use up significant memory or CPU. This caused us to lose significant amounts of data (up to 54%, although most had data losses ~10% or lower) from some of our participants, until we identified the app and asked them to remove it. Another issue we did not account for was the amount of time the phone was off. While both we and the original paper report reasonably high proximity numbers from our studies, these numbers drop significantly when time when the phone is off is considered. Participants in our study had their phones off or our framework off 22% of the time. This results in our arm+room proximity to drop from 88% to 69%, when taken into account. As off time can be considerable, especially for some users (*e.g.*, paramedic, teacher, pregnant participant, foreign travel), off time needs to be considered when designing mobile applications that make assumptions about phone availability.

CONCLUSION AND FUTURE WORK

We have presented a field data collection-based study of 28 smart phone users to understand whether their phones can serve as proxies for their context and availability. We found that when their phones are on, they are only within arm's reach 53% of the time, but within arm+room 88% of the time. Based on these results, we build on the work of Patel *et al.*, and show how mobile application designers can leverage smart phones as proxies for users' environmental context, availability for delivering information and availability for accessing information. We demonstrate that we can reasonably predict user proximity with easily collected features about user activity, and when combined with knowledge about individual users and their normal proximity, we are very accurate (greater than 90%). In the future, we intend to collect and leverage additional features regarding activity and user context to further improve our predictive ability. We also will build this ability into mobile applications as a demonstration of its effectiveness.

ACKNOWLEDGMENTS

This work was supported in part by the National Science Foundation under grants 0746428 and 0910754.

REFERENCES

1. Banjo, O., Hu, Y. and Sundar, S.S. Cell phone usage and social interaction with proximate others: Ringing in theoretical model. *The Open Communication Journal*, 2, 2008: 127-135.
2. Brandt, J., Weiss, N., and Klemmer, S. R. Lowering the burden for diary studies under mobile conditions. *CHI '07* extended abstracts. 2007. 2303-2308.
3. Consolvo, S., *et al.* Activity sensing in the wild: a field trial of ubifit garden. *CHI '08*. 2008. 1797-1806.
4. Cozza, R. Forecast: Mobile Communications Devices by Open Operating System, Worldwide. Gartner Report. 2011.
5. Cozza, R., *et al.* A. Market Share Analysis: Mobile Devices, Worldwide, 4Q10 and 2010. Gartner Report. 2011.
6. Eagle, N. and Pentland, A.S. Reality mining: sensing complex social systems. *Personal Ubiquitous Computing*, 10 (March 2006): 255-268.
7. Entner, R. Smartphones to Overtake Feature Phones in U.S. by 2011, Nielsen Wire, http://blog.nielsen.com/nielsenwire/consumer/smartphones-to-overtake-feature-phones-in-u-s-by-2011/, March 26, 2010.
8. Garzonis, S. Mobile Service Awareness Via Auditory Notifications. Doctoral thesis, University of Bath, June 2010.
9. Györb'ıró, N., Fábián, Á. and Hományi, G. An activity recognition system for mobile phones. *Mobile Networks and Applications*, 14 (February 2009): 82-91.
10. Hall, M., *et al.* The WEKA Data Mining Software: An Update. *SIGKDD Explorations*, 11(1), 2009: 10-18
11. Helal, S., *et al.* Smart phone based cognitive assistant. UbiHealth 2003, Workshop on Ubiquitous Computing for Pervasive Healthcare Applications. 2003.
12. Henderson-Summet, V. Facilitating Communication for Deaf Individuals with Mobile Technologies. Doctoral thesis, Georgia Institute of Technology, 2010.
13. Kahneman, D., *et al.* A Survey Method for Characterizing Daily Life Experience: The Day Reconstruction Method. *Science,* 306 (December 2004): 1776-1780.
14. Kellogg, D. Among Mobile Phone Ussrs, Hispanics, Asians are Most-Likely Smartphone Owners in the U.S. Nielsen Wire, http://blog.nielsen.com/nielsenwire/consumer/among-mobile-phone-users-hispanics-asians-are-most-likely-smartphone-owners-in-the-u-s, February 2, 2011.
15. Krause, A., Smailagic, A., Siewiorek, D.P. Context-Aware Mobile Computing: Learning Context-Dependent Personal Preferences from Wearable Sensor Array. *IEEE Transactions on Mobile Computing*, 5(2) Feb. 2006 pp. 113-127
16. Krumm, J. Ubiquitous Advertising: The Killer Application for the 21st Century. *IEEE Pervasive Computing*, 10 (January 2011): 66-73.
17. Laasonen, K. Clustering and prediction of mobile user routes from cellular data, 2005. *Knowledge Discovery in Databases*. 2005. 569-576.
18. Massimi, M., Baecker, R.M., and Wu, M. Using participatory activities with seniors to critique, build, and evaluate mobile phones. *ASSETS 2007*. 2007, 155-162.
19. Partridge, K. and Golle, P. On using existing time-use study data for ubiquitous computing applications. In *UbiComp'08*, 2008, 144-153.
20. Patel, S.N., *et al.* Farther Than You May Think: An Empirical Investigation of the Proximity of Users to Their Mobile Phones. *UbiComp '06*. 2006, 123-140.
21. Preuveneers, D. and Berbers, Y. Mobile phones assisting with health self-care: a diabetes case study. *MobileHCI '08*. 2008, 177-186.
22. Satyanarayanan, M. Swiss army knife or wallet? *IEEE Pervasive* 4(2), Jan.-Mar., 2005, 2-3.
23. Varshavsky, A. and Patel, S. Location in Ubiquitous Computing. In Krumm, J. (ed.), *Ubiquitous Computing Fundamentals*, Taylor and Francis Group, Florida, (2010) Chapter 8, 285-319.

The Danger of Loose Objects in the Car: Challenges and Opportunities for Ubiquitous Computing

Daniel Avrahami[1], Michael Yeganyan[2], Anthony LaMarca[1]

[1]Intel
Seattle, WA 98105 USA
{daniel.avrahami, anthony.lamarca}@intel.com

[2]University of California, Irvine
6210 Donald Bren Hall, Irvine, CA 92697
michaely23@gmail.com

ABSTRACT

Every year, loose objects inside cars during crashes cause hundreds of serious injuries and even deaths. In this paper, we describe findings from a study of 25 cars and drivers, examining the objects present in the car cabin, the reasons for them being there, and driver awareness of the potential dangers of these objects. With an average of 4.3 potentially dangerous loose objects in a car's cabin, our findings suggest that despite being generally aware of potential risks, considerations of convenience, easy access, and lack of in-the-moment awareness lead people to continue to place objects in dangerous locations in cars. Our study highlights opportunities for addressing this problem by tracking and reminding people about loose objects in cars.

Author Keywords

Loose objects, in-car safety, unrestrained cargo, awareness.

ACM Classification Keywords

H5.0. Information interfaces and presentation: General.

General terms: Design, Human Factors.

INTRODUCTION

Every year, loose objects inside cars cause hundreds of serious injuries and even deaths during crashes. Recent innovations in depth cameras and object recognition algorithms enable a technical solution that could recognize and notify drivers of possible risk. But before building such a system, one must understand drivers' awareness and attitude towards these risks and whether such a technical solution would be useful in practice. In this paper, we describe findings from a study of drivers and cars looking at the reasons for the presence of objects in the car, whether drivers are at all aware of the dangers that loose objects pose to them and their passengers, and whether or not they act on such awareness. This paper provides two primary contributions: 1) empirically demonstrating the disparity between awareness of the danger of loose objects and the quantity of in-vehicle objects present, and 2) highlighting opportunities for in-vehicle object tracking and awareness for addressing this problem.

A car crash is often described as having two phases: a *first collision*, between the vehicle and other objects, followed by a *second collision* (or "second impact") between the person and the vehicle or other objects in the vehicle [9]. Most efforts into reducing the effects of this second collision have focused on the impact between passenger and vehicle (*e.g.*, improved seatbelt technology, airbags, side curtains and the ISOFIX/LATCH system for restraining child seats). However, injuries related to unrestrained cargo or other unrestrained passengers are some of the major contributors to total harm in traffic accidents [7].

In an ongoing US study of children involved in crashes, researchers found that of 12,513 children injured by something inside the vehicle, more than 3,000 collided with loose objects, other passengers or both [1]. Unrestrained cargo may even cause death in a frontal crash by striking an occupant's seatback [6]. In fact, loose objects can become lethal not only in a collision but even in emergency braking. The threat posed by objects is not limited only to inanimate objects; in an analysis of 73,893 accidents in Japan, Ichikawa *et al.* show, for example, that an unrestrained passenger in the rear increases five-fold the risk of death for restrained front seat occupants [5]. Finally, the danger that objects pose is not restricted to particularly large and heavy objects. During a collision, impact from a loose object will have a relative force equal to the object's weight multiplied by the speed in which it travels. While prior research has examined the placement and organization of objects and people in vehicles to understand their dynamics during frontal impacts [5] and to estimate their effects on the vehicle's center of mass and stability [2], very little work has been conducted into the rationale for *ad hoc* placement of everyday objects in the car. Thus, in this work, we sought to answer the following questions: Are drivers aware of the dangers that objects pose to them and their passengers? What loose objects do people keep in their car's cabins and where? Why do they choose to place these objects inside the car? How could technology be used to alleviate the problem? How should such technology address the conflicting goals of safety and in-car object use?

THE STUDY

To better understand people's awareness of the dangers of loose objects in the car, whether or not they act on this awareness and why, and also to highlight possible technical solutions for this problem, we conducted a two-part study with 25 drivers. Each driver first participated in an object inventory and open-ended interview, followed by completing a survey of awareness and attitudes. Each session started with logging of objects in the car and their location in the cabin. Pictures of the car's interior were taken. Drivers were then asked for the reason that different objects were in the car and in their particular locations. For safety reasons, sessions took place when cars were parked. We thus asked participants about other objects that they frequently carried in the car, such as their work bag, purse, laptop, or grocery bags. In this first part we intentionally *avoided* asking about the danger of loose objects in the car, so that we don't bias participants' explanations for the reasons they kept objects in the car.

In the second part of each session, participants were asked to complete a short survey either on paper or online. Participants marked their agreement with a series of statements on a 7-point scale. In this survey we captured participants' stated awareness of the risk from loose objects, their attitudes towards basic safety features (seatbelts), seatbelt warning indicators, and finally an indication of their willingness to adopt a system that will warn them of objects that are dangerous to them and their passengers. Participation in the study was voluntary.

Participants

Twenty-five drivers, 10 women and 15 men, participated in the study. Six of the drivers (4 women, 2 men) were parents to children younger than driving age. Kids' ages ranged from 7 months to 8 years, with a median of 4.1 years. The 25 vehicles observed included 15 sedans, 3 SUVs, 3 hatchbacks, 2 coupes, and 2 pickup trucks. 14 of the participants were co-workers (none of whom work on this project) and 11 were recruited through our social network.

RESULTS

In this section, we first describe the types (and quantity) of objects found in the cars. We then describe where these objects were found and the reasons given for their placement in the cabin versus the trunk (almost none of which related to safety). Finally, we report people's stated awareness of the dangers that objects pose to them and their passengers, contrasting with their observed behavior, and we describe people's attitudes towards in-vehicle safety and safety reminders. The disparity between awareness and action, shown by our study, highlights the need and the potential for a real-time awareness system.

Objects in the Car

We recorded 145 objects in the 25 vehicles' cabins, of which 44 objects were both loose and have the potential to become dangerous to driver and passengers in a collision (M=1.8, SD=1.5), while 8 objects were secured (those included child-seats, and car-racing instruments). The remaining objects include clothing, empty plastic bottles, papers, food, tissue boxes, etc. In addition to the objects present in the cars at the time of the study, participants listed 63 (M=2.5, SD=1.1) objects that they frequently carry in the car, such as laptops, briefcases, and groceries, bringing the total of potentially dangerous objects to 107 (M=4.3, SD=1.9). We focus our results on these objects.

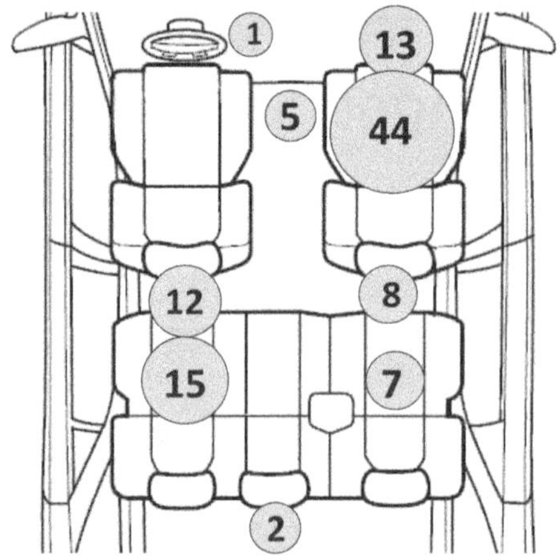

Figure 1. The total number of objects in each location in our study participants' cars.

Many of the loose objects were everyday items (*e.g.,* drink bottles, bags, groceries) or things commonly found in cars (*e.g.,* tool-boxes, car-battery chargers). Others were less expected (large books, and even a 17" LCD monitor). Many of these objects were placed in the car, typically in the rear, and left there for a long time rather than being moved to the (safer) trunk. Because these objects stay in the rear of the car for extended times, awareness of their presence and the danger they pose could subside. This dangerous habituation suggests the potential for an awareness system that reminds drivers of objects' presence.

Mobile and Portable Technology

Phones, laptops, GPS, music players and cameras, accounted for 18 of the 107 objects (17%). All 18 objects were placed in the front of the cabin (15 of them on the passenger seat). The main reasons participants cited for placing these objects next to them were convenience and ability to quickly access information. However, placing such devices next to the driver can prove deadly in a side collision [8,10]. An implication is, thus, that enabling drivers to access their information and devices (phone calls, music, etc.) through alternate channels would allow these devices to be placed in a more secure location.

Groceries and Other Bags

Twenty participants reported that if they only have one or two grocery bags, they tend to place them in the cabin rather than the trunk. As one participant said, *"For groceries, if I just have a couple bags, I put them in the back seat..."* (P11). However, a bag of groceries in the car can be fatal (for example, when a 2kg bag of rice flies through the car during a collision [4]). Similarly, other bags, such as backpacks, briefcases, and purses could easily be dangerous to driver and passengers. In our data, 15 of 25 bags in the cabins typically contained a participant's laptop.

This particular category of objects poses a technical challenge for an in-car awareness system because a grocery bag (or any other bag) is a *collection* of items, some of which may by dangerous while others, possibly those visible on top, may be light and harmless. Different approaches may overcome this problem, such as the use of weight sensors (similar to sensors in front passenger seats), mm wave radio to distinguish dense from light objects, or volume-based visual recognition, such that a grocery bag is represented as a single large item on an awareness display.

The Location of Objects in the Car

The placement of an object in the car and its physical relation to driver and passenger plays a critical role in the threat of the object. Figure 1 shows the location of observed and listed objects in participants' cars. We describe a number of themes that emerged from the interviews and highlight implications for system design.

Easy access during the drive: The need for easy access to an object was cited as a key reason for placing it inside the cabin. *"I place it on the front passenger seat next to me if I'm in a hurry and need quick and easy access to it. It's convenient that way."* (P4). Primary locations for objects in these cases were the front passenger seat (n=44), and rear foot-wells (n=12). However, these objects can pose a direct threat to the driver if they need to be within arm's reach. This is important since these objects are unlikely to be stored in the trunk.

In-and-out: The desire to enter and leave the car quickly is another reason for the choice of object placement. *"It's too much work to open the trunk. I put it on the seat behind my seat so that I can get out, open that door then leave."* (P11) Typical behavior included dropping a bag in the rear behind the driver seat, or "flinging the bag" over to the front passenger seat when entering the car; *"For the passenger seat, I'll just throw the backpack in...throw it across the middle thing to the passenger side, I just don't want to have to go to the passenger side to do anything."* (P13). Obviously, the danger of the two locations (front passenger seat vs. rear left passenger seat) differs significantly.

External constraints: Finally, for some, the choice of where to place objects was imposed by external factors. As one participant said: *"I have little space to open my trunk at home, so I'm used to placing [the grocery bags] on the back seats"* (P15). For others, small parking spaces actually led to safer behavior in putting objects in the trunk. The implication, however is that an awareness system should warn, but not nag, since moving objects to the trunk is not always possible.

Awareness and Attitudes

We now turn to participants' responses to the survey filled out in the second part of the study. Table 1 summarizes participants' responses to the 11 survey statements S1-S11.

Statement	Agreement (1..7) mean [sd]
1. How aware are you that certain objects in the car can become dangerous during a car-crash?	**5.0** [1.4]
2. I take into account the danger of objects when I decide whether to place objects in the cabin or trunk.	**3.7** [1.8]
3. I put objects in the trunk because I am safer this way.	**3.4** [1.8]
4. I wear a seat-belt to keep me safe.	**6.8** [0.7]
5. I wear a seat-belt because it is the law.	**5.3** [2.1]
6. I ensure passengers in the front wear a seat-belt.	**6.7** [0.6]
7. I ensure passengers in the back seat wear a seat-belt.	**6.0** [1.4]
8. I find the seat-belt audible reminder annoying.	**4.3** [2.2]
9. I find the seat-belt audible reminder useful.	**4.9** [2.0]
10. If your car warned you of objects in the car that could be dangerous to you, how likely are you to move it to a safer location (e.g., the trunk)?	**5.6** [1.0]
11. If your car warned you of objects in the car that could be dangerous to your passengers, how likely are you to move it to a safer location (e.g., the trunk)?	**5.8** [1.1]

Table 1. Survey responses. Ratings are on a scale of 1=Completely Disagree/Unware...7=Completely Agree/Aware.

Awareness vs. Behavior

Generally, participants indicated awareness of the danger of loose objects. In response to statement S1 "*How aware are you that certain objects in the car can become dangerous during a car-crash?*" 18 of the 25 participants reported at least some awareness of the danger: 7 selected "5 - *Somewhat Aware*", 8 selected "6 - *Aware*", and 3 selected "7 - *Completely Aware*" with an average of 5.0. This is surprising given the large number of objects we observed earlier. To contrast, participants expressed low agreements with S2 "*I take into account the danger of objects when I decide whether to place objects in the cabin or trunk.*" (M=3.7) and S3 "*I put objects in the trunk because I am safer this way.*" (M=3.4). A planned paired-samples t-test showed that participants claimed to be aware of the danger significantly more than they claimed to act on it (S1 vs. S2: $t(24)=3.89$, $p<.001$; S1 vs. S3: $t(24)=4.07$, $p<.001$)[1]. Additionally, we found no correlation between reports of awareness and the number of objects in the car ($p=.2$, *n.s.*).

Attitudes towards Seatbelts and Seatbelt Reminders

We next asked participants about their use of seatbelts (S4-S7) – since those are the most common in-car safety system – and attitudes towards seatbelt reminders (S8 and S9). A comparison shows that safety was rated significantly higher (M=6.8) than requirement by law (M=5.3) as motivator for using seatbelts ($t(24)=3.49$, $p<.001$). This is encouraging since an awareness system for objects in the cabin is

[1] Testing with only participants aware of the danger of loose objects (rating>=5) showed similar significant differences ($t(24)=3.62$, $p<.001$ and $t(24)=4.04$, $p<.001$).

unlikely to be required by law. Participants indicated that they ensure passengers in the front wear a seatbelt (S6; M=6.7 with all response at least „*Somewhat Agree*') more than passengers in the back seat (S7; M=6.0; t(24)=2.52, p<.001), possibly again suggesting reduced awareness of the back seats. The parents of small children showed a marginally significant difference from the rest of the drivers in ensuring that passengers in the back seat wear seatbelts (M=6.8 vs. M=5.7; F[1,23]=3.22, p=0.086). We found no significant difference between finding seat-belt audible reminders to be useful (M=4.9) or annoying (M=4.3).

DISCUSSION

As we've shown, despite being generally aware of potential risks, considerations of convenience, easy access, and lack of in-the-moment awareness led our participants to continue to place objects in dangerous locations in their cars. Our study suggest that merely increasing drivers' general awareness (e.g., through an always present warning label in the car) would not solve the problem. Instead, an awareness system that tracks and warns drivers of loose objects in the car may be necessary. Our results also show the frequent presence of backpacks, purses, and grocery bags in cars, the presence of which presents a technical challenge for a vision system. Thus, we envision a system that would, for example, track objects and people in the car using a combination of depth cameras and weight sensors (see Figure 2 for an illustration), label them as secure or loose (using seatbelt sensors) and warn drivers, for instance, using the car's console.

Just as a well positioned sign can get people to choose taking the stairs instead of the escalators (c.f., [3]), so might an awareness system of loose objects lead drivers to safer behavior. While the design of such a system is an area for future work, our findings provide a number of insights as to when, and how often to alert the driver. For example, our data show that ease of access is a key factor in the choice of placement of objects in the car. This finding has two implications: First, since convenience is a dominant factor in object placement, alerting drivers when they turn on the car, after they are seated and likely buckled up, may be too late (although such a notification may still affect future behavior). Second, if easy access to an item is important (e.g., to be able to hand to a child in the back) then drivers are unlikely to use the trunk and a system must notify, but not nag, lest drivers start ignoring it.

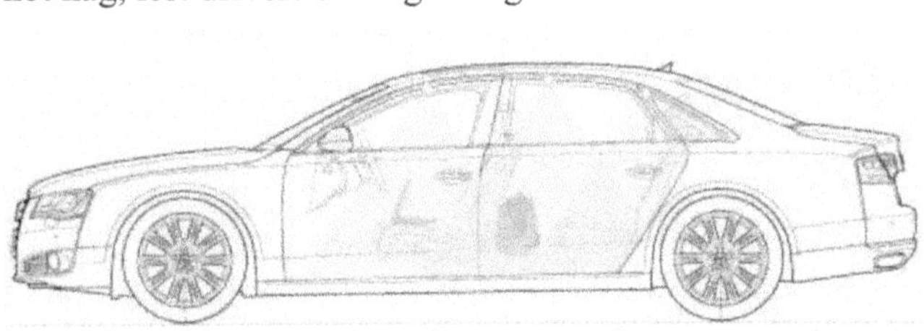

Fig 2. System illustration: Cameras and sensor monitor the cabin to identify loose objects (e.g.: a laptop and backpack)

CONCLUSIONS

This paper presented findings from a field study that details reasons for the presence of loose objects in the car, and demonstrates the disparity between drivers' awareness of the problem in general, and their actions in practice. These findings provide an understanding of the problem of loose objects in the car and challenges ubicomp researchers to solve this important problem. We highlighted both technical and behavioral challenges, such as the need to correctly distinguish between secure and loose objects, or accommodating users' desire for quick access to belongings during a drive. While the cost of a technical solution must be weighed, reducing the number of injuries and deaths caused by loose objects could outweigh such costs.

REFERENCES

1. Adlam, E. Hidden Dangers in your Car: When everyday objects turn deadly. *Readers Digest.* (2003), 550-557.
2. Arndt, M.W., Dickerson, C.P., Arndt, S.M., Mowery, G.A. and Shapiro, S.C. Effects of Passenger and Cargo Loading on a Motor Vehicle's Mass Properties. *Society of Automotive Engineers.* SAE Paper #952676. 1995.
3. Brownell K. D., Stunkard A. J., Albaum J. M. (1980) Evaluation and modification of exercise patterns in the natural environment. *AJP*, 137:1540-1545.
4. Hudson, J. (2007) Reverse the toll. *The Sydney Morning Herald*, February 23, 2007.
5. Ichikawa, M., Nakahara, S. and Wakai, S. Mortality of Front-Seat Occupants Attributable to Unbelted Rear-Seat Passengers in Car Crashes. *The Lancet 359, 9300* (2002), 43-47.
6. Samuel P. Mandell, S.P, Kaufman, R., Mack, C.D. and Bulger, E.M. Describing a Problem: Rear Seatback Failure and Unsecured Cargo. *Prehospital and Disaster Medicine 25, 2* (2010).
7. Schaper D. and Zech G. (1986). Cargo Retention in Passenger Cars Under Accident Conditions. *Society of Automotive Engineers* SAE Paper# 860206. 1986.
8. Unrestrained Objects Deadly While Driving. *ABC News.* January 2010. http://abcnews.go.com/GMA/story?id=128062
9. Waters, W., Macnabb, M.J. and Brown B. A Half Century of Attempts to Re-Solve Vehicle Occupant Safety: Understanding Seatbelt and Airbag Technology. In *Proc. Enhanced Safety of Vehicles (ESV'98)*. 1337-1346.
10. Woman killed by laptop in Surrey crash. *CBC News.* http://www.cbc.ca/canada/british-columbia/story/2009/04/15/bc-surrey-laptop-crash-kills-woman.html

Who's Your Best Friend? Targeted Privacy Attacks In Location-sharing Social Networks

Vassilis Kostakos, Jayant Venkatanathan, Bernardo Reynolds
Madeira Interactive Technologies Institute
University of Madeira
{vk, vjayant, bernardo.reynolds}@m-iti.org

Norman Sadeh, Eran Toch
School of Computer Science
Carnegie Mellon University
{sadeh, eran}@cs.cmu.edu

Siraj A. Shaikh
Faculty of Engineering and Computing
Coventry University
s.shaikh@coventry.ac.uk

Simon Jones
Department of Computer Science
University of Bath
s.jones2@bath.ac.uk

ABSTRACT
This paper presents a study that aims to answer two important questions related to targeted location-sharing privacy attacks: (1) given a group of users and their social graph, is it possible to predict which among them is likely to reveal most about their whereabouts, and (2) given a user, is it possible to predict which among her friends knows most about her whereabouts. To answer these questions we analyse the privacy policies of users of a real-time location sharing application, in which users actively shared their location with their contacts. The results show that users who are central to their network are more likely to reveal most about their whereabouts. Furthermore, we show that the friend most likely to know the whereabouts of a specific individual is the one with most common contacts and/or greatest number of contacts.

Author Keywords
Location sharing, privacy, privacy attacks.

ACM Classification Keywords
H5.m. Information interfaces and presentation (e.g., HCI): Miscellaneous.

General Terms
Experimentation, Human Factors.

INTRODUCTION
The study tries to answer two important questions relating to targeted location-sharing privacy attacks. First, given a group of users and the social ties amongst them, is it possible to predict which of these users is likely to reveal the most about their whereabouts? Second, given an individual user within a particular social network, is it possible to predict which of her friends knows most about her whereabouts? To answer these, the paper presents a longitudinal study of real-time location sharing whereby the patterns of information exchange and privacy policies of a large group of users are analysed and modelled.

Real-time location sharing applications are gaining wide adoption, with a number of commercial systems now available on the market, including Foursquare, Facebook Places, and Google Latitude. Such services are frequently used in the context of online social networks (OSN), whereby one's real-time location becomes yet another sharable aspect of one's online profile. With the increasing adoption of online location sharing services, understanding the privacy implications and potential targeted attacks enabled by this new technology, becomes crucial.

A conventional approach for engineering a privacy attack is to attempt to gain ongoing access to the target's whereabouts, thereby building up a profile of that user's behaviour. In this paper, we assume that location sharing practices are likely to follow the trend of other OSN profile properties and propagate through the network of friends. The key assumption, therefore, is that a target's location can be visible to friends of friends. From the attacker's perspective, this has the benefit that they do not get "too close" to the target while still they are able to collect information about the target's location on an ongoing basis.

The two questions that this paper addresses are key in instrumenting a targeted attack against users. Such an attack would first identify a suitable target amongst a set of users. Once this has been achieved, the attacker then identifies a "weak link" in the target's list of friends. The "weak link" is a friend of the target whom the attacker will attempt to befriend in order to gain direct access to the target's whereabouts by becoming a friend of a friend. Therefore, the attacker is likely to seek for weak links who are most likely to have full access to the whereabouts of the target.

RELATED WORK

Sharing perceptions and strategies

Substantial research shows that people approach for developing rules and ultimately policies for sharing information with others are strongly related to the presentation of self [13], and also relate to the formulation of dialectic and dynamic behavioural mechanisms depending on circumstantial context [2] or the conjugation of disclosure, identity and temporal boundaries [24]. What was once achieved with walls, doors and other physical or architectural constraints is still to be adapted to today's communication means [34]. Privacy management is an intricate process and is further augmented in a computer mediated environment. On social networking sites, privacy regulation is a socio-technical activity involving interaction with the technological system and the group context. Individuals' privacy behaviour in such systems involves a mixture of technical and mental strategies. For instance, a technical strategy may involve the use of privacy settings to regulate content distribution to select audiences [30], while research has also shown that considering tie strength is another strategy for developing rules for disclosure [36].

Despite the evidence suggesting that users adopt objective strategies for controlling their privacy online, previous work has identified a discrepancy between people's privacy attitudes towards sharing information and their actual sharing patters [1,23]. This behaviour has been termed the "privacy paradox". For instance, a study revealed a high discrepancy between stated concerns and actual behaviour towards sharing static profile information on Facebook [1]. Other studies have further established the privacy paradox on social networking sites [34].

While it is not clear whether the privacy paradox also applies to people's perceptions towards location sharing, it certainly highlights the needs for collecting quantitative data on people's location-sharing behaviour rather than relying purely on subjective data.

Location-sharing privacy

There is an increasing amount of work on understanding users' location-privacy needs in ubiquitous and location-aware systems relying on techniques such as diary studies [4], interviews [14], surveys [17], scenarios [16, 35] and lab and field observations [5]. Research suggests that users may start with relatively coarse and conservative preferences [28]. Over time, they take advantage of controls exposed to them and exhibit more sophisticated sharing behaviours, controlling the availability of the data through mechanisms such as disabling the service [4] or obtaining feedback about which users can see or have seen their information [14,16,28,33]. Users are also sceptical about the usefulness of location sharing in day-to-day activities, suggesting that current practices (such as calling somebody up) are sufficient [4]. However, the usefulness of such services was acknowledged in more stressful situations involving unfamiliar environments or in crisis and safety scenarios in general [14]. In such situations, information usefulness outweighs privacy concerns. Furthermore, prior work has shown that people's presence in different physical environments is likely to affect their willingness to trust and actually engage in interaction with location-based services [18].

Research investigating sophisticated privacy mechanisms, such as customizable privacy policies, has indicated that, without new interface technologies, they can present significant challenges for users. One recent study reports participants failing to implement their desired policies with a high degree of accuracy [28]. Furthermore, it also noted that although participants varied considerably in the time they spent defining their policies (between 5 and 8 minutes), the duration of this period was not strongly correlated to final policy accuracy.

It has also been observed that the recipients of the location data are typically more significant to users than the locations being shared. Perhaps unsurprisingly, users are more willing to share information with friends than acquaintances or strangers [5,33]. While recipient identity seems to be the strongest factor influencing one's willingness to share her location [10,20] time and location restrictions have been shown to also be important in capturing people's preferences [5]. Research has also shown that users are sensitive to the reactions of recipients if location information is denied or not made available [14, 28], suggesting that systems need to incorporate an element of plausible deniability. However, users do make distinctions in sharing particular locations: additional privacy is required at home when compared to work [31].

Privacy attacks on OSNs

Targeted privacy attacks on OSNs have been demonstrated in the past. Attempts to construct social graphs for individuals from available public listings are already shown to be feasible [6]. Once achieved, social graphs can be clustered for segregating groups into sub-groups in terms of different spheres of activity for an individual [37,15]. Further results show that even hidden communities can be detected with reasonable effort [22]. This work shows that given an individual of interest, it is possible to identify a close group around that person, which may potentially be used in order to get closer to the target. To some extent, this is already done by authorities targeting criminals coordinating their activities using OSNs [7,9], and it usually involves some level of active probing [29] which in the context of OSNs may mean striking friendships with individuals close to the target so as to avoid detection.

The characteristics of privacy attacks in the context of location sharing differ from privacy attacks online social networks because of two reasons. Location-sharing applications include information about users' physical whereabouts, which can lead to access to one's physical self. Empirical evidence show that users fear that revealing their location to people they do not trust may lead to physical and property harm [32]. Furthermore, users' decisions on location sharing may differ considerably than decisions taken in the context of social networks, making this subject worthwhile of investigation.

Identifying "weak links"

Prior work on social networks may be used to derive some hypotheses about who is likely to share information with whom on a social network. For instance, Petronio's theory of Communications Privacy Management (CPM) describes an iterative process of rule development, boundary coordination and boundary turbulence [25]. Rule development can be defined as the process of developing regulations about who to tell what. These regulations guide our everyday disclosures, and are a function of our context and disclosure goals. Ties of differing strength have varying disclosure norms, thus Stutzman theorizes rule development is a function of network composition [30]. For example, a network that is more heavily focused on strong ties may require higher levels of privacy, as disclosures among strong ties are more personal in nature [36]. This suggests that network structure may be used as a basis for attempting to predict disclosures amongst individuals.

Recent work on sharing ephemeral information shows that rule development is a function of tie strength [27]. In order to test CPM's rule development process on the context of posting content to Facebook, users were presented various scenarios of information disclosure and were prompted to decide how and with whom to share that information with. Results show users are more prone to share with stronger ties as opposed to weak ties. These findings where uniform across the various scenarios of information disclosure presented to participants. Intended and expected audience for both profile and ephemeral information was a function of tie strength [27,30]. Both authors report that users' perceived audience for the information they share is mostly composed of strong ties.

STUDY

Definitions

The following are definitions of metrics used in the study that follows.

- *Social Graph*: A set of individuals and the explicit friendship ties amongst them.
- *Degree Centrality* : The degree centrality of a user is the number of direct connections (or "friends") that the user has in the social graph. These were the friends of the user on Facebook that were also users of Locaccino.
- *Betweenness Centrality* : The betweenness centrality of a user is the number of shortest paths between all pairs of nodes in the social graph that pass through the node representing the user. For a more thorough description of the betweenness centrality, the reader is directed to [11].
- *Openness* : The *openness* of the ordered pair (A, B) of users is the percentage of simulated location requests made to A by B that were granted by A's policies.
- *Trust* : The *trust* of a user A is the mean of the openness values (A, B) where B ranges over all of A's friend. i.e. it is the average openness of user A towards all her friends.
- *Trustworthiness* : The trustworthiness of a user A is the mean of the openness values (B, A) where B ranges over all of A's friends. i.e. it is the average openness of A's friends towards A.
- *Trust Rank :* Given a user A and a user B who is a friend of A, the *trust rank of B with respect to A* is *i* if there are precisely *i-1* friends $C_1, C_2 \ldots C_{i-1}$ of A such that the openness of (A, C_j) , $1 \leq j < i$, is greater than the openness of (A, B). i.e. the trust rank is obtained by ranking A's friends in terms of how much they are trusted by A.
- *Degree Rank* : Given a user A and a user B who is a friend of A, the *degree rank of B with respect to A* is *i* if there are precisely *i-1* friends $C_1, C_2 \ldots C_{i-1}$ of A such that the degree centralities of $C_1, C_2 \ldots C_{i-1}$ are greater than that of B. i.e. the degree rank is obtained by ranking A's friends in terms of their degree centralities.
- *Mutual Rank* : Given a user A and a user B who is a friend of A, the *mutual rank of B with respect to A* is *i* if there are precisely *i-1* friends $C_1, C_2 \ldots C_{i-1}$ of A such that the number of common friends A has with each of C_1, $C_2 \ldots C_{i-1}$ is greater than the number of common friends that A has with B. i.e. the mutual rank is obtained by ranking A's friends in terms of how many mutual friends they have with A.

Hypotheses

Previous work suggests a relationship between social network structure, tie strength and the patterns of disclosure amongst individuals (e.g. [30]). In attempting to identify which individual is more likely to reveal information about their whereabouts, one may hypothesise that individuals who are more central to the network are more likely to do so. A possible explanation would be that such individuals are more likely to engage in collaboration and coordination activities, therefore it may be more likely that they are willing to share their real-time location with others. This reasoning provides ground for the first experimental hypothesis:

- H1: Individuals who are more central to the social graph are likely to reveal the most about their location.

Upon determining a suitable person to target, the next step in a potential attack would be to befriend someone from the target's social network. Considering that previous literature suggests that reciprocity is an important driving force in social networks [26], one can expect that the target is likely to share their location with someone in the social network out of their desire to reciprocate. Hence, the friend of the target with the most number friends, who by means of H1 is likely to share their own location, is someone with whom the target may wish to share their location in order to reciprocate. That person is therefore a potential "weak link" whom the attacker might befriend in order to get closer to the target. This leads to the second experimental hypothesis:

- H2: The target's friend with the highest degree has higher probability of knowing more about the target.

Finally, it can be argued that shared membership and being part of the same community would be suggestive of two individuals who may be possibly involved in joint activities requiring coordination. In addition, literature on homophily has shown that individuals who share mutual friends are more likely to be alike, thus likely to engage in joint activities [21,8]. It is therefore plausible to hypothesise that individuals who belong to the same group are more likely to share their real-time location with each other, thus becoming candidate "weak links". This leads to the third experimental hypothesis:

- H3: The target's friend with most common ties with the target knows most about the target.

To test these hypotheses, the location-sharing system described next was deployed and used by a large group of users longitudinally.

System

The study was conducted by deploying Locaccino, a real-time location sharing application integrated in the OSN Facebook. The application consists of two components: a Web application component and a mobile component. Various version of the mobile component were developed to run on multiple mobile platforms: windows and apple laptops, and Symbian smartphones. The purpose of this component is to collect in real-time a user's location and then upload it to a central server.

The Web application component of Locaccino (Figure 1) allows users to set preferences regarding how their location is shared with their Facebook contacts. Users are given the option to create policies in order to manage their location sharing. Policies specify the conditions under which the location should be revealed to another user. These conditions include the identity of the recipient of the information, the time and day, and the actual location where the user is. For instance, one may specify a policy to allow work colleagues to obtain one's location only during work hours and when they are in town.

Participants were recruited on campus using advertisements on-line and via email, as well as through national press covering the features of our system.

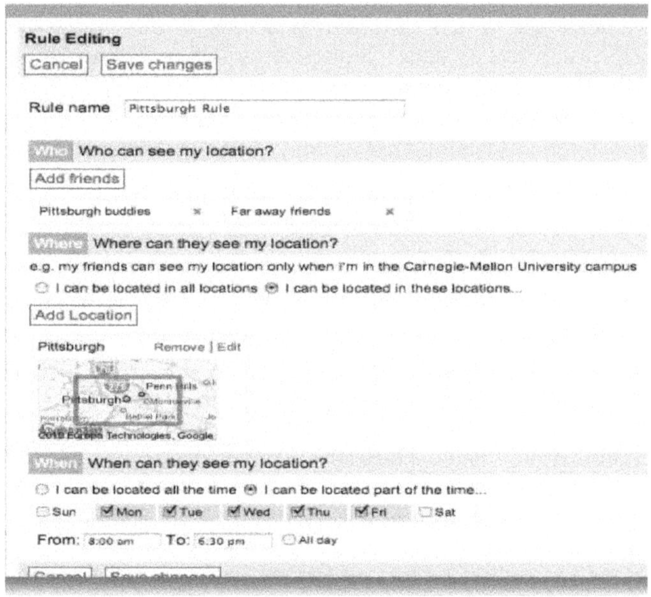

Figure 1. Screenshot of Locaccino's functionality that allows users to construct their location sharing policy rules.

The system was used longitudinally and more than 300 users installed the application and actively begun using it to share their location with colleagues. For the purposes of the study presented here, the following information was collected about users:

- Social graph: An undirected unweighted graph describing the friendship between all the participants. In this graph, a node represents a user, and two nodes are connected if they are friends on Facebook.
- Policy graph: A directed weighted graph describing the privacy policies between the users. In this graph each node represents a user, and user A is connected to user B if user if these two users are friends on Facebook. In addition, the weight of the edge from user A to user B is a value between 0 and 1 based on the "openness" of user A towards user B. The weight of the opposite edge, i.e. the openness of user B towards user A, is independent and may be a different.

The openness value of (A,B) was calculated as the percentage of B's possible requests that were granted by A's policies. The openness value from one user towards another represents the extent to which a user is willing to share their location with another user. In our case we rely on users' policies to capture and quantify this feature. Specifically, to generate a value representative of the openness between two users we conducted the following procedure. For each pair of users (A,B) in the dataset we ran a simulation whereby user B repeatedly requested the location of user A. These simulated requested were processed by the policies of user A, and the result was either positive or negative, thereby either showing or hiding user A's location respectively. During this analysis the

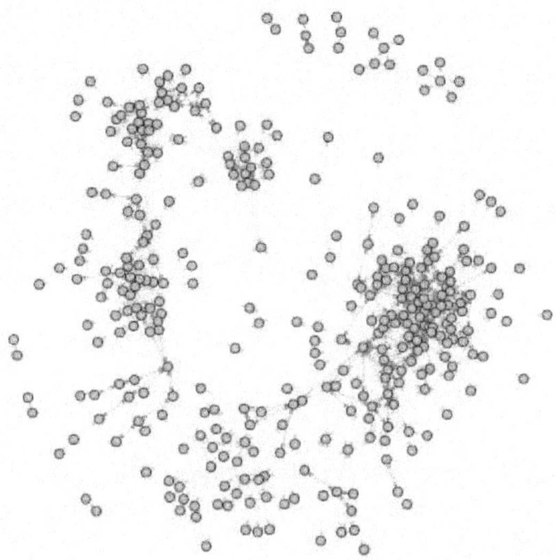

Figure 2. The graph representing the participants (nodes) and their trust relationships as directed edges. Mutually open relationships are highlighted in red.

movement of user A was the same as recorded during the study.

RESULTS

The study ran for a month with 340 users who were already users of Facebook. The derived policy graph contained 1778 policy rules, two for each of the 889 friendship ties within the user population (Figure 2).

Each policy described the openness of one user towards other users, ranging from 0 to 1. For each user the average openness that they show towards their friends was calculated (referred to as "trust" towards others) and is summarised in Figure 3, while the average openness that a user was shown by his friends (i.e. their "trustworthiness") is shown in Figure 4.

Hypothesis testing

H1: Individuals who are more central to the social graph are likely to reveal the most about their location.

A Kruskal_Wallis non-parametric test of independent samples [e.g. 12] showed that there was a significant effect of a node's betweenness on that node's trust towards its direct connections ($H(45)=82.111$, $p<0.001$) but not on that node's trustworthiness ($H(45)=56.168$, $p=0.123$). Furthermore, there was a significant effect of degree centrality on node trust ($H(23)=82.076$, $p<0.0001$) and also on node trustworthiness ($H(23)=35.276$, $p<0.05$).

H2: The target's friend with the highest degree has higher probability of knowing more about the target.

To test this hypothesis all users with less than 2 friends in the dataset were discarded from the analysis, leaving 247 users. This data was discarded because no comparison can

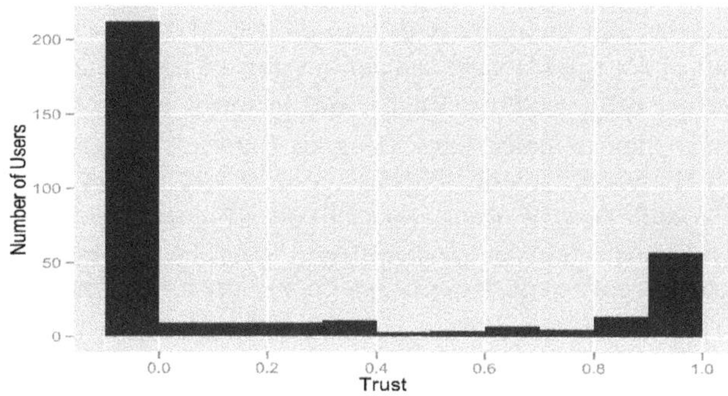

Figure 3. Histogram of distribution of nodes' average openness (i.e. the average of all outgoing ties for each node)

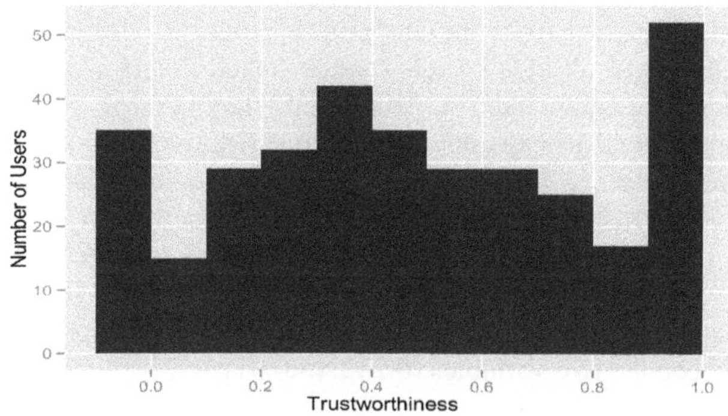

Figure 4. Histogram of nodes' average trustworthiness (i.e. the average of all incoming ties for each node).

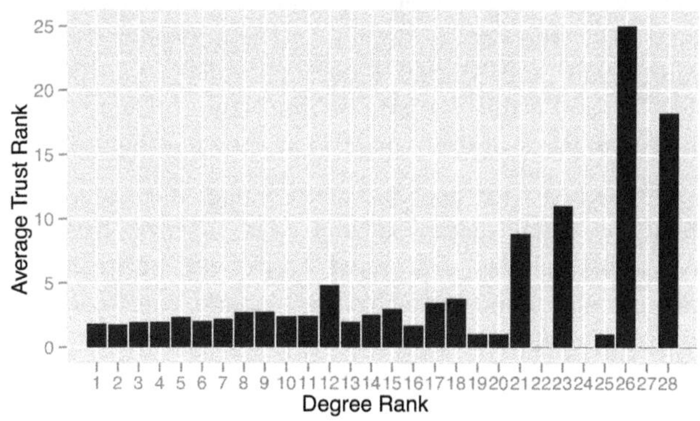

Figure 5: Degree rank of nodes (x-axis) versus the average trust rank (y-axis) for all nodes of a specific degree rank

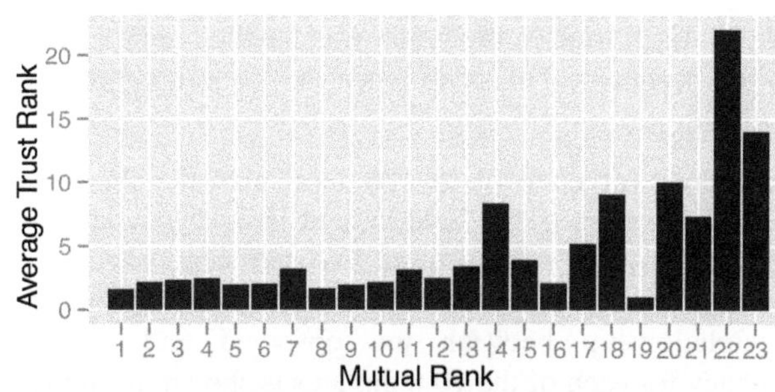

Figure 6. Histogram of Mutual rank (x-axis) vs. average trust rank (y-axis) for all nodes of a specific CommonFriends rank.

be carried out for users with a single friend. For each user A, all of A's friends were ranked in terms of how much they are trusted by A (Trust Rank), and in terms of how many friends they actually have (Degree Rank). This gave for each friendship relationship in the data two values: Trust Rank and Degree Rank respectively (Figure 5). A chi-square test showed a significant relationship between Degree Rank and Trust Rank (x^2=3981.723, dF=744, p<0.001) while there was a positive correlation between the two variables (0.239, p<0.01).

H3: The target's friend with most common ties with the target knows most about the target.

To test this hypothesis all users with less than 2 friends were discarded from the analysis, leaving 247 users. For each user A, all of A's friends were ranked in terms of how much they know about A (Trust Rank), and in terms of how many mutual friends they have with A (Mutual Rank). This gave us for each friendship relationship in the data two values: Trust Rank and Mutual Rank respectively (Figure 6). A chi-square test showed a significant relationship between Mutual Rank and Trust Rank (x^2=3210.841, dF=682, p<0.001), while there was a positive correlation between the two variables (0.252, p<0.01).

Structural analysis

Finally, an analysis was conducted to assess the extent to which friends with the highest degree are the same as friends with a large number of common friends. A chi-square test showed a significant relationship between Degree Rank and Mutual Rank (x^2=6548.051, dF=528, p<0.001), and a positive correlation between Degree Rank and Mutual Rank of 0.81 (p<0.01) as shown in Figure 7.

Furthermore, a triad analysis was conducted, to assess the extent to which there exists a bias in how trust and trustworthiness was distributed across the network. The analysis was conducted by first classifying each bi-directional edge in one of three possible states: balanced-high (meaning both people are sharing in full or partially), balanced-low (meaning that both people are not sharing), and unbalanced (meaning that one person is sharing while the other is not). Given the three possible labels for each edge, there exist 10 possible "templates" for triads, depending on the combination of its bidirectional edges (see Table 1). Each triad in the graph was labelled appropriately, and the frequency of occurrence of each template was calculated.

In addition, for each of the 10 templates the theoretical expected frequency of occurrence was calculated, as described in [19], by assuming that the same edges were randomly distributed on a graph with identical topography. The relationship between the observed and expected frequency for each of the 10 templates is shown in Figure 8. The figure shows a modest correlation (R^2=0.75), with the exception of the data point at (119,225) corresponding to

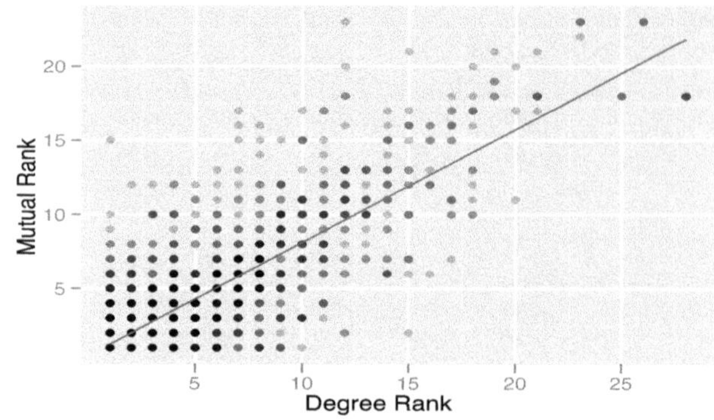

Figure 7. X-axis: degree rank of a neighbour wrt another node. Y-axis: common friends rank of a neighbour wrt another node. Darker dots indicate overlapping points.

Template	Expected Frequency	Observed frequency
1	292	209
2	142	119
3	119	225
4	23	22
5	39	10
6	1	19
7	16	5
8	3	1
9	3	0
10	0.7	28

Unbalanced Balanced-Low Balanced-High

Table 1. Expected frequency (given a random model) and observed frequencies for each of the 10 possible triad templates.

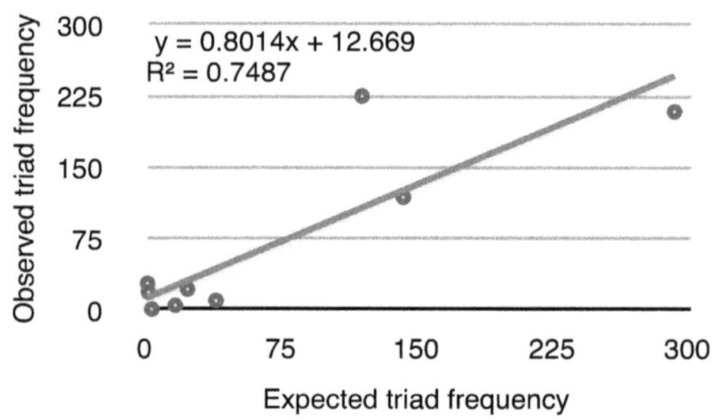

Figure 8. Correlation between the expected and observed frequencies for each of the 10 possible triad templates.

the template "Balanced-high, Unbalanced, Unbalanced". Removal of this point would substantially improve the correlation (R^2=0.96).

DISCUSSION

Targeted location-sharing privacy attacks

This paper proposes a threat model related to location-sharing privacy, whereby the attacker attempts to collect data about a target's longitudinal movements. To do this, the attacker first needs to identify suitable targets such that his chances of success are maximised. Once a suitable target is identified, then the attacker attempts to gain access to the target in order to collect data about the target's location, but not "too close" to avoid detection. Therefore, even though a strategy for collecting data on a target's whereabouts would be to attempt to befriend the target directly, that increases the chances of the attacker being noticed. This paper assumes that the attacker can attempt to collect data about the target by befriending one of the target's friends, i.e. a "weak link". This will make the attacker a "friend of a friend" of the target, which is arguably adequate to gain access to the target's location. In order to achieve this, the attacker needs to figure out which of the target's friend are more likely to have access to the target's location data, and are therefore a more suitable person to befriend. The results from Figure 3 show that, on average, nodes exhibit a bimodal distribution of trust which is weighted towards not sharing at all. Hence, if the attacker picks a target's friend at random, they are about four times more likely to not gain access at all to the target's data.

To assess the extent to which such an attack can be engineered, the study presented here answers two important questions relating to this kind of targeted location-sharing privacy attacks. First, given a group of users and the friendship ties amongst them, is it possible to predict which of these users is likely to reveal the most about their whereabouts? Second, given an individual user within a particular social network, is it possible to predict which of her friends know most about her whereabouts?

The study presented here captured a measure of "openness" between individuals, which reflects the probability that a request for someone's real-time location is likely to be satisfied. An advantage of using a generic measure, which we refer to us trust (when a person of interest is open towards someone else) and trustworthiness (when someone else is open towards a person of interest), is that it can be applied across multiple features of online social networks. Therefore, while commercial location-sharing systems vary in features and their capabilities evolve over time, the measure of trust and trustworthiness is likely to remain an underlying driver in guiding users' decision to share their location with others.

Identifying a suitable target

The motivation for H1 was to suggest a way in which the attacker can identify users who are more likely to share their location with friends. The hypothesis was that individuals who are more central to the social network reveal the most about themselves, motivated by the observation that such individuals are more likely to engage in collaboration and coordination activities. Our results suggest that a user's network centrality as measured by betweenness and degree centrality had a significant effect on the amount of trust that user was willing to show towards their friends, thus supporting hypothesis.

The results suggest that individuals who are more central to their network are more likely to be willing to share their location with others, and therefore they are good targets for a potential attacker. Hence, an attacker can conduct a basic analysis of the network structure to identify central nodes, and then attempt to target more central nodes since they are more likely to share their location. It can be argued that individuals who are more central to the network are more socially active, and maintain more social relationships. This is likely to require them to take part in more social activities, and therefore it can be argued that these conditions require more coordination on their part. This offers one explanation as to why the findings in this study suggest that more central users did in fact share their location more often.

How to target individuals

Once the attacker has identified a target who is likely to be open and share their location, the next step is to develop a strategy for targeting that individual. The threat model discussed in this paper assumes that the attacker will not attempt to befriend the target directly, since that bears a high risk of being detected. Instead, the attacker can attempt to befriend someone from the target's friends since that can give them access to the target's location data without bringing them "too close" to the target. Therefore, the next step for the attacker is to identify a "weak link" in the target's list of friends, or a person who is likely to be granted access to the target's location data. The study tested two possible strategies for identifying weak links: based on the number of friends that a weak link may have (H2), and based on the number of common friends that the weak link may have with the target (H3).

Prior studies have shown the importance of reciprocity in social interactions, thus providing the motivation for H2. More specifically, studies have shown that when an individual performs a favour or act that bestows trust upon another individual, that individual is likely to feel obliged to reciprocate the favour or act. The motivation for H2 comes from this perceived obligation and from H1. The results show a positive correlation between the amount of trust that an individual bestows on each of his friends and the number of friends of those friends. This suggests that the attacker can identify a suitable "weak link" of the target by considering the target's list of friends and identifying those individuals with the highest number of friends of their own. Such individuals are more likely to be social active, and are therefore more likely to choose to share their location with the target (see H1). The target, by virtue of reciprocity, is therefore more likely to share their location with such individuals.

A competing, and possibly complementary hypothesis for identifying weak links is H3, which states that the target's friend with most common ties with the target knows most about the target's whereabouts. This can be due to the fact that the existence of common friends can indicate shared membership in a community or organisation. The results show that there is a significant positive correlation between the trust of a target towards each of his friends and the rank of that friend in terms of the number of mutual friends he has with the target. The results provide a clear strategy for how an attacker can identify a "weak link", which entails identifying who from the target's list of friends has the highest number of common friends with the target. One explanation for these findings is that individuals who share many friends, and are thus likely to belong to the same social groups, are more likely to share their location in order to coordinate their activities better, as well as to maintain an increased awareness of each other's ongoing activities.

Finally, it should be pointed out that the analysis provides evidence that H2 and H3 are directly related. Since both hypotheses were supported by the analysis, this is not surprising. The results show a strong positive correlation between H2 and H3 in that a target's friends who have many friends are also likely to have a lot of common friends with the target. One explanation for this relationship may be that individuals who have many friends of their own are more likely to be extroverts who socialise and engage in multiple social interactions activities. Their behaviour therefore increases the likelihood of them being friends with mutual friends with the target simply because they have a lot of friends.

Triads and small group privacy

The results of the structural analysis presented here offer insights into how, in the context of location-sharing, triads of users distribute and balance trust and trustworthiness. In addition to being useful in understanding the behaviour of our participants, these results are also useful in situations where only partial information may be known about the network.

The structural analysis shows that even though under a completely random model we expected to observe only one triad where all three members trust each other (template 10 in Table 1), we actually observed 28 such triads. Furthermore, the correlation analysis highlights triad template 3 as being substantially different from the overall correlation pattern between expected and observed frequencies. In this case, this result shows that we observed quite often situations where two people trust each other but both maintain unbalanced relationships with a third individual. This is a balanced situation and expected to be more frequent in a realistic setting than in a purely random environment [e.g. 11].

The results from this analysis coincide with prior work in that people tend to avoid unbalanced situations and prefer the comfort of balanced triads . Furthermore, these results can be used to make predictions in situations where incomplete information has been collected about individuals. This is possible since given three individuals and 2 of the 3 relationships between them, we may be able to predict the third relationships. For example, given a triad with two balanced-high relationships, the chances of the third relationship being balanced-low is very close to zero, unbalanced is 15%, and balanced-high is 85%.

Protection against such privacy attacks

The attack described here assumes that the attacker is trying to gain longitudinal access to the target's whereabouts, and does so by avoiding detection since they do not need to befriend the target directly, but only one of their friends. Assuming that on average users have about 150 friends in a social network, then the attacker's strategy ensures that he is one of about 22000 people who are friends-of-friends of the target, making detection much harder.

One strategy that the platform could follow in case of a pull-based location-sharing model would be to ensure that individuals are notified if anyone is making too many location-sharing requests. This could be implemented in the form of a user-defined threshold or as a nudging mechanism intended to help people refine their sharing preferences [3]. In the case of a push-based model, the users can ensure that their information is visible only to their friends directly, and to no-one beyond that. Similarly, limits could be imposed on how often a user can update their location, hence offering an upper bound on how much users can reveal about their whereabouts. However, such solutions seem to contradict the needs of commercial systems which appear to strive for increasing the amount of shared information.

Making useful predictions

While the work described here was framed in the context of a privacy attack, the hypotheses that were tested may be useful in developing user-friendly features that can automatically provide useful suggestions to users. For instance, the hypotheses discussed earlier provide an indication on how to identify a person who is likely to know the whereabouts of an individual of interest. It may be the case that the individual of interest has not logged into the location-sharing system to update their location, due to technical difficulties, time constraints, or any other plausible difficulty. Under such circumstances, the system may be able to make automated suggestions about who to ask regarding the whereabouts of the person of interest based on a simplistic network-structure analysis. Therefore, in cases of high urgency it is possible to offer such recommendations as a fall-back strategy.

Limitations of the study

In a realistic environment there may be multiple factors affecting the sharing of information, many of which are inadvertently manipulated by users. For instance, battery life and group norms may be important factors that urge users to hide or share their location. These were not taken into account in this study.

Furthermore, this study presents and tests a generic strategy for engineering such an attack. Clearly, the fine details of the social platform where this information is recorded and shared are important, and may facilitate or hinder the success of such an attack. For instance, being friend of a friend may be "too close" or "too far" to obtain location information, while some auditing mechanism may allow users to see who is viewing their location information repeatedly.

Finally, it is important to take into consideration here the fact that users of this location sharing application start with a default privacy policy of not sharing their location information with anybody in the network. We cannot rule this out a contributing factor to our result that more central nodes trust more, as they are also likely to be seasoned users of the system and hence have invested more time to articulate their location sharing preferences.

CONCLUSION

This paper presents a study that aims to answer two important questions related to targeted location-sharing privacy attacks: (1) given a group of users and their social graph, is it possible to predict which among them is likely to reveal most about their whereabouts, and (2) given a user, is it possible to predict which among her friends knows most about her whereabouts.

The results show that users who are more central to their social network (both locally and globally) are more likely to share information about their location, and hence are more "vocal". In addition, the findings show that given a target, that target's friend who either has many friends or many common friends with the target is more likely to be trusted by the target.

The findings of this study are important both in understanding how privacy attacks can be engineered and how they can be prevented. An important next step for this work is the application of these insights for the development of automated protection and suggestion mechanisms that will make the sharing of real-time location safer and more useful.

ACKNOWLEDGEMENTS

This work is funded by NSF grants CNS-0627513, CNS-0905562, CNS-1012763, by CyLab at Carnegie Mellon under grants DAAD19-02-1-0389 and W911NF-09-1-0273 from the Army Research Office. Additional support has been provided by Google and the CMU/Portugal Information and Communication Technologies Institute and the Portuguese Foundation for Science and Technology (FCT) grant CMU-PT/SE/0028/2008 (Web Security and Privacy). The authors would also like to acknowledge the entire Locaccino team, including Jason Hong, Lorrie Cranor, Paul Hankes Drielsma, Justin Cranshaw, Patrick Gage Kelley, Jialiu Lin and Michael Benisch for their contributions.

REFERENCES

1. Acquisti, A. and Gross, R. (2006). Imagined communities: awareness, information sharing, and privacy on the Facebook. Proc. PET 2006, Springer, 36-56.
2. Altman, I. (1977). Privacy Regulation: Culturally Universal or Culturally Specific? Journal of Social Issues, 33 (3), 66-84.
3. Balebako, R., Leon, P.G., Mugan, J., Acquisti, A., Cranor, L.F., Sadeh, N. (2011) Nudging Users Towards Privacy on Mobile Devices, CHI 2011 workshop article, May 2011
4. Barkhuus, L. (2004). Privacy in location-based services, concern vs. coolness. Mobile HCI 2004 workshop: Location System Privacy and Control.
5. Benisch, M., Kelley, P.G., Sadeh, N., Cranor, L.F., (2010). Capturing Location-Privacy Preferences: Quantifying Accuracy and User-Burden Tradeoffs. Personal and Ubiquitous Computing (PUC). Forthcoming.
6. Bonneau, J., Anderson, J., Anderson, R. and Stajano, F. (2009) Eight Friends Are Enough: Social Graph Approximation via Public Listings. SNS'09.
7. Choo, K-K. R. and Smith, R. G. (2008). Criminal Exploitation of Online Systems by Organised Crime Groups. Asian Criminology (2008) 3:37–59
8. Christakis, N., Fowler, J.H. (2008). The collective dynamics of smoking in a large social network. The New England journal of medicine 358(21): 2249-58.
9. CISC (2010) Report on Organized Crime. Criminal Intelligence Service Canada. Available At: http://www.cisc.gc.ca [Last Accessed 25th October 2010]. ISBN 978-1-100-51931-9.
10. Consolvo, S., Smith, I. E., Matthews, T., LaMarca, A., Tabert, J., and Powledge, P. (2005). Location disclosure to social relations: why, when, & what people want to share. CHI 2005, 81-90.

11. Easley, D., and Kleinberg, J. (2010). Networks, Crowds, and Markets: Reasoning About a Highly Connected World. Cambridge University Press.

12. Gibbons, J.D. (1993). Nonparametric statistics: An introduction. Sage University Paper series on Quantitative Applications in the Social Sciences, 07-090.

13. Goffman, E. (1959). The presentation of self in everyday life. Garden City, NY: Doubleday Anchor.

14. Hong, J. I. and Landay, J. A. (2004) An architecture for privacy-sensitive ubiquitous computing. MobiSys '04, 177-189.

15. Jones, S., and O'Neill, E. (2010). Feasibility of structural network clustering for group-based privacy control in social networks. In Proceedings of the Sixth Symposium on Usable Privacy and Security (SOUPS '10). ACM, New York, NY, USA, , Article 9 , 13 pages

16. Kelley, P. G., Hankes Drielsma, P., Sadeh, N., and Cranor, L. F. (2008). User-controllable learning of security and privacy policies. AISec 2008, 11-18.

17. Khalil, A. and Connelly, K. (2006). Context-aware telephony: privacy preferences and sharing patterns. CSCW '06, 469-478.

18. Kostakos, V. and Oakley, I. (2009). Designing Trustworthy Situated Services: an Implicit and Explicit Assessment of Locative Images' Effect on Trust. CHI, Boston, USA, pp. 329-332.

19. Kostakos, V. and Venkatanathan, J. (2010). Making friends in life and online: Equivalence, micro-correlation and value in spatial and transpatial social networks. IEEE SocialCom, Minneapolis, USA, pp. 587-594.

20. Lederer, S., Mankoff, J., and Dey, A. K. (2003). Who wants to know what when? privacy preference determinants in ubiquitous computing. CHI 2003, ACM Press, 724-725.

21. McPherson, Miller, Lynn Smith-Lovin, and James M Cook. "Birds of a Feather: Homophily in Social Networks." Annual Review of Sociology 27(1):415-444.

22. Nagaraja, S. (2008) The economics of covert community detection and hiding. WEIS: Workshop on the Economics of Information Security.

23. Norberg, Patricia A, Daniel R. Horne, and David A. Horne (2007). The Privacy Paradox: Personal Information Disclosure Intentions versus Behaviors. Journal of Consumer Affairs, 41(1):100-126.

24. Palen, L., Dourish, P. (2003). Unpacking Privacy for a Networked World. In Proc. of the Conference on Human Factors and Computing Systems: CHI 2003, ACM Press 129–136.

25. Petronio, S. (2002). Boundaries of Privacy: Dialectics of Disclosure. SUNY, Albany, NY

26. Regan, D.T. (1971). Effects of a favor and liking on compliance. Journal of Experimental Social Psychology, 7(6):627-639.

27. Reynolds, B., Venkatanathan, J., Goncalves, J., and Kostakos, V. (2011). Sharing Ephemeral Information in Online Social Networks: privacy perceptions and behaviours. In proceedings of INTERACT.

28. Sadeh, N., Hong, J., Cranor, L., Fette, I., Kelley, P., Prabaker, M., and Rao, J. (2008). Understanding and capturing people's privacy policies in a mobile social networking application. Personal and Ubiquitous Computing 13, 6, 401-412.

29. Shaikh, S. A., Chivers, H., Nobles, P., Clark, J. A. and Chen, H. (2008). Network reconnaissance. Network Security, 2008(11):12-16.

30. Stutzman, F., Kramer-Duffield, J. (2010) Friends only: examining a privacy-enhancing behavior in Facebook In Proc. of the Conference on Human Factors and Computing Systems: CHI 2010, ACM Press 1553-1562.

31. Toch, E., Cranshaw, J., Drielsma, P.H., Tsai, J. Y., Kelley, P. G., Cranor, L., Hong, J., Sadeh, N. (2010) Empirical Models of Privacy in Location Sharing, in Proceedings of the Twelfth International Conference on Ubiquitous Computing. Ubicomp 2010

32. Tsai, J., Kelley, P.G., Cranor, L.F., and Sadeh N. (2010). Location- Sharing Technologies: Privacy Risks and Controls. Journal of Law and Policy for the Information Society, 2010.

33. Tsai, J.Y., Kelley, P., Drielsma, P., Cranor, L.F., Hong, J., and Sadeh, N. (2009). Who's viewed you?: the impact of feedback in a mobile location-sharing application. CHI '09, 2003–2012.

34. Tufekci Z. (2008). Can You See Me Now? Audience and Disclosure Management in Online Social Network Sites. Bulletin of Science and Technology Studies. Volume 11, Number 4, June 2008 , pp. 544-564(21).

35. Wagner, D., Lopez, M., Doria, A., Pavlyshak, I., Kostakos, V., Oakley, I., Spiliotopoulos, T. (2010). Hide And Seek: Location Sharing Practices With Social Media. MobileHCI '10, 55-58.

36. Wellman, B. and Wortley, S. (1990). Different Strokes from Different Folks: Community Ties and Social Support. American Journal of Sociology 96, 3, 558-588.

37. Xu, X., Yuruk, N., Feng, Z. and Schwieger, T. A. J. (2007) SCAN: a structural clustering algorithm for networks. Proceedings of the 13th ACM SIGKDD international conference on Knowledge discovery and data mining, 824-833.

On the Limitations of Query Obfuscation Techniques for Location Privacy

Sai Teja Peddinti
Computer Science and Engineering
Polytechnic Institute of New York University
Brooklyn, NY USA
psaiteja@cis.poly.edu

Nitesh Saxena
Computer and Information Sciences
University of Alabama, Birmingham
Birmingham, AL USA
saxena@cis.uab.edu

ABSTRACT
A promising approach to location privacy is query obfuscation, which involves reporting $k-1$ false locations along with the real location. In this paper, we examine the level of privacy protection provided by the current query obfuscation techniques against adversarial location service providers. As a representative and realistic implementation of query obfuscation, we focus on SybilQuery. We present two types of attacks depending upon whether or not a short-term query history is available. When history is available, using machine learning, we were able to identify **93.67%** of user trips, with only **2.02%** of fake trips misclassified, for the security parameter $k = 5$. In the absence of history, we used trip correlations to form a smaller set of trips effectively increasing the user query identification probability from 20% to about **40%**. Our work demonstrates that the use of aggregate statistical information alone is not sufficient to generate simulated trips. We identify areas for improvement in the existing query obfuscation techniques.

Author Keywords
Anonymity, Location Privacy, Query Obfuscation, Machine Learning

ACM Classification Keywords
K.6.5 Management of Computing and Information Systems: Security and Protection.; K.4.1 Computers and Society: Public Policy Issues—*Privacy*

General Terms
Security, Experimentation, Human Factors

INTRODUCTION
Location based services (LBSs) are quite common on modern mobile and wireless devices, ranging from smart phones to automobile systems. These services open up new opportunities for ordinary end users. They can be used for navigation from current location to a given destination, locating nearby businesses, restaurants or friends, and receiving geographic alerts (e.g., about traffic or weather conditions) or advertisements, to name a few. The LBSs are clearly very appealing, but unfortunately they violate users' location privacy. These services require the users to transmit their locations to the server in a sporadic or periodic manner, depending on the service being offered. This enables the service provider to track the whereabouts of the user, map user's daily commute, identify his home or work locations, thereby gaining insight into the user's personal life. Consequently, privacy conscious users do not wish to disclose their locations to the LBSs. This seriously limits the acceptance of LBSs, which is reflected in the low adoption of E-ZPass [4] toll collection, and the New York City cab drivers' denial of equipping all cabs with GPS tracking devices [5].

Many techniques have been proposed to protect the location privacy of the end users. A straight-forward approach is to strip the user queries of any user identifying information (i.e., anonymizing them) and assigning a pseudonym. Such methods have been proven to be ineffective allowing the attacker to locate the home of a user from the pseudonymized GPS tracks [19]; when associating this information with the street address listings, one can obtain the name of the individual [21]. Even when completely anonymized queries were used with no pseudonyms, it has been shown that all the queries belonging to a trip could be related, effectively forming a pseudonym for each trip [16]. Another privacy-preserving approach is to distort the actual users locations by adding random noise [9]. However, the amount of random noise necessary to prevent tracking attacks is large [21].

Instead of adding random noise, one can degrade the location information to query for a region, so that the condition of k-anonymity is satisfied. In these k-anonymity based spatial cloaking [15, 6, 12] methods, regions are presented to the LBS instead of actual locations, such that at least k users of the service exist in each region. When the LBS returns the response for the entire region, based on each user's location the results are filtered and forwarded appropriately. As the LBS only sees a region containing k users, it does not have any information as to where the users might be within the region. Here the value k is the security parameter, which determines the level of anonymity. These k-anonymity techniques, however, rely on the presence of a third party server, which handles the generation of the cloaked regions and demultiplexing of the returned responses. Moreover, the cloaking and uncloaking needs to be performed for every user query, resulting in performance and scalability issues. The third-party server must be careful while generating the cloaked regions so as to prevent any correlation attacks [13], whereby the LBS can break the k-anonymity by keeping track of the regions sent by the server. Furthermore, the third party servers become single points of failure and easy attack targets.

As an alternative, peer-to-peer solutions to location privacy have been developed. These require the participation of at least k peers to ensure k-anonymity [7, 14]. However, relying on other users is not always possible and reduces the autonomy of the system. Private Information Retrieval (PIR) protocols, such as [13, 20, 18], offer provable privacy protection to the user. However, current PIR protocols are not feasible to be deployed in practice due to their high computation and communication overhead.

The focus of this paper is on decentralized and autonomous k-anonymity based solutions [22, 26]. In these solutions, several false queries are posed to the LBS, along with the real user query. The LBS responds to each of these queries, and the user simply selects the response matching the real query and discards all other responses. By ensuring that a sufficient number of these fake queries are posed and that they look realistic, the probability of a LBS identifying the real query could be reduced to a desired level. In contrast to the aforementioned solutions, such query obfuscation approaches are more attractive because they do not require any infrastructural changes, third party servers or rely on other users, and are available for ready deployment by privacy conscious users.

Our Contributions

A higher level goal of our paper is to examine the effectiveness of the decentralized query obfuscation approach in protecting users' privacy against adversarial LBSs. Specifically, we consider two types of adversaries with different capabilities, trying to identify the real user location queries from the pool of fake queries and user queries. The first LBS adversary (referred to as the *Strong Adversary*) has access to the user's previously recorded short-term location query history. This history does not constitute any out-of-band information, but rather only the previous queries posed by the user that the LBS recorded. The second adversary (referred to as the *Weak Adversary*) does not have any query history pertaining to the user.

Of the two currently available query obfuscation tools [22] [26], we concentrate on SybilQuery [26]; however, we believe that our results could be extended to the other tool as it is based on similar principles. In order to begin our evaluation, we first recreated the SybilQuery system as described in [26, 25] using traces of 540 cabs obtained from [3]. We then selected mobility traces of 85 cabdrivers over a period of one month, and treated them as users of SybilQuery. We collected the pool of fake/sybil queries and real queries produced by the tool, for each of these users when their mobility traces were simulated. We then evaluate the feasibility for an adversarial location service provider to identify the user queries from the query pool.

Since the strong adversary has access to the user location history, we applied machine learning to identify the real queries. The results of our *classification attacks* indicate that SybilQuery obfuscation approach is fairly weak. We show that, when using $k = 5$, on an average user trips could be identified with accuracies as high as **93.67%** and rate at which sybil trips are misclassified as user trips is about **2.02%**. Although we found that increasing the security parameter k does provide better privacy, the performance of the classifiers only degrades gradually with this parameter. For example, for one of our classification approaches, the user accuracy only decreased from about 80% to 63%, and the sybil misclassification rate changed from about 6% to 5%, when k was changed from 5 to 11. In the context of the weak adversary, since the user location history is not available, we correlate trips to filter out few sybil queries. Using our trip *correlation attacks*, we were able to reduce the problem size to a smaller set, effectively increasing the average user query identification probability from 20% to about **40%**, for $k = 5$.

Our results demonstrate that aggregate statistical information, used for generating the sybil/fake queries, is not sufficient to hide the user queries, if the adversary has access to the location history. This is because the user query patterns tend to stand out among the pool of sybil and user queries. Moreover, the sybil queries need to be consistent across trips to prevent correlation attacks. On a broader note, we believe that these insights drawn from our work will help guide the design of future query obfuscation tools, better resistant to automated privacy attacks. In fact, we identify areas for improvement in the existing query obfuscation tools, making them more robust to such automated attacks.

SYBILQUERY BACKGROUND

SybilQuery is a k-anonymity based location anonymization tool that is decentralized and works from the client side without any server side modifications. It works by generating $k - 1$ statistically similar sybil location queries for every user query to the LBS. All the k location queries are sent to the LBS at the same time.

In the SybilQuery model [26], an LBS is a database that stores $< l, v >$ tuples, where l is a geographic location and v represents value(s) associated with that location. When a user queries the LBS with a location, the values associated with that location are returned to the user. Also, in the model, the users periodically send queries to the LBS during a trip.

If SybilQuery just reports random $k - 1$ locations for each user query sent to the LBS, it becomes easy to separate the real locations. This is because real locations will follow a real path between a source and a destination, whereas random queries do not map to such paths. Moreover, the reported random locations might end up in highly unlikely places, such as mountains or oceans. Therefore, the sybil queries being generated should also follow a valid path, i.e. starting from a source and ending at a destination. To this end, the SybilQuery tool requires the user to enter the trip source and destination, so that it can generate similar looking sybil source and destinations, and simulate the user movement between them as realistically as possible. Also, the tool requires the users to specify the k parameter, allowing the user to select the level of privacy they desire. Larger the value of k, stronger is the privacy protection. Recall that a real query can be identified from a pool of all the queries (sybil and real) by making a random guess with a probability $1/k$.

The SybilQuery tool has three modules, namely an endpoint generator, a path generator and a query generator. The endpoint generator produces $k-1$ pairs of sybil sources and destinations, which have similar statistical properties to that of the user source and destination. For this, the tool requires a database of past traffic information across a given geographic region. The endpoint generator processes the database for location clusters that are similar to the user source and destination, and while picking up each sybil source and destination from these clusters, it makes sure that the euclidean distance between the sybil source and destination are within a threshold of the euclidean distance between the actual user source and destination.

Once the $k-1$ end points are generated, the path generator uses any existing navigation system like Bing maps/Microsoft Multimap [1], to generate paths between the end points. Each path is represented as a sequence of way points. The query generator uses this way point information to simulate the user movement along the sybil paths. When the user initiates a query with his current location l, the query generator is triggered. It uses this location l to estimate the user offset along his path, and simulates the motion along each of the $k-1$ sybil paths using similar offsets, and generates $k-1$ sybil locations. All these k locations (real and sybil) are then queried to the LBS at the same time.

RECREATING SYBILQUERY

A prototype implementation of SybilQuery has been reported in [26], geared towards providing privacy for vehicular networks (cabs equipped with GPS systems). This prototype uses PostgreSQL database with PostGIS spatial extensions as the endpoint generator and an off-the-shelf mapping service, Microsoft Multimap [1], as the path generator. Because the prototype is not publicly available, we had developed our own implementation of Sybilquery following the instructions in [26] and [25]. In doing so, we tried to be as close as possible to the original prototype so that our observations are not restricted to the prototype we developed.

For populating the regional traffic database, we obtained real mobility traces of cabs in the San Francisco Bay area. The Cabspotting [3] service, which tracks the location of the cabs using on-board GPS devices, has provided us with these cab traces. Each cab involved with the project, sends its location to the server periodically. These updates are a tuple of the form *<cab-id, current latitude, current longitude, status, timestamp>*; (*status* indicates whether the cab was empty or metered). All the metered readings in a sequence correspond to a trip made by the cab. The cab traces, we obtained, were spread over two periods of 45 days and 25 days. The first dataset was used to pre-process the traffic database and the second dataset of 25 days is used to test the efficiency of the query obfuscation approach. There is a time gap of one month between the two datasets.

We implemented the end point generator using the PostgreSQL database with PostGIS Spatial extensions enabled and a python client to communicate with the database. The trips' information gathered from the cab updates for the initial 45 days was stored in the PostgreSQL database, which facilitates making spatial queries. These trips are used in the pre-processing step and during the generation of endpoints. Our trip database had a total of 596,496 trips for 540 cabs.

Pre-Processing Stage

For generating sybil endpoints, we need annotated databases which contain tags to identify locations with similar properties or features. As manually labelling the data is hard, SybilQuery uses a pre-processing step to process the database and automatically extract the features for the locations. The two features described in [26] are traffic density τ and the probability distribution function (PDF) π. Based on the density values, the locations are separated into clusters or buckets. All the locations within the same cluster were found to share similar properties. Since these features vary with the time of the day and the week, SybilQuery identifies six temporal patterns [26]. Thus, for a given location, there are 6 values of density and 6 values of PDF.

In SybilQuery a geographic location l is represented as a rectangular region or block instead of a geographic point, to represent the map in a finite number of locations. SybilQuery [26] adopts an adaptive data structure such as Quadtree [10] to represent blocks of uniform density. A block is considered uniform if every $25m \times 25m$ sub-block lying in it has density values within some threshold of each other. If the region is not uniform, it is broken uniformly into 4 smaller blocks. This is continued iteratively until the smallest block size is reached or the block has uniform density.

In our implementation, we used the same features and the temporal patterns. The smallest block size was chosen as $100m \times 100m$. We have used the threshold value of 250 to determine the uniformity of adjacent blocks. At the end of the pre-processing stage, with the parameters we have chosen, the San Francisco Bay area could be represented using 16,384 blocks, close to what was reported in [26].

Sybil End Point Generation

When the user provides his source and destination points, we identify the regions/blocks that contain these endpoints. All the regions that have the similar traffic densities and similar PDF π to user source are identified as possible sybil sources. All the regions having similar traffic densities to that of the user destination are identified as possible sybil destinations. From these source and destination clusters, we select regions such that the distance between the sybil source and destination regions is comparable to the actual user trip length. Once the regions are identified, we select random locations (to be specific, the nearest street addresses) within the regions to generate sybil endpoints. In our implementation, we followed the above approach and utilized the 'Snap To' feature already provided by the Microsoft Multimap Routing API [1], which snaps the location coordinates to the nearest road automatically.

Path Generation

For path generation between user endpoints and sybil endpoints, we use the Microsoft Multimap API [1] as specified in [26]. The API takes as an input a source and destination pair, and generates the shortest path between the endpoints as a sequence of waypoints through which the user needs to pass in order to reach the destination.

Query Generation

SybilQuery tool simulates the user movement along sybil paths to generate sybil locations for the queries. Off-the-shelf routing services, such as [1], provide the estimated time to reach the destination based on the distance to be covered and the projected speeds along the paths. Using these, we estimate the speed of the user along the sybil paths. Additionally, the mapping service may also take into consideration the current traffic information to estimate the trip time. When the user initiates a query, the time elapsed since the start of the trip and the estimated speed along the sybil paths is used to generate his position along the sybil paths. For every user location query, we estimate user's positions along the sybil paths and generate k location queries, which are sent at the same time to the LBS.[1]

ATTACK PRELIMINARIES

Attacker Model

In our attack model, the adversary is the LBS itself. This malicious LBS wants to track the users from their location queries for its own personal reasons, ranging from causing physical harm to performing a robbery, or even selling the information to third party advertisers. With the use of query obfuscation techniques, the LBS receives many fake queries. The LBS intends to filter the real user queries to continue with user profiling and to reduce the server overhead due to the sybil queries (once identified, the server could simply respond with dummy responses to sybil queries, for example). We assume that the adversary is passive and only tracks the locations sent by the user without manipulating the responses returned to the user. Moreover, we make an assumption that the user is not making use of an anonymizing network, such as Tor, or proxy servers which hide the query source from the LBS. Note that if the mobile network service provider itself acts as a proxy or if an anonymizing network is used, and if there are no user identifiers associated with the queries, then the user already enjoys a certain level of anonymity obviating the need for query obfuscation tools. We aim to evaluate the query obfuscation approach when it is used independently of any network anonymizers, and when the attacker can relate all the queries coming from a user's device (using identifiers).

We consider two types of adversaries, based on the usage scenarios of the query obfuscation tools:

1. **Strong Adversary:** If the query obfuscation technique is released as a software update or an application onto the mobile or navigational devices, then we can assume that the LBS possesses a short-term history of location-based queries posed by a user prior to using the query obfuscation tool (i.e., when no privacy protection was available and the LBS could associate a user's identity with the user's queries). Equipped with this information, the attacker then tries to filter the sybil trips and identify the real user trips from a pool consisting of sybil and user queries (i.e., obtained after the user started employing the privacy tool). This scenario is realistic, since we can not expect the users to reinvest in new devices just for protecting their privacy.[2]

2. **Weak Adversary:** If the query obfuscation technique is available to new users or new devices alone, then the LBS does not possess any user history and is forced to filter the sybil queries just by analysing the received user and sybil queries. This situation arises when the user starts using the query obfuscation tool prior to communicating with the LBS for the first time.

In our attack model, we assume that the attacker does not use any external or out-of-band information (like searching Google about a user or knowing a user's address through yellow pages) apart from the locations in the queries sent by the user and the time stamps. We intend to work with the information directly available to the attacker obtained by observing the user queries. Incorporating any additional and meaningful side information can only increase the accuracy of our attacks, and thus our results will be representing a lower bound of accuracies achievable in identifying the user queries.

Overview of Attacks

Since the strong adversary has access to user history (training data), we utilize machine learning classification techniques to identify user query patterns and filter out the current queries (test data) which do not comply to these query patterns as sybil queries. To this end, we have selected Weka [11], an open source machine learning software for our needs. These machine learning classification techniques apply labels (user or sybil) to the test data after learning the features of each label from the training data.

For the weak adversary, we try to correlate trips to identify the user queries. SybilQuery tool uses caching, but it treats each user trip independently while selecting the sybil end-

[1] We do not incorporate current traffic conditions because we are working with older trips. Instead, we only use the time and distance information provided by the path generators to simulate the user movement.

[2] We note that such an attacker model has previously been incorporated in the context of web search privacy [24].

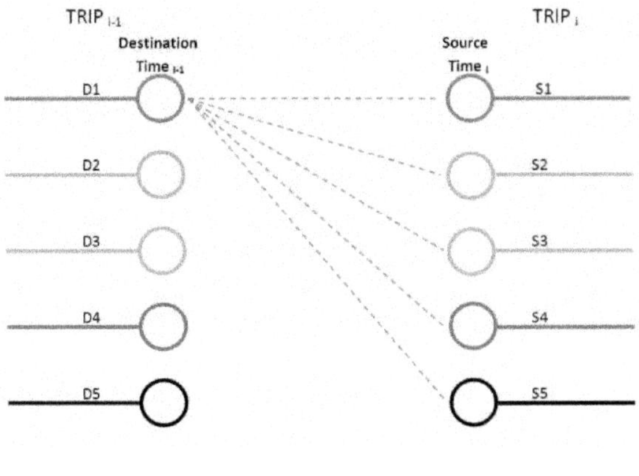

Figure 1. Correlating Trips

points. Because of this, the new sybil sources selected for the following trip, might be very far from the destinations of the previous trip in few cases, allowing us to identify them as sybil queries. Consider a simple example shown in Figure 1. Let us say the user is using SybilQuery with $k = 5$, and completed $Trip_{i-1}$ at $Time_{i-1}$ and reached destinations D_1, D_2, D_3, D_4 and D_5. After a while, at time $Time_i$, he started another trip from sources S_1, S_2, S_3, S_4 and S_5. The adversary only knows that one of these destinations is the actual user destination and one of these sources is the actual user source. Considering the previous locations and the times reported by the user, the adversary can obtain an assessment of the highest movement speed of the user. Now, the adversary can identify all the valid (D_m, S_n) pairs (where $1 \leq m, n \leq 5$), such that the distance between D_m and S_n can be covered in time $(Time_i - Time_{i-1})$ with the recorded highest speed of the user (plus some threshold speed, to accommodate increase in maximum user speeds). Of all valid (D_m, S_n) pairs, we consider k pairs - one for each destination (since user could be along any of the k destinations and can go to only one source). We use two simple methods (described in the following section) to identify the optimal k pairs from the valid (D_m, S_n) pairs.

We begin with k empty trip sequences, each indicating the probable sequence of trips taken by the user. We initialize the trip sequences with the first set of k trips. For every new received set of k trips, we obtain the last destination of each trip sequence D_m and the sources S_n of the new k trips and find the optimal (D_m, S_n) pairs, and add the trips to the trip sequences appropriately. Situations may arise, where the last destination of a trip sequence does not have any valid mapping with sources in the new set. This is because the destination is very far away from the sources of the trips in the new set, and can not be covered in $(Time_i - Time_{i-1})$ time going at the maximum user speed – thereby ending the trip prematurely. Hence, after processing the last set of k trips, in most cases, we are left with only p complete trip sequences (where $p \leq k$) – effectively reducing the complexity of the problem. Based on the algorithm for determining the optimal (D_m, S_n) pairs, we can have few user trips and few sybil trips in each of the p trip sequences.

For our experiments, we work with trips instead of individual location queries received from the user, because trips convey more information and are easier to study. Given a sequence of location queries, we identify trips based on the timing information associated with the queries. As per the SybilQuery model [26], clients periodically sends queries to the LBS as they move from source to destination. So, if there is more than 10 minutes of inactivity between subsequent location queries, we consider the user began a new trip. Also, since the queries are user initiated, the registered location queries at the LBS convey the approximate source and destination of the trip. This can be understood from Figure 2, where the red colored crosses indicate the locations registered by the LBS, when the actual trip made by the user is indicated by the blue line.

For each user, we use two metrics to measure the efficiency of our attacks: (1) *user accuracy*, i.e., the percentage of correctly identified user trips, and (2) *sybil misclassification rate*, i.e., the percentage of sybil trips identified as user trips.[3] Let us assume there are u user trips and s sybil trips, as reported by the sybil query tool, for a given user. On using the classifiers, let us say $u' + s'$ trips were identified as user queries, where u' corresponds to user trips identified as user trips and s' corresponds to sybil trips identified as user trips. Then our metrics are going to be u'/u and s'/s, which we shall henceforth call as accuracy and misclassification rate. The classifier is said to perform better, if the value of u'/u is close to 1 i.e. close to 100%, and s'/s is close to 0 i.e. close to 0%. So the adversary's goal is to identify as many of the user trips as possible while making few mistakes in (mis)identifying sybil trips as user trips.

Dataset Employed

We have collected cabspotting data for two periods of 45 days and 25 days. Of this, we have utilized the 540 cabs' trip data over a period of 45 days for preprocessing the database and identifying the uniform regions in the San Francisco Bay area. We have selected 85 cabs at random from the total 540 as the SybilQuery users. For each of these 85 users' trips during the later 25 days, we generated the sybil trips from our SybilQuery implementation with the default security parameter of $k = 5$. In the case of strong adversary, the Cabspotting data collected for the initial 45 days would be used as the user training data and the query pool of the remaining 25 days would serve as the test data. The weak adversary only has access to the pool of queries received during the 25 day period.

EXPERIMENTAL PRELIMINARIES

The Preliminaries for Classification Attacks

Selecting the Classifiers

We have chosen Support Vector Machines (SVM) classifier for our machine learning needs, because of its wide spread use in many user identification scenarios like [17], [2] and [8]. There are many SVM implementations in Weka [11],

[3]In traditional machine learning terminology, the two metrics are known as the *true positive rate* and the *false positive rate*, respectively.

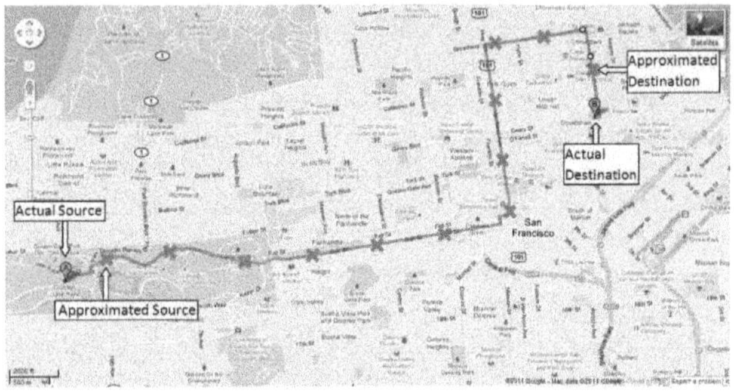

Figure 2. Trip formed from the Approximate Source and Destination points

and we have chosen One-class SVM and C-SVC classifier implementations. One-class SVM is used when we have the training data for only one class, and its instances need to be identified when mixed with outliers or non-class instances. Since we had the training data for the users and the test data contained user queries mixed with sybil queries (outliers), we used one-class SVM to identify the user queries.

C-SVC classifier is a binary classifier, which needs the training data for both the classes. Since the training data set is not available for the sybil trips, we wanted to test if the sybil trips generated for a known set of user trips helped in the classification process. To this end, for a randomly selected set of 10 users (cabs), whose user trips are known to us, we generated the sybil trips using SybilQuery. For these 10 users, we fixed the value of parameter k as 10, so as to maximize the feature extraction from sybil trips. The generated sybil queries are used as the sybil training data set for binary classification.

Selecting the Attributes

Every trip is represented as a sequence of locations representing the source, in between waypoints and the destination. Since the endpoints alone convey a lot of information about the trips, we decided to compare the classification accuracies with and without including the waypoints. The data provided to the classifier is of the format: <cab-id, start location, (waypoint1, waypoint2,...), end location, temporal, class>. Here, the class label (either user or sybil) will be provided for instances in the training data, and is to be estimated for the instances in the test data. In one experiment, we varied the number of waypoints to check its effect on the accuracies.

SVM treats each data instance (i.e., trip) to be independent and tries to classify it as a user or sybil trip based on the attribute values. However, there is an additional restriction in our scenario that states that only one user trip can exist in a set of k trips reported to the LBS at one given time (because $k-1$ trips are sybil trips). To incorporate this feature into the classification, we tweaked the standard Weka SVM library. SVM provides the posterior probabilities to each label (user or sybil) for each data instance/trip. In default SVM classification, a data instance is labelled user or sybil based on which probability is greater. We tweaked the classification algorithm to consider the user class probabilities of all the trips in a set, and label the trip with maximum user class probability as the user trip and the rest as sybil trips.

We also wanted to test if varying the security parameter k has any effect on the level of privacy (theoretically, larger k should provide better protection). To this end, we determine the user accuracies and the misclassification rates for a set of 48 users, with k set as 5, 7, 9, and 11.

The Preliminaries for Trip Correlation Attacks

After finding valid set of (D_m, S_n) pairs, as described before, we need to find at most k optimal pairs such that each destination is mapped to one source. We consider two simple approaches to obtain these k optimal pairs. In the first approach, we map each destination D_m to the nearest source S_n, such that (D_m, S_n) is present in the valid set of pairs. In the second approach, we map each destination D_m to the source S_n which could be reached with speeds closest to the average speed of the user, in time $(Time_i - Time_{i-1})$. We can find the average speed of the user in the same way as finding the highest speed of the user (based on previously reported locations and time stamps).

EXPERIMENTAL RESULTS

Classification Attacks

To recall, our first experiment involves the one-class SVM classifier wherein we train the classifier with the user training data alone, and try to distinguish the user trips from the sybil trips by considering them as data outliers. For the remaining four experiments, we perform C-SVC binary classification using the sybil query training data generated from known user trips. In the second experiment, we represent a trip with just the source and the destination pair. In the third experiment, the trips are represented as a sequence of locations including the source, destination and few waypoints in between. The fourth experiment is a slight variation of the second experiment, where we modify the C-SVC classification mechanism to consider the restriction that only one user trip can exist in a set of trips reported by the SybilQuery at a particular time. The fifth experiment is a variation of the third experiment with this additional restriction.

The average user accuracies and the sybil misclassification rates obtained after running each of these five experiments are reported in Table 1. In all these experiments, the value of k was 5, and the trips in experiments three and five were represented as a sequence of source, destination and 3 waypoints along the path from source to destination. Looking at Table 1, we observe that, of all the experimental methods, the restricted classification approach with just the trip endpoints seems to outperform the rest – with a quite high user accuracy of about 93.67% and very low sybil misclassification rate of only about 2.02%. We also find that incorporating waypoints seems to have an adverse effect on the performance.

As discussed earlier, we were also interested in testing the effect of security parameter k on the level of privacy provided to the users. To achieve this, we used SybilQuery to obfuscate the queries of 25 users (independent of the 85

Experiment Type	Average User Accuracy	Average Sybil Misclassfication Rate
#1: One-Class Classification using SVM	44.63%	36.1%
#2: Binary Classification with Trip Endpoints	44.93%	5.02%
#3: Binary Classification with Waypoints	16.57%	7.03%
#4: Restricted Classification with Trip Endpoints	93.67%	2.02%
#5: Restricted Classification with Waypoints	79.29%	5.18%

Table 1. Comparison of Average Accuracies for Different Experiments (by default, k is 5 and number of waypoints is 3 whenever applicable)

Value of k	Average User Accuracy	Average Sybil Misclassfication Rate
5	80.17%	6.13%
7	74.04%	5.46%
9	67.93%	5.25%
11	63.13%	5.02%

Table 2. Comparison of Average Accuracies for Different Values of Security Parameter k (using restricted classification with 3 waypoints)

users selected for previous set of experiments) using the values of k as 5, 7, 9 and 11. We then applied one of our previous classification approach, i.e., restricted classification using three waypoints along the path. For each of these 25 users, and for each value of k, we calculated the user accuracies and sybil misclassification rates. The average values are depicted in Table 2. As expected, the performance of the classifiers indeed goes down with the increase in the security parameter. However, even with a value as large as 11, the user accuracy is reasonably high standing at over 60% and sybil misclassification rate is quite low at about 5%.

Since the performance of our methods degraded when we incorporated more information about the trips (i.e., the waypoints), as can be seen from Table 1, we conducted an additional experiment on a set of randomly chosen 25 users (a subset of the previous 85 test users) by varying the number of waypoints between the trip source and destination. The restricted classification approach was used and the value of parameter k was set to the default 5 for this experiment. The results of this experiment are shown in Table 3. Increasing the number of waypoints appears to work favourably to the performance of classifiers. The results seems to be approaching the accuracies and misclassification rates corresponding to our best approach so far, i.e., restricted classification with trip endpoints only (Table 1).

Trip Correlation Attacks

As described earlier, we intend to correlate trips based on two metrics – distance and average speed. We start with the first set of k trips and form k trip sequences containing one trip each. For every new set of k trips received, we determine the mappings between these new trips and the last trip

Number of Waypoints	Average User Accuracy	Average Sybil Misclassfication Rate
3	81.40%	5.67%
4	86.20%	4.21%
5	91.58%	2.53%

Table 3. Comparison of Average Accuracies for Different Number of Waypoints (using restricted classification with $k = 5$)

in each of the k trip sequences. Based on the mappings, we add these new trips to the trip sequences. If there are no mappings between the new trips and the last trip of a trip sequence, then that trip sequence ends prematurely. After processing all the trip sets received, we are left with p complete trip sequences, where $0 \leq p \leq k$. In some cases, the value of p is zero because all the trip sequences can end prematurely. This happens when the last trip in each of the k trip sequences is a sybil trip and the sources in the next set of trips are very far away. Also, these p trip sequences are not completely disjoint and contain user or sybil trip overlappings. These p trip sequences form a smaller set P of user and sybil trips. We consider trip correlations to be successful if the random probability of picking a user trip from the set P is better than the random probability to pick a user trip from the complete set of user and sybil trips.

The results for the trip correlations based on the two metrics are depicted in Table 4. Here, columns 4 and 5 represent the percentage of total user trips and percentage of the total sybil trips that fall in the set P. While using distance metric to identify the optimal (D_m, S_n) pairs, we have a large number (56) of users whose trip sequences ended prematurely. However, for the rest 29 users, the trip sequences contained about 42.89% of total user trips and 15.2% of total sybil trips. The probability of a random trip, picked from this set P, to become a user trip is 0.414 which is about twice the random probability when $k = 5$. By using the average speed metric, we were able to reduce the number of users whose trip sequences end prematurely to 43, but the percentage of total user trips reduced to 33.57% and the percentage of sybil trips increased to 17.38%. The random probability of picking a user trip from this smaller subset is 0.326 (still higher than random probability across the complete set).

INTERPRETATION OF RESULTS AND DISCUSSION

Comparison with Prior Evaluation of SybilQuery

An analysis of SybilQuery tool had been performed in [25], but it was restricted to only a user study and certain statistical measures. The SybilQuery authors performed a study with 15 users, by visually showing them a combined set of real and user trips and asking them to identify the real trips. The results of this study showed that a user can not differentiate between a real and a sybil trip with a probability any better than $1/k$ (random guessing). The authors of SybilQuery also devised a statistical metric PATHCMP [25], to measure the similarity between real and sybil paths. This analysis showed that the real and the sybil paths are very close to each other, based on the PATHCMP metric, thereby making it hard to statistically separate the two. It is mentioned in

	Total Number of Users	Number of users with p=0	Average % of user queries in Set P	Average % of Sybil queries in Set P
Distance Metric	85	56	42.89%	15.20%
Speed Metric	85	43	33.57%	17.38%

Table 4. Correlation Experiment Results

[26] that SybilQuery can not defend against adversarial LBS which has some out-of-band background information about the users, like their daily commuting patterns or about the specific places the user visits such as home and office. We note that our attacks against query obfuscation utilize not out-of-band information, but rather the user's queries themselves that were posed to the LBS prior to employing SybilQuery.

Our work analyzes whether the sybil and the real queries can be separated if we take into consideration the user behaviour. Every cab driver, the user in our case, may follow a particular pattern while making trips around the city. While generating the sybil endpoints, the SybilQuery tool does not take this important user aspect into account, and hence the sybil endpoints and the user trip endpoints are very likely to differ.

Performance of Classification Methods

When we have user history, it is easier to use off-the-shelf machine learning techniques as compared to manually coming up with a function which helps us in separating user and sybil trips. Finding relation between data instances based on the data fields is a hard task. Support Vector Machines map the data instances into points in high dimensional/kernel spaces, which makes it easier to identify relations among the data instances. So, when a test data instance is supplied, it is converted to a point in kernel space and based on its proximity to points of different classes, the test data instance is classified as a user or sybil query.

Classification algorithms should perform better than naive identification techniques, like query/trip repetition between the test set and the training set. A trip repetition occurs when a trip in the user training set appears again in the user test set. Identification of such user trips is trivial. Moreover, just the repetition of source or the destination locations can indicate that it corresponds to a real user query. For assessing the influence of query repetitions in our experiments, we tried to identify such trip repetitions.

We considered two trips to be repeating or identical, if the sources (starting points) of both the trips lie within a $25m \times 25m$ region, and the destinations also obey the same condition. We tried to identify the trip repetitions for all the 85 users we experimented with, and the average number of repeated user trips is found to be only 1.48%. The average source repetition was 32.64% and the destination repetition was 28.58%. It is possible that the sybil trips (or sources or destinations) are also identical to the user trips (or sources or destinations). We found that such an overlap between the sybil trips and the user trips was close to 0%, but the sybil source overlap was 7.84%, and the sybil destination overlap was 7.56%. Using this naive classification approach, we were able to obtain user accuracies close to 62%, while the sybil misclassification rate was close to 16%. We can clearly see that our restricted classification approaches perform much better than the naive approach (Table 1).

One-class SVM tries to identify the distribution of the user class, i.e., the regions with large fraction of training data in the kernel space [23]. All those test instances lying within the region are classified as user instances and the rest are labelled as outliers. Since the classifier did not have information about the sybil class, it could not accurately differentiate between a user query and a sybil query, thereby resulting in poor performance. In the case of binary classification (experiments 2,3,4 and 5), we find a marginal hyperplane that separates the binary class instances belonging to user and sybil classes. We generated the sybil training data from known queries of 10 users. Since all SybilQuery instances use the same database for generating the trip endpoints, we are able to gather some details about the underlying database when we try to generate the Sybil query training set. Thus, by using the sybil training dataset, we were able to reduce the number of misclassifications, but the user accuracies did not improve. When we tried to increase the amount of trip information, by adding the details about three waypoints along the user trip, the accuracies decreased further. This could be because three waypoints are not sufficient to represent the entire trip and incorporating the waypoints introduced more noise into the training data.

As discussed before, SVMs treat the data instances (i.e. trips) to be independent. To impose the restriction that only one user trip can exist in k trips, we obtained the class probabilities returned by the SVM classifier when it is trying to classify a data instance. For every data instance SVM tries to check these probabilities, and assigns the label which has more probability ($>$ 0.5). For every set of k trips sent to the LBS, we pick the one with the highest user class probability and label it as the user trip and the rest as the sybil trips. There is a substantial improvement when we added this restriction to the SVM classification. This is because – in simple SVM classification all trips in a set could be labelled as sybil trips, but in the restricted version one trip (the one with highest user class probability, even if it is less than 0.5) should definitely be labelled as user trip and the rest as sybil trips. When only end points were used to represent the trips, we were able to attain the best performance with 93.67% average user accuracy and 2.02% misclassification rate. On adding the waypoint information, the accuracies decreased due the same reason discussed in the case of regular binary classification.

Effect of Security Parameter
Table 2 shows that the accuracies are decreasing with increase in k value. This is expected, because more the number of sybil trips, better is the level of privacy protection. Notice that when we increase the number of sybil trips, the probability that these sybil trips overlap with the user locations (in the user history) is also increased. As per our modified restricted SVM classifier, if these sybil trips have a higher user class probability, they are labelled as user trips resulting in the actual query being classified as the sybil query. Hence, the user accuracies decrease when the value of k is increased. Although the misclassification percentages from the table might appear to be slightly decreasing, the actual number of misclassifications are increasing (since k is increasing).

Effect of Waypoints
Having few waypoints may not be sufficient to represent the entire trip. These waypoints are generated when the user initiates a query to the LBS, so they are different from the important locations which govern the trip between the source and the destination, like places where the user needs to change his direction. Hence the waypoints registered by the adversary add more noise to the trip information conveyed by the endpoints, resulting in a decrease in accuracy (as seen in Table 1). As these number of waypoints increase, we get more information about the trip resulting in an improvement in user accuracies and decrease in the misclassification rates (as we can observe from Table 3).

Performance of Correlation methods
Even though we do not receive any queries from users in between trips, the user must have travelled between the destination of one trip and the source of the next trip. Taking cue from this, we try to relate trips together and form a trip sequence indicating a probable path the user might have taken. The main purpose of this evaluation was to check if we can eliminate some sybil trips and increase the random probability of selecting user trips. Our results in Table 4 show that we were successful in doubling the probability of selecting a user trip using simple approaches – distance and average speed. Using any better approach to identify optimal mappings is surely bound to reduce the number of users with $p = 0$ and the sybil trip percentages, and also increase the percentage of user trips.

Extensibility of Data
The data that we utilized in our experiments came from real cabs while no privacy-preserving tool was being used by the devices equipped on the cabs. In using this data for our purposes, we have assumed that the user's querying pattern is independent of whether the obfuscation technique, like SybilQuery, is employed or not. This is because the users may not be aware that such privacy mechanisms are enabled. This is especially true in the case of cab drivers or everyday mobile users. Moreover, it is highly unlikely for the user to purposefully make sensitive queries when these services are enabled, and make insensitive queries when they are disabled. This is a valid assumption because the tools such as SybilQuery offer better protection when they are enabled all the time. Therefore, our results capture realistic usage of the underlying tool, i.e., SybilQuery.

Extensions to Other Applications and Tools
Our methods indicate that attaching statistically similar trips to the user trips can not always provide anonymity, when the user possesses behavioural patterns which make his trips stand out within the pool of real and fake trips. The approach is not specific to the cab mobility traces and could be generalized to any implementation of SybilQuery, ranging from mobile or smart phone deployments to regular GPS navigational device implementations adopted for personal cars. In fact, it is our hypothesis that using obfuscation tools like SybilQuery on personal devices can further increase the identification accuracies. This is because on personal devices, the user's behavioural traits will be much more prominent when compared to those on passenger vehicles or cabs. The classification approaches and experimental methodology are also applicable and can be used to evaluate the effectiveness of other query obfuscation tools, such as [22]. We anticipate that our performance results might be very similar in case of [22] due to the fact that this tool also does not take into account the user behavior while generating fake queries.

IMPROVING THE QUERY OBFUSCATION TECHNIQUES
Based on our results, we propose a few simple, yet important changes to the query obfuscation techniques to make them more robust. The query obfuscation tool should not just be developed from aggregate statistical information, but it needs to consider the user query patterns to generate fake queries resembling real user queries. These user query patterns could be obtained by recording the user queries for a short period. While generating the sybil queries, the obfuscation tool can utilize both the statistical information and the user query patterns to generate sybil queries.

To prevent the machine learning attacks in the case of strong adversary, the obfuscation tool can repeat few locations the user previously visited in order to form the sybil queries. We can make sure that either the source or the destination of the sybil trips have occurred in the history and try to bring in or add in more locations that the user might visit. And, later we could use these new locations introduced to generate future fake trips. Since these locations occur in the user history, the machine learning classifier would classify them as user queries effectively increasing the sybil misclassifications and raising the level of the privacy protection provided. However, repeating locations from the user history might raise privacy issues because now we will be leaking both current and past information instead of the current information alone. Hence, this approach would be helpful if we can guess what part of the user query history the attacker possesses, and we can restrict the location repetitions to that part alone.

The trip correlation was able to filter out few sybil trips because the obfuscation tool is treating each user trip independently and selecting sybil trip sources very far from the previous sybil destinations. To prevent these attacks, we need to make these trip sequences (not just individual trips) to closely mimic the user behaviour. For this, we need to consider previous sybil destinations while generating sybil trips for the next user trip. If the user travelled distance x from the previous trip destination, and took time τ before making another trip, then the sybil sources need to lie within a distance of $x + c$, where c is a constant, from the previous sybil destinations – such that the distance $x + c$ can be covered in time τ with the highest user speed recorded. This would make it harder for the adversary to filter out any sybil trips, because now all the (D_m, S_n) pairs become valid, effectively making the probability to pick a user trip close to $1/k$.

CONCLUSIONS

In this paper, we analyzed and tried to quantify the level of location privacy provided by query obfuscation tools, specifically focusing on one practical implementation named SybilQuery. We recreated the SybilQuery system using real mobility traces of 540 cabs over a period of 70 days, and we generated sybil trips corresponding to the real traces. We demonstrated that a strong adversary, one having knowledge of the user location queries from the past, can effectively use machine learning techniques to identify the user trips. We also made an attempt to identify the reasons behind the machine learning accuracies, and tried to answer why they vary with different parameters, such as k, and the number of waypoints. In addition, we showed that even a weak adversary, one who does not have access to previous user locations, can correlate trips and filter out a certain fraction of the sybil trips. Using correlation attacks, we were able to double the random probability to identify a user trip.

Based on these results, we can conclude that existing query obfuscation techniques, based on aggregate statistical information alone, will be ineffective in protecting users' location privacy. The strength of our attacks lies in the fact that we use minimal information available to the adversary as well as off-the-shelf and simple approaches in identifying the user and sybil queries. The results could be improved further by using additional out-of-band information such as current traffic distributions. We therefore conclude that obfuscation tools need to take into account the user location patterns, so as to generate real looking sybil queries. We proposed some improvements which could be incorporated to make these obfuscation techniques more robust. On a broader note, we believe that the insights drawn from our work will help guide the design of future query obfuscation tools, better resistant to automated privacy attacks.

Acknowledgments

We would like to thank the Cabspotting service for providing us with the cab traces to conduct our evaluation, and Ambarish Karole for his help with the experiments.

REFERENCES

1. Microsoft multimap api. http://classic.multimap.com/openapidocs/1.2/demos/index.htm.
2. S. Ben-Yacoub, Y. Abdeljaoued, and E. Mayoraz. Fusion of face and speech data for person identity verification. *Neural Networks, IEEE Transactions on*, 10(5):1065 –1074, Sept. 1999.
3. Cabspoting. http://cabspotting.org/.
4. C. Caldwell. A pass on privacy?, Jul 2005. http://www.nytimes.com/2005/07/17/magazine/17WWLN.html?_r=1.
5. J. Choe. Nyc cab drivers say "nothanks" to gps installation, Mar 2007. Available at http://www.nytimes.com/2005/07/17/magazine/17WWLN.html?_r=1.
6. C.-Y. Chow, M. Mokbel, and X. Liu. Spatial cloaking for anonymous location-based services in mobile peer-to-peer environments. *GeoInformatica*, pages 1–30, 2009.
7. C.-Y. Chow, M. F. Mokbel, and X. Liu. A peer-to-peer spatial cloaking algorithm for anonymous location-based service. In *ACM international symposium on Advances in geographic information systems*, 2006.
8. O. de Vel, A. Anderson, M. Corney, and G. Mohay. Mining e-mail content for author identification forensics. *SIGMOD Rec.*, 30:55–64, 2001.
9. M. Duckham and L. Kulik. A formal model of obfuscation and negotiation for location privacy. In *Pervasive Computing*, pages 152–170. 2005.
10. R. A. Finkel and J. L. Bentley. Quad trees a data structure for retrieval on composite keys. *Acta Informatica*, 4:1–9, 1974.
11. I. W. . E. Frank. *Data Mining–Practical Machine Learning Tools and Techniques, Second Edition*. Elsevier, 2005.
12. B. Gedik and L. Liu. Protecting location privacy with personalized k-anonymity: Architecture and algorithms. *IEEE Transactions on Mobile Computing*, 7:1–18, 2008.
13. G. Ghinita, P. Kalnis, A. Khoshgozaran, C. Shahabi, and K.-L. Tan. Private queries in location based services: anonymizers are not necessary. In *SIGMOD international conference on Management of data*, 2008.
14. G. Ghinita, P. Kalnis, and S. Skiadopoulos. Mobihide: a mobilea peer-to-peer system for anonymous location-based queries. In *Conference on Advances in spatial and temporal databases*, 2007.
15. M. Gruteser and D. Grunwald. Anonymous usage of location-based services through spatial and temporal cloaking. In *Conference on Mobile systems, applications and services*, pages 31–42, 2003.
16. M. Gruteser and B. Hoh. On the anonymity of periodic location samples. In *Security in Pervasive Computing*, volume 3450, pages 179–192, 2005.
17. M. Hearst, B. Schvlkopf, S. Dumais, E. Osuna, and J. Platt. Trends and controversies - support vector machines. *IEEE Intelligent Systems*, 13(4):18-28, 1998.
18. U. Hengartner. Hiding location information from location-based services. In *Mobile Data Management, 2007 International Conference on*, pages 268–272, May 2007.
19. B. Hoh, M. Gruteser, H. Xiong, and A. Alrabady. Enhancing security and privacy in traffic-monitoring systems. *IEEE Pervasive Computing*, 5:38–46, 2006.
20. A. Khoshgozaran, H. Shirani-Mehr, and C. Shahabi. Spiral: A scalable private information retrieval approach to location privacy. In *Mobile Data Management Workshop*, pages 55–62, Apri 2008.
21. J. Krumm. Inference attacks on location tracks. In *Proceedings of the 5th international conference on Pervasive computing*, PERVASIVE'07, pages 127–143, 2007.
22. J. Krumm. Realistic driving trips for location privacy. In *Pervasive Computing*. 2009.
23. L. M. Manevitz and M. Yousef. One-class svms for document classification. *J. Mach. Learn. Res.*, 2:139–154, 2002.
24. S. T. Peddinti and N. Saxena. On the privacy of web search based on query obfuscation: A case study of trackmenot. In *Privacy Enhancing Technologies Symposium (PETS)*, 2010.
25. L. I. Pravin Shankar, Vinod Ganapathy. Privately querying location-based services with sybilquery- technical report, 2009. Available at: http://www.cs.rutgers.edu/~vinodg/papers/technical_reports/tr652/.
26. P. Shankar, V. Ganapathy, and L. Iftode. Privately querying location-based services with sybilquery. In *International conference on Ubiquitous computing*, 2009.

Are You Close with Me? Are You Nearby? Investigating Social Groups, Closeness, and Willingness to Share

Jason Wiese, Patrick Gage Kelley, Lorrie Faith Cranor,
Laura Dabbish, Jason I. Hong, John Zimmerman
Carnegie Mellon University
{wiese, pkelley, lorrie, dabbish, jasonh, johnz}@cs.cmu.edu

ABSTRACT
As ubiquitous computing becomes increasingly mobile and social, personal information sharing will likely increase in frequency, the variety of friends to share with, and range of information that can be shared. Past work has identified that whom you share with is important for choosing whether or not to share, but little work has explored which features of interpersonal relationships influence sharing. We present the results of a study of 42 participants, who self-report aspects of their relationships with 70 of their friends, including frequency of collocation and communication, closeness, and social group. Participants rated their willingness to share in 21 different scenarios based on information a UbiComp system could provide. Our findings show that (a) self-reported closeness is the strongest indicator of willingness to share, (b) individuals are more likely to share in scenarios with common information (e.g. we are within one mile of each other) than other kinds of scenarios (e.g. my location wherever I am), and (c) frequency of communication predicts both closeness and willingness to share better than frequency of collocation.

Author Keywords
Privacy, social networking, relationships, tie strength

ACM Classification Keywords
H5.m. Information interfaces and presentation (e.g., HCI): Miscellaneous.

General Terms
Design, Human Factors

INTRODUCTION
The increasing intersection between mobile and social computing provides many new ways for people to interact with one another. Evidence of this can be seen in the actions of the more than 250 million users who accessed Facebook from a mobile device as of April 2011 [18]. Mobile access allows users to share thoughts and images as they happen, as well as keep up on the minutiae of their friends' lives while out and about in the world.

UbiComp' 11, September 17-21, 2011, Beijing, China.

An ever-increasing number of mobile applications are making it easier for people to share their current location, activity, and other contextual information across many different social networking applications. Some of these applications share information automatically [27,35,41,42, 43]. For example, Google Latitude is a location-sharing service with over 10 million members [24], and allows people to continuously share their location with friends without requiring them to "check-in." This kind of automatic sharing removes the need for people to explicitly indicate they want to share a piece of private information with specific people in their social network.

These new modes for explicit, implicit, and automated sharing raise new concerns about privacy in terms of (i) accidental sharing of information [1,17], (ii) presentation of different versions of self to different social communities [3,4,22,36,39], and (iii) the ever increasing burden of configuring privacy and sharing policies across more and more applications and services [28,31]. These issues represent a growing problem as well as an opportunity area for ubiquitous computing. We posit that UbiComp products and services could help us manage information sharing if they had a model of the interpersonal relationships between different people, one that is better than the social graph we have today where everyone is simply a "friend."

Numerous researchers have identified the importance of interpersonal relationship in expressing sharing preferences [8,32,43]; however, little work has been done to understand which characteristics of interpersonal relationships most influence different kinds of sharing. Is a person's sex associated with the kinds of information they are willing to share? Does frequency of collocation or frequency of communication correlate with a preference for sharing location information or photos from family vacations? Understanding the most salient and predictive characteristics associated with sharing presents an opportunity for UbiComp: this knowledge enables UbiComp systems to aid in the management of privacy settings (and the converse, i.e. sharing policies).

Our work develops the role of UbiComp in understanding dimensions of interpersonal relationships, and further to use this as a method for managing personal information sharing. We conducted a study in which 42 participants provided details about their relationship with 70 friends and their willingness to share different kinds of information with each of those friends. We conducted a mixed-model analysis of variance based on this self-reported data to examine associations between relationship context and closeness, and willingness to share personal information.

Our results show that how close somebody feels to another person is a stronger predictor of a willingness to share than social group; that frequency of communication is a better predictor of closeness than frequency of collocation; and that people are more willing to share information when it is seen as an exchange of information between both people. In this paper we provide an overview of related work, details of our study design, our findings, and insights for the development of new UbiComp technologies to help automate or semi-automate configuration of privacy and sharing preferences.

RELATED WORK

Past Work in Privacy and Sharing

There has been extensive work examining sharing and social relationships. Belk's exhaustive review of many disciplines' literature on sharing helped him distinguish sharing as a distinct behavior from commodity-exchange and gift-giving as it does not result in compensation or thanks [2]. He draws out "demand sharing" as a behavior found in most families. For example, parents feed, cloth, and shelter their children with no expectation of compensation or thanks. In addition, Belk distinguishes two sharing motives. When "sharing-in" people share things with people they feel close to or desire to feel closer to, as a way of strengthening this relationship. "Sharing-out" involves interactions with people outside of close social boundaries and is generally more like gift-giving or commodity-exchange.

With respect to past work on privacy and sharing in UbiComp, one popular thread of work focuses on sharing one's location. A field study of the Locaccino location sharing application found 79% accuracy in user-specified rules for disclosing their own location [43]. However, this study also found that individual policies are likely to change over time and that these policies will require maintenance, echoing concerns about the potential pitfalls of static policies [39]. Work by Kelley *et al.* explored several friend-grouping interfaces as an instrument for creating privacy rules [29]. They found that different interfaces for producing friend lists affect both the strategies that users employ in creating groups as well as the makeup of the groups themselves. They also found that the groupings their participants created were inadequate for expressing privacy preferences, even just after creation time. Our work explores grouping as one of several features that may predict sharing. Our findings suggest that free-form grouping may not be the most effective method for expressing sharing preferences.

Several pieces of work have found that when sharing location or other contextual information, the person to be shared with is the most important factor in deciding whether or not to share [8,30,32], and in determining the detail/granularity of the information to be shared [33]. Olson *et al.* [37] conducted a study examining 40 different types of personal information and 19 general social "types" that people might share personal information with. In addition to finding that an individual's willingness to share depends on who they are sharing the information with, they clustered "friends" based on similarity of answers, revealing several distinct groups: family, co-workers, public (e.g. salesmen), and spouse. They also found clusters of information that are shared (or not shared); however, they could not succinctly label these categories.

Building on these findings, our work connects characteristics of social relationships with sharing preferences. In contrast with the studies above, we collect information about specific ongoing relationships the participant is a part of, and preferences for sharing information with the other party in that relationship. Most important is that our participants are rating specific individuals that they know, and that they provide explicit details about the nature of each relationship. See Table 1 for a list of the information we capture.

Past Work in Tie Strength

Tie strength is an area of strong interest for online social network (OSN) researchers. While there is still some discussion on the definition of tie strength, Granovetter proposed four dimensions: amount of time, intimacy, intensity, and reciprocal services [25].

Many studies have shown that the vast majority of interaction on social network sites is with small numbers of strong ties. For example, two recent studies suggest that the average number of friends on Facebook is around 180 [5,23], though many users have many more. However, most people on Facebook only interact regularly with 4 to 6 people [44]. A different study examined people who posted and tagged pictures of each other on Facebook, and found that on average people had 6.6 such "friends" [7].

Gilbert and Karahalios took seven dimensions of tie strength (the four proposed by Granovetter and three more) and predicted with 85% accuracy whether a tie between two people was strong or weak [21]. Note that this work only predicts a binary category (strong or weak tie) and has no prediction for role or group. Using a different approach, Xiang *et al.* [45] developed an unsupervised model that could predict a range of tie strengths based on activities on OSNs, though this was not empirically validated with users' perceptions. A different line of work looks at tie stability, analyzing mobile phone data of 2M people over a year [26]. De Choudhury *et al.* pose an interesting question regarding what exactly is a tie, showing that different definitions in an email corpus led to different kinds of results [12]. Our work captures a simplified version of tie strength expressed as closeness. We use closeness as a feature to predict sharing preference and discuss it as an attribute UbiComp systems could sense. Because of the scope of data we collect, our work allows us to examine closeness in relation to different properties than the work described above.

In summary, rather than investigating new ways of measuring or inferring tie strength, we examined the influence of tie strength on location and activity sharing preferences. We also demonstrate that using a single self-reported measure of closeness as a proxy for tie strength can be effective in predicting sharing preferences.

Friend Grouping, Affiliation, and Social Structure

In his seminal work on impression management, Goffman proposed that people perform different roles in order to manage their presentation of self to different groups [22]. More recent work has explored challenges for managing online self presentation. Binder, Howes, and Sutcliffe found that diversity of an individual's Facebook network predicts online tension, and that this tension is between social spheres (such as "work" and "college friends"), not within them [3]. Spencer and Pahl examine individual social structure in detail, exploring differences between "given" and "chosen" relationships and descriptive characteristics of individual personal networks [40].

Farnham and Churchill describe the situation of having conflicting social spheres as "faceted identity" and found through a survey of 631 respondents that faceted identity is common, that these facets are in some cases incompatible, and that one approach for managing some of these facets is to use different media to communicate with different facets [20]. A subsequent qualitative study identified three main facets, or life modes: family, work, and social. This work proposes dealing with these modes online with the concept of focused sharing, where individuals can select subsets of their social network to share with [38]. They also emphasized the ubiquity of smartphones as an important tool for managing relationships and connectedness in social media. We used these same three main facets in our analysis. Our work also extends this past work by exploring faceted identity as one of the factors that can influence sharing of personal information, in the form of different social groups.

There has also been past work looking at automatically clustering groups of online friends based on interactions on OSNs. Past work found manually organizing one's friends into groups to be a high burden [28]. Some proposed solutions include automatically inferring the social context of information on OSNs using a person's social structure [11], privacy wizards that use active learning for configuring privacy policies on OSNs [19], and network clustering algorithms for organizing people into groups [28]. By capturing explicit friend groupings in addition to a variety of other information, we can characterize individual groups and compare the utility of grouping to other features.

Researchers have begun using sensors to infer information about people and their social networks, using audio data [6] and collocation data [10]. Eagle *et al*, studied and modeled human social structure using data from mobile phones [14,15,16]. They collected data on call logs, Bluetooth devices in proximity, cell tower IDs, application usage, and phone status, and compared this data to self-reports. They found that self-reports of physical proximity were heavily dependent on recency and salience of the interactions, and thus did not always match mobile phone data. They were also able to infer 95% of friendships based on call records and proximity.

Our work explores the value of developing a more enhanced social graph that includes notions of groups and roles. We do this using individual self-reports as ground truth. This approach, contrasted with those above, has two main benefits. First, we can make observations that describe a more complete relationship between individuals instead of their relationships within the context of a specific service. Second, this approach does not require the participation of friends whose relationships are being described, thereby mitigating concerns about adoption, ecological validity, and critical mass. Our work looks broadly at the members of our participants' perceived personal network and at an aggregate picture of each relationship, as opposed to one fragmented by technology.

STUDY ON FEATURES OF RELATIONSHIPS AND SHARING PREFERENCES

The goal of this study was to reveal salient features of interpersonal relationships that predict willingness to share information relevant to UbiComp applications, such as location, proximity to another person, and activity. Specifically, we wanted to understand the association between factors such as collocation frequency, communication frequency, closeness, and social group, with preferences for sharing specific kinds of information. We conducted an online study where participants provided basic demographic information and a list of friends. They then associated each friend with relevant social groups, rated their perception of closeness with each friend (tie strength), and stated a willingness to share information with each individual for 21 different sharing scenarios.

Participants

We recruited participants by posting ads in several nationwide online bulletin boards and through two study recruiting websites. Prospective participants were selected based on several criteria:

Age (20 - 50): We wanted people in different life stages, especially with respect to either having or being a child within an immediate family.

Occupation (non-student): We chose to exclude students because they do not easily allow distinctions between work and school groups.

Social network membership (members of Facebook with at least 50 Facebook friends): This was a source for generating friends' names for the study. Additionally, membership in a social networking site indicates that participants are more likely to want to share information about themselves with people they know, allowing us to observe differences in their sharing preferences (as opposed to a person who does not want to share at all).

Mobile device usage (must have a smartphone): We felt that participants with smartphones were more likely to understand the potential values and risks of our UbiComp scenarios.

Participants were compensated $20 for completing task 1, and $60 for completing tasks 2 and 3 (see below). The data collection took place online and participants were given two weeks to complete all parts of the study.

Method

We engaged participants in three distinct activities:

1. Generating a lists of friends
2. Describing each friend in terms of closeness and affiliation with different groups
3. Stating willingness to share different kinds of information with each friend

Friends Lists

We wanted to ensure that participants would answer questions about friends who varied in social group and in closeness, so we asked participants to provide two lists. The first was a list of people based on several categories, which we derived based on qualitative work on relationships [34,40]. The groups were:

- people you currently live with (5 people maximum)
- immediate family members (5)
- extended family members (10)
- people you work with (10)
- people you are close to (10)
- people you do hobbies or activities with (10).

We instructed participants to avoid duplicates. The second list was a list of all of their Facebook friends. We provided participants with instructions on how to download this information from Facebook.

We included everyone from the first list (typically less than 40). We then randomly sampled from their Facebook friend list to reach 70 total friend names, excluding duplicates and names that the participant did not recognize. From here on we will refer to this list of 70 names as the "friend list."

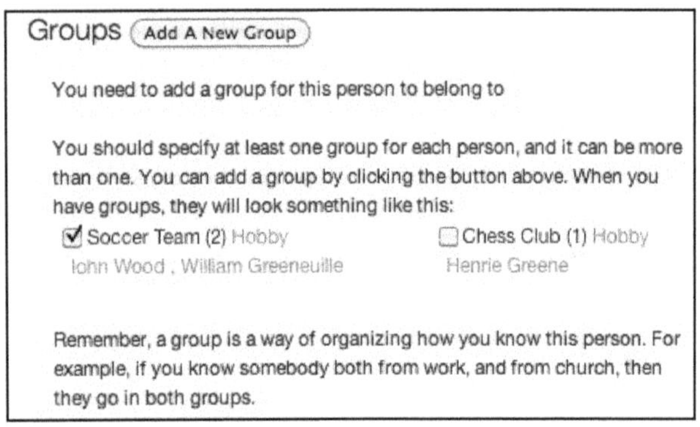

Figure 1: The grouping instructions a participant saw before they had created any groups.

	Data collected	Data type
Observable features	Friend sex	Male/Female
	Friend age	Rounded to nearest year
	Years known	
	Frequency seen	Likert 0-7: Less than yearly (0), yearly, yearly-monthly, monthly, monthly-weekly, weekly, weekly-daily, daily (7)
	Frequency communicated with electronically	
Non-Observable	Closeness (strength of tie)	Likert 1-5: very distant (1), distant, neither distant nor close, close, very close (5)
	Group	Participant-dependent, however each group was put in a pre-specified category

Table 1: Data collected for each friend. Data in the top half ("observable features") is data that we felt was potentially observable by a UbiComp system or social networking site. Data on the bottom half would either be inferred from the observable features or manually inputted by the user

Describing each relationship

We next asked participants to provide information about their relationship with each person on their friend list. The complete list of data collected per friend is in Table 1. We organized this information into two categories: data that we felt would be easily observable from within a UbiComp system or social networking site, and data that would require more work either to infer from observable features or for the user to express manually. Although there are several scales for quantifying tie strength, we opted for a simple measure, asking "How close do you feel to this person?" on a 1-5 Likert scale. This approach is similar to the one taken in work by McCarty [34]. In this paper we refer to this measure as "closeness."

Next, participants detailed their shared affiliations with each friend by placing them into groups that they specified to represent those affiliations. Our interface (see Figure 1) allowed participants to create groups. In addition, it required them to classify each group into one of 12 pre-determined categories: neighborhood, religious, immediate family, extended family, family friend, know through somebody else, work, school, hobby, significant other, trip/travel group, and other. We developed these categories based on a combination of literature sources [34] and data from previous work on grouping friends in social network sites [29]. We instructed participants to indicate at least one group affiliation for each friend, and we encouraged them to indicate multiple group affiliations when relevant. For example, if a person and their friend went to college together, and they both attend or attended the same church, the participant would place them in two groups. The result is a set of affiliations, and all of the people on the friend list who are associated with each affiliation.

n=2370	Mean (SD)	Sharing M=2.83(0.66)							closeness
friend sex = female	55.5%					0.01	0.01	0.01	0.01
friend age	32.7 (12.3)					-0.01***	-0.004***	-0.005***	-0.01***
frequency seen	1.8 (2.2)					0.06***	-0.03	-0.03*	0.21***
frequency comm	2.5 (2.4)					0.17***	0.03**	0.04***	0.34***
years known	10.5 (9.8)					0.03***	0.02	0.01**	0.03***
user age × person age						-0.0004	-0.0004*	-0.0002	0.0001
user sex = female × friend sex = female						0.02	0.01	0.02	0.02
freq seen × freq comm						-0.02***	0.004	0.003	-0.05***
user age × years known						-0.0007**	-0.0004	0.00005	-0.001**
friend closeness	2.7 (1.4)		0.45***		0.40***		0.41***	0.37***	
is family	23.2%			0.59***	0.24***			0.22***	
is social	66.9%			0.14***	0.03			0.03	
is work	18.0%			0.18***	-0.02			-0.001	
Intercept		2.86***	1.62***	3.25***	1.89***	2.33***	1.66***	1.99***	1.61***
R^2 (variance explained)		0.36	0.63	0.48	0.65	0.57	0.65	0.66	0.70
Model Name		User	Close	Mode	Non-Obs	Obs	Obs+close	All	

Table 2: Linear regression models predicting sharing and closeness (last column only), controlling for each participant. Each column is a different model and data in the table are non-standardized β coefficients, except for R^2 in the last row, which can be compared across models to demonstrate the variance explained. For example, the "close" model (fourth column) includes one effect, friend closeness, and this model accounts for 63% of the variance in sharing preferences. Gray cells indicate effects that were not included for that particular model. The data indicate both that closeness is the best predictor of sharing, and that observable features can predict closeness. Significance: *p<0.05; **p<0.01; ***p<0.001

Sharing scenarios

Next, we asked participants to indicate their willingness to share information with each friend in the context of 21 different information-sharing scenarios (see Table 3).

We developed these scenarios using a brainstorming process followed by a broad survey on scenario similarity. First, we brainstormed over 100 different UbiComp scenarios in which individuals could share information, such as location, activity, calendar, history, photos, etc. We grouped scenarios into 11 categories based on the type of information being shared. We assembled these scenarios in a survey that we posted on Amazon's Mechanical Turk, where we asked two questions for each scenario:

- how often do you currently share this information now (whether with one person or with many people): never, seldom, sometimes, frequently, constantly
- how useful is it to you to share this information with somebody you know, answering for maximum usefulness: totally useless, somewhat useless, neither useless nor useful, somewhat useful, totally useful

Using the results from this survey as a guide, we reduced the list of 100 scenarios down to 21 specific scenarios. The resulting list fit into five different categories: current personal location (7), personal location history (5), calendar and location plans (7), communication activity (1), and social graph information (1). See Table 3 for a list of the final set of scenarios used.

For each of the 21 scenarios, we asked participants to indicate their willingness to share information with each of their 70 friends using a 5-point Likert scale (labels: 1-definitely not, 3-no preference, 5-definitely). We adapted this method based on past work by Olson *et al.* [37].

FINDINGS

Forty-two participants completed our study. Their occupations ranged from education and engineering to administration and legal. We eliminated three problematic respondents who each demonstrated no variance for more than 65 out of the 70 friends; each individual friend had the same rating for each of the sharing scenarios. These participants seemed to have simply rated the sharing scenarios as quickly as possible. Of our remaining 39 participants, there were 28 female and 11 male, with ages ranging from 21 to 49 (M=29.8, SD=6.4).

Willingness to Share Location and Activity Information

We were first interested in whether the relationship characteristics that we captured were associated with a willingness to share. Participants were distributed in their mean sharing answer, representing a range of individual privacy/sharing preferences (M = 2.83 out of 5 where 5 is "definitely willing to share this information with this person", SD = 0.66). To address this question we conducted a mixed-model analysis of variance predicting sharing as the outcome variable (see Table 2, note that the variables user age and user sex refers to our study participants). We chose this analysis to account for the non-independence of observations within each participant. This analysis allowed us to explain and compare the variation in sharing using different combinations of independent variables. The goal in doing this analysis was to identify which characteristics of a relationship were most effective for predicting sharing.

All following regressions were done on a per-friend level of analysis; for these models, we took the mean sharing value across all scenarios for each friend (n=2730) and used features that described each relationship as effects in the models. We included the participant in the model as a random effect to account for non-independence of ratings within each participant. The first column shows means and standard deviations for all continuous effects in the model, and percentages of women for the sex data type.

The next column (model name = user) is a model that has no effects except for the effect of the participant (which accounts for individual differences). The result shows that certainly some amount of the variance relates to individual differences, likely preferences for sharing in general (R^2 = 0.36). We also examined models for participant-level effects of sex and age, but the models performed poorly.

Non-Observable Features

The next three columns are models with effects that only include the non-observable data. For these analyses, we pooled together group categories into the three descriptive "life modes" identified by Ozenc and Farnham, (family, work, and social) [38], which they suggest are the primary areas of a person's life.

Closeness by itself turns out to be a very strong predictor of sharing preferences (model name = close, R^2 = 0.63) with each 1-point gain in closeness accounting for a 10% increase of the sharing outcome. This means that a friend who is at closeness 5 (top closeness) is 50% more likely to be shared with. The regression that only had life modes as a predictor did not account for as much of the variance as closeness alone did (model name = mode, R^2 = 0.48), with membership in family, work, and social modes accounting for a 12%, 3%, and 3% increase in likelihood to share respectively (note that all friends were categorized into at least one of these modes). This means that just knowing that somebody is in one of these categories is not particularly helpful in expressing sharing preferences. Finally, adding groups to closeness resulted in only a slight increase in performance over just closeness (model name = non obs, R^2 = 0.65), and resulted in a loss of significance for the "not social" and "not work" effects: closeness and family were all that mattered in this model.

Observable Features

Next, we wanted to explore how well the different observable features (see Table 1) of the relationship predicted sharing, including friend age, sex, years known, frequency seen, and frequency communicated with. Again, we call these observable because we felt that UbiComp systems could capture these features by gathering them from existing social network data, or capturing them automatically using sensor and communication logs. As such, by testing these features, we can evaluate how well a fully automated system might perform for predicting sharing preferences. This model performed well (model name = obs, R^2= 0.57), though still not as well as the model with just closeness. Significant effects included friend age (0.2% less likely to share per year), frequency seen (1.4% more likely to share per point increase), frequency communicated with (3.6% more likely to share per point increase), years known (0.6% increase per year known). The only feature that was not predictive was friend sex.

We included four interactions in the model as well. First, we included the interaction between participant and friend sex and the interaction between participant and friend age to see if homophily accounted for sharing preferences (are men more likely to share with men or women with women, and are people more likely to share with people who are closer in age?), but neither of these were significant.

The next interaction we included was between years known and participant age, which we included because we hypothesized that the duration of a person's life that they have know another person might be a useful indicator. This did have a very small effect, indicating that younger participants were more greatly influenced by how long this person had known them.

Finally, we included an interaction between frequency seen and frequency communicated with. We hypothesized that there are people that are important to us who we communicate with much more often than we see (e.g. family who do not live nearby); similarly, that there are people who are less important to us that we see often but do not exchange as much communication (coworkers who you see often, but with whom you otherwise do not communicate). This interaction was also significant, revealing that communication is a stronger indicator of willingness to share when collocation is less frequent.

Observables and Non-Observables

Next, we wanted to look at models that include observables and non-observables. First we looked at the same model as the previous one but with the addition of closeness. This model improves the explained variance (model name = obs+close, R^2= 0.65). Closeness has nearly the same effect as in the closeness only model, with each point in closeness increasing the likelihood to share by 8.8%. Frequency seen is no longer significant in this model, neither is the interaction between frequency seen and frequency communicated with. Additionally, frequency communicated with has less of an effect in the model (0.8% more likely to share per point increase, down from 3.6%).

Finally, we included all effects in the model. There was no difference in the variance in sharing behavior (R^2= 0.66), and the model behaved nearly identical to the previous model. As a check, we did run a model with all 12 group categories instead of being grouped into the 3 life modes, and the model did not differ (R^2= 0.67).

Overall, the models with closeness did better than any of the models without closeness, and adding closeness results in the loss of significance for other effects in the model.

Predicting Closeness using Observables

With closeness being such a predictive feature, we wanted to examine how well the observable features of each relationship explain closeness. We used the same approach as before of a mixed-model analysis of variance controlling for participant as a random effect, but this time with closeness as the outcome. We included all observable effects from the other models. This model was quite

Scenario	Pearson's r with closeness	Mean Sharing	Std Dev	Tukey-Kramer HSD			
The next calendar event that we have in common	0.39	3.45	1.42	A			
All calendar events that we have in common	0.39	3.40	1.42	A			
I am with a person who we both know	0.43	3.36	1.39	A			
I'm within 1 mile of this person	0.49	3.26	1.46		B	C	
Details of who my family connections/family relationships are	0.46	3.17	1.39		B	C	D
My personal travel plans that mean we will be in the same place	0.43	3.17	1.54			C	D
My location when I am closer to this person than we normally are	0.35	3.06	1.60			C	D
Everywhere I have travelled to	0.47	3.02	1.36	E			D
My location when I am on vacation	0.53	3.02	1.38	E	F		
I've been to the place that this person currently is	0.42	2.94	1.43	E	F		
My work travel plans that mean we will be in the same place	0.36	2.94	1.62		F	G	
All places that I've been to that this person has also been to	0.42	2.92	1.42		F	G	H
My location when this person has been here before	0.41	2.84	1.37	I		G	H
Everywhere that I have gone out to eat	0.38	2.80	1.34	I			H
I'm at home during a normal weekend	0.50	2.71	1.31	I			
When I am usually at work	0.40	2.45	1.29		J		
My location wherever I am	0.39	2.39	1.34		J		
My tentative plan for the day	0.36	2.23	1.24			K	
I'm in a call on my cell phone	0.25	2.19	1.30			K	L
When the next thing on my calendar starts	0.33	2.10	1.18				L
All details of the next event on my personal calendar	0.33	1.93	1.19	M			

Table 3: Summary of data for each sharing scenario, sorted by overall mean sharing. The first column reports the correlation with closeness, and all correlation coefficients are significant to p<.001. The Tukey-Kramer test compares the overall means for sharing in each scenario: scenarios that have the same letter are not significantly different from each other.

effective (R^2 = 0.70, last column of Table 2). Significant effects in this model included: friend age (0.2% less close per year), frequency seen (4.2% closer per point increase), frequency communicated with (6.8% closer per point increase), years known (0.6% closer per year). The interaction between frequency seen and frequency communicated was also significant, showing that communication has a much stronger effect when collocation is infrequent. The interaction between participant age and years known was significant with a

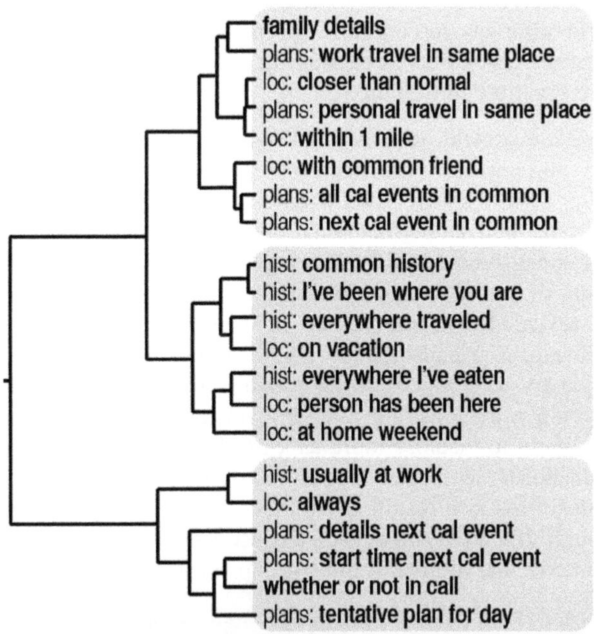

Figure 2: Hierarchical clustering using average linkage distance. Horizontal position of the branches is directly proportional to the calculated distance between each cluster. Scenarios are shorthand for the same ones in Table 3.

small effect as before. Friend sex and the interactions of participant and friend age and participant and friend sex were not significant.

Sharing Across Different Scenarios

The finding that closeness was such a strong predictor for sharing across all scenarios led us to further investigate how closeness related to the different scenarios. That is, is closeness a strong predictor for certain scenarios only, or for all scenarios? Our analysis indicates that closeness is correlated with sharing for all scenarios with Pearson's correlation values ranging from $r=0.25$ to $r=0.53$, all $p<0.001$ (see Table 3 for all values).

By asking about sharing across 21 different scenarios, we were able to investigate differences in sharing as a function of scenario type. All scenarios were significantly and positively correlated with each other ($r=0.40$ to 0.96, Cronbach's $\alpha = 0.97$).

We examined these similarities further by performing a hierarchical cluster analysis using the average linkage distance formula, a standard technique for examining groupings among items which Olson *et al.* also used in their analysis of privacy and sharing [37]. We chose to use mean sharing per level of closeness as the input because of the strength of closeness in explaining the variance of sharing responses. The dendrogram in Figure 2 shows the clusters. The horizontal scale for the dendrogram is linearly related to the cluster distance at each point where a pair of clusters was merged. For example, in the middle of the dendrogram "hist:common hist" and "hist:I've been where you are" were more closely clustered than the next two "hist:everywhere traveled" and "loc:on vacation", which you can tell by the fact that the first cluster is formed closer to the right side than the second one. Note that the scenarios are shorthand for the same scenarios in Table 3.

These clusters demonstrate an interesting grouping. If we consider the scenarios split into three clusters, the clusters can be roughly labeled as scenarios based on sharing using information about something that we have in common (see Figure 2 top, e.g. loc:within 1 mile); location-history-related scenarios (see Figure 2 middle, e.g. hist:everywhere traveled); and scenarios that reveal sensitive information (see Figure 2 bottom, e.g. loc:always).

To ensure that the means were in fact significantly different, we performed a Tukey-Kramer HSD across all of the means (see Table 3, there was no significant difference across scenarios that are connected by the same letter). This revealed 13 groups (some of which overlap) of scenarios with no mean difference. From the table, we can see that the seven highest-mean sharing scenarios all involve sharing personal information that has something in common with the friend's information, for example shared calendar events or location proximity with the friend.

DISCUSSION

Closeness for expressing sharing preferences

A main focus of our work was to understand which of the collected features are most useful for predicting individual sharing preferences. Our results show that our simple 1-5 Likert scale for closeness was clearly the most useful feature for predicting sharing, outperforming grouping and all other models that do not include closeness.

An examination of the literature indicates that there has been much emphasis on privacy controls that focus on grouping [11,19,28]. In addition, commercial OSNs all seem to either provide grouping controls (e.g. Facebook and LinkedIn), or else require users to specify sharing preferences on a per-friend basis (e.g. Google Latitude's "send my location" feature). We also cannot find a single example of a system (location-based or otherwise) that lets users express closeness for their friends. Not asking about closeness may be a missed opportunity as it is a simple question to ask and is quite predictive of sharing. While it is true that a grouping paradigm does not prevent individuals from constructing groups based on closeness, on the surface it seems easier for users to simply express closeness.

An advantage of using closeness to aid privacy controls is that expressing closeness also expresses a sense of order. That is to say, with group-based privacy controls there is no natural ordering between groups; they are nominal. The ordinal nature of closeness can be useful for expressing privacy controls, as users could simply express "don't share with anybody below medium closeness" (closeness = 3). We could also imagine tiered rules, like "closest friends (5) can always see my location, medium-close friends (3 and 4) can only check up to twice a day, nobody else (1 and 2) can see it without requesting."

To be clear, we are not making the argument that friend grouping is not useful and that researchers and system designers should abandon their focus on this structure. We can imagine systems and types of information that could benefit from an accurate description of groups. In addition, there are many sharing scenarios that we did not ask about in this study (e.g. pictures, status updates, etc), and we did not ask participants about sharing a specific piece of information that might have a more singular group focus. Instead we had them rate classes of information to share. Nevertheless, we do argue that systems would benefit in allowing users to express closeness.

Given our results, it seems that researchers and system designers might find it valuable to investigate automated or semi-automated approaches to inferring closeness.

Sharing scenarios and information "in common"

The scenarios that triggered the highest overall willingness to share all involve an exchange of information that the user and their friend have in common, referred to here as "in-common information." For example, in the 3rd highest ranked scenario (I am with a person who we both know), and the 4th highest (I'm within 1 mile of this person), the sharing scenarios are dependent on the in-common information: we both know this person in the former case and we're within 1 mile of each other in the latter. Compare this to "My location wherever I am," for example, where the sharing is not dependent on in-common information.

First, consider the differences between the clusters in the three-cluster set in Figure 2. The top cluster is mostly focused on in-common information that addresses current or future information (plans). The middle cluster deals mostly with scenarios that have in-common information and a location history component, or scenarios that do not involve in-common information. The bottom cluster does not involve any in-common information, and the scenarios represent less constrained sharing, or scenarios that reveal more sensitive information.

There are several reasons that might explain why scenarios with in-common information resulted in an increased willingness to share. First, people share in order to initiate, maintain, and strengthen relationships with others within their social boundary [2]. Sharing in our scenarios is also a means of self-disclosure, and past work on self-disclosure has revealed the importance of symmetry or equity of disclosure in friendships [9]. These studies have shown that people try to compensate for inequity in sharing practices: if person A demonstrates higher levels of disclosure, person B is likely to disclose more as a result. Similarly, if person A discloses less than person B, person B is likely to disclose less as a result. If we look at the sharing scenarios through this equity-in-self-disclosure lens, perhaps it is the symmetry that motivates the willingness to share.

Another explanation is that people want to maintain privacy (control of their self-disclosures) [13], and that there is some aspect of in-common information that is useful for this purpose. Possible explanations are:

- **utility:** people are more willing to share common information because the information is more useful
- **frequency:** people are more willing to share in these situations because they were less likely to occur
- **no new information:** people are more likely to share in these situations because they are revealing information that the friend might already know

Though these factors are by no means mutually exclusive, it would be valuable to understand which qualities (these or others) make sharing in-common information a more attractive paradigm than sharing other kinds of information. This presents a significant opportunity for future work.

The immediate implication is that there are important considerations for the design of sharing control mechanisms: choosing to support sharing controls that specify in-common information may encourage sharing.

This finding also motivates further work to develop secure and reliable methods for detecting in-common information and only revealing the information (and the associated identities) when particular information does in fact overlap.

Collocation and Communication Frequency

While collocation is clearly a type of in-common information, it did not predict sharing or closeness nearly as well as frequency of communication. This finding seems to support work by Cranshaw *et al.,* which reported that collocation alone was not a useful feature in predicting friendship between two individuals [10]. They found that other features of the collocation history, such as the entropy of a location, significantly improved predictions. Our finding also suggests further work is necessary to determine what features of collocation and communication correspond to features of relationship and to sharing preferences.

One possible explanation for why communication frequency outperforms collocation is that people cannot always choose whom they are near. People are frequently near people that they know, be it coworkers, commuters, acquaintances, or classmates, all of whom they may not feel close to. On the other hand, frequency of communication seems to support more control, especially for the initiator of the communication. Again, there may be communication with work colleagues or others with whom a person is not close. We believe it may be possible for UbiComp systems to differentiate these kinds of communication, for example based on time of day or location, to add richer structure in inferring the nature of the communication, and ultimately the nature of the relationship and closeness.

Limitations

It is important to acknowledge that this data is entirely self-reported, and that further work is required to demonstrate the real-world application of these findings. By conducting the study online and anonymously, we expect that experimenter effects were minimized. Furthermore, individuals are the ground truth on measures such as felt closeness. However, some of the answers may have been idealized responses (e.g. people they call less frequently than reported), or participants may have been unable to answer (e.g. cannot answer for all places I've been to).

CONCLUSION

Social conventions around sharing are being strongly affected by the proliferation of mobile UbiComp technologies, in terms of what information can be shared, how we share it, and how we consume it. With this, the burden of managing one's sharing behavior with the variety of social relationships that one maintains is greater than before, and the systems that we design have the ability to either improve this, or to exacerbate the situation.

This work is a step towards improving that situation. In our study, we found that of all of the data we collected describing 2730 social relationships, self-reported closeness was the best indicator of whether or not to share a piece of information, and common information is more likely to be shared. Also, frequency of communication performs better than frequency of collocation in predicting whether or not to share and in predicting closeness. These results have implications for the design of systems to improve the experience of sharing, and show promise that systems could automatically or semi-automatically predict useful defaults for individual sharing preferences. By automating the process of expressing sharing preferences, we can reduce the burden that systems impose on users and increase the utility of these systems, empowering the user to share information with those whom they would like to share, and otherwise to maintain their privacy.

ACKNOWLEDGMENTS

This work was supported in part by a Yahoo Key Scientific Challenge Award, Google, The Alfred P. Sloan Foundation, and NSF DGE-0903659. The authors wish to thank Ian Li and Rebecca Balebako for their assistance in this work.

REFERENCES

1. Adams, P. The Real Life Social Network. *Voices that Matter Web Design Conference*, 2010. http://www.slideshare.net/padday/the-real-life-social-network-v2.
2. Belk, R. Sharing. *Journal of Consumer Research 36*, 5 (2010), 715-734.
3. Binder, J., Howes, A., and Sutcliffe, A. The problem of conflicting social spheres: effects of network structure on experienced tension in social network sites. *In Proc. CHI '09*, (2009), 965-974.
4. boyd, d.m. and Ellison, N.B. Social Network Sites: Definition, History, and Scholarship. *JCMC 13*, 1 (2008)
5. Burke, M., Marlow, C., and Lento, T. Social network activity and social well-being. *In Proc CHI '10* (2010)
6. Choudhury, T. and Basu, S. Modeling conversational dynamics as a mixed-memory markov process. *In Proc. NIPS '04*, (2004).
7. Christakis, N.A. and Fowler, J.H. *Connected: The Surprising Power of Our Social Networks and How They Shape Our Lives*. 2009.

8. Consolvo, S., Smith, I.E., Matthews, T., LaMarca, A., Tabert, J., and Powledge, P. Location Disclosure to Social Relations: Why, When, & What People Want to Share. *In Proc. CHI '05*
9. Cozby, P., Self-disclosure: A literature review. Psychological Bulletin, Vol 79(2), Feb 1973, 73-91
10. Cranshaw, J., Toch, E., and Hong, J. Bridging the Gap Between Physical Location and Online Social Networks. *In Proc. Ubicomp '10*
11. Danezis, G. Inferring Privacy Policies for Social Networking Services. *In Proc. AISec '09*
12. De Choudhury, M., Mason, W.A., Hofman, J.M., and Watts, D.J. Inferring relevant social networks from interpersonal communication. *Proc. WWW '10*, 2010
13. Derlega, V.J. and Chaikin, A.L. Privacy and Self-Disclosure in Social Relationships. *Journal of Social Issues 33*, 3 (1977), 102-115.
14. Eagle, N., Pentland, A., and Lazer, D. Inferring Social Network Structure using Mobile Phone Data. *The National Academy of Sciences (PNAS) 106*, 36 (2009), 15274-15278.
15. Eagle, N. and Pentland, A. Eigenbehaviors: Identifying Structure in Routine. *Behavioral Ecology and Sociobiology 63*, 7 (2009), 1057-1066.
16. Eagle, N. Mobile Phones as Social Sensors. *The Handbook of Emergent Technologies in Social Research*, (2010).
17. Elgan, M. The five stages of Facebook grief. *Computerworld*, 2010. http://www.computerworld.com/s/article/9179258/The_five_stages_of_Facebook_grief.
18. Facebook. Statistics. http://www.facebook.com/press/info.php?statistics.
19. Fang, L. and LeFevre, K. Privacy wizards for social networking sites. *In Proc. WWW '10*
20. Farnham, S.D. and Churchill, E.F. *Faceted identity, faceted lives. In Proc. CSCW '11*
21. Gilbert, E. and Karahalios, K. Predicting tie strength with social media. *In Proc. CHI '09*
22. Goffman, E. *The Presentation of Self in Everyday Life*. Doubleday, 1959.
23. Golder, S.A., Wilkinson, D., and Huberman, B.A. Rhythms of Social Interaction: Messaging within a Massive Online Network. *In Proc. C&T '07*
24. Google. Check in with Google Latitude. http://googlemobile.blogspot.com/2011/02/check-in-with-google-latitude.html.
25. Granovetter, M. The Strength of Weak Ties: A Network Theory Revisited. *Sociological Theory 1*, (1983), 201-233.
26. Hidalgo, C.A. and Rodriguez-Sickert, C. The dynamics of a mobile phone network. *Physica A: Statistical Mechanics and its Applications 387*, 2008
27. Hsieh, G., Tang, K.P., and Hong, J.I. The Design and Evaluation of Privacy Controls and Feedback Mechanisms for Contextual Instant Messaging. (2007)
28. Jones, S. and O'Neill, E. Feasibility of Structural Network Clustering for Group-Based Privacy Control in Social Networks. *In Proc. SOUPS '10*
29. Kelley, P.G., Brewer, R., Mayer, Y., Cranor, L.F., Sadeh, N. An Investigation into Facebook Friend Grouping. *In Proc. INTERACT '11.*
30. Khalil, A. and Connelly, K. Context-aware telephony: privacy preferences & sharing patterns. *Proc. CHI '06*
31. Lampinen, A., Tamminen, S., and Oulasvirta, A. All My People Right Here, Right Now: management of group co-presence on a social networking site. *In Proc. CSCW '09*
32. Lederer, S., Mankoff, J.C., and Dey, A.K. Who Wants to Know What When? *In Proc. CHI '03*
33. Lin, J., Xiang, G., Hong, J.I., and Sadeh, N. Modeling People's Place Naming Preferences in Location Sharing. *In Proc. Ubicomp '10*
34. McCarty, C. Structure in Personal Networks. *Journal of Social Structure 3*, (2005).
35. Miluzzo, E., Lane, N.D., Fodor, K., et al. Sensing Meets Mobile Social Networks: The Design, Implementation and Evaluation of the CenceMe Application. *In Proc. SenSys '08*
36. Odom, W., Zimmerman, J., and Forlizzi, J. Teenagers and Their Virtual Possessions: Design Opportunities and Issues. *In Proc. CHI '11*
37. Olson, J., Grudin, J., and Horvitz, E. A study of preferences for sharing and privacy. *In Proc. CHI '05*
38. Ozenc, F.K. and Farnham, S.D. Life " Modes " in Social Media. *In Proc. of CHI '11*
39. Palen, L. and Dourish, P. Unpacking "Privacy" for a Networked World. *CHI Letters 5*, 1 (2003), 129-136.
40. Spencer, L. and Pahl, R.E. *Rethinking friendship: hidden solidarities today*. Princeton University Press, 2006.
41. Tang, J.C., Yankelovich, N., Begole, J., Kleek, M.V., Li, F., and Bhalodia, J. ConNexus to awarenex: extending awareness to mobile users. *In Proc.CHI '01*
42. Tang, K.P., Keyani, P., Fogarty, J., and Hong, J.I. Putting people in their place: an anonymous and privacy-sensitive approach to collecting sensed data in location-based applications. *In Proc. CHI '06*
43. Tsai, J., Kelley, P., Drielsma, P.H., Cranor, L.F., Hong, J., and Sadeh, N. Who's viewed you? the impact of feedback in a mobile-location system. *In Proc. CHI '09*
44. Wilson, C., Boe, B., Sala, A., Puttaswamy, K.P.N., and Zhao, B.Y. User interactions in social networks and their implications. *In Proc. EuroSys 09.*
45. Xiang, R., Neville, J., and Rogati, M. Modeling relationship strength in online social networks. *In Proc. WWW '10*

Understanding How Visual Representations of Location Feeds Affect End-User Privacy Concerns

Karen P. Tang
Department of Informatics
University of California, Irvine
kptang@ics.uci.edu

Jason I. Hong, Daniel P. Siewiorek
Human-Computer Interaction Institute
Carnegie Mellon University
{jasonh, dps}@cs.cmu.edu

ABSTRACT
While past work has looked extensively at how to design privacy configuration UIs for sharing *current* location, there has not yet been work done to examine how visual representations of *historical* locations can influence end-user privacy. We present results for a study examining three visualization types (text-, map-, and time-based) for social sharing of past locations. Our results reveal that there are important design implications for location sharing applications, as certain visual elements led to more privacy concerns and inaccurate perceptions of privacy control.

Author Keywords
location, visualization, privacy concerns, location sharing.

ACM Classification Keywords
H5.m. Information interfaces and presentation (e.g., HCI): Miscellaneous.

General Terms
Design, Human Factors.

INTRODUCTION
The breadth of location-based services (LBSs) continues to grow and is aided by rapid advances in location sensing technology that is embedded in nearly every mobile phone today. LBSs are no longer just for navigational assistance or localized search results. Recently, LBSs have shifted away from simply *consuming* location to *sharing* locations; we refer to these LBSs as location-sharing applications (LSAs).

Many LSAs today operate by sharing the user's current location with those in her social network. To visually represent locations, these LSAs usually opt for a *map*-based visualization (e.g., Loopt, Google Latitude) or a *text*-based representation (e.g., Twitter). However, a growing number of LSAs also support sharing of location *feeds*, a historical list of a user's past locations. Figure 1 (a, c) shows examples of these feed-based LSAs, which all support *text*-based representations of location information.

The disadvantage of a text-based location feed is that it can be much more difficult to *extract* certain location properties, such as a place's spatial orientation. But the tradeoff with making these properties more salient is that information becomes more accessible to others, which introduces new privacy risks for end-users. This dilemma is similar to the privacy reaction that Facebook faced when it introduced its newsfeed feature. The newsfeed made it much easier to read through people's profile information, but the increased exposure led users desire for better privacy controls [11]. Thus, when proposing new visualizations for location feeds, it is important for visualizations to balance end-user privacy needs with the social and functional utility needed to support LSAs.

To better understand how visualizing location feeds can impact users' perceived privacy concerns, we interviewed 12 participants as part of a two-week long GPS logging study. There has already been much work done on location privacy, including work on computational location privacy [3], as well as work on designing usable privacy configuration interfaces for location sharing [7, 13, 18]. However, to date, there has not been any work done to explore users' privacy preferences and attitudes towards location *visualizations*. To address this issue, we collected actual location traces from our participants and conducted a within-subject comparison of three types of visualizations. Our study examines the following research questions:

- **Sharing Location Feeds**. Are participants willing to share their actual location feeds with others? Does this willingness change depending on what visualizations are used to present the location information to others?
- **Automated Generation of Location Visualizations**. We examine the practicality of automating visualizations for LSAs. We specifically look at the process for creating location labels using existing database sources.
- **Privacy Sensitivities towards Location Visualizations**. What makes a particular visualization more privacy invasive than another? Which visual elements, if any, lead to more privacy concerns from end-users?
- **Privacy Reasoning towards Sharing Visualizations.** How do users reason about the privacy-preserving properties of one visualization over another? Are users well-informed in their visualization choices?

We found that many of our participants were willing to share their location feeds, but different visualizations led users to *different* decisions about who to share their location feeds with. Based on interview feedback, participants mostly preferred sharing map-based visualizations. Participants also expressed significant concerns about sharing temporal properties of their location feeds. In creating our visualization, we encountered several technical challenges that we put forth as future challenges for LSAs. We conclude our paper with a discussion of our observations about the interaction between privacy and location visualizations, paying particular attention to the implications for LSAs that wish to share location feeds.

RELATED WORK

Westin defined information privacy as an individual's claim to when, how, and to what extent information about them is shared with others [27]. Location privacy can be similarly framed. Past work has already provided a thorough discussion of how to design privacy feedback and controls so that users can more effectively specify their preferences for how their location information should be shared with others [13]. Equally important to specifying privacy preferences is the necessity for designing appropriate visualizations for conveying location information.

Work by Tufte and Cleveland have demonstrated how visualizations can influence people's interpretation of data [6, 24]. We posit there are similar effects with location visualizations. But, unlike charts, visualizing one's location (and sharing those visualizations with others) has important privacy implications for users. Prior work has identified many ways in which privacy considerations can affect one's social relationships [17]. However, these studies mostly examine privacy concerns with an implicit understanding that location is shared occasionally, rather than continuously [1, 7, 13, 14, 18]. Also, most of the previously studied LSAs have focused primarily on sharing of *current* locations. Some LSAs support varying degrees of historical logging, but it is usually not its primary goal; thus, little attention has been shown for sharing of *historical* locations.

Our study is most similar to work done by Brush et al [3], who examined users' preferences for sharing location traces. Though we both use location visualizations in our study, Brush et al. primarily used them to convey different types of location obfuscation techniques. Users then specified their obfuscation preference when sharing past locations with a commercial entity (e.g., Microsoft). In our study, location visualizations are examined in much more detail, as we probe how different visual elements influence users' decisions to share their past locations with others.

Current LSAs predominantly represent locations with text or a map (Figure 1b). Each representation has its pros and cons, particularly when applied to sharing of historical locations. On one hand, text can allow easier integration into existing information newsfeeds. However, textual representations of location are often less informative, as it buries many properties of location feeds. For example, while text affords a more compact visualization, it is harder to determine the spatiality of a place. Maps are better suited for this, but they are not without fault. For example, Figure 1d shows a mash-up of Google Maps and Foursquare's check-ins (text). Having the map instantly provides more spatial awareness, but it is difficult to discern the temporal properties (like the order in which the places were visited).

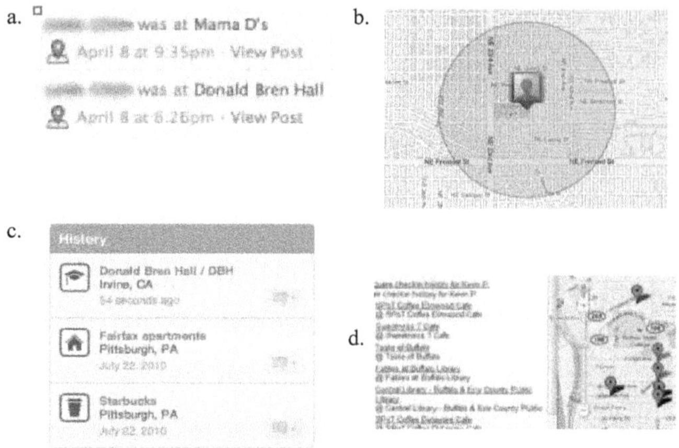

Figure 1. Examples from current LSAs that use text (a, Facebook Places; c, Foursquare) and maps (b, Google Latitude). (d) Mash-up of Foursquare (text) & Google Maps.

PROPERTIES OF SHARING LOCATION FEEDS

Adding more information to either a text- or map-based visualization is not difficult. In this section, we describe different dimensions of location feeds and how we represented them in our study. Note that our goal is not to design an optimal visualization. Instead, we focus on creating different styles of visualizations, making them as isomorphic as possible (i.e. having the same content), and then comparing how users interpret and react to them from a privacy perspective. This kind of analysis is new to the domain of sharing *historical* locations and can provide important insights for future LSAs, particularly given the rather homogenous types of LSA visualizations seen today.

When sharing current locations, we consider the following:

1) **Spatiality**: a place's physical location, in absolute terms (GPS coordinates) or where a place is located relative to a known landmark (e.g., "in south LA")
2) **Label**: how a user refers to the place (e.g., the user at "Starbucks", "a coffee house", or simply "in LA")
3) **Arrival**: when a user arrives at a place

Unsurprisingly, there is only one temporal variable that's accessible when sharing current location (arrival). When sharing location *feeds*, there is a richer set of temporal information that can be shared, including:

4) **Departure**: when a user leaves a place
5) **Duration**: how long a user stays at a place
6) **Sequence**: the order in which a user visited each place
7) **Frequency**: how often a user visits a place

There are certainly other features that one could include in a location visualization. However, for our study, we limit our exploration of the design space to these seven features.

Generating Location Labels

The second property in our list (a location's *label)* presents an interesting layer of complexity that is worth describing in more detail. Existing LSAs provide varying levels of

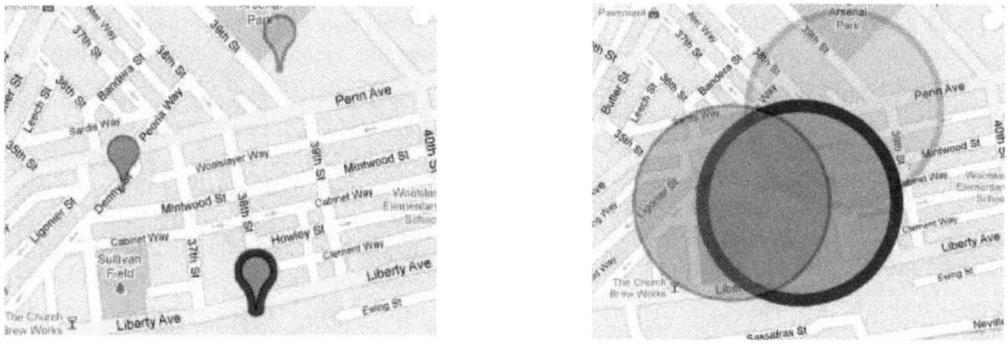

Figure 2. Shows three visualization techniques (post-pilot). The two marker styles represent same locations; (left) halos use random blurring technique, where midpoint is not necessarily actual location. Both images show transparency (to show sequence, faintest=oldest), color (red=most recent place), border width (thickest=most frequented place)

support for creating location labels. Many LSAs, like Facebook Places and Foursquare, operate by having users specify the business name or a personal label for each place they check-in at. These labels are then implicitly associated to a physical place through an address or GPS coordinates.

Past work has proposed that location labels can be classified using a taxonomy that distinguishes between geographic and semantic descriptions [16], and general and specific descriptions [22]. In our study, we use these two dimensions to create four different types of labels:

- **General geographic labels**: referencing the city and/or neighborhood that a place is in (e.g., "I'm in NYC")
- **Specific geographic labels**: a street address or an intersection (e.g., "I'm at Fifth & Main")
- **General semantic labels**: referencing the kind of place somewhere is (e.g., "I'm at a coffee shop")
- **Specific semantic labels**: a business name or specific place name (e.g., "at Starbucks", "at the White House")

Based on these categories, we note that LSAs with manual check-ins are using two types of labels: a specific geographic label (because check-ins are always tied to an address or GPS coordinate) and a semantic label (whatever string the user provides to describe their check-in). However, the types of semantic references that users provide vary greatly [5]; thus, in our study, we provide an initial exploration to see if different place descriptions affect privacy preferences and, in particular, whether labels change how users perceive different location visualizations.

VISUALIZING LOCATIONS IN TEXT, MAPS, AND TIME

Existing LSAs use either a text- or map-based visualization, and LSAs that support sharing of historical data typically only use textual representations. In our study, we study both of these types to better understand how location visualizations affect users' privacy preferences. We also include a third (time-based) visualization type.

Text-Based Representations

In text-based representations (**Figure 3**a), each row has a timestamp showing arrival and the length of stay. We chose to use relative timestamps ("5 minutes ago") for times that are < 3 hours from when the visualization is viewed. For visits that occur before then, we use absolute timestamps ("13:25pm"). This mimics current LSA behaviors (Fig 1c).

What is visually important about the text-based representation is that every location is treated the same. In other words, every row in the visualization is visually no different than any other row. The text-based representation emphasizes specific temporal features of location feeds: the *sequential order* of past visits and the *arrival* information for each place. Thus, we can use this visualization to probe whether these properties are an important factor in how end-users reason about their privacy concerns for sharing their historical locations with others.

What is less obvious in a text-based representation is the frequency that one visits a place and the spatial properties of each place. However, one could glean this information by analyzing the historical data, manually gathering appropriate statistics (for frequency information) or reverse geocoding location labels (for a place's spatial property).

Map-Based Visualizations

Most map-based visualizations (Figure 1d) mark a user's location using a pushpin at specific GPS coordinates. This style is conducive for describing locations with geographic labels. However, to support different kinds of semantic labels, we also use a halo marker (**Figure 3**b) that shows a user's true location as somewhere within the boundaries of the halo. The halo is more ambiguous and supports plausible deniability, which past work has shown to be an important privacy feature for LSAs [14]. When adding a halo to a map, we randomly add noise to the true location up to +/- 300m (Figure 2), reflecting a blurring of up to three city blocks (which, on average, are ~100m long). Generally speaking, this amount of blurring is most useful when using semantic labels. Given the urban area that we conducted our study in, we feel that a 3-block blurring radius provides sufficient support for plausible deniability.

While randomized blurring affects the location of the halo marker, we also manipulated the size of the halo to account for potential inconsistencies between location labels and the preciseness of the halo marker. For example, with specific geographic location labels, it does not make sense to have large-sized halo markers, as the label's precise description takes away the possibility for plausible deniability. Thus, we adjusted the diameter of the halo markers depending on the level of specificity provided by the location label. For markers associated with general geographic labels (e.g., city or neighborhood), we set the diameter to be two miles wide. For halo markers associated with semantic labels (e.g., "coffee shop", "Starbucks"), we set a smaller diameter (0.25 miles) and used the randomized blurring technique. The exact sizes of the halo's diameter were chosen based on the particular city in which our study was conducted and was influenced by the typical size of neighborhoods in the area as well as the surrounding area's urban density.

We added basic interactivity to our map-based visualization, letting users click on the halo markers to show temporal features like when the user arrived and left, and how long the user stayed (per visit). The pop-up window also includes one of the four location labels we previously described. To show the remaining temporal variables (sequential order and frequency), we manipulated the marker's visual properties. Card et al [4] and Ware [26] argue there are at least nine visual properties that can convey information: an object's position, size, orientation, grayscale, color, texture, shape, animation, & transparency. Using these design guidelines, Figure 2 describes some of the visual mappings we used in our study.

Generally speaking, the most salient feature for map-based visualizations is the *spatial* information. By visually manipulating the marker's transparency, size, and border width, we have also emphasized certain temporal features. However, the set of markers and their placement on the map is arguably more prominent in comparison. Thus, we can use this visualization to probe how sensitive users are to sharing the spatiality of their historical locations.

Time-Based Visualizations

We also introduced a third visualization type, as we noticed that there were still some temporal features (duration and departure) not emphasized in either the text- or map-based visualizations. In the time-based visualization (Figure 3c), we use a timeline and color-coded blocks to show when a user arrives and leaves a place. The colors of each block are randomly assigned. Similarly colored blocks indicate that the user has returned to a particular location.

The time- and map-based visualizations are isomorphic, containing the same information. Users can click on a particular block to show a map with a halo marker placed according to the same rules as for the map-based visualization. It is important to note that, in addition to the map, we also show the precise arrival, duration, and departure information to ensure that we provide the same descriptiveness in both visualizations.

In the time-based visualization, the most salient features are the colored blocks in the timeline, which show how much time a user spends at their past locations. The visualization draws the user's attention to locations with repeated visits because of the similarly colored blocks. On the other hand, spatial information is less emphasized, as users must click on the colored blocks to see map-related information. Thus,

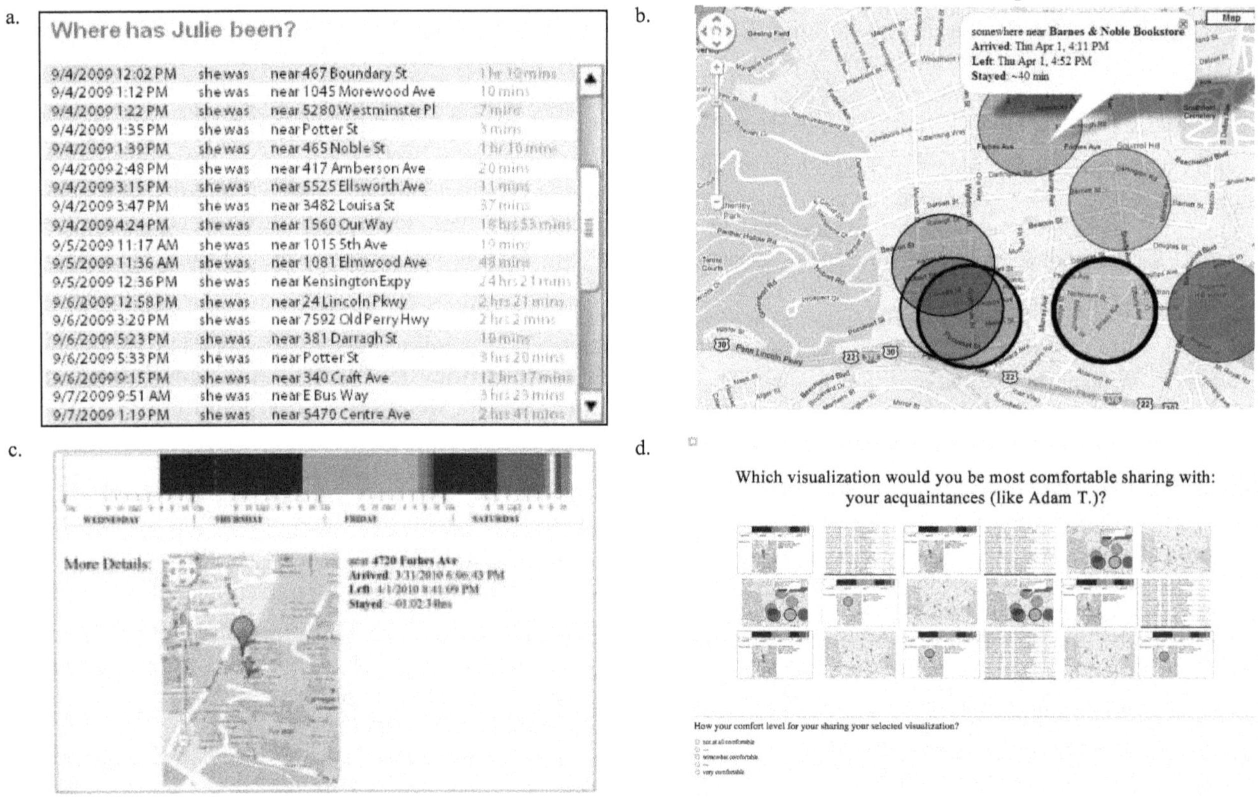

Figure 3: Examples of our 3 visualizations, post-piloting. (a) Text-based shows arrival, labels, & duration. (b) Map-based shows arrival, departure, duration, labels, spatiality, frequency, & sequence. (c) Time-based shows same features as (b). Visualizations made to be isomorphic. (d) Prompt shown to participants for choosing and evaluating visualizations.

we can use the time-based visualization to probe whether the duration and arrival/departure properties adversely affect users' privacy preferences for sharing location feeds.

PILOT STUDY FOR REFINING VISUALIZATIONS

While our text-based representation is straightforward, we wanted to make sure that our map-based visualization would not overwhelm our users or be difficult to comprehend. Thus, as a sanity check, we conducted a pilot study with 30 users to provide feedback on a sample screenshot of a map-based visualization.

Each visualization contained week-long location feeds for three individuals. The map-based visualization showed the three location trails, differentiated by differently colored markers. In the text-based representation, the three location feeds were intertwined, ordered by arrival times and demarked by differently colored text. These two visualizations were designed to be isomorphic. That is, one could convert the text-based representation into the map visualization (and vice versa) with some effort, but without needing any additional information. The order of the visualizations was counter-balanced. Participants were asked to explain each visualization to the best of their ability and choose which visualization they would be most comfortable sharing, if it were incorporated into a LSA.

Based on participants' qualitative feedback, we found that differences in transparency levels were not easy to discern. Participants reported that it was hard to pick out the most opaque marker (the most recent location) for each of the location feeds. We referred back to Card [4] and Ware's [26] suggestions and opted to use a combination of color and transparency to indicate sequential ordering of location visits. To represent the most recent location, we used a red-colored halo. All other markers were marked using a different color (blue); for these markers, we continued to use transparency levels to indicate older locations (Fig 2).

One implication for this design choice, though, was that we could now only display one user's location feed at a time (as color is now associated with sequential order and cannot be used to indicate different location feeds). In light of this change, we decided that the thickness of a marker's border (how often a user visits a place) would be computed in relative terms. In our original visualizations (as shown in the pilot study), we mapped border widths (thin, medium, thick) to certain frequencies (1-2, 3-6, and 7+ times), which were the same across different location feeds. However, since our new visualizations show only one user, we opted to calculate the border widths based on percentages instead. For example, if a user visited three places equally often (say, 5 times a week), then there would have originally been five markers, all with medium-width borders. In our new scheme, the markers each have a thin border, as the user spent equal time at each place. By using percentages, we normalize the visual features so that there are fewer thick borders in the visualization, reducing visual clutter. This change was also in response to participants' worry that our visualizations might be overwhelming with more data.

Our participants reported a clear preference for the map-based visualization for *viewing* their friends' locations (76.7%). However, when picking which visualization they would like to *share* with their friends, their preferences shifted to the text-based representation (63.3%). This statistically significant difference ($p<0.01$) suggests that there are indeed important privacy considerations for LSAs that go beyond designing adequate privacy controls and are related to how information is *visualized* to others. Armed with these results, we redesigned our visualizations and conducted a second, more controlled study.

STUDY DESIGN FOR EVALUATING VISUALIZATIONS

In our main study, our primary manipulation was between the three types of visualizations (text-, map-, time-based). For each visualization, we varied the location labels (general or specific, geographic or semantic). Within the map- and time-based visualizations, we also varied the marker type (the traditional marker style or a halo). In total, there were twenty possible combinations of these visualization variables (3 visualization types x 4 label types x 2 marker styles – 4 since text visualization does not use markers). In this study, we evaluated 18 combinations. We excluded two visualizations since they present an illogical combination, where the halo marker is paired with a specific geographic label. The intention behind using the halo is that, by providing a larger marker, users are afforded plausible deniability. However, when using the halo with a fully precise label (like an address), the halo's ambiguity is much less useful. As such, these two pairings are excluded.

Participants

Using a university-wide mailing list, we recruited twelve participants, ranging from 23-51 years old ($\mu=30.8$, $\sigma=6.2$). Five participants were female. Seven participants were graduate students, the rest were university staff members. Half the participants were from non-technical backgrounds. We did not advertise that our study was about privacy, nor did we mention this in the entrance survey. Instead, participants were recruited under the pretense that they would be evaluating different information visualizations.

Entrance Survey and Data Collection

Participants completed a 10-minute survey to collect basic demographic and social network information. For their social networks, participants provided examples (names) for four relationship groups: family, acquaintances, supervisors, and close friends. We told participants that their examples must live in the same city. We later used these names to frame the privacy questions for evaluating the visualizations. By controlling for geographical distance, we avoid it potentially biasing participants' preferences.

To ensure that participants realistically considered their privacy concerns when evaluating the visualizations, we collected two weeks of *actual* GPS traces from each participant. Participants were given mobile phones (Nokia N95s) to carry and use as their primary phone during the study period. This incentivized them to keep their phones on at all times, though participants were not penalized if they momentarily turned it off for privacy reasons.

The phones were equipped with location-logging software to record participants' actual location traces (modeled after the software used in [2]). The software ran continuously in the background and collected GPS and Wi-Fi positioning data. To reduce power consumption, we used the phone's accelerometer to selectively sample locations. The logging data was stored on the phone and we required participants to upload their data (through a website) twice during the study: midway through and at the end.

Automatically Generating Location Labels

Before each interview, we analyzed each participant's location trace. For times when there was no GPS readings (e.g., when indoors), we used Skyhook's API [21] to translate the Wi-Fi readings into GPS coordinates. We then computed the distance and speed between consecutive GPS readings to determine if the participant was moving. Places that the participant stayed for more than five minutes were marked as "significant". Using the coordinates for each significant place, we *programmatically* generated the four label types (geographic vs. semantic, general vs. specific).

To generate the general geographic label, we queried a publicly available database to first reverse geocode the GPS coordinates to a zip code. We then used the zip code to lookup the nearest neighborhood. To generate the specific geographic description, we used Geonames [9] to perform reverse geocoding using their `findNearestAddress()` and `findNearestIntersection()` webservice calls.

To generate the semantic labels, we used the specific geographic labels (the street address & nearest intersection) to query the Google Maps API and obtain a list of the nearest POIs. Each POI result includes information about the type of place it is (e.g., "Restaurant", "Shopping") and the name of the place (typically a business name, like "Starbucks"). We record the top result, as the API dictates that it should be the POI that is closest to the address provided. As an alternate source of labels, we also queried other publicly available sources, including Microsoft's Mappoint webservice and Wikipedia. To use Wikipedia, we first scraped Wikipedia for their geo-tagged articles and then used these tags to create a local database mapping GPS coordinates to corresponding article titles (which would serve as the location label). Among the three database sources, we choose the label belonging to the POI closest to the given address, within the bounds of the halo marker.

The challenge behind automatically generating location labels is that there is no guarantee that the generated label is actually correct. In fact, there are several ways in which the label generation process is susceptible to errors.

- **Sensing Errors**: All generated labels ultimately depend on having accurate GPS coordinates. However, there are times when GPS readings are not available and we must rely on Wi-Fi readings, which can be less accurate. Also, switching between GPS and Wi-Fi sensing consumes a non-trivial amount of battery power [25]. Thus, even for the most diligent participants, there were times when their phones did not record data due to poor battery life.
- **Triangulation Errors**: For Wi-Fi readings, we rely on Skyhook's API to generate appropriate GPS coordinates. This process is, by definition, only an approximation of the user's true GPS coordinates. The accuracy of these coordinates is also highly dependent on how up-to-date Skyhook's database is. For a more detailed discussion of the shortcomings of Wi-Fi localization, we refer the reader to any one of several Place Lab papers (e.g., [19]).
- **Interpolation Inaccuracies**: Even with perfectly accurate GPS coordinates, our process relies on webservices to provide accurate reverse geocoding. However, by definition, reverse geocoding only returns a best estimate. For example, to determine the exact street number for a given set of coordinates, reverse geocoding often relies on interpolating between two known street addresses. Thus, slight variations in GPS coordinates can result in very different reverse geocoding results.
- **Sparse and/or Stale Databases**: Assuming that we can record an accurate GPS reading from the phone and we can retrieve a perfectly interpolated address via reverse geocoding, we still depend on public database sources to be up-to-date. Since we use these databases to find the nearest POIs (and their associated semantic names), we are essentially at the mercy of these services. Two problems that we frequently encountered in running this study are: 1) some databases contain out-of-date entries, and 2) databases often have fewer entries for suburban areas. In both cases, the generated label will be incorrect and, in the latter case, the generated label may end up outside the boundaries of the halo marker (resulting in no label being added to our visualization).

Based on several weeks' worth of pre-study test data, we were able to consistently and reliably translate the recorded GPS sensor readings into *geographic* place labels (with 98.7% accuracy) using the process we described. However, automatically generating *semantic* place labels proved to be much more difficult. For this study, since creating place naming algorithms (e.g., using machine learning techniques) was not the goal of this study, we opted instead to use a human-in-the-loop approach to get accurate labels.

User Validation of Location Labels

We required participants to verify our generated labels twice: midway through the two-week data collection and at the end of the study. Once participants uploaded their sensor readings through our website, we extracted the GPS coordinates, identified the significant places, and used our previously described steps to automatically generate the two labels (specific semantic and specific geographic names) for each place. We then emailed this list of labels, along with their corresponding arrival times, to each participant. In the email form, we asked participants to verify and correct, if necessary, any obviously incorrect labels. We also asked participants to provide labels for any locations that did not appear in the list (but should have). In these cases, the phone may have been off, resulting in there being no sensor readings, or our heuristics may not have generated any labels due to database errors.

This human-in-the-loop approach requires extra work from users, but results in much more accurate location labels. We felt that this tradeoff was acceptable, as we did not want participants to evaluate our visualizations based on their accuracy. Instead, we want to probe participants' *privacy reactions* to visual differences. Thus, we wanted to reduce, as much as possible, factors like label inaccuracies.

Evaluating Location Visualizations

At the end of the two-week study, we interviewed each participant about their location feeds. For each interview, we randomly ordered the visualization manipulations (for visualization type, as well as marker and label types). For the first visualization shown, we asked participants if there were any surprises or locations missing. Also, because the labels are often not as visually prominent at first glance, we made sure to point out the differences between label types when they first occurred. Otherwise, no other features were explicitly called out to the participant, though the experimenter did address any questions that the participants asked. This allowed our researcher to ensure participants properly understood each visualization and could ask follow-up questions to provide further qualitative feedback.

Recall that at the pre-study interview, we asked participants to provide names of four relationship groups (family, close friends, acquaintances, supervisors). We used these names to frame the sharing questions and, for each relationship, participants choose one of the 18 visualizations that they were most comfortable sharing (**Figure 3**d). After indicating their preferences, participants verbally explained their choices. The interview lasted one hour; feedback was recorded and later transcribed. At the end of the interview, participants were compensated with a $30 gift card.

RESULTS

In total, we identified 139 unique places, with each participant visiting, on average, 11.6 unique places (σ=3.1). In response to the completeness of our visualizations, nearly all of our participants responded that there were no omissions in their visualization. Only one participant was surprised by the inclusion of some places on her visualization, though she quickly recalled the relevant events and realized that the visualization was correct.

We were able to automatically generate geographic labels for all 139 identified places. We generated semantic labels for 71.3% of the places. Following the human-in-the-loop approach, participants corrected 10.2% of those labels. Locations that the participant was not able to label were removed and not included in any of the visualizations.

Sharing Location Feeds

As Table 1 shows, depending on who the visualization is shared with, participants generally preferred either the text- or map-based visualization. Prior work has shown that, when sharing *current* locations, users are significantly influenced by who is asking [7, 15]. Our results are similar, but apply to sharing of *historical* locations.

By choosing different types of location labels, participants implicitly control the granularity of their shared location feeds. Consolvo et al. showed that users are likely to share location at a granularity useful to the requester [7]. In our study, we found that participants did *not* consistently choose the same granularity for each group. For example, when sharing with family members, participants were split between sharing specific geographic (addresses, 66.7%) and general geographic labels (neighborhood or city). For acquaintances, we found that participants were split between general semantic (business types, 66.7%) and general geographic names. Only close friends and bosses elicited consistent granularity preferences of general semantic labels and general geographic labels, respectively.

These results suggest that, when there are potential power dynamics involved (e.g. sharing with family members or supervisors), participants prefer the lowest granularity (general geographic labels). When with more intimate relationships (such as close friends), they are comfortable sharing a more descriptive location (general semantic).

When explaining their preference, participants most commonly cited concerns about their physical privacy, where they wanted to avoid being unexpectedly found.

> *"I like being able to go someplace and know that other people can't find me. If you have [specific geographic labels], then you can't really do that anymore. It makes it super easy for people to bother you whenever they want. So yeah, I'd rather share the [general geographic labels]. If someone really knows you, then they might still know where to find you. But those people are OK...they know you well enough to figure it out, so it probably means they're a good friend so if they find you, it's not a big deal. But that's why you need something general, so you don't have to worry about those other people." –P3*

> *"I can see how [specific geographic labels] might help spontaneous meetings [and that] might be cool. But I think I'd only like it every once and while. I'd rather someone just call me if they want to find me. Giving them [general semantic labels] means they'll still need to ask me to find me. Sure, it's more work for me, but I prefer to know that someone is looking for me, rather than have them just show up and surprise me." –P9*

Previous studies have mentioned the issue of power dynamics [20] and users' fear of unknowingly being tracked [23]. Our results suggest that the same concerns for sharing historical locations but also, more importantly, that there are ways to overcome these privacy concerns by *visually* manipulating how location information is shared.

Visualization Preferences and Reactions

There were two main visualization preferences that we observed. First, participants unanimously disliked sharing the time-based visualization. Based on interview feedback, participants felt that it was too privacy-invasive. In particular, several participants showed concerns that visualizing the time information might make others more curious about a place than they might have otherwise been.

> *"If [others] see that I was somewhere for a long time, like for more than a day, they're going to want to click on [the timeline]. You know, so that they can find out more. I mean, that's what I would do if I were looking at someone else's timeline. I'd be curious why someone would spend so much time at a place." –P2*

Similarly, many participants felt that revealing the temporal information may lead others to draw incorrect inferences about what they may have been doing at a place.

> *"You just don't know what kinds of conclusions people are going to jump to when they see how much time you spend at certain places. I mean, what if I was at home for a whole week? Maybe I was feeling sick. But someone else might think 'gosh he's such a lazy bum' and totally get the wrong picture of me." –P5*

> *"Actually, it's not that I mind people knowing I was [at the store]. It's more that I mind people knowing that I was there for so long. I guess I don't want to have to explain to people what I was doing, if they ask. Isn't it enough that they know where I was at?" –P11*

Our second observation was that, when choosing a map-based visualization, participants' preferences for which marker to use was often not consistent with their choice of location labels. For example, one would expect that when choosing either general geographic (city/neighborhood) or general semantic labels (business type), participants will prefer a visualization with halo markers, since using general names and the halo provides more plausible deniability. For example, combining a specific semantic label (like Starbucks) with a halo marker is nearly as informative as a pushpin marker with an exact address, especially if the person viewing the map is familiar with the area and knows that there is only one Starbucks there.

Yet, the majority of our participants selected this mismatched label+marker combination for sharing their location feeds with their close friends and acquaintances. To understand this preference, recall that halos are, by definition, randomly centered. The participant's true location is only guaranteed to be somewhere inside the halo and not necessarily at the center of the marker. Because of this design, it is possible for two locations to be somewhat far from each other, yet appear close together with the halos (Figure 2). Thus, some participants mentioned that their preference for pushpin markers was because they felt that the pushpins conveyed more mobility than halo markers.

> *"I know [the pushpin markers] are kind of revealing, but I like that the points are more scattered around. It feels like [the halo markers] just make my life seem kind of boring. They often overlap and makes it look like I'm not really moving around much." –P10*

Some participants also selected this combination for sharing their location feeds with family. However, this percentage is much smaller than with close friends and acquaintances.

DISCUSSION

We now discuss the strengths and limitations of our study methodology, the implications of how visualizations can impact end-user privacy preferences sharing location feeds, and the remaining challenges for LSAs to design privacy-aware visualizations for socially sharing location feeds.

Strengths and Limitations of the Study Design

In our study, we use participants' *actual* location traces, so that participants can better reflect on the potential consequences of sharing their location feeds with others. But, despite this realism, there are some confounding factors that our results should be considered against.

First, all the disclosure decisions posed to our participants were hypothetical. Participants did not actually share their visualizations with others. However, to help ground their decision making, we provided real names of people in their social network when framing disclosure questions. Also, based on interview feedback, we felt that participants were indeed thoughtfully answering and carefully reflecting. Second, our sample size was quite small. This is due to the effort and equipment needed to collect GPS data. A larger sample size would be helpful in future studies, in addition to recruiting more users from outside the university.

Sensitivity Towards Temporal Features

Relationship Group	Visualization Type			Label Type				Marker Type		% of Participants	Comfort Rating (median)
	Text	Map	Time	Specific Geographic	General Geographic	Specific Semantic	General Semantic	Pushpin	Halo		
Family Members											
Combination #1		X			X				X	50.0%	5
Combination #2		X		X				X		33.3%	4
Combination #3		X			X			X		16.7%	4
Close Friends											
Combination #1		X					X	X		83.3%	4
Combination #2		X					X		X	16.7%	4
Acquaintances											
Combination #1		X					X	X		66.7%	3
Combination #2		X			X				X	33.3%	3
Supervisors											
Combination #1	X				X			N/A		83.%	4
Combination #2		X			X				X	16.7%	4

Table 1. Visualizations preferences, grouped by the different relationship groups. Comfort ratings indicate how comfortable participants felt sharing a particular visualization combination with a specific relationship type.

When examining location sharing, past work has almost exclusively focused on sharing of *current* locations [1, 7, 13, 14, 18] and has only recently begun to consider *social* location sharing [22]. In our study, we provide initial insights into how users make privacy decisions about sharing *visualizations* of their *historical* locations. Based on participants' responses, we found that certain dimensions of location feeds are much more privacy sensitive than others.

In our visualizations, we choose to emphasize 7 location variables: spatiality, name (label), arrival, departure, duration, frequency, and sequential order. Some of these emphasize the physical properties of a place (spatiality and label), while the rest are temporal features. Generally speaking, participants felt that temporal properties were more privacy sensitive. In fact, of the five temporal features, participants reported that they were least comfortable sharing duration (median=1) and arrival (median=2). These self-reported comfort scores are based on a 5-point Likert scale, where 1=not at all comfortable.

Participants' discomfort is because they felt that some temporal features were often tightly associated with what they were *doing* at a particular place. This suggests that users are more concerned about sharing their *activities* rather than their location. This finding is interesting as prior work suggests that users are willing to share their activity information [22]. We reason that our results are different because, in Tang et al's study, participants were allowed to manually specify a place's label. In our study, labels are automatically generated and are always tied to the physical properties of a place. As such, activity information is never explicitly conveyed through the visualization; it is only inferred based on the label, spatiality, and time information.

Technically, as the visualizations are isomorphic, these inferences should be possible with any of the three visualization types. However, participants had the strongest (negative) reaction to the time-based visualization because it exposes the very information that is most suggestive of one's activity at a particular place. Thus, our results suggest that, when sharing location feeds, users should be given an option to *not* share certain temporal information. Otherwise, LSAs should allow users to additionally tag locations with their own activity information, so that there will fewer chances that others will improperly judge the user.

Perceived Perceptions of Control

In the interviews, participants hinted at issues of control and how some visualizations took control away from them.

> *"I can't really control what the timeline [in the time-based visualization] will look like to other people, so I just don't feel comfortable sharing it." –P7*

> *"I chose this visualization because I feel like it's the most flexible. Like, it shows just enough that people can know what I'm up to, but it's vague enough that I can spin another story, if I want to." –P5*

While P5's comment is somewhat related to the issue of plausible deniability, it is also indicative of the importance for LSAs to support *flexible* visualizations that empower users to feel in control of *how* their locations are perceived by others. In our study, we automatically generated labels for users' past locations. This automation led users to feel less control over *what* location information might be shown to others. Thus, to compensate for this loss, users chose visualizations that allowed them to share information only in broad strokes, though they still wanted it to be helpful.

> *"I don't think I'd share [the text visualization] with my close friends. It's just not that useful in that format, but I also don't want to share everything on the map either. But, by using the general labels, I feel like the map won't be too revealing." –P10*

P10's comment suggests that having the right spectrum of location labels is an important feature for LSAs to consider when supporting automated sharing of location feeds.

But labels are not the only way that participants try to control their location disclosures. All the participants agreed that the text-based representation was the least revealing of the three visualization types. This is an interesting response, as the visualizations were designed to be as close to isomorphic as possible. However, most participants believed that presenting location in text form was less susceptible to further probing by others.

> *"The text[-based visualization] just seems more innocent. You can't immediately tell if a place is sketchy unless you look really hard and google it or something. And people are usually way too busy so they aren't going to bother with all that work." –P4*

P4's belief is that, by removing sensitive location information to be one-click away, he is afforded more privacy. This perceived privacy control is important to note, as it reinforces the link between *information control* and *information access*, both important concepts that LSAs should heed in supporting privacy-sensitive sharing. Specifically, when users feel like it is harder to access information, then they are more likely to feel comfortable sharing a particular visualization. However, this also suggests that LSA should remind users that access is not always as elusive as they may believe.

Social Dimension of Perceived Privacy Concerns

Recent studies in social location sharing have suggested that impression management factors into users' decisions about how they name their locations [22]. We have similar findings in our study and have evidence to suggest that users give significant consideration how a visualization may be interpreted by others. In particular, several participants opted for pushpin markers over the halo markers for this very reason, commenting that the pushpins gave them the sense that they were more mobile and, consequently, would appear more interesting to others.

This type of feedback strongly suggests that there are indeed ways for visualizations to manipulate end-user perceptions about *what* and *how* information is shared. The consequence of choosing pushpin markers is that, at least visually speaking, readers are given a much more precise indication of where a user was located. Thus, LSAs again must carefully consider how they design visualizations so that they can responsibly inform users of both the social benefits, as well as the potential privacy issues.

Challenges: Scalability and Value of Automated Sharing

Our study examines the privacy concerns relating to *automated* sharing of *historical* locations. One may question whether this type of location sharing is worth studying, given current trends in LSAs. Foursquare, a LSA with one of the largest user base, has over 6 million users and has reported over 1 million check-ins per day [10]. While these numbers do suggest Foursquare is growing, it also shows that the users are only contributing, on average, about one place every week. LSAs are often seen as a service that mainstream has not fully embraced yet [12].

One potential reason for this is that there may not be enough location data being recorded and shared, so services are seen as less useful. To address this, LSAs could easily begin incorporating automated location updates, and some LSAs already in fact support this sharing mode. Thus, it is critical for us to be ahead of the technology curve and begin understanding how we can appropriately design LSAs to share these location feeds. Designing *privacy-sensitive visualizations* and understanding their effect on users' perceived privacy concerns has not yet been discussed for LSAs, though we have seen previous visualization studies done in other domains (e.g., [8]). Based on our observations, we have found that there are indeed important domain-specific issues to consider when considering how users are influenced by visual representation of locations.

Moving forward, there are still many challenges to address. For example, our study only considers a small section of the design space for location visualizations. There are many other variations that should be further explored. In addition, our visualizations were all designed to support only a single user and only two week's worth of data. For future work, these visualizations should address scalability issues so that they can support multiple users and varying time windows.

CONCLUSION

In summary, our study has focused on users' perceptions of different visualizations for sharing location feeds. While we have not exhaustively explored the design space of location visualizations, we believe that this study is a step forward in understanding how visual representations of location information can affect a user's perception of privacy. Based on our findings, we describe several design implications for LSAs that wish to support sharing of past locations.

REFERENCES

1. Anthony, D., Kotz, D. and Henderson, T. (2007). Privacy in Location-Aware Computing Environments. IEEE Pervasive Computing, 6 (4), 64-72.
2. Benisch, M., Kelley, P.G., Sadeh, N., et al. (2008). The Impact of Expressiveness on the Effectiveness of Privacy Mechanisms for Location Sharing. Technical Report, CMU-ISR-08-141R, Carnegie Mellon University, Institute of Software Research.
3. Brush, A.J., Krumm, J. and Scott, J. (2010). Exploring End User Preferences for Location Obfuscation, Location-Based Services, and the Value of Location. In Ubicomp '10, 95-104.
4. Card, S.K., Mackinlay, J. and Shneiderman, B. Readings in Information Visualization: Using Vision to Think Morgan Kaufmann, San Francisco, 1999.
5. Cheng, Z., Caverlee, J., Lee, K., et al. Exploring Millions of Footprints in Location Sharing Services. In ICWSM '11.
6. Cleveland, W.S. The Elements of Graphing Data. Wadsworth, Monterey, CA, USA, 1985.
7. Consolvo, S., Smith, I., Matthews, T., et al. (2005). Location Disclosure to Social Relations: Why, When, & What People Want to Share. In CHI '05, 82-90.
8. Cranor, L.F., Guduru, P. and Arjula, M. (2006). User Interfaces for Privacy Agents. ACM Trans. Comput.-Hum. Interact., 13 (2), 135-178.
9. Geonames. http://www.geonames.org/export/ws-overview.html
10. Grove, J. Foursquare Nearing 1 Million Checkins Per Day. http://mashable.com/2010/05/28/foursquare-checksin/
11. Hoadley, M.C., Xu, H., Lee, J., et al. (2010). Privacy as Information Access and Illusory Control: The Case of the Facebook News Feed Privacy Outcry. Electronic Commerce Research and Applications, 9 (1), 50-60.
12. Hong, J.I. Privacy & Security in the Location-Enhanced World Wide Web. In Workshop on Privacy at Ubicomp '03.
13. Hsieh, G., Tang, K.P., Low, W.Y., et al. Field Deployment of Imbuddy: A Study of Privacy Control and Feedback Mechanisms for Contextual Im. In Ubicomp '07, 91-108.
14. Iachello, G., Smith, I., Consolvo, S., et al. Control, Deception, & Communication: Evaluating the Deployment of a Location-Enhanced Messaging Service. In Ubicomp '05, 213-231.
15. Lederer, S., Mankoff, J. and Dey, A.K. (2003). Who Wants to Know What When? Privacy Preference Determinants in Ubiquitous Computing. In CHI '03, 724-725.
16. Lin, J., Xiang, G., Hong, J.I., et al. Modeling People's Place Naming Preferences in Location Sharing. Ubicomp '10, 75-84.
17. Palen, L. and Dourish, P. (2003). Unpacking "Privacy" for a Networked World. In CHI '03, 129-136.
18. Sadeh, N., Hong, J.I., Cranor, L., et al. (2008). Understanding and Capturing People's Privacy Policies in a Mobile Social Networking Application. Pers & Ubiq Comp, 13 (6), 401-412.
19. Schilit, B.N., LaMarca, A., Borriello, G., et al. (2003). Challenge: Ubiquitous Location-Aware Computing and the "Place Lab" Initiative. In WMASH '03, 29-35.
20. Shklovski, I., Vertesi, J., Troshynski, E., et al. (2009). The Commodification of Location: Dynamics of Power in Location-Based Systems. In Ubicomp '09, 11-20.
21. Skyhook Wireless. http://skyhookwireless.com/locationapps/
22. Tang, K.P., Lin, J., Hong, J.I., et al. (2010). Rethinking Location Sharing: Exploring the Implications of Social-Driven Vs. Purpose-Driven Location Sharing. In Ubicomp '10, 85-94.
23. Tsai, J., Kelley, P., Cranor, L., et al. (2009). Location-Sharing Technologies: Privacy Risks and Controls. In TPRC '09.
24. Tufte, E.R. The Viual Display of Quantitative Information. Graphics Press, 1983.
25. Wang, Y., Lin, J., Annavaram, M., et al. (2009). A Framework of Energy Efficient Mobile Sensing for Automatic User State Recognition. In MobiSys '09, 179-192.
26. Ware, C. Information Visualization: Perception for Design. Morgan Kaufman, San Francisco, 1999.
27. Westin, A.F. Privacy and Freedom. Atheneum, NY, 1967.

Employing User Feedback for Semantic Location Services

Donnie H. Kim, Kyungsik Han, Deborah Estrin
UCLA CSD CENS
{dhjkim, kshan, destrin}@cs.ucla.edu

ABSTRACT
Just as coordinate-oriented location-based applications have exploded recently with mapping services, new semantic location services will be critical for the next wave of killer applications. People are going to want everyday applications to have location-awareness that goes beyond simple numerical latitude and longitude. Loci is a new semantic location service layer that employs user feedback to bridge the gap between machine-learned and human-defined places. Advances in place learning techniques have provided us the tools to detect nearly 95% of the visits we make to places and the distances we travel. The difficulty of recovering the remaining 5% comes from designing parameters that work for every user in every place. Based on a user study with 29 participants over three weeks, we show that the level of user feedback required by the service is acceptable and most of the users are willing to provide help to improve their experiences with the service. Our results suggest that user feedback has the potential to significantly improve semantic location services, but requires well-timed prompting mechanisms to improve the quality of the feedback.

Author Keywords
Semantic Location, User Feedback

ACM Classification Keywords
H.5.m Information interfaces and presentation (e.g., HCI): Miscellaneous.

General Terms
Design, Human Factors, Management

INTRODUCTION
Mobile phones are increasingly expected to do more than make phone calls. A growing number of mobile devices can now determine their own physical location, and various location-based mobile applications are on the rise. In addition to applications that require instantaneous locations (*e.g.*, navigation, emergency response, and local search), many applications can benefit from continuously understanding the user's location context. Ranging from personal applications such as geo-reminders and location-diaries [27], to social applications such as whereabout-sharing and ride-sharing [3, 29], numerous emerging applications want colloquial places and paths rather than just coordinates. As people normally think and speak locations in terms of places like "my home" or "Ed's office", location-aware applications will encounter the problem of translating coordinates provided by today's positioning systems to semantic places. Track-based applications for map building, traffic estimation, and trace sharing, can also benefit from automatically parsed paths that are sequences of coordinates between places.

Unfortunately, current location-aware applications must handle the coordinates directly. Absence of a universal place database forces developers to ask users to define places one-by-one by drawing circles (or polygons) on a map for each application. Paths are also parsed by post-processing algorithms from day-long location traces or by depending on users to manually start and stop location tracking. However, such schemes fail in describing many interesting indoor places and poorly scale. Creating indoor localization systems in every building is currently far-fetched, and relying on users to delineate places from scratch can omit many interesting places. Moreover, continuously estimating absolute positions significantly impacts battery-life on the mobile device, preventing these applications from penetrating into a wider population. Current applications either cope with a fixed sampling interval with a lower resolution or depend on users to manually check-in to places and track paths.

Place learning is one way to move from coordinates to semantic locations. Several algorithms have been developed for extracting significant locations by post-processing complete location traces offline [1, 18]. More recently, algorithms that learn and recognize semantic places from pervasive Wi-Fi access points enable discovering many indoor places in real-time [12, 14]. Furthermore, researchers have shown that semantically interpreting location context also helps designing an energy-efficient location tracking mechanism by leveraging people's tendency of staying at indoor places for the majority of the time [15]. The state-of-the-art technique can accurately detect over 95% of the place visits and the travel distance while using significantly less energy than collecting coordinates at a fixed rate. These techniques

This work was supported in part by Intel PhD Fellowship.

have been shown to be effective in capturing people's concept of a place most of the time. However, machine-learned places are not always same as human-defined places.

This paper presents Loci, a service layer that abstracts a user's location context as places and paths. The service learns new places, suggests potentially meaningful places, recognizes registered places, and tracks paths connecting places using previously proposed techniques [15]. To overcome the problem of when machine-learned places are different from user-defined places, Loci employs user feedback. User feedback comes in two forms: 1) managing suggested places, and 2) telling when the service detects places incorrectly. We sought to understand how often user feedback is needed, what helps a user manage suggested places, and how we can encourage a user to provide feedback to the service.

To answer these questions, we conducted a three-week user study with 29 participants. We found that the amount of user feedback required by Loci is acceptable and many of our participants were willing to provide feedback to the service. Comments made by study participants suggest that the places found by Loci were easily understood and were close to how they perceive places most of the time. Our results also suggest that well-timed notifications and system feedback motivate users to provide more input. Overall, our study points towards the feasibility of engaging users for improving semantic location services.

RELATED WORK

Place Learning

Place learning algorithms extract semantic places from raw sensor signals and can be divided into two classes by input data: geometry and fingerprint.

Geometry-based algorithms find significant locations by clustering coordinates from location traces. For example, Ashbrook *et al.* and Toyama *et al.* used a variant of the k-means clustering algorithm and found clusters by GPS signal losses [1, 28]. Liao *et al.* introduced a supervised learning approach using a hierarchical CRF model to recognize high level activities and places from GPS traces. Parameters were fit by training on a labeled data set [18]. Zhou et al. proposed a density-based clustering algorithm that can discover clusters of arbitrary shape [30]. Harihanran *et al.* and Kang *et al.* used a temporal and spatial stay threshold to find places from location traces [11, 13]. Unlike other approaches that required an entire trace, their heuristics based on time and distance are computationally inexpensive and can be used in real-time. These approaches extract building-level or outdoor places, as GPS is usually not available inside buildings. Marmasse *et al.* defined a place as an area where GPS is unavailable [22].

Fingerprint-based algorithms use ambient signals to identify a specific place, and work better than coordinate-based approaches in discovering indoor places. RF-based fingerprints (*e.g.*, cell tower, Wi-Fi, Bluetooth) are the most common while other ambient signals such as sound, color, light texture information are also used [21, 2]. RF-based algorithms infer a single visit to a place by detecting stable radio environments. Laasonen *et al.* found cliques by clustering cell towers while Froehich *et al.* identified places by prompting users when the currently connect cell tower changes [17, 9]. Hightower *et al.* used newly detected Wi-Fi access points to determine a place visit [12]. Kim *et al.* further improved the place detection accuracy by using selected strong access points to detect a place visit [14]. These algorithms can be applied to any RF beacon signals but relying on Wi-Fi provided better resolution than cell towers.

Place Labeling

Several research efforts have been made to understand how people assign place names. Zhou *et al.* analyzed how people describe places and suggested five categories of descriptions [31]. Barkhuus *et al.* proposed four different types of location labels namely geographic references, personally meaningful labels, activity-related labels, and hybrid [3]. Lin *et al.* refined the categories by imposing a hierarchy with more fine-grained subcategories [19]. Patterson *et al.* studied the use of place labels as meaningful status messages for instant messaging (IM) applications [26]. Monibi *et al.* used collaborative filtering techniques for recommending place labels for IM status based on history data from multiple users [23].

Continuous Localization

Tradeoff between energy consumption and location accuracy has been extensively studied for continuous localization. Several approaches assumed that a set of positioning systems with varying accuracy and energy consumption are available while others used low power sensors to find GPS sleep opportunities. Constandache *et al.* intermixed positioning systems by solving an optimization problem using dynamic programming [8]. Lin *et al.* assumed that the accuracy requirement changes as a user moves around and used an HMM model to select positioning systems [20]. Kjaergaard *et al.* assumed that applications define their distance error limits, used accelerometer to turn off GPS, and predicted next GPS sampling time based on speed estimation [16]. Paek *et al.* and Zhuang *et al.* also similarly used accelerometer data to adaptively sample GPS coordinates [24, 32]. These approaches tried to continuously estimate absolute locations within a distance error-bound while reducing the energy cost. Kim *et al.* took a different approach by interpreting location context in a more semantically meaningful way which helped to reduce the energy cost for continuously sensing locations [15].

User Feedback to create Indoor Location Systems

Over the years, several localization techniques relying on existing Wi-Fi infrastructure have been proposed. Due to the complex nature of indoor signal propagation, signal mapping has been a more practical and accurate solution than signal modeling. However, constructing a signal map (often called as *training phase*) requires a large amount of human labor for measuring signal strengths in every corners of a building. To bypass this, a couple of systems depending on user input to create the database have been proposed.

ActiveCampus uses a hill-climbing algorithm to approximate

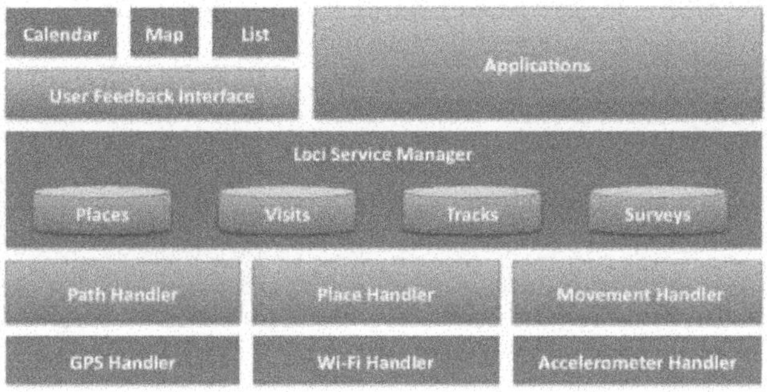

Figure 1. Loci semantic location service architecture

a user's location and employs a correction mechanism to improve its accuracy [10, 5]. When a user's location is incorrectly estimated, the user corrects the location by clicking on the right spot on a map. RedPin also avoids a costly offline training phase and generates location fingerprints from user input [6]. In contrast to ActiveCampus's geometric approach, RedPin generates symbolic location identifiers with room-level accuracy. The authors later proposed detecting intervals of immobility (using an accelerometer) to collect fingerprints while stationary and allow users to label data in a more appropriate time referring to the starting time and duration of the interval [7]. This interval method reduced the influence of second-by-second signal fluctuations that may be severe when fingerprints are instantaneously collected when a user dedicates to label a fingerprint on-site. Barry *et al.* conducted a year-long study of a similar crowd-sourcing localization system and showed its utility [4]. OIL additionally conveys graphical feedback about spacial uncertainties derived from discrete Voronoi diagrams and weeds out erroneous user contributions [25]. It prompts the user for feedback when the spatial uncertainty is too high (large Vornonoi region), and the user can postpone or turn off prompting.

However, these systems instantaneously localize a user in a particular building as opposed to continuously understanding a user's everyday location context.

THE LOCI SEMANTIC LOCATION SERVICE

Loci runs as a background service on a mobile device and abstracts a user's location context as places and paths rather than just coordinates. Visits to a place are recognized by detecting enter and exit events at a particular place. Paths are tracked by collecting a series of position fixes (a bundle of time, latitude, longitude, and optionally altitude, speed, accuracy, heading) that a user creates while moving from one place to another. Figure 1 shows the architecture of our service, which is comprised of a user feedback interface, a service manager, and three components handling place visits, path travels, and user movements. We first give an overview of how the service is used by a user and then explain the details of each component.

Places are managed by the user through a single interface directly provided by Loci and shared with various applications. When the user begins using Loci, no places are registered with the service. However, as the user carries around the mobile device running Loci, new places are gathered as potential everyday places waiting to be reviewed and confirmed. Places are suggested when the user visits them for the first time and spends a substantial amount of time (in our case, defined as more than 5 minutes). Loci automatically infers entrance to and exit from a place using Wi-Fi fingerprints collected during the stay. These Wi-Fi fingerprints are stored and used to identify places in the future. Recent visit times (as enter and exit times), approximate position of the place, and a list of neighboring Wi-Fi access point (AP) names are provided as hints to assist the user in deciding if a place is valid and should be saved or is spurious and should be discard.

At a convenient time, the user can decide which suggested places to register, add to existing place, delete, or block. As Loci uses Wi-Fi fingerprints to recognize a place, registering a place involves assigning a set of Wi-Fi fingerprints to a place. A Wi-Fi fingerprint is defined as a list of APs visible by the device and their received signal strength (RSS). Places are suggested when the Wi-Fi environment stabilizes for a period of time indicating a stay but does not match with any previously registered places. Adding a suggested place to an existing place allows user to register several Wi-Fi fingerprints to a single place. Some places may have more than one fingerprint. A user can define a place as a large space (e.g., markets, warehouses, etc.) where a single Wi-Fi fingerprint cannot cover the entire place, or the Wi-Fi environment of a place can change over time due to indoor signal interference and network reconfigurations. Loci also estimates the approximate position of the place using position fixes acquired around the visit time while tracking paths[1]. If a place is blocked, it will never be suggested as a place again, while a deleted place can be. Once a place is registered, Loci recognizes it using Wi-Fi scans. The user can also manually register a place when a visit to a new place was not successfully suggested (*e.g.*, brief visits or incorrect recognitions).

In the following sections, we describe Loci's user interfaces, embedded survey tools we designed for our user study, and its operational architecture.

User Interface

Loci offers a set of user interfaces for managing places, viewing location histories, and providing feedback. The user interface is organized primarily around a tab bar at the top of the screen that provides instance access to three main views: a *calendar view*, a *map view*, and a *list view*.

Calendar View

Calendar view allows a user to view place visit histories in a calendar which consists of a *monthly view* (Figure 2(a)) and a *daily view* (Figure 3(g)). The user can click on a date presented on the *monthly view* (which is shown when the *calendar view* is selected) to open a *daily view*. This takes the

[1]Path tracking is initiated when a user leaves a place and is suspended as the next destination is reached.

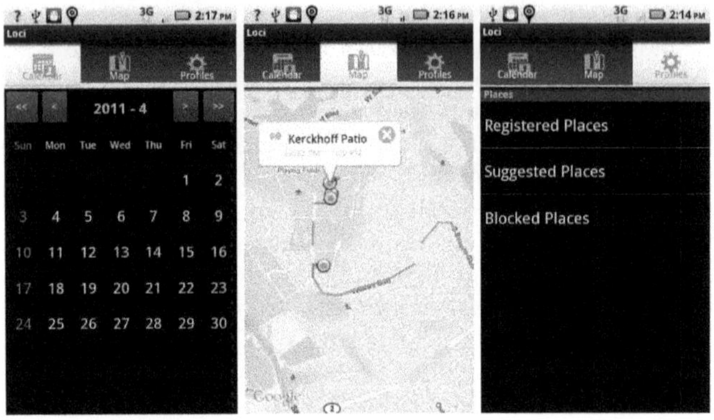

(a) Calendar (b) Map (c) List

Figure 2. Loci's user interface consists of three main tabs. *Calendar view* shows visit histories in time-order. *Map view* shows daily place visits and travel paths. *List view* categorizes places as registered, suggested, and blocked.

user to a screen which presents all visit activities of that particular day on a list. A list entry displays information about a single visit including enter time, exit time, and place name. When a new place is visited and suggested by Loci, the place name is presented as "New Place #X". The user can click on a list entry (representing a visit instance) to view more information about that particular visit (Figure 3(b)) such as stay duration and the Wi-Fi fingerprint collected during the visit (Figure 3(c)). This screen also provides an interface to register a new place (if recognized as a visit to a new place), edit a place's profile (if recognized as a visit to a registered place), or correct a misclassification (if recognized as a visit to a wrong place) through a single button labeled as "Edit". Correcting misclassification allows users to either register a new place using the Wi-Fi fingerprint collected during the visit, or add it to an existing place. Short visits to an unrecognized place is hidden by default in a daily view as they are mostly transient locations. However, the user can reveal these hidden visits and select a visit instance to manually register a new place using the saved fingerprint (Figure 3(g)).

Map View

Map view lets a user view location trajectories of a selected day on a map (both in satellite and map mode) (Figure 2(b)). The user can either select to display every single GPS point or a subset of filtered points (to reduce loading overhead) of a particular day. When the filtering option is selected, GPS points are filtered based on a selected time interval t, and displays one position per every t. Color of a line connecting each pair of points is defined by speed provided by the GPS module. Green, yellow, red, and gray are used when the estimated speed is above 10 m/s, between 5-10 m/s, between 1.5-5 m/s, and below 1.5 m/s respectively. A place is displayed as a dot on the map and uses the coordinate associated with the place when the place was registered. The user can zoom and pan the map and navigate the locations. Clicking on a place dot populates a popup bubble showing the place name and every visit instance during the day (showing enter and exit times). Clicking on the bubble takes the user to a *place info* screen (Figure 3(a)). If the selected place dot is a new place (suggested and waiting to be registered), the user can handle the suggested place instead.

List View

List view allows a user to view places by its status: *registered*, *suggested*, and *blocked* (Figure 2(c)). The three place lists are shown by choosing the *Profiles tab* (figure 2(c)). The *suggested place list* displays places suggested by Loci but not reviewed by the user yet (Figure 3(e)). Suggested places are given a temporary name such as "New Place #X". Selecting a new place will take the user to a screen where visit times, a position, and neighboring Wi-Fi APs are presented as hints (*calendar* and *map view* also arrive to the same place view). Tapping the map allows the user to enlarge the map for a better view (Figure 3(d)). The user can register, add to existing place, delete, or block the suggested place. Registering a place requires assigning a unique name and optionally correcting the estimated position of the place to the exact location. A place is shown as a circle, and a map tool is provided so the user can move the center or adjust the radius. The circle is currently not used to detect places, but is presented as an additional information about the place[2]. When the *registered place list* is viewed, every registered place are listed in an alphabetical order and the time elapsed since the last visit is shown (Figure 3(f)). Selecting a place from the list takes the user to a screen where the user can view and edit the place (Figure 3(a)). The *blocked place list* displays all blocked places. The user can unblock places by selecting a blocked place on this list.

Embedded Survey Tools

We embedded two survey tools in Loci to understand its performance in the field and the amount of feedback about place failures a user may provide to the service in everyday use. We directly asked users to tell us when a place found by Loci differs from their perception of a place using these tools.

Place Surveys

Place surveys are used to characterize places based on user feedback. Users can take a survey about a particular place by choosing a place from the *registered place list*. On a *place survey*, a user can select a name category of the chosen place name [19], add keywords, report place-detection failures that happened during visits, and provide free-text comments. *Place survey* is initiated by the user. We have primarily used this tool to understand place characteristics that lead to a specific place-detection failure and discuss potential solutions. Users can edit the place survey anytime they want. The embedded nature of the survey tool allows the users to provide *in-situ* feedback. We categorized place failures as 1) *missed* visits, 2) one visit *divided* into multiple visits, 3) two or more visits to different places *merged* into a single visit to a single place, and 4) *wrong* place recognition. When a machine-logged visit duration is significantly shorter than human-remembered duration, we asked the user to categorize them as a *divided* visit. Users can report on these four different failure types by answering how often each failure

[2]Circles can be used for detecting large outdoor places such as parks, beaches, or large superstores in low-rise buildings.

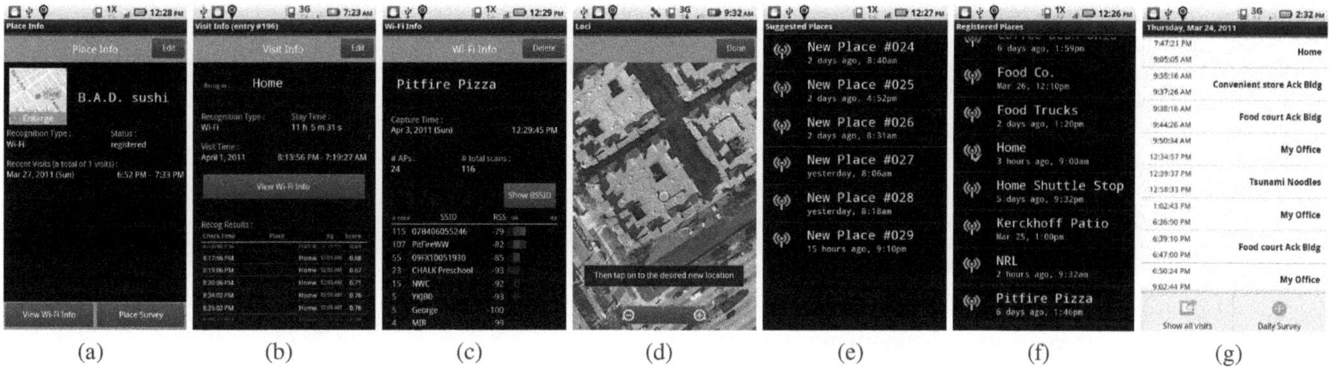

Figure 3. User interfaces for viewing and managing places. Screen shots of place info screen, visit info screen, Wi-Fi info screen, map edit screen, suggested place list, registered place list, and daily view are shown from left to right.

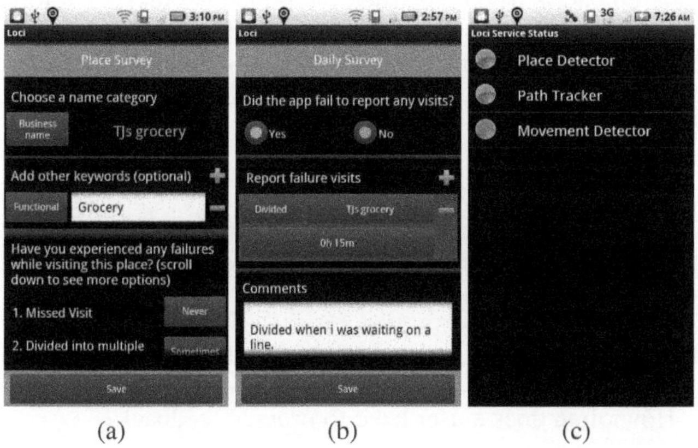

Figure 4. Embedded survey tools and status screen. Daily surveys are used to report place detection failures by day. Place surveys are used to report failures by place. Status screen illustrates activated components.

occurred. Frequency options include *never*, *sometimes* (less than a half of the visits), *often* (equal or more than a half of the visits), and *always*. Users can also additionally provide contextual information about the failure in the comment box.

Daily Surveys

To understand how often a user may need to report about failures, *daily surveys* are used to get feedback from the user. If any discrepancies between what Loci detects and what the user remembers are noticed during a day, they are reported in the *daily surveys*. On a *daily survey*, the user can report a failure by selecting a place from a list of registered places, a failure type, and a visit duration. Any number of failures can be added to the survey. If a place suggestion fails, the user can select "new place" from the place list and provide information about the detection failure during the first visit. A comment box is used to collect any additional information the user may wish to share about the failures.

Service Architecture

The service consists of three main building blocks to keep track of locations in a semantically meaningful way while reducing its energy expenditure: place handler, path handler, and movement handler (Figure 1). Loci service manager on top of these blocks controls the components, manages location history data, and provides a gateway to the user interface modules and applications. Our service architecture is built upon previously proposed ideas [15]. We briefly describe how each component works and interacts.

Place Handler

Place handler periodically scans neighboring Wi-Fi APs to detect place visits (for every 10 seconds in our case). Once the neighboring radio environment stabilizes (receiving c=3 consecutive similar scans), an entrance to a place is declared, and the service manager consults with the local database to recognize the place. If the Wi-Fi fingerprint similarity of the visited place against every registered places is lower than a threshold, the place is saved as a potentially new personal place in *place database*. Similarity of two Wi-Fi fingerprints is measured by computing a *Tanimoto coefficient* of the two signal strength vectors. *Place handler* continuously checks if the latest scan and the accumulated scans during a visit are similar. To suppress noisy signals misleading to prematurely declaring a departure, a subset of steady beacons (based on the response rate[3]) are used to measure similarity. If the scans are similar for longer than a predefined amount of time (5 minutes), place handler triggers the movement handler to find opportunities to sleep. If no movement is detected, place detector suspends until a movement is detected again. A departure from a place is detected when the similarity score is below a threshold for more than c scans. The visit information (a place name, enter and exit times, and a Wi-Fi fingerprint) is saved and *path handler* is initiated as the user leaves the place.

Path Handler

Path handler starts tracking positions using the GPS module on the mobile device as the user leaves a place. The sampling interval for acquiring position fixes is a tunable parameter defined by the application needs (we set as 15 seconds). Every position fixes acquired while the path handler is on are coupled with a timestamp and stored in *track database*.

[3]Response rate is the ratio of the detection count and the total number of scans.

Path handler signals *place handler* to suspend itself through the service manager when it detects that the user is traveling in high speed and is unlikely to arrive at a place any time soon. This avoids unnecessary Wi-Fi scans. When the average speed over a non-overlapping time window (30 seconds) is higher than 2 m/s[4], *place handler* is notified to sleep until the average speed drops below the same threshold. The speed information of each position fix is supplied by the GPS module.

Movement Handler

Movement handler is turned on to find opportunities to save energy while the device is staying at a place and immobile. Hinted by *place handler* that the user is staying at a place and the surrounding radio environment is stable, it powers the accelerometer on board and starts to monitor the motion of the device. The accelerometer is duty-cycled 50% (using a duration and a period set to 3 and 6 seconds) and is set at a low sampling rate (3-7Hz) to further save energy used for detecting movements. The variance of acceleration magnitude (to tolerate random orientation) is computed during the 3 seconds on-time window to determine a motion state. *Place handler* is put into sleep when the variance is consistently below a threshold for more than 30 seconds, and awaken when its above the threshold for more than 12 seconds. A shorter wait time is used for resuming *place handler* as the energy used for a couple of more Wi-Fi scans is negligible while a more conservative waiting time can lead to missing an exit event.

Data Storage

Loci manages four databases to maintain places, visit histories, tracks, and survey answers. *Place database* stores suggested places, registered places, and blocked places. For each place, a place name, a geographical area (as a circle on a map), a list of Wi-Fi fingerprints, and additional information associated with the place is saved. A new place is added to the database when *place handler* learns a new place (marked as suggested until the user confirms) or when a user manually registers a place using a particular Wi-Fi fingerprint. A place can be manually created by selecting a Wi-Fi fingerprint collected during a particular visit[5] and saved in *visit database*. When a user reviews a potential place to register (both from suggestions and manual entries), positions collected within the visit time (saved in *track database*) are used to estimate the geographical location of the place. Loci uses the most accurate position fix among the coordinates acquired during a stay. If no position with a timestamp that is within the stay time is available, it uses a position with the closest timestamp. *Visit database* maintains visit histories including enter and exit times, place name, and a Wi-Fi fingerprint collected during the stay. *Track database* stores positions collected while *path handler* was active. A position is a tuple of timestamp, latitude, longitude, altitude, speed, accuracy, and bearing (which are provided by the GPS module). Finally, survey answers provided by the user are saved in *survey database* until they are uploaded.

[4]Average human walking speed is 1.3-1.5 m/s.

[5]A short visit disqualified to be suggested as a place or a visit incorrectly labeled to another place can be used.

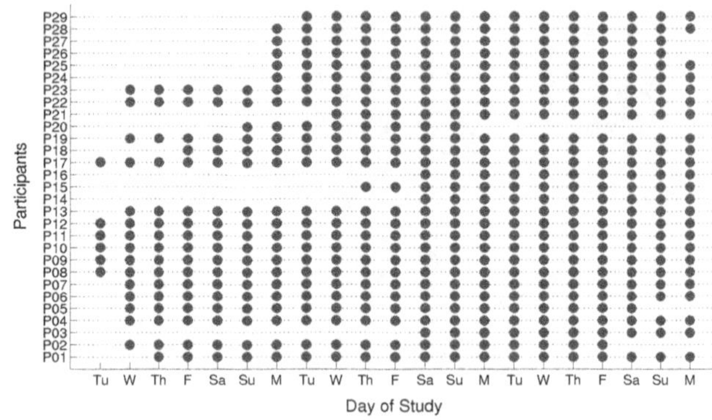

Figure 5. User study participation dates

Upload Handler

Data upload is triggered when the phone is plugged-in to a power outlet to conserve energy. Currently, upload handler is specifically designed for remotely collecting user study data, but can be extended to back-up the above described databases.

USER STUDY RESULTS

We conducted a user study with 29 participants living in four major cities and three continents to understand how people use Loci and adopt an interactive semantic location service.

Three research questions guided our study design:

1. How often does a user need to provide feedback?
2. What helps a user manage suggested places?
3. How can we motivate a user to provide feedback?

To address our research questions, we asked participants to use Loci for at least two weeks which preferably ran on their primary mobile phone, but we provided a secondary smart phone when necessary. The entire user study spanned for three weeks while each participant had different start dates and periods. However, a couple of participants experienced device failures or made unintentional errors during the study (*e.g.,* uninstalling before an upgrade), thus, couldn't provide a full two weeks of data (Figure 5). We present these partial experiment results as well as the results from the other participants who collected more than two weeks worth of data.

Procedure

Study sessions began by gathering a study consent form and providing a short tutorial about Loci. Users were required to enable GPS and Wi-Fi on their phone, then to download and install Loci (provided as an Android app) by visiting a URL. Once the participants successfully installed and used Loci for a couple of days, we requested that they complete an entrance survey posted online. The entrance survey probed the participants' commute distance, average number of visited places during weekdays and weekends, and their interests in location-based applications. Participants were expected to carry the phone most of the time, clear all suggested places everyday, make sure to recharge the phone every night, and use the embedded survey tools to report all place detection failures. We explained the three different user interfaces (calendar, map, and list) that can be used to access suggested places, and encouraged them to use the most convenient method. We also informed participants how to manually register places that were not successfully suggested (including brief visits or incorrectly recognized visits). The participants were advised to continue the study for at least two weeks. When the study concluded, we asked the participants to complete an exit survey. The exit survey asked about their experience and desired new features.

Participants

We collected data from 29 participants (21 males and 8 females) aged between 25 and 55 (median 30) who volunteered to participate. Among the participants, 11 were grad students, 6 were undergraduates, and the other 12 had different professions. Most of the participants used their own mobile phone and five participants were provided a secondary smart phone (Samsung 18, HTC 6, Motorola 5). Based on the entrance survey, commute distance for 79% of our participants were within 10 miles. For both weekdays and weekends, most of the participants selected between 3 and 6 as their number of unique places they visit per day (86% for weekdays and 71% for weekends). We also asked about their interests in location-based services. Location-based reminders were the most popular application (71%), followed by location diary apps (67%), place suggestion apps (57%), contributing data for urban planning (38%), and social apps (33%). Multiple choices were allowed.

Results

To measure how often a user needs to provide feedback to the service, we first investigate the suggested places a user receives everyday. We also examine how often users may report about place detection failures and help the service meet their needs. We then take a look at what factors help users to recognize a suggested place and provide correct user input. Finally, we discuss about possible methods for encouraging users to provide feedback to the service, and briefly analyze the resource usage of Loci.

User Feedback Demands

Loci requests user input for 1) handling suggested places (deciding to either register, add to existing place, delete, or block), 2) assigning a name when registering a place, and 3) manually registering a place when necessary. Since the service automatically recognizes registered places, user input is required primarily when a new place is visited. Another occasion is when Loci has trouble detecting a place as a user expects. The answers, gathered through the embedded survey tools, help to highlight when a gap exists between machine-learned and human-defined places. As we analyze the survey answers, many failures can be recovered by tuning the parameters of a place detection algorithm at challenging places. The difficulty comes from designing the parameters so that detections work everywhere. Having user feedback allows the parameters to be sub-optimally tuned so that the detection works reasonably well without overly burdening the user. We examine these two types of user inputs to measure how much feedback Loci demands from its user.

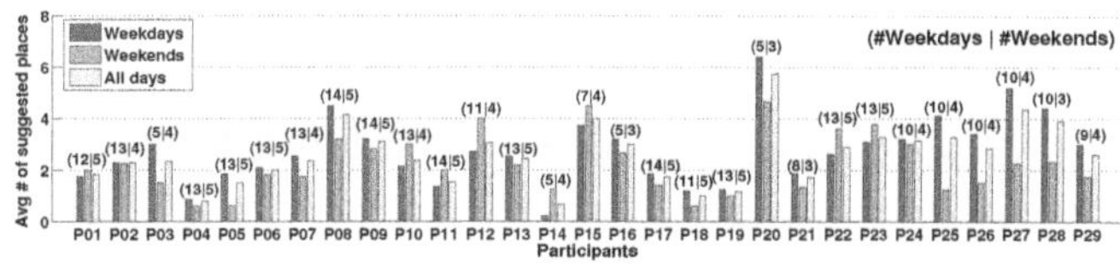

Figure 6. Average number of suggested places a user received by weekdays, weekends, and all days. About one third of the participants got more new place suggestions during weekends than weekdays.

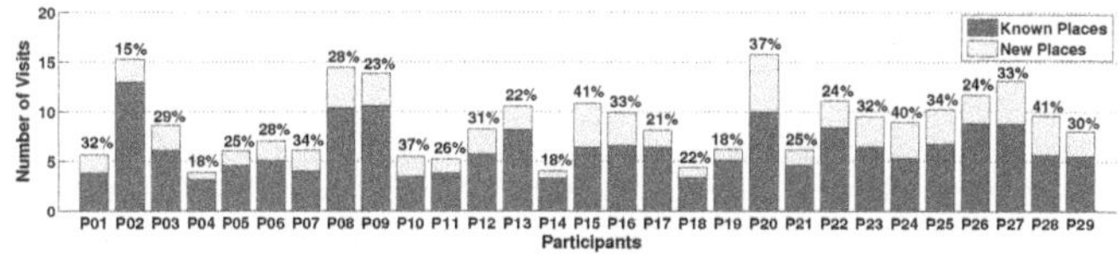

Figure 7. Average number of visits per day by user. The percentage on top of each bar indicates the percentage visits that require user input (visits to new places).

A) Registering new places.

Figure 6 illustrates the average number of suggested places a participant received for a day by weekdays, weekends, and all days. The number on top of each bar depicts the number of days used to calculate the average (weekdays and weekends). Participation dates varied from 8 days to 21 days. Overall, participants received 2.51 new places each day on average (weekends 2.18 and weekdays 2.64), and the number varied by users between 0.26 and 6.40. The maximum number of suggested places a participant received within a day was 11 and the minimum was 0. Among 29 participants, 9 users got more suggestions during weekends compared to weekdays.

To examine what influenced the number of suggestions a participant received, we first compare the average number of place visits per day by user (Figure 7). A visit is a single instance of a user staying at one place, and a place can be visited several times during a day. The percentage provided on top of each bar indicates the ratio of visits that required user input as the visited place was new to the service. P15 and P20 show a high ratio as the participant visited many new places over a weekend, but only provided week-long data sets. P23 exhibits a relatively high ratio due to a travel to another city during the first week of the study. In general, people with less place visits had to review less newly suggested places, but having more place visits did not always lead to a higher ratio (*e.g.*, P02). Some people occasionally traveled between a smaller set of places, increasing the number of visits but not new places, while others visited slightly more diverse places and less repeated places.

Next, we selected three participants and plotted how the number of suggested places changed over time. P08 registered the largest number of places during the study (over 85 unique places for three weeks), and visited 7-12 unique places each day. In the first few days, the percentage of new places were

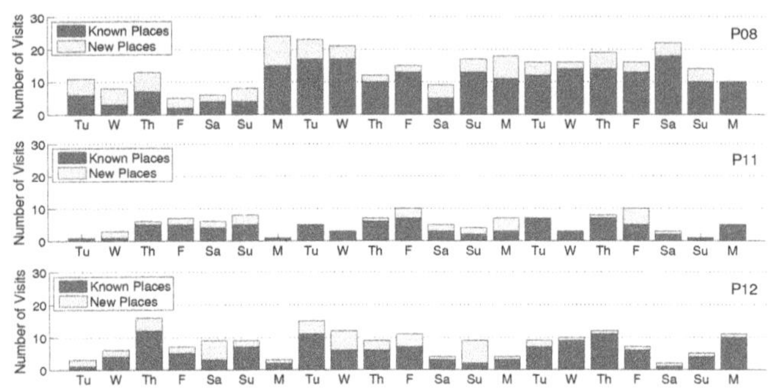

Figure 8. The number of place suggestions by participation date. P08 registered the largest number of places. P11 had place visits fewer than average. P12 visited average number of places. All participants generally experienced decreasing number of suggested places over time.

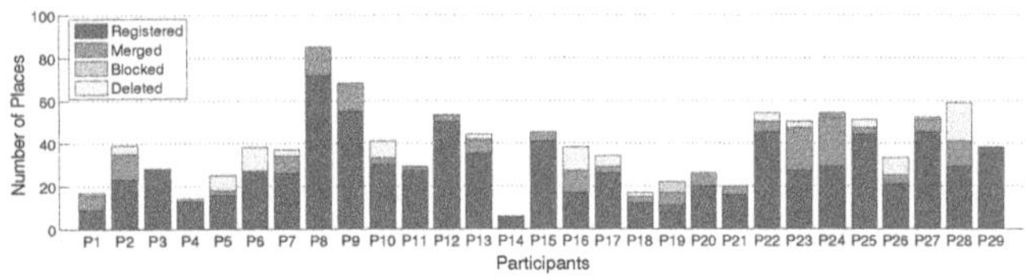

Figure 9. Quality of the suggested places. Overall, 75% of the suggested places were registered, 16% were merged, and 8% were deleted.

comparatively higher than the following days. However, regardless of the participant's high level of activity, many visits were recognized and new places were gradually learned over time. P11 made less place visits than the average and didn't have to deal with new places for 6 days out of 21 days. New places were mostly found over the weekends. P12 had average place visits and the number of suggested places went down as the participant entered the third week. Most participants experienced decreasing number of suggested places in general.

Finally, we analyzed how the participants decided to process each suggestion to understand the quality of our suggestions. Figure 9 breaks down the suggested places by its latest status: *registered*, *merged*, *deleted*, and *blocked*. Overall, 75% of the suggested places were registered, 16% were merged, and 8% were deleted. A *registered* suggestion is confirmed as a valid new place by the participant while a *merged* one is added to an existing place. P23 and P24 had noticeably more merged places as P23 merged many suggested places into "Disneyland" and two airport names while P24 defined places as buildings and merged many rooms. When a place was *deleted*, we asked why and saved the answers. Participants deleted suggestions mostly when Loci picked up a congested road as a place or when they couldn't recognize the suggested place. Some people blocked an open space where they often walked.

B) Reporting place failures.

When a place visit detected by Loci is incorrect, we asked participants to report such failures on both the *daily survey* and the *place survey*. We used *daily surveys* to gauge how often a user experienced place detection failures. We collected

Freq.	Missed		Divided		Merged		Wrong	
Never	845	(97.3%)	793	(91.4%)	844	(97.2%)	850	(97.9%)
Sometimes	20	(2.3%)	54	(6.2%)	20	(2.3%)	16	(1.8%)
Often	3	(0.4%)	17	(1.9%)	3	(0.4%)	1	(0.1%)
Always	0	(0%)	4	(0.5%)	1	(0.1%)	1	(0.1%)
Total	868	(100%)	868	(100%)	868	(100%)	868	(100%)

Table 1. Distribution of the place detection failures reported from the *place surveys*. Overall, *divided* failures were most common, followed by *merged*, *missed*, and *wrong* failures.

a total of 112 *daily surveys* from 29 participants during the study. However, we found that some failures were partially reported to one of the survey tools and not both. We manually fixed the discrepancies between the data sets from the two survey tools. As a result, the total increased to 176 *daily surveys*. First, we calculated the average number of *daily surveys* per day by individual user. About 51% of the participants submitted the *daily survey* every other day or less often, 27% reported once a day more, and 21% submitted none. However, this included repeating failures occurring while revisiting the same place. Thus, assuming that a failure can be fixed once it is reported, we excluded repeating reports and calculated the average again. In this case, every participant would report less than one failure per day. We also projected that the number will even get lower as the participant uses the service for a longer period. However, we also admit that the number we provide here may underestimate the failures as the participants may not have reported some failures.

With the *place survey*, the participants reported on how often a particular failure occurred at a place and, optionally, provided the context of the failure using a text box. We further analyzed place detection failures using these reports. For the 868 places registered by 29 participants during the study, *divided* failures happened most often, followed by *merged*, *missed*, and *wrong* failures (Table 1). Place visits were *divided* at relatively large spaces where a single Wi-Fi fingerprint couldn't cover the entire space (*e.g.*, department store, music hall). Next common places were in homes and offices where the participants stayed for extended time. Instantaneous failures occurred when strong APs briefly disappeared or radio signals fluctuated enough to trigger premature exits. *Divided* visits can be reduced by using a less sensitive similarity threshold or using several Wi-Fi fingerprints as a single place. Places were *merged* especially when a user directly moved from one place to another separated by a single floor or a hallway, These were also often incorrectly recognized places, resulting *wrong* failures. A solution for discriminating proximate places is manually separating the fingerprints for challenging places with a more aggressive similarity threshold. Finally, places were often *missed* when Wi-Fi wasn't available. These places are usually outdoors or in rural areas, where GPS may work better to detect places.

Managing Suggested Places

To understand how users dealt with suggested places, we logged which user interface was used to review suggested places and received additional feedback from exit surveys.

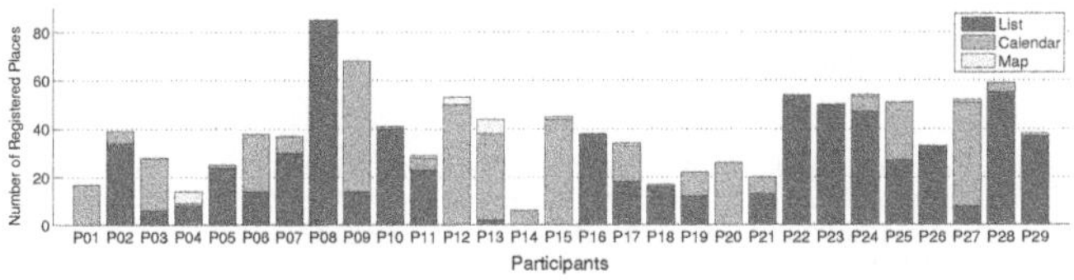

Figure 10. User interfaces selected for viewing and registering suggested places. Calendar view and list view were commonly used while map view was rarely used.

As illustrated in Figure 10, participants usually selected either *calendar view* or *list view* to review new places and stuck with one interface. *Map view* was used rarely. People who chose *calendar view* thought viewing place visits in a chronological order was helpful in remembering places, while others found it easier to view every suggested places in one place using the *list view*. About 38% of our participants answered that they preferred *calendar view* and 48% favored *list view*. We asked when the participants usually reviewed suggested places. 45% said they reviewed suggested places within a couple of hours after they left a new place and 31% reviewed new places at the end of the day. Others cleared the items right after they left the place (3%) or a couple of days later (3%). When we asked in what order they consulted the hints we provided (visit times, a map position, and visible Wi-Fi APs), 42% answered time-map-wifi and 31% answered map-time-wifi. While viewing the surrounding APs helped in some cases, participants found time (54% as the first consultant) and map (43%) more helpful to remember places. However, 71% of the participants thought that managing places became difficult when they couldn't recognize the suggested place, while assigning a name to each place (36%) or taking the time to handle them (18%) were less of an issue. It was also mentioned that map failed to provide enough information in cases where the GPS provided largely inaccurate indoor position estimations.

Encouraging User Feedback

Finally, we asked participants about their experience during the user study through exit surveys and sought for suggestions. We wanted to highlight two key implications to the semantic location services that resulted from the field study results: 1) people are generally open to providing feedback to improve the service, and 2) well-timed notifications and informative feedback motivates users to provide more input.

Based on the post-study exit survey, participants were mostly positive about receiving suggested places and managing personal places, M=7.32, (based on a Likert scale from 1 to 10, from annoying to fun). We also asked the maximum number of suggested places a participant will handle per day before giving up. 32% of the participants said that the number of suggested places doesn't really matter as long as they are reminded to review suggestions before the place is forgotten. 50% chose four or above and 28% chose three or below. People suggested that providing other contextual information about the visit (*e.g.*, phone calls made) or adding a social component (*e.g.*, sharing places with friends) may encourage them to engage more. However, the most desired

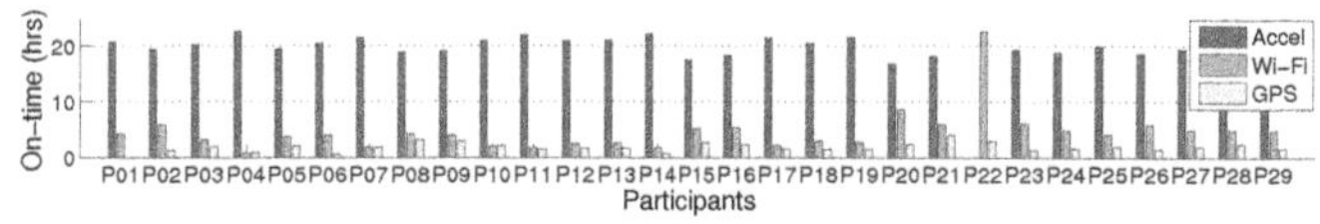

Figure 11. Daily average sensor on-time by participant

feature was getting reminders about new suggestions. 75% of the participants thought they would register more places if Loci prompted when new places appeared. 46% wanted to be prompted while they were at the new place and 36% preferred to be prompted when arriving at home in the evening. Others favored being prompted when staying at some place for a long time (11%) or while in transit (7%).

Participants were also willing to provide feedback when Loci fails to correctly detect place visits as they expected. About 96% of the participants answered that they can tell Loci when it's not correctly detecting places so that it can do a better job for the next visit. Based on their experience using Loci, 25% thought they will have to provide place failure feedback once every other day, 39% as twice a week or less, and 35% as once a day or more. Lastly, 69% told us that visualizing and providing feedback about how Loci detects enter and exits as well as showing how it recognizes known places will have positive influence on getting more user feedback.

Resource Usage

Lastly, we analyze Loci's daily energy consumption and memory usage, which are greatly affected by the user's mobility pattern. We logged the time each sensor was activated to estimate power usage as different phones have different power profiles. As illustrated in Figure 11, on average, accelerometer, Wi-Fi, and GPS were activated for 19.9, 3.9, and 1.7 hours, respectively. Samsung Galaxy S lasted for about 15 hours while Motorola Droid X lasted for about 36 hours. As the accelerometer had the longest active time, in general, we suspect that the two models have significantly different power profile for their accelerometers. Loci required 0.25 MB per day on average (min: 0.05 MB, max: 0.53 MB) to save location histories.

CONCLUSIONS AND FUTURE WORK

Loci is a personal semantic location manager that helps users to identify everyday places and paths. Location-based applications can take advantage of the personal places registered by the service, much as the contact list of the user is currently used by social applications. Loci employs a place learning algorithm to help users identify semantic places. Places are gradually learned and suggested as users visit new places, instead of asking them to define places one-by-one ahead of time. Paths between places can also be traced for track-based applications. We investigated the amount of user feedback required by Loci when used everyday. Our three-week study with 29 participants indicates that the number of suggested places could vary from 0 to 10 or more per day depending on the user's activity level but gradually decreased overall as the service was used for a longer period of time. About 75% of the suggested places were registered as a new place while 16% were added to an existing place. Place detection failures were reported once every other day on average, assuming that a failure at a particular place can be fixed once it is reported. Most of the user study participants felt positive about providing feedback to the service for better performance. Finally, on a Likert scale from 1-10, where 1 stands for "Never" and 10 for "Absolutely", response to "Will you use a service like this?" had a mean of 7.28 and standard deviation of 2.36.

Our results provided us with a foundation for two new research agendas. First, we plan to investigate how user feedback can be transformed into system parameters and improve place detection performance. Adaptively intermixing place learning techniques based on Wi-Fi and GPS may also allow us to cover more places. Designing user interfaces that intuitively convey the cause of place detection failures and requests minimum user effort in providing feedback is also critical. This will help users to define and tune places as they want. Next, we plan to focus on identifying a rich class of location-based applications and implementing the service at a larger scale.

REFERENCES

1. D. Ashbrook and T. Starner. Using gps to learn significant locations and predict movement across multiple users. *Personal Ubiquitous Comput.*, 7(5):275–286, 2003.
2. M. Azizyan, I. Constandache, and R. Roy Choudhury. Surroundsense: mobile phone localization via ambience fingerprinting. In *MobiCom '09: Proceedings of the 15th annual international conference on Mobile computing and networking*, pages 261–272, New York, NY, USA, 2009. ACM.
3. L. Barkhuus, B. Brown, M. Bell, S. Sherwood, M. Hall, and M. Chalmers. From awareness to repartee: sharing location within social groups. In *Proceeding of the twenty-sixth annual SIGCHI conference on Human factors in computing systems*, CHI '08, pages 497–506, New York, NY, USA, 2008. ACM.
4. A. Barry, B. Fisher, and M. L. Chang. A long-duration study of user-trained 802.11 localization. In *Proceedings of the 2nd international conference on Mobile entity localization and tracking in GPS-less environments*, MELT'09, pages 197–212, Berlin, Heidelberg, 2009. Springer-Verlag.
5. E. S. Bhasker, S. W. Brown, and W. G. Griswold. Employing user feedback for fast, accurate, low-maintenance geolocationing. In *Proceedings of the Second IEEE International Conference on Pervasive Computing and Communications (PerCom'04)*, PERCOM '04, pages 111–, Washington, DC, USA, 2004. IEEE Computer Society.
6. P. Bolliger. Redpin - adaptive, zero-configuration indoor localization through user collaboration. In *Proceedings of the first ACM international workshop on Mobile entity localization and tracking in GPS-less environments*, MELT '08, pages 55–60, New York, NY, USA, 2008. ACM.
7. P. Bolliger, K. Partridge, M. Chu, and M. Langheinrich. Improving location fingerprinting through motion detection and asynchronous interval labeling. In *Proceedings of the 4th International Symposium on Location and Context Awareness*, LoCA '09, pages 37–51, Berlin, Heidelberg, 2009. Springer-Verlag.
8. I. Constandache, S. Gaonkar, M. Sayler, R. R. Choudhury, and L. P. Cox. Enloc: Energy-efficient localization for mobile phones. In *INFOCOM*, pages 2716–2720. IEEE, 2009.
9. J. Froehlich, M. Y. Chen, I. E. Smith, and F. Potter. Voting with your feet: An investigative study of the relationship between place visit behavior and preference. In *Ubicomp '06*, pages 333–350, 2006.
10. W. Griswold, P. Shanahan, S. Brown, R. Boyer, M. Ratto, R. Shapiro, and T. Truong. Activecampus: experiments in community-oriented ubiquitous computing. *Computer*, 37(10):73–81, 2004.
11. R. Hariharan and K. Toyama. Project lachesis: Parsing and modeling location histories. In M. J. Egenhofer, C. Freksa, and H. J. Miller, editors, *GIScience*, volume 3234, pages 106–124. Springer, 2004.
12. J. Hightower, S. Consolvo, A. LaMarca, I. E. Smith, and J. Hughes. Learning and recognizing the places we go. In *Ubicomp '05*, pages 159–176, 2005.
13. J. H. Kang, W. Welbourne, B. Stewart, and G. Borriello. Extracting places from traces of locations. In *WMASH '04*, pages 110–118, New York, NY, USA, 2004. ACM.
14. D. H. Kim, J. Hightower, R. Govindan, and D. Estrin. Discovering semantically meaningful places from pervasive rf-beacons. In *Ubicomp '09: Proceedings of the 11th international conference on Ubiquitous computing*, pages 21–30, New York, NY, USA, 2009. ACM.
15. D. H. Kim, Y. Kim, D. Estrin, and M. B. Srivastava. Sensloc: Sensing everyday places and paths using less energy. In *Proceedings of the 8th ACM Conference on Embedded Networked Sensor Systems*, SenSys '10, pages 43–56, New York, NY, USA, 2010. ACM.
16. M. B. Kjaergaard, J. Langdal, T. Godskand, and T. Toftkjaer. Entracked: energy-efficient robust position tracking for mobile devices. In *MobiSys '09: Proceedings of the 7th international conference on Mobile systems, applications, and services*, pages 221–234, New York, NY, USA, 2009. ACM.
17. K. Laasonen, M. Raento, and H. Toivonen. Adaptive on-device location recognition. In *Pervasive '04*, pages 287–304, 2004.
18. L. Liao, D. Fox, and H. Kautz. Extracting places and activities from gps traces using hierarchical conditional random fields. *Int. J. Rob. Res.*, 26(1):119–134, 2007.
19. J. Lin, G. Xiang, J. I. Hong, and N. Sadeh. Modeling people's place naming preferences in location sharing. In *Proceedings of the 12th ACM international conference on Ubiquitous computing*, Ubicomp '10, pages 75–84, New York, NY, USA, 2010. ACM.
20. K. Lin, A. Kansal, D. Lymberopoulos, and F. Zhao. Energy-accuracy aware localization for mobile devices. In *Proceedings of the 8th International Conference on Mobile Systems, Applications, and Services (MobiSys'10)*, 2010.
21. H. Lu, W. Pan, N. D. Lane, T. Choudhury, and A. T. Campbell. Soundsense: scalable sound sensing for people-centric applications on mobile phones. In *MobiSys '09: Proceedings of the 7th international conference on Mobile systems, applications, and services*, pages 165–178, New York, NY, USA, 2009. ACM.
22. N. Marmasse and C. Schmandt. Location-aware information delivery with commotion. In *HUC '00*, pages 157–171. Springer-Verlag, 2000.
23. M. Monibi and D. J. Patterson. Getting places: Collaborative predictions from status. In *Proceedings of the European Conference on Ambient Intelligence*, AmI '09, pages 60–65, Berlin, Heidelberg, 2009. Springer-Verlag.
24. J. Paek, J. Kim, and R. Govindan. Energy-efficient rate-adaptive gps-based positioning for smartphones. In *Proceedings of the 8th International Conference on Mobile Systems, Applications, and Services (MobiSys'10)*, June 2010.
25. J.-g. Park, B. Charrow, D. Curtis, J. Battat, E. Minkov, J. Hicks, S. Teller, and J. Ledlie. Growing an organic indoor location system. In *Proceedings of the 8th international conference on Mobile systems, applications, and services*, MobiSys '10, pages 271–284, New York, NY, USA, 2010. ACM.
26. D. J. Patterson, X. Ding, S. J. Kaufman, K. Liu, and A. Zaldivar. An ecosystem for learning and using sensor-driven im status messages. *IEEE Pervasive Computing*, 8:42–49, 2009.
27. T. Sohn, K. A. Li, G. Lee, I. E. Smith, J. Scott, and W. G. Griswold. Place-its: A study of location-based reminders on mobile phones. In M. Beigl, S. S. Intille, J. Rekimoto, and H. Tokuda, editors, *Ubicomp '05*, volume 3660 of *Lecture Notes in Computer Science*, pages 232–250. Springer, 2005.
28. N. Toyama, T. Ota, F. Kato, Y. Toyota, T. Hattori, and T. Hagino. Exploiting multiple radii to learn significant locations. In *LoCA '05*, pages 157–168, 2005.
29. Y. Zheng, L. Zhang, X. Xie, and W.-Y. Ma. Mining interesting locations and travel sequences from gps trajectories. In *Proceedings of the 18th international conference on World wide web*, WWW '09, pages 791–800, New York, NY, USA, 2009. ACM.
30. C. Zhou, D. Frankowski, P. Ludford, S. Shekhar, and L. Terveen. Discovering personally meaningful places: An interactive clustering approach. *ACM Trans. Inf. Syst.*, 25(3):12, 2007.
31. C. Zhou, P. Ludford, D. Frankowski, and L. Terveen. Talking about place: An experiment in how people describe places. 2005.
32. Z. Zhuang, K.-H. Kim, and J. P. Singh. Improving energy efficiency of location sensing on smartphones. In *MobiSys '10: Proceedings of the 8th international conference on Mobile systems, applications, and services*, pages 315–330, New York, NY, USA, 2010. ACM.

Nurturing Natural Sensors

Stacey Kuznetsov, William Odom, James Pierce, Eric Paulos
Human-Computer Interaction Institute
Carnegie Mellon University
Pittsburgh, PA, USA
{stace, wodom, jjpierce, paulos}@cs.cmu.edu

ABSTRACT
Sensing has played a significant role in the evolution of ubiquitous computing systems, enabling many of today's compelling interactive and ubiquitous experiences. In this paper, we argue for expanding the current landscape of sensing to include living organisms such as plants and animals, along with traditional tools and digital devices. We present a comprehensive field study of ten individuals who routinely work with living organisms such as plants, fish, reptiles and bees, and rely on these organisms as well as analog instruments and digital sensors to infer environmental conditions and inform future actions. Our findings offer a new perspective on everyday biomarkers, and we use the lens of organic and non-digital sensing to reflect on current sensing paradigms in ubiquitous computing. We conclude with three opportunity areas to help frame future work in ubiquitous sensing: (1) incorporating traditional technologies and living systems into ubiquitous sensing applications, (2) developing information technologies that teach new ways of 'seeing', and (3) supporting richer forms of metadata to unite stakeholders through their actions, interests and concerns.

ACM Classification Keywords
H5.m. Information interfaces and presentation (e.g., HCI): Miscellaneous

General Terms Design.

INTRODUCTION
Over the past few decades, UbiComp and HCI communities have explored a range of sensing systems to support our interactions with local environments, as well as the people, technologies and artifacts inhabiting them. While a sensor can be broadly defined as any device that responds to a physical stimulus, the majority of prior and ongoing research in UbiComp has understandably focused on electronic instantiations of sensing devices. In this paper, we present the practices of gardeners, beekeepers, zoologists and other 'experts' in the domain of organic and non-digital sensing to reflect on the question, *when is an electronic sensor appropriate or necessary in a given context*?

Visionary research has often turned to groups outside 'mainstream' user populations to productively inform new areas of inquiry within the UbiComp community [*e.g.*, 39, 40]. Similarly, we explore the values and practices of individuals who use *everyday biomarkers*- common biological organisms that express information about an ecosystem or its many parts. We present a comprehensive field study of 10 participants who routinely work with living organisms such as plants, fish, reptiles or bees. While many people might make inferences about the environment (*e.g.*, a cloudy sky suggests the possibility of rain), we expect our sample of participants to be more attuned to environmental processes as their work explicitly engages with living systems. Specifically, we focus on participants' use of digital devices, traditional tools and living organisms to infer environmental conditions and inform actions related to local ecosystems. In doing so, we reflect on current sensing paradigms in ubiquitous computing through the lens of organic and non-electronic sensing.

Figure 1. Everyday biomarkers: reptile posture suggesting a disturbance to the environment (top left); scale larvae signifying a pest problem (top right); bee behavior reflecting local weather and bloom cycles (bottom left); fish appearance indicating water quality and parasite levels (bottom right).

Our findings offer new insights into everyday biomarkers and serve to expand UbiComp visions of sensing to include more traditional instruments as well as the living organisms themselves. We conclude with three opportunity areas to help critically frame future work in ubiquitous sensing: (i) leveraging non-digital sensors, (ii) designing technologies that teach new ways of *'seeing'*, and (iii) enriching practices of data collection and sharing.

WHAT IS A SENSOR?

In what follows, we present several categories of electronic sensing technologies that emerged in UbiComp and HCI literature. Although these categories are by no means exhaustive or exclusive, they help contextualize the diverse range of sensors currently studied by these communities.

Input techniques

Early visions of sensing in HCI focused on detecting human actions to manipulate computer systems. For instance, Card, *et al.*'s taxonomy of input devices [8] quantifies sensing in terms of expressiveness and effectiveness. Kurtenbach and Buxton emphasize 'direct manipulation', contributing a suite of touch and gesture sensing technologies [24]. More recently, novel input techniques have appropriated everyday objects, surfaces or the body to capture human input [*e.g.*, 19]. Many of these new, more natural input techniques fall under the moniker of Natural User Interfaces (NUI). To be clear, "natural" terminology used in NUI refers to the interactive experience "feeling natural" (not to natural organisms as parts of the system).

Activity recognition/ infrastructure sensing

Another area of research explores sensing human behavior implicitly. For instance, wearable sensors support tracking routine actions [27]; or sensor-enabled mobile phones monitor physical exercise [10]. Ubiquitous systems are also designed to infer human behavior by sensing surrounding infrastructure, for example by sensing and tracking interactions with common appliances in the home [16, 18].

Active participatory sensing

New, often low-cost and DIY (do it yourself) technologies enable people (typically 'non-experts') to actively measure a range of environmental factors through participatory sensing [41]. Examples include handheld air quality monitors [14, 30], or mobile phones for tracking water quality [22], among many other others.

Passive environmental monitoring

An alternative body of sensing applications does not require continuous human involvement to monitor the environment. Examples include air quality monitors deployed on street sweepers [1] and autonomous robots [21]; or sensors left in public spaces [26] and private homes [23]. Here, humans may still interact with the collected data (*e.g.*, via map or graph) without explicitly engaging in the sensing process.

RELATED LITERATURE

As interest within the sensing community expands beyond indoor settings (home or office), new technologies are designed to promote deeper engagement with urban and rural environments. New applications are emerging to augment human interactions with organic materials, including sensor networks to support agricultural production in vineyards [3, 6], networks for non-invasive quality inspection of agricultural produce [37], or smart garden watering to promote conservation practices [30]. Other research focuses on context-aware computing to offer agricultural information [1], and, more generally, the educational potential of mobile sensor-based applications for learning about outdoor environments [7, 35, 38].

Critiques of sensing technologies emphasize expanding the scope of environmental sensing and, in some cases, drawing attention to possible unintended consequences. Aoki *et al.* [1] illustrate how the framing of environmental sensing and data collection can be expanded to encourage participation in public discussion of political issues. Similarly, DiSalvo *et al.*'s [14] review of related works articulates how political participation represents a key future dimension for sensing-based research to consider. Leshed *et al.* [28] critically investigate how GPS navigation systems can disengage people from the environments through which they navigate. Others describe the potential unproductive outcomes technical interventions might have on community organization and practices that otherwise sustain small-scale food production efforts [*e.g.*, 29].

Research exploring existing practices

Another body of research explores existing practices in order to inform the design of future ubiquitous technologies [*e.g.*, 42]. For example, Chetty *et al.* [9] and Dillahunt *et al.* [11] both study home resource consumption to draw out implications for the design of ubiquitous energy sensing; and Wyche, *et al.* examine how Pentecostals use communication technologies, suggesting interventions for supporting alternative value systems in UbiComp [43]. We build on these respective works by exploring the tools and practices of individuals working with living systems.

METHODS

We conducted semi-structured interviews (2-3 hours) with 10 participants who work with organic organisms (plants, reptiles, bees, fish, *etc.*) in and around a mid-sized city in the United States. Participants (ages 20's to late 60's; 3 female, 7 male) were recruited through local gardening and beekeeping communities, and the city zoo. Interviews took place at participants' respective sites of work (garden, zoo, apiary, *etc.*) to support rich, *in situ* reflections. We asked participants to walk through their daily routines (in regards to gardening, beekeeping, *etc.*) and, in doing so, show us their tools and local settings. Additionally, open-ended questions probed common uses of digital and non-digital sensors (and other technologies, such as computers, mobile phones, *etc.*); participants' knowledge of the environment based on tools and living systems; and how this information is shared with fellow practitioners or other stakeholders.

We audio recorded all interviews and took field notes, documentary photographs and select videos. The research team repeatedly reviewed the audio and all field materials to draw out underlying themes. Interview audio recordings were transcribed and coded using these themes. We also created conceptual models and affinity diagrams to reveal themes and unexpected connections across our data.

FINDINGS

We begin our findings by introducing the participants. We then detail our data in regards to: 1) *monitoring practices*—participants' use of technology, tools and observation to monitor the environment; 2) *types of living indicators*— how participants use living organisms as environmental indicators; 3) *collection, sharing and speculation*— patterns of discussion and speculation around biomarker data.

Participants

We recruited 10 diverse participants who routinely work with living organisms, including: beekeepers who maintain hives at home and throughout the city as a part of local community initiatives; an Integrated Pest Management (IPM) scientist who controls pest populations in a tropical greenhouse through organic means, such as beneficial insects that consume pests; a horticulturist who innovates, builds and maintains bioshelters (self-sustaining greenhouses, *"designed on the model of a cell- like a living cell that looks like a living organism*", H); organic farmers and gardeners who work independently or with urban agriculture groups; and reptile and fish overseers at a local zoo that acutely examine animal behaviors to inform their daily work. We reference data owing to individuals from each domain as follows:

- Organic farming, urban agriculture group [F1, F2, F3]
- Organic gardening, independent [G]
- IPM (integrated/organic pest management), city zoo [I]
- Beekeeping, urban beekeeping community [B1, B2]
- Horticulture, independent [H]
- Aquarium and fish keeping, city zoo [A]
- Reptile keeping, city zoo [R]

Participants' backgrounds

All participants have worked in their domain for several years, and most have been involved for decades: 8 participants have lived on farms or worked in gardens, zoos or aquariums for over 20 years. 7 participants earned professional degrees in biology, sustainable community development, etymology, zoology or a related field. However, all participants emphasize learning their craft through a mentor ("*Beekeeping is kind of an art or a craft, you really do need a mentor... you really need somebody local that can really tune you in with what's going on locally*", B1) or hands-on experience (*"just a function of working with fish a really long long time—you start to get kind of a zen feel for, ok something is not right there*", A).

Motivations

Participants rely on their work for income, either by selling equipment or produce, through education initiatives (radio shows, books, *etc.*), or employment at an urban agriculture community or the city zoo. However they also emphasize enjoyment ("*I enjoy growing- personally that's the most rewarding thing for me*", F1; "*the fact of seeing something go from just a little ity bity thing all the way to fruition*", G) and the broader benefits of their practice ("*every third bite of food that we eat as a society is attributed to the honey bee*", B1) as primary motivations behind their work.

Monitoring practices

Despite differences in their specific domains, all participants' work revolves around regular check-ups to track the health of the organisms their work relates to. From daily 'rounds' at tanks and aquariums ("*The first thing we do when we start is to check on our animals, we do rounds*", R; "*You just stand and watch them* [fish] *for a little bit and you see... Am I noticing anything that's off*", A) to weekly inspections of select plants (*"Every Wednesday we go and inspect certain plants",* I) or the bi-weekly examination of beehives ("*I check my hives once in 12 to 14 days*", B2), participants routinely monitor their environment. We continue by detailing participants' monitoring practices, organized by technological complexity, starting with practices that rely on technology as a primary means of data collection, and ending with practices that draw on more traditional instruments or do not involve any tools ('naked' human observation).

Technology-mediated monitoring

Predictably, some monitoring practices fundamentally rely on technology (Figure 2). Digital sensors are used routinely, occasionally (to clarify an anomaly), or early on (before participants acquire a skill and abandon the technology).

Routine digital sensing

Participants draw on certain technologies on a regular basis. A thermometer is used twice a day in aquariums ("*if you can catch the temperature before the chiller has been off for too long maybe you can save the animals*", A); daily at greenhouses, reptile tanks and bioshelter ("*if it's cold* [we] *build the fire and open and close vents as needed*", H), and weekly in IPM:

> *We try to look at the temperature and humidity and see how that affects the population of pests... we know that certain insects like spider mites, they love hot dry temperature.* (I)

Weather is also checked regularly (online, TV, *etc.*), for instance, to infer soil conditions ("*we're always looking at the weather, like you shouldn't do this when the ground is wet, you should do this*", F2) or availability of pollen:

> *I watch to see what the weather is like: the flowers may be open, but maybe raining and the plant flowers can't secrete nectar, the bees can't get to the flowers, maybe too cold maybe very dry, there's not an excess moisture for the flowers to secret a lot of nectar.* (B1)

Figure 2. Technologies used by participants: ORP probe, routinely used to monitor ozone levels in aquariums (top left), scale for weighing reptiles (top right), refractometer, occasionally used to check honey before harvesting (bottom left); thermometer, checked daily (bottom right).

Moreover, A checks ORP sensors twice a day to ensure proper function of the ozone generator ("*check in's and check out's. Spend a good hour and a half of my day*", A) and runs water quality tests weekly ("*we do monitor it* [water] *once a week to make sure the carbon is still removing the chlorine*", A). R uses a scale to weigh reptiles while they are quarantined ("*we do weights, measurements, we want to make sure the animal is thriving in quarantine*", F). F1, F2 and F3 take annual soil tests as part of their farming community's standards but do not notice drastic differences as most soil is imported compost ("*the nutrients would change a little bit, your nitrogen would jump up and down cause plans use to much of it*", F1).

Occasional digital sensing

In addition to the digital tools employed during routine monitoring, some technologies are used only occasionally, to clarify an anomaly or confirm an observation. For example, although G does not routinely test the soil, he would use a test if his plants were not growing properly:

> *I've never tested the soil here, I'm getting everything I want out of my garden so I'm not gonna worry about it. It's more if you're having problems… if your beets aren't heading up, you know probably a pH problem or a nutrient deficiency* [test the soil to] *figure out what it is.* (G)

Similarly, when F1 noticed dust accumulating from nearby dump trucks, he sent a sample to a local lab for testing:

> *The biggest air quality concern is the dump trucks full of slag that drive by… there's this like black dust that collects in the street and we scooped some of that up recently and sent it away for testing. I'm curious to see…* (F1)

The aquarist participant relies on water quality testing when he notices unusual fish behavior ("*we just start checking everything to see where's the problem, what's wrong*", A). Water quality sensors include a pH meter, a spectrophotometer, which can run up to "*400 different chemical analysis*", and a dissolved oxygen meter:

> *We have a dissolved oxygen meter in the lab, we don't go around and check all the exhibits once a week… if there's a problem… we'll bring the DO* [dissolved oxygen] *meter out. We'll check that it's not too low or too high.* (A)

Likewise, before harvesting honey, B2 occasionally uses a handheld refractometer to check its water content ("*anything above 18% tends to ferment, anything below 18% doesn't ferment*", B2). Thus, while technologies such as a DO meter or refractometer are not part of routine practice, participants tend to draw on them when their observations suggest ambiguous outcomes.

Abandoned digital sensing

Lastly, in several instances, digital sensing is used early on but is eventually abandoned. F2 no longer uses a sprinkler timer since it caused a pipe to "*burst*", and participant I does not trust the Fogstat system to correctly water the greenhouse due to faulty humidity sensing ("*it hasn't been calibrated in a while so it's way off*", I). Additionally, some sensors were abandoned when a participant acquired a certain skill. For instance, participant I stopped testing her soil when she learned to infer soil quality from plant growth:

> *I used to* [test soil] *every year but it kept coming back pretty much the same. I guess I'm just sort of working off how everything looks- everything seems to be green and growing pretty well.* (I)

Our findings thus suggest that while some technologies are regularly or occasionally used to monitor the environment, several types of sensors have been abandoned either due to malfunction or lack of useful data once a skill was acquired.

Traditional tools and observation-based monitoring

We discovered that a wide range of participants' monitoring practices do not involve digital sensing to understand environmental processes and states. Participants rely equally (although in different ways) on naturally occurring phenomena and non-digital 'measurement' tools.

Magnification and counting tools

Participants routinely use counting and magnification tools to infer environmental conditions (Figure 3). In beekeeping, a "*monitoring tray*"—a tray imprinted with a square inch grid—is placed under a hive. B2 accesses the infestation by counting the number of mites (pests) fallen on each square:

> *This is a monitoring tray… I'll slide it in there* [under a hive]*… We can either do a 24-hour count or a 15 min count. I just do a 15 min count. I'd look at it, and go ok there's 6* [mites] *in that one and on average there's 5 or 6 mites, which is heavy per square… So then I can determine whether I want to do a treatment.* (B2)

Similarly, F2 uses handmade traps (notecards covered with a sticky substance) to monitor pests based on the amount of caught insects:

Figure 3. Magnification and counting tools: monitoring tray (left); hand lens (center); handmade sticky trap (right).

> *"To see them* [pest insects], *we set sticky traps... you can go and you stick them in the dirt and you can go and see what you have... I don't count them* [insects], *but I kinda look at it. Like what's been caught on these cards*-[F2 looks at card] *it's not a ton, but it's definitely a lot."* (F2)

In IPM, a magnifying hand lens helps observe larvae stages on leaves to determine if beneficial insects are thriving:

> *If you look at this* [larvae] *under a hand lens, it has a really white wooly covering to it... getting to know the larval stages helps recognize that your beneficial insect is getting established.* (I)

Likewise, high-resolution magnification is used to monitor fish and reptiles. A microscope is used for annual checkups ("*the vet department will look at it* [fecal matter] *under a microscope and look for various parasites*", R), or inspections of fish, often cross-referenced with "*pictures of different parasites*":

> *We'll open up the gill cover take a little snip of the filament put that on the slide with the skin scrape look at it on the scope look for things that are crawling around.* (A)

Participants thus regularly use magnification and counting tools to reveal information that is invisible to the naked eye.

Monitoring through physical engagement and action

In another set of practices aimed at exploring information that is not accessible through passive observation (hearing, sight, *etc.*), participants become active agents in their environment. For instance, the whitefly pest tends to reside on leaves and is not easily discernable to the naked eye. To access this infestation F2 habitually taps her plants, causing noticeable clouds of whitefly to emerge ("*they* [whitefly] *come off in like a big cloud when you run your hand over it* [plant]", F2). Similarly, since nectar is not visible from outside the hive, B1 and B2 routinely 'tip' each beehive to gauge its weight and infer whether the amount of nectar is sufficient:

> *You just pick up—you tip the hive. You pick up one end and you can tell by the weight how many stored pounds of honey there is in the hive and that's something we do this time of the year to see if the bees are starving.* (B1)

In the bioshelter, H uses his finger to track moisture at various soil depths, accessing 'data' that might be unreliable or inaccessible through other means:

> *The human skin is a lot more sensitive than the gauges* [moisture sensors]. *When you want to know how moist the soil is at the bottom of the pot or the top of the pot... stick your finger in the pot and you know how far down it is.* (H)

Our aquarist participant shares an analogous practice, scuba diving into exhibits to monitor aspects of fish appearance and behavior that might be invisible from outside the tank:

> *I would love to be in my exhibits more... when I go scuba diving I can get this close to the animal, I can see a lot more. Because of the way the windows filter the light and the animals react to the light and everything... there are things you just miss that if you get in you can see.* (A)

These and other examples across all of our studied practices suggest physical action (tapping, tipping, inserting, *etc.*) as a means of gathering richer information, inaccessible through 'naked' and passive observation.

Monitoring through 'naked' observation

Finally, participants regularly infer information about the environment through 'naked' observations. Our findings include examples of the use of all five senses: smell ("*if the water is really bad you can actually smell the ammonia*", A); sight ("*parsnip starts to sprout so that usually means the soil gets to 70 degrees... by* [seeing] *what's germinating I can tell the temperature*", H); taste ("*some old time beekeepers... can taste that droplet of nectar and identify the flower that way, based on the taste*", B1); hearing ("*red belly woodpecker calling that's when a lot of my spring stuff is going* [to be planted]... *he's not gonna start mating calls till the weather is—till the light is in a certain way*", G); and touch ("*soft scale* [pest]... *exude a sugary substance called honeydew, so it's kind of a way of finding them— when a lot of leaves are getting sticky*", I). These instances illustrate how the human senses alone serve to inform participants of a range of processes and factors in the environment.

Types of everyday biomarkers

All 10 participants shared numerous experiences and habits of inferring environmental factors by observing elements of living systems. The everyday biomarkers used by participants can be classified as showing one specific factor (*one-to-one*); showing several possible factors (*one-to- many*); or showing the status of the ecosystem as a whole (*ecosystem*).

One to one

Biomarkers in this category map to concrete phenomena: a "*chicken coop smell*" in a beehive is used to detect foulbrood—a deadly bacterial infestation (B2); green water in a fish tank suggests an ozone deficiency ("*I can look at this water and tell that the ozone system hasn't been working for 2 weeks on this... because it's green*", A); particles resembling '*saw dust*' at the bottom of vine plants help identify a squash vine borer pest (F1); hydrangea color (pink or blue) is matched with low or high soil pH (I); a piping sound signals "*that a [new] queen is getting ready to emerge*" and a colony will soon split (B1); accentuated leaf growth in fruit plants is correlated with "*too much nitrogen in the soil*" (F2). Input from these and a multitude of other one-to-one biomarkers is nearly always mapped to a single cause and a subsequent associated practice.

One-to-many

One-to-many biomarkers inform our participants of several possible factors as opposed to one conclusive state. For instance, interveinal chlorosis, a yellowing "*between veins of leaves*" suggests nutrient deficiency or pH imbalance ("*a lot of times pH effects the availability of nutrients*", I); blossom end rot in tomatoes is "*caused by a lack of calcium*" (F1), or "*the calcium's there but the plant isn't able to accept it because of the moisture content*" (G); a 'sliming' fish suggests poor water quality or a parasite:

> *If a fish is sliming really heavily that's a good sign that something's wrong. It could be- water quality and the slime is trying to protect the animal* [or] *if there's a parasite that's causing the fish to slime really heavily to push that parasite off.* (A)

Similarly, bees returning to the hive trembling indicate a contamination, but do not imply one specific chemical:

> *If you have bees that are flying normally and coming back and trembling and dying they've obviously either got sprayed by something or got contaminated...* (B2)

Thus, one-to-many biomarkers typically lead to further reflection and investigation on behalf of our participants in order to infer the cause or actions that should follow.

Ecosystem

Lastly, participants rely on numerous biomarkers to learn about the ecosystem as a whole. For example, B1 infers local drought and blooming cycles by observing his bees:

> *One of the neat things about beekeeping is that it kinda gets you in touch with your local ecosystem. When there's a drought I can tell, the bees aren't bringing in much nectar, you can tell when the bees are bringing in pollen by observing the hive so you know when the first flowers are blooming in the spring, you can tell what flowers they're working based on the color of the pollen.* (B1)

Similarly, our IPM participant monitors the greenhouse by tracking the balance between pest and beneficial insects:

> *You always want to reach a balance, you never want to totally eradicate an insect... If you wanna sustain a population of beneficial insects, you always wanna have a baseline or a lower level of the pest insect - because they'll keep your beneficial* [insect] *around.* (I)

Alternatively, organisms are also used to infer problems in the ecosystem: coral reef bleaching as *"a response to stress, it's not necessarily any specific stress*", (A); algae on reefs suggesting "*a disturbance to the system... nutrients are very tightly cycled, algae indicates that they're not so tightly cycled*", (A); the endangerment of the Philippine crocodile, suggesting "*pollution, habitat loss, people kill them out of fear",* (R); or diseases prevailing on unhealthy plants ("*when a plant is stressed, a whole host of things can then be multiplied, diseases.. and pests will spread more easily*", F2). These examples illustrate how biomarkers are used to learn about complex processes within the ecosystem or infer information about the ecosystem as a whole.

Data collection, sharing and speculation

Participants maintain a variety of records of their practice (Figure 4) including: daily logs of water quality and feedings (A, R); an extensive log and computer database of pest infestations (I); recipes of honey products (B1, B2); schedules and layouts for crop rotations (F1, F2, F3); or a gardening journal that combines planting information with mementos from personal life ("*I'm hoping that my grandkids and great grandkids will be able to read that stuff*", G). While G was hesitant to share his journal due to an interweaving of sentimental material with garden data, all other participants were eager to show us their records. However, in practice, they rarely saw value in sharing everyday data with people outside their work ("*the only time that we really drew these graphs and all is when we were doing a PowerPoint doing a talk about the program*", I; "*what I do every day I don't think should be on the report- cleaning and feeding and the sort of mundane things*", R). Records thus serve to inform aspects of the work (*e.g.*, where to plant crops, what chemicals to add to the water), but are not typically shown to others.

Sharing Mechanisms

Nevertheless, participants do routinely share aspects of their work. Day to day information is discussed with other community members by word of mouth ("*people call me... I lend out an extractor to people and they come and pick it up and they tell me what's going on*", B1; "*casual conversation*", F1). More serious concerns, *e.g.* a mosquito spraying, might be posted to community listserves:

> *The mosquito spraying for instance, we put out a big email blast that said hey this is happening we're gonna monitor our hives, we suggest you do the same and we will let you know if anything came up we just kept everybody updated, we said nothings happening, nothings happening and everybody else reported the same... and it's good, watch out for each other.* (B2)

Twitter and Facebook are utilized to broadcast community events ("*tweet about things like- we're delivering this and this to the restaurant*", F2); while mediums such as books, blogs and radio shows offer gardening information and advice to the general public (G, H). Alternatively, R speaks directly to zoo visitors to correct misunderstandings:

> *I'm always listening in on people when they talk and I try to interject with the correct information in a way that I don't insult them... maybe tell them more about the animal they didn't know and try to make them understand.* (R)

Participants thus rely on a range of mediums, from conversation to Twitter and mailing lists, to share aspects of their practice in and outside of their communities.

Speculation

Participants tend to actively discuss the implications and causes of unusual environmental phenomena. For instance, all farming participants commented on a recent stinkbug infestation that affected the east coast of the United States. F2 wondered if it was caused by weather patterns and discussed the matter with other farmers:

> *I think there's something in the weather pattern that allowed them* [stink bugs] *to reproduce at those rates... a lot of*

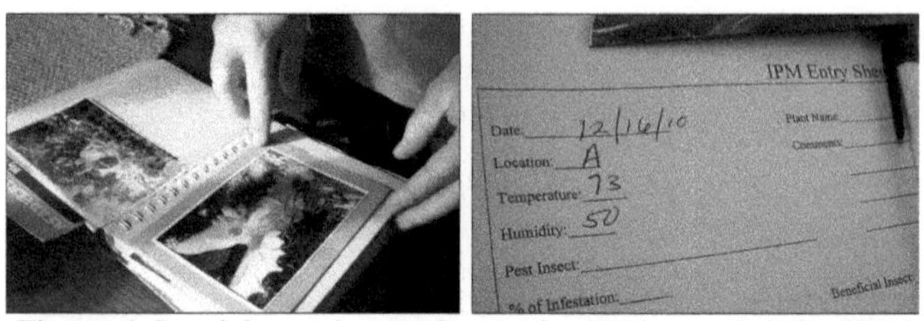

Figure 4. Participants' records: gardening journal (left); IPM data entry sheet (right).

farmers we spoke to had whole crops that were destroyed and that was very strange because we've never even seem the attack food crops. (F2)

Consequently, numerous community members began to experiment and share possible solutions to the problem:

> *I got them on my blog—this woman sent me a picture* [of] *a mouse going onto her deck and eating stink bugs... then another woman called me... she gathered all the stinkbugs that she found and threw them out on the deck and here come the turkeys eating the stinkbugs. This is really great news, because to this point we didn't know if local birds would eat stinkbugs and now they're discovering it.* (G)

Likewise, urban water quality emerged as an issue of concern for many participants: G prefers to water his plants with rainwater ("*just because there's no chlorine in it, fluoride and all that other crap*", G), H uses a private well, and city water is filtered prior to entering A's aquariums. In particular, A notes the lack of accessible information about urban water ("*you can call them and ask, or you can just test it*", A), noting that certain chemicals are lethal for fish:

> *They* [the city] *can change the chemicals they use for disinfection* [of water]*... now a lot of facilities are switching to chloramine... so if it gets into your fish tank it really wreaks havoc.* (A)

Moreover, the rise in colony collapse disorder—a national die-off in honeybees—has spurred a debate on pesticide use in beekeeping communities, locally and internationally. B2 showed us numerous posts on an online international forum (*e.g.*, "*document shows EPA allow bee toxic pesticide despite their own scientists' red flags*", B2), suggesting pesticides and genetically modified plants as likely causes:

> *...all these self pollinating plants, or synthetically modified plants they don't need pollinators anymore, so that's taking away a food source, on top of that they're spraying the shit with chemicals that's killing the bees.* (B2)

Both B1 and B2 also blame lack of government regulation ("*In Europe they banned neonicotinoids because they believe it is hurting the bee population, but in this country, they haven't been able to prove it's a problem, but a lot of beekeepers think it is a problem*", B1). Similarly, G speculates that commercial advertisements promoting stylized images of green lawns led people to use chemical sprays on their yards, resulting in nitrogen soil deficiencies ("*clover takes the nitrogen out of the air and puts it in the soil... it wasn't until advertisers told us that we don't want clover in our lawns that were taught not to have clover in our lawns*", G). To counter such advertisements, G endorses organic practices on his blog, radio show and in numerous publications: "*this is what I teach people- there is no reason to use any chemical in your garden*" (G).

Likewise, R is also taking action in his field— collaborating with another zoo to breed and reintroduce the endangered Louisiana Pine Snake into the wild. He notes the broader processes, which may have contributed to the endangerment:

> *They* [Louisiana Pine Snakes] *feed primarily on... the pocket gopher, and when it went they went with it, and the reason the pocket gopher went is cause they specialize in certain types of grass—a lightening would burn an area where these things would grow—the grass would grow first... well with forest management now there is no burning... that's what started the problems* (R)

The above instances illustrate a range of reflections based on ambiguous or unexpected inputs from living systems. The resulting speculations are often projected to broader groups to infer potential meaning(s) as well as to consider (and in some cases even organize) collective action aimed at the responsible or intervening social and political forces.

DISCUSSION

Our findings detail the practices of 10 individuals who directly and indirectly work with living organisms on a daily basis. We highlight participants' proficiency with and access to a range of technologies, which range from social media such as mailing lists, blogs, forums and Twitter, to digital information systems such as a database of records or online weather reports, to highly technical sensors for soil and water quality. While our participants skillfully draw on these digital technologies throughout their practice, they also habitually rely on living systems (biomarkers) to infer information about the environment and shape their course of action. We highlight two unique themes that emerge from participants' use of everyday biomarkers.

Biomarker systems

Our findings suggest that biomarkers are perceived to be and used as integral components of larger systems. Some practices revolve around systems that are purely organic: designing a bioshelter "*on the model of a living cell*", or using *one-to-many* and *ecosystem* biomarkers (fish appearance, bee behavior, balance between pest and beneficial insects, *etc.*) to infer complex processes within an ecosystem, or gain a glimpse into its well-being as a whole. Other practices confirm or clarify 'naked' perceptions of living organisms with data from analog and digital tools, resulting in systems of interdependencies between technological and biological inputs. More broadly, participants' collective practices reveal larger, socio-political systems that shape their work: regional water quality treatment, national policies to preserve or destroy snake habitats, or international regulations on pesticide use.

Active engagement with context

Consequently, biomarkers not only cue participants to environmental states, but also serve as points of engagement with underlying contexts. In the most direct sense, participants physically interact with the environment—from tapping on plant leaves, tipping a beehive, inserting a finger into the soil, or diving into an aquarium, they are active and immersed in their surroundings. On a higher level, participants become involved in the social and political processes that shape their practices. Examples such as beekeepers debating EPA regulations on international forums, farmers experimenting with natural remedies for stinkbugs, a gardener advising the general public against using commercially advertised chemical sprays, and a reptile keeper collaborating across state lines to preserve endangered snakes, all suggest that biomarkers serve to inspire active participation in broader contexts.

DESIGN IMPLICATIONS AND OPPORTUNITIES

We conclude with three design implications emerging from our data. We draw on our findings to expand the UbiComp community's conceptualization of 'sensor' and present new opportunity areas for the design of future sensing systems.

Leveraging non-digital inputs

Earlier, we outlined several popular categories of sensing in UbiComp and HCI research, whereby a sensor is typically conceptualized and studied as an electronic device. Our work suggests examples of both traditional tools (hand lens, *etc.*) and living organisms that may be construed as 'sensors'. Our participants effectively monitor factors such as soil temperature ("*by seeing what's germinating*"), ammonia levels (by smelling the water), amount of stored honey (by tipping the hive), or pest infestation levels (through counting and magnification tools) without the use of soil sensors, water quality monitors or IR insect tracking. When participants do rely on digital sensing, they often employ such technologies only as a secondary measure (*e.g.*, chemical analysis of water when fish do not appear healthy; testing the soil if plants are not growing properly).

Our findings, which include a range of sensing practices that do not involve digital sensors. As new research emerges to question technology-focused approaches in HCI (*e.g.*, "could technology be replaced by an equally viable low-tech or non-technological approach?" [2]), and their implications (*e.g.*, sustainable disposal of digital artifacts [5]), we argue for expanding the UbiComp community's vision of sensing beyond electronic devices, to include living organisms and traditional tools.

Throughout our fieldwork we discovered that sensors (digital, analog or organic) are rarely if ever used in isolation. Instead participants fluidly navigate across a hybrid *system* of biomarkers, traditional tools and digital devices to gain insights into environmental processes and inform future actions. Our findings suggest an opportunity to shift from designing sensing technologies to designing ubiquitous *systems* that incorporate living organisms and traditional tools along with digital devices. In particular, this paradigm could open a rich design space for *active participatory sensing* or *passive environmental monitoring*, for instance by expanding prior work in public air quality sensing (*e.g.*, [1]) to integrate inputs from plants [24] and insects, or monitoring water quality (*e.g.*, [22]) based on fish activity. Alternatively, entirely new ubiquitous systems could emerge to broaden our understanding of the ecosystem as a whole (rather than specific aspects such as water or air quality) by integrating inputs from plants, insects and animals along with analog tools and digital sensors into holistic representations of the environment. For instance, a system might track the well-being of a neighborhood by visualizing noise, air and water quality along with insect activity and appearance of street plants.

Designing technologies that teach new ways of *seeing*

Our data suggests that over time, participants developed a "*zen feel*" for the complex processes in their environment. Occasionally, highly skilled and nuanced ways of "reading" biomarkers were accompanied by the use of more advanced technologies. However, such technologies were sometimes abandoned after participants developed a skill (*e.g.*, "*working off how everything looks*" instead of testing the soil), or were used infrequently and only to help resolve a problem that more traditional tools could not (*e.g.*, D.O. meter to verify water quality when fish appear sick). These findings suggest a new model for designing digital sensors: sensing technologies as tools that support new ways of 'seeing' or engaging with the environment. Such sensors move away from 'smart' technology and towards systems that encourage human awareness, refection and wonderment about our living world [32].

Embracing low-fidelity signals. Digital sensing tools can offer remarkable degrees of precision, and the collected data lends itself to powerful methods of analysis. Graphs, charts and other scientific presentations are common throughout HCI sensing applications ranging from *activity recognition* to *input sensing*. These approaches contrast with the numerous 'imprecise' sensing practices of our participants: biomarkers (plant growth, reptile activity levels, *etc.*) and more traditional tools (*e.g.*, monitoring tray) often provided highly useful and reliable information without the degrees of precision characteristic of digital sensors. Imprecision often prompted our participants' physical involvement with the materials being sensed: tipping a beehive, inserting a finger into soil, or tapping a plant leaf. These and similar actions can inspire future *input techniques* to support indiscreet and fluid interactions with digital systems. More broadly, ubiquitous systems can draw on 'imprecise' digital sensing to embrace "ambiguity as a resource for design" [17] or "design for doubt" [31]. For instance, as an alternative to providing concrete measurements such as time and duration of electrical appliance use [18], *activity recognition* systems might explore imprecise sensing to facilitate more critical explorations of human behavior. Similarly, research supporting outdoor learning experiences [*e.g.* 35] might use imprecise sensing to encourage inquiry into ambiguously represented environmental phenomena.

Peripheral engagement. The use of imprecise biomarkers and tools also inspired participants' engagement with context that is peripheral to the phenomena being sensed: by looking at larval stages, the IPM participant assessed the "*balance*" and well-being of the entire greenhouse; by tracking bee behavior, a beekeeper became "*in touch with* [the] *local ecosystem*"; by observing algae on a reef, A inferred a "*disturbance to the system*". While often subtle to articulate, this type of engagement seemed to play essential roles in developing a sensibility for understanding the environment. In addition, peripheral engagement was at times suggested as a source of meaning. Whether by directly "*seeing something* *go from just a little ity bity thing all the way to fruition"* or taking pride in the fact that "*every third bite of food is attributed to the honey bee*", participants drew experiential value from their practice.

These findings highlight the importance of the degree to which a digital sensor either facilitates or hinders peripheral engagement. For example, as noted in a recent CHI panel on food and sustainability [20], a system that senses soil moisture and waters plants remotely may discourage active presence in the garden. Consequently, the user may neglect or never learn important cues about the health of plants.

However, digital sensing also has the potential to support new and exciting forms of peripheral engagement, especially with phenomena that are difficult or impossible to sense with 'naked' human perception. For example, water quality sensing systems used in *infrastructure* and *environmental sensing* [*e.g.*, 16] can reveal relationships between the home water system and local water source. Similarly, air quality monitoring can connect users with processes that contribute to air pollution in the home or neighborhood. On a higher level, considering peripheral engagement in the design of sensing systems can support more holistic interactions, including engagement with broader phenomena aside from ones directly being sensed.

Scaffolding. Through "*years of experience*" and insights from mentors, our participants developed highly nuanced sensibilities to infer information such as complex air or water quality from cues as subtle as a sliming fish or a trembling bee. With some participants viewing their practice as "*an art or a craft*", our findings suggest opportunities for new scaffolding tools that train individuals and groups to 'sense' better and differently. For instance, a body of research in *activity recognition* and *participatory sensing* appropriates mobile phones as digital sensing devices [10, *etc.*]. Complimentary to this work, mobile phones and other ubiquitous platforms can be used to direct people to their local environments, providing information that supports 'reading' natural or artificial biomarkers, such as appearances of plants and behaviors of animals. Some information technologies can serve as scaffolding tools that are needed less frequently or not at all after a sufficient level of skill has been developed. Others can be designed to nurture mentor/apprentice relationships in communities, encouraging sensing as a "conjoint practice" [26] and tool for community togetherness [14].

Enriching practices of data collection and sharing

Our participants routinely record environmental data in logs, databases, and personal journals. While these documents are not directly shown to other stakeholders, the participants actively share aspects of their practice, from day-to-day events discussed with local practitioners through "*causal conversation"*, or telling zoo visitors "*more about the animal*", to broadcasting issues of local concern on community listserves and speculating about large-scale phenomena on international forums. As new *citizen science* and *environmental monitoring* applications continue to explore data sharing [*e.g.*, 23, 21], we see a range of opportunities for collecting and presenting inputs from living systems and analog tools as well as digital sensors.

On one hand, we see opportunities for existing and future citizen science applications to incorporate a new user group: individuals working with living systems. Technologies can combine routine information collected by beekeepers, aquarists, reptile keepers, or gardeners with rich forms of metadata, for example: augmenting mite counts with observations of bee behavior; supplementing water quality data with images of fish appearance; integrating gardening data with mementos from personal life; or more broadly correlating inputs from organic systems with users' insights into the surrounding environmental processes. Alternatively, metadata might be embedded into the organic materials themselves (similar to augmenting fabric with storytelling [36]). For instance, a beehive could be annotated with current flower conditions or weather patterns; a plant bed might show crop rotation history, *etc.*

On a higher level, data collected from living organisms, coupled with personal or group annotations, can serve to further issues of community concern and political interest. As HCI research emerges to encourage collective action around shared issues [14], we see opportunities for supporting activism around the well-being of living systems (similar to technologies that sustain 'publics' [12]). For example, local beekeepers could capture and share videos of bee flights, attributing metadata to draw attention to potential pesticide spraying in the area (as per [7]). Similarly, gardeners and aquarists might upload images of fish and plants to track possible changes in urban water quality. Moreover, using the scaffolding tools outlined earlier, everyday citizens could be involved in the collection and sharing of biomarker data. Examples include mobile applications that enable photographs and annotations of nature reserves to assess snake habitats, or insect counting tools to track local pest populations. Resulting data could be shared within and across communities of local residents, individuals working with living systems, or government officials thus supporting "politics of scale" [15] by linking people through their collective actions in the service of broader social change.

CONCLUSION

We presented the environmental monitoring practices of 10 individuals who routinely engage with living organisms. Our participants draw on independent and interrelated systems of biomarkers, traditional tools and digital sensors to infer information about the environment and inform actions related to local ecosystems. We use our findings to reflect on current sensing paradigms and explore approaches for incorporating living organisms, traditional tools and digital devices into future sensing systems. We propose (1) leveraging non-digital inputs in ubiquitous systems, (2) designing technologies that teach new ways of 'seeing', and (3) enriching practices of data collection and sharing as opportunities for expanding and guiding future research in this area. Ultimately, we hope our work inspires a broader framing of and a more hybrid approach towards sensing infrastructures that support the diversity and richness of human and environmental ecosystems.

REFERENCES

1. Aoki, P. et al. 2009. A Vehicle for Research: Using Street Sweepers to Explore the Landscape of Environmental Community Action. Proc. of CHI '09.
2. Baumer E., Silberman, S. 2011. When the implication is not to design (technology). Proc. of CHI 2011.
3. Beckwith, R., Teibel, D., Bowen, P. 2004. Report from the Field: Results from an Agricultural Wireless Sensor Network. In Proceedings of LCN '04, 471-478.
4. Bidwell, N., Browning, D. 2010. Pursuing genius loci: interaction design and natural places. *Personal Ubiquitous Comput. 14, 1* (January 2010), 15-30.
5. Blevis, E. 2007. Sustainable interaction design. CHI '07
6. Burrell, J., Brooke, T., Beckwith, R. 2004. Vineyard Computing: Sensor Networks in Agricultural Production. IEEE Pervasive Computing 3, 1 (January 2004), 38-45.
7. J. Campbell, L. Mummert, R. Sukthankar. Video Monitoring of Honey Bee Colonies at the Hive Entrance. Visual observation & analysis of animal & insect behavior, ICPR'08.
8. Card, S. K., Mackinlay, J. D., Robertson, G. G. 1990. The design space of input devices. CHI '90.
9. Chetty, M., Tran, D., Grinter, R. E. 2008. Getting to green: understanding resource consumption in the home. UbiComp'08.
10. Consolvo, S., *et al.* 2008. Activity sensing in the wild: a field trial of ubifit garden. CHI '08.
11. Dillahunt, T., Mankoff, J., Paulos, E., Fussell, S.. 2009. It's not all about "Green": energy use in low-income communities. In Proceedings of UbiComp '09.
12. DiSalvo, C. 2009. "Design and the Construction of Publics." Design Issues, Vol. 25, No. 1 (2009): 48-63.
13. DiSalvo, C., Boehner, K., Knouf, N. A., Sengers, P. Nourishing the Ground for Sustainable HCI: Considerations from Ecologically Engaged Art. CHI '09.
14. DiSalvo, C. Marti, L., Coupland, J., Steiner, M. A 2009. "Local Issues, Local Uses: Tools for robotics and sensing in community contexts." C&C'09: Creativity & Cognition.
15. Dourish, P. 2010. HCI and Environmental Sustainability: The Politics of Design and the Design of Politics. DIS'10
16. Froehlich, J. E., *et al.* 2009. HydroSense: infrastructure-mediated single-point sensing of whole-home water activity. In Proceedings of UbiComp '09.
17. Gaver, W. W., Beaver, J., Benford, S. 2003. Ambiguity as a resource for design. In Proc. of the SIGCHI '03.
18. Gupta, S., Reynolds, M. S., Patel, S. N. 2010. ElectriSense: single-point sensing using EMI for electrical event detection and classification in the home. UbiComp '10.
19. Harrison, C. Desney Tan, and Dan Morris. 2010. Skinput: appropriating the body as an input surface. CHI '10.
20. Hirsch, T., Sengers, P., Blevis, E., Beckwith, R., Parikh, T. 2010. Making food, producing sustainability. CHI EA '10.
21. Jeremijenko, N., Arnold, J. J., Kavesh, W. Feral Robotic Dogs. 2009.
22. Kim, S., Robson, C., Zimmerman, T., Harber, E., Pierce, J. 2011. Creek Watch: Pairing Usefulness and Usability for Successful Citizen Science. CHI 2011
23. Kim, S., Paulos, E. inAir: Sharing Indoor Air Quality Measurements and Visualizations. CHI 2010
24. Kuribayashi, S., Sakamoto, Y., Tanaka, H. 2007. I/O plant: a tool kit for designing augmented human-plant interactions. Ext. Abs. of of CHI '07, 2537-2542.
25. Kurtenbach, G., Buxton, W. 1991. Issues in combining marking and direct manipulation techniques. In Proceedings of UIST '91.
26. Kuznetsov, S., Davis, G. N., Cheung, J. C., Paulos, E. 2011. Ceci N'est Pas Une Pipe Bombe: Authoring Urban Landscapes with Air Quality Sensors. CHI 2011, to appear
27. Lee, M.L., Dey, A.K. 2008. Lifelogging Memory Appliance for People with Episodic Memory Impairment. Proceedings of UbiComp'08.
28. Leshed, G., Velden, T., Rieger, O., Kot, B., Sengers, P. 2008. In-car gps navigation: engagement and disengagement from the environment. CHI '10, 1675-1684.
29. Odom, W. 2010. "Mate, we don't need a chip to tell us the soil's dry": opportunities for designing interactive systems to support urban food production. In Proc. of DIS '10.
30. Paxton, M., Benford, S. 2009. Experiences of participatory sensing in the wild. Proc of UbiComp '09, 265-274.
31. Paulos, E. 2009. Designing for Doubt: Citizen Science and the Challenge of Change. Engaging Data, MIT, Cambridge.
32. Paulos, E., Jenkins, T., Joki, A., Vora. P. 2008. Objects of wonderment. DIS '08, New York, NY, USA, 350-359.
33. Pearce, J., Smith, W., Nansen, B., Murphy, J. 2009. Smart Garden Watering: experiences of using a garden watering simulation. Proc. of OZCHI '09, 217-224.
34. Rana, R. K., Chou, C. T., Kanhere, S. S., Bulusu, N., Hu, W. (2010). Ear-phone: an end-to-end participatory urban noise mapping system. ACM/IEEE IPSN '10.
35. Rogers, Y. *et al.* 2004. Ambient wood: designing new forms of digital augmentation for learning outdoors. IDC '04, 3-10.
36. Rosner, D. K., Ryokai, K. 2008. Spyn: augmenting knitting to support storytelling and reflection. UbiComp '08.
37. Ruiz-Altisent, M. et al. 2010. Review: Sensors for product characterization and quality of specialty crops-A review. Comput. Electron. Agric. 74, 2 (November 2010), 176-194.
38. Ryokai et al. GreenHat: Exploring the Natural Environment Through Experts' Perspectives. CHI '11.
39. Satchell, C. and Dourish, P. 2009. Beyond the User: Use and Non-Use in HCI. Proc. Australasian Conf. Computer-Human Interaction OzCHI 2009, 9-16.
40. Shklovski, I., Vertesi, J., Troshynski, E., Dourish, P. 2009. The commodification of location: dynamics of power in location-based systems. In Proceedings of UbiComp '09.
41. Willett, W., Aoki, P., Kumar, N., Subramanian, S., Woodruff, A. (2010) Common Sense Community: Scaffolding Mobile Sensing and Analysis for Novice Users. Pervasive'10
42. Woodruff, A., Hasbrouck, J., Augustin, A. 2008. A bright green perspective on sustainable choices. SIGCHI'08.
43. Wyche, S. P., Magnus, C. M., Grinter, R. E. 2009. Broadening UbiComp's vision: an exploratory study of charismatic pentecostals and technology use in Brazil. In UbiComp '09

Red Balloon, Green Balloon, Sensors in the Sky

Stacey Kuznetsov[1], George Noel Davis[2], Eric Paulos[1], Mark D. Gross[3], Jian Chiu Cheung[2]

Human-Computer Interaction Institute[1]
Carnegie Mellon University
Pittsburgh, PA, USA
{stace, paulos}@cs.cmu.edu

Department of Electrical and Computer Engineering[2]
Carnegie Mellon University
Pittsburgh, PA, USA
{gnd, jccheung}@andrew.cmu.edu

Computational Design Lab[3]
School of Architecture
Carnegie Mellon University
Pittsburgh, PA, USA
mdgross@cmu.edu

ABSTRACT
Spectacle computing is a novel strategy for vibrantly projecting information into the public sphere using expressive and tangible media. We demonstrate an example of this computing meme with large, glowing balloons that change color based on input from attached air quality sensors (exhaust, diesel, or volatile organic compounds). In two public installations (city street and public park) and a deployment with six everyday citizens, we invited stakeholders to playfully explore and actively participate in visualizing surrounding air quality. We also created a do-it-yourself (DIY) kit that includes a printed circuit board, electronic parts and instructions for building the air quality balloons. In a workshop, six non-expert users successfully assembled functional balloons, validating our technology as a DIY tool for public air quality visualization. Our deployments and workshop highlight play and spectacle as essential elements for public participation and activism. We outline design guidelines for future spectacle computing projects that engage stakeholders with environmental data and empower them to transform urban landscapes.

Author Keywords
Spectacle computing, participatory sensing, air quality

ACM Classification Keywords
H5.m. Information interfaces and presentation (e.g., HCI): Miscellaneous.

General Terms
Design.

INTRODUCTION
Low cost sensors, DIY (do-it-yourself) methods and bottom-up initiatives have expanded environmental sensing beyond the domain of scientists and experts, enabling ordinary citizens to measure, analyze, and share information about their environment. An emerging body of HCI and ubicomp research has explored this mode of distributed data collection by non-experts, referred to as *participatory sensing* [8] or *citizen science* [39]. Recently,

UbiComp 11, September 17–21, 2011, Beijing, China.

Figure 1. Air quality balloons in public park (top left), diesel balloon inflated (top right), DIY diesel kit fully assembled (bottom left), and a VOC balloon close-up (bottom right).

citizen science projects have focused on handheld devices such as cellphones and data loggers [*e.g.*, 11] to collect environmental data, and visualizations such as graphs, charts, and maps [*e.g.*, 16] to present this data to communities of users. We introduce *spectacle computing* as a playful and powerful approach to enable non-experts to view environmental data and project this information into the public sphere.

We developed large, glowing, air-quality sensing balloons as a vehicle for stakeholders to explore and reflect on urban air quality (Figure 1). The balloons change color in response to one of exhaust gas, diesel, or VOC's (volatile organic compounds). These three pollutants continue to exacerbate urban air quality problems, especially in the city where we conducted this research, where air quality has been rated as among the worst in the United States [4]. Diesel exhaust consists of fine particulate matter emitted by engines and industrial processes [44]; exhaust gas—a mixture of carbon monoxide, nitrogen dioxide, and hydrocarbons—is produced by gasoline engines [9]; and VOC's (volatile organic compounds) originate from paints, pesticides, or certain types of fuels [45]. Exposure to any of these substances can lead to chronic respiratory illnesses, not to mention the pollutants' role in global climate change.

Research objectives

The following section describes social phenomena that inspired spectacle computing and reviews related ubicomp and HCI literature. We then detail the design of our air quality balloons and present findings from two public installations and deployments with six everyday citizens. Finally, we introduce our DIY kit, which we distributed in a workshop where six non-expert users successfully assembled functional air quality sensing balloons. Our findings offer insights into questions such as: 1) how do playful *spectacles* influence public perceptions of air quality; 2) how do everyday citizens use tangible media to broadcast their concerns about air quality; and 3) what are the implications of tangible media as a supporting material for DIY making and grassroots activism?

SPECTACLE COMPUTING

Artists have a long history of integrating "the spectacle" into their work: from Allan Kaprow's *Happenings* [27] and the writings of Guy Debord and the Situationists in the 1960's [14], to more contemporary tactical media artists such as The Yes Men, Critical Art Ensemble, RTMark, Preemptive Media, and Institute for Applied Autonomy. The Situationists differentiated between passive subjects—consumers of the spectacle—and those who transform their own ideas, concerns, and passions into the spectacle itself. This movement applied concepts of commodity fetishism [33] to contemporary mass media to expose the common politics of its day. *Spectacle computing* intentionally and overtly foregrounds these ideas, using expressive technologies to inspire new thinking, curiosity and beliefs. Stakeholders who otherwise may not be aware of or care about an issue are drawn into the spectacle.

Contrary to contemporary rhetoric of "invisible" interfaces and seamless computing, we argue for a complementary strategy explicitly designed to generate spectacles. First and foremost, spectacles are difficult to ignore. The barrier to engagement is thereby effectively lowered because individuals need not download an application or carry specific hardware. The spectacle is intentionally designed to distract the individual or group's attention. Moreover, it invites people to engage in otherwise socially unacceptable behaviors such as overt public voyeurism, gossip and curiosity. Finally, it presents an acceptable context for individuals to participate in the spectacle, in the spirit of a *Happening*, even if such participation involves odd, unusual, or socially awkward activities (*i.e.* willingly taking and carrying around a glowing balloon).

We view these insights as experience design opportunities. We observe how spectacle computing moves people from a personal and private context, through public voyeurism, and into readily carrying balloons around the city, thereby creating their own spectacle. To be clear, spectacle computing is not intended to mimic the experience of yelling "fire" in a crowded theater, but to more tactfully and expressively engage public audiences in issues of personal or societal concern. While this approach is tangentially related to FlashMobs, which draw large groups of people to suddenly assemble and perform unusual acts in public places, the goal of spectacle computing is to foster discourse between stakeholders, technology and space through the use of dynamic computing elements. Also unlike FlashMobs, which may create a feeling of inclusion and exclusion, spectacle computing invites open participation from everyone.

Balloons

We use balloons as an expressive medium for creating air quality spectacles. Balloons are inherently playful: they remind us of birthday parties, water balloon fights, street fairs, weddings, or carnivals. Balloons are also functional: for decades they have enabled scientific endeavors, ranging from the NASA superpressure balloon which successfully flew over Antarctica [34] to the National Weather Service radiosondes (sensor packages) deployed on weather balloons [36], as well as a milieu of grassroots aerial photography projects [*e.g.,* 19]. Lastly, balloons are compelling and visual: they have shaped artistic and political expressions, including the popular song *99 Luftballons* [35], Lamorisse's film *The Red Balloon* [32], the literary work *More Sky* [41], and most recently, interactive balloon installations such as *Open Burble* [20]. This vast range of artistic and functional balloon projects inspired us to utilize large glowing weather balloons as a playful expression of a serious concern—public air quality.

RELATED WORK

Ubicomp and HCI communities have explored a range of participatory sensing platforms to enable citizens to monitor their environment. Examples include handheld sensing devices [10] cellphones [23] sensors installed in private homes [28], or sensors deployed on moving vehicles [3], bicycles [16] and pigeons [12]. Most projects employ conventional visualization methods: line graphs [28], maps [11] or numeric data [16]. More expressive and public visualizations include WearAir—a T-shirt that responds to air quality with interactive lights [29], CO2RSET—a corset that constricts when the air becomes toxic [37], the pollution e-sign, which hijacks passersby mobile phones with air quality data [24], and *Air de Paris Balloon*—a giant balloon tethered over the city of Paris to show data collected from several sensing stations [1]. Unlike prior work, our balloon visualization enables stakeholders to transform and produce urban lightscapes with sensor data.

Urban lightscapes

Public displays and installations such as BlueTone [13], Aarhus by Light [10], Amphibious Architecture [2], and many others have enabled stakeholders to alter urban lightscapes through sound, body movement or text messages. Modular technologies including LED Throwie's [18], Light Bodies [43], and WallBots [31] allow individuals (ranging from ordinary passersby to artists and activists) to move and place interactive elements in urban spaces. Drawing from this prior work, we created modular sensors and reactive lights carried by weather balloons. Our project is inspired by other creative balloon installations: *Burble*- a floating cloud of balloons that is controlled by moving a handlebar [20], and *Wire and Balloon Installation*, which responds to touch with sound [40], to name a few.

Support tools for DIY practices

A range of HCI initiatives have focused on technologies that involve communities of non-experts in hands-on making. Examples include Sketching in Hardware—a creative workshop for physical prototyping [22]; Simple Haptics—a suite of tools for creating haptic interfaces; or numerous e-textile workshops with the LilyPad as a ubiquitous tool for education [*e.g.*, 5, 6]. In addition, prior work has explored the values and practices of DIY communities through conference workshops [*e.g.*, 7, 26], surveys [30], or qualitative fieldwork [42]. We contribute to this research by introducing a low-cost DIY kit that enables non-experts to assemble their own interactive air quality balloons. We evaluate our approach by conducting a DIY balloon-making workshop with hobbyists from a local DIY community.

AIR QUALITY BALLOONS

Our circuit is powered by a rechargeable lithium polymer battery and relies on one of two inexpensive sensors from Figaro: a VOC sensor or a dual function Diesel/Exhaust sensor [17]. The latter measures either diesel or exhaust on separate balloons, and each balloon is labeled with the corresponding pollutant ('voc', 'diesel', or 'exhaust'). PICAXE [38], a low-cost ($1.50) microcontroller, processes sensor data and controls a tri-colored LED. This LED is inserted into the balloon; the sensor, microcontroller, and battery are mounted outside using wire and electrical tape. Balloons are illuminated based on surrounding air quality, glowing green, yellow, or red to indicate 'low', 'average', or 'high' pollution levels. Balloons are inflated using helium and their latex material naturally diffuses LED light, resulting in a large, evenly 'glowing', floating orb.

Ambient light thresholds

To support Do-It-Yourself (DIY) principles of easy access to materials and methods for creation by non-experts, we constrained the design of our system by choosing low-cost and low-fidelity sensors. We empirically determined our illumination thresholds (sensor values for green, yellow, or red balloon lighting) by gathering sensor data around Pittsburgh over the course of one week. We visited five different neighborhoods and collected readings indoors, outdoors, and at varying distances from busy streets, as well as in (traffic-free) parks. We used the observed variance in sensor output to determine thresholds below, within, and above the average sensor output for green, yellow, and red lighting respectively. Consequently, our balloons show air quality relative to the data collected in our city. Our display choice appropriately affords open interpretation through relative threshold lighting than exact numbers.

AIR QUALITY SPECTACLE

We deployed about thirty balloons throughout the city of Pittsburgh, Pennsylvania, USA over the course of one night. The authors tethered balloons around two different locations (in a public park and along a city street), observing public interactions with the installation. In addition, six stakeholders were invited to participate in our project, placing and photographing air quality balloons in public spaces throughout the city.

Installations

We selected two locations to install our air quality balloons: a public park and a city street (Figure 2), expecting to see a range of balloon colors due to different amounts of traffic, people, etc. in the two spaces. Our installation coincided with extreme humidity (over 80%) and a PM2.5 (fine particulate matter) alert, causing many of the balloons to turn red. We inflated the balloons on site, tethering them to trees and benches (in public park) and on parking meters, cars and street signs along a city block. In addition to observing public interactions with our project we interviewed individuals who approached us and invited them to take some balloons. The installation was after dusk (around 9.30pm), so we encountered few people in the public park but numerous passersby approached us along the city block. We spent about one hour in each location.

Public reactions

Consistent with our framing of spectacle computing, nearly everyone who saw our installation was compelled to stop or slow down. In the public park and along the city block people expressed curiosity about the large, mysteriously glowing balloons. Most initial reactions suggested awe at the size and illumination: *"I thought there was a party down the street", "My kids love your balloons", "Awesome balloons", etc.* Most people understood the significance of the red-yellow-green lighting upon closer inspection—when they read the balloon labels, or after they asked us to confirm that the balloons 'showed air quality'. People reacted positively: *"Keep it up, I dig it!", "Diesel exhaust-that's a very bad thing"* or, *"Awesome, so how can we make money with this?"* Not surprisingly, individuals who

Figure 2. Air quality balloon installations in public park (top left & right); and city street (bottom left & right).

Figure 3. Interview setup: participant drawing on map transparency prior to sorting air quality factors (cards).

lived in the neighborhoods where we placed our installations related more intimately, with one person commenting:

> *This is my neighborhood and I know everybody, so I would probably put them [balloons] wherever I wanted. I think you should have more people with balloons...*

Several people asked us if they could take a few balloons. One person excitedly pointed out:

> *I think anything that's big and shiny will get America's attention... I know a little bit about VOCs so I can spread the word... Word, I feel powerful now, can she [friend] have one?*

Thus, when first noticing the installation, passersby reacted with excitement and curiosity. Upon further reflection, however, stakeholders began to more critically discuss the visualization, the environment, and their neighborhood. Some further speculated on the role they can play in '*spreading the word*'.

TAKE A BALLOON AND EXPLORE THE CITY

In addition to our public installations, we recruited six individuals by advertising our project on Craigslist (a general-purpose classified advertising website) and local biking forums. We invited participants for a semi-structured interview exploring their relationships with urban spaces. We asked them to mark locations on a map of Pittsburgh associated with words such as "work", "play", "unhealthy", "alienating", "personal", "boring", "interesting", *etc.* In addition, participants identified places where they would like to monitor and broadcast air quality (Figures 3 & 4). Lastly, participants completed a card sorting exercise, ordering air quality factors such as traffic, household cleaning products, pollen, pesticides, industrial byproducts, etc., from most to least harmful for their health.

Upon completing the interview, we showed participants the air quality balloons and offered them up to three (choosing between VOC, diesel, exhaust). We encouraged participants to photograph and use the balloons as they saw fit during the course of the night: to carry them all night, leave them temporarily or permanently in a place, *etc.* All participants returned for a follow-up interview to share their pictures of, and experiences with, the air quality balloons. We recorded interview audio, and reference data owing to individual study participants as P1-6.

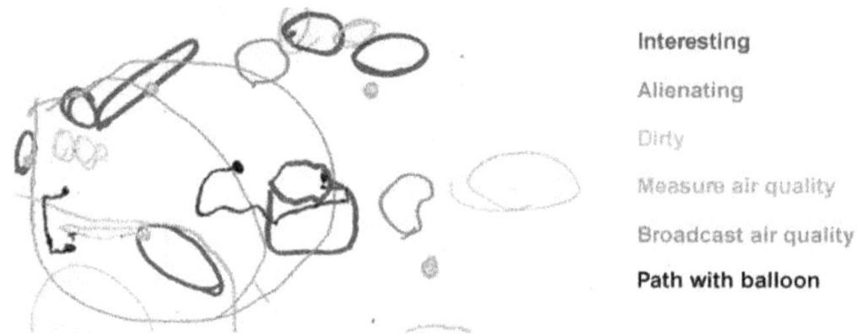

Figure 4. A subset of transparency maps drawn by a participant.

Stakeholders and spaces

Our pre-balloon interviews reveal a wide range of participants' concerns, values, and relationships with public spaces in Pittsburgh. P1 and P2 (a couple) are graduate students who spend time outdoors biking, running and playing sports such as rugby. P3 is working on a medical residency, commuting regularly by bicycle along bike trails, parks, and city streets. P4 and P5 are artists (also a couple), and P6 is a student; all three traverse the city by bus. None view themselves as political or environmental activists, and only one sporadically attends social eco-themed events. The six participants occupy very different neighborhoods, working and living in four distinct regions of Pittsburgh. Participants also have divergent perceptions of urban spaces: for instance, P1 and P2 hang out in an '*interesting*' neighborhood that P3 and P4 consider '*alienating*'.

Despite these differences, all participants frequent the same public parks and expect air quality to be cleaner there. They also consider the same neighborhoods to be unhealthy spaces, describing them as '*rundown*', '*industrial*', or having '*construction*', '*traffic*', or '*bad smell*'. Moreover, everyone identifies vehicle traffic as the most harmful factor for health in terms of air quality. Pesticides, trash, dust, and pollen are considered least harmful because participants are less frequently exposed to these factors.

Sensing and broadcasting air quality

When asked to identify places where they would sense air quality, all participants mentioned sites they considered dirty, polluted, or unhealthy. In addition, several people wanted to monitor places they felt were clean ("*I was thinking that- probably is clean there... At [park] would be more positive*", P1). All participants wanted to broadcast air quality data to the general public, for instance via a 'blimp' (P4), or atop a bridge (P6), cultural district (P3), or downtown (P1& P2). Many also suggested locations that target specific audiences. For instance, P1 and P2 suggested spaces most visible to other students:

> *These two* [pointing on map] *would be college students, because that would be the target demographic for people who'd want to change it.* (P1)

Meanwhile, P3 suggested an 'eco-friendly' neighborhood:

> P3: *Lawrenceville, because it's full of eco-people that might be a little more aware of it. Like a little more open and receptive towards it, so people that are more*

active in it and might be more receptive to the message.

I: More receptive how? What are you thinking?

P3: *People that are more willing to change behavior- so to do things about it or to tell other people about it.*

Balloons in the hands of urban stakeholders

When offered the three types of balloons, five of the six participants wanted to measure VOC. P3 explained:

That's something that you can't get an idea of just visually... 'cause you know, when you're sucking in car exhaust—at least high levels, you notice that you're sucking in car exhaust. But with organic compounds, it is what it is—like you don't know. (P3)

The two couples (P1&P2 and P4&P5) and P6 also took an exhaust or diesel balloon. Participants brought balloons to different parts of the city: public park and downtown city center (P4&P5), to her home and later to a party (P3), along a city street to a neighborhood where participants tend to hang out (P1&P2), and around a college campus (P6). All six participants made an effort to visit a part of the city outside of their evening plans *because* of the balloons.

Curiosity

Participants reported that their balloons changed colors based on location and activity, with most people finding these changes '*interesting*' or '*surprising*'. Participants tended to rationalize balloon behavior: for instance, P1 and P2 noticed that the diesel balloon turned red whenever they put it inside their house, proposing several explanations:

P1: *We came up with theories but none of them that... not necessarily impossible, but none of them even borderline likely.*

I: A-ha, like what?

P1: *Like the stove- the gas that we use for the stove could be producing diesel... but that doesn't make any sense. The other theory was that there's a lot of humidity in the house- like much more than outside, and the humidity... affects a lot of things.*

Likewise, P3 told us that her VOC balloon reacted to doors opening and closing in her house:

I left it in my house for a couple of hours and the interesting thing was- it was red when my door was closed and green when my door was open. (P3)

P3 noted that perhaps VOC's tend to accumulate in her house due to poor ventilation:

It does make me wonder if my house worse because it's not like aerated or ventilated. (P3)

P3's friend also pointed out that the VOC balloon reacted to hair spray:

I was going to a costume party, and I was a giraffe so I had lots of hair spray going on... and then I like- stood near it and it suddenly went like really red.

Later that night, P3 and her friends noticed the balloon turning red outside of a bar. P3 suggested that this was caused by chemicals from a nearby children's hospital.

Public attention: wanted

All six participants intentionally brought the balloons to places where they would encounter more people, reflecting positively on public attention. P2 told us:

I think they [public reactions] were pretty positive, everybody seemed pretty excited about the balloons.

Similarly, P4 noted people's immediate reaction to red balloon colors:

It caught a lot of attention, it got people almost instant awareness, especially if it was red at the time they saw it: they're like Wow! That's... concerning!!

All participants interacted with strangers, asking them to help photograph the balloons and explaining the project to passersby. Consequently, observers (passersby) began to reflect on other air quality issues in their lives. For instance:

P1: *We got pictures with people, we were like 'here can you hold these' and we explained what we were doing to them'.. and then [laughing] towards the end of the night people had progressively more interest in it. We had one group ask us like in detail what we were doing and we talked to them for like 5-10 minutes.*

I: And what did they say when you told them?

P1: *They were like oh, that's interesting... and then one guy explained how the levels in his hometown were above what they're supposed to be because of the corporations.*

Moreover, balloons inspired discussion about other expressions of air quality. P5 detailed her experience with a passerby who suggested logging and storing the data:

Figure 5. Air quality balloons placed by study participants: diesel balloon downtown (top left), VOC balloon near public hospital (top right), VOC & diesel balloons in an underpass (bottom left), and VOC balloon in public park (bottom right).

P5: *One guy recommended having... an actual digital log of how it changes color, and then just having certain paths all ready that you go down. And then you could record the changes over a period of time...*

P5: *...and then that would really track how things change, because I mean, just walking form one place to another, we were seeing changes left and right.*

Activism

We asked participants what they would do if they could use our balloons for longer periods of time. One person (P3) wanted to place balloons all around a children's hospital to monitor VOC levels, and another suggested to permanently insteall balloons at street intersections and in public parks. Participants were skeptical about reporting this data to local authorities, with one person explaining:

I guess we usually say that we'd want to show it to the mayor, except I don't really believe in it. (P5)

Instead, people wanted to broadcast the data they collected to as many people as possible:

If you show it to just one person who's either back higher [in the government]... *would just toss it away but if you get more- dozens, hundreds, thousands, millions of people, then you can get a movement. You need a ton of people to start a revolution, you can't just have one person start a revolution.* (P6)

Ultimately, participants wanted to have more balloons for longer periods of time in order to collect and share data with the general public. Most participants also suggested showing data on a map, with P3 emphasizing visual (non-numeric) representations:

I don't wanna read things like- this is however many parts per million... I just want to say like- this is bad, this is better, this needs to be better because that's all you really wanna boil it down to. (P3)

In addition, participants wanted to show data specifically to people whose behavior might be causing poor air quality:

We pretty much rely on either public transportation or a mode of walking or biking or whatever, there's really not much we can do to make less exhaust or volatile chemicals individually... But like I said, we can spread it to people who we know that may be in cars. (P4)

To summarize, our deployment with six diverse individuals inspired participants to explore new (non-routine) spaces with the balloons, as well as seek public attention and discuss the project with strangers. Reflecting on the study, participants expressed interest in using balloons for longer periods of time and in showing the visualization to other stakeholders such as eco-friendly neighborhoods or those who might be causing poor air quality.

DIY AIR QUALITY BALLOON WORKSHOP

Lastly, we created a DIY kit to enable non-experts to assemble functional air quality balloons. Here, we describe our kit and circuit board, and a workshop where six participants assembled their own working balloons.

Figure 6. PCB board for the DIY balloon kit (left) and instruction booklet for assembling the board (right).

DIY balloon kit

Our DIY balloon kit includes a custom circuit board that can be populated with a VOC or exhaust/diesel sensor. For the dual-function exhaust/diesel sensor, one of two pairs of solder pads must 'shorted' (soldered across) to supply input from either the exhaust or the diesel pin of the sensor. The board is powered by a regular 9 volt battery or two rechargeable 3.7 volt lithium ion polymer (LiPo) batteries. The circuit relies on two PICAXE-8M chips, with each modulating the pulse width of a red or a green LED channel based on input from the sensor. The PCB also supports an optional piezo vibration sensor in order to alter balloon brightness based on movement (*e.g.*, tug on the balloon string). Similar to our earlier design, a tri-colored LED resides inside the weather balloon, connected to the PCB, which hangs below the balloon neck. The board is intentionally designed for a non-expert to assemble, with ample spacing between through-hole solder pads and all components clearly labeled (Figure 6, left). In addition, we created a booklet with step-by-step picture instructions for assembling the board (Figure 6, right). Each DIY kit costs under $25 (VOC) or $35 (exhaust/diesel) and includes the PCB, instruction booklet and all components (including an air quality sensor, weather balloon, tri-colored LED, piezo, two pre-programmed PICAXE chips, battery, and resistors).

DIY balloon workshop

Working with a local DIY community in Pittsburgh, we conducted a free air quality balloon-making workshop with six participants (Figure 7). The workshop began with brief discussion about attendees' backgrounds and motivations for participating. Each participant then chose one of VOC, exhaust or diesel balloon kits. Participants worked independently to assemble kits by following the included instructions, with most completing a board in about 30 minutes. Workshop organizers then assisted participants in inflating balloons and attaching batteries to the PCB (with tape). A few days later, an informal follow-up interview was conducted by phone or email to gather participants' feedback. Participants were compensated $15 for completing this interview. We recorded audio and photographed the workshop; we reference data owing to individual workshop participants as W1-6.

Participants

Our workshop was hosted by a local community that sponsors projects ranging from: creating hacky sack footbags by filling balloons with sand; to working with electroluminescent (EL) wire; to "*yarn bombing and trying to incorporate social feedback and small bits of electronics into it*" (W6); or "*high altitude weather balloons to take pictures of the curvature of the earth*" (W1). Workshop participants (ages mid 20's to late 30's, 5 male, 1 female) have been involved with the DIY organization for various amounts of time: more than 2 years (W1); over a year (W2, W3, W6); 6 months (W4), and just under a month (W5). Participants' backgrounds varied, including degrees and work in design, engineering and English. Participants had some familiarity with soldering and different degrees of proficiencies with electronics—from relative beginner ("*other kits I've assembled were much simpler*", W6; "*my first introduction to soldering was the class that* [DIY community] *had in like September* [6 months ago]", W4), to working on electronics projects on a weekly basis over the past few years (W1, W2, W3). None of the participants had previously worked with the PICAXE chip or Figaro air quality sensors. One participant owns a similar carbon monoxide sensor, but had not yet used it in a project.

Motivation

All participants indicated that they were drawn to the workshop for personal enjoyment: "*a project that integrates balloons with technology is just kinda fun for us*" W1; "*I just thought it sounds like a really neat project*" W3. Although participants were not environmental activists, some have previously thought about air quality in Pittsburgh. W5 was concerned with air and soil near his workplace:

> *I always kinda wonder about the soil- you know, like the lead... I wanna put this* [balloon] *at* [work place] *so people can see it as they drive over the* [bridge name] *bridge because it's got a lot of visibility.* (W5)

Similarly, W2 noted, "*I've just come to accept that Pittsburgh air quality sucks*", while W3 was interested in sharing the project with his daughter:

> *I have a 3-year old and I'm really curious if it clicks... the concept of air pollution doesn't really mean much to her but I'm curious to see if see if with the colors it kinda clicks.* (W4)

Assembling the DIY balloon kit

Most participants fully assembled their board in about 30 minutes, with only one participant taking over an hour due to a malfunctioning transistor. Throughout the workshop, participants asked several questions about the hardware ("*we'll want more information about the kit—just even like the components or the source code... just because it's kinda who we are, we like to explore things.*" W5,), as well as a few clarification questions about the instructions (*e.g.*, why are the steps in a certain order; or why/how to solder across the pads for the diesel/exhaust sensors). Participants were excited to turn on their balloons for the first time ("*Testing the balloon! I felt like six* [years old] *all over again*", W3; "*It was really fun to see the balloon light up for the first time, to see them all together in the dark at the shop*", W6)

W4 also noted that unlike kits, which require programming after assembly, the balloon kit worked immediately:

> *The neat thing about this kit is you come out with a functional product. We were able to play with it immediately. It wasn't like... here's the product now go write the software that does something cool.* (W4)

Participants' experiences with balloons

After assembling the kits, participants were encouraged to interact with their balloons throughout the night as they saw fit. Several participants took the balloons to a restaurant, but "*it was really late and we couldn't figure out where we could take them where people would be*" (W5). W4 brought his balloon home to show his daughter the following day:

> *She and I spent some time talking about it, I tried to explain it to her... I did the exhaust, so we did talk a little bit about the smoke that comes out of cars* (W4)

W3 tried to use long exposure photographs to capture his balloon changing color as he walked from a street intersection into the park (Figure 7, bottom right):

> *I walked from the intersection with traffic to the playground in the park to see how the colors would change. Also I figured it would make some cool pictures with long exposure...* (W3)

W2 discussed the project with his friends in India:

> *All of us agreed that it would be a great idea to have this at several locations thorough-out Bangalore. The air quality is noticeably different in different parts of the city and the weather forecasts give pollution readings only from a few places.* (W2)

Likewise, W5 hoped to initiate dialogue by sharing his

Figure 7. Workshop participant assembling a DIY balloon kit (top left); kit fully assembled (top right); fully-functional balloons built by workshop participants (bottom left); participants' long exposure photo of balloon (bottom right).

images (*"I'm hoping I can get some people responding on my Flickr pool... I think people would ask me what it's about"*, W5). W6, whose balloon deflated by the following afternoon speculated on using it for a whole day, *"to see how and if it changed in the various places, and it would be fun to see people's reactions to it as well"*. Lastly, participants had numerous ideas for modifying the kit, from adding data logging (*"so you could look back and see how things changed"*, W6), to incorporating the kit into a *"semi-permanent system using plastic globes (lawn lights) on pipes"* (W2). In summary, our workshop enabled six participants to assemble their own functional balloons, and interactions with the project led to exploration and speculation on expanding the project to include other functionality or be deployed in different regions.

DISCUSSION

We presented the design of our air quality sensing circuit, which was mounted on weather balloons and distributed to stakeholders to visualize concentrations of VOC's, exhaust and diesel around our city. We detailed three deployments of this technology: 1) public installations in city street and park; 2) deployment with six urban stakeholders; and 3) a workshop where six DIY hobbyists who were previously unfamiliar with the project and its underlying technology assembled functional balloons.

Limitations

We intentionally chose low-cost sensors and pursued DIY methods in order to position our technology as a tool for bottom-up movements by ordinary citizens. Admittedly, this approach does not achieve precise air quality measurements, and our work faces the limitations of inexact and un-calibrated sensors. Our visualization appropriately represents sensor readings by illuminating balloons green, yellow, or red based on whether the sensors read below, at, or above average values that were collected throughout the city. We believe there is tremendous value in communicating even these *relative* measurements of air quality to the public (as noted by one participant who did not want to read more detailed 'parts per million' data).

DESIGN IMPLICATIONS

We conclude with three implication areas that emerged from our work, suggesting opportunities for future research in this exciting domain of spectacle computing.

The importance of play

Our work inspired participants who were not environmental activists to assemble and interact with air quality balloons by incorporating elements of *play*.

Playful DIY making

Our balloon kit appealed to a local DIY community as a project that is *"just kinda fun for us"*. The simple, clearly-labeled PCB and step-by-step image instructions enabled non-expert users to create what they considered to be *"functional products"*, emphasizing the *"fun"* of *"seeing the balloon light up"* or feeling *"like 6* [years old] *again"*. Our findings suggest involving users in playful DIY making as an approach for inspiring environmental exploration.

Future systems can support easy assembly and modification of the underlying technology to prompt ideas for creatively augmenting the project or speculations about broader issues such as air quality, as we saw in our workshop. New, even more flexible, easy-soldering or solderless kits that can be populated with a range of sensors might spur the interest of people outside technically-minded DIY communities. Alternatively, sensors with complex underlying circuits might support easy alteration of device appearance, display, or form factor. A parallel body of research can explore intuitive instruction methods, including images, video, or in-person demonstrations. More broadly, these approaches can serve to playfully engage everyday citizens in designing and building ubiquitous technologies that monitor issues of personal concern.

Playful media

In addition, our light-hearted and playful medium (balloons) led participants to explore and discuss air quality throughout the city. During our public installations, observers began to think about air quality in their neighborhood (*"diesel exhaust—that's very bad thing"*). In our deployment with six everyday citizens, participants visited a park and downtown area, walked through a nearby neighborhood, and tethered the balloon to a bicycle, describing their experiences as *'fun'*, *'interesting'*, or *'surprising'*. Moreover, the balloons inspired participants to question and propose theories about air quality in their surroundings: P1 and P2 wondered whether the gas from their stove was emitting diesel exhaust; P3 hypothesized that VOC levels were higher due to poor ventilation or a nearby hospital; while W3 wanted to *"see how the colors would change"* as he walked away from traffic.

Whereas current applications tend to rely on participants' interest in the environment, community values, or monetary compensation as motivations for sensing [*e.g.*, 15], an alternative body of work can encourage grassroots data collection through tangible and playful media. Future systems can explore incorporating play into the experience of environmental sensing. Balloons, for instance, can be used in range of new applications: balloons tethered to a map showing data for a region; balloons that visualize other environmental factors (*e.g.*, water quality); or large-scale projections that respond to onlookers' balloons.

Moreover, other playful objects can be appropriated as sensors to support explorations of overlooked or hard-to-reach spaces (similar to Wallbots [31]). For instance, air quality sensors embedded in kites can encourage engagement with and monitoring of air quality while playing on a beach; remote-controlled boats, outfitted with water quality sensors might inspire fun investigations of local water sources; or digging toys that include soil sensors could support interactive play with soil. Future applications may also leverage familiar platforms (*e.g.*, mobile phones) to distribute games and contests that motivate playful engagement with and reflection on the environment.

The power of spectacle

Air quality balloons enabled us and our participants to create *spectacles*. Our installations in public locations have attracted onlookers to approach the exhibit, ask questions, and voice their opinions. Participants who received working balloons actively sought attention by bringing balloons to busier streets and inviting strangers to photograph and discuss the project. Moreover, our workshop participants who assembled their own balloons, tried to bring them *"where people would be"*, sharing the project with friends, family and strangers (through Flickr). The balloons served as boundary objects, engaging people from different communities, backgrounds, and geographic locations in environmental discourse: one observer recommended recording *"changes over a long period of time"* to P5, another passerby told P1 about '*the levels in his hometown*'; W4 used the balloon to illustrate the "*concept of air pollution*" with his daughter, while W2 and his friends discussed having balloons in "*several locations thorough-out Bangalore*"; passersby who saw our public installations suggested having "*more people with balloons*", requesting to take balloons to "*spread the word*".

Our unconventional, vibrant, and public balloons served as entry points for environmental discourse among a diverse range of stakeholders. The installations and participants' experiences with balloons encouraged speculations about air quality between parents and children, local and international groups of friends, as well as complete strangers, either in person or by commenting on online repositories of images. These findings suggest opportunities to leverage spectacle computing for supporting new interactions between people, technology, and space.

For instance, people with vested interests in a location (*e.g.*, homeowners) might prefer longer-term environmental spectacles in their neighborhood to facilitate local discourse, or "community togetherness" [15]. Alternatively, individuals who traverse different parts of the city (runners or postal workers) might benefit from modular platforms (*e.g.*, Feral Robotic Dogs [25]), which support spectacles and discussions across locations. Moreover, drawing from our workshop participants' willingness to modify the balloon kit (with data logging, or different form factors such as plastic globes), future systems can allow DIY modification and re-appropriation of the spectacle. Finally, the limitations of spectacles remain to be explored. When (if ever) do glowing balloons and other similar installations cease to be enticing? How can the effectiveness of spectacles be extended to inspire environmental discourse over longer periods of time?

Tangible media as an instrument of change

Emerging HCI research continues to explore the methods and processes of activist groups [*e.g.*, 21] in order to inform the design of technologies for political change. We contribute to this work by introducing a technology that can be assembled by non-experts to make information about air quality not only measurable and visible, but also compelling and hard to ignore. Although none of our participants were activists *per se*, they saw opportunities to use air quality balloons to catalyze change. From wanting to show the balloons to an *"eco-friendly neighborhood"*, *"students"*, and *"drivers"*, to discussing the project with friends abroad or the general public at large, participants hoped to project collected data to other stakeholders who might be willing to take action.

Our findings suggest opportunities to use tangible media as a support tool for grassroots movements. On one hand, other new and unexpected media may effectively entice and empower bottom-up data collection: paper airplanes, remote-control cars, dog collars, baby strollers, tree leaves, or roller skates, to name a few, might serve as novel vehicles for environmental sensing (similar to street sweepers or pigeons [3, 12]). Data collected by such distributed means might be aggregated into more traditional representations (*e.g.,* maps, graphs) to serve as political artifacts.

Alternatively, tangible media might enable users to project data within and across urban spaces in more playful and unconventional ways. Wireless communication between visualizations (*e.g.*, balloons) and sensors can support spectacles that are physically removed from the locations being sensed. Users could place vibrant nodes in remote spaces to draw the attention of activist communities, policy makers or the general public to local issues.

CONCLUSION

We explored spectacle computing as an approach for vibrantly projecting data into the public sphere and inspiring environmental discourse. In two public installations and a deployment with six everyday citizens we evaluated a novel technology—large balloons that glow, based on surrounding air quality. In addition, our kit enabled six members of a local DIY community to assemble their own, fully functional balloons. We leverage our findings to propose play and spectacle as essential elements for inspiring public discussion within and across communities of stakeholders. We hope that our work inspires other spectacle computing projects that engage passive onlookers, routine visitors, and avid activists in political and environmental discourse.

ACKNOWLEDGEMENTS

We thank all our participants for their feedback. Financial support for this research was provided in part by the Heinz Endowment. We thank our reviewers for their thoughtful feedback, which will continue to shape our future research.

REFERENCES

1. Aerophile, S.A. *Air de Paris balloon.* http://aerophile.com/
2. *Amphibious Architecture* by The Living Architecture Lab at Columbia University Graduate School of Architecture, September 17 – November 7, 2009. www.sentientcity.net

3. Aoki, P. M., Honicky, R. J., Mainwaring, A., Myers, C. Paulos, E. Subramanian, S. Woodruff, A. A vehicle for research: using street sweepers to explore the landscape of environmental community action. CHI 2009, p. 375-384.
4. American Lung Association. City Rankings 2010: Most Polluted Cities. http://www.stateoftheair.org/2010/
5. Buechley, L., Eisenberg, M. (2009) Fabric PCBs, Electronic Sequins, and Socket Buttons: Techniques for E-textile Craft. Journal of Personal and Ubiquitous Computing, 13(2), p. 133-150.
6. Buechley, L., Eisenberg, M. (2008). The LilyPad Arduino: Toward Wearable Engineering for Everyone. Wearable Computing Column in IEEE Pervasive, v.7 n.2, p.12-15.
7. Buechley, L., Rosner, D., Paulos, E., and Williams, A. (2009). Workshop: DIY for CHI: methods, communities, and values of reuse and customization. In Proceedings of the 27th international conference extended abstracts on Human factors in computing systems (CHI EA '09). ACM, New York, NY, USA, 4823-4826.
8. Burke, J., Estrin, D., Hansen, M., Parker, A., Ramanathan, N., Reddy, S., Srivastava, M.B. Participatory Sensing. In World Sensor Web Workshop. ACM, 2006.
9. Coalition for Clean Air. Pollutants & Health Effects. http://www.coalitionforcleanair.org.
10. Brynskov, M. Aarhus by Light. 2010. http://www.aarhusbylight.dk/index-english.html
11. Da Costa, B., Schulte, J., and Singer, B. AIR – Area's Immediate Reading. http://www.pm-air.net
12. Da Costa, B., Hazegh, C., Ponto, K. Pigeon blog. http://www.pigeonblog.mapyourcity.net
13. Dearman, D., Truong, K. N. 2009. BlueTone: a framework for interacting with public displays using dual-tone multi-frequency through bluetooth. In Ubicomp '09, p. 97-100.
14. Debord, G. The Society of the Spectacle. Zone, 1994.
15. DiSalvo, C. Marti, L., Coupland, J., Steiner, M. A 2009. Local Issues, Local Uses: Tools for robotics and sensing in community contexts. Creativity & Cognition, p. 245-254.
16. Eisenman, S. B., Miluzzo, E., Lane, N. D., Peterson, R. A., Ahn, G., and Campbell, A. T. 2009. BikeNet: A mobile sensing system for cyclist experience mapping. In Proceedings of SenSys '07. p. 87-101.
17. Figaro Gas Sensors. http://www.figarosensor.com/
18. Graffiti Research Lab. Throwies. graffitiresearchlab.com
19. Grassroots Mapping. Balloon Aerial Photography.
20. Haque, U. *Burble, London, UK 2007*, http://www.haque.co.uk/burblelondon.php
21. Hirsch, T., Henry, J. 2005. TXTmob: text messaging for protest swarms. In CHI '05 extended abstracts on Human factors in computing systems (CHI EA '05), p. 1455-1458.
22. Holmquist, L. E.. 2006. Sketching in hardware. Interactions 13, 1 (January 2006), p. 47-60.
23. Honicky, R., Brewer, E. A., Paulos, E., and White, R. 2008. N-smarts: networked suite of mobile atmospheric real-time sensors. ACM SIGCOMM Workshop on Networked Systems For Developing Regions, 2008.
24. Hooker, B., Gaver, W.W., Steed, A., & Bowers, J. The Pollution e-Sign. Workshop on Ubiquitous Sustainability. Ubicomp, 2007.
25. Jeremijenko, N., Arnold, J. J., Kavesh, W. Feral Robotic Dogs. 2009.
26. Kaye, J., Williams, A., Oehlberg, L. Tinkering, Crafts and Inventive Leisure Practices. In proceedings of the 2011 conference on Computer Supported Cooperative Work.
27. Kaprow, A. Assemblages, Environments & Happenings, Harry N. Abrams, Inc.Publishers, New York, 1966.
28. Kim, S. and Paulos, E. 2009. inAir: measuring and visualizing indoor air quality. Ubicomp '09, p. 81-84.
29. Kim, S., Paulos, E., and Gross, M. D. 2010. WearAir: expressive t-shirts for air quality sensing. In Proceedings of the fourth international conference on Tangible, embedded, and embodied interaction (TEI '10), p. 295-296
30. Kuznetsov, S. Paulos, E.. 2010. Rise of the expert amateur: DIY projects, communities, and cultures. In Proc. of the 6th Nordic Conference on Human-Computer Interaction: Extending Boundaries (NordiCHI '10), p. 295-304
31. Kuznetsov, S., Paulos, E, Gross, M.D. WallBots: Interactive Wall-Crawling Robots In the Hands of Public Artists and Political Activists. In Proc. of the 8th ACM Conference on Designing Interactive Systems (DIS '10). ACM, New York, NY, USA, 208-217.
32. Lamorisse, A. *The Red Balloon.*
33. Marx, L. 1867. The Fetishism of Commodities and the Secret thereof. Das Kapital (1867).
34. NASA. New NASA Balloon Successfully Flight-Tested Over Antarctica, December 2009. www.nasa.gov
35. Nena. *99 Luftballons*. Released in 1983.
36. NOAA National Weather Service. Radiosonde Observations. http://www.ua.nws.noaa.gov/
37. OFriel, K., CO2RSET. itpedia.nyu.edu/wiki/CO2RSET
38. PICAXE. http://www.rev-ed.co.uk/picaxe/
39. Paulos, E., Honicky, R.J., Hooker, B. Citizen Science: Enabling Participatory Urbanism. *Handbook of Research on Urban Informatics,* 2008.
40. Pete's Sonic Art Research. Wire and Balloon Installation. http://petes-sonic-art-research.blogspot.com/
41. Piene, O. More Sky. MIT Press, 1973.
42. Rosner, D., Bean, J. 2009. Learning from IKEA hacking: I'm not one to decoupage a tabletop and call it a day. In Proceedings of the 27th international conference on Human factors in computing systems (CHI '09), p. 419-422.
43. Seitinger, S., Taub, D. M., Taylor, A. S. 2010. Light bodies: exploring interactions with responsive lights. In Proc. of the fourth international conference on Tangible, embedded, and embodied interaction (TEI '10), 113-120.
44. U.S. EPA. Health Assessment Document for Diesel Engine Exhaust. U.S. Environmental Protection Agency, 2002
45. U.S. EPA.Volatile Organic Compounds. http://www.epa.gov/air/emissions/voc.htm

Data Broadcasting using Mobile FM Radio: Design, Realization and Application

Hang Yu[1], Ahmad Rahmati[1], Ardalan Amiri Sani[1], Lin Zhong[1], Jehan Wickramasuriya[2], Venu Vasudevan[2]

[1]Department of Electrical & Computer Engineering
Rice University, Houston, Texas, USA
{hang.yu, rahmati, ardalan, lzhong}@rice.edu

[2]Betaworks, Applied Research Center
Motorola Mobility, Libertyville, Illinois, USA
{jehan, venu}@motorola.com

ABSTRACT
In this work, we offer a novel system, *MicroStation* (*μStation)* that allows ubiquitous data broadcasting applications using the FM radio on mobile devices such as smartphones. μStation includes two key modules to enable data broadcasting based on existing mobile FM radio hardware. *Channel Selector* assigns different FM channels to neighboring μStation broadcasters to avoid collision and guides μStation listeners to find their broadcasting of interest. *Data Codec* realizes bit-level communication between mobile devices through existing FM radio hardware. We describe an implementation of μStation on the Nokia N900 smartphone, and provide low-level APIs and services to support application development. We also demonstrate two representative applications: *Facebook-FM* and *Sync-Flash*. These applications demonstrate the capability of μStation to readily enable a new class of ubiquitous data broadcasting applications on mobile devices.

Author Keywords
FM radio, data broadcasting, mobile devices.

ACM Classification Keywords
C2.0 Computer-Communication Networks: Data communications

General Terms
Design, Experimentation, Measurement.

INTRODUCTION
Peer-to-peer (P2P) and location-based mobile applications have long been an important focus of the ubiquitous computing community. A few recent indicative applications include *Color* [1] which allows a user to share photos with others in their vicinity, and *Cisco StadiumVision* [2] which delivers location-based content and service for sports venues. The proliferation of such applications requires power-efficient and overhead-free mobile broadcasting technologies.

In this work, we exploit the FM radio that is increasingly available on mobile devices to provide a *data broadcasting* system for P2P and location-based applications. We are motivated by a recent and important hardware trend on mobile devices: due to its continuously reduced cost and integration with other wireless technologies (e.g., Wi-Fi and Bluetooth) on a single chipset, the FM radio is becoming increasingly available on mobile devices such as smartphones, tablets and media players. Testimony to this trend includes the hardware requirements of the Windows Phone 7 Platform, which embraces the FM radio [3]. As another example, the Apple iPhone and iPod Touch already incorporate the FM receiver and transmitter hardware, and the software to enable them is reportedly under development [4]. The mobile FM receiver and transmitter are intended to allow users to listen to the broadcasted programs, and stream music to short-range home and automobile stereos, respectively. However, we go beyond such intended uses of the mobile FM radio and enable data broadcasting applications based on existing hardware.

We reveal two challenges toward enabling practical and deployable data broadcasting applications. First, simultaneous broadcasters must not collide. Therefore, they should coordinate with each other to use the available FM channels while remaining quickly identifiable by interested listeners. Unlike radios in white space, FM radio has a much shorter range (~5 meters) and multiple orthogonal channels so that the solution requires special treatment toward the hidden-node problem and channel allocation. Second, the solution must not modify the FM radio hardware, but has to rely on the device's audio interface to realize data broadcasting. Therefore, binary data must be properly converted into audio, and the broadcaster and listener must be symbol-synchronized using software.

We address these challenges with μStation, a software solution that operates without modification to device

UbiComp'11, September 17–21, 2011, Beijing, China.

hardware, operating system, and the FM radio driver. μStation has two key modules: *Channel Selector* and *Data Codec*. First, Channel Selector enables automatic and efficient FM channel allocation, so that nearby broadcasters use orthogonal channels with high probability. Meanwhile, it ensures listeners to find the channel with broadcasting of interest timely, by letting broadcasters periodically announce their presence. Second, Data Codec performs conversion between binary data and audio to compatibly work with the FM radio hardware. More importantly, it effectively achieves symbol synchronization in software by leveraging different sampling frequencies in the FM transmitter digital-to-analog converter (DAC) and FM receiver analog-to-digital converter (ADC).

We have implemented μStation on the Nokia N900 smartphone and provided both low-level APIs and services to support a large set of mobile applications. We have also developed two representative applications using μStation to demonstrate its effectiveness. First, *Facebook-FM* broadcasts a user's Facebook ID so that nearby users can load the corresponding Facebook profile to facilitate social interaction. Second, *Sync-Flash* realizes a synchronized flashing pattern using many smartphone screens from users physically close to each other, e.g., the audience of a concert or a sports game.

As the first publicly reported system that aims to enable ubiquitous data broadcasting applications using existing mobile FM radio hardware, μStation has offered the FM radio, which possibly obtains little attention before, significant potential to facilitate the interaction between physically adjacent mobile devices. We hope our initial endeavor with μStation can enlighten more innovative ways to leverage the FM radio as an important hardware feature on current and emerging mobile devices.

BACKGROUND OF MOBILE FM RADIO

We next provide background of the mobile FM radio.

Spectrum Usage

The spectrum usage of FM radio falls into the UHF band and spans from 87.5 MHz to 107.9 MHz in the U.S. In this case, the spectrum is equally divided into 103 orthogonal channels, each of which is 200 KHz apart from its neighbors. A FM channel can be identified by its center frequency, or by a unique number (e.g., Channel #1 for the channel at 87.5 MHz). In each FM channel, FM radio uses 15 KHz and 30 KHz bandwidth for broadcasting monaural and stereo audios respectively. The remaining bandwidth is used for sideband applications such as the Radio Broadcast Data System (RBDS otherwise known as RDS in Europe) [5], and the currently obsolete Microsoft DirectBand [6].

Both licensed and unlicensed FM broadcasting use the same set of channels. Licensed broadcasting usually comes from radio stations owned by commercial organizations or educational institutions, with a fixed coverage and schedule.

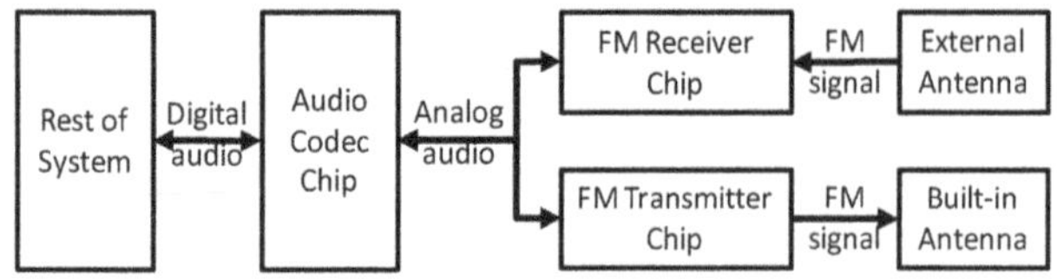

Figure 1: FM radio hardware architecture on mobile devices

As a result, given time and location, licensed broadcastings are often highly predictable, as indicated by [7].

Regulations for Unlicensed Broadcasting

Most countries allow unlicensed FM broadcasting. The US FCC regulates the output power and mandates that the field strength of any unlicensed FM emissions must not exceed 250 microvolt/meter at 3 meters, leading to a maximum output power of approximately 15 nW. The EU regulation is similarly enacted but the maximum allowed output power is 50 nW. Australia allows output power as high as 10 μW, but only if the unlicensed transmission does not interfere with present licensed broadcastings. We note that a few countries such as China do not yet allow unlicensed FM broadcasting; mobile devices used in these countries usually have the FM transmitter disabled. Due to our implementation and experimental constraints, we work under the US FCC regulations.

We define available FM channels in the following way: *a FM channel is available if the channel RSSI under licensed broadcasting is below certain threshold* (e.g., -110dBm in our implementation). We note that a FM channel can be available even with present licensed broadcastings, as long as the licensed broadcasting is sufficiently weak. As a result, checking the availability of a FM channel can be simply done by measuring the channel RSSI, which is supported by mobile FM radio. Our RSSI based definition ensures the quality of unlicensed broadcastings, yet there can be alternative ways to define available FM channels such as using the human perceivable quality of licensed broadcasting. Nonetheless, μStation is agnostic of the definition of channel availability, as we will show later.

Hardware Architecture

We show the hardware architecture of mobile FM radio in Figure 1. We note that the FM transmitter and receiver may be in the same or separate integrated circuits, e.g., the Nokia N900 uses the Silicon Lab Si4713 for the transmitter and Broadcom BCM2048 for the receiver, while the iPhone 4 utilizes the Broadcom BCM4329 including both the transmitter and receiver. Furthermore, some FM radio chipsets have an internal DAC for converting digital audio into analog audio, and an ADC for the opposite conversion. Other chipsets only provide an analog audio interface; an audio codec chip provides the necessary ADC and DAC, and effectively bridges the FM radio hardware with the rest of the system through a digital audio interface. μStation is independent on these implementation issues by interfacing with the digital audio interface provided by either the FM

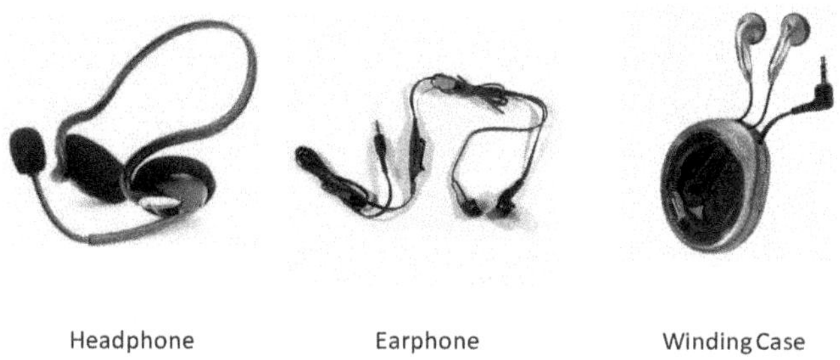

Figure 2: The headphone, earphone and the winding case used in our experiments

radio chipsets or the audio codec. For generality, we use the term *FM radio hardware* to refer to the FM transmitter, FM receiver and audio codec if existing.

Current mobile FM transmitters and receivers employ different antennas. To achieve small antenna loss, the antenna length should be at least a tenth of the carrier wavelength, i.e., about 30 cm for FM radio. Noticeably, this is too big for mobile devices such as smartphone. As a result, the transmitter simply uses a small antenna integrated in the chip, which is sufficient to provide the low permissible output power. The receiver, on the other hand, usually relies on an earphone or headphone as the external antenna, to maintain small antenna loss. But we note that recent FM receiver realizations such as [8] can work with a receive antenna that is built inside the mobile device.

Digital Audio

Digital audio has two important properties, the sampling frequency f_s and the quantization resolution m. The audio can be either monaural or stereo. Stereo audio uses twice the bandwidth as a monaural audio does, i.e., 30 KHz and 15 KHz in each FM channel respectively.

The DAC and ADC in the FM radio hardware can work with any sampling frequency below their maximum, e.g., 96 KHz in the N900. For FM transmission, if the sampling frequency of the digital audio is lower than the maximum, the DAC will perform up-sampling to the input digital audio while maintaining the bandwidth of the output analog audio. For FM reception, the digital audio output always has the maximal sampling frequency but one can further perform down-sampling using software. μStation exploits these properties of the DAC and ADC to address the symbol synchronization challenge.

Other Data Broadcasting Standards

FM radio has a set of benefits compared to other current and emerging wireless technologies supporting broadcasting, such as Wi-Fi, Bluetooth, ZigBee and ANT [9]. First, FM radio is inherently connection-free, unlike all the other technologies that require device pairing. This feature of FM radio prevents extra overhead in connection establishment and maintenance, and thus makes FM radio perfectly fit mobile applications that are short-lived and impromptu. Second, FM radio is power-efficient compared to other technologies especially Wi-Fi, due to its much lower output power under unlicensed regulation. The power efficiency allows an always-on treatment of the FM radio on battery-constrained mobile devices. Third, due to the short range and low frequency nature of mobile FM radio, it can provide an accurate indication of physical proximity with minimum influence from environments. The combination of all the features makes FM radio an outstanding choice for one-way data broadcasting as the focus of this work. For example, to broadcast one's socializing profile as one walks around, device pairing not only is unnecessary but also degrades the throughput significantly; meanwhile broadcasting in Wi-Fi's range would allow a much smaller number of simultaneous broadcastings due to interference.

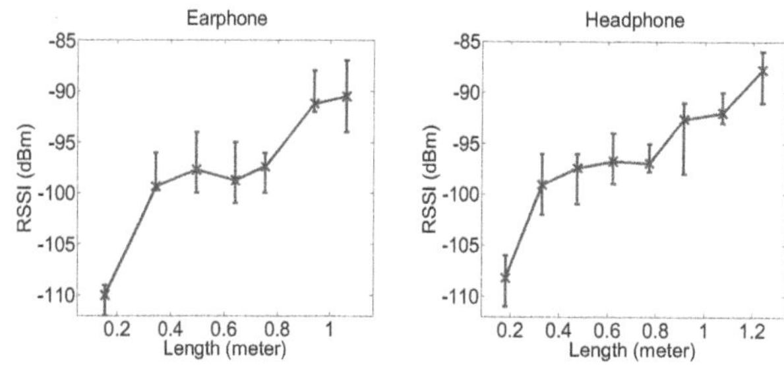

Figure 3: RSSI with different cable lengths of the earphone and headphone

We note that Bluetooth can be alternatively used for broadcasting without device paring, by presenting the message as the device ID in the Bluetooth beacon that is periodically broadcasted. However, this non-standard use of Bluetooth has two limitations. First, each message has a limited length, as the ID is limited to 128 bits. Second, the achievable data rate is limited, e.g., around 1 Kbps for Bluetooth vs. up to 20 Kbps for μStation. The second limitation is made worse when there are multiple Bluetooth broadcasting devices since they have to share the medium for broadcasting beacons.

CHARACTERIZATION OF MOBILE FM RADIO

The mobile FM radio has several distinctive features compared to conventional FM radio from licensed stations, such as limited output power and the use of external antenna for receiving. Since it is relatively new to mobile devices, to the best of our knowledge, there is no published work about its characteristics. Therefore, we next experimentally evaluate the properties of the mobile FM receiver and transmitter with real-life settings, based on the FM radio chipsets in the Nokia N900.

FM Reception

As mentioned earlier, mobile FM receivers employ an external antenna such as a headphone or an earphone. Our measurements show that the choice of the headphone or earphone, and its cable length (within a certain range) has little impact on the quality of FM reception.

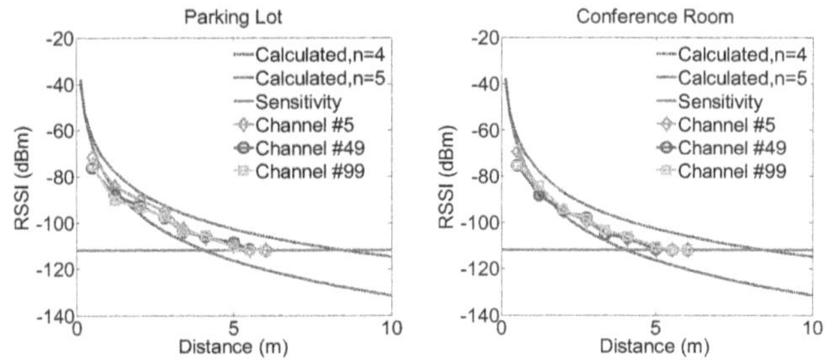

Figure 4: Broadcast range of mobile FM radio

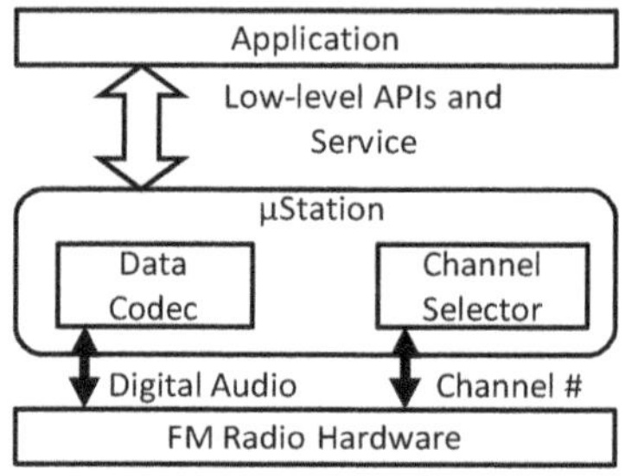

Figure 5: Overview of µStation

Headphones and earphones use a soft cable, which may advertently or inadvertently become coiled. Therefore, we examine the impact of cable length on FM reception quality with real-life settings. To quantify the impact, we measure the received RSSI at the FM receiver first with a 1.9 meters Lenovo P550 headphone, and then with a 1.6 meters Nokia N900 earphone. We use a winding case to adjust the cable length in a controlled manner, as shown in Figure 2. To ensure a fair comparison, we keep other settings fixed, including the output power (15 nW) and the distance between the transmitter and receiver (2.5 meters).

As shown in Figure 3, the RSSI is highly correlated with the length of the headphone/earphone cable. We further make three important observations. First, the RSSI drops with a smaller cable length due to higher antenna loss, and there is a significant drop when the length falls below 20 cm. Second, the two tested antennas exhibit similar characteristics. Last and most importantly, there exists a certain range of the cable length within which the RSSI is approximately constant, e.g., 0.4-0.8 meter. Noticeably, such range is often encountered in real-life situations, e.g., when a user is using a smartphone while wearing an earphone/headphone. Based on these observations, we conclude that the mobile FM reception quality will be relatively independent on the receive antenna. Therefore, for the experiments in the remainder of the paper, we use a 0.5 meter earphone as the receive antenna.

FM Transmission

The broadcast range of the mobile FM radio is important to applications. Our measurements show that the broadcast range is approximately five to six meters under regulation, regardless of the environment or channel number.

We chose two environments to evaluate the broadcast range. The first one is an empty campus parking lot with a line-of-sight (LOS) path and the second one is a conference room with people inside sitting around a table without any LOS path. These two environments have little and rich multipath effect respectively. We performed experiments for three available FM channels at the center and far ends of the spectrum: channel #5, #49, and #99. To see the broadcast range, we measure the RSSI with different distances between the transmitter and receiver. We also compare our measurements with that under a theoretical path loss model $P_r = P_t \cdot [\lambda/(4\pi d)]^n$ where P_t and P_r are the transmit and received power, λ the wavelength, n the power decay factor of the environment, and d the distance.

Our measurement results are summarized in Figure 4. We can see that the broadcast range is limited to about 5-6 meters. The environment and channel number have little impact on the range, due to the good penetration property of FM radio and the closeness of FM channels in the spectrum. The results also indicate a power decay factor between 4 and 5 for the path loss of FM radio.

AN OVERVIEW OF µSTATION

µStation leverages existing FM radio hardware to allow mobile devices with data broadcasting and reception, as the *µStation broadcaster* and *µStation listener* respectively. We assume that each mobile device is, at any given time, either a broadcaster or a listener. Application can choose and quickly switch between these two roles at will. Figure 5 provides an overview of µStation: for both broadcasters and listeners, µStation interacts with the FM radio hardware and presents an interface to applications with low-level APIs and services. There are two key modules in µStation. Channel Selector uses one control channel and multiple data channels so that with a high probability, no two nearby broadcasters will use the same data channel. Furthermore, Channel Selector guarantees listeners to find their broadcasting of interest in a timely fashion, even when devices are mobile. Data Codec converts binary data into an audio stream for transmission and vice versa for reception, in order to compatibly work with the FM radio hardware. Data Codec meanwhile achieves symbol-synchronization between the broadcaster and listener, solely in software.

µSTATION CHANNEL SELECTOR

µStation can be considered as a special incarnation of the extensively researched cognitive radio systems in which collision between coexistent users has to be resolved [10]. µStation Channel Selector enables multiple unlicensed and equally important broadcasters to efficiently share multiple orthogonal FM channels. While apparently the most efficient way to avoid collision is to let the broadcasters use orthogonal channels, achieving it is nontrivial.

µStation Channel Selector is based on one *control channel* and multiple *data channels*, all of which are available FM channels. First, all µStation broadcasters share the control channel. On the control channel, a broadcaster either

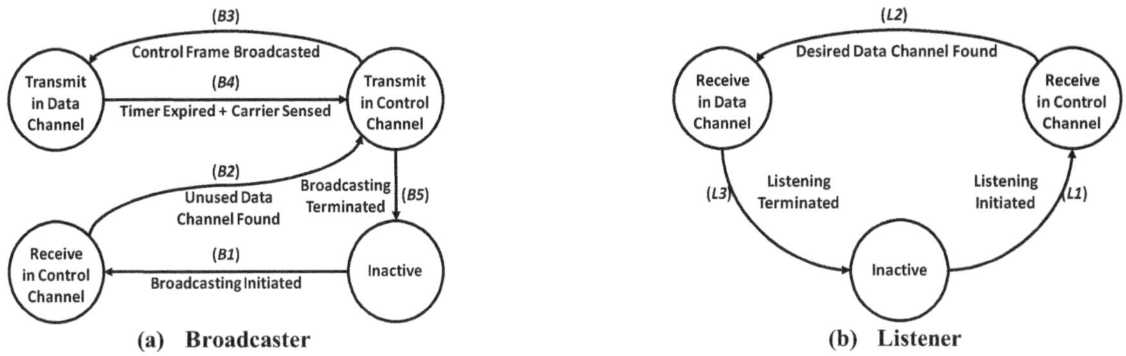

Figure 6: State transition diagrams of μStation Channel Selector

periodically announces which data channel it is using, or finds an unused data channel by listening to the announcement from other broadcasters. Second, only one broadcaster can use each data channel to broadcast application data. Any listener that is interested in the application on a data channel can receive the broadcasting based on the periodical announcement on the control channel.

The control channel enables quick discovery of the data channel usage by broadcasters and their applications. This is important since each device can only listen to one channel at any time. The control channel allows broadcasters to indicate their presence on a single channel to all potential listeners. However, in order to efficiently leverage the spectrum resource of available FM channels, application data broadcasting should utilize individual data channels. Without the control channel, it would take listeners much longer time to scan all the channels to find the right one.

Channel Transition

We illustrate the operation of Channel Selector using state transition diagrams shown in Figure 6. There are four possible states for a broadcaster and three for a listener. We next elaborate the state transitions.

Control Channel

When an application starts, the broadcaster or listener goes from inactive to listening to the control channel (*B1* and *L1*). This is important for two reasons. First, new broadcasters need to monitor the control channel in order to identify an unused data channel for their broadcasting (*B2*). Second, listeners similarly need to monitor the control channel to find the desired data channel (*L2*). Once a broadcaster has identified its data channel, it periodically sends a control frame containing its data channel number, its device ID, and its application ID. This enables listeners to find their data channels of interest by receiving the control frame.

Since multiple broadcasters use the same control channel, we adopt a *Carrier Sense Limited Access* (*CSLA*) mechanism for broadcasters to share the control channel. CSLA avoids collision between broadcasters with carrier sensing, and meanwhile limits the channel usage by each broadcaster to a certain percentage. We note that CSLA is intrinsically similar to p-persistent carrier sense multiple access (CSMA) [11]. We choose not to use 1-persistent CSMA [11] because the notorious hidden-node problem of 1-persistent CSMA may happen frequently due to the short range nature of the mobile FM radio. In accordance to CSLA, a broadcaster announces its presence on the control channel periodically if and only if (*i*) the control channel is free (carrier sensing by checking the RSSI), and (*ii*) it has not broadcasted on the control channel for a certain duration (two seconds in our design).

Data Channel

At any time, a data channel can be occupied by only one broadcaster. The broadcaster can continuously broadcast on its data channel, but must periodically switch to the control channel to announce its presence, as discussed previously (*B3* and *B4*). We leave the decision on how often the broadcaster should utilize the control channel to individual applications, as long as their usage follows the CSLA rule. When the application ends, the broadcaster releases its data channel by stopping broadcasting control frames on the control channel and going back into inactive (*B5*). A listener finds a desired broadcast by listening to the control channel. The listener then tunes to the desired data channel for receiving (*L2*), until the application is terminated (*L3*).

Collision Performance

We next provide an analysis of the collision performance of Channel Selector. That is, we analyze the probability for a listener to successfully receive its broadcasting of interest, with the presence of hidden broadcasters. For simplicity, we assume N broadcasters are in the range of a listener, and K of them are hidden from each other (i.e., the hidden broadcasters cannot hear each other and therefore may collide). We also assume the control frame on the control channel lasts for t seconds, and each broadcaster is allowed to broadcast on the control channel once every T seconds. In this case, when the control channel utilization is small, we can approximate the collision probability on the control channel as:

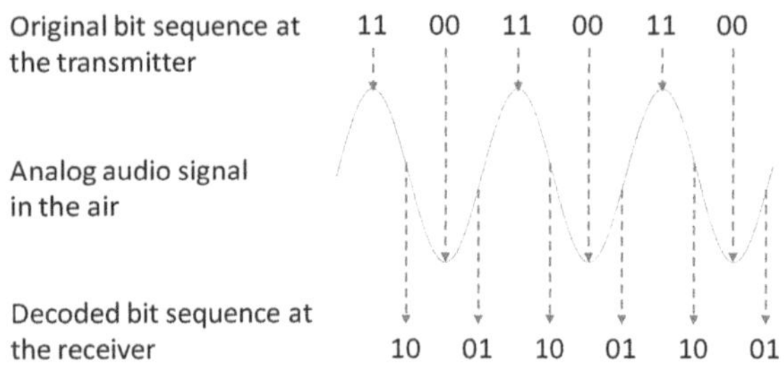

Figure 7: An example of the original and decoded bits without symbol synchronization

$$P_{Control} \cong \frac{2Kt}{T}.$$

When a collision occurs on the control channel, the listener cannot decode the control frame from all of the affected broadcasters.

For the data channels, the hidden node problem appears in a different fashion. Since the hidden broadcasters cannot hear each other, there is a chance that more than one broadcaster is using the same data channel. As a result, the number of unused channels for the K hidden broadcasters is $M'=M-(N-K)$, where M is the total number of data channels. In this case, the probability that more than one broadcaster is using the same data channel is

$$P_{Data} = 1 - \frac{(M')!}{(M'-K)!} \cdot \frac{1}{(M')^K}.$$

From the perspective of listeners, the probability of successfully receiving its desired broadcasting is

$$P = 1 - \frac{K}{N}(P_{Control} + (1 - P_{Control}) \cdot P_{Data}).$$

Assuming the following parameters that are typical in real-life scenarios and adopted in our design

$$t=0.05,\ T=2,\ N=10,\ K=3,\ M=20,$$

we can calculate $P=90\%$. Therefore, Channel Selector ensures successful reception by listeners with a high chance.

Channel Convergence

For Channel Selector to operate correctly, we must ensure that all μStation devices in a particular geographical area converge on the same control channel and have identical lists of data channels. The convergence is easily achievable if all μStation devices have the same set of available FM channels. In this case, the FM channel with the smallest channel number can be treated as the control channel and others as data channels.

In order to achieve channel convergence, we leverage an important property of FM channels. That is, the FM channel availability is time and location-dependent and more importantly, highly predictable, since licensed radio stations often follow a fixed broadcasting schedule. As a result, one can simply construct a mapping from time and location to available FM channels offline, and store it in a remote server which can be accessed in real time. We highlight that the location dependency of FM channel availability is coarse-grained due to the large coverage of licensed broadcastings; a device will usually see the same list of available FM channels even when it moves over certain kilometers. Therefore, localization based on cell towers is more than sufficiently accurate, and device can even locally store the mapping with minimal cost. Additionally, the device only needs to store the mapping with locations where it is used.

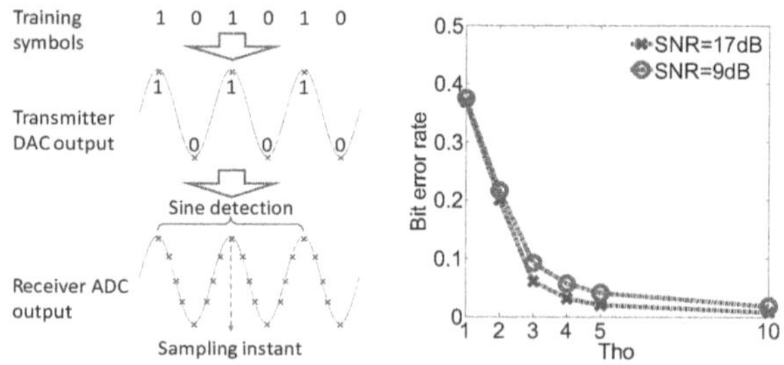

Figure 8: (Left) Symbol synchronization by μStation Data Codec (Right) Bit error rate over different ρ

μSTATION DATA CODEC

Data Codec leverages the existing FM radio hardware to realize bit-level communication between two μStation devices. Here let us consider a single pair of transmitter and receiver. We use the name "transmitter" and "receiver" to generally refer to μStation devices that are transmitting and receiving respectively, but note that a broadcaster needs to both transmit and receive, while a listener only needs to receive. Data Codec interfaces with both the application and the FM radio hardware, by applying conversion between digital data and audio. While the conversion may sound straightforward, Data Codec must properly cope with *symbol (clock) synchronization*, a particular challenge to μStation. By addressing the symbol synchronization challenge with proper design, Data Codec achieves an effective bit rate of up to 10 Kbps for monaural audio.

Bits-Audio Conversion

We use pulse amplitude modulation (PAM) to convert binary bits into audio. PAM is natural and straightforward for our application: one only needs to specify the sampling frequency f_s and quantization resolution m of the audio. Then, m bits are jointly represented as one audio sample with 2^m possible amplitudes, and the audio is streamed to the FM radio hardware with a sampling frequency of f_s. Converting an audio stream to binary bits requires the same procedure in reverse, but encounters an additional challenge, symbol (clock) synchronization, which we will tackle in the next subsection.

Choosing f_s should follow the Nyquist sampling theorem, i.e., f_s can be no greater than twice the available analog audio bandwidth, or $f_s \leq 30$ KHz. Similar to other modulation techniques in digital communication, a larger m will render higher bit error rates, thereby lower reliability. Based on our experimental results, under typical distance between the transmitter and receiver, such as 2.5 meters with a RSSI of -100 dBm, m=2 can offer a good reliability, i.e., a bit error rate of less than 5%.

Symbol Synchronization

Current mobile FM radio is not intended for digital communication; therefore it lacks the dedicated hardware for symbol synchronization, which is critical to PAM. For a receiver to correctly recover the broadcasted bits, the receiver ADC must be symbol-synchronized to the transmitter DAC. That is, the receiver must perform analog-to-digital conversion of the received audio at the right instant. Figure 7 shows an example when the receiver ADC and transmitter DAC are not symbol-synchronized. In the example, a bit sequence of "110011001100" is transmitted with m=2, i.e., each symbol representing two bits. Due to up-sampling, a sine signal will be the analog output of the transmitter DAC. Because the receiver ADC is not symbol-synchronized, it samples the received analog signal with an offset, decoding bits incorrectly.

To achieve symbol synchronization without hardware support, we explore the properties of the DAC and ADC in the FM radio hardware. Similar to the oversampling technique in conventional digital communication but in the software domain, we let the receiver ADC adopt a much higher sampling frequency than that of the transmitter DAC. As a result, the receiver can analyze the approximated analog audio. To achieve symbol synchronization, a transmitter sends a pre-determined sequence of training symbols with alternative symbol "0" and symbol "1" with a sampling frequency of $f_{s,t}$. Due to up-sampling to the input digital signal by the DAC, a sine signal with frequency $0.5f_{s,t}$ will be the analog output and transmitted through FM. On the other hand, the receiver expects a sine signal with its peak corresponding to the symbol "1" in the training symbol sequence. Importantly, the peak also indicates the correct sampling time. The receiver employs a sampling frequency $f_{s,r}$ much higher than $f_{s,t}$ so that the received analog signal can be approximately recovered. Figure 8 (Left) illustrates the symbol synchronization procedure: after getting the samples, the receiver seeks to detect the training symbols which exhibit a sine pattern, and then simply searches for the peak sample and treats it as the right sampling instant.

Noticeably, the ratio of $f_{s,r}$ over $f_{s,t}$, or $\rho=f_{s,r}/f_{s,t}$ determines the symbol synchronization accuracy. In our design, we adopt ρ=5, which is identified experimentally. That is, we measure the bit error rate performance of the broadcasting under different ρ, shown in Figure 8 (Right). We repeat the measurements with two different channel SNRs: 17 dB and 9 dB. One can clearly see that a larger ρ can reduce the bit error rate and the reduction is not linear, i.e., after a certain threshold, e.g., ρ=5, the reduction is trivial. This is because the biggest offset from the right sampling instant is $T_s/2\rho$

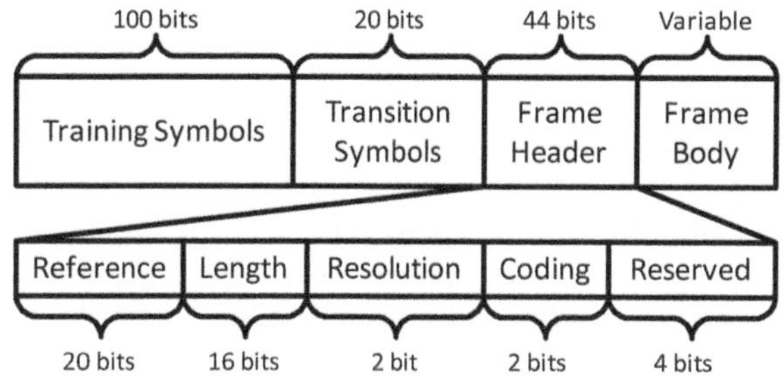

Figure 9: Framing in μStation Data Codec

where T_s is the signal period. As a result, the benefit of increasing ρ decreases with larger ρ, and the BER is mainly affected by channel SNR.

Given ρ=5, the concrete values of $f_{s,r}$ and $f_{s,t}$ in our design are $f_{s,r}$=50 KHz and $f_{s,t}$=10 KHz respectively. While $f_{s,r}$ can be as high as the maximum sampling rate of the receiver ADC, i.e., 96 KHz in N900, we found that it is not only unnecessary, but also hardly achievable. This is due to the insufficient computing capacity of mobile devices for real-time processing, especially when the device is under a heavy workload. Our experimental experience reveals that a maximal $f_{s,r}$ of around 50 KHz can be achieved in N900 without lagging the decoded data from the received audio. It also indicates a $f_{s,t}$ of 10 KHz which is below the maximal sampling frequency allowed by the FM channel.

Framing

Similar to conventional digital communication, to ease bits delivery, Data Codec needs framing to organize binary bits. We next present the frame design. As shown in Figure 9, each Data Codec frame contains four parts: *training symbols*, *transition symbols*, *frame header* and *frame body*.

Training symbols are utilized for two purposes: one is to perform symbol synchronization as we explained previously, and the other is to provide reference amplitude of the symbols so that the rest of the frame can be correctly translated with different quantization resolutions.

Transition symbols partition the training symbols and frame header, in order to avoid the confusion of detecting the starting bit of frame.

Frame header includes various control information for the receiver to decode the bits. It is always translated with m=1 to maximize reliability.

Frame body carries actual data bits given by the application and can have various length.

As shown, the non-data parts of a frame contain 164 bits altogether, while the frame body is allowed to have arbitrary length from 1 to 2^{16}=65536 bits, depending on the application data. For connectionless broadcasting applications, the broadcaster is often continuously and repeatedly streaming data, and therefore the frame body usually has a much longer duration than the other parts do, meaning that the actual application throughput can approach the raw bit rate of µStation.

Reliability Enhancement

µStation assumes one-way broadcasting. While an occasional frame loss and moderate BER might be acceptable for some applications, e.g., location-based services, they can be fatal for applications that have a tight accuracy requirement for data delivery, e.g., synchronization between devices. While the responsibility of maintaining reliability can be left to applications, Data Codec does employ coding to the raw binary bits to assist the application for reliability enhancement. We use linear coding with a rate of 1/2, which is simple and effective.

Bit Rate Performance

Given all the above techniques adopted by Data Codec and the parameters in our design, we can approximately calculate the effective bit rate as

$$R_{bit} = f_{s,t} \times m \times r_{coding},$$

which is 10 Kbps for monaural audio with $f_{s,t}$=10 KHz, m=2 and r_{coding}=1/2. For stereo audio, the achievable bit rate can be up to 20 Kbps.

IMPLEMENTATION

Our design of µStation compatibly works with existing mobile FM radio hardware, and it is largely device independent from an implementation perspective. To offer application developers both flexibility and ease of use, µStation provides both low-level APIs and services. In this section, we first explain the APIs and services, and then present our smartphone-based implementation of µStation.

µStation Low-level API

We encapsulate the basic functionality of µStation as a regular python library, which can be imported by applications and used on any mobile devices through the provided low-level APIs. The core APIs include:

channel_getlist(): list all available FM channels. µStation will gather location information, try to query the remote or local server, and obtain the list of available channels.

channel_find(): find an unused data channel for broadcasting. µStation will treat the device as a broadcaster, tune to the control channel to get a list of unused data channels, and randomly pick one among them.

channel_announce(): announce the application in the control channel. µStation will switch to the control channel and perform carrier sensing. If the medium is free and the broadcaster has not used the control channel in the last T seconds, µStation will broadcast a control frame with its data channel number, device ID and application ID.

channel_bond(app_ID, dev_ID): find the data channel occupied by app_ID and dev_ID. µStation will treat the device as a listener, and keep monitoring the control channel until finding the desired control frame. Then it will tune to the corresponding data channel.

broadcast(bi_data, ch_data): broadcast binary data bi_data in the data channel ch_data. µStation will generate a frame as appropriate, form it as audio, and stream the audio to the FM transmitter for broadcasting.

receive(bi_data[], ch_data): retrieve all the frames in the data channel ch_data and store the decoded binary data in bi_data[]. µStation will keep recording audio from the FM receiver and extract the data within all the frames.

µStation Service

µStation services are built on top of the low-level APIs to further ease application development. Here we show an example service, *inter-device synchronization*, which allows multiple devices to synchronize their system clocks with high accuracy (<0.1 seconds).

µStation leverages the short range property of FM radio to accomplish inter-device synchronization. That is, a "beacon" device as the broadcaster periodically broadcasts reference time signals through µStation. Seeing and then decoding the broadcasted reference time signal, surrounding devices as listeners can adjust their system clocks accordingly. This provides a high-level of accuracy, since the signal latency due to RF propagation is virtually non-existent at the FM radio range, and our measurements show that each device has a small and more importantly, constant signal detection latency. Our experiments show that the accuracy of inter-device synchronization can be less than 0.1 seconds while devices are in range.

Smartphone-based Implementation

To demonstrate the feasibility of µStation, we choose the Nokia N900 smartphone for implementation. The N900 adopts Maemo [12], which is open-source and allows rapid customization and application development. Nonetheless, µStation does not require any hardware, OS or FM radio driver modification.

The N900 implements both the FM transmitter and receiver as Video4Linux radio devices and controls them over the hardware bus I^2C. The FM transmitter integrates a DAC within the chip thereby directly interacts with the system; the FM receiver does not have an ADC and relies on the audio codec for interaction. Hardware configurations such as switching on and off the FM radio or changing the FM channel can be achieved through the standard Video4Linux APIs. The FM radio drivers also expose some information in a virtual file system called *sysfs*, allowing simple configurations such as setting the output power and measuring RSSI. The audio codec and FM transmitter in N900 do not enable very low-level interfacing, e.g., the user cannot directly send or get a digital audio as a binary stream. Nonetheless, µStation indirectly interacts with them using the following methods: for transmission, µStation plays the audio stream as a media which will be automatically captured by the FM transmitter; for reception, μStation records the audio stream from the audio codec with proper sampling frequency, using the *PulseAudio* utility [13] available in Maemo.

Our smartphone-based implementation of μStation is limited by the FM radio hardware and its software interface. As a result, much of the computation of μStation has to be realized using the powerful Application Processor, which inevitably limits the power efficiency of μStation. However, given proper firmware support, μStation can be implemented in the microcontroller within the FM chipset to significantly improve its power efficiency.

APPLICATION

μStation supports a large set of data broadcasting applications on mobile devices, although the broadcast range is limited (5 meters) and the data rate is moderate (20 Kbps). For example, a user can broadcast its profile during a social gathering; a device can broadcast its sensing data to peer devices to support collaborative sensing services; a user can broadcast a product or service advertisement as he or she moves around and encounters other people. Next we present two example applications based on μStation: *Facebook-FM* and *Sync-Flash*.

Facebook-FM

Facebook-FM is a socializing application that allows automatic and rapid sharing of Facebook profiles among a group of users in a small area. To enable the sharing, a device as a broadcaster uses μStation to broadcast the Facebook ID of the user. All the other in-range devices as listeners can simultaneously receive the broadcasting. Each device can switch between broadcasters and listeners so that each user's Facebook ID is shared among others. This application can be particularly useful in public occasions such as a party or a conference to initiate interaction between attendees.

We have implemented Facebook-FM solely based on the μStation low-level APIs, as shown in Figure 10. For broadcasters, the application first calls *channel_getlist()* and *channel_find()* to reserve a data channel, and then repeatedly calls *channel_announce()* to indicate its presence and *broadcast()* to broadcast the user's Facebook ID in its data channel. For listeners, the application first calls *channel_getlist()* and *channel_bond()* to find the data channel used by Facebook-FM. Then it calls *receive()* to retrieve the message for each data channel that is associated with Facebook-FM. The homepage associated with the Facebook ID is further shown in the browser.

Sync-Flash

Another innovative application we create using μStation is called *Sync-Flash*, which coordinates multiple mobile devices to synchronously "flash" using their regular LED flash or screen. It can be used in concerts or sports games where the audiences/fans would like to present certain flashing pattern using their smartphones. Another usage of Sync-Flash can be to provide multiple "slave" flashes for photography, in order to offer additional light or reduce shadows.

Broadcaster	Listener

[ch_control, ch_data_list] = *channel_getlist()*
ch_data = *channel_find()*
bi_data = *enc(*"Facebook ID"*)*
while (true):
    channel_announce()
    *broadcast(*bi_data, ch_data*)*
    if (app terminated):
        break
	[ch_control, ch_data_list] = *channel_getlist()*
	ch_data[] = *channel_bond* *(*"Facebook-FM", N/A*)*
	while (true):
	    for ch in ch_data[]:
	        *receive(*bi_data[], ch*)*
	    if (app terminated):
	        break

Figure 10: Realization of Facebook-FM using the low-level APIs of μStation

We demonstrate Sync-Flash using the concert example shown in Figure 11. Assuming there is a large population of audience and they are uniformly distributed, a flashing pattern can be realized by letting a subset of the audiences, e.g., those in the middle in Figure 11, turn on the screen of their smartphones. Clearly, all the intended audiences should be triggered at the same time and their flashings have to be in the same fashion, e.g., always on or flash every one second, to achieve certain intended pattern. Different fashions can be indicated by different pattern ID.

μStation realizes Sync-Flash using both the low-level APIs and the inter-device synchronization service. The realization involves three steps, as shown in Figure 12. First, a few audiences need to become the initiators, either voluntarily in real time by registration through Internet, or in advance by pre-assignment. The initiators are responsible for triggering the flash and broadcasting the intended flashing pattern. They also act as "beacon" devices for inter-device synchronization. The initiators can be remotely synchronized. Second, when a flashing pattern is desired, the intended initiators, depending on which subset of the audience should flash, broadcast a triggering message to their neighbors. The message has two uses: serving as the reference time signal for inter-device synchronization, and containing a pattern ID which the surrounding audience identify and flash as appropriate. Finally, seeing the triggering message from initiators, all involved audiences simultaneously flash in the same fashion, collectively offering a desired flashing pattern. The pattern stops when the initiator broadcasts a termination message.

RELATED WORK

To the best of our knowledge, μStation is the first work that leverages the mobile FM radio to enable data broadcasting applications. Other uses of mobile FM radio beyond its audio transmission and reception capability are exclusively limited to localization based applications, such as [14].

There exist several systems for radio stations to broadcast small amounts of application specific data alongside FM audio broadcasting, including RBDS [5] and Microsoft DirectBand [6]. Furthermore, the authors of [15] have

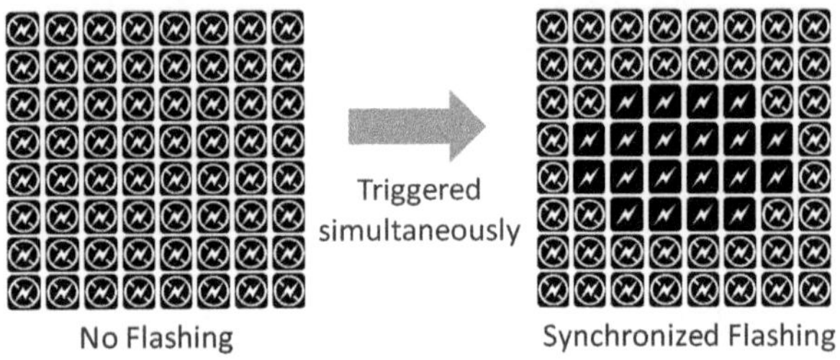

Figure 11: Sync-Flash performed by a concert audience

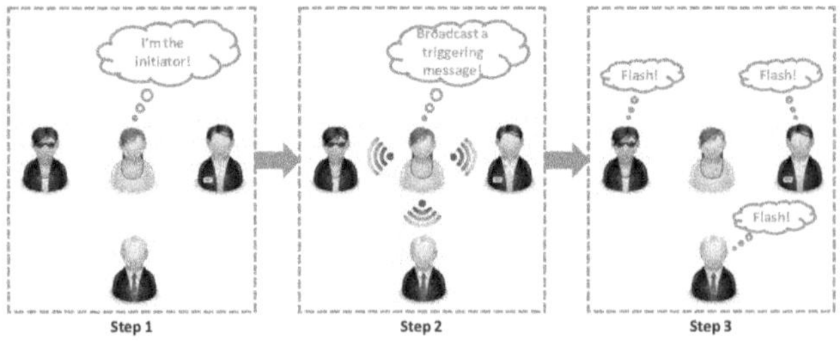

Figure 12: Three steps to realize Sync-Flash with μStation

proposed and evaluated a protocol for radio stations to transfer arbitrary files over RBDS. μStation is fundamentally different. First, μStation targets short-range data broadcasting from mobile devices, as opposed to metropolitan-area radio station broadcastings of RBDS. Second, μStation reuses the frequency band for analog audio broadcasting in each FM channel, while RBDS has its dedicated band allocation. Third and most importantly, μStation only works with the digital audio interface of the mobile FM radio, while the designers of RBDS have access to the radio baseband and are free to develop their own PHY protocols. Our work has its own challenges such as symbol synchronization.

Using voice channels for data communication is an existing concept, e.g., [16-20]. These works primarily focus on how to improve the communication performance while compatibly working with the voice codec in GSM systems. Our work, μStation, has a different focus and targets on data broadcasting from mobile devices, as well as the supported applications. Again, the use of FM radio exhibits its unique challenges such as FM channel selection.

CONCLUSION

In this work, we reported the design, realization and applications of μStation, a data broadcasting system using the mobile FM radio. μStation does not require any modification to device hardware, OS or FM radio driver, and supports efficient channel selection and transmitter-receiver symbol synchronization. μStation enables developers to easily implement a wide range of data broadcasting applications with a compact set of APIs and services, as demonstrated by Facebook-FM and Sync-Flash.

μStation departs from the traditional use of mobile FM radio for audio transmission and reception and is the first publicly reported exploration toward using it for short-range data broadcasting. While we have showed the feasibility of mobile FM radio for ubiquitous applications, its potential invites more serious efforts from both the research community and mobile hardware vendors.

REFERENCES

1. Color, *http://www.color.com/*.
2. Cisco StadiumVision, *http://www.cisco.com/web/strategy/sports/StadiumVision.html*.
3. Windows Phone 7 Series: Everything Is Different Now, *http://gizmodo.com/#!5471805/windows-phone-7-series-everything-is-different-now*.
4. 9 to 5 MAC: In-house Radio.app in the works for iPhone and iPod touch, *http://www.9to5mac.com/10167/In-house-Radio-app-in-the-works-for-iPhone-and-iPod-touch/*.
5. RBDS, *Radio Broadcast Data System*.
6. DirectBand, *Microsoft*.
7. SiriusXM Radio, *http://www.siriusxm.com/frequency*.
8. BlueCore BC7820, *http://www.csr.com/products/10/bluecore-bc7820*.
9. ANT, *http://www.thisisant.com/*.
10. S. Haykin, "Cognitive radio: brain-empowered wireless communications," *IEEE Journal on Selected Areas in Communications (JSAC)*, 2005.
11. P. C. Gupta, *Data Communications and Computer Networks*: PHI Learning Pvt. Ltd., 2011.
12. Nokia Maemo, *http://maemo.org/*.
13. PulseAudio, *http://www.pulseaudio.org/*.
14. A. Matic, A. Papliatseyeu, V. Osmani, and O. Mayora-Ibarra, "Tuning to your position: FM radio based indoor localization with spontaneous recalibration," in *Proc. IEEE PerCom*, 2010.
15. A. Rahmati, L. Zhong, V. Vasudevan, J. Wickramasuriya, and D. Stewart, "Enabling pervasive mobile applications with the FM radio broadcast data system," in *Proc. ACM HotMobile*, 2010.
16. T. Chmayssani and G. Baudoin, "Data transmission over voice dedicated channels using digital modulations," in *Int. Conf. Radioelektronika*, 2008.
17. N. N. Katugampala, K. T. Al-Naimi, S. Villette, and A. M. Kondoz, "Real time data transmission over GSM voice channel for secure voice and data applications," in *Secure Mobile Communications Forum*, 2004.
18. C. K. LaDue, V. V. Sapozhnykov, and K. S. Fienberg, "A Data Modem for GSM Voice Channel," *IEEE Trans. Vehicular Technology,* 2008.
19. M. Rashidi, A. Sayadiyan, and P. Mowlaee, "A Harmonic Approach to Data Transmission over GSM Voice Channel," in *Proc. ICTTA*, 2008.
20. A. Dhananjay, A. Sharma, M. Paik, J. Chen, T. K. Kuppusamy, J. Li, and L. Subramanian, "Hermes: data transmission over unknown voice channels," in *Proc. ACM MobiCom*, 2010.

Myngle: Unifying and Filtering Web Content For Unplanned Access Between Multiple Personal Devices

Timothy Sohn[1], Frank Chun Yat Li[2], Agathe Battestini[1], Vidya Setlur[1], Koichi Mori[1], Hiroshi Horii[1]

[1]Nokia Research Center
Palo Alto, CA 94304
firstname.lastname@nokia.com

[2]Department of Computer Science
University of Toronto
frankli@dgp.toronto.edu

ABSTRACT
Users often engage in tasks that span multiple personal devices. Although many current solutions exist to provide ubiquitous access to one's data, users continue to struggle with cross-device tasks. These solutions often require them to plan ahead for their information needs. In this paper, we present *Myngle*, a device-agnostic system that lets users quickly find the information they are looking for from previously visited web pages without having to plan ahead. *Myngle* provides a unified web history from multiple personal devices, and allows users to filter their history based on high-level categories influenced by common mobile information need categories (*e.g.,* address, phone number). We evaluated *Myngle* with 32 users and found that our category-based method of filtering eases the burden of continuing cross-device tasks.

Author Keywords
Web history revisitation, cross-device interaction, mobile information filtering

ACM Classification Keywords
H5.m. Information interfaces and presentation (e.g., HCI): Miscellaneous.

General Terms
Human Factors

INTRODUCTION
The number of devices a user owns and interacts with is steadily increasing. Mobile phones, tablets, and laptops are now common in a user's ecosystem and introduce opportunities to engage in tasks that span multiple devices. For example, users may look up restaurant reviews and directions on a laptop, but then reenter that same information on a mobile phone to take with them. The lack of tools for continuing tasks across devices boundaries burdens users. As a result, they often resort to cumbersome methods (*e.g.,* writing webpage links on a piece of paper) to resume their task on another device [2,10].

Studies have shown that users could benefit from tools that combine their digital history from multiple devices for easy task resumption [26]. Emerging cloud computing technologies (*e.g.,* Google Docs [20], Evernote [15], and Dropbox [13]) help address some of these problems by making information repositories ubiquitously available. However, these tools are primarily useful when users plan ahead for their information needs (*e.g.,* placing a file in Dropbox). In everyday activities, mobile users rarely plan ahead, and only plan for important or long-term activities, such as a vacation [2]. This gap in supporting the unplanned tendencies of mobile users presents a unique opportunity for systems that can help users quickly address their impromptu mobile information needs.

To address this problem, we present *Myngle*, a system that unifies web history from multiple personal devices and allows users to quickly find the information they are looking for without having to plan ahead. By combining web history, users no longer need to use cumbersome methods to transfer information from one personal device to another. We chose to focus on web history since the information needs of mobile users can often be addressed through online resources [33]. In addition to a unified web history, *Myngle* allows users to comb through their web content with a set of high-level filters (*e.g.,* address, phone number). The categories of filters we chose are influenced by prior research that identified categories of information mobile users typically look for [11,33]. With *Myngle,* users can easily satisfy their information needs without needing to plan ahead or to keep track of web history per device.

Myngle works in Firefox and Chrome web browsers on desktops through browser extensions, as well as in native phone clients that run on Android, iOS, and Nokia Qt devices. We evaluated Myngle with 32 smartphone users over a period of 3 weeks. Our exploration of cross-device web history sharing and filtering demonstrates that category based filtering is an effective method to quickly address information needs. Our results suggest that sharing web history among devices is a successful method of supporting unplanned activities and alleviating the common inconveniences of revisiting previously seen web content.

RELATED WORK

We build on related work from three areas studying search and information retrieval, cross-device interaction, and mobile information needs.

Search and Information Retrieval

Prior research has mostly focused on studying web history revisitation with desktop computers. Studies have shown that web revisitation accounts for 58% [34] to 81% [8] of all desktop website visits. Obendorf *et al.* found that 50% of desktop web revisits occurred within 3 minutes, while the other half took place much later [28]. Adar, Teevan, and Dumais looked deeper into the intent behind revisits and found a variety of revisitation patterns [1]. In order to help users find information they have seen before, Dumais *et al.* created a system for personal information retrieval [14]. However, when studying how users revisit content across devices, the analysis becomes multifaceted. A single piece of content can be accessed through a desktop URL, a mobile URL, or a mobile application. Few studies have been conducted on revisitation patterns where the content can be accessed through a web browser or a smartphone application across multiple devices [2,25].

A number of studies have investigated web search behavior on desktop [24] and mobile devices [23] through query analysis. They reveal that high-end smartphone users (*e.g.*, iPhone) have similar query habits as desktop users. These similar search query habits suggest that revisiting web information may be prevalent across devices for high-end smartphone users; further motivating the need for studying cross device content revisitations.

Cross Device Interaction

Studies on how users manage their life with multiple devices have shown that users frequently migrate tasks across their devices [10,29]. Some studies suggest that sharing web history could alleviate some of the frustrations in interacting with multiple devices [25,26]. Bales *et al.* explored content revisitation patterns among high-end smartphone users and found that revisitation is common from both mobile and desktop devices [2]. These studies reveal the need for systems to combine content from web histories for easy revisitation.

Several systems allow users to revisit previously seen content in a scaled down version on their mobile device by clipping important parts of web pages [4,16,21,27], assembling mashups [17], or searching file systems across devices [30]. Evernote [15] and Dropbox [13] synchronize files and notes in the cloud for access anywhere. Google's Chrome-to-phone extension [7] let users send data from their desktop browser to their phone. In contrast to Myngle, many of these systems require the user to plan ahead for their information needs, which is rarely done by users [2]. Firefox [18] synchronizes bookmarks, tabs, and web history between desktop and mobile Firefox clients so users do not need plan ahead for their information needs. Myngle goes beyond synchronization of web history and enables users to filter their content based on common information needs. Some of the ideas around tagging mobile data types were explored in Gurungo, which sends key data that a user may want to access while mobile to the device through Bluetooth [19]. Myngle builds upon this work by exploring how automatic tagging and sharing of web history among personal devices can help users address their impromptu mobile information needs.

Mobile Information Needs

Studies on mobile information needs have mostly used diary study methods to gather ecologically valid data about the types of content mobile users look for. Several diary studies have identified commonly desired categories of information by mobile users [6,11,33]. These categories tend to cluster around location, maps, and points of interest. Location-based search studies and applications have also shown the power of a user's current location in addressing one's information needs [12,22]. Myngle's filtering system is informed by this prior research by providing users with a tool to filter their web history based on categories of information. This allows users to quickly see the information they are looking for.

MYNGLE ARCHITECTURE

Myngle provides a unified user experience across multiple devices by combining web history from each device. Myngle automatically tags and extracts relevant information from web pages that a user may need later based on high-level categories. The system is designed as a client-server architecture that consists of a backend server, desktop clients, and mobile clients (See Figure 1). The following sections describe each of the components in detail.

Desktop Browser Extensions

Myngle uploads web history from the desktop to the backend server through a browser extension. The extension is designed to be lightweight and to integrate seamlessly with modern web browsers. We currently support Firefox and Chrome as client browsers. The browser extension has two main functions. First, it records the websites that a user visits and uploads each visit to the backend server. Second, it processes each web page and tags content that would be relevant to a mobile user.

The extension is triggered whenever content is loaded within the browser window. This change can be a new page load, or new content being loaded through an HTML iframe on the web page. The extension collects the *URL*, *title*, and *time of visit* of the page and uploads them to the backend. After a page has loaded, the extension classifies the content of the page. The current set of categories that the extension automatically detects is: *addresses, maps,*

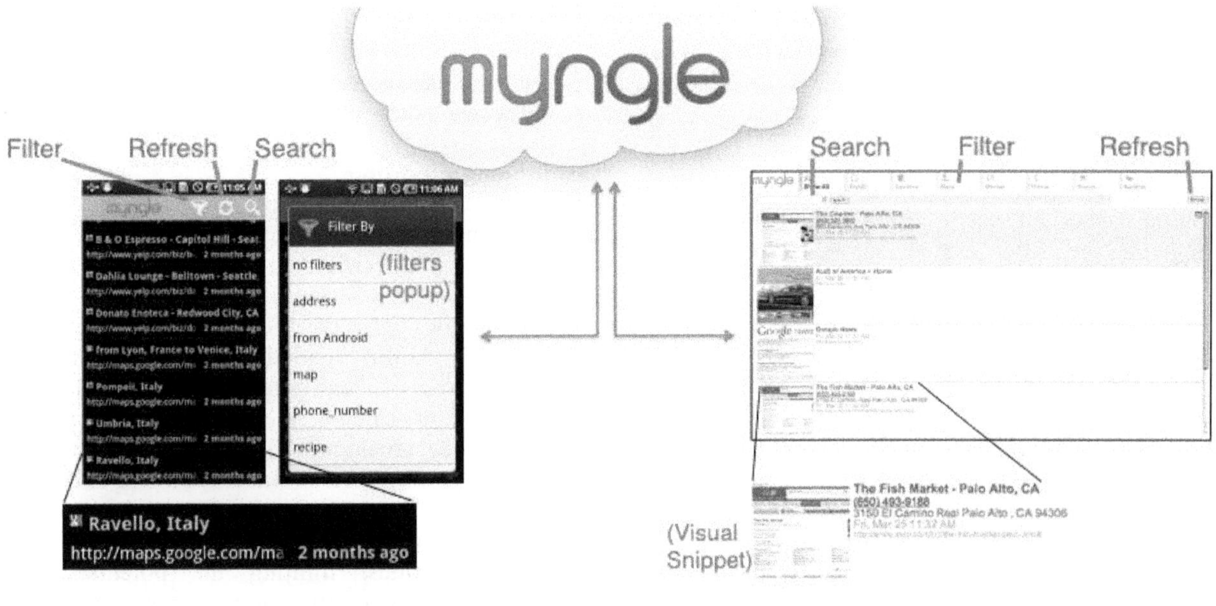

Figure 1. An overview of Myngle. The Myngle server aggregates web history from a user's desktop and mobile devices. Web content is tagged in the client side browser and sent to the server. Users can view their tagged web content through a web application or a mobile application. Myngle offers a native application on three mobile platforms: Nokia Maemo, iOS, and Android.

movie times, shops, phone numbers, and *weather forecasts*. We chose these categories because they were the most common types of information needs that mobile users access through online resources [11,33]. If any of these categories are detected in the content of the page, the extension tags the corresponding URL and sends the tags to the server. Our tagging algorithm is explained in a later section.

There are two benefits to our in-browser tagging approach. First, web page content itself is not uploaded, preserving the privacy of users by not storing sensitive page data (*e.g.*, bank statements, emails). Second, by tagging individual URLs we are able to provide a direct link to pages with the content the user may be looking for. This is especially useful for web-based email because it is one of the primary information stores for users, containing content such as plans for a party or phone numbers for contacts [3]. Instead of manually marking an email as unread or saving it at the top of the inbox, Myngle allows the user to directly access the relevant email. The extension can tag each individual email and give users direct access to the content without having to go to the inbox and then search for the data.

Mobile Applications

Myngle is available as a native application on Android, iOS, and Nokia Maemo devices. Due to API constraints on the native web browser for each platform, not all clients upload web history to the server. In our implementation, only the Android client uploads mobile web history to the server. In this section, we will detail the Android implementation, but the other native clients have similar architectures and user interfaces. The specific capabilities of each individual platform can be found in Table 1.

When a change in the local SQLite browser database is detected, the *URL*, *title*, *time of visit*, and *number of visits* of new web history is uploaded to the backend. The Android browser does not allow browser extensions, thus no tagging is done on web history items uploaded from the mobile clients. Instead, the *mobile* tag is applied to all web history from the mobile clients so that users can have a quick view of all web pages viewed from their mobile device.

The main view of the application has a list of the user's web history in reverse chronological order (see Figure 1). The Android platform allows Myngle to launch other applications on the device, so links do not all need to open in a web browser. A user can choose to open a Google map link in the native map application on her device. Similarly, if a user has Yelp installed, she can open all Yelp links in

	Desktop Browser	*Android*	*iOS*	*Nokia*
History Upload	**Yes**	**Yes**	No	No
History Download	**Yes**	**Yes**	**Yes**	**Yes**
Tagging	**Yes**	No	No	No
Filtering	**Yes**	**Yes**	**Yes**	**Yes**
Launch other apps	No	**Yes**	No	No
Number of Participants	N/A	**7**	**6**	**19**

Table 1. Capabilities and number of users for each platform.

the Yelp application instead. On the other platforms, all links will load in a web view within the Myngle application.

The Myngle application offers basic functionalities such as searching and filtering. A user can performs a case-insensitive text search in the cached URLs and titles (the application caches the user's history for up to a month). Clicking on the filter button shows a popup menu containing all of the possible tags in the user's web history (see Figure 1). Selecting any tags will filter the main list to show only items with the selected tag. For example, selecting addresses will show all history items that were tagged to have an address in the page.

In addition, one of the key goals of the mobile client is to present web history data to the user in a manner that is easily browsable and identifiable. Myngle makes available visual thumbnails of these web pages that are optimized for viewing on various mobile devices. Our thumbnail algorithm, inspired by the Visual Snippets work [35], extracts three main elements from each web page: the title from the web page, the most salient image, and a portion of text surrounding the salient image. Figure 1 shows some sample snippets shown in the Myngle web interface. Visual snippets have been shown to improve recall of websites and provide an alternative method for browsing one's personal web history [35]. These snippets can be useful when combined with our filtering system in both a mobile and desktop web interface to support recall of pages.

Backend Server

Web history items uploaded from the clients are stored as a record in the backend database with the *URL, last visit time*, and *tags* associated with that URL. In our system, the tags represent the categories detected in the user's web browser.

Many sites have different desktop URLs and mobile URLs for the same content. Revisiting a site using a desktop URL on a mobile device can lead to unexpected behaviors, such as a page failing to load or being redirected to a different page. For example, desktop URLs of Gmail will always launch the inbox of the mobile version, not the actual email. To address these issues, the Myngle server automatically translates the desktop URLs to mobile URLs for a few, commonly accessed domains including Facebook and Gmail (more examples in Table 2). Our system allows users to access their content directly without being redirected to unnecessary pages.

Tagging Algorithm

We use the term tagging to represent the process of assigning a label to a web page based on identifying the existence of specific data types (*e.g.,* address) within the page. Analyzing website content has been widely explored through semantic analyses of websites [31]. Our approach builds on this work by exploring the effectiveness of identifying a specific set of tags known to be common categories of mobile information needs. Server side techniques for analyzing web content [5,9] can compromise user privacy by storing and analyzing the contents of the page outside of a user's control. These techniques are also unable to process content behind secure websites, limiting the potential analysis of important content often found in web-based emails. In contrast, Myngle tags web content in the client browser, which maintains user privacy and enables us to analyze and tag password-protected content, but not store the content itself.

Our tags are named after several common categories of information needs that mobile users look for through online resources [33], including *addresses*, *maps*, *movie times*, *phone numbers*, *shops*, and *weather forecasts*. These categories have a contextual component to them that makes them more likely to be accessed while a user is mobile. We considered tagging websites using other categories, such as those found on social bookmarking sites (*e.g.,* delicious.com) that use the power of crowdsourcing to determine what tags should be assigned for a web page. However, our focus is on enabling fast content revisitation of personal web pages, so we decided to start with tags that a user may need again later on other personal devices.

The Myngle extension tags web pages using a combination of regular expressions and heuristics. Our goal is not to create a comprehensive tagging algorithm, but to explore the usefulness of tags on high-level categories. The extension searches the text elements in the DOM model of each page and applies a regular expression search for the existence of a category (*e.g.,* 5 numbers preceded by a state

	Desktop	Mobile
Gmail	https://mail.google.com/mail/***?shva=1***#*inbox/<mail_id>*	https://mail.google.com/mail/***mu/#cv/****inbox/<mail_id>*
Google Docs	https://docs.google.com/***?pli=1#folders/***<*folder_id*>	https://docs.google.com/***m?parent=***<*folder_id*>
Google Voice	https://www.google.com/voice***?pli=1#inbox***	https://www.google.com/voice/***m#~voice:s=inbox&l=inbox***
Facebook	http://***www***.facebook.com/***<name>***	http://***touch***.facebook.com/#/***<name>***
Twitter	http://twitter.com/***#search****?q=<searchText>*	http://twitter.com/***searches****?q=<searchText>*

Table 2. Example translations of desktop URLs to mobile URLs.

may indicate the end of an address, or a degree sign could indicate weather information). If a regular expression matches, the extension then uses several heuristics based on other elements in the page itself and the title to tag the page. For example, movie times were detected by identifying show times and movie ratings (*i.e.,* G, PG, PG-13, etc.) within the page. The heuristics were fine tuned to be conservative and to avoid false positives. Since we only analyze text elements, we would miss a phone number or an address embedded in an image. However, most personal content that a user would likely revisit is often in the text portion of the webpage.

USER EVALUATION

The purpose of our user study was two fold. First, we explored the effects of sharing web history among one's personal devices. We wanted to understand the implications of this approach and how people adapted to thinking about their data as a single source of content instead of by device. Second, we evaluated the usefulness of tagging web history based on the existence of categories of mobile information needs. The following sections describe our methods for conducting the study.

Participants

We recruited 32 participants through several email mailing lists. All of our participants were high-end smartphone users owning three types of phones: Android (7), iPhones (6), and Nokia smartphones (19). We will refer to the participants as [*i,a,n*]<participant number>. All three platforms had access to a native application in addition to the web interface for accessing Myngle, although most Nokia participants used the web interface. Due to platform limitations described earlier, only Android users had mobile web history connected with their desktop browsing history (see Table 1). The participants using the other two platforms were only able to see their desktop web history on their mobile device.

Procedure

Participants used Myngle over a period of three weeks on their phones and laptop/desktop computer. We instructed participants to either use Firefox or Chrome on their laptop/desktop machines for the duration of the study. Participants installed the Myngle plugin on their respective browsers and the native application for each of the respective smartphone platforms. Although each platform has a central application store (*e.g.,* Android Market), we chose to distribute applications to our participants through an ad hoc model in order to track who was using our application.

Through a series of instructional videos, we showed our participants an overview of the Myngle system and demonstrated how to access it on each of the client devices. The videos provided a detailed walkthrough so users could immediately begin using Myngle.

After 1.5 weeks we sent an online survey to our participants asking about their experiences using Myngle and the usefulness of each of the mobile filters. We also asked participants to share example stories where they used Myngle to revisit web pages on multiple devices. Participants who completed the survey were entered in a drawing for a $50 gift card. At the end of the three-week study we sent out another online survey with similar questions as the previous survey and offered a drawing for a $75 gift card.

RESULTS AND OBSERVATIONS

We collected a total of 44,518 unique desktop URL visits and 286 unique mobile URL visits. We observed a total of 143 mobile-to-desktop (*i.e.,* visit a website on a mobile browser then revisiting the same site later on a desktop browser), 127 desktop-to-mobile, 8,318 desktop-to-desktop, and 184 mobile-to-mobile revisits. We measured cross-device revisits by matching URLs and comparing timestamps to determine which access occurred first. This process required matching many of the URLs manually because mobile websites have different URLs than their desktop counterparts. We only considered two URLs a match if the content they referenced was the same.

There were a total of 137 usages of Myngle from a mobile device. In total, participants visited 51 links from the mobile clients.

Uses of a Unified Web History

The largest percentage (31.3%) of the mobile revisits was for locations (*e.g.,* Google maps, Yelp, and restaurant sites). We found this to be one of the key uses of a unified web history. With current technologies, keeping track of location information can be difficult especially if one does not plan ahead to write down restaurant names or addresses. From the survey responses, users noted that Myngle provided an element of security knowing that their locations would be available later.

"I have a friend coming into town and we were talking about all the eateries we wanted to hit up. So I yelped the different places on Chrome and now I have all the different places we want to try stored on my phone for easy access. That way, whenever we're out around town and feel like trying one of the places, I can easily find where it's at." (Participant a4)

This experience also shows that filters can offer a natural grouping of a larger activity. *Participant a4* wanted to know all of the different restaurants that she may want to visit. Filtering through her history based on addresses, would present a time-based grouping of these restaurants for easy access later.

Several participants mentioned the ease of looking up a place right before leaving the house and then grabbing directions on the phone.

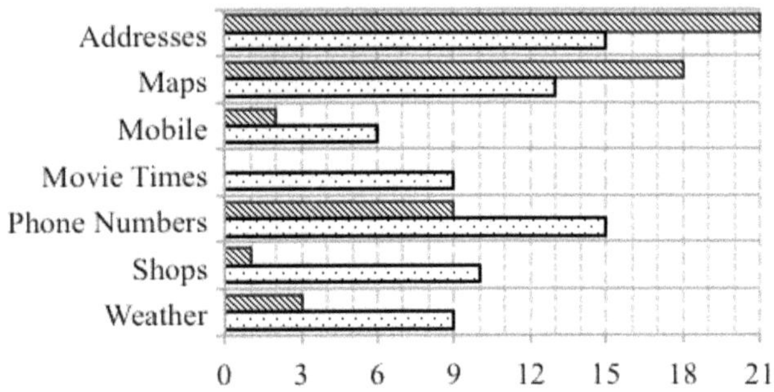

Figure 2. Graph of filters used from mobile (top bar) and desktop (bottom bar).

"I looked up a place for dinner to go with my wife on our home computer. Then figured out where and what place it was and then accessed the information from the car on my Nexus One. It was pretty nice and very easy." (Participant a1)

Google mail (19.6%) and Facebook (9.8%) were another two of the large sources of mobile revisits among our participants. There is currently no easy way to re-read emails on the mobile phone without going through the inbox or search. A common method for users to save emails for later is to mark them unread [26]. Most mobile mail clients only show unread mails and it is time consuming for users to search for previously read emails. Revisiting emails from a unified web history is useful because Myngle automatically translates Gmail web history from desktop versions to mobile versions. Users are able to access the desired email quickly without the clutter in the desktop version of Gmail.

Since Myngle only translates desktop URLs to mobile URLs for a few sites (examples in Table 2), participants would often see desktop versions of a page on their mobile phone. We thought this would be a hindrance for users, but some found it to be advantageous because the mobile version may not always be desired. We observed that in some situations users wanted the version of a page they had seen before. The desktop version of a website can be useful because participants knew where the desired information was on the page. Mobile web pages can be useful since they are optimized for the small screen, but do not always contain the same information and functionality as their desktop counterparts. *Participant a3* expressed joy when he found that Myngle gave him the information he needed through the desktop version of a page instead of the mobile version.

"Yesterday when I was talking to a friend on the phone she told me the name of the place to meet for dinner. I was at my computer so I Googled it and then followed a link to Yelp. When I was walking there, I pulled out my phone and loaded Myngle. It was recent so it was at the top of my list. I didn't want the Yelp page, I wanted the google.com search results because that had a bigger map. What was great is that it gave me the desktop version of my search (which has a map), not the mobile version (which does not have a map)." (Participant a3)

The map was the primary piece of information needed by *Participant a3*, thus having the desktop version with a map was more useful than a properly optimized page. This leads to a larger observation that presenting previously seen websites in their original form to users can be more useful even on a mobile device. Although a mobile version of a webpage can utilize the screen better, one's spatial memory and page recognition can help a user recall pages quickly in their original desktop form.

Uses of Filters

We collected a total of 44,518 unique URLs that were analyzed by our browser extension for tags. Our algorithm tagged a total of 4761 URLs (10.69%) with at least one tag and 2,042 URLs (4.58%) were tagged with two or more different filters. We anticipated only a small subset of the URLs to be tagged given that we focused on identifying certain categories of mobile information needs. Web users browse through many sites that may not fall into any of our tagged categories.

Twenty-one unique participants used mobile filters. Figure 2 shows a graph of the number of times each filter was used by all the participants based on our log data. The most common filters on the mobile device were addresses and maps. Mobility typically means traveling between destinations, thus navigation is a key component of a user's information needs. Participants also found phone numbers to be a useful filter. These web pages typically had phone numbers for businesses or friends that the users needed to call. Accessing the emails directly provided an easy shortcut rather than loading their web mail page and searching for the email.

Our survey results were consistent with the device usage we logged. We asked participants to rate the effectiveness of filters on a five point Likert scale in our survey. In general, participants found the filtering system to be easy to use and helpful (mean: 3.8, SD: 1.3). In addition, participants reported the filters they found most useful; 50% of participants indicated that addresses were most useful, followed by maps (43%) and then phone numbers (29%). One of the more useful filters on the desktop was the *mobile* filter that would show pages seen on the user's mobile device. Mobile users typically revisit content on their PC that they previously viewed on their mobile device because of environmental constraints or technical barriers (*e.g.,* some mobile browsers do not support Flash) [2].

Although some filters were not accessed frequently, users indicated their usefulness in certain situations. The shopping filter empowered participants to quickly do a price comparison between a product they had seen online with one in the store. *Participant n14* said, "*Situations just haven't arisen where I needed it. But, that one [shopping] I talked about above was a great win for the app in my mind.*" Although these predicaments happen infrequently, the ability to quickly recall a previously seen website can alleviate additional mobile interaction, such as remembering query terms for a web search.

Myngle alongside Previous Practices

As participants became more confident in Myngle and its filtering system, they began to trust and use Myngle to replace previous practices.

"Over the weekend, I was planning a day trip in SF and looked up directions and hours/location for various locations on my laptop. Before Myngle, I would've written down the information on a piece of paper / emailed myself the information. Instead, I opened up Myngle on my phone and used the address filter to access the information so I can enter it into my GPS." (Participant i2)

Other participants found Myngle to work well for certain types of websites. They continued to use email as their main source for content synchronization, but they began to rely on Myngle for specific categories of websites.

"I use my computer as usual and then access those pages on my phone. I mainly use email and certain sites like yelp on Myngle." (Participant n1)

Participants agreed that filters were useful, but the success of finding the information depended heavily on the tagging algorithm. Our tagging system worked well for certain websites, but participants had varying levels of success. Some participants began to lose trust in the system when it did not perform to expectations.

"I tried to search for a few spots where I can have dinner in the evening on the PC browser and then access the address of that place on my phone later. Unfortunately it didn't work out, as the address wasn't extracted from the web page." (Participant n14)

In situations where Myngle was not able to help address one's information needs, participants would resort to their usual methods of finding the information such as a web or email search. We view Myngle as a complementary tool that can quicken access of information. Future exploration will involve improving the tagging algorithm so that users can have greater trust in the system.

The tagging algorithm performed well for easily recognizable categories such as maps, where it could search for HTML embed tags that are commonly used to place maps into web pages. However, there were several areas where the tagging algorithm had difficulties. Web pages can have addresses or phone numbers in any part of the page including images embedded in the page. Since our algorithm only analyzes text portions of a page, it was not able to identify content in non-text portions. Non-US addresses were also not identified by the algorithm since our tagging methods were designed for US-based addresses. This affected some of the results because several non-US participants were not able to use the system to its full potential.

Temporal Patterns

Overall participants had a short time span of revisits between their desktop and mobile computers. Revisits occurred within an average time frame of 04:17 (format: hh:mm, SD: 01:46, Min: 00:03, Max: 10 days, 03:13). Participants indicated in their survey responses that they would typically look up an address on their computer and soon after revisit the web page with the information on their mobile device. The average revisit time for addresses was 02:44 (SD: 01:46). Revisit times for other popular categories such as phone numbers and maps were 00:45 (SD: 00:38) and 03:21 (SD: 02:58) respectively. These times are less than the average overall revisit times, indicating that certain categories may have a different lifespan than others. Prioritizing pages based on a category's expected lifespan could allow for improved interaction by showing users pages that would be important to them in their current context (*e.g.*, time of day).

DISCUSSION

In the following section we reflect on the usefulness of our system and opportunities for improvement in addressing the needs of mobile users. We draw on the observations and data from our study.

Usefulness of Myngle

Several studies have suggested the need for a unified web history system [2,26] and we've seen efforts in this space by platforms such as Firefox [18]. Myngle builds on this work by enabling fast synchronization and category filtering of web history to allow quick revisiting of information. Our participants appreciated having Myngle to revisit web pages between their phone and computer.

"Seeing stuff that I viewed on my phone was awesome. When I was looking for something, that didn't have any address, phone number, map or any other filter it took quite a while searching page by page to find it" (Participant a6)

Filtering history helped this participant see their browsed mobile web pages quicker than having to search or browse through their history on the mobile device.

On the other hand, some filters were rarely used by the participants (*e.g.*, movie times in mobile clients). We chose our filters based on the types of mobile information needs that users experience, however some of these information needs may occur infrequently.

"I have to be honest, I did not use Myngle as often as I thought I would. When I first installed the application I envisioned lots of scenarios where I perceived using it. However, in actuality those situations did not really arise." (Participant a5)

Moreover, there are many specialized mobile applications that can satisfy one's information needs (*e.g.,* a specialized application for movie tickets). Some participants found that these specialized mobile applications were sufficient to address their information needs. Myngle provides easy revisitation of web history, but does not tap into the content within applications. In future work, this could be addressed with platforms that allow other applications to communicate across applications silos, which would create a bridge between web and mobile application content.

Introducing a new tool into a user's ecosystem is often difficult especially when they already have certain habits for finding information. Even with these habits, Myngle proved to be used often in certain situations such as shopping comparison, finding addresses, or finding phone numbers. The usefulness of Myngle is that it's a tool for the unplanned situations when standard mobile applications may prove to be too time consuming to use. In the future, we would like to focus on these scenarios where Myngle was successful.

Improvements to the Filtering Mechanism

We have demonstrated that even with an unwieldy personal web history stream, filters designed around mobile information categories can simplify the way users interact with their data. In our work we've focused on the personal filters, but these could be expanded to other data types and filter mechanisms.

Meta-Level Filters

Current methods for finding information tend to center around searching or manually bookmarking websites to access later. Although searching is an easy method to find specific data, the results can be at such a fine-grained level (*e.g.,* single web page) whereas users might want a larger activity-based level (*e.g.,* restaurants to visit with friend). In describing her use of a unified web history, *Participant a4* alluded that one of the benefits of *Myngle* was that the filters would help her focus on the categories she was interested in and would form a natural grouping for her task since she explored web pages chronologically close together. The natural grouping described by our participants occurred because they had accessed the webpages in one sitting. However, there are times when a user may access content sporadically, but still want to group the content together in a meaningful way. This presents an opportunity for a richer tagging and filtering system that could provide semantically meaningful filters based around a specific task or activity. Examples of these task or activity based filters could be "taking my friend to the airport" or "finding an apartment". We can view these as meta-level filters that span across other types of information beyond web history, such as one's calendar, documents, and emails. Our participants saw this as a natural progression of Myngle in supporting their everyday lives.

"I think it would be interesting if Myngle could have a meta-level filter. For example, I've been doing a lot of job search related stuff. Most of which involves phone numbers, addresses, dates, etc. I would want all of that information together under an encompassing filter." (Participant a5)

Using Context

Combining personal web history presents opportunities to prioritize web pages based on contextual information. Users currently access their web history through searching or browsing data in a long time-sorted list. However, mobile users often think of the information they need based on location. Being able to access previously seen data based on the user's current location would allow users to recall information for their current situation.

"For example, if I have a list of places I want to try eating at, I can easily figure out which ones I'm close to. So if I'm on the west side, I can filter out which addresses are close to me so that I can go try one of those places." (Participant a3)

Researchers have explored using location as a proxy for activities that a user may perform at a place [32]. These types of location-based activities could enrich the contextual information and allow users another method for recalling their previously seen web history. For example, the system could present previously seen how-to videos and websites about playing golf while a user is out on the golf course. This could also be extended to incorporate a user's current calendar to further associate previously seen web pages with current activities. We believe further exploration is needed to understand the types of context-based filtering that would be beneficial for users to access their personal history.

CONCLUSION

Cross-device sharing of content is becoming more pervasive as the number of personal devices a user owns increases. This presents an opportunity to create systems that ease the burden of sharing information within one's personal content ecosystem. To explore this area, we presented the design and evaluation of Myngle, a system for cross-device web history sharing and filtering based on high-level categories of information needs. As users browse web pages, Myngle stores them and tags those with information the user may need later. We implemented Myngle in several modern web browsers and high-end mobile platforms. Our results from a three-week user study with 32 participants show that cross-device web revisitation through category-based filters is easier and avoids current cumbersome methods of accessing content. Based on these findings, we suggested several areas to improve cross-device web revisitation through additional types of filters.

ACKNOWLEDGEMENTS

Thanks to the study participants and anonymous reviewers for their helpful comments. We also thank the other members of the NRC IDEA team for their insightful comments with the system and the paper.

REFERENCES

[1] Adar, E., Teevan, J., and Dumais, S. T. Large scale analysis of web revisitation patterns. In *Proceedings of CHI '08*, pp. 1197-1206.

[2] Bales, E., Sohn, T., and Setlur, V. Planning, Apps, and the High-end Smartphone: Exploring the landscape of modern cross-device reaccess. In *Pervasive 2011*, pp. 1-18.

[3] Belotti, V., Ducheneaut, N, Howard, M., and Smith, I. Taking Email to Task: The Design and Evaluation of a Task Management Centered Email Tool. In *Proceedings of CHI'03*, pp. 345-352.

[4] Bila, N., Ronda, T., Mohomed, I., Truong, K.N., de Lara, E. PageTailor: Reusable End-User Customization for the Mobile Web. In *Proceedings of Mobisys'07,* pp. 16-29.

[5] Chakrabarti, D. and Mehta, R. The paths more taken: matching DOM trees to search logs for accurate webpage clustering. In *Proceedings of* WWW '10, pp. 211-220.

[6] Church, K. and Smyth, B. Understanding the intent behind mobile information needs. In *Proceedings Of IUI 2009, pp. 247-256.*

[7] Chrome-to-phone. http://code.google.com/p/chrometophone/

[8] Cockburn, A. and McKenzie, B. What do web users do? An empirical analysis of web use. *International Journal of Human-Computer Studies,* Vol 54 (6), pp. 903-922.

[9] Crescenzi, V., Merialdo, P., and Missier, P. Clustering web pages based on their structure. *Data Knowl. Eng*. Vol 54 (3), pp. 279-299.

[10] Dearman, D. and Pierce, J.S. It's on my other computer!: computing with multiple devices. In *Proceedings of CHI '08*, pp. 767-776.

[11] Dearman, D., Kellar, M., and Truong, K.N. An examination of daily information needs and sharing opportunities. In *Proceedings of CSCW 2008*, pp. 679-688.

[12] Dearman, D., Sohn, T., and Truong, K.N. Opportunities Exist: Continuous Discovery of Places to Perform Activities. In *Proceedings of CHI '11*, pp. 2429-2438.

[13] Dropbox. http://dropbox.com

[14] Dumais, S., Cutrell, E., Cadiz, JJ, Jancke, G., Sarin, R., and Robbins, D.C. Stuff I've seen: a system for personal information retrieval and re-use. In *Proc. of SIGIR* '03, pp. 72-79.

[15] Evernote. http://evernote.com

[16] Fujima, J., Lunzer, A., Hornbaek, K., Tanaka, Y. Clip, Connect, Clone: Combining Application Element to Build Custom Interfaces for Information Access. In *Proceedings of UIST'04*, pp. 175-184.

[17] Hartmann, B., Wu, L., Collins, K., Klemmer, S.R. Programming by a Sample: Rapidly Creating Web Applications with d.mix. In *Proceedings of UIST'07*, pp. 241-250.

[18] Firefox. http://mozilla.com/mobile/sync

[19] González, I.E. and Hong, J. GurunGo: coupling personal computers and mobile devices through mobile data types. In *Proceedings of HotMobile '10, pp.* 66-71.

[20] Google Docs. http://docs.google.com

[21] Harding, M., Storz, O., Davies, N., and Friday, A. Planning ahead: techniques for simplifying mobile service use. In *Proceedings of HotMobile '09.*

[22] Jones, M., Buchanan, G., Harper, R., and Xech, P. Questions not answers: a novel mobile search technique. In *Proceedings of CHI '07*, pp. 155-158.

[23] Kamvar, M. and Baluja, S. A large-scale study of wireless search behavior: Google mobile search. In *Proceedings of CHI '06*, pp. 701-709.

[24] Kamvar, M., Kellar, M., Patel, R., and Xu, Y. Computers and iphones and mobile phones, oh my!: a logs-based comparison of search users on different devices. In *Proceedings of WWW '09*, pp. 801-810.

[25] Kane, S.K., Karlson, A.K., Meyers, B.R., Johns, P., Jacobs, A., and Smith, G. Exploring Cross-Device Web Use on PCs and Mobile Devices. In *Proceedings of INTERACT '09*, pp. 722-735.

[26] Karlson, A.K., Iqbal, S.T., Meyers, B., Ramos, G., Lee, K., and Tang, J.C. Mobile taskflow in context: a screenshot study of smartphone usage. In *Proceedings of CHI '10*, pp. 2009-2018.

[27] Nichols, J., Hua, Z., Barton, J. Highlight: A System for Creating and Deploying Mobile Web Applications. In *Proceedings of UIST'08*, pp. 249-258.

[28] Obendorf, H., Weinreich, H., Herder, E., and Mayer, M. Web page revisitation revisited: implications of a long-term click-stream study of browser usage. In *Proceedings of CHI '07*, pp. 597-606.

[29] Oulasvirta, A., Sumari, L. Mobile kits and laptop trays: managing multiple devices in mobile information work. In *Proceedings Of CHI '07*, pp. 1127-1136.

[30] Pierce, J.S. and Nichols, J. An infrastructure for extending applications' user experiences across

multiple personal devices. In *Proceedings of UIST '08*, pp. 101-110.

[31] Qi, X. and Davison, B. 2009. Web page classification: Features and algorithms. *ACM Computer Survey* 41,2,Article 12 (February 2009).

[32] Shanahan, P. and Griswold, W.G. Inferring the everyday task capabilities of locations. In *Proc. Of LoCa 2007.*

[33] Sohn, T., Li, K.A., Griswold, W.G., and Hollan, J.D. A diary study of mobile information needs. In *Proceedings of CHI '08*, pp. 433-442.

[34] Tauscher, L. and Greenberg, S. How people revisit web pages: empirical findings and implications for the design of history systems. *International Journal of Human-Computer Studies*, 47(1): 97-137, 1997.

[35] Teevan, J., Cutrell, E., Fisher, D, Drucker, S.M., Ramos, G., André, P., and Hu, C. Visual snippets: summarizing web pages for search and revisitation. In *Proceedings of CHI '09*, pp. 2023-2032.

Mechanical Hijacking: How Robots Can Accelerate Ubicomp Deployments

Scott Davidoff
Carnegie Mellon University
research@scottdavidoff.com

Nicolas Villar, Alex S. Taylor, Shahram Izadi
Microsoft Research Cambridge
{ nvillar | ast | shahrami } @microsoft.com

ABSTRACT
The complexities and costs of deploying Ubicomp applications seriously compromise our ability to evaluate such systems in the real world. To simplify Ubicomp deployment we introduce the robotic pseudopod (P.Pod), an actuator that acts on mechanical switches originally designed for human control only. P.Pods enable computational control of devices by hijacking their mechanical switches – a term we refer to as *mechanical hijacking*. P.Pods offer simple, low-cost, non-destructive computational access to installed hardware, enabling functional, real world Ubicomp deployments. In this paper, we illustrate how three P.Pod primitives, built with the Lego MindStorm NXT toolkit, can implement mechanical hijacking, facilitating real world Ubicomp deployments which otherwise require extensive changes to existing hardware or infrastructure. Lastly, we demonstrate the simplicity of P.Pods by observing two middle school classes build working smart home applications in 4 hours.

Author Keywords
Mechanical hijacking, prototyping, evaluation, robotics.

ACM Classification Keywords
H.m Information Systems: Miscellaneous.

General Terms
Design, Economics, Experimentation, Human Factors.

INTRODUCTION
Researchers have posited that domains as varied as automotive [4], the home [10], healthcare [8] and sustainability [1] will benefit from applications of ubiquitous computing (Ubicomp). The complexities and costs of deploying Ubicomp applications in the wild, however, still seriously compromise our ability to explore these domains and ultimately to evaluate these claims [2].

Because deployed Ubicomp systems would interact with social mores [3], it becomes important to examine if benefits *in theory* are achieved *in practice*. As importantly, if Ubicomp applications are to fit into the fabric of our daily lives [5] they will need to *interface* with the hardware infrastructure that already exists in such spaces. These legacy infrastructures, from lighting and heating systems, to bespoke automotive navigation and cooling hardware, to legacy systems in healthcare, and to preexisting appliances in the home, offer no well-defined computational interface.

This paper introduces the term *mechanical hijacking*, an approach to leverage and control legacy hardware systems and infrastructures through mechanical means, instead of through an explicitly defined computational interface. We explore this idea through the design of robotic pseudopods (P.Pods). A P.Pod is an actuator that acts on buttons designed for the human hand. By hijacking the capabilities of existing buttons. P.Pods can offer computational control over any device with a mechanical interface without need to replace or alter existing hardware, Figure 1 shows how P.Pods use the existing buttons to control a thermostat, granting non-invasive computational control of a home's climate control system. A real-world deployment can effectively leverage existing infrastructure.

In this paper, we describe three P.Pod primitives that demonstrate mechanical hijacking, and illustrate how they can simplify application deployment across a number of domains. To demonstrate the simplicity of the P.Pod approach, we invite two middle school classes to each create a functioning "smart home" application. Each class successfully creates one application in just 4 hours. We first turn our attention to P.Pod primitives and their application.

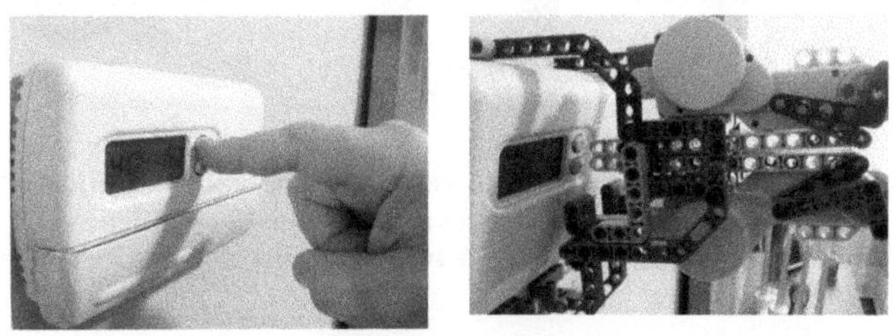

Figure 1. A robot pseudopod (right) mechanically hijacks buttons designed for the human hand, creating non-invasive computational control of a home's existing infrastructure.

APPROACH

Despite a growing belief that understanding the impact of Ubicomp systems requires longitudinal field deployment [2], few systems are actually deployed and rigorously evaluated (*e.g.* [8]). The cost of building custom electronics needed to computationally interface wth installed hardware and infrastructure can deter such deployments[1].

In this section we introduce an alternative approach to ubicomp deployment: *mechanical hijacking*. The alarm clocks, deadbolts, stovetops, light switches, and stereos can already be controlled using the mechanical buttons, knobs and switches built into them for use by human hands. Robot pseudopods (P.Pods) are tiny robots that hijack the mechanical controls on these devices. This provides a mechanical means to control existing hardware, and also a well-defined computational interface by which these robots can be controlled by Ubicomp application developers.

Though only suggestive of a broad vocabulary, we describe three simple P.Pod primitives. Each primitive simulates one capability of the human hand. Though technologically agnostic, we implement P.Pod primitives using the Lego MindStorms NXT[2] toolkit, which includes a wide variety of sensors, a rich mechanical expressivity, and native software interfaces for the Java, RobotC and C# languages.

The piston-like poker (Figure 2, left) simulates finger extension and retraction, hijacking doorbells and on/off switches, buttons that actuate away from the body. The grasping pincher (Figure 2, center) simulates finger flexion and extension, hijacking drill triggers and hole punchers, switches that actuate towards the body, The radial twister (Figure 2, right) operates on sink water flow controls and lighting dimmers, knobs that actuate around rotational axes.

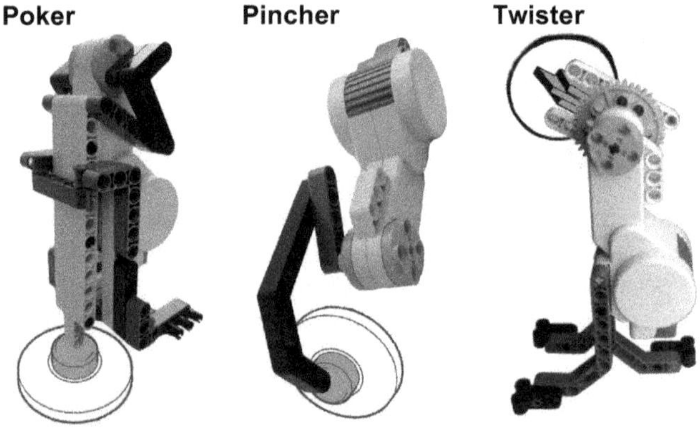

Figure 2. Three P.Pod primitives hijack distinct mechanical controls. The poker (left) controls buttons. The pincher (middle) controls triggers. The twister (right) controls knobs.

[1] Hack a day, http://hackaday.com/tag/thermostat/

[2] Lego MindStorms NXT, http://mindstorms.lego.com

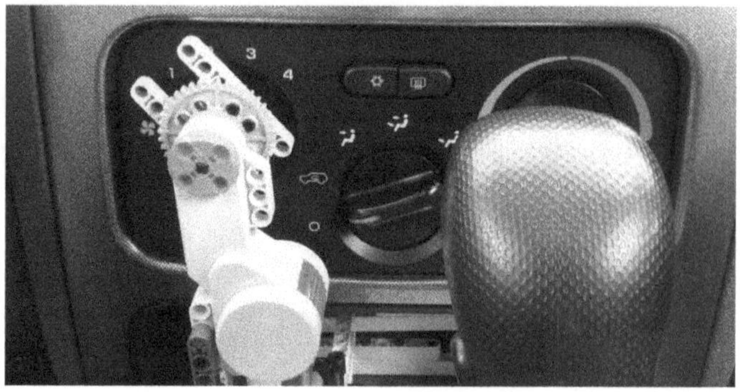

Figure 3. A P.Pod twister hijacking an in-car climate control system's mechanical dial. This P.Pod provides a way to deploy a climate control system in an automtive environment, which is normally hostile to experimentation.

IMPLEMENTATION

To illustrate how mechanical hijacking can accelerate and extend Ubicomp deployments, we illustrate the application of P.Pods in two common Ubicomp research scenarios: sustainability, and domestic robotics.

Deploying to Explore Sustainability

A field deployment of the sustainability models envisioned in [6] require a computational interface to an environment's climate control system. Typically, this is achieved in one of two ways. First, an invasive approach wires the thermostat to a microcontroller that provides network interfaces. Second, a less destructive but more costly approach replaces the thermostat with a networked device that communicates with a home control system (*e.g.* Insteon[3]), and offers built-in network interfaces.

Figure 1 shows how two P.Pod pokers can be configured to access the mechanical controls on the front of an installed thermostat without damaging the device. One P.Pod is aligned over each of the two front-facing buttons, allowing the device as a whole to both raise and lower the desired temperature setting. The two P.Pods are attached to the exterior of the thermostat using an enclosing fixture, which also provides resistance against the force of button-pushing. Figure 3 shows an automotive deployment using a single P.Pod twister. In each case, servomotors communicate with control programs over Bluetooth or USB.

The transparency of the mechanical hijacking approach lowers the technical requirements to deploy a functioning system. Even a high-level microcontroller (*e.g.* Arduino[4]) requires an understanding of thermostat controls and feedback loops. P.Pods can mechanically reproduce any interaction that a human can understand. So understanding the buttons on a thermostat is all that is needed to deploy a functioning system.

[3] Insteon, http://www.insteon.net

[4] Arduino, http://www.arduino.cc/

Figure 4. Three robotic P.Pods together mechanically hijack an i-Robot Roomba. A P.Pod poker uses the on/off button to start or stop the motion of the Roomba. Side-mounted P.Pods pinch the bumpers, giving the Roomba false collision input, causing it to turn away from the side of the pinched bumper.

Deploying to Explore Machine Intelligence

The human relationship with intelligent machines is another area of active Ubicomp research [9]. Efforts are limited because deployments often require custom hardware and are often constrained to fixed locations [7]. Again, we illustrate how P.Pods can *piggyback* on existing hardware to achieve a full range of technical capabilities without their need to be engineered from scratch.

Figure 4 shows how we can configure three P.Pods to mechanically hijack the power and movement of an i-Robot Roomba[5]. A laser-cut grid mounted on the Roomba allows the P.Pods to be placed flexibly on top. A P.Pod poker uses the on/off button to control the movement of the Roomba. We use two P.Pod pinchers to mechanically activate the Roomba's two front bumpers. This signals (falsely) to the Roomba that it has hit an obstacle on that side, causing a change in direction. By pinching the left bumper, the robot goes right. Pinching the right bumper moves the robot left.

Extending the base capabilities of an i-Robot Roomba can allow for much richer interaction with intelligent machines in a prolonged field deployment. While the Roomba has an existing API, this type of low-level, self-contained, and real-time control of the Roomba would be difficult without custom electronics. It also illustrates how other legacy machines could be controlled in this way.

EVALUATION

To demonstrate the simplicity, flexibility and power of P.Pods, we asked two groups of middle school students to create a deployable Ubicomp application over the course of one week. To control learning costs with the MindStorms toolkit, we recruited two groups that participate in the local First Lego Robotics League. Each group contained ten middle school girls, ages 12-15.

Protocol

Researchers explained how P.Pods work, and demonstrated their use with the hijacked Roomba (see Figure 4).

The participants were instructed to use P.Pods to "control anything automatically" and to focus on things what would "make home more fun." Each of the two groups met three times. At 1.5 hours per meeting, each group had 4 hours in total to complete the task. The groups used the last thirty minutes to present and explain their designs.

The two groups elected to each construct a voice-controlled home entertainment system. When the children cheered in unison, the system was to turn on the television, and play a DVD. To implement this concept, the groups had to develop a way to sense the background noise level in the room, and to control the TV in response to the sensed noise level.

Researchers provided no P.Pod specifications to the girls. Nor did the researchers make the Roomba available to use as a model. Participants moved about the class both collaborating and independently solving problems. The researchers observed, and moderated. They did help the participants think through technical stumbling blocks, but always required the girls to solve technical problems using their own ingenuity.

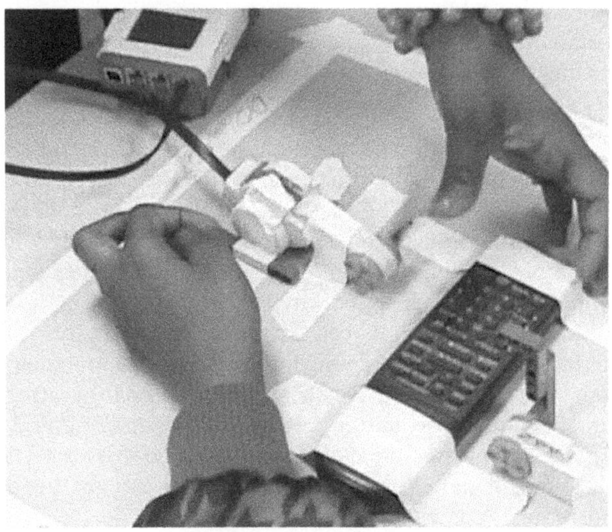

Figure 5. Group 1 focused on the remote control, using one P.Pod to press "On," another to press "Play". They mounted the devices with masking tape.

[5] i-Robot, http://www.irobot.com

FINDINGS

Both groups 1 and 2 successfully created systems that could play a DVD in response to their cheering. After quickly solving the sensing problem, both groups spent most of their time experimenting with P.Pods. Group 1 hijacked the remote controller. Group 2 hijacked the buttons on the front of the TV.

Both groups discovered they could mount the P.Pods using masking tape (see Figure 5). Group 1 initially tried to position a P.Pod poker above the remote control. With the remote's small buttons and dense layout, the poker would often depress multiple buttons. The group adapted the rotational motion of the P.Pod pincher to solve this problem. They used this approach on both the "Power" and "Play" buttons.

With fewer and larger buttons on the front of the TV, Group 2 used the P.Pod poker to more easily gain control of their two buttons.

DISCUSSION

Both our experience, and that of our middle school classes, demonstrates that P.Pods can get prototypes out of the lab and into the field quickly. P.Pods, however, are not the silver bullet of prototyping.

First, mechanical hijacking can only operate on existing controls on off-the-shelf devices. P.Pods cannot support more exploratory applications that operate outside of legacy infrastructures. Also, "deeper" hacks could control devices in more ways than are exposed through physical interfaces.

Second, Lego Mindstorms impose physical limitations on the P.Pod approach. Their relatively large size may require elaborate constructions to actuate controls that lie in close proximity. Additionally, repeated application of servomotors may subject them to drift, requiring periodic adjustment, making long-term deployment difficult.

Even in short-term deployments, P.Pods will block users from interacting with the devices they control. Good P.Pod design can avoid these problems. In one approach, the P.Pod mounting can be designed for portability. The hanging enclosure that mounts the thermostat in Figure 1, for example, allows the P.Pods to be easily removed and then re-mounted. When the environment requires a less flexible enclosure, P.Pods can themselves expose physical or digital interfaces. For physical, semi-direct manipulation, P.Pods can be augmented with external buttons (or other controls). In this case, a user presses a button on the P.Pod, and the P.Pod presses the button on the device. Also a GUI application for mobile phones or tablets can control Lego Mindstorm P.Pods via USB or Bluetooth.

Overall, when researchers are investigating systems that manipulate existing appliances or infrastructures that have mechanical interfaces, P.Pods can accelerate real world deployment by sidestepping the creation of a custom electronic interface.

CONCLUSION

The Ubicomp community continues to move forward under the assumption that systems that sense and take action on behalf of users can provide some kind of improved quality of life. The reality of Ubicomp development is seriously compromised by the real costs and risks to deploy robust, usable systems that fit into the existing hardware and infrastructure ecology of the real world. As long as that gap exists, the proposed benefits of Ubicomp will remain largely theoretical.

The ability to mechanically hijack real world legacy systems and infrastructures using robotic P.Pods presents advances for Ubicomp applications. P.Pods provide the possibility for such applications to now computationally interface with systems such as lights, climate control, or appliances that have previously been off limits to researchers. Our approach allows such legacy systems to be utilized within Ubicomp applications through low-cost and non-destructive means, without the need for any new extensive hardware or custom electronics development.

While the prototyping and creation of research Ubicomp applications represents a considerable investment of time and resources, our hope is that this approach will allow for more rapid prototyping of systems in the wild, and enable new types of applications domains to be explored.

REFERENCES

1. Abrahamse, W. *et al.* (2005). A review of intervention studies aimed at household energy conservation. *J. Env. Psych.*, 25, 273-291.
2. Carter, S., J. *et al.* (2008). Exiting the cleanroom: On Ecological validity and ubiquitous computing. *J. HCI*, 23(1): 47-99.
3. Davidoff, S., *et al.* (2006). Principles of smart home control. *Proc. Ubicomp 2006*, 19-34.
4. Döring. T. *et al.* (2011). Gestural interaction on the steering wheel: reducing the visual demand. *Proc. CHI 2011*, 483-492.
5. Edwards, W.K. & Grinter, R.E. (2001) At home with Ubiquitous computing: Seven challenges, *Proc. Ubicomp 2001*, 256-272.
6. Harle, R. K. & Hopper, A. (2008). The potential for location-aware power management. *Proc. UbiComp 2008*, 302-311.
7. Helmes, J. *et al.* (2011). Rudiments 1, 2 & 3: Design speculations on autonomy. *Proc. TEI 2011*, 145-152.
8. Rowan, J. & Mynatt, E.D. (2005). Digital family portrait field trial: Support for aging in place. *Proc. CHI 2005*, 521-530.
9. Taylor, A. S. (2009). Machine intelligence. *Proc. CHI 2009*, 2109-2118.
10. Taylor, A.S. *et al.* (2007). Homes that make us smart. *Personal & Ubiquitous Computing*, 11(5): 383-393.

MAQS: A Personalized Mobile Sensing System for Indoor Air Quality Monitoring

Yifei Jiang†, Kun Li‡, Lei Tian†, Ricardo Piedrahita*, Xiang Yun§, Omkar Mansata§, Qin Lv†, Robert P. Dick§, Michael Hannigan*, Li Shang‡
† Dept. of CS, ‡Dept. of ECEE, *Dept. of ME, University of Colorado at Boulder, CO 80309, U.S.A.
§ EECS Department, University of Michigan, Ann Arbor, MI 48109, U.S.A.
† * ‡ {yifei.jiang, kun.li, lei.tian, ricardo.piedrahita, qin.lv, hannigan, li.shang}@colorado.edu,
§{xiangyun,omkar}@umich.edu, §dickrp@eecs.umich.edu

ABSTRACT
Most people spend more than 90% of their time indoors; indoor air quality (IAQ) influences human health, safety, productivity, and comfort. This paper describes *MAQS*, a personalized mobile sensing system for IAQ monitoring. In contrast with existing stationary or outdoor air quality sensing systems, MAQS users carry portable, indoor location tracking sensors that provide personalized IAQ information. To improve accuracy and energy efficiency, MAQS incorporates three novel techniques: (1) an accurate temporal n-gram augmented Bayesian room localization method that requires few Wi-Fi fingerprints; (2) an air exchange rate based IAQ sensing method, which measures general IAQ using only CO_2 sensors; and (3) a zone-based proximity detection method for collaborative sensing, which saves energy and enables data sharing among users. MAQS has been deployed and evaluated via user study. Detailed evaluation results demonstrate that MAQS supports accurate personalized IAQ monitoring and quantitative analysis with high energy efficiency.

Author Keywords
Air quality sensing, location based service, smartphone

ACM Classification Keywords
C.3.3 Special-Purpose and Application-Based Systems: Real-Time and Embedded Systems

General Terms
Algorithms, Design, Experimentation, Performance

INTRODUCTION
In recent years, indoor air quality (IAQ) has drawn considerable attention in both the public and scientific domains, due to the fact that most buildings appear to fall far short of reasonable air quality goals [15]. Statistics [28] from the U.S. Environmental Protection Agency (EPA) indicate that, on average, the indoor levels of pollutants are two to five times higher than outdoor levels and people in the U.S. spend about 90% of their time indoors. Bad indoor air quality influences human health, safety, productivity, and comfort [31, 9]. IAQ is important and different people have different exposure to pollutants. Providing personalized IAQ information has the potential to increase public awareness of the relationship between their behavior and air quality; help people to improve their living environments; and also provide valuable information to building managers, policy makers, health professionals, and scientific researchers.

IAQ monitoring is challenging because indoor air pollutants concentration and human motion patterns each vary spatially and temporally within and across rooms. Existing solutions that require stationary sensors or target mobile outdoor sensing scenarios are inappropriate for personalized IAQ monitoring. Stationary sensing [13] has several limitations: (a) it can only measure the IAQ experienced by those who happen to be near the sensors, and there can be substantial variation in IAQ even within one room and (b) when locations or rooms outnumber people, achieving full coverage with stationary sensors is more expensive than doing so with personalized mobile sensors. Outdoor mobile sensing solutions use GPS localization, which fails indoors and is therefore inappropriate for IAQ applications. Furthermore, existing air quality sensing solutions require multiple types of sensors, each of which covers a subset of pollutants. This can be prohibitively expensive for personalized mobile IAQ sensing.

A mobile sensing system designed for personalized IAQ monitoring must address the following three challenges. First, some existing approaches use proprietary radio frequency and ultrasound technologies for room localization, which require investment in infrastructure and special hardware worn by all users. Others use Wi-Fi based fingerprinting, which requires time consuming pre-characterization and is hampered by device or environment heterogeneity. Second, the mobile sensing devices must be inexpensive, portable, and energy efficient. This limits the number and types of sensors that

UbiComp'11, September 17–21, 2011, Beijing, China.

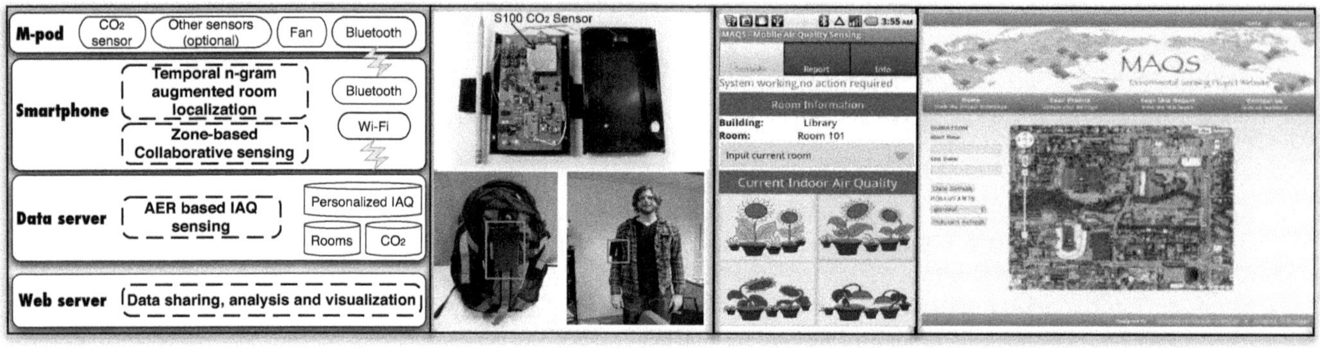

Figure 1. MAQS: A mobile sensing system for personalized indoor air quality (IAQ) monitoring.

can be integrated within each mobile device. Achieving high-quality IAQ monitoring with few sensors is challenging. Third, IAQ sensing depends largely on the motion patterns of individual user. This leads to redundant IAQ information when users are near each other, and may lead to gaps in coverage for users who are not presently carrying sensing devices.

This paper describes *MAQS*[1], a personalized mobile sensing system for IAQ monitoring. MAQS estimates human-dependent air quality factors (e.g., CO_2 and contagious viruses) using CO_2 concentration, and estimates other air quality factors (e.g., volatile organic compounds (VOCs)) using air exchange rates. MAQS integrates smartphones and portable sensing devices to deliver personalized, energy-efficient, IAQ information. MAQS is the first mobile air quality sensing system that achieves high coverage of people in indoor environments. Our work makes the following main technical contributions.

1. A temporal n-gram augmented Bayesian room localization method that is accurate and requires few Wi-Fi fingerprints;
2. An air exchange rate based IAQ sensing method, which measures general IAQ without requiring sensors for various types of air pollutants; and
3. A zone-based proximity detection method for collaborative sensing, which saves energy and enables data sharing among multiple users.

MAQS was evaluated via real-world system deployment and a user study. Our results demonstrate high accuracy (over 96% for room localization and 89% for zone detection) and 2×–8× better energy efficiency. Our quantitative IAQ analysis also reveals that most users are subject to poor IAQ (i.e., high CO_2 concentration and low air exchange rate) in a number of rooms.

SYSTEM OVERVIEW

This section gives a high-level overview of the MAQS system architecture and describes the key components.

As illustrated in Figure 1, MAQS consists of four types of components: (1) *M-pods*, the portable IAQ sensing devices; (2) *smartphones*; (3) a *data server*; and (4) a *web server*. MAQS users carry smartphones and optionally M-pods. The data server communicates with clients and maintains room air quality, CO_2, and personalized IAQ data. The web sever allows users to view, analyze, and share IAQ data. There are three main functional units in MAQS: (a) temporal n-gram augmented room localization, (b) air exchange rate based IAQ sensing, and (c) zone-based collaborative sensing.

A MAQS client runs on each smartphone. It monitors the phone's accelerometer readings to detect room entrance and departure events. For the purpose of IAQ monitoring, rooms are defined as enclosed building units with walls, doors, and windows where people spend substantial time (e.g., office, classroom, bedroom) and we ignore transitional spaces indoor (e.g., hallway). Once the client detects that the user has entered a room, the room localization function collects Wi-Fi signals from nearby access points and uses the subsequences of Wi-Fi signals (spatial information) and the user's mobility pattern (temporal information) to determine the current room. The collaborative sensing unit then uses zone-based proximity detection to select specific sensing devices for (collaborative) IAQ monitoring of the room. This is useful since not all smartphone users carry IAQ sensing devices, and sensing devices close to each other (i.e., in the same zone) are largely redundant. As concentration readings of CO_2, VOCs, and other air pollutants are collected and transmitted to the server, they are stored in databases and combined with room information (e.g., room ID, volume) for air exchange rate calculation and personalized IAQ analysis. MAQS stops IAQ sensing after detecting a room departure and restarts when another room is entered.

M-POD: THE PORTABLE IAQ SENSING DEVICE

In this section, we describe the design of our portable IAQ sensing device, the *M-pod*. The M-pod is a wireless embedded sensing, computation, and communication device based on the Arduino BT [2]. It is capable of sensing the concentrations of a number of air pollutants and either storing these data or transmitting them to nearby smartphones via its Bluetooth interface. The main requirements for the M-pod were to accurately sense pollutant concentrations relevant

[1]MAQS stands for Mobile Air Quality Sensing.

Table 1. M-pod Processor, Wireless Interface, and Sensors

Hardware specs	MCU ATMEGA 168	Bluetooth WT11	Battery CS HDE160XL	Size (inch) 4.8x2.6
On-board sensors	Temperature TMP101	CO_2 S100	Humidity HYT271	Light GL5528

to IAQ and transmit these data, within a compact and long battery life package.

M-pod Hardware Design. The M-pod's major components are an 8-bit, 32-pin microcontroller, a Bluetooth module, and up to ten on-board sensors, which are mounted on a custom-fabricated 4-layer printed circuit board. Table 1 lists the processor, wireless interface, and sensors. The M-pod has a humidity sensor, light sensor, two temperature sensors – one upstream to measure ambient air temperature and the other downstream to measure the temperature near the sensors, a CO_2 sensor, and low-cost metal oxide gas sensors such as Figaro TGS2600 and E2V MICS2611. The S100 is an accurate, low-power non-dispersive infrared based CO_2 sensor. The humidity sensor, temperature sensors, and CO_2 sensor are connected to the microcontroller via the I2C interface. The other sensors are attached to the microcontroller's analog to digital converter interface. The metal oxide gas sensors are power gated using PMOSFETs. The M-pod supports in-system and in-field wireless programming via its Bluetooth interface. When developing and evaluating MAQS, we primarily used data from the M-pod's CO_2 sensor. The M-pod case is a low-cost off-the-shelf enclosure that has been machined for this application. It can be carried using an armband, or attached to a backpack or briefcase. A 5 V DC fan is mounted to the case. The sensors are positioned to enable uniform airflow. When sensing, the fan moves 2 liters of air per minute, thereby minimizing sensing latency when IAQ changes.

Energy Consumption. The M-pod is powered by a 2,200 mA-H Lithium-ion battery, which can be recharged using a standard wall-mounted AC–DC converter. The Lithium-ion battery is protected by an interlock that halts the system when the battery voltage drops below 2.9 V. The M-pod requires 240 mW in low-power mode, in which only the processor and CO_2, humidity, and temperature sensors are enabled. It requires 1,080 mW when, in addition, four metal oxide gas sensors are activated. The fan requires up to 105 mW, but this can be reduced via pulse-width modulation. The Bluetooth interface needs to transmit so infrequently in this application that its power consumption has little impact on battery lifespan. The battery lifespan is approximately 5.5 hours if an M-pod is continuously on and greater than 24 hours when in low-power mode.

Command Processing. The M-pod processes *low power mode, full sensing mode, power state inquiry,* and *transmit data* commands, which are generally received from smartphones. IAQ sensor readings are collected every six seconds and stored in the microcontroller's SRAM.

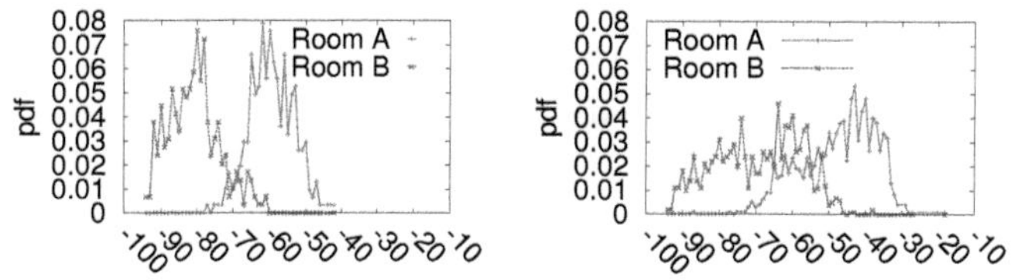

(a) RSS without noise (b) RSS with noise

Figure 2. Wireless RSS distributions in two adjacent rooms: (a) without noise and (b) with environment and device noise.

In the low-power mode, the metal oxide sensors are power gated; these sensors contain resistive heating elements and therefore have high power consumptions. The power state inquiry command causes the current mode (low power or full sensing) to be transmitted to the requester. The data transmit command causes the M-pod to upload stored sensor data to the requester (smartphone), which generally takes three seconds.

ROOM LOCALIZATION

IAQ data is most valuable when it can be associated with the appropriate source room. Room characteristics correlate closely with IAQ and rooms are the basic control units in building management. MAQS users review their IAQ histories and sharing data with others by reference to rooms. Unlike stationary IAQ sensing, M-pods are carried by users, i.e., their locations change as users move. Hence accurate room localization is required for personalized mobile IAQ monitoring.

Researchers have proposed room localization techniques based on Wi-Fi access point received signal strength (RSS) [12, 14]. These methods share two common stages. In the first (training) stage, a database that associates ambient Wi-Fi RSS fingerprints with physical rooms is constructed. In the second (operating) stage, the system identifies the stored Wi-Fi fingerprint that most similar to the one currently being measured, and returns the associated room.

The first stage of our room localization technique is similar to that of Park et al. [12]. All users contribute their Wi-Fi RSS and room information to create a shared database of room fingerprints. This is beneficial as it (1) eliminates the deployment cost for fingerprint pre-sampling and (2) reduces individual users' effort to build the database.

In the second stage, Bayesian room localization models are commonly used [14, 12]. Given a database of fingerprinted rooms R and a Wi-Fi RSS fingerprint represented by a set of access point (AP)-specific signal strengths (w_i for the i-th AP), the mobile device (and user) is most likely in room $\hat{r}$:

$$\hat{r} = \arg\max_{r \in R} \left[\prod_i P(w_i|r)P(r) \right] \quad (1)$$

This model is based on the assumption that the signal strengths observed by the mobile device from different APs are conditionally independent. However, the model fails to address the following two challenges: (1) *device heterogeneity* – different devices may be used for gathering RSS fingerprints and devices might be held differently (e.g., in hand, pocket, or bag) and (2) *environment heterogeneity* – the wireless environment of a room may change over time, due to motion of people and other room contents, influencing the RSS fingerprints gathered by mobile devices. As demonstrated in Figure 2, noise induced by device and environment heterogeneity significantly increase the RSS overlap between adjacent rooms, leading to much lower room localization accuracy. To address these problems, we propose a novel temporal n-gram augmented Bayesian room localization method, which is robust to both environment and device noises.

N-gram Augmented Bayesian Room Localization

Our key observation is that, although the exact RSS values of each AP may change substantially for different devices and environments, *the ordered sequence of APs based on their RSS values tends to be similar for the same room and inconsistent among adjacent rooms.* For example, the ordering may be $[ap_1, ap_2, ap_3, ap_4, ap_5, ap_6]$ at one time, and $[ap_2, ap_1, ap_3, ap_4, ap_5, ap_6]$ at another time, for the same room. The ordered AP sequences of adjacent rooms are less similar, especially when different APs are observed in these rooms. Intuitively, the ordered AP sequence is useful for room localization because: (1) it captures the inherent correlations among APs, which are stable for the same room yet different for adjacent rooms and (2) it uses the order of RSS instead of their exact values, allowing many sources of device variation and wireless environment variation to be tolerated.

Based on the observations above, we propose an n-gram augmented Bayesian room localization model, which works as follows. Let s be a sequence of N APs ordered in descending RSS values:

$$s = (ap_1, ..., ap_N) \quad w_i \geq w_j (1 \leq i < j \leq N), \qquad (2)$$

where w_i is the RSS value of ap_i observed by the mobile device. An n-gram is then defined as a subsequence of length n extracted from the sequence s at position i:

$$ngram_i(s) = (ap_i, \cdots, ap_{i+n-1}). \qquad (3)$$

The most likely room $\hat{r}$ is determined as follows:

$$\hat{r} = \arg\max_{r \in R} \left[\prod_i P(ngram_i(s)|r) P(r) \right]. \qquad (4)$$

In other words, $\hat{r}$ is the room with the highest probability of having the same ordering of APs in subsequence $ngram_i(s)$.

Temporal User Mobility for Room Localization

As shown in the experimental results, our n-gram augmented Bayesian room localization model achieves high accuracy when the room has enough fingerprints (more than 50 or 100). However, when the number of fingerprints is low, the model accuracy is poorer and users tend to be misclassified into nearby rooms. To remove such spatial errors, we propose to incorporate temporal user mobility information. This is motivated by the following observations.

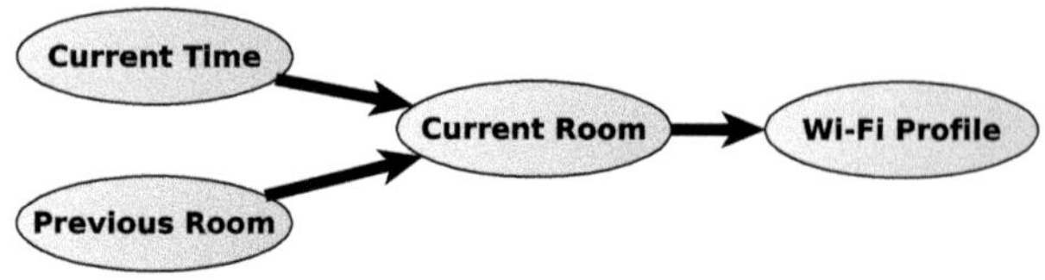

Figure 3. Bayesian network for room localization.

- A user's current room is closely related to time and weekday, e.g., the user has weekly meetings in the conference room on Tuesday mornings.
- Users can only move among adjacent rooms, and their paths tend to contain patterns. For example, a user usually goes to the conference room from her office instead of from a classroom.

Based on these observations, a user's current room can be predicted based on current time and previous room. As shown in Figure 3, the Bayesian network has three layers: current time and user's previous room (first layer) indicate the user's current room (second layer), and user's current room determines the observed Wi-Fi RSS fingerprint. We also define a set of values to represent some semantic concepts of time, including "day of week", "morning", "afternoon", and "evening". Given a Wi-Fi scan observation s, the user's previous room r', and current time t , the user is most likely in room

$$\hat{r} = \arg\max_{r \in R} [P(s, r, t, r')] \qquad (5)$$

$$= \arg\max_{r \in R} [P(s|r)P(r|t, r')P(t)P(r')]. \qquad (6)$$

$P(s|r)$ can be computed using our n-gram augmented Bayesian room localization model. $P(r')$ and $P(r|t, r')$ are calculated from the user's mobility history. $P(t)$ can be ignored since it is the same for any room r.

Room Entrance and Departure Detection

Our room localization method requires Wi-Fi scanning, which can be power intensive. For example, Wi-Fi scanning at 1/6 Hz requires 80 mW on average. Using a lower Wi-Fi scanning frequency improves energy efficiency but increases room localization latency.

To address this problem, our MAQS system leverages the smartphone accelerometer to monitor room entrance and departure, and triggers room localization only when a room entrance event is detected. Previous works have used accelerometer to detect arriving at or departing from a place (e.g., a building or outdoor place) [16] , while our work requires the finer-granularity of indoor room-level entrance/departure detection. Specifically, room entrance/departure detection helps to (1) reduce energy use for room localization; (2) locate rooms in a timely fashion; and (3) start/stop IAQ sensing quickly. We sample acceleration at a low frequency mode, 3–10 samples per second, to reduce the energy consumption of the accelerometer. The magnitude of acceleration is calculated over all three axes and the variance of the magnitude within a 5-second time window is used to detect motion. Variance larger than a threshold θ is taken to indicate motion. The threshold θ was empirically determined based on measured data. If a node is stationary for 60 seconds, a room entrance is detected. if a node is moving for 10 seconds, a room departure is detected. Our experimental results show that this approach achieves high detection accuracy. The false negative rate is 0.01%, which happens when a user moves between two adjacent rooms quickly. The false positive rate is 7% on average, and false positives can be corrected by our room localization algorithm.

AIR EXCHANGE RATE BASED IAQ SENSING

Indoor air quality (IAQ) is influenced by multiple air pollutants and sources, including (1) air pollutants generated indoor, such as volatile organic compounds (VOCs), from combustion and off-gassing of paint and building materials; (2) air pollutants introduced from outside via ventilation, e.g., ozone; and (3) air pollutants generated by people, e.g., CO_2. It is impractical to install sensors on our portable IAQ sensing devices to monitor all pollutants of interest, as the sensing device would become unreasonably large and require too much power. Additionally, not all pollutant sensors are portable yet, and portable sensors are typically less accurate than stationary sensors.

As shown in previous studies [25, 24, 9, 11], CO_2 concentration and ventilation rate are strongly correlated with general IAQ. Therefore, the M-pod monitors CO_2 concentration, which is then used to calculate the air exchange rate, i.e., how quickly air is cycled through a room. This rate is used to estimate general IAQ in a room. Specifically, personalized air exchange rates are modeled using changes in CO_2 concentration and CO_2 generation rate. The rate of change in CO_2 concentration depends on the concentration of in-flowing air, the concentration of the out-flowing air, and the internal generation of CO_2 in a room. The time derivative of the monitored concentration is given by [24]:

$$V\tfrac{dC_t}{dt} = G + QC_{ex} - QC_t, \tag{7}$$

where C_t is the internal concentration of CO_2 at time t, measured in units of ppm (parts per million, i.e., the volume of CO_2 over total volume of air). C_{ex} is the external concentration of CO_2 (ppm). G is the generation rate of CO_2 in the room (cm^3/s). V is the room volume (m^3). Q is the air change rate (m^3/s).

Solving the equation above gives us the formula to calculate air exchange rate Q:

$$Q = \frac{V\frac{dC_t}{dt} - G}{C_{ex} - C_t}, \tag{8}$$

where C_t are the continuous CO_2 readings from the M-pod. External concentration of CO_2, C_{ex}, is set to 390 ppm, the globally averaged CO_2 concentration at the surface [4], unless local outdoor CO_2 concentration is available. To calculate the CO_2 generation rate G, we assume each person's generation rate is equal to 0.0052 L/s[24], which corresponds to an average-sized adult engaged in office work. At this time, we do not incorporate other possible sources of CO_2 such as cooking or smoking. Room volume V can be provided by the user through our system, or it can be calculated from CO_2 data based on the Steady-State Concentration Balance Equation, $\frac{dC_t}{dt} = 0$:

$$Q = \frac{G}{C_{ex} - C_t}. \tag{9}$$

After determining Q, we apply it to the user's data, in which $\frac{dC_t}{dt} \neq 0$ and Q do not change. Then we can calculate the value of V.

The air exchange rate required for good IAQ depends on the size and occupancy of each room. In our system, three metrics are considered for IAQ:

- *Indoor CO_2 concentration* is a surrogate for indoor pollutants emitted by humans and correlates with human metabolic activity. The ASHRAE Standard is at most 700 ppm above outdoor CO_2 concentration [3].
- *Air changes per hour* is a measure of how many times the air within a defined space (normally a room or house) is replaced per hour. Its value equals the air exchange rate of room divided by room volume. The ASHRAE Standard is at least 0.35 1/h [26].
- *Air flow per person* is the room air exchange rate divided by the number of people in the room. The ASHRAE Standard is at least 7.5 l/s/person [26].

ZONE-BASED COLLABORATIVE SENSING

In real-world usage scenarios, multiple users are likely to stay in the same room, e.g., in meeting rooms or the library. Such user groups tend to be concentrated in small areas, leading to similar CO_2 concentration and IAQ within each group. Through collaborative sensing, we aim to reduce the number of sensing devices that have to run concurrently (thus saving energy), and also enable IAQ data sharing with people who do not carry sensing devices (thus increasing system coverage and utility).

Specifically, we propose a zone-based proximity detection and information sharing mechanism. Concentration gradients are driven by transport via molecular diffusion and convection. Both transport processes have random and non-random components. Whatever the process, the spatial gradients dictate that two points close in proximity will likely have more similar concentrations than two points that are more distant. The smaller the distance, the more similar the CO_2 concentration readings. In MAQS, we define an area with

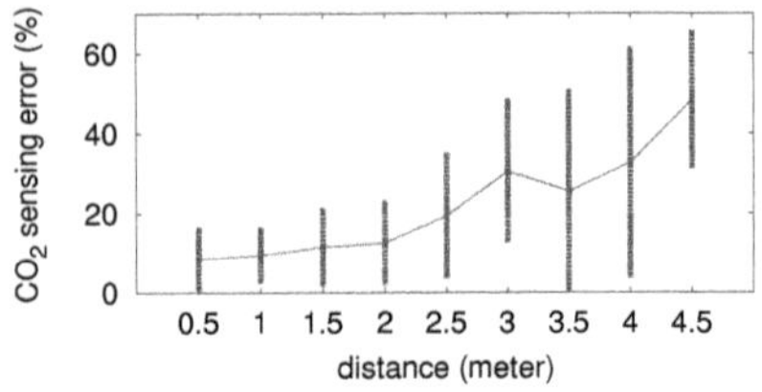

Figure 4. Sensing error of CO_2 concentration at different distances.

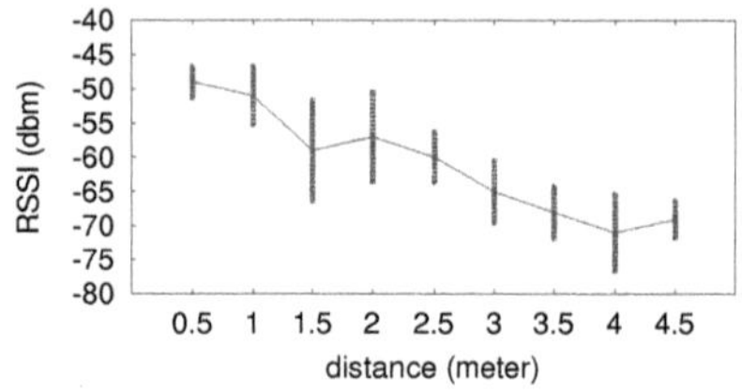

Figure 5. RSSI measurements (*avg* and *stdev*) at different distances.

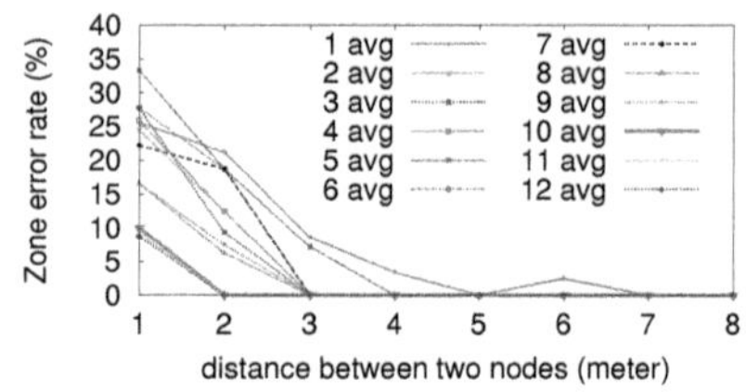

Figure 6. Zone detection error rate decreases by averaging multiple RSSI readings.

high density of people as a *zone*. All people within the same zone can share one M-pod for IAQ monitoring. When a new user without an M-pod joins this zone, the user's smartphone initiates a scan to determine if there is already an M-pod in the zone. If so, a communication link between the phone and the M-pod is established and the IAQ values reported by the M-pod is used to estimate the IAQ of this user.

Zone-based sharing would incur some error, which is defined as the difference between the CO_2 concentration reported by the shared M-pod nearby and the true CO_2 concentration at the user's location. Again, according to the diffusion equation, this error is highly correlated with the distance. Therefore, this error determines the effective range of each zone.

Over 50 experiments have been conducted to determine the relationship between distance and CO_2 error in public rooms, including classrooms and a library. In each experiment, two M-pods are placed 1–10 meters apart for over 20 minutes. The CO_2 readings from both M-pods are monitored and the corresponding air exchange rates are calculated. Figure 4 shows the sensing error rate of CO_2 concentration at different distances. Ranges less than two meters enable better and more consistent results. Two meters is therefore uses as the range threshold of zones in the MAQS system.

Given the zone range threshold (2 meters), each smartphone still needs to determine how far away a specific M-pod is. In MAQS, we use the Received Signal Strength Indication (RSSI) from the Bluetooth radio as the distance metric. The signal power of Bluetooth communication decays proportionally to d^{-2} [18], where d is the distance between transmitter (M-pod) and receiver (smartphone). MAQS is meant to be used in a broad range of unknown environments over long periods of time. It it therefore subject to environment-dependent and time-varying noise. Figure 5 shows the average and standard deviation of RSSI measurements obtained at different distances in real-world experiments. The illustrated noise can result in large errors even for two meter zones. Since this noise can be reasonably well modeled as additive white Gaussian noise, in MAQS, multiple readings are used to detect outliers and average values are used to improve distance estimates. Figure 6 shows that the accuracy of proximity detection can be significantly improved when 10 readings are averaged.

The MAQS zone-based information sharing procedure works as follows. When a user enters a room, the carried mobile phone first identifies the room. Then, the phone scans nearby M-pods 10 times and filters out all M-pods with RSSI readings exceeding a threshold corresponding to 2 meters (-64 dB in our experiments). The remaining M-pod with the smallest RSSI average is selected. The user joins the zone formed by this M-pod and shares its CO_2 concentration and air exchange rate information. Figure 7 illustrates the concept of zone-based information sharing. Numbers along the lines indicate the RSSI between phone and M-pod. In this scenario, phones A and B belong to the zone occupied by M-pod S1, because they are within the required range of S1. Since the RSSI between phone C and M-pod S1 is lower than the threshold, they belong to different zones.

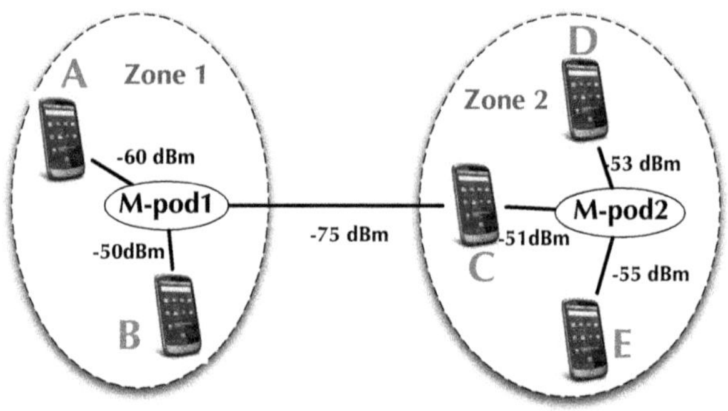

Figure 7. Zone-based collaborative sensing.

In addition to IAQ data sharing by people in the same room, users may also be interested in rooms which they have not yet visited; building managers would like to know the IAQ in their buildings; and medical personnel may need the information to diagnose their patients. MAQS provides a permission control mechanism allowing users to specify the type, location, and time periods of data to be shared publicly. They can also define groups and share their IAQ data with other members in each group, e.g., their family members.

EVALUATIONS

The MAQS system has been implemented and deployed for user study. In this section, we describe the system deployment and user study. We experimentally evaluated the effectiveness and efficiency of the proposed system. We also make some observations based on the data gathered during the user study.

System Deployment and User Studies

The deployed MAQS system includes M-pod sensing devices, Android-based smartphones, as well as the data and web servers. We have conducted two phases of user study with 17 participants, including faculty and graduate students, who share some workplaces and classrooms. The first phase was designed to evaluate our room localization method. In this phase, users were asked to carry their Android phones for 12 weeks. Our MAQS phone application continuously collected Wi-Fi signals, and requested manual labeling when users entered rooms. Weekly meetings with the users were held to verify the accuracy of the motion traces. In addition, users were asked to collect Wi-Fi signals in rooms that are adjacent to those they have visited, which further increased the noise and complexity of our room location task but better represents real-world scenarios.

In the second phase, users carried both their smartphones and the M-pod sensing devices for 3 weeks. The MAQS system collects both room information and IAQ data for all users. This phase of user study allows us to evaluate the entire MAQS system. We collected localization data for 171 rooms, and IAQ data for 56 rooms.

Evaluation of Room Localization Technique

To evaluate our temporal n-gram augmented Bayesian room localization method, we determined the room localization accuracy as a function of the number of Wi-Fi fingerprints. A good room localization method should achieve high accuracy with few fingerprints. Specifically, we conduct experiments to answer the following questions: (1) How does the n-gram length affect overall room localization performance? (2) How does the n-gram augmented Bayesian model perform compared with existing approaches? (3) To what extent does temporal user mobility information improve room localization accuracy?

The subsequence length n of n-gram has an important impact on room localization performance. If n is too small, adjacent rooms may have many similar subsequences and be difficult to distinguish. For example, when $n = 1$, our n-gram augmented model is similar to the original Bayesian model, and the only difference is the binary discretization of signal strength: AP equals 1 (or 0) if its signal can (or cannot) be observed by the device. If n is too big, then the room signature may change for each scan, since longer subsequences have a low probability of being repeated in each scan. For example, when n is set to the total number of APs that can be scanned in a room, it is very unlikely to receive the same sequence for each scan. Therefore, a good n value should make the n-gram signature for each room stable for different scans, and make the n-gram signatures of adjacent rooms distinguishable. Figure 8 shows the accuracy of our n-gram Bayesian model with different n values and different number of fingerprints per room. As shown in the figure, when $n = 2$, our model achieves much better accuracy with fewer fingerprints.

Table 2. Energy Consumption for Room Localization

Method	Wi-Fi (#scans/day)	Acc (#samples/sec)	Energy (mw)
Wi-Fi only	1,440	off	8
Wi-Fi + Acc	5–30	3–10	1–3

We now compare our n-gram augmented Bayesian room localization model with four state-of-the-art algorithms: (1) Bayesian room localization [14, 12], (2) Delta signal Bayesian room localization, which is similar to Bayesian room localization but uses the difference of signal strength (instead of RSS values directly) between each pair of APs to calculate probability, (3) vector-based room localization [5], which uses AP RSS vector as the room signature and Euclidean distance to locate the nearest room, and (4) Delta signal vector-based room localization, which is similar to vector-based room localization but uses the difference in signal strength between each pair of APs to build the vectors. As shown in Figure 9(a), our n-gram augmented Bayesian model achieves the best accuracy, especially when the number of fingerprints per room is above 50.

By incorporating the temporal user mobility information, our temporal n-gram augmented Bayesian model can achieve better accuracy even when the number of fingerprints per room is limited. As shown in Figure 9 (b), our temporal n-gram model further improves the room localization accuracy over our n-gram model, especially when the number of fingerprints per room is less than 50. The Delta Bayesian room localization model, which performed second best in Figure 9(a), can also benefit from the use of temporal user mobility information, but it is still not comparable to our temporal n-gram model.

Finally, we evaluate the energy consumption of our room localization method. By using an accelerometer to detect room entrance/departure and performing a Wi-Fi scan only when entering a new room, we can significantly reduce the energy consumption. As shown in Table 2, our Wi-Fi + accelerometer (Acc) approach consumes only 1–3 mW on the mobile phone, while the Wi-Fi only approach consumes 8 mW.

Evaluation of Air Exchange Rate Based IAQ Sensing

To estimate the general IAQ without using sensors for each specific air pollutant, we propose to calculate the air exchange rate from temporal CO_2 concentration readings, and use this air exchange rate to estimate IAQ. Here, we evaluate the accuracy of the air exchange rate model. We used the *Alnor EBT721 EBT 721 Air Balancing Balometer Flow Capture Hood* [1] to measure the air flow rate directly from vents as the ground truth. During each experiment, we change the forced ventilation rate and the number of people in the room to evaluate

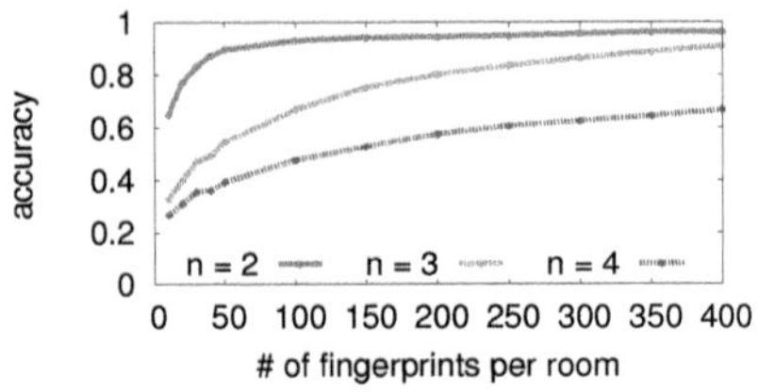

Figure 8. Comparison of different n for n-gram augmented Bayesian model.

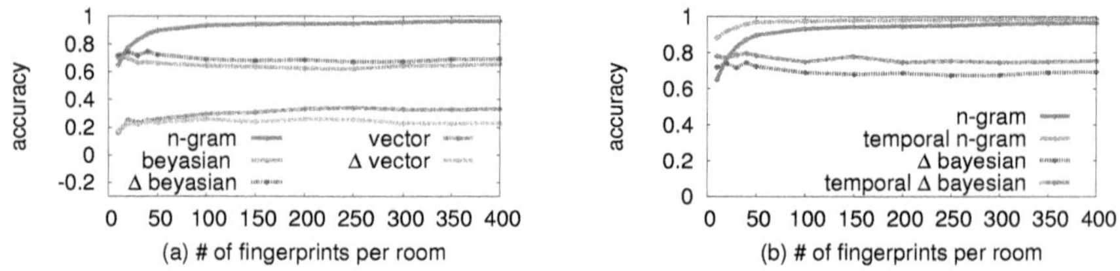

Figure 9. Performance comparison of room localization methods: (a) n-gram model and (b) temporal n-gram model.

Table 3. Zone Detection Accuracy

Seat Map	1	2	3	4	5
Accuracy (%)	97	100	100	78	100
Seat Map	6	7	8	9	10
Accuracy (%)	100	88	100	42	85

the accuracy and responsiveness of our CO_2 based air exchange rate model.

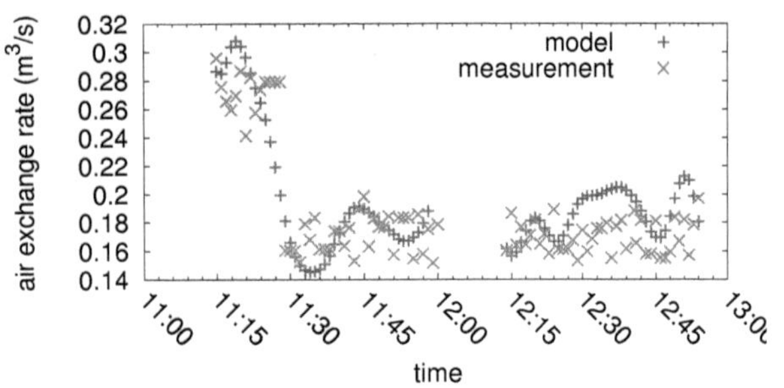

Figure 10. Air exchange rate model evaluation.

Figure 10 shows the results of one experiment. We started at 11:15 with a relatively high forced ventilation rate and lowered the ventilation rate at 11:30. We can see that the air exchange rate calculated by our model followed the actual rate drop quickly and stayed within the same range. Starting from 12:15, we kept the ventilation rate low and changed the number of people in the room every 5 minutes. Again, we can see that the AER calculated by the model well approximates the measured value. It is slightly higher than the measured value, since the door was opened and closed when we changed the number of people in the room, leading to additional air exchange, which is not captured by the vent hood, as it measures only the air exchange at the vent. We conducted multiple experiments in rooms with different sizes and vents, and obtained similar results.

Evaluation of Zone-Based Collaborative Sensing

Zone-based collaborative sensing helps to reduce the number of M-pods needed, saves energy, and allow users to share IAQ data. Since the energy consumption of scanning Bluetooth RSSI for a short period of time (less than 30 seconds) is negligible compared with that of continuous IAQ sensing, a zone with k devices can generally achieve $k\times$ better energy efficiency since only one device needs to be running. Here, we evaluate the accuracy of our zone-based proximity detection, i.e., whether we can identify the correct zone based on the Bluetooth RSSI readings. Given three M-pods and a mobile phone, we selected 10 seat maps that represent real-world user-sitting scenarios. For each seat map, we conducted 10 experiments at different times to capture potential temporal variations. For each experiment, the mobile phone used 10 RSSI readings from each M-pod to determine which zone (i.e., M-pod) it belonged to. The average zone detection accuracy for each seat map is shown in Table 3. We can see that our RSSI-based zone detection method achieved high accuracy for most seat maps with an average of 89%.

IAQ Data Analysis

We analyzed the IAQ distributions for the data gathered during our user study. Specifically, we would like to answer quantitatively what IAQ distributions the study participants experienced. Figure 11 shows the IAQ distributions for all users. The dashed lines indicate the standard limits, blue solid lines represent good IAQ, and red solid lines represent bad IAQ. According to the figure, (1) 67% of the time, indoor CO_2 concentration is higher than the reasonable limit of 1,000 ppm; (2) 30% of the time, air changes per hour do not meet the minimum requirement of 0.35 1/h; and (3) 58% of the time, flow rate per person does not meet the minimum standard of 7 l/s/person. We conclude that our study participants frequently spent time in environments with poor air quality.

Figure 12 shows the distributions of CO_2 concentration, air changes per hour, and air flow per person for different users. The users are ordered by their average CO_2 concentration. We can observe that users are subject to different IAQ at different times, and almost all users are subject to a fairly high percentage of times at which they experienced poor IAQ (high CO_2, low air changes per hour, or low air flow per person).

Figure 13 shows the distributions of CO_2 concentration, air changes per hour, and air flow per person in different rooms. The rooms are ordered by their average CO_2 concentrations. We can see that rooms have dynamic and diverse IAQ profiles. Although the exact fraction is different, many rooms have poor IAQ some of the time. Table 4 compares the IAQ in different types of rooms: office, public place (e.g., library, lobby), classroom, and home (apartment or house). The office has good IAQ in general, since most office rooms are small, sparsely occupied, and have good ventilation systems. IAQ in the other three types of rooms is not good and can be very bad at times (indicated

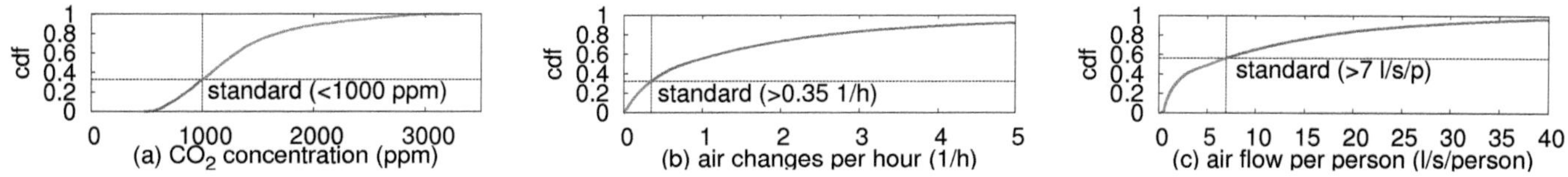

Figure 11. IAQ data distribution for all users: (a) CO_2 concentration; (b) air changes per hour; and (3) flow rate per person.

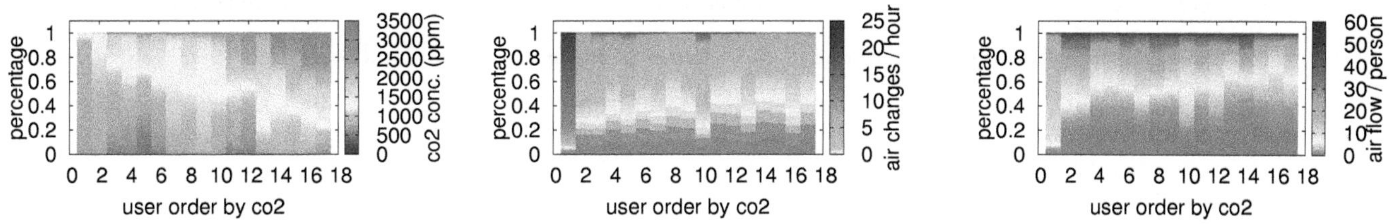

Figure 12. User-specific distributions of CO_2 concentration, air changes per hour, and air flow per person.

Table 4. IAQ Comparison by Room Type

IAQ		Office	Public	Classroom	Home
CO_2	avg	887	1238	1163	1491
	stdev	274	207	303	479
Air changes per hour	avg	2.6	2.9	1.6	1.3
	stdev	3.0	3.8	2.0	1.8
Air flow per person	avg	13.6	11.7	10.5	9.1
	stdev	13.9	14.9	11.5	10.6

by large standard deviation). For example, large classrooms can have insufficient ventilation for large classes. Also, apartments tend to be small and have no or limited forced ventilation, leading to poor IAQ.

RELATED WORK

Our interdisciplinary work of building a personalized mobile system for IAQ monitoring draws upon research in a number of related fields. In this section, we survey research most relevant to ours.

IAQ monitoring. Previous studies [13] have focused on monitoring or identifying air pollutants in different types of rooms, such as classrooms, offices, and residential rooms. However, without knowing when and how long a user stayed in a room, it is difficult to estimate the user's exposure to indoor air pollutants. Moreover, it is difficult to measure all rooms a user stayed in. Other studies have focused on indoor air pollutants in certain areas (e.g., city or countryside) using statistical methods. This approach ignores the fact that users' indoor air pollution exposures differ from each other. Recently, Kim et al. proposed a mobile system for sharing IAQ measurements and visualizations within one's social network [17]. The shared information is room based and not user-specific.

Indoor localization. This has been a topic of active research, some focusing on indoor intra-room positioning and others (such as ours) focusing on inter-room positioning. Proprietary systems based on radio frequency [29], FM radio signal [19, 22] and ultrasound [30] have been implemented. Newer systems include DOLPHIN [23] which is based on ultrasound devices, and the Zigbee-based system proposed by Sugano [27]. They have good accuracy but require substantial investment in infrastructure and special hardware worn by all users. Our system can be deployed in any off-the-shelf smartphones with Bluetooth communication capability. Other techniques are fingerprint-based and leverage existing wireless infrastructure. Haeberlen et al. proposed a localization method over large-scale 802.11 wireless networks, which can be accurate within a few meters in regions with high infrastructure coverage [14] . However, this method has high deployment cost. Other methods leverage user collaboration [7, 8], i.e., users train the system while using it. Issues such as conveying uncertainty, determining when user input is actually required, and discounting erroneous and stale data are addressed by the work of Park et al. [12]. However, none of these methods addresses the challenges associated with environment heterogeneity, device-induced noise, and the requirement for large user inputs.

Proximity detection. Previous peer-based indoor positioning systems attempt to infer either the proximity of a pair of devices, or the actual distances between multiple pairs of devices in order to place them in a virtual map. Most of them techniques use anchors with available position information as references. Other nodes refer to the anchors to determine their own positions. PeopleTones [21] uses a GSM-based approach to detect proximity for mobile phone users. NearMe, proposed by Krumm et al. [20], provides a complete framework for clients equipped with Wi-Fi devices to obtain information about people and things that are physically close (30 to 100 meters). Banerjee et al. proposed Virtual Compass [6], which measures the distances between multiple nearby nodes and generates a map on a 2D plane. In our system, precise absolute position is not required and relative proximity information is sufficient. It is conceptually similar to the reality mining system proposed by Nathan et al. [10]. However, mobile devices within a room are distributed more densely and the amount of noise is greater. We propose zone-based proximity detection to tackle the unique problem of personalized IAQ monitoring.

CONCLUSIONS

This paper has described MAQS, a mobile system for personalized IAQ monitoring. To achieve high accu-

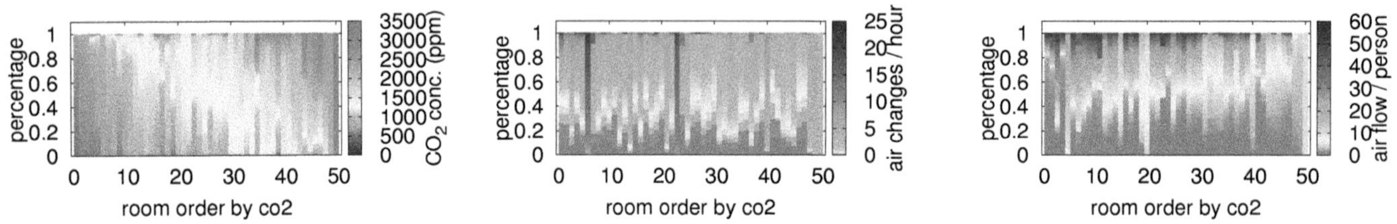

Figure 13. Room-specific distributions of CO_2 concentration, air changes per hour, and air flow per person.

racy and energy efficiency under diverse sensing scenarios, we developed a number of novel techniques: (1) a temporal n-gram augmented Bayesian room localization method that achieves high accuracy with a small number of Wi-Fi fingerprints; (2) an air exchange rate based IAQ sensing method that measures general IAQ using only CO_2 sensors; and (3) a zone-based proximity detection method for collaborative sensing, which saves energy and enables data sharing among multiple users. MAQS has been deployed and evaluated via user study. Detailed evaluation results demonstrate the feasibility, effectiveness, and efficiency of MAQS for personalized IAQ monitoring. We also found that study participants frequently experienced poor IAQ.

ACKNOWLEDGEMENTS

This material is based upon work supported by the National Science Foundation under awards CNS-0910995, CNS-0910816, and CNS-0347941. We thank Simon Olivieri and Lan Bai for help with the experiments. We also thank the anonymous reviewers for constructive comments.

REFERENCES

1. Alnor ebt721 ebt 721 air balancing balometer flow capture hood. http://www.aikencolon.com/Alnor-EBT721-EBT-721-Air-Balancing-Balometer-Flow-Capture-Hood_p_2549.html.
2. Arduino BT. http://www.arduino.cc/en/Main/ArduinoBoardBluetooth.
3. Indoor environmental quality. http://www.cdc.gov/niosh/topics/indoorenv/BuildingVentilation.html.
4. Trends in atmospheric carbon dioxide. http://www.esrl.noaa.gov/gmd/ccgg/trends/global.html.
5. P. Bahl and V. N. Padmanabhan. RADAR: An in-building rf-based user location and tracking system. In *INFOCOM*, pages 775–784, 2000.
6. N. Banerjee, S. Agarwal, P. Bahl, R. Chandra, A. Wolman, and M. Corner. Virtual Compass: Relative positioning to sense mobile social interactions. In *Pervasive Computing*, 2010.
7. E. S. Bhasker, S. W. Brown, and W. G. Griswold. Employing user feedback for fast, accurate, low-maintenance geolocationing. In *PERCOM*, page 111, 2004.
8. P. Bolliger. Redpin - adaptive, zero-configuration indoor localization through user collaboration. In *MELT*, 2008.
9. J. M. Daisey, W. J. Angell, and M. G. Apte. Indoor air quality, ventilation and health symptoms in schools: an analysis of existing information. *Indoor Air*, 13, 2003.
10. N. Eagle and A. (Sandy) Pentland. Reality mining: sensing complex social systems. *Personal Ubiquitous Comput.*, 10, 2006.
11. W. J. Fisk, A. G. Mirer, and M. J. Mendell. Quantitative relationship of sick building syndrome symptoms with ventilation rates. *Indoor Air*, 19, 2009.
12. J. geun Park, B. Charrow, D. Curtis, J. Battat, E. Minkov, J. Hicks, S. Teller, and J. Ledlie. Growing an organic indoor location system. In *MobiSys*, pages 271–284, 2010.
13. C. Godwin and S. Batterman. Indoor air quality in michigan schools. *Indoor Air*, 17(4), 2007.
14. A. Haeberlen, E. Flannery, A. M. Ladd, A. Rudys, D. S. Wallach, and L. E. Kavraki. Practical robust localization over large-scale 802.11 wireless networks. In *MobiCom*, pages 70–84, 2004.
15. C. Huizenga, S. Abbaszadeh, L. Zagreus, and E. Arens. Air quality and thermal comfort in office buildings: Results of a large indoor environmental quality survey. In *Healthy Buildings 2006*, 2006.
16. D. H. Kim, Y. Kim, D. Estrin, and M. B. Srivastava. SensLoc: Sensing everyday places and paths using less energy. In *SenSys*, pages 315–330, 2010.
17. S. Kim and E. Paulos. InAir: sharing indoor air quality measurements and visualizations. In *CHI*, pages 1861–1870, 2010.
18. J. D. Kraus. *Antennas*. McGraw-Hill, 1988.
19. J. Krumm, G. Cermak, and E. Horvitz. Rightspot: A novel sense of location for a smart personal object. In *UBICOMP*, 2003.
20. J. Krumm and K. Hinckley. The NearMe wireless proximity server. In *Ubicomp*, pages 283–300. Springer, 2004.
21. K. A. Li, T. Y. Sohn, S. Huang, and W. G. Griswold. Peopletones: a system for the detection and notification of buddy proximity on mobile phones. In *MobiSys*, pages 160–173, 2008.
22. A. Matic, A. Papliatseyeu, V. Osmani, and O. Mayora-Ibarra. Tuning to your position: Fm radio based indoor localization with spontaneous recalibration. In *IEEE PerCom*, 2010.
23. M. Minami, Y. Fukuju, K. Hirasawa, S. Yokoyama, M. Mizumachi, H. Morikawa, and T. Aoyama. DOLPHIN: A practical approach for implementing a fully distributed indoor ultrasonic positioning system. In *UbiComp*, volume 3205, pages 347–365, 2004.
24. A. Persily. Evaluating building IAQ and ventilation with indoor carbon dioxide. *ASHRAE Transactions*, 1997.
25. O. A. Seppänen, W. J. Fisk, and M. J. Mendell. Association of ventilation rates and co2 concentrations with health and other responses in commercial and institutional buildings. *Indoor Air*, 9, 1999.
26. M. H. Sherman. ASHRAEs first residential ventilation standard. *LBNL-54331*, 2004.
27. M. Sugano. Indoor localization system using rssi measurement of wireless sensor network based on zigbee standard. In *Wireless and Optical Communications*, pages 1–6, 2006.
28. U.S. Environmental Protection Agency Green Building Workgroup. Buildings and their impact on the environment: A statistical summary, 2009.
29. R. Want, A. Hopper, V. Falcão, and J. Gibbons. The active badge location system. *ACM Trans. Inf. Syst.*, 10:91–102, January 1992.
30. A. Ward, A. Jones, and A. Hopper. A new location technique for the active office. *IEEE Personal Communications*, 4:42–47, 1997.
31. D. P. Wyon. The effects of indoor air quality on performance and productivity. *Indoor Air*, 2004.

PreHeat: Controlling Home Heating Using Occupancy Prediction

James Scott[1], A.J. Bernheim Brush[2], John Krumm[2], Brian Meyers[2]
Mike Hazas[3], Steve Hodges[1], Nicolas Villar[1]

[1]Microsoft Research Cambridge
Cambridge, UK
{jws|shodges|nvillar}@microsoft.com

[2]Microsoft Research Redmond
Redmond, WA USA
{ajbrush|jckrumm|brianme}@microsoft.com

[3]Lancaster University
Lancaster, UK
hazas@comp.lancs.ac.uk

ABSTRACT

Home heating is a major factor in worldwide energy use. Our system, PreHeat, aims to more efficiently heat homes by using occupancy sensing and occupancy prediction to automatically control home heating. We deployed PreHeat in five homes, three in the US and two in the UK. In UK homes, we controlled heating on a per-room basis to enable further energy savings. We compared PreHeat's prediction algorithm with a static program over an average 61 days per house, alternating days between these conditions, and measuring actual gas consumption and occupancy. In UK homes PreHeat both saved gas and reduced MissTime (the time that the house was occupied but not warm). In US homes, PreHeat decreased MissTime by a factor of 6-12, while consuming a similar amount of gas. In summary, PreHeat enables more efficient heating while removing the need for users to program thermostat schedules.

Author Keywords

Energy, environment, home heating, sensing, prediction.

ACM Classification Keywords

H5.m. Information interfaces and presentation (e.g., HCI): Miscellaneous.

General Terms

Algorithms, Experimentation, Human Factors.

INTRODUCTION

Home heating uses more energy than any other residential energy expenditure including air conditioning, water heating, and appliances [1]. This makes increasing the efficiency of home heating an important goal for saving money and reducing our ecological footprint. Although programmable thermostats provide the technology to reduce this problem, they are underutilized. Surveys have found that fewer than 50% of US households have programmable thermostats, and even worse, the US Environmental Protection Agency estimates that 30% or more of US households with programmable thermostats are not using their thermostat's programming feature, so they are not saving the 10%-30% claimed for such devices [2, 6].

Fundamentally, home heating is a trade-off between energy use and warmth. By leaving their thermostat set permanently to a warm temperature, households incur increased energy use costs; by using a programmed thermostat to only heat for some of the time, households can use less energy, but occupants may be cold if the program is wrong or while waiting for the house to heat.

Our home heating system, PreHeat, aims both to eliminate the need for manual user programming of a thermostat schedule and to improve the efficiency of home heating (i.e., improving the tradeoff achieved between energy use and time in which occupants are cold). PreHeat uses occupancy sensing and historical occupancy data to estimate the probability of future occupancy, allowing the home to be heated only when necessary.

We experimentally evaluated PreHeat in five family homes. In three US homes, we controlled whole-house forced air heating systems and used active RFID for occupancy sensing. In two UK homes, we controlled radiators and underfloor heating per room, and we sensed occupancy using motion sensors. During the study, we alternated days between using PreHeat and using a schedule, with an average 61 study days per house. We found that PreHeat did indeed achieve a better tradeoff between gas consumption and MissTime [8] – the amount of time someone was home and the house was not warm. US homes used about the same amount of gas, but had a 6x-12x reduction in MissTime. In the UK houses (with per-room control), improvements in both metrics were achieved.

We acknowledge that there are many complementary ways to save energy in home heating, including better insulation, new architectural standards, and persuasive/informative approaches. Our contribution focuses on better heating scheduling. By deploying our system into real homes, and by directly comparing it to the previous control systems, we provide evidence that our novel predictive heating algorithm can improve on the tradeoff between energy consumption and MissTime, and can do so without requiring homeowners to program complex occupancy schedules.

BACKGROUND AND RELATED WORK

In this paper, we focus on the control of two types of *central heating* systems common in Europe and North America. The first type is *hot water space heating*, in which a boiler heats water to 60°C or more and circulates it around the house. Heat in each room is distributed from floor-embedded pipes (*underfloor heating*) or by wall-mounted *radiators*. The second type, more common in North America, is *forced air heating*, in which a furnace heats air and circulates it through ductwork to rooms.

For both types of systems, the temperature is often controlled using a single thermostat located in a central area of the home such as a living room or hallway. The thermostat takes temperature readings and switches the central heating on as needed to maintain a user-defined *setpoint* temperature. Systems with radiators can also be fitted with a thermostatic valve at each radiator, which can be manually set from "1" to "5" to define a separate target temperature for each room. In some houses, particularly those with underfloor heating and some forced-air systems, the system control is split into *zones*, each of which has its own thermostat.

Modern thermostats are typically programmable, allowing the user to specify a *schedule* of times during the day or week when the home should be heated to the setpoint. Outside of these times, the thermostat may use a lower *setback* temperature to reduce the heating energy required, or, as is common in the UK, simply be turned off.

More sophisticated thermostats exist: some are controllable via the Internet; some measure the heat-up latency of the house and compensate the schedule; and others are reactive to occupancy as sensed by entryway or motion sensors. These are expensive, not commonly installed, and as others have reported [3, 8], the latter two tend to heat unnecessarily, actually increasing the energy required.

Researchers have studied the use of domestic heating systems for some time. In 1978, Sonderegger observed that the total energy required by a home's heating system is heavily determined by the particular people living there, dwarfing the effects of insulation or heating infrastructure [9]. Other work has aimed to reduce heating energy using feedback, e.g. via increased frequency and detail of utility bills [10], or real-time energy displays [4]. Feedback and more direct interventions such as "persuasive" interfaces are complementary to our work: while PreHeat may lower energy use by heating less during unoccupied times, a persuasive display may "nudge" an occupant to lower the setpoint and wear a sweater.

Closest to our work are approaches that have aimed to improve control beyond what off-the-shelf products currently offer. Mozer et al. describe a "Neurothermostat" which utilizes a hybrid occupancy predictor, making use of an available daily schedule and a neural network which was trained on five consecutive months of occupancy data [7]. Although real occupancy data from one house is used in the analysis, a first order approximation of the heating system and house is used to model temperature and energy consumption. Mozer et al. show that the Neurothermostat results in a lower unified cost, where energy and occupant "comfort" are expressed as a combined figure, in dollars. We believe that the equivalency of comfort and energy is problematic (the relationship between setpoint deviation and dollars is nonlinear, depends upon the individual, and changes over time), so we prefer to characterize separately the deviation from setpoint temperature at occupied times, and the energy required.

Gupta et al. propose using live data from mobile phones or in-vehicle GPS devices to control home heating and cooling [3]. Their method works by ensuring the home can always be brought to the setpoint in the time it would take the person to travel home from the current location. Using a simulation based on look-up tables extrapolated from three days of temperature readings, they compute the savings possible in four houses based on two months of GPS data. While their scheme does ensure the house is always at setpoint upon arrival, it typically results in lower savings than programmable or manual thermostats.

Lu et al. formulate a hidden Markov model to predict occupancy and control HVAC systems [8]. They collected occupancy data in eight US households for one to two weeks. Using leave-one-out cross-validation to train and test the HMM, they evaluate their approach's MissTime (i.e. total occupied time not at setpoint) and energy savings for each day in a week using the US Dept. of Energy's EnergyPlus simulator. Their forward-looking approach is designed to control specialized two-stage HVAC systems and employs a second "deep" setback (10°C/50°F). By contrast, we show how our system performs in real households using single setback temperatures and single-stage, gas-fired equipment commonly deployed today.

Our occupancy prediction algorithm is itself an improvement over the above approaches: it results in more favorable trade-offs between miss time and energy than the GPS-reactive system [3]. Krumm and Brush [5] also presented an occupancy prediction algorithm that gives probabilities of occupancy at different times of day. However, this algorithm computes a representative Sunday, Monday, etc. for each day of the week, without being able to respond to changing occupancy patterns as PreHeat does.

More broadly, and unlike any of the above work, we evaluate the performance of PreHeat in situ in five houses, using custom embedded sensing and real-time control of the central heating. Previous evaluations have relied upon simulations [3, 7, 8]. While industry standard simulators such as EnergyPlus may go beyond simple first-order approximations, we question the efficacy of simulators for characterizing either (1) the daily energy requirement of heating infrastructure – savings of smaller than 10% can be important, so daily errors of even 3 kWh can muddy analysis; or (2) the deviation from setpoint at occupied

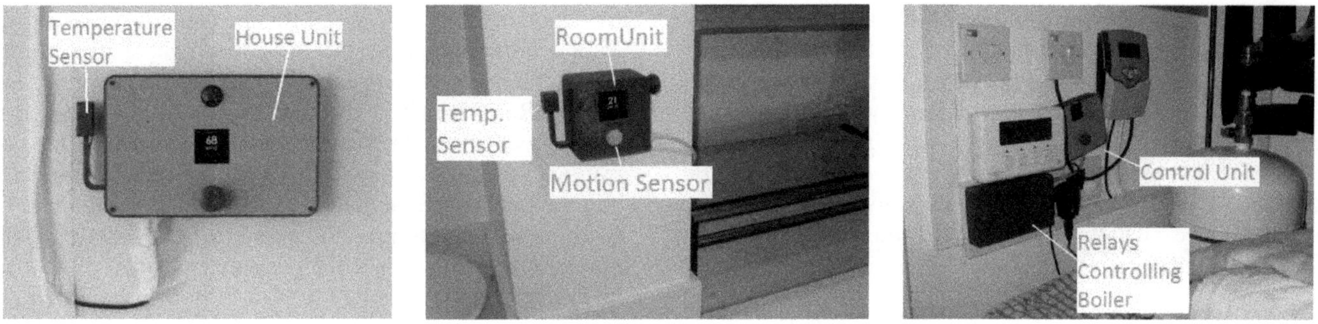

(a) (b) (c)

Figure 1: Photographs of (a) House Unit installed in US house replacing thermostat on wall, (b) Room Unit in UK room, (c) Control Unit beside old house thermostat in UK, wired into boiler control circuitry.

times (i.e. MissTime) – this requires simulator granularity finer than five minutes, better than 1°C, and for individual rooms (when using per-room prediction and control). In contrast, our deployment allows us to characterize PreHeat using real temperatures, gas readings, and occupancy sensors.

EXPERIMENTAL HEATING SYSTEM

We implemented an experimental system, designed to facilitate comparison between PreHeat and existing heating controls. We deployed this system in five homes: three in Seattle, USA (referred to as US1, US2, US3) and two in Cambridge, UK (UK1, UK2) during the winter from January – April, 2011. We chose to deploy in homes of project researchers or our colleaagues, so people knew how to cope if any problems occurred. All of the homes were family homes with two adults and one or more children – ranging from one toddler (UK1) to three school-age children (US1). All US homes used forced air heating, UK1 used both radiators (4 of 10 independently heatable rooms) and underfloor heating (8 of 10 rooms, 2 with radiators too), and UK2 used radiators in all 14 rooms.

Hardware

We built custom hardware, shown in Figure 1, to control the heating systems. In US houses, we replaced the existing thermostat for whole-house control with a "House Unit" built using our in-house-developed prototyping platform, Microsoft .NET Gadgeteer. The core of this unit is a mainboard based on GHI Electronics' Embedded Master module with ARM7 CPU, running custom software in C#. Additionally there were a number of peripheral modules. The House Unit measured temperature using a Sensiron SHT15 sensor (accuracy +/- 0.1°C), and used an Avago ASSR-1611 solid state relay to control the furnace through the existing wiring. It also included a rotary encoder, RGB light level sensor, a 128x128 OLED display and a passive infra-red motion sensor (Panasonic PIR-AMN34111J, 10m max range and 110 degree beam angle).

In UK houses, we controlled the heating on a per-room basis by installing "Room Units" in each space with independent heating. These were similar to "House Units", but instead of a relay had an 868MHz transmitter (TX868-785 from elv.de) to control wireless radiator valves (HHFHT-8V from HouseHeat) which replaced the existing thermostatic radiator valves on the radiators in each room.

In the UK we also deployed "Control Units" that did not have any sensors, but included either Avago ASSR-1611 relays for controlling per-room underfloor heating valves or Omron G6D relays providing 240V control of the house boiler. Turning on heating in any individual room involved activating the boiler (if it was not already active for another room's heating) and per-room valves – either on radiators or for the underfloor heating. These units also controlled the hot water heating for sinks, showers, etc., using a static schedule reflecting the previous hot water schedule.

All hardware was powered through USB mains power adaptors, aside from the battery-powered wireless radiator valves. Power optimization is possible (c.f. battery powered wireless security sensors), but is not our focus. All units had ZigBee radio modules (the "XBee ZB") for wireless mesh communication with a central server PC in each house, running custom software described in the next section.

To evaluate PreHeat, we logged actual gas usage. In the UK, we deployed gas meter readers based on the RFXPulse sensor from RFXCom. In the US, we used daily meter readings provided by the local energy company website.

Occupancy sensing

In US houses, we sensed when occupants were home by using an RFID receiver plugged into the server and placing a small Active RFID tag (RF8315T-s manufactured by Ananiah Electronics) on the house keys of each adult using the house, including the nanny for US3. The option was provided to each household to have RFID tags for kids, but none of the houses accepted this offer, since the kids were in general not expected to be home alone. Visitors were not provided with RFID tags. Each tag sent its identity to the receiver every 5s when in range. The server was placed such that the 8m nominal range included the whole "front hall" area of the house, where we asked participants to leave their keys. We also asked participants to take their keys whenever they left the house (compliance results are described in the Deployment section).

In UK houses, where we could control heating at the room level, we added motion sensors that could determine per room occupancy. These detected motion by any occupant: adults, children or visitors – note that neither UK house had pets. This allowed our predictive system in the UK houses to heat for and predict arrival of any type of occupant, not just those with RFID tags. UK occupants also had RFID tags deployed which were only used during system evaluation, and not for prediction.

Our occupancy sensors (RFID and motion) generated events at discrete points in time. From this data, we derived periods of occupancy by filling in gaps between two sensed events within a certain time difference (2 minutes for RFID, 5 minutes for motion sensing during the day, and 30 minutes for motion sensing during pre-defined sleep hours).

Software

The PC we deployed in each house ran our custom software which managed the network of devices, collected sensor data and ran the heating algorithm. The heating algorithm was provided with a collection of preset parameters. These comprised (for each day of the week): Sleep and Wake times, a Sleep setpoint temperature to use between those times, and Occupied[1] and Away setpoints. In the UK, each room could have its own Occupied temperature. For our experiments, we deployed different heating algorithms, and we switched between algorithms at the preset Sleep time (which all houses chose to be the same time on all seven days of the week). The experimental system was designed so that the only difference between conditions was the algorithm's choice of which setpoint to use at a particular time. Our study used the following algorithms:

Scheduled: Equivalent to a seven-day programmable thermostat, it used preconfigured times for Leave and Return for each of the seven week days. The Away setpoint is used between Leave and Return times, and the Occupied setpoint is used otherwise (other than during Sleep hours).

AlwaysOn: Forced the use of the Occupied setpoint all the time including between Sleep and Wake.

PreHeat: Our prediction algorithm which chooses between Occupied and Away depending on current and predicted occupancy – more details later in this section.

Heating in Anticipation of Occupancy

If a space (whole house in US or room in UK) was deemed occupied by the heating algorithm, this determined the setpoint to use. However, even if a space was not occupied, it may require heating in order to be warm for future need. To achieve this, the system looked ahead up to three hours into the future. If a higher setpoint was expected by the heating algorithm, then the system evaluated the current temperature, target temperature, look ahead duration, and the HeatRate, which is the warming rate of the house in degrees per hour, to decide whether it needed to start heating at the present time. For example, with a HeatRate of 3°C/hour, space temperature of 20°C, and a requirement for 22°C in one hour's time, no heating is yet needed. Twenty minutes later, if the space temperature remained 20°C, then the system would activate the heat in order to warm up in time for the future (predicted or scheduled) occupancy.

User Interface and Overrides

We provided a user interface for occupants on the House Unit/Room Units themselves. This showed the current space temperature and the setpoint. Just as with normal heating controls, we provided a menu option on the units that gave occupants a way to override the system in case they were too cold. We also used the light sensor to automatically dim the screen when the space was dark, to make our system "bedroom friendly".

System Reliability

Since our system ran in real homes, we conducted extensive in-situ testing and implemented a number of features to promote reliability, including the ability to remotely log in to the servers, automatic emails if problems occurred, an auto-restart program to recover from software crashes, etc.

We also implemented a "failsafe mode." In the rare case that the unit was unable to contact the server, while it attempted to recover communication it would act as a local thermostat using the Occupied setpoint. As we later detail, the system achieved an average 99.8% uptime in the study.

PreHeat Occupancy Prediction Algorithm

The PreHeat prediction algorithm works in two ways. First, it uses occupancy-reactive heating; when a space is occupied, it uses the Occupied setpoint (or Sleep setpoint at night). Second, when a space is not occupied, it predicts when it will next be occupied by matching the occupancy data from the current day against historical occupancy data.

We represent space occupancy as a binary vector for each day, where each element represents occupancy in a 15-minute interval, as shown in Figure 2. In the UK such spaces are individual rooms, in the US we use a single whole-house space – no distinction is made by the algorithm. The vector element is 1 if there is any occupancy during the interval or 0 otherwise. As a day progresses, we maintain a partial occupancy vector from midnight up to the current time. To predict future occupancy, we use this partial occupancy vector to find similar days in the past. Specifically, we compute the Hamming distance between the current partial day and the corresponding parts of all the past occupancy vectors. (The Hamming distance simply counts the number of unequal corresponding binary vector elements.) We then pick the K nearest past days for making the prediction. Based on initial experiments, we found K=5 proved to be a good choice for high prediction accuracy.

---

[1] Although our system supported having different morning and evening setpoints (mirroring many US thermostats), all of our households chose the same value for these, so we refer to a single Occupied setpoint to simplify discussion.

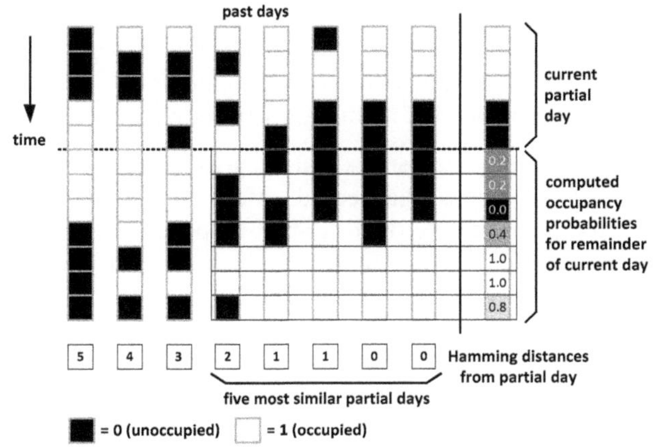

Figure 2: PreHeat prediction algorithm. Each vertical set of blocks represents one day of occupancy split into 15-minute periods. Given a partially observed current day, the algorithm finds the five best matches in the past and averages the remainder of those matched days to compute probabilities for future occupancy.

The predicted occupancy probability for a future time is simply the mean of the corresponding occupancy values in the K nearest past days.

There are two slight variations of this basic algorithm that we implemented to improve accuracy. The first variation distinguishes between weekdays and weekends. Weekday predictions are only computed from past weekdays, and similarly for weekends. This helps accuracy, because households often have quite different occupancy patterns on the two types of days. The second variation augments the beginning of each occupancy vector with four hours of occupancy data from the previous day. This gives predictions near the beginning of the day some extra basis on which to compare to previous days. We also pad the end of each occupancy vector with four hours of occupancy data from the following day. This avoids complexities in making predictions that span midnight.

While in this algorithm we treated every historical day equally for prediction purposes, we could instead automatically adapt to changing occupancy schedules by preferring more recent days when matching.

One advantage of an algorithm like ours is that it gives occupancy probabilities. This gives us the freedom to set a probability threshold for declaring when a space will be occupied. For our experiments, we set this threshold to a neutral value of ½. But, a more environmentally-conscious user may set the threshold higher to ensure that the system is more confident of future occupancy before heating. In contrast, a user more concerned about being warm would choose a lower probability threshold. We demonstrate the effect of this tradeoff in the results section below.

In testing, we found that PreHeat did not perform well in per-room situations for a certain class of rooms – those which are only occupied for very short periods of time and at random intervals, e.g. bathrooms and hallways. These spaces tended to be predicted as "never occupied". We therefore decided to use whole-house occupancy (determined by using the mathematical union of signals from all motion sensors) to predict and heat these rooms. Intuitively, whenever you are home it is possible that you might use the bathroom. In addition to these "whole house spaces", this left 6 individually controlled rooms out of 10 for UK1 and 8 rooms out of 10 for UK2.

DEPLOYMENT

Deployment allowed us to evaluate the heating algorithms using real weather conditions, central heating systems, and human occupancy behavior. Our three phase deployment lasted three to four months in each house, with an average of 61 days per house in Phase 2 (see Table 1), the main comparison between PreHeat and Scheduled heating.

Phase 0: Debug/Acclimatization (≥ 7 days)

In this phase we installed our system running the Scheduled algorithm. We showed adult members of the household how to use the UI and attached RFID tags to keys. To get the most accurate schedule we used the household's current thermostat settings as a baseline and asked household members to update the program if necessary. For per-room heating in the UK we asked participants to provide "Occupied" setpoint temperatures for each room. To model typical systems in the UK which simply turn off between heating periods rather than use a setback, we did not ask for Sleep or Away temperatures, but used a low value of 5°C, which never triggered any heating during our study.

The goal of this phase was to make sure our system was running smoothly in the home and to give people time to adjust their setpoint temperatures or scheduled times if desired. Although changes were permitted in later phases, no household requested to make such a change. We used the average observed heating rate from this phase to set the HeatRate parameter for each house (ranging from 1.5°C/hour in UK1 to 3°C/hour in US2). Phase 0 lasted a minimum of a week and was longest in US1, US2 and UK1 where we did initial in-situ testing.

Phase 1: Initial Data Collection (14 days)

PreHeat's prediction algorithm requires some occupancy history data to work. We therefore ran a 14 day phase without Prediction, which gave the subsequent prediction phase enough historical data to work accurately. In a real deployment of PreHeat, the system might bootstrap by simply heating during all non-sleep hours until it determined that its predictions were accurate enough to start using Away. In our post hoc analysis, however, we found that prediction accuracy was adequate after just one or two days of occupancy data. Given that prior research [3, 8] has used AlwaysOn as a baseline, during Phase 1 we decided to alternate between the AlwaysOn and Scheduled conditions.

Phase 2: PreHeat vs. Scheduled (48-72 days, 61 average)

This comparison was our main focus and comprised the majority of days in the study (see Table 1). In order to balance any effect weather or household schedule changes may have on our study, we alternated each day between two conditions: using PreHeat's prediction algorithm and the Scheduled algorithm. Using neighborhood weather data provided to each US house by their utility company and from nearby public weather stations in the UK, we determined that, for all houses, the average outdoor temperature for PreHeat days differed from Scheduled days by less than 0.3°C.

Our primary metrics for comparing PreHeat and Scheduled were gas consumption and the MissTime metric used by Lu et. al [8]. They defined MissTime as the total time in minutes that the home is occupied but the temperature was more than 1°C below the Occupied setpoint. We used the same definition, but applied it per-space (room in the UK, house in the US). For gas consumption, we used automated meter readings of the volume of gas used as described earlier. Because the system was deployed in our own houses, we purposefully avoided any subjective metrics.

Households US2, US3, and UK2 each went on vacation for about a week during the study. Since at such times it is usual to do some exceptional thermostat programming (e.g. turn it off), we collected a list of such days and excluded them from Phase 2. This is primarily because vacation times are "unfair" to the Scheduled condition which heats regardless. We took advantage of vacation days to run additional AlwaysOn days in these houses. We continued to collect occupancy data during vacations, as PreHeat is robust to having these periods in the historical data set.

Reliability During Deployment

During the study period we had a small number of technical problems which caused us to remove three days from the analysis (N.B. In Table 1 and elsewhere, we have excluded these days already). In UK1, an electrical fuse trip caused two days to be excluded. In UK2, the XBee radio module attached to the PC "hung" and required manual power cycling, causing one day to be excluded.

Of the study days used for analysis, the system was in a not-fully-functional state for an average of three minutes per day (uptime 99.8%). House UK2 had the most problems, averaging eight minutes per day where units were in "failsafe" mode. Most problems were due to XBee, and the system recovered automatically.

Ensuring Occupancy Correctness

Because our MissTime metric is only as valid as the occupancy data used, we took extensive steps to ensure accuracy. Each server directed an email to a house occupant and a project member every morning with a summary of the previous day's per-space occupancy. The recipients looked for any discrepancies, consulting family members if necessary. The documented errors included both "social" failures due to forgetting to carry an RFID tag, and "technical" failures where some aspect of the sensing failed. We also ran data integrity checks on the 37,000 occupancy records generated over the course of the study to find failure cases: In the US, we examined days where RFID tags disappeared many times (a radio range failure). In the UK, we used the RFID data (which was not used for heating prediction purposes) to highlight times when the house was occupied but no motion sensors were active.

Using the documented errors and integrity checks we found a set of 57 issues that could affect the analysis and corrected them in a "ground truth" occupancy table. In the US, there were 17 corrections, of which 14 were "social", and 12 of those occurred in US1. This household had keyless entry so the RFIDs were not as convenient. In the UK, 21/40 corrections were due to occupants being asleep outside the Sleep/Wake period (and thus difficult to detect using motion). In future work, we hope to address sleep detection. Issues with a motion sensor in UK2 not completely covering a room resulted in 18/40 corrections.

We compared the MissTime metric using the original table against the ground truth table and found that only a single instance actually altered the result set (this impacted UK2 - the corrected data is reported in this paper). In the remaining instances, the house was warm enough to prevent the error from impacting the occupants. It is important to note that the PreHeat algorithm did NOT use corrected data; it predicted based on live data that included any errors. This is more representative of a real-life deployment.

PREHEAT VS SCHEDULED RESULTS

Figure 3 and Table 1 summarize how the measured gas consumption and MissTime metrics differ between the Scheduled and PreHeat conditions in each house.

In the UK, PreHeat performed better than Scheduled on both metrics. PreHeat saved energy by not only selecting better heating times, but also by heating rooms different amounts – more details to follow in the Per-Room Heating section. Gas usage decreased from Scheduled by 18% in UK1 and 8% in UK2. In both conditions, the UK houses had comparatively little MissTime, but PreHeat also succeeded in decreasing this by 38% and 60%.

In the US houses, MissTime improved by a large factor (84%, 88% and 92% reductions, a factor of 6-12 decrease!).

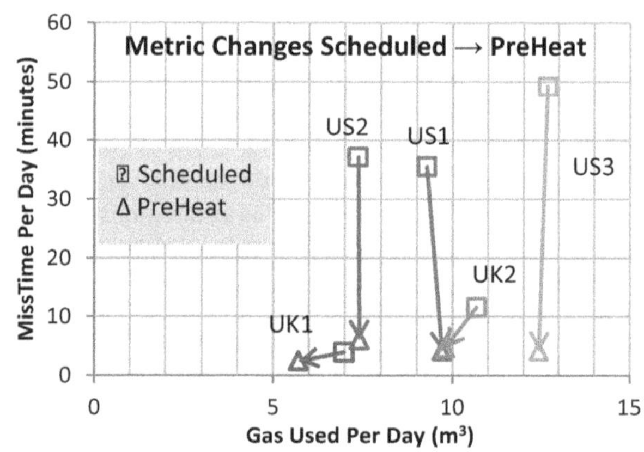

Figure 3: PreHeat improves the trade-off between gas used and MissTime compared to Scheduled

	US1	US2	US3	UK1	UK2
Phase 2 Days (Alternating PreHeat and Scheduled)	72	64	58	62	48
Average Daily Occupancy	89%	69%	67%	73%	68%
Savings in MissTime PreHeat vs. Scheduled	88%	84%	92%	38%	60%
Savings in Gas Used PreHeat vs. Scheduled	-5% (worse)	-1%	2%	18% (better)	8%
Savings in Gas Used PreHeat vs. AlwaysOnModel	3%	17%	10%	27%	35%

Table 1: PreHeat decreased MissTime in all houses. Gas Used decreased in PreHeat in the UK homes with per room heating and was equivalent or slightly higher for the three US homes.

This is further shown by Figure 4 which illustrates that MissTime happens unevenly through the study – over half the days had no MissTime, but one Scheduled day in five (in US houses) had over one hour. PreHeat, unlike a static schedule, is able to dynamically heat day-by-day to more closely match the occupancy. To give one example, in US2, PreHeat heated more on weekends and less on weekdays than Scheduled, while being adaptive to instances of absence on weekends or occupancy on weekdays. PreHeat was able to achieve these large improvements in MissTime while using a similar amount of gas – saving slightly in US3 and using slightly more in US1 and US2. In the Occupancy Prediction section, we discuss how PreHeat could instead be tuned to favor energy savings at the expense of a smaller improvement in MissTime.

Many More Overrides in Scheduled

Our system's user interface allowed occupants to override the current action. We classify overrides into two categories: "time" overrides when the system was not heating and the user overrode it to heat to the normal Occupied temperature, and "temperature" overrides when a non-standard temperature was set. During the study, there were 23 time overrides, 21 of which occurred in the Scheduled condition. The "time" overrides in Scheduled happened when people were home on vacation, sick, or otherwise home at times when Scheduled was not heating the house and they felt cold. The overrides caused more energy to be used, but without these overrides, the MissTime metric would have been (even) higher. The occupancy-reactive element of PreHeat reduces the need for overrides. There were two "time" overrides in the PreHeat condition, which were due to occupancy sensing failures – a guest in US2 who did not have an RFID tag, and a resident of US1 left her RFID tag in the car. The small number of "time" overrides in PreHeat supports our claim that PreHeat requires less programming of a heating schedule by occupants (since overriding is a form of programming).

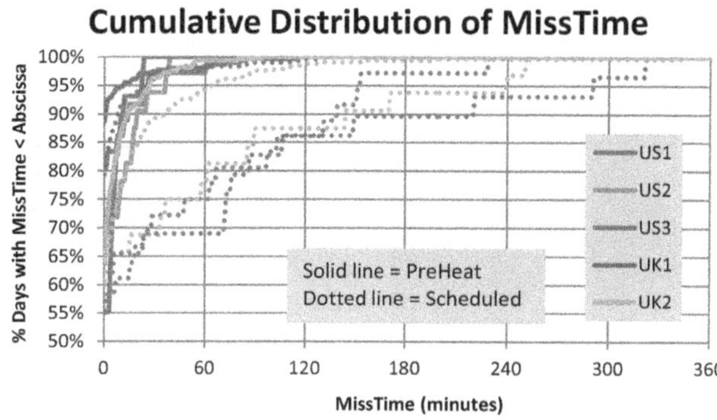

Figure 4: Occurrences of long MissTimes are much reduced with PreHeat, particularly for US houses. (Note Y-axis intercept at 50%)

There were nine "temperature" overrides during Phase 2. These types of overrides can occur in either condition if an occupant wanted a deviation from the normal setpoint. In US3, participants overrode the temperature to be 1-3 degrees higher than the setpoint seven times: three in Scheduled and four in PreHeat. In UK2, an occupant overrode the temperature to be lower than the setpoint twice, both in PreHeat, because it was sunny and he didn't feel the heat needed to be on.

Per-Room Heating

Although we did not study the effect of per-room heating through a direct comparison, we can still get a measure of how well PreHeat tailored its behavior to individual room occupancy patterns.

Figure 5 shows UK1's six per-room-controlled spaces (the other four spaces used whole-house occupancy for heating as previously described), illustrating average occupancy in each space and the amount of time that the Occupied setpoint was used in both PreHeat and Scheduled conditions. We see that Scheduled heats around the same amount in each space (variation is due to turning on a little earlier or later in each space depending on how cold it gets when away/asleep). PreHeat tracks occupancy fairly well.

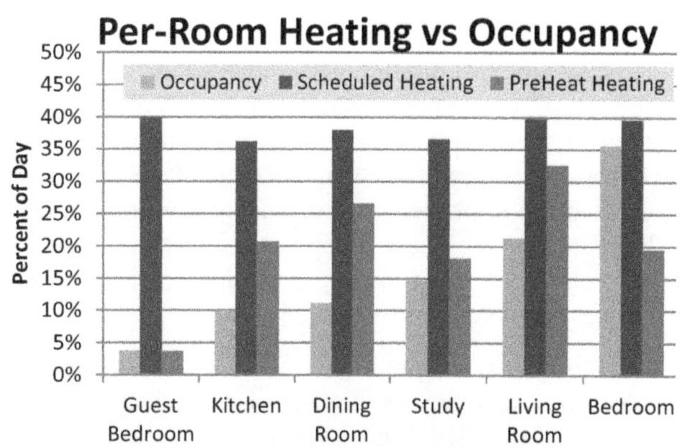

Figure 5: PreHeat heats higher-occupied rooms more, while Scheduled does not adapt per-room.

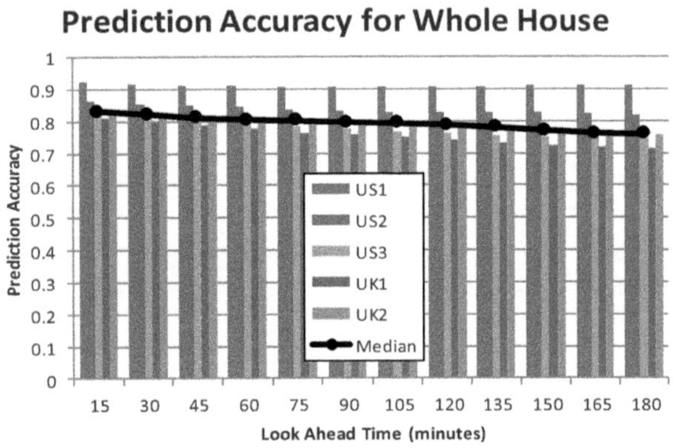

Figure 6: Prediction accuracy varied only slightly with the look ahead time.

Note that the rightmost room is the bedroom where all occupants sleep, so this space needs less heating than occupancy might suggest.

OCCUPANCY PREDICTION

Occupancy prediction is a key part of PreHeat. This section explores how accurate the predictions are compared to actual occupancy.

Figure 6 shows the overall prediction accuracy for different look ahead times for the five houses. We compute accuracy for a given look ahead time as simply the number of correct occupancy predictions (either true or false) divided by the number of attempted predictions. The graph reveals that prediction accuracy for all houses was generally high. The median line shows that prediction accuracy only slightly decreases for longer look ahead times.

Since the system needs advance notice of the need for heat in order for the space to reach the desired setpoint in time, we should evaluate the prediction based on how well it can achieve this goal. Examining each daytime heating instance during Phase 2, we find that 91% of the time, the system needed 90 minutes or less advance notice. For the remainder of our prediction assessments, we evaluate based on this 90-minute look ahead time.

Figure 7 shows the prediction accuracies for 90 minutes into the future. For comparison, it also shows the prediction accuracy of the manually programed Scheduled condition, which was worse by a median 10 percentage points. We suspect that the improvement from using PreHeat would be much greater for the general population, many of whom do not keep up to date programs on their thermostats or do not have programmable thermostats [3].

As one might expect, prediction accuracy varied with the time of day. Accuracy is highest during sleep time and drops during the day when occupancy is naturally less predictable. Because prediction accuracy is high during sleep times, we have eliminated sleep times from all our prediction accuracy assessments. Thus, all our prediction

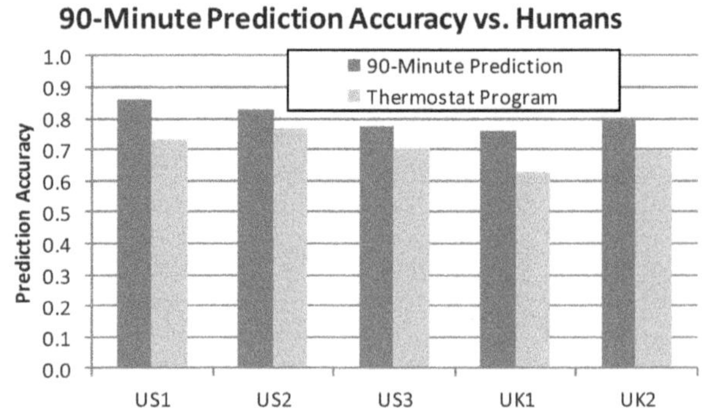

Figure 7: Our prediction algorithm was consistently more accurate than carefully programmed thermostats.

assessments, including those in Figure 6 and Figure 7, pertain only to non-sleep times, eliminating the uninteresting boost in accuracy we would otherwise get.

We also evaluated how prediction accuracy varied with the day of the week. As expected, weekend days are worse, with Sunday being the better of the two. We attribute this to the fact that our households generally had parents with regular working hours and children with regular school hours during the week.

Our prediction algorithm computes occupancy probabilities that are then subjected to a threshold to make a concrete occupancy prediction. For our study, this threshold was set to a neutral value of ½. The effect of this threshold is shown in the receiver operating characteristic (ROC) curve in Figure 8. For different values of the probability threshold, these curves show the tradeoff between false positives (mistakenly predicting positive occupancy when the home would actually be empty) and true positives (correctly predicting positive occupancy). Our selected threshold value is indicated by a dot on each ROC curve.

The ideal operating point is in the upper left corner, where the false positive rate is 0.0 and the true positive rate is 1.0.

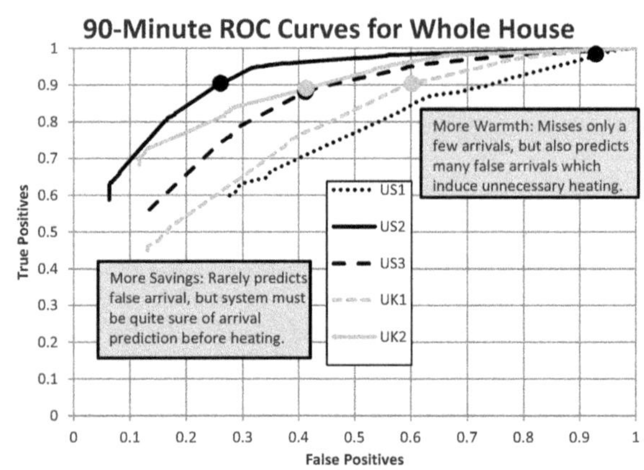

Figure 8: These ROC curves demonstrate the tradeoff in prediction errors due to adjusting the probability threshold.

In reality, as with almost all detection problems, increasing the true positive rate comes at the expense of increasing the false positive rate. An environmentally-conscious user, who is more concerned about energy rather than warmth, would operate with a high probability threshold, which is toward the left side of the ROC curve. This would give fewer mistaken heating events at the expense of missing times when the heat should actually be turned on. A more warmth-sensitive user would operate with a lower probability threshold, which would cause heating more often during times of both occupancy and non-occupancy.

Our study results show that PreHeat improved MissTime in all houses by substantial amounts. This indicates that our selected threshold was generally closer to the "warmth" end of the curves than the "savings" end, as verified in Figure 8. The operating point for US1 is biased far toward warmth. This is because this house was almost continuously occupied, resulting in prediction probabilities that were generally high (including sleep time, US1 was occupied 89% of the day vs. a median of 69% for the other houses). Even with a relatively high false positive rate of 93%, the house was occupied so much that its overall 90-minute prediction accuracy was highest of all the houses at 86%.

Finally, we also looked at prediction on a per-person basis, by applying our algorithm to each individual RFID tag using the tag's unique ID. Running our algorithm in this way showed that our prediction accuracy is even higher, with a median accuracy of 97% compared to a whole-household median of 80%. This means our algorithm could be used to accommodate different temperature preferences when only one of the home's occupants is present.

DISCUSSION

We now discuss how PreHeat compares with AlwaysOn and to occupancy-reactive heating, and share some observations from our experiences of living with PreHeat.

Comparison with Other Heating Algorithms

Our main study directly compared PreHeat with Scheduled based on actual measurements. We now discuss how PreHeat compares to other algorithms.

AlwaysOn

Prior research [e.g. 3, 8] frequently uses the energy necessary to keep the house at a permanent setpoint (AlwaysOn) as a baseline for comparison. Given its past inclusion, we also provide this comparison baseline; however, we believe the comparison between PreHeat and Scheduled to be more meaningful.

Since there were not sufficient days in a single winter to run three conditions, we elected to only gather AlwaysOn data during Phase 1 and vacations. We then used linear regression on this data to model the gas consumed given the average outside daily temperature. The linear regression showed average daily temperature was a very good predictor of gas used for the US houses, where more than 92% of the variance in the data was accounted for in the linear regression equation (all $R^2 > 0.92$). Modeling did not work as well in the UK, with $R^2 = 0.69$ in UK1 and $R^2 = 0.78$ in UK2. However, the models still give us some ability to compare PreHeat to AlwaysOn.

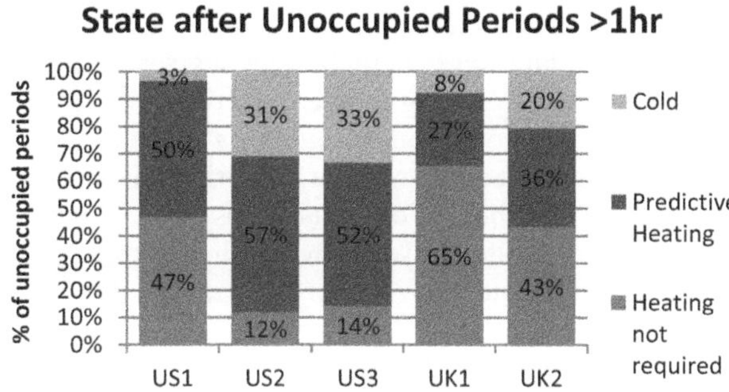

Figure 9: Predictive heating was important in all houses. While occupancy-reactive heating would have sufficed in 36% of cases (average across households) where heating was not required, predictive heating was used to achieve warmth on return for an average of 45% of cases.

For each PreHeat day we used the average daily temperature as input to the linear regression equation. We show the comparison between the model's result and the actual gas used by PreHeat in Table 1. As expected, PreHeat uses less gas than the AlwaysOn model (ranging from a 3% to a 35% decrease). Although the difference in US1 is quite small (3%) we attribute this to the fact that the house was only empty 11% of the day which does not provide much opportunity for savings.

Occupancy-reactive

The PreHeat system incorporates both occupancy-reactive and predictive heating. We wished to evaluate how often just occupancy-reactive heating would have been sufficient in our study, and thereby get a measure of the value of the predictive element. We therefore looked for instances when someone entered a space that had been unoccupied for more than 60 minutes on PreHeat days. As Figure 9 shows, occupancy-reactive heating would have worked 36% of the time (average for all houses) without any MissTime – i.e., the space was still warm enough when someone returned. However, in 45% of the instances PreHeat heated the unoccupied space prior to the person's return and so occupancy-reactive heating would have caused MissTime to occur. Thus we can conclude that predictive heating plays a very significant part in the PreHeat system.

Living With PreHeat

We quantitatively compared the Scheduled and PreHeat algorithms because of the potential for bias when using our own system. However, based on our experience with living with PreHeat, we report a few qualitative examples of how PreHeat gracefully adapted to our homes.

PreHeat Better Handles Weekend Chaos: During the setup phase, we heard that weekend schedules varied more than weekday schedules, and that it was difficult to program the thermostat for weekends. Households adopted one of two strategies for their (previous) thermostat programs, either heating all day on the weekends (US1, US3) or using a shorter away duration than their weekday schedule (US2, UK1, UK2). These strategies were carried over into the study's Scheduled condition. In either case, PreHeat better handled weekend heating without requiring manual effort by household members. For households with a weekend setback, the house stayed warm when they were home on PreHeat days without an override. Households that left the heating on all day had the potential to save energy on weekend days if they left home.

PreHeat Supports More Complicated Occupancy Patterns: Programmable thermostats typically allow people to schedule one away period per day. In contrast, PreHeat can predict multiple away periods. For example, by the end of the study, PreHeat was correctly predicting that US2 would come home and then leave again for a regular Friday evening appointment, and similarly for UK1 on Tuesday evenings. More valuable was PreHeat's ability to predict on a per-room basis in the UK. Even if households had the ability to program on a per room basis, it is unlikely they would make the effort to maintain up-to-date programs in each room separately. We also observed that PreHeat handled occupancy patterns that re-occurred, but not on a weekly basis. For example, PreHeat smoothly handled the fact that a member of US2 arrived home early roughly every other Tuesday afternoon.

PreHeat Adapts to Changing Schedules: In US3, the Nanny who stayed at home after school with the kids took another job during the study. As is likely typical after this type of change, it did not occur to the occupants of US3 that they should change their heating schedule. However, PreHeat adapted over time and began correctly predicting later arrival times at the home.

CONCLUDING REMARKS

By predicting future occupancy from historical data and current occupancy, the PreHeat system provides a better trade-off between energy use and MissTime (the amount of time an occupied space is cold) than a thermostat program, and does so without requiring a user to program an occupancy schedule (which past research has shown that many users fail to do). We evaluated PreHeat using a real deployment in five family homes during winter 2011, alternating days between PreHeat and scheduled heating to provide a direct comparison with measured gas consumption and MissTime.

In three US homes, we found that PreHeat reduced MissTime by a factor of 6-12 while using around the same amount of gas. Across two UK homes, PreHeat halved MissTime and also reduced gas usage by 8% and 18% - this is because UK homes used PreHeat on a per-room basis, so it was able to make additional savings by heating rooms adaptively at different times of day, again without requiring any programming of per-room schedules.

Our research suggests several interesting directions for future work. We want to investigate improvements to the PreHeat algorithm, e.g. using other sources of data such as location from phones, or further exploring per-person predictions. Sleep detection would assist with automatically determining times for setpoint changes. A more sophisticated heating model could also enable more savings, e.g. by predicting departures and "pre cooling" since houses stay warm for some time. Finally, we plan to explore exposing the high-level tradeoffs PreHeat offers between the likelihood of being warm when arriving home unexpectedly and energy consumption to users so they can customize based on their personal preferences.

ACKNOWLEDGEMENTS

Thanks to Kori and Jeff Quinn, and to our families, for being our guinea pigs!

REFERENCES

1. EIA, USE.I.A. Table 2.5 "Household Energy Consumption and Expenditures by End Use and Energy Source, Selected Years 1978 – 2005." Retrieved in April 2011 at http://www.eia.doe.gov/emeu/aer/consump.html.
2. EPA, USE.P.A., Summary of Research Findings From the Programmable Thermostat Market. Available from: http://www.energystar.gov/ia/partners/prod_development/revisions/downloads/thermostats/Summary.pdf
3. Gupta, M., S.S. Intille, and K. Larson. "Adding GPS-Control to Traditional Thermostats: An Exploration of Potential Energy Savings and Design Challenges." *Proc. of Pervasive,* 2009.
4. Hargreaves, T., Nye, M., and Burgess, J. "Making energy visible: A qualitative field study of how householders interact with feedback from smart energy monitors." *Energy Policy* 38:10, pp. 6111-6119, 2010.
5. Krumm, J. and Brush, A. "Learning Time-Based Presence Probabilities", *Proc. of Pervasive 2011*, 2011.
6. Meier, A., Aragon, C., Hurwitz, B., Mujumdar, D., Peffer, T., Perry, D., Pritoni, M. "How People Actually Use Thermostats", *Proc. of ACEEE 2010.*
7. Mozer, M.C., Vidmar, L., and Dodier, R.M. "The Neurothermostat: PreHeat Optimal Control of Residential Heating Systems." *Advances in Neural Information Processing Systems* 9, pp. 953-959, 1997.
8. Lu, J, Sookoor, T., Srinivasan V., Gao, G, Holben, B., Stankovic, J., Field, E., Whitehouse, K. "The Smart Thermostat: Using Occupancy Sensors to Save Energy in Homes." *Proc. of SenSys,* 2010.
9. Sonderegger, R. "Movers and stayers: The resident's contribution to variation across houses in energy consumption for space heating." *Energy and Buildings* 1:3, pp. 313-324, 1978.
10. Wilhite, H. and Ling, R. "Measured energy savings from a more informative energy bill." *Energy and Buildings* 22:2, pp. 145-155, 1995.

How Smart is Your Smartcard? Measuring Travel Behaviours, Perceptions, and Incentives

Neal Lathia, Licia Capra
Department of Computer Science
University College London
Gower Street, London, UK
n.lathia, l.capra@cs.ucl.ac.uk

ABSTRACT
The widespread adoption of automated fare collection (AFC) systems by public transport authorities around the world means that, increasingly, people carry and use passive sensors (embedded inside of public transit tickets) to record their daily movements. Unlike mobile phones, the records held by AFC systems provide a rich and detailed source of data about peoples' transport habits: times of travel, modalities, destinations, trip durations, and fares paid. In this work, we explore the extent that this data offers the possibility to both build and measure future of travel-based ubiquitous computing applications. We focus on two potential end-users: first, how *travellers* may be aided by feedback mechanisms in order to re-align misperceptions of their travel behaviour and leverage this data to change their habits. In particular, we analyse differences between 85 travellers' surveyed perceptions of their public transport habits and their actual usage of the system. Second, how *transport authorities* can use this data to measure and implement incentive mechanisms that produce the expected impact. We use anonymised AFC data to measure the extent that financial incentives implemented by London's transport authority (such as peak-hour fares and student discounts) correlate with measurable changes in millions of travellers' behaviours.

Author Keywords
User Study, Incentive Mechanisms, Behavioural Awareness and Change

ACM Classification Keywords
H.4.m Information Systems Applications: Miscellaneous.

General Terms
Human Factors, Design, Measurement

INTRODUCTION
Many applications of pervasive computing use mobile phones or active sensors embedded into the environment in order to achieve their goals [1]; recent examples include using phones to encourage sustainable travel behaviours [2] and sensors to measure household water usage [3]. The advent and widespread adoption of automated fare collection (AFC) systems by public transport authorities around the world now means that people are also regular carriers of *passive sensors* that they may use when moving about urban spaces. These systems, based on radio-frequency identification (RFID) contactless "smart" cards (e.g., the Pasmo System in Tokyo, Japan, the Oyster card in London, England), not only store each traveller's current tickets, but generate streams of detailed travel records that allow transport operators to construct rich profiles of their passengers' habits [4, 5].

Travellers will often have complex and seemingly contradicting needs with regards to their daily travel habits, including temporal constraints (time to destination), flexibility, cost of travel, as well as being influenced by the availability of public transport and a varying willingness to engage in eco-friendly travel behaviour [2, 6]. By recording peoples' daily travel habits, smart card data implicitly captures how people balance their travel requirements, paving the way for systems that offer personalised [7] and live [8] travel information services. To date, however, this data has been studied in relation to the performance of the public transport system itself: for example, to estimate journey time or model transit demand [9, 10]. By being a system that links *individual* travellers to the public transport network, this data also has the potential to give insights into individuals' habits and test hypotheses relating to many aspects of urban mobility.

In this paper, we demonstrate how AFC records reveal hidden individuals' behaviours and responses to travel incentives. In particular, we use this data to evaluate two hypotheses, relating to two target audiences:

1. **Travellers' perceptions of their usage of public transport do not match their actual behaviour**. Are there any differences between people's perceived and actual transport-usage habits? This question is important for two reasons: (a) travellers will be basing their travel decisions on their perceptions; misperceptions may lead to incorrect decisions, and (b) feedback applications that record and visualise travellers' behaviours may leverage common misperceptions of travel to induce an awareness and encourage travellers to make positive changes in their habits.

In the first part of this paper, we report on the design of, and results from, a survey that, combined with data from smart cards, allows us to compare the differences between how 85 people report that they both purchase tickets and move in a city with how they actually do it. We believe that this is the first in-depth study to not only directly compare self-reported and actual public transport *usage*, but also the perceived relation between usage and payment.

2. **Transport operators offer incentives that do not work.** Public transport systems around the world will each have implicit incentives built into them; for example, they may implement time-varying fares (e.g., charging higher fares for rush-hour travel, to discourage non-essential travel). Do travellers respond to these incentives? We propose to test this question by using AFC data. An understanding of these aspects will be the foundation for any system that aims to stimulate additional behaviours.

   In the second part of this paper, we examine and enumerate a number of incentives that have been implemented by the public transport authority in London, England. We then seek to determine the extent that travellers are responding to these incentives by looking for evidence of the encouraged behaviour in two large, anonymised datasets of trips and ticket purchases of London travellers.

BACKGROUND: TRANSPORT FOR LONDON

The Transport for London (TfL) public transport infrastructure is a vast, multi-modal network of underground trains (11 interconnected lines with 270 stations), overground trains (5 lines with 78 stations) and buses (about 8,000 buses serving 19,000 stops) as well as trams, river services, and other specialised services. At the broadest level, travellers must opt to either use a single, contact-less smart card (the Oyster card) to pay for their journeys, or buy paper-based tickets. Travellers who use an Oyster card must decide between purchasing credit that is then deducted on a per-trip basis (i.e., using "pay as you go") or buying a travel pass (i.e., "travel card"). Pay as you go fares will vary based on the time of day, the locations of the origin and destination, and the travel modality. Travel cards, instead, are valid for unlimited travel within a certain geographic area, for a particular length of time (1 week, 1 month, 1 year), and sometimes for a specific transport modality (i.e., bus only). While these details are certainly specific to London, we note that other cities across the world share similarities. For example, New York's MetroCard allows for purchase of unlimited travel during 7-day and 30-day periods and San Francisco's BART's fares take into account length and speed of trip, as well as differentiating between user groups.

TRAVELLER SURVEY DESIGN

In order to understand how travellers *report* that they move around their city, we designed an online survey. The survey was composed of 25 questions covering two broad areas of interest: how respondents perceive their travel and how they perceive their fare purchasing habits. The first set of questions were about week day and week end travel habits: typical number of trips per day, travel time, modality of choice, whether trips are multi-modal, where their typical origin and destinations are, and how they rate the consistency of their habits (1 star was "very irregular" and 5 stars was "very regular"). The second set of questions dealt with purchasing habits instead. We split the questions into two groups: "when you use pay as you go," and "when you use travel cards." For the former, we asked *how much* credit they tend to purchase (if they ever do), and both *when* and *why* they chose to purchase credit. We also asked what travel card they bought (if they ever do), where they are valid, and why they opt for this purchase.

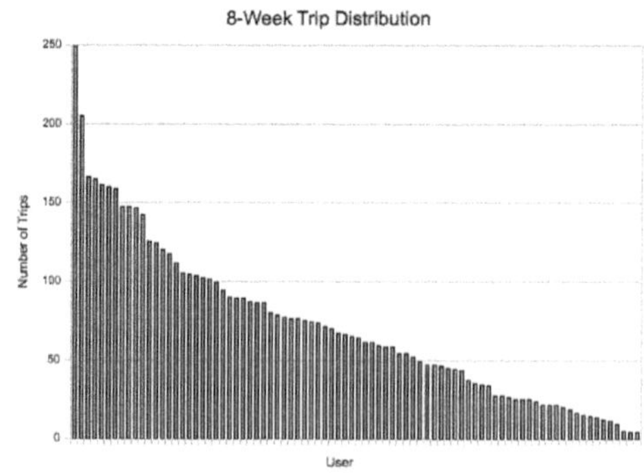

Figure 1. The user-trip distribution over 8-weeks of travel history; our respondents took between 4 and 249 trips.

SURVEY AND SMART CARD DATA COLLECTION

We disseminated the resulting web-form questionnaire online and received 119 responses. The survey data tells us about respondents' perceptions of their own mobility; the next step we took was to obtain the data of their actual trips. Transport for London currently stores eight weeks' travel history for each registered Oyster card; after the eight weeks, the data is anonymised. The last question of our survey thus asked for (a) permission to retrieve the respondent's travel history and (b) the unique identifier on their Oyster card that would enable us to do so. In total, 85 respondents allowed us to retrieve their history. Note that, once we received the data, we assigned a unique identifier to match travel history with survey responses and, in so doing, effectively re-anonymised the data (we cannot link it back to the individual users who responded to the survey). Furthermore, we explicitly did not collect any demographic information (other than the *type* of Oyster card the respondent owned) in order to comply with TfL's privacy requirements relating to disclosing the Oyster card histories. The Oyster card type gives us an indication of the demographic groups we captured in the survey: the majority of respondents (62%) owned adult Oyster cards, while 30% held 18+ student cards (required to have access to student fare discounts), 1% had 60+/Disabled "freedom" cards (which entitle the bearers to free travel), while the other 7% listed "other" or did not input an answer.

In Figure 1 we show the data's distribution of trips. In the data we received, which spans from 11 November 2010 to 1 January 2011, the respondents used their Oyster card between 4 and 249 times. This is an early indication of the widely varying requirements that city residents have with regards to their public transport network: some rely on it for

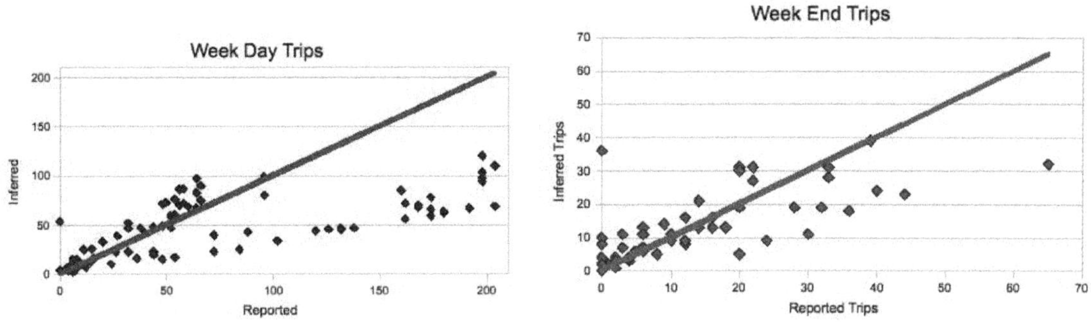

(a) Week Day Trips

(b) Week End Trips

Figure 2. Comparing the survey results and smart card data on trips per day (left, on week days; right, on week ends)

continuous use, while others will be very infrequent users. In order to compensate for seasonal effects (i.e., Christmas and New Year), when travellers habits may be change significantly, we exclude any data after December 23rd from the following analysis.

Transport for London also provided us with two additional, fully anonymised, datasets. The first contains *all* Oyster card records from a one month period (March 2010). The second contains trip, payment and Oyster card details data from a 5% sample of travellers (roughly 300,000 people) over two 83-day periods: 3 May to 25 July 2009 and 18 October 2009 to 9 January 2010. These datasets allow us to compare the results from our survey respondents to the wider population. In the following sections, we refer to these as the 100% and 5% datasets respectively.

COMPARING PERCEIVED AND ACTUAL BEHAVIOUR

The first hypothesis that we test is whether travellers' perceptions of public transport usage match their actual usage of the system. In this section, we compare the *reported* behaviours from our survey to the smart-card recorded trips made by the survey respondents. We decompose the analysis into a number of sections: trips per day, travel times, choice of modality, geographic areas of interest, and fare purchasing habits. Following this comparison, we summarise the key findings and enumerate a number of opportunities for feedback-based systems that leverage this data.

Trips Per Day: Incorrectly Estimating Transport Usage

The first point on which we compare the survey and smart card data is the estimated trips per day. We defined a "trip" as a journey from one place to another using public transport. As an example, we described going from home to work and back home again as two trips. Respondents had to estimate how many trips they take in a typical week day and week end day (Saturday *or* Sunday), and were asked whether their typical trips are multi-modal. We then compute how many trips they have taken per day by looking at their Oyster history. To account for potential multi-modal trips, we only count a smart card swipe as a new trip if it is at least half an hour after the last trip's exit swipe. In Figure 2, we compare the reported and inferred values. In particular, we multiply the reported value (e.g., "2 trips per week day") by the number of (week day) travel days that we observe in the data, and compare this result to the number of actual inferred trips from the data. In this case, making an accurate estimate of one's daily travel habits translates into a value that lies near the $y = x$ line (shown in each figure). We find that a large proportion of users consistently overestimate their usage of public transport: the *inferred* values are less than those that were *reported*. The distance between each point and the $y = x$ line shows the extent that travellers incorrectly estimate their travel habits. By normalising each distance by the number of days each user has travelled, we can get an intuition as to just how far estimation errors arise: in the week day data, travellers are off by 1.77 ± 1.51 trips; on week ends, this value lessens to 0.98 ± 0.88 per user.

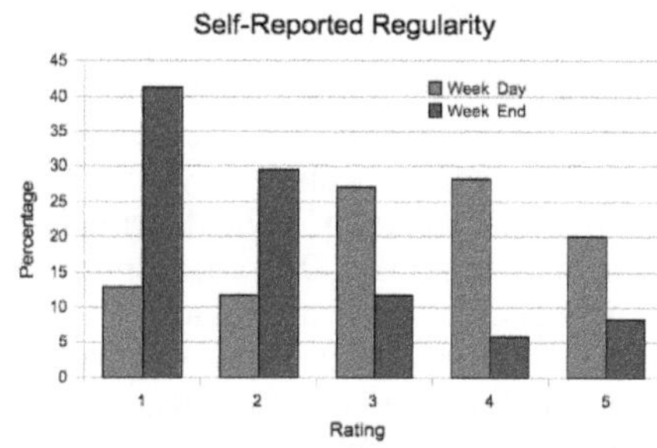

Figure 3. Comparing the survey respondents' self-evaluated trip regularity (where 1* is "very irregular" and 5* is "very regular") for week days and week ends.

Users were also given the option to claim that they never use public transport during week days: 2 of the 85 respondents opted for this answer. However, the smart card data held no evidence of this: all of the respondents used the public transport system in (at least) 1 week day. As per Figure 1, this may be explained by low-frequency travellers (for example, those who used public transport 4 times in the data). The differences between reported and computed average trips per day on week ends (Figure 2(b)) are not as high as the week day data. A total of 18 respondents claimed to not travel during week ends, and 17 smart card histories were missing week end trips. As before, many respondents tend to underestimate the number of trips they take, while overestimating that they only take 1 trip.

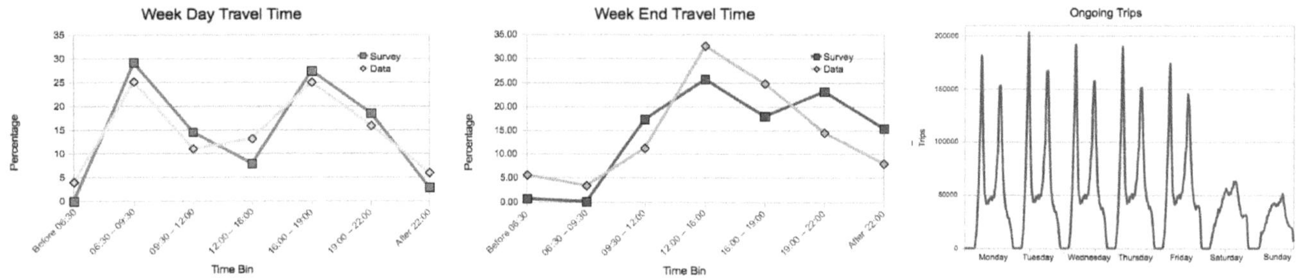

(a) Week Day Trip Times (b) Week End Trip Times (c) 100% Dataset Avg Week

Figure 4. Comparing the survey results and smart card data on trip times per day (left, on week days; middle, on week ends) along with the number of ongoing trips in the anonymised dataset London travellers, clearly showing the commuting trends during week days.

In this case, the data shows that, in general, respondents are unable to accurately estimate how much they use public transport. Respondents were also asked to rate the extent that they believe their week day or week end trips are regular; where a 1 star rating means "very irregular" and a 5 star rating implies "very regular." The distributions of these ratings are shown in Figure 3. Overall, respondents tend to claim that their week day trips are regular (the distribution is biased toward the right), while week end trips are irregular (the distribution leans toward the left). This result contrasts the previous comparisons, where we found that travellers were better at estimating the frequency of their week end trips: it thus seems that travellers are better at estimating their irregular travel habits!

Travel Times and Peak-Time Commutes

The second topic covered in the survey asked about typical travel times. The available answers were split into ranges: before 06:30 AM, 06:30 to 09:30 AM, 09:30 to 12 PM, 12 to 4 PM, 4 to 7 PM, 7 to 10 PM, and after 10 PM. These bins include the two peak-fare times defined by TfL (06:30 to 09:30 AM and 4PM to 7PM), when week day travel, on a single fare, is more expensive. Unlike before, we found that, in this case, respondents' claims were closer to their actual data in the week days rather than week ends (Figures 4(a) and 4(b)). This is likely due to commitments relating to work: the two-spiked commuting pattern clearly emerges in both the survey and travel history data. However, travel outside of peak hours is underestimated; these may include, for example, opportunistic trips taken during lunch-time hours. A difference of a similar magnitude appears in the week end data (Figure 4(b)), where respondents report that they travel later than they actually do.

We also looked into the 100% Oyster card datasets to seek out any differences in the respondents of our survey and the wider population. In Figure 4(c), we show the cumulative ongoing trips over a week. The two-spiked commuting trend is very apparent in this data too, especially when compared to the pattern observed on week end days.

Travel Modality: Flexible or Opportunistic Trips

TfL operates a large multi-modal network. By turning to the smart card data and examining the distribution of travellers' trips with different transport modes (Figure 5(a)), we find that the underground (the "tube") is the most popular transport option, with over 50% of week day trips. However, there is a distinct shift on week ends, when buses carry a higher proportion of travellers than the underground instead (although, compared to week days, there are fewer trips).

The survey included a question of typical transport modality. In this case, we can use the travel modes that people claim to use on typical days to infer trips that may fall outside of their routine, and quantify how much of their travel history represents a-typical trips. We first examined the proportion of users who did not claim to use a particular modality, but actually did during their Oyster history. For example, we looked for respondents who reported to only use the underground during the week, but had week day bus trips registered in their travel history. Of the 85 total users, 47 (55.3%) used modalities that they did not claim to typically use during week days. On week ends, this number fell to 27 (31.8%).

An intuitive explanation of these numbers would be that respondents are telling us what they "typically" do, and this mismatch may arise from irregular, off-the-beaten track trips. If this were the case, we would expect that the proportion of these trips would be low, compared to all the trips by each traveller. In other words, if a person claims to not ride the bus during the week, but has done so, we would expect that the proportion of week day bus trips for this user would be small compared to the total number of trips taken. We therefore computed the distribution of per-user trip proportions that are taken on modalities that they claim to *not* use. The resulting distributions are in Figures 5(b) and 5(c); the corresponding means are 17.17% for week days and 30.70% for week ends. This means that, in our data, respondents take an average of 30.70% of all their week end trips on modalities that they did not claim to normally use on weekends. Both of the figures show a power-law distribution; most notably, there are some users who have taken more than half of their trips on modalities that they did not report to use.

There are two points to note here. First, the travellers with a very high proportion of these trips have a varying number of trips in their history (i.e., some of them are irregular users of public transport). Figures 5(b) and 5(c) include points that denote the total number of trips that each user has. The plots

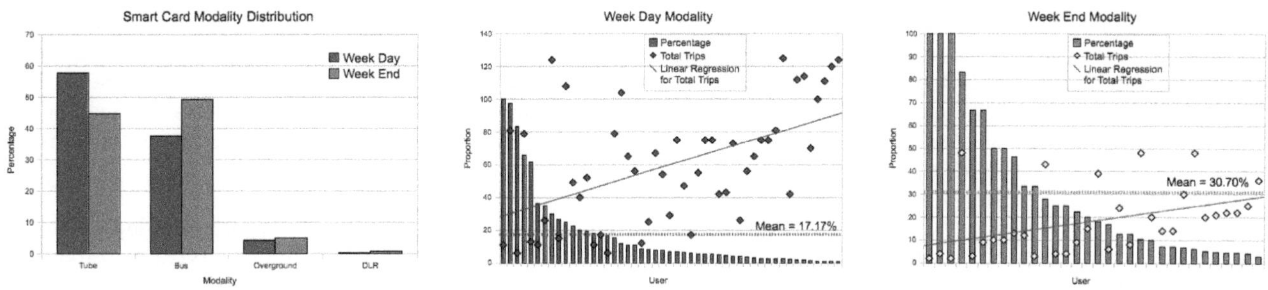

(a) Smart Card Modality Distribution (b) Week Day (c) Week End

Figure 5. Usage of transport modalities: (a) the week day and week end distributions of trips on the underground, buses, overground rail and the Docklands Light Railway (DLR) system based on smart card data, (b) the distribution of the proportion of respondent's week day trips that they spend on modalities they do not typically use, along with the number of trips their smart card data contains, and (c) the same for week end data.

include a trend line, which is a linear regression on the total trips data. Both trend lines have a positive slope: as users have a higher number of trips, the proportion of trips that occur on modalities that they do not report to use decreases. However, there are exceptions to this trend. The dataset includes travellers who have both a high number of historical trips and a high proportion of trips on unreported modalities.

Origins, Destinations, and a-Typical Stations

The survey also asked respondents to list their rail trips' typical origins and destinations (the form itself allowed for an unlimited number of stations to be listed). By comparing these station names to the recorded smart card data, we can discover the extent that users travel between a fixed number of locations. As above, we are interested in comparing two variables: the proportion of trips that include an origin or destination that is *not* listed as a typical place and the total number of trips taken by that user. We note that two respondents used generic terms (e.g., "various," "others") when listing their week end destinations. One respondent even appended a comment to a station name: "when open," reflecting that this station is often closed during week ends due to ongoing construction work. Since we had no means of mapping generic terms to specific locations, we disregarded these users from the analysis.

On average, 64.09% of each respondent's week day rail trips were from or to a station that they did not list as a typical location. On week ends, that average rises to 87.86%. As above, the total number of trips in each user's smart card data is inversely proportional to percentage of user trips that include a-typical origins or destinations. In other words, the survey respondents who were more frequent users of public transport were better at enumerating the stations that they use. The adoption of generic terms further indicates that the respondents themselves seem to be aware of the fact that week end mobility is less likely to be between familiar locations, as they are not constrained by work-related commitments, and more likely to be disrupted by station closures. However, the average week day trips per user that include a-typical stations remains high.

There are two types of trips that may explain this trend: (a) ad-hoc, opportunistic trips that travellers do not consider to be typical, and (b) adaptive travel behaviours (e.g., alighting at an earlier station and walking) when responding to congestion, station closures, or unforeseen events.

Cash-Fare Purchasing Habits: Overestimating Cost

There is currently no system for travellers to relate the way they use public transport to their fare purchasing habits [11]. Recall that travellers can opt to pay for their trips on a per-trip basis by buying travel credit (using *"pay as you go"* fares), or use 7-day, monthly, or annual passes, also called *travel cards*. The act of adding pay as you go credit to an Oyster card is denoted as "topping up," and travellers may do so online, via ticket machines or attendants in stations, or in local shops. In this section, we focus on these cash-fares that are bought by travellers.

In the survey, we asked users how much they typically top-up by each time they do so. The largest groups claimed that they spent between GBP 5 and 10 (33.78%), and between GBP10 and 20 (35.14%) at each purchase. The smart card data contained all the top-up amounts of our respondents; using this, we can compare the amounts that travellers *think* they typically spend at each purchase and how much they actually do, on average, spend each time. The data contained 381 purchases; in Figure 6 we compare the range that users claim to purchase within at each purchase and the actual average of all their purchases. Overall, majority of the

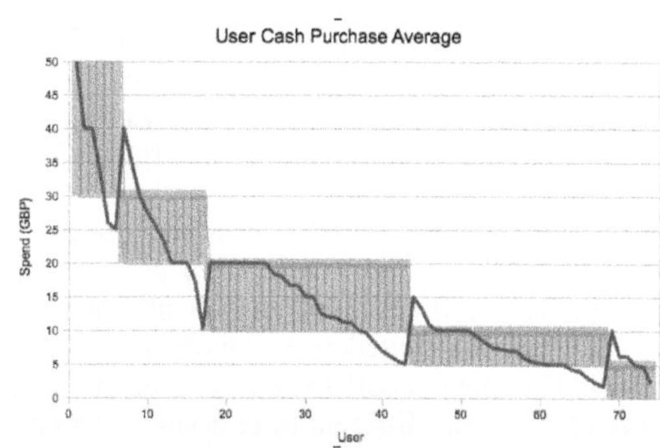

Figure 6. (Blocks) The ranges that users claim to spend when they top up and (line) their smart card average cash purchase: 20.27% of these users claim to spend more than they do.

averages fall within the range claimed by the respondent; we find that 10.81% spend, on average, more than they claim to. However, more importantly, 20.27% of respondents actually spend, on average, less than they claim: the average amount they spend per purchase is less than they claim. This is a substantial group of users who spend less on public transport than they think.

The 5% dataset also contained all of the top-up amounts of the sample of travellers, amounting to 3,379,570 top-up transactions. In these, we found that top-ups of less than GBP 5 accounted for 49.8% of all transactions, and 24.2% were between GBP 5 and 10. The minimum credit card transaction at ticketing machines is GBP 5 (which is also the smallest bank note value): these are thus top-ups made using coins. These figures show a much higher proportion of very small transactions than both our survey and respondents' Oyster histories showed, which reflects on the socio-economic status of the respondents we were able to reach (who were mostly university staff and students–people who have access to the web).

Summary: Opportunities for Feedback Applications

The analysis above displayed a wide variety of traveller behaviours. Differences emerge between travellers (reflecting differences between individuals' travel requirements) and between what survey respondents reported and actually did (misperceptions of travel patterns). In this section, we summarise our findings and relate them to potential applications that may be built from passively collected transport data.

Public Transport Usage Awareness. We noted that, while most respondents are using public transport less than they claim (Figures 2(a) and 2(b)), some clearly over-estimate how much they do, by reporting they take over five trips on a typical day. These results complement research that relate giving feedback to the uptake of public transport: behavioural awareness, in some cases, lead to an increase in public transport by 50% [12].

Regularity of Travel and Real-Time Information. Majority of respondents rated their weekend trips as highly irregular, but provided better estimates of how many trips they take on these days. Regularity thus seems to be a notion that is associated with time of travel (Figures 4(a) and 4(b)) and destinations rather than the amount of travel itself. This result could be used to augment research on real-time travel alerts, where feedback has been shown to reduce waiting time and increase travellers' satisfaction with public transit [13].

Journey Planning by Context. 17.17% of respondents' week day trips and 30.70% of their week end trips were taken on modalities that they did not report to typically use. This result may indicate that travellers are more flexible in their travel habits than they report to be. The clear distinction in modality choice over different time periods is a key piece of information that AFC data can feed into trip planning systems.

Exploring the City. More than half of respondents' week day rail trips included a station that was not listed amongst their typical origins or destinations. Mobility data like this can be used to build recommender systems for city residents, letting them discover locations and social events that may be of interest to them, both in areas that they commonly frequent and unexplored parts of the city [14].

Fare Purchase Awareness. When considering only credit-based purchases, 20.27% of respondents claim to spend more than they actually do. Note that this statistic says nothing about those who buy the incorrect fare (where there was a cheaper option) and do not realise how much they might have saved. Building systems that facilitate the cost-effective use of public transport may also attract those travellers whose primary concern is how much they need to pay [11].

CORRELATING INCENTIVES AND BEHAVIOUR

In the above, we focused on how travellers perceive their behaviour. We now turn to an alternative: how transport operators try to influence travellers' decisions. Travellers' behavioural choices are often guided by conflicting requirements: for example, the need to be at work on time vs. the choice of the cheapest modality; these choices may be swayed in a particular direction by providing different forms of incentives. Much like airlines, transport operators could give "reward miles" to loyal customers that can later be exchanged for free travel; they could also build games and design dynamic fare systems that encourage travellers to make use of their services. Incentives in the public transport domain are already well established: for example, bike sharing users in Paris, France, are given credit for taking bicycles to up-hill stations[1]. In this section, we show how AFC data can also highlight the incentives that travellers are responding to, and those that have no effect. In particular, we focus on the relation between usage and a number of features of the pricing system in London that are aimed to trigger particular travel and purchase behaviours.

Travel Cards: Encouraging Public Transport Usage

Oyster card users can choose to pay for public transport in a variety of ways. As above, the first decision is whether to purchase credit that will then be docked from their smart card on a per-trip basis (pay as you go) or buy a fixed-price pass that allows unlimited travel within a certain geographic area over a specified amount of time (a travel card). Travel cards may also be solely for use on buses or not restricted by modality at all.

The most generic difference between pay as you go and travel cards is that the former entails multiple (incremental) payments, while the latter requires a single payment followed by unlimited use. Since an important concern for travellers who use public transport is cost [2], the implications seems to be that the purchase of a travel card not only reduces the barrier to entry into the system (since, throughout the validity of the travel card, no further financial commitments need to be made) but will also act as an implicit incentive to use the system, in order for travellers to feel that their

[1]http://blog.velib.paris.fr/blog/?p=318

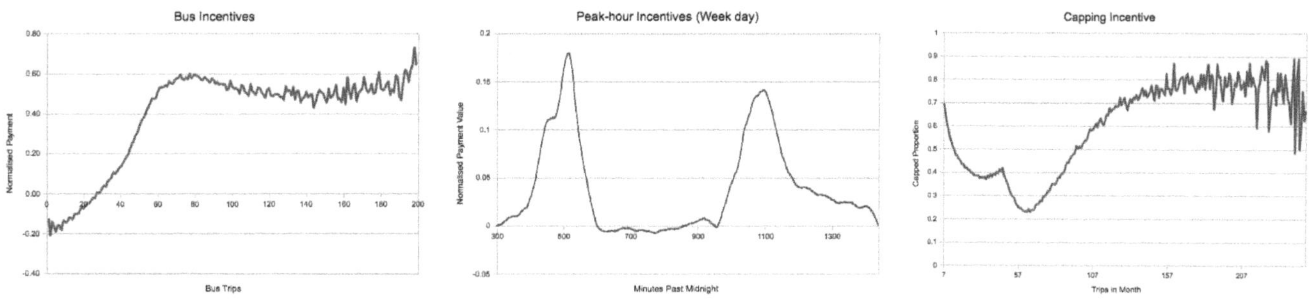

(a) Bus Usage and Payment (b) Week Day Payment Groups (c) Effect of Price Capping

Figure 7. Examining the effect of pricing incentives: positive values indicate a higher proportion of travel card passengers, while negative values represent a higher proportion of pay as you go passengers. Figure (a) shows that travel card owners will use buses more, Figure (b) reproduces the 2-spike commuting pattern and shows that pay as you go passengers tend to avoid peak-times, Figure (c) shows that pay as you go travellers who are given free travel (capped) will travel more.

initial payment is well spent. Does a fixed fare, with unlimited travel, encourage travellers to use public transport more? To examine whether this incentive is reflected in the Oyster data, we focus on bus usage. Buses are not the most popular form of transit, and since they can be used for opportunistic trips (where even walking may be a viable alternative), they are most likely to show whether travel cards correlate with a higher use of the system. Unfortunately, since buses only require travellers to use their smart card upon entry, we cannot know how far each person travelled. The 100% dataset contains a total of 172,286,012 smart card bus trips. We pruned all of those which were taken with bus-only passes, leaving 115,173,544 trips. If travel cards were *not* an incentive to use buses, then we would expect travel card holders to use buses as much as non-travel card holders. More formally, we were able to quantify, for each traveller, how many trips she/he took in that month, and how many of them were taken using pay as you go or a travel card. We binned the data by number of trips; for each number of trips taken in the month i, we have $N_{i,PAYG}$ travellers on pay as you go and $N_{i,TC}$ travellers on travel card. We combined each pair of values as follows:

$$V_i = \frac{N_{i,TC} - N_{i,PAYG}}{N_{i,TC} + N_{i,PAYG}} \quad (1)$$

The normalised values V_i will be -1 when all of the travellers are on pay as you go, $+1$ if all the travellers are using travel cards, and 0 if there is an equal number of each. If travel cards were not an incentive to use buses, then we would expect all of these normalised values to be zero. The results, comparing number of bus trips taken in the month to the normalised value, is shown in Figure 7(a). Not only are none of the values zero, but there is a clear inflection point (from pay as you go to travel cards) at 28 trips in the month (an average of just below 1 bus trip per day): after this point, the use of travel cards vastly exceeds the use of pay as you go on the bus network.

Overall, in the data, 61% of bus trips and 75% of rail trips are completed using travel cards. This is both evidence that per-trip payment reduces the usage of public transport and that low-frequency users of public transport will opt to pay per-trip.

Peak Times: Discouraging Non-Commuters

The public transport authority in London has also implemented time-varying fares: during week days, between 06:30 to 09:30 and 16:00 to 19:00, pay as you go fares are more expensive (on rail services only). The change in price only affects pay as you go users; those commuters who are travelling with travel cards are exempt from fare differences between the peak and off-peak hours. The explicit rule is aimed to act as in incentive for non-essential travel to be avoided, in order to reduce congestion; this may couple with payment since those who are less frequent travellers will (or potentially should) be using pay as you go. However, as Figure 4(c) shows, the spikes in congestion remain unaffected by this rule. Is there any evidence to show that non-essential travel is being avoided (i.e., that this incentive works)?

As above, we can investigate the extent the smart card data holds evidence of the effect of this incentive by grouping travellers. The dataset contains 78,005,747 week day rail trips. From these, we compute two vectors, counting the normalised ongoing trips with travel cards and with pay as you go:

$$T_i = \frac{N_{i,TC}}{max(N_{TC})}; P_i = \frac{N_{i,PAYG}}{max(N_{PAYG})} \quad (2)$$

In this case, we performed the normalisation step first to account for the higher proportion of travel card trips that are taking place. We then combine each pair, in order to see the relative bias towards one fare type (pay as you go or travel card) over the course of a day:

$$V_i = T_i - P_i \quad (3)$$

As above, V_i will be positive when all trips are taken using travel cards and negative when there is a majority of pay as you go being used. If the variable fare structure did not sway travellers' decisions, then we would expect the combined and normalised distribution to be close to zero at all times (i.e., the balance between pay as you go and travel cards would be roughly the same at all times).

First, recall that the two-spiked commuting pattern, the number of ongoing trips over time, was displayed in Figure 4(c). The unnormalised vectors did already show that there are more trips outside of peak hours using pay as you go. The opposite is true for peak hours. After combining and normalising the data, shown in Figures 7(b) (week days), this pattern is highlighted even more clearly: by looking at the relative distribution over time of the fares that travellers use to access public transport, which have, built into them, incentives for peak and off-peak travel, we reproduce two-spiked commuting pattern. The travel data clearly shows that peak-fare pricing does not prevent peak-hours from being the most congested: what these results show is that peak-fare pricing, instead, guides travellers' purchasing decisions rather than their choice to travel.

Daily Capping: Switching to Free Travel

Pay as you go Oyster card usage is also subject to "daily capping:" the amount of credit that will be deducted from the traveller's smart card will not exceed the equivalent price of buying a daily travel card. In other words, once the capping threshold has been reached, travel throughout the rest of the day is free. This switch from paid to free travel should inherently act as an incentive to use public transport. For example, travellers may opt to use a bus (instead of a car, or even instead of walking) for short, opportunistic trips once they have already reached their daily cap.

The 100% dataset contains 91,391,155 trips taken using pay as you go. Of these, 90.37% are uncapped trips; travellers in this fare group often do not reach the capping limit. However, if their behaviour were unchanged when they do, we would expect to see a similar distribution of modality usage across both groups. In the uncapped group, 54.83% of trips are taken with buses. However, if we focus on the capped group, the proportion of bus trips rises to 73.53%. Suddenly, the usage of buses has become much more attractive.

We can examine this further by comparing the number of pay as you go trips that a traveller makes throughout the month with the proportion of those trips that have been capped (and are thus free). We consider *proportions* of trips since travellers need to pay until they reach the cap. Therefore, if they never do reach this cap (even if they still travel often) then a low proportion of their trips will be free. By averaging across all users we can see the trend that emerges across the city. The results are shown in Figure 7(c), where the x-axis denotes number of trips taken in the month and the y-axis is the average proportion of capped trips. The pay as you go travellers who are using the system the most are those who are taking advantage of the free travel they have earned.

Students Do Not Purchase Discounted Fares

The 5% sample data we have contains 184,923 students, identified by the type of Oyster card they use (note that TfL has no requirement that students must have student cards). This card is valid throughout their period of study, and allows them to purchase travel cards at a discounted price (pay as you go is not discounted). We have a total of 10,723,473 trips taken by the students, and 48,888,268 trips taken by everyone else. If students were unaffected by the prospect of a discount for their travel card purchases, we would expect the relative proportion of trips taken with each fare type to be similar. However, we find that students slightly favour pay as you go trips: 35.15% of their trips were credit-based, compared to 31.88% of the pay as you go trips taken by everyone else (a difference of 3.27%). The data seems to show that students are not attracted to buying discounted travel cards.

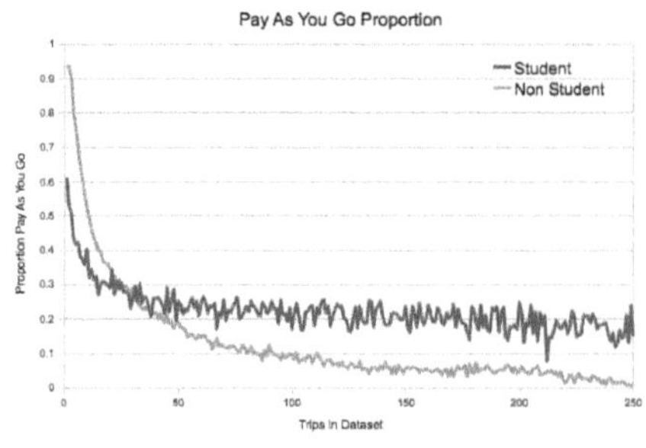

Figure 8. Comparing the number of trips taken in the dataset to the proportions of trips by students and non-students that were made using pay as you go. Although students are offered discounts for travel cards, even those who travel frequently use travel cards less than other travellers.

We can deepen this analysis by comparing students and non-students who have the same travel requirements, or make the same number of trips in the dataset's time period. As before, if two people have the same high levels of travel requirements (expressed as number of trips in a given period) and one is a student, the availability of the discount would seem to imply that the student will be more likely to be using a travel card. In Figure 8, we find that the opposite is true. By plotting number of trips to average per-traveller proportion of trips using pay as you go, we find that the students who take a large number of trips consistently average more pay as you go trips than everyone else.

The data thus suggests that students are, overall, not benefitting from the discounts they are offered. There are a number of potential explanation for this. For example, purchasing a travel card requires a larger one-off payment than pay as you go (even though, cumulatively, more may be spent on pay as you go), and students may not feel to be in a financial position to commit to such a payment. The purchase of a travel card may be unappealing for other reasons too: one survey respondent commented that "as a student with a flexible timetable, it isn't always obvious whether a travel card is a better deal than pay as you go," while another stated that "my travel habits change every semester depending on courses."

Summary: Evidence of Financial Incentives

In this section, we have observed how smart cards can measure the effect of incentives given to travellers. All of the incentives operated by TfL are financial: they balance a ticket type (which has a cost) with an intended behaviour. However, we did not find that the former (ticket type or cost) always affects the latter (travel pattern); in fact, in some cases, the opposite is true. Furthermore, a number of relations emerged:

Accessibility and Balancing Requirements. By allowing passengers to easily access the system (with a one-off payment followed by unlimited travel), travel cards encourage higher use of the system: this is particularly noticed by the significantly higher proportion of bus trips that are taken by these travellers (note that bus stops do not have facilities—like train stations—to recharge Oyster credit).

Free Travel. As expected, those travellers who use pay as you go but reach the daily capping limit (after which travel is no longer charged for) are encouraged to, overall, use the system more. This relates to research by Shampanier, Mazar, and Ariely [15], who looked at the (often drastic) effect that free, or the appearance of free, services have on the purchasing options of customers.

Targeted Discounts. We found that not all students benefit from discounts — due to the fact that the discounted fares (travel cards) either do not match their travel requirements, which are often infrequent, or their budget of available funds. This observation once again highlights the relative importance of various travel requirements to different travellers (and demographic groups).

DISCUSSION

The cornerstone of the analysis above is the rising adoption of automated fare collection systems by public transport authorities, which translates into an ever-increasing number of travellers who carry passive sensors that record their travel behaviours. Although our focus was on London (Oyster), similar systems are in place in Beijing (Yikatong), Hong Kong (Octopus), Washington D.C. (SmarTrip), and Seattle (Orca), as well as many other cities around the world. Each system is designed in a unique way, both in terms of fare structure and geographic layout. However, the homogenising characteristic–the use of contact-less smart-cards–means that all of these systems will be subject to similar analysis.

Although the main task of these smart cards has been to act as a sensing device, to facilitate public transport access and payment, these powerful sources of data now also have the potential to become integral components of technologies aimed at *two* different audiences: towards both the travellers and transport operators. By being a source of long-term, individual public transport usage data for an entire city of commuters, these smart cards are powerful means of measuring how people use public transport (to aide future systems' design), how their perceptions reflect their actual usage (to build feedback applications), and the extent that they respond to incentives that are designed to encourage public transport usage (to measure the effectiveness of policy). In the future, as means for secure access to this data are enabled, a variety of applications may be designed to leverage it and help and promote urban mobility with public transport. The effect of any introduced incentive will be quantifiable using similar analysis on smart card data.

There are a number of dimensions of urban mobility that we did not cover in this work and leave as future work; for example, we did not investigate how users respond to or seek travel information when disruptions or delays occur. London also implemented a road congestion charge in 2003 (and extended it in 2007): drivers must pay a fixed fare to drive into the centre of the city between 7AM and 6PM during week days. Our Oyster data is from 2009 and 2010: earlier samples of the data would indeed show whether drivers were opting to leave their cars at home in exchange for a commute by public transport. However, an important caveat remains: reducing road congestion will eventually encourage travellers to return to their own vehicles [16]. The introduction of shared bicycles in cities around the world[2] now presents the opportunity to also build applications that intertwine exercise, health, and mobility using public transport.

RELATED WORK

Mobility has been a central theme of research into ubiquitous systems; an important theme in this area has been detecting mobility and inferring human activity from mobile phone data [17, 18, 19]. This data can then be leveraged to, for example, build social event recommender systems [14] or understand the design of a city via travel flows [20]. In this paper, we argue that AFC data is equally important for the design of future systems that will guide travel behaviour, manage travellers' individual needs, and provide incentives for sustainable transport. AFC data has the added benefit of not requiring an inference algorithm to operate on it (in order to, for example, classify transport modality [19]): the data itself contains fine grained details of travellers' behaviours.

Recent work has also examined how blind and deaf-blind people use public transit systems [21]. AFC records are also a rich, and non-invasive source of data about how this particular target group (along with all city residents who are ineligible for car licenses) use public transport[3].

The disparity between survey respondents' reports and their actual actions extends beyond transport contexts. Recently, similar investigations into shoppers' behaviours highlighted that shoppers claim to be more ethical in their purchasing choices than they actually are [22]. Our work is also part of a growing literature on voluntary behavioural change relating to public transport usage [23], including mobile-based solutions that visually represent the sustainability of travellers' choices [2, 24]. Mankoff et al. [25] have also investigated the role that social networks play in moulding peoples' decisions. The most direct form of incentive that is often built into mobile applications is based on earning rewards for behaving in a specified way. Often, those rewards are virtual: such is the case in the Ubigreen interface proposed by Froehlich et al. [2].

CONCLUSION

In this paper, we demonstrated how AFC records reveal hidden aspects of individuals' behaviours. To date, research on this data has focused on measuring the transport system's performance: in this work, we show how complimentary analysis can be used to measure the needs and choices of the system's end users.

[2]For example, http://www.tfl.gov.uk/roadusers/cycling/14808.aspx
[3]See: http://www.freedompass.org

We first addressed mis-alignments between self-reported and actual behaviour: we compared travel perceptions and smart card data from 85 London residents, and uncovered a number of differences that pave the way for future feedback-based travel applications. Many respondents were already using public transport more than they claimed to; we also determined that travel regularity is related to destinations and time of travel rather than the amount of travel. We also examined the extent that travellers (a) use modalities and (b) take trips from stations that they do not include in reports of their typical behaviour.

We then examined the extent that smart cards can be used to measure travellers' responses to various incentives, by comparing behavioural patterns with TfL's cost-related incentives. We showed that students do not tend to buy the discounted fares, and that switching to free travel does indeed encourage a higher use of the system. More generally, these results demonstrate that AFC data is a powerful too for measuring the success or failure of travel incentives.

Acknowledgements

The authors would like to thank Angela Sasse and Philip Inglesant for comments on the survey design. The research leading to these results has received funding from the European Community's Seventh Framework Programme (FP7-SST-2008-RTD-1) under Grant Agreement n. 234239.

REFERENCES

1. T. Choudhury et al. The Mobile Sensing Platform: An Embedded System for Capturing and Recognizing Human Activities. *IEEE Pervasive Computing*, 7(2), 2008.
2. J. Froehlich, S. Consolvo, T. Dillahunt, B. Harrison, P. Klasnja, J. Mankoff, and J. Landay. UbiGreen: Investigating a Mobile Tool for Tracking and Supporting Green Transportation Habits. In *ACM CHI*, Boston, USA, April 2009.
3. T. Campbell, E. Larson, G. Cogn, J. Froehlich, R. Alcaide, and S. Patel. WATTR: A Method for Self-Powered Wireless Sensing of Water Activities in the Home. In *ACM Ubicomp*, Copenhagen, Denmark, September 2010.
4. W. Jang. Travel Time and Transfer Analysis Using Transit Smart Card Data. *Transportation Research Board*, 2010.
5. H. Bryan and P. Blythe. Understanding Behaviour Through Smartcard Data Analysis. *Proceedings of the Institution of Civil Engineers: Transport*, 160(4), 2007.
6. L Frank, B Saelens, K. Powell, and J. Chapman. Stepping Towards Causation: Do Built Environments or Neighbourhoods and Travel Preferences Explain Physical Activity, Driving, and Obesity? *Social Science and Medicine*, 65, 2007.
7. N. Lathia, J. Froehlich, and L. Capra. Mining Public Transport Usage for Personalised Intelligent Transport Systems. In *IEEE ICDM*, Sydney, Australia, December 2010.
8. B. Ferris, K. Watkins, and A. Borning. OneBusAway: Results from Providing Real-Time Arrival Information for Public Transit. In *ACM CHI*, Atlanta, GA, 2010.
9. J. Chan. Rail Transit OD Matrix Estimation and Journey Time Reliability Metrics Using Automated Fare Data. Master's thesis, MIT, Department of Civil and Environmental Engineering, June 2007.
10. K. Chu and R. Chapleau. Enriching Archived Smart Card Transaction Data for Transit Demand Modeling. *Journal of the Transportation Research Board*, (2063), 2008.
11. N. Lathia and L. Capra. Mining Mobility Data to Minimise Travellers' Spending on Public Transport. In *ACM KDD*, San Diego, California, August 2011.
12. S. Fujii and A. Taniguchi. Determinants of the Effectiveness of Travel Feedback Programs: A Review of Communicative Mobility Management Measures for Changing Travel Behaviour in Japan. *Transport Policy*, 13, September 2006.
13. K. Dziekan and K. Kottenhoff. Dynamic At-Stop Real-Time Information Displays for Public Transport: Effects on Customers. *Transportation Research Part A*, 41, July 2007.
14. D. Quercia, N. Lathia, F. Calabrese, G. Di Lorenzo, and J. Crowcroft. Recommending Social Events from Mobile Phone Location Data. In *IEEE ICDM*, Sydney, Australia, December 2010.
15. K. Shampanier, N. Mazar, and D. Ariely. Zero as a Special Price: The True Value of Free Products. *Marketing Science*, 26(6):742–757, 2007.
16. S. Cairns, L. Sloman, C. Newson, J. Anable, A. Kirkbride, and P. Goodwin. Smarter Choices: Changing the Way We Travel. *Department for Transport, London*, July 2004.
17. D. Choujaa and N. Dulay. Predicting Human Behaviour from Selected Mobile Phone Data Points. In *ACM Ubicomp*, Copenhagen, Denmark, September 2010.
18. T. Sohn et al. Mobility Detection Using Everyday GSM Traces. In *ACM Ubicomp*, Orange County, USA, 2006.
19. Y. Zheng, Q. Li, Y. Chen, X. Xie, and W. Ma. Understanding Mobility Based on GPS Data. In *ACM Ubicomp*, Seoul, Korea, 2008.
20. C. Roth, S.M. Kang, M. Batty, and M. Barthelemy. Structure of Urban Movements: Polycentric Activity and Entangled Hierarchical Flows. *PLoS ONE*, 6, 2010.
21. S. Azenkot, S. Prasain, A. Borning, E. Fortuna, R. Ladner, and J. Wobbrock. Enhancing Independence and Safety for Blind and Deaf-Blind Public Transit Riders. In *ACM CHI*, Vancouver, Canada, 2011.
22. T. Devinney, P. Auger, and G. M. Eckhardt. Values vs. value. http://bit.ly/eodkAT, March 2011.
23. E. Ampt. Understanding Voluntary Travel Behavior Change. *Australasian Transport Research Forum*, 22, 2003.
24. T. Dillahunt, G. Becker, J. Mankoff, and R. Kraut. Motivating Environmentally Sustainable Behavior Changes with a Virtual Polar Bear. In *Workshop on Pervasive Persuasive Technology and Environmental Sustainability (Pervasive)*, 2008.
25. J. Mankoff, D. Mattews, S. Fussel, and M. Johnson. Leveraging Social Networks to Motivate Individuals to Reduce their Ecological Footprints. In *HICSS*, Waikoloa, Hawaii, 2007.

Mediated Tabletop Interaction in the Biology Lab Exploring the Design Space of The Rabbit

Juan David Hincapié-Ramos, Aurélien Tabard, Jakob E. Bardram
IT University of Copenhagen
{jdhr, auta, bardram}@itu.dk

ABSTRACT
Interactive surfaces like diffuse illumination tabletops (DIT) identify and track objects using multiple techniques like shape and color recognition, fiducial markers, electronic components, and RFID tags. However, tracking becomes more complex when dealing with multiple small objects of similar form. We propose to use tangible mediators for integrating such objects to tabletops. This paper reports on our initial explorations of *mediated tabletop interaction* consisting of a mediator prototype and a design space definition. We built a mediator, the *Rabbit*, a device that translates the value of an RFID tag into a visual 2D code. The *Rabbit* rests on the interactive surface, holds the object, reads its passive RFID tag, and converts the read value into a 2D code that can be read by the DIT's built-in camera. When handling multiple objects, the Rabbit iterates through the generated 2D codes. Through a series of participatory activities with end users (molecular biologists), we collected initial feedback from participants and defined a design space for mediated tabletop interaction.

Author Keywords
Mediated Tabletop Interaction, The Rabbit, Tabletop, Tangible, Interactive Surfaces, RFID

ACM Classification Keywords
H.5.2 Information Interfaces and Presentation: User Interfaces: Input Devices and Strategies, Interaction Styles

General Terms
Design, Human Factors

INTRODUCTION
One of the interesting features of interactive surfaces is the merging of input and output into a single space. This dual-space allows designers to go beyond simple touch interactions, to integrate physical objects as interactive tools on the surface; either to augment objects with digital information and/or use objects as a controllers of the digital system. To achieve this level of integration, objects have to be identifiable by the system, for which several techniques have been proposed: shape and color recognition, RFID tags, active electronic components, and fiducial markers.

UbiComp'11, September 17–21, 2011, Beijing, China.

By working with tabletops in a biology laboratory setting, we uncovered several unexpected constrains for deploying interactive surfaces. Besides supporting extreme usage conditions like radioactivity, designing with reduced UI space and pervasive clutter on the surface, a difficult problem that we faced was the tracking of small objects. Small objects like test tubes are at the core of laboratory work: they do not only contain physical substances, but are now often related to digital information. When biologists order samples from a commercial supplier they also receive spreadsheets describing what they ordered and links to detailed descriptions of the materials. Therefore, integrating test tubes with an interactive laboratory bench could bring to the biology lab some of the benefits the Ubicomp community has explored elsewhere like, for example, better support for the processes of information access and situated data capture. However, test tubes and interactive surfaces cannot be integrated by using existing techniques, because tubes are both too small for attaching fiducial markers to them, too similar and numerous for shape and color recognition, and too expendable for adding active electronic components. These constrains are not unique to biology labs and can also be found elsewhere, e.g. the electronics world where components are also small and have PDF documents or web pages describing them.

In this paper we explore an alternative for integrating everyday objects and tabletops called *mediated tabletop interaction*. In this approach a *mediator* is used to convert the object's tag ID into one that the tabletop can read and use to determine its location and orientation (figure 1). Mediated tabletop interaction derives from our observations that in many cases users engage with small objects through a holder object. Thus, we seek to instrument the holder with communication capabilities in order to enable its integration with the tabletop. In this paper we make three contributions: (1) introduce the notion of mediated tabletop interaction, (2) present a first mediator prototype implementation called the 'Rabbit', and (3) present a collectively defined design space

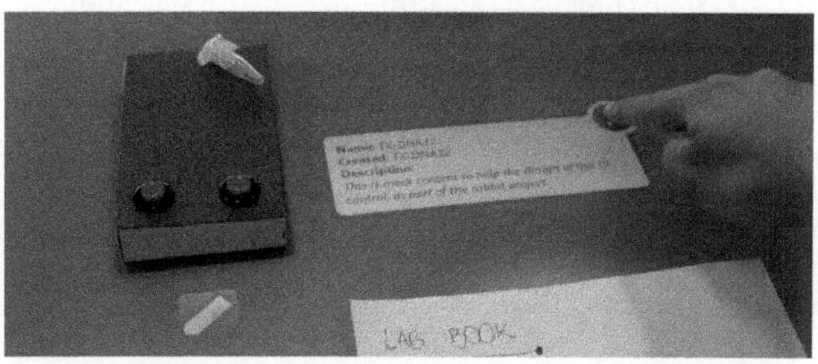

Figure 1. The Rabbit is a *mediator* prototype for integrating small RFID-tagged objects and tabletops.

for mediated tabletop interaction in the biology lab. The paper ends with a discussion on the implications of mediated tabletop interaction, and the conclusions.

RELATED WORK

For integrating physical objects and interactive surfaces (identification and tracking) researchers have looked into different techniques using static means, active means, and RFID tags.

Tracking solutions through static means

Static means relate to the use of physical properties, or passive and un-powered components of objects to determine their identity, location and orientation on an interactive surface. Seminal work in this direction was the DigitalDesk [16] and the metaDESK [13], introducing shape and color recognition for the tracking and augmenting of physical objects. These systems are camera based, and through computer vision algorithms detect physical properties like the color and the 2D contour of the object, which can be used to query a repository in order to determine the object's identity.

Other projects have added special passive components to the objects to aid their recognition. The SenseTable [7] uses electromagnetic pucks to communicate the presence and identity of an object to the interactive surface. Other projects attach fiducial markers to the objects, so they can be recognized with a bottom or overhead camera. A more detailed account of camera-based recognition and tracking techniques can be found in Moeslund et al. [5].

Tracking solutions through active means

Active means relate to the use of dynamic mechanisms in the objects, physical or electronic, that help the interactive surface track them, or that execute the tracking themselves. The SurfaceWare uses a drinking glass with a built-in prism to determine when a refill should be offered [2]. The PhotoelasticTouch uses the elastic properties of transparent materials to enhance touch interaction [11]. Using both static markers and the elastic properties of transparent materials, the SLAP widgets provide controls (keyboard, check box, slider, etc) to interact with the interactive surface [15]. The Madgets maintain the haptic properties of the SLAP widgets and add magnets to them, so that together with an array of electromagnets behind the screen, they become actuators that can change state and even move on the surface [14].

More complex interactions are achieved via electronic active means. For example, the Anoto[1] and Anoto-based projects [3] use a reference grid and a built-in camera into the object, to determine its position on the interactive surface. The QualiTrack system combines IR capable pens with a synchronized IR camera-emitter system to query the ID of the pens [4]. The BlueTable combines BlueTooth and IR light of a cellphone, to enhance the handshaking when establishing a connection between the interactive surface and the phone [17]. In this way the table can match the cellphone's BlueTooth ID with the detected shape on the table. A more comprehensive account of active means and interactive surfaces can be found in Dietz and Eidelson [2].

[1] http://www.anoto.com – Anoto Pen.

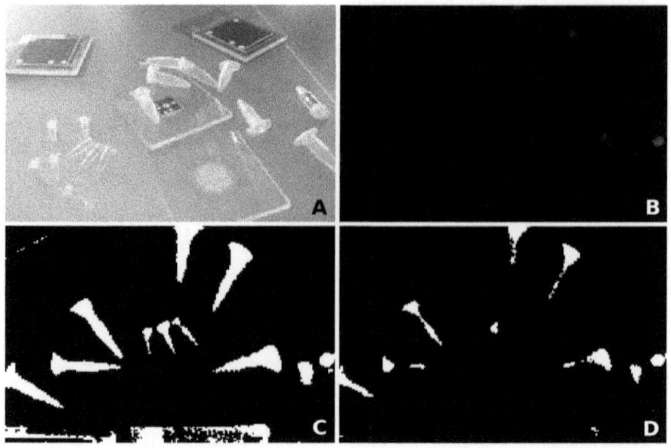

Figure 2. (A) Small objects like test tubes are too small to hold a fiducial marker that can uniquely identify them, and still be readable by the camera. (B) Their reflection in IR light is very poor, and even with a threshold value of (C) 1 and (D) 20, test tubes are indistinguishable by means of shape and color.

Tracking solutions through RFID technology

Radio-frequency identification (RFID) uses radio waves to exchange data between a reader and an electronic tag attached to an object with the purposes of identifying and tracking. RFID-based solutions use the tag's ID, signal strength, and optionally, computer vision to determine the identity, location, and orientation of objects on an interactive surface. The Marked-up Maps project uses RFID tags to mark places of interest in a map, so users can access the information with a hand held RFID reader [9]. The interaction thus takes place in the handheld device and the interactive surface simply acts as an input mechanism. The ePro Board [12] and DataTiles [10] projects use a matrix of readers behind the interactive surface. Objects are tagged with RFID tags, and can then be brought on to the table. However, these configurations of readers cannot determine the objects' orientation.

SurfaceFusion combines activity detection in the RFID and computer vision domains, to establish the identity of the shapes in the scene [6]. SurfaceFusion introduces *Frame Difference Algebra* (FDA) to provide robust and fast detection of objects under the constrain that only one object is manipulated at the time. A more comprehensive account of RF and RFID-based approaches and their integration with interactive surfaces can be found in Olwal and Wilson [6].

Small Objects and Tabletops

Current approaches to object tracking for tabletops do not provide efficient means to identify small objects. For instance, objects like test tubes are too small to carry any static identification like fiducial markers. Figure 2 shows how current vision-based approaches to object tracking in tabletops behave with small indistinguishable objects. Color and shape recognition are not viable, as the tubes' reflection of infra-red light is very poor, and their visual footprints are equal (figure 2B-D). Using active means of identification, like powered electronic components, are too expensive for the mundane and expandable test tubes used in a laboratory environment. Existing RFID-based techniques could be used to identify the objects, but they do not allow for precise location and orientation tracking on the interactive surface. Moreover, the integration small objects with tabletop interaction could extend the reach of applications to new areas. In the biology lab, where biologists work with test tubes, tabletop applications could provide advanced tracking during and after experiments.

MEDIATED TABLETOP INTERACTION

Figure 3 illustrates our proposed notion of *mediated tabletop interaction*, as a way to support tabletop interaction with small objects. The main components of mediated tabletop interaction are *object tags* and the *mediator*. Small objects should be tagged with unique identifiers, in a way that their physical appearance is not radically altered. The mediator acts as a bridge between the physical tag and the tabletop; it can be seen as a conversion mechanism between an object-friendly tagging technology and a technology the tabletop can read. Moreover, the mediator conveys information about the location and orientation of the physical object on the tabletop. With this dataset (location, orientation, and tag value) the tabletop interaction can occur. Optionally, the mediator can communicate information regarding its own state (like battery levels), or user interaction with it (like button pressings).

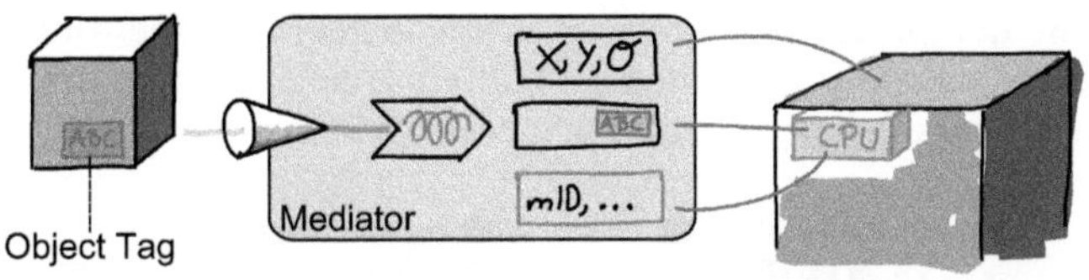

Figure 3. Mediated Tabletop Interaction: The integration between and object and the tabletop is aided by a *mediator*. The mediator reads the object's tag, and interacts with the tabletop to convey location, orientation, the tag value, and optionally, data specific to the mediator.

RESEARCH APPROACH

The goal of our research is to explore both the technical implementation as well as the design implications of *mediated tabletop interactions*. For this purpose, we have engaged in a three-phase research approach. In the first phase, we engaged in an open-ended participatory design process, investigating the need for biologist to integrate physical and digital information while working at the laboratory workbench. In this phase, a series of observations, interviews, and prototyping sessions were conducted. This lead to the design of an artifact for mediating between physical objects – like test tubes – and interactive surfaces – like a future electronic lab bench – as described above.

In the second phase, we did a prototype proof-of-concept implementation of the mediator designed in phase one. This implementation – called *The Rabbit* – is further described below. The aim of this implementation is to prove that such a mediator between physical objects and an interactive surface can actually be implemented in a technical sound manner.

In the third phase, we returned to the explorative participatory design process. In this phase we wanted to explore the design space of mediated tabletop interaction. Our goal was to explore how such a technology could be used in everyday work in a biology laboratory. Therefore, rather than performing a focused usability evaluation of the technical prototype developed in phase two, we decided to deploy mediator design probes in a real biology environment. These probes were not Rabbits, but simple mock-ups. This approach was necessary because the interactive surfaces on which the Rabbit is dependent to run on top of are simply not available in the laboratories yet. This research approach enabled us to map the design space of this kind of technology in much greater details for others to consider in the design of mediators for other application areas.

THE RABBIT

Figure 4 shows *The Rabbit*[2], a mediator device that dynamically converts the value of an object's RFID tag into a 2D code that can be identified and tracked by an interactive surface. The rabbit aims to support objects that cannot be normally augmented on interactive surfaces, because they are very small, yet can hold a passive RFID tag. The key components of the rabbit are an RFID reader and the 2D code display. The rabbit allows the application to present the user with digital information related to the object, and to locate the information according the its location and orientation on the interactive surface.

Figure 4. The rabbit is a device that dynamically conveys the value of an object's RFID tag, its location and orientation to tabletop.

The call-out in Figure 4 illustrates the structure of the 2D code: it's called the *SquareCode*. Similar to other fiducial markers, the SquareCode encodes a value, and its static regions (the three black-dots at square angles) help determine its location and orientation. We created the SquareCode as a new kind of fiducial marker that we could generate dynamically with common electronic components (IR LEDs). Figure 5A shows an RFID-tagged object (●⁘●) approaching the rabbit, the RFID tag is read, and the corresponding 2D code is shown toward the interactive surface. Figure 5B shows a capture of how the SquareCode is seen and recognized by the interactive surface. In addition, as a rabbit can hold multiple RFID-tagged objects, the *SquareCode* provides means to iterate through multiple codes. When an object is no longer sensed within the antenna range, the rabbit removes its code from memory and no longer communicates it to the table. The RFID-tags can be read by one single antenna (with anti-collision support) or by multiple fine-grained antennas. The number of objects that can be tracked is only limited by the RFID reader used and the antenna configuration. Moreover,

[2] *The Rabbit* is the internal code-name for the project seen as the tabletop equivalent to the desktop's *mouse*.

in contrast to the Audiopad [8] and others, the rabbit uses off-the-shelf unmodified passive RFID tags.

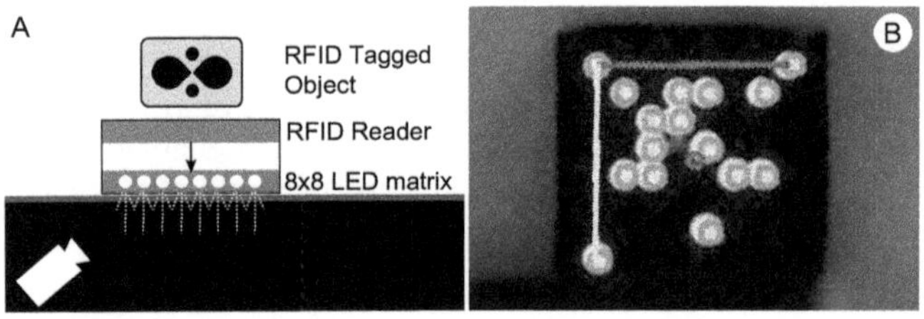

Figure 5. (A) The rabbit translates an RFID code into a SquareCode and displays it to the DIT via infrared LEDs. (B) The DIT reads the code and determines its value, location and orientation.

Another key characteristic of the rabbit is that it can be brought off-the-table to read RFID tags of objects that cannot be brought onto it. The rabbit reads the tag, stores the read code in memory, and communicates it to the tabletop once it is brought back onto the surface. In this kind of rabbit the code remains in the rabbit's memory until it's overwritten by a new code. Also, the rabbit itself uses the interactive surface to communicate issues of its own functioning like low battery levels.

Implementation

The rabbit was built with an *Arduino Pro Mini*, an *Innovation's ID-12* RFID reader, a serial backpack from Sparkfun for LED matrices, a custom IR LED matrix at 850nm (shown in Figure 6), and two buttons. We used standard Eppendorf test tubes with 125kHz RFID glass capsules. The tabletop was a Microsoft Surface, with an API in C# using the Open Computer Vision Toolkit *OpenCV*. The LED matrix encodes values according to the SquareCode, as shown in Figure 7.

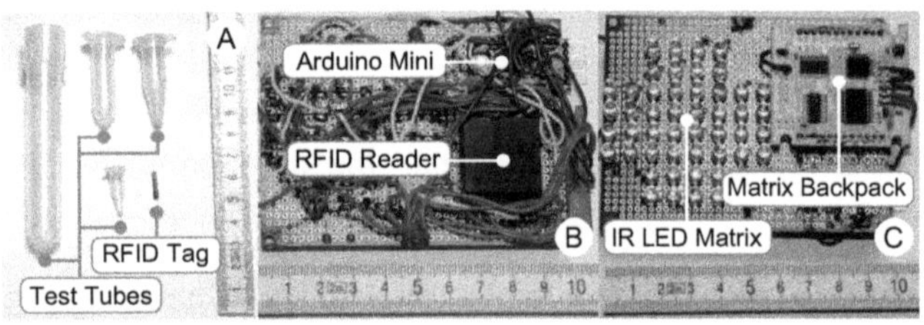

Figure 6. (A) Test tubes, and the 125kHz RFID Glass Capsule. (B) Top-view of the rabbit showing RFID readers and Arduino Mini Pro. (C) Bottom-view of the rabbit showing the serial backpack from Sparkfun, and infra-red LED matrix.

In the current implementation, each test tube is tagged with an RFID glass capsule. The rabbit, normally resting on the Microsoft Surface, continuously reads for nearby RFID tags. When a test tube comes within reading range of the RFID reader (1cm approximately), its RFID identification and checksum are acquired by the reader and transmitted to the Arduino board. The Arduino processor checks the validity of the read identification against the checksum and, if valid, generates a corresponding SquareCode to display through the custom IR LED matrix. The SquareCode also contains information about the state of the buttons (pressed, released). As the IR LED matrix faces down toward the Microsoft Surface, the projected SquareCode can be captured by the surface's infrared camera system.

On the application side, a rabbit-enabled application registers a series of listeners to the provided API (*RabbitObjectEntered*, *RabbitObjectLeft*, *RabbitButtonPressed*, *RabbitButtonReleased*). To trigger these events the API maintains a list of object codes associated with each rabbit. Every captured input image is handed over to the surface application, and from there to our API which processes the image looking for SquareCodes. Then, the API notifies the application about object and button-related events. The object-related events, contain location, orientation, and an object code corresponding the RFID identification of the test tube. Application developers can use this object code to fetch data from local or remote repositories and update the user interface correspondingly.

The LED matrix approach taken for this implementation is not the only possible one, and presents problems when the amount of data to transmit is greater than the capacity of the SquareCode. We considered alternatives to build rabbits; for example using static fiducial markers and BlueTooth to communicate the value of the RFID codes. However, this approach also has several disadvantages compared to the technologies we chose. First, using static markers and BlueTooth requires pairing between the table and the device. Second, wireless connections present interference problems when using multiple rabbits. Third, the static markers and the BlueTooth data are transmitted over different channels, requiring handling of channel fusion (image + wireless).

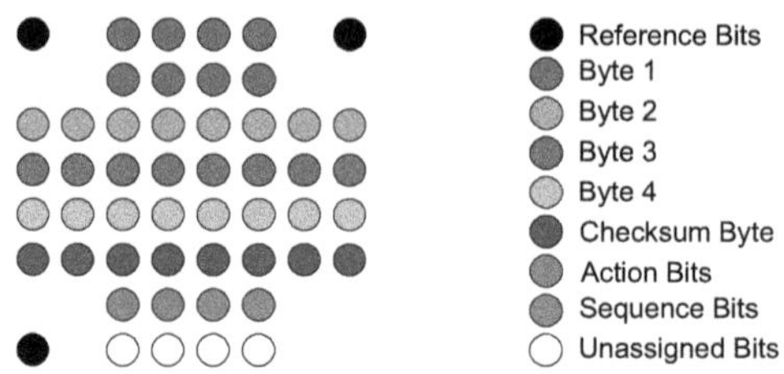

Figure 7. The *SquareCode* contains a 4 byte code value, 1 byte for checksum, 2 action bits for button events, 2 sequencing bits, and 4 unassigned bits.

TECHNOLOGY EXPLORATION

Designing mediators between physical objects and tabletops opens up a whole new design space for bringing surface computing to places like the biology laboratory. In this section we present the user-centered exploration of this new design space involving a group of biologists using 'Rabbit' technology probes in their own biology lab while doing real experiments. This exploration happened in the context of a project with the same biologists devising the design of interactive laboratory benches. Based on this exploration we defined a set of design dimensions along which these tabletop mediators can be designed.

Process

The user-centered design exploration aimed at uncovering factors involved in the application of mediators in a biology laboratory context. In order to introduce the rabbit and tabletop technologies to the biologists, we carried out one participatory design workshop and one focus group. After gathering feedback on our initial designs, we gave a set of *mock* mediator probes to the biologists for them to use during their laboratory work.

Workshops: 6 participants were involved in an early participatory workshop on digital laboratory benches and 12 participants took part in a focus group (8 PhD students and 4 post-docs). All were experienced in laboratory work, and were familiar with digital technologies. In the first workshop, participants created videos whose ideas we used to create video prototypes of possible usages of mediators.

Our video prototypes presented two mediators: the *augmented rack* and the *mobile* mediator. The *augmented rack* is a 4x5 test tubes rack-shaped mediator that can be used as a normal rack and integrates to the interactive surface to support biologists on their interactions with test tubes. The *mobile* mediator reads the RFID code attached to shared laboratory machines allowing biologists to virtually "bring" the machines to the tabletop and access their related digital information. We discussed our videos with the focus group, and invited people to participate in a probe activity.

Probes: In order to have more naturalistic data on how people could use such mediators we gave mock devices (a mock augmented rack and a mock mobile mediator as shown in figure 8) and a disposable film camera to 6 . The devices did not have any electronic components or other functionalities, and were to be used over their existing lab benches. Their physical appearence, however, imitated the rabbit designs we presented in the video prototypes. We asked participants to take pictures during the course of their work, if they had any idea on how to use mediators on a digital bench. The purpose of the mock devices was to inspire and provoke the biologists to come up with ideas in the middle of their daily lab work. Participants received movie tickets for their participation and we asked them to return the cameras within 3 weeks.

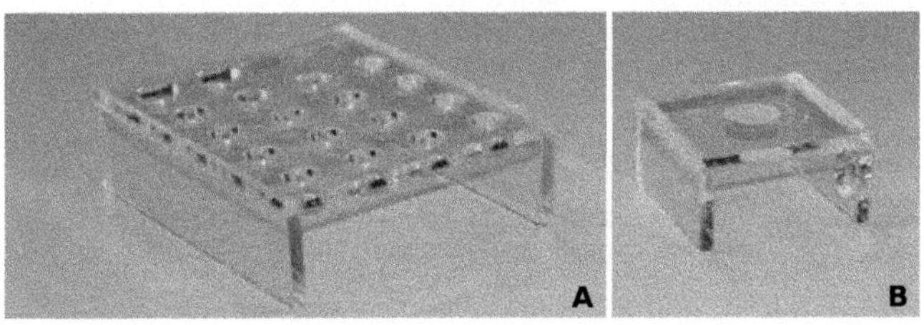

Figure 8. Probes handed to participants A) A rack mediator, shaped as a rack for test tubes. B) A mobile mediator, shaped as a small RFID reader.

Analysis method: Two participants never returned the camera. Overall participants took 35 pictures (avg: 8.7, max: 16, min: 4), out of which 32 had a good enough quality (illumination, focus, etc). To interpret the pictures, we followed a process inspired by grounded theory coding. We attached tags describing the salient characteristics of every picture. For example, the first picture had the following tags: *rabbit in picture, multiple racks, marked tubes, 15+ tubes, small tubes, big tubes, rack with lid, live zone, rack case, storage,* and *rabbit label.* After finishing tagging, we listed the tags and grouped them by topic. Each picture was processed again in order to add missing tags. We created a tag matrix and counted the occurrences of each picture tag. Table 1 shows the 44 tags and 5 categories created during the coding.

Category	Tags
Support Info	physical protocol (6), notebook (3), scrap paper (8), documents (10), digital protocol (2), digital work-flow (1), digital document (3)
Interactive UI	experiment interface (4), sample interface (1), grid like interface (1), text access (10), data analysis (1), linking (3)
Usage Conditions	rack (22), mobile mediator (5), rack empty (3), rack on ice (4), multiple racks (11), mixing (5), marked tubes (23), note-taking (7), 15+ tubes (9)
Tools	small tubes (22), big tubes (5), rack with lid (7), gloves (5), ice box (5), flasks (7), burner (2), machine (14)
Bench	live area (20), lab bench (13), machines bench (8), hazardous bench (1), office bench (3), spacious (10), non-spacious (14)
Storage	rack case (1), storage (3), desk storage (13), freezer (3), rabbit label (13)

Table 1. Tags used to classify the pictures collected (and the number of appearances), and the categories in which they are grouped.

DESIGN DIMENSIONS

Based on our discussions with participants and the categories and tags of the probe activity, we define a series of design dimensions along which mediated tabletop interaction can vary, and which we group in three main themes: (i) mediator design, (ii) object+mediator+surface integration, (iii) and integration with other devices.

Mediator Design

These dimensions present the different ways in which the mediator in itself can be designed. Its form will depend on the content it mediates, or how appropriate a physical shape is for the task at hand.

Capacity

This first dimension refers to objects that are mediated simultaneously. Figure 9 shows the three values for this dimension: *Single* means only one object is mediated at a time. *Bag-like* means that many objects are mediated at once, but without order, and physical location inside the mediator. *Batches* means that multiple objects are mediated simultaneously, with information about the order in which they are read, and their location within the mediator.

Figure 9. Capacity dimension. A *single* mediator. A *bag-like* mediator. A *batched* mediator.

Figure 10 was taken during the probe-phase and shows a biologist with two racks, each containing two lines of 10 tubes. In this case the location of each tube within the rack is important, as their physical location impacts that way tubes relate to each other. As one biologist explained: *You can divide the tubes between archive, primers, and the ones you use to mix.* The different groups of tubes are located in specific parts of the rack for easier handling. Thus, it is meaningful for biologists to keep track of the tubes and their locations.

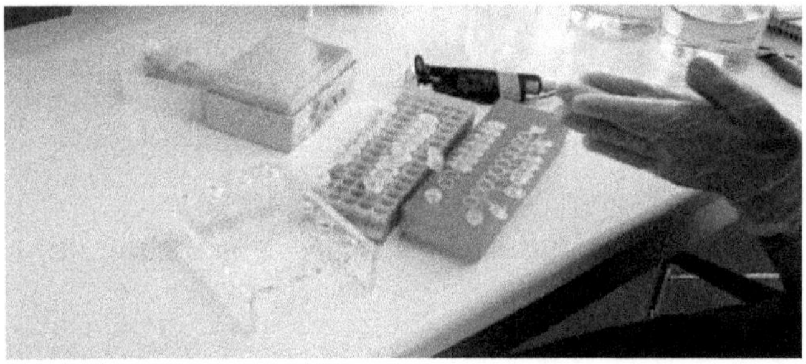

Figure 10. Batches of test tubes in the rack. Biologists organize the tubes inside the rack according to the different conditions they are experimentally testing. In the picture, each line contains a different component, and each tube a different concentration of it.

Embeddedness

This dimension describes the level of replacement of an existing object intended with a specific mediator. This is a continuous value with extremes on *new element* and *replacement*, as shown in figure 11. When a rabbit-like device is a completely new element, alien to the existing uses, users have to incorporate it into their routines. In such situations designers can leverage the mediator to introduce users to new practices. At the other extreme is replacement, which happens when the rabbit is designed to augment an existing object, adding to it the ability to integrate with the interactive surface. Adoption is easier as the object is already part of the work practice. Designers should determine existing practices/objects upon which to build in order facilitate adoption while leaving room for innovation and possibly new activities.

Figure 11. Embeddedness dimension. A new element is completely novel to the users. A replacement element augments an existing tool.

In our technology exploration we saw instances of both extremes. Our proposed idea of augmenting a test tubes rack was well received, with biologists suggesting multiple ways in which the information could be displayed, stored, and related. The fact that integration between the tabletop and the test tubes is through a familiar object increased the biologists interest as they didn't have to adopt yet another technology for their already overloaded space. Moreover, the idea of the *mobile mediator* also received attention, with discussions about new forms of interactions with the existing physical infrastructures in the lab. For instance, a biologist suggested the mobile mediator could be used to move information between lab machines, the tabletop, and his personal computer, as illustrated in figure 20C.

Form Factor

This dimension describes the variety of mediator forms to be supported by the interactive surface (see figure 12). The simplest of cases is for the interactive surface to support mediators with a single physical shape. However, designers might find the need to support objects of different sizes on their interactive surface applications, and therefore building mediators with different physical forms.

Figure 12. Form factor dimension. It describes the multiplicity of mediator shapes that the interactive surface application needs to handle.

Support for multiple shapes has been discussed by authors like Baudisch et al. [1]. In our specific case, we could observe it with test tubes of different sizes and therefore different racks biologists work with. For example, participants captured the diversity of tubes in figure 13, and the diversity of racks can be seen in figures 15A and 10.

Figure 13. An interactive surface application should support mediators of different forms, as they should hold objects of different sizes. The picture shows small size tubes together with bigger ones. Both sizes are normally used in the execution of experiments.

Object+Mediator+Surface Integration

These dimensions present the different ways in which the mediation between tagged-objects and the surface can take place; the mediated objects can be the reference point of the interaction or just additional data to a central digital object. A mediator can also link objects to digital data in different ways, from manual input to embedded sensors.

Reference

This dimension refers to the way that physical objects and digital information are related and the prevalence between them. Figure 14 shows the two values of this dimension: *physical reference* and *digital reference*. Designing for a physical reference, the physical object acts as a container or indexer for the digital data; a common approach in tangible interaction with tabletops. Designing for a digital reference, physical objects are indexed around a digital document.

In our design space exploration we encountered situations where the physical object is one of many resources related

Figure 14. Reference dimension. With *physical* reference, digital information is attached to the physical object. With *digital* reference, physical objects and other digital data are attached to the digital document.

to a master digital object (corresponding to the *digital* reference). Figure 15A shows a biologist relating multiple tubes to a single protocol in his notebook. This relation is later migrated to a digital protocol, and it is this digital protocol which they would refer to when they want to know about the contents of a tube. Figure 15B shows another instance of a digital reference. The image presents a sketch (created by a participant in the probe-phase) representing the protocol as a work-flow showing how each tube was used in the flow.

Figure 15. Reference dimension. A) Biologist keeping track of multiple tubes related to a single experiment. B) UI sketch made by a participant of a experiment work-flow interface, with multiple tubes coming into play at different moments.

Finally, the following quote from the focus group shows how associating several physical objects (test tubes) around a digital one (an agarose gel image) can ease the analysis of information later on:

> *"We normally work with 10 to 20 tubes, and they are all on one [DNA] gel [image]. So, in that way it doesn't make sense to track each small tube. It's the gel that's the focus point now... So, sort of that you click on a band on the gel and you see the tube, and what happened to the tube in history."*

Information Source

This dimension describes the ways in which information is associated to the *reference object* (previous dimension). Figure 16 shows the four association methods: *manual input*, *data integration*, *object integration*, and *contextual*. Manual input requires the user to type in the relevant information. Data integration makes use of existing digital information that a user could simply drag-and-drop. This information can be as simple as document or images files, or more elaborated like database queries using the object code. Object integration creates links between the objects being used simultaneously on the interactive surface. Contextual input adds environmental or situational information to the objects.

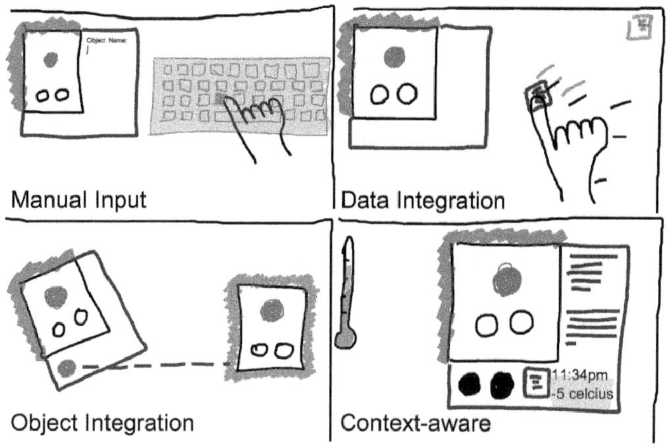

Figure 16. Information source dimension. The figure shows the different sources of digital information for a given physical object.

A biologist could use manual input to type the name and exact ingredients used for a given test tube. Manual input is not rare for biologists, as shown in figure 15A they keep notes on scrap paper and in their paper notebook. However, data integration could have a greater impact given that biologists increasingly use digital data; for example:

> *"It would also be cool if the kits [sets of tubes ordered from suppliers] had this RFID as an optional service. The suppliers generally give a [paper] spreadsheet with the tubes contents and their labels, and a excel file indexing the contents of each tube."*

A interactive surface application could leverage this information and extract the digital information using the RFID code on a given document.

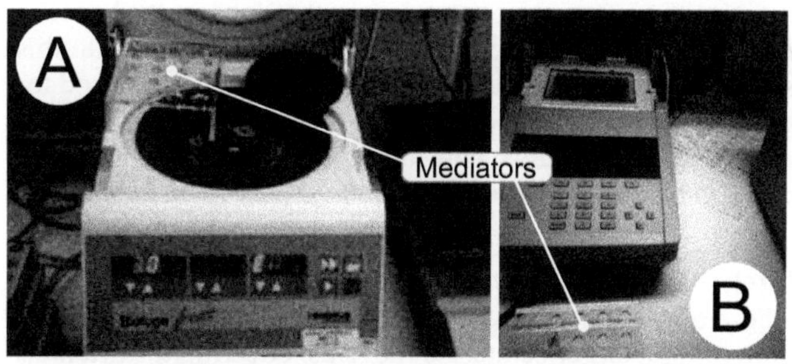

Figure 17. Molecular biologists use plenty of machines for executing their experiments. This machines normally sit on the same benches and most are electronic and programmable. A) shows a centrifuge, and B) shows an UV spectrometer, both are used in most of the experiments.

The picture taking activity documented several instances of object integration. For example figures 15A and 10 show how a tube is used in conjunction with other tubes, and even other racks. Moreover, object integration could also be implemented with other objects that also sit on the interactive surface. Figure 17A and B show different electronic instruments used by the biologists in their work. An interactive surface could integrate with such instruments and collect information from them like the parameters of their execution. Similarly to object integration, the interactive surface could collect contextual information relevant for an experiment like e.g. temperature by integrating to a thermometer.

Output Space

This dimension describes the amount of physical space that is expected to be normally available on the tabletop surface, i.e. space that is not covered by physical objects. Figure 18 shows the two possible values: *spacious* and *non-spacious*. We call it spacious when there are few objects and the designer can expect considerable UI space around them. Moreover, objects on the surface are part of the interaction, and are taken away at the end. In this situation the main purpose of the interactive surface is user interaction. Designers can expect users will reorganize the space so to make room for the UI. We call it non-spacious when there are many objects on the surface, little space between them, and objects remain on the surface for extended periods of time, or even permanently. In this situation the main purpose of the interactive surface is the interaction of the user with the objects; the objects take the central role on the surface. Designers can expect users will not be willing to change the organization of physical objects, and thus the UI has to adjust to the limited space available.

Figure 18. Output space dimension. This figure shows different space availabilities in actual workbenches, influencing the UI design.

The video material we produced for the focus group assumed the interactive surface to be spacious. However, analysis of the participants pictures showed us that laboratory benches are very crowded places. Figure 15A and 10 illustrate this situation. Besides containing tubes racks and bottles used for the current experiment, laboratory benches serve as temporary storage for bottles, new tubes, trashcans, etc. Moreover, often machines are permanently stationed on the benches.

Integration with Other Devices

These dimensions present the different ways in which mediators fit in a larger ecology of devices, covering the artefacts which a mediator can connect to, and also how one mediator can be used alongside others, or shared among many surfaces.

Ecology

This dimension considers the types of objects a mediator interacts with. Figure 19 shows the types we identified in our design space exploration, that, however tied to the domain we studied, we believe are valid for other domains. The types are: *interactive surfaces*, *storage*, *work-specific* machines, and *personal computers*. The general case is a workbench that is enhanced as an interactive surface. In this case the user will be able to access and interact with digital information related to an object. Storage relates to the object or place where the mediator rests while it is not being used on the interactive surface. Work machines relates to specialized machines with electronic properties to which a mediator could integrate to (as shown in *information source → object integration*). Finally, the user could also use his personal computer to access digital data related to an object. In this case the mediator allows the user to access content by connecting to his laptop via, for example, a USB connection.

Figure 19. The ecology dimension. It refers to the types of objects which a mediator interacts with including interactive surfaces, storage places or machines, work specific machines, and personal computers.

Several cases of the ecology of devices where explicit in our exploration activities. Figure 20 shows some of the participants' pictures describing the ecology of devices. Picture 20A shows a mediator rack being stored inside a freezer. Storing test tubes racks in the freezer is a normal practice, and a mediator rack should support it. Picture 20B shows the integration with other machines in the bench. And picture 20C shows a participant pointing the mobile mediator against his laptop computer, as a way to tell us through the picture that the rabbit should integrate with it [3].

The use of a mediator in tandem with other devices opens up a new space for design. For example participants valued the possibility of querying a system to know the current storage location of test tubes that were produced in an experiment months before. One participant pointed out that a mobile mediator could help him managing the shared resources:

> *...one could integrate a machine as a resource into a project [experiment]. So you could say: ok, I use this type of scanner a lot in this project... and then you go to your computer or table and ask: when is this type of machine or scanner booked? And then the system [would] know exactly which one it is, because you scanned one but not the other one. Instead of having to remember a code like i7536VV.*

Surface Coupling

This dimension describes the degree in which a mediator is coupled to a particular interactive surface. Figure 21 shows the possible values: *single surface*, or *shared*. A single surface mediator is tightly coupled to the surface in which it is

[3] The picture is not intended to mean the laptop should read the code from the LED screen, but rather that the mobile mediator could serve as an information link between different devices.

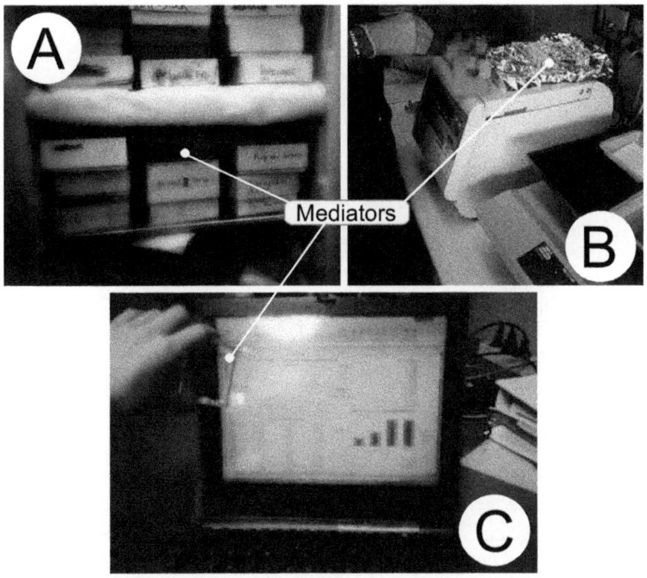

Figure 20. A test tubes rack mediator would have to interact with an ecology of devices. A) The mediator being put to store in a local freezer. B) The mediator on top of a centrifuge. C) A mobile mediator being used to access information from a laptop computer.

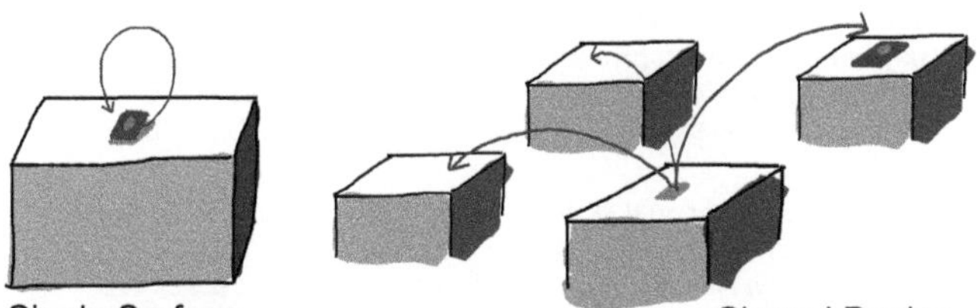

Figure 21. Surface coupling dimension. It describes whether a mediator is expected to be used on a single or multiple interactive surface.

normally used. Tight coupling can be given due to physical connections to the surface, or complicated pairing procedures (like required by BlueTooth). A shared mediator is loosely coupled to the surface in which it is normally used. Loose coupling allows for a mediator to quickly move from one surface to another without any set-up required.

Literature on interactive surfaces often focuses on single surface installations, where coupling is not an issue. However, our technology exploration showed that loose coupling might be necessary for some situations like a biology laboratory. A laboratory is made of multiple workbenches, with some assigned to particular researchers and some shared. Multiple resources including the racks are shared between all the researchers. Thus, a rack can be used by several different researchers during the course of a day. Moreover, a single scientist can move from his personal bench to the shared benches and back within the course of a single experiment. Thus, a mediator rack should support the seamless movement from one bench to the other.

DISCUSSION

Mediated tabletop interaction is our proposal to support tabletop interaction with objects not previously supported (small and big). This notion expands previous research on tangible interaction on tabletops, and opens up for new areas of exploration along the main themes of our design space definition: (i) mediator design, (ii) object+mediator+surface integration, (iii) and integration with other devices.

First, the mediator-related dimensions of *capacity*, *embeddedness* and *form factor* should lead the designer to consider different hardware technologies for building a mediator, and to balance the limitations of the chosen technologies. A highly embedded mediator (i.e. a faithful replacement of an existing holder object), requires the use of small electronics and unobtrusive tagging technologies to support multiple objects in a pre-defined form factor. While a less embedded mediator could let designers explore new form factors or other types of tagging and communication components that, while cheaper, could be bigger and obtrusive.

Second, the set of dimensions related to the object+mediator +surface integration, *reference*, *information source*, and *output space*, should lead the designer to consider the software aspects of the solution. All dimensions bring up interesting questions: does each physical object act as a bag of resources or rather like a resource attached to a digital object? how are the relationships between physical and digital objects created? by manual input? by database lookups? what happens with the digital records of discarded physical objects? how are UI elements organize around physical objects present on the surface? Answering these questions should lead to specific design choices that are reflected in the software, from foreign key relations in databases, to flexible/floating UI controllers.

And third, the dimensions related to the integration with other devices, *ecology* and *surface coupling*, bring to the arena of tabletop interaction traditional topics of distributed systems research. The issues of pairing of devices, standards for data exchange, support for multiple communication channels, and security provisions are all on the table. These topics gain relevancy when bringing mediated tabletop interaction out of the design lab into the everyday settings of users.

From our collaborative exploration in the context of the biology lab, introducing interactive surfaces to the lab requires a mediator implementation designed according to the colored values in figure 22. Rack mediators should support batches of tubes, have an appearance very similar to existing racks, and support tubes of different sizes. The application should index the physical tubes around a master digital object like a experimental protocol, support at least manual and data integration, and expect a rather nonspatious tabletop usage. And racks should initially support integration only with surfaces, but with many of them.

Finally, our explorations in the context of the biology lab could inspire researchers to look into other domains like for example the workbench work with electronic components, or to look into using mediators for purposes other than small objects' integration. In looking into different domains, a useful strategy is to look at instances where users interact with objects by means of an intermediate object like a place-

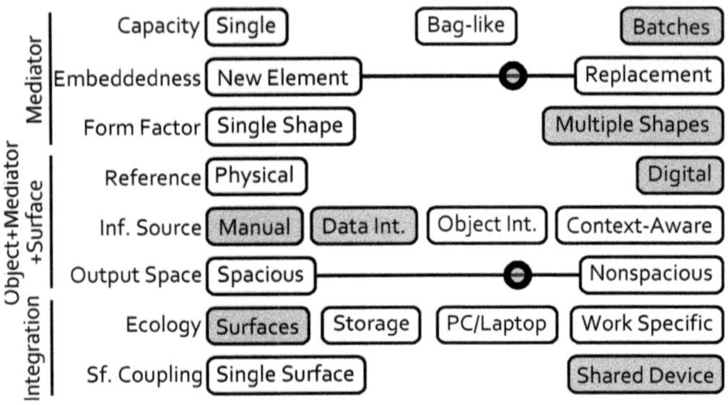

Figure 22. Summary of dimensions and dimension values for a test tubes rack implementation.

holder or an instrument. Like in the biology lab, the intermediate object can become the mediator and fit naturally within the existing working dynamics. As for purposes other than small objects' integration, researchers can look into objects that cannot be normally interacted with through the tabletop, like remote objects, big machines, wrapped objects, etc.

CONCLUSIONS AND FUTURE WORK

Current approaches to integrate objects to tabletops fail at handling small objects. In this paper we present the notion of *mediated tabletop interaction*: an approach to integrating small objects and tabletops, based on the fact that interaction with small objects often happens through a holder object. We explored mediated tabletop interaction by building an RFID+LED-based prototype, and collaboratively defining a design space for mediator solutions in the biology laboratory. Our design space definition introduces dimensions around to three areas: (i) mediator design, (ii) object+mediator+surface integration, (iii) and integration with other devices.

More than reporting final results of a research project, this paper starts the research into mediators and mediated tabletop interaction. Our most immediate path is the construction of multiple mediators with different hardware configurations in order to explore their performance in issues like cost, responsiveness, data transfer, battery consumption, etc. Moreover, we intent to carry out a longitudinal deployment of mediator devices supporting the lab work of molecular biologists. This deployment would shed light on how mediators and tabletop interaction in general can be better designed for everyday experiences. Particular focus would be on the UI layout when multiple physical objects limit the available space, and the UI options when the mediator contains multiple objects.

ACKNOWLEDGEMENT

We thank E. S. Andersen, Z. Sukosd and all the participants from Aarhus University. This research has been funded by the Danish Agency for Science, Technology, and Innovation under the project "PC Mini-Grids for Prediction of Viral RNA Structure and Evolution", #09-061856.

REFERENCES

1. P. Baudisch, T. Becker, and F. Rudeck. Lumino: tangible blocks for tabletop computers based on glass fiber bundles. In *CHI '10: Proceedings of the 28th international conference on Human factors in computing systems*, pages 1165–1174, New York, NY, USA, 2010. ACM.
2. P. H. Dietz and B. D. Eidelson. Surfaceware: dynamic tagging for microsoft surface. In *TEI '09: Proceedings of the 3rd International Conference on Tangible and Embedded Interaction*, pages 249–254, New York, NY, USA, 2009. ACM.
3. M. Haller, P. Br, D. Leithinger, J. Leitner, T. Seifried, and M. Billinghurst. Shared design space: Sketching ideas using digital pens and a large augmented tabletop setup. In *In ICAT 2006, Lecture Notes in Computer Science 4282*, pages 948–959. Springer Verlag, 2006.
4. R. Hofer, T. Nescher, and A. Kunz. Qualitrack: Highspeed tui tracking for tabletop applications. In *INTERACT '09: Proceedings of the 12th IFIP TC 13 International Conference on Human-Computer Interaction*, pages 332–335, Berlin, Heidelberg, 2009. Springer-Verlag.
5. T. B. Moeslund, A. Hilton, and V. Kruger. A survey of advances in vision-based human motion capture and analysis. *Computer Vision and Image Understanding*, 104(2):90–126, November 2006.
6. A. Olwal and A. D. Wilson. Surfacefusion: unobtrusive tracking of everyday objects in tangible user interfaces. In *GI '08: Proceedings of graphics interface 2008*, pages 235–242, Toronto, Ont., Canada, Canada, 2008. Canadian Information Processing Society.
7. J. Patten, H. Ishii, J. Hines, and G. Pangaro. Sensetable: a wireless object tracking platform for tangible user interfaces. In *CHI '01: Proceedings of the SIGCHI conference on Human factors in computing systems*, pages 253–260, New York, NY, USA, 2001. ACM.
8. J. Patten, B. Recht, and H. Ishii. Audiopad: a tag-based interface for musical performance. In *NIME '02: Proceedings of the 2002 conference on New interfaces for musical expression*, pages 1–6, Singapore, Singapore, 2002. National University of Singapore.
9. D. Reilly, M. Rodgers, R. Argue, M. Nunes, and K. Inkpen. Marked-up maps: combining paper maps and electronic information resources. *Personal Ubiquitous Comput.*, 10(4):215–226, 2006.
10. J. Rekimoto, B. Ullmer, and H. Oba. Datatiles: a modular platform for mixed physical and graphical interactions. In *CHI '01: Proceedings of the SIGCHI conference on Human factors in computing systems*, pages 269–276, New York, NY, USA, 2001. ACM.
11. T. Sato, H. Mamiya, H. Koike, and K. Fukuchi. Photoelastictouch: transparent rubbery tangible interface using an lcd and photoelasticity. In *UIST '09: Proceedings of the 22nd annual ACM symposium on User interface software and technology*, pages 43–50, New York, NY, USA, 2009. ACM.
12. M. Sugimoto, F. Kusunoki, and H. Hashizume. Supporting face-toface group activities with a sensor-embedded board. cscw workshop on shared environments to support face-to-face collaboration, 2000.
13. B. Ullmer and H. Ishii. The metadesk: models and prototypes for tangible user interfaces. In *UIST '97: Proceedings of the 10th annual ACM symposium on User interface software and technology*, pages 223–232, New York, NY, USA, 1997. ACM.
14. M. Weiss, F. Schwarz, S. Jakubowski, and J. Borchers. Madgets: Actuating widgets on interactive tabletops. In *Proceedings of UIST '10 (to appear)*, New York, NY, USA, 2010. ACM Press.
15. M. Weiss, J. Wagner, Y. Jansen, R. Jennings, R. Khoshabeh, J. D. Hollan, and J. Borchers. Slap widgets: bridging the gap between virtual and physical controls on tabletops. In *CHI '09: Proceedings of the 27th international conference on Human factors in computing systems*, pages 481–490, New York, NY, USA, 2009. ACM.
16. P. Wellner. Interacting with paper on the digitaldesk. *Commun. ACM*, 36(7):87–96, 1993.
17. A. D. Wilson and R. Sarin. Bluetable: connecting wireless mobile devices on interactive surfaces using vision-based handshaking. In *GI '07: Proceedings of Graphics Interface 2007*, pages 119–125, New York, NY, USA, 2007. ACM.

Hand Shape Classification with a Wrist Contour Sensor:Development of a Prototype Device

Rui Fukui, Masahiko Watanabe, Masamichi Shimosaka, Tomomasa Sato
The University of Tokyo
7-3-1 Hongo, Bunkyo-ku, Tokyo, JAPAN
{fukui, masahiko, simosaka, tsato}@ics.t.u-tokyo.ac.jp

Tomoaki Gyota
Mitsubishi Electronics
325 Kamimachiya Kamakura-shi, Kanagawa, Japan
Gyota.Tomoaki@ct.MitsubishiElectric.co.jp

ABSTRACT
In this paper, we describe a novel sensor device which recognizes hand shapes using wrist contours. Although hand shapes can express various meanings with small gestures, utilization of hand shapes as an interface is rare in domestic use. That is because a concise recognition method has not been established. To recognize hand shapes anywhere with no stress on the user, we developed a wearable wrist contour sensor device and a recognition system. In the system, features, such as sum of gaps, were extracted from wrist contours. We conducted a classification test of eight hand shapes, and realized approximately 70% classification rate.

Author Keywords
Hand shape recognition, classification, wrist contour, gesture interface.

ACM Classification Keywords
H.5.2 User Interfaces: Input devices and strategies.

General Terms
Design, Experimentation, Measurement.

INTRODUCTION
Increasing numbers of companies and researchers are developing natural user interfaces using gestures for human computer interaction[1]. Prominent examples are TV game interfaces such as Wii (Nintendo) and Kinect (Microsoft). Their success made gesture recognition interfaces popular. The most common action used in gesture interfaces is arm movement. However, it requires substantial physical energy and lacks the ability of precise expression. Therefore in this study, we put focus on hand shapes. Hand shapes are used in many scenes such as hand language or hand signals, and we presume that hand shapes are good gestures which can express much information with small actions. Nevertheless,

Figure 1. TV game with wrist contour sensor device.

there are few examples using hand shape recognitions in domestic use because a concise recognition method has not been established yet. There are several hand shape recognition methods[5]; we discuss the features and problems of some major methodologies hereafter.
Wired glove[3]: A wired glove is a glove-like input device that captures the finger bending with sensors mounted on the finger joints. It disturbs the haptic sense of the hand because the glove covers over a whole hand.
Electromyogram signals[6]: Signals are captured by wet or dry type electrodes attached to the surface of the forearm, and the electro signals are used for recognition. Because it is unnecessary to attach a device to a hand, the influence on hand movements is little. However, the electrodes must cover the whole forearm, and it is necessary to compress the arm for reducing the clearance between the electrode and the arm surface. Thus, the stress on the user is a problem.
Camera[4][9]: It trims the hand area from captured images and recognizes the hand shape. It does not disturb the activity and does not stress the user. However, the whole hand must be in the camera view range.
Therefore existing methods may be problematic for domestic use. These problems include the influence on activity, stress on the user, and limitation of circumstances. In this study, we propose the use of "wrist contours" for hand shape recognition. Rekimoto [7] measured wrist contours by capacitive sensors and recognized two hand shapes. We developed a new device using another type of sensor, and it can measure wrist contours more precisely. Figure 1 is a conceptual image of a game interface application. It will capture the ball grip, which any existing interfaces cannot get, and allows players to express a throwing motion more naturally.

WRIST CONTOUR BASIS
We designate a wrist cross-section contour (especially a wrist circumference contour near ulna) as a wrist contour. Figure 2

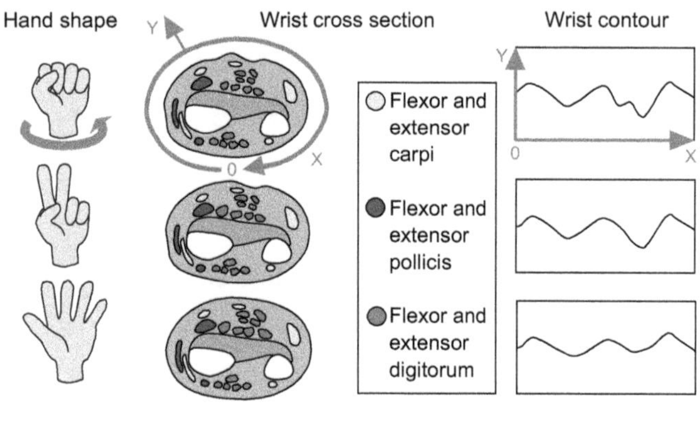

Figure 2. Wrist contour basis.

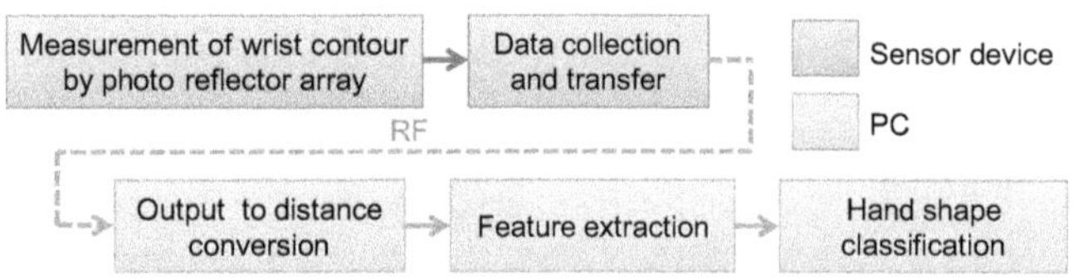

Figure 3. Data flow block diagram.

shows examples of hand shapes and wrist contour sets. Muscles and tendons for finger movements are compacted near the elbow. Around the wrist, however, tendons and muscles are separated to some extent, so they are comparatively observable. We observed the variation of their thicknesses and positions, which vary with finger movements. For example, to bend a finger, a flexor contracts and the nearby wrist surface dents. To straighten a finger, a flexor relaxes and the nearby wrist surface becomes as before. Our approach is to recognize hand shapes from these variations.

WRIST CONTOUR MEASURING SYSTEM

Figure 3 shows our system configuration and data flow diagram. We developed a wrist watch type sensor device (Figure 4) and a recognition system.

Required specification

Human constraints and our design are as follows.

- Human constraints:

(1a) Muscles and tendons for finger movements are approximately 5 mm in diameter. (1b) Radial variation of wrist contour is approximately 5 mm at maximum.
(2a) Wrist circumference is approximately 150∼170 mm.
(2b) Human arm motions should not be interrupted.

- Design:

(1a) Sensor pitch is 2.5 mm around circumference. (1b) Radial resolution of the sensors is 0.1 mm.
(2a) Measurement area is at least 170 mm in circumference.
(2b) The band is narrower than 30 mm.

To achieve the design requirements, we adopted photo reflector sensors and shift register switching method.

Photo reflector as distance sensor

Photo reflector is a combination of infrared LED and photo transistor. LED transmits an infrared signal and Photo transistor detects the intensity of the signal reflected at the surface of the object as shown in Figure 5. We selected a small photo reflector sensor "NJL5901AR-1" (produced by New Japan Radio Co.) to achieve the measurement density 2.5mm. Because an output of photo reflector is non-linear with distance, and sensors have individual differences, raw outputs cannot be used for measuring distances as they are. Then, we calibrated the outputs by prior measurement. We measured range of 0∼10mm with 0.05mm pitch with 1-axis automatic stage to achieve 0.1mm radial resolution. As a result, we achieved 0.1mm resolution in 0∼3.5mm. As figure 6 indicates, the smooth surface of an inclined flat board can be recognized in the range of 0∼3.5mm.

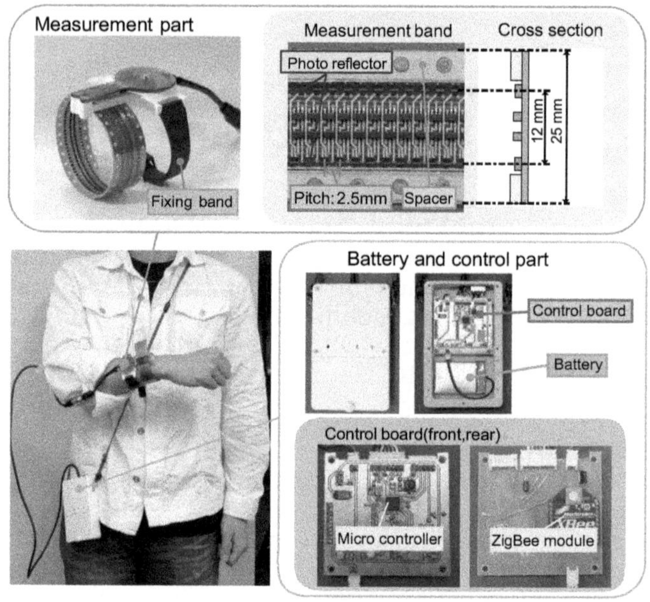

Figure 4. Wrist contour measuring device.

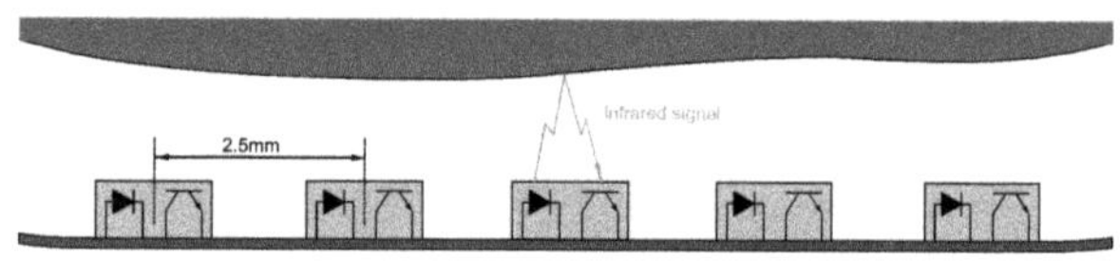

Figure 5. Mechanism of photo reflector.

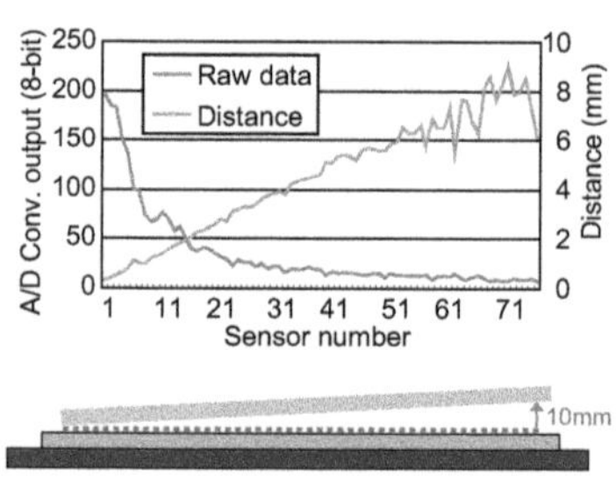

Figure 6. Measuring an inclined board.

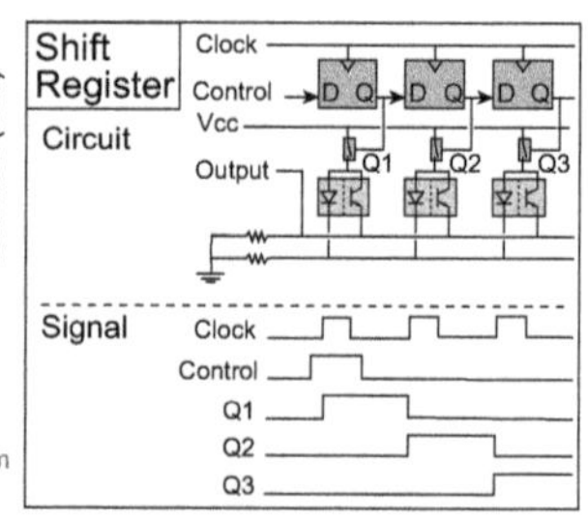

Figure 7. Shift register switching method.

Shift register switching method

To measure the whole circumference of wrist contours, we arranged photo reflector sensors in rows. We mounted them

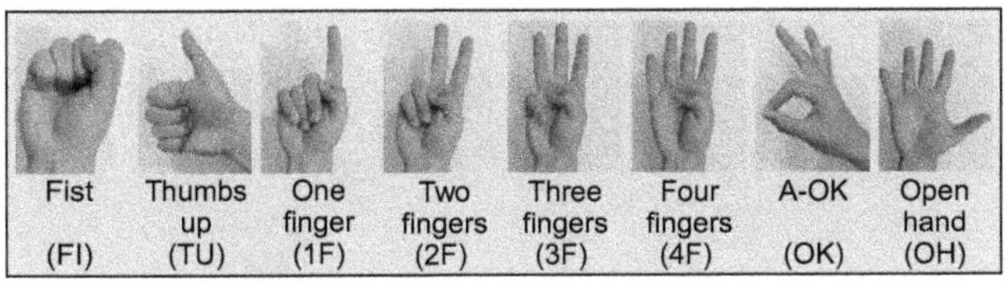

Figure 8. Hand shape eight classes.

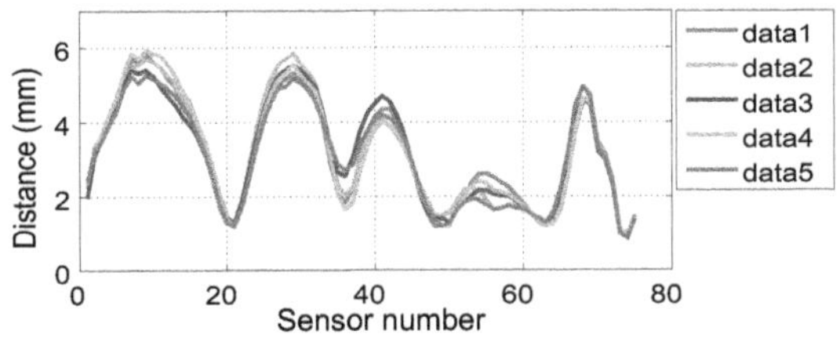

Figure 9. Five data at the same attachment condition.

on a flexible printed circuit board (measuring band). There are two rows in both side of the band and each row has 75 sensors in 2.5mm pitches, so the total number of sensors is 150 and measurement length is 185mm. In this configuration, if all sensors are controlled by one unit, it needs numerous number of signal lines and they make the band wider. Therefore, we utilized the shift register switching method as shown in Figure 7. The D-flip-flops and analog switches realize a sequential measurement by just sending trigger signals. That means only one sensor is active at once.

ANALYSYS OF WRIST CONTOUR

We collected wrist contour data from ten subjects with the device. Subjects are all students, and the wrist device was attached to the right hand. When putting the device on, subjects are guided by an experimenter, but the device is attached by themselves. The device was reattached each time we collected data. We configured eight hand shape classes as shown in Figure 8 and observed differences based on hand shapes, individuals, arm postures and so on. Figure 9 is sample data of one subject, fist class, five iterations, and without reattachment. We confirmed repeatability in the same class and the same posture when the identical subject did not reattach the device.

Individual differences

Figure 10 shows wrist contour data of three hand classes of two subjects. The graph indicates that wrist contours vary not only with hand shapes but also subjects.

Introduction of feature extraction

Variation between subjects executing the same hand shape was large compared with a subject's variation of the contour between hand shapes. So it is difficult to classify using subject-independent models on the raw data. We solved this assignment by introduction of feature extraction.

HAND SHAPE CLASSIFICATION

We didn't adopt regression between finger joint angle and outputs but classification of hand shape. That is because

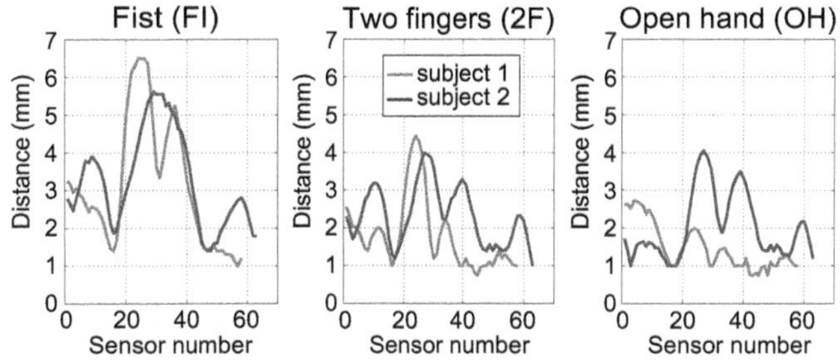

Figure 10. Three hand shape classes of two subjects

Single feature	Sep. Met.		
Sum of gaps	3.104	Differences* of Diff-hist	0.795
Sum of neighbours differences	0.575	Sum ratio (former/latter)	0.020
Number of maximal points	0.042	Max increment width	0.052
Number of minimal points	0.024	Max increment value	0.514
Max gap	0.581	Max decrement width	0.039
Min gap	0.377	Max decrement value	0.320
Differences* of Gap-hist	1.522		

•Adopted features are colored.

*Sum of differences between bins of the class and that of fist class

Histogram feature	Num. of bin	Sep. Met. (Ave.)
Gap Histogram (Gap-hist)	8	0.190
Difference of neighbours histogram (Diff-hist)	8	0.110
Open hand difference histogram	16	0.497

Table 1. Separation metrics of features

muscles and tendons for finger movements are crowded even near the wrist, and it is difficult to recognize the wrist contour variation of independent finger.

Feature extraction

We organized feature candidates (13 single features and 3 histogram features), and evaluated their availabilities. Data of fist class and open hand class were used as the pre-classification calibration data. In evaluation of features, we used separation metrics as an evaluation standard.

$$Separation\ metrics = \frac{Between\ class\ variance}{Within\ class\ variance}$$

We can evaluate effectiveness of features without learning process with the metrics value. Table 1 shows feature candidates and separation metrics of them. Through this analysis, we selected six single features and one histogram feature with high separation metrics. Figure 11 shows the overview and chart of one good feature; max increment value.

Classification method

We designed a classification method using the features as inputs.

Target hand shape classes are eight classes as shown in Figure 8. We utilized "'k-NN method", which can use data similarity effectively, and "boosting", which can make strong classification from weak features [2]. As for boosting, we utilized multi-class method Adaboost.MH [8] with weak learners of features. Each feature is normalized from the calibration data of fist and open hand class, eventually the range between max and min was configured to 2.0.

EXPERIMENT

We conducted hand shape classification experiments. The classification outputs the most probable class. Experiments are sorted into two categories: (1) learning data including

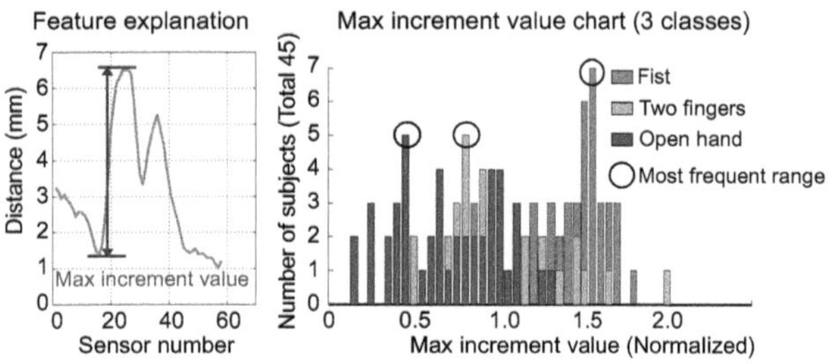

Figure 11. Feature example (max increment value)

the subject's data and (2) learning data excluding the subject's data. In category (1), three data were used for learning and another data was used for test regarding the subject. Learning data included three data of the other six subjects. In category (2), we exerted cross-validation: nine subjects' data out of ten subjects' data were used for learning data and one subject's data was used for test data in rotation.
Figure 12 and Figure 13 show the experimental results. Row classes are input classes (answer classes) and column classes are output classes. The diagonal line indicates correct output classes, larger numbers on the diagonal line mean better performance of the classification. The performance was evaluated in classification rate.

$$Classification\ rate = \frac{Number\ of\ correct\ samples}{Number\ of\ all\ samples}$$

The classification rate (Boosting, k-NN method) are 64.1%, 72.2% in category (1) and 47.8%, 45.6% in category (2). However, in category (2), classification rate changed from 35.8% to 65.4% (Boosting) and from 25.4% to 59.6% (k-NN method) depending on the combination of the data. We thought this is because subjects who have similar wrist contours are exist and high classification rate occurs when one subject is assigned to learning data and the other is assigned to test data. So collecting more learning data may enhance the performance of the classification.

CONCLUDIONS

In this study, we developed a novel hand shape classification system using wrist contours in order to recognize hand shapes with little stress on users.
First, we developed a wrist-watch type wrist contour sensor device. Mounting small distance sensors (photo reflectors) on a flexible band enabled to measure wrist contour with 2.5mm pitch. Second, we observed differences attributed by hand shapes and postures, and then picked up some useful features such as sum of gaps and differences of histogram. In classification, approximately 70% classification rate was marked when the learning data included the subject's data. Additionally, it was confirmed that some subjects have similar wrist contour and it indicates the possibility of pre-learning-free recognition.

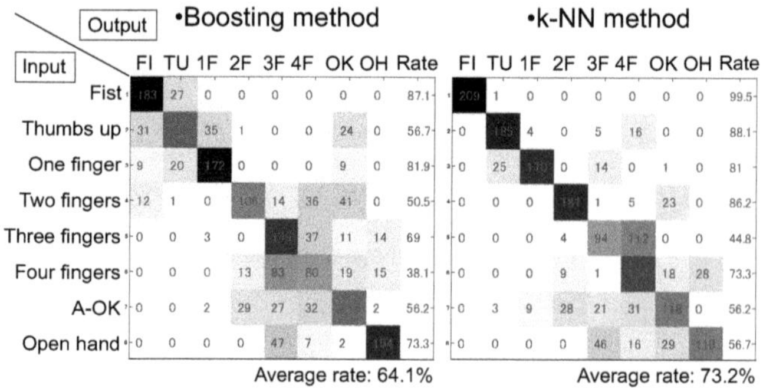

Figure 12. Results 1 (Including subject's data)

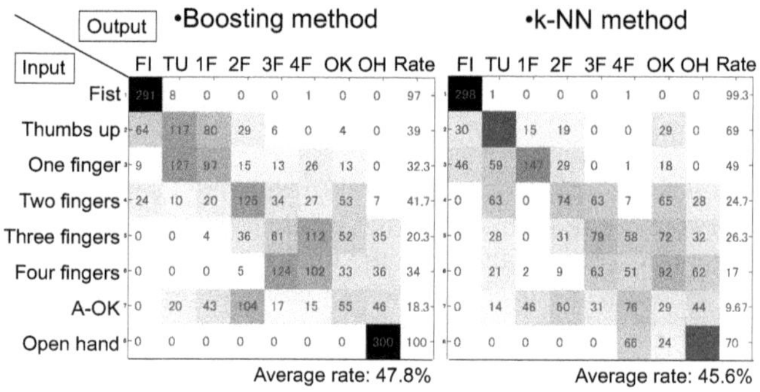

Figure 13. Results 2 (Excluding subject's data)

REFERENCES

1. M. Baldauf et al. Gestural interfaces for micro projector-based mobile phone applications. In *Proc. of the Int. Conf. on Ubiquitous Computing*, 2009.

2. C. M. Bishop. *Pattern Recognition and Machine Learning (Information Science and Statistics)*. Springer, 1st ed. 2006. corr. 2nd printing edition, 2007.

3. CyberGloveSystems. `http://www.cyberglovesystems.com/`.

4. A. Erol et al. A review on vision-based full dof hand motion estimation. In *Proc. of IEEE Computer Society Conf. on Computer Vision and Pattern Recognition*, page 75, 2005.

5. T. S. Huang et al. Hand gesture modeling, analysis, and synthesis. In *Proc. of IEEE Int. Workshop on Automatic Face and Gesture Recognition*, pages 73–79, 1995.

6. K. Nagata et al. A classification method of hand movements using multi channel electrode. In *Proc. of IEEE-EMBS. Annual Int. Conf. of the Engineering in Medicine and Biology Society*, pages 2375 –2378, 2005.

7. J. Rekimoto. Gesturewrist and gesturepad: Unobtrusive wearable interaction devices. In *Proc. of the 5th IEEE International Symposium on Wearable Computers*, IEEE Computer Society Washington, DC, USA, 2001.

8. R. E. Schapire et al. Improved boosting algorithms using confidence-rated predictions. *Machine Learning*, 37:297–336, 1999.

9. T. Starner et al. Real-time american sign language recognition using desk and wearable computer based video. *Pattern Analysis and Machine Intelligence, IEEE Transactions on*, 20(12):1371 –1375, 1998.

Deliberation for Intuition: A Framework for Energy-Efficient Trip Detection on Cellular Phones

Yifei Jiang†, Du Li‡, Guang Yang‡, Qin Lv†, and Zhigang Liu‡
†Dept of Computer Science, University of Colorado, Boulder, Colorado
‡Nokia Research Center, Palo Alto, California
†{yifei.jiang, qin.lv}@colorado.edu, ‡{lidu008, yangguang, zl100871}@gmail.com

ABSTRACT
Trip detection is a fundamental issue in many context-sensitive information services on mobile devices. It aims to automatically recognize significant places and trips between them. The key challenge is how to minimize energy consumption while maintaining high accuracy. Previous works that use GPS/WiFi sampling are accurate but energy efficiency is low and does not improve over time. Learning from the human decision making process, we propose an energy-efficient trip detection framework that consists of two modes: The *deliberation* mode learns cell-id patterns using GPS/WiFi based localization methods; the *intuition* mode only uses cell-ids and learned patterns for trip detection; transition between the two modes is controlled by parameters that are also learned. We evaluated our framework using real-life traces of six people over five months. Our experiments demonstrate that its energy consumption decreases rapidly as users' activities manifest regularity over time.

Author Keywords
Location Based Services, Energy Efficiency, Smart Phones

ACM Classification Keywords
C.3.3 Special-Purpose and Application-Based Systems: Real-Time and Embedded Systems

General Terms
Algorithms, Design, Experimentation, Performance

1. INTRODUCTION
Trip is a common and regular activity in our daily life. According to [5], on average a person makes 4.09 trips every day. Interestingly, most trips are regular in that they are repeated between only a few highly frequented places, e.g., daily commute between home and work.

The proliferation of mobile devices such as cellphones makes it possible to understand these trips more easily and provide information services in context [1]. Those services include single-user apps, e.g., personalized ubiquitous advertising [10], itinerary recommendation and destination prediction [22, 21, 11], transportation mode [18], user tracking for automatic travel diaries and emergency calls, personalized audiovisual narrations to museum visitors, contextualized reminders, pre-caching of data and services. They also include collaborative apps, e.g., road condition and traffic monitoring [14], activity awareness [2], and mining correlated behavior from multiple users' GPS data [24, 23, 3].

Most of the above services require a fundamental function, *trip detection*, to recognize significant places where a person stays or visits frequently and the trips between those places. This information is useful for an application to determine when to start and stop its service. Trip detection is a challenging task for the following three reasons: First, trip detection must be automated. We cannot leave it to the user as it would be annoying and error-prone. Second, it must be energy-efficient. Since the user may start or end a trip anytime and anywhere, the function will be running backstage all the time. Third, the detection must be accurate and timely for the services to be useful to the user.

In this paper, we propose a framework for automatic, accurate, timely, and energy-efficient trip detection on mobile devices. We focus on the detection of when a trip starts and ends with regard to *significant places* where the user spends considerable time, e.g., home and workplace. We synergistically combine the merits of GPS/WiFi based methods, which are more accurate yet energy-consuming, and cell id based methods, which are energy-efficient yet less accurate. Compared with previous GPS/WiFi based works, e.g., [7, 8, 9], our approach exhibits a clear trend of decreasing energy consumption as a user visits the same places and repeats the same trips. Our framework is inspired from human decision theories in psychology [19, 6] with two distinct modes:

• In the *deliberation mode*, we learn cell id patterns from trace data collected by GPS, WiFi, and cell id sensors, and associate those patterns with places and trips learned using existing GPS/WiFi based localization methods. The energy expense will be comparable to previous approaches.

• In the *intuition mode*, we use collected cell id data and the learned cell id patterns for determining whether a user is at a place, entering a place, or departing a place. When it is a repeated place or trip, the energy expense will be minimum because only cell id data is collected.

Section 2 surveys related work. Section 3 motivates and overviews the framework. Section 4 elaborates the deliberation and intuition modes and the transition between them. Section 5 evaluates the framework with real-life traces. Section 6 summarizes contributions and remaining issues.

2. BACKGROUND AND RELATED WORK

2.1 Place Learning

There are generally two approaches to place learning – geometry and fingerprint. [1] and [7] are geometric, in which geo-coordinates belonging to the same meaningful places are clustered. [1] considers locations where GPS signal is lost for some time as potential place candidates, exploiting the fact that GPS reception is poor indoors and around the so-called urban canyons. [7] uses time-based clustering and conceptually can work with any indoor or outdoor positioning technologies as long as they produce geo-coordinates.

Among fingerprint-based approaches, [4][12][20] assume that radio fingerprints of places are stable and unique. By comparing similarity between two fingerprints, we can tell whether they are close or far apart. The BeaconPrint algorithm [4] periodically scans WiFi base stations and GSM cells to form fingerprints. According to [4], the visibility of a beacon is often a better metric than the received signal strength when constructing a fingerprint, an idea inherited in later works [8][9]. Works in [12][20] address mass-market devices by making a harsher assumption that nothing but cellular radio is available. Both adopt simple algorithms to scan traces of timestamped cell ids and cluster those seen as close, using temporal correlations only. Compared to other more advanced methods, although they provide less accuracy, they consume less energy and run on any cellular device.

2.2 Place and Trip Recognition

Geometry-based algorithms recognize places by checking whether the device's current geo-location falls into the geometric shape of any place. Approaches in [12][20] work by comparing the current GSM cell id to each of the cell id clusters. PlaceSense [8] proposes to not only recognize if a user is at a place, but also whether she is arriving at or leaving a place, i.e., place entrance and departure. In addition to revising the original BeaconPrint algorithm in [4], PlaceSense reliably detects place departure by requiring all representative beacons associated with a place to have disappeared for some time, and detects place entrance by buffering scanned fingerprints for parallel entrance/departure detection.

2.3 Energy Efficiency for Location Sensing

Location sensing methods, relying on GPS and/or WiFi, can provide accurate location information but are always power hungry. In order to address the problem, Kim et al. [8, 9] proposed an accelerometer based approach, which uses acceleration reading to detect a user's movement and stops location sensing when the user is stationary. The flip side is two-fold: (1) although accelerometers consume little energy compared to GPS or WiFi, it still incurs extra overhead when always on, and (2) movement detected by accelerometers does not necessarily indicate that the user is in place transition, e.g., she may be walking around in her office.

Lin et al. [13] proposed to select different location sensors to sense locations based on accuracy requirement, energy profile of sensors, and their accuracy at different locations. Paek et al.[16] proposed a rate-adaptive approach for GPS positioning, in which the GPS is adaptively turned on based on estimated velocity of user; further, their approach learns locations of GPS unavailability to avoid turning on GPS in those places. Zhuang et al. [25] proposed an energy efficient location sensing framework that leverages other lower-power location sensors and uses an accelerometer to avoid unnecessary GPS sensing; in addition, it synchronizes the location sensing requests from multiple applications and tunes sensing parameters based on battery level.

2.4 Comparisons

Our work aims to exploit cell ids for trip detection and use GPS/WiFi only for training. Its energy efficiency improves over time as places are re-visited, a trend not demonstrated in previous works to our best knowledge. It resembles [8] in addressing the similar problem of detecting begin and end of a trip; however, [8] resorts to periodic GPS/WiFi scan and does not improve its energy efficiency over time. As in [9, 25], we use accelerometer for energy-efficient data collection in the deliberation mode; however, we only use cell ids in the intuition mode while at familiar places, thus avoiding the overheads and accuracy problems discussed above. Techniques in [13, 16, 25] are complementary to ours, which could be leveraged in our future work for further improvements. Our approach differs from [12][20] in that we use cell ids for recognizing begin/end of a trip, by computing the *time-variant* cell id flipping patterns (probabilities), instead of constructing *time-invariant* cliques as they do.

3. DESIGN OVERVIEW

3.1 Motivating Observations

Our work is motivated by the following four observations that are related to cellular devices: First, each device is assigned to one active cell tower at any time through which its basic telephone capability functions (or none in absence of cellular signals). In a mobile phone application, reading the active cell id is as cheap as reading a system variable. In contrast, it incurs extra costs to read other sensory data such as GPS, WiFi, and Bluetooth that are often used for localization. If a level of accuracy comparable to using those alternative sensors can be achieved, it would be more energy-efficient to use cell id for trip detection.

Second, for reasons such as load balancing and signal attenuation, cells usually overlap. As a result, the active cell id of a device often oscillates between several alternatives even when the device remains still at one place. However, the patterns typically differ when the device is moving within a place, e.g., a building, and when it is moving between two places that are sufficiently far apart. That is, it is possible to use cell id patterns for trip detection.

Third, it is fast to read the active cell id information and detect its changes. Cell id is almost always available, even where WiFi and GPS information is unavailable or noisy. By comparison, WiFi is not always available and takes time to scan; GPS is noisy in the urban canyons and often takes from tens of seconds to a few minutes to warm up, especially after a period of sleep or signal loss, as confirmed in [7].

Last but not least, due to their coarse granularity, cell tower ids alone cannot be used for accurate localization. We must use cell ids in combination with more accurate measures, such as GPS and WiFi beacons, or at least first use those measures to train the cell id based mechanism so as to achieve the desired level of accuracy.

From the above observations, it seems possible and advantageous to use cell id patterns for detecting places and place boundaries (i.e., begin and end of a trip). If this is feasible with high accuracy, then we can rely on cell ids for energy-efficient trip detection. The questions are (1) how to obtain the cell-id patterns for places and their boundaries, (2) how to use these patterns for trip detection, and (3) under what conditions we can or cannot use these patterns.

3.2 Human Decision Making Model

In pursuit of a solution to the trip detection problem, we are inspired by the dual-process theory for human decision making in the psychology literature [19][6]. According to the theory, individuals sometimes make decisions deliberately and sometimes rely on their intuition or gut feeling. Intuition (or associative reasoning) is directly proportional to the similarity of past experiences, relying on temporal and similarity relations to determine reasoning rather than an underlying mechanical structure. On the other hand, deliberation (the true reasoning) functions on logical structure and variables, basing upon rule systems to come to conclusions. In general, deliberation is slower and subject to conscious judgments, while intuition comes to mind quickly and effortlessly.

In spirit of this theory, we treat our mobile phone app as an intelligent agent, which distinguishes deliberation and intuition modes: In the deliberation mode, our system uses more energy-expensive information (e.g., WiFi, GPS, and accelerometer) with heavier computation to make decisions regarding trip detection. Meanwhile, the system will build "experiences," i.e., cell id patterns or probabilities. In the intuition mode, the system uses inexpensive information (the active cell id) and "past experiences" to make decisions through lightweight probabilistic reasoning. Wherever past experiences are insufficient, the system falls back to the deliberation mode to accrue more experiences by learning new patterns, or reinforcing or correcting learned patterns.

3.3 Overall Approach and Scope of Research

Figure 1 gives an overview of our trip detection approach as motivated above. Initially, our system determines the user's current state, whether she is at some significant place or in a trip. By definition, a significant place is where the user has stayed for more than some time (say 10 minutes) or where she frequently visits; a trip is the transition state between two places. In absence of knowledge such as accurate schedule, when the user is at a place, the system has to continuously detect whether the user is leaving the place for a trip to another place, and, when the user is already in a trip, the system has to continuously determine whether she is arriving at some place. This is the so-called problem of trip detection, i.e., to recognize begin and end of a trip [8].

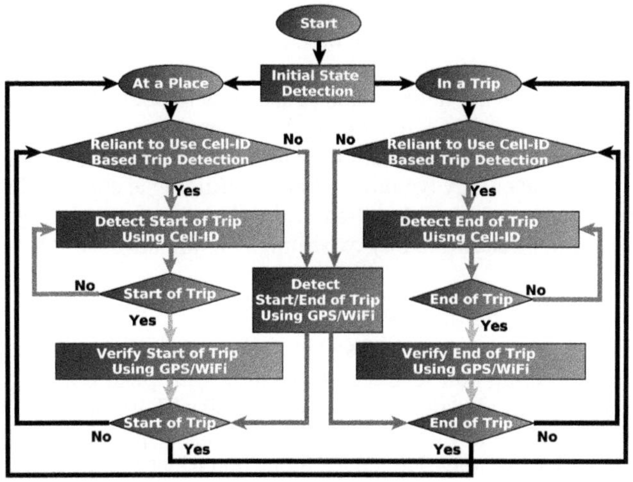

Figure 1. Detecting begin and end of a trip relative to a significant place: Use cell id patterns for "intuitive" detection when possible, and use GPS/WiFi for "deliberate" detection when necessary. Energy saving is achieved when a user visits the same places and repeats the same trips and accordingly the system works in the intuition mode.

In each of the states, at a place or in a trip, the system works in either a deliberation or an intuition mode. In the deliberation mode, sensory data such as GPS and WiFi beacons are collected and used for trip detection and place recognition. Many existing methods could be leveraged here, e.g., [4][7][9]. The method in our system is extended from [7] and [9], which uses GPS/WiFi to infer places/trips and accelerometer based movement detection to reduce power consumption. After the significant places are recognized, we compute the patterns of cell ids at those places.

In the intuition mode, we use cell ids alone for trip detection (and place recognition). We keep a short history of recently observed active cell ids and compute the probability of the history with regard to the patterns learned in the deliberation mode. If the user was last known to be at a place, she is likely departing the place when the probability is low relative to that place, or remains at that place when the probability remains above some threshold. Similarly, if the user was last known to be in a trip, she is likely arriving at a place when the probability is high relative to some known place, or she is still in the trip when no such place is found. It could be a new place when new cell id observations are made; then the algorithm for place/trip learning will step in (Section 2.1).

The two modes are not independent: The intuition mode makes trip detection decisions based on the cell id patterns computed in the deliberation mode. The transition between modes is controlled by system parameters that gauge whether or not the patterns are sufficiently reliant. At a place or in a trip, when a new cell id observation is made that has not been learned, the system falls back to the deliberation mode to collect more data and learn new patterns.

4. DELIBERATION AND INTUITION

This section elaborates the deliberation and intuition modes (phases). Specifically, we will discuss how to compute cell id patterns in the deliberation phase, how to detect begin and end of a trip using cell ids in the intuition phase, and when to transit from the deliberation phase to the intuition phase to harvest the energy benefits without sacrificing accuracy. Key parameters will be identified in the discussions, which will be further determined by experiments in the next section.

4.1 The Deliberation Phase

This phase has three tasks: (1) learning significant places, (2) collecting cell id traces associated with places, and (3) learning cell id patterns. Since we leverage [7, 9] for task (1), we assume that the interesting places and trips are already learned accurately. Hence we focus on tasks (2) and (3).

4.1.1 Collecting Cell ID Traces

In principle, cell phones are able to see all available cells in the vicinity before selecting one to connect to, and some commercial phone models do provide such capability under the so-called "field test" mode. In reality, however, most phone OSs only provide APIs to reveal the active cell to which the phone is currently connected. We assume that only the active cell information may be retrieved, to accommodate mass-market devices that lack a field test mode. The active cell information usually includes mobile country code, mobile network code, local area code, and cell id. To protect user privacy, we hash each observed tuple into an internal id and refer to the hash code as the "cell id".

We associate a time duration to each cell id observation to indicate how long that cell id is continuously observed. For example, if connection to an observed cell id X has lasted δ_X seconds before the phone switches to another cell, we record this observation in a 2-tuple (X, δ_X). If that observation is immediately followed by an observation of cell id Y for δ_Y seconds, they will appear in the trace consecutively as $(X, \delta_X)\,(Y, \delta_Y)$. Modern phone APIs allow an application to register a callback function that is called when the active cell changes. We can record the time difference as δ_X between the moment the active cell changes to X and the moment it changes to something else. In absence of such APIs, we can read the active cell id periodically say every 2 seconds and similarly record the duration of each observed cell id.

4.1.2 Learning Cell ID Patterns

Algorithm 1 sketches how cell id patterns are learned from collected traces. In the input, we assume that each recognized place in *tab_plc* is associated with a sequence of cell id observations, which is a time series. Each cell id observation is labeled with some place Z from *tab_plc*. This provides the basis for supervised learning of cell id patterns. We then calculate the following three sets of probabilities:

1. Pr(Z), the prior probability of place Z, for each place Z;

2. Pr($X, \delta_X | Z$), the conditional probability of observing (X, δ_X) at place Z, for each observation (X, δ_X) at each place Z;

3. Pr($X, \delta_X \rightarrow Y | Z$), the conditional probability of observing cell id Y immediately following the observation of (X, δ_X) at place Z, for each observation (X, δ_X) and each cell id Y at each place Z, where $Y \neq X$.

Algorithm 1 Supervised cell-id pattern learner

global *tab_plc*; ▷ places with cell-id traces – Input
global *tab_ptn*; ▷ cell-id patterns – Output
for each place Z in *tab_plc* **do**
  $tab\_ptn(Z) \leftarrow$ Pr(Z); ▷ prior probability
  for each cell id instance (X, δ_X) in Z **do**
    $tab\_ptn(Z, X, \delta_X) \leftarrow$ Pr($X, \delta_X | Z$);
  end for
  for each consecutive $(X, \delta_X)\,(Y, \delta_Y)$ in Z **do**
    $tab\_ptn(Z, X, \delta_X, Y) \leftarrow$ Pr($X, \delta_X \rightarrow Y | Z$);
  end for
end for

Algorithm 2 Cell-id state predictor(**input** s, q)

global *tab_ptn*; ▷ cell-id patterns
global T_s and T_e; ▷ probability thresholds for places
if last state s is at-a-place(Z) **then**
  Pr($q|Z$) $\leftarrow$ ▷ probability of observed sequence q
    Pr($q_0, \delta_{q_0} | Z$) $\cdot$ Pr($q_0, \delta_{q_0} \rightarrow q_1 | Z$) $\cdot$
    $\cdots \cdot$ Pr($q_{n-1}, \delta_{q_{n-1}} \rightarrow q_n | Z$); ▷ $n{=}|q|$
  if Pr($q|Z$) $\leq T_s(Z)$ **then** ▷ departing place Z
    return start-of-trip;
  end if
else if last state s is in-a-trip **then**
  $\hat{Z} \leftarrow \mathrm{argmax}_{Z \in all\ places}$ Pr($q|Z$) $\cdot$ Pr(Z);
  if Pr($q|\hat{Z}$) $\geq T_e(\hat{Z})$ **then** ▷ arriving at place $\hat{Z}$
    return end-of-trip;
  end if
end if

Given the training set of *tab_plc*, Pr(Z) is calculated by dividing the total stay time at Z by the total stay time at all places. Pr($X, \delta_X | Z$) is calculated by dividing the sum of durations of all (X, δ_X) instances by the total stay time at place Z. Pr($X, \delta_X \rightarrow Y | Z$) is calculated by dividing the number of observation instances where Y appears immediately after some (X, δ_X), by the total number of (X, δ_X) instances at place Z. These probabilities are then saved to *tab_ptn*.

Note that the duration δ_X in each observation (X, δ_X) is a real number. As will be discussed in Section 5, the duration values will all be discretized into a small number of categories. The discretization scheme itself is a system parameter to be determined by experiments.

4.2 The Intuition Phase

Algorithm 2 outlines how we detect the start/end of a trip given the last known state s, either at-a-place or in-a-trip, and an up-to-date sequence q of cell id observations. The length of q is fixed and we keep a sliding window of $|q|$ most recently observed cell ids and their durations. Notation q_i denotes the i-th element in q, where $0 \leq i < |q|$.

When the last system state s is at place Z, Algorithm 2 constantly monitors the active cell id, and calculates $Pr(q|Z)$ every time a new cell id observation is made and added to q. If $Pr(q|Z)$ drops sufficiently low, say below a threshold $T_s(Z)$, a trip start is reported. As shown in Figure 1, GPS/WiFi scan will be turned on to verify this detection. The system state s is changed to in-a-trip if it is confirmed.

When the last state is in-a-trip, Algorithm 2 continues to monitor the active cell id, looking for potential arrival at another place $\hat{Z}$ with the following Bayesian equation:

$$\hat{Z} = \underset{Z \in all\ places}{\text{argmax}}\ Pr(q|Z) \cdot Pr(Z)$$

If $Pr(q|\hat{Z})$ is above threshold $T_e(\hat{Z})$, a trip end is reported. Again GPS/WiFi will be turned on for verification. If it is confirmed, state s is changed to at place $\hat{Z}$.

Assuming that the sliding window size $|q|$ is 3 and the most recent cell id is C. Duration δ_C is not available until the device switches to yet another cell. Let $q = (A, \delta_A)(B, \delta_B)(C, \_)$. By the Bayesian theorem, $Pr(q|Z)$ can be written as:

$$\begin{aligned} Pr(q|Z) &= Pr((A, \delta_A)(B, \delta_B)(C, \_)|Z) \\ &= Pr(A, \delta_A|Z) \times Pr(A, \delta_A \rightarrow B|Z) \\ &\quad \times Pr(A, \delta_A \rightarrow B, \delta_B \rightarrow C|Z) \\ &= Pr(A, \delta_A|Z) \times Pr(A, \delta_A \rightarrow B|Z) \\ &\quad \times Pr(B, \delta_B \rightarrow C|Z). \end{aligned}$$

Note that in the last step we assume a first-order Markov model, which is a widely made assumption. That is, each observation only depends on its immediate preceding observation. Each term on the right-hand side of the equation can be directly retrieved from tab_ptn, which is computed by Algorithm 1. We consider the sliding window size $|q|$ and, for each place Z, the two probability thresholds, $T_s(Z)$ (for detecting start of trip) and $T_e(Z)$ (for detecting end of trip), as parameters yet to be determined by experiments.

4.3 Transition between Two Phases

Obviously, we must deliberate the cell-id patterns before they could be used for intuitive trip detection. For the probabilities to be reliable, they must be computed from a sufficiently large set of data. Otherwise we must fall back to the deliberation mode for more data. The question is how much data would be sufficient and when to switch between modes.

Unfortunately, there is no obvious answer to this obvious question. At any place, for example, the set of cell ids observed and their durations will be dependent on the local cell coverage as well as how active the user is. This has two practical implications: One is that the thresholds for the transition between deliberation and intuition are necessarily different from place to place. The other is that the value space is very large and it would be impractical to require the user to exhaust the value space for data collection.

In order to seek a balance between energy cost and accuracy, our system takes an incremental approach, which is

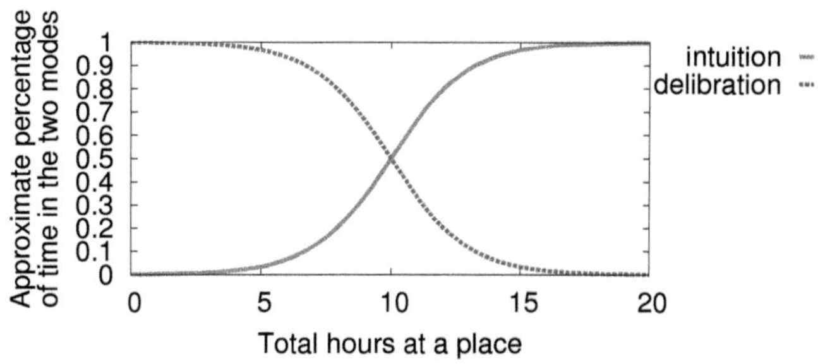

Figure 2. The energy-consuming deliberation phases out after sufficient experience has accrued for intuitive trip detection. The two modes coexist for some period of time for desired accuracy.

illustrated in Figure 2. Initially, the system works in a deliberation mode to aggressively collect data. After spending a few hours at one place, it computes the cell-id patterns for that place. Then, it starts trying to use the cell-id patterns for prediction, while staying in the deliberation mode. Hence there is a period (called dual mode) in which the two phases overlap. In this period, the results yielded from the intuitive predictor are compared to those from the deliberate predictor. When the accuracy of the intuitive predictor is sufficiently high (based on the results of the deliberate predictor), the deliberate predictor will phase out.

On one hand, there are heuristics by which we can estimate how long the user must stay before entering the dual mode. For example, it may deserve a trial if the user has accumulated two hours of data at a place. On the other hand, exceptions may still arise even after it has demonstrated sufficient accuracy at some point and is already in a "pure" intuition mode. This may happen, e.g., when a new cell id X is observed at place Z, or the (discretized) duration δ_X of some X is not yet in the computed patterns. In such cases, our system will temporarily fall back to the dual mode.

5. EXPERIMENTS AND PERFORMANCE EVALUATION

In this section, we evaluate the performance of the proposed framework for energy-efficient trip detection. Specifically, we will answer the following two questions:

- How well does our approach perform trip detection in terms of accuracy, timeliness, and energy efficiency?
- How do the identified parameters affect system performance? How to choose the "best" parameter values?

5.1 Data Collection

We have developed a data collection program which collects GPS, WiFi, accelerometer, and cell id information. GPS and WiFi data are collected every 2 seconds, while cell id data are collected using the "callback" mode and the current cell id is recorded every time it changes. Accelerometer data are sampled at 30 Hz. The data collection program has been deployed on six Nokia N900 devices, each carried by a user in our study. Four users ran it each for four months, and the other two users ran it each for one month. To obtain the ground truth, we asked the users to take notes on all the trips during the data collection period. All trips are also verified on maps using the Google Map API and we have manually marked the start and end of each trip in the collected data.

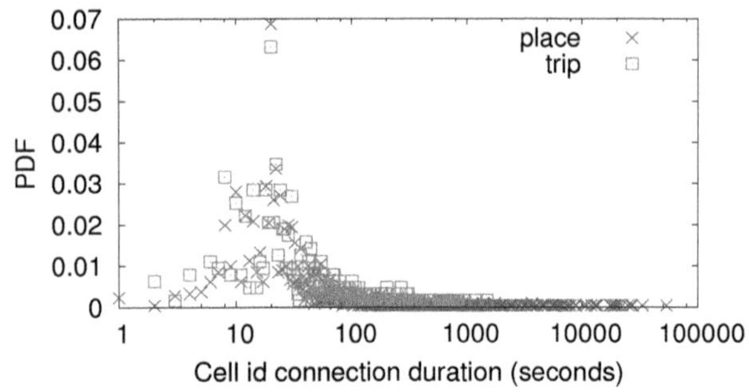

Figure 3. Distribution of cell id connection duration (δ) when at place and in trip. Accordingly, we define 6 discrete categories, i.e., the class is 6 if $\delta > 243$, and $\lceil log_3 \delta \rceil$ if $0 < \delta \leq 243$.

In total, we have collected 1755 trips, among which there are 139 unique trips and 83 unique places. To demonstrate the advantages of our approach, we ignore casual trips and focus only on regular trips, i.e., trips that have been repeated at least once. This leaves us with 1701 trips, which contain 85 unique trips and 43 unique places. On average, a trip is repeated 4.17 times, ranging from 2 to 62 times. The trips range from 1 mile to 32 miles in distance (average 12 miles) and include driving, cycling, and walking trips. Trip duration varies from 5 minutes to 53 minutes, and the average is 24 minutes. The amount of time that our users stay at a place varies from 8 minutes to 16 hours and the average is 5 hours. The regularity in our data set is consistent with [5].

5.2 Parameter Settings

There are three key parameters in our framework: the trip start and end thresholds, $T_s(Z)$ and $T_e(Z)$, for each significant place Z, the discretized duration length δ_X of each cell id connection X, and length $|q|$ of observed cell id sequence q on which we compute probabilities.

5.2.1 Length of Recent Cell-ID Sequence

As shown in Algorithm 2, we compute the probability of a sequence q of recent cell ids. A larger $|q|$ value may yield more accurate probability estimation and better trip detection accuracy, but it may also reduce the timeliness of trip detection and incur higher computation overheads. As will be shown (Figure 6), when $|q| = 3$, the algorithm demonstrates a desired performance tradeoff, and there is no obvious improvement on accuracy when $|q| > 3$. Therefore, we set $|q|$ to 3 in the other experiments and our system.

5.2.2 Discretization of Cell-ID Connection Durations

Figure 3 shows the probability distribution of cell id connection durations in users' places and trips. We see that the connection durations vary significantly from several seconds to a few hours. Equally treating all the possible duration values would result in many zero probabilities. Instead, we need to discretize the duration values into multiple categories which best capture the ranges of connection durations that occur frequently. Our analysis reveals that (1) connection duration goes above 1000 seconds only when a user stays at a place (not during a trip), and (2) connection duration is most frequently around 20 seconds for both trips and places.

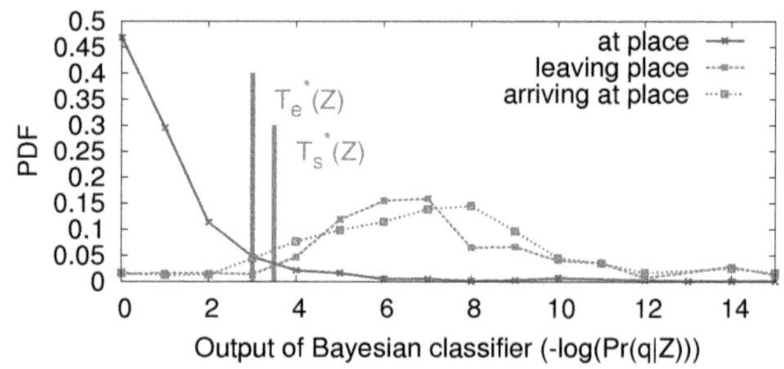

Figure 4. Determination of the probability thresholds $T_s^*(Z)$ and $T_e^*(Z)$ for place Z. Note that the probability $Pr(q|Z)$ decreases as $(-log(Pr(q|Z)))$ increases along the x-axis. To handle small probability values, we compute $-log(Pr(q|Z))$ instead of $Pr(q|Z)$.

Let δ be the duration value of some cell-id connection. We define the discretization function as follows: If $\delta > 243$, the class is 6; or otherwise if $0 < \delta \leq 243$, the class is $\lceil log_3 \delta \rceil$. Then we have finer classes for more frequent durations and coarser classes for less frequent connections. This helps to distinguish start/end of trips from places.

5.2.3 Trip Start/End Thresholds

For each place Z, the thresholds $T_s(Z)$ and $T_e(Z)$ determine at what values of probability $Pr(q|Z)$ should a user be considered at a place or at start/end of a trip. To decide their values, we studied the probability distributions of all users staying, departing and arriving at their significant places and found that they demonstrated similar patterns.

As an example, Figure 4 plots the probability distributions when one user staying at some place Z, leaving place Z (from the user crossing the place boundary till $Pr(q|Z) = 0$), and arriving at place Z (from $Pr(q|Z) > 0$ till user crossing the boundary into Z). When the user stays at place Z, the curve shows higher probabilities for larger values of $Pr(q|Z)$; there is a long tail, however, when the user walks around the boundary of the place and/or some rare cell id observations are made. On the other hand, when the user is leaving or approaching place Z, the probabilities of $Pr(q|Z)$ are relatively low as compared to those when stay at place Z. By the two curves, values of $-log(Pr(q|Z))$ are almost normally distributed around 4-10, where the user is nearby place Z. A few high probabilities happen when user is at the place boundary and a few very low probabilities happen when some rare cell id observations are made.

The goal is to find the optimal threshold $T_s^*(Z)$ or $T_e^*(Z)$ that separates the cases of staying at place Z and leaving (or arriving at) place Z. In spirit of the clustering threshold tuning approach proposed in [17], our optimal threshold $T_s^*(Z)$ or $T_e^*(Z)$ corresponds to the point at which the two corresponding probability distributions intersect. Our experimental results show that $T_s^*(Z)$ and $T_e^*(Z)$ may take different values for the same place Z. For each place Z, our system will recalculate the threshold periodically since both user behavior changes (e.g., switching office room to another side of the building) and cell id changes (e.g., a new cell id observation is made) may entail adjustment to the thresholds.

Monotonicity of $p(q|Z)$ when user is leaving or approaching Z is important because the verification would be triggered many times and thus not "energy-efficient" if value of $p(q|Z)$ changed drastically. However, we found that 85% of $p(q|Z)$ are monotonic when user is leaving or approaching Z. 94% of the 15% non-monotonic values happen below (when leaving Z) or above (when approaching Z) the threshold, which does not need to verify by GPS/WiFi.

5.3 Performance Metrics

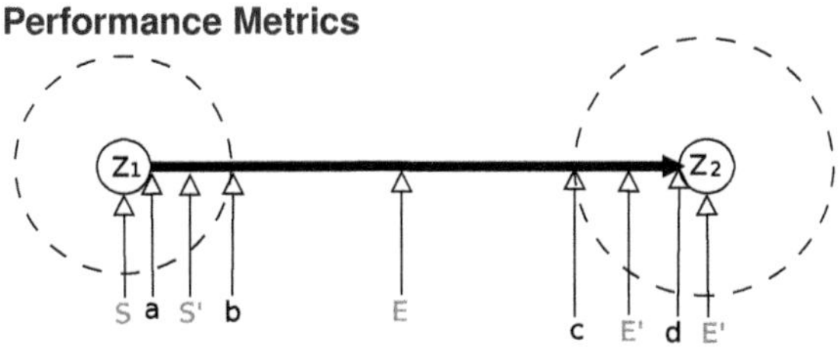

Figure 5. A trip from place Z_1 to place Z_2: a/d is the start/end of trip by ground truth; b/c is where the observation probability $Pr(q|Z_1)/Pr(q|Z_2)$ turns zero when moving away from place Z_1/Z_2.

Figure 5 shows a typical trip in which a user travels from place Z_1 to place Z_2. Consider the following four phases:

- Phase 1: Before a trip starts, the system should report that the user is at place Z_1. It is a false positive if the system reports a trip start (S). Although this type of error will be corrected by verification, a high false positive error will cause frequent verification and thus high energy cost.
- Phase 2: A trip has started, which should be detected (S'); otherwise it is a false negative error if the system still reports at place Z_1. Ideally, the trip start should be detected before $Pr(q|Z_1)$ drops to zero so as to reduce the latency. This is where threshold $T_s(Z_1)$ comes into play.
- Phase 3: During a trip, the system should report in trip. Otherwise, if the system reports end of trip (E), it is a false positive error, which costs energy for verification. Practically, the report of E is allowed to happen anywhere between when S' and E' are reported.
- Phase 4: When arriving at place Z_2, the system should report end of trip (E'). Ideally, to have a timely report, E' should be detected after $Pr(q|Z_2)$ turns greater than zero but before it reaches its maximum or equilibrium. This is where threshold $T_e(Z_2)$ comes into play. Reporting E' either right before d or right after d is considered acceptable (accurate). However, if the system still reports in trip after passing point d, it is a false negative error.

The performance of our trip detection solution can be measured using three key metrics: (1) *accuracy* measures how often our system correctly detects a trip start or end; (2) *timeliness* measures how quickly our system detects a trip start or end; and (3) *energy efficiency* measures the energy overhead incurred by our trip detection system. Ideally, our system should be able to detect trip starts and ends with high accuracy, in a timely manner, and with high energy efficiency. However, these three metrics impact each other and it is our goal to seek an appropriate performance tradeoff. We will explore the three metrics in Sections 5.4-5.6, respectively.

5.4 Accuracy

Since we resort to existing localization methods in the deliberation mode, here we only evaluate the accuracy of our approach in the intuition mode. For each trip and place, we compare our decision with the ground truth in each of the four phases. Our system makes a trip detection decision every time the active cell id changes. We define accuracy in any phase y as the number of correct detections in phase y divided by the total number of detections in phase y.

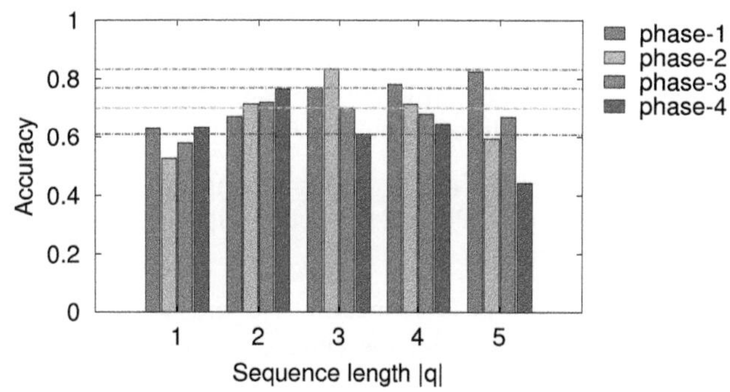

Figure 6. Trip detection accuracy in four phases using different cell id sequence lengths: $|q|$=3 represents a desired performance tradeoff.

Figure 6 compares the trip detection accuracy when different cell id sequence length values are used. We make the following observations:

- Our chosen sequence length $|q| = 3$ achieves the best accuracy overall, and it represents a good balance among accuracy, energy efficiency, and timeliness.
- Longer sequences help improve the accuracy of Phase 1, since people normally stay at a place longer and testing more cell ids will help increase the confidence of decision.
- Accuracy drops for Phase 2 and Phase 4 when $|q| > 3$, since longer sequences are more conservative and make it harder to detect trip start and end in a timely manner.
- Longer sequences result in a slight decrease of accuracy in Phase 3, since people's trips tend to be shorter than when staying at a place, and increasing sequence length may introduce more noise and reduce detection accuracy.

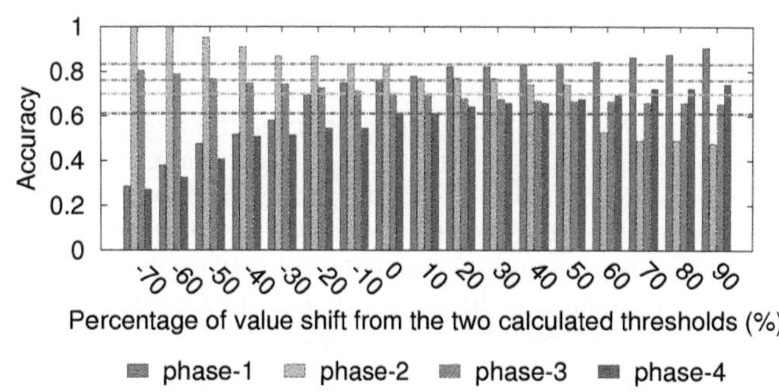

Figure 7. Trip detection accuracy by different classification thresholds.

Figure 7 shows the accuracy of the four phases using different classification thresholds. The x axis is the percentage of shift from the two thresholds automatically calculated as explained in Section 5.2.3: zero means the original thresholds,

10 means that both thresholds are incremented by 10%, and so forth. We can make the following observations:

- Our automatically-determined thresholds balance the false positive and false negative for both start and end of trip detection. This is because the accuracy of Phases 1 and 4 increases while that of Phases 2 and 3 decreases when lowering the thresholds.
- Under our automatically-determined thresholds, higher accuracy is achieved for Phase 1 and Phase 2, i.e., detecting a trip start is stabler than detecting a trip end. This is because the cell id pattern of staying at a place is stabler, while trips may differ in the means of transportation, speed, traffic conditions, and routes.
- For Phase 1 and Phase 2, lowering the thresholds leads to higher accuracy for Phase 2 (detecting trip start) but lower accuracy in Phase 1.
- For Phase 3 and Phase 4, lowering the thresholds leads to lower accuracy for detecting end of trip in Phase 4, but higher accuracy in Phase 3.
- In practice, we could adjust the thresholds to make trip detection more timely or more energy efficient.

Further, we also studied the overall accuracy of trip detection by using metrics of precision and recall. Recall is computed as the fraction of correctly detected trips among all trips that the users had, and precision is computed as the fraction of correctly detected trips among all trips that the algorithm believe to be correct. Based on our data set, we compared our method with four other methods: (1) GSM based, we use PlaceSense [8]; (2) GPS based, we use Kang et al. [7]; (3) GPS + Accelerometer (or GPS+), we use SensLoc [9]; (4) WiFi + Accelerometer (or WiFi+), we use SensLoc [9]. The experimental results are plotted in Figure 8.

As showed in Figure 8, WiFi and GPS based methods both have high precision and recall. For the WiFi based method, the errors in recall are because that several buildings and open places in our data are not covered by WiFi and hence trips from and to those places are not detected; the errors in precision are caused by noise of WiFi signals, when user walked within a building, sometimes the algorithm treats it as a trip start. For GPS based methods, the errors are due to the poor performance in urban canyon and indoor areas. GSM based methods have poor accuracy because single cell id can only work at a very coarse level and it may not be able to detect short trips; oscillation of cell ids at a place makes the precision low. Our method has better performance than WiFi and GPS based methods in recall because the cell id has better coverage than WiFi and GPS. Although the precision of our method is slightly lower, our verification process using WiFi or GPS compensates for the errors.

5.5 Timeliness

Not only do we want to detect trips accurately, the detection must also be made in a timely manner. That is, when a trip starts or ends, our system needs to detect it quickly. The timeliness of trip detection depends on two factors: The first

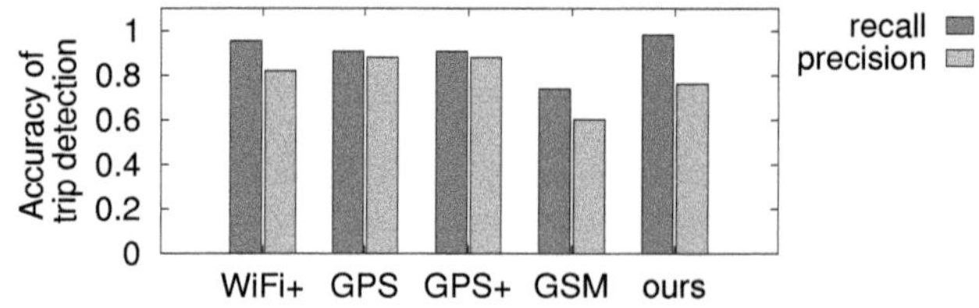

Figure 8. Comparison of overall accuracy of trip detection methods.

is how fast the cell id changes when starting or ending a trip, and the second is how fast we make the decision. The ground truth of trip starts and ends is determined by the time when a user entered or left a building. For open places, such as parks, the trip starts and ends depend on user inputs.

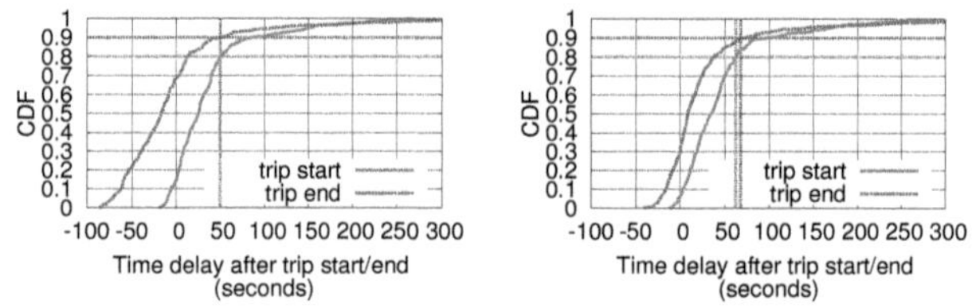

(a) Delay in cell id changes (b) Delay in trip detection

Figure 9. Delays in active cell id changes and intuitive trip detection.

To evaluate how fast the active cell id changes after a user starts or ends a trip, we examine all trips in the collected data. For each trip we extract time of trip start (or end) t from the ground truth, and calculate the time of first cell id change t_c after t. The difference between t and t_c is the inherent delay in our trip detection process. Figure 9(a) plots the cumulative distribution function (CDF) of all $t_c - t$ values calculated from our collected data for trip start and end. It shows that, for 80% (90%) of the time, the cell id changes within 50 seconds after a user starts (ends) a trip.

We then evaluate the average delay in our intuitive trip detection. As shown in Figure 9(b), for 80% (90%) of the time, our system can detect the trip start (end) in less than 62 (68) seconds. It is clear that the actual delays, 12 or 18 seconds, are insignificant. They are caused by trading timeliness for accuracy in our work: Often another cell-id change is awaited for $Pr(q|Z)$ to meet the desired threshold with regard to place Z. Our results are consistent with those in [9] yet we use a more energy-efficient cell-id based method that is, however, insensitive to extra delays as possibly caused by the GPS/WiFi scan period in their work.

We compared timeliness of different methods in Figure 10. As shown in Figure 10(a), our method is comparable to the WiFi based method in that about 80% of trip starts can be detected within 60 seconds. The GPS and GSM based methods have longer delay on trip start detection because GPS takes time to find fixes when the user starts trip and GSM has a coarse granularity in place recognition.

Figure 10(b) compares timeliness of trip end detection in different methods. Similarly to the WiFi based method, which can detect 80% of trip ends within 60 seconds, our method can detect 80% of trip ends within 40 seconds. The GPS

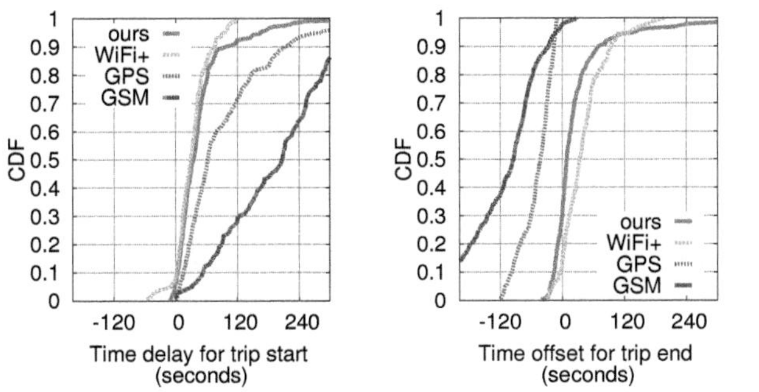

(a) Compare trip start delays (b) Compare trip end delays

Figure 10. Comparison of trip start/end delays in different methods.

and GSM methods can detect trip ends much earlier than our method – more than 90% trip ends are detected 20–240 seconds ahead of time. However, they may lead to premature decisions when the user just passes by the place, which lowers the trip detection accuracy.

In Figure 10, both CDF curves of our method have a long tail, which indicate that 7.5% (5%) of trip detections has a delay of more than 120 seconds. Those delays happened in remote areas due to sparse cellular coverage – the cell ids did not change that frequently. To address the delays, currently we resort to traditional GPS-accelerometer based methods (e.g., [9]) for energy saving at those places.

5.6 Energy Efficiency

To estimate the energy use of our approach, similarly to [9], we make the following assumptions: In the deliberation mode, (a) accelerometer is always on; and (b) GPS is used only when there is no WiFi; (c) neither GPS nor WiFi is on when the user is detected as stationary by accelerometer readings. In the intuition mode, (a) only collect cell id information; and (b) WiFi and accelerometer are always off.

We calculate average power consumption based on the N900 power consumption specification [15]. Specifically, reading cell id costs 0.01mW each time, WiFi scan at 1/6 Hz costs 80mW, GPS reading at 1/2 Hz costs 325mW, and accelerometer reading at 30 Hz costs 25 mW. In addition, we have conducted in-field power consumption measurements. These numbers are slightly higher than the spec but generally consistent, which do not affect the overall energy efficiency improvement we report here.

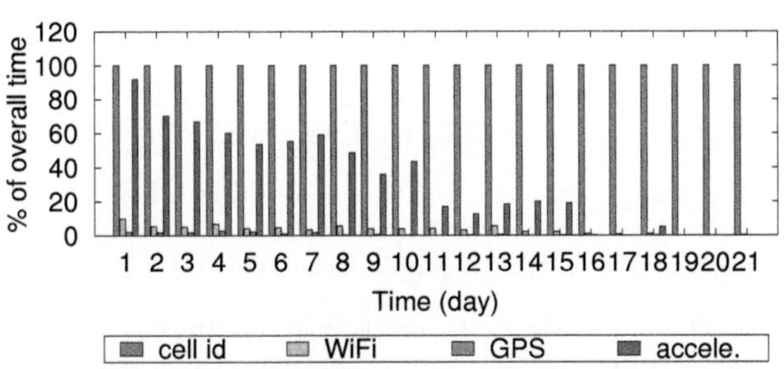

Figure 11. Average sensing time of cell id, WiFi, GPS, and accelerometer by 6 users in the first 21 days.

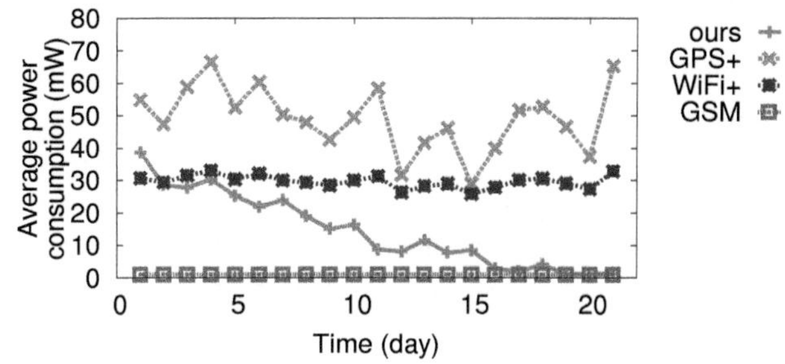

Figure 12. Average energy consumption of 6 users in the first 21 days.

It is our observation from the data that a user's mobility heavily affects power consumption. For instance, if a user is stationary most of the time, the system consumes very little energy even when running in the deliberation mode. If a user stays at a place all day and patterns at that place are already learned, then our system will run in the intuition mode most of the time and the power consumption will also be very low. However, if a user visits many new places, then the cell phone will run in the deliberation mode most of the time and the power consumption will be very high.

Figure 11 shows the average percentage of sensing time based on the total daily system running time of 6 users. We consider the sensing time of cell id, GPS, WiFi, and accelerometer over the first 21 days. During the first several days, the system runs mostly in the deliberation mode, accelerometer and WiFi are turned on most of the time. After a few days, for some places, the system starts to work in the intuition mode, then the daily working time of WiFi and accelerometer decreases generally, but still go up when a user visits new places. The working time of GPS is dependent on how much time a user spends in places without WiFi coverage.

Figure 12 shows the average power consumption of 6 users over the first 21 days. It shows that, overall, the average power consumption decreases quickly over time as our system learns about more places and spends more time in the intuition mode. In some days, the average power consumption increases, as a result of users making more trips or visiting new places. By comparison, other methods do not have a similar trend of decreasing power consumption over time.

Over the first 21 days, the average power consumption is 49.1 mW for the GPS based method, 29.6 mW for the WiFi based method, 1 mW for the GSM based method, and 14.5 mW for ours. Hence, our approach saves 70% energy compared to the GPS based method and 51% to the WiFi based method. Furthermore, the longer a user runs our system, the more energy they will save. In a long run, the power consumption of our system will be close to the GSM based approach because only cell id is used most of the time.

6. CONCLUSIONS AND FUTURE DIRECTIONS

This paper makes the following two novel contributions:

- We propose a 2-phase framework for energy-efficient trip detection on mobile devices: The deliberation phase uses sensors such as GPS and WiFi as in previous work for training a cell-id learner, and the intuition phase solely uses cell-id patterns for predicting start/end of a trip. The goal is to save energy by intuition when a user revisits familiar places or repeats familiar trips.

- We have collected real-life traces from six users over five months and used the data to evaluate the framework in terms of accuracy, timeliness, and energy efficiency. Our experiments demonstrated 51-70% energy savings over previous GPS/WiFi based methods and, moreover, an obvious trend in decreasing power consumption after a period of deliberation, with considerable accuracy and timeliness in intuitive trip detection. We also showed how the system parameters are tuned and how they impact the system performance tradeoffs among the three metrics.

Our framework can be implemented in either application (backstage service) or OS level to provide trip status information for applications. It is possible for people who live/work nearby to share the learned cell-id patterns and collaboratively construct a database of patterns. This would be useful, e.g., for better coverage of data and faster bootstrap of system. We plan to address related issues in future work.

ACKNOWLEDGEMENT

This work was supported in part by the National Science Foundation under Grant No. CNS-0910995.

REFERENCES

1. D. Ashbrook and T. Starner. Using GPS to learn significant locations and predict movement across multiple users. *Personal Ubiquitous Computing*, 7(5):275–286, 2003.
2. E. Bales, K. A. Li, and W. Griwsold. CoupleVIBE: Mobile implicit communication to improve awareness for (long-distance) couples. In *ACM CSCW*, pages 65–74, Mar. 2011.
3. X. Cao, G. Cong, and C. S. Jensen. Mining significant semantic locations from gps data. *Proc. VLDB Endow.*, 3:1009–1020, September 2010.
4. J. Hightower, S. Consolvo, A. LaMarca, I. E. Smith, and J. Hughes. Learning and recognizing the places we go. In *ACM Ubicomp*, pages 159–176, 2005.
5. P. Hu and T. Reuscher. Summary of travel trends, 2001 national household travel survey. Technical report, U.S.F.H.A. U.S. Department of Transportation, 2004.
6. D. Kahneman. A perspective on judgment and choice: mapping bounded rationality. *American Psychologist*, 58(9), Sept. 2003.
7. J. H. Kang, W. Welbourne, B. Stewart, and G. Borriello. Extracting places from traces of locations. *ACM SIGMOBILE Mobile Computing Communication Review*, 9(3):58–68, 2005.
8. D. H. Kim, J. Hightower, R. Govindan, and D. Estrin. Discovering semantically meaningful places from pervasive RF-beacons. In *ACM Ubicomp*, pages 21–30, 2009.
9. D. H. Kim, Y. Kim, D. Estrin, and M. B. Srivastava. SensLoc: Sensing everyday places and paths using less energy. In *ACM SenSys*, pages 315–330, 2010.
10. J. Krumm. Ubiquitous advertising: The killer application for the 21st century. *IEEE Pervasive Computing*, 10:66–73, 2011.
11. J. Krumm and E. Horvitz. Predestination: Where do you want to go today? *IEEE Computer*, 40(4):105–107, 2007.
12. K. Laasonen, M. Raento, and H. Toivonen. Adaptive on-device location recognition. In *Pervasive*, pages 287–304. 2004.
13. K. Lin, A. Kansal, D. Lymberopoulos, and F. Zhao. Energy-accuracy trade-off for continuous mobile device location. In *ACM MobiSys*, 2010.
14. P. Mohan, V. N. Padmanabhan, and R. Ramjee. Nericell: Rich monitoring of road and traffic conditions using mobile smartphones. In *ACM SenSys*, pages 323–336, 2008.
15. N900 hardware power consumption. http://wiki.maemo.org/N900_Hardware_Power_Consumption.
16. J. Paek, J. Kim, and R. Govindan. Energy-efficient rate-adaptive gps-based positioning for smartphones. In *ACM MobiSys*, 2010.
17. J.-g. Park, B. Charrow, D. Curtis, J. Battat, E. Minkov, J. Hicks, S. Teller, and J. Ledlie. Growing an organic indoor location system. In *ACM MobiSys*, 2010.
18. D. J. Patterson, L. Liao, D. Fox, and H. Kautz. Inferring high-level behavior from low-level sensors. In *UbiComp*, pages 73–89, 2003.
19. S. A. Sloman. The empirical case for two systems of reasoning. *Psychological Bulletin*, 119, 1996.
20. G. Yang. Discovering significant places from mobile phones: a mass market solution. In *MELT*, pages 34–49, Berlin, Heidelberg, 2009. Springer-Verlag.
21. H. Yoon, Y. Zheng, X. Xie, and W. Woo. Smart itinerary recommendation based on user-generated gps trajectories. In *Ubiquitous Intelligence and Computing (UIC)*, pages 19–34. Springer-Verlag, 2010.
22. J. Yuan, Y. Zheng, C. Zhang, W. Xie, X. Xie, G. Sun, and Y. Huang. T-drive: Driving directions based on taxi trajectories. In *ACM GIS*, pages 99–108, 2010.
23. Y. Zheng, Q. Li, Y. Chen, X. Xie, and W.-Y. Ma. Understanding mobility based on gps data. In *UbiComp*, pages 312–321. ACM, 2008.
24. Y. Zheng, L. Zhang, X. Xie, and W.-Y. Ma. Mining interesting locations and travel sequences from gps trajectories. In *WWW*, pages 791–800. ACM, 2009.
25. Z. Zhuang, K.-H. Kim, and J. P. Singh. Improving energy efficiency of location sensing on smartphones. In *ACM MobiSys*, 2010.

SiFi: Exploiting VoIP Silence for WiFi Energy Savings in Smart Phones

Andrew J. Pyles
College of William & Mary
ajpyles@cs.wm.edu

Zhen Ren
College of William & Mary
renzh@cs.wm.edu

Gang Zhou
College of William & Mary
gzhou@cs.wm.edu

Xue Liu
Univ. of Nebraska Lincoln
xueliu@cse.unl.edu

ABSTRACT
Since one-third of a smart phone's battery energy is consumed by its WiFi interface, it is critical to switch the WiFi radio from its active or Constantly Awake Mode (CAM), which draws high power (726mW with screen off), to its sleep or Power Save Mode (PSM), which consumes little power (36mW). Applications like VoIP do not perform well under PSM mode however, due to their real-time nature, so the energy footprint is quite high. The challenge is to save energy while not affecting performance. In this paper we present SiFi: Silence prediction based WiFi energy adaptation. SiFi examines audio streams from phone calls and tracks when silence periods start and stop. This data is stored in a prediction model. Using this historical data, we predict the length of future silence periods and place the WiFi radio to sleep during these periods. We implement the design on an Android Smart phone and acheive 40% energy savings while maintaining high voice fidelity.

Author Keywords
Silence prediction, VoIP, energy efficiency, WiFi, smart phone.

ACM Classification Keywords
C.2.1 Computer-Communication Networks: Network Architecture and Design—*Wireless communication*; C.4 Performance of Systems: Design studies

General Terms
Design, Algorithm, Performance, Measurement, Experimentation.

INTRODUCTION
As demonstrated in [25], there is a tradeoff between the cellular data network and WiFi communication that both exist in currently widely used smart phones. Compared to the WiFi interface, the cellular data network incurs a lower penalty to stay connected, but much higher energy price per MB of data transfer. In addition, the cellular data network has higher latency and may incur additional airtime charges. Towards improving battery lifetime and enhancing user experience and productivity [26] [24] [5], many newly developed smart phone related applications choose to involve the WiFi radio communication [25] [21] [3] [19] [32].

Even though WiFi radio is energy efficient when communicating a large amount of data, it is expensive just to stay connected. For example, the Sprint HTC Hero [30] consumes 726mW (with screen off) in the Constantly Awake Mode (CAM). So, it is essential to put WiFi to the Power Save Mode (PSM) which consumes 20 fold less energy (36mW in Sprint HTC Hero). In the research community, a large number of efforts have been proposed to reduce energy consumption. For example, [15] [9] [1] propose to save WiFi energy by exploiting periods of idleness, while [28] improves scheduling on the WiFi Access Point (AP). [14] shows a general purpose 802.11 protocol changes to save energy for general real-time applications, and [23] analyzes the VoIP network traffic playout deadline to determine when to put the radio to sleep. Also, the Adaptive PSM [28] commonly deployed saves energy by monitoring throughput through the WLAN. The radio stays in PSM by default, but switches to CAM when traffic is observed.

However, none of the aforementioned existing work examines the RTP payload to exploit silence period for WiFi energy savings during a VoIP call, even though it has been shown that up to 60% [10] of a typical human conversation is made up of silence. Therefore, we are motivated to address the research challenges towards exploiting silence period for energy saving during a smart phone VoIP call: (1)how to model and predict VoIP silence periods of a phone call at runtime? and (2)how to apply silence prediction to the existing WiFi infrastructure of an Android phone to save energy?

To address the first challenge, we first developed a light weight silence detection algorithm that is able to distinguish silence from voice in RTP packets during a phone call. Then, once an adequate set of silence periods are obtained during runtime, a running statistical model is built to characterize the silence periods distribution in an accurate and energy efficient way. Finally, when the statistical model is observed stable enough, runtime prediction of the future silence period length is conducted based on statistical analysis.

To address the second challenge, we propose SiFi, a silence prediction based WiFi energy adaptation framework for smart phones. SiFi is carefully designed so that it fits well with existing mobile phone constraints as discussed in [20], namely OS limitations, API and operational limitations, energy management limitations, etc. SiFi is able to incorporate the statistical modeling and prediction theory and realize it in the limited smart phone WiFi infrastructure and demonstrates more than 40% energy saving.

Our main contributions can be summarized as follows:

- With lightweight digital signal processing, and statistical modeling and prediction, we successfully exploit during runtime the silence periods of a VoIP call which forms a solid base for runtime WiFi energy saving. To ensure high accuracy and low cost for the runtime silence exploitation, different modeling and prediction techniques including empirical cumulative distribution function and time series analysis are compared, and important statistical issues like runtime training length and confidence of prediction are thoroughly explored.
- To apply the statistical silence exploitation technique we develop, we propose a silence prediction based WiFi energy adaptation framework, called SiFi, for smart phones energy saving. By making modifications to the low level system architecture as well as application components, SiFi is able to directly control the WiFi power save mode based on silence prediction, and fits well with the limited Android phone infrastructure.
- We deploy SiFi on a real system with Sprint HTC Hero that runs VoIP application and obtain more than 40% power savings during runtime. We achieve high call fidelity by sleeping during silence periods and being active during voice periods. Our real system evaluation also demonstrate SiFi's resilience to network congestion, and its robustness in different phone call scenarios like with different phone call lengths, different languages, different number of speakers, and different genders of speakers.

The rest of the paper is organized as follows. We explain background knowledge followed by related work. Next, we present details of detecting, modeling and predicting VoIP silence periods of a phone call at runtime. Then, a detailed design of the SiFi framework is given followed by details of the SiFi implementation on an Android phone. Real system performance evaluation with Sprint HTC Hero is illustrated next. Finally, we present the conclusions.

BACKGROUND

Session Initiation Protocol (SIP) is widely used in Internet Telephony. It is used to establish and tear down calls where Real Time Protocol (RTP) media is streamed. To illustrate how SIP works, imagine two phones A and B, where A would like to call B. Once a call has been established, RTP packets are sent bi-directionally until a call is terminated with a BYE message. Detailed description of SIP is outside the scope of this paper, and interested readers are referred to [27]. When a call is initiated with an INVITE packet, phone A notifies phone B which UDP port it is listening for RTP packets. Phone B responds soon after with a 200 OK message. The 200 OK message will notify phone A which UDP port it will listen for RTP packets. During this negotiation phase, the two parties also agree on the codec to use and also whether or not Voice Activity Detection (VAD) and Comfort Noise (CN) is supported.

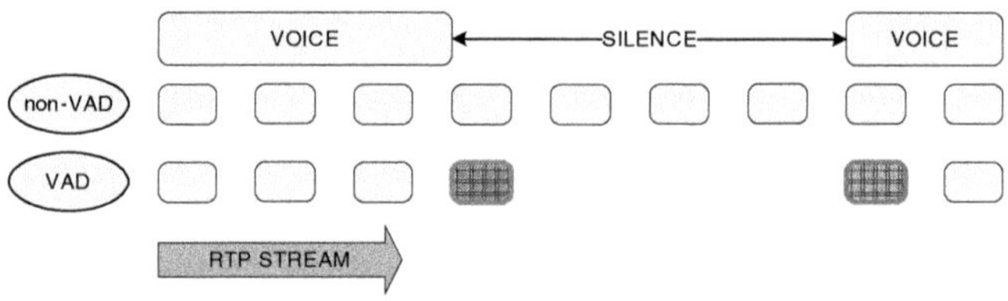

Figure 1. VAD and RTP

RTP packets are usually sent at evenly spaced intervals that the two parties agree upon during the codec negotiation phase. For instance, if two parties use the G.711 codec, typically a 20ms RTP interval is used. Figure 1 shows a typical RTP flow. RTP packets that do not use VAD, that is silence packets are transmitted the same as voice packets, we define as non-VAD. However during silence periods, VAD has a different behavior. When the silence period starts at the sender end, the next scheduled RTP packet is a Comfort Noise (CN) packet. When the CN packet is received at the receiver side, it knows that a silence period has begun. When the period of silence has stopped, a normal RTP packet with the Marker bit is set. When the this RTP packet is received, the silence period has ended and a new voice period has begun.

RELATED WORK

A large amount of research attention has been recently paid to the problem of WiFi energy saving in mobile devices. Here we discuss the work most relevant to SiFi.

Exploiting Idle opportunities. Considerable work has been done finding idle opportunities within WLAN to exploit for power savings. In Bounded Slowdown [15], idle periods between TCP establishment are exploited to switch WiFi between CAM and PSM modes. Time periods between slow start and between Web transactions are used. Beacon intervals are dynamically adjusted to minimize PSM overhead.

Micro Power Management [18] exploits small time periods (μ seconds) between MAC frames to save energy. Micro power sleep periods are effective since the speed of WLANs are typically much greater than the WLAN up-link speed. This approach is complimentary to SiFi. SiFi examines the payload of RTP packets and based on the prediction methods, puts the radio to sleep. Micro power management could be combined with SiFi to gain additional energy savings.

Another approach, Catnap [9] stores data into blocks that are combined at the AP, then the blocks can be transmitted efficiently to the STA allowing for additional power savings. This approach is not applicable to real-time applications such as VoIP due to the added delay incurred.

Self-Tuning [1] provides an API to application developers to identify network traffic that is considered background or foreground traffic. Using these hints, the kernel driver can schedule background traffic into PSM mode while foreground traffic can be scheduled at a higher priority. Self-Tuning is not a good fit for the real-time nature of VoIP for two reasons. First, in the case of non-VAD RTP traffic, the same traffic pattern exists for voice and silence RTP packets which is difficult for Self-Tuning to attach different traffic hints. Second, unlike SiFi that directly controls the WiFi driver, the Self-Tuning kernel module may introduce delay that impacts VoIP performance.

VoIP Specific Approaches w/o Idle Exploitation. There are several other VoIP specific approaches that do not exploit idle opportunities for saving WiFi energy. The GreenCall algorithm [23] uses a deadline approach that does not consider silence periods. By examining the inter-arrival times of the packets, they determine the play-out deadline. As long as the play-out deadline has not been reached, the WiFi radio is put into PSM mode. Our approach is complimentary to this approach with the following distinction. We place special emphasis on putting the radio to sleep particularly during silence periods. The play-out deadline for silence packets is not as important as for voice packets.

AP Modification. Some AP centric approaches are also developed for WiFi energy. Napman [28] focuses on modifying the AP scheduler so that PSM traffic and CAM traffic are treated fairly. Specific care is given to Adaptive PSM implementations on the latest smart phones such as the iPhone and Android based approaches. By adjusting the TCP window size, PSM-Throttling [31] increases the burstiness of multimedia streaming traffic causing energy saving to be realized.

IEEE 802.11e U-APSD. IEEE 802.11e also introduces U-APSD [14] to provide an extra layer of QoS while saving energy. When the AP receives a frame from the STA, the AP will send all buffered data to the client without requiring the PS-POLL mechanism. This works when upstream and downstream RTP streams are complimentary as in the non-VAD case. However, in cases such as VAD, the upstream and downstream RTP streams can be asymmetric and the downlink frames will not be triggered.

In [7] an exponential backoff scheme is employed during silence periods of VoIP calls to determine the maximum period to put the radio into sleep mode. For long silence periods, this scheme has the potential problem of over sleeping causing delay. By using training data, SiFI can more accurately determine the length of the silence period, to prevent extended oversleeping.

SILENCE MODELING & PREDICTION

In this section, we use a lightweight threshold based algorithm to detect silence RTP packets from voice RTP packets. Then, we compute the length of silence periods between consecutive voice packets and also use statistical analysis to characterize the silence data. We finally present an algorithm to predict the future silence period length based on observed silence history. Such prediction will be used in the next section for saving WiFi energy in smart phones.

Lightweight Silence Detection

It has been shown that approximately 60% of a typical conversation is made up of silence [10]. Intuitively, during a silent period of a conversation we should not need to transmit any packet and therefore maximize the energy savings of the WiFi radio used. Our approach is to look for mutual silence where at time t, all RTP streams are silent from both parties. That is, the payload in the RTP packets have no meaningful data. This can correspond to a short silence period between two consecutive words in a sentence or a pause in a conversation, for example.

Although some codecs such as g.729b and G.273.1 3GPP provide Silence suppression [11], these codecs are not always available. By implementing a lightweight silence detection on the phone, this allows greater flexibility and allows SiFi to be used with any voice codec.

In order to find the start of a period of mutual silence, we have two cases to deal with. The first case is that the remote end of the conversation supports VAD. In this case the silence detection is dealt with by the sender. By examining the RTP packets, we can easily determine when the silence starts. For the second case where VAD is not in use, we implemented a simple Digital Signal Processing (DSP) algorithm. This algorithm and its associated problem, which is well studied in the Speech and Language Processing research area, is known as Endpoint Detection. However, most recent Endpoint Detection algorithms [13] [17], although highly accurate, are very computational expensive. Since the end result of our research is to save energy, we decided upon a lightweight threshold based algorithm that relies upon the amplitude of the audio stream which from our analysis performs reasonably well.

The DSP algorithm we use is as follows. We set a threshold th. th is configured manually to the noise level of a normal conversation. When the average audio level (over the past k samples) are less than th, $Silence = true$, where k is the number of audio samples in a single RTP packet. When the average audio level equals or exceeds th, $Silence = false$.

For the purpose of simplification, we assume the VAD case in the following discussions unless explicitly stated otherwise. Since we can observe the start of the mutual silence period we need to determine how long the silence period will be so that we can maximize the radio sleep time.

ECDF Based Silence Prediction

In this subsection, we discuss in detail how to design the silence length prediction. An accurate but simple (less computationally intensive) silence length prediction algorithm is important as this helps achieve better conversation quality while at the same time saves more energy.

To this end, we first analyze 7 Skype call traces which last 5 hours and 41 minutes in total and contain 52,929 silence periods (65% of the call time). These Skype calls are conducted by 3 different groups of participants. Group 1 and Group 2 each has three participants using two Skype clients: one participant at one end, and two at the other end. We collected 3 traces from Group 1, and 2 traces from Group 2. In Group 3, 4 participants use 4 Skype clients respectively for conference calls, and we collected 2 traces. The silence period lengths from the traces are used to build the empirical cumulative distribution function (ECDF) as shown in Figure 3. From the ECDF, we observe that the length of the silence period can range from 20ms to more than one minute, with variation as large as more than 900ms. With this observation, we propose a staged prediction algorithm that utilizes the conditional probability. The call traces were gathered from conference calls with students as well as personal calls provided by student volunteers.

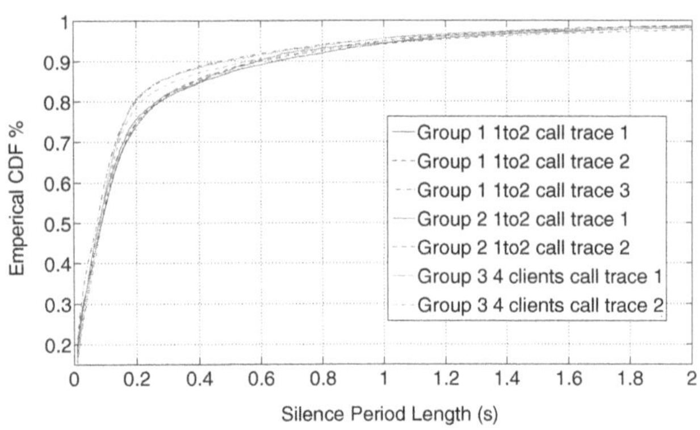

Figure 2. ECDF of Silence Length

Let X denotes the length of the silence period, and $P(\alpha) = P(X \leq \alpha)$ be the probability that the silence period X lasts less than time α. Then, the probability of the silence period lasting longer than α is $P(X > \alpha) = 1 - P(\alpha)$. Assume that the silence period has already lasted for time α, the conditional probability that it will last longer than $(\alpha + \Delta)$ is:

$$\begin{aligned} P(X > \alpha + \Delta | X > \alpha) &= \frac{P(X > \alpha, X > \alpha + \Delta)}{P(X > \alpha)} \\ &= \frac{1 - P(\alpha + \Delta)}{1 - P(\alpha)} \end{aligned} \quad (1)$$

With the ECDF, our prediction algorithm is able to look for appropriate value of Δ (i.e. new increment in time) that has conditional probability $P(X > \alpha + \Delta | X > \alpha)$ larger than or equal to a given confidence interval β. If such Δ can be found, the algorithm predicts that if the silence period has lasted for time α, it would stay silence for the next period of Δ with high confidence. By the end of each predicted period, the algorithm will predict again if it detects that the silence period continues. The prediction loop breaks when the silence period ends or no Δ value can be found with the confidence bound. This algorithm is shown in algorithm 1.

Algorithm 1 ECDF Based Silence Prediction

Input: confidence interval β, observed silence length α, $ECDF$

Output: predicted silence length Δ

on event that a silence period has lasted for time α, find the maximum Δ that satisfies $P(X > \alpha + \Delta | X > \alpha) \geq \beta$

if no Δ can be found **then**
  $\Delta = 0$
else
  $\alpha = \alpha + \Delta$
end if
return(Δ)

We use R^2 error value to evaluate the accuracy of the prediction, which is commonly used to measure how well statistical models can predict the future outcomes. Let f_i be the predicted value, y_i be the real value, and $\bar{y}$ be the mean of y_i. R^2 is computed using Equation 2. With R^2 value closer to 1, the predictions are more accurate.

$$\begin{aligned} SSE &= \sum_i (y_i - f_i)^2 \\ SST &= \sum_i (y_i - \bar{y})^2 \\ R^2 &= 1 - \frac{SSE}{SST} \end{aligned} \quad (2)$$

We apply the prediction algorithm to the 7 Skype traces with the first half of the traces as training data to build the ECDF, and predict for the second half and test its accuracy. Given $\beta = 65\%$ and α initiated as 50ms, 6 of the prediction results have R^2 value above 0.9 and the other one over 0.8.

Determine the Runtime Training Length

To determine the proper length of the training period, we compute the Kullback-Leibler divergence [16] of the silence period length distribution. When a new call starts, the system begins to collect the training data of silence periods in groups of 50 (usually included in about 20s calling time). If the Kullback-Leibler divergence between the current training set including and excluding the new group of silence periods is larger than a predefined threshold KL_{thres}, the new group of 50 silence periods is added to the training data set, and the training continues. Otherwise, we know that the current training data is enough to build a stable ECDF. When the training period ends, the prediction period begins. KL_{thres} is a design parameter. For example, with $KL_{thres} = 0.02$, in one of our traces the training periods stops after 500 silence periods, which lasts 193s in call time, see Figure 3.

After the training period, we also check whether the ECDF

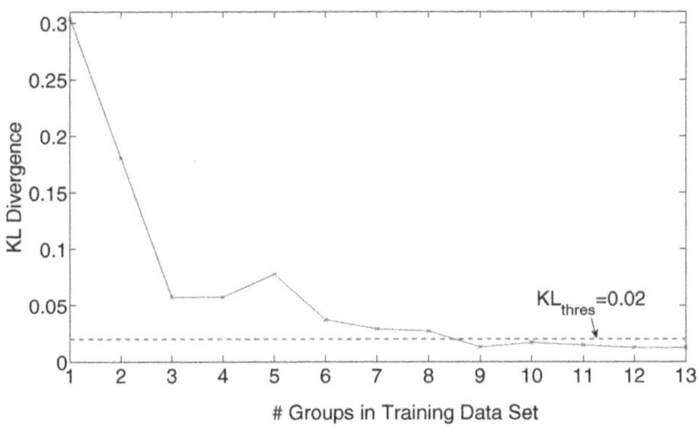

Figure 3. KL Divergence vs. Training Length

needs to be updated with every 50 new silence periods. If the Kullback-Leibler divergence raises above KL_{thres}. The system stops predicting and updates the ECDF with new silence periods. When the Kullback-Leibler divergence is below KL_{thres}, the prediction resumes.

The Observed Silence Length α

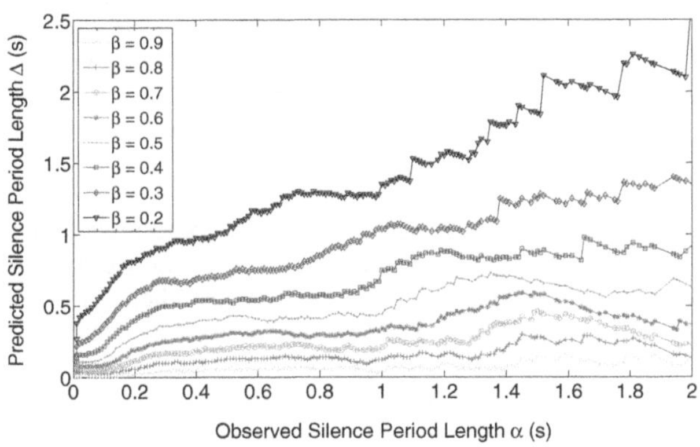

Figure 4. Observed Silence Period Length α vs. Predicted Silence Period Length Δ

Figure 4 show the analysis of the predicted silence period length with different observed silence period lengths. For different values of confidence interval β, we observed that the predicted silence period length Δ generally increases when α increases. When a silence period starts, Algorithm 1 waits for an initial period of α before prediction, with the phone on the CAM mode. If the setting of the initial α is too large, some silence periods may be too short to predict. For longer silence periods, less energy can be saved with the long initial waiting period. If the initial period α is too short, however, the predicted silence period may be too short to save energy. Also, the lightweight silence detection is not very accurate in classifying very short silence periods, even though it is very accurate for longer silence periods.

Therefore, we decide to use a larger value of initial α and do not predict for very short silence periods. We configure the initial value of α so that the first predicted Δ (a sequence of Δ predictions are possible within the same long silence period) is larger than 20ms. In our trace data, the corresponding initial α value is 50ms.

The Confidence of Prediction

β	R^2	Mean Iteration	Mean Δ
0.15	0.0237	1.1155	0.7846
0.20	0.2894	1.1636	0.6215
0.25	0.5778	1.2084	0.4998
0.30	0.6332	1.2641	0.4192
0.35	0.8044	1.3362	0.3509
0.40	0.8448	1.4246	0.3039
0.45	0.8902	1.5262	0.2612
0.50	0.9047	1.6576	0.2260
0.55	0.8965	1.8258	0.1925
0.60	0.9149	2.0046	0.1664
0.65	0.9251	2.2376	0.1425
0.70	0.9187	2.5303	0.1214
0.80	0.8946	4.0082	0.0679
0.75	0.9387	3.1789	0.0905
0.85	0.8750	5.5128	0.0472
0.90	0.7861	9.3979	0.0259

Table 1. Prediction with Different β

For each silence period, our prediction algorithm iterates until the silence period ends or no Δ can be found with the given confidence interval β. We analyze the effect of β on the prediction accuracy in Table 1. R^2 is used to measure the prediction accuracy. We observe that when the confidence interval β increases from 0.10 to 0.65, R^2 increases because each Δ is calculated with higher accuracy. But R^2 fluctuates when β increases after 0.65, and when β equals 0.90, the R^2 drops to 0.7861. This is because the algorithm can not find a Δ prediction for very large α with the given confidence interval.

In order to save more energy, large silence prediction Δ is preferred with a lower confidence interval β, but the prediction also risks large errors which may degrade the quality of the phone call. We can estimate the expected error for each prediction of Δ. If the silence period stops at some time x before the predicted time $(\alpha + \Delta)$, the voice packets arrived after x will be delayed. Also considering the beacon interval I in the Power Save Mode, the delayed packets won't be received until the next beacon. Equation 4 defines the expected error E of prediction which is also the expected delay.

$$d_i = \begin{cases} \alpha + \Delta - x_i, & \text{if } \Delta \le I \\ I - (x_i \bmod I), & \text{if } \Delta > I \end{cases} \tag{3}$$

$$E = \sum_{x_i \in (\alpha, \alpha+\Delta]} \frac{P(X > x_i) - P(X > x_{i-1})}{P(X > \alpha)} * d_i.$$

We find the value of β so that for all possible prediction Δ the expected error is below a threshold. Besides the prediction accuracy, we also consider the cost for the algorithm to wake up and check for each iteration. For each silence period, the prediction algorithm should not wake up too many times. From Table. 1, we can see the mean iterations for predictions within one silence period increases as β increases. Considering both accuracy and cost, in our experiments, we limit β values within the range of 0.25~0.6. We found impericaly that the phone call fidelity was of good quality for β values in that range.

Time series models such as Autoregressive moving average (ARMA) and Autoregressive Integrated Moving Average (ARIMA) [6] were also examined, but the drawbacks were many. We found a weak data correlation and low prediction accuracy, not to mention the higher computation cost. Our ECDF based prediction algorithm is both efficient and can predict the silence period length with high accuracy.

SIFI: SILENCE PREDICTION BASED WIFI ENERGY ADAPTATION

We propose SiFi: silence prediction based WiFi energy adaptation. As shown in figure 5, SiFi is composed of the following main components: Modeling and Prediction, WiFi Manager, and the Silence Classifier. The RTP Media Server is an optional component included here to handle the case of VAD. Each of these components has been added to the SIP user agent on Android.

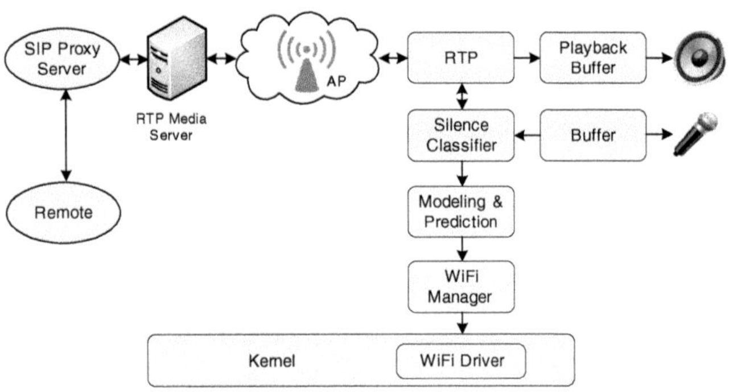

Figure 5. SiFi Architecture

Modeling and Prediction. Based upon the call history, we can determine how long we can sleep for. Modeling has two modes: training and running mode. During training mode, the modeling component is fed the observed silence period lengths from the silence classifier. The cumulative silence period length data is stored in an internal data structure. We transition to the running mode as soon as we have enough silence period lengths. Immediately after entering the running mode, we compute the empirical cumulative distribution function (ECDF) based on this training data. We also calculate an appropriate α based on the ECDF.

The prediction component is idle during the training period. As input, the prediction component receives two arguments: the silence period start event and β. We immediately sleep for the predefined α milliseconds. Then we follow Algorithm 1. Based on the value of β we predict the length of the sleeping period.

WiFi Manager. The WiFi manager is responsible for putting the WiFi radio to sleep. When the current WiFi power mode is switched to active we override the Adaptive PSM and forcibly place the WiFi driver into PSM mode for a specified time period. Once the time period expires, the driver is switched back to Adaptive PSM.

Silence Classifier. This component is responsible for detecting silence in both directions: inbound RTP packets and outbound RTP streams. When RTP packets are received, the silence classifier observes the silence start and silence stop events. We compute the average amplitude level over each received RTP packet. By using a known threshold value, we can detect if the current packet is a start or stop silence event.

Inbound RTP packet processing needs to deal with two separate cases. The first case is when silent packets are embedded into the RTP stream or the non-VAD case. In the non-VAD case, the silence classifier checks every packet. The silence classifier also handles the case when VAD is enabled for a call. In this case, it has the same responsibility for detecting silence, with an additional layer of complexity. In addition to checking every received packet for the average amplitude level as before, the call state is implicitly received through Comfort Noise (CN) packets and those packets with the *marker* bit set. Silence starts when a CN packet is received while silence stops when the Marker bit is set. The silence classifier still computes the amplitude level of every packet, in case the remote VAD implementation is not aggressive enough at detecting silence.

For the silence classifier to handle outbound RTP streams, we sample input from the microphone and detect the average amplitude level. The sample interval is determined by codec negotiation. As before, when the amplitude level drops the threshold th, a silence start event occurs. Similarly, when the amplitude level exceeds the pre-defined threshold, a voice event occurs. If VAD is enabled, we do not send silence packets. Only voice RTP packets are transmitted.

The voice and silence states from both outbound and inbound are combined to produce a joint event we call mutual silence. Mutual silence occurs when there is silence both with the sender and receiver RTP streams. These mutual silence start and mutual silence stop events are sent to the Modeling and Prediction component. To illustrate mutual silence, we consider the following scenario: the receiver RTP stream is silent for three seconds. Starting at time 0, the sender RTP stream alternates between one second of silence, then one second of voice and so on until three seconds. This means the first mutual silence period is between time zero and one. The second is between time two and three.

RTP Media server. Finally, our last component is the RTP Media server. This is an optional component included here to handle the case of VAD. We found an open source RTP Media Server [12] that allows us to relay any RTP traffic including embedded silence in the RTP payload. The media server has its own DSP algorithm and detects when silence occurs. When silence starts, a CN packet is inserted. When voice starts, an RTP packet with the marker bit is sent.

ANDROID PHONE IMPLEMENTATION

We implemented our design on the Sprint HTC Hero [30] with root access. This version contains version 2.1 of Android with HTC enhancements. The Hero has the TI WLAN 1251 driver which is part of the Android source repository that is freely available on top of the 2.6.29 Linux Kernel. The implementation is comprised of two parts: the WiFi system modifications and the application modifications done within the Android virtual machine layer. We first start with the application, followed by system level modifications.

Application Level Modifications

There are a number of VoIP clients available on the Android market. For our research, we wanted one that is well established on the Android Market. A big plus was also to find a package that was open source since we need to make a number of changes. One such SIP User Agent [29], hereafter referred to as SIPua, is available for Android with over 250K downloads from the Android Market and has high user ratings. It provides the ability to make and receive VoIP phone calls using WiFi or a mobile data plan. It is able to handle video and audio and a number of codecs are supported. It is comprised of third party SIP and RTP stacks.

The silence classifier component is shared between the SIPua's RTP sending and receiving threads. We analyze the energy level of the payload of each RTP packet. We first implemented the component in Java. We quickly realized, however, that the energy calculation was too computationally expensive and the performance was unacceptable. Using the Android Native Development Kit (NDK) [2] for a native code implementation, we were able to obtain acceptable performance with a minimal performance penalty. We measured the performance penalty to be a 3% energy overhead. The penalty was realized by comparing a call with the silence classifier enabled for both inbound, outbound streams to a call made with the silence classification disabled.

System Level Modifications

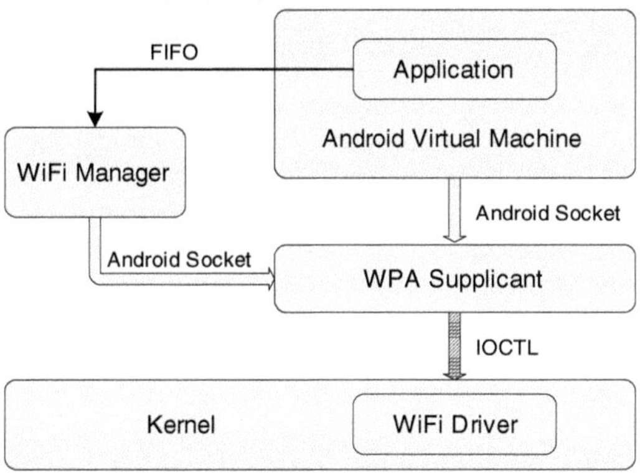

Figure 6. Android WiFi Architecture

We introduce the WiFi Manager implementation. The WiFi Manager has two components: the low level system implementation and the Application API. The latest Android system (as of this writing version 2.2) is missing the functionality to forcibly switch the WiFi radio from adaptive PSM to static PSM from the Android environment. We modified the Android Virtual Machine to include this functionality, but quickly realized this broke other parts of the system. As we discovered, although Android is open source, contributors can add to the system various components that are not. By modifying the Android VM, we would not be able to have a fair comparison since our modified VM would be missing key components. Instead we needed a simpler design that would not require modifications to the Android VM.

Radio Status	Screen ON	Screen Off
CAM	1070.00 mW	726.05 mW
PSM	381.40 mW	36.5 mW
Disabled	345.94mW	4.9 mW

Table 2. Baseline Average Power

Figure 6 describes how the current WiFi subsystem works within Android. When an application makes an API call to the WiFi sublayer, it passes through the VM and connects to the $WPA\_Supplicant$ daemon running on the system. To save energy, when the WiFi radio is inactive, it runs for 15 minutes and then the driver is disabled in the Linux kernel. When the Android system receives an indication that network activity starts again, the driver is then loaded again. During the loading and unloading phase, the $WPA\_Supplicant$ daemon is also started and stopped. The $WPA\_Supplicant$ listens for events through an Android Socket interface. The Android socket is essentially a UNIX socket with some modifications.

We created a separate daemon process called the WiFi Manager. This daemon simply listens on a FIFO interface which our application has access to. Then, when the Android application wants to send a special WiFi command, it can send a FIFO message to the WiFi Manager. We used the Android NDK to implement a native code interface to interact with the WiFi Manager. The WiFi Manager then communicates to the $WPA\_Supplicant$ daemon through the same Android Socket as the VM. We modified the init scripts on the phone such that whenever WiFi is enabled and disabled, WiFi Manager is also started and stopped, respectively.

Once the aforementioned system was in place, it was trivial to implement the sleepforMS() WiFi function. This function an integer millisecond argument and sends a request to the WiFi Manager through the FIFO interface.

We also modified the WPA_supplicant daemon. When it receives the sleepforMS() command, it forcibly puts the radio into PSM mode. Then it pauses for the specified milliseconds before changing the radio back to Adaptive PSM.

Finally, we modify the RTP Media Server. When a silence start event is observed, a CN RTP packet is sent. Prior to our modifications, the RTP Media Server would only set the marker bit when a voice start event occurred. With this change, the Silence Classifier component can easily detect when silence starts and stops when VAD is enabled.

PERFORMANCE EVALUATION

With the implementation in Sprint HTC Hero phone, we present system performance evaluation in the Android platform. Our results demonstrate that our SiFi solution achieves more than 40% energy savings in the smart phone.

Evaluation Setup

Our evaluation setup consists of a Linux server that runs a media server [12] and runs hostapd to serve as a WiFi AP. The media server is configured to host audio recordings.

Threshold	Metric
AutoPowerModeActiveTh	8 packets/sec
AutoPowerModeDozeTh	4 packets/sec
Transition δ	1.5 sec

Table 3. Adaptive PSM Settings in Sprint HTC Hero

When a specific dial string is called the recording is played back. The phone is approximately one meter from the AP. The only delay incurred is isolated to the wireless leg.

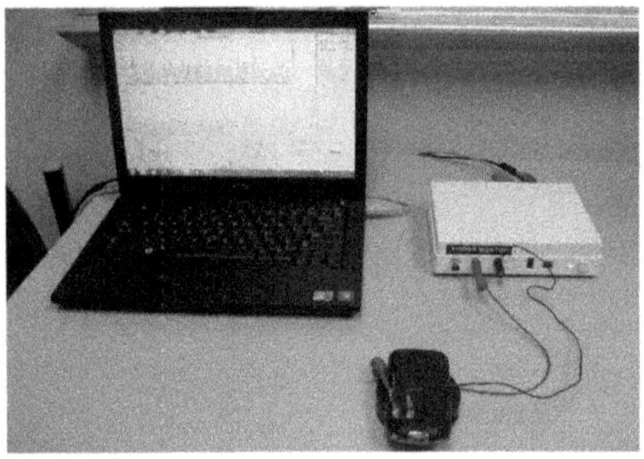

Figure 7. Energy Measurement Setup

We measure the energy use of the phone in real-time using a power meter from Monsoon technologies. Figure 7 shows the setup for energy measurement. A simple circuit is configured such that the positive terminal on the battery is insulated with electrical tape and the positive feed from the power meter is instead connected to the phone's battery terminal. When the phone is powered on, we can measure in real-time the energy usage.

Table 2 shows the baseline power usage of the phone. We measured the power usage by placing the phone in 'airplane mode' which disables all the network interfaces including Bluetooth and mobile radio. Clearly CAM mode is very expensive and should be avoided if possible. Powering the screen is also quite expensive as well. The measurements indicate the power consumed when the radio is idle.

Evaluation Method

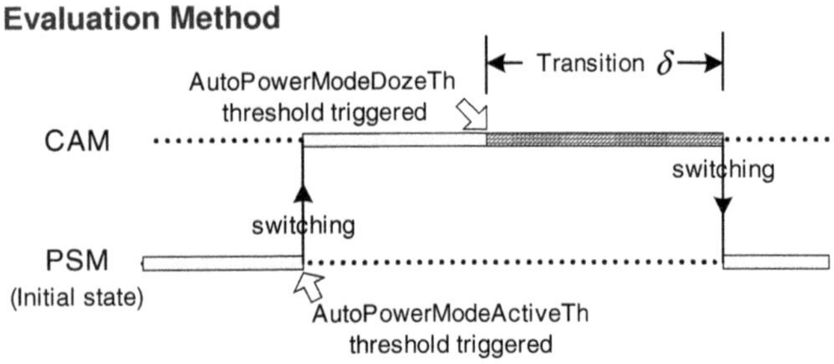

Figure 8. Adaptive PSM State Transitions in Sprint HTC Hero

In the following sections we show the results on how SiFi compares with Adaptive PSM in the VAD case and the NON-VAD case. The Sprint HTC Hero phone uses Adaptive PSM to save energy [15]. Adaptive PSM is complectly controlled by the WiFi kernel driver. The Adaptive PSM sets the default power mode to PSM. When the network interface starts

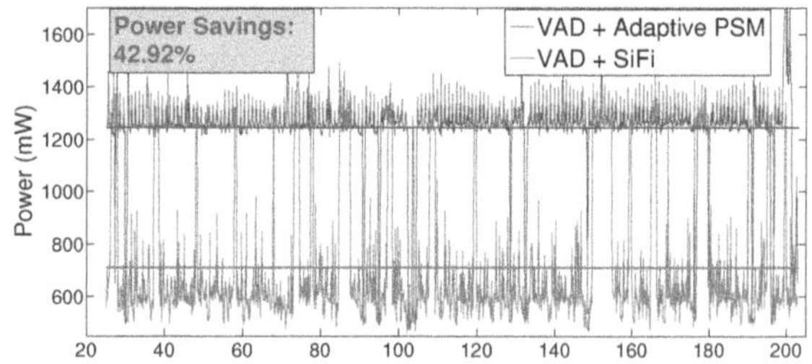

Figure 9. VAD + Adaptive PSM vs. VAD + SiFi

to receive packets, it transitions to CAM mode by sending a NULL:Awake packet to the AP. When the wireless network interface is idle and the driver desires to switch to PSM, it sends a NULL:Sleep packet to the AP.

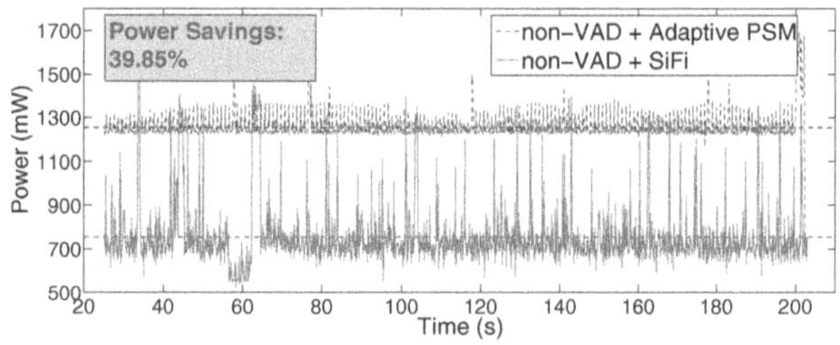

Figure 10. non-VAD + Adaptive PSM vs. non-VAD + SiFi

In Table 3 we see the settings for Adaptive PSM for the Sprint HTC Hero. The *AutoPowerModeActiveTh* parameter refers to the number of packets necessary to trigger the phone to switch from PSM to CAM mode, while the *AutoPowerModeDozeTh* parameter shows the threshold value necessary to switch back to PSM mode. We note these settings are the default settings for this phone. The transition δ parameter is not configurable (without hacking the driver, as we do in the next section). We observed this parameter by sending a small packet burst to the phone that exceeds the $AutoPowerModeActiveTh$ threshold. By watching the kernel logs on the WiFi Access point, we recorded the time difference from when the STA returned to PSM after switching to CAM. We also determined that no other network traffic was sent on the interface.

Although the observed transition δ value might be unique to this phone, others have also observed similar behavior. [28] cites several variations in implementation among common Smartphones. Agressive Adaptive PSM, is when the transition δ is small. Default Adaptive PSM is when the transition δ is longer such as the Sprint HTC Hero. When we refer to Adaptive PSM, we are referring to the default case.

There is tradeoff between the agressive and default adaptive PSM. As noted in [28], Agressive Adaptive PSM can in some cases lose packets, and ultimately consume more energy when the AP is under heavy use and the transmit buffer is full. This is best illustrated by the following example. Suppose the phone is in CAM mode due to a high packet receive rate. Some time later, the AP transmit buffer becomes full from some other traffic. If it takest longer than the transition δ to process the packet through the transmit buffer, the phone will go to sleep and the packet may be lost.

SiFi Energy Savings

In this section we show how SiFi improves both the VAD and non-VAD cases. SiFi is able to efficiently save 40~43% average power over Adaptive PSM.

Figure 9 shows the results of VAD with SiFi enabled. For this call, β was set to .5 and α to 50ms. A 43% power savings was achieved over Adaptive PSM. At certain extended voice periods of the call, for example at 150 seconds, the power levels of Adaptive PSM and SiFi are the same. Similarly when extended silence periods occur, Both Adaptive PSM and SiFi can take advantage. For instance, during the periods right before and after the 100 second mark we see the energy use drop significantly. Adaptive PSM performs poorly due to the long transition δ.

We present the results of non-VAD + SiFi in Figure 10 . β was set to .25 and α to 50ms. When SiFi detects silence and puts the radio into PSM mode, RTP packets continue to queue up at the AP. This results in extra overhead since the phone has to PS-POLL every packet queued at the AP. Therefore, even though β is set to half of the setting used for VAD, the overall power savings are slightly less. Compared to Adaptive PSM, SiFi has 39% power savings. Since RTP packets are always sent even during silence periods, Adaptive PSM never switches to PSM. Once a call is established, there will always be a packet rate that exceeds the $AutoPowerModeActiveTh$ threshold.

To be fair, since the Android phone has a very long transition δ setting, we modified the WiFi driver such that the transition δ was as close to α as possible. Without major modifications to the driver, the lowest setting we were able to maintain was approximately 70ms. Adjusting the transition δ to anything lower than 70 caused stability issues(exceeding the Active threshold did not always keep the driver in CAM). We compared SiFi vs. Aggressive Adaptive PSM and a non-VAD call. In this case, SiFi clearly wins out because the amount of RTP traffic does not change during silence periods, so it will never switch to PSM. Secondly, we compare a VAD call with SiFi vs. a VAD call with Aggressive Adaptive PSM. In this case, SiFi has a 34% improvement (1070 vs 710 mW).

SiFi Application Fidelity

We evaluated the application fidelity of SiFi by using the industry standard for evaluating Voice Quality, the Mean Opinion Score (MOS). The MOS scale ranges from 5-1, with (5) best quality, (4) High quality, (3) Medium quality, (2) Low quality and (1) Completely unusable. VoIP is particularly susceptible to packet loss and delay. The E-model [8] can be used to calculate the MOS rating of a call.

The MOS score was originally designed to be a subjective measurement of call quality. The E-model can be used to estimate the MOS score based on the observed packet loss, one way delay and codec metrics from the codec in use. The E-model computes the R-factor which can then be used to calculate the MOS score as follows: $1 + 0.035R + 7 * 10^{-6}R(R - 60)(100 - R)$.

Description	Length	μOWD(ms)	e_{jitter}	MOS
non-VAD	1 hour	85	1.4%	3.76
VAD	10 minutes	63	1.4%	4.03

Table 4. SiFi Fidelity

Call	SiFi	#People	Duration (min:sec)	μPower (mW)	μOWD (ms)	e_{jitter}	MOS
#1	y	2 people	26:38	615	68.6	0.63%	4.28
#2	y	3 people	48:53	618	69.3	2.03%	4.15
#3	y	4 people	50:00	675	69.3	1.14%	4.25

Table 5. Multiple Longer Call Tests: VAD + SiFi

The R-Factor can be calculated as $R \sim 100 - I_s - I_d - I_{ef} + A$. Where I_d is the delay impairment, I_{ef} the loss impairment, I_s the signal-to-noise impairment and A the expectaton factor. The latter is a subjective measurement that is higher when users expect higher call quality. We set A to zero as in [8, 4] since it is not easily quantified. Since we are using the g.711 codec, the R-Factor can then be simplified to [8]: $R \sim 94.2 - 0.024d - 0.11(d - 177.3)H(d - 177.3) - 30ln(1 + 15e)$. Where d is the mouth-to-ear delay comprised of the codec delay, the delay due to the jitter buffer and the network delay. e is the error rate comprised of total packets lost and late packets dropped by the jitter buffer. H is a heavy-side function where $H(X) = 0, X < 0$ and $H(X) = 1, X \geq 0$.

The g.711 coding delay is 20ms and we assume the jitter buffer delay is 60 ms. Finally, the network delay is calculated as follows: We assume the one way delay across the US is 40ms to account for VoIP calls over the Internet. d is then equal to $d_{net} + 120ms$, where d_{net} is the delay caused by WiFi. d_{net} is computed by measuring the one-way delay from the media server to the phone. We measure the one-way delay by using the same method in [4]. We assume that the delay is identical in both directions and remove the clock skew according to [22].

We calculate the e_{jitter} by assuming any packet with jitter higher than the jitter buffer, that is 60ms is lost. We made a number of 10 minute calls comparing both the non-VAD and VAD and show the results in Table 4. The overall MOS score on the VAD call slightly outperforms the non-VAD call since only voice packets are transmitted. The MOS is calculated by adding the extra 40ms Internet delay to the shown values. The overall results show that SiFi causes minimal call quality degredation.

SiFi Robustness for Longer Calls

In this section, we show the robustness of SiFi for longer calls. Different call scenarios are explored: longer call lengths, different languages, different genders, and different numbers of people in the phone call. Table 5 describes the following scenarios: Call #1 consists of 2 people (both females & using Chinese) conversing for 26 minutes. Call #2 is a 3 person (all males & using English) conference lasting for 48 minutes. Call #3 is a 4 person (all males & using English) conference lasting for 50 minutes. In all three combinations, SiFi shows consistent high power savings. For reference, the average power consumption with VAD + Adaptive PSM enabled on Call #2 and SiFi disabled was recorded as 1263mW. For longer calls, SiFi performs 51% better than VAD + Adaptive PSM. While saving energy, the quality does not suffer as well, the MOS in all cases is well above 4.

We also tested the stability of the training period. First, training was enabled for call #2 as reflected in Table 5. Call # 3 was made using the training data from call #2. Less than a 10% difference in is apparent between the two calls. As was shown in Figure 2, the silence period distributions observed in the traces are similar. This shows that if training from a previous call is re-used, significant energy savings can still be realized while maintaining high fidelity.

CONCLUSIONS

In this paper, with lightweight digital processing, and runtime modeling and prediction, we exploit during runtime the silence periods of a VoIP call. Thorough statistic analysis is conducted to ensure high modeling and prediction accuracy and low cost for the runtime silence exploitation. To apply silence period exploitation to save smart phone WiFi energy, we also propose the design, implementation, and real system evaluation of a silence prediction based WiFi energy saving framework called SiFi. By making modifications to the low level system architecture and also application components, SiFi is able to directly control the WiFi power save mode based on silence prediction. Our real system evaluation running VoIP application demonstrates that SiFi saves more than 40% energy compared to the standard Adaptive PSM solution deployed in Sprint HTC Hero. We achieve high call fidelity by sleeping during silence periods and active during voice periods. Our real system evaluation also demonstrate SiFi is resistant to network congestion and robust in multiple phone call scenarios.

REFERENCES

1. M. Anand, E. B. Nightingale, and J. Flinn. Self-Tuning Wireless Network Power Management. In *ACM MobiCom*, 2003.
2. Android Native Development Kit, 2010. http://developer.android.com/sdk/ndk/index.html.
3. M. Azizyan, I. Constandache, and R. R. Choudhury. SurroundSense: Mobile Phone Localization via Ambience Fingerprinting. In *ACM MobiCom*, 2009.
4. A. Balasubramanian, R. Mahajan, A. Venkataramani, B. N. Levine, and J. Zahorjan. Interactive wifi connectivity for moving vehicles. In *ACM SIGCOMM*, 2008.
5. N. Banerjee, A. Rahmati, M. D. Corner, S. Rollins, and L. Zhong. Users and Batteries: Interactions and Adaptive Energy Management in Mobile Systems. In *ACM UbiComp*, 2007.
6. C. Chatfield. *The Analysis of Time Series: An Introduction, Sixth Edition*. Chapman and Hall/CRC, 2003.
7. H. Choi and J. Lee. Hybrid Power Saving Mechanism for VoIP Services with Silence Suppression in IEEE 802.16e Systems. In *IEEE Communications Letters*, 2007.
8. R. Cole and J. Rosenbluth. Voice over IP performance monitoring. In *ACM SIGCOMM*, 2001.
9. F. R. Dogar, P. Steenkiste, and K. Papagiannaki. Catnap: Exploiting High Bandwidth Wireless Interfaces to Save Energy for Mobile Devices. In *ACM MobiSys*, 2010.
10. P. Drago, A. Molinari, and F. Vagliani. Digital Dynamic Speech Detectors. In *IEEE TON*, 1978.
11. A. Estepa, R. Estepa, and J. Vozmediano. A new approach for VoIP traffic characterization. In *IEEE Communications Letters*, 2004.
12. Freeswitch, 2010. http://www.freeswitch.org.
13. M. Fujimoto, K. K. Ishizuka, and T. Nakatani. A Voice Activity Detection based on the Adaptive Integration of Multiple Speech Features and a Signal Decision Scheme. In *IEEE ICASSP*, 2008.
14. Medium Access Control (MAC) and Physical Layer (PHY) specifications Amendment 8: Medium Access Control (MAC) Quality of Service Enhancements, 2005. ANSI/IEEE Std. 802.11e.
15. R. Krashinsky and H. Balakrishnan. Minimizing Energy for Wireless Web Access with Bounded Slowdown. In *ACM MobiCom*, 2002.
16. S. Kullback and R. A. Leibler. On Information and Sufficiency. In *The Annals of Mathematical Statistics*, 1951.
17. L. Lamel, L. R. Rabiner, A. Rosenberg, and J. Wilpon. An Improved Endpoint Detector for Isolated Word Recognition. In *IEEE TOASSP*, 2003.
18. J. Liu and L. Zhong. Micro Power Management of Active 802.11 Interfaces. In *ACM MobiSys*, 2008.
19. H. Lu, J. Yang, Z. Liu, N. D. Lane, T. Choudhury, and A. T. Campbell. The Jigsaw Continuous Sensing Engine for Mobile Phone Applications. In *ACM SenSys*, 2010.
20. E. Miluzzo, N. D. Lane, K. Fodor, R. Peterson, H. Lu, M. Musolesi, S. B. Eisenman, X. Zheng, and A. T. Campbell. Sensing Meets Mobile Social Networks: The Design, Implementation and Evaluation of the CenceMe Application. In *ACM SenSys*, 2008.
21. E. Miluzzoy, C. T. Corneliusy, A. Ramaswamyy, T. Choudhuryy, Z. Liux, and A. T. Campbelly. Darwin Phones: the Evolution of Sensing and Inference on Mobile Phones. In *ACM MobiSys*, 2010.
22. S. Moon, P. Skelly, and D. Towsley. Estimation and removal of clock skew from network delay measurements. In *IEEE INFOCOM*, 1999.
23. V. Namboodiri and L. Gao. Towards Energy Efficient VoIP over Wireless LANs. In *ACM MobiHoc*, 2008.
24. T. Pering, Y. Agarwal, R. Gupta, and R. Want. Coolspots: Reducing the Power Consumption of Wireless Mobile Devices with Multiple Radio Interfaces. In *ACM MobiSys*, 2006.
25. A. Rahmati and L. Zhong. Context for Wireless: Context-Sensitive Energy-Efficient Wireless Data Transfer. In *ACM MobiSys*, 2007.
26. A. Rahmati and L. Zhong. Human-Battery Interaction on Mobile Phones. In *Pervasive and Mobile Computing*, 2009.
27. J. Rosenberg, H. Schulzrinne, G. Camarillo, A. Johnston, J. Peterson, R. Sparks, M. Handley, and E. Schooler. SIP: Session Initiation Protocol. In *RFC 3261*, 2002.
28. E. Rozner, V. Navda, R. Ramjee, and S. Rayanchu. NAPman: Network-Assisted Power Management for WiFi Devices. In *ACM MobiSys*, 2010.
29. Sipdroid, 2010. http://www.sipdroid.org.
30. Sprint HTC Hero, 2010. www.htc.com/us/support/hero-sprint.
31. E. Tan, L. Guo, S. Chen, and X. Zhang. PSM-throttling: Minimizing Energy Consumption for Bulk Data Communications in WLANs. In *IEEE ICNP*, 2007.
32. Y. Wang, J. Lin, M. Annavaram, Q. A. Jacobson, J. Hong, and B. Krishnamachari. A Framework of Energy Efficient Mobile Sensing for Automatic User State Recognition. In *ACM MobiSys*, 2009.

LEAP: A Low Energy Assisted GPS for Trajectory-Based Services

Heitor S. Ramos
Federal Univ. of Alagoas
Maceió, 57072-970
Brazil
heitor@ic.ufal.br

Tao Zhang
Pennsylvania State Univ.
University Park, PA 16802
USA
zhangtao@cse.psu.edu

Jie Liu
Nissanka B. Priyantha
Aman Kansal
Microsoft Research
Redmond, WA 98052
USA
{liuj,bodhip,kansal}@microsoft.com

ABSTRACT
Trajectory-based services require continuous user location sensing. GPS is the most common outdoor location sensor on mobile devices. However, the high energy consumption of GPS sensing prohibits it to be used continuously in many applications. In this paper, we propose a Low Energy Assisted Positioning (LEAP) solution that carefully partitions the GPS signal processing pipeline and shifts delay tolerant position calculations to the cloud. The GPS receiver only needs to be on for less than a second to collect the sub-millisecond level propagation delay for each satellites signal. With a reference to a nearby object, such as a cell tower, the LEAP server can infer the rest of the information necessary to perform GPS position calculation. We analyze the accuracy and energy benefit of LEAP and use real user traces to show that LEAP can save up to 80% GPS energy consumption in typical trajectory-based service scenarios.

Author Keywords
Assisted GPS, Mobile, Location

ACM Classification Keywords
H.5.m Information Interfaces and Presentations: Misc.

General Terms
Design

INTRODUCTION
GPS receivers are ubiquitous in smart phones today. Location is a dominant user context information for many mobile applications, such as traffic, navigation, search, advertising, social networking, and personal reminders. While some applications are satisfied with a single location fix — e.g. the current latitude and longitude of the device — many context-aware services require or can take advantage of continuous location traces. We call these services *trajectory-based services* (TBS). In TBS, a mobile device collects a time series of location information, and possibly sends them to a cloud server at once, to obtain services.

For example, many crowd sourcing applications for traffic [11], popular destinations [8], or cab sharing [5] require users to upload their trajectory periodically to the server for analysis. In Place-Its [14] and for location based reminders [10], the device needs to continuously monitor the user's location to deliver reminders or offers. In Predestination [7], the authors show the possibility of predicting people's destination based on a short driving trajectory. Base on such prediction, a mobile search engine can return local businesses in users' driving direction rather than those behind them. Trajectories can also help validate users' current locations by imposing physical constraints. When a person "checks in" at a location (e.g. using services like Foursquare[1]), the immediate past trajectory gives the service provider more confidence that the user is not lying about the current location.

There are several ways for a smart phone to obtain its current location, for example through the GPS receiver, WiFi or Bluetooth signatures, Cell tower ID or signal strength triangulation, etc. Among them, GPS-based positioning gives the best accuracy and best out-door coverage. However, it is well known that continuous GPS sensing is energy consuming, and that a typical smart phone will drain its battery completely in less than half a day with always-on GPS [9, 12, 19, 4]. Several techniques are proposed in the literature to reduce the overhead of continuous location sensing: 1) by using alternative sensors if the accuracy requirement is not high [9]; 2) by turning on the GPS only when significant motion is detected [12]; or 3) by combining multiple location requests from the application layer together [19]. However, in all the previous work, a GPS receiver is treated as a black box that outputs user coordinates at certain energy expenses.

In this paper, we take a deep look at the principle and processing stages of GPS receivers and propose a new operation mode for mobile GPS sensing, called *Low Energy Assisted Positioning* (LEAP). In the LEAP mode, a GPS receiver can shut down most of its internal components and

[1]http://www.foursquare.com

UbiComp'11, September 17–21, 2011, Beijing, China.

heavily duty cycle its RF front-end. Instead of decoding time stamps from satellite signals, performing Least Square location computation, and outputting the (latitude, longitude, altitude) locations, LEAP only outputs the sub-millisecond parts of the time-of-flight (ToF) of the GPS signals[2]. These sub-millisecond parts of ToF, called code phases (CP), can be detected easily without decoding any information from the satellite packets.

Using a technique known as coarse-time navigation (CTN) [16], for each set of the CPs from every visible satellite, together with a known location of a nearby object (e.g. the cell tower that the phone locks to), a server can easily compute the locations for the mobile device, or provide location/trajectory-based services. Thus, LEAP does not require any hardware change to current GSP sensors. It only needs accessing low level CP data and controlling receiver duty cycling, which we argue, should be made available by current GPS receivers.

LEAP can be classified as a type of Mobile Station Assisted GPS (MS-A AGPS or AGPS-A). However, compared to typical AGPS-A, which sends either the raw data or decoded pseudorange (full ToF) to a server, LEAP carefully manages which part of GPS sensing and computation must be done in the receiver, while others can be deferred to the cloud. Although the idea applies to any delay tolerant location calculation, such as photo tagging and single instance location-based services, the benefit is most significant for TBS when a set of CPs can be sent to the cloud at once to amortize the communication cost. Given that energy cost of communicating a packet over a 3G link is comparable to obtaining a GPS fix, LEAP is not a replacement for current GPS receivers when the user only needs to obtain a single instantaneous location coordinate locally.

We analyze the duty cycle period for LEAP mode and use real traces to evaluate accuracy and energy savings for using LEAP. We show that with 10 ms code phases, LEAP gives ± 40 m location error. With 300 ms code phases, LEAP can be as accurate as a standalone GPS. For typical TBS such as trace logging and local social networking (such as Google Latitude), LEAP can save up to 80% energy on GPS sensing than regular GPS.

The rest of the paper is organized as following. We first give a brief background on the GPS signals and GPS receiver principles. Then, we present the LEAP solution based on a coarse-time navigation technique. We examine LEAP's energy benefit by analyzing the timing and data rate at each GPS processing stage. LEAP is evaluated both for accuracy depending on receiver active duration and for energy saving using real user traces and two representative TBS scenarios.

GPS BASICS

We start with a brief (and much simplified) description of how GPS systems work. For a more formal treatment of the principles of GPS and A-GPS, please refer to [6, 16].

[2]The time it takes for the GPS signal to travel from the satellite to the GPS receiver is typically 75ms

GPS Signals

A GPS receiver obtains its location from receiving and processing digital communication signals sent from GPS satellites. There are 31 GPS satellites or space vehicles (SVs), each orbiting the earth two cycles a day. A set of ground stations monitor satellites' trajectory and health, and send the satellite parameters to the satellites. In particular, there are two kinds of trajectory information: the *almanac*, which contains the coarse orbit and status information, and the *ephemeris*, which contains the precise information of satellite trajectory. All satellites are time synchronized to within a few nanoseconds.

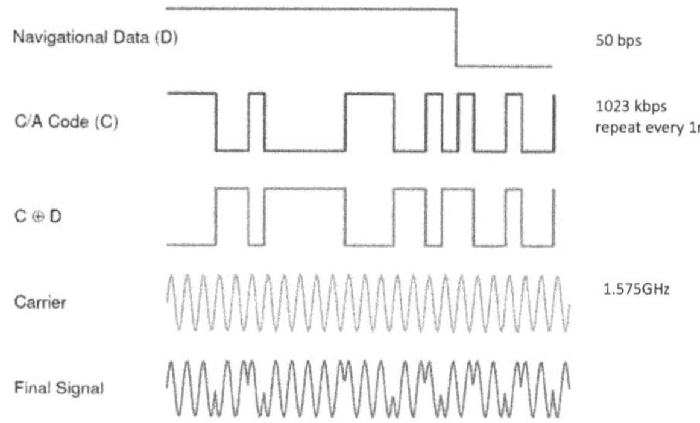

Figure 1. An illustration of GPS signal modulation scheme.

As illustrated in Figure 1, the satellites simultaneously and continuously broadcast time and orbit information through CDMA signals at 1.575 GHz towards the earth. The transmission data rate is at merely 50 bps. Apart from the data, each satellite encodes this signal (CDMA encoding) using a satellite specific C/A code of length 1023 chips at 1023 kbps. Thus, the C/A code repeats every millisecond resulting in 20 repetitions of the C/A code during each data bit sent.

A full data packet from a satellite broadcast is 30 seconds long, containing 5 six-second long frames, as shown in Figure 2. A frame has a preamble, called Telemetry Word (TLM), and a time stamp, called Handover Word (HOW). Ephemeris of the transmitting satellite and the almanac of all satellites are contained in each data packet. In other words, a precise time stamp can be decoded every 6 seconds, and the high accuracy satellite trajectory can be decoded every 30 seconds. The ephemeris information is constantly updated by the ground stations. In theory, the ephemeris data included in the SV broadcast is only valid for 30 minutes.

These data rates explain why standalone GPS may take about 30 seconds or more to obtain a location fix, since all information has to be received and decoded from the satellite signals. In mobile devices, the course-grained satellite trajectory parameters are downloaded from a server. Thus, a low accuracy time to first fix (TTFF) can be reduced to 6s.

GPS Receiving

In order to compute its location, a typical GPS receiver needs three pieces of information: 1) a time stamp [3] 2) the satel-

[3]When the time differences between the receiver and the satellites are within a few seconds, the receiver time can be another variable

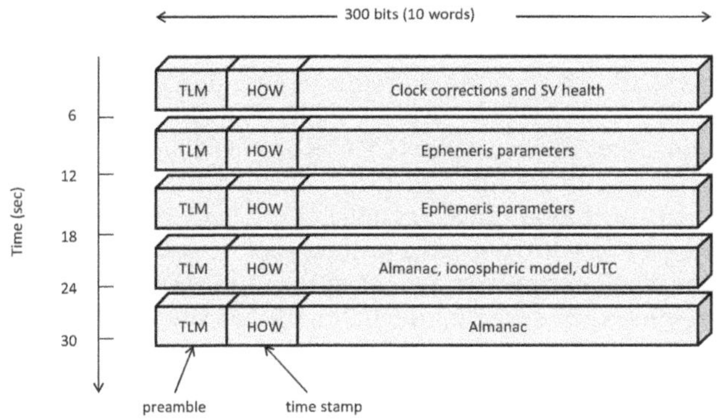

Figure 2. The frame content of a GPS packet of length 1500 bits

lites' orbits at the time, and 3) the approximated distances (called the pseudorange) from each satellite to the receiver at the time. Among those, the key is to obtain the pseudoranges, which are computed from the time of flight of the RF signals from each satellite to the receiver.

The RF signals travel 64 to 89 milliseconds from a satellite to earth surface. Notice that light travels 300 km/ms. So in order to obtain an accurate position, the receiver must track time to the microsecond level. The millisecond part (NMS) and the sub-millisecond (subMS) parts of the propagation time are detected very differently. While NMS is decoded from the packet frames, the subMS propagation time is detected at the C/A code level using correlations.

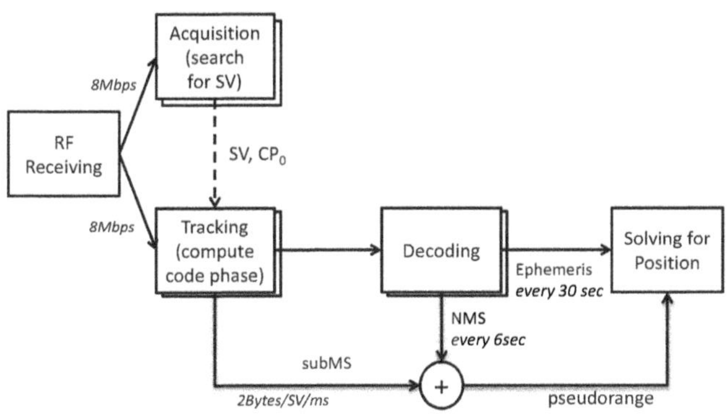

Figure 3. A simplified illustration of GPS processing stages

Figure 3 shows a simplified diagram of different stages of GPS signal processing and location calculation. When the GPS receiver is just turned on, it has no information on what SVs are visible and their code phases [4].

- The *Acquisition* stage is run when the GPS receiver starts up. The goal of the Acquisition phase is to start receiving the data transmitted by the SVs visible to the GPS receiver by correctly decoding the received signal. Acquisition phase also measures the Code Phase values as a byproduct. To decode the data from a given satellite, three unknowns have to be estimated.

  First, it is necessary to determine if the given satellite is visible to the receiver. The presence of a given satellite can be determined by detecting the presence of its C/A code in the received GPS signal. Second, although the satellites transmissions are centered around a 1.575GHz *carrier* frequency, the signals from different satellites received at the GPS receiver deviate from this due to the Doppler frequency shift caused by the relative motion between the satellites and the receiver. It is necessary to determine these Doppler shifts to decode the data from a given satellite. Third, since the satellite signal is encoded by a 1023 bit C/A code, the received signal has to be decoded by multiplying it with the C/A code of the corresponding satellite at the correct time instance (CDMA decodings). Although the C/A codes are well known, the exact timing of when the signals should be multiplied is unknown and it depends on the receiver position. Since the C/A codes repeats every 1 ms this unknown fractional ms time represents the Code Phase of the corresponding satellite.

  If the receiver has no knowledge of the current SV arrangement in the sky and the precise time, it needs to search through all possible C/A codes, Doppler frequency shifts, and code phases. In typical GPS hardware, it can takes 30 seconds to finish acquisition. This is a relatively expensive operation, so A-GPS helps this process by providing the visible SV information off line. However, it is still necessary to complete the frequency and code search for each SV in view.

- Once the satellite signals are acquired, the receiver enters a relatively inexpensive *Tracking* stage, which keeps feedback loops to adjust phase locks and delay locks and maintain the code phases in the receiver in sync with those from the satellites. In the continuous mode, the tracking loop runs every millisecond.

- With correct tracking, the receiver can *decode* the packets sent by the SVs. In general, without assistance information, the receiver needs to decode SV ephemeris every 30 minutes (its valid time span) and time stamps every 6 seconds. Decoding is energy consuming since it has to run tracking continuously for the packet duration in order to receive all the bits. With A-GPS, the receiver is not required to decode ephemeris, but it must still decode HOW.

- Given ephemeris and propagation delays obtained from code phase and HOW, the GPS receiver performs *position calculation* using constraint optimization techniques, such as Least Square minimization. This is usually done on the phone's main processor. With receivers' latitude, longitude, altitude, and precise time, the receiver needs a minimum of 4 SVs in view.

It is important to understand the data rates at each stage of processing. While baseband C/A code has a bit rate of 1.023 Mbps, the signals are typically oversampled at 8 MHz to achieve better code phase estimation. A code phase, referred as subMS, can be computed from any 1 ms of the baseband signal. Once computed, it requires only 2 bytes per satellite (10-bit Code Phase and 6-bit satellite ID) to represent it. On the other hand, it takes 6 or 30 seconds to decode

in Least Square optimization.

[4]in A-GPS, the visible SVs are included in the assisted information, but the receiver still need to acquire the satellites to lock to them.

packet contents from the signals. During which time, the tracking circuits of the receiver cannot be turned off. Thus, as we will realize in the next section, code phases are the most efficient information to represent the device location when other information can be obtained separately.

Energy Analysis

The energy consumption of typical GPS sensing consists of two parts — (1) the GPS receiver that needs to acquire, track, and decode the signals sent from the GPS satellites, and (2) the main processor that controls the receiver and performs position calculation.

As a concrete example, consider the energy use for a GPS receiver on an HTC HD2 smartphone. We placed the mobile phone in a sleep state and ran a background service to use only the GPS receiver and obtain a location fix. The power draw during a location sensing period is shown in Figure 4. In this mode, aside from the nominal power usage of the phone for maintaining network presence (7.3mW in the figure), the only other energy used is that for GPS based location sensing, consisting of the GPS receiver chip-set, the phone's main processor, and the minimal supplemental circuitry required to power the two former components. Ignoring the power bursts during activating and de-activating the system, the power draw during location sensing is 387mW. This is consistent with other measurements of phone based GPS energy consumption performed on other devices. To place this number in perspective, a typical phone battery capacity of 1000mAh will allow such a GPS receiver to operate continuously for only 9.5 hours, assuming that the phone is not used for anything else.

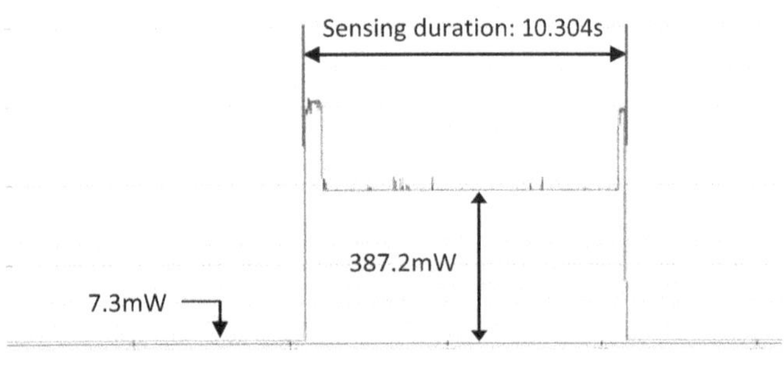

Figure 4. Power trace showing phone energy use for GPS location sensing.

LEAP SOLUTION

The fundamental idea of LEAP is to use coarse-time navigation (CTN) [16] techniques to trade off between local GPS signal processing and communicating sufficient data to the cloud. CTN, also called instant GPS, is a known GPS technique, which have unfortunately received little attention. One reason for this is that standalone GPS does not have a communication link to the cloud. Another reason is that CTN does not necessarily improve TTFF, which has so far been the primary optimization goal for mobile GPS design. However, it provides the best foundation for partitioning GPS receiving stages between the device and the cloud.

Coarse-Time Navigation

Coarse-time navigation does not require decoding any data from satellite packets. Instead, the GPS receiver only needs to compute the code phase (CP) for each visible SV and have a reference to a known "nearby" location. The key insight is that since light travels at 300 km/ms, two locations close enough to each other (e.g. within 150km) will observe the same NMS, modulo the boundary conditions that can be disambiguated by snapping the CP to the nearest integer.

GPS location estimation involves 4 unknowns–the (x, y, z) coordinates of the GPS receiver and the precise time. Solving for these 4 unknowns requires a minimum of 4 visible satellites. However, CTN adds another source of error, called *coarse time error*, due the lack of a precise time reference on the receiver side. Correcting this error requires an additional visible satellite, making it necessary to have 5 visible satellites for computing location. We use the coarse time error model described in [16] to correct this error.

Even though the millisecond part of the pseudorange can be estimated by the initial position and the coarse-time, any small error on this estimate can lead to a very inaccurate position calculation. For instance, an error of 1 ms produces results about 300 km away from the actual location. Integer rollover is the main source of such errors during the estimation process. Van Diggelen [16] proposes the following method to reconstruct the full pseudoranges avoiding the integer rollover problem. The travel time can be written as

$$NMS^{(k)} + \varphi^{(k)} = \tau^{(k)} - \delta_t^{(k)} + b + \epsilon^{(k)} \quad (1)$$

$$= \hat{\tau}^{(k)} - d^{(k)} - \delta_t^{(k)} + b + \epsilon^{(k)} \quad (2)$$

where $NMS^{(k)}$ and $\varphi^{(k)}$ are the millisecond and sub-millisecond components of the transmission delay to the satellite k, respectively, $\tau^{(k)}$ is the actual travel time corresponding to the satellite k, $\delta_t^{(k)}$ is the satellite clock errors obtained from the ephemeris at the a priori coarse time for the satellite k, b is the common bias, and $\epsilon^{(k)}$ represents some unknown errors (tropospheric model error and other stochastic errors).

As $\tau^{(k)}$ is unknown, it can be written as $\tau^{(k)} = \hat{\tau}^{(k)} - d^{(k)}$, where $\hat{\tau}^{(k)}$ is the estimated travel time from the a priori position at the coarse time of transmission, and $d^{(k)}$ is the error in $\hat{\tau}^{(k)}$. The method involves the selection of a reference satellite, $k = 0$, where $NMS^{(0)} = round(\hat{\tau}^{(0)} - \varphi^{(0)})$ is the millisecond part of the pseudorange of the reference SV[5]. This value is used to reconstruct the millisecond travel time of all other satellites relative to the reference satellite. Thus, if we subtract the Eq. (2) from the reference satellite full travel time we get

$$\begin{aligned} NMS^{(k)} &= NMS^{(0)} + \varphi^{(0)} - \varphi^{(k)} \\ &+ \left(\hat{\tau}^{(k)} - d^{(k)} - \delta_t^{(k)} + b + \epsilon^{(k)}\right) \\ &- \left(\hat{\tau}^{(0)} - d^{(0)} - \delta_t^{(0)} + b + \epsilon^{(0)}\right) \quad (3) \end{aligned}$$

[5] [16] recommends the use of the highest satellite in view as reference, and provides a good reason for that

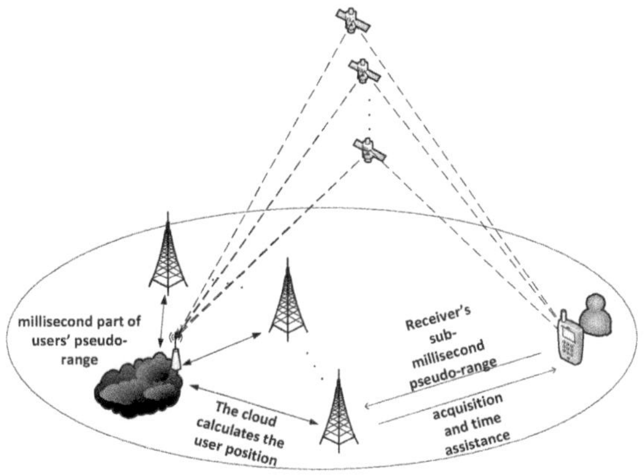

Figure 5. LEAP system overview

We still do not know the values of $d^{(0)}$ and $d^{(k)}$, but considering that we have an initial position and coarse time close to the correct values (about 100 km and 1 min), the order of magnitude of $(-d^{(k)} + \epsilon^{(k)} + d^{(0)} - \epsilon^{(0)})$ is less than about 150 km, thus, we can correctly estimate $NMS^{(k)}$ by

$$NMS^{(k)} = round\Big(NMS^{(0)} + \varphi^{(0)} - \varphi^{(k)} + (\hat{\tau}^{(k)} - \delta_t^{(k)}) - (\hat{\tau}^{(0)} - \delta_t^{(0)})\Big). \quad (4)$$

In summary, the full pseudorange is estimated by using NMS as the millisecond part, and the sub-millisecond is obtained by the code phase estimate. CTN can be computed either on the device or on a back-end server. In order to compute it on the device, the phone needs to periodically update the ephemeris data every 30 minutes, and have a database of the precise locations of a set of landmarks. Alternatively, since the only device dependent data are the code phases for each visible SV, the location computation can be moved completely to the cloud.

LEAP for Trajectory-Based Services

LEAP is a realization of the CTN principle to reduce the energy expense for obtaining trajectory-based services. By not decoding GPS signal and by offloading location calculation to the cloud, LEAP can aggressively duty cycle GPS receivers for energy efficiency.

Mobile devices have two advantages when using the CTN principle. First, they have a fairly good time synchronization due to the requirement from the cellular network. So it is very unlikely to have more than 2 seconds of time error. Secondly, the devices are almost always associated to a cell tower, if there is one within range. Notice that the communication range of a cell tower is typically less than 5 km, which makes the cell towers ideal reference locations for applying CTN.

Figure 5 shows the system overview of the LEAP approach.

- **On the device:** The mobile device receives necessary assistance for SV acquisition phase and has a coarse time synchronized with the cellular system (as in typical AGPS). Whenever a location reading is requested from the application, the device performs a SV acquisition and a few milliseconds of tracking to estimate the code phase for each SV. It stores a *LEAP tuple*, including the code phases, the current time stamp, and the associated cell ID, and then shuts down the receiver. Note that a GPS receiver can see at most 12 SVs at the same time. So each LEAP tuple is at most 40 bytes long, including two bytes for each code phase, 8 bytes for time stamp, and 8 bytes for cell tower ID. When a TBS is requested based on T seconds of history, the device sends the LEAP tuples collected in the last T seconds as part of the service request. A traditional mobile GPS would send three double precision numbers for latitude, longitude, and altitude (total of 24 bytes) and an 8-byte time stamp for each point in a trajectory. So the communication cost between LEAP and traditional mobile GPS is comparable.

- **On the server:** To support the LEAP mode, each TBS server first converts the set of LEAP tuples into a trajectory. This is relatively straightforward using Eq. (4) when the server maintains ephemeris for all SVs and a (rough) location database for all cell towers. Since the locations are computed on the server, mechanisms for improving GPS accuracy, such as Wide Area Augmentation System (WAAS) [1] and differential GPS can be easily applied.

  In US, National Geodetic Survey computes the orbits of GPS satellites and publishes them using the Standard GPS (SP3) Format. The ultra rapid data has a 6-hour latency, which can be extrapolated to estimate real-time orbit information at relatively high accuracy. Obviously, a set of servers can receive and decode the same ephemeris data sent from the satellite for most up to date orbit information.

  While carriers typically do not publish their cell tower locations, there are open source projects, such as OpenCellID[6], that build cell tower databases by crowd sourcing. Note that LEAP does not require precise cell tower locations, since they only provide a rough reference point to compute NMS.

In comparison, a naive method of mobile-station-assisted A-GPS can send raw GPS data, with the amount of 1023 bits/ms to a server. As we will show later, to obtain accurate location comparable to standalone GPS, one may need more than a hundred milliseconds of raw data. Thus, LEAP leverages local computation that GPS receivers already do to reduce the amount of data being sent.

Receiver Duty Cycling

LEAP's energy benefit comes first and foremost from offloading packet decoding and location calculation to the cloud. However, if the RF frontend and the satellite tracking process have to run continuously between consecutive location samples during trajectory collection, then a significant part of the GPS receiver have to remain active all the time.

[6]`http://opencellid.org`

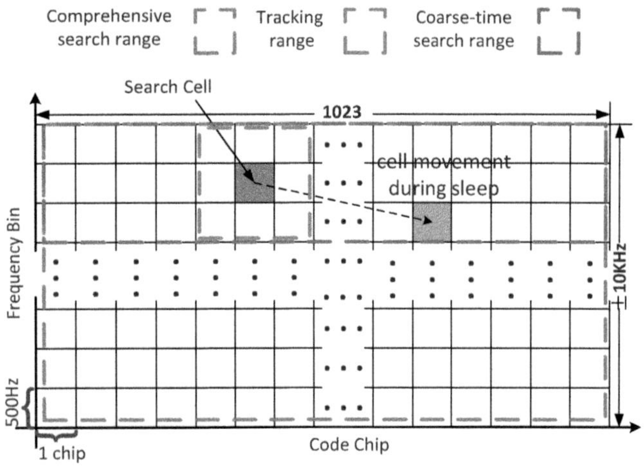

Figure 6. GPS acquisition search range

On the other hand, shutting down and resuming only the satellite tracking component is not as trivial as it seems. The time gap between two tracking processes can cause feedback loop instability, introduce large CP errors, or even lead to a failure to acquire any satellite. So how to duty cycle a GPS receiver must be carefully considered. In this session, we present a mechanism for fast re-acquisition based on previous tracking results, so that the receiver can be turned off completely between readings for better energy saving.

It is necessary to first describe the typical acquisition process when there is no prior knowledge of time or code phases. As shown in Figure. 6, when a GPS receiver starts, it must search in both frequency bins (caused by Doppler effect) and code phase bins (caused by imprecise time) to lock each SV. Given ± 10 KHz frequency uncertainty, 500 Hz frequency bin and code length of $1,023$ chips[7], in the worst case there are $41,943$ search cells in total (the dashed area in Figure. 6). Without acceleration, the search input data rate is 1 ms/cell. Thus a brute-force search process will take more than 40 sec. exhaustively traverse the search space. Much work has been done to speed up the initial acquisition (e.g. massive parallel correlation, parallel frequency search [17], parallel code phase search [18]), however, little has been done on search space reduction based on a previously known SV lock — a process we call *reacquisition* or *reacq* for short.

Assume that the GPS receiver has locked to each visible SV, computed their CPs, and went to the sleep mode for T seconds. When it wakes up, the local carrier frequency and code phase would have changed due to the movement of satellites, of the user, and the local clock bias. The changes of frequency and code phase imply cell movement in Figure. 6. Based on the previously locked cell, and the duration of sleep, the goal is to reduce search space for LEAP to a small neighborhood, rather than searching the whole space again.

The key observation we want to leverage is that a small moving distance of the user in a short period of time only causes small frequency and code phase changes. For example, for less than a 3 km distance, all points fall within ± 3 Hz Doppler frequency shifts and ± 11 chips code phase shifts. Table. 1 sets some parameters for deriving the reacquisition search space. We assume the user moves at a maximum speed of 160 km/h and 8 SVs are visible. We also assume the GPS receiver has 12 correlation channels, which is very conservative comparing to the state-of-art devices.

[7]We simplify the problem description here. In practice, the search unit of code phase is usually half chip, which means totally $2,046$ search cells for one frequency bin.

Table 1. Coarse-time Search Settings (courtesy from [16])

# of Satellites	8
# of Correlation Channels	12
Satellite Velocity	± 3 chips/s(at ± 800 m/s)
GPS Receiver Frequency Drift	3 ppm
Maximum User Speed	160 km/h
Doppler Effect by User Motion	± 468 Hz
Reference Frequency Error	± 157.5 Hz(± 100 ppb)
Vertical Error	± 100 m
Frequency Bin	500 Hz
Code Length	$1,023$ chips
One Tracking Iteration	1 ms

At the maximum 160 km/h(≈ 44.5 m/s) speed, T-second sleep duration results in $\pm 44.5T$ m horizontal location difference. If $44.5T < 3$km, the Doppler shift from the reference position (last position) is less than 3 Hz. In addition, a T-second sleep introduces extra frequency error up to T s$\times 0.8$ Hz/s $= 0.8T$ Hz. By adding these to the local frequency drift and Doppler shift caused by user motion, the maximum assisted-frequency search space is $\pm(157.5 + 468 + 3 + 0.8T) = \pm(628.5+0.8T)$ Hz. For example if $T = 60s$ we can reduce the frequency search space to within -676.5 to $+676.5$ Hz of the previous lock. Considering that each frequency bin is 500 Hz, searching in the nearby 3 bins is sufficient.

Next, the reacq process needs to search all possible code phases, at a minimum rate of 1 s for each frequency bin. If we assume 12 correlation channels searching in parallel, reacq can finish searching the first satellite within 250 ms.

After the first satellite is locked, reacq can use the code phase differences between SVs from previous tracking results to further reduce the code phase search range. Considering ± 11 chips code phase shift due to user motion, ± 11 chips code phase shift due to local clock frequency uncertainty, and ± 3 chips per second code phase shift due to satellite motion, the reference clock error can be estimated as $2 \times 11 + 2 \times 3 \times T$ chips. For example, for $T = 10$ s, we need to search ± 82 chips, while for $T = 60$ s, we need to search ± 382 chips.

Given that bin searching is a relatively simple operation in hardware, reacq can be done in real time. So the time consumed by the receiver is the time it needs to collect the data. Putting everything together when $T = 10$ s, the total reacquisition time is ≤ 414 ms; and for $T = 60$ s, it is $\leq 1,014$ ms.

Based on the analysis above, LEAP uses a three phase duty

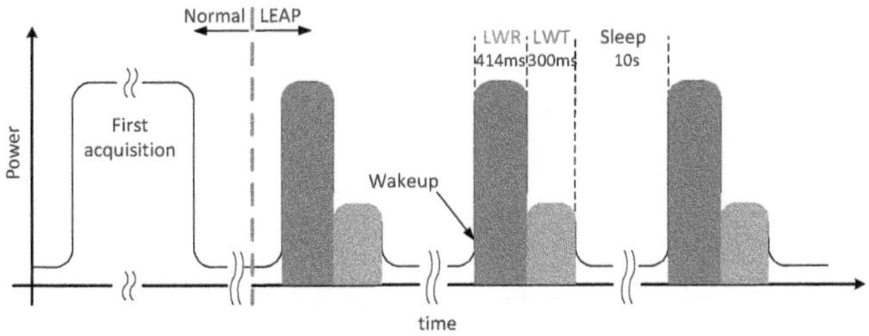

Figure 7. Duty cycling of the GSP receiver in LEAP.

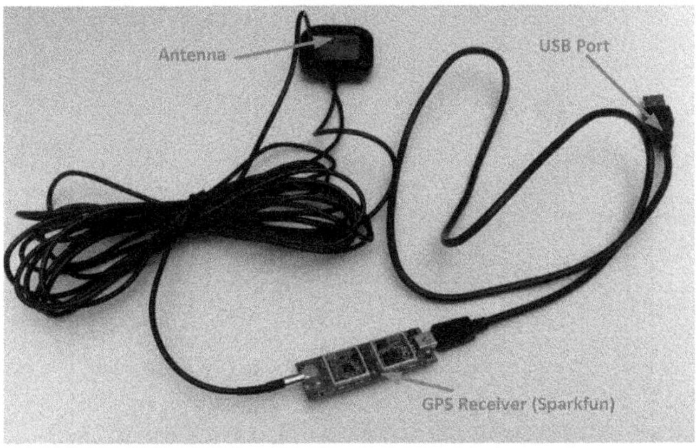

Figure 8. The GSP data collector used for experiments

cycle after the initial full acquisition — sleep, reacquisition, and tracking — as shown in Figure. 7. Assuming maximal vehicle speeds, the longest time that the GPS receiver can sleep is about a minute. Beyond that the small variation assumption is violated and the device must perform an exhaustive search again. After sleeping, LEAP performs a light-weight reacquisition to re-initiate the tracking loop. The length of the tracking loop is determined by the accuracy requirement of the application. One set of code phases is produced by each tracking loop. Due to the noise in the extremely weak GPS signal and the multi-path effect, the receiver must collect sufficient number of CP samples to tease out location errors. In the next section, we will show empirically that 300 ms tracking loops give good enough location outputs.

EVALUATION

Since no off-the-shelf GPS chip outputs low-level code phase information through a programmable interface, we evaluate LEAP using raw GSP data traces and a software-defined GPS implementation [3], which we modified to simulate receiver duty cycles and computation offloading.

We collect about 10 sets of raw GPS data at three different locations using a SiGe GN3S sampler version 2 dongle (available from Sparkfun Electronics[8]), as shown in Figure 8. Each data set includes the baseband GPS signal sampled at 16 MHz for at least 30 second long to cover complete GPS packets.

We use a standalone Garmin GPS Map 60CS[9] device to survey the "ground truth" of these locations, which themselves have about 15 m accuracy. A fourth location is used to simulate a nearby cell tower. During our experiments, the Gamin GPS produces dilution of precision (DOP) values 5 or 6, which are consider good or moderate. Table 2 shows all the positions (latitude and longitude), the precision, and the number of satellites in view at the moment we collected the positions.

For ephemeris data, we used Ultra-Rapid Orbits available on the International GNSS Service (IGS) website[10]. These orbits provide precision estimates of the SV's position and clock rate. Thus, it provides all information required by LEAP.

To evaluate the accuracy of our approach, we calculate the errors between LEAP's output and the outputs from the unmodified software implementing standard GPS processing. It is noteworthy that the values presented here represents how far our approach is from a similar standalone GPS implementation when the same signal trace is used. In addition to regular GPS error sources, LEAP adds the following possible errors: (i) the position is calculated by using code phases samples closer to each other than regular GPS; these samples are more likely to suffer temporary noise, (ii) the LEAP lock loops (PLL and DLL) run for less time than typical GPS; sometimes it may incur to less accurate results, and (iii) the use of CTN technique can also cause numerical errors.

We conduct our experiments with the following LEAP examples: (i) LEAP010, (ii) LEAP050, (iii) LEAP100, (iv) LEAP300, and (v) LEAP500. The numeral suffix corresponds to the amount of milliseconds of the signal used in the tracking phase – 10, 50, 100, and 300 milliseconds.

Given one-millisecond of signal, we are able to estimate a pseudorange for each SV, and therefore the receiver's position. Thus, we compute the final position using two different measures of central tendency: (i) the mean, and (ii) the median of a given number of chunks. Taking average from a set of positions is a common strategy in regular GPS to remove noise. However, median is also known to be resilient to outliers. In our analysis, we consider the maximum of 50 equally spaced chunks used for noise reduction. That is, even when we run 500 tracking loops, a set of code phases are only collected every 10 ms.

The number of satellites

Figure 9 shows the average absolute error with respect to the number of satellites in view, for each location and strategy used (mean or median). It shows that the the number of satellites in view poses a strong influence on the error quality. Observe that, generally, when the receiver can see only five satellites (the minimum for LEAP), all strategies present the largest errors. When the number of satellites increases, the error decreases steeply. We can also see that median values

[8]`http://www.sparkfun.com/commerce/product_info.php?products_id=8238`

[9]`http://www8.garmin.com/products/gpsmap60cs`

[10]`http://igscb.jpl.nasa.gov/`

Table 2. Evaluation Data Points

Location	Latitude	Longitude	Precision (m)	# of Satellites	Distance to the "cell tower"
Assumed Cell Tower	47.64168°	−122.14081°	±5.18	9	–
Location A	47.63006°	−122.14433°	±4.57	10	1.23 km
Location B	47.64337°	−122.13928°	±4.27	10	0.220 km
Location C	47.66941°	−122.14373°	±4.88	8	3.09 km

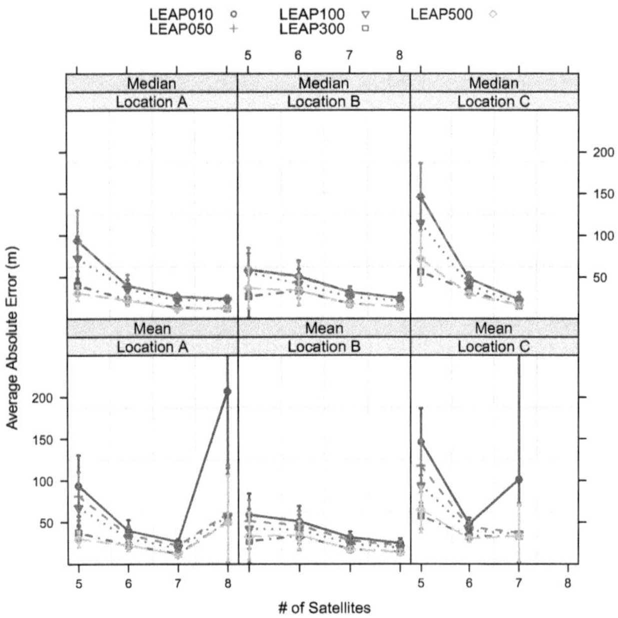

Figure 9. Error in function of the number of satellites and location

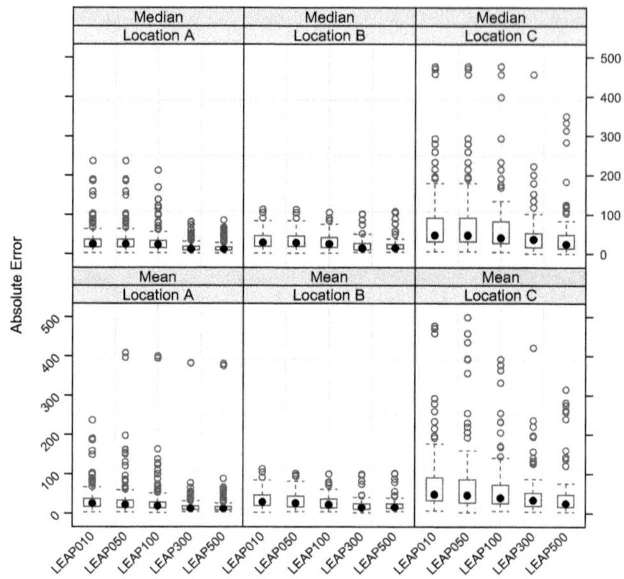

Figure 10. Error in function of the number of chunks and location. About 2% of data were considered outlier and are omited from this plot

Table 3. Outliers Statistics

Min.	1st Qu.	Median	Mean	3rd Qu.	Max.
253.9	314.6	414.8	486.6	517.8	1773.0

are more robust to outliers than the mean values, especially for Locations A and C when LEAP10 is used.

Tracking Time

Figure 10 shows the behavior of the absolute error with respect to tracking time, at various locations and using different strategies (mean or median). In the plot, the lower and upper box limits represent the 1st and 3th quartiles, respectively, the whiskers represent a range 1.5 times the IQR (interquartile range), and the points that eventually appear below or above the whiskers range are considered outliers. The black dots represent the mean value. To better visualize this plot, we removed the most significant outliers with error larger than 250 m. These result in 76 samples among 4000 computed. The noise and distortion in GPS signals are likely to lead to these bad points, which are not uncommon in standard GPS. Some statistics of the outliers are presented in Table 3. These bad conditioned samples can be easily detected and removed in a TBS, for instance, comparing the actual position to prior positions and checking its plausibility.

Observe that LEAP300 leads to absolute errors typically less than 50 m for 75% (above the 3th quartile) of the samples, and the mean values are typically less than 40 m. Moreover, LEAP300 only presents 4 samples into the set of removed outliers, while, for instance, LEAP10 contributes 23 samples. Those results indicate that LEAP300 represents a good trade-off between accuracy, stability, and energy saving. It is noteworthy that the median can help to avoid some outliers and should be used.

So LEAP naturally provides accuracy/energy tradeoff. If the application requires only a city block accuracy, even 10 ms tracking is acceptable. By using 300 and 500 ms, and when the median is used, the error is very similar to regular GPS devices even when the number of satellites in view is low.

Energy Consumption

The energy savings offered by using the LEAP mode in practical usage scenarios are evaluated next using real user location traces. The location traces are collected by asking volunteers to run a data collection application on their mobile devices. This application continuously samples location, stores them locally, and uploads the trace once a day to our server. The trace data set consists of 18 unique users from US, Europe, and Africa, with 1 to 20 days of data per user. Each user's trace has different periods of satellite visibility depending on where they live, work, and travel.

Consider two types of scenarios:

Trajectory Tracking: For this scenario, the user location is tracked continuously throughout the day at a few minutes granularity (once a minute in our runs) at moderate accuracy (40 m). The data is uploaded when the user has wired power, so communication energy is ignored. Such usage is representative to applications that mine user behavior over time, or collect movement patterns over large populations (e.g. skyhook). The location data is not required instantaneously.

Local Social: In this scenarios, location is tracked continuously every few seconds (6 s in our runs) at high accuracy and uploaded to a cloud service every 5 minutes. Such usage represents social networking applications to find friends meeting at a public place, advertisement applications to track user movement and suggest currently relevant local services and/or products, and services that require recent motion trajectory. In this type of scenarios, the communication energy of uploading location is important.

It is tempting to compare LEAP with WiFi-based location services. If we consider proper duty cycling, the amortized energy expense is about the same for the two approaches without hardware optimization for LEAP. And both require communication to the server for location resolution. However, not all places have WiFi coverage. In our dataset, on average 25% locations do not have WiFi in sight, especially when driving on highways. In addition, WiFi services typically provide 30 $\sim$ 100m location accuracy, while LEAP can provide better accuracy 10 $\sim$ 40m with same energy expense. So we focusing on comparing LEAP with standard GPS solutions in this section.

We perform the evaluation based on trace-driven simulation. We assume that location tracking is turned off when the device does not have GPS visibility, such as indoors, and an automated mechanism using a low energy sensor, accelerometer [19], is available to resume GPS use when user movement is detected. This implies that savings from LEAP accrue only when GPS satellite visibility is available, making our comparison disadvantageous for LEAP since savings for other parts of the day are suppressed.

Energy Model: There is no GPS receiver on the market that is optimized for LEAP. For example, in the ideal case, when the GPS receiver is not involved in decoding the satellite packets, corresponding parts should be turned off. To evaluate energy benefits, we take a loose assumption that LEAP uses the same power as a regular GPS receiver when it is active. We assume the same GPS hardware for both LEAP and without LEAP, using an average draw of 400 mW when powered on (brief impulses of higher power are observed for non-LEAP GPS for certain calculations such as least squares phase, and are ignored, making the comparison disadvantageous for LEAP). So the main energy differences come from duty cycling: with LEAP, the GPS only needs to be turned on for 1024 ms for each location sample at 60 s interval and 40 m accuracy. Without LEAP, the GPS requires 5 s for each location sample, every 60 s. When sampling every 6 s with high accuracy, LEAP mode requires 414 ms per sample, while a regular GPS have to stay powered on.

To make the simulation evaluation close to reality, we also measured the energy use for accelerometer sampling (259 mJ for 1s of sampling) for motion detection, and location trace upload (10.1 J for 5 minutes of location trace) relevant to the second scenario.

Figure 11 shows the energy savings provided by LEAP. Since different users have different number of days worth of data and the absolute energy usage varies widely, we normalize the data to the energy usage on non-LEAP mode and plot only the percentage savings. Savings are significant for many users. The users for which savings are small are mostly ones for whom GPS visibility was available only for small time windows during the entire day and the energy use is dominated primarily by the accelerometer sampling. The actual energy use is very different at 60 s sampling and 6 s sampling with upload but the percentage savings are similar. This happens because the communication energy of an upload every 5 minutes is negligible compared to GPS sampling every 6 s.

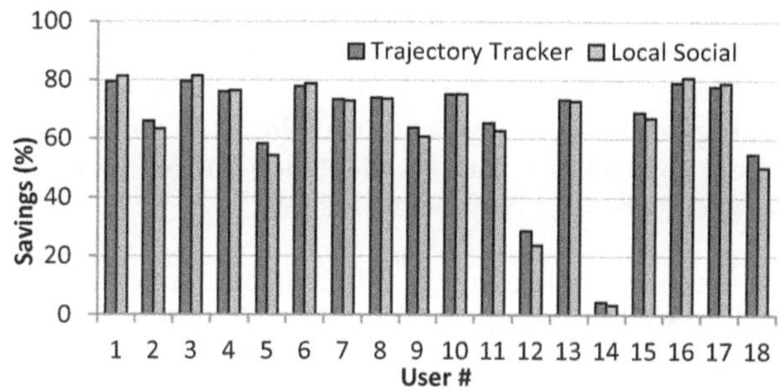

Figure 11. Energy savings from LEAP mode in two representative scenarios. Users #12 and #14 experience less energy saving than others mainly because they have little or almost no GPS visibility during the experimental periods.

RELATED WORK

GPS embraces a rich body of research by itself. Most of them around the receiver design and the signal processing algorithms in them to improve the speed and accuracy of obtaining the first fix. For instance, [15] present a comprehensive survey on signal processing techniques used in AGPS systems. Sirilo [2, 13] and van Diggelen [16] show different approaches on how to model the GPS positioning equations and how to solve them without decode any portion of data when some assistance is provided. Those solutions are useful when the receiver can use assisted data from the network, thus, they can decrease the TTFF and allow the use of GPS devices even when data decoding is not possible such as in presence of noise, shadow and incomplete data. Their work directly motivated us to study the duty cycle and energy efficiency of GPS sensing and lead us to the LEAP solution.

Energy efficiency of location sensing on mobile devices have drawn great attention in recent years. Several pieces of work look into using alternative sensors to infer when to invoke GPS sensing. For example, [9] propose a smart mechanism, namely A-Loc, which automatically determines the dynamic accuracy requirement for mobile search applications. A-Loc chooses the sensor that saves energy while attend the application's accuracy requirements. This approach relies on the idea that location applications do not always need the highest available accuracy. To do so, they use a Bayesian estimation framework to model the location and sensor errors, and thus, choose the most adequate sensor.

Paek et al. [12] propose a rate adaptive GPS-based positioning for smart-phones. They argue that, due the so-called urban canyons problem, even GPS sensor is not able to provide a high accuracy position, thus, the device should be turned off. In those situations, alternatively, they use other location mechanism such as accelerometer, space-time history, cell tower blacklisting and Bluetooth to decrease the active time of GPS devices.

Zhuang et al. [19] present an adaptive location-sensing framework to reduce the use of GPS device in various scenarios. Their framework is based on four design principles: (i) substitution, where alternative location-sensing mechanisms are used instead of GPS device; (ii) suppression, where the information provided by other sensor can suppress the use of the GPS device, for instance, if the accelerometer can identify that the user is not moving, the GPS can be turned off; (iii) piggybacking, that synchronizes location request from different applications, and (iv) adaptation that adjust sensing parameters when the battery level is low.

In comparison, we take a very different, and orthogonal, approach to solving energy efficient location sensing problem by looking into the GPS sensing principle and investigating what can be duty cycled and what can be moved to the cloud. LEAP can be used in combination with other location sensing frameworks transparently.

CONCLUSIONS

This paper presents a low energy GPS sensing solution called LEAP that is particularly suitable for enabling trajectory-based services for mobile devices. By looking into the GPS signal processing stages and applying the coarse-time navigation method, we found a sweet spot to divide GPS sensing between mobile devices and the cloud. As a result, the GPS receiver only needs to perform code phase detection for hundreds of milliseconds and thus can be aggressively duty cycled for energy saving. Through energy analysis and trace-driven simulation, we observe that the energy benefit of LEAP compared to traditional GPS on mobile phones can be up to 80%.

REFERENCES

1. F. A. Administration. Navigation services - wide area augmentation system (waas). `http://www.faa.gov/about/office_org/headquarters_offices/ato/service_units/techops/navservices/gnss/waas/`.
2. D. Akopian and J. Syrjarinne. A fast positioning method without navigation data decoding for assisted gps receivers. *IEEE Transactions on Veicular Technology*, 58(8):4640–4645, 2009.
3. K. Borre, D. M. Akos, N. Bertelsen, P. Rinder, and S. H. Jensen. *A Software-Defined GPS and Galileo Receiver: A Single-Frequency Approach*. Birkhäuser, 2006.
4. S. Gaonkar, J. Li, R. R. Choudhury, L. Cox, and A. Schmidt. Micro-blog: sharing and querying content through mobile phones and social participation. In *Proceeding of the 6th international conference on Mobile systems, applications, and services*, MobiSys '08, pages 174–186, New York, NY, USA, 2008. ACM.
5. M. Haridasan, I. Mohomed, D. Terry, C. A. Thekkath, and L. Zhang. Startrack next generation: a scalable infrastructure for track-based applications. In *Proceedings of the 9th USENIX conference on Operating systems design and implementation*, OSDI'10, pages 1–6, Berkeley, CA, USA, 2010. USENIX Association.
6. E. D. Kaplan and C. J. Hegarty. *Understanding GPS: Principles and Applications*. Artech House, second edition, 2005.
7. J. Krumm and E. Horvitz. Predestination: Inferring destinations from partial trajectories. In *The 18th International Conference on Ubiquitous Computing (UbiComp 2006)*, pages 243–260, 2006.
8. N. D. Lane, S. B. Eisenman, M. Musolesi, E. Miluzzo, and A. T. Campbell. Urban sensing systems: opportunistic or participatory? In *Proceedings of the 9th workshop on Mobile computing systems and applications*, HotMobile '08, pages 11–16, New York, NY, USA, 2008. ACM.
9. K. Lin, A. Kansal, D. Lymberopoulos, and F. Zhao. Energy-accuracy trade-off for continuous mobile device location. In *MobiSys '10: Proceedings of the 8th international conference on Mobile systems, applications, and services*, pages 285–298, New York, NY, USA, 2010. ACM.
10. P. J. Ludford, D. Frankowski, K. Reily, K. Wilms, and L. Terveen. Because i carry my cell phone anyway: functional location-based reminder applications. In *Proceedings of the SIGCHI conference on Human Factors in computing systems*, CHI '06, pages 889–898, New York, NY, USA, 2006. ACM.
11. P. Mohan, V. Padmanabhan, and R. Ramjee. Nericell: using mobile smartphones for rich monitoring of road and traffic conditions. In *Proceedings of the 6th ACM conference on Embedded network sensor systems*, SenSys '08, pages 357–358, New York, NY, USA, 2008. ACM.
12. J. Paek, J. Kim, and R. Govindan. Energy-efficient rate-adaptive gps-based positioning for smartphones. In *MobiSys '10: Proceedings of the 8th international conference on Mobile systems, applications, and services*, pages 299–314, New York, NY, USA, 2010. ACM.
13. N. Sirola. A method for GPS positioning without current navigation data. Master's thesis, Department of Electrical Engineering. Tampere Univeristy of Technology., 2001.
14. T. Sohn, K. A. Li, G. Lee, I. E. Smith, J. Scott, and W. G. Griswold. Place-its: A study of location-based reminders on mobile phones. In *Ubiquitous Computing/Handheld and Ubiquitous Computing*, pages 232–250, 2005.
15. G. Sun, J. Chen, W. Guo, and K. J. R. Liu. Signal processing techniques in network-aided positioning. *IEEE Signal Processing Magazine*, pages 12–23, 2005.
16. F. van Diggelen. *A-GPS: Assisted GPS, GNSS, and SBAS*. Artech House, 2009.
17. D. Van Nee and A. Coenen. New fast gps code-acquisition technique using fft. *Electronics Letters*, 27(2):158 –160, jan. 1991.
18. Y. Zheng. A software-based frequency domain parallel acquisition algorithm for gps signal. In *ASID'10: Proceedings of the internatial conference on Anti-Counterfeiting Security and Identification in Communication*, pages 298 –301, july 2010.
19. Z. Zhuang, K.-H. Kim, and J. P. Singh. Improving energy efficiency of location sensing on smartphones. In *MobiSys '10: Proceedings of the 8th international conference on Mobile systems, applications, and services*, pages 315–330, New York, NY, USA, 2010. ACM.

An Empirical Approach to Smartphone Energy Level Prediction

Earl Oliver, Srinivasan Keshav
David R. Cheriton School of Computer Science
University of Waterloo
Waterloo, ON, Canada
{eaoliver, keshav}@uwaterloo.ca

ABSTRACT

We conduct a large-scale user study to measure the energy consumption characteristics of 20,100 BlackBerry smartphone users. Our dataset is several orders of magnitude larger than any previous work. We use this dataset to build the *Energy Emulation Toolkit* (EET) that allows developers to evaluate the energy consumption requirements of their applications against real users' energy traces. The EET computes the successful execution rate of energy-intensive applications across all users, specific devices, and specific smartphone user types. We also consider active adaptation to energy constraints. By classifying smartphone users based on their charging characteristics we demonstrate that energy level can be predicted within 72% accuracy a full day in advance, and through an *Energy Management Oracle* energy intensive applications can adapt their execution to achieve a near optimal successful execution rate.

ACM Classification Keywords

C.4 Performance of systems

General Terms

Experimentation, Human Factors, Measurement

Author Keywords

smartphone, energy, user study, energy emulation toolkit, energy management oracle

INTRODUCTION

The proliferation of smartphones is driving a rapid growth in mobile applications. The design of these applications is governed by several constraints that are unique to mobile computing environments. Of these constraints, energy is the one resource that when depleted will render all of the applications on the mobile device, including emergency and essential applications such as the phone, inoperable. Unfortunately, while global demand and use of mobile applications continue to expand, the energy density of smartphone batteries has grown at a comparably insignificant rate [18]. Energy is therefore a critical resource that must be carefully considered in the design of mobile applications.

We consider a class of applications that must operate with little or no user-intervention, must operate over long durations, and consume large amounts of energy. Delay tolerant applications, such as [2, 9, 12, 17], are examples of this class of application. Each application must forward data bundles autonomously and operate continuously since being offline negates the possibility of exchanging data with neighbouring devices. These applications also consume large amounts of energy due to their use of wireless network and file I/O during opportunistic connections, and can easily deplete a battery if left unchecked. We are therefore faced with the question of how to maximize benefit to the user while minimizing impact.

We approach this complex question through a large-scale user study that examines the charging characteristics of smartphone users. Using this information, we build the tools and libraries that allow mobile application developers to adapt to increasing energy constraints. The contributions of this work are threefold:

- First, we build a dataset containing the smartphone usage and energy consumption characteristics of 20,100 BlackBerry smartphone users. Our dataset contains over 1150 years of cumulative data from users spanning 23 time zones and every BlackBerry device type released since early 2006.
- Second, we exploit user energy traces in our dataset to build the *Energy Emulation Toolkit* (EET). Using this tool, developers of energy intensive applications can test their applications' energy consumption behaviour against existing energy traces. Developers may then alter their design or tune algorithm parameters to reduce energy consumption and ensure that their application does not deplete users' batteries.
- Third, by classifying users into one of three groups according to their unique energy consumption characteristics, we demonstrate that energy level can be predicted to within 7% error within an hour and within 28% error a full day in advance. Using our prediction algorithm, we build the *Energy Management Oracle* (EMO) library. By querying the EMO before executing an energy intensive operation, applications can adapt their execution to achieve a near optimal successful execution rate.

UbiComp'11, September 17–21, 2011, Beijing, China.

RELATED WORK

Although energy consumption has been widely studied [1, 7, 8, 10, 11, 14, 16], little is known about the charging characteristics of users. Rahmati et al. were the first to qualitatively and quantitatively assess how users consumed energy. They provide preliminary insight into charging behaviour, user interfaces for power-saving settings, user knowledge, and user reaction to battery levels [13]. Their experiment consisted of ten users using unfamiliar devices over a one-month period. Their experiment driver also reduced the life of the device to about 40% of its usual lifetime. Falaki et al. have measured the energy consumption and application usage behaviour of 33 Android and 222 Windows Mobile devices [6]. Our BlackBerry user study complements Falaki's work; however, our dataset is approximately two orders of magnitude larger. Moreover, all of our 20,100 users are running our experiment software on their *personal* devices for periods up to several months in duration. We believe that our work is a more representative study. Finally, our experiment driver is fully event driven, does not record data to flash memory, and consumes less than 1% of additional battery life. Its operation is fully transparent to the user.

Cignetti et al. present the design of an energy model that estimates energy consumption with respect to the actions performed in an application [5]. Given that today's mobile devices are highly concurrent and that energy intensive tasks may take place without user intervention, actions performed by users are insufficient indicators of future energy levels. Bellosa examines OS-directed power management in [3]. In this work, system activity is throttled to achieve a desired energy consumption goal. This work is practical for homogeneous server workloads, but would not work under the heterogeneous workloads of a personal computing environment. Ravi et al. exploit a user's location (via cell tower) to predict when the user will charge their device [14]. Based on this prediction and the current energy consumption rate, their work determines the portion of the battery that can be used by other applications and warns the user of potential battery depletion. Unfortunately, all of these systems require knowledge of the underlying hardware.

SMARTPHONE USAGE STUDY

Our measurement study is focused on understanding how smartphone users interact with their devices and how they consume and replenish energy. We begin with a brief overview of the measurement study driver and data that we collect. We then discuss the top challenges in implementing the driver and producing a large-scale dataset of this kind.

Measurement driver

To the detriment of many user-centric experiments, smartphones are often distributed to a mere 10-30 users: fellow researchers, staff members, or undergraduates. Although this has been a convention for several years of mobile computing research (primarily due to convenience), this method of experimentation has several significant flaws:

- Experiment-enabled devices are typically given to participants on a temporary basis, which can affect users' interaction with the device and degrade the accuracy of user-centric results.
- Participants are often unwilling to use an experiment-enabled device as their primary/personal device. This can further bias the accuracy of an experiment.
- Participants are often intimately aware of their role in an experiment, which may further bias the results both positively and negatively.

Our measurement study is shaped by three high-level objectives. First, to achieve a high degree of accuracy, we require significantly more participants than any previous study [6, 13]. Second, to achieve this goal our measurement driver must run on a heterogeneous set of mobile devices with a diverse set of provisioned capabilities. Finally, our driver runs autonomously on participants' personal mobile devices and must therefore be production-grade software.

We develop two BlackBerry applications to collect the desired data: the Standard Logger and the Background Logger.

Standard Logger

The Standard Logger is an event-driven BlackBerry application that runs continuously in the background of a device. Upon installation, the logger records the following information:

Backlight activity: we infer user-interaction with a device by exploiting the device's LCD backlight being on is a necessary condition of user interaction. Using callbacks from the OS, the logger records the time that the backlight turns on and off.

Idle counter: the OS maintains a counter since the last user gesture. The counter is reset whenever the user presses a button, touches the screen, or moves a trackball on the device. The logger records the counter's value when the backlight turns off to determine the duration that the backlight is on but the user is not interacting with the device.

Charging activity: users' battery charging behaviour can be determined by recording when a device is plugged and unplugged from an external power source such as a USB cable or power adapter.

Battery level: the logger records the battery level every ten minutes to determine how users consume energy throughout the day.

Soft shutdown: the logger records signals that the device is powering on and off to account for inconsistencies in the data. For example, a user may power off a device when the battery is low, plug it in, unplug it at a later time, and power on at a full charge.

Device type: to differentiate BlackBerry devices we record the device type and OS version.

Background Logger

The Standard Logger alone was not capable of achieving our desired scale. We therefore partnered with a major BlackBerry software developer to augment their existing software quality logging tools with a simplified version of the Standard Logger. We refer to this augmentation as the Background Logger. The Background Logger collects the same information as the Standard Logger and uploads the data to the company's servers each week. In the remainder of this paper, we will refer to both loggers generically as the *Logger*.

Assumptions
The Logger makes one fundamental assumption: that the user does not run applications that programmatically enable and disable the device's backlight while resetting the device's idle time by simulating user input (keystroke injections). Given that application developers rarely use both operations, we consider these to be reasonable assumptions in our study; however, we do take steps to detect and discard invalid data.

Challenges
Achieving our three high-level experiment objectives was challenging. We believe that other mobile researchers can benefit from our insight on the following top four challenges.

Volatile file systems
Logging data to a file is a standard technique to ensure persistent storage in the presence of power failures or other interruptions. However, file systems can be unmounted at any time either manually by the user or automatically when connected to a PC. Adapting to this problem by frequently flushing I/O buffers to persistent storage can have a significant impact on battery life. The Logger therefore exploits two trends among BlackBerry users to provide reliable logging and save energy: users maintain a high battery level and rarely fully power off their devices. Our technique buffers log data in volatile memory until uploading it to our collection server each night.

Energy constraints
An application that has a noticeable impact on energy consumption will not be successful. In preliminary experimentation, we found that users were intimately aware of their device's normal battery life; any noticeable or perceived decrease in battery life would be attributed to the experimental application. As observed in previous studies [13], polling a device's state can have a detrimental impact on battery life. The Logger exploits callbacks from the operating system whenever possible. Unfortunately, an event driven model can produce inconsistent sequences of events. For example, when powering off a BlackBerry, we frequently did not receive an event signaling that the screen was off until after powering the device on. Similar scenarios were observed when charging. When analyzing the output of an event driven application, one must take into account possible race-conditions in the underlying OS.

Third-party application intervention
User-centric studies must take into account intervention by third party applications. For example, an application that records a user's battery consumption can be affected by a spyware application that was accidentally installed on the device [4]. Unfortunately, collecting a manifest of all applications present on the mobile device would be in violation of the user's privacy. Instead, during the analysis phase of our study, we checked for statistical abnormalities, such as increased energy consumption or excessively long activity blocks. When an abnormality was found, the data was flagged for review, manually inspected, and discarded if suspected to be fraudulent.

Non-linear time
Time synchronization, a task often taken for granted, is the most challenging problem to overcome in autonomous logging. A device's clock can be updated through three means. Plugging a device into a personal computer and synchronizing with a 'device manager' can change the clock. Users can manually change the time or time zone at any time. A device may also synchronize its clock with the timestamp broadcasted by the cellular network. Changes to the device clock manifest as the appearance of non-linear time. Unfortunately, there is no way to programmatically detect changes to the device clock. We mitigate errors introduced by time changes by detecting when the device is connected to a computer and analyze these events separately from non-connected events. In a large-scale study, users can also traverse many different time zones. UTC time should be used to provide the absolute time of an event. Experiments must also record the device's time zone and when a time zone change takes place.

Aggregate summary
Over six months of data collection, we constructed a dataset that consists of 1150 years of cumulative interaction and energy consumption behaviour from over 20,100 smartphone users. Approximately 15 years of suspicious data from 213 users (a significant quantity of data in its own right) was discarded due to the reasons previously discussed. Our participants span 23 time zones and all BlackBerry device types released since early 2006 [15]. These devices span a wide range of hardware characteristics and similar devices can be found from other manufactures. Our dataset is approximately two orders of magnitude larger than any previous work.

SUCCESSFUL EXECUTION PREDICTION
Using energy consumption traces stored within our dataset, this section examines how knowledge of user charging characteristics can improve the design and implementation of energy intensive applications. We begin with an overview of the Energy Emulation Toolkit (EET) followed by an evaluation using a simple sample application.

Energy Emulation Toolkit
The EET is designed to predict the *successful execution rate* of energy intensive applications given an energy consumption requirement and a specified duration of execution. An application is considered to have 'successfully executed' if it is able to run to completion without draining a device's battery.

The EET operates by iterating over all smartphone users in a target population of either: all users, users with a specific

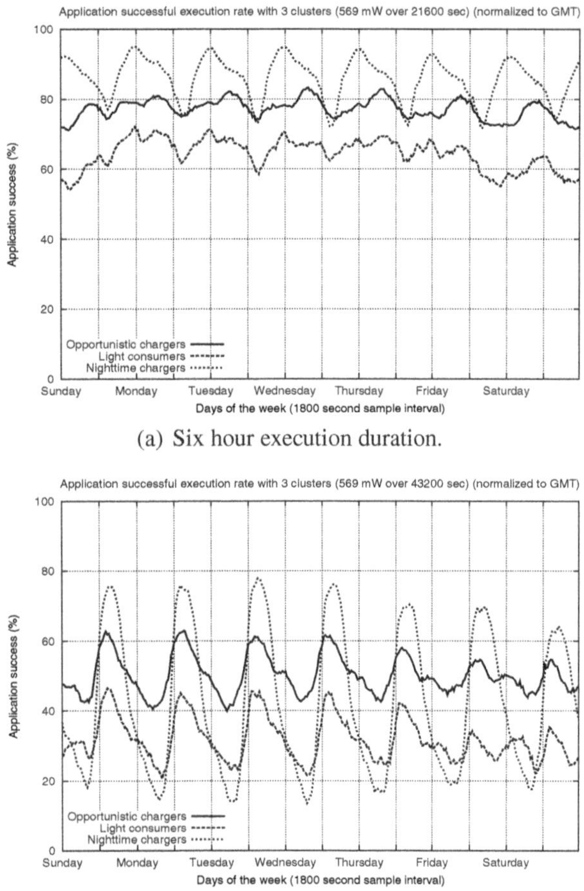

(a) Six hour execution duration.

(b) Twelve hour execution duration.

Figure 1. Successful execution rate by user type.

device type, or users within a specific *user type*. We will examine the characteristics of each user type in the next section. For each user, the EET assembles their energy traces as a linear timeline and begins stepping through in five minute intervals. Through each step of the timeline, the EET initiates a test to determine if an application invoked at the current time, t, with the specified requirements would succeed. A value of 1 or 0 is recorded for the 30 minute bucket corresponding to t's position in the week to represent a successful or failed execution. The successful execution rate of an application can therefore be provided as a function of the starting time or as an aggregate mean rate.

Implementation

We implement the EET as a stand-alone PERL module that can be imported into any existing PERL program/script. The EET module is initialized with the root directory of the dataset and invoked using a single function call that accepts the energy consumption requirements, the duration of execution, and a value that indicates the target population. Because the EET scans energy trace files linearly it accumulates little state during execution; the EET's runtime footprint when traversing the entire dataset is approximately 46 MB.

Application	Duration	Rate
GSM phone call (900 mW)	1 hour	95.2%
Video playback (1.1 W)	2 hour	84.3%
Bluetooth Class 2 (idle) (2.5 mW)	24 hours	100%
Bluetooth scan (1 min. period) (75 mW)	24 hours	100%

Table 1. Sample successful execution rates.

Evaluation

The EET can be applied to both simple and complex applications. Table 1 provides examples of simple applications and their mean successful execution rate.

We demonstrate the use of the EET through an application that mimics the energy consumption behaviour of existing mobile delay tolerant network applications. It consists of a thread that scans for neighbouring Bluetooth devices every one minute. On every second scan, the application connects to a server on the Internet over WiFi and uploads 100 KB of memory-resident data. Once per hour the application reads a 100 MB file from flash memory and uploads the contents to the server. It then downloads 100 MB of data from the server and subsequently writes the data to persistent flash memory. We implement the simple application, run it across a testbed of BlackBerry devices, and measure the energy consumed. Assuming that the energy consumed by the hourly network and flash memory I/O is amortized over the full hour and found that the average consumption rate is 569 mW. We illustrate the successful execution rate for the sample application over a six hour and twelve hour duration for each user type in Figure 1(a) and Figure 1(b) respectively. We will not analyze these sample figures because the results for each user type will be obvious to the reader later in this paper.

ENERGY PREDICTION

The EET can provide developers useful insight into the expected behaviour of the application when deployed across real devices. Using the EET, developers can alter their software design or tune parameters to reduce energy consumption and the likelihood that the application will deplete the user's battery. Unfortunately, the EET cannot benefit applications whose energy consumption rate is not known *a priori*. We address this problem using the EMO library.

We begin our design of the EMO by first describing the following high-level energy characteristics. We then describe our user classification method, user types, and present an analysis of our user classification based energy level predictor. We conclude this section with an analysis of the EMO library.

Energy characteristics

Charge/discharge durations: The charge and discharge durations are the quantities of time that a device is plugged into or unplugged from an external power source. This property has a direct impact on a device's battery life. Devices that charge for longer durations could have a higher expected battery level than those that do not. Similarly, devices that discharge for long durations could have a battery level that is lower than expected.

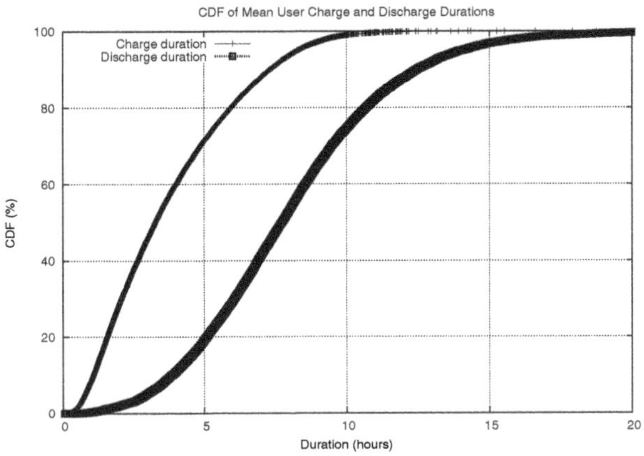

Figure 2. CDF of participants' mean charge/discharge duration.

Charge initiation time/level: The charge initiation time is the time of day when the user begins to charge their device. Regularity in charge initiation time could be used to infer when energy is likely to be replenished. A relationship between charge initiation and battery level could also be used to predict battery level.

Battery level: Patterns in battery level over the course of a day or week could be an ideal parameter for predicting future battery life.

Charge/discharge rates: The charge and discharge rates are the percentage of total battery capacity that is replenished or depleted while plugged or unplugged from a power source. We observed a significant correlation between the discharge rate, device type, and the time of day. This result is not surprising considering the energy consumption disparity between a device sitting idle at night and a device that is used frequently throughout the day.

Other characteristics: Although our dataset contains a rich body of smartphone interaction data, we found that there was little correlation between energy consumption and user interaction. We plan to explore user interaction characteristics in future work.

Classification method

Our user classification method is an iterative process to determine the subset of high-level energy characteristics that best differentiate users. Our metric to determine the utility of a characteristic selection is the mean prediction error derived by clustering users on the selected parameters. Given that the choice of prediction algorithm is dependent on the choice of input parameters, a circular dependency exists. We therefore begin our process by defining a fixed prediction algorithm.

Prediction algorithm

The design of our prediction algorithm was shaped by one high-level goal: to provide predictions over long durations that can easily traverse multiple charge/discharge cycles. The prediction algorithm must therefore adapt to three dominant

Algorithm 1 Predict($t_{curr}, b_{curr}, t_{last}, t_{pred}, \gamma$)

Require: $t_{last} \leq t_{curr}, t_{curr} < t_{predict}$
  $b_{pred} \leftarrow b_{curr}$
  while $t_{curr} < t_{predict}$ **do**
    # Retrieve current cycle duration
    if γ (CHARGING) **then**
      $t_{duration} \leftarrow \delta_{charge}(\mathit{bucket}(t_{last}))$
    else if $\not\gamma$ (DISCHARGING) **then**
      $t_{duration} \leftarrow \delta_{discharge}(\mathit{bucket}(t_{last}))$
    end if
    if $t_{last} < t_{curr}$ **then**
      # Algorithm invoked mid-cycle
      $t_{duration} \leftarrow t_{duration} - (t_{curr} - t_{last})$
    end if
    for bucket $\beta \in t_{duration}$ **do**
      # Increment/decrement predicted battery level
      if γ (CHARGING) **then**
        $b_{pred} \leftarrow min(100, b_{pred} + \rho_{charge}(\beta) * |\beta|)$
      else if $\not\gamma$ (DISCHARGING) **then**
        $b_{pred} \leftarrow max(0, b_{pred} - \rho_{discharge}(\beta) * |\beta|)$
      end if
    end for
    # Advance time by duration of cycle
    $t_{curr} \leftarrow t_{curr} + t_{duration}$
    # The end of a cycle is the beginning of another
    $t_{last} \leftarrow t_{curr}$
    # Alternate the charging state
    $\gamma \leftarrow \not\gamma$
  end while
  return b_{pred}

trends identified during an aggregate analysis of our dataset. First, the charge/discharge durations vary widely among users. The CDF of each mean duration is illustrated in Figure 2. These durations are also time-varying throughout the week. Second, the mean discharge rate varies significantly over the course of day: a device sitting idle at night consumes energy at a lower rate than a device that is active throughout the day. Moreover, there is a large disparity between the mean charge rate (46.8%/hour) and the mean discharge rate (4.2%/hour).

Our prediction algorithm is specified formally in Algorithm 1. We sub-divide each week into 336 discrete 30 minute buckets and initialize the algorithm with four vector parameters: δ_{charge}, $\delta_{discharge}$, ρ_{charge} and $\rho_{discharge}$. The δ vector contain the mean charge/discharge durations for cycles initiated during a specific bucket. If δ is undefined in a given bucket, then the algorithm uses the mean value of the target population. The ρ vector contains the mean charge/discharge rate for each bucket. Again, if a value within ρ is undefined then the mean charge/discharge rate over the target population is used. Each invocation of the algorithm requires the following parameters: the current charge/discharge state (γ), the time that the current charge/discharge cycle (t_{last}) began, the current time (t_{curr}), the current battery level (b_{curr}), and the desired prediction time (t_{pred}). Using the time that the current charge/discharge cycle began, the algorithm examines δ to determine the expected durations of the cycle and the time that the next cycle will begin. While stepping through each

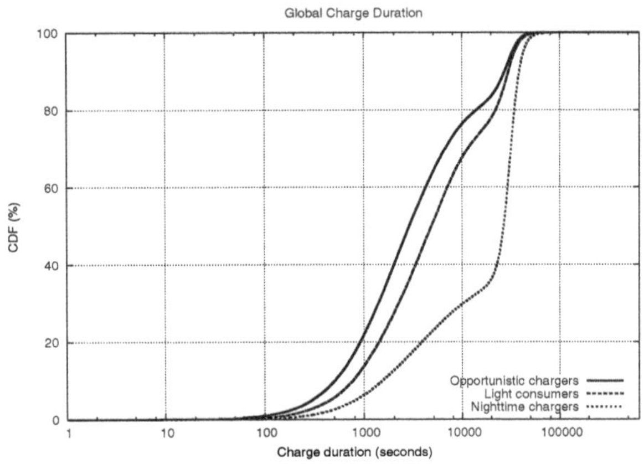

(a) CDF of charge duration.

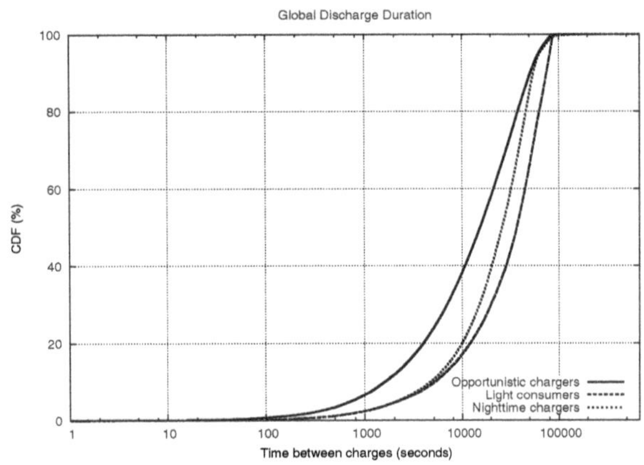

(b) CDF of discharge duration.

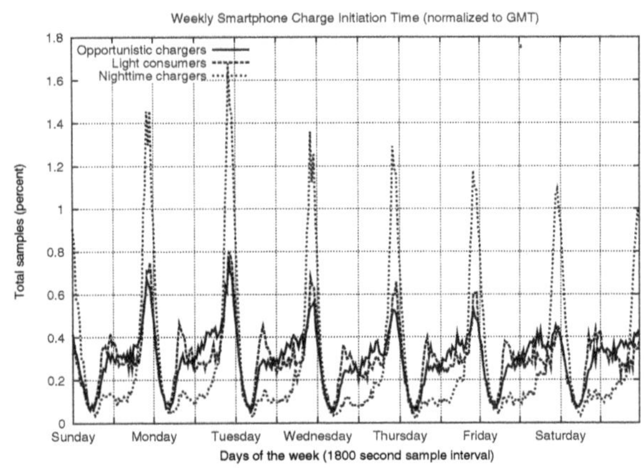

(c) PDF of charge initiation time.

Figure 3. Statistics by user type.

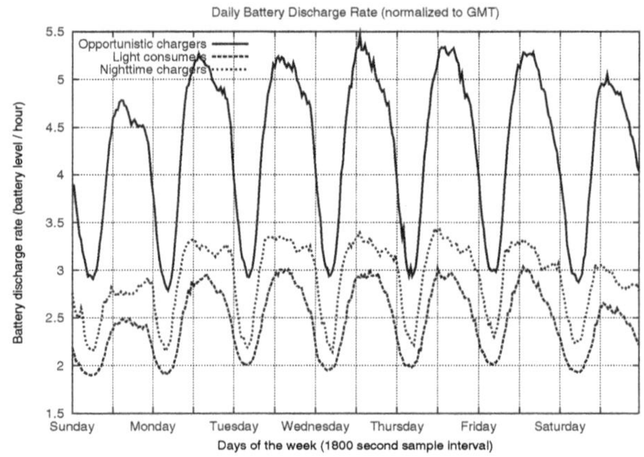

(a) Discharge rate over the week.

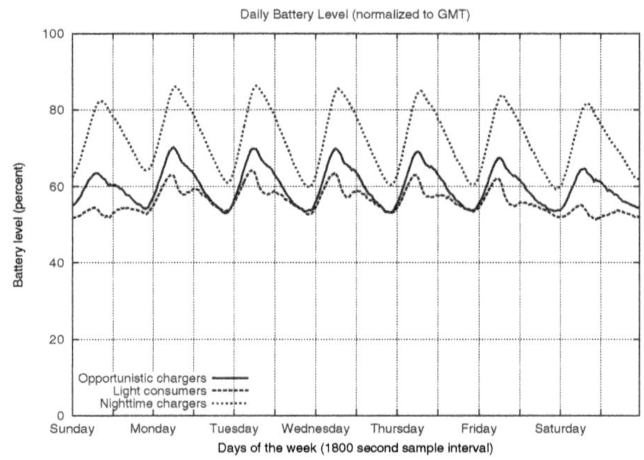

(b) Mean battery level over the week.

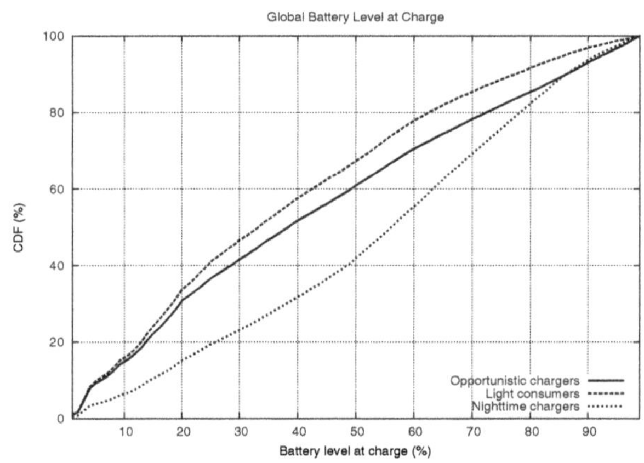

(c) CDF of battery level when initiating a charge.

Figure 4. Statistics by user type.

cycle, our algorithm increments (charge) or decrements (discharge) the predicted battery level (b_{pred}) at the rate specified in ρ.

Clustering strategy

With a fixed prediction algorithm we now evaluate the prediction accuracy derived by different user classifications. This iterative process involves selecting a subset of energy characteristic, clustering users, and applying the prediction algorithm to each cluster. At the end of each iteration we evaluate the gain/loss in prediction accuracy and select a new subset of characteristics.

Clustering was performed using the k-means algorithm with the mean Euclidean distance between variables as our distance metric. In each iteration we loop through the values

$k = [2, 6]$ clusters. The prediction algorithm is applied to each user clustering for $t_{pred} = \{1, 2, 6, 12, 18, 24\}$ hours using three-way cross validation. We calculate prediction error by iterating through each user's energy trace file in five minute steps and apply the algorithm using the file's current state. The prediction error for each prediction is taken as the absolute difference between the predicted battery level and the true battery level in the underlying dataset. The mean prediction error over all trials and users is averaged over each cross validation stage to produce the mean prediction error for a given subset of characteristics and cluster count (k).

At the end of this iterative process we found that clustering users by their mean weekday and weekend charge/discharge durations yielded the highest prediction accuracy. Prediction accuracy converged at three clusters.

User classification

Before a formal evaluation of the predictor, we briefly describe each user type and their differentiating characteristics.

Opportunistic chargers: Opportunistic chargers are the most common type of smartphone users and represent approximately 63% of the population. These users are primarily characterized by frequent, short charge durations during the hours of 8am to 5pm. The CDF of charge duration for opportunistic chargers is illustrated in Figure 3(a). Of the three user types, these users are the most aggressive energy consumers, consuming nearly 4.8% of their device's energy per hour. The discharge rates for each user type throughout the week are illustrated in Figure 4(a).

Light consumers: Light consumers have the lowest energy discharge rate among all three user types. These users represent approximately 20% of the population. These users charge for longer durations than opportunistic chargers, but discharge their devices over a longer duration. The CDF of discharge duration is illustrated in Figure 3(b). Despite having the lowest discharge rate, light consumers surprisingly maintain the lowest mean battery level of 56.0% as illustrated in Figure 4(b). These users also allow their battery to drop to its lowest level before initiating a charge. On average, a light consumer initiates a charge when their battery level has dropped to 34%. The CDF of battery level when a charge is initiated is illustrated in Figure 4(c).

Nighttime chargers: Our final class of user is those that charge at night. These users represent 17% of the population. The charging behaviour of the user is best illustrated in Figure 3(c) as the PDF of the time that users initiate a charge. The daily spike between the hours of 10pm to 11pm illustrate that these users initiate a charge (probably) before going to bed. Given that these users charge predominantly during the night, their mean charge duration is significantly higher than the other two groups, as illustrated in Figure 3(a). Although nighttime chargers consume only 0.5% more of their battery per hour than light consumers, their long charging durations serve to maintain a mean battery level of 72.5%. Similarly, nighttime chargers initiate a charge at an average battery level of 56%.

Device independence

We briefly address the impact of device hardware on our two clustering parameters: charge and discharge duration. Using a t-test, we found that there was no significant different between device types at a 99% CI. These results are illustrated in Figure 5(a). With the exception of the 8700, nearly every 99% CI contains the each cluster's population mean. We observe similarly results in the discharge case, as illustrated in Figure 5(b). Although there is more variation among the CIs for each device, we observe that nearly ever CI contains the cluster's population mean. The user's charge/discharge characteristics are clearly independent of the device type used.

Predictor analysis

We evaluate the accuracy of user classification-based prediction (*Clustered Predictor*) by comparing it to predictions based on the entire participant population (*Simple Predictor*), device type (*Device Predictor*), and predictions made on an individual basis (*Individual Predictor*). With a fixed prediction algorithm, alternating between predictors is performed by initializing the algorithm with the δ and ρ statistics of the training population. Although there are an innumerable number of possible predictors, we believe that this set successfully demonstrates the benefit of a user classification-based prediction scheme.

We evaluate each prediction algorithm through three-way cross validation of our dataset. For the Simple Predictor, we divide the dataset into three equal sized random subsets. We train each predictor on two thirds of the population, the *training set*, and apply the predictor to the remaining third of the dataset, the *target set*. Applying the predictor on a participant's traces requires that we iterate through all energy trace files in five minute steps. At each step through the trace log, we apply each predictor, store the future predicted battery level, and compare the current true value with a previous prediction. We store the absolute error for each prediction for the current bucket. This process is repeated for two remaining portions of the dataset. After applying the predictor to each third of the dataset, we compute the mean absolute error for each bucket in the week.

We evaluate the Clustered Predictor by dividing the training set and target set into two sets of three clusters. Given that clusters are unordered sets, we order the clusters to ensure a maximal overlap with the user types previously described. For each of the three user types, we train the predictor on the cluster in the training set and apply it to the corresponding cluster in the target set. As before, the absolute error for each battery level prediction is stored in a bucket as previously discussed, and the mean absolute error can be computed over the course of the week. Figures 6(a) and 6(b) illustrate the mean absolute prediction error for one and 24 hour predictions for each of the four prediction algorithms. These figures illustrate several important findings. Predictions based on global statistics perform the worst. This is not surprising given that we have shown that users differ. As previously illustrated, there is more variability in the cluster parameters between user types than between users of the same device type. It is therefore not surprising that the Device Predictor

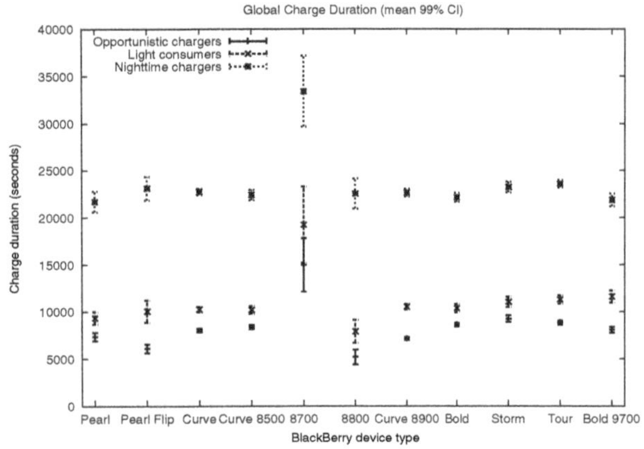

(a) Charge duration for each user type and device type.

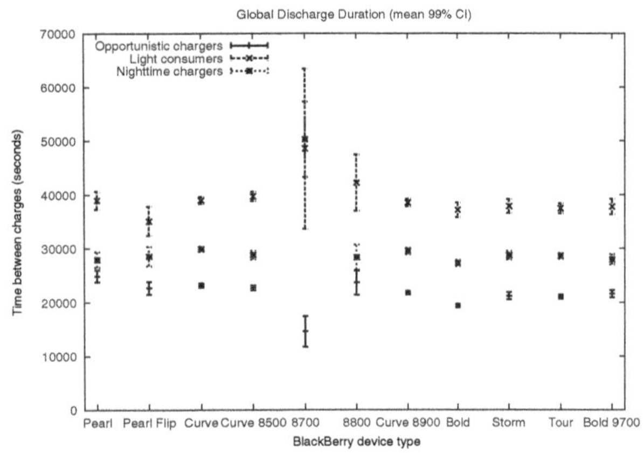

(b) Discharge duration for each user type and device type.

Figure 5. Durations by user and device type.

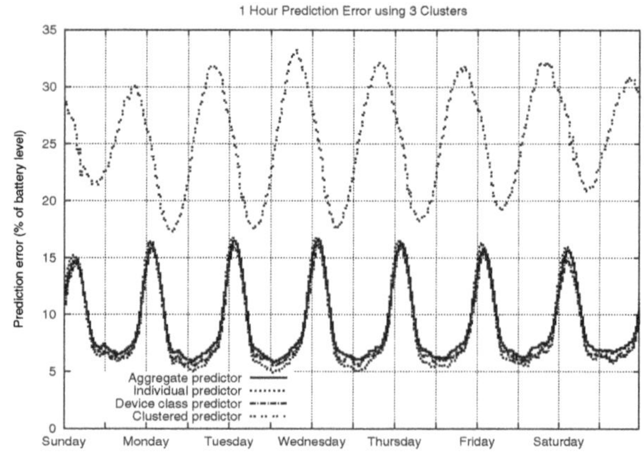

(a) One hour absolute prediction error.

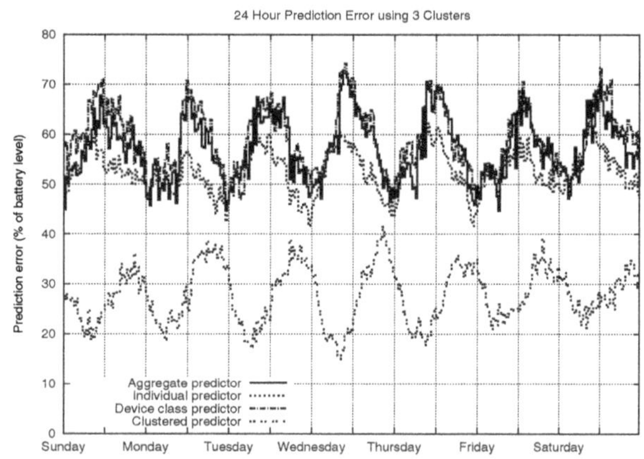

(b) Mean absolute one day prediction error.

Figure 6. Mean absolute prediction error.

also performs poorly. The relationship between the Individual and Clustered Predictors was not expected. Over short durations, predictions made on an individual basis are significantly more accurate than user type predictions. Conversely, over long durations the Clustered Predictor significantly outperforms individual predictions. At predictions of approximately 12 hours, the predictors yield equivalent results.

Over long durations, the Clustered Predictor outperforms the Individual Predictor due to a reduced error accumulation rate. In the individual case, the δ vector is calculated over few samples and has a correspondingly high standard deviation. In the clustered case, δ is calculated as the mean of the δ of each constituent user (a mean of a mean), which is a closer approximation of the population mean, with a reduced standard deviation window and lower propensity to accumulate error. We illustrate this explanation in Figure 7. The peaks in mean error in the evenings of each graph are attributed to the order of magnitude in disparity between the charge and discharge rates. Recall from Figure 3(c) that all three user types tend to charge their device at night. Our algorithm operates by estimating the duration of a charge/discharge cycle. An incorrect estimation of either duration results in a rapid gap between the predicted and true battery level.

Drawing from these observations, we introduce a fifth predictor, the *Hybrid Predictor*, that combines the short-term accuracy of the Individual Predictor with the long-term accuracy of the Clustered Predictor. The Hybrid Predictor is initialized with both an individual user's energy characteristics, the characteristics of all three user types, and the centroid coordinate of each user type's cluster. For predictions of less than 6 hours, the Hybrid Predictor yields the same results as the Individual Predictor. For predictions over six hours, the Hybrid Predictor examines the individual user's δ values and selects the user's type based on the closest cluster centroid. The predictor then exploits the statistics underlying the user type to provide predictions as if they were from the Clustered Predictor. In practice, both the energy characteristics of the three user types and their centroid coordinates would be hard coded into the predictor; allowing the code to be embedded into an energy-intensive application to actively predict the device's future energy level. We illustrate the mean prediction error up to 24 hours in advance from all five predictors in Figure 8.

Energy Management Oracle

Using the Hybrid Predictor, and the ability to predict the future battery level, we now present the design and analysis of

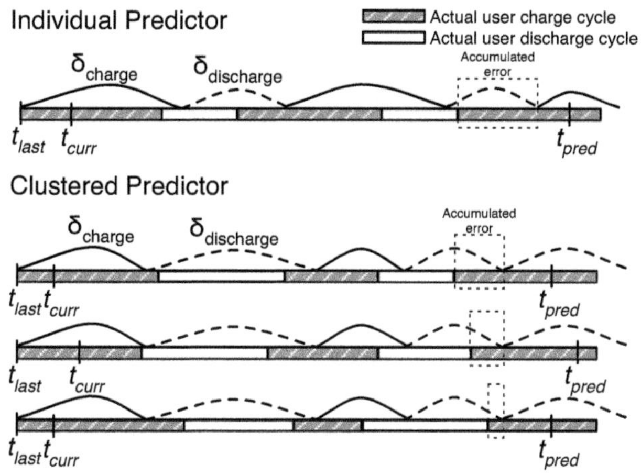

Figure 7. Accumulation of error.

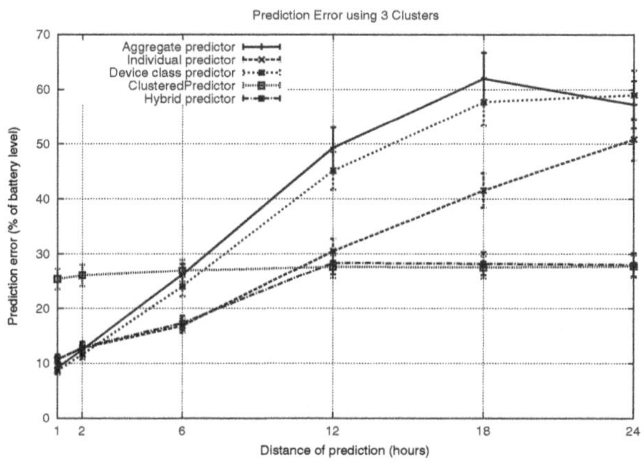

Figure 8. Mean absolute prediction error.

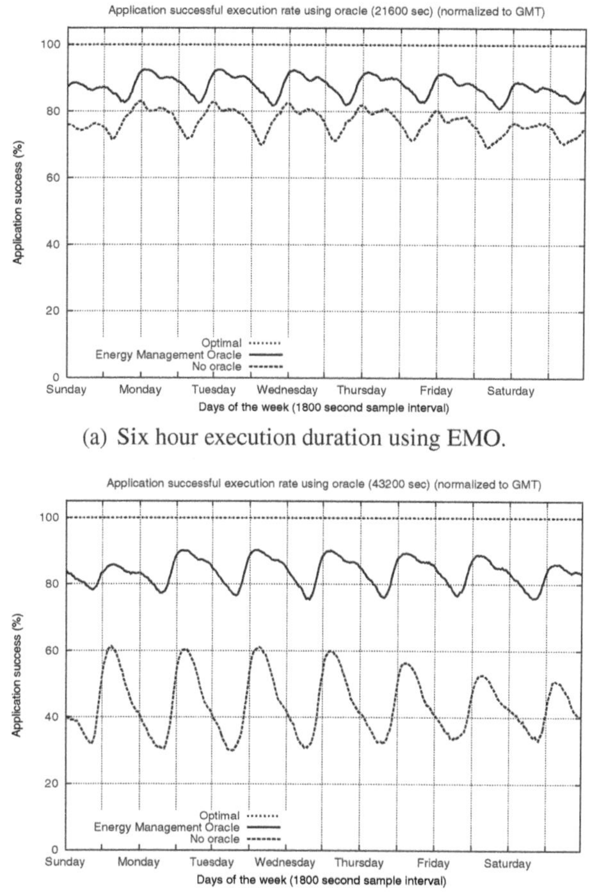

(a) Six hour execution duration using EMO.

(b) Twelve hour execution duration using EMO.

Figure 9. Evaluation of EMO.

the EMO library. The EMO is designed to provide energy-aware hints to applications at runtime. Using the library, applications query the EMO prior to initiating an energy intensive operation. Upon each query, the EMO decrements the current battery level by the energy consumed by the operation and initiates a 24 hour battery level prediction. The EMO query returns 'true' if the application can safely execute the operation, or 'false' if the operation will result in the depletion of the battery.

Implementation

Our implementation of the EMO modifies the Hybrid Predictor slightly by halting the prediction if the predicted battery level drops to zero. Like the EET, the EMO is implemented as a stand-alone PERL module that can be imported into any PERL program/script. PERL is supported on a wide range of mobile devices. For devices such as the BlackBerry and iPhone that do not support PERL, the algorithms underlying the EMO could be implemented in Java or Objective C in two or three days.

Evaluation

We evaluate the EMO through simulation of the sample application previously described. Recall that the application has two energy intensive operations: uploading 100 MB and downloading 100 MB to file. We will refer to these jointly as the *optional operation*, which consumes approximately 1727 Joules of energy when executed. If the optional operation is performed, the application will consume energy at a *standard rate* of approximately 322 J/hour by scanning neighbouring devices and uploading memory resident data.

Our simulation engine consists of a modified version of the EET that decrements the battery level at the standard rate over a specified execution duration. Like the EET, the simulator steps through each energy trace file in five minute steps. In each step, it initiates a simulated execution of the application. During each simulated hour, the application queries the EMO to decide if it should perform the optional operation. The simulator will decrement the battery level by 1727 Joules if and only if the EMO returns 'true'. Like the EET, the simulator records a success or failure for each bucket, which allows us to compute the successful execution rate as a function of the starting time of the application.

We compare the results of the simulation with two additional scenarios that demonstrate the upper and lower bounds on the execution success rate. The first, optimal scenario utilizes an oracle with perfect future knowledge; this oracle scans ahead in the trace file and returns 'true' if and only if the application will succeed. The lower bound is determined by running the EET as normal, where the simulated application executes without the benefit of battery prediction and the EMO. Figure 9(a) and Figure 9(b) illustrates the aggregate successful execution rate of the sample application over a six and twelve hour period respectively. Over six hours, the EMO is able to increase the successful execution rate from 76.7% to 87.6%; a 46.5% reduction in failures. Over long durations, the gain is more substantial. Without the EMO, the application exhibits a successful execution rate of only 43.8%. Applying the EMO increases this rate to 84.6%, which amounts to a 93.1% improvement. We therefore believe that the EMO can add significant value to energy intensive applications.

CONCLUSION

This paper has detailed the design and deployment of a large-scale smartphone user study that examines how users interact with and consume energy on their personal mobile devices. Our dataset contains over 1150 years of cumulative data for 20,100 users from around the globe. Although this work focuses exclusively on energy consumption, we believe that it contains a wealth of knowledge outside this context; spanning areas such as interaction design, battery provisioning, and non-technical domains such as addictology, polysomnography, and psychology.

As the scale and complexity of mobile applications continue to increase, we believe that energy consumption will become a new dimension in mobile software evaluation. Applications that consume large amounts of energy over long durations will be practical for only a subset of the user population with compatible energy characteristics. We predict that in the future, software will be distributed with a specified energy demand in the same way that resources such as CPU speed, memory/disk capacity, and network bandwidth requirements are specified in today's software. The Energy Emulation Toolkit is perfectly positioned to support this trend by providing developers with tools to evaluate their applications across all users, device hardware, and user types.

Smartphone users, like all complex objects, can be classified by an innumerable number of variables. Our work differentiates users on the basis of their daily battery charge and discharge characteristics, and has identified three user-types: opportunistic chargers, light consumers, and night-time chargers. This classification scheme provides 72% accuracy on predictions between 12 to 24 hours in advance. Using our predictor we built the Energy Management Oracle library, which can be queried by applications prior to the execution of an energy intensive operation. Using the oracle, we demonstrate that applications can achieve a near optimal successful execution rate. Using our dataset, we expect that other researchers will discover more efficient energy prediction techniques and that user differentiation will continue to yield similar improvements in prediction accuracy.

REFERENCES

1. Y. Agarwal, R. Chandra, A. Wolman, P. Bahl, K. Chin, and R. Gupta. Wireless wakeups revisited: energy management for voip over wi-fi smartphones. In *MobiSys '07*, pages 179–191, New York, NY, USA, 2007. ACM.
2. G. Ananthanarayanan, V. N. Padmanabhan, L. Ravindranath, and C. A. Thekkath. Combine: leveraging the power of wireless peers through collaborative downloading. In *MobiSys '07*, pages 286–298, New York, NY, USA, 2007. ACM.
3. F. Bellosa. The benefits of event: driven energy accounting in power-sensitive systems. In *SIGOPS European Workshop '2000*, pages 37–42, New York, NY, USA, 2000. ACM.
4. BlackBerry Spyware Wasn't Ready for Prime Time. Last visited: 29/09/2009. *http://www.wired.com/threatlevel/2009/07/blackberry-spyware/*.
5. T. L. Cignetti, K. Komarov, and C. S. Ellis. Energy estimation tools for the palm. In *MSWIM '00: Proceedings of the 3rd ACM international workshop on Modeling, analysis and simulation of wireless and mobile systems*, pages 96–103, New York, NY, USA, 2000. ACM.
6. H. Falaki, R. Mahajan, S. Kandula, D. Lymberopoulos, R. Govindan, and D. Estrin. Diversity in smartphone usage. In *Proceedings of the 8th international conference on Mobile systems, applications, and services*, MobiSys '10, pages 179–194, New York, NY, USA, 2010. ACM.
7. D. Kim, J. J. Garcia-Luna-Aceves, K. Obraczka, J.-C. Cano, and P. Manzoni. Routing mechanisms for mobile ad hoc networks based on the energy drain rate. *IEEE Transactions on Mobile Computing*, 2(2):161–173, 2003.
8. K. Lahiri, S. Dey, D. Panigrahi, and A. Raghunathan. Battery-driven system design: A new frontier in low power design. In *ASP-DAC '02*, page 261, Washington, DC, USA, 2002. IEEE Computer Society.
9. L. McNamara, C. Mascolo, and L. Capra. Media sharing based on colocation prediction in urban transport. In *MobiCom '08*, pages 58–69, New York, NY, USA, 2008. ACM.
10. R. Neugebauer and D. McAuley. Energy is just another resource: Energy accounting and energy pricing in the nemesis os. In *HOTOS '01*, page 67, Washington, DC, USA, 2001. IEEE Computer Society.
11. T. Pering, Y. Agarwal, R. Gupta, and R. Want. Coolspots: reducing the power consumption of wireless mobile devices with multiple radio interfaces. In *MobiSys '06*, pages 220–232, New York, NY, USA, 2006. ACM.
12. A.-K. Pietiläinen, E. Oliver, J. LeBrun, G. Varghese, and C. Diot. Mobiclique: middleware for mobile social networking. In *WOSN '09*, pages 49–54, New York, NY, USA, 2009. ACM.
13. A. Rahmati, A. Qian, and L. Zhong. Understanding human-battery interaction on mobile phones. In *MobileHCI '07*, pages 265–272, New York, NY, USA, 2007. ACM.
14. N. Ravi, J. Scott, L. Han, and L. Iftode. Context-aware battery management for mobile phones. In *PerCom '08*. Citeseer, 2008.
15. Research in Motion. Last visited: 29/09/2009. *http://www.rim.com*.
16. E. Shih, P. Bahl, and M. J. Sinclair. Wake on wireless: an event driven energy saving strategy for battery operated devices. In *MobiCom '02*, pages 160–171, New York, NY, USA, 2002. ACM.
17. J. Su, J. Scott, P. Hui, J. Crowcroft, E. de Lara, C. Diot, A. Goel, M. Lim, and E. Upton. Haggle: Seamless Networking for Mobile Applications.
18. J. Tarascon and M. Armand. Issues and challenges facing rechargeable lithium batteries. *Nature*, 414(6861):359–367, 2001.

Enabling Large-scale Human Activity Inference on Smartphones using Community Similarity Networks (CSN)

Nicholas D. Lane†, Ye Xu*, Hong Lu*, Shaohan Hu*
Tanzeem Choudhury‡, Andrew T. Campbell*, Feng Zhao†

*Dartmouth College, Hanover, New Hampshire, USA
‡Cornell University, Ithaca, New York, USA
†Microsoft Research Asia, Beijing, China

ABSTRACT

Sensor-enabled smartphones are opening a new frontier in the development of mobile sensing applications. The recognition of human activities and context from sensor-data using classification models underpins these emerging applications. However, conventional approaches to training classifiers struggle to cope with the diverse user populations routinely found in large-scale popular mobile applications. Differences between users (e.g., age, sex, behavioral patterns, lifestyle) confuse classifiers, which assume everyone is the same. To address this, we propose *Community Similarity Networks (CSN)*, which incorporates inter-person similarity measurements into the classifier training process. Under CSN every user has a unique classifier that is tuned to their own characteristics. CSN exploits crowd-sourced sensor-data to personalize classifiers with data contributed from other similar users. This process is guided by similarity networks that measure different dimensions of inter-person similarity. Our experiments show CSN outperforms existing approaches to classifier training under the presence of population diversity.

Author Keywords

Mobile Phone Sensing, Activity Recognition, Community Learning.

ACM Classification Keywords

H.5.2 User/Machine Systems; I.5 Pattern Recognition

General Terms

Experimentation, Performance.

INTRODUCTION

The popularity of smartphones with embedded sensors is growing at rapid pace. At the same time, research in the area of mobile phone sensing [17] is expanding the boundaries of mobile applications [12, 25, 22, 21]. Advances in human centric sensing is being fueled by the combination of: i) raw sensor-data, which is now practical to sample from large user populations; and ii) classification models that extract human activities, events and context from low-level sensor-data.

As user populations of mobile sensing applications increase in size the differences between people cause the accuracy of classification to degrade quickly – we call this the *population diversity problem*. In this paper, we demonstrate that the population diversity problem exists and classification accuracy varies widely even as the user population is scaled to up as little as 50 people. To address this problem, we propose *Community Similarity Networks (CSN)*. CSN is a classification system that can be incorporated into mobile sensing applications to address the challenge to robust classification caused by the population diversity problem. The conventional approach to classification in mobile sensing is to use the same classification model for all users. Using CSN, we construct and continuously revise a personalized classification model for each user over time. Typically, personalized models require all users to perform manual sensor-data collection where users provide hand annotated examples of them performing certain activities while their devices gather sensor-data (i.e., labeling data). This is both burdensome to the user and wasteful as multiple users often collect nearly identical data but the training of each model occurs in isolation of each other. The key contribution of CSN is that it makes the personalization of classification models practical by significantly lowering the burden to the user through a combination of crowd-sourced data and leveraging networks that measure the similarity between users.

CSN exploits crowd-sourcing to acquire a steady stream of sensor-data and user input, either corrections to classification errors or the more common hand annotated examples of sensor-data when performing an activity (i.e., labeling). Under CSN training classifiers becomes a networked process where the effort of individual users benefits everyone. However, the use of crowd-sourced data must be done carefully. Crowd-sourced data must only selectively be used during training so the resulting model is optimized for the person using the model. CSN solves this problem by maintaining similarity networks that measure the similarity between people within the broader user population. We do this by proposing three different similarity metrics (i.e., physical, lifestyle/behavior and purely sensor-data driven) that measure different aspects of inter-person diversity which influence classifier performance. The CSN model training phase then utilizes forms of boosting and co-training to allow these different types of similarity to each contribute to improving the accuracy of the personalized classifier.

The contributions of this paper are as follows:

- CSN is the first system to propose embedding inter-person similarity within the process of training activity classifiers. To the best of our knowledge, CSN represents the only activity recognition system designed specifically to cope with the population diversity problem, which would otherwise jeopardize large-scale deployments of mobile sensing systems.
- We propose similarity metrics and a classification training process that support: i) the extraction of similarity networks from raw sensor-data and additional end-user input and ii) a learning process that adapts generic classification models through careful exploitation of crowd-sourced data guided by similarity networks.
- We have evaluated our system with two large-scale mobile sensing datasets, each comprising of approximately 50 people. We measure the robustness of our classifiers and the ability of CSN to cope with population diversity.

COMMUNITY-SCALE CLASSIFICATION

In this section we discuss a key difficulty in realizing large-scale mobile sensing applications. Specifically, we examine how population diversity can cause classification to become unreliable and inaccurate.

One Size Does Not Fit All. As mobile sensing prototype systems are deployed to an increasing number of users their diversity increases as well. These users differ from one another in a variety of ways, a concrete example being physical dissimilarities as measured by sex, weight, height or the level of physical fitness. Beyond these visually obvious differences there are differences based on lifestyle and background. People come from different ethnic and social-economic origins, live and work in different locations and while they may perform the same core collections of activities (e.g., socializing, exercising, working) they may do these activities in significantly different ways.

Inter-personal differences can manifest as differences in the discriminative patterns contained in sensor-data that are used to classify activities, events and contexts. For example, the features from accelerometer data that allow classifiers to distinguish between the basic activities of walking and running can be completely different between a group of older adults (older than 65 years) and a group of people who are in their 20s and 30s. Figure 1 visualizes this difference when these two groups are walking. We plot the first two PCA components on each axis of the figure based on a range of already validated activity recognition accelerometer features [18]. The very clear distinction between sensor-data sourced from these two groups is surprising, particularly given the homogeneity you would expect in a simple activity like walking.

To further quantify this problem we build a LogitBoost classification model [9] and reuse the same previously validated activity recognition features. This model is trained using labeled data from the group of people in their 20s and 30s. Using this model classification accuracy while they walk and climbed stairs ranges between 80% to 90% for each person. However, when this same classifier is used by the group of aged people the average accuracy dropped to nearly 60%. Clearly, a one size fits all approach to classification models will not scale to large user populations which will contain many such groups.

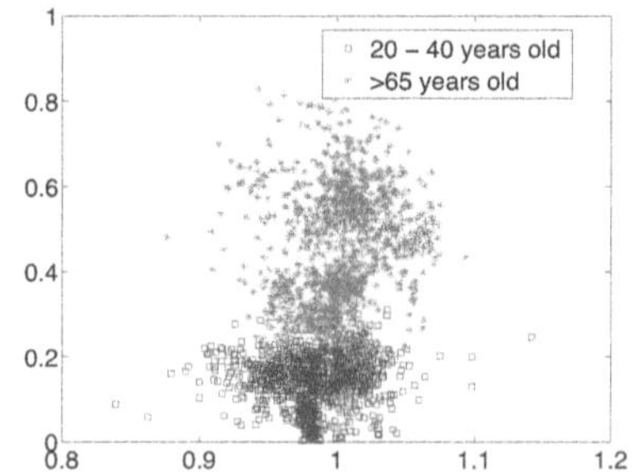

Figure 1. We visualize the differences in features under an identical activity, walking, for two distinct community sub-groups. One group contains people over 65 years old, the other group contains people in their 20s and 30s. Here we show just the first two components of the PCA of these features.

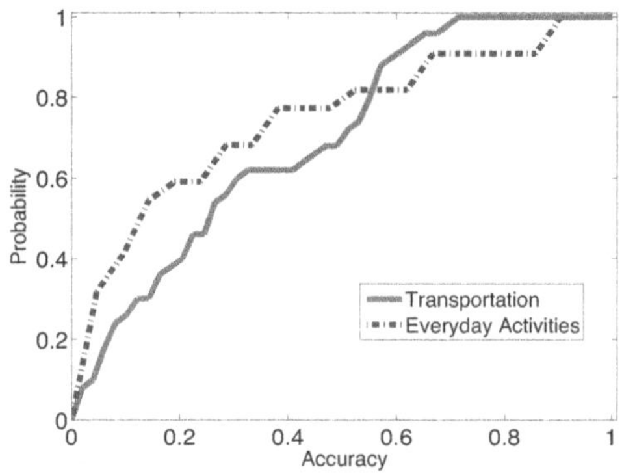

Figure 2. Classification accuracy varies significantly within a large-scale user population for two datasets, one containing everyday activities and the other transportation modes.

This effect is not only limited to strictly physical behavior (e.g., walking, running or climbing stairs) but extends to a broader range of behavioral inferences. We investigate the breadth of this problem by performing an experiment on two distinct mobile sensing datasets. The first dataset (obtained from the authors of [29, 30]) contains GPS sensor data for 51 people performing 4 different transportation modes (e.g., driving a car or riding a bike). The second is comprised of multi-modal sensor-data (e.g., microphone and accelerometer data) for 41 people performing a range of everyday activities (e.g., walking up stairs, exercising, brushing teeth). For both datasets we train a single classifier and evaluate the accuracy for each user, by applying the classifier to test data sourced only from that user. Figure 2 is the Cumulative Distribution Function (CDF) of accuracy for these experiments, and shows the spread of accuracy within the user population under both datasets. Accuracy levels for the transportation mode dataset are as low as approximately 40% for the bottom performing 60% of end-users and as high as 90% for the top 7%. Similarly, we find for the everyday activities dataset for 40% of the users the accuracy is only 12%, even for 80% of users the accuracy raises only marginally to 55%.

Limitations of Current Practice. The de-facto standard practice in incorporating classification into mobile sensing systems centers around a single unchanging classification model which is trained prior to deployment. Due to the reasons of population diversity this model works for some people, but not others; the accuracy of the system remains difficult to predict and increasingly unreliable as the user population grows.

Ideally the classifier would capture the distinctions between certain activities performed by different subgroups in the population as different activities entirely (e.g., walking when performed by two sub-groups could be two different classes); whenever these distinctions impact the classification process. However, this would significantly increase the amount of examples required for the same logical activity. Acquiring these examples is manually intensive (requiring careful labeling of data segments), making this approach impractical as it simply does not scale.

A promising direction being actively explored is the personalization of classification models to improve accuracy (e.g., [19, 26, 20, 15]). These models are tuned to sensor-data generated or encountered by the individual. Typically tuning occurs based on input from the user. For example, the user corrects classification errors or provides additional examples of activities by labeling sensor-data with the ground-truth activity occurring during the sampling of the data. The classifier is then retrained using sensor-data collected and labeled only by the user.

The limitation of such personalization of classification models is that accuracy *only* improves when and if people take the effort to manually provide additional sensor-data examples. Independent of effort it will also take time for people to encounter certain situations that are good discriminative examples to incorporate into the model. The key problem with this type of gradual improvement is that it leads to enormous amounts of redundant effort. Classification models are improved in *isolation* and each user potentially has to repeat steps that have already been done by other users to improve their own personal model.

COMMUNITY SIMILARITY NETWORKS

In this section we describe the system components and the core algorithms used at each stage of CSN. The CSN system is designed to construct and periodically update personalized classification models for each user. A key novelty of CSN is that it achieves personalization by using only a small amount of a specific user's training data and combining it with training data selectively recruited from others with whom the user shares similar traits.

Framework

Figure 3 illustrates stages of the CSN framework that produce personalized classification models for each user. Each of these stages occur either in one of two architectural components, the Mobile Phone Client software or the Mobile Cloud Infrastructure.

The Mobile Phone Client software samples sensor-data to recognize human behavior and contexts by performing inference using classification models. While inference occurs locally the models themselves are downloaded from the Mobile Cloud Infrastructure. The client software also collects training data comprised of both raw sensor-data and data segments that have been labeled by CSN users with the ground-truth activity or context.

The Mobile Cloud Infrastructure is responsible for training classification models. Sensor data is used to construct similarity networks where network edges indicate the level of similarity between two users. CSN employes multiple dimensions of similarity (e.g., sensor-data, physical and lifestyle) to quantify the various ways users can differ. Several similarity networks are generated for each user, one for each of the similarity dimensions. Similarity-sensitive Boosting trains a classifier for each of the different similarity networks (that correspond to a different similarity dimension). Similarity Network Multi-training performs semi-supervised learning and improves every model by recruiting additional labels from the pool of unlabeled data. The final step of multi-training unifies each of the independent classifiers, trained by Similarity-sensitive Boosting, into a single ensemble classifier ready to be installed on the phone of the user.

Mobile Phone Client

In the following subsection we describe the functions performed by the Mobile Phone Client, specifically we detail: i) the classification pipeline, ii) implementation specifics, and iii) the collection of sensor-data and ground-truth labels from users.

Classification Pipeline. The classification pipeline includes sensor-data sampling, feature extraction, and recognition of an activity, event or context.

We use the accelerometer, microphone and GPS sensors to make a variety of proof-of-concept inferences. Our choice of features were based on observations made in prior work [30, 21, 29, 20]. For the accelerometer and microphone we use the same feature set described in [21] which include a variety of time domain and frequency domain features effective for general activity recognition. For the GPS we adopt features that were specifically designed in [30, 29] for transportation mode inference based on time-series GPS readings. Classification is done using a boosted ensemble [23] of naive Bayes classifiers [9]. Inference results are temporally smoothed using a simple Markov model. Although in our client the stages of the classification pipeline (i.e., features and the classification model) remain fixed the parameters of the model are determined, and updated periodically, by the Mobile Cloud Infrastructure.

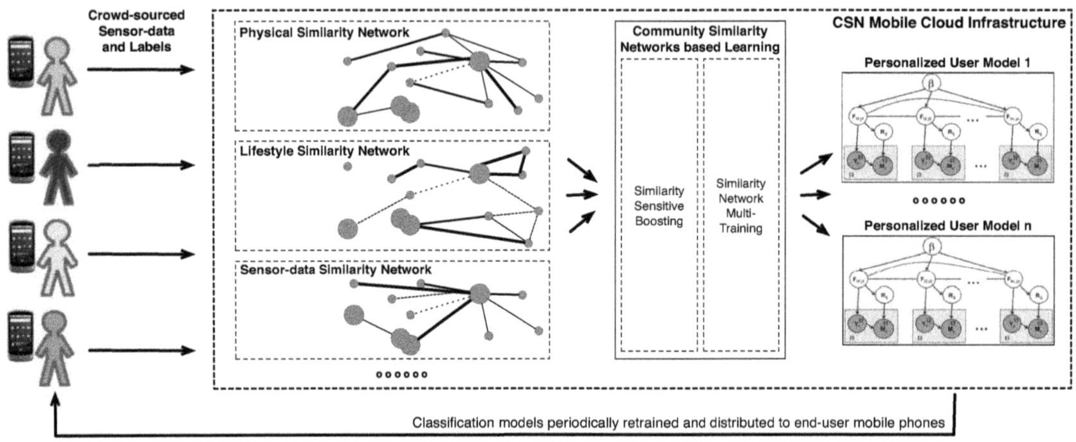

Figure 3. The processing phases within Community Similarity Networks

Implementation. Our prototype client is implemented on the Google Android Nexus One [2]. The design of the phone client is split between a portable classification pipeline library written in C++ and set of device specific supporting service (e.g., sensor sampling, end-user GUI). The library provides core classification pipeline components, including feature extraction and model inference. The device specific components are written in Java and connected with the library via a JNI bridge.

CrowdSourcing. CSN exploits the crowd-sourcing of both sensor-data and user input to improve classification models. User input provides the ground-truth activity to segments of sensor-data. Two specific types of user input is supported. First, users can be asked to confirm or deny a class inference. For example, asking the user a question – *'Are you currently exercising?'*. Such responses are used later as positive or negative examples of certain activities. Second, users can explicitly label data as being an example of an activity or event. For example, users indicate the ground-truth activity when a segment of sensor-data was sampled by selecting it from a list presented on the phone GUI. These types of interactions with users can be incorporated into applications in various ways. As an example, simple binary yes/no questions can be presented when the user unlocks their phone. Alternatively, more involved interaction, such as when users are selecting activities from a list, can be framed as software configuration or *calibration*. Similar forms of user interaction already occur in real products, for example, reading training sentences into speech recognition software or running for precisely one mile to calibrate a single activity recognition system like Nike+[3].

Mobile Cloud Infrastructure

In this section we describe how the Mobile Cloud Infrastructure: i) computes similarity networks and ii) uses these networks to train personalized classification models that are distributed to all users.

Implementation. Our prototype implementation makes extensive use of Amazon Web Services [5] (AWS) which offer a number of generic components useful in building a distributed system. CSN utilizes the AWS message queues (SQS), binary storage (S3) and the simple query-able hash table service (SimpleDB). Each stage of the model training performed by the cloud is implemented either as python scripts or C++ modules depending on available library support given the required functionality. These stages run on a pool of linux machines as part of the Amazon Elastic Cloud product and interact with the individual AWS services as needed. Once a classification model is trained it is serialized into a JSON-like format and written to the binary storage (S3), ready to be downloaded by the client.

Similarity Networks

Each similarity network within CSN is constructed from the perspective of a single target CSN user. Nodes in the network represent other CSN users and edge-weights measure the degree to which the target user is similar to the other users. The CSN framework is designed to leverage multiple similarity measurements, which capture different dimensions of affinity between people. Depending on the activities or contexts that are to be recognized different dimensions may be utilized. In this paper we propose the use of three dimensions of inter-person similarity: sensor-data similarity, physical similarity and lifestyle similarity. We demonstrate the effectiveness of each of these different dimensions in classifying different categories of activities and contexts in the Evaluation section. However, CSN is agnostic as to the exact similarity dimensions used.

We now describe the different similarity dimensions included within the CSN framework.

Physical Similarity. Physical differences between people (e.g., weight, height, age, level of physical fitness or wellbeing) will vary greatly from person to person within a large user population. Such differences can alter the way people move and perform certain physical activities. For example, as we detailed in the earlier section on community-scale classification differences in age can effect the recognition of seemingly simple activities like walking upstairs or jogging.

To compute a single physical similarity value between a pair of users CSN employs five types of physical information: age, height, weight, and the scores from two well established physical well-being surveys (Yale Physical Activity Survey [13] and SF-36 physical activity score [4]). Each of these five values act as elements in a vector that represents a single user. The physical similarity between users (i, j) is based on the mahalanobis distance between the two vectors for each person, as shown here,

$$sim(i,j)^{phy} = exp(-\gamma(\boldsymbol{x}_i - \boldsymbol{x}_j)^\top \Sigma^{-1}(\boldsymbol{x}_i - \boldsymbol{x}_j)) \quad (1)$$

where, $\boldsymbol{x}_i$ and $\boldsymbol{x}_j$ are the physical vectors for user i and user j, Σ is the covariance matrix and γ is an empirically determined scaling parameter.

Lifestyle Similarity. The lifestyle similarity metric attempts to capture the diversity in how people lives their lives, examples of which include: occupation, diurnal patterns (e.g., are they an early morning person or active late at night), the distribution of activities performed, mobility patterns and significant places [8] (e.g., where they work and live). Occupation and the location of work alter, for instance, the accelerometer and audio patterns occurring during social interactions (e.g., meetings and conversations). The time of day and significant places can effect the background context in which people perform activities. For example, late at night or early in the morning different locations will have different background activities that alter the sampled data (e.g., noise from people or cars). Collectively, these factors can change the distribution of features and shift discriminative boundaries for recognizing classes of activities.

We compute lifestyle similarity using three types of information: mobility and diurnal patterns in combination with the distribution of activities performed by users. Mobility patterns are based on GPS location estimates, which are tessellated into m distinct square tiles of equal size. Diurnal patterns are captured as a series of timestamps that are recorded whenever the user is inferred to be non-stationary by the classification pipeline. These timestamps are rounded, and are represented as the particular hour in the week in which they occur (e.g., they range between hour 0 at the start of the week to hour 167 on the final hour of the final day). The distribution of activities is based on the duration users are inferred to be performing each activity classes (e.g, walking, socializing) detected by the classification pipeline. We construct three histograms for each of these types of lifestyle information for every user, normalizing the frequencies across all histograms. For each pair of users (i, j), we compute the lifestyle based similarity by the following equation:

$$sim(i,j)^{life} = \sum_{f \in \mathcal{F}} \mathbf{T}_f(i)^\top \mathbf{T}_f(j) \quad (2)$$

where $\mathbf{T}_f(i)$ is a histogram vector for user i of type f and $\mathcal{F}$ contains each type of lifestyle histogram. Lifestyle similarity between two users is the sum of the inner product of the histograms for each type of lifestyle information used by CSN.

Sensor-data Similarity. Differences between users lifestyle, behavioral patterns, or location will likely manifest as differences in their sensor-data. Sensor-data similarity, unlike lifestyle similarity, does not require feature engineering to extract particular dimensions from the data. Similarly, unlike physical similarity it does not require additional information to be provided by the user (e.g., age). Instead, measuring inter-person similarity based on sensor-data is inherently purely a data-driven approach. Later, we report its effectiveness across a wide range of classification tasks. However, it requires much larger amounts of computation to determine similarity between users than computing lifestyle or physical similarity.

Computing similarity based on the raw sensor-data will be effected by noise and capture too many insignificant variations in the data. Instead, we compute sensor-data similarity between the features extracted from the raw data. For this purpose CSN employes the same features used by the classification pipeline, described earlier in this section. Individual users will accumulate varying amounts of sensor-data based on how frequently they use their device. Consequently, we compute "set" similarity whereby any duplicate feature vector for a user is ignored and only the unique vectors generated from the data of a person are used. For our similarity measurement we adopt a commonly used formulation [28] where the similarity between two users is,

$$sim(i,j)^{data} = \frac{1}{N_i N_j} \sum_{l=1}^{N_i} \sum_{m=1}^{N_j} sim(\boldsymbol{x}_{il}, \boldsymbol{x}_{jm}) \quad (3)$$

where, $\{\boldsymbol{x}_{il}, l = 1 : N_i\}$ is the data of user i, and $\{\boldsymbol{x}_{jm}, m = 1 : N_j\}$ is the data of user j.

However, this pairwise computation quickly becomes impractical as the number of unique features per user increases. To cope with this problem, we adopt Locality Sensitive Hashing (LSH) [7] to construct a histogram to characterize the "set" of data from each user and then compute the similarity between a pair of users by employing this histogram representation. Our method obviates the need to compute the pairwise relations of data from two users as required by the traditional "set" similarity, which has a linear time complexity with the average data size of each user. The basic idea of the LSH method is that a hashing function family can capture the similarity between data. In other words, similar data have a high probability to share the same value after hash mapping.

$$Pr_{h \in \mathcal{H}}[h(\boldsymbol{x_1}) = h(\boldsymbol{x_2})] = s_{\mathcal{H}}(\boldsymbol{x_1}, \boldsymbol{x_2}) = E_{h \in \mathcal{H}}[s_h(\boldsymbol{x_1}, \boldsymbol{x_2})] \quad (4)$$

Therein, $\boldsymbol{x_1}, \boldsymbol{x_2} \in \mathcal{X}$ are two data, $\mathcal{H}$ is a LSH family, h is the hash function sampled from $\mathcal{H}$, and $s_{\mathcal{H}}$ is a similarity measure of $\mathcal{X}$, which is induced by the LSH family $\mathcal{H}$ [7].

In CSN, we randomly choose B independent $0/1$ valued hashing functions $\{\boldsymbol{h_i}\}$ from the *random projection for $\mathcal{L}_2$ distance LSH family* [7] and form a $B-$bit hash function $f = (\boldsymbol{h_1}, \boldsymbol{h_2}, , ..., \boldsymbol{h_B})$. The number of functions B controls the tradeoff between efficiency and accuracy [7].

We apply the $B-$bit hash function to build histograms for each user, whose size is 2^B. Now, we formalize how to construct a histogram from the features of the user. According to the description, let $\mathcal{X}$ be the data space, $\mathcal{F}$ be the B-bit hash functions family mapping from $\mathcal{X}$ to $\mathcal{D} = \{0, 1, \ldots, 2^B - 1\}$, and $\{\mathbf{e}[i] \mid i \in \mathcal{D}\}$ be the standard basis of the $|2^B|$-dimensional vector space. Hence, given $h \in \mathcal{H}$, the histogram T_f for any user i is defined as follows,

$$\mathbf{T}_f(i) = \sum_{\boldsymbol{x}_{il} \in i} \boldsymbol{e}[f(\boldsymbol{x}_{il})] \quad (5)$$

here, $\{\boldsymbol{x}_{il}, l = 1 : N_i\}$ is data of user i, and $\mathbf{T}_f(i)$ is determined by the hash function f sampled from $\mathcal{F}$.

Thus each element of the histogram vector $\mathbf{T}_f(i)$ can be regarded as a bin to record the frequency at which data from user i is mapped into it. As the value of the hash function indicates the probability that two data share the same value after mapping, two users that have many "matched" values in the corresponding bins of histograms implies a high similarity between them. The inner product of the two histogram vectors is next applied to compute the similarity metric for the two users:

$$sim(i, j)^{data} = \mathbf{T}_f(i)^\top \mathbf{T}_f(j) \quad (6)$$

To estimate the expectation shown in Eq. 5, we construct several histograms $f \in \mathcal{F}$ for each user and compute an average value using Eq. 6.

The time complexity of computing the LSH based similarity metric is linear with the average quantity of data for each user. Compared with the pairwise computing method shown in Eq. 3 which is quadratic, the LSH based similarity metric is very efficient.

Community Similarity Networks based Learning

Learning personalized classification models for each user occurs in two stages under CSN. First, Similarity-sensitive Boosting trains three separate classifiers, one for each type of similarity network that is maintained for every user. Each of the classifiers are personalized to the characteristics of the specific individual who will use them. Further, each have different strengths when recognizing specific categories of activity depending on the similarity network used (e.g., physical similarity performs well with physical activities like climbing stairs). Second, Similarity Network Multi-training occurs which: i) uses a semi-supervised approach to recruit additional labels from the unlabeled pool of sensor-data leveraging the different strengths of each separate classifier; and ii) unifies the three classification models trained by Similarity-sensitive Boosting into a single ensemble classifier, ready to be installed on the phone of the user.

Similarity-sensitive Boosting. A personalized classification model emphasizes the particular characteristics found in a target user to increase accuracy. CSN accomplishes personalization using a modified online boosting algorithm [23]. Boosting is a common learning technique that builds a model that is a composite of several weak classifiers trained over multiple iterations. At each iteration certain data segments are weighted higher than others. Under conventional boosting these weights are only altered based on the classification performance of the weak learner trained during the previous iteration. Those data segments that were incorrect are weighted higher than others so the weak classifier produced in the next iteration will be better able to classify these previously incorrect segments. CSN modifies this process by imposing an additional term to the weight at the initial iteration. This weight is based on the similarity between the user i, whose personalized model is being trained, and the user which provides the data,

$$weight^{(0)}(\boldsymbol{x}_k) = sim(i, k) \quad (7)$$

where, k indicates the user who produces the data $\boldsymbol{x}_k$. We define $sim(i, k)$ as the edge weight between these two individuals within the similarity network being used during the boosting process. As a consequence only data segments from user i or any users who are highly similar to user i will be weighted highly and so able to have strong influence over the learned classification boundaries. In subsequent iterations the weighting of data segments is left to fluctuate based solely on classification performance. As boosting is an ensemble technique the CSN framework remains flexible, the weak learner can be replaced with any alternative supervised classifier based on the requirements of intended classification task.

Similarity Network Multi-Training. The three varieties of similarity networks currently used in CSN capture different dimensions of similarity between users. For example, some users being highly similar in terms of physical characteristics but polar opposites when it comes to lifestyle. Using Similarity-sensitive Boosting in conjunction with any of these different networks will result in different classification models. Each network will emphasize different partitions of the training data. This diversity is valuable as the different similarity networks produce models that are highly effective for some classes of activity but not others (see evaluation section). A simple example of this being those activities that are closely connected to the physical characteristics of the person, e.g., running and exercising, benefit from a classification model trained using a physical similarity network.

CSN exploits the strengths of each similarity network by adopting the technique of multi-training (a variation of co-training proposed in [31]). Multi-training is a semi-supervised training algorithm designed to utilize multiple complementary views of the same labeled training data to generate additional labels, which are assigned to data segments within the pool of unlabeled data. This approach is appropriate for CSN given that crowd-sourcing generates large amounts of unlabeled data. People will only infrequently take the time to provide any manual user input; but since simply collecting data is transparent to the user then large pools of unlabeled data quickly can accumulate. Employing a multi-training approach allows CSN to use the diversity provided by the different similarity networks to make use of a plentiful and otherwise wasted resource, unlabeled data.

The multi-training process begins by initially using the three classifiers trained by Similarity-sensitive Boosting. Each of these classification models maintains an independent logical copy of the labeled and unlabeled data. An iterative process is applied whereby the classification models are used to in turn to "label" unlabeled portions in the logical datasets maintained by each of the other models. At the end of each

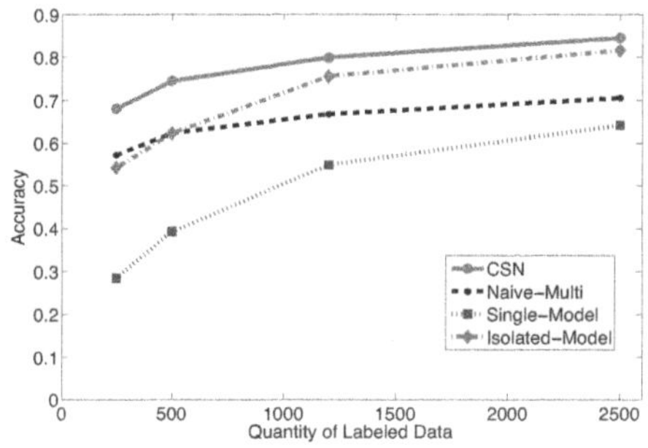

(a) Accuracy

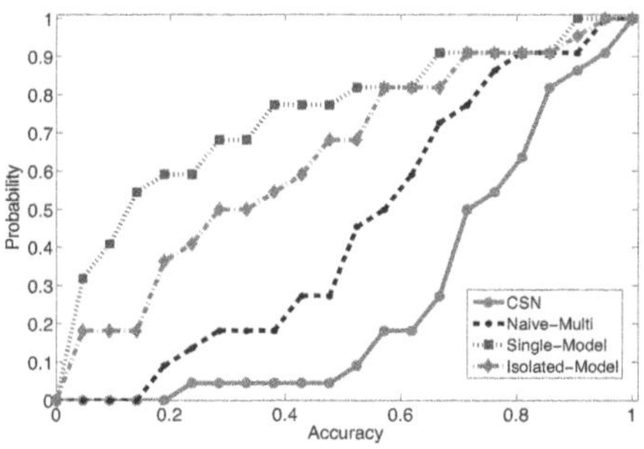

(b) CDF

Figure 4. Classification accuracy for the Everyday Activities dataset under CSN and three baselines.

iteration the classifiers are then retrained (using Similarity-sensitive Boosting) based on the combination of the labeled data from the previous iteration along with any new additional labels. Acquiring labels in this way can be an error-prone process, as a result labels are only accepted when there is agreement with more than half of the classification models. Judging the quality of a proposed new label, based on a majority decision, is only one of many ways that quality can be assessed. Multi-training continues to iterate for several rounds until a stopping condition is met. CSN uses currently a stopping condition based on how many labels are accepted at each iteration. If the number of recruited labels is too low for too many iterations then multi-training stops.

EVALUATION

In this section we evaluate the effectiveness and design choices of CSN. Our experiments show that by incorporating similarity networks among users into the classification process CSN is better equipped to cope with the population diversity problem, compared to existing techniques.

Experimental Methodology

To evaluate CSN we use two large real-world datasets and three representative baselines.

Datasets. Our two datasets require a variety of the activity inferences frequently used in mobile sensing applications. The first dataset, *Everyday Activities*, contains a broad range of routine human activities that have been used to support application domains such as mobile health [12]. The other dataset, *Transportation*, is much more focused on a single category of activity, transportation modes, which are building blocks of various mobile applications, e.g., applications that promote green transportation [14]. We collect the data for *Everyday Activities* as part of a series of internal experiments. The data comprises both simple activities: $\{walk,\ run,\ stationary\}$ and high-level behaviors: $\{meeting\ ,studying,\ exercising,\ socializing\}$. A total of 41 people contribute to this dataset using a Nexus One smartphone sampling sensor-data from the accelerometer, microphone and GPS. People carry the device for variable lengths of time that range between one and three weeks. For *Transportation* we use an external source [29, 30], with the dataset containing only different transportation modes, specifically: $\{bike,\ bus,\ car,\ walk\}$. This dataset comprises 51 people who carry for three months one of a variety of devices that are equipped with a GPS, including, phones, PDAs and personal navigation devices.

Benchmarks. We compare the performance of CSN against three benchmarks, *single*, *isolated* and *naive-multi*. Our benchmarks use the same features and apply the same classification model as CSN but differ significantly in how they approach classifier training. The benchmarks of *single* and *isolated* correspond with the two types of common practice we detailed in the earlier section on community-scale classification. In *single* the same generic model is provided to all users. Unlike CSN after the release of the system the model does not change and new training data is not collected. Under *isolated* every user has their own model. Each user model is personalized by using training data sourced directly from the user. The weakness is that each classification model is considered in isolation of one another. No co-operation or sharing of training data occurs among users. Finally, *naive-multi* allows us to demonstrate the benefit of CSN solely attributable to the use of similarity networks. During training *naive-multi* performs boosting and multi-training, the same techniques used in CSN. However, *naive-multi* uses the conventional versions of these learning techniques without the use of similarity networks. Specifically, the differences are: i) during boosting the weighting of training data at each iteration only changes based on classification performance instead of inter-personal similarity and ii) during multi-training the classifiers used are not based on dimensions of similarity but based on classifiers trained with equally-sized random subgroups of the training data.

Robust Classification with Low User Burden

Our first set of experiments finds, under both datasets, CSN provides more robust classification than any of the benchmarks. Not only is CSN able to achieve higher classification accuracy but we observe classification accuracy is also more evenly distributed throughout the user population. Under CSN the burden to provide training data is lowered, thus, accuracy numbers comparable to the benchmarks can be achieved with smaller quantities of data. In what follows, we report accuracy values resulting from five fold cross-validation.

Figures 4(a) and 5(a) show the results of experiments where we assume users contribute different amounts of labeled data. For each quantity of labeled data we measure the average

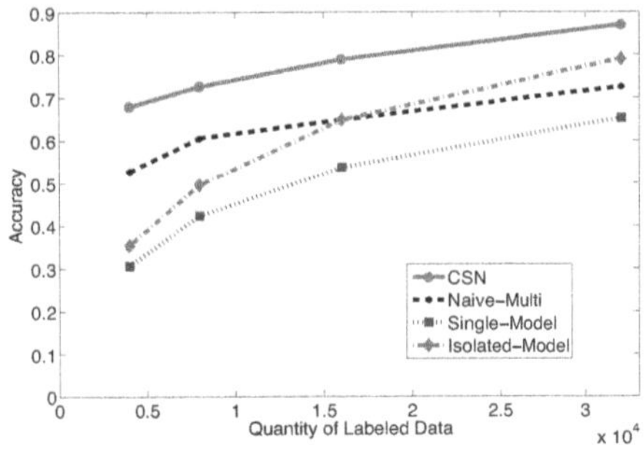

(a) Accuracy

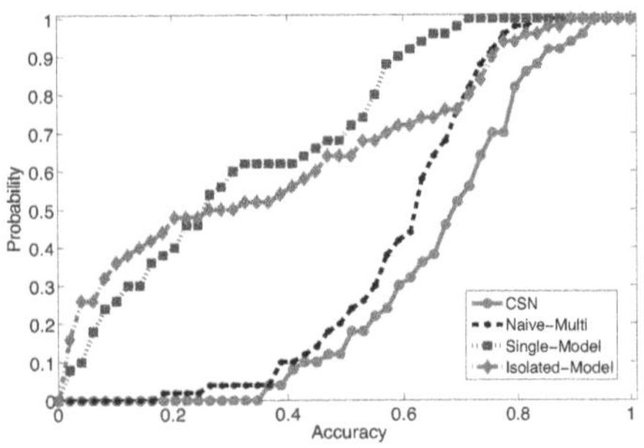

(b) CDF

Figure 5. Classification accuracy for the Transportation dataset under CSN and three baselines.

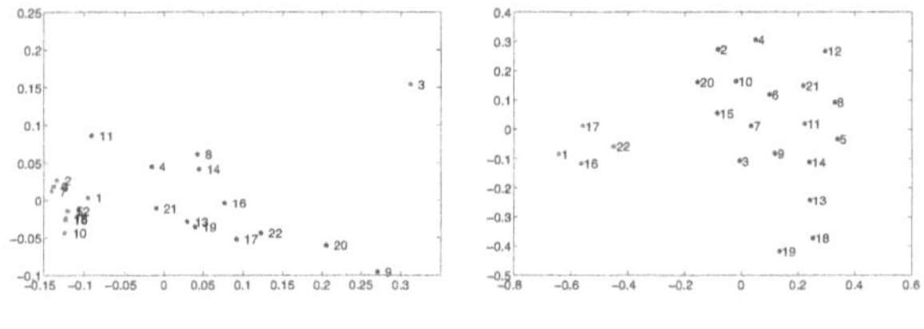

(a) Physical (b) Lifestyle

Figure 6. MDS projection of physical and lifestyle similarity networks used by CSN.

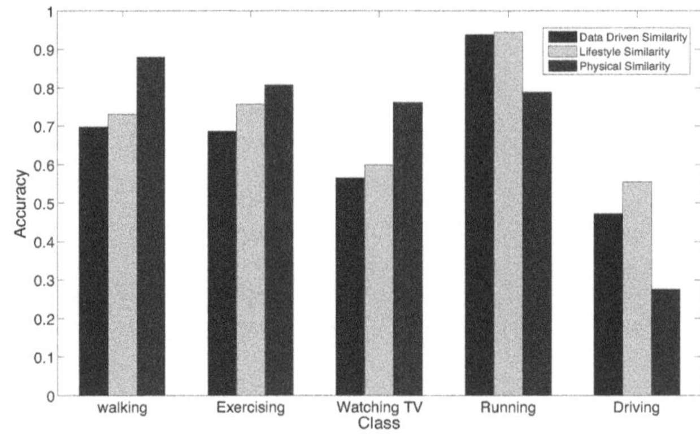

Figure 7. The classification accuracy of each activity class under different dimensions of similarity using the Everyday Activities dataset. It shows different dimensions of similarity are effective for different activities.

per person accuracy of classification for models trained under CSN and the three other benchmarks. Figure 4(a) uses *Everyday Activities*, and Figure 5(a) repeats the experiment using *Transportation*. In both figures the accuracy of CSN outperforms all baselines for each quantity of training data tested. For example, Figure 4(a) shows if 500 labeled data segments are used (approx. 15 minutes of training data per user) then CSN outperforms *naive-multi* and *isolated* by 22%. Similarly, from Figure 5(a) we see if 1.6 x 10^4 labeled data segments are used (approx. 137 minutes of training data from each user) the accuracy of CSN exceeds *single* by 47% and *naive-multi* by 32%.

From Figures 4(a) and 5(a) we also learn that CSN is able to lower the user burden of contributing training data. As an example, Figure 4(a) shows *isolated* requiring 36 minutes of training data from a user to achieve 74% accuracy. CSN can provide approximately this same accuracy for only 15 minutes of training data, a data reduction of 58%. Alternatively, if we consider Figure 5(a) *isolated* is able to perform with 77% accuracy but requires 270 minutes of training data. Again, CSN can provide approximately this level of accuracy but with 49% less data, only needing 137 minutes of data per user. Under CSN users are better rewarded for contributing data due to it having a higher ratio of classification accuracy to crowd-sourced training data, than the other benchmarks.

Figures 4(b) and 5(b) present CDFs of per user accuracy. We illustrate the fraction of the user population who experience different classification accuracy under CSN and all benchmarks. Figure 4(b) uses *Everyday Activities* and assumes users provide 15 minutes of training data each, while Figure 5(b) assumes users provide 137 minutes of labeled data and uses the *Transportation*. Ideally all users should receive the same level of accuracy, otherwise classification performance will be unpredictable when deployed. Better performance is indicated in these figures by curves that are furtherest to the right. We observe from each figure CSN has the most even distribution of accuracy compared to all benchmarks. For example, Figure 4(b) shows for 75% of users that CSN provides 82% accuracy compared to just 65% for *isolated*, 48% for *single* and 52% for *naive-multi*. Figure 5(b) reinforces this finding and indicates for again 75% of users CSN provides 77% accuracy instead of the 68%, 53% and 66% accuracy offered by *isolated*, *single* and *naive-multi* respectively.

Benefits of Leveraging Similarity Networks

With the following experiments we investigate the effectiveness of the similarity networks used by CSN.

To test if the similarity networks used by CSN are capturing meaningful differences between people, we collected additional demographic information from 22 individuals who contributed to *Everyday Activities*. Figures 6(a) and 6(b) plot the result of applying multidimensional scaling (MDS) to two similarity matrices for these people using physical and lifestyle similarity. Distances between points in these figures are proportional to differences in similarity. Figure 6(a) shows two clear groupings. We find these groups correspond to people with similar physical characteristics. The people in the tight cluster near the left of the figure are all over 30 years old, all male, and have similar physical fitness levels.

In contrast, the looser clump of people near the middle are in the same age range (22 - 26) but are all more diverse in terms of sex, and fitness. The outlier in Figure 6(a) is a 50 year old woman and is distinct due to her sex and exceptional fitness. The clusters in Figure 6(b) also correspond to our interview ground truth. The tight cluster to the left are a small group of people who live off campus and maintain regular 9 a.m. to 5 p.m. working hours. They are in sharp contrast to the very loose cluster on the right of the figure. This cluster contains students who, although they live very close to each other, also have erratic sleeping and activity patterns which results in them being grouped but not as tightly as the nearby cluster.

In Figure 7 we can see the value of using multiple similarity dimensions. The figure illustrates the different levels of classification accuracy achieved when using each of our three similarity dimensions to classify classes found in *Everyday Activities*. None of the three similarity metrics has the highest accuracy across all the activities. We find a similar pattern exists within *Transportation*. By exploiting all of these forms of similarity CSN is able to better handle a wide range of classification tasks. This result supports the design choice to use multiple dimensions of similarity and leverage them all when training classification models.

Cloud Scalability with Low Phone Overhead

Our remaining results report on the overhead to smartphones in adopting CSN, along with the ability for CSN to scale to large user populations.

We profile the computation and energy consumption of our CSN client on the Android Nexus One. We find resource consumption comparable to prior implementations of classification pipelines on phones (e.g., [22, 21]). As this overhead is not specific to CSN but found in any mobile sensing application we do not report further details. Overhead specific to CSN includes the transmission of sensor-data and the downloading of classifiers trained in the cloud. We find typical file sizes for our classification models are on the order of $1 \sim 2$ KBs, which means the cost of downloading classification models is minor. However, a significant cost to the phone can accrue when uploading sensor-data. To eliminate this cost our client implements an uploading strategy that waits until the phone is recharging before uploading data, effectively removing any burden to the battery.

The computational demands of computing the three CSN similarity dimensions range from being light-weight to very demanding. We quantify this by profiling the computational overhead for computing similarity networks for all people within *Everyday Activities*. This raw dataset is more than 400GB (mainly due to audio data). Using our CSN Mobile Cloud Infrastructure, configured with only one linux machine in the node pool the computational time for each variety of similarity is, $\approx$200 minutes, $\approx$9 minutes and $\approx$3 minutes respectively for sensor-data, lifestyle and physical similarity. The sensor-data similarity is the most costly of these three as it requires pairwise calculations between users.

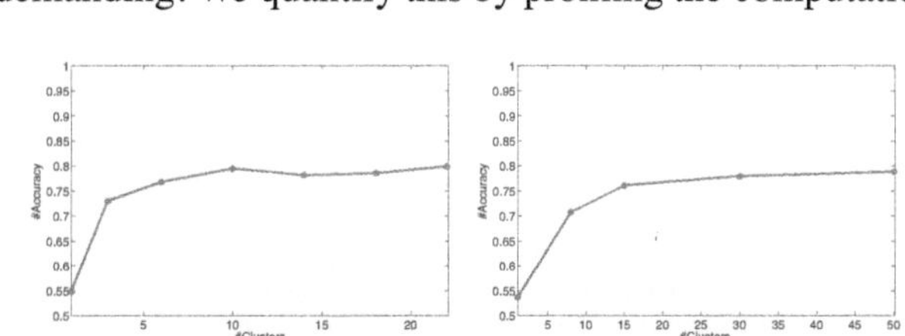

(a) Everyday Activities (b) Transportation

Figure 8. The accuracy of CSN when we group the users into different number of clusters under both datasets.

Personalized models are trained by CSN for each user, however, this can become a bottle-neck. The workload of the Mobile Cloud Infrastructure increases with population size due to: i) the pairwise calculation of similarity between users and ii) each new user requires a new model to be trained. For this reason we designed our Mobile Cloud Infrastructure to effectively leverage a variable sized pool of cloud nodes, so additional nodes could be added when required. However, we experiment with an alternative approach that requires a simple extension to CSN. Instead of training a model for each user, users are first grouped together by clustering. Similarity networks are then built not between people but between these groups, with a model trained for each group. We investigate this trade-off and cluster people with k-means using the least computationally costly similarity dimensions, lifestyle and physical. By lowering the number of groups we can reduce the Mobile Cloud Infrastructure workload. This trade-off is seen in Figure 8. These figures illustrate how accuracy falls as the cluster size (the k in k-means clustering procedure) is reduced. Reducing the number of models dilutes the similarity between people in the cluster. Consequently, the model used by the entire group is less appropriate for everyone. Still, as the cluster number decreases the overhead to the mobile cloud is reduced, since fewer models need to be maintained. This approach allows us to regulate resource consumption by CSN irrespective of the size of the user population.

RELATED WORK

Applications that use mobile phone sensors have been steadily rising (e.g., [10, 12, 11, 6, 22]) and accurate classification of sensor-data is becoming increasingly important.

Researchers investigating sensor-enabled mobile phone applications frequently encounter the limits of activity classification. It is becoming obvious that conventional approaches that rely on supervised learning and carefully controlled training experiments are not suitable. In recognition researchers are considering alternatives. Current research directions point towards models that are adaptive and incorporate people in the process. Automatically broadening the classes recognized by a model is studied in [19] where active learning (where the learning algorithm selectively queries the user for labels) is investigated in the context of heath care. In SoundSense [20] a supervised classification process for a fixed category of sounds is augmented with a human-in-the-loop guided unsupervised process for learning novel sounds.

Research, such as [19, 20], focuses primarily on the individual to assist with classification. CSN leverages the user but also exploits communities of people (rather than just isolated individuals). Researchers are beginning to explore this new direction. [16] proposes a community-based technique that groups people based on their social clique and partitions their data accordingly to improve learning. However, the grouping is based on self-reported social-networks and is evaluated only under a location-based classification scenario. Community-guided Learning (CGL) [24] builds models of human behavior with training data provided by non-expert low-commitment mobile device users. CGL overcomes the challenge presented by noisy labels being introduced to the training process by using data similarity in combination with the crowd-sourced labels.

The potential for crowd-sourcing has been long recognized with interest in the area being established by Luis Von Ahn [27]. Now, commercially available systems including Amazon's Mechanical Turk [1] have made it simple to exploit the power of using thousands of people. The use in CSN of crowd-sourcing builds directly on these existing directions. We see CSN as part of an exciting area of hybrid systems that intelligently combine the effort of the masses towards a task that neither computers nor humans can perform on their own.

CONCLUSION

In this paper, we have proposed Community Similarity Networks (CSN), a classification system designed to address the population diversity problem. We demonstrated that the population diversity problem appears when using conventional techniques with as few as 50 users. CSN combines the crowd-sourcing of labels and sensor-data with multiple similarity networks that capture user similarities across different dimensions. The similarity networks guide the process of selectively merging data from different individuals to produce personalized classifiers at a much lower per-user cost. Finally, the generality, flexibility, and effectiveness of CSN are demonstrated using two distinct mobile sensing datasets.

REFERENCES

1. Amazon Mechanical Turk. `http://www.mturk.com`.
2. Google Nexus One. `http://www.google.com/phone/detail/nexus-one`.
3. Nike+. `http://www.apple.com/ipod/nike/run.html`.
4. SF-36.org. A Community for Measuring Health Outcoming using SF Tools. `http://www.sf-36.org/tools/SF36.shtml`.
5. Amazon Elastic Cloud Computing. `http://aws.amazon.com/ec2`.
6. T. Abdelzaher, Y. Anokwa, P. Boda, J. Burke, D. Estrin, L. Guibas, A. Kansal, S. Madden, and J. Reich. Mobiscopes for Human Spaces. *IEEE Pervasive Computing*, 6(2):20–29, 2007.
7. A. Andoni and P. Indyk. Near-optimal Hashing Algorithms for Approximate Nearest Neighbor in High Dimensions. *Communications of the ACM*, 51(1):117–122, 2008.
8. D. Ashbrook and T. Starner. Using GPS to Learn Significant Locations and Predict Movement Across Multiple Users. *Personal and Ubiquitous Computing*, 7(5):275–286, 2003.
9. C. M. Bishop. *Pattern Recognition and Machine Learning (Information Science and Statistics)*. Springer, August 2006.
10. J. Burke, D. Estrin, M. Hansen, A. Parker, N. Ramanathan, S. Reddy, and M. B. Srivastava. Participatory Sensing. In *Workshop on World-Sensor-Web: Mobile Device Centric Sensor Networks and Applications*, WSW '06, pages 117–134, 2006.
11. A. T. Campbell, S. B. Eisenman, N. D. Lane, E. Miluzzo, and R. A. Peterson. People-centric Urban Sensing. In *Proceedings of the 2nd Annual International Wireless Internet Conference*, WICON '06, pages 18–es., 2006.
12. S. Consolvo, D. W. McDonald, T. Toscos, M. Y. Chen, J. Froehlich, B. Harrison, P. Klasnja, A. LaMarca, L. LeGrand, R. Libby, I. Smith, and J. A. Landay. Activity Sensing in the Wild: A Field Trial of UbiFit Garden. In *Proceedings of the 26th Annual SIGCHI Conference on Human Factors in Computing Systems*, CHI '08, pages 1797–1806, 2008.
13. L. Dipietro, C. Caspersen, A. Ostfeld, and E. Nadel. A Survey for Assessing Physical Activity Among Older Adults. *Medicine and Science in Sports and Exercise*, 25:628–628, 1993.
14. J. Froehlich, T. Dillahunt, P. Klasnja, J. Mankoff, S. Consolvo, B. Harrison, and J. A. Landay. UbiGreen: Investigating A Mobile Tool for Tracking and Supporting Green Transportation Habits. In *Proceedings of the 27th International Conference on Human Factors in Computing Systems*, CHI '09, pages 1043–1052, 2009.
15. A. Kapoor and E. Horvitz. Experience Sampling for Building Predictive User Models: A Comparative Study. In *Proceedings of the 26th Annual SIGCHI Conference on Human Factors in Computing Systems*, CHI '08, pages 657–666, 2008.
16. N. D. Lane, H. Lu, S. B. Eisenman, and A. T. Campbell. Cooperative Techniques Supporting Sensor-based People-centric Inferencing. In *Proceedings of the 6th International Conference on Pervasive Computing*, Pervasive '08, pages 75–92, 2008.
17. N. D. Lane, E. Miluzzo, H. Lu, D. Peebles, T. Choudhury, and A. T. Campbell. A Survey of Mobile Phone Sensing. *Comm. Mag.*, 48:140–150, September 2010.
18. J. Lester, T. Choudhury, N. Kern, G. Borriello, and B. Hannaford. A Hybrid Discriminative/generative Approach for Modeling Human Activities. In *Proceedings of the International Joint Conference on Artificial Intelligence*, IJCAI '05, pages 766–772, 2005.
19. B. Longstaff, S. Reddy, and D. Estrin. Improving Activity Classification for Health Applications on Mobile Devices using Active and Semi-Supervised Learning. In *Proceedings of ICST Conference on Pervasive Computing Technologies for Healthcare*, PervasiveHealth '10, pages 1–7, 2010.
20. H. Lu, W. Pan, N. D. Lane, T. Choudhury, and A. T. Campbell. Soundsense: Scalable Sound Sensing for People-centric Applications on Mobile Phones. In *Proceedings of the 7th International Conference on Mobile Systems, Applications, and Services*, Mobisys '09, pages 165–178, 2009.
21. H. Lu, J. Yang, Z. Liu, N. D. Lane, T. Choudhury, and A. T. Campbell. The Jigsaw Continuous Sensing Engine for Mobile Phone Applications. In *Proceedings of the 8th International Conference on Embedded Networked Sensor Systems*, Sensys '10, pages 71–84, 2010.
22. M. Mun, S. Reddy, K. Shilton, N. Yau, J. Burke, D. Estrin, M. Hansen, E. Howard, R. West, and P. Boda. PEIR, the Personal Environmental Impact Report, as a Platform for Participatory Sensing Systems Research. In *Proceedings of the 7th International Conference on Mobile Systems, Applications, and Services*, MobiSys '09, pages 55–68, 2009.
23. N. C. Oza and S. Russell. Online Bagging and Boosting. In *Proceedings of the 8th International Workshop on Artificial Intelligence and Statistics*, AISTAT '01, pages 105–112, 2001.
24. D. Peebles, H. Lu, N. Lane, T. Choudhury, and A. Campbell. Community-guided Learning: Exploiting Mobile Sensor Users to Model Human Behavior. In *Proceedings of the 24th National Conference on Artificial Intelligence*, AAAI '10, pages 1600–16006, 2010.
25. K. K. Rachuri, M. Musolesi, C. Mascolo, P. J. Rentfrow, C. Longworth, and A. Aucinas. Emotionsense: A Mobile Phones based Adaptive Platform for Experimental Social Psychology Research. In *Proceedings of the 12th ACM International Conference on Ubiquitous Computing*, Ubicomp '10, pages 281–290, 2010.
26. M. Stikic, K. Van Laerhoven, and B. Schiele. Exploring Semi-supervised and Active Learning for Activity Recognition. In *Proceedings of the 12th IEEE International Symposium on Wearable Computers*, ISWC '08, pages 81–88, 2008.
27. L. von Ahn, B. Maurer, C. Mcmillen, D. Abraham, and M. Blum. reCAPTCHA: Human-Based Character Recognition via Web Security Measures. *Science*, pages 1465–1468, 2008.
28. C. T. Y. Rubner and L. J. Guibas. The Earth Movers Distance as a Metric for Image Retrieval. *IJCV*, 40(2):99–121, 2000.
29. Y. Zheng, Q. Li, Y. Chen, X. Xie, and W.-Y. Ma. Understanding Mobility based on GPS Data. In *Proceedings of the 10th ACM International Conference on Ubiquitous Computing*, Ubicomp '08, pages 312–321, 2008.
30. Y. Zheng, L. Zhang, X. Xie, and W.-Y. Ma. Mining Interesting Locations and Travel Sequences from GPS Trajectories. In *Proceedings of the 18th International Conference on World Wide Web*, WWW '09, pages 791–800, 2009.
31. X. Zhu and A. B. Goldberg. *Introduction to Semi-Supervised Learning*. Morgan and Claypool, 2009.

Sundroid: Solar Radiation Awareness with Smartphones*

Thomas Fahrni, Michael Kuhn, Philipp Sommer, Roger Wattenhofer, and Samuel Welten
Computer Engineering and Networks Laboratory
ETH Zurich, Switzerland
firstname.lastname@tik.ee.ethz.ch

ABSTRACT
While the sun is important for our health, overexposure to sunlight carries significant health risks ranging from sunburn to skin cancer. Although people know about these risks, sunlight related skin damages have increased over the past decades. We have conducted a survey that sheds light on this phenomenon and suggests that the missing natural sense for UV radiation negatively influences people's sun related behavior. To address this issue, we have implemented *Sundroid.* Sundroid measures the incident UV radiation using a body-worn sensing unit that communicates wirelessly with the user's smartphone. The phone thereby acts as a user interface to present the measured data in an intuitive manner, and to notify the user once a critical amount of sunlight has been reached. Sundroid can also be applied in other contexts, such as behavioral research or medicine. We show that after calibration, errors are within 5% compared to a high-precision reference signal.

Author Keywords
Personal Health Monitoring, Wearable Sensor, Solar Radiation, UV Exposure, Dosimetry, Survey

ACM Classification Keywords
J.3 Life and Medical Sciences: Health.

General Terms
Design, Experimentation, Measurement, Reliability

INTRODUCTION
Sunlight is a driving force for life and, amongst others due to its role in the production of vitamin D, indispensable for our health. However, over the past decades an increasing number of studies warned against the risks of excessive sunlight exposure. A vast majority of people has already experienced the unpleasant feeling of sunburn after having stayed in the sun too long. Unfortunately, the harmful effects can go beyond unpleasant feelings. Long-term damage, such as premature skin aging and skin cancer are severe implications that can result from an overexposure to sunlight, even if no immediate signs of sunburn are visible [3].

*The authors of this paper are alphabetically ordered.

Both, sunburn as well as the mentioned long-term damages are caused by the ultraviolet (UV) radiation contained in the sunlight. In fact, most of the non-melanoma skin cancers are associated with exposure to ultraviolet radiation [29]. A considerable fraction of people is aware of the risks originating from the sun. Nevertheless, the number of such skin cancer cases in the United States has constantly increased over the past years [30]. Even though most people know about appropriate protective measures, a large fraction of the population gets sunburned from time to time. A first contribution of this paper is a survey that sheds light on the reasons for this phenomenon. A relevant finding of our survey is that inattention and the inability to correctly assess the UV intensity are two major reasons for excessive UV exposure and therefore for people to get sunburned.

Contributions. Following these findings, the main contribution of this paper is a wearable prototype system that tracks the wearer's sunlight exposure in real-time. This is in contrast to existing wearable UV dosimeters, that are designed for offline analysis only. The proposed system is designed in a modular fashion and consists of two parts: (1) A small sensor unit that measures the UV radiation and is equipped with a Bluetooth module. (2) A smartphone application that collects and processes the sensor unit's measurements. The phone thereby acts as a generic processing platform, which makes the system adjustable to a wide range of applications. The application presents the measured solar radiation data in a user-friendly manner. Moreover, it is able to notify the user of the imminent danger due to UV radiation when appropriate, thereby taking into account critical factors such as the specific skin type of the user or sunscreen applied.

The modular design of our sensor system reduces the effort to address other usage scenarios, as basically only the smartphone application needs to be modified. In fact, we also envision applications that go beyond personal UV radiation monitoring. Discussions with a dermatologist have shown that our system could prove advantageous in several medical settings. Moreover, we see various usage scenarios in research and large-scale sensing.

For the discussed usage scenarios, it is essential that the sensor unit works reliably and provides accurate data. We have thus paid particular attention to the technical soundness of our system. By independently tracking UVA (400 nm - 315 nm) and UVB (315 nm - 280 nm) radiation, we can well approximate the action spectrum relevant to a given application. An example is the erythema action spectrum, which describes the radiation relevant to sunburn that is absorbed by the skin. The system has been calibrated using two six hours traces recorded at the World Radiation Center in Davos, Switzerland. The comparison with the reference measurements shows that our sensor module is able to accurately measure the radiation absorbed by the skin at the position of the sensor. In separate experiments we have investigated the effect of a diffuser to reduce angle dependencies. Furthermore, we have conducted two pilot studies in each of which we have recorded real-world data of a person wearing the system during a specific outdoor activity.

RELATED WORK

Existing research efforts have investigated various aspects relevant to our work both in medicine and in the field of ubiquitous computing. In the following, we will briefly review major achievements and results from these different areas and sketch how our work relates to or was influenced by these findings.

UV Dosimeters. A variety of wearable UV dosimeters based on different technologies have been proposed in the past. A rough categorization distinguishes between chemical, biological, and electronic methods to measure UV radiation [15]. While electronic measurements facilitate the post-processing of various sensor inputs to approximate a desired action spectrum, biological and chemical dosimeters are more restricted with respect to the spectral response. Biological dosimeters typically agree well with the DNA damage spectrum [15]. An example of the use of a biological dosimeter is a study on long-term UV exposure of mountain guides [24].

As opposed to biological and chemical dosimeters that exhibit an integral characteristic, electronic systems based on photodiodes can measure the UV intensity at a given point in time. They thus do not only provide higher flexibility with respect to post-processing, but are also well suited to creating plots of the UV intensity over time. Examples for such systems are [1], [6], and [12]. Like our sensor system, these devices are designed to be worn by humans. However, all of them measure UV intensity using a single sensor and thus fail to take advantage of the flexibility given by post-processing of individual UVA and UVB values. Moreover, they are primarily designed for the use in medical studies, and thus do neither provide a direct feedback to the user, nor do they support real-time monitoring. As a consequence the intensity data can only be retrieved after a measurement series has been completed, which is in contrast to our system that constantly transmits the sensor values to a mobile phone, and thus can directly take influence on the user's behavior. Beside these limitations, the system described in [12] was used in a medical study to record the exposure to UV radiation [36] of over 300 subjects. They found that sunburn is correlated with risk behavior.

Mobile phones. We have chosen the mobile phone as a processing platform as it provides high flexibility with respect to applications. Besides the powerful post-processing possibilities, the advantages of a phone are its communication capabilities that make it a perfect gateway to transmit sensor data to servers [37], the permanent reachability by the user [27] and the wide variety of sensors readily available [23]. For these reasons mobile phones have been said to be an ideal platform for context-driven reminders and alerts [34, 17], and for the use in large-scale sensing studies [23, 37].

Reminders. In a recent study, it was shown that the overall adherence to sunscreen use can be improved by daily text-message reminders [2]. As overly frequent reminders are likely to be disturbing over time, in this paper we propose to take the context into account to only issue reminders when required. Such context aware reminders have been proposed before, both, for medical scenarios [22, 20, 35, 28] and in everyday settings [34, 17, 18, 21, 8, 32, 13]. For everyday settings, location-based reminders have been examined particularly well, and have been found useful in several user studies [21, 17, 34]. These studies underline that people are interested in and amenable to context-aware reminders. We thus expect that the context dependent reminders issued by Sundroid can achieve a similar improvement of sunscreen adherence as reported by [2] in a much less obtrusive way.

Medical applications. Many of the usage scenarios we envision are related to health related contexts, such as sunburn warning or long-term behavioral training with respect to sunlight exposure. A variety of studies proposes remote and self-monitoring systems in medical contexts and/or investigates their success. Examples include diabetes self-care [10, 20, 35, 26], asthma management [28], context-aware pill reminders [22] and generic remote monitoring frameworks [5, 25]. User studies thereby on the one hand show that people are open to such systems [28, 35] and on the other hand indicate a positive effect on the patients' health and/or comfort [26, 22, 28, 10, 20]. Several authors highlight the advantages of mobile phones and PDAs as a platform and information hub [20, 10, 35, 28, 26, 25, 5] and the usefulness of context-driven reminders [20, 22, 26, 28, 35], for example triggered when the monitoring system detects low activity or the need to take medication. Moreover, visual feedback of the monitored data has said to be helpful by different studies [10, 26], in particular when it comes to train the user's awareness of, or behavior in a given context. A design evaluation of Logan et al. [20] further investigates relevant requirements as seen by the end users. In particular, they state that user intervention should be avoided for data-gathering, messages must be user understandable (i.e. in laymen terms), and that the system's user interface needs be intuitive. Moreover, Nachman et al. [26] conclude that a wearable sensor system should be unobtrusive, contain as few components as possible, and should not attract attention to the wearer in the public. When designing the prototype implementation of the Sundroid system, we have taken these different factors into account as far as possible given the hardware constraints.

SURVEY

As mentioned in the introduction, the number of skin cancer cases has constantly increased over the past years and most of the non-melanoma skin cancers are associated with exposure to ultraviolet radiation [29]. Moreover, a study in New Zealand showed that 17.8% of the skin cancer cases can directly be attributed to sunburn [33]. Despite the warnings of health departments from all around the world, most people have already experienced sunburn. In the following we present an online survey that investigates possible reasons for the mismatch between information and action, i.e. why people get burned even though they know about the severe health risks.

The online survey was conducted amongst 785 students (52% male, 48% female) from different departments at our university. We wanted to know how often people get burned, and why this happens. For this purpose we have also investigated how well people are informed about the risks of sunburn and protective measures. In addition, we wanted to know whether they believe that a warning system could prevent some of the sunburns they suffer, and whether they would be willing to use such a system. We first asked four control questions related to sunburn and its risks. As expected the participants are generally well informed. Roughly three quarter answered all questions correctly, and even 95% know that sunburn increases the risk of skin cancer.[1]

Despite this knowledge, roughly two thirds of the respondents experience sunburn at least once a year, and almost everybody (96%) has already been sunburned. For the rest of this section, the 4% of participants who never suffered sunburn are excluded. From the remaining participants almost all (96%) consider sunburn somewhat (38%) or very (58%) annoying. To understand why people are suffering sunburn despite the risks and the potential annoyance, we further asked for the reasons for getting sunburned. To get an unbiased picture, the question was formulated openly, i.e. replies were given in free form text. For evaluation, we manually grouped the answers into semantic categories. A single answer could have been assigned to more than one category. The most frequent answers are summarized in Table 1.

It seems that several of the issues mentioned in Table 1, such as the misjudgment of radiation intensity and staying in the sun too long, could be overcome if people were warned before the critical dose of UV radiation has been reached. To find out if people agree with this presumption we asked them whether they believe that a warning system would reduce the number of sunburns. More than two thirds of the respondents confirmed this. Those denying could state why such a warning would not help. People mainly said they knew when to react themselves, and/or could not take appropriate measures in the relevant situations anyways.

We further wanted to know what type of sunburn warning system people might use. The corresponding question was only given to those participants who previously confirmed that a warning system might help. More than half of the respondents could imagine to use a corresponding smartphone application. Roughly a third would feel comfortable to wear a dedicated sensor device and even more than half could imagine to use such a device if it was unobtrusively integrated into accessories or clothing.

[1] These numbers might be slightly biased as they reflect the answers of our participants that tend to be well educated people.

	Category of answer	Percentage
1.	Misjudgment the solar radiation	23%
2.	No sunscreen at hand	19%
3.	Staying in the sun for too long	18%
4.	Incorrect/insufficient application of sunscreen	13%
5.	Forgot to apply sunscreen	13%
6.	Did not pay attention	10%
7.	Sport activities	10%
8.	The skin was not yet accustomed to the sun (mostly in spring)	8%
9.	Did not apply sunscreen (reason unknown)	8%
10.	Sleeping in the sun	6%

Table 1. Most popular reasons for sunburn according to our survey. A single answer could have been assigned to more than one category. Therefore percentage numbers do not sum up to 100%.

The main findings of our survey can be summarized as follows:

- A significant fraction of the people (67%) suffer a sunburn regularly (at least once a year), despite their knowledge of the risks and countermeasures.
- A lot of the reasons for getting sunburned are related to inattention and misjudgment of the sun's intensity, and could be overcome by an adequate warning mechanism.
- Many people are willing to use such a warning system in form of a smartphone application and/or dedicated sensor device.

Following these findings, we propose *Sundroid*, a prototype system that is able to warn its user once a critical dose of sunlight has been absorbed, and can help to improve people's awareness of the incident radiation in different situations. It thereby acts as a replacement for a missing human sense for UV radiation that could naturally warn us, similarly as our sense of smell warns us of inappropriate food.

SYSTEM DESIGN

In this section, we describe the design and implementation of Sundroid, a wearable system to measure solar radiation. The current prototype system targets a broad range of application scenarios for solar radiation awareness. Sundroid consists of two separate components, as shown in Figure 1: A dedicated sensor unit to measure UV radiation, and a smartphone as a universal computing platform. To provide data relevant to its user, the sensor unit needs to be body wearable. Moreover, to find widespread acceptance, it is inevitable to make the corresponding device as unobtrusive as possible and available at low cost.

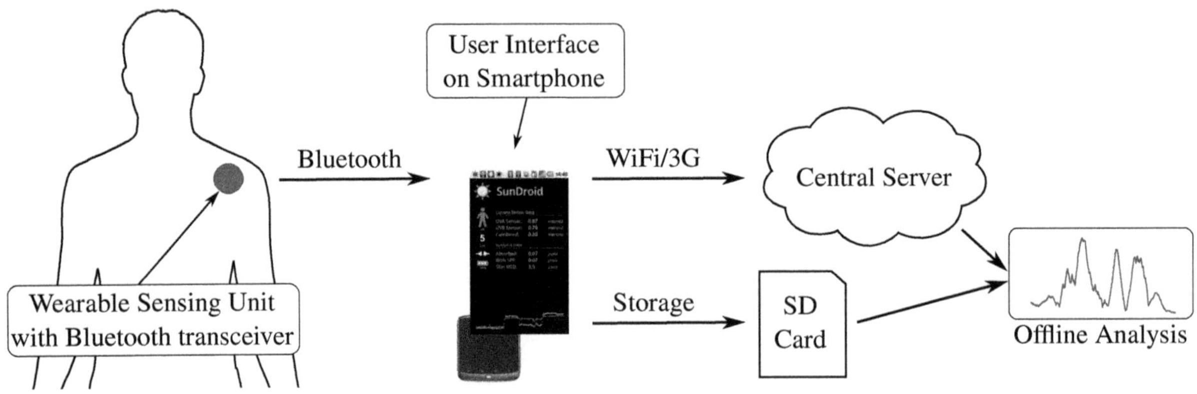

Figure 1. Schematic overview of the Sundroid system: A wearable sensing unit containing UV sensors is attached to a user's clothes or accessories. Sensor data is transferred using Bluetooth to a smartphone, which serves as a graphical user interface. Optionally, measurement data can be transferred to a central server or stored on a SD card for offline analysis by researchers or medical personnel.

Due to application specific action spectra, we decided to independently measure UVA and UVB intensities. This design provides maximal flexibility for the approximation of different spectra. An example is the erythema action spectrum in case of sunburn, which describes the wavelength dependent sensitivity of skin relevant to sunburn. Other examples include the action spectra for DNA damage [31] or skin cancer [7].

To further improve the flexibility with respect to possible applications, we rely on the user's smartphone as a generic information hub. The phone can on the one hand provide further context, such as location and activity patterns, and is on the other hand used for data processing, presentation and communication. Data exchange between the sensor unit and the smartphone is realized over a Bluetooth wireless link in real-time. An important requirement is that the system continually monitors the solar radiation to which the user is exposed, even when the user is temporarily not in the proximity of the phone. Depending on the application, the phone can either log the data and present it to the user, or forward it to a central infrastructure, e.g., for analysis by experts such as researchers or medical personnel.

Wearable Sensing Unit

The wearable sensing unit consists of a custom made printed circuit board (see Figure 2) and a plastic enclosure. It features a TI MSP430 low-power microcontroller with 4 KBytes program flash and 512 Bytes of RAM, which is connected to a Roving Networks RN-42 low-power Bluetooth module. All components are standard parts available at low prices (tens of dollars). The sensing unit is supplied with power by a 3.7 V lithium-polymer rechargeable battery.

UV Sensors. We equipped the wearable sensing unit with a UVA photodiode (Genicom GUVA-S10GD) and a UVB photodiode (Genicom GUVB-S10GD). Each of the two photodiodes gives an estimation of the current sunlight intensity in their intrinsic spectrum. Depending on the use case we are interested in different spectra. Some medical applications, for example, require the measurement of UVA only. In the context of sunburn, we are interested in the erythema action spectrum, which can be approximated using a weighted linear combination of the values of the UVA and UVB sensors. We found that a combination of 9% UVA estimation and 91% UVB estimation can accurately approximate the erythema action spectrum in our setting, as shown in Figure 3.

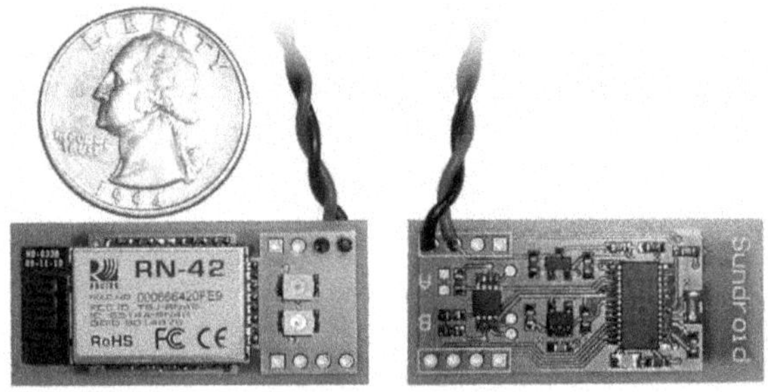

Figure 2. The wearable sensing unit consists of a double-sided printed circuit board. The Bluetooth module and the UV photodiodes are mounted on the top layer (left), while the microcontroller and the analog circuits are on the bottom layer (right).

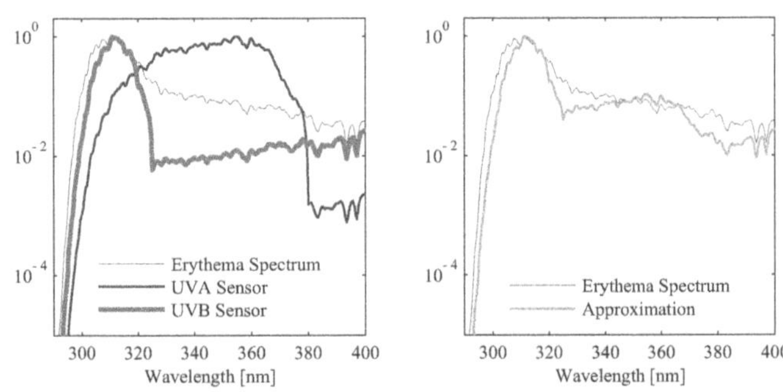

Figure 3. Normalized sensor responses for sunlight (left). The erythema action spectrum can be approximated by combining the values of the UVA and UVB sensors (right).

Data Acquisition and Buffering. Measurement of UV radiation using photodiodes can be accomplished with a simple analog circuit. The energy of the incoming light within the active area of the photodiode is converted into a small current. The magnitude of this current depends on the intensity of the light and the wavelength dependent sensitivity of the photodiode with respect to the incoming light's spectrum. Since the resulting currents are very small, we use a transimpedance amplifier circuit to convert the photocurrent into a corresponding voltage, which is continually sampled using the 10-bit analog-digital converter of the microcontroller. Both sensors can be sampled multiple times per second. Depending on the availability of a Bluetooth connection to the user's smartphone, measurement data is either transferred immediately to the phone or buffered locally in the memory of the microcontroller. This helps to avoid data loss when the user temporarily leaves the connection range of the phone. The storage capacity of the microcontroller allows to store several minutes of samples at the highest resolution using a circular buffer. Furthermore, we also accumulate the sum of the sensor readings which have not yet been transferred to the phone. This assures that we can track the total absorbed radiation even if no Bluetooth connection is available for longer periods. However, we might loose some of the individual sensor readings since they have been overwritten in the local buffer with new data.

Power Consumption

Prolonging battery lifetime is a crucial aspect for wearable applications. Therefore, we carefully designed the sensor unit for low-power operation. The analog sensor circuit and the microcontroller can be put into low-power mode most of the time to reduce the overall power consumption. As a result, the biggest part of the power budget is assigned to the Bluetooth module. By duty-cycling the Bluetooth module when connected (sniff-mode), the total current drawn of the sensor unit can be reduced significantly from 27 to 6 mA, as shown in Figure 4. However, the Bluetooth low-power mode has to be supported by both master (phone) and client (sensor). Given the nominal battery capacity of 110 mAh, the sensor unit can be operated up to 18 hours before it has to be recharged. To prevent a sudden power failure, the battery voltage is measured continuously and displayed on the smartphone. While the current hardware design supports operation of the wearable sensing unit during an interval which is in the order of a typical recharge cycle of a modern smartphone, next generation hardware supporting the upcoming Bluetooth 4.0 low energy standard will allow to tremendously prolong the operation time of the sensor unit using even smaller batteries.

SMARTPHONE APPLICATION

Measurement data from the wearable sensor unit is transferred over Bluetooth to a smartphone running the Google Android operating system. The phone runs a background service, which handles the Bluetooth communication with the sensor device. The wearable sensing unit is polled periodically for new sensor measurements. All sensor readings from the UVA and UVB photodiodes are stored together with the corresponding timestamp and location information provided by the phone. These measurements are made available to the user via the phone in real-time. This is in contrast to existing UV dosimeters which only allow for offline analysis (see section on related work). Furthermore, data is written to the phone's SD card for further analysis. If needed, sensor readings can also be sent to a web server, if the phone provides Wifi or 3G connectivity.

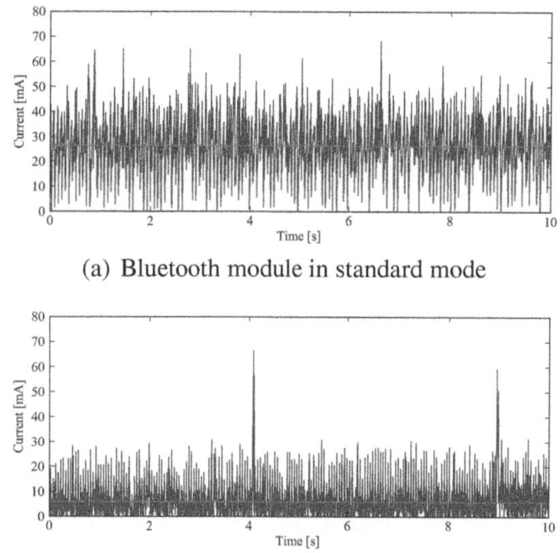

(a) Bluetooth module in standard mode

(b) Bluetooth module in low-power mode

Figure 4. Current consumption of the sensing unit with an active Bluetooth connection for the standard (a) and low-power operation mode (b). The horizontal line indicates the average power consumption measured for the normal operation mode (27 mA) or the low-power mode (6 mA).

Data Processing and Visualization

A considerable difference between stand-alone sensors and smartphone based sensors systems is that the data processing and displaying can be easily adapted to the needs of the use case on smartphone based systems. In the case of Sundroid, this allows us to adapt the system to various applications. In the following we shortly describe two user interfaces we have implemented for Sundroid.

Simple View. The first use case is the one of a person that has an outdoor job or likes to do outdoor sports and wants to avoid skin damage by UV radiation. This user is mainly interested in not being sunburned and avoiding long term skin damage. In order to asses the danger of the accumulated UV radiation to a person, we refer to the commonly used method of Fitzpatrick's skin typing [16]. It classifies a persons skin, based on external features, such as pigmentation, tanning history, and eye color to estimate a minimal erythema dose (MED) for that skin type. The minimal erythema dose is defined as the minimal solar radiation energy that results in a reddening of the skin, that is not induced by heat (i.e. sunburn) [16].

On top of the screen, a simple diagram informs the user about the incident UV radiation he was exposed to that day (see Figure 5). The plain energy value of the accumulated incident UV radiation in J/cm^2 would not be a valuable information for most users. Therefore we display aggregated radiation energy in terms of the percentage of the user's minimal erythema dose. As the minimal UV dose a person can

Skin type	Description	MED in $\frac{mJ}{cm^2}$
1	White, very fair skin	20 - 35
2	White, fair skin	30 - 45
3	Beige skin	40 - 55
4	Beige to brown skin	50 - 80
5	Dark brown skin	70 - 100
6	Black skin	100

Table 2. The skin type and the corresponding minimal erythema doses based on Fitzpatrick's skin typing.

be exposed to without getting a sunburn depends mainly on the skin type and the sun protection factor of the applied sunscreen, these parameters can be set in the application and are taken into account to asses the correct moment to issue a warning. When the accumulated radiation intensity exceeds 80% of the MED (multiplied with the sun protection factor of the applied sunscreen) the users is warned about the acute danger of a sunburn through a notification on the phone (see Figure 6).

To inform the user about the current radiation intensity in an easily understandable manner, the values of the UVA and the UVB radiation are not displayed directly, but are combined to match the erythema action spectrum. The resulting radiation intensity is transformed into the according UV-index[2] and displayed on the center of the screen (see Figure 5, left). On the bottom of the screen the user can see the radiation history of the day, which can serve as an educational component, to learn in which situations the skin was exposed to the highest radiation intensities. Beside processing the data of the external sensors, the use of a smartphone allows to gather more context information. For example, Sundroid fetches the UV-index forecast of the day from the Internet. The predicted UV-index can be used to inform the user on time about necessary precautions, such as to take along appropriate sunscreen or clothing.

Advanced View. The second user interface shows a more technical view, which can be seen in Figure 5 on the right. This view is mainly intended to be used by technical experts (e.g. physicians, researchers or medical staff). It displays the exact values of the incident UVA, UVB and accumulated radiation. The graph on the bottom of the screen displays the UVA and UVB radiation intensities separately. The live feedback on the screen and the possibility to send the sensor data to a central server in real time make it a useful tool for UV-radiation related research (see Application Scenarios).

Data Fusion

The advantages of smartphones as a generic processing platform are manifold. On the one hand, they are personal devices that are almost always with their user. On the other hand, they exhibit a variety of readily available sensors, such as 3D compass, accelerometers, GPS, light sensor, camera,

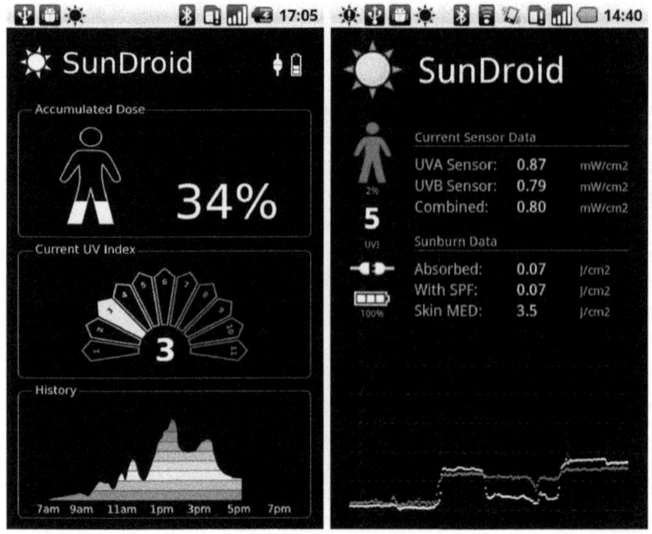

Figure 5. Sundroid activity screens on the smartphone: The *Simple View* displays the accumulated UV dose, the current UV index, and the time line of UV exposure (left). The *Advanced View* shows more detailed information about the current and accumulated UV radiation (right).

Figure 6. A notification window is shown when the absorbed UV radiation exceeds a critical value for the specified skin type and sunscreen.

and microphone, from which the user's context can be inferred. In addition, state-of-the-art smartphones feature enormous computing and communication capabilities, which provides a flexible way to process and distribute the gathered sensor data. Currently, we assign the current timestamp and location of the user as provided by the GPS to each sensor reading, which provides valuable context information for the analysis of the measurement data.

EVALUATION

In this section, we evaluate several aspects of the Sundroid system. First, we compare the accuracy of UV measurements against reference values. Second, we investigate the sensitivity of the sensors with different incident angles of sunlight.

Sensor Calibration

To ensure high accuracy of UV measurements, we have calibrated the sensor units against the erythema specific reference signal of the World Radiation Center (WRC) in Davos, Switzerland. For the measurements, our sensor devices were horizontally mounted on the roof of the WRC building, next to the reference probes. Figure 7 compares the erythema specific responses measured by the high-precision reference equipment with those of our sensor devices during two days. The first measurement was conducted during a partly cloudy day in autumn with some rain around 2.30 pm, and the second measurement took place during a sunny day in winter.

[2]The UV-index is a common measure to communicate UV radiation intensity to the general public. It is defined to be the incident UV radiation irradiance in the erythema action spectrum, divided by $25\frac{W}{cm^2}$.

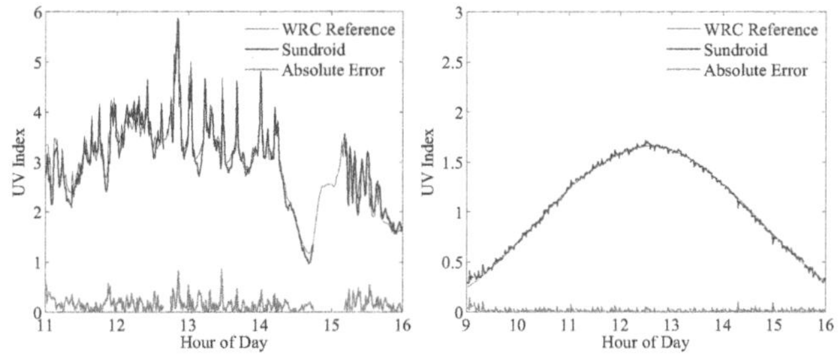

Figure 7. Sensor calibration: The sensors have been calibrated against the reference measurement for the erythema action spectrum at the World Radiation Center (WRC). The calibration measurements were conducted on a partly cloudy day in autumn (left) and on a sunny day in winter (right).

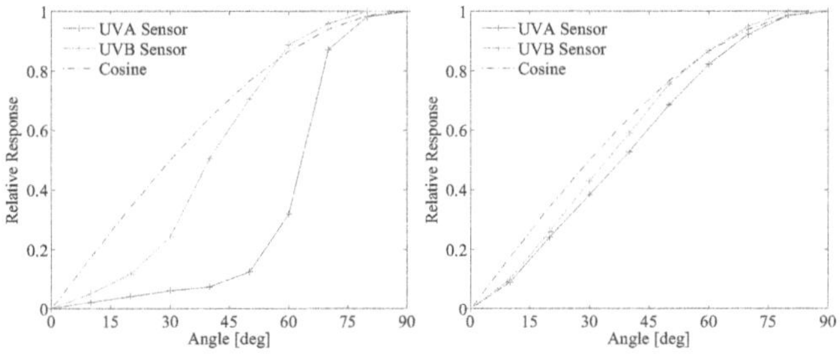

Figure 8. Relative response of the UVA/B photodiodes when exposed to sunlight at different incident angles (left). Placing a PTFE diffuser foil on top of the sensors results in a response which approaches the ideal cosine curve (right).

Due to a bug in the recording software, a small number of sensor readings have been lost during the first measurement day. Nevertheless, the good match of our sensor data with the reference curve after calibration shows that our sensor unit is able to accurately measure the UV radiation relevant to erythema. In fact, the resulting relative error after calibration is less than 5%. The linear correction factor used for calibration needs to be known by the Sundroid application to convert the raw UV measurements into the human readable UV index scale.

Angle Dependencies

Clearly, the sensor sensitivity is dependent on the direction of the incident radiation. Ideally, the response follows a cosine curve, similarly as the response of the human skin. Unfortunately, this curve is not well matched by the raw photodiodes, as shown in Figure 8 (left). To overcome this problem, we integrated a diffuser made from Polytetrafluoroethylene (PTFE). PTFE, also known as Teflon, has been used as a material for UV diffusers in similar contexts before [6, 1]. After applying a diffuser, the dependency on the angle closely follows the ideal cosine curve as shown in Figure 8 (right). The figure shows that the use of a diffuser mitigates angle dependencies, such that the (ideal) cosine response is closely approximated. For these plots, we assumed that at 0 degrees (perpendicular to the incident sunlight) there is only diffuse radiation. The corresponding intensity value has been subtracted from the entire measurement series to account for directed light only.

APPLICATION SCENARIOS

The modular design of the Sundroid system facilitates the use not only as a personal assistant to track absorbed UV radiation in everyday life, such as in personal informatics systems [19], but also opens possibilities in a variety of other settings. This section describes how Sundoid can be used in a variety of contexts.

Behavioral Research. We believe that the real-time reporting capabilities, together with the possibility to grasp the context of a given user, can considerably improve our understanding of the impact of UV radiation throughout different activities. Using time and GPS information, for example, we can precisely match the detected solar irradiation to a person's location. Using the phone's 3D compass, the sun's incident angle becomes known, under the assumption that the user keeps the phone in the same place on the body most of the time. Furthermore, acceleration data, microphone, etc. help to infer the user's current activity. This additional information might help to answer previously unanswered questions. Holman et al. [14], for example, speculate that some of the differences they found compared to a manikin based study [9] originate from the fact that people tend to turn away from the sun. The additional sensor data (GPS, compass) provided by the Sundroid system could help to prove or disprove this conjecture.

Participatory Sensing. Our survey suggests a general interest in using Sundroid as a personal assistant and warning device, in particular when the sensor part is unobtrusively integrated into clothing and/or accessories. If such a system indeed happens to find widespread use, information about UV radiation can enter the domain of participatory sensing [4]. Participatory sensing aims at collecting and sharing sensor data gathered by the everyday use of mobile devices. In the context of UV radiation, large scale UV maps could be drawn at a much finer resolution than currently possible, thereby for example taking time, shadow, and reflection effects into account.

Applications in Therapy. In discussions with a dermatologist, we were pointed to a variety of medical application scenarios. Examples include the different use cases in the context of photodynamic therapy, UV induced immunosuppression, and the treatment of light allergies. Moreover, it could be used to research the positive effects of sunlight, for example in the production of vitamin D, circadian rhythm regulation, or seasonal affective disorder. In particular, a wearable UV sensing device could help both, physicians as well as patients to monitor the irradiation and user activity over a longer period of time, thereby facilitating a more precise treatment at lower cost, as part of the monitoring task is shifted from the physician to the patient. Via the mobile network infrastructure the sensor data can be transmitted to a physician in real-time, who can directly take adequate actions if required. Long-term irradiation traces can further be used to improve people's awareness of sunlight intensity in different situations and are thus well suited for health related behavior training.

Figure 9. Positioning of the three wearable sensor units during the field experiments: Unit 1 is attached on the helmet, Unit 2 is attached on the shoulder, and Unit 3 is attached near the chest. The sensor units are enclosed within a plastic housing to protect them from snow.

PILOT STUDY

In order to demonstrate the practical usability of the system and to investigate the effects of sensor placement in a real-world setting, we have conducted a small scale pilot study. The study encompassed two different outdoor sport activies: snowboarding and climbing. In both experiments the incident UV radiation on a single test subject was measured over several hours.

Scenario 1: Snowboarding

The snowboarding experiment was conducted in a large ski resort. We have attached three Sundroid sensor units to the test subject: One on the helmet, facing upwards, one on the shoulder, facing upwards, and one on the chest, facing frontwards, as shown in Figure 9. The test subject's task was to use all the ski lifts and slopes freely. Beside the UV intensity values we tracked the location of the person using GPS. The location and the UV data was logged on the Android mobile phone carried by the person. From the location, an elevation profile was derived that can be seen in Figure 10 along with the plot of the measured UV radiation of the three sensor units. In the plot, one can clearly see two periods of zero UV radiation; the first of them, around 12 pm, was caused by a lunch break in a restaurant. The second one, around 1.30 pm, was caused by a trip in a closed cabin gondola lift.

This day trace provides a good example of how the Sundroid system can be used in scientific experiments. One can gain different insights by analyzing the UV radiation traces.

For instance the role of the sensor placement (i.e. where a user is wearing the sensing unit) can be studied. Prior research using a rotating manikin has shown that the weather conditions (i.e. amount of clouds) affect the overall UV intensity, but play a minor role for the proportions of sunlight absorbed by different sites of the body [9]. Further studies on living subjects have shown high and relatively stable values for measurements on the shoulder for different outdoor occupations, namely gardener, roof carpenter, bricklayer [14]. The reported values show that roughly 70% of the total ra-

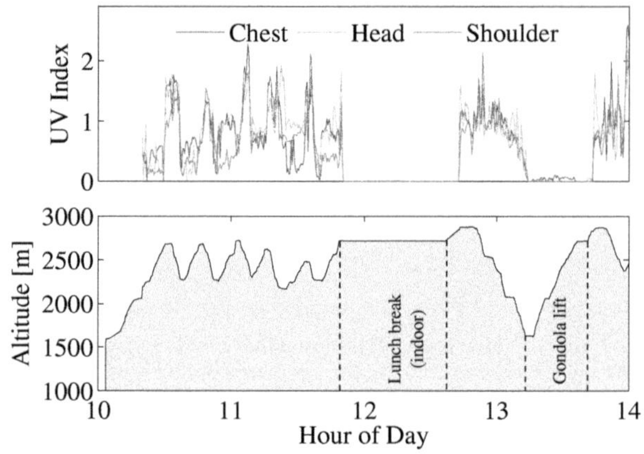

Figure 10. The elevation profile of the test subject during one day of snowboarding in a ski resort (bottom) and the measured UV intensity of the different Sundroid sensors (top).

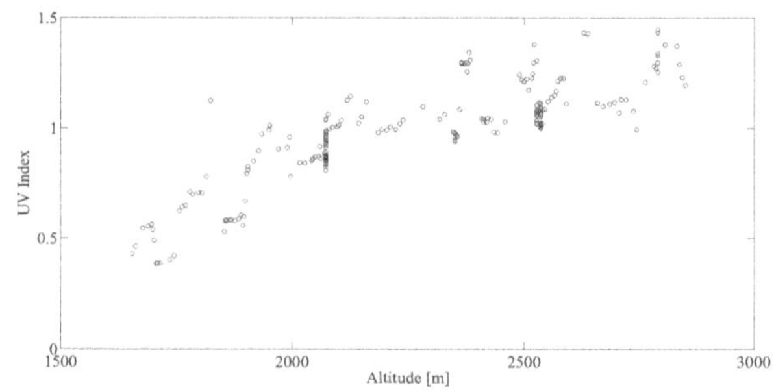

Figure 11. UV intensity versus altitude of the test subject during the ride on the longest ski slope. The correlation of altitude over mean sea level and UV radiation is clearly visible.

diation, as measured by a horizontally placed dosimeter, is received at the shoulder, which is slightly less than the doses measured at the vertex of the head. Moreover, under lightly cloudy weather conditions, the incident radiation at the chest is stated to be about two thirds of the radiation measured at the shoulder.

However in the case of the snowboard trip, the measured intensity ratios of the three sensors (on the head, shoulder and chest), differ significantly from the values reported in [14]: In particular, the sensor mounted on the chest absorbed about 10% more energy than the sensor mounted on the head. These differences can, presumably, be explained by the low position of the sun during winter days and the substantial amount of UV reflection by the snow. Such factors have shown to have a relevant impact by Gröbner et al. [11].

Another interesting observation discussed in [11] is the dependency between UV radiation and the altitude above sea level. The data of the longest downhill drive (around 1 pm) confirms such a dependency. Figure 11 shows the measured intensities versus the current altitude of the test subject. It is important to note that the measured decrease of UV intensity at lower altitudes cannot be explained by the elevation level alone. Other effects, such as an increased amount of shadow in lower areas, or the direction of the slope are also likely to have an influence.

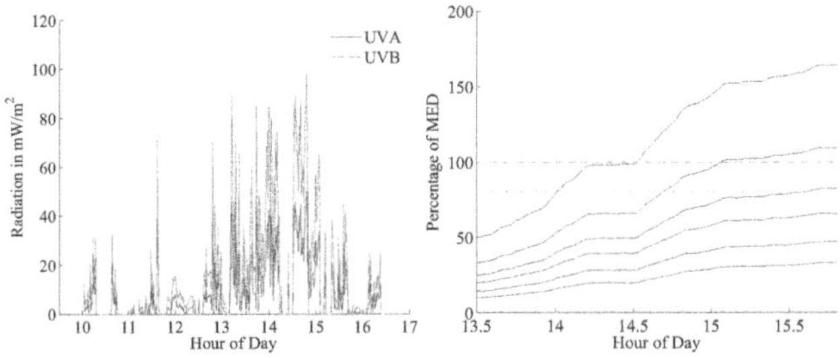

Figure 12. The left plot shows the incident radiation during one day of climbing on a sunny spring day. On the right, one can see the accumulated radiation energy, expressed as percentage of the MED for the different skin types. The blue line on top is skin type 1, whereas the blue line on the bottom is skin type 6.

This experiment demonstrates that the Sundroid system can be used to gain insights into the effects of sensor placement in different environments and to improve the understanding of the surface albedo in various settings. Moreover, the relatively cheap hardware allows to realize studies with a large number of participants.

Scenario 2: Climbing

Another measurement series were conducted during one day of climbing on a sunny spring day. We attached one Sundroid sensor at the climber's harness, which measured the incident sun radiation on the back of the test person. Plots of the recorded UVA and UVB radiation can be seen in Figure 12 (left). Figure 12 (right) plots the accumulated energy in the erythema action spectrum as percentage of the minimal erythema dose for the skin types 1 to 6. The lowest blue line corresponds to the percentage of the MED, a person with skin type 6 would have been exposed to, whereas the highest blue line corresponds to the percentage of the MED of a person with skin type 1.

The UV forecast of the national meteorological institute for that day was UV index 5. As one can see, the radiation was high enough to exceed the minimal erythema dose for skin type 1 and skin type 2. However, a person with skin type 1 would have been warned around 2 pm about the high radiation energy (80% of the MED), which would have allowed the person to apply sunscreen, or seek shadow in time. Similarly, a person with skin type 2 would have been warned around 40 minutes later, which again would have been early enough to take precautions.

CONCLUSIONS AND OUTLOOK

We have presented Sundroid, a wearable prototype system designed to increase the awareness of solar radiation by means of body worn sensors. Our experiments show that despite the use of low cost components, the accuracy reached by our sensor unit is comparable with the one of high-precision infrastructure. In a survey we could further show that a relevant fraction of people could imagine using such a system to reduce sun-related health problems. Our prototype demonstrates the potential of combining wearable sensors with a smartphone. If the Sundroid sensor is worn during everyday activities, it can notify people in time about the imminent risk of a sunburn. The modular design featuring a smartphone as a versatile platform facilitates the use in several other settings, such as medical therapies and research. We are convinced that technological advances will empower the seamless integration of a variety of sensors in clothing and accessories, making systems such as Sundroid a ubiquitous part of our daily life.

ACKNOWLEDGMENTS

We would like to thank Dr. Günter Hofbauer from the Department of Dermatology at the University Hospital Zurich for his useful advice and feedback on the prototype platform. Furthermore, we thank Dr. Julian Gröbner of the World Radiation Center in Davos, Switzerland for his support during the calibration measurements.

REFERENCES

1. M. Allen and R. McKenzie. Dosimeter badges to monitor personal UV doses. In *NIWA UV Workshop*, 2010.

2. A. Armstrong, A. Watson, M. Makredes, J. Frangos, A. Kimball, and J. Kvedar. Text-message reminders to improve sunscreen use: a randomized, controlled trial using electronic monitoring. *Archives of dermatology*, 145(11):1230, 2009.

3. D. E. Brash, J. A. Rudolph, J. A. Simon, A. Lin, G. J. Mckenna, H. P. Baden, A. J. Halperin, and J. Ponten. A role for sunlight in skin cancer: UV-induced p53 mutations in squamous cell carcinoma. *Proceedings of the National Academy of Sciences of the United States of America*, 88(22):10124–10128, 1991.

4. J. Burke, D. Estrin, M. Hansen, A. Parker, N. Ramanathan, S. Reddy, and M. Srivastava. Participatory sensing. In *WSW*, 2006.

5. G. Chen, B. Yan, M. Shin, D. Kotz, and E. Berke. MPCS: Mobile-phone based patient compliance system for chronic illness care. In *MobiQuitous*, 2009.

6. S. David. Personal UV Dosimeter Badges: Mark II. In *NIWA UV Workshop*, 2010.

7. F. de Gruijl, H. Sterenborg, P. Forbes, R. Davies, C. Cole, G. Kelfkens, H. van Weelden, H. Slaper, and J. van der Leun. Wavelength dependence of skin cancer induction by ultraviolet irradiation of albino hairless mice. *Cancer research*, 53(1):53, 1993.

8. A. Dey and G. Abowd. Cybreminder: A context-aware system for supporting reminders. In *HUC*, 2000.

9. B. Diffey, M. Kerwin, and A. Davis. The anatomical distribution of sunlight. *British Journal of Dermatology*, 97(4):407–410, 1977.

10. S. Forjuoh, M. Reis, G. Couchman, and M. Ory. Improving Diabetes Self-Care with a PDA in Ambulatory Care. *Telemedicine and e-Health*, 14(3):273–279, 2008.

11. J. Gröbner, D. Pavel, H. G., and B. M. Effect of snow albedo and topography on UV radiation. In *NIWA UV Workshop*, 2010.
12. J. Heydenreich and H. Wulf. Miniature Personal Electronic UVR Dosimeter with Erythema Response and Time-stamped Readings in a Wristwatch. *Photochemistry and photobiology*, 2005.
13. J. Ho and S. Intille. Using context-aware computing to reduce the perceived burden of interruptions from mobile devices. In *CHI*, 2005.
14. C. Holman, I. Gibson, S. M., and B. Armstrong. Ultraviolet irradiation of human body sites in relation to occupation and outdoor activity: field studies using personal UVR dosimeters. *Clinical and Experimental Dermatology*, 8(3):269–277, 1983.
15. G. Horneck. Quantification of the biological effectiveness of environmental UV radiation. *Journal of Photochemistry and Photobiology B: Biology*, 31(1-2):43–49, 1995.
16. F. Im, A. Eisen, K. Wolff, A. Kf, G. La, and S. Katz. Fitzpatrick's dermatology in general medicine, 2000.
17. A. Kessell and C. Chan. Castaway: a context-aware task management system. In *CHI*, 2006.
18. O. Kwon and S. Choi. Applying associative theory to need awareness for personalized reminder system. *Expert Systems with Applications*, 2008.
19. I. Li, A. Dey, and J. Forlizzi. A stage-based model of personal informatics systems. In *CHI '10: Proceedings of the 28th international conference on Human factors in computing systems*, pages 557–566. ACM, 2010.
20. A. Logan, W. McIsaac, A. Tisler, M. Irvine, A. Saunders, A. Dunai, C. Rizo, D. Feig, M. Hamill, M. Trudel, et al. Mobile Phone-Based Remote Patient Monitoring System for Management of Hypertension in Diabetic Patients. *American journal of hypertension*, 20(9):942–948, 2007.
21. P. Ludford, D. Frankowski, K. Reily, K. Wilms, and L. Terveen. Because I carry my cell phone anyway: functional location-based reminder applications. In *CHI*, 2006.
22. J. Lundell, T. Hayes, S. Vurgun, U. Ozertem, J. Kimel, J. Kaye, F. Guilak, and M. Pavel. Continuous activity monitoring and intelligent contextual prompting to improve medication adherence. In *EMBS*, 2007.
23. E. Miluzzo, N. Lane, K. Fodor, R. Peterson, H. Lu, M. Musolesi, S. Eisenman, X. Zheng, and A. Campbell. Sensing meets mobile social networks: the design, implementation and evaluation of the cenceme application. In *SenSys*, 2008.
24. M. Moehrle, B. Dennenmoser, and C. Garbe. Continuous long-term monitoring of UV radiation in professional mountain guides reveals extremely high exposure. *International Journal of Cancer*, 103(6):775–778, 2003.
25. M. Morón, J. Luque, A. Botella, E. Cuberos, E. Casilari, and A. Díaz-Estrella. J2ME and smart phones as platform for a Bluetooth Body Area Network for Patient-telemonitoring. In *EMBS*, 2007.
26. L. Nachman, A. Baxi, S. Bhattacharya, V. Darera, P. Deshpande, N. Kodalapura, V. Mageshkumar, S. Rath, J. Shahabdeen, and R. Acharya. Jog Falls: A Pervasive Healthcare Platform for Diabetes Management. *Pervasive Computing*, 2010.
27. S. Nylander, T. Lundquist, A. Brännström, and B. Karlson. "It's Just Easier with the Phone"–A Diary Study of Internet Access from Cell Phones. *Pervasive Computing*, 2009.
28. H. Pinnock, R. Slack, C. Pagliari, D. Price, and A. Sheikh. Understanding the potential role of mobile phone-based monitoring on asthma self-management: qualitative study. *Clinical & Experimental Allergy*, 37(5):794–802, 2007.
29. E. D. Pleasance et al. A comprehensive catalogue of somatic mutations from a human cancer genome. *Nature*, 463(7278):191–196, Dec. 2009.
30. H. W. Rogers, M. A. Weinstock, A. R. Harris, M. R. Hinckley, S. R. Feldman, A. B. Fleischer, and B. M. Coldiron. Incidence Estimate of Nonmelanoma Skin Cancer in the United States, 2006. *Arch Dermatol*, 146(3):283–287, Mar. 2010.
31. R. Setlow. The wavelengths in sunlight effective in producing skin cancer: a theoretical analysis. *Proc. of the National Academy of Sciences of the United States of America*, 71(9):3363, 1974.
32. D. Siewiorek, A. Smailagic, J. Furukawa, A. Krause, N. Moraveji, K. Reiger, J. Shaffer, and F. Wong. Sensay: A context-aware mobile phone. In *Wearable Computers*, 2003.
33. M. Sneyd and B. Cox. The control of melanoma in New Zealand. *Journal of the New Zealand Medical Association*, 119:1242, 2006.
34. T. Sohn, K. Li, G. Lee, I. Smith, J. Scott, and W. Griswold. Place-its: A study of location-based reminders on mobile phones. *UbiComp*, 2005.
35. S. Sultan and P. Mohan. myDR: Improving the Self-Care Process for Caribbean Patients with Diabetes through Mobile Learning. *International Journal of Education and Development using Information and Communication Technologies*, 5(4), 2009.
36. E. Thieden, P. A. Philipsen, J. Sandby-Moller, and H. C. Wulf. Sunburn related to uv radiation exposure, age, sex, occupation, and sun bed use based on time-stamped personal dosimetry and sun behavior diaries. *Arch Dermatol*, 141(4), 2005.
37. D. Trossen and D. Pavel. Building a ubiquitous platform for remote sensing using smartphones. In *MobiQuitous*, 2005.

Accurate and Privacy Preserving Cough Sensing using a Low-Cost Microphone

Eric C. Larson[1], TienJui Lee[1], Sean Liu[2], Margaret Rosenfeld[3], Shwetak N. Patel[1,2]

[1]Electrical Engineering,
[2]Computer Science & Engineering,
DUB Institute, University of Washington
Seattle, WA 98195
{eclarson, tienlee, sysliu, shwetak}@uw.edu

[3]Seattle Children's Hospital
Center for Clinical and Translational Research
4800 Sand Point Way NE
Seattle, WA 98105
margaret.rosenfeld@seattlechildrens.org

ABSTRACT
Audio-based cough detection has become more pervasive in recent years because of its utility in evaluating treatments and the potential to impact the quality of life for individuals with chronic cough. We critically examine the current state of the art in cough detection, concluding that existing approaches expose private audio recordings of users and bystanders. We present a novel algorithm for detecting coughs from the audio stream of a mobile phone. Our system allows cough sounds to be reconstructed from the feature set, but prevents speech from being reconstructed intelligibly. We evaluate our algorithm on data collected in the wild and report an average true positive rate of 92% and false positive rate of 0.5%. We also present the results of two psychoacoustic experiments which characterize the tradeoff between the fidelity of reconstructed cough sounds and the intelligibility of reconstructed speech.

Author Keywords
Cough detection, health, mobile phones, signal processing, sensing, privacy.

ACM Classification Keywords
H5.m. Information interfaces and presentation (e.g., HCI): Miscellaneous.

General Terms
Algorithms, Experimentation, Performance, Security.

INTRODUCTION
Coughing is a common, distressing symptom that results in significant health care costs, medical consultations, and medication use [15]. According to the U.S. Department of Health and Human Services, coughing is the most frequent symptom mentioned by people when seeking medical advice [7, 19, 38]. Although the importance of diagnosing and managing cough is well recognized [15, 20], evaluation is limited by the lack of objective measures of ambulatory cough frequency and severity [40]. Efforts to develop objective cough monitoring systems date to the 1950s [3], but have intensified in recent years due to technological advances [40]. As such, the medical community has setup guidelines for objective cough monitoring systems [14, 20, 30]. They recommend using systems that have automated cough recognition, can distinguish cough from other sounds, permit 24-hour recording, and provide digital processing of cough recordings; other critical and desirable features include privacy preservation, mobility, compactness, and unobtrusiveness. Although recent advances in audio cough monitoring have begun to make the process more automated [2, 4 26], current systems do not meet all of these requirements. Most worryingly, current audio based methods expose private information about users' speech.

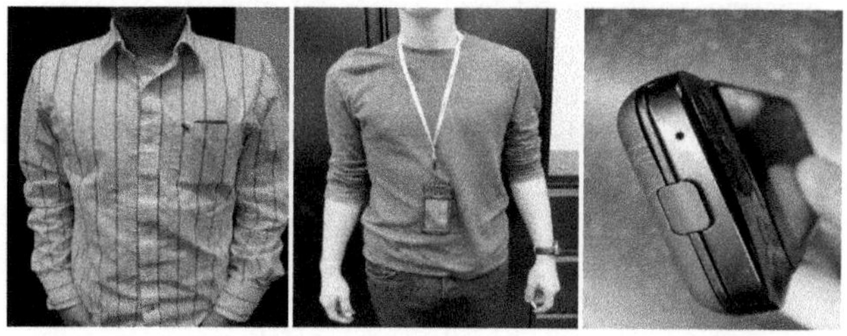

Figure 1. (Left) Participants carrying the mobile phone in their shirt pocket or using a neck strap. (Right) The built-in microphone facing up in the direction of the mouth.

In this paper, we describe our mobile phone-based solution for detecting and counting personal coughs. Our system attempts to meet all of the requirements for objective cough monitoring as outlined by the medical community. Our approach reliably detects cough sounds while preserving the audio privacy of the patient and bystanders. We show our method to have three unique contributions to the research community: (1) it advances the current state of the art in audio cough classification (with average true positive rate of 92% and false positive rate of 0.5%) and allows for classification of individual cough sounds within a coughing episode, (2) it also allows for cough sounds to be reconstructed with good fidelity so that they can be assessed by a physician or to further remove false positives, and (3) it simultaneously prevents other sounds from being reconstructed with useful fidelity (i.e., speech sounds are unintelligible). Our methodology can be used as a general framework for other audio-based UbiComp sensing applications that need to reconstruct sounds of interest while simultaneously suppressing private audio, such as speech.

Our approach uses principal components analysis (PCA) of the audio spectrogram for classification and for the prevention of speech reconstruction. We found that using 10 components was sufficient for classification. For reconstructing cough sounds, we found that 25 components produces a "good" fidelity cough sound while simultaneously disguising 84% of spoken words.

The remainder of the paper is organized as follows: We first motivate our work, highlighting the privacy vulnerabilities of existing audio-based health sensing classification methods. Second, we review and summarize related bodies of work. We then introduce our methodology using eigenvector projections of the audio spectrogram. Finally, we present the results of two experiments: the first evaluates the accuracy of our classifier on *real world* audio data collected from mobile phones for 17 subjects experiencing cough episodes. The second uses subjective ratings and speech dictations to characterize the tradeoff between clarity of reconstructed coughs and the intelligibility of speech.

MOTIVATION

Ambulatory cough sensing combined with the capabilities of modern smart phones is a particularly interesting UbiComp application. The integration can allow individuals to keep a baseline cough frequency on their digital health record and help increase compliance and effectiveness of treatment regimens. Moreover, using mobile phones as sensing platforms could enable large-scale epidemiological studies, such as using cough frequency across cities to identify and track influenza outbreaks. Finally, because of the relatively low cost of commodity phones, this approach may be of particular interest in developing countries where physicians have limited resources to track coughing and lung function (e.g., preventing suffocation fatalities from complications of pneumonia [45]).

Value of Ambulatory and Objective Cough Sensing

Self-report of cough frequency and severity is notoriously unreliable, particularly in patients with chronic respiratory conditions [14, 22, 31]. Thus, objective ambulatory monitoring of cough frequency has the potential for substantial clinical benefits. First, it would allow early detection of respiratory exacerbations in patients with chronic respiratory diseases such as asthma, cystic fibrosis, and chronic obstructive pulmonary disease (COPD)—allowing earlier and therefore more effective treatment. Early intervention in exacerbations of these conditions has been shown to decrease hospitalization rates and improve long-term outcomes, including survival [29, 37, 39, 41]. For example, a potential correlation may exist between cough frequency throughout a daily period and the severity of asthma in patients, even before other warning signs are present [8]. Secondly, objective cough monitoring would allow improved evaluation of treatment efficacy in many diseases, including tuberculosis, pneumonia, bronchiolitis, asthma, cystic fibrosis and COPD, with the associated ability to change treatment algorithms as needed. Finally, there is great interest in developing cough monitors as sensitive endpoints for clinical trials of therapies in patients with many of these diseases [21]. Cough patterns have been used as a metric to evaluate various treatments regimens, in conditions such as gastro esophageal reflux and COPD [17, 40].

The potential utility of ambulatory cough quantification, however, has been limited to date by the cumbersome and expensive monitoring systems available. Formative research on the benefits of cough detection is in its infancy—better tools for automatic cough detection are sorely needed in order to establish larger, more conclusive studies. Current studies, for example, can only recruit 15-20 participants because of the overhead in extracting cough events reliably [27, 40].

Challenges with Existing Cough Sensing Approaches

Researchers have recently created systems that use machine learning to automatically detect coughs from recorded audio streams [2, 4, 13, 26, 27]. The most limiting criterion of audio approaches is robustness to outside noise sources. Because continuous audio streams are high data rate, the specificity of the systems must be extremely high. Otherwise the number of false positives may exceed the actual cough rate of the individual. To gain such high specificity, these systems do not use *one* model for cough classification—in the case of one algorithm, they need *hundreds* of models [4, 26]—or require models to be adjusted for each user. This is a common limitation of audio based classification methods: while the feature extraction may be able to run on a mobile device, the classification may be better suited to reside on a server somewhere in the cloud or database, where these algorithms and models can be continually updated. Moreover, some of the existing algorithms opt to be semi-automated to reduce the false positive rate. A trained annotator cleans the dataset by listening to segments of audio where the algorithm thinks a cough occurred.

In this way, data transfer, cloud computing, and semi-automation can all compromise the privacy of recorded audio. Audio based cough detection systems, however, have historically not focused on maintaining the privacy of an individual's recordings. As such, little work has been done on optimizing the tradeoffs between privacy vulnerabilities and algorithmic methods. Table 1 outlines several classification architectures and the tradeoffs for each. Architectures which use non-invertible transforms, for example, do not provide audio for the physician to evaluate, nor do they provide a mechanism for semi-automation to reduce false positives. Architectures which use ubiquitous speech features, such as mel-frequency Cepstral coefficients (MFCCs), potentially expose a wide range of private speech information including content, identity, and prosody [46].

The advantages of our approach are four-fold:

(1) The features that are transmitted correspond to the weights of components, and the actual components

Architecture	Privacy Tradeoffs	Clinical Tradeoffs
Send raw audio to classification server	(-)Health professionals have access to private audio	(+)Physician can listen to cough sounds (+)Reviewer can remove false positives
Send non-invertible features (like MFCC's)	(-)MFCCs are ubiquitous to speech recognition and carry information about speech content	(-)Physician cannot listen to cough sounds (-)False positives cannot be removed
Send unique, non-invertible features	(+)Private audio is protected	(-)Physician cannot listen to cough sounds (-)False positives cannot be removed
Our algorithm	(+)Speech is unintelligible	(+)Physician can listen to cough sounds (+)Reviewer can remove false positives

Table 1. Tradeoffs between different audio cough sensing system architectures.

needed to reconstruct the audio only exist on the phone and the server.

(2) These features generalize across subjects so that no initial calibration is needed.

(3) Once the weights arrive at the server, they can be used to reconstruct the cough event with good quality, allowing physicians to listen to and diagnose the cough sounds, in addition to allowing the system to be semi-automated to further reduce false positives, if needed.

(4) The patient need not worry about health professionals inadvertently hearing private conversations since speech is wholly disguised.

RELATED WORK

Our related work falls into five categories: (1) mobile phone-based health applications, (2) general cough detection, (3) audio-based cough detection, (4) audio privacy, and (5) eigenvector feature selection in machine learning.

Mobile Phone-based Health Applications

Many ubicomp researchers have investigated the possible use of mobile phones as a sensing and/or feedback platform to enhance people's health conditions. Chiu *et al.* created a mobile phone-based system called the Playful bottle [10]. They used the phone's built-in camera and accelerometer to detect how much water people consume during a day and persuade them to drink healthy quantities of water using hydration games. Consolvo *et al.* proposed a UbiFit garden system that employs a pager-size sensor called MSP (Mobile Sensing Platform) to recognize people's activity levels and provide feedback using a garden display on their mobile phone [12]. AsthmaMD is an iPhone application that allows people to quickly and easily log their asthma activity, medication, and causes of an asthma attack in the form of a diary [1]. This aggregated, anonymous data is sent to the cloud, providing researchers with information regarding the causes and external variables contributing to asthma and other illnesses. We share similar goals with these research projects and applications–using a commodity mobile phone as the sensing platform for collecting and distributing data to health professionals and, in doing so, increasing people's awareness of their own health conditions.

General Cough Detection

The most common technique for estimating cough frequency is to have patients self report using numeric scoring (0-5) or Visual Analog Scoring (VAS) [36]. However, numerous studies have shown self-report to be highly inaccurate, including the study presented in this paper (see [40] for a summary). The number of coughs a patient self-reports, for instance, has been shown to be significantly influenced by the placebo effect and the patient's perception of their cough severity [40]. Moreover, patients cannot accurately track trends in their cough frequency from hour to hour, or when they are asleep. For these reasons, more objective methods have been developed for counting coughs. Many require expensive, cumbersome equipment (e.g., the chest wall device in [25]) or require paid annotators to listen to recordings and manually annotate cough sounds [40].

There are a number of sensing systems that automatically assess cough frequency. Dating back to the 1950s, researchers developed methods of measuring thoracic pressure changes (airflow from the mouth) in order to obtain unbiased measures of cough frequency [3]. Semi-autonomous methods exist that require individuals to parse through a pre-segmented list of possible cough sounds. The "Overnight Cough Monitoring System" is such a system, which attached an air-coupled microphone to the chest wall or over the trachea when the participant is sleeping [16]. Kraman *et al.* created another accelerometer-based system that placed an accelerometer at the participant's chest wall [25], but required researchers to manually count coughs based on the visualization of the accelerometer data.

The VivoMetrics Lifeshirt [13] is a commercial product that incorporates various physiological sensors to monitor breathing rate, heart rate, activity, posture, and skin temperature. It can be used to detect coughs with an extra throat microphone and the existing sensor array. The reported true positive rate is 78.2% and the false positive rate is 0.4%. VitaloJAK [27] is another commercial product that uses a piezoelectric sensor attached to the chest wall to detect coughs. The reported true positive rate was 91.3-99.5% after an initial calibration. Each method suffers from the same paradigm: users must wear specialized sensors on the chest wall or around their body, which adds expense, is cumbersome, and limits the system in ambulatory settings.

Audio Based Cough Detection

Audio based systems, on the other hand, are easy to deploy in an ambulatory setting and can be made extremely low cost. These systems have become more accurate and lower cost over recent years. Barry *et al.* created a system called the Hull Automated Cough Counter (HACC) [2], using a lapel microphone and wearable recording device. The feature set used was motivated by speech recognition; namely, mel-frequency cepstral coefficients (MFCCs) and linear

Algorithm (Author)	Sensing	Subjects	Recording Environment	Automation	Initial Calibration?	Mean True Positive Rate	Mean False Positive Rate	Mean False Alarms / Hr
LifeShirt	Throat Mic. +sensor array	N=8	Lab, 24 hours	Automatic	Yes	78%	0.4%	Not reported
VitaloJak	Piezo Sensor	N=10	Lab, 24 hours	Automatic	Yes	97.5%	2.3%	Not reported
HACC	Lapel Mic.	N=15	Clinic, 1 hour	Semi	Yes	80%	4%	Not reported
LCM (Matos)	Lapel Mic.	N=19	In Wild, 6 hours	Semi	Yes	71-82%	Not reported	13
LCM (Birring)	Lapel Mic.	N=19	In Wild, 2-6 hours	Semi	Yes	91% *	<1%	2.5‡
Our algorithm	Phone Mic. on necklace	N=17	In Wild, 2-6 hours	Automatic	No	92%	0.5%	17

Table 2. Summary of related work in audio based cough detection. *It is not clear if these rates are reported with or without a 95% energy threshold. ‡These rates are reported after review by an annotator.

predictive cepstral coefficients (LPCC). They applied a Neural Network classifier and achieved an 80% (55-100%) true positive rate and 4% (2-8%) false positive rate. However, they recorded audio signals in an outpatient clinic for only one hour per person, which is a relatively controlled and noise-reduced environment.

Similarly, Matos *et al.* created a system called the Leicester Cough Monitor (LCM) [26], which uses a lapel microphone with a portable audio recorder. They used MFCCs (with derivatives) as features to a Hidden-Markov Model (HMM). Their average true positive rate was 71% (50% - 99%) and a false alarm rate of 13 cough events per hour (false positive rate not reported). After applying an energy threshold to discard low intensity coughs, the average true positive rate for LCM could be boosted to 82% and false alarms reduced to 2.5 events per hour. However, the tradeoff was to discard on average 29% (6-72%) of the cough events for each subject, and the energy thresholds were required to be computed per individual. Recently, LCM has reported a true positive rate of 91% and false positive rate ~1% [4]. However, this has received unfavorable criticism by the medical community [28], who point out that their most recent publications are not forthcoming about whether the true positives are reported with or without the energy threshold and the system is only evaluated on a small subset of their audio data. They also point out that to get such a low false positive rate, the system requires hired annotators to listen to the low confidence coughs and the annotators must provide a portion of hand segmented cough examples in order to prime the algorithm. As such, the system should actually be coined as semi-automated.

Our system uses principal components analysis (PCA) and a random forest classifier. It has comparable accuracies to existing detection algorithms (92% mean true positive rate), but does not require any automation in order to prime or retrain the models. We note that a direct comparison between our approach and HACC or LCM is impossible. Many of these systems consider their algorithms as propriety, so there is limited information on many of the actual details. Instead, we must opt to compare algorithms on the published accuracies, albeit different datasets. Table 2 summarizes and compares the classification rate of ambulatory cough detection algorithms.

Audio Privacy

Prior work in audio privacy has largely dealt with hiding certain cues about the speakers and conversations around them so that a machine learning algorithm cannot reconstruct valuable information from the feature sets. It is generally accepted that MFCCs are poor features for maintaining privacy, as they reveal not only speech, but also inflection, and prosody [46]. As such Wyatt *et al.* have devised audio features that can successfully hide speech intelligibility, while simultaneously providing cues for prosody and recognition of conversations [46]. Most of the related audio privacy work attempts to preserve certain quantities while providing poor features for modern speech recognizers [32]. Chen *et al.*, on the other hand, use linear prediction to replace vowels in speech, while keeping environmental noises such as cars and running water intelligible to subjects [9]. Our work in this paper, similar to [9], attempts to make the speech unintelligible, but also make it possible to reconstruct cough sounds. Our methodologies however, are quite different.

Eigenvector Feature Selection

The most common application of eigenvectors in machine learning is called principal components analysis (PCA). PCA uses orthogonal components (i.e., eigenvectors) of a particular feature space to reduce dimensionality. Components can be sorted in terms of their corresponding Eigenvalue, which ranks the components by how much variation they can explain in the data. Traditional PCA is limited by the assumptions that the optimal transformation of the feature space is linear and orthogonal, which is not true in general. Even so, PCA has been successfully applied in many domains, the best known of which is face recognition (i.e., Eigenfaces [42]) and gene mapping dimensionality reduction [23]. The use of PCA on audio spectrograms is not new. Pinkowski successfully used PCA to develop a model of the spectrogram for different English vowels sounds [35]. Our work also uses PCA on spectrograms, except our model is made for coughing sounds.

PHYSIOLOGY OF COUGHING

This section provides a background on the physiology behind the cough reflex and the generation of cough sounds. We also discuss how coughs manifest in an audio stream using spectrograms, motivating the design of our model.

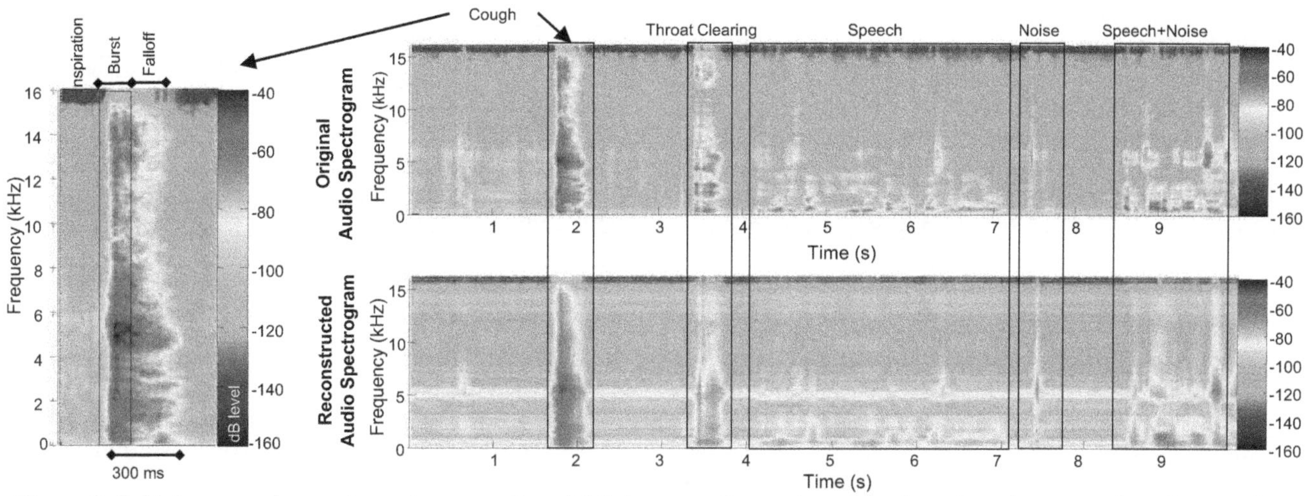

Figure 2. (left) An example cough spectrogram. (top right) An example spectrogram of cough and non-cough audio sounds. (bottom left) An example of the reconstructed spectrogram using principal components analysis.

Cough Reflex

The irritation of afferent cough receptors in the airways triggers the cough reflex. Once triggered, the cough reflex consists of four phases: (1) an initial deep inspiration and glottal closure, (2) contraction of the expiratory muscles against the closed glottis, (3) a sudden glottis opening with an explosive expiration, (4) a wheeze or "voiced" sound [24, 40]. During the initial inspiration, the glottis temporarily narrows and closes. Previous studies show that the glottis closure and expulsive phase can be repeated several times without any inspiration [34].

Audio Analysis

The third and fourth phases of the cough reflex manifest audibly as a cough sound. All cough sounds share common attributes: relatively loud intensity, a quick burst of sound, and a predictable duration and falloff. These are illustrated in Figure 2, where it is easy to identify the cough sound from the audio spectrogram. Notice the overall energy is very strong relative to the surrounding environment and that the initial burst of air causes significant energy well into the 15 kHz range. Despite these common aspects, previous studies [40] show that the pathological processes in the lungs can determine the characteristics of coughing sounds, depending on how lung tissue and vocal resonances are affected. This is why people with different pathological conditions can have different cough sounds.

Figure 2 also shows a close-up of the cough spectrogram. Notice the substantial amount of high frequency content after the burst of sound. This is due to the fourth stage of the cough reflex in which the remaining air from the initial impulse is pushed out of the vocal tract [24, 40]. The differences in cough sounds between different people are largely isolated to the segment of time during this fourth stage. Lastly, notice the cough duration is approximately 300 ms. Empirical measures show coughs range in duration from 300-500 ms [24]. In our approach we leverage the fact that the first 150 ms of a cough sound corresponds only to the explosive phase of the cough reflex and is generally consistent across observers. We only model this explosive stage of the cough reflex so that our model can generalize across observers.

Quantifying Coughs

According to the European Respiratory Society [30], coughing can be quantified in four different ways: (1) *Explosive cough sounds*: the number of characteristic explosive cough impulses. (2) *Cough seconds*: the number of seconds per hour containing at least one explosive cough sound. (3) *Cough breaths*: the number of breaths containing at least one cough. (4) *Cough epochs*: the number continuous cough sounds where each cough is separated by no more than two seconds. The effectiveness of any one of these metrics over the other is still ongoing research. We focus on *explosive cough sounds* because the other three measures can be inferred from this quantity.

DATA COLLECTION AND ANNOTATION

We now turn our attention to creating a labeled audio corpus for evaluating our approach. Participants experiencing coughing episodes were recruited and told to wear a mobile phone (either in shirt pocket or around the neck) that continually recorded their surrounding audio throughout their normal day. These audio streams were manually annotated, labeling all events as one of nine categories, described below in detail.

Data Collection

Seventeen participants, symptomatic of cough before enrollment, were recruited from a local health center. Participants ranged in age from 18 to 60 years old, and 7 of them were females. Their causes of cough include common cold (n=8), asthma (n=3), allergies (n=1) and chronic cough (n=5) due to various reasons including smoking. Table 3 shows these demographic details.

The participants first came to the lab and we explained the recording process. We provided each with an Android G1 mobile phone and asked them to carry the mobile phone around their neck or in their shirt pocket and continue their daily routines. The audio recording software was turned on to record all of the sounds around the participants at 32 kHz using 16 bits. Figure 1 shows our experimental set-up. In all, 72 hours of audio were recorded, resulting in 2,558 cough sounds which occur inside 1,016 coughing episodes. This cough dataset is comparable in size to the datasets used in prior work, however our dataset incorporates a more diverse set of cough events [2, 13, 27]. See Table 2 for a summary of other dataset used in prior work.

Annotation

In order to obtain accurate annotations of the 72 hours of audio recordings, we recruited 6 linguistic students to manually annotate the audio recordings using Praat [5], a scientific software tool for analyzing phonetic sounds and annotate them. The linguists were asked to annotate all sounds with one of the following nine labels: cough (n=2558, 12.2 min), speech (n=5404, 15.8 hr), laughter (n=819, 14 min), breathing (n=522, 11.2 min), throat-clearing (n=1210, 10.23 min), sneezing (n=53, 35 sec), sniffing (n=1289, 9.2 min), other people's cough (n=901, 5.66 min), and environmental noise (n=7296, 28.5 hr). A total of 278 hours were spent completing the annotation of the 72 hours of audio recordings. It took almost 3.9 hours to annotate each hour of audio recording because 62% of the recordings contained ambiguous audio activity which often required the annotators to listen to the clip multiple times. In addition, some ambiguous sounds required discussion among the annotators, researchers, and experts before it was classified into one of the nine categories. If a conclusion could not be made, the event was labeled as unknown and excluded from further analysis. After a sound was labeled by an annotator, it was then verified by a researcher for accuracy. This careful attention was taken to ensure that the annotations were as accurate as possible.

Self Report

We also explicitly asked subjects to keep track of how many times they coughed during the recording process and report this to us after they returned. No correlation existed between self report and the annotated number of coughs. As shown in Table 3, when comparing self report with the annotations, the average difference was 22.8 cough sounds per hour with a standard deviation of 33 cough sounds per hour (i.e., most subjects severely underreported their cough occurrences). The minimum difference was 6 cough sounds per hour while the maximum difference was 149 cough sounds per hour. This highlights the inherent inaccuracy of self report even when patients are primed to monitor their cough for part of the day.

ALGORITHM METHODOLOGY

We use our cough event corpus to inform the design of our cough detection algorithm. Recall that our design objectives were to create an accurate classifier that used features which could also be used to reconstruct the cough sounds, but could not be used to reconstruct other sounds, such as speech. A key element of the design is to retain the fidelity of coughs so that a physician can asses them for diagnosis, and so that false positives can be removed audibly, if needed. During evaluation, we divide the corpus into five folds across the participants. Each fold contains all of the audio data for three or four participants.

Subject Demographics and Dataset		
# Subjects	17	7 Female,10 male
Age Range	18 – 60,	μ.=27, *mode*=25
Diagnosis	3 Asthma, 5 Chronic, 8 Cold, 1 Allergy	
Audio Recorded per Subject	3 – 6.5 hrs	μ =4.2, *mode*=3
Coughs per Subject	33 – 894,	μ =150, *mode*=79
Coughs/Hour	10 – 178,	μ =33, *mode*=15
Difference from Self Report	6 – 139 cough/hr	μ =22.8, *mode*=20
Total Coughs	2558 coughs	1016 epochs

Table 3. Demographic information and number of coughs collected of all the participants.

The algorithm can be divided into four parts: (1) cough model generation, (2) event extraction, (3) cough classification, and (4) cough reconstruction. Before any processing we remove all audio data from the corpus for participants in a given fold. In subsequent discussion we refer to the removed data as the test fold and the remaining data as the training fold. In this way, the cough detection for a single participant's coughs was not trained upon using any audio data from that participant.

Cough Model Generation

During this step of the algorithm we create a cough model for the training fold using PCA on the audio spectrogram [18]. Recall that our audio is recorded at a 32 kHz sampling rate. We first take the magnitude spectrogram of the entire audio sequence (using a hamming window size of 16 ms, 50% overlap, and 512 point FFT). We then select, at random, 40 annotated coughs from each participant in the training fold. For each cough we place the first 150 ms of cough into a single column vector and normalize the vector. We then concatenate each column vector to create a matrix of cough spectrograms, $\boldsymbol{X}$. PCA is run on $\boldsymbol{X}$, yielding a matrix of eigenvectors (components). We save the N components with the largest eigenvalues. This becomes our cough model, $\widehat{\boldsymbol{X}}_N$, where the subscript, N, denotes the number of components in the model. This is similar to the approach used in the face recognition algorithm called "Eigenfaces" [42]; the components in our cough model are analogous to "Eigenface" components.

We then reconstruct the training data spectrograms from $\widehat{\boldsymbol{X}}_{10}$ saving the projection weights used for reconstruction, along with the residual error of the reconstructed spectrogram (11 features). In addition, we also calculate three energy measures of the spectrogram. Namely, the mean decibel energy of the entire FFT, the mean decibel energy of the FFT coefficients above 16 kHz, and below 16 kHz. The energy values, component weights, and residual error are hereafter referred to as our feature set (14 features). For classification of the cough sounds, we found that our model only needed 10 components for reliable classification.

However, the fidelity of the reconstructed coughs can be increased by using a larger number of components, at the expense of making speech more intelligible. We quantify this tradeoff later.

Event Extraction

We use the feature set of our training fold to create a simple extraction algorithm based on thresholds. The algorithm prunes the audio stream, searching for potential events. For each feature, we calculate the threshold at which 98% of the coughs in the training fold are retained regardless of the false positives. We then select five features (out of all 14) with the lowest false positive rates on the training fold. The thresholds of these five features are saved so that they can be used in pruning the audio of the test fold during evaluation. On average, the event extraction retained 96% of the coughs in the training fold, while letting between 5% and 16% of other audio through.

Cough Classification

After event extraction, we train a random forest (RF) classifier [6] on the feature set of extracted events in the training fold. All features are used to train the classifier. The RF classifier is set to weight cough errors more during the building of the forest, and the majority voting threshold for the cough class is set three times lower than non-cough sounds. The max number of trees was set to 500 (as over fitting is rarely a problem in RF classifiers). These parameters, however, were not investigated extensively because of the prohibitive time involved in training and evaluating the models. We ran a few variations on a small subset of the data (about two hours of audio from two participants) and found these parameters to work well. Many different classifiers could be used—we use a RF classifier because it has empirically been shown to work as well as support vector machines and neural networks, but is less sensitive to parameter variation [6].

Cough Sound Reconstruction

For audio reconstruction (if the actual cough sound needs to be replayed), we use the optimal PCA reconstruction method, designed to minimize mean-squared error between the reconstruction and vector of interest [33]. That is, for a given spectrogram, we stack 150 ms of adjacent columns into a normalized column vector, $\boldsymbol{a}$. The reconstruction is

$$\widehat{\boldsymbol{a}} = \widehat{\boldsymbol{X}}_N \widehat{\boldsymbol{X}}_N^{\,T}(\boldsymbol{a} - \bar{a}) + \bar{a}$$

where $\bar{a}$ is the mean of $\boldsymbol{a}$ and $\widehat{\boldsymbol{X}}_N^{\,T}(\boldsymbol{a} - \bar{a})$ are the projection weights (an N element row vector). This provides us with an estimate of the overall spectrogram magnitude for a 150 ms segment of audio. We then remove the stacking and normalization, and reapply the phase of the original spectrogram. We then convert the spectrogram back to the time domain signal by: (1) performing the inverse short time Fourier transform (ISTFT) and (2) applying an inverse hamming window. Figure 2 shows an example reconstruction. We note that to perform reconstruction a mobile platform must send the mean, $\bar{a}$, normalization constant, and phase of the spectrogram in addition to the projection

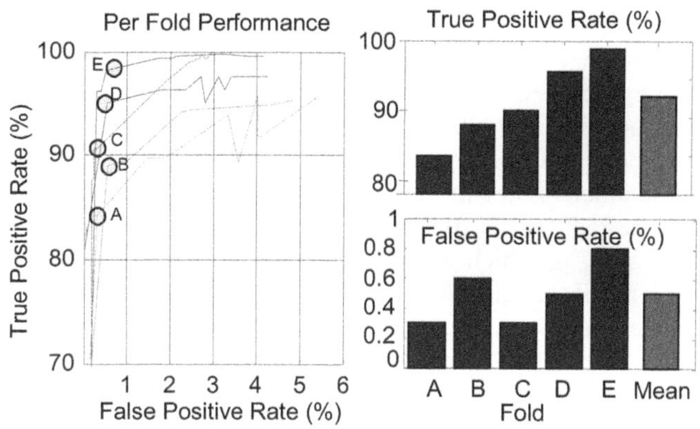

Figure 3. Receiver operating characteristic (ROC) for models trained on five folds of our dataset. "Good" tradeoff points in the ROC are also graphed to the right in column form.

weights. These quantities do not increase the privacy vulnerabilities of the system because phase and mean have historically been found to have little use in speech or speaker recognition. In fact, most recognition algorithms ignore phase or only use it in conjunction with the magnitude [e.g., 32, 45].

CLASSIFICATION PERFORMANCE

We evaluate our random forest classification method using five-fold cross-validation, across subjects, as discussed previously. We obtain receiver operating characteristic (ROC) curves for each test fold by varying parameters of the RF models. This results in changes to the false positive rate and true positive rate that can be plotted to show the tradeoffs in adjusting each RF model. Figure 3 shows the tradeoff in performance for each fold. We define a true positive to be any explosive cough sound that contains at least two consecutive classifier identifications in the same 300 ms window (this is the finest resolution we can achieve as dictated by our PCA and spectrogram implementations). We define a false positive to be any consecutive classifier identifications that do not occur within 10 seconds of an actual explosive cough sound. This is divided by the total number of overlapping 10 second windows in our test folds. This is a standard measure of false positives used in cough detection [4, 26]. Notice that all but one fold rapidly approaches a 90% true positive rate while false positives are below 1%. Also note that we report true and false positive rates using all audio from the database, *not* just events that are pruned from the "event extraction" phase.

Detection Rate and False Alarms

If we take the "best" performance of each classifier to be the highest true positive rate achieved while simultaneously having a false positive rate less than 1% we achieve sensitivities of 85%, 89%, 91%, 96%, and 99% for each fold with a mean of 92%. The respective false positive rates are 0.3%, 0.6%, 0.3%, 0.5%, and 0.8% with a mean of 0.5%. These points are marked in Figure 3 with a circle and graphed across each fold, A-E. When comparing to other cough detection algorithms, however, the false positive rates cannot be directly compared. This is because each algorithm uses a slightly varied sampling window of the audio data. Instead, the false alarms per hour are a better indication of the number of falsely classified sounds one can expect. The respective number of false alarms per hour for each fold is 7, 20, 17, 29, and 12 with a mean of 17. We also note that one can reduce this value by trading off model parameters. For instance, the mean false alarms per hour can be reduced to 10.7 by trading off a mean true positive rate of 82%, which is comparable to the state of the art in automated cough detection [4, 26, 27]. Alternatively, a trained annotator can review the collected events and discard false positive sounds, as is done with some of the existing cough detection systems. For our dataset this would require reviewing, on average, 1.4 minutes of audio per hour of recording. This time could be further reduced by having the annotator only review identifications that had low confidences from the classifier.

Confusions

An analysis of the false positives in the dataset reveals that coughs are most often confused for "noise" labels (56% of the actual false positive) and for "speech" labels (43% of the false positives). The remaining 1% of false positives are distributed among "breathing" and "laughter" events. This further stresses the importance of disguising or suppressing the audio for false positives. Roughly half of the false positives to be reviewed would be speech that the wearer never intended to be heard, even by a medical professional.

PRIVACY AND FIDELITY CHARACTERIZATION

We now turn our discussion to assessing how well the components actually disguise speech, while also preserving the fidelity of received coughs. We designed two psychoacoustic experiments aimed at quantifying each design goal. Although our classifier only required 10 bases for high precision, we used 5, 10, 15, 25, and 50 bases in the reconstruction to fully characterize the privacy/fidelity tradeoff.

Experiment 1: Speech Intelligibility

During the first experiment, listeners were asked to dictate the words in 8 segments of speech from our audio corpus. Each segment was 5 seconds long and contained a different speaker (4 male, 4 female). The complication of the speech audio ranged from 4 words up to 21, in various environmental settings from study group conversations, people walking and talking, to quiet settings with almost no environmental noises. Listeners performed the test using a custom interface. They were allowed to listen to the speech segment as many times as they wanted and review and change their dictations at any time. Listeners were also encouraged to give their best guess at the speech, even if they felt it was not wholly intelligible. For instance, if they could only spot a few keywords, they were asked to write those dictations in and any words that they could possibly discern from the context of the keyword.

Each listener heard either a clean version of the speech segment (baseline) or one of five reconstructed versions using 5, 10, 15, 25 or 50 components. 24 observers dictated the speech with, on average, each degraded recording being listened to by 4 listeners. Each listener reported that they

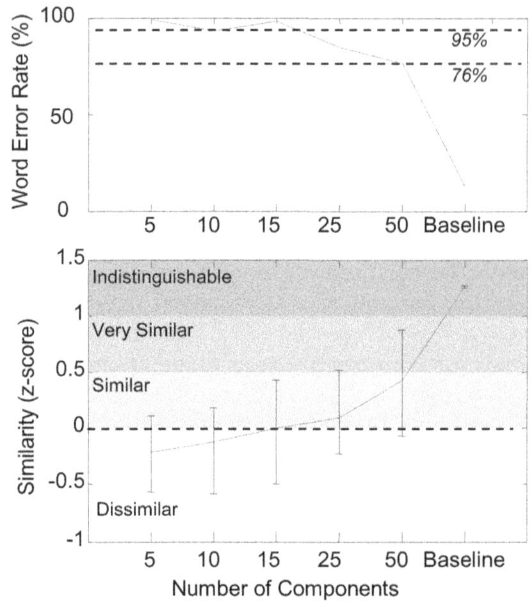

Figure 4. (Top) Word error rate plotted versus the number of model components. (Bottom) Similarity scores (z-scores) of reconstructed cough sounds; error bars are the interquartile range.

were English speakers (n=20) or fluent in the English language (n=4). After completion, two reviewers (one author, one third-party) analyzed all the dictations assessing the number of words that listener's dictated incorrectly. There was good agreement between reviewers; out of the 1,932 words looked at by each reviewer there were only 32 discrepancies.

Intelligibility Results

Figure 4 shows the results of the word error rate as a function of the number of eigenvectors used in reconstruction. The privacy of speech is well protected when using 15 or less components (i.e., >95% of the words are unintelligible). At 25 components, the word error rate begins to drop. However, even at 50 components, the listener's are still only able to spot keywords in the phrases for a total word error rate of 76%. We found on average, that longer speech segments were more difficult to reconstruct. Even at 50 components, if the number of words in the phrase was greater than 15, one can expect a word error rate of about 92%. The shorter phrases (less than 7 words) can sometimes be guessed by spotting keywords and inferring surrounding words, with error rates of about 65% using 50 components.

Experiment 2: Assessing Cough Fidelity

In the second experiment users performed a single stimulus two-alternate forced choice (2-AFC) task in which they were presented with two cough sounds. One was a clean version of the original cough sound, and the other was a reconstructed version of the same cough sound. The order of the cough sounds was randomized. Users where given two tasks: (1) they were asked to judge which cough sounded more natural, and (2) they were asked to rate the similarity of the coughs in terms of fidelity on a five point scale which ranged from "very different," "somewhat different," "somewhat similar," "very similar," to "same cough sound." If they decided the coughs were the same, their judgment of which cough sounded more natural was discarded. Preferences were entered using radio buttons that defaulted to a position of "not set" for each 2-AFC trial. The listeners could go back and forth between tests (the interface remembers and displays their answers as they go backwards and forwards through each forced choice) and they could listen to any trial as many times as they wished even as they reviewed their responses. The listeners were informed that the cough sounds were of the same recording, but with varying degrees of distortion. For some trials the listener was presented with two reference cough sounds.

A total of 12 cough recordings were chosen for the experiment (6 male, 6 female) which occurred in a variety of environments from conference rooms and atriums to outdoor settings. The length of the audio segments ranged from 1-2 seconds. Half of the sounds were chosen at random from the corpus and half were selected by hand to be sure a wide range of cough types were chosen. Each cough sound was reconstructed using 5, 10, 15, 25, and 50 components, resulting in 60 different cough recordings in addition to the 12 original. One reason we chose a small, but diverse number of cough sounds was so we could investigate whether any particular cough is always reconstructed with high or poor fidelity using a relatively small number of listeners. Each listener reviewed 30 cough sounds per session. After the experiment, we converted each observer's similarity selections into z-scores. We removed the first five responses from each listener to account for any learning curve the listener may have had. In all, 27 listeners participated for a total of 810 subjective ratings. On average, each degraded cough sound was rated by 13 listeners.

Fidelity Results

Figure 4 shows the results of the second experiment. The mean similarity (z-score) is plotted versus the number of components used in the reconstruction. Error bars are shown around the 25th and 75th percentiles of the z-scores. In all cases the participants could distinguish which cough sounds had been reconstructed and which were natural (i.e., no cough sound was rated as indistinguishable). This result is not wholly surprising. Manipulating the spectrogram often results in audible artifacts that are easy for the listener to cue in upon [32, 46]. The degree of similarity, then, becomes the quantity of interest.

The threshold of similarity was found to be about 15 components. Coughs reconstructed with less than 15 components were found to almost always be rated as dissimilar. Coughs with 25 to 50 components were found to almost always be rated similar or very similar. A Wilcoxon rank test [43] can be used to validate when there is a significant jump in the median similarity score (at 95% confidence). The test reveals that there is a significant difference in the median scores for using 5-10 components versus 25-50. There is also a significant difference for cough sounds with 5-25 versus 50 components. All other comparisons reveal the null hypothesis cannot be rejected with high confidence.

These findings reveal, at 15 components, one can expect about half the coughs to have "good" fidelity while simultaneously making almost all speech unintelligible. Higher similarities can be achieved, however, if one is willing to sacrifice the privacy of some keywords in their conversations. At 50 components, for example, the resulting cough will almost always be "similar" or "very similar," while making only certain words intelligible. It is likely that the context of the conversation will remain hidden to a listener. This is in contrast to the cough event detection, which only required 10 components.

DISCUSSION AND LIMITATIONS

It is of note that the classifier never confused a bystander's cough for a cough of the subject. This is likely because of the mobile phone placement. One of the reasons we chose to deploy the mobile phone around our participants' neck or in the shirt pocket is because these positions provide a short distance between the microphone and subject's mouth and should receive the best audio quality. However, they might not be the best positions in terms of comfort. According to our participants, the best positions in terms of comfort would be the pants pocket or in bags/purses. Audio signals recorded at these positions will likely require the use of a lapel microphone or Bluetooth headset.

One limitation of this study is that we only look at the details of a cough detection algorithm, without a complete system. We are currently porting our feature extraction algorithm over to a T-Mobile G1 mobile phone platform (rather than an offline calculation). Our initial cough extraction is threshold based and should easily run on a mobile device. This simple extraction algorithm prevents us from sending frivolous features to our server for classification. However, this does not account for *battery life* of the phone, only the real time aspects. We are currently looking at hardware accelerations and algorithmic approximations that can extend the battery life of a system running our algorithm. Additionally, we are exploring using our algorithm on phones as they charge overnight to assess the cough frequency patterns of subjects while they sleep. Traditionally, listening devices in the bedroom or at home have been considered invasive, but our algorithm, because it preserves speech privacy, may mitigate these concerns.

This last point brings up an interesting opportunity for future work. Our algorithm has been shown to preserve speech privacy, but there are other forms of private audio information that may still be vulnerable. For instance, environmental noises may still be intelligible, exposing location or activities. Also, it is unclear whether our algorithm can hide *who* is speaking in an audio stream and the gender of speakers. These are important avenues for future research.

Although we were able to show that subjective listening tests reveal increasing sound similarity, our work is largely informed by working with pulmonologist. More work is still needed to find the effective tradeoff for cough quality from the medical community. It is important to quantify the number of components that can capture key features of the cough that physicians consider important for diagnosis.

CONCLUSION

In this paper, we present a mobile phone-based sensing and inference technique for detecting and counting individual coughs using a commodity mobile phone's built-in microphone in a real world environment. We implement PCA on audio spectrograms for classification and for retaining cough fidelity, while simultaneously disguising and suppressing speech sounds. Our system attempts to address all of the design goals for an objective cough monitoring system as outlined by the medical community: accuracy, low false positives, privacy preservation, mobility, compactness, and unobtrusiveness [14, 20, 30].

REFERENCES

1. AsthmaMD, http://www.asthmamd.org
2. Barry SJ, Dane AD, Morice AH, and Walmsley AD (2006). The automatic recognition and counting of cough. *Cough*.
3. Bickerman HA and Itkin SE (1958). The effect of a new bronchodilator aerosol on the airflow dynamics of the maximal voluntary cough of patients with bronchial asthma and pulmonary emphysema. *J Chron Dis*.
4. Birring SS, Fleming T, Matos S, Raj AA, EvansDH, and Pavord ID (2008). The Leicester Cough Monitor: preliminary validation of an automated cough detection system in chronic cough. *Eur Respir J*.
5. Boersma P and Weenink D. Praat: doing phonetic by computer, http://www.praat.org
6. Breiman, L (2001). Random Forests. *Machine Learning*, 5–32.
7. Cerry DK, Hing E, Woodwell D, and Rechtsteiner E (2006). *National Ambulatory Medical Care Survey: Summary*.
8. Chang AB and Gibson PG (2002). Relationship between cough, cough receptor sensitivity and asthma in children. *Pulm. Pharmacol. Ther.*
9. Chen F, Adcock J, and Krishnagiri J (2008). Audio Privacy: Reducing Speech Intelligibility while Preserving Environmental Sounds. *MM'08*.
10. Chiu MC, Chang SP, Chang YC, Chu HH, Chen CC, Hsiao FH, and Ko JC (2009). Playful Bottle: a Mobile Social Persuasion System to Motivate Healthy Water Intake, *Proceedings of UbiComp*.
11. Chung K and Pavord I (2008). Prevalence, pathogenesis, and causes of chronic cough. *The Lancet*, 1364-1374.
12. Consolvo S, Mcdonald D, Toscos T, Chen M, Froehlich J, Beverly H, Klasnja P, LaMarca A, Legrand L, Libby R, Smith I, and Landay J (2008). Activity Sensing in the Wild: A Field Trial of UbiFit Garden, *Proceedings of CHI*.
13. Coyle MA, Keenan DB, Henderson LS, *et al.* (2005). Evaluation of an ambulatory system for the quantification of cough frequency in patients with chronic obstructive pulmonary disease. *Cough*.
14. Decalmer SC, Webster D, Kelsall AA, McGuinness K, Woodcock AA, and Smith JA (2007). Chronic cough: how do cough reflex sensitivity and subjective assessments correlate with objective cough counts during ambulatory monitoring? *Thorax*, 329-34.
15. Gibson PG, Chang AB, Glasgow NJ, Holmes PW, Katelaris P, Kemp AS, Landau LI, Mazzone S, Newcombe P, Van Asperen P, and Vertigan AE (2010). CICADA: Cough in Children and Adults: Diagnosis and Assessment. *Australian cough guidelines summary statement. Med J Aust*, 265-71.
16. Gross V, Reinke C, Dette F, and Koch R (2007). Mobile nocturnal long-term monitoring of wheezing and cough. *Biomed Tech*,73–76.
17. Hoglung NJ and Michaelson M (1905). A method for determining the cough threshold with, some preliminary experiments on the effect of codeine. *Acta Physical Scand*, 168-173.
18. Hotelling H (1933). Analysis of a Complex of Statistical Variables Into Principal Components, *Journal of Educational Psychology*, 417-520.
19. Information Resources Inc. (2008) *OTC Market Size Statistics*.
20. Irwin RS, Bolser DC, Braman SS, *et al.* (2006). Diagnosis and Management of Cough Executive Summary: *ACCP Evidence-Based Clinical Practice Guidelines. Chest*. Suppl. 1S–23S.
21. Kerem E, Hirawat S, Harmoni S, Yaakov Y, Shoseyov D, Cohen, *et al.* (2008). Effectiveness of PTC124 treatment of cystic fibrosis caused by nonsense mutations: a prospective phase II trial. *Lancet*, 719-27.
22. Kerem E, Wilschanski M, Miller NL, Pugatsch T, Cohen T, Blau H, Rivlin J, Shoseyov D, Reha A, Constantine S, Ajayi T, Hirawat S, Elfring GL, Peltz SW, and Miller LL (2011). Ambulatory quantitative waking and sleeping cough assessment in patients with cystic fibrosis. *J Cyst Fibros*.
23. Khan J, Wei1 J, Ringnér M, Saal L, Ladanyi M, Westermann F, Berthold F, Schwab M, Antonescu C, Peterson C, and Meltzer P (2001). Classification and diagnostic prediction of cancers using gene expr-ession profiling and artificial neural networks. *Nature Medicine*.
24. Korpas J, Sadlonova J, and Vrabec M (1996). Analysis of the cough sound: an overview. *Pulm Pharmacol*, 261–268.
25. Kraman SS, Wodicka GR, Pressler GA, Pasterkamp H (2006). Comparison of lung sound transducers using a bioacoustic transducer testing system. *J Appl Physiol*, 469–476.
26. Matos S, Birring SS, Pavord ID, and Evans DH (2006). Detection of cough signals in continuous audio recordings using hidden Markov models. *IEEE Trans Biomed Eng*, 1078–1083.
27. McGuinness K, Kelsall A, Lowe J, Woodcock A, and Smith JA (2007). Automated cough detection: a novel approach. *Am J Resp Crit Care Med*
28. McGuinness K, Morice A, Woodcock A and Smith J (2010). The Leicester Cough Monitor: a semi-automated, semi-validated cough detection system? *European Respiratory Journal*, 529-530.
29. Miravitlles M, Murio C, Guerrero T, and Gisbert R (2002). Pharmacoeconomic evaluation of acute exacerbations of chronic bronchitis and COPD. *Chest*, 1449-55.
30. Morice AH, Fontana GA, Belvisi MG, Birring SS, Chung, KF, Dicpinigatis PV, Kastelik JA, Smith JA, Tatar M, and Widdicombe J (2007). *ERS guidelines on the assessment of cough, Eur Respir J.*
31. Newcombe PA, Sheffield JK, Juniper EF, Petsky HL, Willis C, and Chang AB (2010). Validation of a parent-proxy quality of life questionnaire for pediatric chronic cough (PC-QOL). *Thorax*. 819-23.
32. Pathak M (2010). *Privacy Preserving Techniques for Speech Processing*. PhD Thesis. Carnegie Melon.
33. Pearson K (1901). On lines and planes of closest fit to systems of points in space, *Philosophical Magazine*, 559-572.
34. Piirila P and Sovijarvi ARA (1995). Objective assessment of cough, *Eur Respir J*, 1949-1956.
35. Pinkowski B (1997). Principal Components Analysis of Spectrogram Images. *Pattern Recognition*, 777-787.
36. Raj A and Birring S (2007). Clinical assessment of chronic cough severity, *Pulmonary Pharmacology and Therapeutics*, Vol. 20, Issue 4.
37. Sanders DB, Hoffman LR, Emerson J, Gibson RL, Rosenfeld M, and Redding GJ (2010). Return of FEV1 after pulmonary exacerbation in children with cystic fibrosis. *Pediatr Pulmonol.*, 127-34.
38. Schappert S, Burt C, and Ed E (2006). Ambulatory Care Visits to Physician Offices, Hospital Outpatient Departments, and Emergency Departments: United States 2001-02, *Vital Health Stat 13,* 1-66.
39. Seemungal TA, Donaldson GC, Bhowmik A, Jeffries DJ, and Wedzicha JA (2000). Time course and recovery of exacerbations in patients with chronic obstructive pulmonary disease. *Am J Respir Crit Care Med*. 1608-13.
40. Smith JA and Woodcock A (2008). New development in the objective assessment of cough, *Lung,* 186.
41. Spencer S and Jones PW (2003). Time course of recovery of health status following an infective exacerbation of chronic bronchitis. *Thorax,* 589-93.
42. Turk M and Pentland A (1991). Face recognition using eigenfaces. *Proc. IEEE Conf on Comp. Vision and Patt. Rec.* 586–591.
43. Wilcoxon F (Dec 1945). Individual comparisons by ranking methods. *Biometrics Bulletin*, 80–83.
44. Witten I. and Frank E (2005). Data Mining: Practical machine learning tools and techniques, 2nd Edition, Morgan Kaufmann, San Francisco.
45. World Health Organization (2001). *Cough and cold remedies for the treatment of acute respiratory infections in young children*. Geneva, Switzerland: World Health Organization.
46. Wyatt D, Choudhury T, and Blimes J (Aug 2007). Conversation Detection and Speaker Segmentation in Privacy Sensitive Situated Speech Data. *Proceedings of Interspeech*

Passive and In-situ Assessment of Mental and Physical Well-being using Mobile Sensors

Mashfiqui Rabbi*
Dept. of Information Science
Cornell University
ms2749@cornell.edu

Shahid Ali
Community and Family Medicine
Dartmouth Medical School
shahid.a.ali@dartmouth.edu

Tanzeem Choudhury*
Dept. of Information Science
Cornell University
tanzeem.choudhury@cornell.edu

Ethan Berke
Community and Family Medicine
Dartmouth Medical School
ethan.berke@tdi.dartmouth.edu

ABSTRACT
The idea of continuously monitoring well-being using mobile-sensing systems is gaining popularity. In-situ measurement of human behavior has the potential to overcome the short comings of gold-standard surveys that have been used for decades by the medical community. However, current sensing systems have mainly focused on tracking physical health; some have approximated aspects of mental health based on proximity measurements but have not been compared against medically accepted screening instruments. In this paper, we show the feasibility of a multi-modal mobile sensing system to simultaneously assess mental and physical health. By continuously capturing fine-grained motion and privacy-sensitive audio data, we are able to derive different metrics that reflect the results of commonly used surveys for assessing well-being by the medical community. In addition, we present a case study that highlights how errors in assessment due to the subjective nature of the responses could potentially be avoided by continuous mobile sensing.

Author Keywords
mental health, physical health, activity inference, mobile sensing, machine learning.

ACM Classification Keywords
H.1.2 User/Machine Systems; I.5 Pattern Recognition; J.3 Life and Medical Sciences.

General Terms
Algorithms, Experimentation.

INTRODUCTION
One of the pillars of population health is to improve overall quality of life by promoting cognitive, physical and mental well-being [1, 2]. Everyday behaviors are often reflective of physical and mental health and can be predictive of future health problems. The standard practice for collecting behavioral data in the health sciences relies on observational data collected in laboratory settings or through periodic recall surveys or self-reports. These proxy measures have several limitations: (i) the time and resource requirements are too high to simultaneously gather data from a large number of individuals; (ii) the measurements are prone to considerable bias and the manual and sporadic recording of information often fails to capture the finer details of behavior that may be important; and (iii) the end user effort is too high to be suitable for continuous long-term monitoring.

With continued rises in medical costs, the need for a model that screens and facilitates early diagnosis, as well as increased efforts in prevention, is an essential concern for health-care providers and administrators. Consequently, a growing number of studies are demonstrating potential of behavior monitoring devices to assist in one or more of the three clinical applications mentioned above [3, 4, 5]. The ultimate vision is to develop a mobile sensing system that can contribute significantly to cognitive, physical and mental well-being while maintaining easy and universal applicability, security and patient privacy protection, and low cost.

BACKGROUND
Monitoring physical activity and mental health has been extensively investigated in the past via a variety of traditional recall surveys or Ecological Momentary Assessments (EMA) [6]. Paper-based surveys like Yale Physical Activity Survey (YPAS) [7], SF-36 [8], and Center for Epidemiological Studies - Depression (CES-D) [9] are examples of commonly accepted surveys and are some of the primary metrics for assessing physical and mental well-being in medicine. These paper-based surveys utilize recall techniques to capture daily, weekly, and seasonal patterns of behavior, but may require in-person administration and are limited by recall bias, memory dependence, current mood, and their obtrusive nature [10, 11]. Furthermore, answers to the paper-based survey questions are subjective, with risk of social de-

UbiComp'11, September 17–21, 2011, Beijing, China.

* The work presented here was done while both the authors were in the Computer Science department at Dartmouth College.

sirability bias, and sometimes suffer from issues like "backfilling" due to non-adherence to time-sensitive protocols (i.e. completing daily surveys at end of the week [6]). Electronic survey tools such as digital diaries, smart-phone and web-based surveys allow investigators to tailor and improve survey questions dynamically, reduce recall bias by collecting responses close in time to one's experience, and avoid backfilling by digitally time-stamping the submitted surveys. However, recall surveys and EMA, both paper-based and electronic, do not capture activities continuously and rely on the subjects to be responsive, can be cumbersome, and may require periodic re-administration, thereby hindering their consistent use in the primary care setting.

More recently, a variety of sensor-based systems have emerged with great potential of circumventing recall limitation and subjective dependence of aforementioned techniques. These sensor-based systems differ in their mobility, placements, numbers, and continuity in data capture, and have their own advantages and limitations. For example, video camera and RFID equipped rooms have been used to capture physical activity and sleep patterns for users [12]. These systems usually capture a portion of user's daily life and can be prohibitively costly for mass use. In contrast, wearable single-sensor devices such as pedometers and monoaxial accelerometers have been used to measure physical activity continuously and unobtrusively while observing subjects in their natural environment [13, 14, 15]. Although useful, single-sensor based systems are limited in the types of activities they can capture. To overcome this limitation, investigators have used a combination of multiple sensors placed on different locations of the body to learn more about subject behavior [16]. These systems can capture a richer set of activities and can yield higher accuracy in recognizing activities. Another approach investigators have explored is the use of single mobile devices equipped with multiple types of sensors. Devices such as Actigraph [17], Sensewear [18], the Mobile Sensing Platform (MSP) [19] and LifeShirt system (Vivometrics, Ventura, CA) [20] provide versatility by detecting different modalities ranging from light and directional acceleration to physiological signals. These devices and new sensor-equipped smartphones have been used in a wide range of applications ranging from measurement of physical activity and energy expenditure to providing context-aware instantaneous feedback with goal of preventing future health complications. Furthermore, a network of wearable sensors communicating with a central server has demonstrated the potential benefits of monitoring and assisting in the care of the aged, a rapidly growing subset of population [21].

In contrast, the use of automated sensing techniques in assessing mental health has been very limited. Mental illness costs $30.7 billion/year [22] in the US alone. Depression, a common psychiatric disorder, has a prevalence of 5-25% [23, 24] and contributes significantly to the cost of healthcare [25, 26]. Previous research has shown that increased social activity correlates negatively with depressive behavior and can even improve depressive symptoms [27, 28]. Others have demonstrated using subjective methods that physical activity delays cognitive decline [29]. Some aspects of mental health have been approximated using proximity measurements [30]. We feel proximity based approach has three potential limitations: (i) its inability to detect reduction in physical activity and speech limits availability of useful information for clinicians to treate and manage mental dysfunction, (ii) interactions inferred from speech and colocation have been shown to be different [31], thus it is possible that behavioral indicators of social isolation may be manifesting itself but not being detected by colocation, and (iii) the system has not been compared against medically approved screening techniques validated in the medical literature and used in practice. Nonetheless, purely proximity based approaches may be a useful tool to screen for mental health risk but we believe a detailed measure of *behavior* will be more useful to practitioners for diagnosis purposes and is a worthy line of investigation. There is also a growing body of evidence supporting the use of acoustical properties of speech to detect changes in emotional health [32], variations in mood [33, 34] and periods of stress [35]. Furthermore, voice analysis can detect changes in verbal initiation (difficulty in starting sentences) and perseveration, characteristics highly associated with changes in mental health and inability to perform Instrumental Activities of Daily Living [36]. We believe these results, together with the fact that face-to-face conversations, are still perceived as a common and important medium for social communication [37], make the continuous study of human speech in people's daily life a valuable line of investigation for mental health assessment.

CONTRIBUTIONS

In this paper we present an automated system for measuring mental well-being from behavioral indicators in natural everyday settings, in addition to measuring physical well-being. We describe the sensing and activity recognition system and its deployment in a real-world setting of older adults. We assess its reliability, its feasibility in this population, and its validity with established health instruments.

We hypothesized that continuous recording of daily audio patterns, specifically relating to the amount of human speech, would be linked to social and mental well-being. To address the challenges of survey implementation and test our hypothesis, we used a previously developed mobile multimodal sensor platform for continuous and objective evaluation of mental health in a small group of elders. Specific contributions include:

- Automatic analysis of the amount of speech occurring in natural settings while avoiding raw audio collection for privacy protection. Correlation between the total amount of human speech sensed and the well-established paper-based surveys for mental health like CES-D score, SF-36, and Friendship Scale, approached statistical significance for CES-D and showed statistically significant correlation for SF-36 Mental Health Component and Friendship Scale.
- In addition to mental health, an overall physical activity score was computed, based on a weighted count of sim-

ple physical activity categories including stationary (sitting/standing), walking on flat surface, walking up and down inclines. This physical activity score showed significant correlation with Yale Physical Activity Survey (YPAS), a survey commonly used by the medical community.

- Presentation of a case study that illustrates how automated sensing could potentially lead to improved screening of mental health disorders and can overcome some of the limitations of current paper-based surveys. Specifically, in a subject whose CES-D scores were well below those that would indicate depressive symptoms, the sensor-based measurements were in closer agreement with observational assessment by the physician and the medical trainee on the research team.

STUDY OVERVIEW: ASSESSING MENTAL AND PHYSICAL WELL-BEING

Fine-grained sensor data were collected continuously from a group of older adults living in a continuing care retirement community. Located at the bottom of a hill, the retirement community includes a variety of facilities including a dining center, a library, group meeting rooms, and a fitness center. Apartment buildings surround the community center and are situated at a relatively higher elevation. Sloping roads connect the community center to the apartments.

Letters were sent to resident mailboxes and posted on major announcement boards across the retirement community requesting unpaid volunteers to participate in a study on automatic sensing of mental and physical well-being. Interested residents were interviewed by the team physician to establish availability for the entirety of pilot, comfort level with electronic devices, and were selected on a first come basis as a convenience sample. Eight self-selected adults were recruited: 4 singles and 2 couples; 50% male and female. The length of the pilot study was 10 consecutive days in August 2009 from 7am to 7pm; inter-individual variability was roughly ± 2 hours for pickup and drop off times. One participant dropped from the study one day before the start of study due to personal reasons unrelated to the study protocol. Investigators found a replacement but lost one day of observation due to recruitment delay for that subject. All participants were informed of their right to leave the study at any time and briefed on the Institutional Review Board (IRB) approved pilot design, its goals, and the extent of use of the collected data. All participants accepted the terms and conditions by signing a written informed consent form during their face-to-face time with project investigators. Four surveys (CES-D, YPAS, SF-36, and Friendship Scale) [9, 7, 8, 38] were administered before and after the pilot and a usability survey was administered post-study only to evaluate participants' experience with the device, surveys, and to receive comments and concerns about the technology's potential and privacy concerns.

During data collection, each participant wore a 2-inch waist-mounted device equipped with multiple sensors: 3-axis accelerometer, barometer, light sensors, temperature sensor, humidity sensor, compass and microphone. Each device was equipped with a clip so the subject could wear it comfortably around the waist. Participants were trained one day prior to the start of the pilot on basic usage of the device. To tackle scenarios where the participants may feel uncomfortable to record, they were shown how to turn on and off the device and where to contact the medical trainee, who was always present on-site during the study. Also, acceptable ways of wearing the device were demonstrated. Participants were instructed to avoid placing the device in pockets and wet environments as the device is not waterproof. Participants received no special instruction on changing their daily routine, and were allowed to travel outside the facility with the device. At the start and end of the protocol (i.e., on two different days), participants completed a series of activities (short walk, walking up and down inclines) and engaged in casual conversation in different parts of the retirement community that amounted to approximately 80 minutes of total data (8-15 minutes of data for each subject). This data is later used to compare the recognition accuracy with previous published results [39, 40, 41, 42]. Devices were collected daily every evening, data was extracted, and batteries were recharged. Participants were asked to occasionally monitor the recording LED and were provided instructions to seek assistance from on-site support or contact one of the principal investigators (a computer scientist and a family medicine physician) in case there was an issue or if device stopped recording.

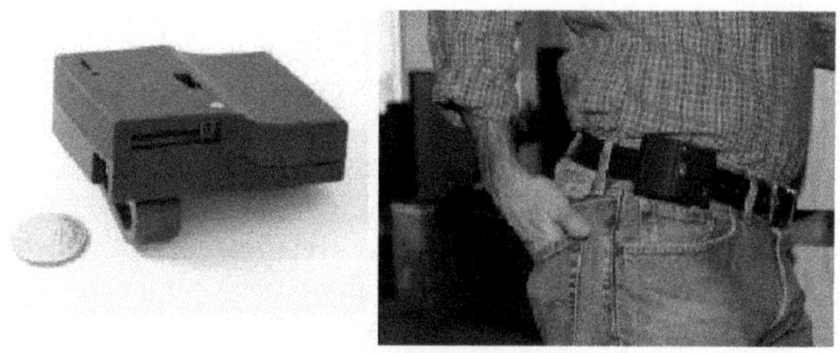

Figure 1: Mobile sensing device

Raw audio was not recorded because of privacy reasons (a detailed description of the recorded audio features are in Overview of Speech and Conversation Detection section). Although the recorded features do not allow reconstruction of audio afterwards, they enabled us to infer when human voice was present and whether there was conversation. This information is also sufficient for estimating who was speaking when, and how a specific subject was speaking (energy and pitch) [41, 43]. In this context, it is worth mentioning that during the study we learned that the privacy sensitive audio data collection was very well accepted by users, since there was no incident of a participant turning off the device or seeking assistance for turning off the device due to privacy concerns. It can be argued that we could have recorded raw audio for further analysis given such a pilot study. But we want to argue that privacy sensitive features enable us to collect data in realistic environments continuously in unobtrusive way. Furthermore, it is still possible to do interesting analysis related to health and mental well-being using non-verbal aspects of speech (e.g., pitch, speaking rate, loudness) and are supported by previous research [44, 45, 46]. In addition, the Health Insurance Portability and Accountability Act (HIPAA) provides strict guidelines on protecting personal health information. Since this act prevents access and use of health information without explicit consent of all patients, recording of raw health information becomes extremely challenging, since it is almost impossible to control when unconsented individuals in the background gets recorded. Even for our experiments, the management authority of the retirement community would not have approved continuous recording of audio. Although focused recording in pre-specified rooms may have been a possibility, it defeats the goal of our study, which aims to assess mental health from passive sensing of everyday speech in naturalistic conditions.

Participant ID	Marital Status	Age (years)
SU01	Single	90
SU02	Single	89
SU03	Married	83
SU04	Married	82
SU05	Single	93
SU06	Single	81
SU07	Married	84
SU08	Married	86

Table 1: Subject profile

Overview of Speech and Conversation Detection
Audio is processed on-the-fly to extract and record features that are informative for inferring the presence and style of speech and conversations but not enough to reconstruct the words that are spoken. We utilize the privacy-sensitive speech processing methods developed in [47, 42]. Features that are recorded include: (i) non-initial maximum auto-correlation peak, (ii) the total number of auto-correlation peaks, and (iii) relative spectral entropy – these features have been shown to be particularly useful for detecting the structure of voiced speech and are more robust than energy based methods.

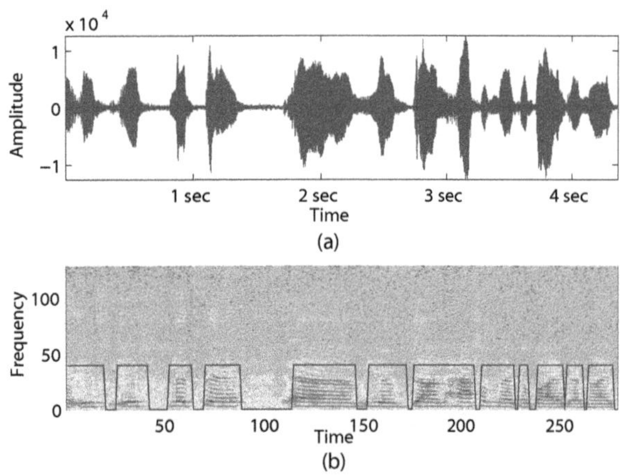

Figure 2: (a) amplitude values for 5 second recording of audio (b) spectrogram of the recording with blue lines depicting inferred human speech

The first step in the inference pipeline involves finding audio segments that contain human voice. A two-state hidden Markov model (HMM) is used to classify speech vs. non-speech segments using the aforementioned three recorded features. For each hidden state, the observation probability is modeled using a multi-variate Gaussian distribution (for a detailed description of the classification approach please see [47]). Upon detection of human voice, mutual information between voicing segments for each pair of microphones is used to find conversations among subjects. If two individuals are in the same physical environment and engaged in a conversation, they will take turns in speaking, which will result in high mutual information between the two sensor streams. If a third individual, who also happens to be wearing a device, also takes part in the conversation with the two, our method will also put the third person in conversation with the first two because conversation detection method will compute mutual information for each pair of users who are wearing the devices (for detailed discussion of the conversation detection technique please see [48, 42]).

Overview of Physical Activity Detection
Physical activities such as walking on flat surface, walking up and down on inclines, and stationary (includes both sitting and standing) were detected based on features extracted from accelerometer and barometric pressure data. We segmented the data into quarter second segments and manually labeled the activity for supervised learning and testing. The features included energy, mean, variance, and suite of spectral features for the accelerometer data, and variance and signed change in pressure over various time windows for the barometric pressure data. We use simple boosted decision-stump classifiers [49] in our current experiments to train binary activity classifiers. Boosted decision stumps have been successfully used in a variety of classification [50] tasks including human activity recognition [39, 51]. For each activity A_i, we iteratively learn an ensemble of weak binary classifiers $C^i = {c_1}^i, {c_2}^i, {c_3}^i, ..., {c_M}^i$ and their associated weights ${\alpha_m}^i$ using a variation of the AdaBoost algorithm [52]. The final output is a weighted combination of the weak classifiers. The prediction of classifier C_i is:

$$C_i = sign(\sum_m {\alpha_m}^i {c_m}^i) \quad (1)$$

The classification approach is based on the approach previously developed and validated by Lester, *et. al.*. We refer the reader to [39, 51] for further details.

Overview of Survey Instruments
Four common surveys for measuring well-being used by healthcare practitioners were administered in a pre-post study design. Subjects completed these paper-based surveys one day prior to study commencement and repeated again one day after the study was concluded (three subjects took the post-study surveys two days after the conclusion of the study). Conducetd surveys are as follows:

Friendship Scale is a self-administered [38] survey that measures six dimensions of social isolation and connectedness. Each question can be scored from 0-4 points and adds up to a total of 24 points. High scores indicate social connectedness and low scores near indicate social isolation.

SF-36 [8] is a self-administered and commonly used survey for evaluating overall well-being. Its eight sections are weighed together to produce a mental health and a physical health score. We focused on the SF-36 Mental Health Score and compared it with sensed audio measures. As an example, we present in Table 2 the questions used to obtain the mental health score based on five out of the total eight sections.

CES-D (Center for Epidemiological Study Depression Scale) is one of the most frequently used surveys to screen for depressive symptoms and behaviors. Each question is scored from 0-3 points with a maximum of 60 points. Individuals with scores 16 or higher are considered to have symptoms indicative of clinical depression [9].

YPAS (Yale Physical Activity Survey) [7] is a survey requiring administration that recalls activities performed during a typical period in the previous month. The validated survey estimates energy expenditure (kcals/week), total time spent doing vigorous or leisure activities, and provides a total activity summary index.

Dimension	Summary of Questions Used To Evaluate Dimensions
Social Functioning	During the past 4 weeks, to what extent has your physical health or emotional problems interfered with your normal social activities with family, friends, neighbors, or groups? (Not at all, slightly, Moderately, Quite a bit, Extremely) During the past 4 weeks, how much of the time has your physical health or emotional problems interfered with your social activities (like visiting friends, relatives, etc.)? (all the time, most of the time, a good bit of the time, some of the time, little of the time, none of the time)
Role Emotional	During the past 4 weeks, have you had any of the following problems with your work or other regular daily activities as a result of any emotional problems (such as feeling depressed or anxious)? 1.Cut down the amount of time you spent on work or other activities 2. Accomplished less than you would like 3. Didnt do work or other activities as carefully as usual
Mental Health	How much of the time during the past 4 weeks (all the time, most of the time, a good bit of the time, some of the time, little of the time, none of the time) 1. been a very nervous person? 2. felt so down in the dumps nothing could cheer you up? 3. felt calm and peaceful? 4. felt downhearted and blue? 5. been a happy person?
General Health	In general, would you say your health is (Excellent, Very Good, Good, Fair, Poor?) - I seem to get sick a little easier than other people (definitely true, mostly true, I dont know, mostly false, definitely false) - I am as health as anybody I know (definitely true, mostly true, I dont know, mostly false, definitely false) - I expect my health to get worse (definitely true, mostly true, I dont know, mostly false, definitely false
Vitality	How much of the time during the past 4 weeks (all the time, most of the time, a good bit of the time, some of the time, little of the time, none of the time) 1. did you feel full of pep? 2 .did you have a lot of energy? 3. did you feel worn out? 4. did you feel tired?

Table 2: Questions asked in different components of the Mental Health Score of SF-36

Evaluation Methodology

Evaluation of data collected in everyday environment is challenging as it is often impossible to have "ground-truth" for every single data point recorded. In order to be confident in our analysis and findings, we took a multi-pronged approach to evaluation. The first step was to label some data from the subjects in the retirement community and compare the physical activity and speech classification accuracy with the accuracy numbers on labeled datasets collected from other individuals in different geographical locations and from different age groups. For speech classification, the comparison dataset included more than twenty-five individuals ranging between 18-50 years of age and about an hour of labeled speech [48, 42]. For activity classification, the comparison dataset included ten individuals ranging between 20-30 years of age and with more than ten hours of labeled data [39, 40]. The labeled data from the retirement community was much smaller in size but was collected in two different days and in different locations of the facility. The speech data was labeled at a very fine granularity to accurately label human voice that changes in the order of milliseconds. We had 16,000 labeled data points collected from the retirement community amounting to little over 4 minutes of audio. For the activity data, we had slightly over 19,000 labeled data points amounting to 80 minutes of data. Our approach for validation was to ensure consistency in classification results across data sets. Since neither the sensing device nor the algorithms changed, we believe it is sufficient to ensure that the new results are consistent with previous results and it is not necessary to collect an extensive new labeled dataset for this population, which is not feasible given the age of our subjects and their willingness to generate such a dataset.

In addition to verifying the consistency of our classification accuracy with existing results, a family care practitioner interviewed each subject during recruitment and a medical trainee was present on-site everyday throughout the day while the study was ongoing. The medical trainee was trained by the physician to administer the surveys to ensure reliability and compliance. The trainee typically had brief interactions with the subjects when he handed out the sensing devices every morning and collected them every evening. He also had occasional interactions with the elders if they chose to come by his room during the day for any questions related to the study. A few subjects used this opportunity to stop by for social interactions. This provided us with some opportunistically collected observational data and indication to whether the survey responses from the subjects were consistent with the medical trainee and the physician's observations.

RESULTS AND DISCUSSION

In this section, we present the classification accuracy of the various activity classifiers as well as our findings related to the in-situ assessment of physical and mental well-being.

Classification Accuracy

As mentioned previously, a small amount of labeled data is used to test whether our performance is similar to previously published results on larger datasets [48, 42] and evaluate if it is robust across diverse scenarios in the retirement community and across subjects. According to our previous research [48, 42], the typical accuracy numbers for inferring human speech ranged between 85%-95% and conversation detection was approximately 95%. For activity recognition, detection accuracy numbers ranged from 80%-95% for stationary, walking on a flat surface, walking up and walking down inclines [39, 40].

As described in the Evaluation Methodology section, four minutes of raw audio included speech both inside the meeting room and around the retirement center. These data are manually labeled for the speech and non-speech segments. Three minutes of this data is used for training and the remaining for testing. Testing performance of the human speech classifier in the meeting room is: accuracy 85%, precision 84%, recall 82%, and along the corridors of retirement center was: accuracy 83%, precision 92%, recall 84%. Overall accuracy is 83.7%, precision 90%, recall 84%.

	SU01	SU02	SU03	SU04	SU05	SU06	SU07
SU01		12	20	4	24	10	12
SU02	12		70	10	48	12	30
SU03	20	70		108	42	38	32
SU04	4	10	108		12	10	8
SU05	24	48	42	12		20	26
SU06	10	12	38	10	20		12
SU07	12	30	32	8	26	12	
TOTAL	82	182	310	152	172	102	120

Table 3: Pairwise and total conversation times in minutes for different subjects over 10 day study period

However, one concern is that the speech/non-speech classifier can overhear the sound of TV programs and classify human speech in TV programs as speech. Since in subsequent analysis, we plan to use the amount of human speech in a subject's conversational vicinity for mental health assessment, we discuss how we filter out speech sounds that occur in TV programs. In a preliminary test of a TV recording that included movie and news (including commercials), the speech inference algorithm classified 19% of the recording as speech. To filter out TV speech, we use two energy features derived from the audio signal. During speech in conversational vicinity there is a broader spread in the energy intensity in the voiced region due to non-fixed location of the speech sound (as opposed to fixed location of TV) and the energy values of voiced regions for TV are more uniform across time. Thus, the entropy of energy intensity is higher for human speech occurring in the same physical space compared to the human speech occurring on TV. And entropy of energy distribution over time will be lower for speech in the same physical space compared to speech in TV. These features are computed for every three minute windows. Thirty-three minutes of conversation data and fifty seven minutes of TV program data is used (comprising of a short movie segment and news program) to train a model. A simple Gaussian classifier, where one gaussian is trained for TV and one gaussian for conversation, is used for classification. On a separate testing dataset that included one hundred and three minutes of conversation and forty-two minutes of TV data, the classifier have a 100% classification accuracy for TV and 94% accuracy for human voice occurring in the same location of the subject. The conversation data used for training and testing in this experiment were collected from a research group meeting, casual conversation between colleagues in the department and during the orientation session at the retirement community. We apply this filtering algorithm after the speech inference step to eliminate instances of TV speech.

Table 5 shows the number of minutes inferred as human speech across different subjects for the entire 10 day data collection. During our analysis, we found that subject 08's microphone was faulty and the audio recorded by the device was unusable for speech and conversation detection. Furthermore, subject 04 stopped recording on several occasions before the afternoon and most of the data collection was heavily skewed towards the morning. We omitted subject 04's data when computing correlation with the survey scores as the amount and distribution of data collection from him was substantially different than the rest of the study group. Figure 4 shows data availability for different subjects.

Conversation is detected only between the study participants as the detection algorithm assumes that each of the conversation participant will be carrying their own microphones. The mutual information between the inferred speech streams are calculated for each pair of subjects for every two minute of data and conversation is identified using a threshold on the mutual information score that was obtained via cross-validation [48, 42]. Table 3 shows the number of minutes of conversation that took place between each pair of subjects over the 10 day period. One particular point to note is that subject 03 and 04 are a couple and they have the highest amount of conversation between them (the other couple in the experiment is not presented here because that couple includes subject 08 whose audio data, as stated above, was unusable for further analysis). In this context, conversation analysis is presented here not just for sanity checking our data but to show that it reveals important interpersonal information among the subjects of the experiment. Also conversation analysis is pivotal for speaker segmentation [42] and subsequent user specific speech analysis, like pitch, speaking rate etc., which will be used for future research.

For physical activity recognition, a total of 80 minutes of physical activity data was collected from the subjects. Out of this data, 25 minutes of data is labeled for stationary, walking on flat surface, walking up and down inclines. During labeling, it is ascertained that data from every subject is represented and all classes have roughly the same number of labeled data points. Leave one subject out cross-validation results are reported in Table 4. Here, we expect the performance numbers on the small test dataset to be higher and the actual performance will be closer to previously published results [39, 40]. We would like to reiterate that these evaluations are mainly used to check that the classification accuracy is consistent with the performance of prior systems. Furthermore, cross-validation establishes that the classification worked robustly across individuals and device placement variations.

Actiivty	Precision	Recall	Accuracy
stationary	92.4%	100%	96.05%
walking flat surface	100%	75.86%	93.1%
walking up	94.9%	100%	99.6%
walking down	86.7%	100%	97.4%

Table 4: Performance numbers for physical activity classifier

Automated Measurement of Mental Well-Being

To determine the relationship between sensed speech and mental well-being, we calculated the fraction of time human speech was present within conversational proximity for each subject (as shown in table 5). Fraction of time refers to the ratio of the time human speech was present within conversational proximity and the total duration of recording. We use fraction rather than total amount of speech for the subjects because of unequal data length across different subjects. Univariate regression analysis comparing the sensed speech with SF-36 Mental Health Score revealed a positive correlation R= 0.82 (p=0.048). In order to interpret this result, it is worth delving into the SF-36 Mental Health Score. It is the average of five out of eight sections of the survey, which include Social Functioning, Role Emotional, Mental Health, and Reported Health. Table 2 contains the questions used in these five sections. The Social Functioning dimension is concerned with issues that interfere with subjective perception of General Health, and Vitality. Role Emotional is concerned with emotions that interfere with daily social and occupational activities. The Mental Health dimension captures subjective self-perception, which can be clouded by pathologic negative interpersonal interactions and subject's current mood, especially in those with mood disorders [53, 54, 55]. The General Health represents subjective perception of health compared to others. Lastly, Vitality captures the subjective perception of energy and stamina. Thus, a comprehensive look at mental health score accounts for emotional or physical stressors that interfere with socialization and seeks to quantify the effect on the emotional integrity of the participant. Directly capturing amount of human speech present in an individual's close vicinity can indicate whether an individual is socially engaged and provide valuable information about metal health. Although, the measurement of speech alone is unlikely to be a conclusive or comprehensive measurement of mental health, it can serve as a continuous indicator and early warning system.

Regression analysis comparing fraction of human speech sensed in conversational proximity and CES-D scores revealed a negative correlation R= -0.73 (p=0.096), which is slightly outside the statistical significance range in this small sample. Note that higher CES-D scores indicate increased presence of depressive symptoms. In addition to CES-D and SF-36, regression analysis comparing fraction of human speech sensed in conversation vicinity and friendship scales revealed a strong correlation of R= 0.96 (p=0.002).

Anecdotal qualitative observations provide support that sensed measurements can be used to assess mental health and are often used as one of the early screening methods for depression. Table 5 shows that subject 01 scored above 25 on CES-D and had a much lower SF-36 Mental Health score. Comparing this score to the interaction-based assessment of the participant by the medical trainee and the physician in the team (before survey results were obtained) confirmed concerns that the participant appeared socially isolated, and avoided large groups, and was dysthymic (exhibiting depressive symptoms without a formal diagnosis of depression) and unhappy. Automatically inferred speech duration for subject 01 was low compared to what was observed for the rest of the group. We also discuss another example in section below.

Subject	Amount of Human speech (%)	SF-36 Mental Health Score	CES-D Score	Friendship Scale
SU01	2.6	68	25	14.5
SU02	9.9	90	13	22
SU03	11.6	90	0.5	21
SU04	6.3*	96	1.5	22
SU05	15.3	90	5.5	24
SU06	6.9	88	4.5	18
SU07	12.03	88	5.5	21
SU08	Faulty Mic.	96	2	24

Table 5: Percentages of sensed human speech during the 10 day study and mental health scores from the surveys. (*ignored for further analysis because of lack of data throughout the day)

Subject	Stationary (%)	Walking (%)	Going Up (%)	Going Down (%)	Unknown (%)	Assistive Devices
SU01	63.41	3.98	10.81	6.24	15.56	No
SU02	57.29	11.20	6.39	5.08	20.04	Walker /Cane
SU03	62.76	18.43	1.24	3.17	14.39	No
SU04	65.20	9.71	0.66	7.70	16.72	Cane
SU05	54.60	2.72	14.49	11.42	16.77	No
SU06	66.13	2.95	3.58	17.54	9.80	No
SU07	73.39	4.83	1.82	2.12	17.84	Wheelchair /Cane
SU08	62.85	3.25	7.42	11.62	14.85	No

Table 6: Percentages of different physical activities for subjects during the 10 day study (Going up and going down refers to walking up and walking down inclines respectively)

Automated Measurement of Physical Well-Being

Table 6 shows the breakdown of classified activities, namely walking on flat surface, walking up and down inclines, and being stationary (sitting and standing). The *unknown* category contained all segments of the data that were not associated with the four classified types of activity. Comparing the percentage of time spent doing a specific activity with daily patterns and physical limitations of individual subjects shows good qualitative correlation. Subject 05 reported walking and participating in other physical activities multiple hours daily and had the highest amount of climbing up, down and walking and the lowest percentage of stationary data in the group. Lastly, subject 07 had a neurological disease that limited the person's ability to walk and take part in other physical activities. This is reflected in the amount of stationary activity that is inferred–the highest in the group–and also by the lower values for all other activities. Furthermore, it is worth mentioning that the retirement community is situated on a hilly area with sloping pathways. A few of the subjects took long daily walks along those path and as a result have high percentages of walking up and walking down inclines.

To demonstrate the potential to partly capture the information gathered by surveys using automatically sensed behavior, we compute a weighted sum of physical activity measure inferred using Equation 2 and compare it to the YPAS Activity Index. In the equation, a_i (in percentage) represents different types of activities (stationary, walking, walking up inclines, walking down inclines) and w_i corresponds to the weights of different activities in the overall inferred activity score A.

$$A = \sum_i w_i a_i \quad (2)$$

A multi-dimensional linear regression is utilized to determine relations between YPAS scores and the measures computed from the sensed data. Coefficients (or weights) generated by this regression are as follows: 0.6 for stationary, 3.0 for walking, 5.0 for walking up inclines, 1.0 for walking down inclines, and -1.5 for unknown. These weights for different activities make intuitive sense and reflect the increasing intensity of activity and calories burnt as one goes from stationary, walking down, walking on flat surface to walking up. Furthermore, possible explanation for the negative weight for *unknown* is two fold: (i) it may represent activities that do not correspond to any physical activity; (ii) a high relative proportion of *unknown* makes the values for other physical activities lower than usual (i.e., it has a negative effect on other physical activities).

The total minutes for different activities inferred from sensor measurements can be found in Table 6 and the weighted sum can be computed based on Equation 2 to obtain the activity score. The *inferred activity score* demonstrates a correlation of R=0.88 with p=0.01 with the YPAS activity index. Of note, subject 04's data is not included in the correlation analysis because of lack of data throughout the day.

An unexpected finding was observed for subject 02 regarding the relationship between inferred activity score (A) (from equation 2) and the YPAS activity score. Direct observation of the person's daily activities indicated that the subject spent most of the day being active as a volunteer and also spent time cooking/cleaning her home. The inferred activity level was comparable to the rest of the group and this paralleled observational assessment by the medical trainee who was always at the facility during data collection. However, YPAS reported a much lower estimate of their physical activity level. Despite being administered by the medical trainee, inaccurate recall of daily activities, human error in calculating amount of time spent doing a specific activity, and limitation of the survey in capturing the time spent participating in the specific volunteer task the person engaged in may have contributed to this discrepancy.

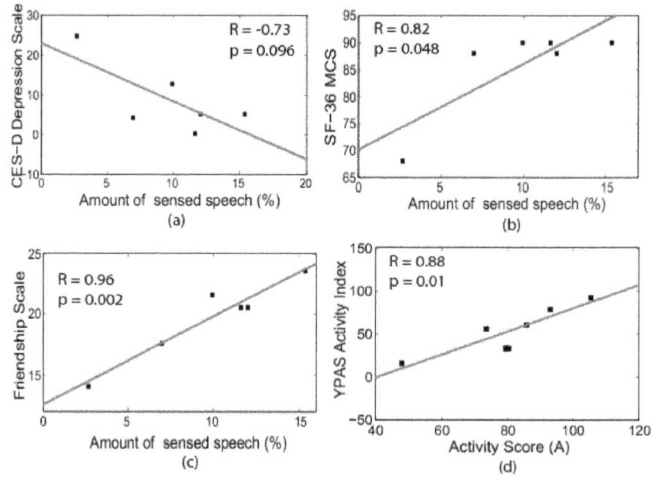

Figure 3: Correlation between (a) sensed human speech and CES-D (b) sensed human speech and SF-36 Mental Health Score (c) sensed human speech and friendship scale (d) physical activity score A and YPAS

Case Study: Limitations of Survey-based Assessment

Our primary goal was to validate sensor-based measurement of in-situ behavior with paper-surveys, the current gold standards in health industry for assessing mental and physical health. We also wanted to explore the potential limitations of self-reported measurement of behavior and how continuous sensing of behavior using easily wearble mobile sensors can supplement and improve currently available tools and methods in health behavioral sciences. Analysis of total amount of speech for subject 06 provides a case example illustrating the limitations of the standard methods for measuring mental health and suggests that automated measurements could potentially overcome these limitations. A comparison of subject 06's CES-D and the Mental Health component of the SF-36 scores and the inferred activities indicate that: (i) there are no major mental health concerns detected by CES-D and SF-36 and (ii) the surveys disagree with the measurement made using the mobile sensors (6.9% of human speech sensed in conversation vicinity, which is second lowest after subject 01), and raised concerns of social isolation, a major risk factor for emotional well-being [56]. The sensor based measurement was in agreement with direct observations made by the medical trainee. This subjective measurement of mental health could have been inappropriately influenced by one or more factors including skewed self-perception, misinterpretation of questionnaires, and purposeful misrepresentation. Thus, continuos sensing could be utilized in preventing exclusive dependence on subject for accurate recall, interpretation and response to questions.

LIMITATIONS AND SHORTFALLS

Our study has several of limitations. The sample size was small and it is difficult to draw definitive conclusions and should be viewed as a promising pilot study. Similarly, this study was focused on older adults. Additional investigation needs to be performed on other populations to see if findings are generalizable. While we did collect a small amount of observational data, we did not perform continuous direct observation. Although this strategy would have made comparison between subjective behavior and actual behavior easier, it would have likely biased observations by disrupting the natural setting of participants.

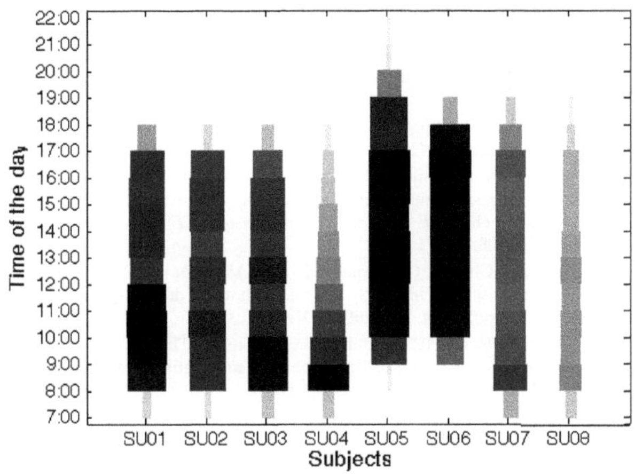

(a)

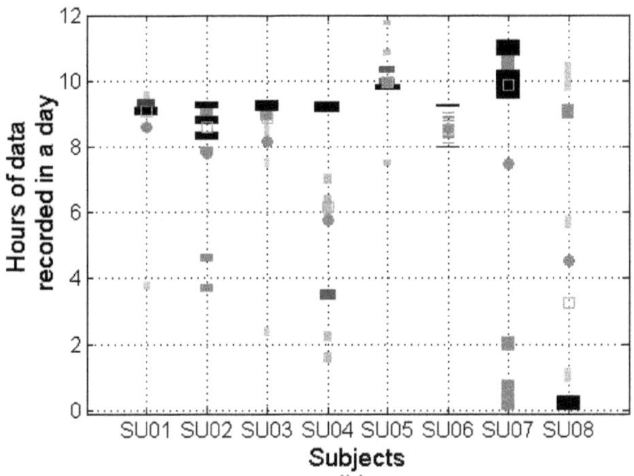

(b)

Figure 4: Amount of data recorded for different subjects through out the 10 day pilot study. (a) shows the amount of recorded data at different parts of a day. Wider and darker horizontal bars represent more recording during that part of the day. (b) shows distribution of the hours of data recorded on each day for a given subject. For example, subject 02 recorded close to 9 hours of data on most days but has a couple of days where she records between 3.5-4.5 hours of data. The red dot represent the mean and the green square represents the median number of recorded hours per day for each subject.

Figure 4 shows the amount of data recorded at different parts of the day during the 10 day study. It highlights the fact that subject 08 provided the least amount of data because he choose not to wear the device during voluntary duties outside the retirement facility. Subject 04 provided data mostly in the morning and his data distribution is heavily skewed towards the morning as can also be seen in Figure 4. To increase reliability and decrease user burden, participants dropped off the sensing devices at the end of the day and picked them up the following morning. This enabled offloading of data and recharging of the batteries overnight. Due to picking up and returning the device at different times, unequal amount of data was collected for different subjects. Finally, significantly less data were collected on day 8 due to insufficient charging of the devices during the previous night. Despite these limitations, this pilot work demonstrates the power and potential of utilizing commonly available sensors with sophisticated processing techniques to improve the detection of specific physical and behavioral activities. As more people are carrying sensors as part of everyday mobile devices, the potential to detect health problems and monitor treatment could become more efficient and effective.

CONCLUSION

In this paper, we demonstrated that daily human behaviors, inferred from mobile sensors, correlate highly with well-established survey metrics, including measures of depressive symptoms, in older adults. In an informal usability survey, most study participants stated that they found the device easy to use, comfortable to wear, and all participants thought the sensor based approach was preferable to surveys. Though the strong quantitative results combined with qualitative acceptance is encouraging, there are scopes for future improvements in scalability, usability, robustness and in detecting finer aspects of mental health. We are currently focusing on implementing our sensing and inference system on smartphones. We believe that the recent proliferation and pervasiveness of smartphones can enable us to truly scale the passive objective well-being system for the masses. These smartphones will not only improve usability but also enable us to collect large amount of data in diverse environments and create models that are robust across scenarios. In addition to data collection, we plan to focus on different aspects of mental health, for example aspects that change rapidly overtime (e.g., non-chronic stress, mood) and that are less transient (e.g., personality). We believe this work highlights a first step towards our goal by showing that passive and continuous sensing of activity and behavior is feasible and comparable to traditional, more cumbersome methods of assessment for an increasing population like older adults. With continued advancement of these technologies, there is great potential to improve early detection of changes in well-being and overall quality of life.

ACKNOWLEDGMENTS

This work was supported by NSF IIS-0845683, NSF CNS-0910842 and National Institute on Aging 1K23AG036934.

REFERENCES

1. R. Camicioli, MM Moore, G. Sexton, DB Howieson, and JA Kaye. Age-related brain changes associated with motor function in healthy older people. *Journal of the American Geriatrics Society*, 47(3):330, 1999.
2. P.L. Sheridan, J. Solomont, N. Kowall, and J.M. Hausdorff. Influence of executive function on locomotor function: divided attention increases gait variability in Alzheimer's disease. *Journal of the American Geriatrics Society*, 51(11):1633–1637, 2003.
3. Daniel Olguin Olguin, Benjamin N Waber, Taemie Kim, Akshay Mohan, Koji Ara, and Alex Pentland. Sensible organizations: technology and methodology for automatically measuring organizational behavior. *IEEE Transactions on Systems, Man, and Cybernetics, Part B: Cybernetics*, 39(1):43–55, 2009.
4. Megan P Rothney, Emily V Schaefer, Megan M Neumann, Leena Choi, and Kong Y Chen. Validity of physical activity intensity predictions by actigraph, actical, and rt3 accelerometers. *Obesity (Silver Spring)*, 16(8):1946–52, 2008.
5. S. Consolvo, D.W. McDonald, T. Toscos, M.Y. Chen, J. Froehlich, B. Harrison, P. Klasnja, A. LaMarca, L. LeGrand, R. Libby, et al. Activity sensing in the wild: a field trial of ubifit garden. In *Proceeding of the twenty-sixth annual SIGCHI conference on Human factors in computing systems*, pages 1797–1806, 2008.

6. Susan J Wenze and Ivan W Miller. Use of ecological momentary assessment in mood disorders research. *Clinical psychology review*, 2010.
7. L. Dipietro, C.J. Caspersen, A.M. Ostfeld, and E.R. Nadel. A survey for assessing physical activity among older adults. *Medicine and science in sports and exercise*, 25:628–628, 1993.
8. Sf-36, http://www.sf-36.org, 2008.
9. E M Andresen, J A Malmgren, W B Carter, and D L Patrick. Screening for depression in well older adults: evaluation of a short form of the ces-d (center for epidemiologic studies depression scale). *American Journal of Preventive Medicine*, 10(2):77–84, 1994.
10. A A Stone, J E Schwartz, J M Neale, S Shiffman, C A Marco, M Hickcox, J Paty, L S Porter, and L J Cruise. A comparison of coping assessed by ecological momentary assessment and retrospective recall. *Journal of Personality and Social Psychology*, 74(6):1670–80, 1998.
11. J E Schwartz, J Neale, C Marco, S S Shiffman, and A A Stone. Does trait coping exist? a momentary assessment approach to the evaluation of traits. *Journal of personality and social psychology*, 77(2):360–9, 1999.
12. Sunlee Bang, Minho Kim, Sa-Kwang Song, and Soo-Jun Park. Toward real time detection of the basic living activity in home using a wearable sensor and smart home sensors. *Proc IEEE Engineering in Medicine and Biology Society*, pages 5200–3, 2008.
13. DM Bravata, C Smith-Spangler, V Sundaram, AL Gienger, N Lin, R Lewis, CD Stave, I Olkin, and JR Sirard. Using pedometers to increase physical activity and improve health: a systematic review. *JAMA*, 298(19):2296, 2007.
14. C. Tudor-Locke, S.B. Sisson, T. Collova, S.M. Lee, and P.D. Swan. Pedometer-determined step count guidelines for classifying walking intensity in a young ostensibly healthy population. *Applied Physiology, Nutrition, and Metabolism*, 30(6):666–676, 2005.
15. R Bergman and D Bassett Jr. Validity of 2 devices for measuring steps taken by older adults in assisted-living facilities. *Journal of physical activity & health*, 5:S166, 2008.
16. L. Bao and S.S. Intille. Activity recognition from user-annotated acceleration data. *Pervasive Computing*, pages 1–17, 2004.
17. Actigraph, http://www.theactigraph.com/.
18. Sensewear, http://sensewear.com/.
19. T Choudhury, G Borriello, S Consolvo, D Haehnel, B Harrison, B Hemingway, and J Hightower. The mobile sensing platform: An embedded activity recognition system. *IEEE Pervasive Computing*, pages 32–41, 2008.
20. Ansgar Conrad, Frank H Wilhelm, Walton T Roth, David Spiegel, and C Barr Taylor. Circadian affective, cardiopulmonary, and cortisol variability in depressed and nondepressed individuals at risk for cardiovascular disease. *Journal of psychiatric research*, 42(9):769–77, 2008.
21. S. Reder, G. Ambler, M. Philipose, and S. Hedrick. Technology and Long-term Care (TLC): A pilot evaluation of remote monitoring of elders. *Gerontechnology*, 9(1):18–31, 2010.
22. Revenues and expenditures reports from 2006.
23. L J Kirmayer, J M Robbins, M Dworkind, and M J Yaffe. Somatization and the recognition of depression and anxiety in primary care. *American Journal of Psychiatry*, 150(5):734–41, 1993.
24. M Olfson, B Fireman, M M Weissman, A C Leon, D V Sheehan, R G Kathol, C Hoven, and L Farber. Mental disorders and disability among patients in a primary care group practice. *American Journal of Psychiatry*, 154(12):1734–40, 1997.
25. G Simon, J Ormel, M VonKorff, and W Barlow. Health care costs associated with depressive and anxiety disorders in primary care. *American Journal of Psychiatry*, 152(3):352–7, 1995.
26. H J Henk, D J Katzelnick, K A Kobak, J H Greist, and J W Jefferson. Medical costs attributed to depression among patients with a history of high medical expenses in a health maintenance organization. *Archives of General Psychiatry*, 53(10):899–904, 1996.
27. Vivian Isaac, Robert Stewart, Sylvaine Artero, Marie-Laure Ancelin, and Karen Ritchie. Social activity and improvement in depressive symptoms in older people: a prospective community cohort study. *American Journal of Geriatric Psychiatry*, 17(8):688–96, 2009.
28. Hayden B Bosworth, Judith C Hays, Linda K George, and David C Steffens. Psychosocial and clinical predictors of unipolar depression outcome in older adults. *International journal of geriatric psychiatry*, 17(3):238–46, 2002.
29. W.W. Walk. A prospective study of physical activity and cognitive decline in elderly women. *Arch Intern Med*, 161:1703–1708, 2001.
30. Anmol Madan, Manuel Cebrian, David Lazer, and Alex Pentland. Social sensing for epidemiological behavior change. In *Ubicomp '10: Proceedings of the 12th ACM international conference on Ubiquitous computing*, pages 291–300, New York, NY, USA, 2010. ACM.
31. Danny Wyatt, Tanzeem Choudhury, James Kitts, , and Jeff Bilmes. Inferring Colocation and Conversation Networks from Privacy-sensitive Audio with Implications for Computational Social Science. *To appear in ACM Transactions on Intelligent Systems and Technology*, 2010.
32. D.J. France, R.G. Shiavi, S. Silverman, M. Silverman, and M. Wilkes. Acoustical properties of speech as indicators of depression and suicidal risk. *IEEE Transactions on Biomedical Engineering*, 47(7):829–837, 2002.
33. R. Cowie and E. Douglas-Cowie. Automatic statistical analysis of the signal and prosodic signs of emotion in speech. In *Spoken Language, 1996. ICSLP 96. Proceedings., Fourth International Conference on*, volume 3, pages 1989–1992, 2002.
34. R.W. Frick. Communicating Emotion:: The Role of Prosodic Features. *Psychological Bulletin*, 97(3):412–429, 1985.
35. Elliot Moore, Mark A Clements, John W Peifer, and Lydia Weisser. Critical analysis of the impact of glottal features in the classification of clinical depression in speech. *IEEE Transactions on Biomedical Engineering*, 55(1):96–107, 2008.
36. D.N. Kiosses, S. Klimstra, C. Murphy, and G.S. Alexopoulos. Executive dysfunction and disability in elderly patients with major depression. *American Journal of Geriatric Psych*, 9(3):269, 2001.
37. B.L. Kirkman, B. Rosen, P.E. Tesluk, and C.B. Gibson. The impact of team empowerment on virtual team performance: The moderating role of face-to-face interaction. *The Academy of Management Journal*, 47(2):175–192, 2004.
38. G Hawthorne. Measuring social isolation in older adults: Development and initial validation of the friendship scale. *Social Indicators Research*, pages 1–28, 2006.
39. Jonathan Lester, Tanzeem Choudhury, Nicky Kern, Gaetano Borriello, and Blake Hannaford. A hybrid discriminative/generative approach for modeling human activities. In *In Proc. of the International Joint Conference on Artificial Intelligence (IJCAI)*, pages 766–772, 2005.
40. Jonathan Lester, Tanzeem Choudhury, Gaetano Borriello, and Blake Hannaford. A practical approach to recognizing physical activities. In *Proc. of Pervasive*, 2006.
41. D. Wyatt, T. Choudhury, J. Bilmes, and J.A. Kitts. Inferring colocation and conversation networks from privacy-sensitive audio with implications for computational social science. *ACM Transactions on Intelligent Systems and Technology (TIST)*, 2(1):7, 2011.
42. D. Wyatt, T. Choudhury, and J. Bilmes. Conversation detection and speaker segmentation in privacy sensitive situated speech data. In *Proceedings of Interspeech*, pages 586–589, 2007.
43. D. Wyatt, J. Bilmes, T. Choudhury, and J.A. Kitts. Towards the automated social analysis of situated speech data. In *Proceedings of the 10th international conference on Ubiquitous computing*, pages 168–171. ACM, 2008.
44. F. Dellaert, T. Polzin, and A. Waibel. Recognizing emotion in speech. In *Spoken Language, 1996. ICSLP 96. Proceedings., Fourth International Conference on*, volume 3, pages 1970–1973. IEEE, 1996.
45. D. Gatica-Perez, I. McCowan, D. Zhang, and S. Bengio. Detecting group interest-level in meetings. In *Proc. IEEE Int. Conf. on Acoustics, Speech and Signal Processing (ICASSP)*. Citeseer, 2005.
46. R.T. Hurlburt, M. Koch, and C.L. Heavey. Descriptive experience sampling demonstrates the connection of thinking to externally observable behavior. *Cognitive Therapy and Research*, 26(1):117–134, 2002.
47. S. Basu. A linked-HMM model for robust voicing and speech detection. In *Proceedings of International Conference on Acoustic, Speech, and Signal Processing (ICASSP)*, 2003.
48. Tanzeem Choudhury and Sumit Basu. Modeling conversational dynamics as a mixed-memory markov process. In *Proc. of NIPS*, 2004.
49. Jerome Friedman, Trevor Hastie, and Robert Tibshirani. Additive logistic regression: a statistical view of boosting. *Annals of Statistics*, 28:2000, 1998.
50. Antonio Torralba and Kevin P. Murphy. Sharing visual features for multiclass and multiview object detection. *IEEE Transactions on Pattern Analysis and Machine Intelligence*, 29(5):854–869, 2007.
51. Ulf Blanke and Bernt Schiele. Daily routine recognition through activity spotting. In *LoCA '09: Proceedings of the 4th International Symposium on Location and Context Awareness*, pages 192–206, Berlin, Heidelberg, 2009. Springer-Verlag.
52. P. Viola and M. Jones. Robust real-time object detection. *International Journal of Computer Vision*, 57(2):137–154, 2002.
53. J.B. Nezlek, R.M. Kowalski, M.R. Leary, T. Blevins, and S. Holgate. Personality moderators of reactions to interpersonal rejection: Depression and trait self-esteem. *Personality and Social Psychology Bulletin*, 23(12):1235, 1997.
54. T L Simoneau, D J Miklowitz, and R Saleem. Expressed emotion and interactional patterns in the families of bipolar patients. *Journal of Abnormal Psychology*, 107(3):497–507, 1998.
55. Saul Shiffman, Arthur A Stone, and Michael R Hufford. Ecological momentary assessment. *Annual review of clinical psychology*, 4:1–32, 2008.
56. T E Seeman. Social ties and health: the benefits of social integration. *Annals of Epidemiology*, 6(5):442–51, 1996.

The Place for Ubiquitous Computing in Schools: Lessons Learned from a School-Based Intervention for Youth Physical Activity

Erika Shehan Poole[1], Andrew D. Miller[2], Yan Xu[2], Elsa Eiriksdottir[3], Richard Catrambone[3], and Elizabeth D. Mynatt[2]

College of Information Sciences and Technology[1]
The Pennsylvania State University
University Park, PA 16802 USA
epoole@ist.psu.edu

College of Computing[2] and School of Psychology[3]
Georgia Institute of Technology
Atlanta, GA 30332 USA
{andrew.miller, elsa, yxu7, rc7, mynatt}@gatech.edu

ABSTRACT
With rising concerns about obesity and sedentary lifestyles in youth, there has been an increasing interest in understanding how pervasive and ubiquitous computing technologies can catalyze positive health behaviors in children and teens. School-based interventions seem like a natural choice, and ubiquitous computing technologies hold much promise for these interventions. Yet the literature contains little guidance for how to approach school-based ubicomp deployments. Grounded in our analysis of a large-scale US school-based intervention for promoting youth physical activity, we present an approach to the design and evaluation of school-based ubicomp that treats the school as a social institution. We show how the school regulates students' daily lives, drawing from work in the sociology of schools to create a framing for planning, executing and analyzing school-based ubicomp deployments. These insights will assist other researchers and designers engaging in deployments of ubiquitous computing systems in settings with established institutional structures.

Author Keywords
children, health, physical activity, school-based interventions, ubiquitous computing

ACM Classification Keywords
H5.m. Information interfaces and presentation (e.g., HCI): Miscellaneous.

General Terms
Human Factors

INTRODUCTION
The increasing number of overweight and obese children and adolescents is a key health challenge in 21st century America. Since the 1980s, rates of overweight adolescents have doubled, and rates of obese adolescents have tripled [19,42]. Medical research has also uncovered a phenomenon known as the "adolescent slump"; around age 12, physical activity levels drop dramatically, and in many cases never recover [40]. Adolescent obesity is the single biggest predictor of adult obesity, and the crisis has disproportionately affected lower-income and minority communities. There is general agreement in the literature that such a complex societal problem requires a holistic approach, and that successful health behavior change interventions must address adolescents' everyday lives [19].

In response, many interventions in this space choose the school as their deployment environment. Schools reach the majority of youth, regardless of the particulars of their home life. Schools have facilities and existing programming for physical activity, serve children 1-2 meals daily, and have trained adults available to facilitate health-related behavior change. Schools might be particularly adept at reaching children less accessible via parent and family-only interventions. Historically, most of these interventions have not included a computing technology component, but often require large commitments of staff, time, or space [41].

Ubiquitous computing technologies seem a natural fit for school-based health interventions. Ubicomp deployments have the potential to integrate with schools and the school day, leveraging computing power to let teachers, parents and students concentrate on the behavioral objectives of the deployment. They can extend sensing and feedback beyond the classroom and into students' lives after school and at home. Yet prior work offers little guidance for the design and study of ubiquitous computing deployments in schools. To address this need, we describe a case study of a school-based ubiquitous computing application aimed at increasing adherence to a behavior strongly correlated with risk reduction for obesity and a number of chronic diseases: engaging in regular low-to moderate- intensity physical activity.

This program, the American Horsepower Challenge (AHPC), was used over the course of three semesters by over 1400 American children in 61 schools. In studying this program, we saw that although many of the challenges facing all school-based interventions (even the ones with minimal or no advanced technology) also apply to school-based ubicomp, these deployments in schools offer new opportunities for engagement and have their own unique needs.

In this paper, we present an approach to the design and evaluation of school-based ubicomp intervention that treats the school as a social institution, one that regulates interactions through space, time, ritual and social hierarchy. We argue that schools—as established institutions with a set of rituals and norms—require new ways of designing and deploying ubiquitous computing interventions than what has been previously discussed in the literature.

In building this argument, we draw from studies of school sociology to show how ubiquitous computing technologies fit into school settings. We describe the rituals of the school day, including temporal, spatial, differentiating and integrating rituals, and show how each of these impacts ubicomp technologies. Throughout, we ground our discussion in our experiences studying a large-scale longitudinal school-based ubicomp deployment, providing real-world examples and data. We address the potential for school-based ubicomp deployments to extend beyond the school, and describe the challenges such deployments face in moving beyond the schoolhouse. Although our US-based study necessarily restricts our specific observations to American school settings, our findings will have relevance for researchers and designers in many countries. We conclude with a set of design recommendations for the design of ubicomp deployments in schools. Finally, while the focus of our study was a school-based technological intervention for increasing daily physical activity of American youth, the experiences, analysis, and guidelines presented in this paper apply to other ubiquitous computing technologies seeking a fit within established institutional cultures.

RELATED WORK

Our discussion of school-based deployments relies on related work from several disciplines. First, we discuss relevant work in technological interventions aimed at improving health behaviors, and the limitations of these systems when they used in K-12 environments. We then turn to a discussion of the sociology of education, and how it may provide guidance for the design and evaluation of ubiquitous computing in schools and other institutions with established norms.

Technology Interventions for Health Behavior Change

School-based health interventions come in a number of formats, and have been met with mixed success; many predate work in ubiquitous computing research [41]. Of particular interest is McCaughtry et al's [34] study of a cohort of elementary school PE teachers as they integrated analog pedometers into their classrooms over a period of six months. Despite initial teacher enthusiasm, over time they struggled with technical malfunctions and classroom disruptions related to the interfaces on the pedometers.

Technology-focused research projects have examined how exercise video games ("exergames") [3], mobile phone applications [14,15,22,24,33,37,39,44,47], and sensors [20,34,36] can be used to support positive health behavior changes in children and adults in a number of settings. Typically, these systems provide benefits through social support, reduction of monotony and boredom, or by providing new knowledge that can be incorporated into one's daily life. In addition to these research-focused applications, the past decade has borne a number of commercial fitness gaming systems, such as Konami Dance Dance Revolution, Sony EyeToy, Nintendo Wii Fit, and Xbox 360 Kinect; all claim to make video gaming a more healthy and active experience. In addition to promoting general health and wellness in broad cross sections of the population, specialized applications have been developed for the purposes of stroke rehabilitation [9,11,18,38,43], physical therapy [28], mental health care [46], increasing nutrition knowledge in low-income communities [22,23,24,25], and chronic disease management for conditions such as diabetes, cystic fibrosis, and asthma [5,10,33]. Despite the creation of research and commercial systems aimed at promoting positive lifestyle changes, it has been difficult to effectively integrate them into a typical K-12 school environment.

In particular, a focus on the use of mobile and sensor-based technologies in behavior change applications offers new challenges when integrated into K-12 schools. On one hand, mobile and ubiquitous computing technologies for encouraging healthy behavior changes seem like a reasonable medium because they are heavily used. In the United States, over 75% of teens have mobile phones, 93% are online, 87% use email, 60% have their own computer, and 97% play video/computer games [31,32].

On the other hand, using these technologies at school raises questions about liability and cultural norms. Studies of mobile phone-based deployments in schools have suggested that including these devices in the institutional setting of a school requires a radical paradigm shift from how "schooling is done" [16]. Although mobile technologies are used nearly ubiquitously among American children, schools have been reluctant to allow usage during the school day for educational or other purposes. Mobile technologies blur the boundary between the educational world and the outside world, and are difficult to monitor. Cramer and Hayes, for example, [16] note that mobile technologies have been viewed with suspicion and panic, starting with pager bans in the 1980s to current day concerns over using text messaging to send sexually suggestive content ("sexting"). Above all else, schools focus on making sure that students are protected. Mobile technology can be seen as a threat in some ways, especially to schools concerned with minimizing their potential liability. However, these concerns are not unique to mobile deployments; indeed all school-based ubicomp deployments must make the case for their potential utility compared with their disruptive potential. In the following section, we turn to a discussion of the sociology of education to as a framing to understand the opportunities and constraints of deploying ubiquitous computing technologies in schools.

Schools as Institutions: Using Sociology of Education to Understand Ubicomp Deployments

The sociological perspective on education, which views the school as an institution, provides many insights for understanding ubiquitous computing deployments in educational settings. Not only are schools places for learning intellectual skills, they are also are places for building political allegiance, assimilating cultural groups, and more broadly teaching the norms, laws, values, and behaviors of society [6,17]. Moreover, schools play an economic role in society by preparing children for eventual participation in the labor market [35]. Schools are in many ways variable in nature; there might be quite a bit of difference between the day-to-day functions of any two schools [2,6], particularly in the United States due to decentralized, local control of school operations [35]. However unique an individual school might be, schools as societal institutions have shared organizational characteristics. In particular, schools—across age groups and geographic boundaries—are places that are selective in what is taught, have a sequenced curriculum, and have distinct boundaries to the outside world [6].

For the discussion that follows, we have identified three particular facets of sociological research on education: status hierarchies, spatiotemporal rituals, and differentiating/integrating rituals.

Status Hierarchies

Schools are places with status hierarchies, where status can be obtained through either academic or non-academic means. They have standardized membership categories–e.g., "freshman" or "high school graduate"—allowing individuals who might have very different skills and abilities to be treated as equals [6].

Temporal and Space-Related Rituals

Schools have temporal rituals marking individual days as well as longer periods of time (semesters or a school year). So too are physical spaces arranged in a ritualistic manner. There is some amount of separation between students and staff (e.g., through teachers' lounges and playgrounds), and movement between spaces is highly regulated for students and visitors [6].

Differentiating and Integrating Rituals

Schools have other rituals that contribute to the maintenance of a moral order within the school setting. *Differentiating rituals* seek to celebrate students who conform to school norms and values (e.g., an honor roll). In contrast, *integrating rituals* produce a collective school identity (e.g., pep rallies or school dances) [4,6].

Ubiquitous Computing in Schools

With this framework in mind, let us consider existing ubiquitous computing projects in school settings. There have been a number of deployments that focus on everything from note taking in college classrooms [8] to behavior management in K-12 special education classrooms [27,29]. In neurotypical K-12 classrooms, ubicomp technologies have been explored for behavioral tracking of classroom activities [30], transmitting information about emotions between students and teachers [1] and using multi-touch or large collaborative displays for small-group collaboration in academic projects and storytelling activities [7,12,26]. Often these projects are built into the classroom, or designed for classroom-only use [1]. Other times, they have been explicitly built to be incorporated into existing school rituals. The Playful Toothbrush project, for example, was integrated into an existing tooth brushing break in a kindergarten to teach children how to brush teeth properly [13]. Similarly, Ervasti et al's study of a technology for automating taking attendance in schools relied on existing rituals in the classroom [21]. In contrast to this prior work, we discuss a ubiquitous computing technology that addresses an important societal problem, but does not necessarily fit neatly into the day-to-day educational objectives of a school.

AMERICAN HORSEPOWER CHALLENGE: A UBICOMP INTERVENTION IN U.S. MIDDLE SCHOOLS

The American Horsepower Challenge (AHPC) is a pedometer-based pervasive health game for middle school students (approximately ages 9-13). This game, which aims to increase daily physical activity, was intended to broaden opportunities for children—even those with little skill in traditional sports—to compete in an athletic competition for their school. Developed by Humana Games For Health and sponsored by the Humana Foundation[1], the AHPC takes real-world step data and feeds it into a virtual environment. Through a combination of Bluetooth-enabled pedometers, an automatic upload station located within a school classroom, and a web-based game that showed a school vs. school race as well as individual performance statistics, the AHPC tracked students' daily physical activity over several months and translated it into points in a virtual race among schools enrolled in the program. Unlike other exercise video games in which points are earned through interacting with the game system itself (e.g., Dance Dance Revolution, Wii Fit), players' interaction with the AHPC online game portion did not earn them any points. Instead, all points came from real-world physical activity measured by the wearable pedometers; students were rewarded equally for low-, moderate-, and high-intensity activities. The design of the technology was intended such that it could transcend *status hierarchies* in the school; as long as a child could walk, he or she could participate equally in the game.

[1] The philanthropic arm of Humana, Inc., a health benefits company.

Game Technology

Humana distributed 20 pedometers and a base station to each school, and normally about 20 students at each school participated at any given time. Students joined or left the program for various reasons, including student transience and teacher preference (teachers often lost daily access to students when they started a new school year, and some teachers recruited new students for the second school year).

Steps from the wireless pedometers were automatically uploaded to the base station when in range (within a few feet) and available on the website within eight hours. Students could use the web interface to check their steps, and see their school's total compared to other schools. The website featured a "horserace" metaphor; each student's avatar was a customizable cartoon horse, and the horses sat in a customizable school bus, which traveled around a racetrack with other schools in the competition. The relative position of the school bus indicated a school's standing in the competition. Teachers had their own version of the website that allowed them to customize the school's bus, keep track of students' step counts, and perform basic administrative tasks.

Participant Recruitment

After several prototype deployments, Humana conducted a large-scale field trial with 61 schools in 2009 and 2010, inviting our research team to study the game's impact and effectiveness during this period. After a one week pre-game baseline period in which baseline step data was collected, the game played out over two phases: Phase I occurred in Spring 2009 and Phase II spanned Fall 2009 and early Winter 2010. The top performing schools in each phase received grants to purchase fitness equipment. At the end of Phase II, 37 schools remained in the challenge.

All participating schools were Title I schools (a US federal funding program targeted at "public schools with high numbers or percentages of poor children"[45]); many with a substantial portion of the student body receiving free or reduced priced meals. The schools were situated in a range of environments, from large cities to rural areas. Thirty-seven schools continued in the AHPC across both phases of the game. Overall 1465 students participated in the game. Most of the students were in US 6th grade (11-12 years old) when they began the challenge, and continued it into 7th grade (12-13 years old).

Research Methods

As part of a larger research initiative, our group independently evaluated the AHPC; full details of this evaluation are available in our tech report [20]. Note that our research team did not create the game, recruit schools, choose players, or take responsibility for the upkeep of the game. Nor did we have control over the length of time the game was played or the ways it was distributed to the schools.

In the course of the AHPC, we used surveys to collect information from the students, their parents, and the teachers involved in the challenge about participation in physical activities, attitudes toward non-exercise physical activities and structured exercise, perceived social support for participating in the challenge, demographic information, and neighborhood characteristics. In total, 577 students (33%), 380 parents (22%) and 19 teachers (51%) responded to our surveys. We also gathered website usage and pedometer log data from each child to supplement self-reports. In total, we examined 14 weeks of individual and aggregate data from two school years. To supplement the survey and log data, members of our research team also visited 15 schools participating in the AHPC, speaking with over 200 students and teachers. The profile of the 15 schools we visited is representative of the overall group socioeconomically, demographically and regionally. At each school, we conducted a student-only focus group, teacher interviews, and individual student interviews and wrote field notes with observations of interest. We analyzed these data using an iterative, inductive qualitative analysis approach in which all members of the research team worked to achieve consensus.

(a) Accelerometer is worn on shoe, storing the number of steps per day for up to seven days.

(b) Base station in high-traffic area of the school automatically collects data, uploads to web server

(c) Updated school position in the race and individual performance stats are shown on program website within 8 hours of upload.

Figure 1. Overview of the deployment technology

Results

Overall, the participants' physical activity levels increased during the game. The AHPC-enrolled students increased their daily step-counts during the game relative to a pregame baseline. The average student participant in the

AHPC recorded 4,193 steps per day ($SD = 2347$) during the deployment, as compared to an average of 3,416 steps during the pregame data collection period ($SD = 3420$ steps). We found a significant difference between the pregame baseline step counts and each round of the competition. Step counts in Phase I were significantly greater than the pregame baseline ($t(6764) = 24.48, p < .001$ (two-tailed); so is the first month in Phase II ($t(9018) = 12.99, p < .001$ (two-tailed)) and second month in Phase II ($t(13930) = 4.84, p < .001$ (two-tailed)).

Digging deeper, we found a diversity of approaches and local implementation strategies. As we analyzed the data, we started to see patterns emerge, ways in which these seemingly disparate practices were connected to a common set of needs and underlying social structures. In the sections that follow, we show how these sociological phenomena presented themselves in the case of the AHPC, and draw implications for the place of ubicomp in schools.

SPATIAL AND TEMPORAL RITUALS

The highly structured nature of school days leaves little room for additional activities including health interventions. In this light, ubiquitous computing technologies may have an advantage for incorporation into the daily rituals of schools. For example, pervasive sensors reduce the need to interrupt the school day to enter data, and mobile interfaces allow students to interact with the system between classes. Our analysis of the AHPC, however, shows a more nuanced picture. In the AHPC, the sensors collected data instantly and constantly, but students would often go days without viewing or analyzing the data. Additionally, because the AHPC was a behavioral intervention, the sensors were not there merely to capture existing behavior but to motivate students to increase desired behaviors. In schools where students gained the most steps, this dual purpose motivated the introduction of new rituals into the school day: both to acquire more steps and to collectively view and analyze progress.

Sensing and Feedback

The AHPC's design is, in a sense, minimally disruptive to the school day. Wireless base stations that students had to pass in order to upload steps were placed in high-traffic locations already visited by the students in their daily schedules; they did not need to interact with an explicit interface in order to participate in data collection. Compared to analog pedometers or mobile phone interfaces that have been found to be distracting in school environments [16][34], the AHPC sensors have a minimally distracting physical design. The sensors contain no displays themselves, and feedback is provided via a website, which allowed schools to control whether and when students could interact with the interface during the school day.

How, then, did students become aware of their individual and collective progress? This information was available on the program website, accessible on any Internet-connected computer. From our interviews and site visits, we suspect that many students logged onto the site once or twice a week during the challenge (specific data on logins was not available from the project sponsor). On average, the students logged in to the AHPC website 9.2 times from Nov. 16, 2009 to Feb 5, 2010 ($SD = 12.9$). Few students reported logging in from home; for most students, access to feedback was determined by when they could go to a computer lab or use the classroom computer. Students would often go days without seeing if their steps had been uploaded correctly. In contrast, personal health informatics systems often rely on regular daily use. Diabetics, for example, often take several readings per day, and must code and interpret their blood glucose readings [33]. Fitness interventions, for example many commercial pedometers and the Ubifit Garden project [15], include a passive, pervasive information display.

The sensing and feedback mechanisms the AHPC present an issue of import to deployments in schools. On one hand, the lack of display on the sensors combined with tightly controlled access to feedback sessions can reduce disruption from existing activities within the school (for example, students comparing steps during lessons, as has been found in other pedometer-based interventions [34]). On the other hand, this style of sensing and feedback required the teachers to create technological workarounds as well as regular rituals surrounding physical activity and feedback about performance.

Structuring Time

Schools where the AHPC worked well, that is, where we saw little participation drop-off and step-counts were above average, answered the challenge of making time for successful gameplay by inventing more opportunities for physical activity during the boundaries of the school day. During the deployment, teachers in these schools would open the gym before school, during recess and lunch breaks, and even during regular instruction hours. As just one part of students' lives, the AHPC constantly faced the threat of being lost in the shuffle. Regular rituals served as reminders to participate in physical activity and provided reaffirmations of purpose.

In some cases, students lacked any recess time during the school day. At one school we visited, the students' lunch break was their only real free time during the entire school day. These lunch breaks provided a unique opportunity to encourage more physical activity. As their teacher told us:

> *[Students'] lunches are 40 minutes and most students will eat lunch in the first 15 minutes and that's pushing it. Usually they're done within the first 10. So whenever the weather is decent...they have four square stations and basketball.*

Additionally some teachers also opened the gym before school, making it available to any student but particularly encouraging the AHPC students to get in some steps during that time:

> *7:15 they'll come rolling in and unfortunately we don't know how many students are coming in one day to the next so it's hard to plan but we kind of think off of our toes real quick and come up with something. We average about a dozen that come in.*

This practice of opening up the gym was not uncommon, and teachers were able to be fairly creative with strategies for getting steps. At one school, the PE teacher opened up the gym to AHPC students during their study hall, even if another PE class was going on during that time.

The motivation by teachers and schools to extend the school day is, in some ways, unsurprising. Schools are very good at regulating time and coordinating activities within their own spaces. Schools did this in two main ways: through differentiating rituals and integrating rituals.

DIFFERENTIATING AND INTEGRATING RITUALS

Literature in the sociology of education distinguishes *differentiating rituals*, which seek to celebrate students who conform to school norms and values (e.g., an honor roll), as well as *integrating rituals,* which produce a collective school identity (e.g., pep rallies or school dances) [4,6]. In the AHPC, we saw evidence of both.

Differentiating Rituals

The AHPC technology was designed such that there were few differentiating rituals. Students could not view one another's step counts (unless physically looking over the shoulder of another student at a computer). Yet we saw differentiating rituals occurring, particularly in recruitment practices within the school. At one school, the AHPC teacher even ran the AHPC as a team, hiring and firing students based on performance. He "hired" and "fired" participants according to their performance in the Challenge. He found the strategy an effective one.

> *I'd say, 'You're fired.' And I'd give the chip to someone else. I'd say, 'Now you're hired.' So I probably had to do that to maybe four kids last year. And that worked.*

In other schools we visited, teachers described how they chose students based on characteristics such as "responsibility" and whether they were "good athletes." In these schools, participation in the AHPC was, to some extent, a reward for meeting some desirable criteria. Yet sometimes, student selection choices were not made because the student would benefit the most from being in the program. For instance, given the lack of replacement pedometers and the long duration of the study, one teacher remarked that she chose students whose families were long-time residents in the local community, as well as students who were athletes or otherwise active in extracurricular activities.

> *I wanted kids who I knew would return the stuff [permission slips], and who would return the pedometer.*

The teacher knew that she was excluding students who could have most benefited from participating in the program. Yet given the long time span of the deployment, she intentionally chose students who would be most likely to succeed individually, lest their irresponsibility lead the program as a whole to collapse.

Integrating Rituals

Most schools attempted to deploy AHPC by making use of existing in-school rituals, for example, by placing their base stations in high-traffic areas. However, we found that top-performing teachers went beyond this step, and used integrating rituals—those that encourage a collective school identity—to encourage students in the program. In particular, we observed a school in which the two teachers in charge of the program were teachers of elective subjects. By incorporating AHPC-specific elements into their classes, the teachers automatically gained access to the rituals of school life, such as a regular meeting time and the legitimacy of an elective course. The teachers asked the children to walk past the access point during class if they had yet to do so, and then as a group, the teachers and children viewed their current standing in the competition by having the AHPC website projected at the front of the room. Through this daily ritual, the teacher and children watched the progress of a nearby school, to ensure that they were staying ahead of their rivals.

Additionally, because there were more children in the two classes than there were slots on the AHPC "team," the teachers at the school mentioned above created a parallel opportunity for the remaining students to wear analog pedometers during the hour they were in this class; at the end of each hour, they would record their step counts onto a sheet of paper. Thus all children, whether enrolled in AHPC or not, had a chance to participate as a group in this physical activity monitoring experience.

UBICOMP AND SCHOOL SCHEMAS

The school is an institution, but it is also a stakeholder, one whose interests should ultimately align with the goals of a school-based ubicomp deployment. As a stakeholder, the school is organized to deal with certain kinds of activities, and will attempt to incorporate new activities based on their conformity to known categories. Schools are equipped to deal with curriculum, clubs, sports, after-school programs; deployments that fit this *schema* will have an easier time becoming part of everyday school life.

But as disruptive embedded technologies, ubicomp deployments might not fit into existing schemas. The AHPC itself is a good example. By combining features of several kinds of deployments, the AHPC relied more heavily on schools' ability to incorporate it into their everyday schedule, and not all schools were able to do so. But more broadly, the deployment did not fit neatly into an existing schema for school activities. Was the AHPC a team sport? A club? A fundraising challenge? A part of the PE curriculum? A part of the Social Studies curriculum? We encountered schools that handled the AHPC in all these ways, and often found different answers within the same school. This designed ambiguity gave schools the ability to customize the deployment to their own needs, but also forced them to fit it into a pre-existing schema.

Ubicomp as Team Sport

The AHPC fits in a space between traditional games and fitness programs. In some ways, the AHPC operates like a school-based fundraising program, where the school receives a package of materials and, with a limited amount of support from the sponsor, runs the program themselves. However, the emphasis on performance and school rivalry sets the AHPC up to appear more like a sport. If anything, the AHPC most resembles a decentralized asynchronous cross-country team.

Teachers' inclinations to create rituals and AHPC-related experiences touches on an issue that pervasive fitness applications might face, particularly if they are deployed in school settings: the lack of "events." The AHPC uses racing metaphors and language—each cycle is a called a "heat," and virtual buses zoom around a virtual racetrack—but includes no support for the in-person practices central to most sports. A majority (72%) of student survey respondents agreed that their school collaborated as a team, yet many told us in interviews that AHPC was not a sport. While not exactly a contradiction, this difference is striking. Students generally felt they were "on a team" but that did not necessarily translate into feeling AHPC was a sport. Part of this was the lack of access to students in other schools. Students saw each other only at the end, when schools in the same metropolitan area gathered to receive prizes. As one student put it:

> *The only time we actually saw [students from other schools] was when we received the check, and nobody talked to each other. They just like stopped in, the people in the other school…it would be nice to know who you're competing against.*

We described earlier how the AHPC teacher at one school treated the deployment as a team sport explicitly, hiring and firing students and instilling a strong team spirit. This strategy seems at odds with the AHPC's goals of using technology to help ordinary students get additional physical activity throughout the day, and although it appears to have increased motivation in this case, the strategy has an obvious downside in its potential for humiliation or shame.

Ubicomp as Curricular Project

Another approach was to treat the AHPC as a class project. Teachers were sometimes able to integrate the AHPC into their curriculum. This integration was especially important for non-PE teachers, who often felt they had to justify spending class time on the AHPC. One particularly innovative example of curriculum integration came from a school we visited. The AHPC teacher at this school was a Social Studies teacher. She worked an AHPC challenge into a lesson on the Civil War. Students re-enacted the Battle of Gettysburg, which involved literally walking a mile in the soldiers' shoes. Said one student:

> *It was a mile off from where the Confederates were from the Union…we walked through a mile of fields and we pretended to get shot.*

It would be interesting to see how the AHPC would change if it was presented as an extra-curricular activity. Even if the actual step accumulation took place outside the regular meetings, we suspect that engagement and retention would improve, and that schools would be able to more easily administer it. On the other hand, the AHPC would then directly compete with other activities such as sports practices, musical ensemble rehearsals, or tutoring programs that are particularly common in Title I schools.

It might not always be possible to find a genre of school-based activity that exactly matches the features and patterns of use of a ubicomp deployment. But understanding the school's schemas can help smooth a technological introduction into the school environment.

DISCUSSION AND DESIGN RECOMMENDATIONS

Within schools where the AHPC was deployed, typically 1-2 teachers took responsibility for administering the AHPC program; other teachers might have been supportive of the program but had no day-to-day responsibilities. The teachers in charge performed much of the stakeholder coordination required for the AHPC to function. They selected students, worked with administrators for gym or computing resources, contacted project managers at Humana to coordinate technology, set up the base stations and distributed pedometers, and monitored students' progress using the website. As authority figures with a limited ability to adjust the daily schedule, the AHPC teachers became instrumental in finding ways around time and space constraints embedded in the school day.

Fit Into the School Day

We found two factors that characterized teachers who led successful deployments: whether the teacher had regular access to the students, and whether this interaction occurred in a single class or was distributed throughout the day. Schools used a variety of methods to choose students for participation. Some schools enrolled all children in one classroom; in other schools, the children might not have had a single class as a group. The variety of enrollment practices afforded us the ability to see opportunities and constraints associated with incorporating physical activity interventions into school settings. We found that when all of the AHPC students met in a single class, the teacher had an easier time providing opportunities for structured physical activity options, as well as access to computer resources. In sum, daily access allowed the teacher to make arrangements for computer availability, monitor technology malfunctions, and to create meaningful rituals surrounding the program.

One issue with physical education in K-12 schools in the United States is that there is no guarantee that children *have* PE classes on a regular basis. PE requirements are determined at the state level, and even with state requirements, schools may interpret and enact requirements in different ways. Most schools we visited experienced more severe funding constraints for PE relative to academic subjects. The teacher survey indicated that although the student population in the AHPC schools ranged from 140 to 2000, the number of PE teachers ranged from 1-3, creating an average student-to-teacher ratio of 247:1. Thus, if physical activity interventions are to reach a maximum number of children, we might consider alternatives to the traditional PE class, particularly for schools that might not be able to offer each student daily physical education.

Where in the school day might AHPC fit other than PE class? On our site visits, we saw indications that participants were most satisfied with AHPC when it was incorporated into classes that have some degree of curriculum flexibility. We spoke to teachers in "non-core" subjects (e.g., those not subject to standardized testing requirements) who had more flexibility incorporating AHPC into their classroom activities. We found that teachers of topics less frequently subjected to standardized testing scrutiny (e.g., history, science), with support from the school's administration, might have flexibility to include physical activities into daily lessons. For instance, they might take children on a nature walk in a science class or have them re-enact a historical battle outdoors in a history class.

Overall, due to the teacher's central role in managing the school environment and schedule, it is imperative that regular student-teacher contact be prioritized for ubicomp deployments in schools, and that for physical activity interventions, there is sufficient flexibility to teach in ways that allow for activity.

Participation Boundaries: School-Based vs. -Delimited

One of the benefits of school-based ubicomp is the ability to deploy holistic interventions that meet youth where they already are. The AHPC was intended to reach into kids' lives by being school-based but extending into after-school and weekend life. However, our research indicates that it might have had limited effects outside the school environment. Despite the mobile nature of the sensors and the social support provided by parents, the AHPC appeared to minimally impact the home environment, and although many students told us they worked together to get steps, we saw little evidence of regular after-school play or exercise routines directed specifically at the AHPC. Instead, schools that obtained the most steps tended to be ones that had made provision for in-school step-accruing practices.

We heard this distinction in our qualitative interviews and site visits, but indications of this limitation can be found in the step data as well. The step data, binned into 24-hour periods, revealed higher physical activity levels during school days compared to weekends. Participants consistently took more steps on weekdays than weekends before and during the AHPC (during Pre-game baseline period: $t(1857) = 12.63, p < .001$ (two-tailed); during Phase I : $t(9213) = 39.36, p < .001$ (two-tailed); during the first month in Phase II: $t(4252) = 29.89, p < .001$ (two-tailed); during the second month in Phase II: $t(3729) = 28.90, p < .001$ (two-tailed)).

One might expect the opposite pattern of activity; students typically have more leisure time on the weekends, and the structures of the school environment that might inhibit step-counts (sitting in class, little time for recess) are not present. But these findings indicate that the students who wore the pedometers on weekends did less physical activities during days off than they did during schooldays. Whether the reason for fewer steps logged during weekends compared to weekdays is due to opportunities and organization of physical activities or competition with other leisure activities (or a combination of both), we have to consider whether in-home ambient displays might be interesting for short term competitions, or whether one should just not expect the program to extend beyond the school day. That being said, these results indicate that there still is a larger space for increasing activity levels during weekends.

When considering ubicomp deployments for schools, in addition to thinking about the school itself, researchers and designers also must consider the negative space: the school's blind spots and limitations. The school extends its influence outside its physical boundaries in many ways: homework, clubs, or sports teams, for example. But just because a deployment is mobile or pervasive does not guarantee it will cross the boundaries of the schoolhouse.

Designing For Group Experiences

The AHPC, as it was designed, does not impose any specific physical activity events or goal setting on participants. It is up to the participants to set their own goals, collect steps, and use the website. This flexibility is both a benefit and a problem. On the one hand, it allows teachers to integrate the program into the school day in whatever ways best meets local needs. On the other hand, if teachers are not proactive about providing ways for the children to participate, then the burden is on the students. Given the highly structured nature of a secondary school day, this burden might create a higher threshold for participation as the students have to be especially enthusiastic to create the time and space to participate.

In schools that left the AHPC as an individual experience—for instance, where students could use the website on a classroom computer when they were finished with other school work—we did not see as much enthusiasm about the program as compared to those with teacher-sponsored group experiences. These experiences, which typically involved the teacher leading the students in examining some aspect of their performance as a group (e.g., comparing aggregate step counts to a rival school), reinforced participation and excitement about the program.

Teacher-centered rituals that are brief and frequent work well in schools; they overcome technological and time constraints (e.g., not enough computers in a classroom or having to make special and disruptive arrangements to visit a computer lab). Teacher-centered rituals also control the experience of the game; they remove any potential of outside-world communication that might be perceived as threatening or harmful to students (e.g., like scares over social network safety for minors).

CONCLUSIONS

In this paper, we provided guidance for introducing ubiquitous computing technologies in institutions with established norms and rules, based on a study of a school-based health intervention for American youth. Drawing from work in the sociology of schools, we showed how the school regulates students' daily lives, and how this regulation impacts the planning, execution, and analysis of school-based ubiquitous computing deployments. We then provided recommendations including designing for group experiences, tempering expectations surrounding out-of-school impact, and supporting teachers in "making space" for the technology in a typical school day.

ACKNOWLEDGMENTS

We are deeply appreciative to Humana Games for Health and the Humana Foundation for their guidance and support. We would also like to thank the students, teachers, and parents who took our surveys, participated in focus groups and interviews and welcomed us into their schools.

REFERENCES

1. Balaam, M., Fitzpatrick, G., Good, J., and Luckin, R. Exploring affective technologies for the classroom with the subtle stone. *Proc. ACM CHI 2010*, 1623-1632.
2. Barr, R. and Dreeben, R. *How Schools Work.* University Of Chicago Press, 1991.
3. Berkovsky, S., Coombe, M., Freyne, J., Bhandari, D., and Baghaei, N. Physical activity motivating games. *Proc. ACM CHI 2010*, 243-252.
4. Bernstein, B. *Class, Codes and Control.* Routledge and Kegan Paul, 1977.
5. Bingham, P.M., Bates, J.H.T., Thompson-Figueroa, J., and Lahiri, T. A breath biofeedback computer game for children with cystic fibrosis. *Clinical Pediatrics 49*, 4 (2010), 337-342.
6. Brint, S. *Schools and Societies*. Pine Forge Press, 2006.
7. Brodersen, C. and Iversen, O.S. eCell - Spatial IT design for group collaboration in school environments. *Design*, (2005), 227-235.
8. Brotherton, J.A. and Abowd, G.D. Lessons Learned From eClass: assessing automated capture and access in the classroom. *ACM Transactions on Computer-Human Interaction (TOCHI)* 11, 2 (2004), 121-155.
9. Brown, R., Sugarman, H., and Burstin, A. Use of the Nintendo Wii Fit for the treatment of balance problems in an elderly patient with stroke: A case report. *International Journal of Rehabilitation Research 32*, (2009), S109.
10. Brown, S.J., Lieberman, D. a, Gemeny, B. a, Fan, Y.C., Wilson, D.M., and Pasta, D.J. Educational video game for juvenile diabetes: results of a controlled trial. *Informatics for Health and Social Care 22*, 1 (1997), 77-89.
11. Bruin, E.D. de, Schoene, D., Pichierri, G., and Smith, S.T. Use of virtual reality technique for the training of motor control in the elderly.: some theoretical considerations. *Zeitschrift für Gerontologie und Geriatrie : Organ der Deutschen Gesellschaft für Gerontologie und Geriatrie 43*, 4 (2010), 229-34.
12. Cao, X., Lindley, S.E., Helmes, J., and Sellen, A. Telling the whole story: anticipation , inspiration and reputation in a field deployment of TellTable. *Proc. ACM CSCW 2010,* 251-260.
13. Chang, Y.-chen, Lo, J.-ling, Huang, C.-ju, et al. Playful toothbrush: ubicomp technology for teaching tooth brushing to kindergarten children. *Proc. ACM CHI 2008,* 363-372.
14. Consolvo, S., Everitt, K., Landay, J.A., and Smith, I. Design requirements for technologies that encourage physical activity. *Proc. ACM CHI 2006*, 457-466.
15. Consolvo, S., McDonald, D., and Toscos, T. Activity sensing in the wild: a field trial of ubifit garden. *Proc. CHI 2008*, 1797-1806.
16. Cramer, M. and Hayes, G. Acceptable use of technology in schools: risks, policies, and promises. *IEEE Pervasive Computing 9*, 3 (2010), 37-44.
17. DeMarrais, K.B. and LeCompte, M.D. *The Way Schools Work : A Sociological Analysis Of Education*. Longman, 1995.
18. Deutsch, J.E., Robbins, D., Morrison, J., and Guarrera Bowlby, P. Wii-based compared to standard of care balance and mobility rehabilitation for two individuals post-stroke. *Proc. IEEE Virtual Rehabilitation International Conference 2009*. 117-120.
19. Ebbeling, C.B., Pawlak, D.B., and Ludwig, D.S. Childhood obesity: public-health crisis, common sense cure. *Lancet* 360, 9331 (2002), 473-82.
20. Eiriksdottir, E., Poole, E.S., Miller, A.D., Xu, Y., Kestranek, D., Catrambone, R., and Mynatt, E.D. Assessing health games in secondary schools: an investigation of the american horsepower challenge 2009-2010. *GVU Center Technical Report, Georgia Institute of Technology*, 2010.
21. Ervasti, M., Isomursu, M., and Kinnula, M. Bringing technology into school: NFC-enabled school attendance supervision. *Proc. ACM MUM 2009,* 10 pages.
22. Grimes, A., Bednar, M., Bolter, J.D., and Grinter, R.E. EatWell: sharing nutrition-related memories in a low-income community. *Proc. ACM CSCW 2008*, 87–96.

23. Grimes, A. and Grinter, R.E. Designing persuasion: Health technology for low-income African American communities. *Proc. PERSUASIVE'07*, 24-35.
24. Grimes, A. and Harper, R. Celebratory technology. *Proc. ACM CHI 2008,* 467-476.
25. Grimes, A., Landry, B.M., and Grinter, R.E. Characteristics of shared health reflections in a local community. *Proc. ACM CSCW 2010,* 435-444.
26. Harris, A., Rick, J., Bonnett, V., et al. Around the table: Are multiple-touch surfaces better than single-touch for children's collaborative interactions? *Proc. CSCL'09,* 335-344.
27. Hayes, G.R., Gardere, L.M., and Abowd, G.D. CareLog : a selective archiving tool for behavior management in schools. *Proc. ACM CHI 2008,* 685-694.
28. Herndon, C.D., Decambre, M., and McKenna, P.H. Interactive computer games for treatment of pelvic floor dysfunction. *The Journal of Urology,* 166, 5 (2001), 1893-1898.
29. Hirano, S.H., Yeganyan, M.T., Marcu, G., Nguyen, D.H., Boyd, L.A., and Hayes, G.R. vSked : evaluation of a system to support classroom activities for children with autism. *Proc. ACM CHI 2010,* 1633-1642.
30. Hwang, I., Jang, H., Nachman, L., Song, J., Corporation, I., and Clara, S. Exploring inter-child behavioral relativity in a shared social environment : a field study in a kindergarten. *Proc. Ubicomp 2010,* 271-280.
31. Kennedy, T.L.M., Smith, A., Specialist, R., et al. Networked families. *Pew Internet & American Life Project*, (2008).
32. Lenhart, A., Kahne, J., Middaugh, E., Macgill, A., and Vitak, J. Teens, video games, and civics. *Pew Internet & American Life Project*, 2008.
33. Mamykina, L., Mynatt, E., Davidson, P., and Greenblatt, D. MAHI: investigation of social scaffolding for reflective thinking in diabetes management. *Proc. CHI 2008*, 477-486.
34. Mccaughtry, N., Dillon, S.R., Martin, J.J., and Oliver, K.L. Teachers' perspectives on the use of pedometers as instructional technology in physical education: a cautionary tale. *Journal of Teaching in Physical Education*, 21, 1, (2008), 83-99.
35. Meyer, J.W. and Rowan, B. The structure of educational organizations. In M. Meyer, ed., *Environments and organizations*. Jossey-Bass, 1978, 78-109.
36. Morgan Jr., C.F., Pangrazi, R.P., and Beighle, A. Using pedometers to promote physical activity in physical education. *JOPERD: The Journal of Physical Education, Recreation & Dance* 74, 7 (2003), 33-39.
37. Music, J. and Murray-Smith, R. Virtual hooping: teaching a phone about hula-hooping for fitness, fun and rehabilitation. *Proc. MobileHCI 2010*, 309-312.
38. Perry, J.C., Andureu, J., Cavallaro, F.I., Veneman, J.F., Carmien, S.P., and Keller, T. Effective game use in neurorehabilitation: user-centered perspectives. In *Handbook of Research on Improving Learning and Motivation through Educational Games*. IGI Global, 2010, 1-44.
39. Prévost, L., Liechti, O., Lyons, M.J., et al. Design and Implementation of a Mobile Exergaming Platform. In *Intelligent Technologies for Interactive Entertainment,* Springer Berlin Heidelberg, 2009, 213-220.
40. Rotwein-Pivnick, R. Getting kids and adolescents excited about exercise. *IDEA Fitness Journal* 3, 2 (2006), 5 pages.
41. Strong, W.B., Malina, R.M., Blimkie, C.J.R., et al. Evidence based physical activity for school-age youth. *The Journal of Pediatrics* 146, 6 (2005), 732-737.
42. Suskind, R.M., Blecker, U., Udall, J.N., et al. Recent advances in the treatment of childhood obesity. *Pediatric diabetes 1*, 1 (2000), 23-33.
43. Taylor, A., Backlund, P., Engstrom, H., Johannesson, M., and Lebram, M. The birth of elinor: a collaborative development of a game based system for stroke rehabilitation. *Proc. IEEE Visualisation 2009*, 52–60.
44. Toscos, T., Faber, A., Connelly, K., and Upoma, A. Encouraging physical activity in teens Can technology help reduce barriers to physical activity in adolescent girls? *Proc. IEEE PervasiveHealth 2008,* 218–221.
45. US Department of Education. Title I, Part A Program. 2010. http://www2.ed.gov/programs/titleiparta.
46. Wilkinson, N., Ang, R.P., and Goh, D.H. Online Video Game Therapy for Mental Health Concerns: A Review. *International Journal of Social Psychiatry* 54, 4 (2008), 370-382.
47. Wylie, C.G. and Coulton, P. Mobile exergaming. *Proc. ACE 2008,* 338–341.

Understanding My Data, Myself: Supporting Self-Reflection with Ubicomp Technologies

Ian Li[1], Anind K. Dey[1], Jodi Forlizzi[1,2]
[1]Human Computer Interaction Institute, [2]School of Design
Carnegie Mellon University, Pittsburgh, PA 15213
ianli@cmu.edu, {anind, forlizzi}@cs.cmu.edu

ABSTRACT
We live in a world where many kinds of data about us can be collected and more will be collected as Ubicomp technologies mature. People reflect on this data using different tools for personal informatics. However, current tools do not have sufficient understanding of users' self-reflection needs to appropriately leverage Ubicomp technologies. To design tools that effectively assist self-reflection, we need to comprehensively understand what kinds of questions people have about their data, why they ask these questions, how they answer them with current tools, and what kinds of problems they encounter. To explore this, we conducted interviews with people who use various kinds of tools for personal informatics. We found six *kinds of questions* that people asked about their data. We also found that certain kinds of questions are more important at certain times, which we call *phases*. We identified two phases of reflection: *Discovery* and *Maintenance*. We discuss the kinds of questions and the phases in detail and identify features that should be supported in personal informatics tools for which Ubicomp technologies can play an important role.

Author Keywords
Personal informatics, reflection, phases, discovery, design features, visualizations

ACM Classification Keywords
H5.m. Information interfaces and presentation (e.g., HCI): Miscellaneous.

General Terms
Design, Human Factors

INTRODUCTION
The abundance of computers, mobile devices, sensors, and access to information via the Internet enables the recording of a myriad of personal data (*e.g.*, physiological data, behaviors, habits, and thoughts). All of this data can be used for self-reflection to help people become more aware of their own behavior [5], make better decisions [8], and change behavior in domains ranging from health to energy conservation [7,28]. More tools are being developed that people use for *personal informatics*, which help people collect and reflect on personally relevant data for the purpose of self-knowledge [17]. Many Ubicomp tools have been created for personal informatics, such as Fish'n'Steps [18], Ubigreen [10], and mobile apps for diabetes [24].

However, we believe current tools for personal informatics were not designed with sufficient understanding of users' self-reflection needs. For example, a tool might show the user's current step counts, but the user might prefer a historical view of her average step counts to inform her how to increase her steps. To appropriately design these tools, we need a comprehensive understanding of what kinds of questions people want to answer about their data, why they ask these questions, how they answer them with current tools, and what kinds of problems they encounter. By doing so, developers and designers can better take advantage of Ubicomp technologies to help users self-reflect.

To explore these issues, we conducted a study in which we interviewed people who used tools for personal informatics. We identified six *kinds of questions* that people asked about their data: *Status*, *History*, *Goals*, *Discrepancies*, *Context*, and *Factors*. We discuss the tools that people used to answer these kinds of questions and the problems that they encountered. We also discovered that people's information needs change, which we called *phases of reflection*: *Discovery* and *Maintenance*. These phases differ by how frequently people asked the different kinds of questions. An important aspect of the phases is that people transitioned between them. People transitioned from *Maintenance* to *Discovery* when they were unable to reach their goals or when they had to redefine their goals because they experienced a new set of problems. On the other hand, people transitioned from *Discovery* to *Maintenance* when they had identified their goal and had learned the steps they needed to take to achieve their goal.

The importance of this work to Ubicomp is threefold. First, this work describes the kinds of questions that people ask about their data, which suggests how data should be presented to inform users of proper actions towards behavior change. Second, this work identifies features that Ubicomp tools should have, so that users can get the

UbiComp'11, September 17–21, 2011, Beijing, China.

information they need to make better decisions towards behavior change. Lastly, this work describes how Ubicomp technologies can appropriately support people to answer the questions they ask within the phases and help them transition between the phases. This work shows that Ubicomp technologies can play an important role in helping people become more self-aware, which is valuable in making good decisions and changing behavior.

This paper is organized in the following manner. First, we discuss what we mean by personal informatics and discuss related work in personal informatics. Second, we describe our interviews, which explore what questions people ask about their data and how they answer these questions with current tools. We then discuss our findings: the six main questions people asked about their data and the two phases of reflection that they transitioned between. We present a list of features that Ubicomp tools should support to help users with reflection, and discuss their implications.

Defining Personal Informatics

We extend the definition of personal informatics [17] from a class of tools to an *activity* where people collect and reflect on personal data to gain a better understanding of their own behavior. People can and will use almost any tool for personal informatics. Tools can vary by form factor (paper, web sites, devices, *etc.*) and level of support (manual *vs.* automated). However, the limitations of tools that people use can make the activity of personal informatics cumbersome and time-consuming [17]. Therefore, Ubicomp technologies have an opportunity to assist the people in their personal informatics activity.

Data for personal informatics include data about behavior (*e.g.*, frequency of exercise) and physiology (*e.g.*, heart rate). They may include current and historical data and may be quantitative or qualitative (*e.g.*, step counts *vs.* moods). In addition to personal information, external data can be used when it is personally relevant, *e.g.*, weather data might be personally relevant if the user is interested in knowing how the weather affects her physical activity.

As we will discuss later, our exploration found that people collected personal data for other reasons other than personal informatics, such as reminiscing about the past [21], aiding memory [14], and personal information management [16]. In this paper, we focus on collection of personal data for the purpose of gaining insights and understanding oneself. There is much research that shows that reflection plays an important role in changing behaviors [see 7 for a review].

RELATED WORK

This work builds on top of other research that has looked into investigating appropriate feedback for users. This paper focuses on supporting users' reflection needs, which is one of the stages of the model of personal informatics systems [17]: *Preparation*, *Collection*, *Integration*, *Reflection*, and *Action*. The model describes the different types of support that tools must provide to assist users through their personal informatics activity. The model also highlights that the stages are inter-related, *i.e.*, problems from the earlier stages affect the later stages. This implies that the person's ability to reflect on her data and the value of the reflection are affected by how and what data she collects. Thus, the support that Ubicomp technologies can provide in improving how data is collected and in increasing the types of data that can be collected can help with self-reflection.

Related to the PI model is the Transtheoretical Model of Behavior Change (TTM) [25], which also consists of five stages: *Precontemplation*, *Contemplation*, *Preparation*, *Action*, and *Maintenance*. Unlike the PI model, which describes the different types of support needed to assist personal informatics activities, the TTM describes people's different levels of motivation and ability to change behavior. The TTM is used to classify people's readiness to change behavior, which is useful for tailoring interventions, such as, designing feedback to encourage environmentally friendly behavior [13]. Others have also explored other behavioral theories. Consolvo and colleagues used various psychological theories to describe eight design strategies to support behavior change [6]. Froehlich and colleagues described different ways of designing eco-feedback technologies [10]. While these models suggest the need for Ubicomp technologies, they do not define how tools should be designed based on people's changing information needs when engaging in personal informatics activities.

There is plenty of research on effective information visualization techniques to explore data for insights [see 4 for an extensive review], but they are not all focused on personal data. Some projects have applied exploration techniques on personal data. For example, Frost and Smith used visualizations to help diabetic patients explore the relationship between their blood glucose level and the types of food they consumed [11]. Commercial products, such as Mint (expenditures), Nike+ (physical activity), and Wattson (electricity), use information visualizations to assist users in exploring their data for patterns and trends. Some information visualizations, such as ambient displays [22], glanceable displays [19], and information art [20], are less focused on exploration of historical information. Instead, they increase awareness of one's current status (*e.g.*, you've got mail, your stock portfolio is currently up, your bus is arriving) while minimizing cognitive load. This work explores how people use these existing tools to answer their questions about themselves and what problems they encounter. We use this exploration to define users' specific information needs and to describe how Ubicomp technologies can provide support.

In the next section, we describe our interviews of people who used tools for personal informatics. We analyzed the responses for the kinds of questions they asked and how they used existing tools to answer them.

INTERVIEWS

The goal of the interviews was to study how people explore and reflect on the data they collect for personal informatics.

We conducted interviews with people who were already self-tracking and reflecting on collected data. This helped us see behavior in a natural setting where people's routines around tracking and reflecting were focused on their own needs, rather than forcing people to use a system we designed. In the following sections, we describe how we recruited participants and conducted the interviews.

Recruitment

We advertised the study on Craigslist, the Quantified Self blog, and a campus recruiting web site. The recruitment letter stated that we were looking for users of self-tracking/personal informatics tools, such as Mint, Nike+, MoodJam, *etc.* People interested in the study completed a pre-questionnaire that asked what type of data they collect, for how long, and contact information. They had to be currently using a tool for personal informatics and must have used it for a month or more. We recruited a diverse group of people from around the nation and our city. Given that we were only going to be able to talk to a limited number of people, the pre-questionnaire helped us ensure that we recruited a set of participants using a range of tools for a range of types of data.

91 people responded to the pre-questionnaire (local: 76, remote: 15). We selected 15 people (P1-P15) from all the respondents to participate in the study. Ten lived locally within the city limits and five lived remotely. A third were male (5 vs. 10 females). The age ranges and their respective counts were 20-25 (6), 25-30 (4), 30-35 (1), and over 50 (4). Additionally, half were professionals (8) and the rest were students (graduate: 4, undergraduate: 3).

Procedure

We invited participants for a one-hour interview in either our lab or over Skype, depending on whether they lived locally or remotely. Local participants were required to bring the tools they used for personal informatics (e.g., laptop, devices, notebooks) to the interview. Remote participants used Skype's Screen Sharing and Video features to show us the tools they used.

At the beginning of the interview, we introduced participants to the study. Participants signed the study consent form and completed an online survey that asked about their general personal informatics usage. The questionnaire is a condensed version of the survey described in [17]. We sat with the participants in front of their laptop or mobile phone and asked them to describe their general usage. We observed participants as they used their tools. We asked them how they reflected on their data and to show us how they reviewed their data: What were they looking for? What questions did they have? Why did they ask these questions? How did they answer their questions using their tools? What problems did they experience while trying to answer their questions?

Participants were compensated $10 (in cash or as Amazon gift certificates) for the one hour they spent with us. The interviews were videotaped.

RESULTS

We transcribed the interview recordings. We analyzed the interviews by coding the responses line by line. We did not have a pre-determined coding scheme before the analysis. Instead, we identified themes from the data as we processed the responses. The themes emerged after we organized the codes using affinity diagrams. During the analysis, we focused on the reasons people reflected on their data, what questions people were trying to answer when reflecting on their data, how the tools they used supported or prevented finding answers to their questions), and what design features in the tools they used supported their personal informatics activity.

Participant Information

To help focus our interviews, we asked participants to describe the *primary data* about themselves that they collected [Table 1]. The participants varied in the types of information they collected. The primary data that participants collected were: financial expenditures (3), sleep (3), weight (2), blood glucose level (2), exercise (1), productivity (1), web history (1), books read (1), and life events (1). Half of the participants collected one or more types of data. For example, P7, who collected the widest variety of data, used Daytum and your.flowingdata to track television shows and movies that she watched, restaurants she dined at, and places she visited. She recorded her eating habits with DailyBurn. Because of periods of insomnia, she used Fitbit to record her sleep patterns and physical activity levels. She also complemented her sleep tracking by taking notes about the quality of her sleep in YawnLog. There was also a diversity of experiences in self-tracking. Four participants had been self-tracking for a month or two; seven participants, for a year or two; and three participants, for more than three years. P3, who has diabetes, had been tracking her blood glucose level for 15 years. For several years, she used a fingerstick blood glucose meter that required piercing the skin to draw blood 3 to 10 times a day. In the past year, she started using a Dexcom device, which has a sensor that adheres to the body and continuously takes blood glucose readings very 5 minutes.

ID	Primary Data	Multiple Types?	Reason
P1	expenses	No	Behavior Change
P2	weight	Yes	Behavior Change
P3	blood glucose	Was	Behavior Change
P4	exercise	Was	Behavior Change
P5	expenses	Yes	Behavior Change
P6	blood glucose	Was	Behavior Change
P7	sleep	Was	Behavior Change
P8	sleep	Yes	Behavior Change
P9	sleep	Yes	Behavior Change
P10	life events	No	Reminiscence
P11	weight	Was	Behavior Change
P12	expenses	No	Coordination
P13	productivity	No	Behavior Change
P14	web history	No	Retrieval
P15	books	No	Sharing

Table 1. The participants, their primary data, whether they collected multiple types of data, and their reasons for collection.

Reasons

Participants cited different reasons for collecting personal data. Many participants (11 out of 15) self-tracked to reflect on the data, because they wanted to change or maintain a behavior. For example, P1 used Mint to maintain a budget after moving to a new city. P8 tracked her sleep patterns and various factors that might affect the quality of her sleep using the Sleeptracker watch and laptop application. Four participants collected data for other uses. P14 collected his web history with Google Web History for *later retrieval*. P15 collected book information in GoodReads to *share* with other people. P12 recorded his grocery and utility expenditures in Buxfer to easily *coordinate* expenses with his roommates. P10 wrote about life events in online journals to better *remember* her past. These four participants' usage of personal informatics tools is more closely in line with other types of applications (in order): personal information management, social networking, coordination, and reminiscence. In the following section, we focus our discussion on the 11 participants who wanted to change or maintain their behavior, because personal informatics tools are useful when they help people gain self-knowledge that improves decision-making and assists in behavior change.

QUESTIONS

In this section, we discuss the 6 kinds of questions that people asked about their personal information: *Status*, *History*, *Goals*, *Discrepancies*, *Context*, and *Factors*. We describe in detail what participants were looking for and how they answered their questions.

Status

People were interested in data that revealed their current status. For example, P7 checked her Fitbit device several times a day to determine her current physical activity level. Checking one's status doesn't have to happen several times a day; P5 checked her finances using Mint and her bank web site at the end of each day.

People also checked their current status to determine whether they were meeting their goal and whether they should act to correct their behavior. For example, P7 checked her step count to determine whether she took enough steps for the day. If not, she would go out for a walk. P5 checked her finances to make sure that she is staying within her daily budget. If not, she tried to spend less the subsequent days.

How often people checked their status is dependent on what kind of data they were tracking and how they were tracking it. For example, P3 and P6 have diabetes, and used blood glucose meters to measure their current blood sugar level. P3 wore a Dexcom continuous blood glucose meter, which measured her blood glucose level every 5 minutes. However, P6 used a fingerstick device, so he could only check 3 to 6 times a day.

For some kinds of data, participants did not use a device to measure their current status; instead, they used their own senses. For example, P9 who was interested in her sleep quality recorded the quality of her sleep and whether leg cramps occurred. P8 used the SleepTracker watch to measure her sleep, but she used her senses to record information related to sleep, such as mood and stress.

History

Beyond looking at one's current status, participants were also interested in seeing their data over the long term. Instead of looking at one piece of data or a short time's worth of data (an hour to a day), people wanted to see their data over a long range to find trends and patterns. Trends (whether the data is going up, going down, or remaining steady) are especially important to figure out whether they are making progress towards a particular goal. For example, P4 looked for trends in her physical activity data to make sure that she was maintaining her goal of regular physical activity over a long period of time. P5 also looked at trends to make sure that she was reducing her monthly expenditures to save for a trip abroad.

People experienced different kinds of problems in understanding their history. One problem is that the ability to see trends and patterns largely depends on having collected data over a long period of time. Thus, the person has to first put in the effort of collecting data before the value of the data becomes evident. For example, P5 started using Mint when her mom introduced her to the site. She could not make any significant conclusions regarding her spending trends because she had only been collecting data for a month prior to the interview. Another problem is that tools do not provide adequate support to allow reflection over the long term. P8 experienced this problem with the SleepTracker watch, which she had been using for several months. The watch had a desktop interface to review her past history. However, the software just listed her sleep quantity on a spreadsheet-like interface, which made it difficult to see trends. She said a simple bar graph would have been helpful.

A related question is: *how does data from one time range compare with another?* Viewing one's data over a long period of time allows the person to answer this question. For example, P1 compared her spending between two different months. She was particularly interested in seeing how her recent move affected her spending.

Goal

In addition to wanting to know their status and their history, people also wanted to figure out what goals would be appropriate to pursue. Sometimes, people started self-tracking without knowing their goal and they used self-tracking as way to 1) determine what actions they should take to fix a problem or 2) establish a "baseline" of their activities to determine whether they have a problem.

Before we go into detail about this question, we need to define what kind of goals we are talking about, because the distinction between the different kinds of goals is important. Powers [23] described goals as a hierarchical structure ranging from abstract to more specific. The four levels are *system concept*, *principle*, *program*, and *sequence*. The *system-concept goal* refers to the sense of an idealized self, an idealized relationship, or an idealized society, and, as such, is very abstract. The next level of goals is the *principle level*, which refers to the set of goals (or guiding principles) that one tries to achieve to reach an ideal. Some examples of principle-level goals are: be physically fit, be thrifty, and be productive. This level is still quite abstract; a person does not just become physically fit or thrifty or productive, one has to exhibit such qualities by doing specific activities or *programs* [26]. Some example of *program-level goals* are: 1) running three times a week to become physically fit; 2) spending money within a budget to become thrifty; and 3) minimizing the amount of time spent browsing social media websites to become productive. To perform a program-level goal, a person does *sequences* of specific actions. For example, the *sequence-level goals* to complete the goal of running three times a week may consist of putting on shoes, going outside, running a specified route, *etc.*

In the rest of this paper, we are talking about "program-level goals" when we refer to "goals". Program-level goals are more specific than principle- or system-concept level goals, so they are more actionable or more ready to be acted upon. We found that people use personal informatics tools to help them set and complete program-level goals. For example, P4 used SparkPeople because she wanted to become physically fit (principle-level goal), but the value of the tool was in helping her track her progress in accomplishing her program-level goals: running three times per week and eating within a specified amount of calories.

Knowing one's goals had an effect on the number of kinds of data the participants collected. For example, P9 had problems sleeping because of her leg cramps. She wanted to address the problem to improve her sleep (principle-level goal), but she did not know what caused her leg cramps. She tracked what she ate and her physical activity to see if these were causing the leg cramps, so she could make program-level goals, such as "avoid X kind of food" or "don't do physical activity X hours before sleeping."

Once participants identified their program-level goals, they changed their data collection habits. For example, when P3 was diagnosed with diabetes, she did not know the appropriate program-level goals to manage her diabetes, such as what specific foods to avoid, how active she could be, *etc.* To figure out her goals, she collected multiple kinds of data: what she ate, what physical activity she did, as well as her blood sugar level. She is a "brittle diabetic" (her blood sugar fluctuates to dangerous levels quickly), so figuring out the effects of food and physical activity was critical, but difficult to do. She did this for two years until she understood her blood sugar fluctuations better and she was able to set appropriate food and physical activity goals. When this happened, she stopped collecting the other pieces of data because she already knew their effects. She still tracks her blood sugar level, but she just takes mental notes of the meal, physical activity, and sleep quality prior to her blood sugar level measurement.

Discrepancies

Once people know their goal, they compare their current status with their goal [5]. We also observed this in our interviews. Participants checked their current status then compared it with their goal: Is there a difference between my current status and my goal? How big is the difference? And what should I do to reduce the difference? For example, P4 wanted to become more physically active, so she set a goal of exercising every other day or about three times a week. She looked at her weekly physical activity using SparkPeople. She checked how much her current status differed from the goal. When she found a difference, she modified her schedule to compensate for her missed physical activity. Also, how participants addressed discrepancies changed over time. At the beginning, P4 was very strict at meeting her goals, so she immediately addressed missing her goal by exercising the same day. A year after her physical activity tracking she became less strict about meeting her goal. She allowed herself to miss days, and instead of exercising immediately, she postponed physical activity until the end of the week when she had more time. Another example is P11 who compared her daily food consumption with a range of calories, a goal that she had set in the DailyPlate tool. Every day she checked whether she was within the range of her allotted daily consumption. When her consumption was below her goal, she increased her consumption for that day. If she was within range, she made sure that she did not go over. Both P4 and P11 found that comparing their current status with their goal helped them make immediate decisions to address any differences. If they were meeting their goal, they could focus on maintaining it.

A problem with this question is that it is largely dependent on knowing what the program-level goal is. If the goal is undefined, the person cannot act on fixing their problem. This is what happened with P9. She knew her principle-level goal: fix her leg cramps when she goes to sleep. Unfortunately, she did not understand the causes of her leg cramps well enough to set appropriate program-level goals, such as avoiding certain foods or certain physical activity.

Context

Participants also wondered what other things were happening at or near the same time as their current information-seeking context. They were curious about how other events may explain what was happening to them *in the present*. For example, P3 kept in mind other events at or near the time she checked her blood sugar level (*e.g.*, what she ate, what physical activity she did), so she could act on problems appropriately. P6 noted his current mood and stress level along with his blood sugar level. He thought that his blood sugar level might explain how he was feeling.

How participants answered this question was dependent on their access to additional data. Some people depended on other devices. For example, P6 used Fitbit and Zeo to automatically record his physical activity and sleep quality. He used the data from these devices to figure out the relationship of his physical activity and sleep with his blood sugar level. Some people used written notes (on paper or a web site) to remind themselves of other events that happened at a particular time. P8 used the annotation feature in the SleepTracker software to record her mood, stress level, and caffeine intake, which may be related to her sleep quality. P5 kept a journal of her activities to remind her of what she did when she spent her money. Sometimes, people just depended on their memory to remind them of what happened. For example, P4 diligently recorded her data at the start of her self-tracking, but after a while she just used her memory. She explained, "I just depend on my memory…I didn't want to become, like, OCD (obsessive-compulsive) about it." However, one problem with dependence on memory is that one's memory of events can be unreliable and degrades over time.

Factors

Unlike the previous question, which asks what influences a person's current status, this question asks what influences behavior *over a long period of time*. Factors collected over time help to identify and monitor trends. For example, P4 was curious how her physical activity and nutrition affected her overall health over a long period of time.

Participants were interested in how other factors may be affecting their behavior. For example, it is not sufficient to say that one wants to lose weight; it is important to know how one's physical activity level and food consumption affect one's weight. By knowing the factors, people can act on those factors to change their behavior. This is especially important when other things could cause the behavior. For example, P2 was interested in losing weight. To help her accomplish this goal, she tracked several types of information in addition to her weight: exercises she did, what she ate, total calories, and water drank. She used the CalorieTracker Android app to help her compute the calories of her food and DailyPlate to store all the data online. She used the DailyPlate graphs and charts to see the trends in her weight and how they were affected by other factors. When her weight went up, she reduced her food intake and increased her physical activity. She also made sure that her weight went down at a "healthy rate of decline", so that she lost weight in a healthy way. P2 also wrote in a journal to record her goals and how she felt about her progress. She said, "I look for things that I have done well. Places where I might have made a misstep, either I've done too much exercise in one day or I've done too little. Or maybe I didn't meet all of my exchanges or maybe I met all of my exchanges, calorie-wise."

One problem with this kind of question is that a tool did not exist that could help users explore their data holistically. Instead, they had to look at their data one at a time. Even when data was stored in the same tool, they had to look at different graphs separately (*e.g.*, Daytum). Using different tools for different types of data exacerbated this problem. For example, P6 used Fitbit for physical activity and Zeo for sleep and there was not an easy way to look at these data together. P7 used Fitbit for both sleep and physical activity tracking, so she was able to explore both types of data together. However, she also collected other types of data using Daytum and your.flowingdata, which she could not easily review along with her Fitbit data. Some participants managed to explore their data together by using paper graphs (P9 and P6) or by painstakingly reviewing logs of their data (P2 and P8). However, participants experienced other setbacks: exploring multiple types of data was confusing and understanding the influences of the factors on their behavior was difficult.

PHASES OF REFLECTION

We noticed that participants asked some questions more often than others at different times. We analyzed our data further by looking at when participants asked certain questions. We identified two distinct phases when participants asked different sets of questions: Maintenance and Discovery. We also found that participants did not remain in one phase; instead they transitioned between the two. We discuss the properties of each phase and the transitions between the phases in the next sections.

Maintenance Phase

The Maintenance phase is marked with participants mostly asking *Status* and *Discrepancy* questions. In this phase, participants used their collected data to maintain awareness of their status relative to a goal and to maintain their behavior. When in the Maintenance phase, participants can be characterized in the following way: 1) they already knew the goal they were trying to meet and 2) they have identified how different factors affected their behavior. We describe each of these characteristics below.

Participants in the Maintenance phase have already identified their program-level goals. In this phase, they self-track to determine whether their current actions are in line with their goals. P13 wanted to be more productive (principle-level goal), and had already determined his program-level goal: limit his visits to social media websites to 20 minutes a day. While his StayFocusd Chrome browser extension stored his total web site visit times over a week and a month, he did not look at those numbers; he just needed the tool to alert him when he went above his goal. P1 used Mint to keep track of her expenditures to make sure that she is meeting several budgets that she had already set for various categories of expenditures (program-level goals). When she showed us her Mint account, she had set budgets for 14 categories!

Also, participants in the Maintenance phase already knew the relationships between their behavior and factors that affect their behavior. They collected information about their behavior; they did not collect other types of data that might affect their behavior because they were not useful anymore. For example, P13 just tracked the minutes that he spent on Facebook, Twitter, and other social media sites, because he already knew how browsing such web sites affected his productivity. He did not track other factors that might affect his productivity (*e.g.*, sleep quality, interruptions). P1 did not use the exploratory tools within Mint to see how much she had spent on different categories and what she purchased. Instead, she primarily used the main screen where her budget was prominently displayed to check whether she was within her monthly budget.

During the Maintenance phase, participants only tracked one or a few types of data. They have already defined their goal and were collecting just enough information that would allow them to tell whether they were meeting their goal. For example, P1 and P5 only reflected on their expenses and P13, on his productivity.

Discovery Phase

The Discovery phase is marked with participants mostly asking *History*, *Goals*, *Context*, and *Factors* questions. When in the Discovery phase, participants can be characterized in the following way: 1) they did not know the goal they were trying to meet and/or 2) they have not identified the factors that influenced their behavior. We describe each of these characteristics below.

Participants in the Discovery phase were still trying to figure out what their program-level goals were. When P3 was newly diagnosed with diabetes, she knew that she had to manage her blood sugar level (principle-level goal), but she did not know specifically what kinds of foods to avoid or how much physical activity she could perform (program-level goals). P8 tracked the quality of her sleep so that she feels better rested (principle-level goal). She explored her sleep data to "spot trends for which I can take corrective action." She wanted to figure out the specific program-level goals that would improve her sleep quality, such as eating dinner earlier or refraining from coffee or alcohol. She also added that she was "trying to take a long-term view", so that the solution is "not a quick-fix approach."

Also, participants in the Discovery phase did not know how different factors affected their behavior. Because of this lack of knowledge, participants collected different types of data, so they could figure out the correlations between them. P3 tracked food consumption and physical activity along with her blood glucose levels because she wanted to figure out how her eating and exercise habits affected the fluctuations in her blood glucose level. P9 had leg cramps while sleeping. She had several hypotheses about what caused her leg cramps. She talked to her doctor who said the leg cramps might be due to an electrolyte imbalance, so she tracked the types of food she ate. She also used FitBit to see if her amount of physical activity had an effect on the occurrence of her leg cramps.

Transitions Between Phases

We found in our interviews that people did not stay in one phase; instead, they transitioned between the two phases. Several participants who were in the Maintenance phase at the time of the interviews were in the Discovery phase earlier in their self-tracking regimen. P6 initially tracked his blood sugar level, his food consumption, and mood until he found that "it turns out one of the things I do to manage stress is eat something, because blood sugar feels good. So if things are unsettled or high pressure, eating something feels good." P6 described his transition to gaining control of his diabetes, "In the initial phase, three and a half years ago, over about six months, I learned to control my blood sugar down to a level from 300 to about 180. Then I escaped there and measurement became less interesting because there was no progress to be made; it was steady state stuff." P3 had a similar experience in dealing with her diabetes. She said, "When I first became diabetic, I needed to keep track of everything. At this point in my life, I've had diabetes for about 15 years, and I no longer write anything down." Now, she just wears a continuous blood glucose monitoring device to alert her whether her blood glucose is too high or too low. Her reason for transitioning was two-fold: 1) tracking all the information "would be onerous" and 2) "it wasn't helping me anymore. I was remembering. Not the exact numbers, but I was remembering trends."

P4 tracked her physical activity and food consumption diligently at the beginning, but became more lax later and did not track her food consumption. She said, "I feel like I have a handle on it. I have accomplished the goals of creating a healthy lifestyle for myself. As long as I stay like this I'm good. It's more maintenance." She still kept track of her physical activity, but for her food tracking, she just "keeps a mental note of it and just overall have become more self aware of what I eat and stuff."

Sometimes people have difficulty transitioning to the Maintenance phase because they could not find an actionable goal. P9 described that she still did not know what caused the leg cramps when she sleeps. She said, "They're not completely gone, but they're not as bad as they were. But I still don't know exactly what's caused them." She added that she still recorded the recurrence of the leg cramps, "It may always be sort of a mystery, and so I still have data for every night I've had leg cramps."

All the participants who were in the Maintenance phase at the time of the study described anecdotes when they might go back to the Discovery phase. For example, while looking at her budget, P1 saw that she made a purchase of $24 for a gift and she asked herself, "What was that?" She said since she did not remember, she explored her data to find an explanation. Since Mint provided enough detail about her purchases, she easily found that the gifts were bought at a local mall, which reminded her that she recently purchased a gift for a friend there. Sometimes the explanatory data was not immediately available, so the participant had to restart data collection of influencing factors. For example, P7 who had recurrent insomnia tracked her sleep using FitBit. Patterns of insomnia or weird dreams would appear intermittently and she would again note factors that may have caused the problem.

FEATURES

We have identified the questions that people asked and the phases in which people asked these different questions. Now, we discuss the features that should be supported in building personal informatics tools and how Ubicomp technologies can help. We also describe opportunities for Ubicomp to explore.

Supporting the Maintenance Phase

Supporting the Maintenance Phase is not as difficult as the Discovery phase because many personal informatics tools already support collecting the user's current status. Additionally, if a Ubicomp technology can sense simple things about a user's behavior, it is not difficult to display the information back to the user. However, there are some opportunities to better support the Maintenance phase.

Alert the user when they are not meeting their goal

During the Maintenance phase, it is possible for a user to know how to fix their problem, but still not fix the problem. For example, a pedometer user may know that they can get plenty of steps while walking their dog at the park, but the user may still not consistently walk their dog. In cases like this, feedback about progress towards goals can have a positive effect on self-efficacy and achievement [27]. Additionally, Ubicomp technologies can help by identifying whether the user is meeting their goal. Because alerts can sometimes be unwelcome, Ubicomp technologies, such as just-in-time feedback [15], can help determine the opportune time to alert the user of discrepancies.

Participants were more interested in their current status during the Maintenance phase compared to during the Discovery phase. Most tools for personal informatics have daily reminders of the user's current status, but this may become bothersome if the status is the same as the past several days. Instead, tools should reserve alerts for when special circumstances arise (*e.g.*, the user's step counts changed significantly). Tools can better support this by giving users control of when they are alerted.

Assist the user when they don't meet their goal

The phases of reflection do not address the question of how users could act on their newfound insights to change their behavior. Thus, it is possible for a user in the Maintenance phase to still not meet their goal. When the user does not meet her goal, the tool can be proactive in assisting her in resolving the problem. One idea is to analyze the user's history to create suggestions for resolution. For example, an automated analysis can reveal the causes of the problem. The tool can say "when you drink coffee at 6pm, you have a hard time sleeping, so avoid drinking coffee at 6pm". Automated analysis can also remind users of what they did before to resolve the problem. For example, "last time when you weren't being active you were sitting on the couch watching TV. During the other times you were active, you decided to walk your dog around the neighborhood."

Supporting the Discovery Phase

There are many opportunities for support in the Discovery phase because 1) there are many questions that are asked during this phase; 2) some questions require data collected over a long time; and 3) some questions can be answered using multiple types of data.

Collect data anytime, anywhere, and often

People in the Discovery phase try to better understand their behavior by collecting sufficient data to yield insights during reflection. Getting sufficient data may require tracking over a long period of time, over different contexts, and with great frequency. For example, understanding how one's environment affects physical activity may require tracking over a couple of weeks, at multiple locations, throughout the day. Many barriers to personal informatics are associated the burden of collecting data [17]. Automated data capture as exemplified by many Ubicomp technologies (*e.g.*, [1,12]) can reduce this burden by automating the data collection and storing large amounts of data about the user. By reducing the burden of data collection, users can focus on exploring their data.

There is a caveat about user involvement in reflection that is important. In the Discovery phase, user involvement is critical. People want to discover the relationships between data. Automation can diminish users' engagement with their data. This does not mean that automation should not be supported. It just means that automation should be balanced with ways to keep users engaged with their data. One way to do this is to force users to interact with their data daily, either by sending reports or alerts. On the other hand, user involvement in the Maintenance phase is not as critical. Users are just trying to maintain their behavior. Telling people that they are doing well can become annoying. Instead, the Ubicomp tool should be there to notify the user if anything unusual happens.

Support different kinds of collection tools

Corollary to the previously discussed need, understanding behavior may require exploring the relationships between multiple types of data. For example, understanding how one's environment affects physical activity may require collection of multiple types of data, such as location, type of activity, and weather. However, most tools for personal informatics only support collection of one or a few types of data. One thing to do is to wait for an "ultimate" data collection tool that can collect any kind of the data that a user wants to collect. However, this might just be a pipe dream or could be too far off into the future. More realistically, users should be allowed to use different kinds of collection tools, and then a system or a service can help users integrate data from the different collection tools. There is a proliferation of APIs available, and we can take advantage of this. Recently, Fitbit and Zeo partnered with RunKeeper to share data with each other. This is a good development because people can now use different tools to collect data. However, this is still incomplete because there is a plethora of tools that are not interoperable. Device interoperability has been part of Ubicomp since Weiser started the field [29], so the expertise exists in Ubicomp to help develop and establish standards for interoperation between self-tracking devices and systems.

Data should be presented together

One of the consequences of needing multiple types of data during the Discovery phase is that people have to use different kinds of tools. Unfortunately, the current state of personal informatics systems is that they tend to be *silos of data*, that is, they do not share data with other systems. When they do share data, they do so in a limited fashion, only supporting a few tools. One of the many complaints that people had was that they had to go to different applications/web sites to answer their questions. They wished that they could explore their data in a single interface. Again, Ubicomp technologies can help here. There has been plenty of research in Ubicomp on how to integrate data together [9,12]. The technology is already available to help people collect and see their data from multiple sources at once.

Reduce the upfront cost of data collection

People in the Discovery phase are interested in relationships between different kinds of personal data. This presents two kinds of problems. First, users have to spend a significant amount of time collecting data. One solution is to support lifelong automated data collection of personal data, which many Ubicomp research projects are exploring [12,14]. The second problem is that users cannot predict whether they are collecting all of the data they need. This problem is called the *relevance paradox* [2]. For example, people often do not decide to self-track because the data is not important to them. However, when the data becomes important (*e.g.*, they get sick or they want to develop new habits), they do not have the necessary data to start reflecting immediately. Thus, they have to invest plenty of upfront cost to bootstrap their data collection. With lifelong data collection, once the user needs the data, Ubicomp tools can provide the necessary data for the user to figure out what their goal should be or what factors are influencing their behavior.

Supporting Transitions between Phases

Since people transition between the two phases, personal informatics tools should not be designed for just one phase, but should be flexible to support both. This is important because it prevents a potential problem with any personal informatics tool: people may stop using the tool because their information needs are not appropriately supported.

Identify which phase the user is in

Personal informatics tools should identify what phase the user is in and change its reflection features appropriately. Without this support, people might find the tool useless because of too little information during the Discovery phase, or people may be burdened with too much information during the Maintenance phase. It is an interesting Ubicomp research challenge to automatically determine what phase the user is in, based on sensed data.

Help users transition from Discovery to Maintenance quickly

The Discovery phase is data intensive and can be burdensome to users. Personal informatics tools should help users who are in the Discovery phase to identify program-level goals and how different factors affect their behavior, so users can transition quickly to the Maintenance phase. This would be interesting future work to explore how Ubicomp technologies help users understand their data.

Continuous data collection throughout the phases

The amount of data that users need decreases when users transition from the Discovery phase to the Maintenance phase. However, this does not mean that tools should collect less data during the Maintenance phase. Instead, only the amount of data presented to the user should decrease. We suggest tools should continue collecting as much data in the Maintenance phase as during the Discovery phase. This ensures that if a user who is in the Maintenance has to transition to the Discovery phase because of a new problem, the user can immediately reflect on her data.

CONCLUSIONS

This paper explores the different questions that people ask about their data and why they ask these questions. We identified six types of questions: *Status*, *History*, *Goals*, *Discrepancies*, *Context*, and *Factors*. We discuss how people answered these questions using existing tools and the problems that they encountered. Identifying these questions is important because they require different answers and different kinds of data, which have implications on how tools should support them. Ubicomp technologies play a big role in addressing these needs because what data is collected and how data is collected affect how people reflect on their data.

We also discovered that these questions are not asked at the same time. We identified two distinct phases in which people ask certain questions more often than others: Discovery and Maintenance. The distinction between the phases is important because it highlights the need for personal informatics tools to support different information needs, and to be better tailored to users' current needs, instead of providing them all the tools to answer all six questions at once (when they do not need all of them). Additionally, the phases are not static; people's information needs change. They transition from Discovery to Maintenance, and vice versa. Again, Ubicomp can play a big role here supporting the different information demands of the two phases and the transitions between them.

Though we did not conduct a controlled study to observe how the questions differ between the phases because it is out of the scope of this research, the identification of the questions and the phases is an important first step towards the development of future controlled studies. For example, we could create visualizations for each of the questions then observe whether people use certain visualizations more often than others based on what phase they are in. We expect that people in the Discovery phase will heavily use visualizations that answer *History*, *Goals*, *Context*, and *Factors* questions, while people who are in the Maintenance phase will use visualizations that answer *Status* and *Discrepancy* questions.

As evidenced by articles on personal informatics [3,30] and the growing Quantified Self community around the world (http://quantifiedself.com/), more and more people are using personal informatics tools. However, current personal informatics tools are not designed with a sufficient understanding of users' self-reflection needs. This study takes one step towards an understanding of these needs. We identified six main questions, which people ask in varying frequency between two phases. We presented features that should be supported in personal informatics tools and discussed ways that Ubicomp can provide the necessary support. We believe that this work will help developers and designers more appropriately build personal informatics tools and take better advantage of Ubicomp technologies to help users self-reflect.

ACKNOWLEDGMENTS

This work is based on research supported by the National Science Foundation under Grant No. IIS-0325351 and EEEC-0540865.

REFERENCES

1. Abowd, G.D. & Mynatt, E.D. Charting Past, Present, and Future Research in Ubiquitous Computing. *TOCHI*, 2000, pp. 29-58.
2. Andrews, D. *The IRG Solution - Hierarchical Incompetence and How to Overcome It.* Souvenir Press: London, 1984.
3. Brophy-Warren, J. "The New Examined Life." *Wall Street Journal*, 6 Dec 2008.
4. Card, S.K., Mackinlay, J.D., & Shneiderman, B. *Readings in information visualization: using vision to think.* Morgan Kaufman: 1999.
5. Carver, C. & Scheier, M.F. *On the self-regulation of behavior.* Cambridge University Press, 2001.
6. Consolvo, S., McDonald, D.W., & Landay, J. Theory-Driven Design Strategies for Technologies that Support Behavior Change in Everyday Life. *CHI'09*, pp. 405-414.
7. DiClemente, C.C., Marinilli, A.S., Singh, B., & Bellino, E. The Role of Feedback in the Process of Health Behavior Change. *American Journal of Health Behavior*, 25(3), 2000, pp. 217-227.
8. Endsley, M.R. The Role of Situation Awareness in Naturalistic Decision Making. *Naturalistic Decision Making*, 1997, pp. 269-282.
9. Freeman, E. & Gelernter, D. Lifestreams: A Storage Model for Personal Data. *SIGMOD Record*, 25(1), 1996, pp. 80-86.
10. Froehlich, J., Dillahunt, T., Klasnja, P., Mankoff, J., Consolvo, S., Harrison, B., & Landay, J.A. Ubigreen: Investigating a Mobile Tool for Tracking and Supporting Green Transportation Habits. *CHI'09*, pp. 1043-1052.
11. Frost, J. and Smith, B.K. Visualizing Health: imagery in diabetes education. *DUX'03*, pp. 1-14.
12. Gemmell, J., Bell, G., and Lueder, R. MyLifeBits: a personal database for everything. *Communications of the ACM*, 2006, pp. 88-95.
13. He, A.H., Greenberg, S., & Huang, E.M. One Size Does Not Fit All: Applying the Transtheoretical Model to Energy Feedback Technology Design. *CHI'10*, pp. 927-936.
14. Hodges, S., Williams, L., Berry, E., *et al.* SenseCam: A Retrospective Memory Aid. *Ubicomp'06*, pp. 177-193.
15. Intille, S.S., Rondoni, J., Kukla, C., Ancona, I., & Bao, L. A Context-Aware Experience Sampling Tool. *CHI'03*, pp. 972-973.
16. Jones, W., & Teevan, J. *Personal Information Management.* UW Press, 2007.
17. Li, I., Dey, A.K., & Forlizzi, J. A Stage-Based Model of Personal Informatics Systems. *CHI'10*, pp. 557-566.
18. Lin, J.J., Mamykina, L., Lindtner, S., Delajoux, G., & Strub, H.B. Fish'n'Steps: Encouraging Physical Activity with an Interactive Computer Game. *Ubicomp'06*, pp. 261-278.
19. Matthews, T., Rattenbury, T., & Carter, S. Defining, designing, and evaluating peripheral displays: an analysis using Activity Theory. *Human-Computer Interaction Journal*, 22(1), 2007.
20. Miller, T. & Stasko, J. Artistically Conveying Information with the InfoCanvas: A Highly, Personalized, Elegant Awareness Display. *AVI'02*.
21. Peesapati, S.T., Schwanda, V., Schultz, J., Lepage, M., Jeong, S., & Cosley, D. Pensieve: Supporting Everyday Reminiscence. *CHI'10*, pp. 2027-2036.
22. Pousman, Z. & Stasko, J. A Taxonomy of Ambient Information Systems: Four Patterns of Design. *AVI'06*, pp. 67-74.
23. Powers, W.T. *Behavior: The control of perception.* Chicago: Alidine, 1973.
24. Preuveneers, D. & Berbers, Y. Mobile Phones Assisting With Health Self-Care: a Diabetes Case Study. *MobileHCI'08*, pp. 177-186.
25. Prochaska, J.O., Velicer, W.F. The Transtheoretical Model of health behavior change. *American Journal of Health Promotion*, 12(1), 1997, pp. 38-48.
26. Schank, R.C. & Abelson, R.P. *Scripts, plans, goals, and understanding.* Hillsdale, NJ: Erlbaum, 1977.
27. Schunk, D. H., & Swartz, C. W. Goals and progress feedback: Effects on self-efficacy and writing achievement. *Contemporary Educational Psychology*, 18(3), 1993, pp. 337-354.
28. Seligman, C., & Delay, J.M. Feedback as a Means of Decreasing Residential Energy Consumption. *Journal of Applied Psychology*, 62(4), 1977, pp. 363-368.
29. Weiser, M. The Computer for the 21st Century. *SIGMOBILE*, 3(3), July 1991, pp. 3-11.
30. Wolf, G. "The Data-Driven Life." *The New York Times*, 28 April 2010.

Investigating Intelligibility for Uncertain Context-Aware Applications

Brian Y. Lim, Anind K. Dey
Human-Computer Interaction Institute
Carnegie Mellon University
5000 Forbes Ave., Pittsburgh, PA 15213
{byl, anind}@cs.cmu.edu

ABSTRACT
Context-aware applications use sensing and inference to attempt to determine users' contexts, and take appropriate action. However, they are prone to uncertainty, and this may compromise the trust users have in them. Providing intelligibility has been proposed to help explain to users how context-aware applications work in order to improve user impressions of them. However, we hypothesize that intelligibility may actually be harmful for applications that are very uncertain of their actions. We conducted a large controlled study of a location-aware and a sound-aware application, investigating the impact of intelligibility on understanding, and user impression of applications with varying certainty. We found that intelligibility impacts user impressions, depending on the application's certainty and behavior appropriateness. Intelligibility is helpful for applications with high certainty, but it is harmful if applications behave appropriately, yet display low certainty.

Author Keywords
Context-awareness, intelligibility, explanations, user study.

ACM Classification Keywords
H.m. Information systems: Miscellaneous.

General Terms
Human Factors, Reliability.

INTRODUCTION
Context-aware applications make use of sensing and intelligent inference to automatically learn users' contexts and adapt their behavior [7]. However, much of the context sensing is done invisibly [21], and the context inferencing is growing increasingly complex (*e.g.*, numerous rules, hidden Markov models). Lay users may not understand how these applications make their decisions, let alone be aware when decisions are made and actions are taken. This can lead to user frustration, and loss of trust in the applications [18]. Therefore, context-aware applications should be *intelligible* (also called transparent, comprehensible, scrutable), capable of generating explanations of their behavior [3]. Towards this endeavor, much research has shown the positive effects of providing users with explanations from applications. In several domains including decision-making [9], end-user debugging [12], and user modeling [5], explanations have increased user trust and acceptance of applications. In context-aware systems, Lim *et al.* [14] found that some explanation types were more effective than others in improving understanding and trust, and later investigated more explanation types that end-users of context-aware applications are interested in [15].

Even though these studies show great promise for the efficacy of intelligibility in context-aware applications, they have assumed the use of systems that have reasonably high certainty in their actions, and that, while fallible, generally take appropriate actions. Intelligibility would enhance the positive impression a user may have of an application, and reveal how it intelligently tries to figure out what is happening even for difficult sensing and inference situations. Unfortunately, because of these difficulties in sensing and inference, applications can be uncertain of their actions, often resulting in users having a negative impression of these applications. It is hoped that intelligibility would help bring up this shortfall, and raise a user's impression of a context-aware application. However, is there a certainty below which intelligibility would not help, but may actually *harm* a user's impression of the application? If this were the case, the user could lose even more trust in the application's capability and precision. So an application with sufficiently low certainty would not benefit from adding intelligibility, and instead, the developer should focus on improving its certainty instead.

In this paper, we present two scenario-driven lab studies where we investigate the interaction between intelligibility and application uncertainty. For the first study, we manipulated the provision of Intelligibility in three levels (None, Certainty-only, Full), and Certainty in six levels (50, 60, 70, 80, 90, 100%), in a *between-subject* design for an online survey. We designed two context-aware applications (location-aware, and sound-aware) to explore the impact of certainty on intelligibility for applications with differing complexity. In a follow-up study, we ran a think-aloud study using a reduced form of the online survey, seeking to

UbiComp'11, September 17–21, 2011, Beijing, China.

add greater context to our quantitative findings. Our contributions are:

1. Understanding how users respond to intelligibility in context-aware applications under different levels of certainty; and
2. Identifying when, how, and why intelligibility is helpful or harmful as a result of application certainty.

INTELLIGIBILITY AND UNCERTAINTY

In this section, we provide background and related work on intelligibility, uncertainty in context-aware applications, and the impact of showing uncertainty to end-users.

Displaying Uncertainty in Context-Aware Applications

Context-aware applications are prone to uncertainty, and one common strategy for dealing with this involves user mediation where the user resolves uncertainty [8]. Furthermore, these applications should represent to their users what they know [3], not hide this ambiguity or uncertainty [10], and reveal the "seams" of their underlying systems [4]. Currently, some context-aware applications are able to model uncertainty due to their underlying probabilistic models (*e.g.*, [12, 20]), but few display the system certainty (*e.g.*, [5]).

Conversely, many studies have also explored various ways to display uncertainty, and the benefits of doing so. Antifakos and colleagues showed that uncertainty improved task performance speed of participants when certainty is high [1], and that participants verified automatic settings made by a context-aware system less often when its certainty was high or medium [2]. Similarly, Rukzio *et al.* found that displaying uncertainty slowed down user performance, because users would double-check fields with lower certainty [19]. In studies of presenting location information, visualizations of location certainty were found to improve user performance with location-based services [6, 13]. Though not explicitly investigating about uncertainty, Yan *et al.* found that displaying higher trust and reputation values of mobile applications increased users' willingness to continue using them [22].

Our work adds to the research on displaying uncertainty by carefully varying uncertainty to identify a certainty threshold below which displaying uncertainty becomes harmful instead of helpful, in two different contexts — location and sound. Furthermore, we extend the displaying of uncertainty to include other explanations that provide users with a fuller form of intelligibility.

Intelligibility in Context-Aware Applications

For this work, we use the definition of intelligibility defined by Lim *et al.* [14, 15], which classifies explanations in terms of questions that users may ask of context-aware applications. Specifically, we developed interfaces for explanations of the following questions:

1. **What** is the current value of the context?
2. **Certainty**: how certain is the application of this value?
3. **Why** is this context the current value?

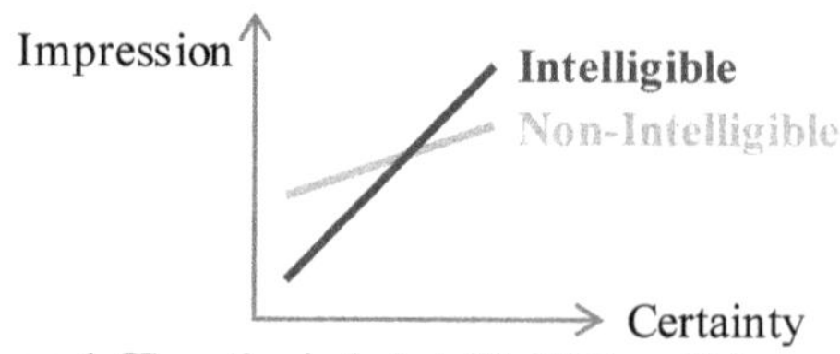

Figure 1. Hypothesis 1: Intelligibility will improve user impressions when an application is certain of its actions, but it will harm impressions when it is uncertain. Only interaction effect suggested, not linearity of trends.

4. **Why Not**: why isn't this context value Y, instead?
5. **Inputs**: what factors affect this context?

We describe how to provide explanations for these questions in a later section (Application Platforms).

HYPOTHESES

While we do not assert it here, we believe the user's impression of an application impacts her trust of it. We define that a user has a good *impression* of a context-aware application when she perceives it to be highly **certain** of its inference, feels that it generally behaves **appropriately**, and she **agrees** with what it is doing. As illustrated in Figure 1, we hypothesize that:

H1a: Above a certainty threshold, intelligibility improves a user's impression of a context-aware application.
H1b: Below the threshold, intelligibility harms the user's impression of the application. This could be due to the user realizing how poorly the application is performing.

We hypothesize that this effect on impression is due to the increased understanding provided by intelligibility:

H2: Providing intelligibility helps increase a user's understanding of the application.

While H2 has been shown to be true in [14], we seek to verify those results, as H1 depends on this. Thus, H2 in combination with H1b hypothesizes that a *gain* of understanding about a low certainty application leads to a *loss* in impression. Next, we describe a large-scale, between-subjects lab study to test these hypotheses.

METHOD

We are primarily interested in the interaction between the provision of intelligibility, the certainty of the application, and the impact on understanding and impression. We chose to investigate this effect using a large-scale, controlled lab study. The study was deployed online through Amazon Mechanical Turk (MTurk) to allow us to collect input from a large number of participants and span many levels of certainty and intelligibility (as in [14, 15]). For generality, we designed two context-aware applications and varied their certainty, and intelligibility levels. We exposed participants to several canonical situations of these applications through 10 different scenarios.

Experimental Conditions

We varied Intelligibility and application Certainty as independent variables in a *between-subject* experiment, across two applications, for a total of $3\times6\times2=36$ conditions.

Intelligibility (3 conditions: None, Certainty-only, Full)
We varied whether participants were provide with explanations where they only saw the application inference (None), or additionally saw a rich explanation visualization (Full). We included an intermediate intelligibility level, where we provided just Certainty percentage only, to investigate how much value the explanation visualizations add over just showing certainty.

Certainty (6 conditions: 50%, 60%, 70%, 80%, 90%, 100%)
We varied certainty as six intervals (rather than a dichotomy) to be able to observe any trends that may arise.

Measures

We are interested in measuring how much participants understand the application for each intelligibility condition, and whether this affects their perception of certainty, feeling of whether the application behaved appropriately, and how much they agree with the application's inference.

Understanding. For each scenario, we asked participants *why* the application inferred what it did, and *why not* something else (free-text). We asked these questions for all scenarios to prime participants to think about the underlying inference of the application. We analyzed the responses from the sixth of 10 scenarios presented, as we expected participants to be sufficiently familiarized with the application through previous scenarios, but not overly tired of providing feedback. We validated that this was true through a sampling of the responses.

Perceived Certainty. For each scenario, we asked participants how certain they believed the application was in its inference (as numerical input 0 to 100%). After the scenarios, we asked for their overall sense of the certainty.

Perceived Appropriateness. For each scenario, we measured what the participant felt about the appropriateness of the application behavior, on a 7-point Likert scale from Very Inappropriate to Very Appropriate.

Agreement. For each scenario, we measured how much the participant agreed with the application's inference, given the ease or difficulty of making the inference; on a 7-point Likert scale from Strongly Disagree to Strongly Agree.

APPLICATION PLATFORMS

To investigate the interaction between intelligibility and uncertainty, we designed two applications — LocateMe and HearMe — and varied their certainty and intelligibility levels. Derived from design explorations of intelligibility in [16], both applications are mobile phone applications, but deal with different contexts (location, and sound activity, respectively), different inference mechanisms, and different explanation interfaces. While real, physical prototypes were not used in this study, these applications have been prototyped, and their described functionality are feasible and indicative of real applications and their associated uncertainty. We describe these applications, how they sense and make inferences, their basis for uncertainty, and how they visualize their inferences.

Each application has three different levels of intelligibility. The None version would just show the output of the application (*e.g.*, "You are at the Washroom", "You were in a Conversation"). The Certainty version adds a certainty percentage (*e.g.*, 89%, 62%). The Full version adds an explanation visualization (see Table 1 and Table 2).

LocateMe

LocateMe is a location-aware mobile phone application that uses GPS, Wi-Fi and cellular networks to triangulate where the user is, and match that to a predetermined set of locations to infer which *place* the user is at. It then uses this inference to take actions such as sending a reminder, or identifying the nearest printer. In the scenarios, LocateMe is used for indoor and outdoor situations.

Basis for uncertainty. Due to the probabilistic model of the user's location (as a Gaussian area), LocateMe infers the user being at places with varying levels of certainty. Its certainty depends on how much the user's estimated area "overlaps" with the area of the named place, and is computed into a probability. The larger the area of the named place, and/or the closer the user's area is to that place, the higher the certainty. Uncertainty is also affected by sensing errors due to GPS signal occlusion (*e.g.*, being indoors), Wi-Fi or Cell network signal strength, *etc.*

HearMe

HearMe is a sound-aware mobile phone application that uses the phone's microphone to sense and infer one of three activities: whether the user is (i) in a conversation, (ii) listening to music, or there is mostly (iii) ambient noise. It uses several features extracted from processing the microphone signal, such as: frequency bandwidth, spectral entropy, low-energy frame rate, Mel-Frequency Ceptral Coefficients (see [16] for more details about features used). HearMe uses a trained naïve Bayes model to infer whether the sound heard was one of the three activities.

Basis for uncertainty. HearMe models uncertainty of its inference from the probabilistic uncertainty of the naïve Bayes model. This depends on the sound samples used to train the original model. HearMe does not model the error due to the microphone signal for uncertainty.

Due to the ubiquity of GPS devices and location sensing in smart phones, LocateMe is likely more familiar to users than HearMe which uses machine learning inferences that are less common-place in devices available to consumers.

SCENARIOS

Similar to [1, 14, 15], we use scenarios to let participants learn about and experience our applications. However, rather than present 5-second video clips to help participants experience a scenario, we provided users with a precise representation to understand the ground truth of each scenario. For LocateMe, we showed a map or floorplan indicating where the participant would actually be in the scenario. For HearMe, we played an audio clip of what the participant and her phone would supposedly have heard.

<table>
<tr><th></th><th>LocateMe</th><th>HearMe</th></tr>
<tr><td>Situation description and Ground truth</td><td>(a) You are in the washroom taking care of some business, just before your meeting with your neighboring coworker, Damien.
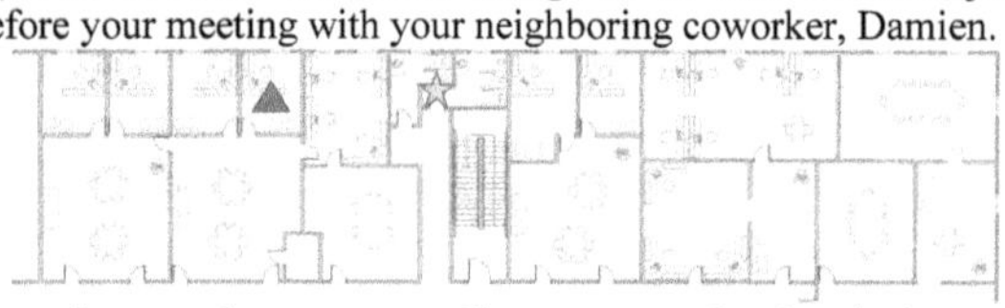
Star denotes where you actually are at; purple triangle denotes Damien's office (RM102).</td><td>(d) At the coffee shop, you find Michelle, a coworker, there, and have a chat with her.

Participant listens to an auto-started audio clip of ambient noise in a coffee shop, with a female voice occasionally talking.
H6-groundtruth.mp3</td></tr>
<tr><td>Application behavior (Certainty 90%)</td><td>(b) You receive a text message from Damien, who tells you he is waiting for you at his office. You check LocateMe:
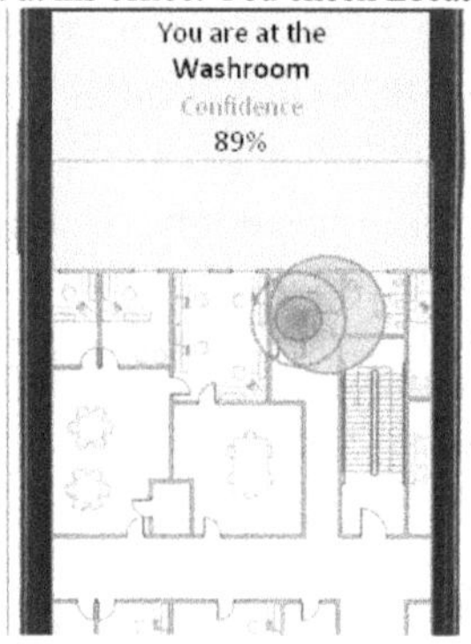
</td><td>(e) You are not interrupted for 12 min, and when the conversation ends, you receive a notification message from HearMe:
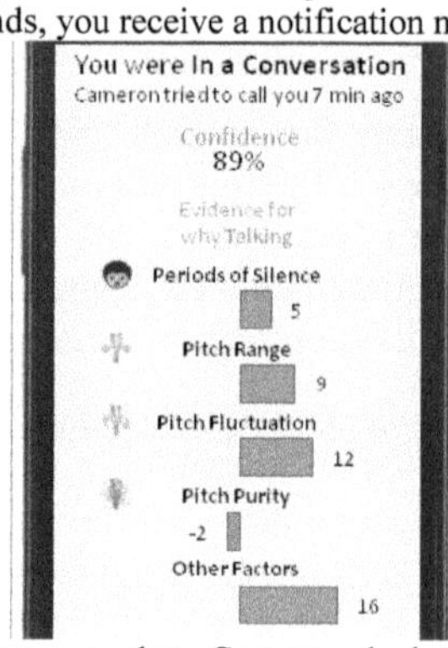

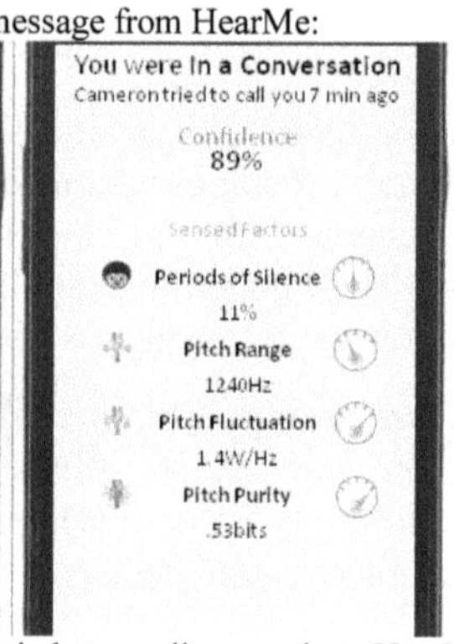

You see that Cameron had tried to call you, but HearMe suppressed his call since it interpreted you as uninterruptible.</td></tr>
<tr><td>(Certainty 60%)
Wrong inference, in this case</td><td>(c) Damien calls to ask where you are since LocateMe said you are in his office, which is obviously false. You check LocateMe:
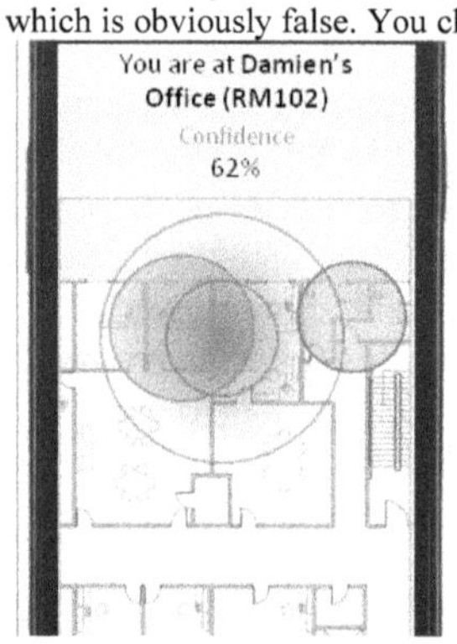
</td><td>(f) You are not interrupted for 12 min, and when the conversation ends, you receive a notification message from HearMe:
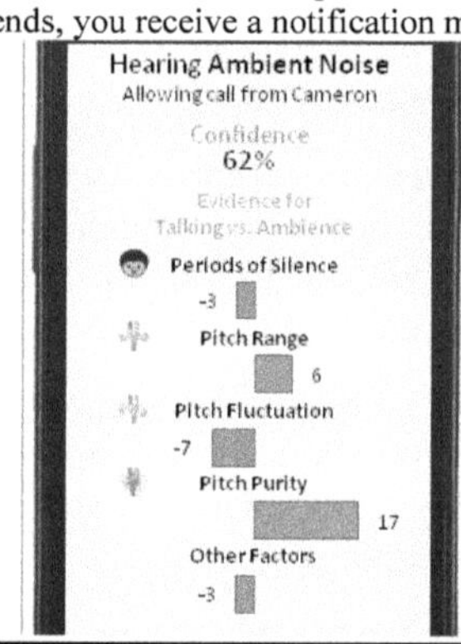

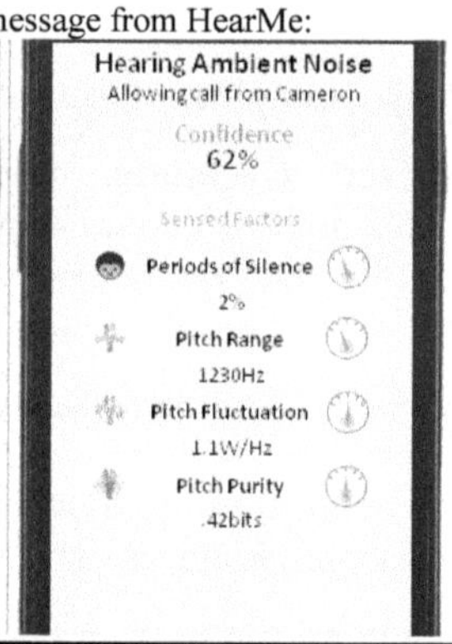
</td></tr>
<tr><td>Explanation UI Description</td><td>LocateMe uses "bubbles", to determine and show where the user is, rather than showing pin-point positions. The user's sensed location is represented by two blue concentric circles, and a Gaussian blue area. He is most likely to be in the center of the area, but less likely the further away from it. The bounds indicate thresholds of certainty (50, 90%) that the user is within the bounds. Places are represented with uniform circular areas of varying size. E.g., Washroom is defined with a circle, with the center where the room is, and the size is how large the room is.

The user is inferred to be at a place if his blue bubble "overlaps" with the place's bubble. A green bubble indicates the place where the user is inferred to be; a red bubble indicates where he is not inferred to be. (b) shows a green bubble over the washroom overlapping with the user's blue bubble to explain why he is inferred to be there. The large overlap suggests a high certainty (in this case, 89%). (c) explains why the user is not inferred to be at the washroom but at Damien's office instead, by showing: a red bubble for the washroom, a green bubble for Damien's Office. The blue bubble overlaps with the green bubble more than with the red bubble, indicating 62% certainty.</td><td>HearMe uses two types of visualizations to explain what it senses, and how it infers an activity, with a Sensed State and Evidence visualization, respectively. We substitute the technical names of the input factors with metaphorical terms (e.g., Periods of Silence for low-energy frame rate, Pitch Purity for spectral entropy), and aggregate the remaining factors as Other Factors. We explain the meanings of each factor and implications of their values, e.g.: Periods of Silence indicates what percentage of the sound sample was relatively silent compared to the rest of it; talking would have higher percentage. The Sensed Factors viz (right diagram) shows the values of the factors, and a gauge icon indicating whether each value is at, below, or above the average values for that factor.

The Evidence viz (left diagram) shows a bar chart indicating if each factor votes for (blue towards right) or against (red towards left) the inference, and by how much. This viz can be used to compare one output against all others (e), or specifically contrast between two outcomes (f). The balance of the bars indicate how certain the application is about its inference. If it is more certain, the bars are weighted more towards the right, and if less certain, the bars are equally weighted to the right and left.</td></tr>
</table>

Table 1. Scenario scripts, application interfaces showing Full intelligibility, and their interpretation of Scenario 6.

	Description / Function	LocateMe	HearMe
What	Show the current inference of the context and consequent action.	Reports inferred place, and shows blue bubble of the user in map visualization.	Reports inferred sound activity.
Certainty	Show the certainty of the application's inference of the current context value.	Shows a certainty percentage, and size of bubbles in map visualization (larger sizes show lower certainty).	Shows a certainty percentage, and sense of balance of bars in evidence viz (more balance show lower certainty).
Why	Show a model-based explanation of how the application inferred the current context value.	Shows the overlap between the inferred place (as a green bubble) and the user's blue bubble.	Shows evidences for the inference due to each input factor in a bar chart visualization.
Why Not	Show a model-based explanation distinguishing how the application did not infer the alternative inference.	In addition to the Why visualization, shows the lack of overlap between the place (as a red bubble) and blue bubble.	Shows the evidence visualization, contrasting the current inference against the alternative inference.
Inputs	Show the current values of input context / features.	Visually shows the user's position by positioning the blue bubble in a map.	Lists current input factor values, and provides a gauge of its relative value.

Table 2. Explanation types. LocateMe uses a map and bubbles visualization for its explanations about its location inference. HearMe uses lists the current values of its sensed factors, and their corresponding evidence to explain its sound activity inference.

We presented 10 scenarios as a chronological sequence of events happening through a single day. As in [15], the scenarios were written to span five *themes* typical of what context-aware applications are used for: interruption management, social awareness, reminders, recommender, exploration / learning. Each theme is *repeated* twice (not consecutively) to provide repeated exposure. Collectively, the scenarios are *representative* of the application certainty (*e.g.*, for 60%, the application behaved appropriately for 6 out of 10 scenarios). Hence, participants in the None intelligibility condition could perceive the certainty of the application. The certainties presented (for Certainty and Full intelligibility) also reflected the certainty condition, but with small *randomized* differences (*e.g.*, 60, 63, 59, 60, 58, 62, 61, 57, 60, 60%), to prevent participants from ignoring the values had they been constantly shown 60% repeatedly.

Table 1 shows the scripts and diagrams shown to participants in the LocateMe (left), and HearMe (right) surveys for a scenario, S6. Next, we describe what participants were asked to do for each application survey.

PROCEDURE

After consenting to participate in the survey (either LocateMe or HearMe), the participant was randomly assigned to a Certainty condition and an Intelligibility condition. He read instructions on how the application works, and how to interpret its display. As recommended by [10], we then asked two verification questions (multiple-choice) to ensure comprehension. The participant next went through 10 scenarios to experience the application under various situations. For each scenario, he read (i) a scenario description, and (ii) the subsequent response of the application which may or may not be appropriate for the situation. He was then (iii) asked verification questions to ensure he had carefully read and understood the scenario. Next we asked questions for our measures of (iv) perception of certainty, (v) application behavior appropriateness, and (vi) agreement. Finally, he was asked about his (vii) understanding of the application inference. After the scenarios, he was asked about his background with using smart phones, and for demographic information.

PARTICIPANTS AND DATA CLEANSING

We recruited participants from Amazon Mechanical Turk. There were 397 incomplete HITs (human intelligence tasks), and 584 completed HITs. We rejected 76 HITs because each participant had low verification score, rushed through the survey too quickly, and/or was unconscientious (gave reasons that were gibberish, repetitive, or irrelevant). Of the remaining 508 participants, their survey completion time was Median=33 minutes (8.9 to 109), and their verification score was Median=20 (7 to 22) out of 22. Some participants had low verification scores, which indicates poor understanding of the scenarios and application, but their free-text reasons indicated conscientious effort in the survey. So they were included in our population sample to represent users who have greater comprehension difficulty. We had participants across 36 conditions (3 Intelligibility × 6 Certainty × 2 Application) in our experiment (M=14.1, 11 to 17 in each condition). We paid each participant $2.

DATA ANALYSIS AND RESULTS

In this section, we present the analysis we performed on the survey results, related to our hypotheses. Before we investigate whether intelligibility influences users' impressions of a context-aware application, first we analyze whether intelligibility improves understanding of how the application works (H2). We assume that understanding is not influenced by the certainty of the application.

Understanding of Application Inference

As a measure of understanding, we coded the free-text responses about how they thought the application made its inferences for S6. We counted how many of the reasons *about the application* that they provided were correct. A reason is considered correct if it relates to an actual factor that the application uses (*e.g.*, GPS, latitude, distance threshold, bubbles; Periods of Silence, Pitch Purity, noisiness). We eliminated repeated and redundant reasons

Intelligibility	None	Certainty	Full
LocateMe	.73 ± .10	.81 ± .10	.97 ± .09*
HearMe	.72 ± .08	.82 ± .08	1.57 ± .09**

Table 3. Number of correct reasons (Mean ± Standard Error) counted from participant free-text reasons of how the application made its inference in S6. Contrast of None *vs.* Full: p<.01 for HearMe, p=.08 for LocateMe*.**

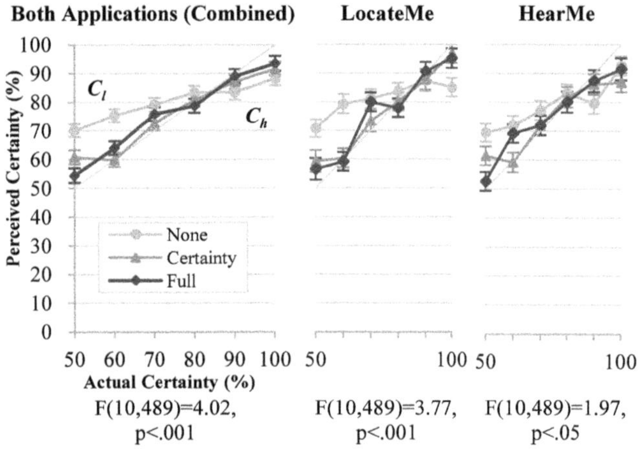

Figure 2. Perception of Overall Certainty: combined analysis (Left), and for individual applications (Middle and Right). Participants with Full intelligibility perceived a higher certainty when the application had high actual certainty, but perceived a lower certainty when it had low actual certainty.

App	Combined		LocateMe		HearMe	
Actual Certainty	Low 50-70%	High 90-100%	Low 50-60%	High 100%	Low 50-70%	High 80-100%
None ***vs.*** **Full**	p<.001	p<.05	p<.001	p<.05	p<.01	p=n.s.
None ***vs.*** **Certainty**	p<.001	p=n.s.	p<.001	p<.05	p<.01	p=n.s.

Table 4. Pre-hoc contrast between Intelligibility types for low and high actual certainty. These groups were chosen after visually inspecting the interaction graphs.

Certainty (%)	50	60	70	80	90	100
Certainty	<.01	n.s.	n.s.	n.s.	.05	.01
Full	.02	n.s.	<.01	n.s.	n.s.	<.01

Table 5. Means testing of whether perceptions of overall certainty are different from actual certainties. *t*-test p-values suggest copying if p=n.s.

(*i.e.*, paraphrasing of the same idea), and accepted language that demonstrated an approximate idea of valid concepts.

We fit a mixed model with: correct reason count as the dependent variable, intelligibility and application as independent variables, interaction × application as an interaction effect, certainty as a control variable, and participant as a random variable (nested in intelligibility, application, and certainty). We found that participants with Full intelligibility gave more correct reasons than those with None, especially regarding HearMe (see Table 3).

Next, we analyze whether and how this increase in understanding influences how participants perceived the certainty of the application. We annotate some figures to indicate notable findings in our results (*e.g.*, C_l, $C_{\neg a,l}$, A_a).

Perceived Overall Certainty

We asked each participant about their perception of the overall (average) certainty of the application, after completing all 10 scenarios. To examine differences in this perception for each application separately, we fit a mixed model with: perceived overall certainty as dependent variable, intelligibility and certainty as independent variables, intelligibility × certainty as an interaction effect,

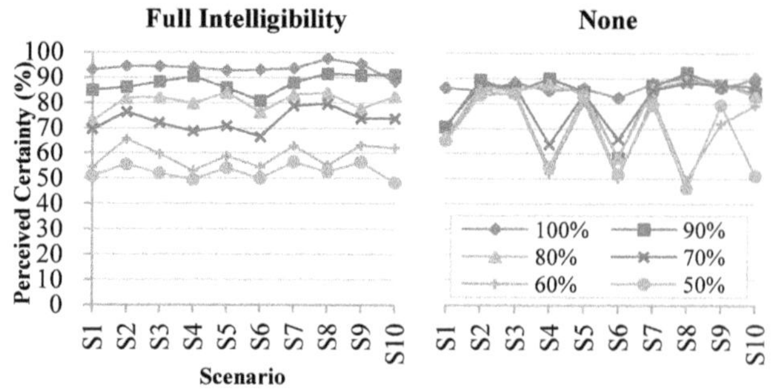

Figure 3. Perceived certainty influenced by application appropriateness across scenarios. The application behaved appropriately for at least one Certainty condition in S1, S4, S6, S8, and S10, more so for lower certainty conditions.

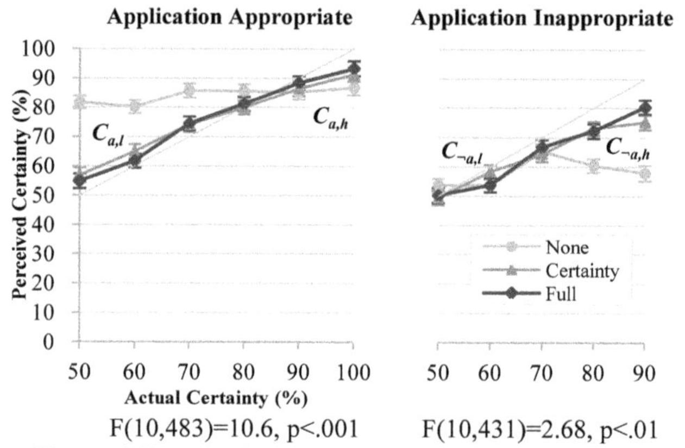

Figure 4. Perceived certainty across actual certainty by application appropriateness. Note: no inappropriate scenarios for 100% certainty condition.

App Behavior	Appropriate		Inappropriate	
Actual Certainty	50-70%	80-90%	50-70%	80-90%
None ***vs.*** **Full**	p<.001	p<.05	p=n.s.	p<.001
None ***vs.*** **Certainty**	p<.001	p=n.s.	p=n.s.	p<.001

Table 6. Contrast between Intelligibility types for low and high actual certainty grouped by application behavior.

and participant as a random variable (nested in intelligibility and certainty). We also combined data from both applications, and fit a similar mixed model but also with application as a control variable. These results are presented in Figure 2 and Table 4. Our results show that, for high actual certainty, participants with intelligibility perceived a higher certainty than those without (C_h); for low actual certainty, participants with intelligibility perceived a lower certainty than those without (C_l). Alternatively, an interpretation may be participants with intelligibility just copied the certainty displayed. Means testing suggests that this could be so (see Table 5), but we further investigate this in a follow-up study (see later).

While our results show that participants' perceived overall certainty *across* different certainty levels is influenced by intelligibility, we next show that their perception also varies based on how the application behaved per scenario.

Perceived Certainty by Application Appropriateness

To investigate perception of certainty across scenarios, we analyzed the repeated measure of how certain participants

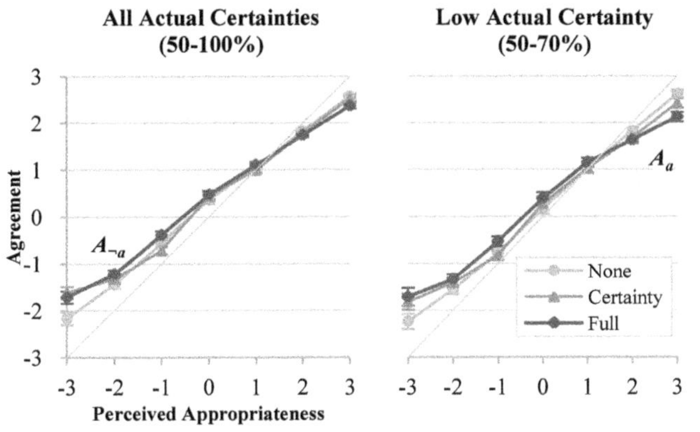

F(12,4984)=2.92, p<.001 F(12, 1645)=3.31, p<.001

Figure 5. Agreement across Perceived Appropriateness, grouped by actual certainty. The effect of *finding 4_h* is only significant for low actual certainty.

Actual Certainty	All (50-100%)		Low (50-70%)	
Appropriateness	Not (<0)	High (2-3)	Not (<0)	High (2-3)
None *vs.* Full	p<.01	p<.05	p<.01	p<.01
None *vs.* Certainty	p=.052	p=n.s.	p=n.s.	p<.05

Table 7. Contrast between Intelligibility types for low and high appropriateness grouped by actual certainty.

felt the application was for each scenario. Figure 3 (Right) shows the fluctuation of perceived certainty as participants with no intelligibility (None) go through the scenarios, depending on whether the application behaved appropriately in the scenario. When participants received Full intelligibility (Figure 3, Left), their perceived certainty was more stratified, and less fluctuating.

We group our results by application appropriateness, and fit two mixed models with: perceived certainty as dependent variable, intelligibility and certainty as independent variables, intelligibility × certainty as an interaction effect, and participant as a random variable (nested in intelligibility and certainty). Our results (see Figure 4 and Figure 5) show that, for appropriate application behaviors, participants with intelligibility perceived lower certainty than those with None when encountering actual low certainty ($C_{a,l}$), and conversely perceived higher certainty when encountering actual high certainty ($C_{a,h}$). For inappropriate application behaviors, there was no difference in perception for actual low certainty ($C_{\neg a,l}$), but participants with intelligibility perceived higher certainty for actual high certainty, than participants without ($C_{\neg a,h}$).

Agreement by Perceived Appropriateness

Given the difference in perception due to application appropriateness, we are interested to see if participants' opinion of how appropriately the application behaved, and how much they agree with its inference were affected by intelligibility. These self-reported, repeated measures for every scenario were obtained with the following questions:

Perceived Appropriateness with "How appropriately or inappropriately did the application behave in this situation?" (7-point Likert scale)

Agreement with "How much do you agree or disagree with the application's inference, given how easy or difficult it is to infer this?" (7-point Likert scale)

We did not compare perceived certainty, because, as expected, it varied independently of appropriateness.

We fit a mixed model with: agreement as dependent variable, appropriateness and agreement as independent variables, appropriateness × agreement as an interaction effect, and participant as a random variable (nested in appropriateness and agreement). Our results (see Figure 5 and Table 7) show that participants tended to agree with the application when they perceived it behaved appropriately, and *vice versa*. When participants felt the application behaved inappropriately (<0), those with intelligibility agreed with the application more than those with None ($A_{\neg a}$). However, when participants perceived the application behaved very appropriately (2-3), participants using an application with low certainty and intelligibility agreed less with it than those with None (Figure 5, Right; A_a).

Summary of Findings

We summarize our findings in terms of our hypotheses. Participants with Full intelligibility gave more correct reasons of how the application works, than those without (satisfies **H2**). *Finding C_h* satisfies **H1a** that intelligibility improves user impression of a context-aware application if its certainty is high. This is more pronounced when the application behaved inappropriately ($C_{\neg a,h}$) than appropriately ($C_{a,h}$). Conversely, *finding C_l* satisfies **H1b** that intelligibility harms user impression if its certainty is low; particularly, when the application behaved appropriately ($C_{a,l}$), or when it displays a low certainty despite being appropriate (A_a). However, participants with intelligibility disagreed less with the application inference when they felt that it behaved inappropriately ($A_{\neg a}$). To gain better insights into our results, we ran a follow-up study where we engaged participants face-to-face.

FOLLOW-UP: THINK-ALOUD STUDY

At this point, our results positively support our hypotheses that intelligibility *exaggerates* the perception of certainty compared to not receiving any explanation. However, this could be because our participants with intelligibility could just be copying the certainty value they were shown (see Table 5). Do participants mindlessly copy these values, or do they weigh their opinion with previous experiences with the application (from previous scenarios)? Furthermore, *finding A_l* suggests that Full intelligibility provides some additional benefit of improving the perception of certainty than showing Certainty-only. How does Full intelligibility help to reinforce the Certainty information provided?

Method and Procedure

Answering these questions will help us examine the link between the information provided through Certainty-only and Full intelligibility, the user's understanding, and their subsequent impression of the application. It will also help us explore whether and how Full intelligibility influences

Certainty	Low (S6:52%, S9:49%)				High (S6:89%, S9:92%)			
Application	LocateMe		HearMe		LocateMe		HearMe	
Participant	1	5	2	8	3	5	4	7

Table 8. Distribution of participants in think-aloud study. Each participant saw S6 (appropriate behavior) and S9 (inappropriate), iterated within-subjects with intelligibility types in the order: None, Certainty, Full.

the user compared to Certainty-only. To explore this, we ran a follow-up *think-aloud* study where we presented all three intelligibility conditions *within-subject*, focusing on a subset of Certainty conditions (low: 50%; high 90%). We continued to use both applications (*between-subject*) due to their differences in complexity, and participant reliance on their explanations. Hence, we have four conditions. Due to the time-consuming nature of the think-aloud study (one-hour long), we presented only two scenarios (S6, S9) to our participants, counter-balanced for application correctness. S6 has been described in Table 1. For S9, LocateMe correctly infers the user in Meeting Room B and automatically loads the meeting agenda; HearMe correctly infers conversation during a group meeting, and allows the user to retrieve the audio and save it. In the follow-up study, the application always behaves incorrectly for S6, but correctly for S9, regardless of certainty.

We recruited two participants per condition (total 8), 4 females, mean age 28.1 years old (21 to 58). We presented three iterations of the survey starting with None, Certainty, then Full, so as to avoid a training effect. Each scenario has the same format and questions as the original survey. Additionally, we asked them to think-aloud and provide reasons for their answers. This way, we learned about how they thought the application made its inferences, and how they constructed opinions of the application's behavior. We used paper surveys, so participants could refer to previous surveys, compare previous phone displays, their previous answers, and discuss why they changed or did not change their opinions. Table 8 shows which conditions participants P1 to P8 were in. We discuss our findings in the next section in the context of our original quantitative results.

DISCUSSION

We discuss the results from both experiments in terms of how intelligibility affects understanding (H2), and how it affects users' impression of context-aware applications (H1).

H2: Intelligibility Increases Understanding of Context-Aware Applications

As expected, Full intelligibility allowed participants to better express an understanding of the applications. This was particularly significant for HearMe, because the explanations listed relevant factors, increasing the participants' vocabulary to describe how the application works. In the think-aloud study, participants could analyze and interpret the values of HearMe's sensed factors, and their corresponding evidences, and LocateMe's bubble visualization. However, because the input factors were not explicitly stated in LocateMe as they were for HearMe, participants gave reasons for how LocateMe works by describing names of technologies, *e.g.*, GPS, "position-specific sensing" (P3), a "grid in the building" (P6), or in terms of the situation, *e.g.*, signal blocked by nearby stairs (P5), or improved signal because of proximity to windows (P5). Full intelligibility only marginally increased the correct ideas that participants had about how LocateMe works. For HearMe, without Full intelligibility, participants considered the "noisiness" of the audio, along with speaker identification (especially that of the user) as the most important factors for inference, but with Full intelligibility, they tended to discard their original understanding and described the inference in terms of the factors shown. We can interpret the differences between the applications as due to their *complexity* and the users' *familiarity* with them. These findings reinforce those in [14] that prior knowledge about an application domain (in this case, LBS) reduces the impact of intelligibility on understanding.

By providing more information, intelligibility also helps provide participants with an increased awareness of what the application was inferring, and what it understood. This consequently impacted their impression of it.

H1: Impact of Intelligibility on User Impressions

Without Intelligibility, MTurk participants are influenced by whether the application behaved appropriately to perceive its certainty (see Figure 3, Right). They perceived a modestly high certainty (~85%) when it is behaved appropriately, and how often it behaved appropriately (Figure 2), but perceived a low certainty otherwise (~60%). Their overall perceived certainty is also impacted by the cumulative application behavior, gently increasing from ~70 to ~90% as actual certainty increases from 50 to 100% (Figure 3). With intelligibility, participants' perceived certainty aligned more closely with the actual certainty.

But, do participants just copy the application certainty (as suggested in Table 5)? In the think-aloud study, though influenced by the displayed value, *all* participants did not outright adhere to it. They continued to be influenced by their perception of how difficult it was to make the inference, and whether the application behaved appropriately, but adjusted their certainty rating depending on the presented value. Hence, if a low certainty was presented, participants lowered their certainty estimate, and while if a high certainty was displayed, participants raised their certainty estimate, but not all the way to the presented value for both cases. Furthermore, participants reevaluated their certainty rating when given Full intelligibility. Next, we discuss and interpret our results (shown in Figure 4 and Figure 5) in terms of hypotheses H1a and H1b. We found a caveat to H1b which we denote as H1b'. Table 9 summarizes these positive and negative impacts that intelligibility has on user impressions.

H1a: Intelligibility Increases User Impressions of Context-Aware Applications with High Certainty

For context-aware applications with **high certainty**, our results verify previous findings of [14, 15] that intelligibility improves users' impression of the applications (*finding* C_h). With intelligibility, participants perceived a higher certainty from the application, particularly when it **behaved appropriately** (*finding* $C_{a,h}$). After seeing the Certainty-only intelligibility, P4 raised her original rating (85% with None) to "just below" what was shown (92%), despite feeling that HearMe was "overconfident," because of her "overall understanding" of the conversation that she heard in the audio clip. With Full intelligibility, participants felt the explanations "reinforced" the high certainty (P3), or even raised their certainty of the application (P6).

Intelligibility had a more significant impact on perceived certainty if the application **behaved inappropriately**, since MTurk participants had a lower baseline certainty rating (about 60% instead of ~85%). Though not to as high a level for appropriate application behavior, intelligibility raised their confidence rating by a larger margin (by 15% to ~75%; *finding* $C_{\neg a,h}$). With Certainty-only intelligibility, P3 liked that LocateMe was "honest," and trusted it more. P4 felt that HearMe "would know its own certainty better than [she] would" and raised her certainty to 75-85%, which was between what she had imagined and what was presented. P6 insisted that LocateMe's certainty should not have been so high, but raised her rating by 5%. With Full intelligibility, participants reevaluated their opinion. P4 and P7 were more accepting of HearMe's certainty, and raised their ratings.

H1b: Intelligibility Decreases Impressions of Applications with Low Certainty when they behave Appropriately

For context-aware applications with **low certainty**, intelligibility revealed how uncertain they were, and compromised the impressions participants had of them (*finding* C_l). This was particularly notable when the application **behaved appropriately** (*finding* $C_{a,l}$). In the think-aloud study, participants were surprised to discover the low certainty. For LocateMe, P5 thought that the location in S9 was easier to infer than in S6, and felt that the certainty should have been higher (60%) than the presented 49%. For HearMe, P2 felt that the conversation in S9 was "so clear" that the certainty should be higher at 60-65%. Furthermore, the unexpectedly low presented certainty caused participants to disagree more with the application inference (*finding* A_h). P1 and P5 lowered their agreement rating from 7 (None) to 2 (Certainty), and P8 from 6 to 4. With Full intelligibility, P8 became convinced by HearMe's displayed 50% certainty by examining the bar chart of evidences and noting they were very balanced; she consequently lowered her certainty rating.

H1b': Intelligibility Increases Impressions of Applications with Low Certainty when they behave Inappropriately

Contrary to H1b, intelligibility was helpful for an application with **low certainty** when it **behaved inappropriately** (*finding* A_a), even though it did not influence perceived certainty (*finding* $C_{\neg a,l}$). Participants appreciated the difficulty of inference, forgave the application, and disagreed less with it (A_l). P5 conceded that it was "very difficult" for LocateMe to estimate the

		Certainty	
		Low	**High**
	Overall	**Harmful (H1b)** Decreases perceived overall accuracy (*finding* C_l).	**Helpful (H1a)** Increases perceived overall accuracy (*finding* C_h).
Behavior Appropriateness	**Appropriate**	**Harmful (H1b)** Decreases perceived accuracy (*finding* $C_{a,l}$), and Decreases agreement with inference (*finding* A_a).	**Helpful (H1a)** Increases perceived accuracy (*finding* $C_{a,h}$).
	Not	**Helpful (H1b')** Increases agreement with inference (*finding* $A_{\neg a}$).	**Helpful (H1a)** Increases perceived accuracy (*finding* $C_{\neg a,h}$).

Table 9. Impact of Intelligibility on user impressions of a context-aware application depends on application certainty and whether it behaved appropriately.

certainty, and thought "it got it almost right"; she agreed more with the application, changing her rating from 4 (None) to 5 (Certainty). With Full intelligibility, participants more clearly saw how uncertain the applications were: large margins of error (LocateMe), or a high amount of ambiguity (HearMe). This allowed P8 to understand how HearMe "misjudged the environment," and "agree with its logic based on the parameters."

DESIGN RECOMMENDATIONS

There are two ways to apply our findings in terms of application certainty: regarding *overall* certainty, or *per situation* certainty. Considering overall certainty, our findings recommend providing intelligibility as long as the application usually has high certainty. However, our findings caution that intelligibility is harmful if certainty is too low, so intelligibility should not be provided for such applications; their certainty should be improved first. While the precise threshold for what is a *sufficiently* high overall certainty depends on the application and domain, our results (see Figure 2) suggest it falls within the range of about 80-90% for a non-critical, "everyday" application.

Considering certainty per situation, we note that an application that usually has high certainty may still occasionally have situations with low certainty. Fortunately, in the majority of times with high certainty, we still recommend providing intelligibility even if it is ultimately wrong and behaves inappropriately. On the other hand, our recommendation is not immediately clear with low certainty. The impact of intelligibility on impression also depends on whether the application behaves appropriately.

If the application behaves appropriately, showing intelligibility compromises the original good impression the user may have had, causing her to lower her impression. If it behaves inappropriately, intelligibility can help her realize how difficult the inference task is, and improve her impression. Unfortunately, an application will not be able to know if it will act appropriately beforehand. It will be safer to not show intelligibility before it acts, when certainty is low. After it acts, if the user asks questions, especially if a *why not* question, it is likely the application behaved inappropriately, where it is beneficial to show intelligibility. Therefore, just show intelligibility *on demand*, when situation certainty is low. Our results (see Figure 4, Left) indicate that our participants have a baseline belief that the application is about 80-85% certainty when it behaved appropriately. This suggests that, for each situation, a context-aware application may safely provide intelligibility automatically when it is at least 80% certain, but should provide intelligibility on demand when it is less certain.

Carefully designing explanations can provide an alternative solution to deal with intelligibility as a double-edged sword for low certainty. Intelligibility should focus on convincing the user how difficult the inference task is, and how the application is intelligently tackling it, rather than implying that the application is incompetent. This could mean not revealing the low certainty in explanations. For example, HearMe's Sensed Factors visualization explains what *input values* it knows, but does not betray HearMe's uncertainty.

CONCLUSION AND FUTURE WORK

We have described a large controlled study investigating the impact of intelligibility on understanding and user impressions of context-aware applications with varying certainty from low to high. This was conducted using lab-based, scenario-driven surveys of two context-aware applications (location-aware, and sound-aware). Our results show that intelligibility can positive or negatively impact user impressions, depending on the application's certainty and behavior appropriateness. Intelligibility is helpful for applications with high certainty, but it is harmful for applications with low certainty, because the user loses even more trust in its capability. Still, intelligibility can help users appreciate and forgive applications if they behave inappropriately and have low certainty. This work explicitly cautions the necessity for a context-aware application to be sufficiently certain before it leverages intelligibility.

In this study, we have focused on a *passive* display for intelligibility, and did not have users act on the information; they could only use intelligibility to judge their impression of the application. However, users could also *interactively* use intelligibility for debugging and finding out why the application faltered (*e.g.* [12]). Perhaps, this could make intelligibility useful instead of harmful to user impression.

This work provides a stepping stone to understanding how intelligibility affects a user's impression of a context-aware application. For future work, we plan to gain more lucid and nuanced insights into the use of intelligibility and how that affects users in real-world situations through deploying an intelligible prototype in a longitudinal field trial.

ACKNOWLEDGMENTS

This work was funded by the National Science Foundation under grant 0746428, and the Agency for Science Technology And Research, Singapore. We also thank Matt L. Lee, Tawanna Dillahunt, Denzil Ferreira, and Jin-Hyuk Hong for their helpful discussions; Gabriela Marcu for her involvement in the think-aloud study; and our reviewers for their insightful feedback.

REFERENCES

1. Antifakos, S. *et al.* (2004). Evaluating the Effects of Displaying Uncertainty in Context-Aware Applications. *Ubicomp 04*, 54-69.
2. Antifakos, S. *et al.* (2005). Towards improving trust in context-aware systems by displaying system confidence. *MobileHCI 05*, 9-14.
3. Bellotti, V. & Edwards, W.K. (2001). Intelligibility and Accountability: Human Considerations in Context-Aware Systems, *Human-Computer Interaction*, 16(2-4): 193-212.
4. Chalmers, M. & MacColl, I. (2003). Seamful and seamless design in ubiquitous computing. *In Workshop: At the Crossroads: The Interaction of HCI and Systems Issues, Ubicomp 03*.
5. Cheverst, K. *et al.* (2005). Exploring issues of user model transparency and proactive behavior in an office environment control system. *UMUAI 05*, 15(3-4), 235-273.
6. Dearman, D. *et al.* (2007). An exploration of location error estimation. *Ubicomp 07*, 181-198.
7. Dey, A.K., Abowd, G.D. & Salber, D. (2001). A conceptual framework and a toolkit for supporting the rapid prototyping of context-aware applications. *HCI Journal*, 16(2–4): 97–166.
8. Dey, A. *et al.* (2002). Distributed mediation of ambiguous context in aware environments. *UIST 02*, 121–130.
9. Dzindolet, M. *et al.* (2003). The role of trust in automation reliance, *International Journal of Human-Computer Studies*, 58(6): 697-718.
10. Greenberg, S. (2001). Context as a dynamic construct. HCI 16(2), 257–268.
11. Kittur, A. *et al.* Crowdsourcing user studies with Mechanical Turk. *CHI 08*, 453-456.
12. Kulesza, T. *et al.* (2009). Fixing the Program My Computer Learned: Barriers for End-users, Challenges for the Machine. *IUI 09*, 187-196.
13. Lemelson, H., *et al.* (2008). A Study on User Acceptance of Error Visualization Techniques. *HUCUBIS 08*.
14. Lim, B.Y. *et al.* (2009). Why and why not explanations improve the intelligibility of context-aware intelligent systems. *CHI 09*, 2119-2128.
15. Lim, B.Y., Dey, A.K. (2009). Assessing Demand for Intelligibility in Context-Aware Applications. *Ubicomp 09*, 195-204.
16. Lim, B.Y., Dey, A.K. (2011). Design of an Intelligible Mobile Context-Aware Application. To appear in *MobileHCI 11*.
17. Lu, H. *et al.* (2009). SoundSense: scalable sound sensing for people-centric applications on mobile phones. *MobiSys 09*, 165-178.
18. Muir, B. (1994). Trust in automation: Part i. theoretical issues in the study of trust and human intervention in automated systems. *Ergonomics*, 37(11): 1905–1922.
19. Rukzio, E. *et al.* (2006). Visualization of uncertainty in context aware mobile applications. *MobileHCI 06*, 247-250.
20. Tullio, J. *et al.* (2007). How it works: A field study of non-technical users interacting with an intelligent system. *CHI 07*, 31-40.
21. Weiser, M. & Brown, J.S. (1997). The coming age of calm technology. *Beyond Calculation: the Next Fifty Years*, 75-85.
22. Yan, Z. *et al.* (2010). Effects of displaying trust information on mobile application usage. *ATC 10*, 107-121.

PANDAA: Physical Arrangement Detection of Networked Devices through Ambient-Sound Awareness

[1]Zheng Sun, [1]Aveek Purohit, [2]Kaifei Chen, [2]Shijia Pan, [3]Trevor Pering, [1]Pei Zhang
[1]Electrical and Computer Engineering, Carnegie Mellon University
[2]Computer Science and Technology, University of Science and Technology of China
[3]Independent
{zhengs, apurohit, peizhang}@cmu.edu, {kaifei.chen, shijia.pan, grafnu}@gmail.com

ABSTRACT
Future ubiquitous home environments can contain 10s or 100s of devices. Ubiquitous services running on these devices (i.e. localizing users, routing, security algorithms) will commonly require an accurate location of each device. In order to obtain these locations, existing techniques require either a manual survey, active sound sources, or estimation using wireless radios. These techniques, however, need additional hardware capabilities and are intrusive to the user. Non-intrusive, automatic localization of ubiquitous computing devices in the home has the potential to greatly facilitate device deployments.

This paper presents the PANDAA system, a zero-configuration spatial localization system for networked devices based on ambient sound sensing. After initial placement of the devices, ambient sounds, such as human speech, music, footsteps, finger snaps, hand claps, or coughs and sneezes, are used to autonomously resolve the spatial relative arrangement of devices using trigonometric bounds and successive approximation. Using only time difference of arrival measurements as a bound for successive estimations, PANDAA is able to achieve an average of 0.17 meter accuracy for device location in the meeting room deployment.

ACM Classification Keywords
C.3 Special-purpose and application-based systems: Signal processing systems.

General Terms
Algorithms, Design, Experimentation.

Author Keywords
Arrangement detection, networked devices, localization.

INTRODUCTION
PANDAA (Physical Arrangement Detection of Networked Devices through Ambient-Sound Awareness) is a spatial localization technique that uses ambient sounds. By forming a collective understanding across a set of nodes of the time-of-arrival for ambient audio events, PANDAA can automatically determine the physical arrangement of nodes without prior calibration of their locations. After initial deployment, ambient sounds, such as human speech, music, footsteps, finger snaps, hand claps, or coughs and sneezes, are used to autonomously resolve the spatial relative arrangement of the devices using trigonometric bounds and successive approximation.

Automatic localization of ubiquitous computing devices has the potential to greatly facilitate the introduction of technology into consumer or other "non administrated" environments. For example, consider the simple case of a consumer purchasing a new smart television for their home. Manual configuration would entail the user specifying which room the device is in, information that should be easily discernible by the system itself. Consider, then, the difficulty in configuring a ubiquitous computing environment that contains 10s or 100s of devices. As the number of devices increases, so does the need for very-low overhead configuration mechanisms. Fortunately, an increase in the number of devices also increases the potential for collaborative techniques to handle configuration.

Once devices are accurately positioned, the system can also be used to localize the source of audio events themselves. This can enable the automatic deployment of a variety of context-aware applications, such as audio surveillance [11], speaker localization [10], activity detection [5], and patient and elderly monitoring [25]. In these applications, locations of audio events being monitored are of great importance causing a pronounced "chicken-and-egg" problem where sensing can be used to determine the location of ambient acoustic events, but only after the location of the sensors is known.

The PANDAA system leverages microphones that already exist in various consumer devices, such as laptops, tablets, mobile phones, home theaters, smart TVs, etc. One single microphone per device is used to detect usable segments of ambient sound generated in a room. Next, the time difference of sound arrival (TDoA) between devices is calculated and used to iteratively estimate inter-device distances. These distances are then used to determine the overall arrangement of devices. Finally multiple TDoA measurements are combined to improve arrangement detection accuracy over time.

The implementation and evaluation of the PANDAA system

UbiComp'11, September 17–21, 2011, Beijing, China.

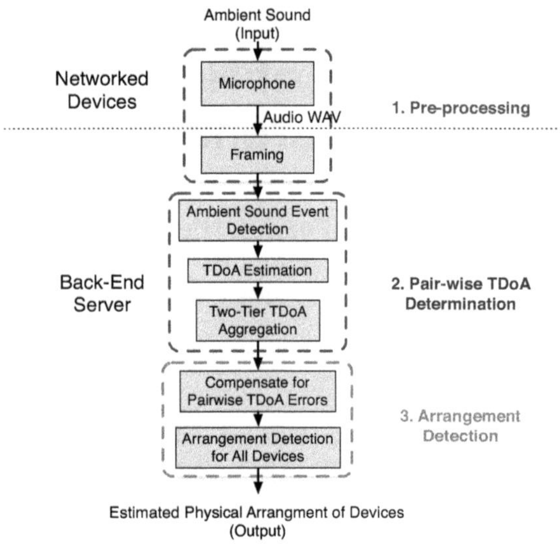

Figure 1. The system architecture of PANDAA.

shows that calibration-free device localization is possible. To cover broad ranges of ambient sounds, we tested the system under different distribution of ambient sound locations with cough, speech, and two types of music that commonly exist in office and home environments. To deal with time-varying indoor noises and compensate for reflections from walls and obstacles, we tested how sound event detection, aggregation and noise modeling techniques can be applied to improve system performance. We show that PANDAA can achieve 0.17m arrangement detection accuracy in real indoor environments. And with such accuracy, the system is able to localize sound sources to within 0.5m 80% of the time, yielding an error level that is comparable to previous work that used manual surveys [10, 25].

The key contributions of this paper are as follows:

1. We provide a proof of concept for a zero-configuration spatial localization of nodes based on ambient sound sensing.
2. We design a set of algorithms that leverages multi-node collaboration to compensate for indoor ambient sound effects, such as echos and ambient noise.
3. We design an algorithm that iteratively determines and improves the relative arrangement of the sensing nodes over time.

The following sections provide a detailed description of the PANDAA system, along with experimental evaluations to show its efficacy. Then we highlight the difference between related work and PANDAA. Finally, we conclude our work and summarize our contributions.

THE PANDAA SYSTEM

The system architecture of PANDAA is shown in Figure 1. Each sensor node is assumed to have a microphone that captures ambient sound, a microprocessor for basic signal processing, and a radio for communicating results back to a central server. In this paper, we assume all devices in the room are placed in a 2-D plane. However, the algorithms presented can be easily extended to cover 3-D cases. No further assumptions are made about the 2-D physical location of the devices and ambient sound sources. The devices themselves are assumed to be wirelessly connected to the central server. Additionally, it is assumed that the devices themselves do not move. Time synchronization is achieved over the local wireless network.

The PANDAA system addresses the major challenges of ambient sound-based arrangement detection as follows.

1. **Choosing Usable Ambient Sound Segments.** Ambient sounds, such as music played on a radio, human speech, noise from a working vacuum cleaner or a barking dog, may vary significantly in signal-to-noise ratio (SNR). In addition, varying proximity to the sound source can lead to significant difference in SNR. PANDAA addresses this challenge using an algorithm that can automatically detect *impulsive sounds*. Impulsive sounds are short duration sounds with relatively higher amplitude, such as human cough, finger snaps, or beats in a song.
2. **Correcting Inaccurate TDoA Measurements.** In indoor environments, TDoA measurements can be affected by environmental factors, such as reflections, non-line-of-sight (LoS) path, or ambient noise. These effects are location-dependent and time-variant. Consider a resident walking in the room. His/her changing location may temporarily cause a few devices to lose LoS, which can cause erroneous TDoA measurements. To compensate for TDoA errors, PANDAA uses a novel two-tier TDoA aggregation algorithm that identifies sounds originating from the same sound source and averages TDoA measurements over them.
3. **Localizing Devices From TDoA Measurements.** TDoA measurements from one single sound event are insufficient for estimating distance between two devices. PANDAA addresses this challenge by considering TDoA measurements from multiple ambient sound sources over time, to estimate inter-device distances and iteratively improve accuracy.

The following sections describe in detail the algorithm design of the PANDAA system.

Choosing Usable Ambient Sound Segments

PANDAA uses a frame-based impulse detection approach to automatically detect impulsive sounds that are distinct and have high signal-to-noise ratios (SNR). This approach consists of two steps.

First, compensating for hardware variation among devices by eliminating each microphone's circuit noise. This is achieved by recording a period of ambient sound under quiet conditions, which is described in step two below.

Second, since circuit noise can be assumed independent to environmental sound levels, we calculate the root mean square (RMS) of framed audio signals as an indicator of current local loudness from the microphone. The minimum RMS κ_i^c of the recorded audio under quiet conditions is used to quantify circuit noise on device D_i. For each device pair D_i and D_j, the circuit noise levels $\kappa_{i(j)}^c$ are subtracted from the RMS values $\kappa_{i(j)}$ of each incoming frame on the two devices to obtain ambient sound levels. The results are then com-

Algorithm 1 Ambient Sound Event Detection

for each device pair D_i and D_j **do**
  Compute $\kappa_{i(j)}$ for the current frame on D_i and D_j
  $\kappa_{i(j)} \leftarrow \kappa_{i(j)} - \kappa^{c}_{i(j)}$
  if $InEvent$ = NO **then**
    if for either D_i or D_j, or both, $\kappa_{i(j)} \geq \kappa^{aver}_{i(j)} \cdot \alpha_\kappa$ **then**
      $InEvent \leftarrow$ YES // *A sound event starts*
      Save the current frame on D_i and D_j into buffer
    else
      $\kappa^{aver}_{i(j)} \leftarrow \frac{\kappa^{aver}_{i(j)} + \kappa_{i(j)}}{2}$
    end if
  else
    if for either D_i or D_j, $\kappa_{i(j)} \geq \kappa^{aver}_{i(j)} \cdot \alpha_\kappa$ **then**
      Save the current frame on D_i and D_j into buffer
    else
      $InEvent \leftarrow$ NO // *A sound event ends*
    end if
  end if
end for

pared with iteratively updated admission thresholds $\kappa^{aver}_{i(j)}$. If

$$\kappa_{i(j)} - \kappa^{c}_{i(j)} \geq \kappa^{aver}_{i(j)} \cdot \alpha_\kappa \tag{1}$$

holds for either D_i or D_j, or both, an impulsive sound is detected, indicating a sound event starts; otherwise, the frame is discard as ambient noise. A sound event ends when Eq. (1) does not hold for incoming frames on either device D_i or D_j.

The value $\kappa^{aver}_{i(j)}$ tracks the average level of ambient noise at each device, and is updated as a moving average of the current $\kappa^{aver}_{i(j)}$ and the RMS value of the latest discarded frame. α_κ is an RMS ratio between impulsive sounds and ambient noises.

Using this impulsive sound detection approach, PANDAA can automatically extract high SNR sound events from a variety of ambient sound types. We observe that a smaller α_κ reduces probability of missing usable sound events, but increases computational cost. During the experiments, we empirically set α_κ to 1.80 to reduce probability of missing distant impulsive sounds. However, an adaptive threshold could also be applied to further reduce computation. Algorithm 1 outlines the ambient sound event detection process.

Time Difference of Arrival Estimation

After detecting a sound event, each pair of devices use audio frames in the detected event to compute time difference of sound arrivals (TDoA).

We denote the distance between a sound source and the two devices as d_{si} and d_{sj}, then the TDoA of device D_i and D_j is computed as

$$\tau_{ij} = \frac{d_{si} - d_{sj}}{v} \tag{2}$$

where v is the speed of sound. TDoA can be estimated by maximizing the cross-correlation of received audio signals on the two devices. Due to its effectiveness for non-stationary signals in the presence of noise and echos, we choose the generalized cross-correlation (GCC) algorithm, which estimates TDoA by solving

$$\tau_{ij} = \underset{\tau \in \mathcal{R}}{\arg\max} \frac{1}{K} \sum_{k=0}^{K-1} \Psi_{ij}[k] C_{ij}[k] e^{jk\frac{2\pi}{K}\tau}, \tag{3}$$

where $\Psi_{ij}[k]$ is a weighting function, and $C_{ij}[k] = X_i[k]X'_j[k]$ is the cross-spectrum of audio frames on device D_i and D_j, respectively [7, 8]. K is the number of audio samples in one frame.

The solution to Eq. (3) can be found by using linear-search. One variant of GCC algorithm defines the weighting function using a *phase transform* (GCC-PHAT) [23], and performs considerably better than its counterpart version under an echo-rich indoor environment. The GCC-PHAT algorithm defines the weighting function as $\Psi^{phat}_{ij}[k] = \frac{1}{|C_{ij}[k]|}$.

To reduce effects from ambient noise, such as low and steady hum from air conditioning in the room, we apply a bandpass filter to suppress the energy components with frequencies lower than 300Hz or higher than 6KHz. The filter is defined as

$$\Psi^{bandpass}_{ij}[k] = \begin{cases} 1 & 300 \leq \frac{k}{K} \cdot f_s \leq 6000 \\ 0 & \text{otherwise} \end{cases}, \tag{4}$$

where f_s is the sampling rate of each microphone on the devices. Finally the entire weighting function is defined as $\Psi_{ij}[k] = \Psi^{phat}_{ij}[k] \times \Psi^{bandpass}_{ij}[k]$.

Correcting Inaccurate TDoA Measurements

To compensate for TDoA errors caused by reflections and ambient noises, PANDAA uses a two-tier TDoA aggregation algorithm.

Lower Tier: Since sound events are typically tens of milliseconds in length, the locations of sound sources can be assumed to be stationary within a single sound event [8]. Based on this assumption, the lower tier aggregates cross-spectrums $C_{ij}[k]$ over successive frames in the same sound event to suppress any frame-to-frame effects that are uncorrelated. First, each device pair D_i and D_j uses all frames in the current sound event to compute *aggregated* cross-spectrum

$$C_{ij}[k] = \frac{1}{N} \sum_{n=0}^{N-1} X_{i,n}[k] X'_{j,n}[k], \tag{5}$$

where N is the number of frames in the current event. Then, each pair uses Eq.(3) to compute TDoA for the current sound event.

Upper Tier: While the lower-tier aggregation is sufficient for reducing uncorrelated frame-level noise, longer lasting ambient effects, such as a moving person blocking acoustic LoS of several nodes, can also significantly alter the TDoA measurements. To handle such effects, that are uncorrelated between consecutive events, we design an upper-tier aggregation that averages TDoA estimates over multiple consecutive sound events belonging to the same sound source.

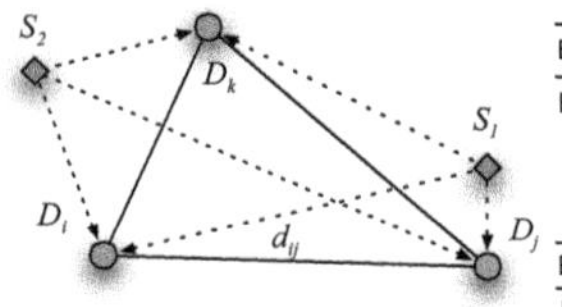

TDoA of S_1(ms)

	Di, Dj	Di, Dk	Dj, Dk
Event 15	20.4	1.2	-17.1
Event 16	19.7	1.9	-15.9

TDoA of S_2(ms)

	Di, Dj	Di, Dk	Dj, Dk
Event 17	-6.8	0.2	21.2
Event 18	-7.3	0.5	20.1

Aggregate (Events 15, 16) / Seperate (Events 16, 17) / Aggregate (Events 17, 18)

Figure 2. As locations of sound sources can be physically apart, TDoA measurements of consecutive sound events from the same source tend to be similar (such as the ones of Event 15 and 16), whereas those from different sources are dissimilar (such as the ones of Event 16 and 17). This information can be used to aggregate TDoA measurements from the same sound source and separate those from different sources.

The major challenge of the upper-tier aggregation is in separating sound events originating from different sound sources. Solitary devices cannot differentiate between multiple sound sources. However, as networked systems usually have multiple devices in a room, a group of networked devices can generate multiple TDoA measurements. For example, in Figure 2, TDoA measurements from the same sound source tend to be similar whereas those from different sources are more dissimilar. Considering TDoA measurements of multiple device pairs as a high-dimensional space, sound events from different sources can thus be separated by computing distances between TDoA measurements.

We note that there are two types of TDoA distances that should be considered. First, for the same sound source, different device pairs may experience different SNR measurements. According to the ambient sound detection algorithm, some of the device pairs may be able to detect the impulsive sounds whereas others may not. We consider this issue as the *hearability* difference between device pairs.

Second, if one device pair is able to make multiple TDoA measurements from the current sound source, it tends to get similar measurements with relatively small variation. We consider this as the TDoA *similarity*. Sound events from the same sound sources should be consistent in hearability and generate TDoA values with high similarity.

Based on this intuition, we define a hearability-vector to quantize the hearability difference between consecutive sound events, i.e.

$$\overrightarrow{\beta} = \{\beta_{1,2}, \beta_{1,3}, ...\beta_{2,3}, \beta_{2,4}, ...\}_{i,j}, \quad (6)$$

where $\beta_{i,j}$ equals 1 if a devise pair D_i, D_j is able to compute TDoA from the current sound event; otherwise 0. We also define a TDoA-vector to contain all the pairwise TDoA values for the current sound event, i.e.

$$\overrightarrow{\tau} = \{\tau_{1,2}, \tau_{1,3}, ...\tau_{2,3}, \tau_{2,4}, ...\}_{i,j}, \quad (7)$$

where $\tau_{i,j}$ is the TDoA value for the device pair D_i, D_j computed through the lower-tier aggregation. Both the hearability-vector and the TDoA-vector have $\frac{N_D(N_D-1)}{2}$ dimensions, where N_D is the total number of devices deployed in a room.

Then, the Hamming distance between the hearability-vectors of the current sound event, $\overrightarrow{\beta_{cur}}$, and that of the previous sound event, $\overrightarrow{\beta_{prev}}$, is computed to quantize consistency in hearability, i.e.

$$d_{\mathrm{H}} = \frac{\#(\overrightarrow{\beta_{cur}} \neq \overrightarrow{\beta_{prev}})}{\#\text{ of device pairs}}. \quad (8)$$

Meanwhile, the Euclidean distance between the TDoA-vectors of the current and previous sound events is computed to quantize the similarity in TDoA values.

Since difference in hearability may result in missing elements in the two TDoA-vectors, the common elements that *both* TDoA-vectors possess and which are valid, are first determined. Then, the Euclidean distance is computed *only* based on these common elements and finally normalized, i.e.

$$d_{\mathrm{E}} = \frac{\|\overrightarrow{\tau_{cur}} - \overrightarrow{\tau_{prev}}\|}{\#\text{ of common elements}}. \quad (9)$$

Finally, the per-dimensional hybrid distance is computed as the product of the two distances

$$d_{\mathrm{ALL}} = d_{\mathrm{H}} \cdot d_{\mathrm{E}}, \quad (10)$$

which is compared with a threshold d_{thr} to determine if the two consecutive sound events are considered as from the same source. If so, the TDoA values of the two events are averaged to suppress effect from ambient noise. Otherwise, the sound events are separated and treated as if they are from different sources. Algorithm 2 shows the two-tier TDoA aggregation process.

Algorithm 2 Two-Tier TDoA Aggregation

```
Lower-tier aggregation:
for each device pair D_i and D_j do
    Aggregate cross-spectrums within the current sound event according to Eq. (5).
    Compute TDoA values for the current sound event using Eq.(3).
end for

Upper-tier aggregation:
for each sound event do
    Create the hearability-vector β_cur for the current sound event according to Eq.(6); compute the Hamming distance d_H between β_cur and β_prev according to Eq.(8).
    Create the TDoA-vector τ_cur using TDoA values of the current event according to Eq.(7).
    In the TDoA-vector, determine common elements in which both the current and previous events have valid TDoA values, and compute the per-dimensional Euclidean distance d_E between τ_cur and τ_prev according to Eq.(9).
    Compute hybrid distance d_ALL = d_H · d_E
    if d_ALL ≤ d_thr then
        τ_ij = (τ_ij + τ'_ij)/2, where τ'_ij is the TDoA value of device pair D_i,D_j for the previous sound events
    end if
end for
```

Localizing Devices From TDoA Measurements

To determine the physical arrangement of networked devices, PANDAA utilizes a two step approach. 1) obtain the pairwise TDoA values as an estimate of the lower bound of the inter-device distances, and 2) use the distribution of TDoA collected over time to estimate the true inter-device distances, from which device arrangement is derived.

Determine Pairwise Distance Using TDoA Noise Model

Consider two devices D_i and D_j in a room, as shown on Figure 2. When a sound source S_1 generates a sound, TDoA measurements of the device pair D_i and D_j can be found using Eq.(2). Denote $\tau_{ij} \cdot v$ in Eq.(2) as $\hat{d}_{ij,1}$, which is the difference in distances from S_1 to D_i and D_j. According to the triangle inequality, $\hat{d}_{ij,1}$ sets a lower bound of the real inter-device distance d_{ij} such that $d_{ij} \geq |\hat{d}_{ij,1}|$. As the system detects more sounds from multiple sound sources, multiple distance differences establish a tighter lower bound of d_{ij} such that

$$d_{ij} \geq \max_{\forall m \in M}(|\hat{d}_{ij,m}|), \tag{11}$$

where $\hat{d}_{ij,m}$ is the difference in distances from the mth sound source to D_i and D_j, and M is the total number of sound sources that have generated ambient sounds.

As the number of sound sources increases, the maximum absolute value of all distance differences, i.e. $\max(|\hat{d}_{ij,m}|)$, will increase. Given an infinite number of uniformly distributed sound sources, $\max(|\hat{d}_{ij,m}|)$ will finally equal to the true inter-device distance d_{ij} if TDoA measurements have no errors. Thus $\max(|\hat{d}_{ij,m}|)$ can be regarded as a good estimate of d_{ij}. However, in a real indoor environment, TDoA measurements are corrupted by effects from reflections, obstacles and other ambient noises, and sound sources may not be uniformly distributed in the room. These factors make the value $\max(|\hat{d}_{ij,m}|)$ deviate significantly from the true value of d_{ij}.

To examine these effects during the estimation of inter-device distances d_{ij}, we build a geometry model in which sound sources are assumed uniformly distributed in the 2-D plane.

Two devices are located at $(-\frac{d_{ij}}{2}, 0)$ and $(\frac{d_{ij}}{2}, 0)$. We find that the probability density function (*pdf*) of the values of $\hat{d}_{ij}$ has three properties: 1) The *pdf* concentrates at values close to d_{ij} and $-d_{ij}$; 2) At values between $(-d_{ij}, d_{ij})$, the *pdf* resembles a uniform distribution; 3) At values outside $[-d_{ij}, d_{ij}]$, the *pdf* is 0.

To approximate this distribution, we define an empirical distribution such that: 1) In $(-d_{ij}, d_{ij})$, the values of $\hat{d}_{ij}$ are uniformly distributed; 2) At $\pm d_{ij}$, the probability equals ϵ times of that inside $(-d_{ij}, d_{ij})$; 3) Elsewhere, the probability is 0. Since the integration of the entire probability density function should be 1, we derive the probability distribution of $\hat{d}_{ij}$ as follows.

$$f_X(x) = \begin{cases} \frac{\epsilon}{2d_{ij}+2\epsilon} & x = \pm d_{ij} \\ \frac{1}{2d_{ij}+2\epsilon} & -d_{ij} < x < d_{ij} \\ 0 & \text{otherwise} \end{cases}. \tag{12}$$

For high SNR, TDoA values estimated by the GCC-PHAT algorithm are shown to be normally distributed with zero mean [15]. Therefore, we assume an additive Gaussian noise model $f_Y(y) \sim \mathcal{N}_{0,\sigma}$ for $\hat{d}_{ij}$ to take ambient noise into account. Together, the probability distribution of the noise-corrupted $\hat{d}_{ij}$ is the convolution of $f_X(x)$ and $f_Y(y)$, which is derived as

$$\begin{aligned} f_Z(z) &= \int_{-\infty}^{+\infty} f_X(z-y) f_Y(y) dy \\ &= \frac{\epsilon}{2d_{ij}+2\epsilon} \cdot (\mathcal{N}_{0,\sigma}(z-d_{ij}) + \mathcal{N}_{0,\sigma}(z+d_{ij})) \\ &+ \frac{1}{2}\left[\text{erf}\left(\frac{z-d_{ij}}{\sqrt{2}}\right) - \text{erf}\left(\frac{z+d_{ij}}{\sqrt{2}}\right)\right], \end{aligned} \tag{13}$$

where erf(.) denotes the error function.

Arrangement Detection for All Devices

Eq.(13) provides a parametric noise model of the distribution of $\hat{d}_{ij}$. It is determined by three parameters: 1) the actual inter-device distance d_{ij}, 2) the value of ϵ, and 3) the standard deviation of the Gaussian noise distribution σ. Therefore, we cannot simply take the maximum TDoA value as the true inter-device distance. However, given multiple TDoA measurements and thus multiple distance differences $\{\hat{d}_{ij,1}, \hat{d}_{ij,2},...,\hat{d}_{ij,m}\}$, d_{ij} can be estimated using a maximum likelihood estimator (MLE) that optimizes the following nonlinear optimization problem

$$\{d_{ij}, \epsilon, \sigma\}_{\text{MLE}} = \arg\max_{d_{ij},\epsilon,\sigma \in \mathcal{R}} \prod_{m=1}^{M} f_Z(\hat{d}_{ij,m}|d_{ij}, \epsilon, \sigma). \tag{14}$$

Maximization of Eq.(14) can be solved using various nonlinear optimization techniques, such as the Levenberg-Marquardt algorithm [4]. The process of solving Eq.(14) is out of the scope of this work. Interested readers are referred to [4, 18].

One common problem with most nonlinear optimization techniques is that the optimization does not guarantee finding the global optimum unless given good initial starting points. Therefore, we create a heuristic algorithm that finds a close approximation of the real d_{ij} value. To begin with, each device pair D_i and D_j makes a histogram of all the historical $\hat{d}_{ij}$ values computed from all sound sources that have generated sound events. The algorithm consists of the following four steps, which are illustrated on Figure 3. First, each pair selects $a\%$ bins with the highest $\hat{d}_{ij}$ values to determine the location of the uniformly-distributed region. Second, the value of the largest absolute x-coordinate of all the selected bins is determined, which is denoted as p. The value of p can approximate the area where the Gaussian noise affects. Third, the value of the largest absolute x-coordinate of all the historical $\hat{d}_{ij}$ values is determined, which is denoted as q. The difference between p and q can approximate the standard deviation of the Gaussian noise. Finally, each pair uses $\frac{p+q}{2}$ as a starting point for the MLE process.

This heuristic algorithm cannot generate the actual value of d_{ij}, but since it's lightweight and provides a good estimate of d_{ij}, we use it to generate a starting point in the MLE process. Algorithm 3 outlines the process of generating the starting point.

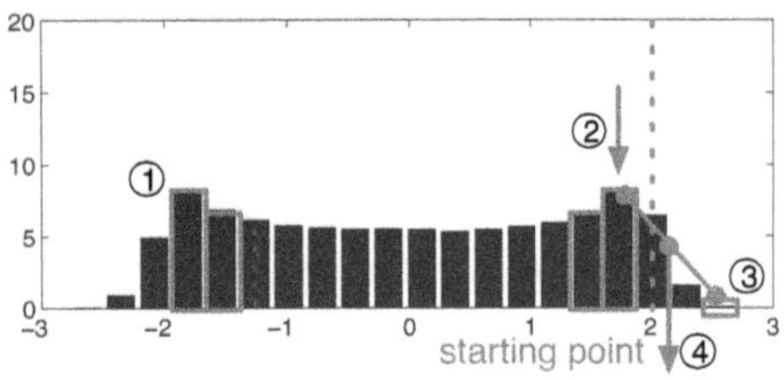

Figure 3. The four steps of the heuristic algorithm to determine the starting point for the MLE. Note that the histogram of the historical $\hat{d}_{ij}$ values shown is simulated based on the pair-wise TDoA noise model. In this example, the real inter-device distance d_{ij} is 2.

Algorithm 3 Starting Point Determination Algorithm

for each device pair D_i and D_j **do**
  Make histogram of all historical $\hat{d}_{ij}$ values
  Select $a\%$ bins that have the highest $\hat{d}_{ij}$ value (Step 1)
  Let the value of the largest absolute x-coordinate of all the selected bins be p (Step 2)
  Let the value of the largest absolute x-coordinate of all historical $\hat{d}_{ij}$ values of the pair be q (Step 3)
  Determine the starting point as $\frac{p+q}{2}$ (Step 4)
end for

After the MLE process computes inter-device distances for all pairs, we compute the physical arrangement of all devices in the network using the multidimensional scaling (MDS) techniques [21]. Originally applied in the psychological field, the MDS is a set of statistical techniques for exploring similarities and dissimilarities in data. It takes a distance matrix that quantizes inter-point dissimilarity. In our case, the dissimilarity between points is given by the inter-device distances d_{ij}, which is estimated by $\hat{d}_{ij}$. The MDS creates a configuration of relative coordinates for the points, between which the Euclidean distances can approximately represent the original distance matrix. We use these output relative coordinates as the final estimates of the physical arrangement of the devices in the room.

SYSTEM IMPLEMENTATION AND EVALUATION

To evaluate the arrangement detection techniques, we present real experiments with a few sound source locations (fixed speakers to localize), and many locations (ambient sound localization). We implemented the PANDAA system using acoustic sensing nodes and deployed them in indoor environments. Each node is built upon an LPC-P2148 prototyping board, featuring an ARM7 60MHz CPU and 48KB memory, with an inexpensive microphone (Knowles MD9745APZ-F [1]) and a Bluetooth radio for diagnosis. Figure 4 (left) shows a PANDAA sensor node.

Experimental Traces and Setup

We conducted experiments in a $7.80 \times 5.96 \times 2.84$ m^3 meeting room in our building. The meeting room is a generic rectangular shape as well as it contains furniture including tables, chairs, a HDTV, a blackboard, and an electrical control desk. A picture of the room is shown on Figure 4 (right) and a floor plan of the room is shown on Figure 5. Eight PANDAA nodes were placed on a table at approximately

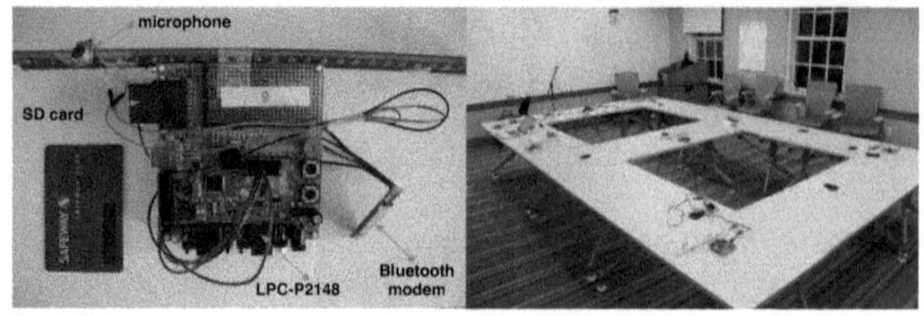

Figure 4. Left: A PANDAA acoustic sensing node placed next to a credit card. The microphone is fixed on a plastic ruler. Right: The meeting room where our controlled and full-scale experiments were done.

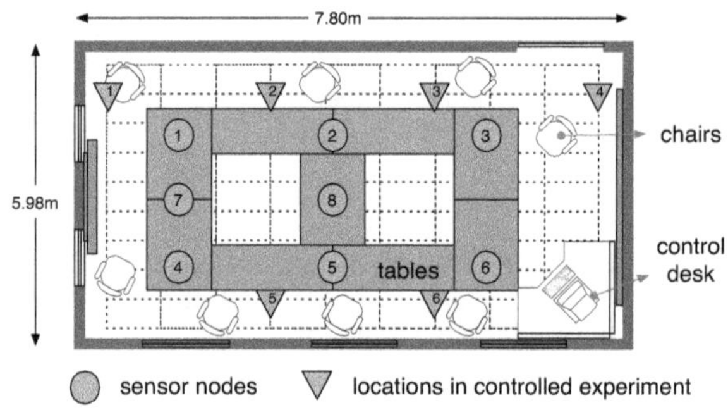

Figure 5. A floor plan of the meeting room. A total of 100 locations were marked as a grid (shown by dotted lines) in the meeting room and used as ground-truth locations of sound sources.

0.8m height as shown by the numbers in Figure 5. In order to make the system evaluation repeatable, a total of 100 locations were marked in the room, the intersection of the grid in Figure 5 shows the location of where ambient sounds were located.

To evaluate the system's ability of operating with different types of ambient sound, we selected cough, speech, and two genres of music as representative sound types common in indoor environments. All the sound was captured at 16KHz using a 10bit A/D converter on each of the eight PANDAA nodes. At the beginning of the experiments, a loud acoustic impulse was generated using a loudspeaker to synchronize all the nodes. During the experiments, one student was wandering inside the meeting room as well as a few chairs had been moved purposefully, generating time-varying ambient effects including noises and acoustic non-LoS.

Controlled Experiment

In order to test the capability of the system with a few fixed but repeatable sound locations (i.e. a few fixed speakers), we first performed a controlled experiment in the meeting room with six locations, as shown on Figure 5. At each location 160 human coughs were played using a loudspeaker. The pairwise TDoA values computed from the coughs were then used to analyze the TDoA errors. Figure 6 shows the distributions of errors, which approximately follow Gaussian distributions with zero mean. The standard deviations (std) for different device pairs changed slightly, with average std value of 1.27ms. Given the speed of sound, assumed to be 343m/s in the experiments, this std value translates to about 0.44m errors in inter-device distance estimation when sound sources are fixed but repeatable.

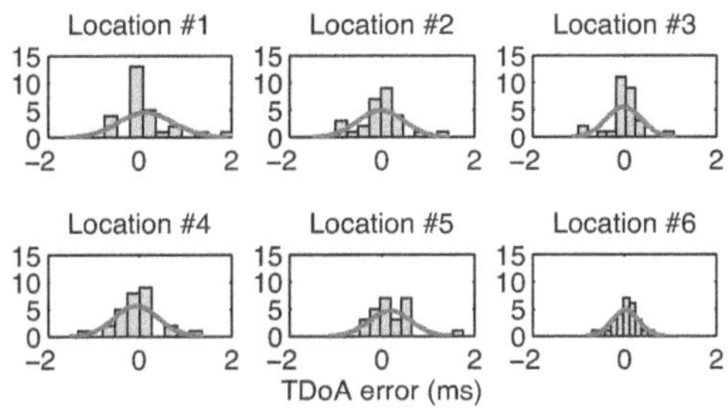

Figure 6. Distribution of pairwise TDoA errors for each sound source location with Gaussian fitting curves. Note that the number of devices is 8, so each histogram represents $\frac{8\times(8-1)}{2} = 28$ pairwise TDoA errors. The errors approximately follow Gaussian distributions.

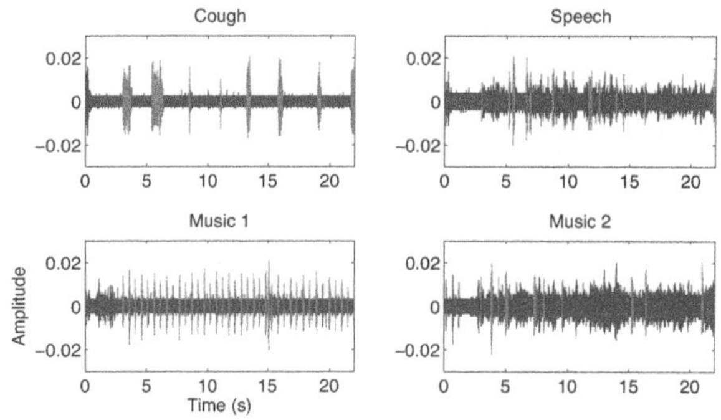

Figure 7. Sound events detected from the four sound clips. Blue: original sound clips. Red: detected sound events. While different sound types differ in time and spectrum properties, the event detection algorithm managed to detect and extract useful sound events from all the four tested sound clips.

Full-Scale Deployment

To evaluate performance of arrangement detection using unpredictable ambient sounds, we then tested in full-scale deployments using the 100 locations in the grid.

Performance of Sound Event Detection

To leverage a variety of ambient sounds, PANDAA detects impulsive sound events from different ambient sound signals recorded on each device. We selected coughs, speech and two different genres of music. The first genre was rock music (i.e. we chose Michael Jackson's "Billie Jean"), which features numerous clear rhythmic pulses that intuitively serve well to generate sufficient impulsive sounds; in contrast, the second genre was slower pop music (i.e. we chose Paul Simon and Garfunkel's "The Sound of Silence"), which was relatively smooth and melodic. In total, we tested all the four sound clips at each of the 100 locations in the full-scale experiments, which are summarized in Table 1.

Table 1. Ambient sounds used in the experiment

Type	Duration (s)	Note
Cough	32	12 coughs recorded by 6 individuals, including 2 males and 4 females
Human speech	21	A conversation between a male and a female
Music #1	21	"Billie Jean"
Music #2	21	"The Sound of Silence"

Table 2. Frequency and duration of detected sound events

Type	Freq. (events)	Avg. Duration (s)
Cough	1.10/cough	0.58
Human speech	0.67/s	0.24
Music #1 ("Billie Jean")	1.80/s	0.08
Music #2 ("The Sound of Silence")	0.55/s	0.17

Experimental results show that, the sound event detection algorithm is generalizable enough to handle the four different sound clips. Figure 7 shows the detection of impulsive sounds from one of the eight sensor nodes and Table 2 summarizes the frequency of detections and the durations of the detected events from all the nodes. Generally, every cough was considered by the nodes as a single sound event because of its distinct impulsive waveform. In addition, the "Billie Jean" song generated a large amount of sound events. This is explainable by considering its strong bass line. As a contrast, the "The Sound of Silence" song and human speeches generated considerably less sound events, but still achieved about one event per two seconds. On average, cough sounds generated 1 event/cough, and the other three sound clips generated 1 event/s. This frequency is sufficiently high to guarantee the system to acquire a large number of sound events quickly for arrangement detection. Using the detected sound events from each of the sound types, we computed TDoA values. Given the same sound source and device locations, the standard deviations of the TDoA measurements among different sound types were similar to those observed in the controlled experiments. Therefore, the following evaluations are based on the combination of different sound types.

Performance of TDoA Aggregation and Separation

As shown in the controlled experiment, raw TDoA values from the sound events contain considerable measurement errors due to indoor echoes and ambient noises. In PANDAA, the two-tier TDoA aggregation algorithm is aimed to suppress the time-domain uncorrelated noisy effects. In the upper-tier aggregation, accurately separating two consecutive sound events that come from different sound sources is important in improving TDoA performance. During the full-scale experiment, we randomly selected two locations from the grid to generate ambient sounds, forming a *sound-pair*. The ambient sounds were selected among the four sound clips. Then, multiple sound-pairs were considered by the system for aggregation or separation. Figure 8 shows the aggregation and separation results after the system considered 1000 randomly generated sound-pairs. The top graph indicates that there is a high positive correlation between the per-dimensional hybrid distances d_{ALL} of sound events and the real physical distances between the sound sources that have generated the events. The bottom graph shows that as the percentage of accurately aggregated sound events increases, the accuracy of sound events separation drops. This allows us to determine a value of the threshold d_{thr} such that the number of accurate aggregation can be maximized while maintaining a low false separation rate. During the experiment, we empirically set d_{thr} to 1.80. This led to 92.5% aggregation accuracy and 93.9% separation accuracy. After aggregating consecutive sound events, the standard deviation of TDoA errors are reduced by about 36%. Table 3 summa-

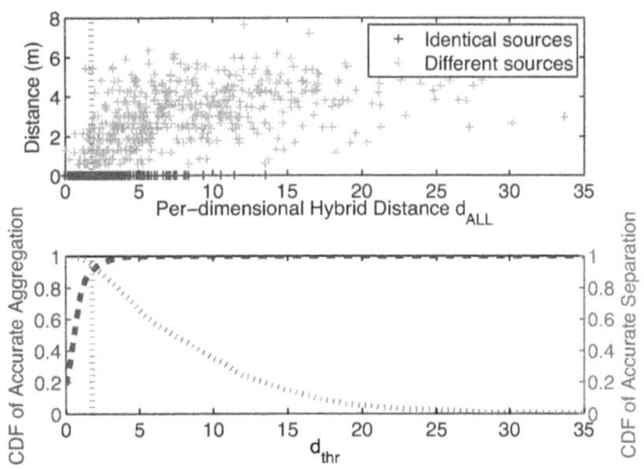

Figure 8. Upper-tier TDoA aggregation. Top: Per-dimensional hybrid distances between consecutive sound events vs. the physical distances between sound sources that generate the events. Note that if the two sound sources are identical, their physical distance (i.e. the y-coordinate) is 0. Bottom: Value of d_{thr} affects the accuracy of aggregating TDoAs from identical sources as well as separating TDoAs from different sources.

rizes the results comparing the standard deviation of TDoA errors between using and without using the TDoA aggregations.

Table 3. Comparison of pairwise TDoA estimation performance between using and without using the two-tier aggregation

Std. of TDoA errors (ms)	No Aggregation	With Aggregation
Cough	1.86	1.16
Human speech	2.14	1.02
Music #1	1.95	1.40
Music #2	2.18	1.64

Pairwise TDoA Error Rejection Performance

During the experiment, sound sources were randomly located at the 100 grid points shown in the room. After a sound source was selected, its ambient sound type was chosen from the four sound clips and a sound duration was set as a random value between 0s to the maximum clip durations shown in Table 1. The two-tier aggregation was enabled to improve accuracy of TDoA measurements. Figure 9 shows the performance of arrangement detection. Four approaches to compensating TDoA errors were compared:

1. Max: using the maximum historical pairwise TDoA measurements as estimates of inter-device distances d_{ij}. This approach was used as a baseline.
2. Heuristic: using the starting points computed in Algorithm 3 as estimates of d_{ij}.
3. MLE: using the starting points to initialize the MLE and use the MLE to estimate d_{ij}.
4. MLE ($\epsilon = 0$): assuming $\hat{d}_{ij}$ is uniformly distributed.

The figure shows that, as the number of sound sources increases, the errors of coordinate estimations drop quickly. For approaches except the Max baseline, the estimation performance becomes stable after about 10 sound sources having generated ambient sounds. After the estimation becomes stable, the baseline approach achieves the highest estimation

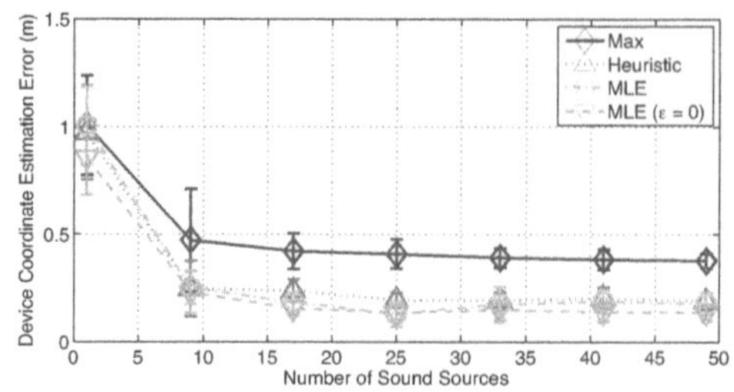

Figure 9. Performance of arrangement detection when using different methods to determine the inter-device distance.

error. Since pairwise TDoA errors are compensated in the second and third approaches, both of these two approaches reduce errors by at least 35%.

During the experiments we observed that the performance of MLE varied considerably between different evaluation runs. This was due to the fact that the MLE method tended to over-fit the multiple TDoA measurements given that the number of sound sources was small, which caused the value of d_{ij} to oscillate significantly. Many techniques can be applied to mitigate over-fitting in the MLE, such as the penalty-based approaches or reducing the number of parameters [6]. After testing different approaches, we chose an efficient approach that reduced the number of parameters in MLE by setting ϵ to 0. This change actually makes the values of $\hat{d}_{ij}$ to be uniformly distributed between $[-d_{ij}, d_{ij}]$. As shown on Figure 9, the fourth approach "MLE ($\epsilon = 0$)" leads to the highest accuracy of coordinate estimations, which is 0.17m. This performance is about 2.5X better than the baseline Max approach.

Performance with Different Numbers of Sensor Nodes

We evaluate the performance limit of PANDAA when the number of nodes is limited. Since at least three nodes are needed to uniquely define a 2-D plane, we start to evaluate the system by using 4, 6, and 8 nodes. Figure 10 shows the accuracy improvement as the system evolves under different node numbers. In the 4-node case, the convergence of coordinate estimation accuracy is slower than those under 6- and 8-node cases, which requires about 20 sound sources. This is because under fewer node numbers, the system requires more sound sources to make accurate estimation of inter-device distances. In contrast, we do not observe significant difference in the ultimate accuracy among the three cases. This is because as the number of sound sources increases, eventually the system will always have high probability of accurately estimating inter-device distances for every device pair. This result shows that the performance of PANDAA is robust against changes in the number of devices and is mostly determined by estimation accuracy of inter-device distances.

Performance Under Skewed Source Distributions

In real scenarios, different furniture layouts, room shapes and resident life patterns may cause sound sources to not be uniformly distributed (i.e. people might only walk in one part of the room). We would like to evaluate how the performance of arrangement detection changes given skewed distributions of source locations.

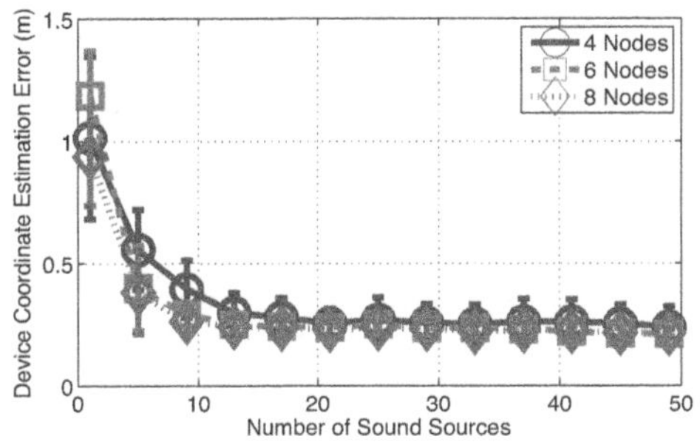

Figure 10. Performance comparison when using different numbers of sensor nodes.

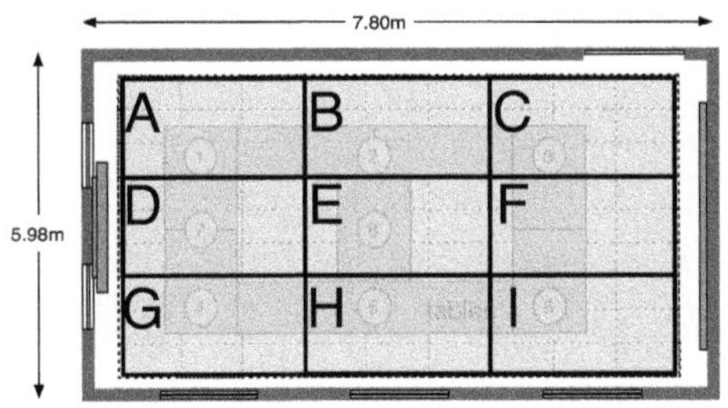

Figure 11. The location grid is divided into nine blocks to evaluate effects from skewed source distributions.

Therefore, we first divide the grid into nine blocks, as shown on Figure 11, and group them into symmetrical groups. We define four Side regions (for example, block A, B, and C form the Up-Side region), four Corner regions (for example, block A, B, D, and E form the Up-Left Corner region), and Center regions (containing block B, D, E, F, and H). Then, we select sound source locations *only* from within one of these regions to evaluate the system. Table 4 summarizes the performance under different cases.

To consider the convergence process and wait for the performance of arrangement detection to become stable, the estimation accuracy is determined after 20 sound sources have generated sounds. For all cases, skewed distribution of sound sources had higher errors than that of the uniformly distribution case described earlier. In particular, sound sources that are limited to only one side of the room (Side regions) have higher errors due to most limited diversity of sound source locations. However, we observe that PANDAA still achieved better than 0.4m estimation accuracy.

Table 4. Accuracy of arrangement detection under skewed source distributions (Accuracy is determined after 20 sound sources as the performance tends to be stable)

Cases	Avg. Error (m)	Std. Error (m)
Side Regions	0.39	0.17
Corner Regions	0.21	0.08
Center Regions	0.27	0.06

Using PANDAA to Determine Source Locations

As shown in previous evaluation, under uniformly distributed sound sources, PANDAA achieves up to 0.17m in accuracy. We would like to investigate how the performance of arrangement detection affects that of sound source localization. Figure 12 shows that, as the number of sensor nodes

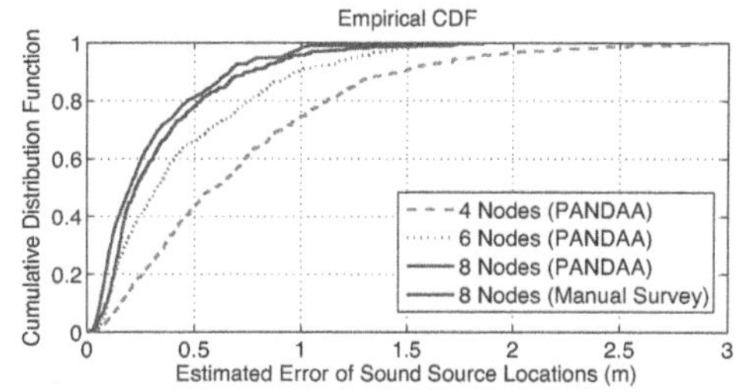

Figure 12. Sound source localization performance when using the PANDAA system.

increases in the system, the accuracy of source localization improves significantly. Using full sound source distributions, with 8 sensor nodes, PANDAA can localize a sound source to within 0.5m 80% of the time, and within 0.9m 95% of the time. This performance is comparable to previous work that localizes sound sources based on manually surveyed sensor node locations [10, 25]. Meanwhile, we compare PANDAA's performance with that of manually surveyed device locations. Under the 8-node case, the performance of manually surveyed locations is only about 10.5% better than PANDAA.

RELATED WORK AND DISCUSSION

There are many techniques that have been previously explored for indoor localization. The Global Positioning System (GPS) [3] is only available outdoors and provides limited accuracy. In indoor settings, researchers have developed RF radio-based positioning techniques like Radio Signal Strength (RSS) ranging, RSS fingerprinting, Angle-of-Arrival, RF Time Difference of Arrivals (TDoA), and Time of Flight (ToF) [16]. However, localization is not good enough for sub-meter accuracy required in many applications. Some work using ultrasonic sensing provides higher accuracy [12, 19], but is limited due to the use of specialized sensors, which are not ubiquitously available on electronic devices, and often require specialized configuration or setup to produce results.

Other work has shown audible sound can be a good resource for localizing devices. However, most of the previous work uses on-device loudspeakers to actively emit known finite-length repeatable signals, such as chirps or peaks [9, 17, 20]. This approach can be intrusive and sometimes annoying if the systems require frequent location updates of their devices.

Ambient sounds have also been used in outdoor environments to passively determine locations of devices [14]. While they report 0.58m average microphone localization error in open outdoor scenarios, their simulations show that the system generates large errors (>2m) when sound sources are close to the microphones indoors. In contrast, PANDAA deals with indoor ambient effects by selectively using impulsive sounds to compute TDoA, and leveraging multi-node collaboration to improve measurement accuracy. Scott and Dragovic also describe an audio location sensing technique that uses impulsive sounds [22], however it is not clear how the system deals with indoor acoustic effects, such as echoes and non-LoS.

TDoA is a common technique to self-localize devices in microphone arrays [2]. Prior work has discussed this technique using both close-formed [13] or iterative methods [26] theoretically. For distributed sensor networks, Raykar et al. present an approximate solution combined with nonlinear optimization [20]. However, they make an additional assumption that some loudspeakers are co-located with microphones. In contrast, PANDAA assumes no a priori knowledge of ambient sound types or locations of sound sources, and we present generalizable impulsive sound event detection and TDoA aggregation algorithms to leverage ambient sound in arrangement detection. Other TDoA approaches for sound source localization have also been explored. Guo and Hazas make comprehensive comparisons between TDoA estimation techniques in terms of sound type, accuracy, power and bandwidth requirements [10], but assume fixed microphones with known locations.

This paper focuses on the design and evaluation of PANDAA, thus implementation details are not fully addressed due to the page limit and are presented elsewhere [24].

CONCLUSION

In this paper, we presented PANDAA, a novel autonomous physical arrangement detection technique that determines device locations using ambient sounds generated in indoor environments. Using ambient sounds commonly existing in the office and home environments (i.e. coughs, human speech, and music), the system is able to accurately measure device location. To show the performance of PANDAA in real deployments, we deployed our system in a meeting room environment under different source distributions, and with different sound types. Using only TDoA as a bound for its successive measurements, PANDAA was able to achieve an average of 0.17m device location accuracy. In addition, based on this estimation, PANDAA is able to localize sound sources to within 0.5m 80% of the time, well within comparable error level to previous work that is based on manual surveys.

By autonomously resolving the spatial relative arrangement using trigonometric bounds and successive approximation, PANDAA is less intrusive and more accurate than existing techniques. We propose our system can be used to solve the device localization problem for many emerging indoor ubiquitous computing applications. Furthermore, our automatic localization of ubiquitous computing devices has the potential to greatly facilitate device deployments in future smart home environments.

REFERENCES

1. Knowles microphone, www.knowles.com/search/prods_pdf/MD9745APZ-F.pdf, 2011.
2. P. Aarabi. Self-Localizing Dynamic Microphone Arrays. *IEEE Transactions on Systems, Man and Cybernetics*, 32(4):474–484, Nov. 2002.
3. A. Ali, S. Asgari, T. Collier, M. Allen, L. Girod, R. Hudson, K. Yao, C. Taylor, and D. Blumstein. An Empirical Study of Collaborative Acoustic Source Localization. In *Proc. of the 6th International Conference on Information Processing in Sensor Networks*, volume 57, pages 415–436. Springer, Nov. 2007.
4. D. P. Bertsekas. *Nonlinear Programming*. Athena Scientific, 1999.
5. X. Bian, G. Abowd, and J. Rehg. Using sound source localization to monitor and infer activities in the Home. In *Proc. of the 3rd International Conference on Pervasive Computing*, Munich, Germany, 2005. Springer.
6. C. Bishop. *Pattern Recognition and Machine Learning*, volume 4. Springer New York, 2006.
7. M. Brandstein and H. Silverman. A Practical Methodology for Speech Source Localization with Microphone Arrays. *Computer Speech & Language*, 11(2):91–126, Apr. 1997.
8. J. DiBiase. *A High-Accuracy , Low-Latency Technique for Talker Localization in Reverberant Environments Using Microphone Arrays*. PhD thesis, 2000.
9. L. Girod, V. Bychkovskiy, J. Elson, and D. Estrin. Locating Tiny Sensors in Time and Space: A Case Study. In *Proc. of the IEEE International Conference on Computer Design: VLSI in Computers and Processors 2002*, pages 214–219. IEEE, 2002.
10. Y. Guo and M. Hazas. Localising Speech, Footsteps and Other Sounds Using Resource-Constrained Devices. In *Proc. of the 10th International Conference on Information Processing in Sensor Networks*, number 2, pages 330 – 341, Chicago, Illinois, USA, 2011. IEEE.
11. A. Harma, M. McKinney, and J. Skowronek. Automatic Surveillance of the Acoustic Activity in Our Living Environment. In *Proc. of the IEEE International Conference on Multimedia and Expo 2005*, volume 1, pages 1–4, Zurich, Switzerland, 2005. IEEE.
12. M. Hazas, C. Kray, H. Gellersen, H. Agbota, G. Kortuem, and A. Krohn. A Relative Positioning System for Co-located Mobile Devices. In *Proc. of the 3rd International Conference on Mobile Systems, Applications, and Services*, pages 177–190, New York, New York, USA, 2005. ACM.
13. K. Ho. An Approximately Efficient TDOA Localization Algorithm in Closed-Form for Locating Multiple Disjoint Sources with Erroneous Sensor Positions. *IEEE Transactions on Signal Processing*, 57(12):4598–4615, Dec. 2009.
14. T. Janson, C. Schindelhauer, and J. Wendeberg. Self-Localization Application for iPhone Using Only Ambient Sound Signals. In *Proc. of the International Conference on Indoor Positioning and Indoor Navigation 2010*, number September, pages 1–10. IEEE, 2010.
15. C. Knapp and G. Carter. The Generalized Correlation Method for Estimation of Time Delay. *IEEE Transactions on Acoustics, Speech and Signal Processing*, 24(4):320–327, 1976.
16. H. Liu, H. Darabi, P. Banerjee, and J. Liu. Survey of Wireless Indoor Positioning Techniques and Systems. *IEEE Transactions on Systems Man and Cybernetics*, 37(6):1067–1080, 2007.
17. C. Peng, G. Shen, Y. Zhang, Y. Li, and K. Tan. BeepBeep: A High Accuracy Acoustic Ranging System Using COTS Mobile Devices. In *Proc. the 5th International Conference on Embedded Networked Sensor Systems*, pages 1–14, Sydney, Australia, 2007. ACM.
18. W. H. Press, B. P. Flannery, S. A. Teukolsky, and W. T. Vetterling. *Numerical Recipes in C: The Art of Scientific Computing*. Cambridge University Press, 1992.
19. N. Priyantha, A. Chakraborty, and H. Balakrishnan. The Cricket Location-Support System. In *Proc. of the 6th International Conference on Mobile Computing and Networking*, volume 2000, pages 32–43, Boston, Massachusetts, USA, 2000. ACM.
20. V. Raykar, I. Kozintsev, and R. Lienhart. Position Calibration of Microphones and Loudspeakers in Distributed Computing Platforms. *IEEE Transactions on Speech and Audio Processing*, 13(1):70–83, Jan. 2005.
21. S. Schiffman, M. L. Reynolds, and F. W. Young. *Introduction to Multidimensional Scaling: Theory, Methods, and Applications*. Emerald Group Publishing Limited, 1981.
22. J. Scott and B. Dragovic. Audio Location: Accurate Low-Cost Location Sensing. In *Proc. of the 3rd International Conference on Pervasive Computing*, pages 1–18, Munich, Germany, 2005. Springer.
23. M. Silverman. A Robust Method for Speech Signal Time-Delay Estimation in Reverberant Rooms. In *Proc. of the IEEE International Conference on Acoustics, Speech and Signal Processing 1997*, pages 375–378. IEEE, 1997.
24. Z. Sun, A. Purohit, P. De Wagter, I. Brinster, C. Hamm, and P. Zhang. PANDAA: A Physical Arrangement Detection Technique for Networked Devices through Ambient-Sound Awareness. In *Proc. of the ACM SIGCOMM 2011*, pages 1–2, Toronto, Canada, 2011.
25. Z. Sun, A. Purohit, K. Yang, N. Pattan, D. Siewiorek, I. Lane, and P. Zhang. CoughLoc : Location-Aware Indoor Acoustic Sensing for Non-Intrusive Cough Detection. In *Proc. of the International Workshop on Emerging Mobile Sensing Technologies, Systems, and Applications 2011*, pages 1–6, San Francisco, California, USA, 2011.
26. D. J. Torrieri. Statistical Theory of Passive Location Systems. *IEEE Transactions on Aerospace and Electronic Systems*, pages 183– 198, July 1984.

Exploring Micro-Incentive Strategies for Participant Compensation in High-Burden Studies

Mohamed Musthag, Andrew Raij†, Deepak Ganesan, Santosh Kumar‡, Saul Shiffman⋆
Univ. of Massachusetts Amherst, Univ. of South Florida†, Univ. of Memphis‡, Univ. of Pittsburgh⋆
{musthag,dganesan}@cs.umass.edu, raij@usf.edu, skumar4@memphis.edu, shiffman@pinneyassociates.com

ABSTRACT
Micro-incentives represent a new but little-studied trend in participant compensation for user studies. In this paper, we use a combination of statistical analysis and models from labor economics to evaluate three canonical micro-payment schemes in the context of high-burden user studies, where participants wear sensors for extended durations. We look at how these strategies affect compliance, data quality, and retention, and show that when used carefully, micro-payments can be highly beneficial. We find that data quality is different across the micro-incentive schemes we experimented with, and therefore the incentive strategy should be chosen with care. We think that adaptive micro-payment based incentives can be used to successfully incentivize future studies at much lower cost to the study designer, while ensuring high compliance, good data quality, and lower retention issues.

Author Keywords
micro-payments, micro-incentives, user study.

ACM Classification Keywords
H.5.m Information interfaces and presentation (e.g., HCI): Miscellaneous.

General Terms
Economics, Experimentation, Human Factors, Performance

INTRODUCTION
A growing segment of the health and science community is turning to ubiquitous computing technologies, such as wearable sensors and smartphones, to conduct studies in natural environments [4, 8, 15, 16, 20, 21]. These studies are providing new understanding of the human condition in the real world rather than the lab, and leading to more ecologically valid mechanisms to measure, evaluate, and improve health.

Often, such health and science field studies are characterized by high burden on the participant. They may ask participants to wear sensors on their body for days at a time or provide frequent self-reports (e.g., 10-20 times per day) that interrupt the normal flow of daily life. This burden has consequences. It reduces participant compliance with the study protocol (not wearing the sensors one day or ignoring questionnaires) and can even lead to participant dropouts. By reducing compliance and retention, burden effectively reduces the amount and quality of the data, and by extension, its validity and statistical power.

Incentives are a powerful and common mechanism to counteract the effects of burden [6, 28, 29]. Initially, they are used to entice people to participate in a study. During the study, they encourage participants to follow the study protocol (compliance), remain in the study (retention), and provide high quality data [5]. Incentives come in many forms, including money or gift cards, free health care services, and the knowledge that one's participation can advance science and/or improve the human condition [10, 13, 19].

Monetary incentives are typically distributed in fixed bulk amounts for completing study milestones. In some studies, there is only one milestone, reaching the end of the study. Other studies might have several milestones, spaced days or weeks apart (e.g., completion of the first lab study, completion of 1 day of monitoring, etc.). Each incentive is then used to encourage the participant to reach the next milestone and reward the participant for continued participation. How often to award incentives (number and schedule of milestones), how much each award should be per milestone, and how much to offer in total for the entire study is decided based on the goals of the study, importance of each milestone, the overall burden to the participant, and the budget available to the study designers.

While traditional high-burden user studies have largely relied on such coarse-grained, bulk payments, the use of mobile phones and other devices offer significant new flexibility in terms of when, what, and how much incentives are offered. For example, amounts offered could be varied based on the number of hours a participant wore a sensor, upon completion of individual self-report questionnaire, or even upon completion of a single question within a questionnaire. They could also be varied by the day of the study, time of day, type of question asked, consistency or quality of answers, extent of burden, and so on. Perhaps the amounts offered could be tailored to the individual, and use personalized pricing while simultaneously reducing the overall cost of running the study. In addition, the frequency with which incentives are provided could be varied, or the presentation of incentives could be manipulated. For example, incentive amounts could only be revealed after a question is answered, making the act of compliance more like playing a lottery.

The increased flexibility offered by micro-incentive strategies poses a significant challenge to the study designer. What micro-incentive strategy should be chosen to improve compliance? At what granularity should incentives be provided? What effect does varying incentives have on compliance, data quality, and retention? Does one micro-incentive strategy work for all participants, or should they be personalized to the individual? What are common pitfalls of micro-incentive strategies? To what extent can micro-incentives lead to unintended adverse consequences? While the possibilities are tantalizing, the dearth of studies on micro-incentive strategies complicates the design of user studies.

This paper is an initial exploration of the spectrum of micro-payment design choices facing study designers as more field studies become mobile-based and put larger burdens on participants. While it is infeasible to cover the space of micro-incentives strategies, we use three canonical mechanisms to explore the benefits and pitfalls of these approaches. We look at a high-burden study that involves wearing a chest-band with several on-board sensors for three days. Throughout, participants experience roughly 20 interruptions from experience sampling questionnaires per day. The three micro-incentive mechanisms that we compare are simple, intuitive choices that a study designer might make: the *Uniform* strategy pays the same amount per questionnaire, the *Variable* strategy pays different amounts for each questionnaire based on a prior distribution of rewards, and the *Hidden* strategy also has different amounts per questionnaire but includes a lottery component by hiding the amount earned until the user completes the questionnaire.

Our study enables us to answer several key questions including: 1) which micro-incentive schemes perform well or poorly?, 2) how does the amount of micro-incentive impact compliance and data quality?, 3) do micro-incentive strategies encourage adverse behavior from participants?, 4) how do micro-incentive schemes impact retention? and 5) do users perceive micro-incentives favorably?

We use a combination of statistical analysis and models from labor economics to answer these questions, and draw several implications from the data. We find evidence that micro-incentives are a powerful tool for the study designer, and have a significant impact on participant behavior. We think that adaptive micro-incentives can be used to reduce the cost of future studies, while providing high-quality results. However, we also find evidence that poorly chosen micro-incentive amounts can lead to adverse behavior from participants. For example, higher micro-incentive amounts may motivate lying on questionnaires to earn more money. The results from our study lead to several valuable insights that can be useful for study designers in the future.

RELATED WORK

The availability of micro-incentive based task markets such as the Amazon Mechanical Turk (AMT [1]) has led to several incentive-based studies. Mason and Watts found that higher micro-payments led to higher task completion rates on AMT [17]. However, the quality of the data provided by participants was not affected by the size of the incentive. Similarly, Heer et al [11] used AMT to conduct a visualization study and found that larger incentives led to quicker completion times, but again, no difference in the quality of data provided across different incentive amounts. Micro-payments have also been used to monetize downloads from peer-to-peer networks [31] and websites [27], as well as motivate environmental stewardship [30].

Micro-payments are being increasingly used in mobile phone-based user studies. For example, Consolvo et al awarded participants $1 for each questionnaire completed in a seven-day field study [8]. Similar to our study, Reddy et al studied micro-payment incentives in the context of participatory sensing [25]. Their study tested multiple micro-payment amounts as well examined how game-like characteristics affect the compliance and data quality. Participants were divided into five groups, and were assigned to take pictures of the contents of waste bins around a University campus. The first group was paid a fixed amount at the end of the study, three groups were paid a uniform micro-payment for each valid picture, and the last group was awarded a variable amount for valid images, depending on their ranking with respect to other participants.

Our study differs from [25] in three important ways: a) we examine micro-payments for *carefully controlled scientific field studies* where motivation is more difficult because of significant burden (wearable sensors, and several interruptions from questionnaires per day), rather than for more voluntary, unstructured participatory sensing tasks, b) we analyze results using labor economic models of reservation wages, which gives greater insight into the population, and c) motivated by concepts from behaviorism and "gamification" [18, 2, 9, 22, 12, 23, 7, 26], we include *Variable* and *Hidden* incentives schemes to understand the effect of different incentive strategies on compliance, data quality, and retention (discussed in the next section).

STUDY DESIGN

We designed a study to examine the effect of micro-payment incentives on high-burden experience sampling studies. Specifically, the study is designed to measure how compliance, data quality, and the perceived burden of participation are affected by three different schemes for distributing micro-payments, *Uniform*, *Variable*, and *Hidden*. In the *Uniform* scheme, participants are awarded a fixed amount for completing a micro-task. In the *Variable* scheme, awards vary randomly based on a prior distribution. In the *Hidden* scheme, awards again vary randomly, but the amount is not revealed until after the micro-task is completed. Both of these schemes are inspired by the variability and unknowns typical in game dynamics, and are intended to elicit more engagement, and ultimately, more compliance and better data quality.

To enable an analysis of these micro-incentive schemes within a realistic context, we integrate them into an existing field study. The study's primary goal was to collect physiological, psychological, and behavioral measures of stress from people in natural environments, specifically when exposed to interruptions in daily life (results reported separately). The study had several characteristics typical of recent ubiquitous computing and health science field studies and applications [4, 8, 15, 16, 20, 21], and was thus ideally suited to meeting the goals of this paper. These characteristics include:

- **Experience Sampling Questionnaires:** Participants provided frequent self-reports. They were prompted to complete 20 questionnaires per day, with each questionnaire having between 21 and 25 questions. Each question in a questionnaire was an opportunity to encourage compliance, data quality, and retention using micro-incentives.
- **Three Days:** The study required three consecutive days of participation, allowing analysis of the effect of waning interest in the study as the study progresses, and whether micro-incentive structures can offset this waning interest.
- **Wearable Sensors:** Participants in the study wore sensors around their chest for 10-12 hours each day of the study, not unlike other UbiComp and behavioral science applications and studies.
- **High Burden:** The above characteristics - frequent questionnaires, monitoring with wearable sensors, and for several days at a time - represent a significant burden to participants. Adding to this burden, participants had to return to the lab each day to exchange used batteries for new ones. We believe this level of burden represents the upper end of what participants in field studies are usually exposed to. Thus, our results will provide insight into appropriate incentive schemes for high-burden field studies.

Incentive Structures

We ran a between-subjects study, where participants were assigned to one of three incentive schemes, *Uniform*, *Variable*, and *Hidden*. Each scheme paid the participant a micro-payment for completing a single question in a questionnaire. We incentivize each question in a questionnaire, because a question is the finest-grain opportunity to measure compliance and data quality in experience sampling studies. *Uniform* participants were paid a fixed amount of four cents per question completed. Thus, if participants answer all 25 questions in a questionnaire, they earned $1. This level of compensation is similar to that given in [8], where $1 was awarded for each questionnaire completed.

Variable and *Hidden* participants were paid a variable amount, between 2 and 12 cents per question. This amount changed from questionnaire to questionnaire according to a random distribution. The distribution was biased such that smaller micro-payments were offered more frequently than larger ones. For example, 2-cent awards were offered 30% of the time, 4-cent awards were offered 10% of the time, and 12 cent awards were offered 1% of the time. If a *Variable* participant was offered 12 cents per questions, they stood to earn as much as $3 if they completed all questions - three times as much as *Uniform*.

The distribution was also chosen such that the expected amount earned for completing all 25 questions in a questionnaire was approximately $1, the same amount earned by *Uniform*. Thus, even though *Variable* and *Hidden* could occasionally earn far more than *Uniform* on a questionnaire, on average all three groups could earn the same amount of money (assuming they completed all questionnaires presented). Guaranteeing similar potential earnings across all three groups ensured all participants were compensated similarly and fairly. The only difference between *Variable* and *Hidden* incentives is that *Hidden* was not told the amount each question was worth until they completed an entire questionnaire.

Justification of Incentive Structures: The design space of micro-incentive schemes is large, with many options available to the study designer. From this space, we chose to study the *Uniform*, *Variable*, and *Hidden* micro-incentive structures described above for several reasons.

The *Uniform* scheme represents a likely choice for a study designer interested in incentivizing micro-tasks in a study. Uniform micro-payments are simple to implement (they do not require calculation of individual micro-incentives) and are a natural evolution of bulk payment schemes that are already familiar to study designers. Indeed, this evolution is apparent in two recent studies [25, 8] that adopted or examined uniform micro-payments. Furthermore, since the *Uniform* scheme is a likely choice for study designers aiming to incentivize micro-tasks (e.g., question completion), we use it as a pseudo-control condition for comparison to the *Variable* and *Hidden* incentive structures.

The *Variable* incentive scheme was chosen because of the effectiveness of variable rewards in sustaining behavior in games [2, 18, 12] and broader behavioral contexts [9, 22]. In addition, variable incentives allow examination of the influence of reward sizes on desired outcomes (high compliance, data quality, etc.).

Lastly, the *Hidden* incentive scheme was chosen because it is akin to playing the lottery or gambling where the exact reward is not always known [2, 23]. Lotteries usually offer higher rewards (jackpots) at far lower frequencies than lower rewards. The contrast between low and high rewards and their frequencies create a sense of scarcity that artificially increases the perceived value of the reward [7], and by extension, the motivation to play. Furthermore, the occasional higher reward or near-miss of a higher reward creates the impression that high rewards are possible, thus encouraging the player to continue playing [26]. We note that participating in our study is not the same as gambling. Unlike gambling, our participants always earn money and cannot lose money for answering a question.

Procedure

36 participants were recruited from the student population at the University of Memphis in the United States using flyers and word-of-mouth. Participants received compensation according to one of the three incentive structures to which they were randomly assigned. 12 participants were assigned to each incentive structure. Earned incentives were paid in full when participants completed the study.

Day 1 Start: After providing informed consent, participants were introduced to the wearable sensor suite they wore about their chest underneath their clothes throughout the study. They were also provided smartphones, which they used to complete the experience sampling questionnaires in the field. They were asked to wear the sensors and carry the phone with them during waking hours (10-12 hours per day). The participant was then randomly assigned to one of the three incentive schemes. The study coordinator explained the assigned incentive scheme and how participants could keep track of their earned incentives (see below). Participants were not told about the other incentive schemes. All participants were told they could earn approximately $60 if they complete all questionnaires requested of them (Average of $1 per questionnaire × 20 questionnaires per day × 3 days). Participants returned to the lab each day at a scheduled time to replace sensor batteries, provide backups of data collected, and mark down the incentives earned each day.

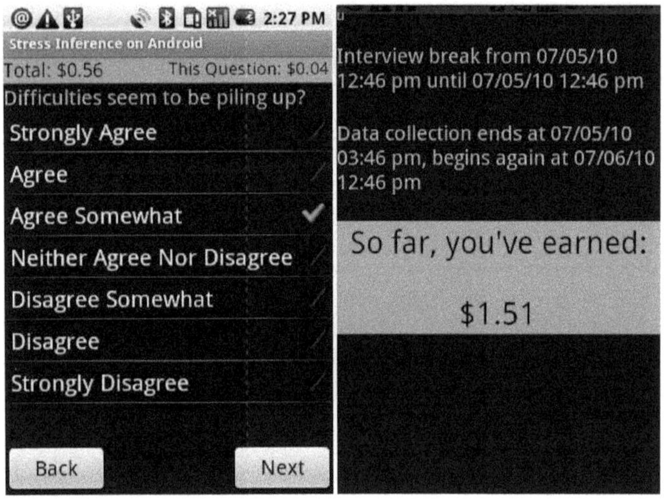

Figure 1. Left - The user interface for the experience sampling questionnaires (left) and the display shown on the phone when participants were not completing questionnaires (right). The questionnaire interface updates incentives in real-time as questions are completed.

Field Study: In the field, participants were prompted to complete questionnaires 20 times per day. Ten appeared when the participant's stress or speaking state changed (context-aware experience-sampling [14]), as detected on the smartphone using data collected by the sensor suite [20, 24]. The remaining ten questionnaires were scheduled to appear 55 minutes after the last questionnaire (whether triggered by inferences or scheduled). To keep participant burden within reason, participants did not receive questionnaire prompts within 30 minutes of a previous prompt. The mobile phone vibrated and played an audible tone to alert the participant to a new questionnaire. To encourage timely completion, time limits were imposed on questionnaires. If the participant could not attend to the questionnaire immediately, he/she could choose a one-time delay of ten minutes.

To help participants keep track of awarded micro-payments, the smartphone software included several reminders of the incentives available and already earned. Before starting the questionnaire, a message appears informing the participant how much money they could earn per question answered ("Each question you answer in this interview will earn you _____." In the case of the *Hidden* group, the blank was filled with "???" followed by the statement: "We'll tell you what you earned after the interview." Next, the first question in the questionnaire would appear and participants could answer by selecting choices from a list (Figure 1 - Left). In the case of the *Uniform* and *Variable* groups, the top of the questionnaire screen also showed the amount the participant could earn for the current question and the amount earned on the current questionnaire thus far. The amount earned thus far changed as soon as the participant answered the question, providing instant positive feedback of compliance. After completing all questions, a summary screen would appear displaying the amount earned per question, the total earned for the just-completed questionnaire, and the total amount earned since the beginning of the study (Figure 1 - Right). For the *Hidden* group, this was the first and only time they were made aware of the amount earned per question and the total earned for the just-completed questionnaire. The main application screen also provided a persistent display of the total amount earned since the beginning of the study.

Field Questionnaire: The field questionnaire contained questions that assess stress levels and situational information about the user at the time of the administration. Sample questions include "Angry/Frustrated?," "Happy?," and "Talking?" Metadata useful for assessing compliance and data quality were also collected, including the start and completion time of each question and questionnaire, the number of questions answered, and whether the questionnaire was delayed.

The questionnaire also includes gateway questions, which if answered in a particular way leads to one or more optional questions. For example, if the user responds "yes" to "Talking?," three additional questions appear: "If talking, on the phone?," "If talking, with whom?" (men and/or women), and "If talking, with whom?" (significant other, children, relatives, etc.). Micro-payments are also earned for these optional questions, providing an opportunity to assess how incentives affect compliance and data quality for optional questions. Micro-incentives could encourage participants to answer these questions more but they could also lead to inaccurate responses to earn more money.

End-of-Study: Participants returned to the lab and returned equipment at the end of three days. They then completed an end-of-study questionnaire to gather subjective feedback about the incentive scheme and their perception of the burden they experienced during the study.

RESULTS

We analyzed participant data with respect to the goals of the study as discussed in the preceding section. We now discuss the results and their interpretation. We use mixed-effects regressions analyses, which account for correlation of observations within individuals, to test for significant differences. Where space allows, p-values are reported with the means and confidence bounds of the corresponding distributions.

Compliance

Compliance is the extent to which participants execute the study protocol. The compliance for an experience sampling questionnaire is measured using two metrics: the completion rate, and the number of questions answered. Completion rate refers to the percentage of questionnaires completed of the total prompted to participants. The number of questions answered refers to the total number of questions answered on completed questionnaires. This can vary across participants due to the presence of optional questions.

Completion Rate

We look at completion rates along two axes: the overall completion rate across different micro-payment sizes, and across different incentive mechanisms.

First, we look at the *Variable* scheme and ask if the likelihood of questionnaires being completed varied with the size of the micro-payment offered on questionnaires. Note that only participants in *Variable* observed a changing micro-payment incentive from survey to survey. Surprisingly, we do not find any evidence to indicate that the likelihood of questionnaires getting completed was affected by the offered micro-payment size for the *Variable* group. In fact, the EMAs with lowest micro-payment were just as likely to be completed as the EMAs with highest micro-payment.

The influence of incentives on completion rate is, perhaps, better articulated by using the notion of reservation wage of an individual [3]. In Labor Economics, the *reservation wage* refers to the minimum amount an individual has to be paid for the individual to complete some task. The reservation wage of an individual is the product of the individual's assessment of the benefit and cost of participation in the particular task. Depending on the individual's preferences, this assessment process could take in to consideration things like the private value to him of contributing to the advancement of Science. Based on his budget, the study designer chooses how much to pay the participant, i.e. he has to choose w_j, which is the per question incentive offered to participants for each questionnaire j. The participant then decides whether to complete the questionnaire or not, based on w_j and r_i, where r_i is the *reservation wage* of individual i. Note that r_i can be modeled as a small range for practical purposes. Thus, the individual will choose to complete the questionnaire only if $w_j \geq r_i$.

One conclusion from this result is that we overpaid individuals for their EMAs *i.e.* that the reservation wage for most individuals was below even the lower threshold that we had chosen. This implies that, for our sample, we could have reduced the incentives by significant amounts without reducing the completion rate. In fact, the results also suggest that we may have offered too much for the *Uniform* strategy ($4c$ per question); if we had instead offered an amount of $2c$ (low end of the *Variable* strategy), we would have reduced overall costs by roughly 50% with similar completion rates.

Second, we look at overall completion rates across different incentive mechanisms. Table 1 shows the completion rates we observe in our study, over all participants, and across different incentive mechanisms. We find high completion rates, over all participants, with the mean completion rate standing at 85%. We find no statistically significant difference in completion rates across the groups, although notable is the fact that *Hidden* performs worst amongst the three schemes – a trend that we see across several analyses.

Groups	Mean (%)
Overall	85.03 ± 1.61
Uniform	86.28 ± 2.58
Variable	86.92 ± 2.70
Hidden	81.68 ± 3.12

Table 1. Completion rate across groups. (Participant Avg % ± 95% CI)

Number of questions answered

In order to see if particular incentive schemes encouraged participants to answer more questions, we pose several optional questions in each questionnaire. A questionnaire is considered completed if all required questions have been answered. Thus, for completed questionnaires, the number of questions answered varies only to the extent the number of optional questions answered varies. We analyze the optional questions data in three ways: across different micro-payment sizes, over time, and across different incentive schemes.

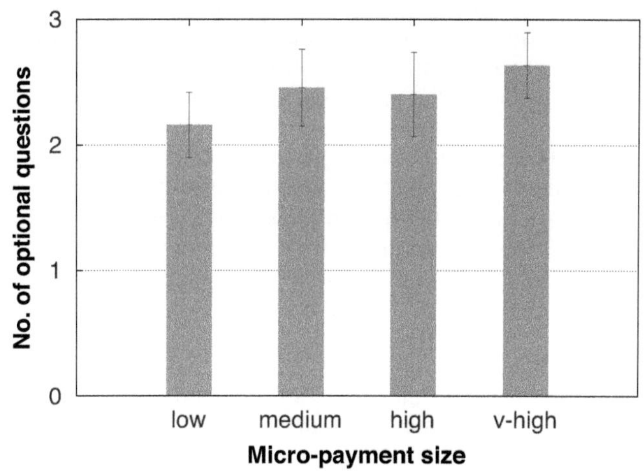

Figure 2. Number of optional questions answered vs. micro-payment size for *Variable*. The bins are quartiles — low $2c$; medium $3c$; high $4c$; v-high $> 4c$

First, we ask if the micro-payment offered on questionnaires had an effect on the number of optional questions answered by participants in *Variable*. We find a statistically significant positive effect of the size of the micro-payment incentive on the number of optional questions answered, i.e. larger micro-payment incentives encouraged participants in *Variable* to answer more optional questions ($p < 0.013$). Figure 2 shows the average number of optional questions answered broken down by the size of the micro-payment incentive offered on questionnaires, for the *Variable* incentive scheme.

On this surface, incentivizing participants to answer more optional questions appears useful, but this depends on the truthfulness of the answers provided. To understand this behavior, we turn to a model from Labor Economics. The decision making process can be explained as a simplistic two player game between the study designer and the participant. The study designer has to decide how much to pay the participant, i.e. he chooses w_j, which is the per question incentive offered to participants for each questionnaire j. The participant then decides whether to answer honestly or dishonestly on the gateway question, that would lead to one or more subsequent optional questions, based on w_j and r_i, where r_i is the *reservation wage* of individual i.

	$w_j < r_i$	$w_j = r_i$	$w_j > r_i$
Talking	NT	T	T
Not Talking	NT	NT	T

Table 2. Choice matrix facing an individual when considering answering the gateway question "Are you Talking?"

Table 2 shows the choice matrix facing the individual, when he is considering answering one of the several gateway questions in the questionnaire, "Are you Talking?". If the individual answers "Yes", that leads to three additional questions that can be answered to earn more on the questionnaire. There are three cases to consider:

- When $w_j < r_i$, the individual does not feel that the reward is sufficient for the burden of answering the optional questions. Therefore, to avoid answering the subsequent optional questions, he might be tempted to answer in the negative (NT), even if he was in fact talking (T).
- When $w_j = r_i$, the individual is indifferent between answering, or not answering the subsequent optional questions. There is no incentive for him to be dishonest, so he will tend to answer gateway question truthfully.
- When $w_j > r_i$, the reward outweighs the burden of answering the optional questions. Therefore, in order to maximize his reward, he would be tempted to answer in the affirmative (T), even if he was, in fact, not talking (NT).

The lack of ground truth validation makes it difficult to determine the truthfulness of results provided by users in our study. However, the trend in Figure 2 does indicate that users are more incentivized to answer high-paid optional questions, suggesting that the above model may indeed have some validity. These observations have important implications for study design. In particular, we think that when using micro-payment strategies together with optional questions, it is important to have ground truth validation. For instance, sensors on a smartphone may be used to collect context about whether an individual is talking or not. This can help check if the gateway question was answered correctly, and a study designer can be confident that micro-payment incentives have played a positive role in nudging the participant to answer more questions. In our study, we were unable to make this correlation since the data from our sensors were too noisy for accurate activity classification. In cases where accurate ground truth estimation is not possible, we recommend that any optional branches pay out identical sums, so that the individual has no incentive to pursue one of the branches.

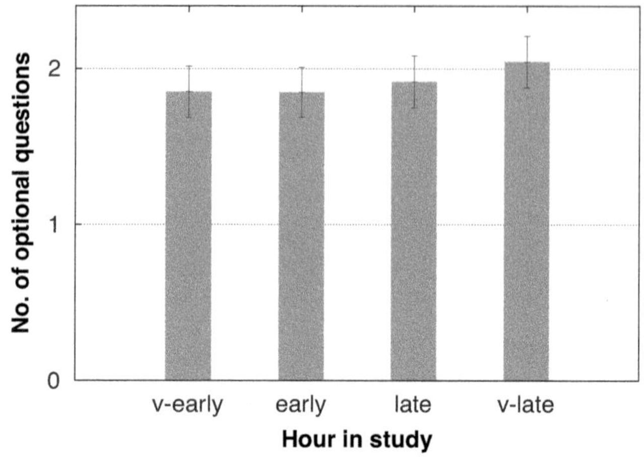

Figure 3. Number of optional questions answered over time for *Variable*. The bins are four quartiles of the study duration.

Second, we look at the trend in answering optional questions over time to see whether there was any notable change. Curiously, we find that participants do indeed tend to answer more optional questions over time ($p < 0.055$). Figure 3 shows a breakdown by quartile. This result is not easy to explain — is it due to honest reporting or are users taking advantage of optional questions as they become more familiar with the study design? Again, these results make the case for using context inference to judge the validity of the data provided by users.

Groups	Mean
Uniform	2.08 ± 0.14
Variable	2.09 ± 0.14
Hidden	1.55 ± 0.14

Table 3. Number of optional questions answered across groups. (Participant Avg $\pm$ 95% CI)

Third, we check to see if the number of optional questions answered differed across incentive schemes. Table 3 shows the number of optional questions participants answered across different incentive schemes. We find that participants in the *Hidden* incentive scheme are likely to answer fewer optional questions than participants in the *Uniform* ($p < 0.045$) and the *Variable* ($p < 0.060$) incentive schemes.

Data Quality

Data quality is the extent to which questionnaire answers are truthfully completed. We measure data quality using a consistency score that we compute by comparing answers on questionnaires which implicitly capture the same information. Specifically, we consider two opposing question-pairs to compute consistency: 1) Happy vs. Sad, and 2) Cheerful vs. Sad. We argue that these two metrics are reasonable for measuring questionnaire consistency because they represent different extremes in the valence of emotion, i.e. a participant is extremely unlikely to be both "Happy" and "Sad", or "Cheerful" and "Sad" at the same time.

The pairs of questions in the consistency metrics above are *inversely-related*, in that a high score on one question should imply a low score on the other. Participants choose an answer amongst these choices: 1 'Strongly Disagree'; 2 'Disagree', 3 'Disagree Somewhat', 4 'Neither Disagree Nor Agree', 5 'Agree Somewhat', 6 'Agree', 7 'Strongly Agree'. Let $r_{jq} \in \{1, 2, 3, 4, 5, 6, 7\}$ be the response to question q in questionnaire j. The consistency score, $cs_{jqq'}$, for a pair of *inversely-related* questions, q and q', on questionnaire j is computed as follows:

$$cs_{jqq'} = \begin{cases} 1 & \text{if } (r_{jq} > 4 \text{ and } r_{jq'} < 4) \text{ or } (r_{jq} < 4 \text{ and } r_{jq'} > 4) \\ 0 & \text{otherwise} \end{cases}$$

Groups	Happy vs. Sad (%)	Cheerful vs. Sad (%)
Uniform	94.74 ± 1.68	92.99 ± 1.92
Variable	95.70 ± 1.62	94.21 ± 1.87
Hidden	87.56 ± 2.66	87.06 ± 2.70

Table 4. Happy vs. Sad and Cheerful vs. Sad consistency across groups. (Participant Avg % $\pm$ 95% CI)

Table 4 shows the proportion of surveys that are consistent as measured using Happy vs. Sad and Cheerful vs. Sad consistency metrics, respectively. In terms of the Happy vs. Sad metric, we find that questionnaires completed by participants in *Hidden* are less likely to be consistent than questionnaires completed by participants in both *Uniform* ($p < 0.007$) and *Variable* ($p < 0.005$). In terms of the Cheerful vs. Sad metric, we find that questionnaires completed by participants in *Hidden* are less likely to be consistent than questionnaires completed by participants in both *Uniform* ($p < 0.040$) and *Variable* ($p < 0.018$).

If we look at the *Hidden* group more closely, we see that participants in this group do not know how much they would earn by completing the questionnaire at hand. This could perhaps frustrate this group and lead to the behavior we observe here.

Groups	Mean (hours)
Uniform	62.77 ± 10.48
Variable	62.46 ± 7.54
Hidden	62.84 ± 10.35

Table 5. Retention across incentive schemes. (Participant Avg (h) % $\pm$ 95% CI)

Groups	Completed (%)	Delayed (%)
v-early	87.87 ± 3.07	4.81 ± 2.01
early	85.56 ± 3.21	4.31 ± 1.36
late	84.40 ± 3.39	7.40 ± 2.13
v-late	82.61 ± 3.39	6.00 ± 2.13

Table 6. Completion rate and Delay rate over time. Each bin shows a quartile. v-early (Q1) $< 10h$; $10 \leq$ early (Q2) $< 30h$; $30h \leq$ late (Q3) $< 52h$; v-late (Q4) $\geq 52h$. (Participant Avg (h) % $\pm$ 95% CI)

Next, we drill further down, and examine *how* inconsistent the inconsistent questionnaires were. We breakdown inconsistent behavior into three bins: mildly, moderately, and highly inconsistent. An inconsistent question-pair is: a) *mildly* inconsistent when participants 'Agree Somewhat' or 'Disagree Somewhat' to both questions, b) *highly* inconsistent when one of the answers is 'Strongly Disagree' or 'Strongly Agree', and c) *moderately* inconsistent otherwise. Figures 4 and 5 show a breakdown for Happy vs. Sad and Cheerful vs. Sad, respectively. The figures show that *Hidden* has the highest level of inconsistency, with 6% of all questionnaires completed being highly inconsistent, and 5% being moderately inconsistent. This, perhaps, reinforces our hypothesis that participants in *Hidden* may be getting frustrated.

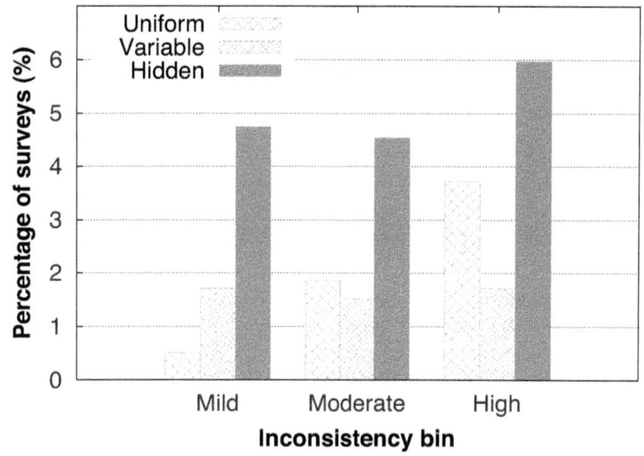

Figure 4. Happy vs. Sad - Degree of failure

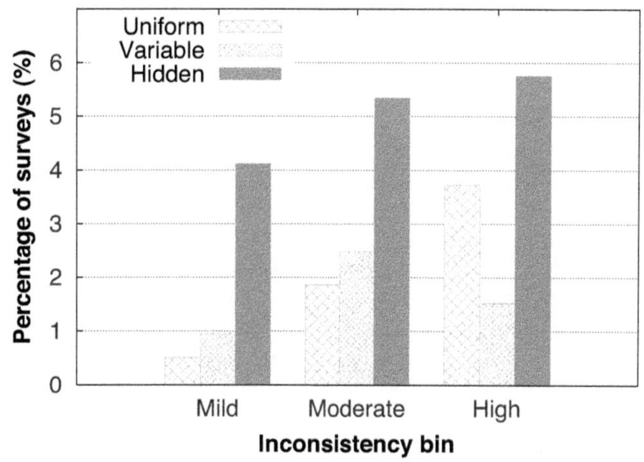

Figure 5. Cheerful vs. Sad - Degree of failure

Retention

Retention is the extent to which participants remain active over the course of the study. Here, we measure retention as the number of hours participants remain in the study, *i.e.* the difference between the time of the last and first questionnaires they answered. While this metric does not account for periods of inactivity within this duration, previously discussed compliance metrics already capture this effect.

	Question	*Uniform*	*Variable*	*Hidden*
1	I felt more engaged in the study because of micro-payments	3.08 ± 0.57	3.17 ± 0.53	2.92 ± 0.63
2	I'd rather receive $50 bulk-payment, than micro-payments for each question	2.83 ± 0.60	2.42 ± 0.74	2.83 ± 0.60
3	The phone interfered with my daily activities	2.25 ± 0.39	2.17 ± 0.60	2.08 ± 0.57
4	The phone interfered with my social interactions	2.67 ± 0.49	2.25 ± 0.61	2.00 ± 0.54
5	Overall, the phone was a nuisance	1.83 ± 0.46	2.0 ± 0.66	1.92 ± 0.50
6	The chestband interfered with my daily activities	2.08 ± 0.42	2.67 ± 0.56	2.33 ± 0.56
7	The chestband interfered with my social interactions	2.17 ± 0.53	2.08 ± 0.74	1.67 ± 0.41
8	Overall, the chestband was a nuisance	2.00 ± 0.54	2.58 ± 0.57	2.58 ± 0.50

Table 7. Participant Perception. Participants responded on a scale of 1 to 4. 1 - 'Strongly Disagree'; 2 - 'Disagree'; 3 - 'Agree'; 4 - 'Strongly Agree'. (Participant Avg $\pm$ 95% CI)

#	Age group	Interruptions	Duration	Payment	Completion rate
1	23-50y	Every 45min, take measurement, and complete 58-item survey.	6 days	$42/day	81% completed at least 75% of prompts.
2	50-70y	Every 45min, take measurement, and complete 45-item survey.	6 days	$33/day	88% completed at least 57% of prompts.
3	17-30y	Roughly every 45min, complete 25-item survey.	3 days	$20/day	81% completed at least 75% of prompts, and 100% completed at least 57% of prompts.

Table 8. Comparison to two other studies with similar burden that use bulk-payment incentives.

Table 5 shows that retention was similar across different incentive schemes. However, Table 6 shows a result that may be indicative of waning interest over time. We find a negative effect trending towards significance on the effect of time on completion rate, i.e. completion rate falls over time ($p < 0.096$). The mean completion rate drops from 88% in the 'v-early' period to 83% in the 'v-late' period. We do not find evidence that participants delayed more questionnaires over time. However it is interesting to note that the mean likelihood that a questionnaire is delayed is considerably lower in the first two quartiles (4.81% and 4.31%) than in the last two quartiles (7.40% and 6.0%).

Participant perception

Upon completion of the study, participants complete an End-of-Study questionnaire, which we use to gather subjective feedback about the incentive schemes. Because these responses are collected per-participant, we do not have sufficient data to make statistical inferences in many cases. Nonetheless, we present this data here because we feel it provides insights for study designers into how participants perceive micro-incentive approaches.

Rows 1 and 2 in Table 7 show responses from the participants that relate specifically to micro-payments based incentive schemes. 75% of participants felt more engaged in the study because of the micro-payments attached to each questionnaire, which is encouraging and explains the high compliance that we obtained. However, 53% of participants also would have preferred to receive $50 at the end of the study, instead of receiving smaller amounts for each question. Intuitively, this makes sense since committing to a micro-payment based study generally implies more risk than committing to a bulk-payment based study, and thus risk-averse individuals are likely to prefer the safer alternative. Furthermore, we note that participants in *Hidden* appear to prefer bulk payments more than the other groups, implying they perceived more burden than the other groups.

Rows 3 to 5 in Table 7 show the responses that relate specifically to the impact of the *phone* on participants' lives. Most participants did not feel that the phone adversely affected their daily activities or social life, and most participants did not find the phone a nuisance to use. Rows 6 to 8 in Table 7 show the responses that relate specifically to the impact of the *chestband* on participants' lives. Most participants did not feel that the chestband had an adverse effect on their daily activities or social life. Furthermore, *Uniform* participants felt that the chestband was not a nuisance, but participants in *Variable* ($p < 0.03$) and *Hidden* ($p < 0.03$) did see the chestband as a nuisance. This could, perhaps, be attributed to the occasional frustrations *Variable* and *Hidden* participants experienced when they were paid low wages on some questionnaires.

Comparison with bulk-payment based incentives

We now look at how the completion rates we observed in our micro-payment based study compares against the completion rates of bulk-payment based studies. Comparing studies with different population, burden, total payment, questionnaires, devices, etc. is difficult, if not impossible to make in a rigorous manner. Therefore our comparison is merely a high-level comparison of these studies.

Table 8 compares our study against two studies that seem to involve a similar amount of burden [15, 21]. Participants in [21] were required to take measurements, using an on-body sensor, and complete a 58-item questionnaire every 45minutes, during waking hours. Participants got prompted roughly 18-20 questionnaires per day, for which they were compensated about $42 per day. The study was split into three days for training and feedback, and three for actual data collection. Of the 157 participants in the study, the authors report that 81% of participants completed at least 75% of all prompts. [15] was a similar study, with the main differences being a slightly shorter questionnaire (45 items), and lower compensation ($33 per day). This study comprised of 2 periods of 3 day monitoring. The authors report that 88% completed at least 57% of all prompts. Our study offered $20 per day, which is less than what the others offered. However, our study lasted only 3 days rather than six days, and our questionnaires were shorter and involved only 25 items.

Comparing completion rates across these studies, we see that our compliance is similar to that reported in [21] (81% of participants completed at least 75% of all prompts), and higher than numbers from [15] (they reported 88% of participants completing at least 57% of prompts, whereas ours was 100% for the same metric). This is despite the fact that our study did not involve any pre-screening of participants to enroll only compliant participants unlike [15, 21].

These observations indicate that the completion rates that we obtain are at least comparable, if not better, than those from other bulk payment studies. However, we note that making an authoritative comparison between micro-payment and bulk-payment incentive schemes will require a careful study designed to experiment with both types of incentive schemes under identical conditions.

IMPLICATIONS AND LIMITATIONS

Uniform vs Variable incentives: In terms of overall performance, we see that both incentive schemes perform very well across the board. While one could conclude that this implies the *Uniform* incentive scheme is good enough, the *Variable* incentive scheme can be useful to measure the reservation wage of the population, which can be used to enable better parameter settings for future studies for similar users. For example, we found that the overall cost of the *Uniform* strategy could have been reduced by 50% by using information gleaned from the *Variable* study that similar compliance could be achieved by lower incentives. Thus, we feel that *Variable* is a more powerful incentive strategy than *Uniform*: it provides insight into the relationship between wages and compliance for the population, is robust to poor choices of remuneration, and can be used strategically to improve compliance.

Hidden incentives: The *Hidden* incentive scheme was designed to create a sense of anticipation for larger rewards in participants. However, our results clearly showed that it did not perform well. Participants in this group were less attentive to the questions resulting in lower consistency, and perhaps the frustration over finishing a questionnaire only to find out that the remuneration was less than they had hoped carried over to future questionnaires. One explanation for this is that unlike a lottery where the payoffs are large, the potential payoffs with micro-incentive strategies are relatively modest. Overall, the lack of good performance from the *Hidden* incentive scheme is consistently seen across our results, and suggests that this was, in retrospect, not such a good idea.

Personalized micro-payments: Our analyses show that variable micro-payment incentive schemes provide powerful knobs that study designers can tune in order to affect different performance metrics. One can even imagine taking this one step further and using dynamic pricing models to personalize micro-payment incentives. The incentives can adapt to individuals' reservation wages in order to obtain high levels of compliance while minimizing cost to the study designer. Similarly, micro-payments may be adapted over time to improve compliance and retention for longer studies. We believe that our work lays the foundation for future studies that explore personalization at greater depth, and we plan to pursue these directions in future work.

Optional questions: Our analysis shows several ways in which micro-payments and optional questions interact. Response rate for optional questions can be increased by careful selection of micro-incentives, but variable micro-payments may also lead to adverse behavior. Optional questions can be used, but we recommend some fraction of them be validated through context inferencing on the phone. Examples include: "Are you talking now?", and "Are you walking?", where accurate context inferencing can be performed using accelerometer or other sensor data. Such questions can help determine if an individual is more likely to lie or tell the truth, and can help provide confidence in the data. Our future studies will explore the effectiveness of such techniques.

Limitations and Implications for Future Work: While our study reveals several unanticipated considerations with micro-incentives, it also has several limitations. Perhaps the key limitation of our study is the size of the participant pool. Since we wished to compare several micro-incentives, we had to divide the participant pool into smaller groups, which gave us less data for some comparisons. In addition, this limited us to an exploration of three incentive models; clearly, there are several variants of these models as well as other incentive models that could have been attempted. In particular, a comparison of micro-payment schemes to commonly-used bulk payments would help identify what advantages each approach has over the other. In addition, we need to understand the reactivity or impact of micro-payments on the affective state of the participant. Do high rewards increase participant happiness and vice-versa? In studies that involve affect, this could be undesirable, since affect triggered by micro-incentives could confound the data and reduce its ecological validity. Ultimately, our work should be viewed as a pilot that articulated and explored several questions that need to be addressed for designing more robust micro-payment based incentive mechanisms. We hope that future work drills into these considerations through larger studies.

CONCLUSIONS

In conclusion, this paper presents an in-depth look at several micro-incentive based strategies for high-burden user studies. Overall, we find that micro-incentive strategies play a central role in keeping users engaged and attentive in studies. We saw very high levels of compliance, and little if no retention issues, despite the high burden on the individual to participate in our study. Our study also revealed several interesting observations about how incentives impact various aspects of user studies, which we explained using concepts from labor economics. Some of the most interesting observations include: a) our variable incentive strategy allow us to empirically measure if compliance would drop if we had reduced wages, and can be an effective strategy to reduce the cost of user studies, b) we demonstrate that the micro-payment amount and its relation to the reservation wage influences the propensity for users to answer optional questions, and the truthfulness of these answers, and c) we show that the data quality is influenced by the incentive strategy, with consistency of answers likely to suffer if not carefully designed. Our results lay the framework for larger and longer-term incentive studies that we wish to pursue, and more in-depth understanding of how to design micro-incentive strategies that are low-cost and yet provide high compliance, and high data quality.

ACKNOWLEDGEMENTS

We acknowledge the contributions of the following individuals. Anind Dey and Mustafa alAbsi contributed to the study design, while Mary Read, Kelly Peck, Andrew Hoff, Ken Ward, and Satish Kedia helped conduct the study. Emre Ertin, Nathan Stohs, and Siddharth Shah developed the AutoSense sensor suite. Dan Siewiorek, Asim Smailagic, Patrick Blitz, Brian French, and Scott Fisk contributed to the study smartphone software. This work was supported in part by NSF grants CNS-0910878, CNS-0910900, CNS-0855128 funded under the American Recovery and Reinvestment Act of 2009 (Public Law 111-5), CNS-0939652 and NIH Grant U01DA023812 from NIDA.

REFERENCES

1. Amazon mechanical turk. `http://www.mturk.com`.
2. Gamification.org. `http://gamification.org/`.
3. P. Cahuc and A. Zylberberg. *Labor Economics*. MIT Press, 2004.
4. T. Choudhury, G. Borriello, S. Consolvo, D. Haehnel, B. Harrison, B. Hemingway, J. Hightower, et al. The mobile sensing platform: An embedded activity recognition system. *IEEE Pervasive Computing*, pages 32–41, 2008.
5. T. Christensen, L. Barrett, E. Bliss-Moreau, K. Lebo, and C. Kaschub. A practical guide to experience-sampling procedures. *Journal of Happiness Studies*, 4(1):53–78, 2003.
6. A. Church. Estimating the effect of incentives on mail survey response rates: A meta-analysis. *Public Opinion Quarterly*, 57(1):62, 1993.
7. R. Cialdini. *Influence: Science and practice*. Allyn and Bacon, 2001.
8. S. Consolvo and M. Walker. Using the experience sampling method to evaluate ubicomp applications. *IEEE Pervasive Computing*, pages 24–31, 2003.
9. C. Ferster and B. Skinner. *Schedules of reinforcement.* Appleton-Century-Crofts, 1957.
10. C. Grady, N. Dickert, T. Jawetz, G. Gensler, and E. Emanuel. An analysis of US practices of paying research participants. *Contemporary clinical trials*, 26(3):365–375, 2005.
11. J. Heer and M. Bostock. Crowdsourcing graphical perception: using mechanical turk to assess visualization design. In *Proceedings of the 28th international conference on Human factors in computing systems*, pages 203–212. ACM, 2010.
12. J. Hopson. Behavioral Game Design, April 2011. `http://www.gamasutra.com/view/feature/3085/behavioral_game_design.php`.
13. G. Hsieh, I. Li, A. Dey, J. Forlizzi, and S. Hudson. Using visualizations to increase compliance in experience sampling. In *Proceedings of the 10th international conference on Ubiquitous computing*, pages 164–167. ACM, 2008.
14. S. S. Intille, E. M. Tapia, J. Rondoni, J. Beaudin, C. Kukla, S. Agarwal, L. Bao, and K. Larson. Tools for studying behavior and technology in natural settings. In *In Proceedings of UBICOMP 2003*, pages 157–174. Springer, 2003.
15. T. Kamarck, M. Muldoon, S. Shiffman, K. Sutton-Tyrrell, C. Gwaltney, and D. Janicki. Experiences of Demand and Control in Daily Life as Correlates of Subclinical Carotid Atherosclerosis in a Healthy Older Sample. *Health Psychology*, 23(1):24, 2004.
16. S. Magari, J. Schwartz, P. Williams, R. Hauser, T. Smith, and D. Christiani. The association between personal measurements of environmental exposure to particulates and heart rate variability. *Epidemiology*, 13(3):305–310, 2002.
17. W. Mason and D. Watts. Financial incentives and the performance of crowds. *ACM SIGKDD Explorations Newsletter*, 11(2):100–108, 2010.
18. J. McGonigal. *Reality is Broken: Why games make us better and how they can change the world.* Penguin Pr, 2011.
19. R. Nelson and J. Merz. Voluntariness of consent for research: an empirical and conceptual review. *Medical care*, 40(9):V, 2002.
20. K. Plarre, A. Raij, S. Hossain, A. Ali, M. Nakajima, M. Al'absi, E. Ertin, T. Kamarck, S. Kumar, M. Scott, D. Siewiorek, A. Smailagic, and L. Wittmers. Continuous inference of psychological stress from sensory measurements collected in the natural environment. In *Information Processing in Sensor Networks (IPSN), 2011 10th International Conference on*, pages 97 –108, april 2011.
21. D. Polk, T. Kamarck, and S. Shiffman. Hostility explains some of the discrepancy between daytime ambulatory and clinic blood pressure. *Health Psychology*, 21(2):202, 2002.
22. R. Pritchard, D. Leonard, C. Von Bergen, et al. The effects of varying schedules of reinforcement on human task performance* 1. *Organizational Behavior and Human Performance*, 16(2):205–230, 1976.
23. K. Pryor. *Don't shoot the dog!: the new art of teaching and training.* Interpet Publishing, 2002.
24. M. Rahman, A. Ali, K. Plarre, M. al'Absi, E. Ertin, and S. Kumar. mconverse: Inferring conversation episodes from respiratory measurements collected in the field. In *In Proceedings of the 2nd ACM Wireless Health Conference, San Diego, CA*, 2011.
25. S. Reddy, D. Estrin, M. Hansen, and M. Srivastava. Examining micro-payments for participatory sensing data collections. In *Proceedings of the 12th ACM international conference on Ubiquitous computing*, pages 33–36. ACM, 2010.
26. R. Reid. The psychology of the near miss. *Journal of Gambling Studies*, 2(1):32–39, 1986.
27. R. Rivest and A. Shamir. PayWord and MicroMint: Two simple micropayment schemes. In *Security Protocols*, pages 69–87. Springer, 1997.
28. E. Simmons and A. Wilmot. Incentive payments on social surveys: A literature review. *Social Survey Methodology Bulletin*, pages 1–11, 2004.
29. E. Singer. The use of incentives to reduce nonresponse in household surveys. *Survey nonresponse*, pages 163–177, 2002.
30. T. Yamabe, V. Lehdonvirta, H. Ito, H. Soma, H. Kimura, and T. Nakajima. Applying pervasive technologies to create economic incentives that alter consumer behavior. In *Proceedings of the 11th international conference on Ubiquitous computing*, pages 175–184. ACM, 2009.
31. B. Yang and H. Garcia-Molina. PPay: micropayments for peer-to-peer systems. In *Proceedings of the 10th ACM conference on Computer and communications security*, pages 300–310. ACM, 2003.

The Social fMRI: Measuring, Understanding, and Designing Social Mechanisms in the Real World

Nadav Aharony[1], **Wei Pan**[1], **Cory Ip**[1], **Inas Khayal**[1,2], **Alex Pentland**[1]
{nadav, panwei, coryip, ikhayal, pentland}@media.mit.edu
[1]The Media Lab, Massachusetts Institute of Technology, Cambridge, MA, USA
[2]Masdar Institute of Science and Technology, Masdar City, Abu Dhabi

ABSTRACT
A key challenge of data-driven social science is the gathering of high quality multi-dimensional datasets. A second challenge relates to design and execution of structured experimental interventions in-situ, in a way comparable to the reliability and intentionality of ex-situ laboratory experiments. In this paper we introduce the *Friends and Family* study, in which a young-family residential community is transformed into a living laboratory. We employ a ubiquitous computing approach that combines extremely rich data collection in terms of signals, dimensionality, and throughput, together with the ability to conduct targeted experimental interventions with study populations. We present our mobile-phone-based social and behavioral sensing system, which has been deployed for over a year now. Finally, we describe a novel tailored intervention aimed at increasing physical activity in the subject population. Results demonstrate the value of social factors for motivation and adherence, and allow us to quantify the contribution of different incentive mechanisms.

Author Keywords
Social Computing, Mobile Sensing, Social Health

ACM Classification Keywords
H.4.m Information Systems: Miscellaneous; J.9.d Mobile Applications: Pervasive computing

General Terms
Algorithms, Experimentation, Measurement

INTRODUCTION
Imagine the ability to place an imaging chamber around an entire community. Imagine the ability to record and display nearly every facet and dimension of behavior, communication, and social interaction among the members of said community. Moreover, envision being able to conduct interventions in the community, while measuring their effect - by both automatic sensor tools as well as qualitative assessment of the individual subjects. Now, think about doing this for an entire year, while the members of the community go about their everyday lives.

Utilizing ubiquitous computing devices and methodologies, we developed a mobile-phone-centric social and behavioral sensing system that we have deployed with 130 adult members of a young-family living community for over a year now. During this year we have amassed what is, to the best of our knowledge, an unprecedented longitudinal dataset, which we dub the *Friends and Family* dataset. The dataset includes continuous collection of over 25 phone-based signals - including location, accelerometery, Bluetooth-based device proximity, communication activities, installed applications, currently running applications, multimedia and file system information, and additional data generated by our experimental applications. In addition, we collect financial information through receipts and credit card statements, logging of Facebook socialization activities, daily polling of mood, stress, sleep, productivity, and socialization, as well as other health and wellness related information, standard psychological scales like personality tests, and many other types of manually entered data by the participants.

The data enable us to construct multiple network modalities of the community - such as the phone communication network, physical face-to-face encounters network, online social network, self-reported network, and more. We use these networks to investigate questions like how things spread in the community, or how communication activities predict the spread of mobile applications. Another example using both the individuals financial status and social behaviors is understanding the causality question raised by Eagle et al. [15], where we discovered that the causality may go along the opposite direction. However, in the current paper we direct the discussion to an additional aspect of the study, which is the design and execution of experimental interventions while measuring their effect on individual and group behavior.

Out of several interventions conducted over the past year and planned for the upcoming months, in this report we focus on a fitness and physical activity intervention conducted between October to December of 2010. Using an experimental intervention within the Friends and Family study population, we test social mechanism-design principles. In particular, we propose a novel social mechanism in which subjects are rewarded based on their peers' performance and not their own. Results suggest that: (1) Social factors have an effect on the physical activity behavior, motivation, and adherence over time. (2) Social incentives, and particularly our novel Peer-Reward mechanism encouraging social influence among participants, support higher activity returns per dollar invested in the system. (3) Finally, results support the notion of a complex contagion [10] like effect related to pre-existing social ties between participants.

The contributions of the work described in this paper are threefold: We present the Friends and Family study and very rich dataset; We describe the field-proven system that has been deployed and used for over a year, which we intend to release as an open source platform for social and behavioral data collection and feedback; We conducted the fitness intervention and find results that contribute to our understanding of social incentives and motivation in real-world contexts.

In the remainder of this paper, we first review related literature and the contextual underpinning of our proposed vision. We then introduce our approach. In the next section we go into our methodology - the Friends and Family living laboratory and its characteristics. Next we describe our system architecture, and then review the experimental design of our social fitness intervention. We emphasize how our gained familiarity with the community comes into play in the study design. Finally we analyze key results of the intervention.

RELATED WORK AND CONTEXT

Ubiquitous Social Observatories

In recent years the social sciences have been undergoing a digital revolution, heralded by the emerging field of "computational social science". Lazer, Pentland et al. [24]. describe the potential of computational social science to increase our knowledge of individuals, groups, and societies, with an unprecedented breadth, depth, and scale. [24] highlights challenges in terms of scientific approach for observation and intervention when dealing with real people in their living environments, including issues of subject privacy, monitoring, and altering of environments during the discovery process.

Figure 1 gives a high-level qualitative overview of social observatories and datasets, comparing them along axes of sample size, duration, and a very rough notion of "throughput" or the amount of information in the datasets. The idea is that dataset throughput is a function of the data dimensionality (number of different signals collected), its resolution (e.g. raw or aggregate), sampling rate (how often data is collected), and unique information in it (an accelerometer sensor lying on a desk for a week does not collect a lot of information). This diagram illustrates the potential of ubiquitous technologies for the design of social observatories and the collection of very rich datasets. At the bottom of the diagram are traditional sociology studies as well as many of the corporate "donated" datasets. Leading traditional dataset include, for example, the Framingham Heart Study [13], which stands out for its duration and a subject pool of several thousands, however its "throughput" is low as subjects were sampled approximately once in three years.

The pervasiveness of mobile phones has made them ubiquitous social sensors of location, proximity and communications. Because of this, mobile phone records from telecom companies have proven to be quite valuable in particular. Gonzales et al. show that cell-tower location information can be used to characterize human mobility and that humans follow simple reproducible mobility patterns [21]. Eagle et al. find that the diversity of individuals relationships is strongly correlated with the economic development of communities [15]. These and other corporate "donated" datasets are usually characterized by having, on one hand, information on very large numbers of subjects, but on the other hand, this information is constrained to a specific domain (email messages, financial transactions, etc.), and there is very little if any contextual information on the subjects themselves. This is why, although their sample size may be in the millions, they are relatively low on the throughput axis. As example, [22], each sampling point was an aggregated 15-day call summary of anonymous phone users. In addition, domain-limited results might be harder to generalize for the physical world, as discussed by Onnela et al. in context of Facebook data[32]. Finally, there is the offline nature of most existing datasets which are based on previously collected data, making it harder to test cause and effect using these datasets. Yet these datasets are yielding significant contributions to our understanding of society, one might imagine that by increasing the dimensionality and throughput, such datasets could lead to even further advancement.

An alternative approach is a bottom-up one, collecting data at the level of the individual. Eagle and Pentland [16] defined the term"Reality Mining" to describe collection of sensor data pertaining to human social behavior. They show that using call records, cellular-tower IDs, and Bluetooth proximity logs, collected via mobile phones , the subjects' social network can be accurately detected, as well as regular patterns in daily activity [16, 17]. This initial study was then expanded in Madan et al. [27], who conducted a similar experiment and show that mobile social sensing can be used for measuring and predicting the health status of individuals based on mobility and communication patterns. They also investigate the spread of political opinion within the community [28]. Other examples for using mobile phones for social sensing were done by Montoliu et al. [30] and Lu et al. [26]. Most of these were of an observational nature, and have not performed controlled experimental interventions for exploring social mechanism. Other types of sensor-based "social observatories" are the Sociometric Badges by Olguin et al. that capture human activity and socialization patterns via a wearable sensor badge [31]. A key aspect of the Sociable Badges is that they have been deployed in studies where sensor feedback was given to the corporate participants [31].

Physical Activity Sensing and Feedback

In this paper we focus on a specific problem from the domain of health and wellness: Studies have shown a great increase in obesity and related chronic medical conditions over the last several decades. Physical activity has been shown to help alleviate the burden of obesity and other health conditions [6, 8]. Over the past two decades, the accelerometer

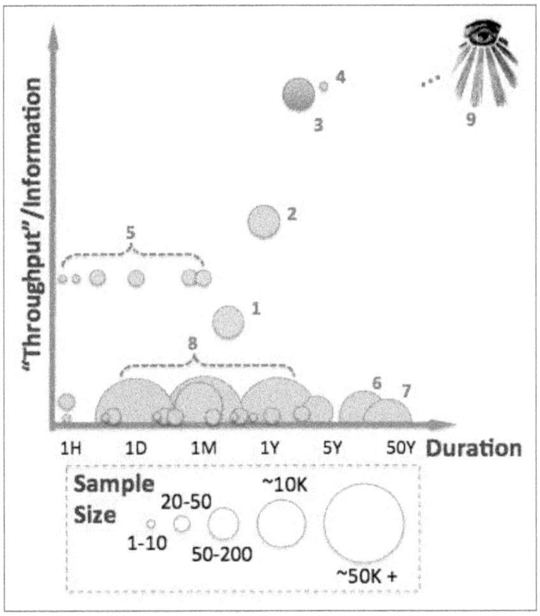

Figure 1. Qualitative Overview of social science "observatories" and datasets, along axes of data collection duration, qualitative"throughput" , and the size of the subject sample.(1)Reality Mining[16], (2) Social Evolution[28], (3) Friends and Family Dataset, (4) rich-data pioneers [3, 20] (5) Sociometric Badge studies [31], (6) Midwest Field Station [5], (7) Framingham Heart Study[13], (8) Large Call Record Datasets [21, 15, 22] , (9) "Omniscient"/All-Seeing View

has been established and refined as a tool for tracking physical activity [9, 18, 35]. Accelerometry-based sensors have been found to provide more accurate estimates than other widely-used proxies for energy expenditure [18]. Although there is some error associated with using accelerometers to track energy expenditure in free-living situations, a significant relationship between accelerometer output and energy expenditure has nevertheless been established [9]. Several studies in the ubiquitous computing literature have targeted this important problem domain. Ubifit [12] is one of the most extensive works investigating ways to encourage physical activity. Other projects include Fish'n'Steps [25] and Houston [11], among others. These works investigate diverse aspects of the problem, such as user interface, goal setting, or techniques for using the accelerometer for accurate expenditure measurement and activity detection.

Of particular relevance are those studies that involve social components [25, 11, 4, 34, 19]. It has long been established that social support is a resource for behavioral change an and indicator for health [7], however here is still much to be learned about the fine-grained *social mechanisms* related to physical activity behavior, as well as how to leverage such insights in *designing better socially-aware interventions and mechanisms* for encouraging healthy behavior change.

For activity measurement, relevant works are and those using unaugmented phone-based activity detection [4, 33], whereas the majority of studies to date used additional measurement devices that need to be carried by subjects. In the consumer world, a growing number of activity measuring mobile applications such as CardioTrainer [1] use the phone's acclerometer, combined with visualization and other feedback to help users increase their physical activity levels. Most applications aim to provide a step count measurement, and ask the users to hold the phone in a certain orientation while exercising in order to deliver accurate measurements.

THE SOCIAL *f*MRI

In the medical realm, Magnetic Resonance Imaging, MRI, is considered one of the most comprehensive diagnostic techniques available, and functional MRI, fMRI, is one of the leading tools used for studying the brain through response to carefully designed stimuli. Analogously, we define Social Mechanism-design and Relationship Imaging, or Social MRI, which allows detailed sensing and imaging of social systems through the use of mobile phones, credit cards, social media, and telecommunications for social and behavioral sensing platform. *Social fMRI* takes it a step further - allowing for specifically designed stimuli and interventions to the social system, while measuring the individual and collective response. Just as fMRI helps us understand the inner workings of the brain, we hope that the Social fMRI approach could help us understand the inner workings of social systems and the way humans interact and react to one another. More than just an aspiration, in this paper we show a proof of concept as to how this could be done.

The general framework of the Social fMRI idea is a combination of a longitudinal living-laboratory/social-observatory type of study, coupled with a supporting system infrastructure that enables the sensing and data collection, data processing, and also a set of tools for feedback and communication with the subject population. The Social fMRI implements and extends the ideas of the Reality Mining approach [16], by (1) adding much greater data richness and dimensionality, combined with (2) a strong element of active interaction and carefully designed experimental stimulation of the study population.

METHODOLOGY

Living Laboratory: The "Friends and Family" Community

Starting March 2010, we initiated a living laboratory study conducted with members of a young-family residential living community adjacent to a major research university in North America. All members of the community are couples, and at least one of the members is affiliated with the university. The community is composed of over 400 residents, approximately half of which have children. The residence has a vibrant community life and many ties of friendship between its members. We shall refer to this residence as the "*Friends and Family*" community.

This study involves a relatively different subject population when compared to previous ubiquitous computing observatory studies. For example, colleagues and co-workers in Reality Mining [16], and undergraduates in [27]. The Friends and Family community includes a much more heterogeneous subject pool, and provides a unique perspective into a phase in life that has not been traditionally studied in the field of ubiquitous computing - married couples and young families.

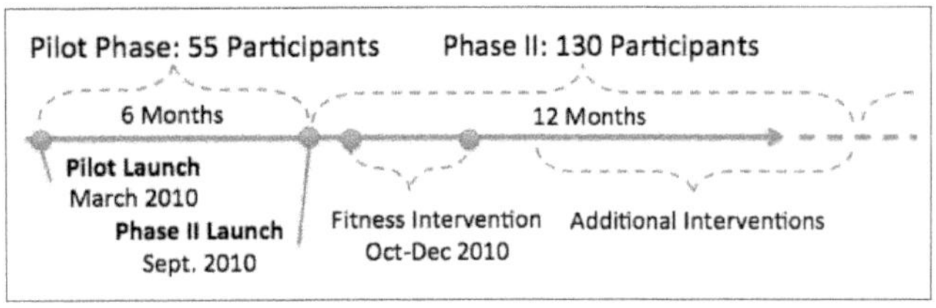

Figure 2. High level timeline for the Friends and Family study.

As depicted in Figure 2, a pilot phase of 55 participants launched in March 2010. In September 2010 phase two of the study included 130 participants, approximately 64 families. Participants were selected out of approximately 200 applicants, in a way that would achieve a representative sample of the community and sub-communities. One of the reasons for keeping the number below 150 is that these numbers fit well with Dunbar's social evolutionary theory regarding the number of people humans are able to maintain a relationship with [14]. Throughout the study we ask about social closeness between all participants in the study, and numbers larger than Dunbar's number could become quite tedious. We refer to experiments in our scale as "Dunbar scale" experiments. The research goals of the longitudinal study touch on many aspects of life, from better understanding of social dynamics to health to purchasing behavior to community organization. The two high-level themes that unify these varied aspects are: (a) how people make decisions, with emphasis on the social aspects involved, and (b) how we can empower people to make better decisions using personal and social tools.

Study Data Collection

One of the key goals of the Social fMRI idea is the collection of multi-modal and highly diverse range of signals from the subject population. We wanted to gather data on numerous network modalities, so that their properties and interrelation could be better understood. We applied a user centric, bottom up approach utilizing the following components:

Mobile Phone Sensing Platform

This is the core of the studys data collection. Android OS based mobile phones are used as in-situ social sensors to map users activity features, proximity networks, media consumption, and behavior diffusion patterns. The mobile phone platform is described in more detail in the next section. We did not sponsor phone plans or data plans - users received a mobile phone that fit their desired provider, and they were responsible to port their existing account to it or open a new account. The condition was that the study phone be their primary phone for the duration of the study.

Surveys

Subjects complete surveys at regular intervals, combining web-based and on-phone surveys. Monthly surveys include questions about self perception of relationships, group affiliation, and interactions, and also standard scales like the Big-Five personality test [23]. Daily surveys include questions like mood, sleep, and other activity logging.

Purchasing Behavior

Information on purchases is collected through receipts and credit card statements submitted at the participants discretion. This component targets categories that might be influenced by peers, like entertainment and dining choices.

Facebook Data Collection Application

Participants could opt to install a Facebook application that logs information on their online-social network and communication activities. About 70% of subjects opted to install.

Subject Protection and Privacy Considerations

The study was approved by the Institutional Review Board (IRB) and conducted under strict protocol guidelines. One of the key concerns in the design of the study was the protection of participant privacy and sensitive information. For example, data is linked to coded identifiers for participants and not their real world personal identifiers. All human-readable text, like phone numbers and text messages are captured as hashed identifiers, and never saved in clear text. Collected data is physically secured and de-identified before being used for aggregate analysis. An second important consideration was for being as unobtrusive as possible to the subject's life routines. Participants are able to keep the phone at the end of the study. For mandatory out-of-routine behavior that asked of participants, like filling out surveys, subjects are compensated (e.g. $10 for completing the monthly survey). Participation in intervention or sub-experiment on top of the main study components is completely optional, and interventions are carefully designed with the interests of the participants in mind.

SYSTEM ARCHITECTURE

Mobile Phone Platform

The phones run our software platform, which periodically senses and records information such as cell tower ID, wireless LAN IDs; proximity to nearby phones and other Bluetooth devices; accelerometer and compass data; call and SMS logs; statistics on installed phone applications, running applications, media files, general phone usage; and other accessible information. Over 25 different types of data signals are currently collected. The system also supports integration of user-level apps, like an alarm clock app we developed, for additional data collection and interventions. The phone system also has a survey application. Sample screenshots can be seen in Figure 3. The configuration is set so that battery-intensive actions (e.g. GPS scans) are performed in intervals allowing usefulness while minimizing battery drain. A remote configuration capability allows for fine-tuning the system, with a goal of enabling a minimum of 16 hours between charges. We are working towards releasing the software, named "Funf", as an open source framework [2].

Data Formats and Server Communications

Phone data is is saved in SQLite file format, with files rotated every three hours to reduce data loss due to file corruption and to allow periodic uploading to the back-end. Since many participants do not have a mobile data service plan, the system was designed in a "delay tolerant" way: In the

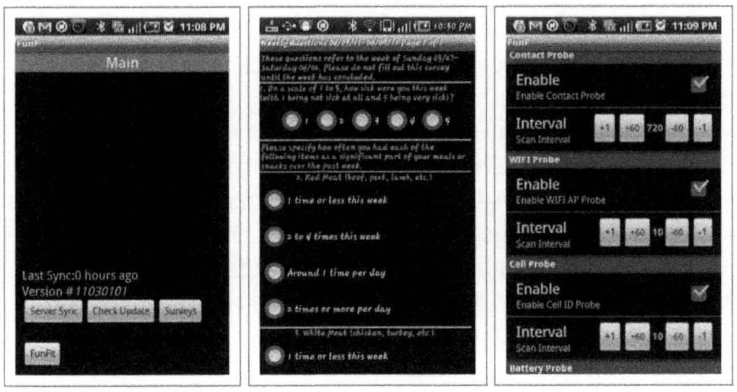

Figure 3. Sample screenshots: Sync-state and version display (left), survey (center), and probe preferences debug screen

absence of network access, the phone accumulates the collected database files locally. Once server connection is made (for example a participant connects to WiFi to browse the web), the system attempts to upload files. Once uploaded, files are also encrypted and saved in a backup directory on the phone, until data integrity is confirmed. In addition, the system downloads from the server parameter configurations files that define which data signals to collect, how often, and additional configuration parameters. It also checks for new versions of itself and notifies the user to update when new versions are available. The system downloads any new surveys that should be presented to the user.

Back-end

The server-side back-end processes all incoming SQLite files and insets them into a central MySQL database. It sends email reports to investigators about status of phones and alerts of any issues. Additional services provide data for interventions and personal data visualization for participants.

FITNESS-CENTERED SOCIAL INTERVENTION DESIGN

Between October-December 2010, an active intervention was carried out with the Friends and Family study pool. Its main goal was to explore the question of understanding social influence and motivation in the context of health and wellness activities. The intervention was presented to participants as a wellness game to help them increase their daily activity levels. 108 out of 123 active subjects at the time elected to participate. Subjects were divided into three experimental conditions: Control, Peer-View, and Peer-Reward (described below), allowing us to isolate different incentive mechanisms related to monetary reward, the value of social information, and social pressure/influence. Following an initial period where baseline activity levels were collected, all intervention subjects were given feedback on their performance in the form of a monetary reward, R, which was calculated as a function of their activity. Reward of up to $5 was allocated every three days. Participants were presented current, past, and total reward accumulated, as shown in Figure 4, and could access their reward page via browser or the phone. Each group received a variant adapted to its condition. The game was not designed as a competition, and every subject had the potential to earn the maximal reward.

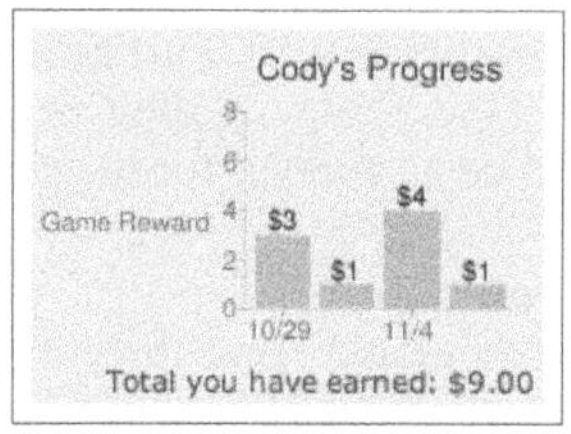

Figure 4. Reward display for participants in the Control condition

Experimental Conditions

Control Condition

All conditions have a baseline of self-monitoring. In the control condition, subjects saw only their own progress as visualized in Figure 4. Also, reward given to the control subjects depended only on their own activity.

Experimental Condition 1: "Peer-View"

In the first experimental condition, "Peer-View", subjects were shown their own progress and the progress of two "Buddies" also in the same experimental group. In turn, the subject's progress was visible to two other peers in the same experimental group. Each subject's reward still depended on his own activity.

Experimental Condition 2: "Peer-Reward"

We propose a novel condition aimed at generating increased incentives for social influence and possibly the leveraging of social capital. In this "Peer-Reward" mechanism, subjects were shown their own progress as well as that of two Buddies, but this time subjects' rewards depended solely on the performance of their Buddies. At the same time, their own performance reward was split between two other peers, to which the current user was a Buddy. If subject A had Buddies B and C, the maximal reward A could receive for this period is still $5 per three-day period: $2.5 from B and $2.5 from C. The Peer-Reward feedback page displays how much reward they received from their Buddies, as well how much reward they are earning for the people they are Buddy to.

Accelerometer-based Activity Measurement

Our investigation of social mechanisms does not require accurate activity classification and step measurement. We decided to implement a less accurate but more robust algorithm for estimating activity levels, which allowed for increased flexibility in the way participants could carry the phone, and reduced the obtrusiveness of the study. Accelerometer scans were sampled in a duty cycle of 15 seconds every 2 minutes. During the 15 seconds, raw 3-axis accelerometer measurements are sampled at 5Hz rate and combined to compute the vector magnitude for each sample. The variance of the the magnitude in each one-second block is then computed [18]. The score was calculated by giving one point for every second, thresholded to three states 1)"still" 2)"moderate activity" 3)"high activity". However, in this paper we are interested in general change in activity levels and therefore combine the two active levels. Participants were not constrained in the way they should carry the phone. [33] found this did not interfere with activity measurement and classification, and our tests suggest this as well. Participants were told that the more they carry the phone on their person, the more of their activity would be accounted for their game score.

Game Reward Calculation

Game reward was calculated every three days, using a reference window of the seven days preceding the current 3-day bin. Average and variance for daily activity count are calculated for the reference window, as well the daily average for the current 3-day bin. Reward depended solely on an individual's performance, and was mapped to be between \$0.50-\$5, in \$0.50 increments between one standard deviation above and below the reference average value. Values above or below the bounds received max or min value, respectively. To avoid discouragement due to zero reward, we did not give less than 50 cents per reward period.

Discussion of Experiment Design Considerations

One of the great advantages of the Social fMRI and other ubiquitous living-laboratory approaches is the ability to conduct interventions and structured experiments with the study population, as they live their everyday life. In contrast to most fitness-related studies who recruit participants specifically for the fitness study and many times pick participants who actively want to increase their physical activity [25, 11, 12], we faced similar challenges to those discussed in [29] for working with general populations in the wild. The sub-experiment had to be tailored to the nature of the subjects and the community, and be unobtrusive and attractive enough that the study population would want to opt-in.

We had to consider a range of attitudes towards physical activity. The intervention was thus designed as an non-competitive game, where each person is judged based on their own performance and performance change. A previously non-active participant could gain the same reward as a highly active one, while the highly active person would need to work harder. We also had to assume subjects might talk to each other and share information about the game. This is one of the reasons we made sure every participant would have potential to earn the same reward amount. Additional practical considerations included the fact that not everyone had data-plans, and data upload could be delayed. Since we needed it for the reward calculation, we added feedback to users about their data upload state, and also designed the accelerometer and reward three-day bins in a way that would allow for backlogged data to reach the server in time.

By creating a network structure rather than closed team structure for the social interventions (A receives reward for B and C's performance, while D and E receive reward for A's), we are able to disambiguate and focus on the diadic and asymmetric relationship of the person doing the activity vs. the person receiving the reward, motivated to convince the first.

PREPARATORY ANALYSIS

Self Reported Closeness

For the social conditions allocation, we wanted to leverage our knowledge of the subjects' network. We decided to use the network of self-perceived closeness since this network is explicit in participant's minds (as opposed to the Bluetooth collocation network, for example), and this was desirable for the experimental conditions. Each participant rated every other participant on a scale of 0-7,from 0(not familiar) to 7(very close). Basic analysis for the intervention participants network shows that it is a fully connected graph except one user. On average, each participant knows 14 other participants. Each participant has, on average, 7 explicit friendship ties (closeness > 2) in the study pool. The mean distance between any two participant is 1.9.

Experimental Condition Allocation

Based on this and marriage ties information, we designed an allocation algorithm to pair each participant in Peer-See and Peer-Reward with two buddies within their group. We wanted to ensure that at least some participants are paired with existing friends, while keeping the desired network topology and avoiding reciprocal pairings. Due to the sparsity of the friendship network, our division to disjoint experimental groups, and our enforced constraints, we formulated an integer programming optimization problem that attempts to prioritize closer friends as buddies with the following constraints: First, each participant should have exactly two Buddies. Second, participants cannot be their own Buddy. The third constrain prohibits two participants from being buddies of each other (reciprocity). Finally we prevented participants from having their spouses as buddies. This decision eliminates the unique and complicated effects resulting from marriage ties, and ensures that our fitness peer monitoring topology is purely constructed of regular friendship ties. The integer programming problem cannot be solved directly, and we applied an iterative approach: In each iteration, we randomized initial values and used the branch-and-bound algorithm to search for reasonable results, and we select the best solution among all iterations to match individual with their Buddies for both social condition groups in our experiment.

POST-INTERVENTION ANALYSIS

Subject Pool

Eleven subjects were removed from the study pool over the course of the intervention (due to prolonged technical issues that prevented reliable activity tracking, long durations of out of town travel, or dropping out of the longitudinal study entirely). Their data has been removed from the analysis, except for cases of analyzing peer effects for their Buddies. For details on the final number of subjects in each study condition, see Table 1.

Condition	Initial	Dropped	Total
Control	18	2	16
Peer-See	45	5	40
Peer-Reward	45	4	41

Table 1. Number of subjects in each condition

Intervention periods for analysis

For analysis of changes in activity level through the intervention, we divided the intervention into three periods: the baseline period before the beginning of the intervention was officially announced , the first 19 days of the intervention , and the second 20 days of the intervention . The periods are summarized in Table 2. For this analysis, the days after the intervention begins are broken up into two periods, and we focus on the latter one to account for any novelty effects and allow us to take a first look at the persistence of any change in behavior. Another timing aspect that should be noted is that when considers the experiment periods in weather and school-year contexts, we can assume that physical activity becomes more challenging as the experiment advances due to the North American winter conditions. In addition, for period 3 we can expect increased end-of-semester workload and stress for the student participants in the subject group.

Period	Dates	Days
1	Oct 5-Oct 27	1-23
2	Oct 28-Nov 15	24-42
3	Nov16-Dec 5	43-62

Table 2. Dates and days of periods used for analysis.

Normalized Activity Values

For analysis purposes, we normalized activity levels to the span of a single sample. For example, a normalized "daily average activity" is calculated by summing all accelerometer samples for the day and then dividing by the total count of accelerometer readings for the day. This gives us the average activity level per reading for that day. This allows us to easily do things like compare between normalized average activity levels in different times of day. It is trivial to convert a normalized value to actual time: For example, a normalized daily average value of 1.0 for an experimental group represents an average activity of 96 minutes per member.

Aggregated Activity Levels

One would reasonably assume that accelerometer readings would not be uniformly distributed throughout the day. A visual inspection of the distribution of non-zero readings indicated that that the day should be split the day into four quarters of six hours each, starting at midnight, in order to explore the difference in average accelerometer score per reading. Table 3 confirms that activity varies greatly throughout the day, and that it correlates with general intuition about the times of high and low activity.

Time of day	Average accelerometer score per reading
Midnight-6AM	0.23
6AM-Noon	1.29
Noon-6PM	2.34
6PM-Midnight	1.31

Table 3. Average accelerometer score by time of day. The average score per reading is much lower during the night and highest in the afternoon, as expected.

We refer to the a day's worth of accelerometer measurement for one person as a "person-day". For a single person, a complete day's worth of data was 720 accelerometer score readings, since accelerometer scans were taken in two-minute intervals. Data was considered "missing" for an interval if there was no accelerometer score logged for that interval. As also assumed in [16], we attribute most missing data to the phone being off, usually during night-time. As the current analysis deals primarily with daily average activity levels and change in daily average activity across time and experimental condition, we precluded person-days that did not have sufficient information for generating a reliable average score for the day. We observed that for days that had more than 50% of the possible readings, the missing datapoints were relatively uniformly spread accross the day, while in days with fewer than 50% of possible readings, they were not uniformally distributed and could not reliably be used. When a person's day had fewer than 50% of the possible readings, that day was not used for the analysis and calculation of averages. Removed measurements account for less than 5.4% of the available measurments.

Activity Levels by Condition

Table 4 presents information about daily average activity levels in a pairwise comparison of the three experimental conditions pre- and post-intervention, using the K-S test, where D is the K-S statistic. For this analysis, the two post-intervention periods are combined into one. Ideally, in the pre-intervention period we expect the null hypothesis to be true. While in the comparison that compares the control group vs. both social conditions the result is statistically significant ($p < 0.05$), in the direct pairwise comparison the test does not exhibit statistical significance, as expected. Conversely, according to the experimental mechanism design hypothesis, we anticipate that the social conditions will do better than the control, and possibly exhibit difference properties when compared to each other. For all comparisons between the social conditions (independently and jointly) and the control group, K-S test shows statistical significance ($p < 0.01$ and $p < 0.005$). However the difference between the two social conditions comes out non-significant under this comparison, possibly due to the inclusion of novelty effects through combining both post-intervention periods. The difference between the two social conditions is not significant, possibly because higher activity levels are increasingly difficult to obtain (e.g., a 'headroom' effect). In any case, in this experiment we do not care about absolute activity levels as much as the *monetary efficiency* of the incentive mechanisms.

Reward efficiency

We are interested in the change in activity levels for each group rather than simple comparison of activity means. Furthermore, we want to evaluate the effectiveness of the exogenous money or energy injected into a system. We define "reward efficiency", η, which represents the activity change per dollar invested in the system. Reward efficiency for condition i is defined as:

$$\eta_i = \frac{\overline{a_{i,3}} - \overline{a_{i,1}}}{\overline{R_{i,3}}}$$

where $\overline{a_{i,k}}$ is the mean activity level for all participants in group i in period k, and $\overline{R_{i,k}}$ is the average reward per participant in group i in period k. Period 3 is used as the refer-

Groups tested	Group 1 mean	Group 2 mean	D	p-value
Pre-Intervention (Period 1)				
Cntrl vs. PS&PR	1.162	1.241	0.3261	0.046*
Cntrl vs. PSee	1.162	1.266	0.3478	0.078
Cntrl vs. PRew	1.162	1.216	0.3043	0.164
PSee vs. PRew	1.266	1.216	0.2609	0.316
Post-Intervention (Periods 2 and 3)				
Cntrl vs. PS&PR	1.207	1.328	0.3718	0.001***
Cntrl vs. PSee	1.207	1.341	0.4193	0.001***
Cntrl vs. PRew	1.207	1.316	0.3590	0.007**
PSee vs. PRew	1.341	1.316	0.1026	0.976

* $p < 0.05$; ** $p < 0.01$; *** $p < 0.005$

Table 4. Pairwise K-S comparison of activity level of the three experimental conditions pre- and post-intervention. The groups which are being compared are listed in the first column. "Group 1 mean" refers to the group listed first and "Group 2 mean" refers to the group listed second. D is the K-S statistic.

Condition	Activity Change from Period 1 to Period 3	Reward in Period 3	Reward Efficiency (Δ/\$)
Overall			
Control	0.037	\$3.00	0.012
Exp 1	0.070	\$2.77	0.0253
Exp 2	0.126	\$3.04	0.0416
Close Buddies (both Buddies score 3 or higher)			
Exp 1	0.118	\$2.68	0.0444
Exp 2	0.269	\$3.00	0.0896
Stranger Buddies (both Buddies score 2 or lower)			
Exp 1	-0.007	\$2.82	-0.0025
Exp 2	0.137	\$2.95	0.0464
Mixed Buddies (one Close, one Stranger)			
Exp 1	0.154	\$2.75	0.0560
Exp 2	0.053	\$3.12	0.0171

Table 5. Reward efficiencies (η). Reward efficiency is defined as the amount of activity level increase per dollar of reward paid.

ence frame since we want to look at longer-term adherence. Tables 5 and 6 present information on reward efficiency for this dataset, based on actual monetary reward paid. Table 6 shows results of pairwise K-S testing of reward efficiency values (D is the K-S statistic), where all but one demonstrate statistical significance. In Table 5 we see that reward efficiency is more than doubled between the control condition and the Peer-See condition, and the efficiency of the Peer-Reward group is even more than the latter when comparing the conditions as a whole. In relative terms, we observe an average activity increase for Control, Peer-See, and Peer-Reward of 3.2%, 5.5%, and 10.4% respectively, counting in data from all times of day, days of week, sick-times, holidays, and so on. For the Peer-Reward condition, this comes down to an average increase of 84 minutes of physical activity per week, per participant.

As the underlying differences between the two social conditions were not clearly apparent, in Table 6 we dive into the social component. We divide the subjects according to their pre-reported closeness level with their Buddies. Although the overall comparison of the social conditions does not present statistical significance, the further grouping according to pre-existing relationships shows that the Peer-Reward condition achieves better results in two out of the three cases (close buddies and stranger buddies), while the Peer-See condition achieves better results for mixed buddies. For all these cases, we get statistical significance ($p < 0.01$). We see a complicated interaction element with regards to the Buddy closeness, which we touch on in the next section.

Discussion

In this analysis we begin investigating the effectiveness of the different motivation and influence mechanisms for encouraging increased physical activity in-situ. We focus on two key metrics: The first is differences in average activity levels, both across conditions and chronological periods of the experiment, and the second is the efficiency of the reward "investment" in the system.

When daily average activity levels are analyzed, they support the hypothesis that the social components of both experimental conditions, together and separately, lead to a statistically significant positive difference. Analysis of the difference of effect between the two socially involved experimental groups is more complex, and dividing the experimental groups based on pre-intervention closeness of the Buddy triads reveals different trends. When reward efficiency is analyzed, we again see a significant difference between the control group on the one hand and the two experimental groups, taken together, on the other.

Results confirm our notions that embedding the social aspects in this non-competitive game adds to physical activity performance and activity adherence over time, compared to the socially isolated control condition An interesting question arises with respect to the social mechanisms. In the Peer-See group, there is social information that traverses the links between peered Buddies, but participants still receives a "selfish" reward. In Peer-Reward, both information and reward traverse the links between peers, and a potential for social influence as motivator. The intensity of pre-existing social relationships seems to play a factor, and results seem to support a complex contagion like phenomena, as described by Centola and Macy [10], especially when observing the interplay in triads where there is a "mix" of close and stranger peers. We have yet to investigate the communication patterns between the peers, and their subjective view of their condition, to try and understand if and how the social influence or pressure was exerted. We hope that by analyzing additional signals already collected, like the communication logs and co-location information, as well as related surveys administered to the participants, we will be able to shed more light on these underlying processes.

Had this intervention been conducted in springtime, one might expect a natural rise in physical activity as weather improves, which might have made it hard to separate the intervention's

Groups being compared	Group 1 reward efficiency	Group 2 reward efficiency	D	p-value
Overall				
Cntrl vs. PSee	0.0120	0.0253	1.000	0.001**
Cntrl vs. PRew	0.0120	0.0416	1.000	0.001**
PSee vs. PRew	0.0253	0.0416	0.429	0.432
Close Buddies (both Buddies score 3 or higher)				
PSee vs. PRew	0.0444	0.0896	1.000	0.002**
Stranger Buddies (both Buddies score 2 or lower)				
PSee vs. PRew	-0.0025	0.0464	1.000	0.001**
Mixed Buddies (one Close, one Stranger)				
PSee vs. PRew	0.0560	0.0171	1.000	0.001**

** $p < 0.01$

Table 6. Pairwise K-S comparison of the differences between reward efficiencies. D is the K-S statistic. All differences are statistically significant, except the difference between the two experimental groups when taken in their entirety.

contribution. By going against the natural trend during winter, we challenge our experimental mechanisms. While results are not fully conclusive, they may suggest that while performance in the control and even Peer-See conditions deteriorates as time passes, the performance in Peer-Reward is slower to start but steadier in increase over time. The observations might support a hypothesis that the Peer-Reward condition induces social capital that takes time to build up, but once in place provides a more sustainable incentive structure than the direct monetary reward, or alternatively, a way to augment the exogenous monetary compensation with indigenous social capital, leading to a higher efficiency, and higher "return" on every Dollar invested in the system.

It is also important to mention that by design choice, we did not perform any external communication "scaffolding" to encourage social interaction. There were no mechanism within the study software for sharing results and promoting discussion - any such actions were done by participants on their own accord using their existing means of interaction. Related studies with social components [19, 11] suggest that adding explicit communication mechanisms to the technical system might add to the social effects of the intervention.

CONCLUSION

In this paper we introduced the Friends and Family Study, which combines high-dimensionality and high-throughput social and behavioral sensing using ubiquitous mobile phones, together with experimental interventions. We described our Android phone centred system that has been deployed in the study for over a year now. We presented initial results of a specific experimental intervention that demonstrates the great potential of the study dataset, its underlying technical system, and the of the general Social fMRI approach for measuring and experimenting with social mechanisms.

Through the fitness intervention example, we demonstrated challenges and benefits of leveraging our prior observations for the experiment design. We presented three key findings through this intervention: First, results support there is a statistically significant effect of social components on the real-world in-situ physical activity levels. Second, results show that our novel Peer-Reward social influence mechanism leveraging social capital can increase the efficiency of exogenous money and resources invested in the system. This could contribute to the design of future policies and intervention. Finally, we see a complex interaction effect related to pre-existing social ties inside the social experimental conditions. This could support hypothesis of a complex contagion like effect that should be further investigated. Immediate future work includes expanding the analysis of the existing data, as well as the design of new experiments based on these initial observations, particularly in the area of quantifying social capital and favor exchange. We hope that isolating and evaluating health related social mechanisms will become part of the toolbox for encouraging healthy behavior, combined with other components such as user interfaces, accurate measurement techniques, and individual goal setting.

In the same way that fMRI techniques help map the interconnections and mechanics of the human brain, we hope that our work will help advocate an evolution from mostly passive observatories to Social fMRI type of studies that can help further our understanding of the interconnections and mechanics of human society.

ACKNOWLEDGEMENTS

We would like to thank Sai Moturu, Cody Sumter, and Maya Orbach for their contribution towards the experimental deployment, surveys, and visualizations, and the undergraduate contributors for their help with the development of the sensing platform. We thank the Ubicomp reviewers for their thoughtful comments. Most importantly, we thank the Friends and Family Study participants. This research was partially sponsored by the Army Research Laboratory under Cooperative Agreement Number W911NF-09-2-0053, and by AFOSR under Award Number FA9550-10-1-0122, by the MASDAR Institute of Science and Technology, and by generous gifts from PG, Best Buy, Motorola, Google, and Samsung. Views and conclusions in this document are those of the authors and should not be interpreted as representing the official policies, either expressed or implied, of the sponsors.

REFERENCES

1. Cardiotrainer. http://www.worksmartlabs.com/cardiotrainer/about.php.
2. Funf: Open sensing framework. http://funf.media.mit.edu.
3. The human speechome project. http://www.media.mit.edu/cogmac/projects/hsp.html.
4. I. Anderson et al. Shakra: tracking and sharing daily activity levels with unaugmented mobile phones. *Mob. Netw. Appl.*, 12:185–199, March 2007.
5. R. Barker and U. of Kansas. Midwest Psychological Field Station. *Ecological psychology: concepts and*

methods for studying the environment of human behavior. Stanford University Press, 1968.

6. A. Bauman. Updating the evidence that physical activity is good for health: an epidemiological review 2000-2003. *Journal of Science and Medicine in Sport*, 7(1, Supplement 1):6 – 19, 2004. Physical Activity.
7. L. Berkman and T. Glass. Social integration, social support, and health. In L. Berkman and I. E. Kawachi, editors, *Social Epidemiology*. 2000.
8. S. N. Blair, Y. Cheng, and S. J. Holder. Is physical activity or physical fitness more important in defining health benefits? *Medicine & Science in Sports & Exercise*, 33(6), 2001.
9. C. V. Bouten, K. T. Koekkoek, M. Verduin, R. Kodde, and J. D. Janssen. A triaxial accelerometer and portable data processing unit for the assessment of daily physical activity. *IEEE Trans Biomed Eng*, Mar.
10. D. Centola and M. Macy. Complex contagions and the weakness of long ties. *The American Journal of Sociology*, 113(3):pp. 702–734, 2007.
11. S. Consolvo, K. Everitt, I. Smith, and J. A. Landay. Design requirements for technologies that encourage physical activity. In *Proceedings of CHI '06*, New York, NY, USA, 2006. ACM.
12. S. Consolvo et al. Activity sensing in the wild: a field trial of ubifit garden. In *Proceeding of CHI '08*, pages 1797–1806, New York, NY, USA, 2008. ACM.
13. T. Dawber. *The Framingham Study. The Epidemiology of Atherosclerotic Disease*. Harvard U. Press, 1980.
14. R. I. M. Dunbar. Co-evolution of neocortex size, group size and language in humans. *Behavioral and Brain Sciences*, 16(4):681–735, 1993.
15. N. Eagle, M. Macy, and R. Claxton. Network diversity and economic development. *Science*, 328(5981), 2010.
16. N. Eagle and A. Pentland. Reality mining: Sensing complex social systems. *Personal and Ubiquitous Computing*, (10):255–268, 2006.
17. N. Eagle, A. S. Pentland, and D. Lazer. Inferring friendship network structure by using mobile phone data. *Proc. Natl. Academy of Sciences*, 106(36), 2009.
18. R. G. Eston, A. V. Rowlands, and D. K. Ingledew. Validity of heart rate, pedometry, and accelerometry for predicting the energy cost of children's activities. *Journal of Applied Physiology*, 84(1):362–371, 1998.
19. D. Foster, C. Linehan, and S. Lawson. Motivating physical activity at work: using persuasive social media extensions for simple mobile devices. *Design*, 2010.
20. J. Gemmell, G. Bell, R. Lueder, S. Drucker, and C. Wong. Mylifebits: fulfilling the memex vision. MULTIMEDIA '02, New York, NY, USA, 2002.
21. M. C. Gonzalez, C. A. Hidalgo, and A.-L. Barabasi. Understanding individual human mobility patterns. *Nature*, 453(7196):779–782, 06 2008.
22. C. A. Hidalgo and C. Rodriguez-Sickert. The dynamics of a mobile phone network. *Physica A: Statistical Mechanics and its Applications*, 387(12), 2008.
23. O. P. John and S. Srivastava. *The Big-Five trait taxonomy: History, measurement, and theoretical perspectives*, volume 2, pages 102–138. Guilford, 1999.
24. D. Lazer, A. Pentland et al. Computational social science. *Science*, 323(5915):721–723, 2009.
25. J. J. Lin, L. Mamykina, S. Lindtner, G. Delajoux, and H. B. Strub. Fish'n'steps: Encouraging physical activity with an interactive computer game. In *Proc. of the International Conf. on Ubiquitous Computing*, 2006.
26. H. Lu et al. The jigsaw continuous sensing engine for mobile phone applications. In *Proceedings of the 8th ACM Conference on Embedded Networked Sensor Systems*, SenSys '10, New York, NY, USA, 2010.
27. A. Madan, M. Cebrian, D. Lazer, and A. Pentland. Social sensing for epidemiological behavior change. In *Proceedings of the 12th ACM international conference on Ubiquitous computing*, Ubicomp '10, pages 291–300, New York, NY, USA, 2010. ACM.
28. A. Madan, K. Farrahi, D. G. Perez, and A. Pentland. Pervasive sensing to model political opinions in face-to-face networks. In *Pervasive'11 (in press)*, 2011.
29. J. Maitland and K. A. Siek. Technological approaches to promoting physical activity. In *Proceedings of the 21st Annual Conference of the Australian Computer-Human Interaction*, New York, 2009. ACM.
30. R. Montoliu and D. Gatica-Perez. Discovering human places of interest from multimodal mobile phone data. In *Proc of 9th Int. Conference on on Mobile and Ubiquitous Multimedia (MUM,',',')*, 12 2010.
31. D. O. Olguín, B. N. Waber, T. Kim, A. Mohan, K. Ara, and A. Pentland. Sensible organizations: Technology and methodology for automatically measuring organizational behavior. *IEEE Transactions on Systems, Man, and Cybernetics, Part B*, 39(1):43–55, 2009.
32. J.-P. Onnela and F. Reed-Tsochas. Spontaneous emergence of social influence in online systems. *Proc. Natl. Academy of Sciences*, 107(43), 2010.
33. S. T. Saponas et al. ilearn on the iphone: Real-time human activity classification on commodity mobile phones. Tech report, University of Washington, 2008.
34. T. Toscos et al. Encouraging physical activity in teens can technology help reduce barriers to physical activity in adolescent girls? In *Pervasive Computing Technologies for Healthcare*, 2008.
35. R. P. Troiano et al. Physical activity in the united states measured by accelerometer. *Med Sci Sports Exerc*, 40(1):181–8, Jan 2008.

Recognition of Visual Memory Recall Processes Using Eye Movement Analysis

Andreas Bulling
Computer Laboratory
University of Cambridge
andreas.bulling@acm.org

Daniel Roggen
Wearable Computing Laboratory
ETH Zurich
droggen@ife.ee.ethz.ch

ABSTRACT
Physical activity, location, as well as a person's psychophysiological and affective state are common dimensions for developing context-aware systems in ubiquitous computing. An important yet missing contextual dimension is the cognitive context that comprises all aspects related to mental information processing, such as perception, memory, knowledge, or learning. In this work we investigate the feasibility of recognising visual memory recall. We use a recognition methodology that combines minimum redundancy maximum relevance feature selection (mRMR) with a support vector machine (SVM) classifier. We validate the methodology in a dual user study with a total of fourteen participants looking at familiar and unfamiliar pictures from four picture categories: abstract, landscapes, faces, and buildings. Using person-independent training, we are able to discriminate between familiar and unfamiliar abstract pictures with a top recognition rate of 84.3% (89.3% recall, 21.0% false positive rate) over all participants. We show that eye movement analysis is a promising approach to infer the cognitive context of a person and discuss the key challenges for the real-world implementation of eye-based cognition-aware systems.

Author Keywords
Visual Memory Recall, Eye Movement Analysis, Cognition-Awareness, Cognitive Context, Electrooculography (EOG)

ACM Classification Keywords
H.1.2 Models and Principles: User/Machine Systems–Human information processing; I.5.2 Pattern Recognition: Design Methodology–Pattern analysis

General Terms
Algorithms, Experimentation, Human Factors

INTRODUCTION
Context-awareness has emerged as a key area of research in ubiquitous computing [12]. Considerable advances in sensing, inferring, and using context information were achieved by investigating different dimensions of context, such as physical activity [10], location [37], or the psychophysiological and affective state of a person [20]. These common contextual dimensions do not provide a complete picture of the context of a person. An important yet not explicitly considered dimension of context is the *cognitive context* of a person. According to the major research fields in experimental psychology, we define the cognitive context to comprise all aspects related to mental processing, such as perception, memory, knowledge, and learning. We define a computing system as *cognition-aware* if it is able to sense, infer, and adapt to the cognitive context of its user.

Current context-aware systems have a hard time assessing the cognitive context in an unobtrusive manner. This is due to the fact that the cognitive context is encoded in complex neural dynamics inside the brain and few obvious cues are accessible by non-invasive measurement techniques. Cognitive neuroscience uses techniques such as functional magnetic resonance imaging (fMRI, [8]) that are not suited for real-world applications. More light-weight techniques potentially useful to get at the cognitive context, such as electroencephalography (EEG, [2]), are not (yet) unobtrusive and robust enough for use in mobile daily life settings.

In earlier work we introduced eye movement analysis as a new modality for activity and context recognition [5, 6]. We showed that the movement patterns the eyes perform during different activities carry information that allows to recognise the activities themselves [6]. A large body of research in experimental psychology has evidenced that, in addition to physical activity, visual behaviour is tightly linked to cognitive processes, such as attention [26], relational memory [18], learning [21], or saliency determination [22]. This link to cognition makes eye movements a particularly promising source of information on the cognitive context of a person - beyond mere physical or visual activities.

To illustrate the vision of eye-based cognition-awareness consider the following scenario: Attendees of a business reception wear eye trackers that are unobtrusively embedded into their goggles. By analysing their eye movement patterns during conversations, cognition-aware memory assistants running on their mobile phones assess whether the involved speakers have met before and still remember each other. Using this information, the systems then automatically provide real-time memory assistance about people fallen into oblivion to prevent from embarrassing situations.

Although this example scenario is not novel per se, current state-of-the-art approaches use image processing techniques to detect whether two people have met before. The assistant envisioned here goes beyond mere detection of conversations or matching of faces to a database. Instead, it needs to detect whether a person actually *remembers* having seen somebody else before. For instance, let's assume that an attendee has met another person before. Consequently, a memory assistant using image processing would indicate that the other person is "known". The attendee, however, may still not remember that other person. Thus, in our scenario, the assistant is required to identify the *process of visual memory retrieval*. This can only be accomplished by extending the current notion of context with a cognitive dimension that reflects the attendee's subjective appraisal of the situation.

Paper Scope and Contributions

As a first step towards our vision of eye-based cognition-awareness, in this work we investigate the feasibility of using eye movement analysis to recognise visual memory recall processes of people looking at familiar pictures (that they have seen before) or unfamiliar pictures (that they see for the first time). The specific contributions are: (1) the introduction of cognition-awareness and the cognitive context as new paradigms in ubiquitous computing; (2) the introduction of eye movement analysis as a promising modality to infer processes of visual cognition, here memory recall, of a person; (3) the concept of a dual user study to investigate automatic recognition of one example cognitive process from eye movements, namely visual memory recall; and (4) the identification and discussion of the key challenges for the real-world implementation of cognition-aware systems.

RELATED WORK

Eye Movement Analysis

Eye movement analysis has long been used as a tool to investigate visual behaviour. In an early study, Hacisalihzade *et al.* used Markov processes to model visual fixations of observers looking at an object [17]. They transformed fixation sequences into character strings and used the string edit distance to quantify the similarity of eye movements. Elhelw *et al.* used discrete time Markov chains on sequences of temporal fixations to identify salient image features that affect the perception of visual realism [15]. They found that fixation clusters were able to uncover the features that most attract an observer's attention. Dempere-Marco *et al.* presented a method for training novices in assessing tomography images [11]. They modelled the assessment behaviour of domain experts based on the dynamics of their saccadic eye movements. Salvucci *et al.* evaluated means for automated analysis of eye movements [32]. They described three methods based on sequence-matching and hidden Markov models that interpreted eye movements as accurately as human experts but in significantly less time.

Eye Movements and Cognition

A growing number of researchers study eye movements in natural environments to better understand the role the visual system plays in the execution of everyday tasks [19]. Human vision research has shown that unconscious eye movements are strongly related to the underlying cognitive and perceptive processes. For example, it has been shown that visual behaviour is a good measure of visual engagement [34], drowsiness [33], and cognitive load [35]. Heisz *et al.* investigated changes in eye movement behaviour across several exposures to pictures of faces [21]. They found that as a face became more familiar, observers looked longer and more often at the eyes and less often at the nose, mouth, or forehead.

Differences in eye movement patterns are also linked to a number of mental disorders. It is for this reason that eye tracking has been investigated for the diagnosis of disorders on the autism spectrum (see [3] for a review). For example, Klin *et al.* showed that people with autism tend to show fewer fixations to the eyes but more fixations to the mouth [24]. Similar links were found for schizophrenia [16] as well as Parkinson's [28] and Alzheimer's disease [9].

All of these studies demonstrate the close link between visual behaviour and cognition and underline the potential of eye movement analysis for assessing the cognitive context of a person. While these studies analysed eye movements they were purely descriptive in nature. They did not attempt to automatically predict from the eye movements whether the object of attention, such as a face, was previously seen and remembered.

EYE MOVEMENT ANALYSIS

Wearable Eye Tracking

Developing sensors to track eye movements in daily life is an active topic of research. Portable video-based eye trackers - such as the Dikablis from Ergoneers or the iView X HED from SensoMotoric Instruments - require auxiliary equipment for the demanding video processing. The size of latest systems, such as the Glasses from Tobii Technology, is more appropriate for mobile settings, however, these eye trackers only allow for recordings over a couple of hours and do not (yet) provide real-time processing and output. Electrooculography (EOG) - the measurement technique used in this work - is an inexpensive method for mobile eye movement recordings; it is computationally light-weight and can be implemented using on-body sensors [27, 4]. These characteristics are crucial with a view to long-term eye movement recordings with real-time feedback in daily life.

Electrooculography

The eye can be modelled as a dipole with its positive pole at the cornea and its negative pole at the retina. Assuming a stable corneo-retinal potential difference, the eye is the origin of a steady electric potential field. The process of measuring changes in this field is called electrooculography. Using two pairs of skin electrodes placed at opposite sides of the eye and an additional reference electrode, two signal components (EOG_h and EOG_v), corresponding to two movement components - a horizontal and a vertical - can be identified. If the eye moves away from the centre position, the retina approaches one electrode while the cornea approaches the opposing one. This change in dipole orientation causes a change in the electric potential field and thus the measured

EOG signal amplitude. By analysing these changes, eye movements can be tracked.

Eye Movement Characteristics

To use eye movement analysis for context-awareness, it is important to understand the different types of eye movements. In earlier work we identified three types that can be robustly detected using EOG: saccades, fixations, and blinks.

Saccades

The eyes do not remain still when viewing a visual scene. Instead, they have to move constantly to build up a mental "map" from interesting parts of that scene. The main reason for this is that only a small central region of the retina, the fovea, is able to perceive with high acuity. The fast movement of the eyes is called a saccade. The duration of a saccade depends on the angular distance the eyes travel during this movement: the so-called saccade amplitude.

Fixations

Fixations are stationary states of the eyes during which gaze is held upon a specific location in the visual scene. Fixations can also be defined as the time between each two saccades.

Blinks

The frontal part of the cornea is coated with a thin tear film. To spread this fluid across the corneal surface, regular opening and closing of the eyelids, or blinking, is required. The average blink rate is influenced by environmental factors such as relative humidity, temperature or brightness, but also by physical activity [6], cognitive load [35], or fatigue [33].

EXPERIMENT

The experiment consisted of user studies: A main study to record natural eye movements during visual memory recall and a validation study to evaluate visual memory recall performance of a second group of participants. The main study was designed with two objectives in mind: (1) to elicit distinct eye movements by using a large screen and well-defined visual stimuli, and (2) to record natural visual behaviour without any active visual search or memory task by not asking participants for real-time feedback. The validation study followed the same protocol as the main study but participants were asked to provide real-time feedback on whether each image had previously been shown. While the main focus of the current work was on visual memory recall of faces, we included additional picture categories for comparison and to investigate the general applicability of our approach.

Apparatus

We created four picture sets, one set for each of the following picture categories: abstract images, landscapes, faces, and buildings. For the faces category, we manually selected 20 mixed-gender pictures (11 male, 9 female) from the CVL Face Database[1]. We chose pictures with frontal view and neutral expression; the face of the person was centred in the picture (see Figure 1). Pictures in the other categories were randomly selected from the Internet. We ensured, however, that these pictures had similar visual features. For example, we selected landscape photographs that showed a lake as their main feature; the building photographs always showed skyscrapers centred in the picture. The pictures were shown on a screen using a beamer resulting in a picture dimension of between 1x1 m and 1.5x1.5 m. A MATLAB script was used to control the display of the pictures as well as to ground truth annotate the experimental procedure.

[1]Database is available online: `http://lrv.fri.uni-lj.si/facedb.html`

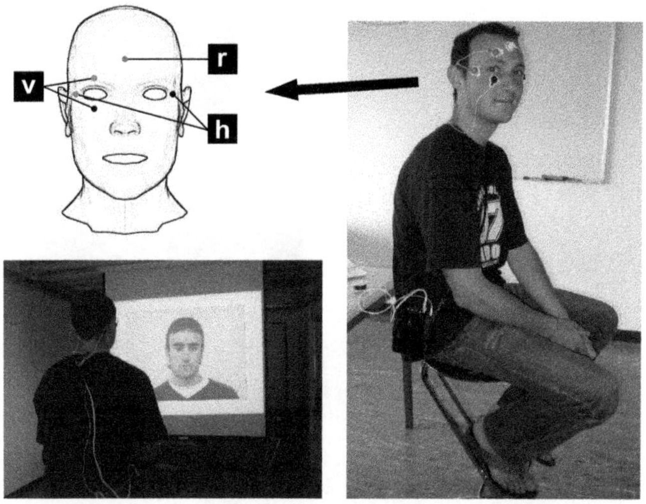

Figure 1: Experimental setup consisting of five electrodes for EOG data collection (h: horizontal, v: vertical, r: reference). The participants' eye movements were recorded while seated in front of a screen in a dimmed office room. No constraints with respect to movements of the upper body or head were imposed.

For EOG data collection we used a commercial system, the Mobi from Twente Medical Systems International (TMSI). The device records a four-channel EOG with a joint sampling rate of 128 Hz. The device was worn on a belt around each participant's waist and transmitted aggregated data via Bluetooth to a laptop placed behind the participant.

EOG signals were picked up using an array of five 24 mm Ag/AgCl wet electrodes from Tyco Healthcare placed around the right eye (see upper left picture in Figure 1). The horizontal signal was collected using one electrode on the nose and another directly across from this on the edge of the right eye socket. The vertical signal was collected using one electrode above the right eyebrow and another on the lower edge of the right eye socket. The fifth electrode, the signal reference, was placed away from the other electrodes in the middle of the forehead. Five participants (three male, two female) had to wear spectacles during the experiment. For these participants, the nose electrode was moved to the edge of the left eye socket to not interfere with the glasses frame. Data recording and synchronisation was handled by the Context Recognition Network (CRN) Toolbox [1].

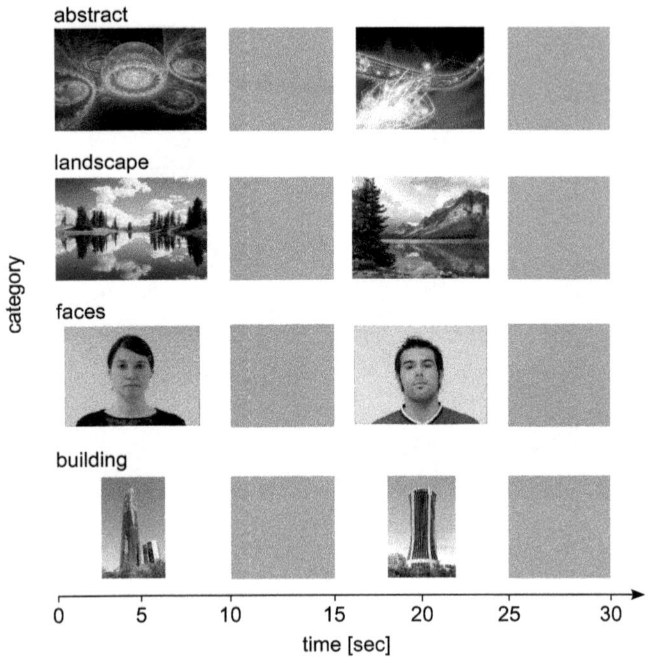

Figure 2: Example pictures from the four categories (abstract, landscape, faces, and buildings) and their sequence of display used in the experiment. Each picture was shown for 10 seconds; pictures with Gaussian noise were shown in between for five seconds.

Participants

We collected eye movement data from seven participants - four male and three female - recruited from the lab. Participants were between 25 and 29 years old (M = 26.4, SD = 1.6). Originally there were eight participants but one was withdrawn due to bad EOG signal quality that prevented robust detection of eye movements. We made sure all participants were well rested and we confirmed that none of them had seen pictures from the CVL database before.

Setup and Procedure

In contrast to [21], participants were only informed about the measurement equipment before the experiment; neither the purpose of the study nor any task were given to them. This was to not influence their visual behaviour by engaging them in an active visual search task. For the same reason, participants were also not asked to provide real-time feedback on whether they remembered each picture during the experiment. Participants were seated in a dimmed office room about 2 m in front of a screen facing its centre. Movements of the upper body were allowed at any time but we encouraged the participants to sit still throughout the experiment (see right picture in Figure 1).

Participants were asked to look at four continuous sequences of pictures. Each sequence was randomly created from pictures of a single picture category (see Figure 2). Within each sequence, 12 pictures were presented only once; five others were presented four times at regular intervals. This resulted in a total number of 32 pictures for each sequence. We randomised both the overall sequence as well as the selection of the repeated pictures across participants. In contrast to [21] we limited the exposure time for each picture to 10 seconds. In between each exposure, a picture with Gaussian noise was shown for five seconds as a baseline measurement and to allow the participants to relax. The total experiment time for each participant was about one hour. At the end of each experiment, the participants were asked on their experiences on the procedure in a short questionnaire.

Validation Study

The validation study used the same picture sets and experimental procedure as the main study. In contrast to the main study, the pictures were shown on a laptop and no eye movements were recorded from the participants. Instead, participants were asked for real-time feedback on whether or not each picture had been shown before by pressing two buttons on the laptop's keyboard. We collected feedback from seven participants disjunct to those of the main study - four male and three female - aged between 23 and 30 years (M = 26.9, SD = 2.9).

METHOD

All methods used in this work were implemented offline using MATLAB and C++. In this section we first describe the EOG signal processing algorithms and provide an overview of the extracted eye movement features (an in-depth description of these algorithms and features is outside the scope of this paper but can be found in [6]). We then introduce the feature selection and classification algorithms, as well as the parameter selection and training procedures.

Noise and Baseline Drift Removal

EOG_h and EOG_v were first stripped of high frequency noise using a median filter. For baseline drift removal, we then performed an approximated multilevel 1-D wavelet decomposition at level nine using Daubechies wavelets on each signal component. The reconstructed decomposition coefficients gave a baseline drift estimation. Subtracting this estimation from the original signals yielded the corrected signals with reduced drift offset (see [36] for further details).

Saccade Detection

In an earlier work we introduced the *Continuous Wavelet Transform - Saccade Detection* (CWT-SD) algorithm [6]. Briefly, CWT-SD detects saccades by thresholding on the continuous 1-D wavelet coefficient vector computed from the de-noised and baseline drift removed EOG_h and EOG_v. CWT-SD takes physiological saccade characteristics into account to increase the robustness of detection [14].

Fixation Detection

Our algorithm for fixation detection exploits the fact that fixation points tend to cluster together closely in time. Thus, by thresholding on the dispersion of these points, fixations can be detected [38]. Based on the output of the CWT-SD algorithm, dispersion and duration values are calculated for each non-saccadic segment. If the dispersion is below a maximum threshold, and the duration above a minimum threshold, a fixation is detected.

Blink Detection

Similar to the algorithm for saccade detection, the *Continuous Wavelet Transform - Blink Detection* (CWT-BD) algorithm uses thresholding of wavelet coefficients to detect blinks in EOG_v. In contrast to saccades, a blink is characterised by a short sequence of two large peaks in the coefficient vector: one positive, the other negative. The time between these peaks is much smaller than for saccades. Thus, blinks are distinguished from saccades by applying a maximum threshold on this time difference.

Analysis of Saccade Sequences

Visual attention while looking at faces is strongly attracted by internal face features (eyes, nose, and mouth) as these convey crucial information about face identity. When viewing unfamiliar faces observers were found to scan more diverse regions of a face compared to familiar faces [21]. This suggests that eye movement features that capture the sequential nature of visual scanning behaviour contain useful information for recognising memory recall processes.

To extract information about saccade sequences we used a wordbook analysis. First, each saccade was encoded into a discrete, character-based representation. A sliding window of length l and a step size of one was used to scan the stream of encoded saccades for saccade sequences. A saccade sequence is given by l successive characters. As an example with $l = 4$, the sequence "LrBd" translates to large left (L) $\rightarrow$ small right (r) $\rightarrow$ large diagonal right (B) $\rightarrow$ small down (d). These sequences were then collected in wordbooks and analysed statistically. Each new sequence was added to the corresponding wordbook Wb_l; for a sequence already included in Wb_l its occurrence count was increased by one.

Feature Extraction and Selection

We considered the two-class recognition problem of discriminating between pictures that were only seen once (class "non-repeated") and pictures that were seen several times (class "repeated") by the participants. We first removed all eye movement data that belonged to Gaussian noise pictures. We then assigned all picture instances (picture and corresponding eye movement data) of all first and single exposures to the "non-repeated" class (17 picture instances), and picture instances of exposures two, three, and four to the "repeated" class (15 picture instances).

Feature extraction was run on all picture instances separately using a sliding window with window size W_{fe} and step size S_{fe}. We extracted four groups of features from the detected saccades, fixations, blinks, and wordbooks (see Table 1). The features were calculated on both EOG_h and EOG_v. Features calculated from saccadic eye movements made up the largest proportion of extracted features. In total, there were 62 such features comprising the mean, variance and maximum EOG signal amplitudes of saccades, and the normalised saccade rates. These were calculated for both EOG_h and EOG_v; for small and large saccades; for saccades in positive or negative direction; and for all possible combinations of these. We calculated five different fixation features: the mean and variance of the EOG signal amplitude within a fixation; the

Group	Features
saccade (*S*-)	mean (mean), variance (var) or maximum (max) EOG signal amplitudes (Amp) or rate (rate) of small (S) or large (L), positive (P) or negative (N) saccades in horizontal (Hor) or vertical (Ver) direction
fixation (*F*-)	mean (mean) and/or variance (var) of the horizontal (Hor) or vertical (Ver) EOG signal amplitude (Amp) within or length (Length) of a fixation or rate of fixations
blink (*B*-)	mean (mean) or variance (var) of the blink duration or blink rate (rate)
wordbook (*W*-)	wordbook size (size) or maximum (max), difference (diff) between maximum and minimum, mean (mean) or variance (var) of all occurrence counts (Count) in the wordbook of length (-lx)

Table 1: Naming scheme for the features used in this work. For a particular feature, e.g. *S-rateSPHor*, the capital letter represents the group - saccadic (S), blink (B), fixation (F) or wordbook(W) - and the combination of abbreviations after the dash describes the particular type of feature and the characteristics it covers.

mean and the variance of fixation duration; and the fixation rate over window W_{fe}. For blinks, we extracted three features: blink rate, as well as the mean and variance of the blink duration. We used four wordbooks. This allowed us to account for all possible eye movement patterns up to a length of four ($l = 4$), with each wordbook containing the type and occurrence count of all patterns found. For each wordbook we extracted five features: the wordbook size, the maximum occurrence count, the difference between the maximum and minimum occurrence counts, and the variance and mean of all occurrence counts. The resulting feature matrices were combined to one large feature matrix per participant, each comprising 32 picture instances.

For feature selection we chose a filter scheme over the commonly used wrapper approaches because of the lower computational costs and thus shorter runtime. We use minimum redundancy maximum relevance feature selection (mRMR, [31]). The mRMR algorithm selects a feature subset of arbitrary size S that best characterises the statistical properties of the given target classes based on the ground truth labelling (see [30] for the MATLAB implementation we used).

Classification and Performance Evaluation

For classification we chose a linear support vector machine (SVM, see [25] for the C implementation we used). All parameters of the saccade, fixation, and blink detection algorithms were fixed to values common to all participants. For evaluation we followed a leave-one-person-out scheme: the datasets of all but one participant were combined and used for training (the "training set"); the dataset of the remaining participant was used for testing (the "test set"). This was repeated for each participant. Feature selection was performed

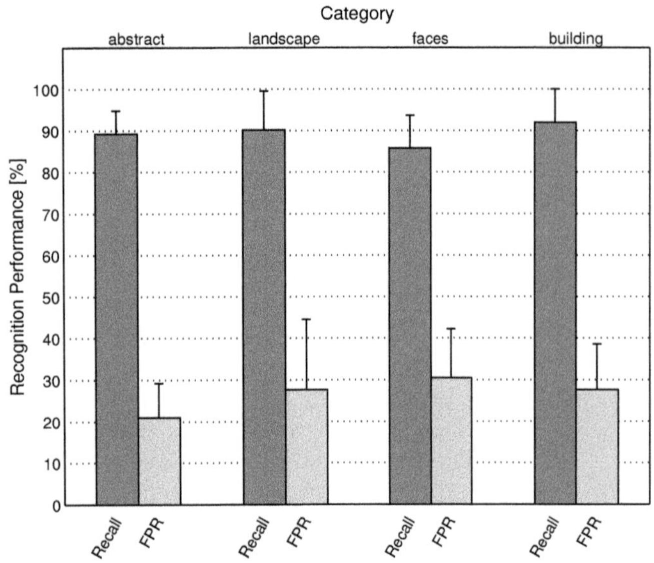

Figure 3: Mean recall and false positive rate (FPR) for the different picture categories using an exposure time $T_{exp} = 10s$. Error bars denote 95% confidence intervals.

solely on the training set. During the classification process the size of the feature set for each leave-one-person-out iteration was optimised with respect to accuracy by sweeping over S, W_{fe}, and S_{fe}. In addition, the prediction vector returned by the classifier for each picture instance was reduced to a single class label ("repeated" or "non-repeated") using majority voting.

RESULTS

Results for Each Picture Category

On average, participants from the validation study were able to correctly identify pictures that had previously been shown with an accuracy of 97.3% for abstract, 97.8% for landscape, 96.4% for faces, and 97.3% for building pictures. Given this high accuracy, in the following analysis we assume that participants in the main study perfectly remember a picture that was shown before.

Based on the data recorded in the main study, Figure 3 summarises the overall recognition performance using person-independent parameters and training for each picture category. The bars contrast true positive rate (recall) ($\frac{TP}{TP+FN}$) to false positive rate (FPR) ($\frac{FP}{FP+TN}$), where TP, FP, TN and FN represent true positive, false positive, true negative and false positive counts, respectively. The figure shows that the recognition system consistently achieves recall values above 85% with the highest recall of 92% for the building (FPR: 27.6%) and the lowest recall of 85.7% for the faces picture category. The FPR is above 20% for all picture categories with the highest FPR of 30.5% for the faces category and the lowest FPR of 21.0% for abstract pictures (recall: 89.3%).

The results for each individual participant show a range of differences in recognition performance (see Table 2). For example, the highest recall result for the faces category is 93.8% (participants 3 and 4) but with a FPR of 46.7%. The worst result was for participant 6, with 68.8% recall but a FPR of only 13.3%. What can be seen from the table, however, is that for all categories the differences do not seem to correlate to the gender of the person.

Further Analysis of the Faces Picture Category

With a view to the cognition-aware memory assistant outlined in the introduction we then analysed the results for the faces picture category in more detail.

Eye Movement Features

We first analysed how mRMR ranked the features on each of the seven leave-one-person-out training sets for the faces category. The rank of a feature is the position at which mRMR selected it within a set. The position corresponds to the importance with which mRMR assesses a feature's ability to discriminate between classes in combination with the features selected before it. Figure 4 shows the top 15 features according to the median rank over all sets (see Table 1 for a description of the type and name of the features). For each feature the vertical bar represents the spread of mRMR ranks for the seven training sets. The most useful features are those found with the highest rank (close to one) for most training sets, indicated by shorter bars. Note that some features are not always included in the final result (e.g. feature 64 only appears in four sets). Equally, a useful feature that is ranked lowly might still improve a classification (e.g. feature 89 is spread between rank two and 21, but is included in six sets).

This analysis reveals that most features are based on horizontal and vertical saccades, e.g. 39 (*sacc-EMRt*), 24 (*sacc-varAmpLPHor*), and 62 (*sacc-propHorVer*). Feature 67 (*fix-varLength*, variance of fixation duration) is used by six sets, four of which rank it highly. Feature 65 (*bl-varLength*, variance of blink duration) is selected for six out of the seven sets, all of which give it a high rank. Three wordbook features are in the top ranks, all of which were selected at least four times and describe eye movements sequences of length three and four: 89 (*str-varCount-l4*), 83 (*str-diffCount-l3*), and 88 (*str-diffCount-l4*).

Analysis of Different Exposure Times

The analysis so far assumed a fixed exposure time $T_{exp} = 10s$. A short exposure time is desired as this directly translates to a low latency of the recognition system. In addition, 10 seconds may be regarded as rather long for real-world environments considering that looking at the faces of others, for example while walking down a street, is a subtle visual activity and may occur on a smaller time scale. In a laboratory setting, Hsiao *et al.* found that the best performance for face recognition was achieved with only two fixations and that performance did not improve with additional fixations [23]. Based on the fixation durations reported there and typical physiological saccade characteristics, two fixations correspond to about one second of exposure.

To analyse the influence of T_{exp} on the recognition performance we sweeped $T_{exp} = 10s, 5s, 3s, 2s, 1s$. For example for $T_{exp} = 3s$, we only used the eye movement data

picture category		P1 (m)	P2 (m)	P3 (f)	P4 (m)	P5 (f)	P6 (m)	P7 (f)	mean	std
abstract	Recall [%]	*81.3*	87.5	87.5	93.8	**100.0**	87.5	87.5	89.3	5.9
	FPR [%]	**6.7**	20.0	26.7	20.0	26.7	*33.3*	13.3	21.0	9.0
landscape	Recall [%]	93.8	**100.0**	93.8	93.8	93.8	87.5	*68.8*	90.2	10.1
	FPR [%]	40.0	33.3	*46.7*	13.3	**6.7**	*46.7*	**6.7**	27.6	18.2
faces	Recall [%]	87.5	87.5	**93.8**	**93.8**	87.5	*68.8*	81.3	85.7	8.6
	FPR [%]	26.7	20.0	*46.7*	*46.7*	26.7	**13.3**	33.3	30.5	12.7
building	Recall [%]	93.8	*75.0*	93.8	93.8	**100.0**	87.5	**100.0**	92.0	8.6
	FPR [%]	20.0	**13.3**	20.0	26.7	26.7	40.0	*46.7*	27.6	11.8

Table 2: Recall and false positive rate (FPR) for each participant and the mean and standard deviation over all. The table also shows the participants' gender (f: female, m: male). Best case results for each picture category are indicated in bold, worst case results in italic.

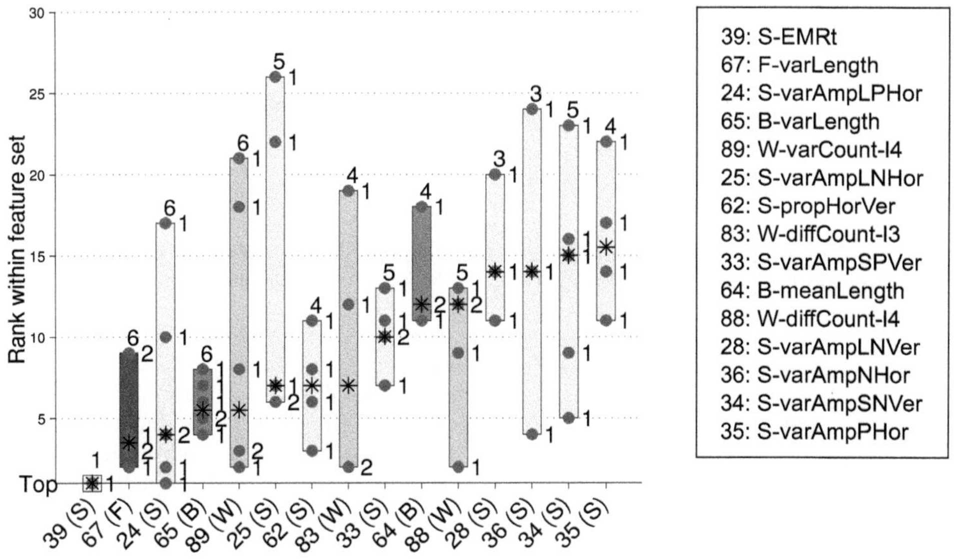

Figure 4: Top 15 eye movement features selected by mRMR for all seven training sets for the faces picture category. X-axis shows feature number and group; the key on the right shows the corresponding feature names as described in Table 1; Y-axis shows the rank (top = 1). For each feature, the bars show: the total number of training sets for which the feature was chosen (bold number at the top), the rank of the feature within each set (dots, with a number representing the set count), and the median rank over all sets (black star). For example, a useful feature is 67 (F) - a fixation feature selected for six sets, in four of which it is ranked four or below; less useful is 28 (S) - a saccade feature used in only three sets and ranked between 11 and 20.

recorded during the first three seconds of each exposure for classification. We calculated the recognition performance again using person-independent parameters and training. As can be seen from Figure 5 the exposure time considerably influences the recognition performance. For $T_{exp} = 10s$ the mean recall is 85.7% (FPR: 30.5%), whereas for $T_{exp} = 1s$ the recall drops to 65.2% with a FPR of 34.3%. It is interesting to note that $T_{exp} = 5s$ yields the best FPR of 21.9% (recall: 77.7%) and while $T_{exp} = 3s$ yields the worst FPR of 38.1% the recall only decreases to 83.9% compared to an exposure time of 10 seconds.

DISCUSSION

Eye Movement Features

The mRMR-based feature ranking provides interesting insights into the type of eye movement features that are useful for assessing visual memory recall of faces (see Figure 4). The saccade and wordbook feature groups were particularly well represented in the study. This result confirms that in addition to eye movement characteristics well-known in experimental psychology, such as the mean fixation duration, saccades and saccade sequences carry useful information on a person's visual behaviour during memory recall tasks. Similar to earlier results for eye-based activity recognition [6] the best recognition performance was only achieved using a mixture of features from different feature groups.

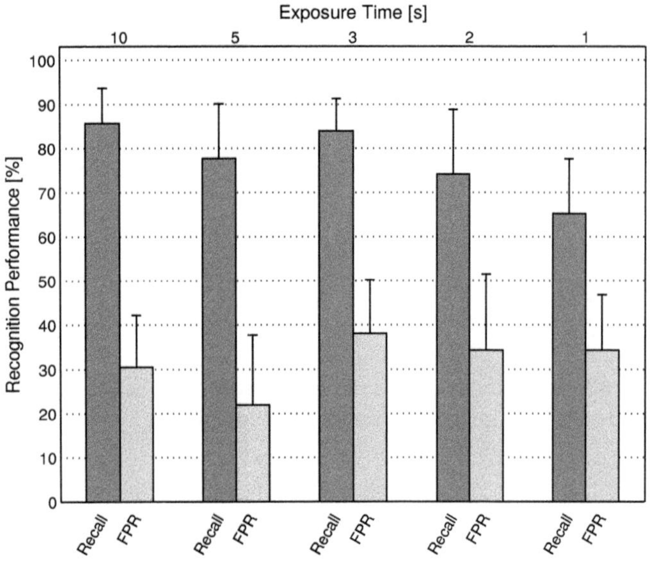

Figure 5: Mean recall and false positive rate (FPR) for different exposure times for the faces picture category. Error bars denote 95% confidence intervals.

Blink features were less well represented in the top ranks. This is most likely due to the short exposure time of only 10 seconds for which participants could not show much blink rate variations as for example while looking at unpleasant visual stimuli [29]. Blink features may be found to be more discriminative for longer duration activities, such as prolonged visual search. In combination with the ease by which they were calculated, we believe that blink features are still promising for future work on cognition-aware systems.

The same applies to the group of fixation features from which only one feature, the variance of the fixation duration, was selected in top ranks for six of the seven sets. It is interesting to note that the mean fixation count - a feature found in [21] to significantly change across exposures - was not among the top 15 features in this study.

Recognition Performance

All parameters of the saccade, fixation and blink detection algorithms were fixed to values common to all participants; the same applies to the parameters of the feature selection and classification algorithms. Using person-independent training, our recognition system achieved best average recall values of between 85.7% and 92%, and FPR of between 21% and 30.5% for all four picture categories (see Figure 3). While such a high FPR may not be problematic for certain use cases, lower FPR are generally preferable and could, for example, be achieved by using person-dependent parameters and training.

The analysis of different exposure times revealed that while a one second exposure yielded a recall well above chance, the recall for three seconds was close to that of a full 10 second exposure (see Figure 5). This lower bound is important for a potential real-world implementation of a cognition-aware memory assistant and may be further lowered by using eye movement features and analysis methods particularly geared towards recognition of visual memory recall.

Additional eye movement characteristics - such as pupil dilation or microsaccades - that are potentially useful for recognising visual memory recall or the other cognitive processes mentioned before were not used here because of the difficulty in measuring them with EOG. These characteristics are still worth investigating in the future as they may carry information that complements that available in the current work.

Experiment

To investigate the feasibility of inferring cognitive processes from eye movements requires an experimental methodology that is more similar to that used in experimental psychology rather than in ubiquitous computing. Human vision experiments typically involve controlled tasks with carefully designed and timed visual stimuli. In contrast, ubiquitous computing aims for real-world applications that involve unconstrained natural behaviour. Techniques from experimental psychology can therefore not directly be adopted for ubiquitous computing. As demonstrated here, a viable approach is to first evoke and infer specific cognitive processes in a similar but less controlled laboratory setting. The experimental design and procedures can then be transferred and gradually extended to cover more complex daily life situations.

In the experiment we faced a trade-off between natural visual behaviour and user-annotated ground truth. We addressed this trade-off by implementing a dual study design with two different groups of participants. In the main study we did not ask participants for real-time feedback on whether they actually remembered each picture. This was to not involve them in an active visual memory task that would have influenced their visual behaviour. In terms of evaluation, this lack of user-annotated ground truth required the assumption that the ground truth labels defined by the experimental procedure reflected the participants' subjective experience. The validation study showed that this assumption may not always hold, i.e. some pictures had been shown before but were not remembered by the participants. Participants' consistently high memory recall performance for all picture categories in the validation study also showed, however, that this occurred in only about 3% of the cases and had negligible influence on the participants' performance in the main study. We plan to compare the dual study design introduced in the current work with other validation techniques such as post-experiment questionnaires or analysis of video footage.

Toward a Real-World Implementation

While the initial results presented here are promising, there are several challenges that we aim to address in future work for a real-world implementation of the envisioned cognition-aware memory assistant.

One of the key challenges for a real-world implementation is the co-influence of (visual) task, situation, and cognitive processes on a person's eye movements. In laboratory settings these influences can be minimised by using a constrained experimental setup and well-defined visual stimuli. Everyday settings can typically not be controlled in a similar fashion. It is therefore crucial to identify and separate these different sources of influence for robust recognition of visual memory recall and other cognitive processes. This problem could be addressed by using a multi-modal approach for context recognition and annotation that incorporates additional modalities to eye tracking, such as proximity sensors, GPS for localisation, inertial measurement units for head movements, or eye contact sensors [13].

This leads to a second challenge. Personal encounters in daily life differ considerably from the situation investigated here. In these settings, facial expressions of conversational partners change continuously, the viewpoint is dynamic, and other visual stimuli may attract attention and lead to "random" saccades to other entities in the surrounding environment. In addition, personal encounters may range from longer face-to-face discussions between two people, over glances to faces of others while in transit, to looking at several faces of a group of people in succession. This will require advanced methods for robust detection of when and how people look at each other's face. One part of a solution to this problem is to augment the analysis of eye movement dynamics - as presented here - with a computer vision system for face detection and a wearable gaze tracker to identify the points in time the person has looked at a face.

The current experiment involved participants to look at a large screen to provoke distinct eye movements that could easily be measured using EOG. It remains to be investigated whether current wearable eye trackers - whether EOG- or video-based - are accurate and robust enough to capture eye movement characteristics that reflect visual memory recall processes on smaller screens (e.g. on a mobile phone) or with the person being in transit.

In the questionnaire participants one and two reported that they got slightly bored and participants one, two, and five reported of getting slightly tired while looking at the pictures. Participants one, three, four, and seven also reported of having lost concentration towards the end of the experiment. These phenomena did not seem to have influenced the recognition performance in the current experiment (see Table 2). Given that blink duration was found to be a reliable indicator of fatigue [7] and that its variance was a high-ranked features for six of the seven training sets (see Figure 4) we still believe that a fatigue detector may prove beneficial for increasing the performance of a real-world implementation of a cognition-aware memory assistant.

Finally, it will be interesting to see how social conventions, such as not to look into the eyes of others for too long or not to scrutinise the faces of others, will influence the available time to analyse eye movements and therefore the recognition performance of the memory assistant.

CONCLUSION

In this work we proposed cognition-awareness as a novel paradigm to describe context-aware computing systems that are able to sense and adapt to a user's cognitive context. We introduced eye movement analysis as a promising method to assess the cognitive context in an unobtrusive manner. Using a dual user study we showed that visual memory recall processes while looking at familiar and unfamiliar pictures can be recognised from eye movements of seven participants with decent performance. These initial results are promising as the described approach may soon be applicable to other stationary real-world setups, e.g. in a cognition-aware picture browser on a desktop computer. They also open up the discussion on the wider applicability of the approach to other cognitive processes and mobile daily life settings.

REFERENCES

1. D. Bannach, P. Lukowicz, and O. Amft. Rapid Prototyping of Activity Recognition Applications. *IEEE Pervasive Computing*, 7(2):22–31, 2008.
2. N. Bigdely-Shamlo, A. Vankov, R. R. Ramirez, and S. Makeig. Brain activity-based image classification from rapid serial visual presentation. *IEEE Transactions on Neural Systems and Rehabilitation Engineering*, 16(5):432 –441, 2008.
3. Z. Boraston and S.-J. Blakemore. The application of eye-tracking technology in the study of autism. *Journal of Physiology*, 581(3):893 –898, 2007.
4. A. Bulling, D. Roggen, and G. Tröster. Wearable EOG goggles: Seamless sensing and context-awareness in everyday environments. *Journal of Ambient Intelligence and Smart Environments*, 1(2):157–171, 2009.
5. A. Bulling, J. A. Ward, and H. Gellersen. Multi-Modal Recognition of Reading Activity in Transit Using Body-Worn Sensors. *ACM Transactions on Applied Perception*, 2011, to appear.
6. A. Bulling, J. A. Ward, H. Gellersen, and G. Tröster. Eye Movement Analysis for Activity Recognition Using Electrooculography. *IEEE Transactions on Pattern Analysis and Machine Intelligence*, 33(4):741–753, 2011.
7. P. P. Caffier, U. Erdmann, and P. Ullsperger. Experimental evaluation of eye-blink parameters as a drowsiness measure. *European Journal of Applied Physiology*, 89(3-4):319–325, 2003.
8. M. J. Chadwick, D. Hassabis, N. Weiskopf, and E. A. Maguire. Decoding individual episodic memory traces in the human hippocampus. *Current Biology*, 20(6):544 – 547, 2010.
9. T. J. Crawford, S. Higham, T. Renvoize, J. Patel, M. Dale, A. Suriya, and S. Tetley. Inhibitory control of saccadic eye movements and cognitive impairment in alzheimer's disease. *Biological Psychiatry*, 57(9):1052–1060, 2005.
10. N. Davies, D. P. Siewiorek, and R. Sukthankar. Special issue: Activity-based computing. *IEEE Pervasive Computing*, 7(2), 2008.

11. L. Dempere-Marco, X. Hu, S. L. S. MacDonald, S. M. Ellis, D. M. Hansell, and G.-Z. Yang. The use of visual search for knowledge gathering in image decision support. *IEEE Transactions on Medical Imaging*, 21(7):741–754, 2002.
12. A. K. Dey. Understanding and using context. *Personal and Ubiquitous Computing*, 5(1):4–7, 2001.
13. C. Dickie, R. Vertegaal, J. S. Shell, C. Sohn, D. Cheng, and O. Aoudeh. Eye contact sensing glasses for attention-sensitive wearable video blogging. In *Extended Abstracts of the ACM SIGCHI Conference on Human Factors in Computing Systems*, pages 769–770, 2004.
14. A. T. Duchowski. *Eye Tracking Methodology: Theory and Practice*. Springer-Verlag New York, Inc., Secaucus, NJ, USA, 2007.
15. M. Elhelw, M. Nicolaou, A. Chung, G.-Z. Yang, and M. S. Atkins. A gaze-based study for investigating the perception of visual realism in simulated scenes. *ACM Transactions on Applied Perception*, 5(1):1–20, 2008.
16. U. Ettinger, M. Picchioni, M.-H. Hall, K. Schulze, T. Toulopoulou, S. Landau, T. J. Crawford, and R. M. Murray. Antisaccade performance in monozygotic twins discordant for schizophrenia: The maudsley twin study. *American Journal of Psychiatry*, 163(3):543–545, 2006.
17. S. S. Hacisalihzade, L. W. Stark, and J. S. Allen. Visual perception and sequences of eye movement fixations: a stochastic modeling approach. *IEEE Transactions on Systems, Man and Cybernetics*, 22(3):474–481, 1992.
18. D. E. Hannula and C. Ranganath. The eyes have it: Hippocampal activity predicts expression of memory in eye movements. *Neuron*, 63(5):592 – 599, 2009.
19. M. M. Hayhoe and D. H. Ballard. Eye movements in natural behavior. *Trends in Cognitive Sciences*, 9(4):188–194, 2005.
20. J. Healey, L. Nachman, S. Subramanian, J. Shahabdeen, and M. Morris. Out of the lab and into the fray: Towards modeling emotion in everyday life. In *Proc. of the 8th International Conference on Pervasive Computing*, pages 156–173, 2010.
21. J. J. Heisz and D. I. Shore. More efficient scanning for familiar faces. *Journal of Vision*, 8(1):1–10, 2008.
22. J. M. Henderson. Human gaze control during real-world scene perception. *Trends in Cognitive Sciences*, 7(11):498–504, 2003.
23. J. H.-w. Hsiao and G. Cottrell. Two fixations suffice in face recognition. *Psychological Science*, 19(10):998–1006, 2008.
24. A. Klin, W. Jones, R. Schultz, F. Volkmar, and D. Cohen. Visual fixation patterns during viewing of naturalistic social situations as predictors of social competence in individuals with autism. *Archives of General Psychiatry*, 59(9):809–816, 2002.
25. C.-J. Lin. LIBLINEAR - a library for large linear classification, 2008. `http://www.csie.ntu.edu.tw/~cjlin/liblinear/`.
26. S. P. Liversedge and J. M. Findlay. Saccadic eye movements and cognition. *Trends in Cognitive Sciences*, 4:6–14, 2000.
27. H. Manabe and M. Fukumoto. Full-time wearable headphone-type gaze detector. In *Extended Abstracts of the ACM SIGCHI Conference on Human Factors in Computing Systems*, pages 1073–1078, 2006.
28. U. P. Mosimann, R. M. Müri, D. J. Burn, J. Felblinger, J. T. O'Brien, and I. G. McKeith. Saccadic eye movement changes in Parkinson's disease dementia and dementia with Lewy bodies. *Brain*, 128(6):1267–1276, 2005.
29. D. Palomba, M. Sarlo, A. Angrilli, A. Mini, and L. Stegagno. Cardiac responses associated with affective processing of unpleasant film stimuli. *International Journal of Psychophysiology*, 36(1):45 – 57, 2000.
30. H. Peng. mRMR Feature Selection Toolbox for MATLAB, 2007. `http://research.janelia.org/peng/proj/mRMR/`.
31. H. Peng, F. Long, and C. Ding. Feature selection based on mutual information criteria of max-dependency, max-relevance, and min-redundancy. *IEEE Transactions on Pattern Analysis and Machine Intelligence*, 27(8):1226–1238, 2005.
32. D. D. Salvucci and J. R. Anderson. Automated eye-movement protocol analysis. *Human-Computer Interaction*, 16(1):39–86, 2001.
33. R. Schleicher, N. Galley, S. Briest, and L. Galley. Blinks and saccades as indicators of fatigue in sleepiness warnings: looking tired? *Ergonomics*, 51(7):982 – 1010, 2008.
34. J. Skotte, J. Nøjgaard, L. Jørgensen, K. Christensen, and G. Sjøgaard. Eye blink frequency during different computer tasks quantified by electrooculography. *European Journal of Applied Physiology*, 99(2):113–119, 2007.
35. E. Stuyven, K. V. der Goten, A. Vandierendonck, K. Claeys, and L. Crevits. The effect of cognitive load on saccadic eye movements. *Acta Psychologica*, 104(1):69 – 85, 2000.
36. M. A. Tinati and B. Mozaffary. A wavelet packets approach to electrocardiograph baseline drift cancellation. *International Journal of Biomedical Imaging*, Article ID 97157, 2006.
37. R. Want, A. Hopper, V. Falcão, and J. Gibbons. The active badge location system. *ACM Transactions on Information Systems*, 10:91–102, 1992.
38. H. Widdel. *Theoretical and Applied Aspects of Eye Movement Research*, chapter Operational problems in analysing eye movements, pages 21–29. Elsevier, 1984.

Author Index

www.ingramcontent.com/pod-product-compliance
Ingram Content Group UK Ltd.
Pitfield, Milton Keynes, MK11 3LW, UK
UKHW051414290926
15471UKWH00009B/1591